Collins

Spanish

Dictionary

HarperCollins Publishers
Westerhill Road
Bishopbriggs
Glasgow
G64 2QT
Great Britain

Eighth Edition/Octava Edición 2009

Reprint 10 9 8 7 6 5 4 3

© William Collins Sons & Co. Ltd
1982, 1989
© HarperCollins Publishers 1993,
1998, 2001, 2004, 2006, 2009

ISBN 978-0-00-728449-8

Collins Gem® is a registered trademark
of HarperCollins Publishers Limited

www.collinslanguage.com

A catalogue record for this book is
available from the British Library

HarperCollins Publishers,
10 East 53rd Street,
New York, NY 10022

COLLINS GEM SPANISH DICTIONARY
Eighth US Edition

ISBN 978-0-06-199517-0

www.harpercollins.com

HarperCollins books may be
purchased for educational, business
or sales promotional use. For
information, please write to: Special
Markets Department, HarperCollins
Publishers, 10 East 53rd Street,
New York, NY 10022

Random House Mondadori, S.A.
Travessera de Gràcia 47–49, 08021
Barcelona

www.diccionarioscollins.com

ISBN 978-84-253-4313-1

Typeset by/Fotocomposición por
Wordcraft, Glasgow

Supplement typeset by/
Fotocomposición de la Guía del viajero
por Davidson Publishing Solutions,
Glasgow

Printed in Italy by/Impreso en Italia
por LEGO Spa, Lavis (Trento)

When you buy a Collins dictionary
or thesaurus and register on
www.collinslanguage.com for the
free online and digital services, you
will not be charged by HarperCollins
for access to Collins free Online
Dictionary content or Collins free
Online Thesaurus content on that
website. However, your operator's
charges for using the internet on
your computer will apply. Costs
vary from operator to operator.
HarperCollins is not responsible for
any charges levied by online service
providers for accessing Collins free
Online Dictionary or Collins free
Online Thesaurus on
www.collinslanguage.com using
these services.

HarperCollins does not warrant
that the functions contained in
www.collinslanguage.com content
will be uninterrupted or error free,
that defects will be corrected, or that
www.collinslanguage.com or the
server that makes it available are
free of viruses or bugs. HarperCollins
is not responsible for any access
difficulties that may be experienced
due to problems with network, web,
online or mobile phone connections.

Acknowledgements
We would like to thank those
authors and publishers who kindly
gave permission for copyright
material to be used in the Collins
Word Web. We would also like to
thank Times Newspapers Ltd for
providing valuable data.

PUBLISHING DIRECTOR/DIRECTORA DE PUBLICACIONES
Catherine Love

MANAGING EDITOR/DIRECCIÓN EDITORIAL
Gaëlle Amiot-Cadey

EDITOR/REDACCIÓN
Genevieve Gerrard

CONTRIBUTORS/COLABORADORES
José Martín Galera
Wendy Lee
Cordelia Lilly
José María Ruiz Vaca
Malihé Sanatian

SERIES EDITOR/COLECCIÓN DIRIGIDA POR
Rob Scriven

ÍNDICE

CONTENTS

INTRODUCCIÓN

Estamos muy satisfechos de que hayas decidido comprar
este diccionario y esperamos que lo disfrutes y que te sirva
de gran ayuda ya sea en el colegio, en el trabajo, en tus
vacaciones o en casa.

Esta introducción pretende darte algunas indicaciones
para ayudarte a sacar el mayor provecho de este diccionario;
no sólo de su extenso vocabulario, sino de toda la información
que te proporciona cada entrada. Esta te ayudará a leer y
comprender – y también a comunicarte y a expresarte –
en inglés moderno. Este diccionario comienza con una lista
de abreviaturas utilizadas en el texto y con una ilustración
de los sonidos representados por los símbolos fonéticos.

EL MANEJO DE TU DICCIONARIO

La amplia información que te ofrece este diccionario
aparece presentada en distintas tipografías, con caracteres
de diversos tamaños y con distintos símbolos, abreviaturas
y paréntesis. Los apartados siguientes explican las reglas y
símbolos utilizados.

ENTRADAS

Las palabras que consultas en el diccionario – las entradas
– aparecen ordenades alfabéticamente y en color para una
identificación más rápida. La palabra que aparece en la
parte superior de cada página es la primera entrada
(si aparece en la página izquierda) y la última entrada
(si aparece en la página derecha) de la página en cuestión.
La información sobre el uso o la forma de determinadas
entradas aparece entre paréntesis, detrás de la transcripción
fonética, y generalmente en forma abreviada y en cursiva

(p. ej.: (*fam*), (*Com*)). En algunos casos se ha considerado oportuno agrupar palabras de una misma familia (nación, nacionalismo; accept, acceptance) bajo una misma entrada que aparece en color.

Las expresiones de uso corriente en las que aparece una entrada se dan en negrita (p. ej.: hurry: [...] **to be in a ~**).

SÍMBOLOS FONÉTICOS

La transcripción fonética de cada entrada inglesa (que indica su pronunciación) aparece entre corchetes, inmediatamente después de la entrada (p. ej. knife [naif]). En las páginas xv-xviii encontrarás una lista de los símbolos fonéticos utilizados en este diccionario.

TRADUCCIONES

Las traducciones de las entradas aparecen en caracteres normales, y en los casos en los que existen significados o usos diferentes, éstos aparecen separados mediante un punto y coma. A menudo encontrarás también otras palabras en cursiva y entre paréntesis antes de las traducciones. Estas sugieren contextos en los que la entrada podría aparecer (p. ej.: alto (*persona*) o (*sonido*)) o proporcionan sinónimos (p. ej.: mismo (*semejante*)).

PALABRAS CLAVE

Particular relevancia reciben ciertas palabras inglesas y españolas que han sido consideradas palabras 'clave' en cada lengua. Estas pueden, por ejemplo, ser de utilización muy corriente o tener distintos usos (de, haber; get, that). La combinación de triángulos y números te permitirá distinguir las diferentes categorías gramaticales y los diferentes significados. Las indicaciones en cursiva y entre paréntesis proporcionan además importante información adicional.

FALSOS AMIGOS
Las palabras que se prestan a confusión al traducir han sido identificadas. En tales entradas existen unas notas que te ayudaran a evitar errores.

INFORMACIÓN GRAMATICAL
Las categorías gramaticales aparecen en forma abreviada y en cursiva después de la transcripción fonética de cada entrada (*vt, adv, conj*). También se indican la forma femenina y los plurales irregulares de los sustantivos del inglés (child, -ren).

We are delighted that you have decided to buy this Spanish dictionary and hope you will enjoy and benefit from using it at school, at home, on holiday or at work.

This introduction gives you a few tips on how to get the most out of your dictionary – not simply from its comprehensive wordlist but also from the information provided in each entry. This will help you to read and understand modern Spanish, as well as communicate and express yourself in the language. This dictionary begins by listing the abbreviations used in the text and illustrating the sounds shown by the phonetic symbols.

USING YOUR DICTIONARY

A wealth of information is presented in the dictionary, using various typefaces, sizes of type, symbols, abbreviations and brackets. The various conventions and symbols used are explained in the following sections.

HEADWORDS

The words you look up in a dictionary – 'headwords' – are listed alphabetically. They are printed in colour for rapid identification. The headwords appearing at the top of each page indicate the first (if it appears on a left-hand page) and last word (if it appears on a right-hand page) dealt with on the page in question.

Information about the usage or form of certain headwords is given in brackets after the phonetic spelling. This usually appears in abbreviated form and in italics (e.g. (fam), (Com)).

Where appropriate, words related to headwords are grouped in the same entry (nación, nacionalismo; accept, acceptance) and are also in colour. Common expressions in which the headword appears are shown in a different bold roman type (e.g. cola: [...] hacer ~).

The phonetic spelling of each headword (indicating its pronunciation) is given in square brackets immediately after the headword (e.g. cohete [ko^{1}ete]). A list of these symbols is given on pages xv-xviii.

Headword translations are given in ordinary type and, where more than one meaning or usage exists, they are separated by a semi-colon. You will often find other words in italics in brackets before the translations. These offer suggested contexts in which the headword might appear (e.g. fare (*on trains, buses*) or provide synonyms (e.g. litter (*rubbish*) o (*young animals*)). The gender of the Spanish translation also appears in italics immediately following the key element of the translation, except where this is a regular masculine singular noun ending in 'o', or a regular feminine noun ending in 'a'.

Special status is given to certain Spanish and English words which are considered as 'key' words in each language. They may, for example, occur very frequently or have several types of usage (e.g. de, haber; get, that). A combination of triangles and numbers helps you to distinguish different parts of speech and different meanings. Further helpful information is provided in brackets and italics.

Words which can be easily confused have been identified in the dictionary. Notes at such entries will help you to avoid these common translation pitfalls.

GRAMMATICAL INFORMATION

Parts of speech are given in abbreviated form in italics after the phonetic spellings of headwords (e.g. *vt, adv, conj*). Genders of Spanish nouns are indicated as follows: *nm* for a masculine and *nf* for a feminine noun. Feminine and irregular plural forms of nouns are also shown (irlandés, esa; luz (*pl* luces)).

abreviatura	*ab(b)r*	abbreviation
adjetivo, locución adjetiva	*adj*	adjective, adjectival phrase
administración	*Admin*	administration
adverbio, locución adverbial	*adv*	adverb, adverbial phrase
agricultura	*Agr*	agriculture
anatomía	*Anat*	anatomy
Argentina	*Arg*	Argentina
arquitectura	*Arq, Arch*	architecture
el automóvil	*Aut(o)*	the motor car and motoring
aviación, viajes aéreos	*Aviac, Aviat*	flying, air travel
biología	*Bio(l)*	biology
botánica, flores	*Bot*	botany
inglés británico	*BRIT*	British English
Centroamérica	*CAM*	Central America
química	*Chem*	chemistry
comercio, finanzas, banca	*Com(m)*	commerce, finance, banking
informática	*Comput*	computing
conjunción	*conj*	conjunction
construcción	*Constr*	building
compuesto	*cpd*	compound element
Cono Sur	*CS*	Southern Cone
cocina	*Culin*	cookery
economía	*Econ*	economics
eletricidad, electrónica	*Elec*	electricity, electronics
enseñanza, sistema escolar y universitario	*Escol*	schooling, schools and universities
España	*ESP*	Spain
especialmente	*esp*	especially
exclamación, interjección	*excl*	exclamation, interjection
femenino	*f*	feminine
lengua familiar (! vulgar)	*fam(!)*	colloquial usage (! particularly offensive)
ferrocarril	*Ferro*	railways
uso figurado	*fig*	figurative use
fotografía	*Foto*	photography
(verbo inglés) del cual la partícula es inseparable	*fus*	(phrasal verb) where the particle is inseparable
generalmente	*gen*	generally
geografía, geología	*Geo*	geography, geology
geometría	*Geom*	geometry

historia	*Hist*	history
uso familiar	*inf(!)*	colloquial usage
(! vulgar)		(! particularly offensive)
infinitivo	*infin*	infinitive
informática	*Inform*	computing
invariable	*inv*	invariable
irregular	*irreg*	irregular
lo jurídico	*Jur*	law
América Latina	LAM	Latin America
gramática, lingüística	*Ling*	grammar, linguistics
masculino	*m*	masculine
matemáticas	*Mat(h)*	mathematics
masculino/femenino	*m/f*	masculine/feminine
medicina	*Med*	medicine
México	MÉX, MEX	Mexico
lo militar, ejército	*Mil*	military matters
música	*Mús, Mus*	music
substantivo, nombre	*n*	noun
navegación, náutica	*Náut, Naut*	sailing, navigation
sustantivo numérico	*num*	numeral noun
complemento	*obj*	(grammatical) object
	o.s.	oneself
peyorativo	*pey, pej*	derogatory, pejorative
fotografía	*Phot*	photography
fisiología	*Physiol*	physiology
plural	*pl*	plural
política	*Pol*	politics
participio de pasado	*pp*	past participle
preposición	*prep*	preposition
pronombre	*pron*	pronoun
psicología, psiquiatría	*Psico, Psych*	psychology, psychiatry
tiempo pasado	*pt*	past tense
química	*Quím*	chemistry
ferrocarril	*Rail*	railways
religión	*Rel*	religion
Río de la Plata	RPL	River Plate
	sb	somebody
Cono Sur	SC	Southern Cone
enseñanza, sistema escolar	*Scol*	schooling, schools
y universitario		and universities
singular	*sg*	singular
España	SP	Spain
	sth	something

sujeto	*su(b)j*	(grammatical) subject
subjuntivo	*subjun*	subjunctive
tauromaquia	*Taur*	bullfighting
también	*tb*	also
técnica, tecnología	*Tec(h)*	technical term, technology
telecomunicaciones	*Telec, Tel*	telecommunications
imprenta, tipografía	*Tip, Typ*	typography, printing
televisión	*TV*	television
universidad	*Univ*	university
inglés norteamericano	*US*	American English
verbo	*vb*	verb
verbo intransitivo	*vi*	intransitive verb
verbo pronominal	*vr*	reflexive verb
verbo transitivo	*vt*	transitive verb
zoología	*Zool*	zoology
marca registrada	®	registered trademark
indica un equivalente cultural	≈	introduces a cultural equivalent

SPANISH PRONUNCIATION

VOWELS

a	[a]	pata	not as long as *a* in far. When followed by a consonant in the same syllable (i.e. in a closed syllable), as in *a*mante, the *a* is short, as in b*a*t
e	[e]	me	like *e* in they. In a closed syllable, as in g*e*nte, the *e* is short as in p*e*t
i	[i]	pino	as in m*ea*n or machine
o	[o]	lo	as in l*o*cal. In a closed syllable, as in c*o*ntrol, the *o* is short as in c*o*t
u	[u]	lunes	as in r*u*le. It is silent after q, and in g*ue*, g*ui*, unless marked g*üe*, g*üi* e.g. antig*üe*dad, when it is pronounced like *w* in wolf

SEMIVOWELS

i, y	[j]	bien hielo yunta	pronounced like *y* in yes
u	[w]	huevo fuento antigüedad	unstressed *u* between consonant and vowel is pronounced like *w* in well. See notes on *u* above.

DIPHTHONGS

ai, ay	[ai]	baile	as *i* in ride
au	[au]	auto	as *ou* in shout
ei, ey	[ei]	buey	as *ey* in grey
eu	[eu]	deuda	both elements pronounced independently [e] + [u]
oi, oy	[oi]	hoy	as *oy* in toy

CONSONANTS

b	[b, β]	boda bomba labor	see notes on *v* below
c	[k]	caja	*c* before *a, o, u* is pronounced as in cat
ce, ci	[θe, θi]	cero cielo	*c* before *e* or *i* is pronounced as in thin
ch	[tʃ]	chiste	*ch* is pronounced as *ch* in chair
d	[d, ð]	danés ciudad	at the beginning of a phrase or after *l* or *n*, *d* is pronounced as in English. In any other position it is pronounced like *th* in the

xv

g	[g, ɣ]	gafas paga	g before *a*, *o* or *u* is pronounced as in *gap*, if at the beginning of a phrase or after *n*. In other positions the sound is softened
ge, gi	[xe, xi]	gente girar	g before *e* or *i* is pronounced similar to *ch* in Scottish *loch*
h		haber	h is always silent in Spanish
j	[x]	jugar	j is pronounced similar to *ch* in Scottish *loch*
ll	[ʎ]	talle	ll is pronounced like the *y* in *yet* or the *lli* in *million*
ñ	[ʃ]	niño	ñ is pronounced like the *ni* in *onion*
q	[k]	que	q is pronounced as *k* in *king*
r, rr	[r, rr]	quitar garra	r is always pronounced in Spanish, unlike the silent *r* in *dancer*. rr is trilled, like a Scottish *r*
s	[s]	quizás isla	s is usually pronounced as in *pass*, but before *b*, *d*, *g*, *l*, *m* or *n* it is pronounced as in *rose*
v	[b, β]	vía	v is pronounced something like *b*. At the beginning of a phrase or after *m* or *n* it is pronounced as *b* in *boy*. In any other position the sound is softened
z	[θ]	tenaz	z is pronounced as *th* in *thin*

f, k, l, m, n, p, t and x are pronounced as in English.

STRESS

The rules of stress in Spanish are as follows:

(a) when a word ends in a vowel or in *n* or *s*, the second last syllable is stressed:
 pat*a*ta, pat*a*tas; c*o*me, c*o*men
(b) when a word ends in a consonant other than *n* or *s*, the stress falls on the last syllable:
 par*e*d, habl*a*r
(c) when the rules set out in (a) and (b) are not applied, an acute accent appears over the stressed vowel:
 com*ú*n, geograf*í*a, ingl*é*s

In the phonetic transcription, the symbol ['] precedes the syllable on which the stress falls.

LA PRONUNCIACIÓN INGLESA

VOCALES

	Ejemplo inglés	Explicación
[ɑ:]	father	Entre a de padre y o de noche
[ʌ]	but, come	a muy breve
[æ]	man, cat	Con los labios en la posición de e en pena y luego se pronuncia el sonido a parecido a la a de carro
[ə]	father, ago	Vocal neutra parecida a una e u o casi muda
[ə:]	bird, heard	Entre e abierta y o cerrada, sonido alargado
[ɛ]	get, bed	Como en perro
[ɪ]	it, big	Más breve que en si
[i:]	tea, see	Como en fino
[ɔ]	hot, wash	Como en torre
[ɔ:]	saw, all	Como en por
[u]	put, book	Sonido breve, más cerrado que burro
[u:]	too, you	Sonido largo, como en uno

DIPTONGOS

	Ejemplo inglés	Explicación
[aɪ]	fly, high	Como en fraile
[au]	how, house	Como en pausa
[ɛə]	there, bear	Casi como en vea, pero el sonido a se mezcla con el indistinto [ə]
[eɪ]	day, obey	e cerrada seguida por una i débil
[ɪə]	here, hear	Como en manía, mezclándose el sonido a con el indistinto [ə]
[əu]	go, note	[ə] seguido por una breve u
[ɔɪ]	boy, oil	Como en voy
[uə]	poor, sure	u bastante larga más el sonido indistinto [ə]

CONSONANTES

	Ejemplo inglés	Explicación
[b]	big, lobby	Como en tumban
[d]	mended	Como en conde, andar
[g]	go, get, big	Como en grande, gol
[dʒ]	gin, judge	Como en la ll andaluza y en Generalitat (catalán)
[ŋ]	sing	Como en vínculo
[h]	house, he	Como la jota hispanoamericana
[j]	young, yes	Como en ya
[k]	come, mock	Como en caña, Escocia
[r]	red, tread	Se pronuncia con la punta de la lengua hacia atrás y sin hacerla vibrar
[s]	sand, yes	Como en casa, sesión
[z]	rose, zebra	Como en desde, mismo
[ʃ]	she, machine	Como en chambre (francés), roxo (portugués)
[tʃ]	chin, rich	Como en chocolate
[v]	valley	Como f, pero se retiran los dientes superiores vibrándolos contra el labio inferior
[w]	water, which	Como la u de huevo, puede
[ʒ]	vision	Como en journal (francés)
[θ]	think, myth	Como en receta, zapato
[ð]	this, the	Como en hablado, verdad

f, l, m, n, p, t y x iguales que en español.

El signo [*] indica que la r final escrita apenas se pronuncia en inglés británico cuando la palabra siguiente empieza con vocal.
El signo ['] indica la sílaba acentuada.

1 Gerund 2 Imperative 3 Present 4 Preterite 5 Future 6 Present
subjunctive 7 Imperfect subjunctive 8 Past participle 9 Imperfect

Etc indicates that the irregular root is used for all persons of the tense,
e.g. oír: 6 oiga, oigas, oigamos, oigáis, oigan

agradecer 3 agradezco 6 agradezca
etc
aprobar 2 aprueba 3 apruebo,
apruebas, aprueba, aprueban
6 apruebe, apruebes, apruebe,
aprueben
atravesar 2 atraviesa 3 atravieso,
atraviesas, atraviesa, atraviesan
6 atraviese, atravieses,
atraviese, atraviesen
caber 3 quepo 4 cupe, cupiste,
cupo, cupimos, cupisteis,
cupieron 5 cabré etc 6 quepa
etc 7 cupiera etc
caer 1 cayendo 3 caigo 4 cayó,
cayeron 6 caiga etc 7 cayera etc
cerrar 2 cierra 3 cierro, cierras,
cierra, cierran 6 cierre, cierres,
cierre, cierren
COMER 1 comiendo 2 come,
comed 3 como, comes, come,
comemos, coméis, comen
4 comí, comiste, comió,
comimos, comisteis, comieron
5 comeré, comerás, comerá,
comeremos, comeréis,
comerán 6 coma, comas, coma,
comamos, comáis, coman
7 comiera, comieras, comiera,
comiéramos, comierais,
comieran 8 comido 9 comía,
comías, comía, comíamos,
comíais, comían
conocer 3 conozco 6 conozca etc
contar 2 cuenta 3 cuento,
cuentas, cuenta, cuentan

6 cuente, cuentes, cuente,
cuenten
dar 3 doy 4 di, diste, dio, dimos,
disteis, dieron 7 diera etc
decir 2 di 3 digo 4 dije, dijiste,
dijo, dijimos, dijisteis, dijeron
5 diré etc 6 diga etc 7 dijera etc
8 dicho
despertar 2 despierta
3 despierto, despiertas,
despierta, despiertan
6 despierte, despiertes,
despierte, despierten
divertir 1 divirtiendo 2 divierte
3 divierto, diviertes, divierte,
divierten 4 divirtió, divirtieron
6 divierta, diviertas, divierta,
divirtamos, divirtáis, diviertan
7 divirtiera etc
dormir 1 durmiendo 2 duerme
3 duermo, duermes, duerme,
duermen 4 durmió, durmieron
6 duerma, duermas, duerma,
durmamos, durmáis, duerman
7 durmiera etc
empezar 2 empieza 3 empiezo,
empiezas, empieza, empiezan
4 empecé 6 empiece, empieces,
empiece, empecemos,
empecéis, empiecen
entender 2 entiende 3 entiendo,
entiendes, entiende, entienden
6 entienda, entiendas,
entienda, entiendan
ESTAR 2 está 3 estoy, estás, está,
están 4 estuve, estuviste,

estuvo, estuvimos, estuvisteis, estuvieron 6 esté, estés, esté, estén 7 estuviera *etc*

HABER 3 he, has, ha, hemos, han 4 hube, hubiste, hubo, hubimos, hubisteis, hubieron 5 habré *etc* 6 haya *etc* 7 hubiera *etc*

HABLAR 1 hablando 2 habla, hablad 3 hablo, hablas, habla, hablamos, habláis, hablan 4 hablé, hablaste, habló, hablamos, hablasteis, hablaron 5 hablaré, hablarás, hablará, hablaremos, hablaréis, hablarán 6 hable, hables, hable, hablemos, habléis, hablen 7 hablara, hablaras, hablara, habláramos, hablarais, hablaran 8 hablado 9 hablaba, hablabas, hablaba, hablábamos, hablabais, hablaban

hacer 2 haz 3 hago 4 hice, hiciste, hizo, hicimos, hicisteis, hicieron 5 haré *etc* 6 haga *etc* 7 hiciera *etc* 8 hecho

instruir 1 instruyendo 2 instruye 3 instruyo, instruyes, instruye, instruyen 4 instruyó, instruyeron 6 instruya *etc* 7 instruyera *etc*

ir 1 yendo 2 ve 3 voy, vas, va, vamos, vais, van 4 fui, fuiste, fue, fuimos, fuisteis, fueron 6 vaya, vayas, vaya, vayamos, vayáis, vayan 7 fuera *etc* 9 iba, ibas, iba, íbamos, ibais, iban

jugar 2 juega 3 juego, juegas, juega, juegan 4 jugué 6 juegue *etc*

leer 1 leyendo 4 leyó, leyeron 7 leyera *etc*

morir 1 muriendo 2 muere 3 muero, mueres, muere, mueren 4 murió, murieron 6 muera, mueras, muera, muramos, muráis, mueran 7 muriera *etc* 8 muerto

mover 2 mueve 3 muevo, mueves, mueve,mueven 6 mueva, muevas, mueva, muevan

negar 2 niega 3 niego, niegas, niega, niegan 4 negué 6 niegue, niegues, niegue, neguemos, neguéis, nieguen

ofrecer 3 ofrezco 6 ofrezca *etc*

oír 1 oyendo 2 oye 3 oigo, oyes, oye, oyen 4 oyó, oyeron 6 oiga *etc* 7 oyera *etc*

oler 2 huele 3 huelo, hueles, huele, huelen 6 huela, huelas, huela, huelan

parecer 3 parezco 6 parezca *etc*

pedir 1 pidiendo 2 pide 3 pido, pides, pide, piden 4 pidió, pidieron 6 pida *etc* 7 pidiera *etc*

pensar 2 piensa 3 pienso, piensas, piensa, piensan 6 piense, pienses, piense, piensen

perder 2 pierde 3 pierdo, pierdes, pierde, pierden 6 pierda, pierdas, pierda, pierdan

poder 1 pudiendo 2 puede 3 puedo, puedes, puede, pueden 4 pude, pudiste, pudo, pudimos, pudisteis, pudieron 5 podré *etc* 6 pueda, puedas, pueda, puedan 7 pudiera *etc*

poner 2 pon 3 pongo 4 puse, pusiste, puso, pusimos, pusisteis, pusieron 5 pondré *etc* 6 ponga *etc* 7 pusiera *etc* 8 puesto

preferir 1 prefiriendo 2 prefiere 3 prefiero, prefieres, prefiere, prefieren 4 prefirió, prefirieron 6 prefiera, prefieras, prefiera, prefiramos, prefiráis, prefieran 7 prefiriera *etc* querer 2 quiere 3 quiero, quieres, quiere, quieren 4 quise, quisiste, quiso, quisimos, quisisteis, quisieron 5 querré *etc* 6 quiera, quieras, quiera, quieran 7 quisiera *etc*

reír 2 ríe 3 río, ríes, ríe, ríen 4 reí, rieron 6 ría, rías, ría, riamos, riáis, rían 7 riera *etc*

repetir 1 repitiendo 2 repite 3 repito, repites, repite, repiten 4 repitió, repitieron 6 repita *etc* 7 repitiera *etc*

rogar 2 ruega 3 ruego, ruegas, ruega, ruegan 4 rogué 6 ruegue, ruegues, ruegue, roguemos, roguéis, rueguen

saber 3 sé 4 supe, supiste, supo, supimos, supisteis, supieron 5 sabré *etc* 6 sepa *etc* 7 supiera *etc*

salir 2 sal 3 salgo 5 saldré *etc* 6 salga *etc*

seguir 1 siguiendo 2 sigue 3 sigo, sigues, sigue, siguen 4 siguió, siguieron 6 siga *etc* 7 siguiera *etc*

sentar 2 sienta 3 siento, sientas, sienta, sientan 6 siente, sientes, siente, sienten

sentir 1 sintiendo 2 siente 3 siento, sientes, siente, sienten 4 sintió, sintieron 6 sienta, sientas, sienta, sintamos, sintáis, sientan 7 sintiera *etc*

SER 2 sé 3 soy, eres, es, somos, sois, son 4 fui, fuiste, fue, fuimos, fuisteis, fueron 6 sea *etc* 7 fuera *etc* 9 era, eras, era, éramos, erais, eran

servir 1 sirviendo 2 sirve 3 sirvo, sirves, sirve, sirven 4 sirvió, sirvieron 6 sirva *etc* 7 sirviera *etc*

soñar 2 sueña 3 sueño, sueñas, sueña, sueñan 6 sueñe, sueñes, sueñe, sueñen

tener 2 ten 3 tengo, tienes, tiene, tienen 4 tuve, tuviste, tuvo, tuvimos, tuvisteis, tuvieron 5 tendré *etc* 6 tenga *etc* 7 tuviera *etc*

traer 1 trayendo 3 traigo 4 traje, trajiste, trajo, trajimos, trajisteis, trajeron 6 traiga *etc* 7 trajera *etc*

valer 2 vale 3 valgo 5 valdré *etc* 6 valga *etc*

venir 2 ven 3 vengo, vienes, viene, vienen 4 vine, viniste, vino, vinimos, vinisteis, vinieron 5 vendré *etc* 6 venga *etc* 7 viniera *etc*

ver 3 veo 6 vea *etc* 8 visto 9 veía *etc*

vestir 1 vistiendo 2 viste 3 visto, vistes, viste, visten 4 vistió, vistieron 6 vista *etc* 7 vistiera *etc*

VIVIR 1 viviendo 2 vive, vivid 3 vivo, vives, vive, vivimos, vivís, viven 4 viví, viviste, vivió, vivimos, vivisteis, vivieron 5 viviré, vivirás, vivirá, viviremos, viviréis, vivirán 6 viva, vivas, viva, vivamos, viváis, vivan 7 viviera, vivieras, viviera, viviéramos, vivierais, vivieran 8 vivido 9 vivía, vivías, vivía, vivíamos, vivíais, vivían

volver 2 vuelve 3 vuelvo, vuelves, vuelve, vuelven 6 vuelva, vuelvas, vuelva, vuelvan 8 vuelto

VERBOS IRREGULARES EN INGLÉS

PRESENTE	PASADO	PARTICIPIO	PRESENTE	PASADO	PARTICIPIO
arise	arose	arisen	dream	dreamed,	dreamed,
awake	awoke	awoken		dreamt	dreamt
be (am, is, are; being)	was, were	been	drink	drank	drunk
			drive	drove	driven
bear	bore	born(e)	dwell	dwelt	dwelt
beat	beat	beaten	eat	ate	eaten
become	became	become	fall	fell	fallen
begin	began	begun	feed	fed	fed
bend	bent	bent	feel	felt	felt
bet	bet,	bet,	fight	fought	fought
	betted	betted	find	found	found
bid (at auction, cards)	bid	bid	flee	fled	fled
			fling	flung	flung
bid (say)	bade	bidden	fly	flew	flown
bind	bound	bound	forbid	forbad(e)	forbidden
bite	bit	bitten	forecast	forecast	forecast
bleed	bled	bled	forget	forgot	forgotten
blow	blew	blown	forgive	forgave	forgiven
break	broke	broken	forsake	forsook	forsaken
breed	bred	bred	freeze	froze	frozen
bring	brought	brought	get	got	got, (us) gotten
build	built	built			
burn	burnt,	burnt,	give	gave	given
	burned	burned	go (goes)	went	gone
burst	burst	burst	grind	ground	ground
buy	bought	bought	grow	grew	grown
can	could	(been able)	hang	hung	hung
cast	cast	cast	hang (suspend)	hung	hung
catch	caught	caught	hang (execute)	hanged	hanged
choose	chose	chosen	have	had	had
cling	clung	clung	hear	heard	heard
come	came	come	hide	hid	hidden
cost (be valued at)	cost	cost	hit	hit	hit
			hold	held	held
cost (work out price of)	costed	costed	hurt	hurt	hurt
			keep	kept	kept
creep	crept	crept	kneel	knelt,	knelt,
cut	cut	cut		kneeled	kneeled
deal	dealt	dealt	know	knew	known
dig	dug	dug	lay	laid	laid
do (does)	did	done	lead	led	led
draw	drew	drawn	lean	leant,	leant,

PRESENTE	PASADO	PARTICIPIO	PRESENTE	PASADO	PARTICIPIO
	leaned	leaned	shine	shone	shone
leap	leapt,	leapt,	shoot	shot	shot
	leaped	leaped	show	showed	shown
learn	learnt,	learnt,	shrink	shrank	shrunk
	learned	learned	shut	shut	shut
leave	left	left	sing	sang	sung
lend	lent	lent	sink	sank	sunk
let	let	let	sit	sat	sat
lie (lying)	lay	lain	slay	slew	slain
light	lit,	lit,	sleep	slept	slept
	lighted	lighted	slide	slid	slid
lose	lost	lost	sling	slung	slung
make	made	made	slit	slit	slit
may	might	–	smell	smelt,	smelt,
mean	meant	meant		smelled	smelled
meet	met	met	sow	sowed	sown,
mistake	mistook	mistaken			sowed
mow	mowed	mown,	speak	spoke	spoken
		mowed	speed	sped,	sped,
must	(had to)	(had to)		speeded	speeded
pay	paid	paid	spell	spelt,	spelt,
put	put	put		spelled	spelled
quit	quit,	quit,	spend	spent	spent
	quitted	quitted	spill	spilt,	spilt,
read	read	read		spilled	spilled
rid	rid	rid	spin	spun	spun
ride	rode	ridden	spit	spat	spat
ring	rang	rung	spoil	spoiled,	spoiled,
rise	rose	risen		spoilt	spoilt
run	ran	run	spread	spread	spread
saw	sawed	sawed,	spring	sprang	sprung
		sawn	stand	stood	stood
say	said	said	steal	stole	stolen
see	saw	seen	stick	stuck	stuck
seek	sought	sought	sting	stung	stung
sell	sold	sold	stink	stank	stunk
send	sent	sent	stride	strode	stridden
set	set	set	strike	struck	struck
sew	sewed	sewn	strive	strove	striven
shake	shook	shaken	swear	swore	sworn
shear	sheared	shorn,	sweep	swept	swept
		sheared	swell	swelled	swollen,
shed	shed	shed			swelled

xxiii

PRESENTE	PASADO	PARTICIPIO	PRESENTE	PASADO	PARTICIPIO
swim	swam	swum	wear	wore	worn
swing	swung	swung	weave (on loom)	wove	woven
take	took	taken			
teach	taught	taught	weave (wind)	weaved	weaved
tear	tore	torn	wed	wedded,	wedded,
tell	told	told		wed	wed
think	thought	thought	weep	wept	wept
throw	threw	thrown	win	won	won
thrust	thrust	thrust	wind	wound	wound
tread	trod	trodden	wring	wrung	wrung
wake	woke,	woken,	write	wrote	written
	waked	waked			

7 (*razón*): **a 30 céntimos el kilo** at 30 cents a kilo; **a más de 50 km/h** at more than 50 kms per hour

8 (*dativo*): **se lo di a él** I gave it to him; **vi al policía** I saw the policeman; **se lo compré a él** I bought it from him

9 (*tras ciertos verbos*): **voy a verle** I'm going to see him; **empezó a trabajar** he started working o to work

10 (+ *infin*): **al verlo, lo reconocí inmediatamente** when I saw him I recognized him at once; **el camino a recorrer** the distance we *etc* have to travel; **¡a callar!** keep quiet!; **¡a comer!** let's eat!

○ PALABRA CLAVE

a [a] (*a* + *el* = *al*) *prep* 1 (*dirección*) to; **fueron a Madrid/Grecia** they went to Madrid/Greece; **me voy a casa** i'm going home

2 (*distancia*): **está a 15 km de aquí** it's 15 kms from here

3 (*posición*): **estar a la mesa** to be at table; **al lado de** next to, beside; V *tb* **puerta**

4 (*tiempo*): **a las 10/a medianoche** at 10/midnight; **a la mañana siguiente** the following morning; **a los pocos días** after a few days; **estamos a 9 de julio** it's the ninth of July; **a los 24 años** at the age of 24; **al año/a la semana** a year/week later

5 (*manera*): **a la francesa** the French way; **a caballo** on horseback; **a oscuras** in the dark

6 (*medio, instrumento*): **a lápiz** in pencil; **a mano** by hand; **cocina a gas** gas stove

abad, esa [a'βað, 'ðesa] *nm/f* abbot/abbess; **abadía** *nf* abbey

abajo [a'βaxo] *adv* (*situación*) (down) below, underneath; (*en edificio*) downstairs; (*dirección*) down, downwards; **el piso de ~** the downstairs flat; **la parte de ~** the lower part; **¡~ el gobierno!** down with the government!; **cuesta/río ~** downhill/downstream; **de arriba ~** from top to bottom; **el ~ firmante** the undersigned; **más ~** lower o further down

abalanzarse [aβalan'θarse] *vr*: **~ sobre** o **contra** to throw o.s. at

abanderado, -a [aβande'raðo] *nm/f* (*portaestandarte*) standard bearer; (*de un movimiento*) champion, leader; (*MÉX: linier*) linesman, assistant referee

abandonado, -a [aβando'naðo, a] *adj* derelict; (*desatendido*) abandoned; (*desierto*) deserted; (*descuidado*) neglected

abandonar [aβando'nar] *vt* to leave; (*persona*) to abandon, desert; (*cosa*) to abandon, leave behind; (*descuidar*) to neglect; (*renunciar a*) to give up; (*Inform*) to quit; **abandonarse** *vr*: **~se a** to abandon o.s. to; **abandono** *nm* (*acto*) desertion, abandonment; (*estado*) abandon, neglect; (*renuncia*) withdrawal, retirement; **ganar por**

abandono to win by default
abanico [aβa'niko] nm fan; (*Náut*) derrick
abarcar [aβar'kar] vt to include, embrace; (*LAM: acaparar*) to monopolize
abarrotado, -a [aβarro'taðo, a] adj packed
abarrotar [aβarro'tar] vt (local, estadio, teatro) to fill, pack
abarrotero, -a [aβarro'tero, a] (*MÉX*) nm/f grocer; **abarrotes** (*MÉX*) nmpl groceries; **tienda de abarrotes** (*MÉX, CAM*) grocery store
abastecer [aβaste'θer] vt: ~ **(de)** to supply (with); **abastecimiento** nm supply
abasto [a'βasto] nm supply; **no dar ~ a** to be unable to cope with
abatible [aβa'tiβle] adj: **asiento ~** tip-up seat; (*Auto*) reclining seat
abatido, -a [aβa'tiðo, a] adj dejected, downcast
abatir [aβa'tir] vt (muro) to demolish; (pájaro) to shoot o bring down; (fig) to depress
abdicar [aβði'kar] vi to abdicate
abdomen [aβ'ðomen] nm abdomen; **abdominales** nmpl (tb: **ejercicios abdominales**) sit-ups
abecedario [aβeθe'ðarjo] nm alphabet
abedul [aβe'ðul] nm birch
abeja [a'βexa] nf bee
abejorro [aβe'xorro] nm bumblebee
abertura [aβer'tura] nf = **apertura**
abeto [a'βeto] nm fir
abierto, -a [a'βjerto, a] pp de **abrir** ▷ adj open
abismal [aβis'mal] adj (fig) vast, enormous
abismo [a'βismo] nm abyss
ablandar [aβlan'dar] vt to soften; **ablandarse** vr to get softer
abocado, -a [aβo'kaðo, a] adj (vino) smooth, pleasant
abochornar [aβotʃor'nar] vt to embarrass
abofetear [aβofete'ar] vt to slap

(in the face)
abogado, -a [aβo'xaðo, a] nm/f lawyer; (notario) solicitor; (en tribunal) barrister (*BRIT*), attorney (*US*); **abogado defensor** defence lawyer o (*US*) attorney
abogar [aβo'xar] vi: ~ **por** to plead for; (fig) to advocate
abolir [aβo'lir] vt to abolish; (cancelar) to cancel
abolladura [aβoʎa'ðura] nf dent
abollar [aβo'ʎar] vt to dent
abombarse [aβom'barse] (*LAM*) vr to go bad
abominable [aβomi'naβle] adj abominable
abonado, -a [aβo'naðo, a] adj (deuda) paid(-up) ▷ nm/f subscriber
abonar [aβo'nar] vt (dinero) to settle; (terreno) to fertilize; (idea) to endorse; **abonarse** vr to subscribe; **abono** nm payment; fertilizer; subscription
abordar [aβor'ðar] vt (barco) to board; (asunto) to broach
aborigen [aβo'rixen] nmf aborigine
aborrecer [aβorre'θer] vt to hate, loathe
abortar [aβor'tar] vi (malparir) to have a miscarriage; (deliberadamente) to have an abortion; **aborto** nm miscarriage; abortion
abovedado, -a [aβoβe'ðaðo, a] adj vaulted, domed
abrasar [aβra'sar] vt to burn (up); (Agr) to dry up, parch
abrazar [aβra'θar] vt to embrace, hug
abrazo [a'βraθo] nm embrace, hug; **un ~** (en carta) with best wishes
abrebotellas [aβreβo'teʎas] nm inv bottle opener
abrecartas [aβre'kartas] nm inv letter opener
abrelatas [aβre'latas] nm inv tin (*BRIT*) o can opener
abreviatura [aβreβja'tura] nf abbreviation
abridor [aβri'ðor] nm bottle opener;

(de latas) tin (BRIT) o can opener

abrigador, a [aβriɣa'ðor, a] (MÉX) adj warm

abrigar [aβri'ɣar] vt (proteger) to shelter; (ropa) to keep warm; (fig) to cherish

abrigo [a'βriɣo] nm (prenda) coat, overcoat; (lugar protegido) shelter

abril [a'βril] nm April

abrillantar [aβriʎan'tar] vt to polish

abrir [a'βrir] vt to open (up) ⊳ vi to open; **abrirse** vr to open (up); (extenderse) to open out; (cielo) to clear; **~se paso** to find o force a way through

abrochar [aβro'tʃar] vt (con botones) to button (up); (zapato, con broche) to do up

abrupto, -a [a'βrupto, a] adj abrupt; (empinado) steep

absoluto, -a [aβso'luto, a] adj absolute; **en ~** adv not at all

absolver [aβsol'βer] vt to absolve; (Jur) to pardon; (: acusado) to acquit

absorbente [aβsor'βente] adj absorbent; (interesante) absorbing

absorber [aβsor'βer] vt to absorb; (embeber) to soak up

absorción [aβsor'θjon] nf absorption; (Com) takeover

abstemio, -a [aβs'temjo, a] adj teetotal

abstención [aβsten'θjon] nf abstention

abstenerse [aβste'nerse] vr: **~ (de)** to abstain o refrain (from)

abstinencia [aβsti'nenθja] nf abstinence; (ayuno) fasting

abstracto, -a [a'βstrakto, a] adj abstract

abstraer [aβstra'er] vt to abstract; **abstraerse** vr to be o become absorbed

abstraído, -a [aβstra'iðo, a] adj absent-minded

absuelto [aβ'swelto] pp de **absolver**

absurdo, -a [aβ'surðo, a] adj absurd

abuchear [aβutʃe'ar] vt to boo

abuelo, -a [a'βwelo, a] nm/f grandfather(-mother); **abuelos** nmpl grandparents

abultado, -a [aβul'taðo, a] adj bulky

abultar [aβul'tar] vi to be bulky

abundancia [aβun'danθja] nf: **una ~** plenty of; **abundante** adj abundant, plentiful

abundar [aβun'dar] vi to abound, be plentiful

aburrido, -a [aβu'rriðo, a] adj (hastiado) bored; (que aburre) boring; **aburrimiento** nm boredom, tedium

aburrir [aβu'rrir] vt to bore; **aburrirse** vr to be bored, get bored

abusado, -a [aβu'saðo, a] (MÉX: fam) adj (astuto) sharp, cunning ⊳ excl: **¡~!** (inv) look out!, careful!

abusar [aβu'sar] vi to go too far; **~ de** to abuse

abusivo, -a [aβu'siβo, a] adj (precio) exorbitant

abuso [a'βuso] nm abuse

acá [a'ka] adv (lugar) here

acabado, -a [aka'βaðo, a] adj finished, complete; (perfecto) perfect; (agotado) worn out; (fig) masterly ⊳ nm finish

acabar [aka'βar] vt (llevar a su fin) to finish, complete; (consumir) to use up; (rematar) to finish off ⊳ vi to finish, end; **acabarse** vr to finish, stop; (terminarse) to be over; (agotarse) to run out; **~ con** to put an end to; **~ de llegar** to have just arrived; **~ por hacer** to end (up) by doing; **¡se acabó!** it's all over!; (¡basta!) that's enough!

acabóse [aka'βose] nm: **esto es el ~** this is the last straw

academia [aka'ðemja] nf academy; **academia de idiomas** language school; **académico, -a** adj academic

acalorado, -a [akalo'raðo, a] adj (discusión) heated

acampar [akam'par] vi to camp

acantilado [akanti'laðo] nm cliff

acaparar [akapa'rar] vt to

monopolize; *(acumular)* to hoard

acariciar [akari'θjar] *vt* to caress; *(esperanza)* to cherish

acarrear [akarre'ar] *vt* to transport; *(fig)* to cause, result in

acaso [a'kaso] *adv* perhaps, maybe; **(por) si ~** (just) in case

acatar [aka'tar] *vt* to respect; *(ley)* obey

acatarrarse [akata'rrarse] *vr* to catch a cold

acceder [akθe'ðer] *vi*: **~ a** *(petición etc)* to agree to; *(tener acceso a)* to have access to; *(Inform)* to access

accesible [akθe'siβle] *adj* accessible

acceso [ak'θeso] *nm* access, entry; *(camino)* access, approach; *(Med)* attack, fit

accesorio, -a [akθe'sorjo, a] *adj, nm* accessory

accidentado, -a [akθiðen'taðo, a] *adj* uneven; *(montañoso)* hilly; *(azaroso)* eventful ▷ *nm/f* accident victim

accidental [akθiðen'tal] *adj* accidental

accidente [akθi'ðente] *nm* accident; **accidentes** *nmpl* *(de terreno)* unevenness *sg*; **accidente laboral o de trabajo/de tráfico** industrial/road o traffic accident

acción [ak'θjon] *nf* action; *(acto)* action, act; *(Com)* share; *(Jur)* action, lawsuit; **accionar** *vt* to work, operate; *(Inform)* to drive

accionista [akθjo'nista] *nmf* shareholder, stockholder

acebo [a'θeβo] *nm* holly; *(árbol)* holly tree

acechar [aθe'tʃar] *vt* to spy on; *(aguardar)* to lie in wait for; **acecho** *nm*: **estar al acecho (de)** to lie in wait (for)

aceite [a'θeite] *nm* oil; **aceite de girasol/oliva** olive/sunflower oil; **aceitera** *nf* oilcan; **aceitoso, -a** *adj* oily

aceituna [aθei'tuna] *nf* olive; **aceituna rellena** stuffed olive

acelerador [aθelera'ðor] *nm* accelerator

acelerar [aθele'rar] *vt* to accelerate

acelga [a'θelxa] *nf* chard, beet

acento [a'θento] *nm* accent; *(acentuación)* stress

acentuar [aθen'twar] *vt* to accent; to stress; *(fig)* to accentuate

acepción [aθep'θjon] *nf* meaning

aceptable [aθep'taβle] *adj* acceptable

aceptación [aθepta'θjon] *nf* acceptance; *(aprobación)* approval

aceptar [aθep'tar] *vt* to accept; *(aprobar)* to approve; **~ hacer algo** to agree to do sth

acequia [a'θekja] *nf* irrigation ditch

acera [a'θera] *nf* pavement (BRIT), sidewalk (US)

acerca [a'θerka]: **~ de** *prep* about, concerning

acercar [aθer'kar] *vt* to bring o move nearer; **acercarse** *vr* to approach, come near

acero [a'θero] *nm* steel

acérrimo, -a [a'θerrimo, a] *adj* *(partidario)* staunch; *(enemigo)* bitter

acertado, -a [aθer'taðo, a] *adj* correct; *(apropiado)* apt; *(sensato)* sensible

acertar [aθer'tar] *vt* *(blanco)* to hit; *(solución)* to get right; *(adivinar)* to guess ▷ *vi* to get it right, be right; **~ a** to manage to; **~ con** to happen o hit on

acertijo [aθer'tixo] *nm* riddle, puzzle

achacar [atʃa'kar] *vt* to attribute

achacoso, -a [atʃa'koso, a] *adj* sickly

achicar [atʃi'kar] *vt* to reduce; *(Náut)* to bale out

achicharrar [atʃitʃa'rrar] *vt* to scorch, burn

achichincle [atʃi'tʃinkle] (MÉX: fam) *nmf* minion

achicoria [atʃi'korja] *nf* chicory

achuras [a'tʃuras] (RPL) *nfpl* offal *sg*

acicate [aθi'kate] *nm* spur

acidez [aθi'ðeθ] nf acidity

ácido, -a ['aθiðo, a] adj sour, acid
▷nm acid

acierto etc [a'θjerto] vb V **acertar**
▷nm success; (buen paso) wise move;
(solución) solution; (habilidad) skill,
ability

acitronar [aθitro'nar] (Méx: fam) vt
to brown

aclamar [akla'mar] vt to acclaim;
(aplaudir) to applaud

aclaración [aklara'θjon] nf
clarification, explanation

aclarar [akla'rar] vt to clarify,
explain; (ropa) to rinse ▷vi to clear
up; **aclararse** vr (explicarse) to
understand; **~se la garganta** to clear
one's throat

aclimatación [aklimata'θjon] nf
acclimatization

aclimatar [aklima'tar] vt to
acclimatize; **aclimatarse** vr to
become acclimatized

acné [ak'ne] nm acne

acobardar [akoβar'ðar] vt to
intimidate

acogedor, a [akoxe'ðor, a] adj
welcoming; (hospitalario) hospitable

acoger [ako'xer] vt to welcome;
(abrigar) to shelter

acogida [ako'xiða] nf reception;
refuge

acomedido, -a [akome'ðiðo, a]
(Méx) adj helpful, obliging

acometer [akome'ter] vt to attack;
(emprender) to undertake; **acometida**
nf attack, assault

acomodado, -a [akomo'ðaðo, a] adj
(persona) well-to-do

acomodador, a [akomoða'ðor, a]
nm/f usher(ette)

acomodar [akomo'ðar] vt to adjust;
(alojar) to accommodate; **acomodarse**
vr to conform; (instalarse) to install o.s.;
(adaptarse) **~se (a)** to adapt (to)

acompañar [akompa'nar] vt to
accompany; (documentos) to enclose

acondicionar [akondiθjo'nar] vt to

arrange, prepare; (pelo) to condition

aconsejar [akonse'xar] vt to advise,
counsel; **~ a algn hacer o que haga
algo** to advise sb to do sth

acontecer [akonte'θer] vi to happen,
occur; **acontecimiento** nm event

acopio [a'kopjo] nm store, stock

acoplar [ako'plar] vt to fit; (Elec) to
connect; (vagones) to couple

acorazado, -a [akora'θaðo, a]
adj armour-plated, armoured ▷nm
battleship

acordar [akor'ðar] vt (resolver) to
agree, resolve; (recordar) to remind;
acordarse vr to agree; **~ hacer algo**
to agree to do sth; **~se (de algo)** to
remember (sth); **acorde** adj (Mús)
harmonious; **acorde con** (medidas etc)
in keeping with ▷nm chord

acordeón [akorðe'on] nm accordion

acordonado, -a [akorðo'naðo, a]
adj (calle) cordoned-off

acorralar [akorra'lar] vt to round
up, corral

acortar [akor'tar] vt to shorten;
(duración) to cut short; (cantidad) to
reduce; **acortarse** vr to become
shorter

acosar [ako'sar] vt to pursue
relentlessly; (fig) to hound, pester;
acoso nm harassment; **acoso sexual**
sexual harassment

acostar [akos'tar] vt (en cama) to
put to bed; (en suelo) to lay down;
acostarse vr to go to bed; to lie down;
~se con algn to sleep with sb

acostumbrado, -a [akostum'braðo,
a] adj usual; **~ a** used to

acostumbrar [akostum'brar] vt: **~
a algn a algo** to get sb used to sth
▷vi: **~ (a) hacer** to be in the habit of
doing; **acostumbrarse** vr: **~se a** to
get used to

acotación [akota'θjon] nf marginal
note; (Geo) elevation mark; (de
límite) boundary mark; (Teatro) stage
direction

acotamiento [akota'mjento] (Méx)

nm hard shoulder (BRIT), berm (US)

acre ['akre] *adj* (olor) acrid; (fig) biting ▷ *nm* acre

acreditar [akreði'tar] *vt* (garantizar) to vouch for, guarantee; (autorizar) to authorize; (dar prueba de) to prove; (Com: abonar) to credit; (embajador) to accredit

acreedor, a [akree'ðor, a] *nm/f* creditor

acribillar [akriβi'ʎar] *vt*: **~ a balazos** to riddle with bullets

acróbata [a'kroβata] *nmf* acrobat

acta ['akta] *nf* certificate; (de comisión) minutes *pl*, record; **acta de matrimonio/nacimiento** (MÉX) marriage/birth certificate; **acta notarial** affidavit

actitud [akti'tuð] *nf* attitude; (postura) posture

activar [akti'βar] *vt* to activate; (acelerar) to speed up

actividad [aktiβi'ðað] *nf* activity

activo, -a [ak'tiβo, a] *adj* active; (vivo) lively ▷ *nm* (Com) assets *pl*

acto ['akto] *nm* act, action; (ceremonia) ceremony; (Teatro) act; **en el ~** immediately

actor [ak'tor] *nm* actor; (Jur) plaintiff ▷ *adj*: **parte ~a** prosecution

actriz [ak'triθ] *nf* actress

actuación [aktwa'θjon] *nf* action; (comportamiento) conduct, behaviour; (Jur) proceedings *pl*; (desempeño) performance

actual [ak'twal] *adj* present(-day), current

> No confundir **actual** con la palabra inglesa *actual*.

actualidad *nf* present; **actualidades** *nfpl* (noticias) news *sg*; **en la actualidad** at present; (hoy día) nowadays; **actualizar** [aktwali'θar] *vt* to update, modernize; **actualmente** [aktwal'mente] *adv* at present; (hoy día) nowadays

> No confundir **actualmente** con la palabra inglesa *actually*.

actuar [ak'twar] *vi* (obrar) to work, operate; (actor) to act, perform ▷ *vt* to work, operate; **~ de** to act as

acuarela [akwa'rela] *nf* watercolour

acuario [a'kwarjo] *nm* aquarium; (Astrología) **A~** Aquarius

acuático, -a [a'kwatiko, a] *adj* aquatic

acudir [aku'ðir] *vi* (asistir) to attend; (ir) to go; (a fig) to turn to; **~ a una cita** to keep an appointment; **~ en ayuda de** to go to the aid of

acuerdo etc [a'kwerðo] *vb* **V acordar** ▷ *nm* agreement; **¡de ~!** agreed!; **de ~ con** (persona) in agreement with; (acción, documento) in accordance with; **estar de ~** to be agreed, agree

acumular [akumu'lar] *vt* to accumulate, collect

acuñar [aku'ɲar] *vt* (moneda) to mint; (frase) to coin

acupuntura [akupun'tura] *nf* acupuncture

acurrucarse [akurru'karse] *vr* to crouch; (ovillarse) to curl up

acusación [akusa'θjon] *nf* accusation

acusar [aku'sar] *vt* to accuse; (revelar) to reveal; (denunciar) to denounce

acuse [a'kuse] *nm*: **~ de recibo** acknowledgement of receipt

acústica [a'kustika] *nf* acoustics *pl*

acústico, -a [a'kustiko, a] *adj* acoustic

adaptación [aðapta'θjon] *nf* adaptation

adaptador [aðapta'ðor] *nm* (Elec) adapter, adaptor; **adaptador universal** universal adapter o adaptor

adaptar [aðap'tar] *vt* to adapt; (acomodar) to fit

adecuado, -a [aðe'kwaðo, a] *adj* (apto) suitable; (oportuno) appropriate

a. de J.C. *abr* (= antes de Jesucristo) B.C.

adelantado, -a [aðelan'taðo, a] *adj* advanced; (reloj) fast; **pagar por ~** to pay in advance

adelantamiento [aðelanta'mjento]

nm (Auto) overtaking

adelantar [aðelan'tar] vt to move forward; (avanzar) to advance; (acelerar) to speed up; (Auto) to overtake ▷ vi to go forward, advance; **adelantarse** vr to go forward, advance

adelante [aðe'lante] adv forward(s), ahead ▷ excl come in!; **de hoy en ~** from now on; **más ~** later on; (más allá) further on

adelanto [aðe'lanto] nm advance; (mejora) improvement; (progreso) progress

adelgazar [aðelɣa'θar] vt to thin (down) ▷ vi to get thin; (con régimen) to slim down, lose weight

ademán [aðe'man] nm gesture; **ademanes** nmpl manners

además [aðe'mas] adv besides; (por otra parte) moreover; (también) also; **~ de** besides, in addition to

adentrarse [aðen'trarse] vr: **~ en** to go into, get inside; (penetrar) to penetrate (into)

adentro [a'ðentro] adv inside, in; **mar ~** out at sea; **tierra ~** inland

adepto, -a [a'ðepto, a] nm/f supporter

aderezar [aðere'θar] vt (ensalada) to dress; (comida) to season; **aderezo** nm dressing; seasoning

adeudar [aðeu'ðar] vt to owe

adherirse [aðe'rirse] vr: **~ a** to adhere to; (partido) to join

adhesión [aðe'sjon] nf adhesion; (fig) adherence

adicción [aðik'θjon] nf addiction

adición [aði'θjon] nf addition

adicto, -a [a'ðikto, a] adj: **~ a** addicted to; (dedicado) devoted to ▷ nm/f supporter, follower; (toxicómano) addict

adiestrar [aðjes'trar] vt to train, teach; (conducir) to guide, lead

adinerado, -a [aðine'raðo, a] adj wealthy

adiós [a'ðjos] excl (para despedirse) goodbye!, cheerio!; (al pasar) hello!

aditivo [aði'tiβo] nm additive

adivinanza [aðiβi'nanθa] nf riddle

adivinar [aðiβi'nar] vt to prophesy; (conjeturar) to guess; **adivino, -a** nm/f fortune-teller

adj abr (= adjunto) encl

adjetivo [aðxe'tiβo] nm adjective

adjudicar [aðxuði'kar] vt to award; **adjudicarse** vr: **~se algo** to appropriate sth

adjuntar [aðxun'tar] vt to attach, enclose; **adjunto, -a** adj attached, enclosed ▷ nm/f assistant

administración [aðministra'θjon] nf administration; (dirección) management; **administrador, a** nm/f administrator, manager(ess)

administrar [aðminis'trar] vt to administer; **administrativo, -a** adj administrative

admirable [aðmi'raβle] adj admirable

admiración [aðmira'θjon] nf admiration; (asombro) wonder; (Ling) exclamation mark

admirar [aðmi'rar] vt to admire; (extrañar) to surprise

admisible [aðmi'siβle] adj admissible

admisión [aðmi'sjon] nf admission; (reconocimiento) acceptance

admitir [aðmi'tir] vt to admit; (aceptar) to accept

adobar [aðo'βar] vt (Culin) to season

adobe [a'ðoβe] nm adobe, sun-dried brick

adolecer [aðole'θer] vi: **~ de** to suffer from

adolescente [aðoles'θente] nmf adolescent, teenager

adonde [a'ðonðe] conj (to) where

adónde [a'ðonðe] adv = **dónde**

adopción [aðop'θjon] nf adoption

adoptar [aðop'tar] vt to adopt

adoptivo, -a [aðop'tiβo, a] adj (padres) adoptive; (hijo) adopted

adoquín [aðo'kin] nm paving stone

adorar [aðo'rar] vt to adore

adornar [aðor'nar] vt to adorn
adorno [a'ðorno] nm ornament; (decoración) decoration
adosado, -a [aðo'saðo, a] adj: **casa adosada** semi-detached house
adosar [aðo'sar] vt (adjuntar) to attach, enclose (with a letter)
adquiero etc vb V **adquirir**
adquirir [aðki'rir] vt to acquire, obtain
adquisición [aðkisi'θjon] nf acquisition
adrede [a'ðreðe] adv on purpose
ADSL nm abr ADSL
aduana [a'ðwana] nf customs pl
aduanero, -a [aðwa'nero, a] adj customs cpd ▷ nm/f customs officer
adueñarse [aðwe'ɲarse] vr: **~ de** to take possession of
adular [aðu'lar] vt to flatter
adulterar [aðulte'rar] vt to adulterate
adulterio [aðul'terjo] nm adultery
adúltero, -a [a'ðultero, a] adj adulterous ▷ nm/f adulterer/ adulteress
adulto, -a [a'ðulto, a] adj, nm/f adult
adverbio [að'βerβjo] nm adverb
adversario, -a [aðβer'sarjo, a] nm/f adversary
adversidad [aðβersi'ðað] nf adversity; (contratiempo) setback
adverso, -a [að'βerso, a] adj adverse
advertencia [aðβer'tenθja] nf warning; (prefacio) preface, foreword
advertir [aðβer'tir] vt to notice; (avisar): **~ a algn de** to warn sb about o of
Adviento [að'βjento] nm Advent
advierto etc vb V **advertir**
aéreo, -a [a'ereo, a] adj aerial
aerobic [ae'roβik] nm aerobics sg; **aerobics** (MÉX) nmpl aerobics
aerodeslizador [aeroðesliθa'ðor] nm hovercraft
aeromozo, -a [aero'moθo, a] (LAM) nm/f air steward(ess)
aeronáutica [aero'nautika] nf aeronautics sg

aeronave [aero'naβe] nm spaceship
aeroplano [aero'plano] nm aeroplane
aeropuerto [aero'pwerto] nm airport
aerosol [aero'sol] nm aerosol
afamado, -a [afa'maðo, a] adj famous
afán [a'fan] nm hard work; (deseo) desire
afanador, a [afana'ðor, a] (MÉX) nm/f (de limpieza) cleaner
afanar [afa'nar] vt to harass; (fam) to pinch
afear [afe'ar] vt to disfigure
afección [afek'θjon] nf (Med) disease
afectado, -a [afek'taðo, a] adj affected
afectar [afek'tar] vt to affect
afectísimo, -a [afek'tisimo, a] adj affectionate; **suyo ~** yours truly
afectivo, -a [afek'tiβo, a] adj (problema etc) emotional
afecto [a'fekto] nm affection; **tenerle ~ a algn** to be fond of sb
afectuoso, -a [afek'twoso, a] adj affectionate
afeitar [afei'tar] vt to shave; **afeitarse** vr to shave
afeminado, -a [afemi'naðo, a] adj effeminate
Afganistán [afɣanis'tan] nm Afghanistan
afianzar [afjan'θar] vt to strengthen; to secure; **afianzarse** vr to become established
afiche [a'fitʃe] (RPL) nm poster
afición [afi'θjon] nf fondness, liking; **la ~** the fans pl; **pinto por ~** I paint as a hobby; **aficionado, -a** adj keen, enthusiastic; (no profesional) amateur ▷ nm/f enthusiast, fan; amateur; **ser aficionado a algo** to be very keen on o fond of sth
aficionar [afiθjo'nar] vt: **~ a algn a algo** to make sb like sth; **aficionarse** vr: **~se a algo** to grow fond of sth

afilado, -a [afiˈlaðo, a] *adj* sharp

afilar [afiˈlar] *vt* to sharpen

afiliarse [afiˈljarse] *vr* to affiliate

afín [aˈfin] *adj* (*parecido*) similar; (*conexo*) related

afinar [afiˈnar] *vt* (*Tec*) to refine; (*Mús*) to tune ▷ *vi* (*tocar*) to play in tune; (*cantar*) to sing in tune

afincarse [afinˈkarse] *vr* to settle

afinidad [afiniˈðað] *nf* affinity; (*parentesco*) relationship; **por ~** by marriage

afirmación [afirmaˈθjon] *nf* affirmation

afirmar [afirˈmar] *vt* to affirm, state; **afirmativo, -a** *adj* affirmative

afligir [afliˈxir] *vt* to afflict; (*apenar*) to distress

aflojar [afloˈxar] *vt* to slacken; (*desatar*) to loosen, undo; (*relajar*) to relax ▷ *vi* to drop; (*bajar*) to go down; **aflojarse** *vr* to relax

afluente [afluˈente] *adj* flowing ▷ *nm* tributary

afmo, -a *abr* (= *afectísimo(a) suyo(a)*) Yours

afónico, -a [aˈfoniko, a] *adj*: **estar ~** to have a sore throat; to have lost one's voice

aforo [aˈforo] *nm* (*de teatro etc*) capacity

afortunado, -a [afortuˈnaðo, a] *adj* fortunate, lucky

África [ˈafrika] *nf* Africa; **África del Sur** South Africa; **africano, -a** *adj*, *nm/f* African

afrontar [afronˈtar] *vt* to confront; (*poner cara a cara*) to bring face to face

afrutado, -a [afruˈtaðo, a] *adj* fruity

after [ˈafter] (*pl* **~s**) *nm* after-hours club; **afterhours** [afterˈaurs] *nm inv* = **after**

afuera [aˈfwera] *adv* out, outside; **afueras** *nfpl* outskirts

agachar [aɣaˈtʃar] *vt* to bend, bow; **agacharse** *vr* to stoop, bend

agalla [aˈɣaʎa] *nf* (*Zool*) gill; **tener ~s** (*fam*) to have guts

agarradera [aɣarraˈðera] (*MÉX*) *nf* handle

agarrado, -a [aɣaˈrraðo, a] *adj* mean, stingy

agarrar [aɣaˈrrar] *vt* to grasp, grab; (*LAM: tomar*) to take, catch; (*recoger*) to pick up ▷ *vi* (*planta*) to take root; **agarrarse** *vr* to hold on (tightly)

agencia [aˈxenθja] *nf* agency; **agencia de viajes** travel agency; **agencia inmobiliaria** (*BRIT*) o real estate (*US*) agent's (office)

agenciarse [axenˈθjarse] *vr* to obtain, procure

agenda [aˈxenda] *nf* diary; **~ electronica** PDA

No confundir **agenda** con la palabra inglesa *agenda*.

agente [aˈxente] *nmf* agent; (*tb*: **~ de policía**) policeman/policewoman; **agente de seguros** insurance agent; **agente de tránsito** (*MÉX*) traffic cop; **agente inmobiliario** estate agent (*BRIT*), realtor (*US*)

ágil [ˈaxil] *adj* agile, nimble; **agilidad** *nf* agility, nimbleness

agilizar [axiliˈθar] *vt* (*trámites*) to speed up

agiotista [axjoˈtista] (*MÉX*) *nmf* (*usurero*) usurer

agitación [axitaˈθjon] *nf* (*de mano etc*) shaking, waving; (*de líquido etc*) stirring; (*fig*) agitation

agitado, -a [axiˈtaðo, a] *adj* hectic; (*viaje*) bumpy

agitar [axiˈtar] *vt* to wave, shake; (*líquido*) to stir; (*fig*) to stir up, excite; **agitarse** *vr* to get excited; (*inquietarse*) to get worried o upset

aglomeración [aɣlomeraˈθjon] *nf* agglomeration; **aglomeración de gente/tráfico** mass of people/traffic jam

agnóstico, -a [aɣˈnostiko, a] *adj*, *nm/f* agnostic

agobiar [aɣoˈβjar] *vt* to weigh down; (*oprimir*) to oppress; (*cargar*) to burden

agolparse [aɣolˈparse] *vr* to crowd

together

agonía [aɣo'nia] nf death throes pl; (fig) agony, anguish

agonizante [aɣoni'θante] adj dying

agonizar [aɣoni'θar] vi to be dying

agosto [a'ɣosto] nm August

agotado, -a [aɣo'taðo, a] adj (persona) exhausted; (libros) out of print; (acabado) finished; (Com) sold out; **agotador, a** [aɣota'ðor, a] adj exhausting

agotamiento [aɣota'mjento] nm exhaustion

agotar [aɣo'tar] vt to exhaust; (consumir) to drain; (recursos) to use up, deplete; **agotarse** vr to be exhausted; (acabarse) to run out; (libro) to go out of print

agraciado, -a [aɣra'θjaðo, a] adj (atractivo) attractive; (en sorteo etc) lucky

agradable [aɣra'ðaβle] adj pleasant, nice

agradar [aɣra'ðar] vt: **él me agrada** I like him

agradecer [aɣraðe'θer] vt to thank; (favor etc) to be grateful for; **agradecido, -a** adj grateful; **¡muy agradecido!** thanks a lot!; **agradecimiento** nm thanks pl; gratitude

agradezco etc vb V **agradecer**

agrado [a'ɣraðo] nm: **ser de tu** etc ~ to be to your etc liking

agrandar [aɣran'dar] vt to enlarge; (fig) to exaggerate; **agrandarse** vr to get bigger

agrario, -a [a'ɣrarjo, a] adj agrarian, land cpd; (política) agricultural, farming

agravante [aɣra'βante] adj aggravating ▷ nm: **con el ~ de que ...** with the further difficulty that ...

agravar [aɣra'βar] vt (pesar sobre) to make heavier; (irritar) to aggravate; **agravarse** vr to worsen, get worse

agraviar [aɣra'βjar] vt to offend; (ser injusto con) to wrong

agredir [aɣre'ðir] vt to attack

agregado, -a [aɣre'ɣaðo, a] nm/f: **A-** = teacher (who is not head of department) ▷ nm aggregate; (persona) attaché

agregar [aɣre'ɣar] vt to gather; (añadir) to add; (persona) to appoint

agresión [aɣre'sjon] nf aggression

agresivo, -a [aɣre'siβo, a] adj aggressive

agriar [a'ɣrjar] vt to (turn) sour

agrícola [a'ɣrikola] adj farming cpd, agricultural

agricultor, a [aɣrikul'tor, a] nm/f farmer

agricultura [aɣrikul'tura] nf agriculture, farming

agridulce [aɣri'ðulθe] adj bittersweet; (Culin) sweet and sour

agrietarse [aɣrje'tarse] vr to crack; (piel) to chap

agrio, -a [a'ɣrjo, a] adj bitter

agrupación [aɣrupa'θjon] nf group; (acto) grouping

agrupar [aɣru'par] vt to group

agua ['aɣwa] nf water; (Naut) wake; (Arq) slope of a roof; **aguas** nfpl (de piedra) water sg, sparkle sg; (Med) water sg, urine sg; (Náut) waters; **agua bendita/destilada/potable** holy/distilled/drinking water; **agua caliente** hot water; **agua corriente** running water; **agua de colonia** eau de cologne; **agua mineral (con/sin gas)** (sparkling/still) mineral water; **agua oxigenada** hydrogen peroxide; **aguas abajo/arriba** downstream/upstream; **aguas jurisdiccionales** territorial waters

aguacate [aɣwa'kate] nm avocado (pear)

aguacero [aɣwa'θero] nm (heavy) shower, downpour

aguado, -a [a'ɣwaðo, a] adj watery, watered down

aguafiestas [aɣwa'fjestas] nmf inv spoilsport, killjoy

aguamiel [aɣwa'mjel] (MÉX) nf fermented maguey o agave juice

aguanieve [aɣwa'njeβe] nf sleet

aguantar [aɣwan'tar] vt to bear, put up with; (sostener) to hold up ▷ vi to last; **aguantarse** vr to restrain o.s.; **aguante** nm (paciencia) patience; (resistencia) endurance

aguar [a'ɣwar] vt to water down

aguardar [aɣwar'ðar] vt to wait for

aguardiente [aɣwar'ðjente] nm brandy, liquor

aguarrás [aɣwa'rras] nm turpentine

aguaviva [aɣwa'βiβa] (RPL) nf jellyfish

agudeza [aɣu'ðeθa] nf sharpness; (ingenio) wit

agudo, -a [a'ɣuðo, a] adj sharp; (voz) high-pitched, piercing; (dolor, enfermedad) acute

agüero [a'ɣwero] nm: **buen/mal ~** good/bad omen

aguijón [aɣi'xon] nm sting; (fig) spur

águila [ˈaɣila] nf eagle; (fig) genius

aguileño, -a [aɣi'leɲo, a] adj (nariz) aquiline; (rostro) sharp-featured

aguinaldo [aɣi'naldo] nm Christmas box

aguja [a'ɣuxa] nf needle; (de reloj) hand; (Arq) spire; (Tec) firing-pin; **agujas** nfpl (Zool) ribs; (Ferro) points

agujerear [aɣuxere'ar] vt to make holes in

agujero [aɣu'xero] nm hole

agujetas [aɣu'xetas] nfpl stitch sg; (rigidez) stiffness sg

ahí [a'i] adv there; **de ~ que** so that, with the result that; **~ llega** here he comes; **por ~** that way; (allí) over there; **200 o por ~** 200 or so

ahijado, -a [ai'xaðo, a] nm/f godson/daughter

ahogar [ao'ɣar] vt to drown; (asfixiar) to suffocate, smother; (fuego) to put out; **ahogarse** vr (en el agua) to drown; (por asfixia) to suffocate

ahogo [a'oɣo] nm breathlessness; (fig) financial difficulty

ahondar [aon'dar] vt to deepen, make deeper; (fig) to study thoroughly ▷ vi: **~ en** to study thoroughly

ahora [a'ora] adv now; (hace poco) a moment ago, just now; (dentro de poco) in a moment; **~ voy** I'm coming; **~ mismo** right now; **~ bien** now then; **por ~** for the present

ahorcar [aor'kar] vt to hang

ahorita [ao'rita] (fam) adv (LAM: en este momento) just now; (MÉX: hace poco) just now; (: dentro de poco) in a minute

ahorrar [ao'rrar] vt (dinero) to save; (esfuerzos) to save, avoid; **ahorro** nm (acto) saving; **ahorros** nmpl (dinero) savings

ahuecar [awe'kar] vt to hollow (out); (voz) to deepen; **ahuecarse** vr to give o.s. airs

ahumar [au'mar] vt to smoke, cure; (llenar de humo) to fill with smoke ▷ vi to smoke; **ahumarse** vr to fill with smoke

ahuyentar [aujen'tar] vt to drive off, frighten off; (fig) to dispel

aire ['aire] nm air; (viento) wind; (corriente) draught; (Mús) tune; **al ~ libre** in the open air; **aire aclimatizado/acondicionado** air conditioning; **airear** vt to air; **airearse** vr (persona) to go out for a breath of fresh air; **airoso, -a** adj windy; draughty; (fig) graceful

aislado, -a [ais'laðo, a] adj isolated; (incomunicado) cut-off; (Elec) insulated

aislar [ais'lar] vt to isolate; (Elec) to insulate

ajardinado, -a [axarði'naðo, a] adj landscaped

ajedrez [axe'ðreθ] nm chess

ajeno, -a [a'xeno, a] adj (que pertenece a otro) somebody else's; **~ a** foreign to

ajetreado, -a [axetre'aðo, a] adj busy

ajetreo [axe'treo] nm bustle

ají [a'xi] (cs) nm chil(l)i, red pepper; (salsa) chil(l)i sauce

ajillo [a'xiʎo] nm: **gambas al ~** garlic prawns

ajo ['axo] nm garlic

ajuar [a'xwar] nm household
furnishings pl; (de novia) trousseau; (de
niño) layette

ajustado, -a [axus'taðo, a] adj
(tornillo) tight; (cálculo) right; (ropa)
tight(-fitting); (resultado) close

ajustar [axus'tar] vt (adaptar) to
adjust; (encajar) to fit; (Tec) to engage;
(Imprenta) to make up; (apretar) to
tighten; (concertar) to agree (on);
(reconciliar) to reconcile; (cuentas,
deudas) to settle ▷ vi to fit; **ajustarse**
vr: **~se a** (precio etc) to be in keeping
with, fit in with; **las cuentas a algn**
to get even with sb

ajuste [a'xuste] nm adjustment;
(Costura) fitting; (acuerdo) compromise;
(de cuenta) settlement

al [al] = **a + el**; V **a**

ala ['ala] nf wing; (de sombrero) brim;
winger; **ala delta** nf hang-glider

alabanza [ala'βanθa] nf praise

alabar [ala'βar] vt to praise

alacena [ala'θena] nf kitchen
cupboard (BRIT) o closet (US)

alacrán [ala'kran] nm scorpion

alambrada [alam'braða] nf wire
fence; (red) wire netting

alambre [a'lambre] nm wire;
alambre de púas barbed wire

alameda [ala'meða] nf (plantío)
poplar grove; (lugar de paseo) avenue,
boulevard

álamo ['alamo] nm poplar

alarde [a'larðe] nm show, display;
hacer ~ de to boast of

alargador [alarxa'ðor] nm (Elec)
extension lead

alargar [alar'xar] vt to lengthen,
extend; (paso) to hasten; (brazo)
to stretch out; (cuerda) to pay out;
(conversación) to spin out; **alargarse** vr
to get longer

alarma [a'larma] nf alarm; **alarma
de incendios** fire alarm; **alarmar** vt
to alarm; **alarmarse** to get alarmed;
alarmante [alar'mante] adj

alarming

alba ['alβa] nf dawn

albahaca [al'βaka] nf basil

Albania [al'βanja] nf Albania

albañil [alβa'ɲil] nm bricklayer;
(cantero) mason

albarán [alβa'ran] nm (Com) delivery
note, invoice

albaricoque [alβari'koke] nm
apricot

albedrío [alβe'ðrio] nm: **libre ~**
free will

alberca [al'βerka] nf reservoir;
(MÉX: piscina) swimming pool

albergar [alβer'xar] vt to shelter

albergue etc [al'βerxe] vb V **albergar**
▷ nm shelter, refuge; **albergue juvenil**
youth hostel

albóndiga [al'βondixa] nf meatball

albornoz [alβor'noθ] nm (de los
árabes) burnous; (para el baño) bathrobe

alborotar [alβoro'tar] vi to make
a row ▷ vt to agitate, stir up;
alborotarse vr to get excited; (mar) to
get rough; **alboroto** nm row, uproar

álbum ['alβum] (pl **-s, -es**) nm
album; **álbum de recortes** scrapbook

albur [al'βur] (MÉX) nm (juego de
palabras) pun; (doble sentido) double
entendre

alcachofa [alka'tʃofa] nf artichoke

alcalde, -esa [al'kalde, esa] nm/f
mayor(ess)

alcaldía [alkal'dia] nf mayoralty;
(lugar) mayor's office

alcance etc [al'kanθe] vb V **alcanzar**
▷ nm reach; (Com) adverse balance; **al ~
de algn** available to sb

alcancía [alkan'θia] nf (para
ahorrar) money box; (para colectas)
collection box

alcantarilla [alkanta'riʎa] nf (de
aguas cloacales) sewer; (en la calle)
gutter

alcanzar [alkan'θar] vt (algo: con
la mano, el pie) to reach; (alguien: en el
camino etc) to catch up (with); (autobús)
to catch; (bala) to hit, strike ▷ vi (ser

suficiente) to be enough; **~ a hacer** to manage to do

alcaparra [alka'parra] nf caper

alcayata [alka'jata] nf hook

alcázar [al'kaθar] nm fortress; (Náut) quarter-deck

alcoba [al'koβa] nf bedroom

alcohol [al'kol] nm alcohol; **alcohol metílico** methylated spirits pl (BRIT), wood alcohol (US); **alcohólico, -a** adj, nm/f alcoholic; **alcoholímetro** [alko'limetro] nm Breathalyser® (BRIT), drunkometer (US); **alcoholismo** [alko'lismo] nm alcoholism

alcornoque [alkor'noke] nm cork tree; (fam) idiot

aldea [al'dea] nf village; **aldeano, -a** adj village cpd ⊳ nm/f villager

aleación [alea'θjon] nf alloy

aleatorio, -a [alea'torjo, a] adj random

aleccionar [alekθjo'nar] vt to instruct; (adiestrar) to train

alegar [ale'xar] vt to claim; (Jur) to plead ⊳ vi (LAM: discutir) to argue

alegoría [alexo'ria] nf allegory

alegrar [ale'xrar] vt (causar alegría) to cheer (up); (fuego) to poke; (fiesta) to liven up; **alegrarse** vr (fam) to get merry o tight; **~se de** to be glad about

alegre [a'levre] adj happy, cheerful; (fam) merry, tight; (chiste) risqué, blue; **alegría** nf happiness; merriment

alejar [ale'xar] vt to remove; (fig) to estrange; **alejarse** vr to move away

alemán, -ana [ale'man, ana] adj, nm/f German ⊳ nm (Ling) German

Alemania [ale'manja] nf Germany

alentador, a [alenta'ðor, a] adj encouraging

alentar [alen'tar] vt to encourage

alergia [a'lerxja] nf allergy

alero [a'lero] nm (de tejado) eaves pl; (guardabarros) mudguard

alerta [a'lerta] adj, nm alert

aleta [a'leta] nf (de pez) fin; (ala) wing; (de foca, Deporte) flipper; (Auto) mudguard

aletear [alete'ar] vi to flutter

alevín [ale'βin] nm fry, young fish

alevosía [aleβo'sia] nf treachery

alfabeto [alfa'βeto] nm alphabet

alfalfa [al'falfa] nf alfalfa, lucerne

alfarería [alfare'ria] nf pottery; (tienda) pottery shop; **alfarero, -a** nm/f potter

alféizar [al'feiθar] nm window-sill

alférez [al'fereθ] nm (Mil) second lieutenant; (Náut) ensign

alfil [al'fil] nm (Ajedrez) bishop

alfiler [alfi'ler] nm pin; (broche) clip

alfombra [al'fombra] nf carpet; (más pequeña) rug; **alfombrilla** nf rug, mat; (Inform) mouse mat o pad

alforja [al'forxa] nf saddlebag

algas ['alxas] nfpl seaweed

álgebra ['alxeβra] nf algebra

algo ['alxo] pron something; anything ⊳ adv somewhat, rather; **¿~ más?** anything else?; (en tienda) is that all?; **por ~ será** there must be some reason for it

algodón [alxo'ðon] nm cotton; (planta) cotton plant; **algodón de azúcar** candy floss (BRIT), cotton candy (US); **algodón hidrófilo** cotton wool (BRIT), absorbent cotton (US)

alguien ['alxjen] pron someone, somebody; (en frases interrogativas) anyone, anybody

alguno, -a [al'xuno, a] adj (delante de nm): **algún** some; (después de n): **no tiene talento** = he has no talent, he doesn't have any talent ⊳ pron (alguien) someone, somebody; **algún que otro libro** some book or other; **algún día iré** I'll go one o some day; **sin interés** = without the slightest interest; **~ que otro** an occasional one; **~s piensan** some (people) think

alhaja [a'laxa] nf jewel; (tesoro) precious object, treasure

alhelí [ale'li] nm wallflower, stock

aliado, -a [a'ljaðo, a] adj allied

alianza [a'ljanθa] nf alliance; (anillo) wedding ring

aliar [a'ljar] *vt* to ally; **aliarse** *vr* to form an alliance

alias ['aljas] *adv* alias

alicatado [alika'taðo] (*ESP*) *nm* tiling

alicates [ali'kates] *nmpl* pliers

aliciente [ali'θjente] *nm* incentive; (*atracción*) attraction

alienación [aljena'θjon] *nf* alienation

aliento [a'ljento] *nm* breath; (*respiración*) breathing; **sin ~** breathless

aligerar [alixe'rar] *vt* to lighten; (*reducir*) to shorten; (*aliviar*) to alleviate; (*mitigar*) to ease; (*paso*) to quicken

alijo [a'lixo] *nm* consignment

alimaña [ali'maɲa] *nf* pest

alimentación [alimenta'θjon] *nf* (*comida*) food; (*acción*) feeding; (*tienda*) grocer's (shop)

alimentar [alimen'tar] *vt* to feed; (*nutrir*) to nourish; **alimentarse** *vr* to feed

alimenticio, -a [alimen'tiθjo, a] *adj* food *cpd*; (*nutritivo*) nourishing, nutritious

alimento [ali'mento] *nm* food; (*nutrición*) nourishment

alineación [alinea'θjon] *nf* alignment; (*Deporte*) line-up

alinear [aline'ar] *vt* to align; (*Deporte*) to select, pick

aliñar [ali'ɲar] *vt* (*Culin*) to season; **aliño** *nm* (*Culin*) dressing

alioli [ali'oli] *nm* garlic mayonnaise

alisar [ali'sar] *vt* to smooth

alistarse [alis'tarse] *vr* to enlist; (*inscribirse*) to enrol

aliviar [ali'βjar] *vt* (*carga*) to lighten; (*persona*) to relieve; (*dolor*) to relieve, alleviate

alivio [a'liβjo] *nm* alleviation, relief

aljibe [al'xiβe] *nm* cistern

allá [a'ʎa] *adv* (*lugar*) there; (*por ahí*) over there; (*tiempo*) then; **~ abajo** down there; **más ~** further on; **más ~ de** beyond; **¡~ tú!** that's your problem!; **¡~ voy!** I'm coming!

allanamiento [aʎana'mjento] *nm* (*LAM: de policía*) raid; **allanamiento de morada** burglary

allanar [aʎa'nar] *vt* to flatten, level (out); (*igualar*) to smooth (out); (*fig*) to subdue; (*Jur*) to burgle, break into

allegado, -a [aʎe'ɣaðo, a] *adj* near, close ▷ *nm/f* relation

allí [a'ʎi] *adv* there; **~ mismo** right there; **por ~** over there; (*por ese camino*) that way

alma ['alma] *nf* soul; (*persona*) person

almacén [alma'θen] *nm* (*depósito*) warehouse, store; (*Mil*) magazine; (*cs: de comestibles*) grocer's (shop); **grandes almacenes** department store *sg*; **almacenaje** *nm* storage

almacenar [almaθe'nar] *vt* to store, put in storage; (*proveerse*) to stock up with

almanaque [alma'nake] *nm* almanac

almeja [al'mexa] *nf* clam

almendra [al'mendra] *nf* almond; **almendro** *nm* almond tree

almíbar [al'miβar] *nm* syrup

almidón [almi'ðon] *nm* starch

almirante [almi'rante] *nm* admiral

almohada [almo'aða] *nf* pillow; (*funda*) pillowcase; **almohadilla** *nf* cushion; (*para alfileres*) pincushion; (*Tec*) pad

almohadón [almoa'ðon] *nm* large pillow; bolster

almorranas [almo'rranas] *nfpl* piles, haemorrhoids

almorzar [almor'θar] *vt*: **~ una tortilla** to have an omelette for lunch ▷ *vi* to (have) lunch

almuerzo *etc* [al'mwerθo] *vb* V **almorzar** ▷ *nm* lunch

alocado, -a [alo'kaðo, a] *adj* crazy

alojamiento [aloxa'mjento] *nm* lodging(s) pl; (*viviendas*) housing

alojar [alo'xar] *vt* to lodge; **alojarse** *vr* to lodge, stay

alondra [a'londra] *nf* lark, skylark

alpargata [alpar'ɣata] *nf* rope-soled

sandal, espadrille

Alpes ['alpes] nmpl: **los ~** the Alps

alpinismo [alpi'nismo] nm mountaineering, climbing; **alpinista** nmf mountaineer, climber

alpiste [al'piste] nm birdseed

alquilar [alki'lar] vt (propietario: inmuebles) to let, rent (out); (: coche) to hire (out); (: TV) to hire (out); (alquilador: inmuebles, TV, coche) to hire; **"se alquila casa"** "house to let (BRIT) o for rent (US)

alquiler [alki'ler] nm renting; letting; hiring; (arriendo) rent; hire charge; **de ~** for hire; **alquiler de automóviles o coches** car hire

alquimia [al'kimja] nf alchemy

alquitrán [alki'tran] nm tar

alrededor [alreðe'ðor] adv around, about; **~ de** around, about; **mirar a su ~** to look (round) about one; **alrededores** nmpl surroundings

alta ['alta] nf (certificate of) discharge

altar [al'tar] nm altar

altavoz [alta'βoθ] nm loudspeaker; (amplificador) amplifier

alteración [altera'θjon] nf alteration; (alboroto) disturbance

alterar [alte'rar] vt to alter; to disturb; **alterarse** vr (persona) to get upset

altercado [alter'kaðo] nm argument

alternar [alter'nar] vt to alternate ▷ vi to alternate; (turnar) to take turns; **alternarse** vr to alternate; to take turns; **~ con** to mix with; **alternativa** nf alternative; (elección) choice; **alternativo, -a** adj alternative; (alterno) alternating; **alterno, -a** adj alternate; (Elec) alternating

Alteza [al'teθa] nf (tratamiento) Highness

altibajos [alti'βaxos] nmpl ups and downs

altiplano [alti'plano] nm = **altiplanicie**

altisonante [altiso'nante] adj high-

flown, high-sounding

altitud [alti'tuð] nf height; (Aviac, Geo) altitude

altivo, -a [al'tiβo, a] adj haughty, arrogant

alto, -a ['alto, a] adj high; (persona) tall; (sonido) high, sharp; (noble) high, lofty ▷ nm (Mús) alto; (Geo) hill ▷ adv (de sitio) high; (de sonido) loud, loudly ▷ excl halt!; **la pared tiene 2 metros de ~** the wall is 2 metres high; **en alta mar** on the high seas; **en voz alta** in a loud voice; **las altas horas de la noche** the small o wee hours; **en lo ~ de** at the top of; **pasar por ~** to overlook; **altoparlante** [altopar'lante] (LAM) nm loudspeaker

altura [al'tura] nf height; (Náut) depth; (Geo) latitude; **la pared tiene 1.80 de ~** the wall is 1 metre 80cm high; **a estas ~s** at this stage; **a estas ~s del año** at this time of the year

alubia [a'luβja] nf bean

alucinación [aluθina'θjon] nf hallucination

alucinar [aluθi'nar] vi to hallucinate ▷ vt to deceive; (fascinar) to fascinate

alud [a'luð] nm avalanche; (fig) flood

aludir [alu'ðir] vi: **~ a** to allude to; **darse por aludido** to take the hint

alumbrado [alum'braðo] nm lighting

alumbrar [alum'brar] vt to light (up) ▷ vi (Med) to give birth

aluminio [alu'minjo] nm aluminium (BRIT), aluminum (US)

alumno, -a [a'lumno, a] nm, a nm/f pupil, student

alusión [alu'sjon] nf allusion

alusivo, -a [alu'siβo, a] adj allusive

aluvión [alu'βjon] nm alluvium; (fig) flood

alverja [al'βerxa] (LAM) nf pea

alza ['alθa] nf rise; (Mil) sight

alzamiento [alθa'mjento] nm (rebelión) rising

alzar [al'θar] vt to lift (up); (precio, muro) to raise; (cuello de abrigo) to turn up; (Agr) to gather in; (Imprenta) to gather; **alzarse** vr to get up, rise; (rebelarse) to revolt; (Com) to go fraudulently bankrupt; (Jur) to appeal

ama ['ama] nf lady of the house; (dueña) owner; (institutriz) governess; (madre adoptiva) foster mother; **ama de casa** housewife; **ama de llaves** housekeeper

amabilidad [amaßili'ðað] nf kindness; (simpatía) niceness; **amable** adj kind; nice; **es usted muy amable** that's very kind of you

amaestrado, -a [amaes'traðo, a] adj (animal: en circo etc) performing

amaestrar [amaes'trar] vt to train

amago [a'maɣo] nm threat; (gesto) threatening gesture; (Med) symptom

amainar [amai'nar] vi (viento) to die down

amamantar [amaman'tar] vt to suckle, nurse

amanecer [amane'θer] vi to dawn ▷ nm dawn; **~ afiebrado** to wake up with a fever

amanerado, -a [amane'raðo, a] adj affected

amante [a'mante] adj: **~ de** fond of ▷ nmf lover

amapola [ama'pola] nf poppy

amar [a'mar] vt to love

amargado, -a [amar'ɣaðo, a] adj bitter

amargar [amar'ɣar] vt to make bitter; (fig) to embitter; **amargarse** vr to become embittered

amargo, -a [a'marɣo, a] adj bitter

amarillento, -a [amari'ʎento, a] adj yellowish; (tez) sallow; **amarillo, -a** [ama'riʎo, a] adj, nm yellow

amarrado, -a [ama'rraðo, a] (MÉx: fam) adj mean, stingy

amarrar [ama'rrar] vt to moor; (sujetar) to tie up

amarras [a'marras] nfpl: **soltar ~** to set sail

amasar [ama'sar] vt (masa) to knead; (mezclar) to mix, prepare; (confeccionar) to concoct

amateur [ama'ter] nmf amateur

amazona [ama'θona] nf horsewoman; **Amazonas** nm: **el Amazonas** the Amazon

ámbar ['ambar] nm amber

ambición [ambi'θjon] nf ambition; **ambicionar** vt to aspire to; **ambicioso, -a** adj ambitious

ambidextro, -a [ambi'ðekstro, a] adj ambidextrous

ambientación [ambjenta'θjon] nf (Cine, Teatro etc) setting; (Radio) sound effects

ambiente [am'bjente] nm atmosphere; (medio) environment

ambigüedad [ambiɣwe'ðað] nf ambiguity; **ambiguo, -a** adj ambiguous

ámbito ['ambito] nm (campo) field; (fig) scope

ambos, -as ['ambos, as] adj pl, pron pl both

ambulancia [ambu'lanθja] nf ambulance

ambulante [ambu'lante] adj travelling cpd, itinerant

ambulatorio [ambula'torjo] nm state health-service clinic

amén [a'men] excl amen; **~ de** besides

amenaza [ame'naθa] nf threat; **amenazar** [amena'θar] vt to threaten ▷ vi: **amenazar con hacer** to threaten to do

ameno, -a [a'meno, a] adj pleasant

América [a'merika] nf America; **América Central/Latina** Central/Latin America; **América del Norte/del Sur** North/South America; **americana** nf coat, jacket; V tb **americano**; **americano, -a** adj, nm/f American

ametralladora [ametraʎa'ðora] nf machine gun

amigable [ami'ɣaßle] adj friendly

amígdala [a'miɣðala] nf tonsil; **amigdalitis** nf tonsillitis

amigo, -a [a'miɣo, a] adj friendly

▷ nm/f friend; (amante) lover; **ser ~ de algo** to be fond of sth; **ser muy ~s** to be close friends

aminorar [amino'rar] vt to diminish; (reducir) to reduce; **~ la marcha** to slow down

amistad [amis'taθ] nf friendship; **amistades** nfpl (amigos) friends; **amistoso, -a** adj friendly

amnesia [am'nesja] nf amnesia

amnistía [amnis'tia] nf amnesty

amo ['amo] nm owner; (jefe) boss

amolar [amo'lar] (MÉX: fam) vt to ruin, damage

amoldar [amol'dar] vt to mould; (adaptar) to adapt

amonestación [amonesta'θjon] nf warning; **amonestaciones** nfpl (Rel) marriage banns

amonestar [amones'tar] vt to warn; (Rel) to publish the banns of

amontonar [amonto'nar] vt to collect, pile up; **amontonarse** vr to crowd together; (acumularse) to pile up

amor [a'mor] nm love; (amante) lover; **hacer el ~** to make love; **amor propio** self-respect

amoratado, -a [amora'taðo, a] adj purple

amordazar [amorða'θar] vt to muzzle; (fig) to gag

amorfo, -a [a'morfo, a] adj amorphous, shapeless

amoroso, -a [amo'roso, a] adj affectionate, loving

amortiguador [amortigwa'ðor] nm shock absorber; (parachoques) bumper; **amortiguadores** nmpl (Auto) suspension sg

amortiguar [amorti'ɣwar] vt to deaden; (ruido) to muffle; (color) to soften

amotinar [amoti'nar] vt to stir up, incite to riot; **amotinarse** vr to mutiny

amparar [ampa'rar] vt to protect; **ampararse** vr to seek protection; (de la lluvia etc) to shelter; **amparo** nm

help, protection; **al amparo de** under the protection of

amperio [am'perjo] nm ampère, amp

ampliación [amplja'θjon] nf enlargement; (extensión) extension

ampliar [am'pljar] vt to enlarge; to extend

amplificador [amplifika'ðor] nm amplifier

amplificar [amplifi'kar] vt to amplify

amplio, -a ['ampljo, a] adj spacious; (de falda etc) full; (extenso) extensive; (ancho) wide; **amplitud** nf spaciousness; extent; (fig) amplitude

ampolla [am'poʎa] nf blister; (Med) ampoule

amputar [ampu'tar] vt to cut off, amputate

amueblar [amwe'βlar] vt to furnish

anales [a'nales] nmpl annals

analfabetismo [analfaβe'tismo] nm illiteracy; **analfabeto, -a** adj, nm/f illiterate

analgésico [anal'xesiko] nm painkiller, analgesic

análisis [a'nalisis] nm inv analysis

analista [ana'lista] nmf (gen) analyst

analizar [anali'θar] vt to analyse

analógico, -a [ana'loxiko, a] adj (Inform) analog; (reloj) analogue (BRIT), analog (US)

análogo, -a [a'naloxo, a] adj analogous, similar

ananá [ana'na] (RPL) nm pineapple

anarquía [anar'kia] nf anarchy; **anarquista** nmf anarchist

anatomía [anato'mia] nf anatomy

anca ['anka] nf rump, haunch; **ancas** nfpl (fam) behind sg

ancho, -a ['antʃo, a] adj wide; (falda) full; (fig) liberal ▷ nm width; (Ferro) gauge; **ponerse ~** to get conceited; **estar a sus anchas** to be at one's ease

anchoa [an'tʃoa] nf anchovy

anchura [an'tʃura] nf width; (extensión) wideness

anciano, -a [an'θjano, a] adj old,

aged ▷ *nm/f* old man/woman; elder

ancla ['ankla] *nf* anchor

Andalucía [andalu'θia] *nf* Andalusia; **andaluz, -a** *adj, nm/f* Andalusian

andamio [an'damjo] *nm* scaffold(ing)

andar [an'dar] *vt* to go, cover, travel ▷ *vi* to go, walk, travel; *(funcionar)* to go, work; *(estar)* to be ▷ *nm* walk, gait, pace; **andarse** *vr* to go away; **~ a pie/a caballo/en bicicleta** to go on foot/on horseback/by bicycle; **~ haciendo algo** to be doing sth; **¡anda!** *(sorpresa)* go on!; **anda por o en los 40** he's about 40

andén [an'den] *nm* (Ferro) platform; *(Náut)* quayside; *(CAM: de la calle)* pavement *(BRIT)*, sidewalk *(US)*

Andes ['andes] *nmpl*: **los ~** the Andes

andinismo [andi'nismo] *(LAM) nm* mountaineering, climbing

Andorra [an'dorra] *nf* Andorra

andrajoso, -a [andra'xoso, a] *adj* ragged

anduve *etc vb V* **andar**

anécdota [a'nekðota] *nf* anecdote, story

anegar [ane'xar] *vt* to flood; *(ahogar)* to drown

anemia [a'nemja] *nf* anaemia

anestesia [anes'tesja] *nf (sustancia)* anaesthetic; *(proceso)* anaesthesia; **anestesia general/local** general/ local anaesthetic

anexar [anek'sar] *vt* to annex; *(documento)* to attach; **anexión** *nf* annexation; **anexo, -a** *adj* attached ▷ *nm* annexe

anfibio, -a [an'fiβjo, a] *adj* amphibious ▷ *nm* amphibian

anfiteatro [anfite'atro] *nm* amphitheatre; *(Teatro)* dress circle

anfitrión, -ona [anfi'trjon, ona] *nm/f* host(ess)

ánfora ['anfora] *nf (cántaro)* amphora; *(MÉX Pol)* ballot box

ángel ['anxel] *nm* angel; **ángel de la**

guarda guardian angel

angina [an'xina] *nf (Med)* inflammation of the throat; **tener ~s** to have tonsillitis; **angina de pecho** angina

anglicano, -a [angli'kano, a] *adj, nm/f* Anglican

anglosajón, -ona [anglosa'xon, ona] *adj* Anglo-Saxon

anguila [an'gila] *nf* eel

angula [an'gula] *nf* elver, baby eel

ángulo ['angulo] *nm* angle; *(esquina)* corner; *(curva)* bend

angustia [an'gustja] *nf* anguish

anhelar [ane'lar] *vt* to be eager for; *(desear)* to long for, desire ▷ *vi* to pant, gasp; **anhelo** *nm* eagerness; desire

anidar [ani'ðar] *vi* to nest

anillo [a'niλo] *nm* ring; **anillo de boda/compromiso** wedding/ engagement ring

animación [anima'θjon] *nf* liveliness; *(vitalidad)* life; *(actividad)* activity; bustle

animado, -a [ani'maðo, a] *adj* lively; *(vivaz)* animated; **animador, a** *nm/f (TV)* host(ess), compère; *(Deporte)* cheerleader

animal [ani'mal] *adj* animal; *(fig)* stupid ▷ *nm* animal; *(fig)* fool; *(bestia)* brute

animar [ani'mar] *vt (Bio)* to animate, give life to; *(fig)* to liven up, brighten up, cheer up; *(estimular)* to stimulate; **animarse** *vr* to cheer up; to feel encouraged; *(decidirse)* to make up one's mind

ánimo ['animo] *nm (alma)* soul; *(mente)* mind; *(valentía)* courage ▷ *excl* cheer up!

animoso, -a [ani'moso, a] *adj* brave; *(vivo)* lively

aniquilar [aniki'lar] *vt* to annihilate, destroy

anís [a'nis] *nm* aniseed; *(licor)* anisette

aniversario [aniβer'sarjo] *nm* anniversary

anoche [a'notʃe] adv last night; **antes de ~** the night before last

anochecer [anotʃe'θer] vi to get dark ▷ nm nightfall, dark; **al ~** at nightfall

anodino, -a [ano'ðino, a] adj dull, anodyne

anomalía [anoma'lia] nf anomaly

anonadado, -a [anona'ðaðo, a] adj: **estar ~** to be overwhelmed o amazed

anonimato [anoni'mato] nm anonymity

anónimo, -a [a'nonimo, a] adj anonymous; (Com) limited ▷ nm (carta anónima) anonymous letter; (: maliciosa) poison-pen letter

anormal [anor'mal] adj abnormal

anotación [anota'θjon] nf note; annotation

anotar [ano'tar] vt to note down; (comentar) to annotate

ansia ['ansja] nf anxiety; (añoranza) yearning; **ansiar** vt to long for

ansiedad [ansje'ðað] nf anxiety

ansioso, -a [an'sjoso, a] adj anxious; (anhelante) eager; **~ de o por algo** greedy for sth

antaño [an'taɲo] adv long ago, formerly

Antártico [an'tartiko] nm: **el ~** the Antarctic

ante ['ante] prep before, in the presence of; (problema etc) faced with ▷ nm (piel) suede; **~ todo** above all

anteanoche [antea'notʃe] adv the night before last

anteayer [antea'jer] adv the day before yesterday

antebrazo [ante'βraθo] nm forearm

antecedente [anteθe'ðente] adj previous ▷ nm antecedent; **antecedentes** nmpl (historial) record sg; **antecedentes penales** criminal record

anteceder [anteθe'ðer] vt to precede, go before

antecesor, a [anteθe'sor, a] nm/f predecessor

antelación [antela'θjon] nf: **con ~** in advance

antemano [ante'mano]: **de ~** adv beforehand, in advance

antena [an'tena] nf antenna; (de televisión etc) aerial; **antena parabólica** satellite dish

antenoche [ante'notʃe] (LAM) adv the night before last

anteojo [ante'oxo] nm eyeglass; **anteojos** nmpl (LAM: gafas) glasses, spectacles

antepasados [antepa'saðos] nmpl ancestors

anteponer [antepo'ner] vt to place in front of; (fig) to prefer

anterior [ante'rjor] adj preceding, previous; **anterioridad** nf: **con anterioridad a** prior to, before

antes ['antes] adv (con prioridad) before ▷ prep: **~ de** before ▷ conj: **~ de ir/de que te vayas** before going/ before you go; **~ bien** (but) rather; **dos días ~** two days before or previously; **no quiso venir ~** she didn't want to come any earlier; **tomo el avión ~ que el barco** I take the plane rather than the boat; **~ de o que nada** (en el tiempo) first of all; (indicando preferencia) above all; **~ que yo** before me; **lo ~ posible** as soon as possible; **cuanto ~ mejor** the sooner the better

antibalas [anti'βalas] adj inv: **chaleco ~** bullet-proof jacket

antibiótico [anti'βjotiko] nm antibiotic

anticaspa [anti'kaspa] adj inv antidandruff cpd

anticipación [antiθipa'θjon] nf anticipation; **con 10 minutos de ~** 10 minutes early

anticipado, -a [antiθi'paðo, a] adj (pago) advance; **por ~** in advance

anticipar [antiθi'par] vt to anticipate; (adelantar) to bring forward; (Com) to advance; **anticiparse** vr: **~se a su época** to be ahead of one's time

anticipo [anti'θipo] nm (Com) advance

anticonceptivo, -a [antikonθep'tiβo, a] adj, nm contraceptive

anticongelante [antikonxe'lante] nm antifreeze

anticuado, -a [anti'kwaðo, a] adj out-of-date, old-fashioned; (desusado) obsolete

anticuario [anti'kwarjo] nm antique dealer

anticuerpo [anti'kwerpo] nm (Med) antibody

antidepresivo [antiðepre'siβo] nm antidepressant

antidóping [anti'dopin] adj inv: **control ~** drugs test

antídoto [an'tiðoto] nm antidote

antiestético, -a [anties'tetiko, a] adj unsightly

antifaz [anti'faθ] nm mask; (velo) veil

antiglobalización [antiɣloβaliθa'θjon] nf anti-globalization; **antiglobalizador, a** adj anti-globalization cpd

antiguamente [antixwa'mente] adv formerly; (hace mucho tiempo) long ago

antigüedad [antixwe'ðað] nf antiquity; (artículo) antique; (rango) seniority

antiguo, -a [an'tixwo, a] adj old, ancient; (que fue) former

Antillas [an'tiʎas] nfpl: **las ~** the West Indies

antílope [an'tilope] nm antelope

antinatural [antinatu'ral] adj unnatural

antipatía [antipa'tia] nf antipathy, dislike; **antipático, -a** adj disagreeable, unpleasant

antirrobo [anti'rroβo] adj inv (alarma etc) anti-theft

antisemita [antise'mita] adj anti-Semitic ▷nmf anti-Semite

antiséptico, -a [anti'septiko, a] adj antiseptic ▷nm antiseptic

antivirus [anti'birus] nm inv (Comput) antivirus program

antojarse [anto'xarse] vr (desear): **se me antoja comprarlo** I have a mind to buy it; (pensar): **se me antoja que ...** I have a feeling that ...

antojitos [anto'xitos] (MÉX) nmpl snacks, nibbles

antojo [an'toxo] nm caprice, whim; (rosa) birthmark; (lunar) mole

antología [antolo'xia] nf anthology

antorcha [an'tortʃa] nf torch

antro [an'tro] nm cavern

antropología [antropolo'xia] nf anthropology

anual [a'nwal] adj annual

anuario [a'nwarjo] nm yearbook

anublado [anu'blaðo] adj overcast

anulación [anula'θjon] nf annulment; (cancelación) cancellation

anular [anu'lar] vt (contrato) to annul, cancel; (ley) to revoke, repeal; (suscripción) to cancel ▷nm ring finger

anunciar [anun'θjar] vt to announce; (proclamar) to proclaim; (Com) to advertise

anuncio [a'nunθjo] nm announcement; (señal) sign; (Com) advertisement; (cartel) poster

anzuelo [an'θwelo] nm hook; (para pescar) fish hook

añadidura [aɲaði'ðura] nf addition, extra; **por ~** besides, in addition

añadir [aɲa'ðir] vt to add

añejo, -a [a'ɲexo, a] adj old; (vino) mellow

añicos [a'ɲikos] nmpl: **hacer ~** to smash, shatter

año [a'ɲo] nm year; **¡Feliz A~ Nuevo!** Happy New Year!; **tener 15 ~s** to be 15 (years old); **los ~s 90** the nineties; **el ~ que viene** next year; **año bisiesto/ escolar/fiscal/sabático** leap/school/ tax/sabbatical year

añoranza [aɲo'ranθa] nf nostalgia; (anhelo) longing

apa [a'pa] (MÉX) excl goodness me!, good gracious!

abapullar [apaβuˈʎar] vt to crush, squash

apacible [apaˈθiβle] adj gentle, mild

apaciguar [apaθiˈɣwar] vt to pacify, calm (down)

apadrinar [apaðriˈnar] vt to sponsor, support; (Rel) to be godfather to

apagado, -a [apaˈɣaðo, a] adj (volcán) extinct; (color) dull; (voz) quiet; (sonido) muted, muffled; (persona: apático) listless; **estar ~** (fuego, luz) to be out; (Radio, TV etc) to be off

apagar [apaˈɣar] vt to put out; (Elec, Radio, TV) to turn off; (sonido) to silence, muffle; (sed) to quench

apagón [apaˈɣon] nm blackout; power cut

apalabrar [apalaˈβrar] vt to agree to; (contratar) to engage

apalear [apaleˈar] vt to beat, thrash

apantallar [apantaˈʎar] (MÉX) vt to impress

apañar [apaˈɲar] vt to pick up; (asir) to take hold of, grasp; (reparar) to mend, patch up; **apañarse** vr to manage, get along

apapachar [apapaˈtʃar] (MÉX: fam) vt to cuddle, hug

aparador [aparaˈðor] nm sideboard; (MÉX: escaparate) shop window

aparato [apaˈrato] nm apparatus; (máquina) machine; (doméstico) appliance; (boato) ostentation; **al aparato** (Tel) speaking; **aparato digestivo** (Anat) digestive system; **aparatoso, -a** adj showy, ostentatious

aparcamiento [aparkaˈmjento] nm car park, parking lot (US)

aparcar [aparˈkar] vt, vi to park

aparear [apareˈar] vt (objetos) to pair, match; (animales) to mate; **aparearse** vr to make a pair; to mate

aparecer [apareˈθer] vi to appear; **aparecerse** vr to appear

aparejador, a [aparexaˈðor, a] nm/f (Arq) master builder

aparejo [apaˈrexo] nm harness;

rigging; (de poleas) block and tackle

aparentar [aparenˈtar] vt (edad) to look; (fingir): **~ tristeza** to pretend to be sad

aparente [apaˈrente] adj apparent; (adecuado) suitable

aparezco etc vb V **aparecer**

aparición [apariˈθjon] nf appearance; (de libro) publication; (espectro) apparition

apariencia [apaˈrjenθja] nf (outward) appearance; **en ~** outwardly, seemingly

apartado, -a [aparˈtaðo, a] adj separate; (lejano) remote ▷ nm (tipográfico) paragraph; **apartado de correos** (ESP) post office box; **apartado postal** (LAM) post office box

apartamento [apartaˈmento] nm apartment, flat (BRIT)

apartar [aparˈtar] vt to separate; (quitar) to remove; **apartarse** vr to separate, part; (irse) to move away; to keep away

aparte [aˈparte] adv (separadamente) separately; (además) besides ▷ nm aside; (tipográfico) new paragraph

aparthotel [aparˈtotel] nm serviced apartments

apasionado, -a [apasjoˈnaðo, a] adj passionate

apasionar [apasjoˈnar] vt to excite; **le apasiona el fútbol** she's crazy about football; **apasionarse** vr to get excited

apatía [apaˈtia] nf apathy

apático, -a [aˈpatiko, a] adj apathetic

Apdo abr (= Apartado (de Correos)) PO Box

apeadero [apeaˈðero] nm halt, stop, stopping place

apearse [apeˈarse] vr (jinete) to dismount; (bajarse) to get down o out; (Auto, Ferro) to get off o out

apechugar [apetʃuˈɣar] vr: **~ con algo** to face up to sth

apegarse [apeˈɣarse] vr: **~ a**

become attached to; **apego** nm attachment, devotion

apelar [ape'lar] vi to appeal; **~ a** (fig) to resort to

apellidar [apeʎi'ðar] vt to call, name; **apellidarse** vr: **se apellida Pérez** her (sur)name's Pérez

apellido [ape'ʎiðo] nm surname

apenar [ape'nar] vt to grieve, trouble; (LAM: avergonzar) to embarrass; **apenarse** vr to grieve; (LAM: avergonzarse) to be embarrassed

apenas [a'penas] adv scarcely, hardly ▷ conj as soon as, no sooner

apéndice [a'pendiθe] nm appendix; **apendicitis** nf appendicitis

aperitivo [aperi'tiβo] nm (bebida) aperitif; (comida) appetizer

apertura [aper'tura] nf opening; (Pol) liberalization

apestar [apes'tar] vt to infect ▷ vi: **~ (a)** to stink (of)

apetecer [apete'θer] vt: **¿te apetece un café?** do you fancy a (cup of) coffee?; **apetecible** adj desirable; (comida) appetizing

apetito [ape'tito] nm appetite; **apetitoso, -a** adj appetizing; (fig) tempting

apiadarse [apja'ðarse] vr: **~ de** to take pity on

ápice [a'piθe] nm whit, iota

apilar [api'lar] vt to pile o heap up

apiñarse [api'narse] vr to crowd o press together

apio ['apjo] nm celery

apisonadora [apisona'ðora] nf steamroller

aplacar [apla'kar] vt to placate

aplastante [aplas'tante] adj overwhelming; (lógica) compelling

aplastar [aplas'tar] vt to squash (flat); (fig) to crush

aplaudir [aplau'ðir] vt to applaud

aplauso [a'plauso] nm applause; (fig) approval, acclaim

aplazamiento [aplaθa'mjento] nm postponement

aplazar [apla'θar] vt to postpone, defer

aplicación [aplika'θjon] nf application; (esfuerzo) effort

aplicado, -a [apli'kaðo, a] adj diligent, hard-working

aplicar [apli'kar] vt (ejecutar) to apply; **aplicarse** vr to apply o.s.

aplique etc [a'plike] vb V **aplicar** ▷ nm wall light

aplomo [a'plomo] nm aplomb, self-assurance

apodar [apo'ðar] vt to nickname

apoderado [apoðe'raðo] nm agent, representative

apoderarse [apoðe'rarse] vr: **~ de** to take possession of

apodo [a'poðo] nm nickname

apogeo [apo'xeo] nm peak, summit

apoquinar [apoki'nar] (fam) vt to fork out, cough up

aporrear [aporre'ar] vt to beat (up)

aportar [apor'tar] vt to contribute ▷ vi to reach port; **aportarse** vr (LAM: llegar) to arrive, come

aposta [a'posta] adv deliberately, on purpose

apostar [apos'tar] vt to bet, stake; (tropas etc) to station, post ▷ vi to bet

apóstol [a'postol] nm apostle

apóstrofo [a'postrofo] nm apostrophe

apoyar [apo'jar] vt to lean, rest; (fig) to support, back; **apoyarse** vr: **~se en** to lean on; **apoyo** nm (gen) support; backing, help

apreciable [apre'θjaβle] adj considerable; (fig) esteemed

apreciar [apre'θjar] vt to evaluate, assess; (Com) to appreciate, value; (persona) to respect; (tamaño) to gauge, assess; (detalles) to appreciate

aprecio [a'preθjo] nm valuation, estimate; (fig) appreciation

aprehender [apreen'der] vt to apprehend, detain

apremio [a'premjo] nm urgency

aprender [apren'der] vt, vi to learn;

~ algo de memoria to learn sth (off) by heart
aprendiz, a [apren'diθ, a] *nm/f* apprentice; *(principiante)* learner; **aprendizaje** *nm* apprenticeship
aprensión [apren'sjon] *nm* apprehension, fear; **aprensivo, -a** *adj* apprehensive
apresar [apre'sar] *vt* to seize; *(capturar)* to capture
apresurado, -a [apresu'raðo, a] *adj* hurried, hasty
apresurar [apresu'rar] *vt* to hurry, accelerate; **apresurarse** *vr* to hurry, make haste
apretado, -a [apre'taðo, a] *adj* tight; *(escritura)* cramped
apretar [apre'tar] *vt* to squeeze; *(Tec)* to tighten; *(presionar)* to press together, pack ▷ *vi* to be too tight
apretón [apre'ton] *nm* squeeze; **apretón de manos** handshake
aprieto [a'prjeto] *nm* squeeze; *(dificultad)* difficulty; **estar en un ~** to be in a fix
aprisa [a'prisa] *adv* quickly, hurriedly
aprisionar [aprisjo'nar] *vt* to imprison
aprobación [aproβa'θjon] *nf* approval
aprobar [apro'βar] *vt* to approve (of); *(examen, materia)* to pass ▷ *vi* to pass
apropiado, -a [apro'pjaðo, a] *adj* suitable
apropiarse [apro'pjarse] *vr*: **~ de** to appropriate
aprovechado, -a [aproβe'tʃaðo, a] *adj* industrious, hard-working; *(económico)* thrifty; *(pey)* unscrupulous
aprovechar [aproβe'tʃar] *vt* to use; *(explotar)* to exploit; *(experiencia)* to profit from; *(oferta, oportunidad)* to take advantage of ▷ *vi* to progress, improve; **aprovecharse** *vr*: **~se de** to make use of; to take advantage of; **¡que aproveche!** enjoy your meal!
aproximadamente [aproksimaða'mente] *adv*

approximately
aproximación [aproksima'θjon] *nf* approximation; *(de lotería)* consolation prize
aproximar [aproksi'mar] *vt* to bring nearer; **aproximarse** *vr* to come near, approach
apruebo *etc vb* V **aprobar**
aptitud [apti'tuð] *nf* aptitude
apto, -a [a'apto, a] *adj* suitable
apuesta [a'pwesta] *nf* bet, wager
apuesto, -a [a'pwesto, a] *adj* neat, elegant
apuntar [apun'tar] *vt* *(con arma)* to aim at; *(con dedo)* to point at o to; *(anotar)* to note (down); *(Teatro)* to prompt; **apuntarse** *vr* *(Deporte: tanto, victoria)* to score; *(Escol)* to enrol

No confundir **apuntar** con la palabra inglesa **appoint**.

apunte [a'punte] *nm* note
apuñalar [apuɲa'lar] *vt* to stab
apurado, -a [apu'raðo, a] *adj* needy; *(difícil)* difficult; *(peligroso)* dangerous; *(LAM: con prisa)* hurried, rushed
apurar [apu'rar] *vt* *(agotar)* to drain; *(recursos)* to use up; *(molestar)* to annoy; **apurarse** *vr* *(preocuparse)* to worry; *(LAM: darse prisa)* to hurry
apuro [a'puro] *nm* *(aprieto)* fix, jam; *(escasez)* want, hardship; *(vergüenza)* embarrassment; *(LAM: prisa)* haste, urgency
aquejado, -a [ake'xaðo, a] *adj*: **~ de** *(Med)* afflicted by
aquel, aquella [a'kel, a'keʎa] *adj* that; **~los(as)** those
aquél, aquélla [a'kel, a'keʎa] *pron* that (one); **~los(as)** those (ones)
aquello [a'keʎo] *pron* that, that business
aquí [a'ki] *adv* *(lugar)* here; *(tiempo)* now; **~ arriba** up here; **~ mismo** right here; **~ yace** here lies; **de ~ a siete días** a week from now
ara ['ara] *nf*: **en ~s de** for the sake of
árabe ['araβe] *adj, nmf* Arab ▷ *nm* *(Ling)* Arabic

Arabia [a'raβja] nf Arabia; **Arabia Saudí** o **Saudita** Saudi Arabia

arado [a'raðo] nm plough

Aragón [ara'yon] nm Aragon; **aragonés, -esa** adj, nm/f Aragonese

arancel [aran'θel] nm tariff, duty

arandela [aran'dela] nf (Tec) washer

araña [a'raɲa] nf (Zool) spider; (lámpara) chandelier

arañar [ara'ɲar] vt to scratch

arañazo [ara'ɲaθo] nm scratch

arbitrar [arβi'trar] vt to arbitrate in; (Deporte) to referee ▷ vi to arbitrate

arbitrario, -a [arβi'trarjo, a] adj arbitrary

árbitro ['arβitro] nm arbitrator; (Deporte) referee; (Tenis) umpire

árbol ['arβol] nm (Bot) tree; (Náut) mast; (Tec) axle, shaft; **árbol de Navidad** Christmas tree

arboleda [arβo'leða] nf grove, plantation

arbusto [ar'βusto] nm bush, shrub

arca ['arka] nf chest, box

arcada [ar'kaða] nf arcade; (de puente) arch, span; **arcadas** nfpl (náuseas) retching sg

arcaico, -a [ar'kaiko, a] adj archaic

arce ['arθe] nm maple tree

arcén [ar'θen] nm (de autopista) hard shoulder; (de carretera) verge

archipiélago [artʃi'pjelaxo] nm archipelago

archivador [artʃiβa'ðor] nm filing cabinet

archivar [artʃi'βar] vt to file (away); **archivo** nm file, archive(s) pl; **archivo adjunto** (Inform) attachment; **archivo de seguridad** (Inform) backup file

arcilla [ar'θiʎa] nf clay

arco ['arko] nm arch; (Mat) arc; (Mil, Mús) bow; **arco iris** rainbow

arder [ar'ðer] vi to burn; **estar que arde** (persona) to fume

ardid [ar'ðið] nm ploy, trick

ardiente [ar'ðjente] adj burning, ardent

ardilla [ar'ðiʎa] nf squirrel

ardor [ar'ðor] nm (calor) heat; (fig) ardour; **ardor de estómago** heartburn

arduo, -a ['arðwo, a] adj arduous

área ['area] nf area; (Deporte) penalty area

arena [a'rena] nf sand; (de una lucha) arena; **arenas movedizas** quicksand sg; **arenal** [are'nal] nm (terreno arenoso) sandy spot

arenisca [are'niska] nf sandstone; (cascajo) grit

arenoso, -a [are'noso, a] adj sandy

arenque [a'renke] nm herring

arete [a'rete] (MÉX) nm earring

Argel [ar'xel] n Algiers; **Argelia** nf Algeria; **argelino, -a** adj, nm/f Algerian

Argentina [arxen'tina] nf (tb: **la -**) Argentina

argentino, -a [arxen'tino, a] adj Argentinian; (de plata) silvery ▷ nm/f Argentinian

argolla [ar'yoʎa] nf (large) ring

argot [ar'yo] (pl **-s**) nm slang

argucia [ar'yuθja] nf subtlety, sophistry

argumentar [aryumen'tar] vt, vi to argue

argumento [aryu'mento] nm argument; (razonamiento) reasoning; (de novela etc) plot; (Cine, TV) storyline

aria ['arja] nf aria

aridez [ari'ðeθ] nf aridity, dryness

árido, -a ['ariðo, a] adj arid, dry

Aries ['arjes] nm Aries

arisco, -a [a'risko, a] adj surly; (insociable) unsociable

aristócrata [aris'tokrata] nmf aristocrat

arma ['arma] nf arm; **armas** nfpl arms; **armas blanca** blade, knife; **arma de doble filo** double-edged sword; **arma de fuego** firearm; **armas de destrucción masiva** weapons of mass destruction

armada [ar'maða] nf armada; (flota) fleet

armadillo [arma'ðiʎo] nm armadillo

armado, -a [ar'maðo, a] *adj* armed;
(*Tec*) reinforced

armadura [arma'ðura] *nf* (*Mil*)
armour; (*Tec*) framework; (*Zool*)
skeleton; (*Física*) armature

armamento [arma'mento] *nm*
armament; (*Náut*) fitting-out

armar [ar'mar] *vt* (*soldado*) to arm;
(*máquina*) to assemble; (*navío*) to fit
out; **~la, ~ un lío** to start a row, kick
up a fuss

armario [ar'marjo] *nm* wardrobe;
(*de cocina, baño*) cupboard; **armario
empotrado** built-in cupboard

armatoste [arma'toste] *nm* (*mueble*)
monstrosity; (*máquina*) contraption

armazón [arma'θon] *nf o m* body,
chassis; (*de mueble etc*) frame; (*Arq*)
skeleton

armiño [ar'miɲo] *nm* stoat; (*piel*)
ermine

armisticio [armis'tiθjo] *nm*
armistice

armonía [armo'nia] *nf* harmony

armónica [ar'monika] *nf* harmonica

armonizar [armoni'θar] *vt* to
harmonize; (*diferencias*) to reconcile

aro ['aro] *nm* ring; (*tejo*) quoit;
(*cs: pendiente*) earring

aroma [a'roma] *nm* aroma, scent;
aromaterapia *n* aromatherapy;
aromático, -a [aro'matiko, a] *adj*
aromatic

arpa ['arpa] *nf* harp

arpía [ar'pia] *nf* shrew

arpón [ar'pon] *nm* harpoon

arqueología [arkeolo'xia] *nf*
archaeology; **arqueólogo, -a** *nm/f*
archaeologist

arquetipo [arke'tipo] *nm* archetype

arquitecto [arki'tekto] *nm*
architect; **arquitectura** *nf*
architecture

arrabal [arra'βal] *nm* poor suburb,
slum; **arrabales** *nmpl* (*afueras*)
outskirts

arraigar [arrai'ɣar] *vt* to establish
▷ *vi* to take root

arrancar [arran'kar] *vt* (*sacar*) to
extract, pull out; (*arrebatar*) to snatch
(away); (*Inform*) to boot; (*fig*) to extract
▷ *vi* (*Auto, máquina*) to start; (*ponerse en
marcha*) to get going; **~ de** to stem from

arranque *etc* [a'rranke] *vb* V
arrancar ▷ *nm* sudden start; (*Auto*)
start; (*fig*) fit, outburst

arrasar [arra'sar] *vt* (*aplanar*) to level,
flatten; (*destruir*) to demolish

arrastrar [arras'trar] *vt* to drag
(along); (*fig*) to drag down, degrade;
(*agua, viento*) to carry away ▷ *vi* to
drag, trail on the ground; **arrastrarse**
vr to crawl; (*fig*) to grovel; **llevar algo
arrastrado** to drag sth along

arrear [arre'ar] *vt* to drive on, urge on
▷ *vi* to hurry along

arrebatar [arreβa'tar] *vt* to snatch
(away), seize; (*fig*) to captivate

arrebato [arre'βato] *nm* fit of rage,
fury; (*éxtasis*) rapture

arrecife [arre'θife] *nm* reef

arreglado, -a [arre'ɣlaðo, a] *adj*
(*ordenado*) neat, orderly; (*moderado*)
moderate, reasonable

arreglar [arre'ɣlar] *vt* (*poner orden*)
to tidy up; (*algo roto*) to fix, repair;
(*problema*) to solve; **arreglarse** *vr* to
reach an understanding; **arreglárselas**
(*fam*) to get by, manage

arreglo [a'rreɣlo] *nm* settlement;
(*orden*) order; (*acuerdo*) agreement;
(*Mús*) arrangement, setting

arremangar [arreman'gar] *vt* to roll
up, turn up; **arremangarse** *vr* to roll
up one's sleeves

arremeter [arreme'ter] *vi*: **~ contra**
to attack, rush at

arrendamiento [arrenda'mjento]
nm letting; (*alquilar*) hiring; (*contrato*)
lease; (*alquiler*) rent; **arrendar** *vt* to
let, lease; to rent; **arrendatario, -a**
nm/f tenant

arreos [a'rreos] *nmpl* (*de caballo*)
harness *sg*, trappings

arrepentimiento
[arrepenti'mjento] *nm* regret,

repentance
arrepentirse [arrepen'tirse] vr to
repent; **~ de** to regret
arresto [a'rresto] nm arrest; (Mil)
detention; (audacia) boldness, daring;
arresto domiciliario house arrest
arriar [a'rrjar] vt (velas) to haul down;
(bandera) to lower, strike; (cable) to
pay out

⚪ **PALABRA CLAVE**

arriba [a'rriβa] adv **1** (posición) above;
desde arriba from above; **arriba de
todo** at the very top, right on top; **Juan
está arriba** Juan is upstairs; **lo arriba
mencionado** the aforementioned
2 (dirección): **calle arriba** up the street
3 **de arriba abajo** from top to bottom;
mirar a algn de arriba abajo to look
sb up and down
4 **para arriba: de 5000 euros
para arriba** from 5000 euros
up(wards)
▷ adj: **de arriba: el piso de arriba** the
upstairs (BRIT) flat o apartment; **la
parte de arriba** the top o upper part
▷ prep: **arriba de** (LAM: por encima de)
above; **arriba de 200 dólares** more
than 200 dollars
▷ excl: **¡arriba!** up!; **¡manos arriba!**
hands up!; **¡arriba España!** long live
Spain!

arribar [arri'βar] vi to put into port;
(llegar) to arrive
arriendo etc [a'rrjendo] vb V
arrendar ▷ nm = **arrendamiento**
arriesgado, -a [arrjes'xaðo, a] adj
(peligroso) risky; (audaz) bold, daring
arriesgar [arrjes'xar] vt to risk;
(poner en peligro) to endanger;
arriesgarse vr to take a risk
arrimar [arri'mar] vt (acercar) to
bring close; (poner de lado) to set aside;
arrimarse vr to come close o closer;
~se a to lean on
arrinconar [arrinko'nar] vt (colocar)

to put in a corner; (enemigo) to corner;
(fig) to put on one side; (abandonar) to
push aside
arroba [a'rroβa] nf (Internet) at (sign)
arrodillarse [arroði'ʎarse] vr to
kneel (down)
arrogante [arro'xante] adj arrogant
arrojar [arro'xar] vt to throw, hurl;
(humo) to emit, give out; (Com) to
yield, produce; **arrojarse** vr to throw
o hurl o.s.
arrojo [a'rroxo] nm daring
arrollador, -a [arroʎa'ðor, a] adj
overwhelming
arrollar [arro'ʎar] vt (Auto etc) to run
over, knock down; (Deporte) to crush
arropar [arro'par] vt to cover, wrap
up; **arroparse** vr to wrap o.s. up
arroyo [a'rrojo] nm stream; (de la
calle) gutter
arroz [a'rroθ] nm rice; **arroz con
leche** rice pudding
arruga [a'rruxa] nf (de cara) wrinkle;
(de vestido) crease; **arrugar** [arru'xar]
vt to wrinkle; to crease; **arrugarse** vr
to get creased
arruinar [arrwi'nar] vt to ruin,
wreck; **arruinarse** vr to be ruined,
go bankrupt
arsenal [arse'nal] nm naval
dockyard; (Mil) arsenal
arte [a'rte] (gen m en sg y siempre f en pl)
nm art; (maña) skill, guile; **artes** nfpl
(bellas artes) arts
artefacto [arte'fakto] nm appliance
arteria [ar'terja] nf artery
artesanía [artesa'nia] nf
craftsmanship; (artículos) handicrafts
pl; **artesano, -a** nm/f artisan,
craftsman(-woman)
ártico, -a [a'rtiko, a] adj Arctic
▷ nm: **el Á~** the Arctic
articulación [artikula'θjon] nf
articulation; (Med, Tec) joint
artículo [ar'tikulo] nm article;
(cosa) thing, article; **artículos** nmpl
(Com) goods; **artículos de escritorio**
stationery

artífice [ar'tifiθe] nmf (fig) architect
artificial [artifi'θjal] adj artificial
artillería [artiλe'ria] nf artillery
artilugio [arti'luxjo] nm gadget
artimaña [arti'maɲa] nf trap, snare; (astucia) cunning
artista [ar'tista] nmf (pintor) artist, painter; (Teatro) artist, artiste; **artista de cine** film actor/actress; **artístico, -a** adj artistic
artritis [ar'tritis] nf arthritis
arveja [ar'βexa] (LAM) nf pea
arzobispo [arθo'βispo] nm archbishop
as [as] nm ace
asa ['asa] nf handle; (fig) lever
asado [a'saðo] nm roast (meat); (LAM: barbacoa) barbecue

● **ASADO**
●
● Traditional Latin American
● barbecues, especially in the River
● Plate area, are celebrated in the
● open air around a large grill
● which is used to grill mainly beef
● and various kinds of spicy pork
● sausage. They are usually very
● common during the summer and
● can go on for several days. The
● head cook is nearly always a man.

asador [asa'ðor] nm spit
asadura [asa'ðura] nf entrails pl, offal
asalariado, -a [asala'rjaðo, a] adj paid, salaried ▷nf wage earner
asaltar [asal'tar] vt to attack, assault; (fig) to assail; **asalto** nm attack, assault; (Deporte) round
asamblea [asam'blea] nf assembly; (reunión) meeting
asar [a'sar] vt to roast
ascendencia [asθen'denθja] nf ancestry; (LAM: influencia) ascendancy; **de ~ francesa** of French origin
ascender [asθen'der] vi (subir) to ascend, rise; (ser promovido) to

gain promotion ▷vt to promote; **~ a** to amount to; **ascendiente** nm influence ▷nmf ancestor
ascensión [asθen'sjon] nf ascent; (Rel): **la A~** the Ascension
ascenso [as'θenso] nm ascent; (promoción) promotion
ascensor [asθen'sor] nm lift (BRIT), elevator (US)
asco ['asko] nm: **¡qué ~!** how revolting o disgusting; **el ajo me da ~** I hate o loathe garlic; **estar hecho un ~** to be filthy
ascua ['askwa] nf ember
aseado, -a [ase'aðo, a] adj clean; (arreglado) tidy; (pulcro) smart
asear [ase'ar] vt to clean, wash; to tidy (up)
asediar [ase'ðjar] vt (Mil) to besiege, lay siege to; (fig) to chase, pester; **asedio** nm siege; (Com) run
asegurado, -a [aseɣu'raðo, a] adj insured
asegurador, a [aseɣura'ðor, a] nm/f insurer
asegurar [aseɣu'rar] vt (consolidar) to secure, fasten; (dar garantía de) to guarantee; (preservar) to safeguard; (afirmar, dar por cierto) to assure, affirm; (tranquilizar) to reassure; (tomar un seguro) to insure; **asegurarse** vr to assure o.s., make sure
asemejarse [aseme'xarse] vr to be alike; **~ a** to be like, resemble
asentado, -a [asen'taðo, a] adj established, settled
asentar [asen'tar] vt (sentar) to seat, sit down; (poner) to place, establish; (alisar) to level, smooth down o out; (anotar) to note down ▷vi to be suitable, suit
asentir [asen'tir] vi to assent, agree; **~ con la cabeza** to nod (one's head)
aseo [a'seo] nm cleanliness; **aseos** nmpl (servicios) toilet sg (BRIT), cloakroom sg (BRIT), restroom sg (US)
aséptico, -a [a'septiko, a] adj germ-free, free from infection

asequible [ase'kiβle] adj (precio) reasonable; (meta) attainable; (persona) approachable

asesinar [asesi'nar] vt to murder; (Pol) to assassinate; **asesinato** nm murder; assassination

asesino, -a [ase'sino, a] nm/f murderer, killer; (Pol) assassin

asesor, a [ase'sor, a] nm/f adviser, consultant; **asesorar** [aseso'rar] vt (Jur) to advise, give legal advice to; (Com) to act as consultant to; **asesorarse** vr: **asesorarse con o de** to take advice from, consult; **asesoría** nf (cargo) consultancy; (oficina) consultant's office

asestar [ases'tar] vt (golpe) to deal, strike

asfalto [as'falto] nm asphalt

asfixia [as'fiksja] nf asphyxia, suffocation; **asfixiar** [asfik'sjar] vt to asphyxiate, suffocate; **asfixiarse** vr to be asphyxiated, suffocate

así [a'si] adv (de esta manera) in this way, thus; (aunque) although; (tan pronto como) as soon as; **~ que** so; **~ como** as well as; **~ y todo** even so; **¿no es ~?** isn't it?, didn't you? etc; **~ de grande** this big

Asia ['asja] nf Asia; **asiático, -a** adj, nm/f Asian, Asiatic

asiduo, -a [a'siðwo, a] adj assiduous; (frecuente) frequent ▷ nm/f regular (customer)

asiento [a'sjento] nm (mueble) seat, chair; (de coche, en tribunal etc) seat; (localidad) seat; (fundamento) site; **asiento delantero/trasero** front/back seat

asignación [asiɣna'θjon] nf (atribución) assignment; (reparto) allocation; (sueldo) salary; **asignación (semanal)** pocket money

asignar [asiɣ'nar] vt to assign, allocate

asignatura [asiɣna'tura] nf subject; course

asilo [a'silo] nm (refugio) asylum,

refuge; (establecimiento) home, institution; **asilo político** political asylum

asimilar [asimi'lar] vt to assimilate

asimismo [asi'mismo] adv in the same way, likewise

asistencia [asis'tenθja] nf audience; (Med) attendance; (ayuda) assistance; **asistencia en carretera** roadside assistance; **asistente** nmf assistant; **los asistentes** those present; **asistente social** social worker

asistido, -a [asis'tiðo, a] adj: **~ por ordenador** computer-assisted

asistir [asis'tir] vt to assist, help ▷ vi: **~ a** to attend, be present at

asma ['asma] nf asthma

asno ['asno] nm donkey; (fig) ass

asociación [asoθja'θjon] nf association; (Com) partnership; **asociado, -a** adj associate ▷ nm/f associate; (Com) partner

asociar [aso'θjar] vt to associate

asomar [aso'mar] vt to show, stick out ▷ vi to appear; **asomarse** vr to appear, show up; **~ la cabeza por la ventana** to put one's head out of the window

asombrar [asom'brar] vt to amaze, astonish; **asombrarse** vr (sorprenderse) to be amazed; (asustarse) to get a fright; **asombro** nm amazement, astonishment; (susto) fright; **asombroso, -a** adj astonishing, amazing

asomo [a'somo] nm hint, sign

aspa ['aspa] nf (cruz) cross; (de molino) sail; **en ~** X-shaped

aspaviento [aspa'βjento] nm exaggerated display of feeling; (fam) fuss

aspecto [as'pekto] nm (apariencia) look, appearance; (fig) aspect

áspero, -a ['aspero, a] adj rough; bitter; sour; harsh

aspersión [asper'sjon] nf sprinkling

aspiración [aspira'θjon] nf breath, inhalation; (Mús) short pause;

aspiraciones nfpl (ambiciones) aspirations

aspirador [aspira'ðor] nm = **aspiradora**

aspiradora [aspira'ðora] nf vacuum cleaner, Hoover®

aspirante [aspi'rante] nmf (candidato) candidate; (Deporte) contender

aspirar [aspi'rar] vt to breathe in ▷ vi: ~ a to aspire to

aspirina [aspi'rina] nf aspirin

asqueroso, -a [aske'roso, a] adj disgusting, sickening

asta ['asta] nf lance; (arpón) spear; (mango) shaft, handle; (Zool) horn; **a media** ~ at half mast

asterisco [aste'risko] nm asterisk

astilla [as'tiʎa] nf splinter; (pedacito) chip; **astillas** nfpl (leña) firewood sg

astillero [asti'ʎero] nm shipyard

astro ['astro] nm star

astrología [astrolo'xia] nf astrology; **astrólogo, -a** nm/f astrologer

astronauta [astro'nauta] nmf astronaut

astronomía [astrono'mia] nf astronomy

astucia [as'tuθja] nf astuteness; (ardid) clever trick

asturiano, -a [astu'rjano, a] adj, nm/f Asturian

astuto, -a [as'tuto, a] adj astute; (taimado) cunning

asumir [asu'mir] vt to assume

asunción [asun'θjon] nf assumption; (Rel): **A~** Assumption

asunto [a'sunto] nm (tema) matter, subject; (negocio) business

asustar [asus'tar] vt to frighten; **asustarse** vr to be (o become) frightened

atacar [ata'kar] vt to attack

atadura [ata'ðura] nf bond, tie

atajar [ata'xar] vt (enfermedad, mal) to stop ▷ vi (persona) to take a short cut

atajo [a'taxo] nm short cut

atañer [ata'ɲer] vi: ~ a to concern

ataque etc [a'take] vb V **atacar** ▷ nm attack; **ataque cardíaco** heart attack

atar [a'tar] vt to tie, tie up

atarantado, -a [ataran'taðo, a] (MÉX) adj (aturdido) dazed

atardecer [atarðe'θer] vi to get dark ▷ nm evening; (crepúsculo) dusk

atareado, -a [atare'aðo, a] adj busy

atascar [atas'kar] vt to clog up; (obstruir) to jam; (fig) to hinder; **atascarse** vr to stall; (cañería) to get blocked up; **atasco** nm obstruction; (Auto) traffic jam

ataúd [ata'uð] nm coffin

ataviar [ata'βjar] vt to deck, array

atemorizar [atemori'θar] vt to frighten, scare

Atenas [a'tenas] n Athens

atención [aten'θjon] nf attention; (bondad) kindness ▷ excl (be) careful!, look out!

atender [aten'der] vt to attend to, look after; (Tel) to answer ▷ vi to pay attention

atenerse [ate'nerse] vr: ~ a to abide by, adhere to

atentado [aten'taðo] nm crime, illegal act; (asalto) assault; (tb: ~ **terrorista**) terrorist attack; ~ **contra la vida de algn** attempt on sb's life; **atentado suicida** suicide bombing

atentamente [atenta'mente] adv: **Le saluda ~** Yours faithfully

atentar [aten'tar] vi: ~ **a o contra** to commit an outrage against

atento, -a [a'tento, a] adj attentive, observant; (cortés) polite, thoughtful; **estar ~** (explicación) to pay attention to

atenuar [ate'nwar] vt (disminuir) to lessen, minimize

ateo, -a [a'teo, a] adj atheistic ▷ nm/f atheist

aterrador, a [aterra'ðor, a] adj frightening

aterrizaje [aterri'θaxe] nm landing; **aterrizaje forzoso** emergency o forced landing

aterrizar [aterri'θar] vi to land

aterrorizar [aterrori'θar] vt to terrify

atesorar [ateso'rar] vt to hoard

atestar [ates'tar] vt to pack, stuff; (Jur) to attest, testify to

atestiguar [atesti'ɣwar] vt to testify to, bear witness to

atiborrar [atiβo'rrar] vt to fill, stuff; **atiborrarse** vr to stuff o.s.

ático ['atiko] nm (desván) attic; (apartamento) penthouse

atinado, -a [ati'naðo, a] adj (sensato) wise; (correcto) right, correct

atinar [ati'nar] vi (al disparar): ~ **al blanco** to hit the target; (fig) to be right

atizar [ati'θar] vt to poke; (horno etc) to stoke; (fig) to stir up, rouse

atlántico, -a [at'lantiko, a] adj Atlantic ▷ nm: **el (océano) A~** the Atlantic (Ocean)

atlas ['atlas] nm inv atlas

atleta [at'leta] nm athlete; **atlético, -a** adj athletic; **atletismo** nm athletics sg

atmósfera [at'mosfera] nf atmosphere

atolladero [atoʎa'ðero] nm (fig) jam, fix

atómico, -a [a'tomiko, a] adj atomic

átomo ['atomo] nm atom

atónito, -a [a'tonito, a] adj astonished, amazed

atontado, -a [aton'taðo, a] adj stunned; (bobo) silly, daft

atormentar [atormen'tar] vt to torture; (molestar) to torment; (acosar) to plague, harass

atornillar [atorni'ʎar] vt to screw on o down

atosigar [atosi'ɣar] vt to harass, pester

atracador, a [atraka'ðor, a] nm/f robber

atracar [atra'kar] vt (Náut) to moor; (robar) to hold up, rob ▷ vi to moor; **atracarse** vr: **~se (de)** to stuff o.s.

(with)

atracción [atrak'θjon] nf attraction

atraco [a'trako] nm holdup, robbery

atracón [atra'kon] nm: **darse o pegarse un ~ (de)** (fam) to stuff o.s. (with)

atractivo, -a [atrak'tiβo, a] adj attractive ▷ nm appeal

atraer [atra'er] vt to attract

atragantarse [atraɣan'tarse] vr: **~ (con)** to choke (on); **se me ha atragantado el chico** I can't stand the boy

atrancar [atran'kar] vt (puerta) to bar, bolt

atrapar [atra'par] vt to trap; (resfriado etc) to catch

atrás [a'tras] adv (movimiento) back(-wards); (lugar) behind; (tiempo) previously; **ir hacia ~** to go back(wards), to go to the rear; **estar ~** to be behind o at the back

atrasado, -a [atra'saðo, a] adj slow; (pago) overdue, late; (país) backward

atrasar [atra'sar] vi to be slow; **atrasarse** vr to remain behind; (tren) to be o run late; **atraso** nm slowness, lateness, delay; (de país) backwardness; **atrasos** nmpl (Com) arrears

atravesar [atraβe'sar] vt (cruzar) to cross (over); (traspasar) to pierce; to go through; (poner al través) to lay o put across; **atravesarse** vr to come in between; (intervenir) to interfere

atravieso etc vb V **atravesar**

atreverse [atre'βerse] vr to dare; (insolentarse) to be insolent; **atrevido, -a** adj daring; insolent; **atrevimiento** nm daring; insolence

atribución [atriβu'θjon] nf attribution; **atribuciones** nfpl (Pol) powers; (Admin) responsibilities

atribuir [atriβu'ir] vt to attribute; (funciones) to confer

atributo [atri'βuto] nm attribute

atril [a'tril] nm (para libro) lectern; (Mús) music stand

atropellar [atrope'ʎar] vt (derribar)

to knock over o down; (*empujar*) to push (aside); (*Auto*) to run over, run down; (*agraviar*) to insult; **atropello** *nm* (*Auto*) accident; (*empujón*) push; (*agravio*) wrong; (*atrocidad*) outrage

atroz [a'troθ] *adj* atrocious, awful

ATS *nmf abr* (*= Ayudante Técnico Sanitario*) nurse

atuendo [a'twendo] *nm* attire

atún [a'tun] *nm* tuna

aturdir [atur'ðir] *vt* to stun; (*de ruido*) to deafen; (*fig*) to dumbfound, bewilder

audacia [au'ðaθja] *nf* boldness, audacity; **audaz** *adj* bold, audacious

audición [auði'θjon] *nf* hearing; (*Teatro*) audition

audiencia [au'ðjenθja] *nf* audience; (*Jur: tribunal*) court

audífono [au'ðifono] *nm* (*para sordos*) hearing aid

auditor [auði'tor] *nm* (*Jur*) judge advocate; (*Com*) auditor

auditorio [auði'torjo] *nm* audience; (*sala*) auditorium

auge ['auxe] *nm* boom; (*clímax*) climax

augurar [auxu'rar] *vt* to predict; (*presagiar*) to portend

augurio [au'xurjo] *nm* omen

aula ['aula] *nf* classroom; (*en universidad etc*) lecture room

aullar [au'ʎar] *vi* to howl, yell

aullido [au'ʎiðo] *nm* howl, yell

aumentar [aumen'tar] *vt* to increase; (*precios*) to put up; (*producción*) to step up; (*con microscopio, anteojos*) to magnify ▷ *vi* to increase, be on the increase; **aumentarse** *vr* to increase, be on the increase; **aumento** *nm* increase; rise

aun [a'un] *adv* even; ~ **así** even so; ~ **más** even o yet more

aún [a'un] *adv*: ~ **está aquí** he's still here; ~ **no lo sabemos** we don't know yet; **¿no ha venido ~?** hasn't she come yet?

aunque [a'unke] *conj* though, although, even though

aúpa [a'upa] *excl* come on!

auricular [auriku'lar] *nm* (*Tel*) receiver; **auriculares** *nmpl* (*cascos*) headphones

aurora [au'rora] *nf* dawn

ausencia [au'senθja] *nf* absence

ausentarse [ausen'tarse] *vr* to go away; (*por poco tiempo*) to go out

ausente [au'sente] *adj* absent

austero, -a [aus'tero, a] *adj* austere

austral [aus'tral] *adj* southern ▷ *nm* monetary unit of Argentina

Australia [aus'tralja] *nf* Australia; **australiano, -a** *adj, nm/f* Australian

Austria ['austrja] *nf* Austria; **austríaco, -a** *adj, nm/f* Austrian

auténtico, -a [au'tentiko, a] *adj* authentic

auto ['auto] *nm* (*Jur*) edict, decree; (: *orden*) writ; (*Auto*) car; **autos** *nmpl* (*Jur*) proceedings; (: *acta*) court record *sg*

autoadhesivo [autoaðe'siβo] *adj* self-adhesive; (*sobre*) self-sealing

autobiografía [autoβjoxra'fia] *nf* autobiography

autobomba [auto'bomba] (*RPL*) *nf* fire engine

autobronceador [autoβronθea'ðor] *adj* self-tanning

autobús [auto'βus] *nm* bus; **autobús de línea** long-distance coach

autocar [auto'kar] *nm* coach (*BRIT*), (*passenger*) bus (*US*)

autóctono, -a [au'toktono, a] *adj* native, indigenous

autodefensa [autoðe'fensa] *nf* self-defence

autodidacta [autoði'ðakta] *adj* self-taught

autoescuela [autoes'kwela] (*ESP*) *nf* driving school

autógrafo [au'toxrafo] *nm* autograph

autómata [au'tomata] *nm* automaton

automático, -a [auto'matiko, a] *adj* automatic ▷ *nm* press stud

automóvil [auto'moβil] *nm*

(motor) car (BRIT), automobile (US);
automovilismo nm (actividad)
motoring; (Deporte) motor racing;
automovilista nmf motorist, driver
autonomía [auto'nomia] nf
autonomy; **autónomo, -a** (ESP),
autonómico, -a (ESP) adj (Pol)
autonomous
autopista [auto'pista] nf motorway
(BRIT), freeway (US); **autopista de
cuota** (ESP) o **peaje** (MÉX) toll (BRIT) o
turnpike (US) road
autopsia [au'topsja] nf autopsy,
postmortem
autor, a [au'tor, a] nm/f author
autoridad [autori'ðað] nf authority;
autoritario, -a adj authoritarian
autorización [autoriθa'θjon] nf
authorization; **autorizado, -a** adj
authorized; (aprobado) approved
autorizar [autori'θar] vt to
authorize; (aprobar) to approve
autoservicio [autoser'βiθjo] nm
(tienda) self-service shop (BRIT) o
store (US); (restaurante) self-service
restaurant
autostop [auto'stop] nm hitch-
hiking; **hacer ~** to hitch-hike;
autostopista nmf hitch-hiker
autovía [auto'βia] nf = A-road
(BRIT), dual carriageway (BRIT), = state
highway (US)
auxiliar [auksi'ljar] vt to help ▷ nf
assistant; **auxilio** nm assistance, help;
primeros auxilios first aid sg
Av abr (= Avenida) Av(e)
aval [a'βal] nm guarantee; (persona)
guarantor
avalancha [aβa'lantʃa] nf avalanche
avance [a'βanθe] nm advance; (pago)
advance payment; (Cine) trailer
avanzar [aβan'θar] vt, vi to advance
avaricia [aβa'riθja] nf avarice, greed;
avaricioso, -a avaricious, greedy
avaro, -a [a'βaro, a] adj miserly,
mean ▷ nm/f miser
Avda abr (= Avenida) Av(e)
AVE ['aβe] nm sf abr (= Alta Velocidad

Española) ≈ bullet train
ave ['aβe] nf bird; **ave de rapiña**
bird of prey
avecinarse [aβeθi'narse] vr
(tormenta: fig) to be on the way
avellana [aβe'ʎana] nf hazelnut;
avellano nm hazel tree
avemaría [aβema'ria] nm Hail Mary,
Ave Maria
avena [a'βena] nf oats pl
avenida [aβe'niða] nf (calle) avenue
aventajar [aβenta'xar] vt
(sobrepasar) to surpass, outstrip
aventón [aβen'ton] nm (MÉX: fam) nm
ride; **dar ~ a algn** to give sb a ride
aventura [aβen'tura] nf adventure;
aventurero, -a adj adventurous
avergonzar [aβerxon'θar] vt to
shame; (desconcertar) to embarrass;
avergonzarse vr to be ashamed; to be
embarrassed
avería [aβe'ria] nf (Tec) breakdown,
fault
averiado, -a [aβe'rjaðo, a] adj
broken down; **"~"** "out of order"
averiarse [aβe'rjarse] vr to break
down
averiguar [aβeri'ɣwar] vt to
investigate; (descubrir) to find out,
ascertain
avestruz [aβes'truθ] nm ostrich
aviación [aβja'θjon] nf aviation;
(fuerzas aéreas) air force
aviador, a [aβja'ðor, a] nm/f aviator,
airman(-woman)
ávido, -a [a'βiðo, a] adj avid, eager
avinagrado, -a [aβina'ɣraðo, a] adj
sour, acid
avión [a'βjon] nm aeroplane, (ave)
martin; **avión de reacción** jet (plane)
avioneta [aβjo'neta] nf light aircraft
avisar [aβi'sar] vt (advertir) to warn,
notify; (informar) to tell; (aconsejar) to
advise, counsel; **aviso** nm warning;
(noticia) notice
avispa [a'βispa] nf wasp
avispado, -a [aβis'paðo, a] adj
sharp, clever

avivar [aβiˈβar] vt to strengthen, intensify

axila [akˈsila] nf armpit

ay [ai] excl (dolor) owl, ouch!; (aflicción) oh!, oh dear!; **¡~ de mí!** poor me!

ayer [aˈjer] adv, nm yesterday; **antes de ~** the day before yesterday; **~ mismo** only yesterday

ayote [aˈjote] (CAM) nm pumpkin

ayuda [aˈjuða] nf help, assistance ▷ nm page; **ayudante** nmf assistant, helper; (Escol) assistant; (Mil) adjutant

ayudar [ajuˈðar] vt to help, assist

ayunar [ajuˈnar] vi to fast; **ayunas** nfpl: **estar en ayunas** to be fasting; **ayuno** nm fast; fasting

ayuntamiento [ajuntaˈmjento] nm (consejo) town (o city) council; (edificio) town (o city) hall

azafata [aθaˈfata] nf air stewardess

azafrán [aθaˈfran] nm saffron

azahar [aθaˈar] nm orange/lemon blossom

azar [aˈθar] nm (casualidad) chance, fate; (desgracia) misfortune, accident; **por ~** by chance; **al ~** at random

Azores [aˈθores] nfpl: **las ~** the Azores

azotar [aθoˈtar] vt to whip, beat; (pegar) to spank; **azote** nm (látigo) whip; (latigazo) lash, stroke; (en las nalgas) spank; (calamidad) calamity

azotea [aθoˈtea] nf (flat) roof

azteca [aθˈteka] adj, nmf Aztec

azúcar [aˈθukar] nm sugar; **azucarado, -a** adj sugary, sweet

azucarero, -a [aθukaˈrero, a] adj sugar cpd ▷ nm sugar bowl

azucena [aθuˈθena] nf white lily

azufre [aˈθufre] nm sulphur

azul [aˈθul] adj, nm blue; **azul celeste/marino** sky/navy blue

azulejo [aθuˈlexo] nm tile

azuzar [aθuˈθar] vt to incite, egg on

B.A. abr (= Buenos Aires) B.A.

baba [ˈbaβa] nf spittle, saliva; **babear** vi to drool, slaver

babero [baˈβero] nm bib

babor [baˈβor] nm port (side)

babosada [baβoˈsaða] (MÉX, CAM: fam) nf drivel; **baboso, -a** [baˈβoso, a] (LAM: fam) adj silly

baca [ˈbaka] nf (Auto) luggage o roof rack

bacalao [bakaˈlao] nm cod (fish)

bache [ˈbatʃe] nm pothole, rut; (fig) bad patch

bachillerato [batʃiʎeˈrato] nm higher secondary school course

bacinica [baθiˈnika] (LAM) nf potty

bacteria [bakˈterja] nf bacterium, germ

Bahama [baˈama]: **las (Islas) ~** nfpl the Bahamas

bahía [baˈia] nf bay

bailar [baiˈlar] vt, vi to dance; **bailarín, -ina** nm/f (ballet) dancer; **baile** nm dance; (formal) ball

baja [ˈbaxa] nf drop, fall; (Mil)

casualty; **dar de ~** (*soldado*) to discharge; (*empleado*) to dismiss

bajada [ba'xaða] *nf* descent; (*camino*) slope; (*de aguas*) ebb

bajar [ba'xar] *vi* to go down, come down; (*temperatura*, *precios*) to drop, fall ▷ *vt* (*cabeza*) to bow; (*escalera*) to go down, come down; (*precio*, *voz*) to lower; (*llevar abajo*) to take down; **bajarse** *vr* (*de coche*) to get out; (*de autobús*, *tren*) to get off; **~ de** (*coche*) to get out of; (*autobús*, *tren*) to get off; **~se algo de Internet** to download sth from the Internet

bajío [ba'xio] (LAM) *nm* lowlands *pl*

bajo, -a [baxo] *adj* (*mueble*, *número*, *precio*) low; (*piso*) ground; (*de estatura*) small, short; (*color*) pale; (*sonido*) faint, soft, low; (*voz*: *en tono*) deep; (*metal*) base; (*humilde*) low, humble ▷ *adv* (*hablar*) softly, quietly; (*volar*) low ▷ *prep* under, below, underneath ▷ *nm* (Mús) bass; **~ la lluvia** in the rain

bajón [ba'xon] *nm* fall, drop

bakalao [baka'lao] (ESP: *fam*) *nm* rave (music)

bala ['bala] *nf* bullet

balacear [balaθe'ar] (MÉX, CAM) *vt* to shoot

balance [ba'lanθe] *nm* (Com) balance; (: *libro*) balance sheet; (: *cuenta general*) stocktaking

balancear [balanθe'ar] *vt* to balance ▷ *vi* to swing (to and fro); (*vacilar*) to hesitate; **balancearse** *vr* to swing (to and fro), to hesitate

balanza [ba'lanθa] *nf* scales *pl*, balance; **balanza comercial** balance of trade; **balanza de pagos** balance of payments

balaustrada [balaus'traða] *nf* balustrade; (*pasamanos*) banisters *pl*

balazo [ba'laθo] *nm* (*golpe*) shot; (*herida*) bullet wound

balbucear [balβuθe'ar] *vi*, *vt* to stammer, stutter

balcón [bal'kon] *nm* balcony

balde ['balde] *nm* bucket, pail; **de ~**

(for) free, for nothing; **en ~** in vain

baldosa [bal'dosa] *nf* (*azulejo*) floor tile; (*grande*) flagstone; **baldosín** *nm* (small) tile

Baleares [bale'ares] *nfpl*: **las (Islas) ~** the Balearic Islands

balero [ba'lero] (LAM) *nm* (*juguete*) cup-and-ball toy

baliza [ba'liθa] *nf* (Aviac) beacon; (Náut) buoy

ballena [ba'ʎena] *nf* whale

ballet [ba'le] (*pl* **~s**) *nm* ballet

balneario [balne'arjo] *nm* spa; (*cs: en la costa*) seaside resort

balón [ba'lon] *nm* ball

baloncesto [balon'θesto] *nm* basketball

balonmano [balon'mano] *nm* handball

balonred [balon'reð] *nm* netball

balsa ['balsa] *nf* raft; (Bot) balsa wood

bálsamo ['balsamo] *nm* balsam, balm

baluarte [ba'lwarte] *nm* bastion, bulwark

bambú [bam'bu] *nm* bamboo

banana [ba'nana] (LAM) *nf* banana; **banano** *nm* (LAM: *árbol*) banana tree; (CAM: *fruta*) banana

banca ['banka] *nf* (Com) banking

bancario, -a [ban'karjo, a] *adj* banking *cpd*, bank *cpd*

bancarrota [banka'rrota] *nf* bankruptcy; **hacer ~** to go bankrupt

banco ['banko] *nm* bench; (Escol) desk; (Com) bank; (Geo) stratum; **banco de arena** sandbank; **banco de crédito** credit bank; **banco de datos** databank

banda ['banda] *nf* band; (*pandilla*) gang; (Náut) side, edge; **banda ancha** broadband; **banda sonora** soundtrack

bandada [ban'daða] *nf* (*de pájaros*) flock; (*de peces*) shoal

bandazo [ban'daθo] *nm* **dar ~s** to sway from side to side

bandeja [ban'dexa] *nf* tray

bandera [ban'dera] *nf* flag

banderilla [bande'riʎa] *nf* banderilla

bandido [ban'diðo] nm bandit
bando ['bando] nm (edicto) edict, proclamation; (facción) faction; **bandos** nmpl (Rel) banns
bandolera [bando'lera] nf: **llevar en ~** to wear across one's chest
banquero [ban'kero] nm banker
banqueta [ban'keta] nf stool; (MÉX: en calle) pavement (BRIT), sidewalk (US)
banquete [ban'kete] nm banquet; (para convidados) formal dinner; **banquete de boda(s)** wedding reception
banquillo [ban'kiʎo] nm (Jur) dock, prisoner's bench; (banco) bench; (para los pies) footstool
banquina [ban'kina] nf (RPL) hard shoulder (BRIT), berm (US)
bañadera [baɲa'ðera] nf (RPL) nf bathtub
bañador [baɲa'ðor] (ESP) nm swimming costume (BRIT), bathing suit (US)
bañar [ba'ɲar] vt to bath, bathe; (objeto) to dip; (de barniz) to coat; **bañarse** vr (en el mar) to bathe, swim; (en la bañera) to have a bath
bañera [ba'ɲera] (ESP) nf bath(tub)
bañero, -a [ba'ɲero, a] (CS) nm/f lifeguard
bañista [ba'ɲista] nmf bather
baño ['baɲo] nm (en bañera) bath; (en río) dip, swim; (cuarto) bathroom; (bañera) bath(tub); (capa) coating; **darse** o **tomar un ~** (en bañera) to have o take a bath; (en mar, piscina) to have a swim; **baño María** bain-marie
bar [bar] nm bar
barahúnda [bara'unda] nf uproar, hubbub
baraja [ba'raxa] nf pack (of cards); **barajar** vt (naipes) to shuffle; (fig) to jumble up
baranda [ba'randa] nf = **barandilla**
barandilla [baran'diʎa] nf rail, railing
barata [ba'rata] nf (MÉX) (bargain)

sale
baratillo [bara'tiʎo] nm (tienda) junkshop; (subasta) bargain sale; (conjunto de cosas) secondhand goods pl
barato, -a [ba'rato, a] adj cheap ▷ adv cheap, cheaply
barba ['barβa] nf (mentón) chin; (pelo) beard
barbacoa [barβa'koa] nf (parrilla) barbecue; (carne) barbecued meat
barbaridad [barβari'ðað] nf barbarity; (acto) barbarism; (atrocidad) outrage; **una ~** (fam) loads; **¡qué ~!** (fam) how awful!
barbarie [bar'βarje] nf barbarism, savagery; (crueldad) barbarity
bárbaro, -a [bar'βaro, a] adj barbarous, cruel; (grosero) rough, uncouth ▷ nm/f barbarian ▷ adv: **lo pasamos ~** (fam) we had a great time; **¡qué ~!** (fam) how marvellous!; **un éxito ~** (fam) a terrific success; **es un tipo ~** (fam) he's a great bloke
barbero [bar'βero] nm barber, hairdresser
barbilla [bar'βiʎa] nf chin, tip of the chin
barbudo, -a [bar'βuðo, a] adj bearded
barca ['barka] nf (small) boat; **barcaza** nf barge
Barcelona [barθe'lona] n Barcelona
barco ['barko] nm boat; (grande) ship; **barco de carga/pesca** cargo/fishing boat; **barco de vela** sailing ship
barda ['barða] (MÉX) nf (de madera) fence
baremo [ba'remo] nm (Mat: fig) scale
barítono [ba'ritono] nm baritone
barman ['barman] nm barman
barniz [bar'niθ] nm varnish; (en loza) glaze; (fig) veneer; **barnizar** vt to varnish; (loza) to glaze
barómetro [ba'rometro] nm barometer
barquillo [bar'kiʎo] nm cone, cornet
barra ['barra] nf bar, rod; (de un bar, café) bar; (de pan) French stick; (palanca)

lever; **barra de labios** lipstick; **barra libre** free bar

barraca [ba'rraka] nf hut, cabin

barranco [ba'rranko] nm ravine; (fig) difficulty

barrena [ba'rrena] nf drill

barrer [ba'rrer] vt to sweep; (quitar) to sweep away

barrera [ba'rrera] nf barrier

barriada [ba'rrjaða] nf quarter, district

barricada [barri'kaða] nf barricade

barrida [ba'rriða] nf sweep, sweeping

barriga [ba'rriɣa] nf belly; (panza) paunch; **barrigón, -ona** adj potbellied; **barrigudo, -a** adj potbellied

barril [ba'rril] nm barrel, cask

barrio ['barrjo] nm (vecindad) area, neighborhood (us); (en afueras) suburb; **barrio chino** (ESP) red-light district

barro ['barro] nm (lodo) mud; (objetos) earthenware; (Med) pimple

barroco, -a [ba'rroko, a] adj, nm baroque

barrote [ba'rrote] nm (de ventana) bar

bartola [bar'tola]: **a ~ de** on the **tumbarse a la ~** to take it easy, be lazy

bártulos ['bartulos] nmpl things, belongings

barullo [ba'ruʎo] nm row, uproar

basar [ba'sar] vt to base; **basarse** vr: **~se en** to be based on

báscula ['baskula] nf (platform) scales

base ['base] nf base; **a ~ de** on the basis of; (mediante) by means of; **base de datos** (Inform) database

básico, -a ['basiko, a] adj basic

basílica [ba'silika] nf basilica

básquetbol ['basketbol] (LAM) nm basketball

○ **PALABRA CLAVE**

bastante [bas'tante] adj **1** (suficiente) enough; **bastante dinero** enough o

sufficient money; **bastantes libros** enough books

2 (valor intensivo): **bastante gente** quite a lot of people; **tener bastante calor** to be rather hot

▷ adv: **bastante bueno/malo** quite good/rather bad; **bastante rico** pretty rich; **(lo) bastante inteligente (como) para hacer algo** clever enough o sufficiently clever to do sth

bastar [bas'tar] vi to be enough o sufficient; **bastarse** vr to be self-sufficient; **~ para** to be enough to; **¡basta!** (that's) enough!

bastardo, -a [bas'tarðo, a] adj, nm/f bastard

bastidor [basti'ðor] nm frame; (de coche) chassis; (Teatro) wing; **entre ~es** (fig) behind the scenes

basto, -a ['basto, a] adj coarse, rough; **bastos** nmpl (Naipes) ≈ clubs

bastón [bas'ton] nm stick, staff; (para pasear) walking stick

bastoncillo [baston'θiʎo] nm cotton bud

basura [ba'sura] nf rubbish (BRIT), garbage (US) ▷ adj: **comida/televisión ~** junk food/TV

basurero [basu'rero] nm (hombre) dustman (BRIT), garbage man (US); (lugar) dump; (cubo) (rubbish) bin (BRIT), trash can (US)

bata ['bata] nf (gen) dressing gown; (cubretodo) smock, overall; (Med, Tec etc) lab(oratory) coat

batalla [ba'taʎa] nf battle; **de ~** (fig) for everyday use; **batalla campal** pitched battle

batallón [bata'ʎon] nm battalion

batata [ba'tata] nf sweet potato

batería [bate'ria] nf battery; (Mús) drums; **batería de cocina** kitchen utensils

batido, -a [ba'tiðo, a] adj (camino) beaten, well-trodden ▷ nm (Culin: de leche) milk shake

batidora [bati'ðora] nf beater, mixer;

batidora eléctrica food mixer, blender

batir [ba'tir] vt to beat, strike; (vencer) to beat, defeat; (revolver) to beat, mix; **batirse** vr to fight; **~ palmas** to applaud

batuta [ba'tuta] nf baton; **llevar la ~** (fig) to be the boss, be in charge

baúl [ba'ul] nm trunk; (Auto) boot (BRIT), trunk (US)

bautismo [bau'tismo] nm baptism, christening

bautizar [bauti'θar] vt to baptize, christen; (fam: diluir) to water down; **bautizo** nm baptism, christening

bayeta [ba'jeta] nf floorcloth

baza ['baθa] nf trick; **meter ~** to butt in

bazar [ba'θar] nm bazaar

bazofia [ba'θofja] nf trash

be [be] nf name of the letter B; **be chica/grande** (MÉX) V/B; **be larga** (LAM) B

beato, -a [be'ato, a] adj blessed; (piadoso) pious

bebé [be'βe] (pl **~s**) nm baby

bebedero [beβe'ðero, a] (MÉX, CS) nm drinking fountain

bebedor, a [beβe'ðor, a] adj hard-drinking

beber [be'βer] vt, vi to drink

bebida [be'βiða] nf drink; **bebido, -a** adj drunk

beca ['beka] nf grant, scholarship; **becario, -a** [be'karjo, a] nm/f scholarship holder, grant holder

bedel [be'ðel] nm (Escol) janitor; (Univ) porter

béisbol ['beisβol] nm baseball

Belén [be'len] nm Bethlehem; **belén** nm (de Navidad) nativity scene, crib

belga ['belɣa] adj, nmf Belgian

Bélgica ['belxika] nf Belgium

bélico, -a ['beliko, a] adj (actitud) warlike

belleza [be'ʎeθa] nf beauty

bello, -a ['beʎo, a] adj beautiful, lovely; **Bellas Artes** Fine Art

bellota [be'ʎota] nf acorn

bemol [be'mol] nm (Mús) flat; **esto**

tiene ~es (fam) this is a tough one

bencina [ben'θina] nf (Quím) benzine

bendecir [bende'θir] vt to bless

bendición [bendi'θjon] nf blessing

bendito, -a [ben'dito, a] pp de **bendecir** ▷ adj holy; (afortunado) lucky; (feliz) happy; (sencillo) simple ▷ nm/f simple soul

beneficencia [benefi'θenθja] nf charity

beneficiario, -a [benefi'θjarjo, a] nm/f beneficiary

beneficio [bene'fiθjo] nm (bien) benefit, advantage; (ganancia) profit, gain; **a ~ de algn** in aid of sb; **beneficioso, -a** adj beneficial

benéfico, -a [be'nefiko, a] adj charitable

beneplácito [bene'plaθito] nm approval, consent

benévolo, -a [be'neβolo, a] adj benevolent, kind

benigno, -a [be'niɣno, a] adj kind; (suave) mild; (Med: tumor) benign, non-malignant

berberecho [berβe'retʃo] nm (Zool, Culin) cockle

berenjena [beren'xena] nf aubergine (BRIT), eggplant (US)

Berlín [ber'lin] n Berlin

berlinesa [berli'nesa] (RPL) nf doughnut, donut (US)

bermudas [ber'muðas] nfpl Bermuda shorts

berrido [be'rriðo] nm bellow(ing)

berrinche [be'rrintʃe] (fam) nm temper, tantrum

berro ['berro] nm watercress

berza ['berθa] nf cabbage

besamel [besa'mel] nf (Culin) white sauce, bechamel sauce

besar [be'sar] vt to kiss; (fig: tocar) to graze; **besarse** vr to kiss (one another); **beso** nm kiss

bestia ['bestja] nf beast, animal; (fig) idiot; **bestia de carga** beast of burden; **bestial** adj bestial; (fam) terrific; **bestialidad** nf bestiality;

(fam) stupidity

besugo [be'suɣo] *nm* sea bream; *(fam)* idiot

besuquear [besuke'ar] *vt* to cover with kisses; **besuquearse** *vr* to kiss and cuddle

betabel [beta'ßel] *(MÉX) nm* beetroot *(BRIT)*, beet *(US)*

betún [be'tun] *nm* shoe polish; *(Quím)* bitumen

biberón [bíße'ron] *nm* feeding bottle

Biblia ['bißlja] *nf* Bible

bibliografía [bißljoɣra'fia] *nf* bibliography

biblioteca [bißljo'teka] *nf* library; *(mueble)* bookshelves; **biblioteca de consulta** reference library; **bibliotecario, -a** *nm/f* librarian

bicarbonato [bikarßo'nato] *nm* bicarbonate

bicho ['bitʃo] *nm (animal)* small animal; *(sabandija)* bug, insect; *(Taur)* bull

bici ['biθi] *(fam) nf* bike

bicicleta [biθi'kleta] *nf* bicycle, cycle; **ir en ~** to cycle

bidé [bi'ðe] *(pl* **-s)** *nm* bidet

bidón [bi'ðon] *nm (de aceite)* drum; *(de gasolina)* can

○ PALABRA CLAVE

bien [bjen] *nm* 1 *(bienestar)* good; **te lo digo por tu bien** I'm telling you for your own good; **el bien y el mal** good and evil

2 *(posesión)* **bienes** goods; **bienes de consumo** consumer goods; **bienes inmuebles** *o* **raíces/bienes muebles** real estate *sg*/personal property *sg*

▷ *adv* 1 *(de manera satisfactoria, correcta etc)* well; **trabaja/come bien** he works/eats well; **contestó bien** he answered correctly; **me siento bien** I feel fine; **no me siento bien** I don't feel very well; **se está bien aquí** it's nice here

2 *(frases)*: **hiciste bien en llamarme** you were right to call me

3 *(valor intensivo)* very; **un cuarto bien caliente** a nice warm room; **bien se ve que ...** it's quite clear that ...

4 **estar bien**: **estoy muy bien aquí** I feel very happy here; **está bien que vengan** it's all right for them to come; **¡está bien! lo haré** all right, I'll do it

5 *(de buena gana)*: **yo bien que iría pero ...** I'd gladly go but ...

▷ *excl*: **¡bien!** *(aprobación)* O.K.!; **¡muy bien!** well done! ▷ *adj inv (matiz despectivo)*: **gente bien** posh people

▷ *conj* 1 **bien ... bien**: **bien en coche bien en tren** either by car or by train

2 *(LAM)*: **no bien**: **no bien llegue te llamaré** as soon as I arrive I'll call you

3 **si bien** even though; V tb **más**

bienal [bje'nal] *adj* biennial

bienestar [bjenes'tar] *nm* well-being, welfare

bienvenida [bjembe'niða] *nf* welcome; **dar la ~ a algn** to welcome sb

bienvenido [bjembe'niðo] *excl* welcome!

bife ['bife] *(cs) nm* steak

bifurcación [bifurka'θjon] *nf* fork

bígamo, -a ['biɣamo, a] *adj* bigamous ▷ *nm/f* bigamist

bigote [bi'ɣote] *nm* moustache; **bigotudo, -a** *adj* with a big moustache

bikini [bi'kini] *nm* bikini; *(Culin)* toasted ham and cheese sandwich

bilingüe [bi'liŋgwe] *adj* bilingual

billar [bi'ʎar] *nm* billiards *sg*; **billares** *nmpl (lugar)* billiard hall; *(sala de juegos)* amusement arcade; **billar americano** pool

billete [bi'ʎete] *nm* ticket; *(de banco)* (bank)note *(BRIT)*, bill *(US)*; *(carta)* note; **~ de 20 libras** £20 note; **billete de ida y vuelta** return *(BRIT)* o round-trip *(US)* ticket; **billete sencillo** *o* **de ida** single *(BRIT)* o one-way *(US)* ticket; **billete electrónico** e-ticket

billetera [biʎeˈtera] nf wallet

billón [biˈʎon] nm billion

bimensual [bimenˈswal] adj twice monthly

bingo [ˈbingo] nm bingo

biodegradable [bioðeˈxraˈðaβle] adj biodegradable

biografía [bjoɣraˈfia] nf biography

biología [bjoloˈxia] nf biology; **biológico, -a** adj biological; (cultivo, producto) organic; **biólogo, -a** nm/f biologist

biombo [ˈbjombo] nm (folding) screen

bioterrorismo [bjoterroˈrismo] nm bioterrorism

biquini [biˈkini] nm o (RPL) f bikini

birlar [birˈlar] (fam) vt to pinch

Birmania [birˈmanja] nf Burma

birome [biˈrome] (RPL) nf ballpoint (pen)

birria [ˈbirrja] nf: **ser una ~** (película, libro) to be rubbish

bis [bis] excl encore!

bisabuelo, -a [bisaˈβwelo, a] nm/f great-grandfather(-mother)

bisagra [biˈsaɣra] nf hinge

bisiesto [biˈsjesto] adj: **año ~** leap year

bisnieto, -a [bisˈnjeto, a] nm/f great-grandson/daughter

bisonte [biˈsonte] nm bison

bisté [bisˈte] nm = **bistec**

bistec [bisˈtek] nm steak

bisturí [bistuˈri] nm scalpel

bisutería [bisuteˈria] nf imitation o costume jewellery

bit [bit] nm (Inform) bit

bizco, -a [ˈbiθko, a] adj cross-eyed

bizcocho [biθˈkotʃo] nm (Culin) sponge cake

blanca [ˈblanka] nf (Mús) minim; **estar sin ~** (ESP: fam) to be broke; V tb **blanco**

blanco, -a [ˈblanko, a] adj white ▷ nm/f white man/woman, white ▷ nm (color) white; (en texto) blank; (Mil, fig) target; **en ~** blank; **noche en ~**

sleepless night

blandir [blanˈdir] vt to brandish

blando, -a [ˈblando, a] adj soft; (tierno) tender, gentle; (carácter) mild; (fam) cowardly

blanqueador [blankeaˈðor] (MÉX) nm bleach

blanquear [blankeˈar] vt to whiten; (fachada) to whitewash; (paño) to bleach ▷ vi to turn white

blanquillo [blanˈkiʎo] (MÉX, CAM) nm egg

blasfemar [blasfeˈmar] vi to blaspheme, curse

bledo [ˈbleðo] nm: **me importa un ~** I couldn't care less

blindado, -a [blinˈdaðo, a] adj (Mil) armour-plated; (antibala) bullet-proof; **coche** (ESP) o **carro** (LAM) **~** armoured car

bloc [blok] (pl **~s**) nm writing pad

blof [blof] (MÉX) nm bluff; **blofear** (MÉX) vi to bluff

blog [bloɣ] (pl **~s**) nm blog

bloque [ˈbloke] nm block; (Pol) bloc

bloquear [blokeˈar] vt to blockade; **bloqueo** nm blockade; (Com) freezing, blocking; **bloqueo mental** mental block

blusa [ˈblusa] nf blouse

bobada [boˈβaða] nf foolish action; foolish statement; **decir ~s** to talk nonsense

bobina [boˈβina] nf (Tec) bobbin; (Foto) spool; (Elec) coil

bobo, -a [ˈboβo, a] adj (tonto) daft, silly; (cándido) naive ▷ nm/f fool, idiot ▷ nm (Teatro) clown, funny man

boca [ˈboka] nf mouth; (de crustáceo) pincer; (de cañón) muzzle; (entrada) mouth, entrance; **bocas** nfpl (de río) mouth sg; **~ abajo/arriba** face down/up; **se me hace la ~ agua** my mouth is watering; **boca de incendios** hydrant; **boca del estómago** pit of the stomach; **boca de metro** underground (BRIT) o subway (US) entrance

bocacalle [bokaˈkaʎe] nf (entrance

to a) street; **la primera ~** the first
turning o street

bocadillo [boka'ðiʎo] nm sandwich

bocado [bo'kaðo] nm mouthful, bite;
(de caballo) bridle

bocajarro [boka'xarro]: **a ~** adv
(disparar) point-blank

bocanada [boka'naða] nf (de vino)
mouthful, swallow; (de aire) gust, puff

bocata [bo'kata] (fam) nm sandwich

bocazas [bo'kaθas] (fam) nm inv
bigmouth

boceto [bo'θeto] nm sketch, outline

bochorno [bo'tʃorno] nm (vergüenza)
embarrassment; (calor): **hace ~** it's
very muggy

bocina [bo'θina] nf (Mús) trumpet;
(Auto) horn; (para hablar) megaphone

boda ['boða] nf (tb: **~s**) wedding,
marriage; (fiesta) wedding reception;
bodas de oro/plata golden/silver
wedding sg

bodega [bo'ðeɣa] nf (de vino) (wine)
cellar; (depósito) storeroom; (de barco)
hold

bodegón [boðe'ɣon] nm (Arte)
still life

bofetada [bofe'taða] nf slap (in
the face)

boga ['boɣa] nf: **en ~** (fig) in vogue

Bogotá [boɣo'ta] n Bogotá

bohemio, -a [bo'emjo, a] adj, nm/f
Bohemian

bohío [bo'io] (CAM) nm shack, hut

boicot [boi'kot] (pl **~s**) nm boycott;
boicotear vt to boycott

bóiler ['boiler] (MÉX) nm boiler

boina ['boina] nf beret

bola ['bola] nf ball; (canica) marble;
(Naipes) (grand) slam; (betún) shoe
polish; (mentira) tale, story; **bolas** nfpl
(LAM: caza) bolas sg; **bola de billar**
billiard ball; **bola de nieve** snowball

boleadoras [bolea'ðoras] nfpl
bolas sg

bolear [bole'ar] (MÉX) vt (zapatos) to
polish, shine

bolera [bo'lera] nf skittle o bowling

alley

bolero, -a (MÉX) [bo'lero] nm/f
(limpiabotas) shoeshine boy/girl

boleta [bo'leta] (LAM) nf (de rifa)
ticket; (CS: recibo) receipt; **boleta de
calificaciones** (MÉX) report card

boletería [bolete'ria] (LAM) nf ticket
office

boletín [bole'tin] nm bulletin;
(periódico) journal, review; **boletín de
noticias** news bulletin

boleto [bo'leto] nm (LAM) ticket;
boleto de ida y vuelta (LAM) round
trip ticket; **boleto electrónico** (LAM)
e-ticket; **boleto redondo** (MÉX) round
trip ticket

boli ['boli] (fam) nm Biro®

bolígrafo [bo'liɣrafo] nm ball-point
pen, Biro®

bolilla [bo'liʎa] (RPL) nf topic

bolillo [bo'liʎo] (MÉX) nm (bread) roll

bolita [bo'lita] (CS) nf marble

bolívar [bo'liβar] nm monetary unit
of Venezuela

Bolivia [bo'liβja] nf Bolivia;
boliviano, -a [bo'liβjano, a] adj, nm/f Bolivian

bollería [boʎe'ria] nf cakes pl and
pastries pl

bollo ['boʎo] nm (pan) roll; (bulto)
bump, lump; (abolladura) dent

bolo ['bolo] nm skittle; (píldora) (large)
pill; **(juego de) bolos** nmpl skittles sg

bolsa ['bolsa] nf (para llevar algo) bag;
(MÉX, CAM: bolsillo) pocket; (MÉX: de
mujer) handbag; (Anat) cavity, sac; (Com)
stock exchange; (Minería) pocket; **de ~**
pocket cpd; **bolsa de agua caliente** hot
water bottle; **bolsa de aire** air pocket;
bolsa de dormir (MÉX, RPL) sleeping
bag; **bolsa de la compra** shopping
bag; **bolsa de papel/plástico** paper/
plastic bag

bolsear [bolse'ar] (MÉX, CAM) vt: **~ a
algn** to pick sb's pocket

bolsillo [bol'siʎo] nm pocket; (cartera)
purse; **de ~** pocket(-size)

bolso ['bolso] nm (bolsa) bag; (de
mujer) handbag

bomba ['bomba] nf (Mil) bomb; (Tec) pump ▷ adj (fam): **noticia ~** bombshell ▷ adv (fam): **pasarlo ~** to have a great time; **bomba atómica/de efecto retardado/de humo** atomic/time/smoke bomb

bombacha [bom'batʃa] (RPL) nf panties pl

bombardear [bombarðe'ar] vt to bombard; (Mil) to bomb; **bombardeo** nm bombardment; bombing

bombazo [bom'baθo] (MÉX) nm (explosión) explosion; (fam: noticia) bombshell; (: éxito) smash hit

bombear [bombe'ar] vt (agua) to pump (out o up)

bombero [bom'bero] nm fireman

bombilla [bom'biʎa] (ESP) nf (light) bulb

bombita [bom'bita] (RPL) nf (light) bulb

bombo ['bombo] nm (Mús) bass drum; (Tec) drum

bombón [bom'bon] nm chocolate; (MÉX: de caramelo) marshmallow

bombona [bom'bona] (ESP) nf (de butano, oxígeno) cylinder

bonachón, -ona [bona'tʃon, ona] adj good-natured, easy-going

bonanza [bo'nanθa] nf (Náut) fair weather; (fig) bonanza; (Minería) rich pocket o vein

bondad [bon'dað] nf goodness, kindness; **tenga la ~ de** (please) be good enough to

bonito, -a [bo'nito, a] adj pretty; (agradable) nice ▷ nm (atún) tuna (fish)

bono ['bono] nm voucher; (Finanzas) bond

bonobús [bono'βus] (ESP) nm bus pass

bonoloto [bono'loto] nf state-run weekly lottery

boquerón [boke'ron] nm (pez) (kind of) anchovy; (agujero) large hole

boquete [bo'kete] nm gap, hole

boquiabierto, -a [bokia'βjerto, a] adj: **quedarse ~** to be amazed o flabbergasted

boquilla [bo'kiʎa] nf (para riego) nozzle; (para cigarro) cigarette holder; (Mús) mouthpiece

borbotón [borβo'ton] nm: **salir a borbotones** to gush out

borda ['borða] nf (Náut) (ship's) rail; **tirar algo/caerse por la ~** to throw sth/fall overboard

bordado [bor'ðaðo] nm embroidery

bordar [bor'ðar] vt to embroider

borde ['borðe] nm edge, border; (de camino etc) side; (en la costura) hem; **al ~ de** (fig) on the verge o brink of; **ser ~** (ESP: fam) to be rude; **bordear** vt to border

bordillo [bor'ðiʎo] nm kerb (BRIT), curb (US)

bordo ['borðo] nm (Náut) side; **a ~** on board

borlote [bor'lote] (MÉX) nm row, uproar

borrachera [borra'tʃera] nf (ebriedad) drunkenness; (orgía) spree, binge

borracho, -a [bo'rratʃo, a] adj drunk ▷ nm/f (habitual) drunkard, drunk; (temporal) drunk, drunk man/woman

borrador [borra'ðor] nm (escritura) first draft, rough sketch; (goma) rubber (BRIT), eraser

borrar [bo'rrar] vt to erase, rub out

borrasca [bo'rraska] nf storm

borrego, -a [bo'rrevo, a] nm/f (Zool: joven) (yearling) lamb; (adulto) sheep ▷ nm (MÉX: fam) false rumour

borrico, -a [bo'rriko, a] nm/f donkey/she-donkey; (fig) stupid man/woman

borrón [bo'rron] nm (mancha) stain

borroso, -a [bo'rroso, a] adj vague, unclear; (escritura) illegible

bosque ['boske] nm wood; (grande) forest

bostezar [boste'θar] vi to yawn; **bostezo** nm yawn

bota ['bota] nf (calzado) boot; (para vino) leather wine bottle; **botas de agua** o **goma** Wellingtons

botana [bo'tana] (MÉX) nf snack, appetizer

botánica [bo'tanika] nf (ciencia) botany; V tb **botánico**

botánico, -a [bo'taniko, a] adj botanical ▷ nm/f botanist

botar [bo'tar] vt to throw, hurl; (Náut) to launch; (LAM: echar) to throw out ▷ vi (ESP: saltar) to bounce

bote ['bote] nm (salto) bounce; (golpe) thrust; (ESP: envase) tin, can; (embarcación) boat; (MÉX, CAM: pey: cárcel) jail; **de ~ en ~** packed, jammed full; **bote de la basura** (MÉX) dustbin (BRIT), trashcan (US); **bote salvavidas** lifeboat

botella [bo'teʎa] nf bottle; **botellín** nm small bottle; **botellón** nm (ESP: fam) outdoor drinking session

botijo [bo'tixo] nm (earthenware) jug

botín [bo'tin] nm (calzado) half boot; (polaina) spat; (Mil) booty

botiquín [boti'kin] nm (armario) medicine cabinet; (portátil) first-aid kit

botón [bo'ton] nm button; (Bot) bud

botones [bo'tones] nm inv bellboy (BRIT), bellhop (US)

bóveda ['boβeða] nf (Arq) vault

boxeador [boksea'ðor] nm boxer

boxeo [bok'seo] nm boxing

boya ['boja] nf (Náut) buoy; (de caña) float

boyante [bo'jante] adj prosperous

bozal [bo'θal] nm (para caballos) halter; (de perro) muzzle

bragas ['braxas] nfpl (de mujer) panties, knickers (BRIT)

bragueta [bra'yeta] nf fly, flies pl

braille [breil] nm braille

brasa ['brasa] nf live o hot coal

brasero [bra'sero] nm brazier

brasier [bra'sjer] (MÉX) nm bra

Brasil [bra'sil] nm (tb: **el ~**) Brazil; **brasileño, -a** adj, nm/f Brazilian

brassier [bra'sjer] (MÉX) nm V **brasier**

bravo, -a ['braβo, a] adj (valiente) brave; (feroz) ferocious; (salvaje) wild;

(mar etc) rough, stormy ▷ excl bravo!; **bravura** nf bravery; ferocity

braza ['braθa] nf fathom; **nadar a ~** to swim breast-stroke

brazalete [braθa'lete] nm (pulsera) bracelet; (banda) armband

brazo ['braθo] nm arm; (Zool) foreleg; (Bot) limb, branch; **luchar a ~ partido** to fight hand-to-hand; **ir cogidos del ~** to walk arm in arm

brebaje [bre'βaxe] nm potion

brecha ['bretʃa] nf (hoyo, vacío) gap, opening; (Mil, fig) breach

brega ['breɣa] nf (lucha) struggle; (trabajo) hard work

breva ['breβa] nf early fig

breve ['breβe] adj short, brief ▷ nf (Mús) breve; **en ~** (pronto) shortly, before long; **brevedad** nf brevity, shortness

bribón, -ona [bri'βon, ona] adj idle, lazy ▷ nm/f (pícaro) rascal, rogue

bricolaje [briko'laxe] nm do-it-yourself, DIY

brida ['briða] nf bridle, rein; (Tec) clamp

bridge [britʃ] nm bridge

brigada [bri'ɣaða] nf (unidad) brigade; (de trabajadores) squad, gang ▷ nm = staff-sergeant, sergeant-major

brillante [bri'ʎante] adj brilliant ▷ nm diamond

brillar [bri'ʎar] vi to shine; (joyas) to sparkle

brillo ['briʎo] nm shine; (brillantez) brilliance; (fig) splendour; **sacar ~ a** to polish

brincar [brin'kar] vi to skip about, hop about, jump about

brinco ['brinko] nm jump, leap

brindar [brin'dar] vi: **~ a o por** to drink (a toast) to ▷ vt to offer, present

brindis ['brindis] nm inv toast

brío ['brio] nm spirit, dash

brisa ['brisa] nf breeze

británico, -a [bri'taniko, a] adj British ▷ nm/f Briton, British person

brizna ['briθna] nf (de hierba, paja)

blade; (de tabaco) leaf

broca ['broka] nf (Tec) drill, bit

brocha ['brotʃa] nf (large) paintbrush;
brocha de afeitar shaving brush

broche ['brotʃe] nm brooch

broma ['broma] nf joke; **de o en ~** in
fun, as a joke; **broma pesada** practical
joke; **bromear** vi to joke

bromista [bro'mista] adj fond of
joking ▷nmf joker, wag

bronca ['bronka] nf row; **echar una ~
a algn** to tick sb off

bronce ['bronθe] nm bronze;
bronceado, -a adj bronze; (por el sol)
tanned (sun)tan; (Tec) bronzing

bronceador [bronθea'ðor] nm
suntan lotion

broncearse [bronθe'arse] vr to get
a suntan

bronquio ['bronkjo] nm (Anat)
bronchial tube

bronquitis [bron'kitis] nf inv
bronchitis

brotar [bro'tar] vi (Bot) to sprout;
(aguas) to gush (forth); (Med) to
break out

brote ['brote] nm (Bot) shoot; (Med,
fig) outbreak

bruces ['bruθes]: **de bruces** adv: **caer
o dar de ~** to fall headlong, fall flat

bruja ['bruxa] nf witch; **brujería** nf
witchcraft

brujo ['bruxo] nm wizard, magician

brújula ['bruxula] nf compass

bruma ['bruma] nf mist

brusco, -a ['brusko, a] adj (súbito)
sudden; (áspero) brusque

Bruselas [bru'selas] n Brussels

brutal [bru'tal] adj brutal; **brutalidad**
[brutali'ðað] nf brutality

bruto, -a ['bruto, a] adj (idiota)
stupid; (bestial) brutish; (peso) gross; **en
~** raw, unworked

Bs.As. abr (= Buenos Aires) B.A.

bucal [bu'kal] adj oral; **por vía ~**
orally

bucear [buθe'ar] vi to dive ▷vt to
explore; **buceo** nm diving

bucle ['bukle] nm curl

budismo [bu'ðismo] nm Buddhism

buen [bwen] adj V **bueno**

buenamente [bwena'mente] adv
(fácilmente) easily; (voluntariamente)
willingly

buenaventura [bwenaβen'tura] nf
(suerte) good luck; (adivinación) fortune

buenmozo [bwen'moθo] (MÉX) adj
handsome

○ **PALABRA CLAVE**

bueno, -a ['bweno, a] adj (antes de nmsg:
buen) adj 1 (excelente etc) good; **es un
libro bueno, es un buen libro** it's a
good book; **hace bueno, hace buen
tiempo** the weather is fine, it is fine;
el banco de Paco good old Paco; **fue
muy bueno conmigo** he was very nice
o kind to me

2 (apropiado): **ser bueno para** to be
good for; **creo que vamos por buen
camino** I think we're on the right track

3 (irónico): **le di un buen rapapolvo**
I gave him a good o real ticking off;
¡buen conductor estás hecho!
some o a fine driver you are!; **¡estaría
bueno que ...!** a fine thing it would
be if ...!

4 (atractivo, sabroso): **está bueno este
bizcocho** this sponge is delicious;
Carmen está muy buena Carmen is
gorgeous

5 (saludos): **¡buen día!, ¡buenos días!**
(good) morning!; **¡buenas (tardes)!**
(good) afternoon!; (más tarde) (good)
evening!; **¡buenas noches!** good night!

6 (otras locuciones): **estar de buenas**
to be in a good mood; **por las buenas**
o **por las malas** by hook or by crook;
de buenas a primeras all of a sudden
▷excl: **¡bueno!** all right!; **bueno, ¿y
qué?** well, so what?

Buenos Aires [bweno'saires] nm
Buenos Aires

buey [bwei] nm ox

búfalo ['bufalo] nm buffalo

bufanda [bu'fanda] nf scarf

bufete [bu'fete] nm (despacho de abogado) lawyer's office

bufón [bu'fon] nm clown

buhardilla [buar'ðiʎa] nf attic

búho ['buo] nm owl; (fig) hermit, recluse

buitre ['bwitre] nm vulture

bujía [bu'xia] nf (vela) candle; (Elec) candle (power); (Auto) spark plug

bula ['bula] nf (papal) bull

bulbo ['bulβo] nm bulb

bulevar [bule'βar] nm boulevard

Bulgaria [bul'ɣarja] nf Bulgaria; **búlgaro, -a** adj, nm/f Bulgarian

bulla ['buʎa] nf (ruido) uproar; (de gente) crowd

bullicio [bu'ʎiθjo] nm (ruido) uproar; (movimiento) bustle

bulto ['bulto] nm (paquete) package; (fardo) bundle; (tamaño) size, bulkiness; (Med) swelling, lump; (silueta) vague shape

buñuelo [bu'nwelo] nm ≈ doughnut (BRIT), ≈ donut (US); (fruta de sartén) fritter

buque ['buke] nm ship, vessel; **buque de guerra** warship

burbuja [bur'βuxa] nf bubble

burdel [bur'ðel] nm brothel

burgués, -esa [bur'ɣes, esa] adj middle-class, bourgeois; **burguesía** nf middle class, bourgeoisie

burla ['burla] nf (mofa) gibe; (broma) joke; (engaño) trick; **burlar** vt (engañar) to deceive ▷ vi to joke; **burlarse** vr to joke; **burlarse de** to make fun of

burlón, -ona [bur'lon, ona] adj mocking

buró [bu'ro] (MÉX) nm bedside table

burocracia [buro'kraθja] nf civil service

burrada [bu'rraða] nf: **decir** o **soltar ~s** to talk nonsense; **hacer ~s** to act stupid; **una ~** (ESP: mucho) a (hell of a) lot

burro, -a ['burro, a] nm/f donkey/she-donkey; (fig) ass, idiot

bursátil [bur'satil] adj stock-exchange cpd

bus [bus] nm bus

busca ['buska] nf search, hunt ▷ nm (Tel) bleeper; **en ~ de** in search of

buscador [buska'ðor] nm (Internet) search engine

buscar [bus'kar] vt to look for, search for, seek ▷ vi to look, search, seek; **se busca secretaria** secretary wanted

busque etc vb V **buscar**

búsqueda [bu'skeða] nf = **busca**

busto ['busto] nm (Anat, Arte) bust

butaca [bu'taka] nf armchair; (de cine, teatro) stall, seat

butano [bu'tano] nm butane (gas)

buzo ['buθo] nm diver

buzón [bu'θon] nm (en puerta) letter box; (en calle) pillar box; **buzón de voz** nm voicemail

C

C. *abr* (= *centígrado*) C; (*compañía*) Co.

C/ *abr* (= *calle*) St

cabal [ka'βal] *adj* (*exacto*) exact; (*correcto*) right, proper; (*acabado*) finished, complete; **cabales** *nmpl*: **no está en sus cabales** she isn't in her right mind

cábalas [ka'βalas] *nfpl*: **hacer ~** to guess

cabalgar [kaβal'ɣar] *vt*, *vi* to ride

cabalgata [kaβal'ɣata] *nf* procession

caballa [ka'βaʎa] *nf* mackerel

caballería [kaβaʎe'ria] *nf* mount; (*Mil*) cavalry

caballero [kaβa'ʎero] *nm* gentleman; (*de la orden de caballería*) knight; (*trato directo*) sir

caballete [kaβa'ʎete] *nm* (*Arte*) easel; (*Tec*) trestle

caballito [kaβa'ʎito] *nm* (*caballo pequeño*) small horse, pony; **caballitos** *nmpl* (*en verbena*) roundabout, merry-go-round

caballo [ka'βaʎo] *nm* horse; (*Ajedrez*) knight; (*Naipes*) queen; **ir en ~** to ride; **caballo de carreras** racehorse; **caballo de fuerza** *o* **vapor** horsepower

cabaña [ka'βaɲa] *nf* (*casita*) hut, cabin

cabecear [kaβeθe'ar] *vt*, *vi* to nod

cabecera [kaβe'θera] *nf* head; (*Imprenta*) headline

cabecilla [kaβe'θiʎa] *nm* ringleader

cabellera [kaβe'ʎera] *nf* (head of) hair; (*de cometa*) tail

cabello [ka'βeʎo] *nm* (*tb*: **~s**) hair; **cabello de ángel** confectionery and pastry filling made of pumpkin and syrup

caber [ka'βer] *vi* (*entrar*) to fit, go; **caben 3 más** there's room for 3 more

cabestrillo [kaβes'triʎo] *nm* sling

cabeza [ka'βeθa] *nf* head; (*Pol*) chief, leader; **cabeza de ajo** bulb of garlic; **cabeza de familia** head of the household; **cabeza rapada** skinhead; **cabezada** *nf* (*golpe*) butt; **dar cabezadas** to nod off; **cabezón, -ona** *adj* (*vino*) heady; (*fam*: *persona*) pig-headed

cabida [ka'βiða] *nf* space

cabina [ka'βina] *nf* cabin; (*de avión*) cockpit; (*de camión*) cab; **cabina telefónica** telephone (*BRIT*) box *o* booth

cabizbajo, -a [kaβiθ'βaxo, a] *adj* crestfallen, dejected

cable ['kaβle] *nm* cable

cabo ['kaβo] *nm* (*de objeto*) end, extremity; (*Mil*) corporal; (*Náut*) rope, cable; (*Geo*) cape; **al ~ de 3 días** after 3 days; **llevar a ~** to carry out

cabra ['kaβra] *nf* goat

cabré *etc* *vb* V **caber**

cabrear [kaβre'ar] (*fam*) *vt* to bug; **cabrearse** *vr* (*enfadarse*) to fly off the handle

cabrito [ka'βrito] *nm* kid

cabrón [ka'βron] *nm* cuckold; (*fam!*) bastard (!)

caca ['kaka] *nf* (*fam*) pooh

cacahuete [kaka'wete] (*ESP*) *nm* peanut

cacao [ka'kao] nm cocoa; (Bot) cacao

cacarear [kakare'ar] vi (persona) to boast; (gallina) to crow

cacería [kaθe'ria] nf hunt

cacarizo, -a [kaka'riθo, a] (MÉX) adj pockmarked

cacerola [kaθe'rola] nf pan, saucepan

cachalote [katʃa'lote] nm (Zool) sperm whale

cacharro [ka'tʃarro] nm earthenware pot; **cacharros** nmpl pots and pans

cachear [katʃe'ar] vt to search, frisk

cachemir [katʃe'mir] nm cashmere

cachetada [katʃe'taða] (LAM: fam) nf (bofetada) slap

cachete [ka'tʃete] nm (Anat) cheek; (ESP: bofetada) slap (in the face)

cachivache [katʃi'βatʃe] nm (trasto) piece of junk; **cachivaches** nmpl junk sg

cacho ['katʃo] nm (small) bit; (LAM: cuerno) horn

cachondeo [katʃon'deo] (ESP: fam) nm farce, joke

cachondo, -a [ka'tʃondo, a] adj (Zool) on heat; (fam: sexualmente) randy; (: gracioso) funny

cachorro, -a [ka'tʃorro, a] nm/f (perro) pup, puppy; (león) cub

cachucha [ka'tʃutʃa] (MÉX: fam) nf cap

cacique [ka'θike] nm chief, local ruler; (Pol) local party boss

cactus ['kaktus] nm inv cactus

cada ['kaða] adj inv each; (antes de número) every; ~ **día** each day, every day; ~ **dos días** every other day; ~ **uno/a** each one, every one; ~ **vez más/menos** more and more/less and less; ~ **vez que** ... whenever, every time (that) ...; **uno de ~ diez** one out of every ten

cadáver [ka'ðaβer] nm (dead) body, corpse

cadena [ka'ðena] nf chain; (TV) channel; **trabajo en** ~ assembly line work; **cadena montañosa** mountain range; **cadena perpetua** (Jur) life imprisonment

cadera [ka'ðera] nf hip

cadete [ka'ðete] nm cadet

caducar [kaðu'kar] vi to expire; **caduco, -a** adj expired; (persona) very old

caer [ka'er] vi to fall (down); **caerse** vr to fall (down); **me cae bien/mal** I get on well with him/I can't stand him; ~ **en la cuenta** to realize; **dejar** ~ to drop; **su cumpleaños cae en viernes** her birthday falls on a Friday

café [ka'fe] (pl ~s) nm (bebida, planta) coffee; (lugar) café ▷ adj (MÉX: color) brown, tan; **café con leche** white coffee; **café negro** (LAM) black coffee; **café solo** (ESP) black coffee

cafetera [kafe'tera] nf coffee pot

cafetería [kafete'ria] nf (gen) café

cafetero, -a [kafe'tero, a] adj coffee cpd; **ser muy** ~ to be a coffee addict

cafishio [ka'fiʃjo] (cs) nm pimp

cagar [ka'ɣar] (fam!) vt to bungle, mess up ▷ vi to have a shit (!)

caída [ka'iða] nf fall; (declive) slope; (disminución) fall, drop

caído, -a [ka'iðo, a] adj drooping

caiga etc vb V **caer**

caimán [kai'man] nm alligator

caja ['kaxa] nf box; (para reloj) case; (de ascensor) shaft; (Com) cashbox; (donde se hacen los pagos) cashdesk; (: en supermercado) checkout, till; **caja de ahorros** savings bank; **caja de cambios** gearbox; **caja de fusibles** fuse box; **caja fuerte** o **de caudales** safe, strongbox

cajero, -a [ka'xero, a] nm/f cashier; **cajero automático** cash dispenser

cajetilla [kaxe'tiʎa] nf (de cigarrillos) packet

cajón [ka'xon] nm big box; (de mueble) drawer

cajuela [ka'xwela] (MÉX) nf (Auto) boot (BRIT), trunk (US)

cal [kal] nf lime

cala ['kala] nf (Geo) cove, inlet; (de barco) hold

calabacín [kalaβa'θin] nm (Bot) baby marrow; (: más pequeño) courgette (BRIT), zucchini (US)

calabacita [kalaβa'θita] (MÉX) nf courgette (BRIT), zucchini (US)

calabaza [kala'βaθa] nf (Bot) pumpkin

calabozo [kala'βoθo] nm (cárcel) prison; (celda) cell

calada [ka'laða] (ESP) nf (de cigarrillo) puff

calado, -a [ka'laðo, a] adj (prenda) lace cpd ▷ nm (Náut) draught

calamar [kala'mar] nm squid no pl

calambre [ka'lambre] nm (Elec) shock

calar [ka'lar] vt to soak, drench; (penetrar) to pierce, penetrate; (comprender) to understand; (vela) to lower; **calarse** vr (Auto) to stall; **~se las gafas** to stick one's glasses on

calavera [kala'βera] nf skull

calcar [kal'kar] vt (reproducir) to trace; (imitar) to copy

calcetín [kalθe'tin] nm sock

calcio ['kalθjo] nm calcium

calcomanía [kalkoma'nia] nf transfer

calculador, a [kalkula'ðor, a] adj (persona) calculating; **calculadora** [kalkula'ðora] nf calculator

calcular [kalku'lar] vt (Mat) to calculate, compute; **~ que ...** to reckon that ...

cálculo ['kalkulo] nm calculation

caldera [kal'dera] nf boiler

calderilla [kalde'riʎa] nf (moneda) small change

caldo ['kaldo] nm stock; (consomé) consommé

calefacción [kalefak'θjon] nf heating; **calefacción central** central heating

calefón [kale'fon] (RPL) nm boiler

calendario [kalen'darjo] nm calendar

calentador [kalenta'ðor] nm heater

calentamiento [kalenta'mjento] nm (Deporte) warm-up; **calentamiento global** global warming

calentar [kalen'tar] vt to heat (up); **calentarse** vr to heat up, warm up; (fig: discusión etc) to get heated

calentón, -ona [kalen'ton, ona] (RPL: fam) adj (sexualmente) horny, randy (BRIT)

calentura [kalen'tura] nf (Med) fever, (high) temperature

calesita [kale'sita] (RPL) nf merry-go-round, carousel

calibre [ka'liβre] nm (de cañón) calibre, bore; (diámetro) diameter; (fig) calibre

calidad [kali'ðað] nf quality; **de ~** quality cpd; **en ~ de** in the capacity of, as

cálido, -a ['kaliðo, a] adj hot; (fig) warm

caliente etc [ka'ljente] vb V **calentar** ▷ adj hot; (fig) fiery; (disputa) heated; (fam: cachondo) randy

calificación [kalifika'θjon] nf qualification; (de alumno) grade, mark

calificado, -a [kalifi'kaðo, a] (LAM) adj (competente) qualified; (obrero) skilled

calificar [kalifi'kar] vt to qualify; (alumno) to grade, mark; **~ de** to describe as

calima [ka'lima] nf (cerca del mar) mist

cáliz ['kaliθ] nm chalice

caliza [ka'liθa] nf limestone

callado, -a [ka'ʎaðo, a] adj quiet

callar [ka'ʎar] vt (asunto delicado) to keep quiet about, say nothing about; (persona, opinión) to silence ▷ vi to keep quiet, be silent; **callarse** vr to keep quiet, be silent; **¡cállate!** be quiet!, shut up!

calle [ka'ʎe] nf street; (Deporte) lane; **~ arriba/abajo** up/down the street; **calle de sentido único** one-way street; **calle mayor** (ESP) high (BRIT) o main (US) street; **calle peatonal**

pedestrianized o pedestrian street; **calle principal** (*LAM*) high (*BRIT*) o main (*US*) street; **callejear** *vi* to wander (about) the streets; **callejero, -a** *adj* street *cpd* ▷ *nm* street map; **callejón** *nm* alley, passage; **callejón sin salida** cul-de-sac; **callejuela** *nf* side-street, alley

callista [ka'ʎista] *nmf* chiropodist

callo ['kaʎo] *nm* callus; (*en el pie*) corn; **callos** *nmpl* (*Culin*) tripe *sg*

calma ['kalma] *nf* calm

calmante [kal'mante] *nm* sedative, tranquillizer

calmar [kal'mar] *vt* to calm, calm down ▷ *vi* (*tempestad*) to abate; (*mente etc*) to become calm

calor [ka'lor] *nm* heat; (*agradable*) warmth; **hace ~** it's hot; **tener ~** to be hot

caloría [kalo'ria] *nf* calorie

calumnia [ka'lumnja] *nf* calumny, slander

caluroso, -a [kalu'roso, a] *adj* hot; (*sin exceso*) warm; (*fig*) enthusiastic

calva ['kalβa] *nf* bald patch; (*en bosque*) clearing

calvario [kal'βarjo] *nm* stations *pl* of the cross

calvicie [kal'βiθje] *nf* baldness

calvo, -a ['kalβo, a] *adj* bald; (*terreno*) bare, barren; (*tejido*) threadbare

calza ['kalθa] *nf* wedge, chock

calzada [kal'θaða] *nf* roadway, highway

calzado, -a [kal'θaðo, a] *adj* shod ▷ *nm* footwear

calzador [kalθa'ðor] *nm* shoehorn

calzar [kal'θar] *vt* (*zapatos etc*) to wear; (*mueble*) to put a wedge under; **calzarse** *vr*: **~se los zapatos** to put on one's shoes; **¿qué (número) calza?** what size do you take?

calzón [kal'θon] *nm* (*ESP*: *pantalón corto*) shorts; (*LAM*: *ropa interior: de hombre*) underpants, pants (*BRIT*), shorts (*US*); (: *de mujer*) panties, knickers (*BRIT*)

calzoncillos [kalθon'θiʎos] *nmpl* underpants

cama ['kama] *nf* bed; **hacer la ~** to make the bed; **cama individual/de matrimonio** single/double bed

camaleón [kamale'on] *nm* chameleon

cámara ['kamara] *nf* chamber; (*habitación*) room; (*sala*) hall; (*Cine*) cine camera; (*fotográfica*) camera; **cámara de aire** (*ESP*) inner tube; **cámara de comercio** chamber of commerce; **cámara de gas** gas chamber; **cámara digital** digital camera; **cámara frigorífica** cold-storage room

camarada [kama'raða] *nmf* comrade, companion

camarera [kama'rera] *nf* (*en restaurante*) waitress; (*en casa, hotel*) maid

camarero [kama'rero] *nm* waiter

camarógrafo, -a [kama'roɣrafo, a] (*LAM*) *nm/f* cameraman/ camerawoman

camarón [kama'ron] *nm* shrimp

camarote [kama'rote] *nm* cabin

cambiable [kam'bjaβle] *adj* (*variable*) changeable, variable; (*intercambiable*) interchangeable

cambiante [kam'bjante] *adj* variable

cambiar [kam'bjar] *vt* to change; (*dinero*) to change ▷ *vi* to change; **cambiarse** *vr* (*mudarse*) to move; (*de ropa*) to change; **~ de idea u opinión** to change one's mind; **~se de ropa** to change (one's clothes)

cambio ['kambjo] *nm* change; (*trueque*) exchange; (*Com*) rate of exchange; (*oficina*) bureau de change; (*dinero menudo*) small change; **a ~ de** in return o exchange for; **en ~** on the other hand; (*en lugar de*) instead; **cambio climático** climate change; **cambio de divisas** foreign exchange; **cambio de marchas** o **velocidades** gear lever

camelar [kame'lar] *vt* to sweet-talk

camello [ka'meʎo] *nm* camel;

(*fam: traficante*) pusher

camerino [kame'rino] *nm* dressing room

camilla [ka'miʎa] *nf* (*Med*) stretcher

caminar [kami'nar] *vi* (*marchar*) to walk, go ▷ *vt* (*recorrer*) to cover, travel

caminata [kami'nata] *nf* long walk; (*por el campo*) hike

camino [ka'mino] *nm* way, road; (*sendero*) track; **a medio ~** halfway (there); **en el ~** on the way, en route; **~ de** on the way to; **Camino de Santiago** Way of St James; **camino particular** private road

● **CAMINO DE SANTIAGO**
●
● The **Camino de Santiago** is a
● medieval pilgrim route stretching
● from the Pyrenees to Santiago de
● Compostela in north-west Spain,
● where tradition has it the body
● of the Apostle James is buried.
● Nowadays it is a popular tourist
● route as well as a religious one.

camión [ka'mjon] *nm* lorry (*BRIT*), truck (*US*); (*MÉX: autobús*) bus; **camión cisterna** tanker; **camión de la basura** dustcart, refuse lorry; **camión de mudanzas** removal (*BRIT*) o moving (*US*) van; **camionero, -a** *nm/f* lorry o truck driver; **camionista** *nmf* lorry o truck driver

camioneta [kamjo'neta] *nf* van, light truck

camisa [ka'misa] *nf* shirt; (*Bot*) skin; **camisa de fuerza** straitjacket

camiseta [kami'seta] *nf* (*prenda*) tee-shirt; (*ropa interior*) vest; (*de deportista*) top

camisón [kami'son] *nm* nightdress, nightgown

camorra [ka'morra] *nf*: **buscar ~** to look for trouble

camote [ka'mote] *nm* (*MÉX, cs: batata*) sweet potato, yam; (*MÉX: bulbo*) tuber, bulb;

(*cs: fam: enamoramiento*) crush

campamento [kampa'mento] *nm* camp

campana [kam'pana] *nf* bell; **campanada** *nf* peal; **campanario** *nm* belfry

campanilla [kampa'niʎa] *nf* small bell

campaña [kam'paɲa] *nf* (*Mil, Pol*) campaign; **campaña electoral** election campaign

campechano, -a [kampe'tʃano, a] *adj* (*franco*) open

campeón, -ona [kampe'on, ona] *nm/f* champion; **campeonato** *nm* championship

cámper ['kamper] *nm o f* caravan (*BRIT*), trailer (*US*)

campera [kam'pera] (*RPL*) *nf* anorak

campesino, -a [kampe'sino, a] *adj* country *cpd*, rural; (*gente*) peasant *cpd* ▷ *nm/f* countryman/woman; (*agricultor*) farmer

campestre [kam'pestre] *adj* country *cpd*, rural

camping ['kampin] (*pl* **~s**) *nm* camping; (*lugar*) campsite; **ir** o **estar de ~** to go camping

campista [kam'pista] *nm/f* camper

campo ['kampo] *nm* (*fuera de la ciudad*) country, countryside; (*Agr, Elec*) field; (*de fútbol*) pitch; (*de golf*) course; (*Mil*) camp; **campo de batalla** battlefield; **campo de concentración** concentration camp; **campo de deportes** sports ground, playing field; **campo visual** field of vision, visual field

camuflaje [kamu'flaxe] *nm* camouflage

cana ['kana] *nf* white o grey hair; **tener ~s** to be going grey

Canadá [kana'ða] *nm* Canada; **canadiense** *adj, nmf* Canadian ▷ *nf* fur-lined jacket

canal [ka'nal] *nm* canal; (*Geo*) channel, strait; (*de televisión*) channel; (*de tejado*) gutter; **canal de Panamá**

Panama Canal; **canal de la mancha** English Canal

canaleta [kana'leta] (LAM) nf (de tejado) gutter

canalizar [kanali'θar] vt to channel

canalla [ka'naʎa] nf rabble, mob ▷ nm swine

canapé [kana'pe] (pl **-s**) nm sofa, settee; (Culin) canapé

Canarias [ka'narjas] nfpl (tb: **las Islas ~**) the Canary Islands, the Canaries

canario, -a [ka'narjo, a] adj, nm/f (native) of the Canary Isles ▷ nm (Zool) canary

canasta [ka'nasta] nf (round) basket

canasto [ka'nasto] nm large basket

cancela [kan'θela] nf gate

cancelación [kanθela'θjon] nf cancellation

cancelar [kanθe'lar] vt to cancel; (una deuda) to write off

cáncer ['kanθer] nm (Med) cancer; **C~** (Astrología) Cancer

cancha ['kantʃa] nf (de baloncesto) court; (LAM: campo) pitch; **cancha de tenis** (LAM) tennis court

canciller [kanθi'ʎer] nm chancellor

canción [kan'θjon] nf song; **canción de cuna** lullaby

candado [kan'daðo] nm padlock

candente [kan'dente] adj red-hot; (fig: tema) burning

candidato, -a [kandi'ðato, a] nm/f candidate

cándido, -a ['kandiðo, a] adj simple; naive

No confundir **cándido** con la palabra inglesa candid.

candil [kan'dil] nm oil lamp; **candilejas** nfpl (Teatro) footlights

canela [ka'nela] nf cinnamon

canelones [kane'lones] nmpl cannelloni

cangrejo [kan'grexo] nm crab

canguro [kan'guro] nm kangaroo; **hacer de ~** to babysit

caníbal [ka'niβal] adj, nmf cannibal

canica [ka'nika] nf marble

canijo [ka'nixo, a] adj frail, sickly

canilla [ka'niʎa] (RPL) nf tap (BRIT); faucet (US)

canjear [kanxe'ar] vt to exchange

canoa [ka'noa] nf canoe

canon ['kanon] nm canon; (pensión) rent; (Com) tax

canonizar [kanoni'θar] vt to canonize

canoso, -a [ka'noso, a] adj grey-haired

cansado, -a [kan'saðo, a] adj tired, weary; (tedioso) tedious, boring

cansancio [kan'sanθjo] nm tiredness, fatigue

cansar [kan'sar] vt (fatigar) to tire, tire out; (aburrir) to bore; (fastidiar) to bother; **cansarse** vr to tire, get tired; (aburrirse) to get bored

cantábrico, -a [kan'taβriko, a] adj Cantabrian

cantante [kan'tante] adj singing ▷ nmf singer

cantar [kan'tar] vt to sing ▷ vi to sing; (insecto) to chirp ▷ nm (acción) singing; (canción) song; (poema) poem

cántaro ['kantaro] nm pitcher, jug; **llover a ~s** to rain cats and dogs

cante ['kante] nm (Mús) Andalusian folk song; **cante jondo** flamenco singing

cantera [kan'tera] nf quarry

cantero [kan'tero] (RPL) nm (arriate) border

cantidad [kanti'ðað] nf quantity, amount; **~ de** lots of

cantimplora [kantim'plora] nf (frasco) water bottle, canteen

cantina [kan'tina] nf canteen; (de estación) buffet; (LAM: bar) bar

cantinero, -a [kanti'nero, a] (MÉX) nm/f barman/barmaid, bartender (US)

canto ['kanto] nm (acto, arte, canción) song; (borde) edge, rim; (de cuchillo) back; **canto rodado** boulder

cantor, a [kan'tor, a] nm/f singer

canturrear [kanturre'ar] vi to sing

sing softly

canuto [ka'nuto] nm (tubo) small tube; (fam: droga) joint

caña ['kaɲa] nf (Bot: tallo) stem, stalk; (carrizo) reed; (vaso) tumbler; (de cerveza) glass of beer; (Anat) shinbone; **caña de azúcar** sugar cane; **caña de pescar** fishing rod

cañada [ka'ɲaða] nf (entre dos montañas) gully, ravine; (camino) cattle track

cáñamo ['kaɲamo] nm hemp

cañería [kaɲe'ria] nf (tubo) pipe

caño ['kaɲo] nm (tubo) tube, pipe; (de albañal) sewer; (Mús) pipe; (de fuente) jet

cañón [ka'ɲon] nm (Mil) cannon; (de fusil) barrel; (Geo) canyon, gorge

caoba [ka'oβa] nf mahogany

caos [kaos] nm chaos

capa ['kapa] nf cloak, cape; (Geo) layer, stratum; **capa de ozono** ozone layer

capacidad [kapaθi'ðað] nf (medida) capacity; (aptitud) capacity, ability

capacitarse [kapaθi'tarse] vi: ~ **para algo** to qualify for sth

caparazón [kapara'θon] nm shell

capataz [kapa'taθ] nm foreman

capaz [ka'paθ] adj able, capable; (amplio) capacious, roomy

capellán [kape'ʎan] nm chaplain; (sacerdote) priest

capicúa [kapi'kua] adj inv (número, fecha) reversible

capilla [ka'piʎa] nf chapel

capital [kapi'tal] adj capital ▷ nm (Com) capital ▷ nf (ciudad) capital; **capital social** share o authorized capital

capitalismo [kapita'lismo] nm capitalism; **capitalista** adj, nmf capitalist

capitán [kapi'tan] nm captain

capítulo [ka'pitulo] nm chapter

capó [ka'po] nm (Auto) bonnet

capón [ka'pon] nm (gallo) capon

capota [ka'pota] nf (de mujer) bonnet; (Auto) hood (BRIT), top (US)

capote [ka'pote] nm (abrigo: de militar) greatcoat; (de torero) cloak

capricho [ka'pritʃo] nm whim, caprice; **caprichoso, -a** adj capricious

Capricornio [kapri'kornjo] nm Capricorn

cápsula ['kapsula] nf capsule

captar [kap'tar] vt (comprender) to understand; (Radio) to pick up; (atención, apoyo) to attract

captura [kap'tura] nf capture; (Jur) arrest; **capturar** vt to capture; to arrest

capucha [ka'putʃa] nf hood, cowl

capuchón [kapu'tʃon] (ESP) nm (de bolígrafo) cap

capullo [ka'puʎo] nm (Bot) bud; (Zool) cocoon; (fam) idiot

caqui ['kaki] nm khaki

cara ['kara] nf (Anat: de moneda) face; (de disco) side; (descaro) boldness; ~ **a** facing; **de** ~ opposite, facing; **dar la** ~ to face the consequences; **¿** ~ **o cruz?** heads or tails?; **¡qué** ~ **(más dura)!** what a nerve!

Caracas [ka'rakas] n Caracas

caracol [kara'kol] nm (Zool) snail; (concha) (sea) shell

carácter [ka'rakter] (pl **caracteres**) nm character; **tener buen/mal** ~ to be good natured/bad tempered

característica [karakte'ristika] nf characteristic

característico, -a [karakte'ristiko, a] adj characteristic

caracterizar [karakteri'θar] vt to characterize, typify

caradura [kara'ðura] nmf: **es un** ~ he's got a nerve

carajillo [kara'xiʎo] nm coffee with a dash of brandy

carajo [ka'raxo] (fam!) nm: **¡~!** shit! (!)

caramba [ka'ramba] excl good gracious!

caramelo [kara'melo] nm (dulce) sweet; (azúcar fundida) caramel

caravana [kara'βana] nf caravan; (fig) group; (Auto) tailback

carbón [kar'βon] nm coal; **papel** ~

carbon paper

carbono [kar'βono] nm carbon

carburador [karβura'ðor] nm carburettor

carburante [karβu'rante] nm (para motor) fuel

carcajada [karka'xaða] nf (loud) laugh, guffaw

cárcel ['karθel] nf prison, jail; (Tec) clamp

carcoma [kar'koma] nf woodworm

cardar [kar'ðar] vt (pelo) to backcomb

cardenal [karðe'nal] nm (Rel) cardinal; (Med) bruise

cardíaco, -a [kar'ðiako, a] adj cardiac, heart cpd

cardinal [karði'nal] adj cardinal

cardo ['karðo] nm thistle

carecer [kare'θer] vi: ~ **de** to lack, be in need of

carencia [ka'renθja] nf lack; (escasez) shortage; (Med) deficiency

careta [ka'reta] nf mask

carga ['karɣa] nf (peso, Elec) load; (de barco) cargo, freight; (Mil) charge; (responsabilidad) duty, obligation

cargado, -a [kar'ɣaðo, a] adj loaded; (Elec) live; (café, té) strong; (cielo) overcast

cargamento [karɣa'mento] nm (acción) loading; (mercancías) load, cargo

cargar [kar'ɣar] vt (barco, arma) to load; (Elec) to charge; (Com: algo en cuenta) to charge; (Inform) to load ▷ vi (Mil) to charge; (Auto) to load (up); ~ **con** to pick up, carry away; (peso: fig) to shoulder, bear; **cargarse** vr (fam: estropear) to break; (: matar) to bump off

cargo ['karɣo] nm (puesto) post, office; (responsabilidad) duty, obligation; (Jur) charge; **hacerse ~ de** to take charge of o responsibility for

carguero [kar'ɣero] nm freighter, cargo boat; (avión) freight plane

Caribe [ka'riβe] nm: **el ~** the Caribbean; **del ~** Caribbean; **caribeño,**

-a [kari'βeɲo, a] adj Caribbean

caricatura [karika'tura] nf caricature

caricia [ka'riθja] nf caress

caridad [kari'ðað] nf charity

caries ['karjes] nf inv tooth decay

cariño [ka'riɲo] nm affection, love; (caricia) caress; (en carta) love ...; **tener ~ a** to be fond of; **cariñoso, -a** adj affectionate

carisma [ka'risma] nm charisma

caritativo, -a [karita'tiβo, a] adj charitable

cariz [ka'riθ] nm: **tener o tomar buen/mal ~** to look good/bad

carmín [kar'min] nm lipstick

carnal [kar'nal] adj carnal; **primo ~** first cousin

carnaval [karna'βal] nm carnival

CARNAVAL

Carnaval is the traditional period of fun, feasting and partying which takes place in the three days before the start of Lent ("Cuaresma"). Although in decline during the Franco years the carnival has grown in popularity recently in Spain. Cádiz and Tenerife are particularly well-known for their flamboyant celebrations with fancy-dress parties, parades and firework displays being the order of the day.

carne ['karne] nf flesh; (Culin) meat; **se me pone la ~ de gallina sólo verlo** I get the creeps just seeing it; **carne de cerdo/cordero/ternera/vaca** pork/lamb/veal/beef; **carne de gallina** (fig) gooseflesh; **carne molida** (LAM) mince (BRIT), ground meat (US); **carne picada** (ESP, RPL) mince (BRIT), ground meat (US)

carné [kar'ne] (ESP) (pl **~s**) nm: **~ de conducir** driving licence (BRIT), driver's license (US); **~ de identidad** identity card; **~ de socio** membership card

carnero [kar'nero] *nm* sheep, ram; *(carne)* mutton

carnet [kar'ne] (*ESP*) (*pl* **~s**) *nm* = **carné**

carnicería [karniθe'ria] *nf* butcher's (shop); *(fig: matanza)* carnage, slaughter

carnicero, -a [karni'θero, a] *adj* carnivorous ▷ *nm/f* butcher; *(carnívoro)* carnivore

carnívoro, -a [kar'niβoro, a] *adj* carnivorous

caro, -a ['karo, a] *adj* dear; *(Com)* dear, expensive ▷ *adv* dear, dearly

carpa ['karpa] *nf* (*pez*) carp; *(de circo)* big top; *(LAM: tienda de campaña)* tent

carpeta [kar'peta] *nf* folder, file; **carpeta de anillas** ring binder

carpintería [karpinte'ria] *nf* carpentry, joinery; **carpintero** *nm* carpenter

carraspear [karraspe'ar] *vi* to clear one's throat

carraspera [karras'pera] *nf* hoarseness

carrera [ka'rrera] *nf* (*acción*) run(ning); (*espacio recorrido*) run; *(competición)* race; *(trayecto)* course; *(profesión)* career; *(licenciatura)* degree; **a la ~** at (full) speed; **carrera de obstáculos** *(Deporte)* steeplechase

carrete [ka'rrete] *nm* reel, spool; *(Tec)* coil

carretera [karre'tera] *nf* (*main*) road, highway; **carretera de circunvalación** ring road; **carretera nacional** = A road *(BRIT)*, = state highway *(US)*

carretilla [karre'tiʎa] *nf* trolley; *(Agr)* (wheel)barrow

carril [ka'rril] *nm* furrow; *(de autopista)* lane; *(Ferro)* rail; **carril-bici** cycle lane

carrito [ka'rrito] *nm* trolley

carro ['karro] *nm* cart, wagon; *(Mil)* tank; *(LAM: coche)* car; **carro patrulla** *(LAM)* patrol o panda *(BRIT)* car

carrocería [karroθe'ria] *nf* bodywork, coachwork

carroña [ka'rroɲa] *nf* carrion *no pl*

carroza [ka'rroθa] *nf* (*carruaje*) coach

carrusel [karru'sel] *nm* merry-go-round, roundabout

carta ['karta] *nf* letter; *(Culin)* menu; *(naipe)* card; *(mapa)* map; *(Jur)* document; **carta certificada/urgente** registered/special-delivery letter

cartabón [karta'βon] *nm* set square

cartearse [karte'arse] *vr* to correspond

cartel [kar'tel] *nm* (*anuncio*) poster, placard; *(Escol)* wall chart; *(Com)* cartel; **cartelera** *nf* hoarding, billboard; *(en periódico etc)* entertainments guide; **"en cartelera"** "showing"

cartera [kar'tera] *nf* (*de bolsillo*) wallet; *(de colegial, cobrador)* satchel; *(de señora)* handbag; *(para documentos)* briefcase; *(Com)* portfolio; **ocupa la ~ de Agricultura** she is Minister of Agriculture

carterista [karte'rista] *nmf* pickpocket

cartero [kar'tero] *nm* postman

cartilla [kar'tiʎa] *nf* primer, first reading book; **cartilla de ahorros** savings book

cartón [kar'ton] *nm* cardboard; **cartón piedra** papier-mâché

cartucho [kar'tutʃo] *nm* (*Mil*) cartridge

cartulina [kartu'lina] *nf* card

casa ['kasa] *nf* house; *(hogar)* home; *(Com)* firm, company; **en ~** at home; **casa consistorial** town hall; **casa de campo** country house; **casa de huéspedes** boarding house; **casa independiente** detached house; **casa de socorro** first aid post; **casa rodante** *(CS)* caravan *(BRIT)*, trailer *(US)*

casado, -a [ka'saðo, a] *adj* married ▷ *nm/f* married man/woman

casar [ka'sar] *vt* to marry; *(Jur)* to quash, annul; **casarse** *vr* to marry, get married

cascabel [kaskaˈβel] *nm* (small) bell

cascada [kasˈkaða] *nf* waterfall

cascanueces [kaskaˈnweθes] *nm inv* nutcrackers *pl*

cascar [kasˈkar] *vt* to crack, split, break (open); **cascarse** *vr* to crack, split, break (open)

cáscara [ˈkaskara] *nf* (*de huevo, fruta seca*) shell; (*de fruta*) skin; (*de limón*) peel

casco [ˈkasko] *nm* (*de bombero, soldado*) helmet; (*Náut: de barco*) hull; (*Zool: de caballo*) hoof; (*botella*) empty bottle; (*de ciudad*): **el ~ antiguo** the old part; **el ~ urbano** the town centre; **los ~s azules** the UN peace-keeping force, the blue berets

cascote [kasˈkote] *nm* rubble

caserío [kaseˈrio] (*ESP*) *nm* farmhouse; (*casa*) country mansion

casero, -a [kaˈsero, a] *adj* (*pan etc*) home-made ▷ *nm/f* (*propietario*) landlord/lady; **ser muy ~** to be home-loving; **"comida casera"** "home cooking"

caseta [kaˈseta] *nf* hut; (*para bañista*) cubicle; (*de feria*) stall

casete [kaˈsete] *nm o f* cassette

casi [ˈkasi] *adv* almost, nearly; **~ nada** hardly anything; **~ nunca** hardly ever, almost never; **~ te caes** you almost fell

casilla [kaˈsiʎa] *nf* (*casita*) hut, cabin; (*Ajedrez*) square; (*para cartas*) pigeonhole; **casilla de correo** (*cs*) P.O. Box; **casillero** *nm* (*para cartas*) pigeonholes *pl*

casino [kaˈsino] *nm* club; (*de juego*) casino

caso [ˈkaso] *nm* case; **en ~ de** in case of; **en ~ de que ...** in case ...; **el ~ es que ...** the fact is that ...; **en ese/todo ~** in that/any case; **hacer ~ a** to pay attention to; **venir al ~** to be relevant

caspa [ˈkaspa] *nf* dandruff

cassette [kaˈsete] *nm o f* = **casete**

castaña [kasˈtaɲa] *nf* chestnut

castaño, -a [kasˈtaɲo, a] *adj* chestnut(-coloured), brown ▷ *nm* chestnut tree

castañuelas [kastaˈɲwelas] *nfpl* castanets

castellano, -a [kasteˈʎano, a] *adj, nm/f* Castilian ▷ *nm* (*Ling*) Castilian, Spanish

castigar [kastiˈɣar] *vt* to punish; (*Deporte*) to penalize; **castigo** *nm* punishment; (*Deporte*) penalty

Castilla [kasˈtiʎa] *nf* Castile

castillo [kasˈtiʎo] *nm* castle

castizo, -a [kasˈtiθo, a] *adj* (*Ling*) pure

casto, -a [ˈkasto, a] *adj* chaste, pure

castor [kasˈtor] *nm* beaver

castrar [kasˈtrar] *vt* to castrate

casual [kaˈswal] *adj* chance, accidental

> No confundir **casual** con la palabra inglesa *casual*.

casualidad *nf* chance, accident; (*combinación de circunstancias*) coincidence; **da la casualidad de que ...** it (just) so happens that ...; **¡qué casualidad!** what a coincidence!

cataclismo [kataˈklismo] *nm* cataclysm

catador, a [kataˈðor, a] *nm/f* wine taster

catalán, -ana [kataˈlan, ana] *adj, nm/f* Catalan ▷ *nm* (*Ling*) Catalan

catalizador [kataliθaˈðor] *nm* catalyst; (*Auto*) catalytic convertor

catalogar [kataloˈɣar] *vt* to catalogue; **~ a algn (de)** (*fig*) to categorize sb (as)

catálogo [kaˈtaloɣo] *nm* catalogue

Cataluña [kataˈluɲa] *nf* Catalonia

catar [kaˈtar] *vt* to taste, sample

catarata [kataˈrata] *nf* (*Geo*) waterfall; (*Med*) cataract

catarro [kaˈtarro] *nm* catarrh; (*constipado*) cold

catástrofe [kaˈtastrofe] *nf* catastrophe

catear [kateˈar] (*fam*) *vt* (*examen, alumno*) to fail

cátedra [ˈkateðra] *nf* (*Univ*) chair, professorship

catedral [kate'ðral] nf cathedral

catedrático, -a [kate'ðratiko, a] nm/f professor

categoría [katexo'ria] nf category; (rango) rank, standing; (calidad) quality; **de ~** (hotel) top-class

cateto, -a ['kateto, a] (ESP: pey) nm/f peasant

catolicismo [katoli'θismo] nm Catholicism

católico, -a [ka'toliko, a] adj, nm/f Catholic

catorce [ka'torθe] num fourteen

cauce ['kauθe] nm (de río) riverbed; (fig) channel

caucho ['kautʃo] (ESP) nm rubber

caudal [kau'ðal] nm (de río) volume, flow; (fortuna) wealth; (abundancia) abundance

caudillo [kau'ðiʎo] nm leader, chief

causa ['kausa] nf cause; (razón) reason; (Jur) lawsuit, case; **a ~ de** because of; **causar** [kau'sar] vt to cause

cautela [kau'tela] nf caution, cautiousness; **cauteloso, -a** adj cautious, wary

cautivar [kauti'βar] vt to capture; (atraer) to captivate

cautiverio [kauti'βerjo] nm captivity

cautividad [kautiβi'ðað] nf = **cautiverio**

cautivo, -a [kau'tiβo, a] adj, nm/f captive

cauto, -a ['kauto, a] adj cautious, careful

cava ['kaβa] nm champagne-type wine

cavar [ka'βar] vt to dig

caverna [ka'βerna] nf cave, cavern

cavidad [kaβi'ðað] nf cavity

cavilar [kaβi'lar] vt to ponder

cayendo etc vb V **caer**

caza ['kaθa] nf (acción: gen) hunting; (: con fusil) shooting; (una caza) hunt, chase; (de animales) game ▷ nm (Aviac) fighter; **ir de ~** to go hunting; **caza mayor** game hunting; **cazador, a**

[kaθa'ðor, a] nm/f hunter; **cazadora** nf jacket; **cazar** [ka'θar] vt to hunt; (perseguir) to chase; (prender) to catch

cazo ['kaθo] nm saucepan

cazuela [ka'θwela] nf (vasija) pan; (guisado) casserole

CD nm abr (= compact disc) CD

CD-ROM [θeðe'rom] nm abr CD-ROM

CE nf abr (= Comunidad Europea) EC

cebada [θe'βaða] nf barley

cebar [θe'βar] vt (animal) to fatten (up); (anzuelo) to bait; (Mil, Tec) to prime

cebo ['θeβo] nm (para animales) feed, food; (para peces, fig) bait; (de arma) charge

cebolla [θe'βoʎa] nf onion; **cebolleta** nf spring onion

cebra ['θeβra] nf zebra

cecear [θeθe'ar] vi to lisp

ceder [θe'ðer] vt to hand over, give up, part with ▷ vi (renunciar) to give in, yield; (disminuir) to diminish, decline; (romperse) to give way

cederom [θeðe'rom] nm CD-ROM

cedro ['θeðro] nm cedar

cédula ['θeðula] nf certificate, document; **cédula de identidad** (LAM) identity card; **cédula electoral** (LAM) ballot

cegar [θe'ɣar] vt to blind; (tubería etc) to block up, stop up ▷ vi to go blind; **cegarse** vr: **~se (de)** to be blinded (by)

ceguera [θe'ɣera] nf blindness

ceja ['θexa] nf eyebrow

cejar [θe'xar] vi (fig) to back down

celador, a [θela'ðor, a] nm/f (de edificio) watchman; (de museo etc) attendant

celda ['θelda] nf cell

celebración [θeleβra'θjon] nf celebration

celebrar [θele'βrar] vt to celebrate; (alabar) to praise ▷ vi to be glad; **celebrarse** vr to occur, take place

célebre ['θeleβre] adj famous

celebridad [θeleβri'ðað] nf fame; (persona) celebrity

celeste [θe'leste] adj (azul) sky-blue

celestial [θeles'tjal] adj celestial, heavenly

celo¹ ['θelo] nm zeal; (Rel) fervour; (Zool): **en ~** on heat; **celos** nmpl jealousy sg; **dar ~s a algn** to make sb jealous; **tener ~s** to be jealous

celo²® ['θelo] nm Sellotape®

celofán [θelo'fan] nm cellophane

celoso, -a [θe'loso, a] adj jealous; (trabajador) zealous

celta ['θelta] adj Celtic ▷ nmf Celt

célula ['θelula] nf cell

celulitis [θelu'litis] nf cellulite

cementerio [θemen'terjo] nm cemetery, graveyard

cemento [θe'mento] nm cement; (hormigón) concrete; (LAM: cola) glue

cena ['θena] nf evening meal, dinner; **cenar** [θe'nar] vt to have for dinner ▷ vi to have dinner

cenicero [θeni'θero] nm ashtray

ceniza [θe'niθa] nf ash, ashes pl

censo ['θenso] nm census; **censo electoral** electoral roll

censura [θen'sura] nf (Pol) censorship; **censurar** [θensu'rar] vt (idea) to censure; (cortar: película) to censor

centella [θen'teʎa] nf spark

centenar [θente'nar] nm hundred

centenario, -a [θente'narjo, a] adj (chaqueta, pantalón) tight(-fitting)

ceñir [θe'ɲir] vt (rodear) to encircle, surround; (ajustar) to fit (tightly)

ceño ['θeɲo] nm frown, scowl; **fruncir el ~** to frown, knit one's brow

cepillar [θepi'ʎar] vt to brush; (madera) to plane (down)

cepillo [θe'piʎo] nm brush; (para madera) plane; **cepillo de dientes** toothbrush

cera ['θera] nf wax

cerámica [θe'ramika] nf pottery; (arte) ceramics

cerca ['θerka] nf fence ▷ adv near, nearby, close; **~ de** near, close to

cercanías [θerka'nias] nfpl (afueras) outskirts, suburbs

cercano, -a [θer'kano, a] adj close, near

cercar [θer'kar] vt to fence in; (rodear) to surround

cerco ['θerko] nm (Agr) enclosure; (LAM: valla) fence; (Mil) siege

cerdo, -a ['θerðo, a] nm/f pig, pork

cereal [θere'al] nm cereal; **cereales**

station; **central telefónica** telephone exchange

centralita [θentra'lita] nf switchboard

centralizar [θentrali'θar] vt to centralize

centrar [θen'trar] vt to centre

céntrico, -a ['θentriko, a] adj central

centrifugar [θentrifu'xar] vt to spin-dry

centro ['θentro] nm centre; **centro comercial** shopping centre; **centro de atención al cliente** call centre; **centro de salud** health centre; **centro escolar** school; **centro juvenil** youth club; **centro turístico** (lugar muy visitado) tourist centre; **centro urbano** urban area, city

centroamericano, -a [θentroameri'kano, a] adj, nm/f Central American

ceñido, -a [θe'ɲiðo, a] adj (chaqueta, pantalón) tight(-fitting)

centenario, -a [θente'narjo, a] adj (edad) hundred-year-old ▷ nm centenary

centeno [θen'teno] nm (Bot) rye

centésimo, -a [θen'tesimo, a] adj hundredth

centígrado [θen'tixraðo] adj centigrade

centímetro [θen'timetro] nm centimetre (BRIT), centimeter (US)

céntimo ['θentimo] nm cent

centinela [θenti'nela] nm sentry, guard

centollo [θen'toʎo] nm spider crab

central [θen'tral] adj central ▷ nf head office; (Tec) plant; (Elec) exchange; **central eléctrica** power station; **central nuclear** nuclear power

nmpl cereals, grain *sg*

cerebro [θe'reβro] *nm* brain; (fig) brains *pl*

ceremonia [θere'monja] *nf* ceremony; **ceremonioso, -a** *adj* ceremonious

cereza [θe'reθa] *nf* cherry

cerilla [θe'riʎa] *nf* (fósforo) match

cerillo [θe'riʎo] (MÉX) *nm* match

cero ['θero] *nm* nothing, zero

cerquillo [θer'kiʎo] (CAM, RPL) *nm* fringe (BRIT), bangs *pl* (US)

cerrado, -a [θe'rraðo, a] *adj* closed, shut; (con llave) locked; (tiempo) cloudy, overcast; (curva) sharp; (acento) thick, broad

cerradura [θerra'ðura] *nf* (acción) closing; (mecanismo) lock

cerrajero [θerra'xero] *nm* locksmith

cerrar [θe'rrar] *vt* to close, shut; (paso, carretera) to close; (grifo) to turn off; (cuenta, negocio) to close ▷ *vi* to close, shut; (noche) to come down; **cerrarse** *vr* to close, shut; **~ con llave** to lock; **~ un trato** to strike a bargain

cerro ['θerro] *nm* hill

cerrojo [θe'rroxo] *nm* (herramienta) bolt; (de puerta) latch

certamen [θer'tamen] *nm* competition, contest

certero, -a [θer'tero, a] *adj* (gen) accurate

certeza [θer'teθa] *nf* certainty

certidumbre [θerti'ðumbre] *nf* = **certeza**

certificado, -a [θertifi'kaðo, a] *adj* (carta, paquete) registered; (aprobado) certified ▷ *nm* certificate; **certificado médico** medical certificate

certificar [θertifi'kar] *vt* (asegurar, atestar) to certify

cervatillo [θerβa'tiʎo] *nm* fawn

cervecería [θerβeθe'ria] *nf* (fábrica) brewery; (bar) public house, pub

cerveza [θer'βeθa] *nf* beer

cesar [θe'sar] *vi* to cease, stop ▷ *vt* (funcionario) to remove from office

cesárea [θe'sarea] *nf* (Med)

Caesarean operation *o* section

cese ['θese] *nm* (de trabajo) dismissal; (de pago) suspension

césped ['θespeð] *nm* grass, lawn

cesta ['θesta] *nf* basket

cesto ['θesto] *nm* (large) basket, hamper

cfr *abr* (= confróntese) cf.

chabacano, -a [tʃaβa'kano, a] *adj* vulgar, coarse

chabola [tʃa'βola] (ESP) *nf* shack; **barrio de chabolas** shanty town

chacal [tʃa'kal] *nm* jackal

chacha [tʃatʃa] (fam) *nf* maid

cháchara [tʃatʃara] *nf* chatter; **estar de ~** to chatter away

chacra [tʃakra] (cs) *nf* smallholding

chafa ['tʃafa] (MÉX: fam) *adj* useless, dud

chafar [tʃa'far] *vt* (aplastar) to crush; (plan etc) to ruin

chal [tʃal] *nm* shawl

chalado, -a [tʃa'laðo, a] (fam) *adj* crazy

chalé [tʃa'le] (pl ~s) *nm* villa, = detached house

chaleco [tʃa'leko] *nm* waistcoat, vest (US); **chaleco de seguridad** (Aut) reflective safety vest; **chaleco salvavidas** life jacket

chalet [tʃa'le] (pl ~s) *nm* = **chalé**

chamaco, -a (MÉX) [tʃa'mako, a] *nm/f* (niño) kid

chambear [tʃambe'ar] (MÉX: fam) *vi* to earn one's living

champán [tʃam'pan] *nm* champagne

champiñón [tʃampi'ɲon] *nm* mushroom

champú [tʃam'pu] (pl **-es, ~s**) *nm* shampoo

chamuscar [tʃamus'kar] *vt* to scorch, sear, singe

chance ['tʃanθe] (LAM) *nm* chance

chancho, -a [tʃantʃo, a] (LAM) *nm/f* pig

chanchullo [tʃan'tʃuʎo] (fam) *nm* fiddle

chandal [tʃanˈdal] nm tracksuit

chantaje [tʃanˈtaxe] nm blackmail

chapa [ˈtʃapa] nf (de metal) plate, sheet; (de madera) board, panel; (RPL Auto) number (BRIT) o license (US) plate; **chapado, -a** adj: **chapado en oro** gold-plated

chaparrón [tʃapaˈrron] nm downpour, cloudburst

chaperón [tʃapeˈron] nm: **hacer de ~** to play gooseberry; **chaperona** (LAM) nf: **hacer de chaperona** to play gooseberry

chapopote [tʃapoˈpote] (MÉX) nm tar

chapulín [tʃapuˈlin] (MÉX, CAM) nm grasshopper

chapurrear [tʃapurreˈar] vt (idioma) to speak badly

chapuza [tʃaˈpuθa] nf botched job

chapuzón [tʃapuˈθon] nm: **darse un ~** to go for a dip

chaqueta [tʃaˈketa] nf jacket

chaquetón [tʃakeˈton] nm long jacket

charca [ˈtʃarka] nf pond, pool

charco [ˈtʃarko] nm pool, puddle

charcutería [tʃarkuteˈria] nf (tienda) shop selling chiefly pork meat products; (productos) cooked pork meats pl

charla [ˈtʃarla] nf talk, chat; (conferencia) lecture; **charlar** [tʃarˈlar] vi to talk, chat; **charlatán, -ana** [tʃarlaˈtan, ana] nm/f (hablador) chatterbox; (estafador) trickster

charol [tʃaˈrol] nm varnish; (cuero) patent leather

charola [tʃaˈrola] (MÉX) nf tray

charro, -a [tʃaˈrro, a] (MÉX) nm typical Mexican

chasco [ˈtʃasko] nm (desengaño) disappointment

chasis [ˈtʃasis] nm inv chassis

chasquido [tʃasˈkido] nm crack; click

chatarra [tʃaˈtarra] nf scrap (metal)

chatear [tʃateˈar] vi (Internet) to chat

chato, -a [ˈtʃato, a] adj flat; (nariz) snub

chaucha [ˈtʃautʃa] (RPL) nf runner (BRIT) o pole (US) bean

chaval, a [tʃaˈβal, a] (ESP) nm/f kid, lad/lass

chavo, -a [ˈtʃaβo] (MÉX: fam) nm/f guy/girl

checar [tʃeˈkar] (MÉX) vt: **~ tarjeta** (al entrar) to clock in o on; (: al salir) to clock off o out

checo, -a [ˈtʃeko, a] adj, nm/f Czech ▷ nm (Ling) Czech

checoslovaco, -a [tʃekoslo'βako, a] adj, nm/f Czech, Czechoslovak

Checoslovaquia [tʃekoslo'βakja] (Hist) Czechoslovakia

cheque [ˈtʃeke] nm cheque (BRIT), check (US); **cobrar un ~** to cash a cheque; **cheque al portador** cheque payable to bearer; **cheque de viaje** traveller's cheque (BRIT), traveler's check (US); **cheque en blanco** blank cheque

chequeo [tʃeˈkeo] nm (Med) check-up; (Auto) service

chequera [tʃeˈkera] (LAM) nf chequebook (BRIT), checkbook (US)

chévere [ˈtʃeβere] (LAM: fam) adj great

chícharo [ˈtʃitʃaro] (MÉX, CAM) nm pea

chichón [tʃiˈtʃon] nm bump, lump

chicle [ˈtʃikle] nm chewing gum

chico, -a [ˈtʃiko, a] adj small, little ▷ nm/f (niño) child; (muchacho) boy/girl

chiflado, -a [tʃiˈflaðo, a] adj crazy

chiflar [tʃiˈflar] vt to hiss, boo

chilango, -a [tʃiˈlango, a] (MÉX) adj of o from Mexico City

Chile [ˈtʃile] nm Chile; **chileno, -a** adj, nm/f Chilean

chile [ˈtʃile] nm chilli pepper

chillar [tʃiˈʎar] vi (persona) to yell, scream; (animal salvaje) to howl; (cerdo) to squeal

chillido [tʃiˈʎiðo] nm (de persona) yell, scream; (de animal) howl

chimenea [tʃimeˈnea] nf chimney; (hogar) fireplace

China ['tʃina] nf (tb: **la ~**) China

chinche ['tʃintʃe] nf (insecto) (bed)bug; (Tec) drawing pin (BRIT), thumbtack (US) ▷ nmf nuisance, pest

chincheta [tʃin'tʃeta] nf drawing pin (BRIT), thumbtack (US)

chingada [tʃin'gaða] (MÉX: fam!) nf: **hijo de la ~** bastard

chino, -a ['tʃino, a] adj, nm/f Chinese ▷ nm (Ling) Chinese

chipirón [tʃipi'ron] nm (Zool, Culin) squid

Chipre ['tʃipre] nf Cyprus; **chipriota** adj, nmf Cypriot

chiquillo, -a [tʃi'kiʎo, a] nm/f (fam) kid

chirimoya [tʃiri'moja] nf custard apple

chiringuito [tʃirin'xito] nm small open-air bar

chiripa [tʃi'ripa] nf fluke

chirriar [tʃi'rrjar] vi to creak, squeak

chirrido [tʃi'rriðo] nm creak(ing), squeak(ing)

chisme ['tʃisme] nm (habladurías) piece of gossip; (fam: objeto) thingummyjig

chismoso, -a [tʃis'moso, a] adj gossiping ▷ nm/f gossip

chispa ['tʃispa] nf spark; (fig) sparkle; (ingenio) wit; (fam) drunkenness

chispear [tʃispe'ar] vi (lloviznar) to drizzle

chiste ['tʃiste] nm joke, funny story

chistoso, -a [tʃis'toso, a] adj funny, amusing

chivo, -a ['tʃiβo, a] nm (billy-/nanny-)goat; **chivo expiatorio** scapegoat

chocante [tʃo'kante] adj startling; (extraño) odd; (ofensivo) shocking

chocar [tʃo'kar] vi (coches etc) to collide, crash ▷ vt to shock; (sorprender) to startle; **~ con** to collide with; (fig) to run into, run up against; **¡chócala!** (fam) put it there!

chochear [tʃotʃe'ar] vi to be senile

chocho, -a ['tʃotʃo, a] adj doddering,

senile; (fig) soft, doting

choclo ['tʃoklo] (cs) nm (grano) sweet corn; (mazorca) corn on the cob

chocolate [tʃoko'late] adj, nm chocolate; **chocolatina** nf chocolate

chofer [tʃo'fer] nm = **chófer**

chófer ['tʃofer] nm driver

chollo ['tʃoʎo] (ESP: fam) nm bargain, snip

choque etc ['tʃoke] vb V **chocar** ▷ nm (impacto) impact; (golpe) jolt; (Auto) crash; (fig) conflict; **choque frontal** head-on collision

chorizo [tʃo'riθo] nm hard pork sausage, (type of) salami

chorrada [tʃo'rraða] (ESP: fam) nf: **¡es una ~!** that's crap! (!); **decir ~s** to talk crap (!)

chorrear [tʃorre'ar] vi to gush (out), spout (out); (gotear) to drip, trickle

chorro ['tʃorro] nm jet; (fig) stream

choza ['tʃoθa] nf hut, shack

chubasco [tʃu'βasko] nm squall

chubasquero [tʃuβas'kero] nm lightweight raincoat

chuchería [tʃutʃe'ria] nf trinket

chuleta [tʃu'leta] nf chop, cutlet

chulo ['tʃulo] nm (de prostituta) pimp

chupaleta [tʃupa'leta] (MÉX) nf lollipop

chupar [tʃu'par] vt to suck; (absorber) to absorb; **chuparse** vr to grow thin

chupete [tʃu'pete] (ESP, CS) nm dummy (BRIT), pacifier (US)

chupetín [tʃupe'tin] (RPL) nf lollipop

chupito [tʃu'pito] (fam) nm shot

chupón [tʃu'pon] nm (piruleta) lollipop; (LAM: chupete) dummy (BRIT), pacifier (US)

churrería [tʃurre'ria] nf stall or shop which sells "churros"

churro ['tʃurro] nm (type of) fritter

chusma ['tʃusma] nf rabble, mob

chutar [tʃu'tar] vi (Deporte) to shoot (at goal)

Cía abr (= compañía) Co.

cianuro [θja'nuro] nm cyanide

cibercafé [θiβerka'fe] nm cybercafé

cibernauta [θiβer'nauta] nmf web

surfer, Internet user

ciberterrorista [θiβerterro'rista] *nmf* cyberterrorist

cicatriz [θika'triθ] *nf* scar; **cicatrizarse** *vr* to heal (up); form a scar

ciclismo [θi'klismo] *nm* cycling

ciclista [θi'klista] *adj* cycle *cpd* ▷ *nmf* cyclist

ciclo ['θiklo] *nm* cycle; **cicloturismo** *nm* touring by bicycle

ciclón [θi'klon] *nm* cyclone

ciego, -a ['θjeɣo, a] *adj* blind ▷ *nm/f* blind man/woman

cielo ['θjelo] *nm* sky; (Rel) heaven; **¡~s!** good heavens!

ciempiés [θjem'pjes] *nm inv* centipede

cien [θjen] *num* V **ciento**

ciencia ['θjenθja] *nf* science; **ciencias** *nfpl* (Escol) science *sg*; **ciencia-ficción** *nf* science fiction

científico, -a [θjen'tifiko, a] *adj* scientific ▷ *nm/f* scientist

ciento ['θjento] *num* hundred; **pagar al 10 por ~** to pay at 10 per cent; V *tb* **cien**

cierre *etc* ['θjerre] *vb* V **cerrar** ▷ *nm* closing, shutting; (con llave) locking; (Lam: cremallera) zip (fastener)

cierro *etc* *vb* V **cerrar**

cierto, -a ['θjerto, a] *adj* sure, certain; (un tal) a certain; (correcto) right, correct; **por ~** by the way; **~ hombre** a certain man; **ciertas personas** certain o some people; **sí, es ~** yes, that's correct

ciervo ['θjerβo] *nm* deer; (macho) stag

cifra ['θifra] *nf* number; (secreta) code; **cifrar** [θi'frar] *vt* to code, write in code

cigala [θi'ɣala] *nf* Norway lobster

cigarra [θi'ɣarra] *nf* cicada

cigarrillo [θiɣa'rriʎo] *nm* cigarette

cigarro [θi'ɣarro] *nm* cigarette; (puro) cigar

cigüeña [θi'ɣweɲa] *nf* stork

cilíndrico, -a [θi'lindriko, a] *adj* cylindrical

cilindro [θi'lindro] *nm* cylinder

cima ['θima] *nf* (de montaña) top, peak; (de árbol) top; (fig) height

cimentar [θimen'tar] *vt* to lay the foundations of; (fig: fundar) to found

cimiento [θi'mjento] *nm* foundation

cincel [θin'θel] *nm* chisel

cinco ['θinko] *num* five

cincuenta [θin'kwenta] *num* fifty

cine ['θine] *nm* cinema; **cinematográfico, -a** [θinemato'ɣrafiko, a] *adj* cine-, film *cpd*

cínico, -a ['θiniko, a] *adj* cynical ▷ *nm/f* cynic

cinismo [θi'nismo] *nm* cynicism

cinta ['θinta] *nf* band, strip; (de tela) ribbon; (película) reel; (de máquina de escribir) ribbon; **cinta adhesiva/aislante** sticky/insulating tape; **cinta de vídeo** videotape; **cinta magnetofónica** tape; **cinta métrica** tape measure

cintura [θin'tura] *nf* waist

cinturón [θintu'ron] *nm* belt; **cinturón de seguridad** safety belt

ciprés [θi'pres] *nm* cypress (tree)

circo ['θirko] *nm* circus

circuito [θir'kwito] *nm* circuit

circulación [θirkula'θjon] *nf* circulation; (Auto) traffic

circular [θirku'lar] *adj, nf* circular ▷ *vi, vt* to circulate ▷ *vi* (Auto) to drive; **"circule por la derecha"** "keep (to the) right"

círculo ['θirkulo] *nm* circle; **círculo vicioso** vicious circle

circunferencia [θirkunfe'renθja] *nf* circumference

circunstancia [θirkuns'tanθja] *nf* circumstance

cirio ['θirjo] *nm* (wax) candle

ciruela [θi'rwela] *nf* plum; **ciruela pasa** prune

cirugía [θiru'xia] *nf* surgery; **cirugía estética** o **plástica** plastic surgery

cirujano [θiru'xano] *nm* surgeon

cisne ['θisne] *nm* swan

cisterna [θis'terna] *nf* cistern, tank

cita ['θita] *nf* appointment, meeting; (de novios) date; (referencia) quotation

citación [θita'θjon] *nf* (Jur) summons sg

citar [θi'tar] *vt* (gen) to make an appointment with; (Jur) to summons; (un autor, texto) to quote; **citarse** *vr*: **se ~on en el cine** they arranged to meet at the cinema

cítricos ['θitrikos] *nmpl* citrus fruit(s)

ciudad [θju'ðað] *nf* town; (más grande) city; **ciudadano, -a** *nm/f* citizen

cívico, -a ['θiβiko, a] *adj* civic

civil [θi'βil] *adj* civil ▷ *nm* (guardia) policeman; **civilización** [θiβiliθa'θjon] *nf* civilization; **civilizar** [θiβili'θar] *vt* to civilize

cizaña [θi'θaɲa] *nf* (fig) discord

cl. *abr* (= centilitro) cl.

clamor [kla'mor] *nm* clamour, protest

clandestino, -a [klandes'tino, a] *adj* clandestine; (Pol) underground

clara ['klara] *nf* (de huevo) egg white

claraboya [klara'βoja] *nf* skylight

clarear [klare'ar] *vi* (el día) to dawn; (el cielo) to clear up, brighten up; **clarearse** *vr* to be transparent

claridad [klari'ðað] *nf* (de día) brightness; (de estilo) clarity

clarificar [klarifi'kar] *vt* to clarify

clarinete [klari'nete] *nm* clarinet

claro, -a ['klaro, a] *adj* clear; (luminoso) bright; (color) light; (evidente) clear, evident; (poco espeso) thin ▷ *nm* (en bosque) clearing ▷ *adv* clearly ▷ *excl*: **¡~ que sí!** of course!; **¡~ que no!** of course not!

clase ['klase] *nf* class; **dar ~(s)** to teach; **clase alta/media/obrera** upper/middle/working class; **clases particulares** private lessons o tuition sg

clásico, -a ['klasiko, a] *adj* classical

clasificación [klasifika'θjon] *nf* classification; (Deporte) league (table)

clasificar [klasifi'kar] *vt* to classify

claustro ['klaustro] *nm* cloister

cláusula ['klausula] *nf* clause

clausura [klau'sura] *nf* closing, closure

clavar [kla'βar] *vt* (clavo) to hammer in; (cuchillo) to stick, thrust

clave ['klaβe] *nf* key; (Mús) clef; **clave de acceso** password; **clave lada** (MÉX) dialling (BRIT) o area (US) code

clavel [kla'βel] *nm* carnation

clavícula [kla'βikula] *nf* collar bone

clavija [kla'βixa] *nf* peg, dowel, pin; (Elec) plug

clavo ['klaβo] *nm* (de metal) nail; (Bot) clove

claxon ['klakson] (*pl* **~s**) *nm* horn

clérigo ['klerixo] *nm* priest

clero ['klero] *nm* clergy

clicar [kli'kar] *vi* (Internet) to click; **~ en el icono** to click on an icon; **~ dos veces** to double-click

cliché [kli'tʃe] *nm* cliché; (Foto) negative

cliente, -a ['kljente, a] *nm/f* client, customer; **clientela** [kljen'tela] *nf* clientele, customers *pl*

clima ['klima] *nm* climate; **climatizado, -a** [klimati'θaðo, a] *adj* air-conditioned

clímax ['klimaks] *nm inv* climax

clínica ['klinika] *nf* clinic; (particular) private hospital

clip [klip] (*pl* **~s**) *nm* paper clip

clítoris ['klitoris] *nm inv* (Anat) clitoris

cloaca [klo'aka] *nf* sewer

clonar [klo'nar] *vt* to clone

cloro ['kloro] *nm* chlorine

clóset ['kloset] (MÉX) *nm* cupboard

club [klub] (*pl* **~s** o **~es**) *nm* club; **club nocturno** night club

cm *abr* (= centímetro, centímetros) cm

coágulo [ko'aɣulo] *nm* clot

coalición [koali'θjon] *nf* coalition

coartada [koar'taða] *nf* alibi

coartar [koar'tar] *vt* to limit, restrict

coba ['koβa] *nf:* **dar ~ a algn** (*adular*) to suck up to sb

cobarde [ko'βarðe] *adj* cowardly ▷ *nm* coward; **cobardía** *nf* cowardice

cobaya [ko'βaja] *nf* guinea pig

cobertizo [koβer'tiθo] *nm* shelter

cobertura [koβer'tura] *nf* cover; **aquí no hay ~** (*Tel*) I can't get a signal

cobija [ko'βixa] (LAM) *nf* blanket; **cobijar** [koβi'xar] *vt* (*cubrir*) to cover; (*proteger*) to shelter; **cobijo** *nm* shelter

cobra ['koβra] *nf* cobra

cobrador, -a [koβra'ðor, a] *nm/f* (*de autobús*) conductor/conductress; (*de impuestos, gas*) collector

cobrar [ko'βrar] *vt* (*cheque*) to cash; (*sueldo*) to collect, draw; (*objeto*) to recover; (*precio*) to charge; (*deuda*) to collect ▷ *vi* to be paid; **cobrar al entregar** cash on delivery; **¿me cobra, por favor?** how much do I owe you?, can I have the bill, please?

cobre ['koβre] *nm* copper; **cobres** *nmpl* (*Mús*) brass instruments

cobro ['koβro] *nm* (*de cheque*) cashing; **presentar al ~** to cash

cocaína [koka'ina] *nf* cocaine

cocción [kok'θjon] *nf* (*Culin*) cooking; (*en agua*) boiling

cocer [ko'θer] *vt, vi* to cook; (*en agua*) to boil; (*en horno*) to bake

coche ['kotʃe] *nm* (*Auto*) car (BRIT), automobile (US); (*de tren, de caballos*) coach, carriage; (*para niños*) pram (BRIT), baby carriage (US); **ir en ~** to drive; **coche celular** police van; **coche de bomberos** fire engine; **coche de carreras** racing car; **coche comedor** dining car; **coche-escuela** (*AM inv*) learner car; **coche fúnebre** hearse; **coche-cama** (*pl* **coches-cama**) *nm* (*Ferro*) sleeping car, sleeper

cochera [ko'tʃera] *nf* garage; (*de autobuses, trenes*) depot

coche restaurante (*pl* **coches restaurante**) *nm* (*Ferro*) dining car, diner

cochinillo [kotʃi'niʎo] *nm* (*Culin*) suckling pig, sucking pig

cochino, -a [ko'tʃino, a] *adj* filthy, dirty ▷ *nm/f* pig

cocido [ko'θiðo] *nm* stew

cocina [ko'θina] *nf* kitchen; (*aparato*) cooker, stove; (*acto*) cookery; **cocina eléctrica/de gas** electric/gas cooker; **cocina francesa** French cuisine; **cocinar** *vt, vi* to cook

cocinero, -a [koθi'nero, a] *nm/f* cook

coco ['koko] *nm* coconut

cocodrilo [koko'ðrilo] *nm* crocodile

cocotero [koko'tero] *nm* coconut palm

cóctel ['koktel] *nm* cocktail; **cóctel molotov** petrol bomb, Molotov cocktail

codazo [ko'ðaθo] *nm:* **dar un ~ a algn** to nudge sb

codicia [ko'ðiθja] *nf* greed; **codiciar** *vt* to covet

código ['koðixo] *nm* code; **código civil** common law; **código de barras** bar code; **código de circulación** highway code; **código de la zona** (LAM) dialling (BRIT) o area (US) code; **código postal** postcode

codillo [ko'ðiʎo] *nm* (*Zool*) knee; (*Tec*) elbow (joint)

codo ['koðo] *nm* (*Anat, de tubo*) elbow; (*Zool*) knee

codorniz [koðor'niθ] *nf* quail

coexistir [koe(k)sis'tir] *vi* to coexist

cofradía [kofra'ðia] *nf* brotherhood, fraternity

cofre ['kofre] *nm* (*de joyas*) case; (*de dinero*) chest

coger [ko'xer] (ESP) *vt* to take (hold of); (*objeto caído*) to pick up; (*frutas*) to pick, harvest; (*resfriado, ladrón, pelota*) to catch ▷ *vi:* **~ por el buen camino** to take the right road; **cogerse** *vr* (*el dedo*) to catch; **~se a algo** to catch hold of sth

cogollo [ko'ɣoʎo] *nm* (*de lechuga*) heart

cogote [ko'ɣote] *nm* back o nape of

the neck

cohabitar [koaβi'tar] vi to live together, cohabit

coherente [koe'rente] adj coherent

cohesión [koe'sjon] nm cohesion

cohete [ko'ete] nm rocket

cohibido, -a [koi'βiðo, a] adj (Psico) inhibited; (tímido) shy

coincidencia [koinθi'ðenθja] nf coincidence

coincidir [koinθi'ðir] vi (en idea) to coincide, agree; (en lugar) to coincide

coito ['koito] nm intercourse, coitus

coja etc vb V **coger**

cojear [koxe'ar] vi (persona) to limp, hobble; (mueble) to wobble, rock

cojera [ko'xera] nf limp

cojín [ko'xin] nm cushion

cojo, -a etc ['koxo, a] vb V **coger** ▷ adj (que no puede andar) lame, crippled; (mueble) wobbly ▷ nm/f lame person, cripple

cojón [ko'xon] (fam!) nm: ¡**cojones**! shit! (!); **cojonudo, -a** (fam) adj great, fantastic

col [kol] nf cabbage; **coles de Bruselas** Brussels sprouts

cola ['kola] nf tail; (de gente) queue; (lugar) end, last place; (para pegar) glue, gum; **hacer ~** to queue (up)

colaborador, a [kolaβora'ðor, a] nm/f collaborator

colaborar [kolaβo'rar] vi to collaborate

colada [ko'laða] (ESP) nf: **hacer la ~** to do the washing

colador [kola'ðor] nm (para líquidos) strainer; (para verduras etc) colander

colapso [ko'lapso] nm collapse

colar [ko'lar] vt (líquido) to strain off; (metal) to cast ▷ vi to ooze, seep (through); **colarse** vr to jump the queue; **~se en** to get into without paying; (fiesta) to gatecrash

colcha ['koltʃa] nf bedspread

colchón [kol'tʃon] nm mattress; **colchón inflable** air bed o mattress

colchoneta [koltʃo'neta] nf (en gimnasio) mat; (de playa) air bed

colección [kolek'θjon] nf collection; **coleccionar** vt to collect; **coleccionista** nmf collector

colecta [ko'lekta] nf collection

colectivo, -a [kolek'tiβo, a] adj collective, joint ▷ nm (ARG: autobús) (small) bus

colega [ko'leɣa] nmf colleague; (ESP: amigo) mate

colegial, a [kole'xjal, a] nm/f schoolboy(-girl)

colegio [ko'lexjo] nm college; (escuela) school; (de abogados etc) association; **colegio electoral** polling station; **colegio mayor** (ESP) hall of residence

● COLEGIO
●
● A **colegio** is normally a private
● primary or secondary school.
● In the state system it means a
● primary school although these
● are also called **escuelas**. State
● secondary schools are called
● **institutos**.

cólera ['kolera] nf (ira) anger; (Med) cholera

colesterol [koleste'rol] nm cholesterol

coleta [ko'leta] nf pigtail

colgante [kol'xante] adj hanging ▷ nm (joya) pendant

colgar [kol'xar] vt to hang (up); (ropa) to hang out ▷ vi to hang; (Tel) to hang up

cólico ['koliko] nm colic

coliflor [koli'flor] nf cauliflower

colilla [ko'liʎa] nf cigarette end, butt

colina [ko'lina] nf hill

colisión [koli'sjon] nf collision; **colisión frontal** head-on crash

collar [ko'ʎar] nm necklace; (de perro) collar

colmar [kol'mar] vt to fill to the brim; (fig) to fulfil, realize

colmena [kol'mena] *nf* beehive
colmillo [kol'miʎo] *nm* (*diente*) eye tooth; (*de elefante*) tusk; (*de perro*) fang
colmo ['kolmo] *nm*: **¡es el ~!** it's the limit!
colocación [koloka'θjon] *nf* (*acto*) placing; (*empleo*) job, position
colocar [kolo'kar] *vt* to place, put, position; (*dinero*) to invest; (*poner en empleo*) to find a job for; **colocarse** *vr* to get a job
Colombia [ko'lombja] *nf* Colombia; **colombiano, -a** *adj, nm/f* Colombian
colonia [ko'lonja] *nf* colony; (*agua de colonia*) cologne; (*MÉX de casas*) residential area; **colonia proletaria** (*MÉX*) shantytown
colonización [koloniθa'θjon] *nf* colonization; **colonizador, a** [koloniθa'ðor, a] *adj* colonizing ▷ *nm/f* colonist, settler
colonizar [koloni'θar] *vt* to colonize
coloquio [ko'lokjo] *nm* conversation; (*congreso*) conference
color [ko'lor] *nm* colour
colorado, -a [kolo'raðo, a] *adj* (*rojo*) red; (*MÉX chiste*) smutty, rude
colorante [kolo'rante] *nm* colouring
colorear [kolore'ar] *vt* to colour
colorete [kolo'rete] *nm* blusher
colorido [kolo'riðo] *nm* colouring
columna [ko'lumna] *nf* column; (*pilar*) pillar; (*apoyo*) support; (*tb*: **~ vertebral**) spine, spinal column; (*fig*) backbone
columpiar [kolum'pjar] *vt* to swing; **columpiarse** *vr* to swing; **columpio** *nm* swing
coma ['koma] *nf* comma ▷ *nm* (*Med*) coma
comadre [ko'maðre] *nf* (*madrina*) godmother; (*chismosa*) gossip; **comadrona** *nf* midwife
comal [ko'mal] (*MÉX, CAM*) *nm* griddle
comandante [koman'dante] *nm* commandant
comarca [ko'marka] *nf* region

comba ['komba] (*ESP*) *nf* (*cuerda*) skipping rope; **saltar a la ~** to skip
combate [kom'bate] *nm* fight
combatir [komba'tir] *vt* to fight, combat
combinación [kombina'θjon] *nf* combination; (*Quím*) compound; (*prenda*) slip
combinar [kombi'nar] *vt* to combine
combustible [kombus'tiβle] *nm* fuel
comedia [ko'meðja] *nf* comedy; (*Teatro*) play, drama; **comediante** [kome'ðjante] *nmf* (*comic*) actor/actress
comedido, -a [kome'ðiðo, a] *adj* moderate
comedor, a [kome'ðor, a] *nm* (*habitación*) dining room; (*cantina*) canteen
comensal [komen'sal] *nmf* fellow guest (o diner)
comentar [komen'tar] *vt* to comment on; **comentario** [komen'tarjo] *nm* comment, remark; (*literario*) commentary; **comentarios** *nmpl* (*chismes*) gossip *sg*; **comentarista** [komenta'rista] *nmf* commentator
comenzar [komen'θar] *vt, vi* to begin, start; **~ a hacer algo** to begin o start doing sth
comer [ko'mer] *vt* to eat; (*Damas, Ajedrez*) to take, capture ▷ *vi* to eat; (*ESP, MÉX: almorzar*) to have lunch; **comerse** *vr* to eat up
comercial [komer'θjal] *adj* commercial; (*relativo al negocio*) business *cpd*; **comercializar** *vt* (*producto*) to market; (*pey*) to commercialize
comerciante [komer'θjante] *nmf* trader, merchant
comerciar [komer'θjar] *vi* to trade, do business
comercio [ko'merθjo] *nm* commerce, trade; (*tienda*) shop, store; (*negocio*) business; (*fig*) dealings *pl*;

comercio electrónico e-commerce; **comercio exterior/interior** foreign/domestic trade

comestible [komes'tiβle] adj eatable, edible; **comestibles** nmpl food sg, foodstuffs

cometa [ko'meta] nm comet ⊳ nf kite

cometer [kome'ter] vt to commit

cometido [kome'tiðo] nm task, assignment

cómic ['komik] nm comic

comicios [ko'miθjos] nmpl elections

cómico, -a ['komiko, a] adj comic(al) ⊳ nm/f comedian

comida [ko'miða] nf (alimento) food; (almuerzo, cena) meal; (de mediodía) lunch; **comida basura** junk food; **comida chatarra** (MÉX) junk food

comidilla [komi'ðiʎa] nf: **ser la ~ del barrio** o **pueblo** to be the talk of the town

comienzo etc [ko'mjenθo] vb V **comenzar** ⊳ nm beginning, start

comillas [ko'miʎas] nfpl quotation marks

comilona [komi'lona] (fam) nf blow-out

comino [ko'mino] nm: **(no) me importa un ~** I don't give a damn

comisaría [komisa'ria] nf (de policía) police station; (Mil) commissariat

comisario [komi'sarjo] nm (Mil etc) commissary; (Pol) commissar

comisión [komi'sjon] nf commission; **Comisiones Obreras** (ESP) Communist trade union

comité [komi'te] (pl ~s) nm committee

comitiva [komi'tiβa] nf retinue

como ['komo] adv as; (tal ~) like; (aproximadamente) about, approximately ⊳ conj (ya que, puesto que) as, since; **¡~ no!** of course!; **~ no lo haga hoy** unless he does it today; **~ si** as if; **es tan alto ~ ancho** it is as high as it is wide

cómo ['komo] adv how?, why? ⊳ excl

what?, I beg your pardon? ⊳ nm: **el ~ y el porqué** the whys and wherefores

cómoda ['komoða] nf chest of drawers

comodidad [komoði'ðað] nf comfort

comodín [komo'ðin] nm joker

cómodo, -a ['komoðo, a] adj comfortable; (práctico, de fácil uso) convenient

compact [kom'pakt] (pl ~s) nm (tb: ~ **disc**) compact disk player

compacto, -a [kom'pakto, a] adj compact

compadecer [kompaðe'θer] vt to pity, be sorry for; **compadecerse** vr: **~se de** to pity, be o feel sorry for

compadre [kom'paðre] nm (padrino) godfather; (amigo) friend, pal

compañero, -a [kompa'ɲero, a] nm/f companion; (novio) boy/girlfriend; **compañero de clase** classmate

compañía [kompa'ɲia] nf company; **hacer ~ a algn** to keep sb company

comparación [kompara'θjon] nf comparison; **en ~ con** in comparison with

comparar [kompa'rar] vt to compare

comparecer [kompare'θer] vi to appear (in court)

comparsa [kom'parsa] nmf (Teatro) extra

compartimiento [komparti'mjento] nm (Ferro) compartment

compartir [kompar'tir] vt to share; (dinero, comida etc) to divide (up), share (out)

compás [kom'pas] nm (Mús) beat, rhythm; (Mat) compasses pl; (Náut etc) compass

compasión [kompa'sjon] nf compassion, pity

compasivo, -a [kompa'siβo, a] adj compassionate

compatible [kompa'tiβle] adj

compatible

compatriota [kompa'trjota] nmf
compatriot, fellow countryman/
woman

compenetrarse [kompene'trarse]
vr to be in tune

compensación [kompensa'θjon] nf
compensation

compensar [kompen'sar] vt to
compensate

competencia [kompe'tenθja]
nf (incumbencia) domain, field; (Jur,
habilidad) competence; (rivalidad)
competition

competente [kompe'tente] adj
competent

competición [kompeti'θjon] nf
competition

competir [kompe'tir] vi to compete

compinche [kom'pintʃe] (LAM) nmf
mate, buddy (US)

complacer [kompla'θer] vt to
please; **complacerse** vr to be pleased

complaciente [kompla'θjente] adj
kind, obliging, helpful

complejo, -a [kom'plexo, a] adj,
nm complex

complementario, -a
[komplemen'tarjo, a] adj
complementary

completar [komple'tar] vt to
complete

completo, -a [kom'pleto, a] adj
complete; (perfecto) perfect; (lleno) full
▷ nm full complement

complicado, -a [kompli'kaðo,
a] adj complicated; **estar ~ en** to be
mixed up in

cómplice ['kompliθe] nmf
accomplice

complot [kom'plo(t)] (pl **~s**) nm plot

componer [kompo'ner] vt (Mús,
Literatura, Imprenta) to compose; (algo
roto) to mend, repair; (arreglar) to
arrange; **componerse** vr: **~se de** to
consist of

comportamiento
[komporta'mjento] nm behaviour,

conduct

comportarse [kompor'tarse] vr
to behave

composición [komposi'θjon] nf
composition

compositor, a [komposi'tor, a]
nm/f composer

compostura [kompos'tura] nf
(actitud) composure

compra ['kompra] nf purchase;
hacer la ~ to do the shopping; **ir de ~s**
to go shopping; **comprador, a** nm/f
buyer, purchaser; **comprar** [kom'prar]
vt to buy, purchase

comprender [kompren'der] vt to
understand; (incluir) to comprise,
include

comprensión [kompren'sjon] nf
understanding; **comprensivo, -a** adj
(actitud) understanding

compresa [kom'presa] nf (para
mujer) sanitary towel (BRIT), napkin
(US)

comprimido, -a [kompri'miðo, a]
adj compressed ▷ nm (Med) pill, tablet

comprimir [kompri'mir] vt to
compress; (Internet) to zip

comprobante [kompro'βante] nm
proof; (Com) voucher; **comprobante de
compra** proof of purchase

comprobar [kompro'βar] vt to
check; (probar) to prove; (Tec) to
check, test

comprometer [komprome'ter]
vt to compromise; (poner en peligro)
to endanger; **comprometerse** vr
(involucrarse) to get involved

compromiso [kompro'miso] nm
(obligación) obligation; (cometido)
commitment; (convenio) agreement;
(apuro) awkward situation

compuesto, -a [kom'pwesto, a]
adj: **~ de** composed of, made up of ▷ nm
compound

computadora [komputa'ðora]
(LAM) nf computer; **computadora
central** mainframe (computer);
computadora personal personal

computer

cómputo ['komputo] *nm* calculation

comulgar [komul'γar] *vi* to receive communion

común [ko'mun] *adj* common
▷ *nm*: **el ~** the community

comunicación [komunika'θjon] *nf* communication; (*informe*) report

comunicado [komuni'kaðo] *nm* announcement; **comunicado de prensa** press release

comunicar [komuni'kar] *vt, vi* to communicate; **comunicarse** *vr* to communicate; **está comunicando** (*Tel*) the line's engaged (*BRIT*) o busy (*US*); **comunicativo, -a** *adj* communicative

comunidad [komuni'ðað] *nf* community; **comunidad autónoma** (*ESP*) autonomous region; **Comunidad (Económica) Europea** European (Economic) Community; **comunidad de vecinos** residents' association

comunión [komu'njon] *nf* communion

comunismo [komu'nismo] *nm* communism; **comunista** *adj, nmf* communist

○ **PALABRA CLAVE**

con [kon] *prep* **1** (*medio, compañía*) with; **comer con cuchara** to eat with a spoon; **pasear con algn** to go for a walk with sb

2 (*a pesar de*): **con todo, merece nuestros respetos** all the same, he deserves our respect

3 (*para con*): **es muy bueno para con los niños** he's very good with (the) children

4 (+ *infin*): **con llegar a las seis estará bien** if you come by six it will be fine
▷ *conj*: **con que: será suficiente con que le escribas** it will be sufficient if you write to her

concebir [konθe'βir] *vt, vi* to conceive

conceder [konθe'ðer] *vt* to concede

concejal, a [konθe'xal, a] *nm/f* town councillor

concentración [konθentra'θjon] *nf* concentration

concentrar [konθen'trar] *vt* to concentrate; **concentrarse** *vr* to concentrate

concepto [kon'θepto] *nm* concept

concernir [konθer'nir] *vi* to concern; **en lo que concierne a ...** as far as ... is concerned; **en lo que a mí concierne** as far as I'm concerned

concertar [konθer'tar] *vt* (*Mús*) to harmonize; (*acordar: precio*) to agree; (: *tratado*) to conclude; (*trato*) to arrange, fix up; (*combinar: esfuerzos*) to coordinate ▷ *vi* to harmonize, be in tune

concesión [konθe'sjon] *nf* concession

concesionario [konθesjo'narjo] *nm* (licensed) dealer, agent

concha ['kontʃa] *nf* shell

conciencia [konθjen'θja] *nf* conscience; **tomar ~ de** to become aware of; **tener la ~ tranquila** to have a clear conscience

concienciar [konθjen'θjar] *vt* to make aware; **concienciarse** *vr* to become aware

concienzudo, -a [konθjen'θuðo, a] *adj* conscientious

concierto *etc* [kon'θjerto] *vb V* **concertar** ▷ *nm* concert; (*obra*) concerto

conciliar [konθi'ljar] *vt* to reconcile; **~ el sueño** to get to sleep

concilio [kon'θiljo] *nm* council

conciso, -a [kon'θiso, a] *adj* concise

concluir [konklu'ir] *vt, vi* to conclude; **concluirse** *vr* to conclude

conclusión [konklu'sjon] *nf* conclusion

concordar [konkor'ðar] *vt* to reconcile ▷ *vi* to agree, tally

concordia [kon'korðja] *nf* harmony

concretar [konkre'tar] *vt* to make concrete, make more specific; **concretarse** *vr* to become more definite

concreto, -a [kon'kreto, a] *adj*, *nm* (LAM: *hormigón*) concrete; **en ~** (*en resumen*) to sum up; (*especificamente*) specifically; **no hay nada en ~** there's nothing definite

concurrido, -a [konku'rriðo, a] *adj* (*calle*) busy; (*local, reunión*) crowded

concursante [konkur'sante] *nmf* competitor

concurso [kon'kurso] *nm* (*de público*) crowd; (*Escol, Deporte, competencia*) competition; (*ayuda*) help, cooperation

condal [kon'dal] *adj*: **la Ciudad C~** Barcelona

conde ['konde] *nm* count

condecoración [kondekora'θjon] *nf* (Mil) medal

condena [kon'dena] *nf* sentence; **condenación** [kondena'θjon] *nf* condemnation; (*Rel*) damnation; **condenar** [konde'nar] *vt* to condemn; (*Jur*) to convict; **condenarse** *vr* (*Rel*) to be damned

condesa [kon'desa] *nf* countess

condición [kondi'θjon] *nf* condition; **a ~ de que ...** on condition that ...; **condicional** *adj* conditional

condimento [kondi'mento] *nm* seasoning

condominio [kondo'minjo] (LAM) *nm* condominium

condón [kon'don] *nm* condom

conducir [kondu'θir] *vt* to take, convey; (*Auto*) to drive ▷ *vi* to drive; (*fig*) to lead; **conducirse** *vr* to behave

conducta [kon'dukta] *nf* conduct, behaviour

conducto [kon'dukto] *nm* pipe, tube; (*fig*) channel

conductor, a [konduk'tor, a] *adj* leading, guiding ▷ *nm* (*Física*) conductor; (*de vehículo*) driver

conduje *etc vb* V **conducir**

conduzco *etc vb* V **conducir**

conectado, -a [konek'taðo, a] *adj* (*Inform*) on-line

conectar [konek'tar] *vt* to connect (up); (*enchufar*) plug in

conejillo [kone'xiλo] *nm*: **~ de Indias** guinea pig

conejo [ko'nexo] *nm* rabbit

conexión [konek'sjon] *nf* connection

confección [konfe(k)'θjon] *nf* preparation; (*industria*) clothing industry

confeccionar [konfekθjo'nar] *vt* to make (up)

conferencia [konfe'renθja] *nf* conference; (*lección*) lecture; (ESP Tel) call; **conferencia de prensa** press conference

conferir [konfe'rir] *vt* to award

confesar [konfe'sar] *vt* to confess, admit

confesión [konfe'sjon] *nf* confession

confesionario [konfesjo'narjo] *nm* confessional

confeti [kon'feti] *nm* confetti

confiado, -a [kon'fjaðo, a] *adj* (*crédulo*) trusting; (*seguro*) confident

confianza [kon'fjanθa] *nf* trust; (*seguridad*) confidence; (*familiaridad*) intimacy, familiarity

confiar [kon'fjar] *vt* to entrust ▷ *vi* to trust; **~ en algn** to trust sb; **~ en que** ... to hope that ...

confidencial [konfiðen'θjal] *adj* confidential

confidente [konfi'ðente] *nmf* confidant/e; (*policial*) informer

configurar [konfiɣu'rar] *vt* to shape, form

confín [kon'fin] *nm* limit; **confines** *nmpl* confines, limits

confirmar [konfir'mar] *vt* to confirm

confiscar [konfis'kar] *vt* to confiscate

confite [kon'fite] *nm* sweet (BRIT), candy (US); **confitería** [konfite'ria] *nf*

(*tienda*) confectioner's (shop)
confitura [konfi'tura] *nf* jam
conflictivo, -a [konflik'tiβo, a] *adj*
(*asunto, propuesta*) controversial; (*país, situación*) troubled
conflicto [kon'flikto] *nm* conflict;
(*fig*) clash
confluir [kon'flwir] *vi* (*ríos*) to meet;
(*gente*) to gather
conformar [konfor'mar] *vt* to
shape, fashion ▷ *vi* to agree;
conformarse *vr* to conform;
(*resignarse*) to resign o.s.; **~se con algo**
to be happy with sth
conforme [kon'forme] *adj*
(*correspondiente*). **~ con** in line with; (*de acuerdo*) **estar ~s (con algo)** to be in
agreement (with sth) ▷ *adv* as ▷ *excl*
agreed! ▷ *prep*: **~ a** in accordance with;
quedarse ~ (con algo) to be satisfied
(with sth)
confortable [konfor'taβle] *adj*
comfortable
confortar [konfor'tar] *vt* to comfort
confrontar [konfron'tar] *vt* to
confront; (*dos personas*) to bring face to
face; (*cotejar*) to compare
confundir [konfun'dir] *vt* (*equivocar*)
to mistake, confuse; (*turbar*) to
confuse; **confundirse** *vr* (*turbarse*) to
get confused; (*equivocarse*) to make a
mistake; (*mezclarse*) to mix
confusión [konfu'sjon] *nf* confusion
confuso, -a [kon'fuso, a] *adj*
confused
congelado, -a [konxe'laðo, a] *adj*
frozen; **congelados** *nmpl* frozen
food(s); **congelador** *nm* (*aparato*)
freezer, deep freeze
congelar [konxe'lar] *vt* to freeze;
congelarse *vr* (*sangre, grasa*) to
congeal
congeniar [konxe'njar] *vi* to get on
(BRIT) o along (US) well
congestión [konxes'tjon] *nf*
congestion
congestionar [konxestjo'nar] *vt*
to congest

congraciarse [kongra'θjarse] *vr* to
ingratiate o.s.
congratular [kongratu'lar] *vt* to
congratulate
congregar [kongre'ɣar] *vt* to gather
together; **congregarse** *vr* to gather
together
congresista [kongre'sista] *nmf*
delegate, congressman/woman
congreso [kon'greso] *nm* congress
conjetura [konxe'tura] *nf* guess;
conjeturar *vt* to guess
conjugar [konxu'ɣar] *vt* to combine,
fit together; (*Ling*) to conjugate
conjunción [konxun'θjon] *nf*
conjunction
conjunto, -a [kon'xunto, a] *adj*
joint, united ▷ *nm* whole; (*Mús*) band;
en ~ as a whole
conmemoración
[konmemora'θjon] *nf*
commemoration
conmemorar [konmemo'rar] *vt* to
commemorate
conmigo [kon'miɣo] *pron* with me
conmoción [konmo'θjon] *nf* shock;
(*fig*) upheaval; **conmoción cerebral**
(*Med*) concussion
conmovedor, a [konmoβe'ðor, a]
adj touching, moving; (*emocionante*)
exciting
conmover [konmo'βer] *vt* to shake,
disturb; (*fig*) to move
conmutador [konmuta'ðor] *nm*
switch; (LAM: *centralita*) switchboard;
(: *central*) telephone exchange
cono ['kono] *nm* cone; **Cono Sur**
Southern Cone
conocedor, a [konoθe'ðor, a] *adj*
expert, knowledgeable ▷ *nm/f* expert
conocer [kono'θer] *vt* to know;
(*por primera vez*) to meet, get to know;
(*entender*) to know about; (*reconocer*) to
recognize; **conocerse** *vr* (*una persona*)
to know o.s.; (*dos personas*) to (get to)
know each other; **~ a algn de vista** to
know sb by sight
conocido, -a [kono'θiðo, a] *adj*

conocido | 70

(well-)known ▷ nm/f
(well-)known ▷ nm/f acquaintance

conocimiento [konoθi'mjento]
nm knowledge; (Med) consciousness;
conocimientos nmpl (saber)
knowledge sg

conozco etc vb V **conocer**

conque ['konke] conj and so, then

conquista [kon'kista] nf conquest;
conquistador, a adj conquering ▷ nm
conqueror; **conquistar** [konkis'tar]
vt to conquer

consagrar [konsa'ɣrar] vt (Rel) to
consecrate; (fig) to devote

consciente [kons'θjente] adj
conscious

consecución [konseku'θjon] nf
acquisition; (de fin) attainment

consecuencia [konse'kwenθja] nf
consequence, outcome; (coherencia)
consistency

consecuente [konse'kwente] adj
consistent

consecutivo, -a [konseku'tiβo, a]
adj consecutive

conseguir [konse'ɣir] vt to get,
obtain; (objetivo) to attain

consejero, -a [konse'xero, a] nm/f
adviser, consultant; (Pol) councillor

consejo [kon'sexo] nm advice; (Pol)
council; **consejo de administración**
(Com) board of directors; **consejo de
guerra** court martial; **consejo de
ministros** cabinet meeting

consenso [kon'senso] nm consensus

consentimiento [konsenti'mjento]
nm consent

consentir [konsen'tir] vt (permitir,
tolerar) to consent to; (mimar) to
pamper, spoil; (aguantar) to put up with
▷ vi to agree; **~ que algn
haga algo** to allow sb to do sth

conserje [kon'serxe] nm caretaker;
(portero) porter

conservación [konserβa'θjon]
nf conservation; (de alimentos, vida)
preservation

conservador, a [konserβa'ðor,
a] adj (Pol) conservative ▷ nm/f
conservative

conservante [konser'βante] nm
preservative

conservar [konser'βar] vt to
conserve, keep; (alimentos, vida) to
preserve; **conservarse** vr to survive

conservas [kon'serβas] nfpl canned
food(s) pl

conservatorio [konserβa'torjo] nm
(Mús) conservatoire, conservatory

considerable [konsiðe'raβle] adj
considerable

consideración [konsiðera'θjon] nf
consideration; (estimación) respect

considerado, -a [konsiðe'raðo, a]
adj (atento) considerate; (respetado)
respected

considerar [konsiðe'rar] vt to
consider

consigna [kon'siɣna] nf (orden)
order, instruction; (para equipajes) left-
luggage office

consigo etc [kon'siɣo] vb V
conseguir ▷ pron (m) with him; (f)
with her; (Vd) with you; (reflexivo)
with o.s.

consiguiendo etc vb V **conseguir**

consiguiente [konsi'ɣjente] adj
consequent; **por ~** and so, therefore,
consequently

consistente [konsis'tente] adj
consistent; (sólido) solid, firm; (válido)
sound

consistir [konsis'tir] vi: **~ en**
(componerse de) to consist of

consola [kon'sola] nf (mueble)
console table; (de videojuegos)
console

consolación [konsola'θjon] nf
consolation

consolar [konso'lar] vt to console

consolidar [konsoli'ðar] vt to
consolidate

consomé [konso'me] (pl **~s**) nm
consommé, clear soup

consonante [konso'nante]
adj consonant, harmonious ▷ nf
consonant

consorcio [kon'sorθjo] *nm* consortium

conspiración [konspira'θjon] *nf* conspiracy

conspirar [konspi'rar] *vi* to conspire

constancia [kons'tanθja] *nf* constancy; **dejar ~ de** to put on record

constante [kons'tante] *adj, nf* constant

constar [kons'tar] *vi* (*evidenciarse*) to be clear o evident; **~ de** to consist of

constipado, -a [konsti'paðo, a] *adj*: **estar ~** to have a cold ▷ *nm* cold
No confundir con **constipado** con la palabra inglesa *constipated*.

constitución [konstitu'θjon] *nf* constitution

constituir [konstitu'ir] *vt* (*formar, componer*) to constitute, make up; (*fundar, erigir, ordenar*) to constitute, establish

construcción [konstruk'θjon] *nf* construction, building

constructor, a [konstruk'tor, a] *nm/f* builder

construir [konstru'ir] *vt* to build, construct

construyendo *etc vb* V **construir**

consuelo [kon'swelo] *nm* consolation, solace

cónsul ['konsul] *nm* consul; **consulado** *nm* consulate

consulta [kon'sulta] *nf* consultation; (*Med*): **horas de ~** surgery hours; **consultar** [konsul'tar] *vt* to consult; **consultar algo con algn** to discuss sth with sb; **consultorio** [konsul'torjo] *nm* (*Med*) surgery

consumición [konsumi'θjon] *nf* consumption; (*bebida*) drink; (*comida*) food; **consumición mínima** cover charge

consumidor, a [konsumi'ðor, a] *nm/f* consumer

consumir [konsu'mir] *vt* to consume; **consumirse** *vr* to be consumed; (*persona*) to waste away

consumismo [konsu'mismo] *nm* consumerism

consumo [kon'sumo] *nm* consumption

contabilidad [kontaβili'ðað] *nf* accounting, book-keeping; (*profesión*) accountancy; **contable** *nmf* accountant

contactar [kontak'tar] *vi*: **~ con algn** to contact sb

contacto [kon'takto] *nm* contact; (*Auto*) ignition; **estar/ponerse en ~** to be/to get in touch with sb

contado, -a [kon'taðo, a] *adj*: **~s** (*escasos*) numbered, scarce, few ▷ *nm*: **pagar al ~** to pay (in) cash

contador [konta'ðor] *nm* (*ESP: aparato*) meter ▷ *nmf* (*LAM Com*) accountant

contagiar [konta'xjar] *vt* (*enfermedad*) to pass on, transmit; (*persona*) to infect; **contagiarse** *vr* to become infected

contagio [kon'taxjo] *nm* infection; **contagioso, -a** *adj* infectious; (*fig*) catching

contaminación [kontamina'θjon] *nf* contamination; (*polución*) pollution

contaminar [kontami'nar] *vt* to contaminate; (*aire, agua*) to pollute

contante [kon'tante] *adj*: **dinero ~ (y sonante)** cash

contar [kon'tar] *vt* (*páginas, dinero*) to count; (*anécdota, chiste etc*) to tell ▷ *vi* to count; **~ con** to rely on, count on

contemplar [kontem'plar] *vt* to contemplate; (*mirar*) to look at

contemporáneo, -a [kontempo'raneo, a] *adj, nm/f* contemporary

contenedor [kontene'ðor] *nm* container

contener [konte'ner] *vt* to contain, hold; (*retener*) to hold back, contain; **contenerse** *vr* to control o restrain o.s.

contenido, -a [konte'niðo, a] *adj* (*moderado*) restrained; (*risa etc*) suppressed ▷ *nm* contents *pl*, content

contentar [konten'tar] *vt* (*satisfacer*) to satisfy; (*complacer*) to please; **contentarse** *vr* to be satisfied

contento, -a [kon'tento, a] *adj* (*alegre*) pleased; (*feliz*) happy

contestación [kontesta'θjon] *nf* answer, reply

contestador [kontesta'ðor] *nm* (*tb*: ~ **automático**) answering machine

contestar [kontes'tar] *vt* to answer, reply; (*Jur*) to corroborate, confirm

No confundir **contestar** con la palabra inglesa *contest*.

contexto [kon'te(k)sto] *nm* context

contigo [kon'tiɣo] *pron* with you

contiguo, -a [kon'tiɣwo, a] *adj* adjacent, adjoining

continente [konti'nente] *adj, nm* continent

continuación [kontinwa'θjon] *nf* continuation; **a** ~ then, next

continuar [konti'nwar] *vt* to continue, go on with ▷ *vi* to continue, go on; ~ **hablando** to continue talking *o* to talk

continuidad [kontinwi'ðað] *nf* continuity

continuo, -a [kon'tinwo, a] *adj* (*sin interrupción*) continuous; (*acción perseverante*) continual

contorno [kon'torno] *nm* outline; (*Geo*) contour; **contornos** *nmpl* neighbourhood *sg*, surrounding area *sg*

contra [ˈkontra] *prep, adv* against ▷ *nm inv* con *o* **pro**: **la C~** (*de Nicaragua*) the Contras *pl*

contraataque [kontraa'take] *nm* counter-attack

contrabajo [kontra'βaxo] *nm* double bass

contrabandista [kontraβan'dista] *nmf* smuggler

contrabando [kontra'βando] *nm* (*acción*) smuggling; (*mercancías*) contraband

contracción [kontrak'θjon] *nf*

contraction

contracorriente [kontrako'rrjente] *nf* cross-current

contradecir [kontraðe'θir] *vt* to contradict

contradicción [kontraðik'θjon] *nf* contradiction

contradictorio, -a [kontraðik'torjo, a] *adj* contradictory

contraer [kontra'er] *vt* to contract; (*limitar*) to restrict; **contraerse** *vr* to contract; (*limitarse*) to limit o.s.

contraluz [kontra'luθ] *nm* view against the light

contrapartida [kontrapar'tiða] *nf*: **como** ~ (**de**) in return (for)

contrapelo [kontra'pelo]: **a** ~ *adv* the wrong way

contrapeso [kontra'peso] *nm* counterweight

contraportada [kontrapor'taða] *nf* (*de revista*) back cover

contraproducente [kontraproðu'θente] *adj* counterproductive

contrario, -a [kon'trarjo, a] *adj* contrary; (*persona*) opposed; (*sentido, lado*) opposite ▷ *nm/f* enemy, adversary; (*Deporte*) opponent; **al** *o* **por el** ~ on the contrary; **de lo** ~ otherwise

contrarreloj [kontrarre'lo] *nf* (*tb*: **prueba~**) time trial

contrarrestar [kontrarres'tar] *vt* to counteract

contrasentido [kontrasen'tiðo] *nm* (*contradicción*) contradiction

contraseña [kontra'seɲa] *nf* (*Inform*) password

contrastar [kontras'tar] *vt, vi* to contrast

contraste [kon'traste] *nm* contrast

contratar [kontra'tar] *vt* firmar un acuerdo para, to contract for; (*empleados, obreros*) to hire, engage

contratiempo [kontra'tjempo] *nm* setback

contratista [kontra'tista] *nmf* contractor

contrato [kon'trato] nm contract

contraventana [kontraβen'tana] nf shutter

contribución [kontriβu'θjon] nf (municipal etc) tax; (ayuda) contribution

contribuir [kontriβu'ir] vt, vi to contribute; (Com) to pay (in taxes)

contribuyente [kontriβu'jente] nmf (Com) taxpayer; (que ayuda) contributor

contrincante [kontrin'kante] nmf opponent

control [kon'trol] nm control; (inspección) inspection, check; **control de pasaportes** passport inspection; **controlador, a** nm/f controller; **controlador aéreo** air-traffic controller; **controlar** [kontro'lar] vt to control; (inspeccionar) to inspect, check

contundente [kontun'dente] adj (instrumento) blunt; (argumento, derrota) overwhelming

contusión [kontu'sjon] nf bruise

convalecencia [kombale'θenθja] nf convalescence

convalecer [kombale'θer] vi to convalesce, get better

convalidar [kombali'ðar] vt (título) to recognize

convencer [komben'θer] vt to convince; **~ a algn (de o para hacer algo)** to persuade sb (to do sth)

convención [komben'θjon] nf convention

conveniente [kombe'njente] adj suitable; (útil) useful

convenio [kom'benjo] nm agreement, treaty

convenir [kombe'nir] vi (estar de acuerdo) to agree; (venir bien) to suit, be suitable

> No confundir **convenir** con la palabra inglesa convene.

convento [kom'bento] nm convent

convenza etc vb V **convencer**

convergir [komber'xir] vi = **converger**

conversación [kombersa'θjon] nf conversation

conversar [komber'sar] vi to talk, converse

conversión [komber'sjon] nf conversion

convertir [komber'tir] vt to convert

convidar [kombi'ðar] vt to invite; **~ a algn a una cerveza** to buy sb a beer

convincente [kombin'θente] adj convincing

convite [kom'bite] nm invitation; (banquete) banquet

convivencia [kombi'βenθja] nf coexistence, living together

convivir [kombi'βir] vi to live together

convocar [kombo'kar] vt to summon, call (together)

convocatoria [komboka'torja] nf (de oposiciones, elecciones) notice; (de huelga) call

cónyuge ['konjuxe] nmf spouse

coñac [ko'na(k)] (pl **~s**) nm cognac, brandy

coño ['kono] (fam!) excl (enfado) shit! (!); (sorpresa) bloody hell! (!)

cool [kul] adj (fam) cool

cooperación [koopera'θjon] nf cooperation

cooperar [koope'rar] vi to cooperate

cooperativa [koopera'tiβa] nf cooperative

coordinadora [koorðina'ðora] nf (comité) coordinating committee

coordinar [koorði'nar] vt to coordinate

copa ['kopa] nf cup; (vaso) glass; (bebida) drink; **tomar una ~** (to have a) drink; (de árbol) top; (de sombrero) crown; **copas** nfpl (Naipes) = hearts

copia ['kopja] nf copy; **copia de respaldo** o **seguridad** (Inform) back-up copy; **copiar** vt to copy

copla ['kopla] nf verse; (canción) (popular) song

copo ['kopo] nm: **~ de nieve** snowflake; **~s de maíz** cornflakes

coqueta [ko'keta] *adj* flirtatious, coquettish; **coquetear** *vi* to flirt

coraje [ko'raxe] *nm* courage; (*ánimo*) spirit; (*ira*) anger

coral [ko'ral] *adj* choral ▷ *nf* (*Mús*) choir ▷ *nm* (*Zool*) coral

coraza [ko'raθa] *nf* (*armadura*) armour; (*blindaje*) armour-plating

corazón [kora'θon] *nm* heart

corazonada [koraθo'naða] *nf* impulse; (*presentimiento*) hunch

corbata [kor'βata] *nf* tie

corchete [kor'tʃete] *nm* catch, clasp

corcho ['kortʃo] *nm* cork; (*Pesca*) float

cordel [kor'ðel] *nm* cord, line

cordero [kor'ðero] *nm* lamb

cordial [kor'ðjal] *adj* cordial

cordillera [korði'ʎera] *nf* range (of mountains)

Córdoba ['korðoβa] *n* Cordova

cordón [kor'ðon] *nm* (*cuerda*) cord, string; (*de zapatos*) lace; (*Mil etc*) cordon; **cordón umbilical** umbilical cord

cordura [kor'ðura] *nf*: **con ~** (*obrar, hablar*) sensibly

corneta [kor'neta] *nf* bugle

cornisa [kor'nisa] *nf* (*Arq*) cornice

coro ['koro] *nm* chorus; (*conjunto de cantores*) choir

corona [ko'rona] *nf* crown; (*de flores*) garland

coronel [koro'nel] *nm* colonel

coronilla [koro'niʎa] *nf* (*Anat*) crown (of the head)

corporal [korpo'ral] *adj* corporal, bodily

corpulento, -a [korpu'lento, a] *adj* (*persona*) heavily-built

corral [ko'rral] *nm* farmyard

correa [ko'rrea] *nf* strap; (*cinturón*) belt; (*de perro*) lead, leash; **correa del ventilador** (*Auto*) fan belt

corrección [korrek'θjon] *nf* correction; (*reprensión*) rebuke; **correccional** *nm* reformatory

correcto, -a [ko'rrekto, a] *adj* correct; (*persona*) well-mannered

corredizo, -a [korre'ðiθo, a] *adj* (*puerta etc*) sliding

corredor, a [korre'ðor, a] *nm* (*pasillo*) corridor; (*balcón corrido*) gallery; (*Com*) agent, broker ▷ *nm/f* (*Deporte*) runner

corregir [korre'xir] *vt* (*error*) to correct; **corregirse** *vr* to reform

correo [ko'rreo] *nm* post, mail; (*persona*) courier; **Correos** *nmpl* (*Esp*) Post Office *sg*; **correo aéreo** airmail; **correo basura** (*Inform*) spam; **correo electrónico** e-mail, electronic mail; **correo web** webmail

correr [ko'rrer] *vt* to run; (*cortinas*) to draw; (*cerrojo*) to shoot ▷ *vi* to run; (*líquido*) to run, flow; **correrse** *vr* to slide, move; (*colores*) to run

correspondencia [korrespon'denθja] *nf* correspondence; (*Ferro*) connection

corresponder [korrespon'der] *vi* to correspond; (*convenir*) to be suitable; (*pertenecer*) to belong; (*concernir*) to concern; **corresponderse** *vr* (*por escrito*) to correspond; (*amarse*) to love one another

correspondiente [korrespon'djente] *adj* corresponding

corresponsal [korrespon'sal] *nmf* correspondent

corrida [ko'rriða] *nf* (*de toros*) bullfight

corrido, -a [ko'rriðo, a] *adj* (*avergonzado*) abashed; **un kilo ~** a good kilo

corriente [ko'rrjente] *adj* (*agua*) running; (*dinero etc*) current; (*común*) ordinary, normal ▷ *nf* current ▷ *nm* current month; **estar al ~ de** to be informed about; **corriente eléctrica** electric current

corrija *etc vb* V **corregir**

corro ['korro] *nm* ring, circle (of people)

corromper [korrom'per] *vt* (*madera*) to rot; (*fig*) to corrupt

corrosivo, -a [korro'siβo, a] *adj* corrosive

corrupción [korrup'θjon] *nf* rot,

decay; (*fig*) corruption

corsé [kor'se] nm corset

cortacésped [korta'θespeð] nm lawn mower

cortado, -a [kor'taðo, a] adj (*gen*) cut; (*leche*) sour; (*tímido*) shy; (*avergonzado*) embarrassed ⊳ nm coffee (with a little milk)

cortafuegos [korta'fweɣos] nm inv (*en el bosque*) firebreak, fire lane (*us*); (*Internet*) firewall

cortalápices, cortalápiz [korta'lapiθes, korta'lapiθ] nm inv (pencil) sharpener

cortar [kor'tar] vt to cut; (*suministro*) to cut off; (*un pasaje*) to cut out ⊳ vi to cut; **cortarse** vr (*avergonzarse*) to become embarrassed; (*leche*) to turn, curdle; **~se el pelo** to have one's haircut

cortauñas [korta'uɲas] nm inv nail clippers pl

corte ['korte] nm cut, cutting; (*de tela*) piece, length ⊳ nf: **las C~s** the Spanish Parliament; **corte de luz** power cut; **corte y confección** dressmaking

cortejo [kor'texo] nm entourage; **cortejo fúnebre** funeral procession

cortés [kor'tes] adj courteous, polite

cortesía [korte'sia] nf courtesy

corteza [kor'teθa] nf (*de árbol*) bark; (*de pan*) crust

cortijo [kor'tixo] (*esp*) nm farm, farmhouse

cortina [kor'tina] nf curtain

corto, -a ['korto, a] adj (*breve*) short; (*tímido*) bashful; **~ de luces** not very bright; **~ de vista** short-sighted; **estar ~ de fondos** to be short of funds; **cortocircuito** nm short circuit; **cortometraje** nm (*Cine*) short

cosa ['kosa] nf thing; **~ de** about; **eso es ~ mía** that's my business

coscorrón [kosko'rron] nm bump on the head

cosecha [ko'setʃa] nf (*Agr*) harvest; (*de vino*) vintage; **cosechar** [kose'tʃar] vt to harvest, gather (in)

coser [ko'ser] vt to sew

cosmético, -a [kos'metiko, a] adj, nm cosmetic

cosquillas [kos'kiʎas] nfpl: **hacer ~** to tickle; **tener ~** to be ticklish

costa ['kosta] nf (*Geo*) coast; **a toda ~** at all costs; **Costa Brava** Costa Brava; **Costa Cantábrica** Cantabrian Coast; **Costa del Sol** Costa del Sol

costado [kos'taðo] nm side

costanera [kosta'nera] (*cs*) nf promenade, sea front

costar [kos'tar] vt (*valer*) to cost; **me cuesta hablarle** I find it hard to talk to him

Costa Rica [kosta'rika] nf Costa Rica; **costarricense** adj, nmf Costa Rican; **costarriqueño, -a** adj, nm/f Costa Rican

coste ['koste] nm = **costo**

costear [koste'ar] vt to pay for

costero, -a [kos'tero, a] adj (*pueblecito, camino*) coastal

costilla [kos'tiʎa] nf rib; (*Culin*) cutlet

costo ['kosto] nm cost, price; **costo de (la) vida** cost of living; **costoso, -a** adj costly, expensive

costra ['kostra] nf (*corteza*) crust; (*Med*) scab

costumbre [kos'tumbre] nf custom, habit; **como de ~** as usual

costura [kos'tura] nf sewing, needlework; (*zurcido*) seam

costurera [kostu'rera] nf dressmaker

costurero [kostu'rero] nm sewing box o case

cotidiano, -a [koti'ðjano, a] adj daily, day to day

cotilla [ko'tiʎa] (*esp: fam*) nmf gossip; **cotillear** (*esp*) vi to gossip; **cotilleo** (*esp*) nm gossip(ing)

cotizar [koti'θar] vt (*Com*) to quote, price; **cotizarse** vr: **~se a** to sell at, fetch; (*Bolsa*) to stand at, be quoted at

coto ['koto] nm (*terreno cercado*) enclosure; (*de caza*) reserve

cotorra [ko'torra] nf parrot

coyote [ko'jote] nm coyote, prairie wolf

coz [koθ] nf kick

crack [krak] nm (droga) crack

cráneo ['kraneo] nm skull, cranium

cráter ['krater] nm crater

crayón [kra'jon] (MÉX, RPL) nm crayon, chalk

creación [krea'θjon] nf creation

creador, a [krea'ðor, a] adj creative ▷ nm/f creator

crear [kre'ar] vt to create, make

creativo, -a [krea'tiβo, a] adj creative

crecer [kre'θer] vi to grow; (precio) to rise

creces ['kreθes]: **con ~** adv amply, fully

crecido, -a [kre'θiðo, a] adj (persona, planta) full-grown; (cantidad) large

crecimiento [kreθi'mjento] nm growth; (aumento) increase

credencial [kreðen'θjal] nf (LAM: tarjeta) card; **credenciales** nfpl credentials; **credencial de socio** (LAM) membership card

crédito ['kreðito] nm credit

credo ['kreðo] nm creed

creencia [kre'enθja] nf belief

creer [kre'er] vt, vi to think, believe; **creerse** vr to believe o.s. (to be); **~ en** to believe in; **creo que sí/no** I think/don't think so; **¡ya lo creo!** I should think so!

creído, -a [kre'iðo, a] adj (engreído) conceited

crema ['krema] nf cream; **crema batida** (LAM) whipped cream; **crema pastelera** (confectioner's) custard

cremallera [krema'ʎera] nf zip (fastener)

crepe ['krepe] (ESP) nf pancake

cresta ['kresta] nf (Geo, Zool) crest

creyendo etc vb V **creer**

creyente [kre'jente] nm/f believer

creyó etc vb V **creer**

crezco etc vb V **crecer**

cría etc ['kria] vb V **criar** ▷ nf (de animales) rearing, breeding; (animal)

young; V tb **crío**

criadero [kria'ðero] nm (Zool) breeding place

criado, -a [kri'aðo, a] nm servant ▷ nf servant, maid

criador [kria'ðor] nm breeder

crianza [kri'anθa] nf rearing, breeding; (fig) breeding

criar [kri'ar] vt (educar) to bring up; (producir) to grow, produce; (animales) to breed

criatura [kria'tura] nf creature; (niño) baby, (small) child

cribar [kri'βar] vt to sieve

crimen ['krimen] nm crime

criminal [krimi'nal] adj, nm/f criminal

crines ['krines] nfpl mane

crío, -a ['krio, a] (fam) nm/f (niño) kid

crisis ['krisis] nf inv crisis; **crisis nerviosa** nervous breakdown

crismas ['krismas] (ESP) nm inv Christmas card

cristal [kris'tal] nm crystal; (de ventana) glass, pane; (lente) lens; **cristalino, -a** adj crystalline; (fig) clear ▷ nm lens (of the eye)

cristianismo [kristja'nismo] nm Christianity

cristiano, -a [kris'tjano, a] adj, nm/f Christian

Cristo ['kristo] nm Christ; (crucifijo) crucifix

criterio [kri'terjo] nm criterion; (juicio) judgement

crítica ['kritika] nf criticism; V tb **crítico**

criticar [kriti'kar] vt to criticize

crítico, -a ['kritiko, a] adj critical ▷ nm/f critic

Croacia [kro'aθja] nf Croatia

croissant, croissan [krwa'san] nm croissant

cromo ['kromo] nm chrome

crónica ['kronika] nf chronicle, account

crónico, -a ['kroniko, a] adj chronic

cronómetro [kro'nometro] nm stopwatch

croqueta [kro'keta] nf croquette

cruce etc ['kruθe] vb V **cruzar** ▷ nm (para peatones) crossing; (de carreteras) crossroads

crucero [kru'θero] nm (viaje) cruise

crucificar [kruθifi'kar] vt to crucify

crucifijo [kruθi'fixo] nm crucifix

crucigrama [kruθi'xrama] nm crossword (puzzle)

cruda ['kruða] (MÉX, CAM: fam) nf hangover

crudo, -a ['kruðo, a] adj raw; (no maduro) unripe; (petróleo) crude; (rudo, cruel) cruel ▷ nm crude (oil)

cruel [krwel] adj cruel; **crueldad** nf cruelty

crujiente [kru'xjente] adj (galleta etc) crunchy

crujir [kru'xir] vi (madera etc) to creak; (dedos) to crack; (dientes) to grind; (nieve, arena) to crunch

cruz [kruθ] nf cross; (de moneda) tails sg; **cruz gamada** swastika

cruzada [kru'θaða] nf crusade

cruzado, -a [kru'θaðo, a] adj crossed ▷ nm crusader

cruzar [kru'θar] vt to cross; **cruzarse** vr (líneas etc) to cross; (personas) to pass each other

Cruz Roja nf Red Cross

cuaderno [kwa'ðerno] nm notebook; (de escuela) exercise book; (Náut) logbook

cuadra ['kwaðra] nf (caballeriza) stable; (LAM: entre calles) block

cuadrado, -a [kwa'ðraðo, a] adj square ▷ nm (Mat) square

cuadrar [kwa'ðrar] vt to square ▷ vi: **~ con** to square with, tally with; **cuadrarse** vr (soldado) to stand to attention

cuadrilátero [kwaðri'latero] nm (Deporte) boxing ring; (Geom) quadrilateral

cuadrilla [kwa'ðriʎa] nf party, group

cuadro ['kwaðro] nm (Arte) painting; (Teatro) scene; (diagrama) chart; (Deporte, Med) team; **tela a**

~s checked (BRIT) o chequered (US) material

cuajar [kwa'xar] vt (leche) to curdle; (sangre) to congeal; (Culin) to set; **cuajarse** vr to curdle; to congeal; to set; (llenarse) to fill up

cuajo ['kwaxo] nm: **de ~** (arrancar) by the roots; (cortar) completely

cual [kwal] adv like, as ▷ pron: **el** etc **~** which; (persona sujeto) who; (: objeto) whom ▷ adj such as; **cada ~** each one; **déjalo tal ~** leave it just as it is

cuál [kwal] pron interr which (one)

cualesquier, a [kwales'kjer(a)] pl de **cualquier(a)**

cualidad [kwali'ðað] nf quality

cualquier [kwal'kjer] adj V **cualquiera**

cualquiera [kwal'kjera] (pl **cualesquiera**) adj (delante de nm y f **cualquier**) any ▷ pron anybody; **un coche ~ servirá** any car will do; **no es un hombre ~** he isn't just anybody; **cualquier día/libro** any day/book; **eso ~ lo sabe hacer** anybody can do that; **es un ~** he's a nobody

cuando ['kwando] adv when; (aún si) if, even if ▷ conj (puesto que) since ▷ prep: **yo, ~ niño ...** when I was a child ...; **~ no sea así** even if it is not so; **~ más** at (the) most; **~ menos** at least; **~ no** if not, otherwise; **de ~ en ~** from time to time

cuándo ['kwando] adv when; **¿desde ~?** since when?

cuantía [kwan'tia] nf extent

○ **PALABRA CLAVE**

cuanto, -a ['kwanto, a] adj **1** (todo): **tiene todo cuanto desea** he's got everything he wants; **le daremos cuantos ejemplares necesite** we'll give him as many copies as o all the copies he needs; **cuantos hombres la ven** all the men who see her

2 unos cuantos: **había unos cuantos periodistas** there were a few journalists

3 (+ *más*): **cuanto más vino bebes peor te sentirás** the more wine you drink the worse you'll feel ▷ *pron*: **tiene cuanto desea** he has everything he wants; **tome cuanto/cuantos quiera** take as much/many as you want ▷ *adv*: **en cuanto: en cuanto profesor** as a teacher; **en cuanto a mí** as for me; *V tb* **antes** ▷ *conj* **1 cuanto más gana menos gasta** the more he earns the less he spends; **cuanto más joven más confiado** the younger you are the more trusting you are **2 en cuanto: en cuanto llegue/ llegué** as soon as I arrive/arrived

cuánto, -a ['kwanto, a] *adj* (*exclamación*) what a lot of; (*interr: sg*) how much?; (: *pl*) how many? ▷ *pron, adv* how; (: *interr: sg*) how much?; (: *pl*) how many?; **¡cuánta gente!** what a lot of people!; **¿~ cuesta?** how much does it cost?; **¿a ~s estamos?** what's the date?

cuarenta [kwa'renta] *num* forty

cuarentena [kwaren'tena] *nf* quarantine

cuaresma [kwa'resma] *nf* Lent

cuarta ['kwarta] *nf* (*Mat*) quarter, fourth; (*palmo*) span

cuartel [kwar'tel] *nm* (*Mil*) barracks *pl*; **cuartel de bomberos** (*RPL*) fire station; **cuartel general** headquarters *pl*

cuarteto [kwar'teto] *nm* quartet

cuarto, -a ['kwarto, a] *adj* fourth ▷ *nm* (*Mat*) quarter, fourth; (*habitación*) room; **cuarto de baño** bathroom; **cuarto de estar** living room; **cuarto de hora** quarter (of an) hour; **cuarto de kilo** quarter kilo; **cuartos de final** quarter finals

cuatro ['kwatro] *num* four

Cuba ['kuβa] *nf* Cuba

cuba ['kuβa] *nf* cask, barrel

cubano, -a [ku'βano, a] *adj, nm/f* Cuban

cubata [ku'βata] *nm* (*fam*) large drink (*of rum and coke etc*)

cubeta [ku'βeta] (*ESP, MÉX*) *nf* (*balde*) bucket, tub

cúbico, -a [ku'βiko, a] *adj* cubic

cubierta [ku'βjerta] *nf* cover, covering; (*neumático*) tyre; (*Náut*) deck

cubierto, -a [ku'βjerto, a] *pp de* **cubrir** ▷ *adj* covered ▷ *nm* cover; (*lugar en la mesa*) place; **cubiertos** *nmpl* cutlery *sg*; **a ~** under cover

cubilete [kuβi'lete] *nm* (*en juegos*) cup

cubito [ku'βito] *nm* (*tb*: **~ de hielo**) ice-cube

cubo ['kuβo] *nm* (*Mat*) cube; (*ESP: balde*) bucket, tub; (*Tec*) drum; **cubo de (la) basura** dustbin (*BRIT*), trash can (*US*)

cubrir [ku'βrir] *vt* to cover; **cubrirse** *vr* (*cielo*) to become overcast

cucaracha [kuka'ratʃa] *nf* cockroach

cuchara [ku'tʃara] *nf* spoon; (*Tec*) scoop; **cucharada** *nf* spoonful; **cucharadita** *nf* teaspoonful

cucharilla [kutʃa'riʎa] *nf* teaspoon

cucharón [kutʃa'ron] *nm* ladle

cuchilla [ku'tʃiʎa] *nf* (*large*) knife; (*de arma blanca*) blade; **cuchilla de afeitar** razor blade

cuchillo [ku'tʃiʎo] *nm* knife

cuchitril [kutʃi'tril] *nm* hovel

cuclillas [ku'kliʎas] *nfpl*: **en ~** squatting

cuco, -a ['kuko, a] *adj* pretty; (*astuto*) sharp ▷ *nm* cuckoo

cucurucho [kuku'rutʃo] *nm* cornet

cueca ['kweka] *f* Chilean national dance

cuello ['kweʎo] *nm* (*Anat*) neck; (*de vestido, camisa*) collar

cuenca ['kwenka] *nf* (*Anat*) eye socket; (*Geo*) bowl, deep valley

cuenco ['kwenko] *nm* bowl

cuenta *etc* ['kwenta] *vb V* **contar** ▷ *nf* (*cálculo*) count, counting; (*en* *café, restaurante*) bill (BRIT), check (US); (Com) account; (de collar) bead; **a fin de ~s** in the end; **caer en la ~** to catch on; **darse ~ de** to realize; **tener en ~** to bear in mind; **echar ~s** to take stock; **cuenta atrás** countdown; **cuenta corriente/de ahorros** current/savings account; **cuenta de correo (electrónica)** (*Inform*) email account; **cuentakilómetros** nm inv ~ milímetro; (de velocidad) speedometer

cuento etc ['kwento] vb V **contar** ▷ nm story; **cuento chino** tall story; **cuento de hadas** a fairy tale

cuerda ['kwerða] nf rope; (fina) string; (de reloj) spring; **dar ~ a un reloj** to wind up a clock; **cuerda floja** tightrope; **cuerdas vocales** vocal cords

cuerdo, -a ['kwerðo, a] adj sane; (prudente) wise, sensible

cuerno ['kwerno] nm horn

cuero ['kwero] nm leather; **en ~s** stark naked; **cuero cabelludo** scalp

cuerpo ['kwerpo] nm body

cuervo ['kwerβo] nm crow

cuesta etc ['kwesta] vb V **costar** ▷ nf slope; (en camino etc) hill; **~ arriba/abajo** uphill/downhill; **a ~s** on one's back

cueste etc vb V **costar**

cuestión [kwes'tjon] nf matter, question, issue

cuete ['kwete] adj (MÉX: fam) drunk ▷ nm (LAM: cohete) rocket; (MÉX, RPL: fam: embriaguez) drunkenness; (MÉX: Culin) steak

cueva ['kweβa] nf cave

cuidado [kwi'ðaðo] nm care, carefulness; (preocupación) worry ▷ excl carefull, look out!; **eso me tiene sin ~** I'm not worried about that

cuidadoso, -a [kwiða'ðoso, a] adj careful; (preocupado) anxious

cuidar [kwi'ðar] vt (Med) to care for; (ocuparse de) to take care of, look after ▷ vi: **~ de** to take care of, look after; **cuidarse** vr to look after o.s.; **~se de hacer algo** to take care to do sth

culata [ku'lata] nf (de fusil) butt

culebra [ku'leβra] nf snake

culebrón [kule'βron] (fam) nm (TV) soap(-opera)

culo ['kulo] nm bottom, backside; (de vaso, botella) bottom

culpa ['kulpa] nf fault; (Jur) guilt; **por ~ de** because of; **echar la ~ a algn** to blame sb for sth; **tener la ~ (de)** to be to blame (for); **culpable** adj guilty ▷ nmf culprit; **culpar** [kul'par] vt to blame; (acusar) to accuse

cultivar [kulti'βar] vt to cultivate

cultivo [kul'tiβo] nm (acto) cultivation; (plantas) crops

culto, -a ['kulto, a] adj (que tiene cultura) cultured, educated ▷ nm (homenaje) worship; (religión) cult

cultura [kul'tura] nf culture

culturismo [kultu'rismo] nm body-building

cumbia ['kumbja] nf popular Colombian dance

cumbre ['kumbre] nf summit, top

cumpleaños [kumple'aɲos] nm inv birthday

cumplido, -a [kum'pliðo, a] adj (abundante) plentiful; (cortés) courteous ▷ nm compliment; **visita de ~** courtesy call

cumplidor, -a [kumpli'ðor, a] adj reliable

cumplimiento [kumpli'mjento] nm (de un deber) fulfilment; (acabamiento) completion

cumplir [kum'plir] vt (orden) to carry out, obey; (promesa) to carry out, fulfil; (condena) to serve ▷ vi: **~ con** (deber) to carry out, fulfil; **cumplirse** vr (plazo) to expire; **hoy cumple dieciocho años** he is eighteen today

cuna ['kuna] nf cradle, cot

cundir [kun'dir] vi (noticia, rumor, pánico) to spread; (rendir) to go a long way

cuneta [ku'neta] nf ditch

cuña ['kuɲa] nf wedge

cuñado, -a [ku'ɲaðo, a] nm/f brother-/sister-in-law

cuota ['kwota] *nf (parte proporcional)* share; *(cotización)* fee, dues *pl*

cupe *etc vb* V **caber**

cupiera *etc vb* V **caber**

cupo ['kupo] *vb* V **caber** ▷ *nm* quota

cupón [ku'pon] *nm* coupon

cúpula ['kupula] *nf* dome

cura ['kura] *nf (curación)* cure; *(método curativo)* treatment ▷ *nm* priest

curación [kura'θjon] *nf* cure; *(acción)* curing

curandero, -a [kuran'dero, a] *nm/f* quack

curar [ku'rar] *vt (Med: herida)* to treat, dress; *(: enfermo)* to cure; *(Culin)* to cure, salt; *(cuero)* to tan; **curarse** *vr* to get well, recover

curiosear [kurjose'ar] *vt* to glance at, look over ▷ *vi* to look round, wander round; *(explorar)* to poke about

curiosidad [kurjosi'ðað] *nf* curiosity

curioso, -a [ku'rjoso, a] *adj* curious ▷ *nm/f* bystander, onlooker

curita [ku'rita] (LAM) *nf* (sticking) plaster (BRIT), Bandaid® (US)

currante [ku'rrante] (ESP: fam) *nm/f* worker

currar [ku'rrar] (ESP: fam) *vi* to work

currículo [ku'rrikulo] = **currículum**

currículum [ku'rrikulum] *nm* curriculum vitae

cursi ['kursi] (fam) *adj* affected

cursillo [kur'siʎo] *nm* short course

cursiva [kur'siβa] *nf* italics *pl*

curso ['kurso] *nm* course; **en ~** *(año)* current; *(proceso)* going on, under way

cursor [kur'sor] *nm (Inform)* cursor

curul [ku'rul] (MÉX) *nm (escaño)* seat

curva ['kurβa] *nf* curve, bend

custodia [kus'toðja] *nf* safekeeping; custody

cutis ['kutis] *nm inv* skin, complexion

cutre ['kutre] (ESP: fam) *adj (lugar)* grotty

cuyo, -a ['kujo, a] *pron (de quien)* whose; *(de que)* whose, of which; **en ~ caso** in which case

C.V. *abr* (= caballos de vapor) H.P.

---

d

D. *abr* (= Don) Esq

dado, -a ['daðo, a] *pp de* **dar** ▷ *nm* die; **dados** *nmpl* dice; **~ que** given that

daltónico, -a [dal'toniko, a] *adj* colour-blind

dama ['dama] *nf (gen)* lady; *(Ajedrez)* queen; **damas** *nfpl (juego)* draughts *sg*; **dama de honor** bridesmaid

damasco [da'masko] (RPL) *nm* apricot

danés, -esa [da'nes, esa] *adj* Danish ▷ *nm/f* Dane

dañar [da'ɲar] *vt (objeto)* to damage; *(persona)* to hurt; **dañarse** *vr (objeto)* to get damaged

dañino, -a [da'ɲino, a] *adj* harmful

daño ['daɲo] *nm (objeto)* damage; *(persona)* harm, injury; **~s y perjuicios** *(Jur)* damages; **hacer ~ a** to damage; *(persona)* to hurt, injure; **hacerse ~** to hurt o.s.

dañoso, -a [da'ɲoso] *adj* harmful

○ **PALABRA CLAVE**

dar [dar] *vt* **1** *(gen)* to give; *(obra de*

teatro) to put on; (*film*) to show; (*fiesta*) to hold; **dar algo a algn** to give sth o sth to sb; **dar de beber a algn** to give sb a drink; **dar de comer** to feed
2 (*producir: intereses*) to yield; (*fruta*) to produce
3 (*locuciones + n*): **da gusto escuchar** it's a pleasure to listen to him; V tb **paseo**
4 (*+ n: = perífrasis de verbo*): **me da asco** it sickens me
5 (*considerar*): **dar algo por descontado/entendido** to take sth for granted/as read; **dar algo por concluido** to consider sth finished
6 (*hora*): **el reloj dio las 6** the clock struck 6 (o'clock)
7: **me da lo mismo** it's all the same to me; V tb **igual, más**
▷ *vi* 1 **dar con**: **dimos con él dos horas más tarde** we came across him two hours later; **al final di con la solución** I eventually came up with the answer
2: **dar en** (*blanco, suelo*) to hit; **el sol me da en la cara** the sun is shining (right) on my face
3: **dar de sí** (*zapatos etc*) to stretch, give
darse *vr* 1: **darse por vencido** to give up
2 (*ocurrir*): **se han dado muchos casos** there have been a lot of cases
3: **darse a**: **se ha dado a la bebida** he's taken to drinking
4: **se me dan bien/mal las ciencias** I'm good/bad at science
5: **dárselas de**: **se da de experto** he fancies himself o poses as an expert

dardo ['darðo] *nm* dart

dátil ['datil] *nm* date

dato ['dato] *nm* fact, piece of information; **datos personales** personal details

dcha. *abr* (= *derecha*) r.h.

d. de C. *abr* (= *después de Cristo*) A.D.

○ **PALABRA CLAVE**

de [de] (*de + el = del*) *prep* 1 (*posesión*) of; **la casa de Isabel/mis padres** Isabel's/my parents' house; **es de ellos** it's theirs
2 (*origen, distancia, con números*) from; **soy de Gijón** I'm from Gijón; **de 8 a 20** from 8 to 20; **salir del cine** to go out o leave the cinema; **de 2 en 2** by 2, 2 at a time
3 (*valor descriptivo*): **una copa de vino** a glass of wine; **la mesa de la cocina** the kitchen table; **un billete de 10 euros** a 10 euro note; **un niño de tres años** a three-year-old (child); **una máquina de coser** a sewing machine; **ir vestido de gris** to be dressed in grey; **la niña del vestido azul** the girl in the blue dress; **trabaja de profesora** she works as a teacher; **de lado** sideways; **de atrás/delante** rear/front
4 (*hora, tiempo*): **a las 8 de la mañana** at 8 o'clock in the morning; **de día/ noche** by day/night; **de hoy en ocho días** a week from now; **de niño era gordo** as a child he was fat
5 (*comparaciones*): **más/menos de cien personas** more/less than a hundred people; **el más caro de la tienda** the most expensive in the shop; **menos/más de lo pensado** less/more than expected
6 (*causa*): **del calor** from the heat
7 (*tema*) about; **clases de inglés** English classes; **¿sabes algo de él?** do you know anything about him?; **un libro de física** a physics book
8 (*adj + de + infin*): **fácil de entender** easy to understand
9 (*oraciones pasivas*): **fue respetado de todos** he was loved by all
10 (*condicional + infin*) if; **de ser posible** if possible; **de no terminarlo hoy** if I *etc* don't finish it today

d

dé [de] *vb* V **dar**

debajo [de'βaxo] *adv* underneath; **~ de** below, under; **por ~ de** beneath

debate [de'βate] *nm* debate; **debatir** *vt* to debate

deber [de'βer] *nm* duty ▷ *vt* to owe ▷ *vi*: **debe (de)** it must, it should; **deberes** *nmpl* (Escol) homework; **deberse** *vr*: **~se a** to be owing o due to; **debo hacerlo** I must do it; **debe de ir** he should go

debido, -a [de'βiðo, a] *adj* proper, just; **~ a** due to, because of

débil ['deβil] *adj* (persona, carácter) weak; (luz) dim; **debilidad** *nf* weakness; dimness

debilitar [deβili'tar] *vt* to weaken; **debilitarse** *vr* to grow weak

débito ['deβito] *nm* debit; **débito bancario** (LAM) direct debit (BRIT) o billing (US)

debutar [deβu'tar] *vi* to make one's debut

década ['dekaða] *nf* decade

decadencia [deka'ðenθja] *nf* (estado) decadence; (proceso) decline, decay

decaído, -a [deka'iðo, a] *adj*: **estar ~** (abatido) to be down

decano, -a [de'kano, a] *nm/f* (de universidad etc) dean

decena [de'θena] *nf*: **una ~** ten (or so)

decente [de'θente] *adj* decent

decepción [deθep'θjon] *nf* disappointment

> No confundir **decepción** con la palabra inglesa *deception*.

decepcionar [deθepθjo'nar] *vt* to disappoint

decidir [deθi'ðir] *vt, vi* to decide; **decidirse** *vr*: **~se a** to make up one's mind to

décimo, -a ['deθimo, a] *adj* tenth ▷ *nm* tenth

decir [de'θir] *vt* to say; (contar) to tell; (hablar) to speak ▷ *nm* saying; **decirse** *vr*: **se dice que** it is said that; **es ~** that is (to say); **~ para sí** to say to o.s.;

querer ~ to mean; **¡dígame!** (Tel) hello!; (en tienda) can I help you?

decisión [deθi'sjon] *nf* (resolución) decision; (firmeza) decisiveness

decisivo, -a [deθi'siβo, a] *adj* decisive

declaración [deklara'θjon] *nf* (manifestación) statement; (de amor) declaration; **declaración fiscal** o **de la renta** income-tax return

declarar [dekla'rar] *vt* to declare ▷ *vi* to declare; (Jur) to testify; **declararse** *vr* to propose

decoración [dekora'θjon] *nf* decoration

decorado [deko'raðo] *nm* (Cine, Teatro) scenery, set

decorar [deko'tar] *vt* to decorate; **decorativo, -a** *adj* ornamental, decorative

decreto [de'kreto] *nm* decree

dedal [de'ðal] *nm* thimble

dedicación [deðika'θjon] *nf* dedication

dedicar [deði'kar] *vt* (libro) to dedicate; (tiempo, dinero) to devote; (palabras: decir, consagrar) to dedicate, devote; **dedicatoria** *nf* (de libro) dedication

dedo ['deðo] *nm* finger; **hacer ~** (fam) to hitch (a lift); **dedo anular** ring finger; **dedo corazón** middle finger; **dedo (del pie)** toe; **dedo gordo** (de la mano) thumb; (del pie) big toe; **dedo índice** index finger; **dedo meñique** little finger; **dedo pulgar** thumb

deducción [deðuk'θjon] *nf* deduction

deducir [deðu'θir] *vt* (concluir) to deduce, infer; (Com) to deduct

defecto [de'fekto] *nm* defect, flaw; **defectuoso, -a** *adj* defective, faulty

defender [defen'der] *vt* to defend; **defenderse** *vr* (desenvolverse) to get by

defensa [de'fensa] *nf* defence ▷ *nm* (Deporte) defender, back; **defensivo, -a** *adj* defensive; **a la defensiva** on the defensive

defensor, a [defen'sor, a] *adj* defending ▷ *nm/f (abogado defensor)* defending counsel; *(protector)* protector

deficiencia [defi'θjenθja] *nf* deficiency

deficiente [defi'θjente] *adj (defectuoso)* defective; **~ en** lacking *o* deficient in; **ser un ~ mental** to be mentally handicapped

déficit ['defiθit] *(pl* **~s)** *nm* deficit

definición [defini'θjon] *nf* definition

definir [defi'nir] *vt (determinar)* to determine, establish; *(decidir)* to define; *(aclarar)* to clarify; **definitivo, -a** definitive; **en definitiva** definitively; *(en resumen)* in short

deformación [deforma'θjon] *nf (alteración)* deformation; *(Radio etc)* distortion

deformar [defor'mar] *vt (gen)* to deform; **deformarse** *vr* to become deformed; **deforme** *adj (informe)* deformed; *(feo)* ugly; *(malhecho)* misshapen

defraudar [defrau'ðar] *vt (decepcionar)* to disappoint; *(estafar)* to defraud

defunción [defun'θjon] *nf* death, demise

degenerar [dexene'rar] *vi* to degenerate

degradar [deɣra'ðar] *vt* to debase, degrade; **degradarse** *vr* to demean o.s.

degustación [deɣusta'θjon] *nf* sampling, tasting

dejar [de'xar] *vt* to leave; *(permitir)* to allow, let; *(abandonar)* to abandon, forsake; *(beneficios)* to produce, yield ▷ *vi:* **~ de** *(parar)* to stop; *(no hacer)* to fail to; **~ a un lado** to leave *o* set aside; **~ entrar/salir** to let in/out; **~ pasar** to let through

del [del] *(=* **de + el)** V **de**

delantal [delan'tal] *nm* apron

delante [de'lante] *adv* in front; *(enfrente)* opposite; *(adelante)* ahead; **~**

de in front of, before

delantera [delan'tera] *nf (de vestido, casa etc)* front part; *(Deporte)* forward line; **llevar la ~ (a algn)** to be ahead *(of sb)*

delantero, -a [delan'tero, a] *adj* front ▷ *nm (Deporte)* forward, striker

delatar [dela'tar] *vt* to inform on *o* against, betray; **delator, a** *nm/f* informer

delegación [deleɣa'θjon] *nf (acción, delegados)* delegation; *(Com: oficina)* office, branch; **delegación de policía** *(MÉX)* police station

delegado, -a [dele'ɣaðo, a] *nm/f* delegate; *(Com)* agent

delegar [dele'ɣar] *vt* to delegate

deletrear [deletre'ar] *vt* to spell (out)

delfín [del'fin] *nm* dolphin

delgado, -a [del'ɣaðo, a] *adj* thin; *(persona)* slim, thin; *(tela etc)* light, delicate

deliberar [deliβe'rar] *vt* to debate, discuss

delicadeza [delika'ðeθa] *nf (gen)* delicacy; *(refinamiento, sutileza)* refinement

delicado, -a [deli'kaðo, a] *adj (gen)* delicate; *(sensible)* sensitive; *(quisquilloso)* touchy

delicia [de'liθja] *nf* delight

delicioso, -a [deli'θjoso, a] *adj (gracioso)* delightful; *(exquisito)* delicious

delimitar [delimi'tar] *vt (función, responsabilidades)* to define

delincuencia [delin'kwenθja] *nf* delinquency; **delincuente** *nmf* delinquent; *(criminal)* criminal

delineante [deline'ante] *nmf* draughtsman/woman

delirante [deli'rante] *adj* delirious

delirar [deli'rar] *vi* to be delirious, rave

delirio [de'lirjo] *nm (Med)* delirium; *(palabras insensatas)* ravings *pl*

delito [de'lito] nm (gen) crime; (infracción) offence

delta ['delta] nm delta

demacrado, -a [dema'kraðo, a] adj: **estar ~** to look pale and drawn, be wasted away

demanda [de'manda] nf (pedido, Com) demand; (petición) request; (Jur) action, lawsuit; **demandar** [deman'dar] vt (gen) to demand; (Jur) to sue, file a lawsuit against

demás [de'mas] adj: **los ~ niños** the other o remaining children ▷ pron: **los/las ~** the others, the rest (of them); **lo ~** the rest (of it)

demasía [dema'sia] nf (exceso) excess, surplus; **comer en ~** to eat to excess

demasiado, -a [dema'sjaðo, a] adj: **~ vino** too much wine ▷ adv (antes de adj, adv) too; **~s libros** too many books; **¡esto es ~!** that's the limit!; **hace ~ calor** it's too hot; **~ despacio** too slowly; **~s** too many

demencia [de'menθja] nf (locura) madness

democracia [demo'kraθja] nf democracy

demócrata [de'mokrata] nmf democrat; **democrático, -a** adj democratic

demoler [demo'ler] vt to demolish; **demolición** nf demolition

demonio [de'monjo] nm devil; demon; **¡~s!** hell!, damn!; **¿cómo ~s?** how the hell?

demora [de'mora] nf delay

demos ['demos] vb V **dar**

demostración [demostra'θjon] nf (Mat) proof; (de afecto) show, display

demostrar [demos'trar] vt (probar) to prove; (mostrar) to show; (manifestar) to demonstrate

den [den] vb V **dar**

denegar [dene'var] vt (rechazar) to refuse; (Jur) to reject

denominación [denomina'θjon]

nf (acto) naming; **Denominación de Origen** see note

densidad [densi'ðað] nf density; (fig) thickness

denso, -a ['denso, a] adj dense; (espeso, pastoso) thick; (fig) heavy

dentadura [denta'ðura] nf (set of) teeth pl; **dentadura postiza** false teeth pl

dentera [den'tera] nf (grima): **dar ~ a algn** to set sb's teeth on edge

dentífrico, -a [den'tifriko, a] adj dental ▷ nm toothpaste

dentista [den'tista] nmf dentist

dentro ['dentro] adv (interior) ▷ prep: **~ de** in, inside, within; **por ~** (on the) inside; **mirar por ~** to look inside; **~ de tres meses** within three months

denuncia [de'nunθja] nf (delación) denunciation; (acusación) accusation; (de accidente) report; **denunciar** vt to report; (delatar) to inform on o against

departamento [departa'mento] nm sección administrativa, department, section; (LAM: apartamento) flat (BRIT), apartment

depender [depen'der] vi: **~ de** to depend on; **depende** it (all) depends

dependienta [depen'djenta] nf saleswoman, shop assistant

dependiente [depen'djente] adj dependent ▷ nm salesman, shop assistant

depilar [depi'lar] vt (con cera) to wax; (cejas) to pluck

deportar [depor'tar] vt to deport

deporte [de'porte] nm sport; **hacer ~** to play sports; **deportista** adj sports cpd ▷ nmf sportsman/woman; **deportivo, -a** adj (club, periódico) sports cpd ▷ nm sports car

depositar [deposi'tar] vt (dinero) to deposit; (mercancías) to put away, store; **depositarse** vr to settle

depósito [de'posito] nm (gen) deposit; (almacén) warehouse, store; (de agua, gasolina etc) tank; **depósito de cadáveres** mortuary

depredador, a [depreða'ðor, a] adj predatory ▷ nm predator

depresión [depre'sjon] nf depression; **depresión nerviosa** nervous breakdown

deprimido, -a [depri'miðo, a] adj depressed

deprimir [depri'mir] vt to depress; **deprimirse** vr (persona) to become depressed

deprisa [de'prisa] adv quickly, hurriedly

depurar [depu'rar] vt to purify; (purgar) to purge

derecha [de'retʃa] nf right(-hand) side; (Pol) right; **a la ~** (estar) on the right; (torcer etc) to the right

derecho, -a [de'retʃo, a] adj right, right-hand ▷ nm (privilegio) right; (lado) right(-hand) side; (leyes) law ▷ adv straight, directly; **siga todo ~** carry o straight on; **derechos** nmpl (de aduana) duty sg; (de autor) royalties; **tener ~ a** to have a right to; **derechos de autor** royalties

deriva [de'riβa] nf: **ir o estar a la ~** to drift, be adrift

derivado [deri'βaðo] nm (Com) by-product

derivar [deri'βar] vt to derive; (desviar) to direct ▷ vi to derive, be derived; (Náut) to drift; **derivarse** vr to derive, be derived; to drift

derramamiento [derrama'mjento] nm (dispersión) spilling;

derramamiento de sangre bloodshed

derramar [derra'mar] vt to spill; (verter) to pour out; (esparcir) to scatter; **derramarse** vr to pour out

derrame [de'rrame] nm (de líquido) spilling; (de sangre) shedding; (de tubo etc) overflow; (pérdida) leakage; **derrame cerebral** brain haemorrhage

derredor [derre'ðor] adv: **al o en ~ de** around, about

derretir [derre'tir] vt (gen) to melt; (nieve) to thaw; **derretirse** vr to melt

derribar [derri'βar] vt to knock down; (construcción) to demolish; (persona, gobierno, político) to bring down

derrocar [derro'kar] vt (gobierno) to bring down, overthrow

derrochar [derro'tʃar] vt to squander; **derroche** nm (despilfarro) waste, squandering

derrota [de'rrota] nf (Náut) course; (Mil, Deporte etc) defeat, rout; **derrotar** vt (gen) to defeat; **derrotero** nm (rumbo) course

derrumbar [derrum'bar] vt (edificio) to knock down; **derrumbarse** vr to collapse

des etc vb V **dar**

desabrochar [desaβro'tʃar] vt (botones, broches) to undo, unfasten; **desabrocharse** vr (ropa etc) to come undone

desacato [desa'kato] nm (falta de respeto) disrespect; (Jur) contempt

desacertado, -a [desaθer'taðo, a] adj (equivocado) mistaken; (inoportuno) unwise

desacierto [desa'θjerto] nm mistake, error

desaconsejar [desakonse'xar] vt to advise against

desacreditar [desakreði'tar] vt (desprestigiar) to discredit, bring into disrepute; (denigrar) to run down

desacuerdo [desa'kwerðo] nm disagreement, discord

desafiar [desa'fjar] vt (retar) to

challenge; (enfrentarse a) to defy
desafilado, -a [desafi'laðo, a]
adj blunt
desafinado, -a [desafi'naðo, a]
adj: **estar ~** to be out of tune
desafinar [desafi'nar] vi (al cantar) to
be o go out of tune
desafío etc [desa'fio] vb V **desafiar**
▷ nm (reto) challenge; (combate) duel;
(resistencia) defiance
desafortunado, -a
[desafortu'naðo, a] adj (desgraciado)
unfortunate, unlucky
desagradable [desaɣra'ðaβle]
adj (fastidioso, enojoso) unpleasant;
(irritante) disagreeable
desagradar [desaɣra'ðar] vi
(disgustar) to displease; (molestar) to
bother
desagradecido, -a [desaɣraðe'θiðo,
a] adj ungrateful
desagrado [desa'ɣraðo] nm
(disgusto) displeasure; (contrariedad)
dissatisfaction
desagüe [des'aɣwe] nm (de un líquido)
drainage; (cañería) drainpipe; (salida)
outlet, drain
desahogar [desao'ɣar] vt (aliviar)
to ease, relieve; (ira) to vent;
desahogarse vr (relajarse) to relax;
(desfogarse) to let off steam
desahogo [desa'oɣo] nm (alivio)
relief; (comodidad) comfort, ease
desahuciar [desau'θjar] vt (enfermo)
to give up hope for; (inquilino) to evict
desairar [desai'rar] vt (menospreciar)
to slight, snub
desalentador, a [desalenta'ðor, a]
adj discouraging
desaliño [desa'liɲo] nm slovenliness
desalmado, -a [desal'maðo, a] adj
(cruel) cruel, heartless
desalojar [desalo'xar] vt (expulsar,
echar) to eject; (abandonar) to move out
of ▷ vi to move out
desamor [desa'mor] nm (frialdad)
indifference; (odio) dislike
desamparado, -a [desampa'raðo,

a] adj (persona) helpless;
(lugar: expuesto) exposed; (desierto)
deserted
desangrar [desan'grar] vt to bleed;
(fig: persona) to bleed dry; **desangrarse**
vr to lose a lot of blood
desanimado, -a [desani'maðo,
a] adj (persona) downhearted;
(espectáculo, fiesta) dull
desanimar [desani'mar] vt
(desalentar) to discourage; (deprimir) to
depress; **desanimarse** vr to lose heart
desapacible [desapa'θiβle] adj (gen)
unpleasant
desaparecer [desapare'θer] vi (gen)
to disappear; (el sol, el luz) to vanish;
desaparecido, -a adj missing;
desaparición nf disappearance
desapercibido, -a [desaperθi'βiðo,
a] adj (desprevenido) unprepared; **pasar
~ to** go unnoticed
desaprensivo, -a [desapren'siβo, a]
adj unscrupulous
desaprobar [desapro'βar] vt
(reprobar) to disapprove of; (condenar) to
condemn; (no consentir) to reject
desaprovechado, -a
[desaproβe'tʃaðo, a] adj (oportunidad,
tiempo) wasted; (estudiante) slack
desaprovechar [desaproβe'tʃar]
vt to waste
desarmador [desarma'ðor] (Méx)
nm screwdriver
desarmar [desar'mar] vt (Mil, fig) to
disarm; (Tec) to take apart, dismantle;
desarme nm disarmament
desarraigar [desarrai'xar] vt to
uproot; **desarraigo** nm uprooting
desarreglar [desarre'xlar] vt
(desordenar) to disarrange; (trastocar) to
upset, disturb
desarrollar [desarro'ʎar] vt (gen) to
develop; **desarrollarse** vr to develop;
(ocurrir) to take place; (Foto) to develop;
desarrollo nm development
desarticular [desartiku'lar] vt
(hueso) to dislocate; (objeto) to take
apart; (fig) to break up

desasosegar [desasose'ɣar] vt
(inquietar) to disturb, make uneasy
desasosiego etc [desaso'sjeɣo] vb
V **desasosegar** ▷ nm (intranquilidad)
uneasiness, restlessness; (ansiedad)
anxiety
desastre [de'sastre] nm disaster;
desastroso, -a adj disastrous
desatar [desa'tar] vt (nudo) to untie;
(paquete) to undo; (separar) to detach;
desatarse vr (zapatos) to come
untied; (tormenta) to break
desatascar [desatas'kar] vt (cañería)
to unblock, clear
desatender [desaten'der] vt (no
prestar atención a, to disregard;
(abandonar) to neglect
desatino [desa'tino] nm (idiotez)
foolishness, folly; (error) blunder
desatornillar [desatorni'ʎar] vt to
unscrew
desatrancar [desatraŋ'kar] vt
(puerta) to unbolt; (cañería) to clear,
unblock
desautorizado, -a [desautori'θaðo,
a] adj unauthorized
desautorizar [desautori'θar]
vt (oficial) to deprive of authority;
(informe) to deny
desayunar [desaju'nar] vi to have
breakfast ▷ vt to have for breakfast;
desayuno nm breakfast
desazón [desa'θon] nf anxiety
desbarajuste [desβara'xuste] nm
confusion, disorder
desbaratar [desβara'tar] vt
(deshacer, destruir) to ruin
desbloquear [desβloke'ar] vt
(negociaciones, tráfico) to get going
again; (Com: cuenta) to unfreeze
desbordar [desβor'ðar] vt
(sobrepasar) to go beyond; (exceder)
to exceed; **desbordarse** vr (río) to
overflow; (entusiasmo) to erupt
descabellado, -a [deskaβe'ʎaðo, a]
adj (disparatado) wild, crazy
descafeinado, -a [deskafei'naðo, a]
adj decaffeinated ▷ nm decaffeinated

coffee
descalabro [deska'laβro] nm blow;
(desgracia) misfortune
descalificar [deskalifi'kar] vt to
disqualify; (desacreditar) to discredit
descalzar [deskal'θar] vt (zapato) to
take off; **descalzo, -a** adj barefoot(ed)
descambiar [deskam'bjar] vt to
exchange
descaminado, -a [deskami'naðo,
a] adj (equivocado) on the wrong road;
(fig) misguided
descampado [deskam'paðo] nm
open space
descansado, -a [deskan'saðo, a] adj
(gen) rested; (que tranquiliza) restful
descansar [deskan'sar] vt (gen) to
rest ▷ vi to rest, have a rest; (echarse)
to lie down
descansillo [deskan'siʎo] nm (de
escalera) landing
descanso [des'kanso] nm (reposo)
rest; (alivio) relief; (pausa) break;
(Deporte) interval, half time
descapotable [deskapo'taβle] nm
(tb: **coche ~**) convertible
descarado, -a [deska'raðo, a] adj
shameless; (insolente) cheeky
descarga [des'karɣa] nf (Arq, Elec,
Mil) discharge; (Náut) unloading;
descargable adj downloadable; **descargar**
[deskar'ɣar] vt to unload; (golpe) to
let fly; **descargarse** vr to unburden
o.s.; **descargarse algo de Internet** to
download sth from the Internet
descaro [des'karo] nm nerve
descarriar [deska'rrjar] vt
(descaminar) to misdirect; (fig) to lead
astray; **descarriarse** vr (perderse) to
lose one's way; (separarse) to stray;
(pervertirse) to err, go astray
descarrilamiento
[deskarrila'mjento] nm (de tren)
derailment
descarrilar [deskarri'lar] vi to be
derailed
descartar [deskar'tar] vt (rechazar)

to reject; (*eliminar*) to rule out;
descartarse *vr* (*Naipes*) to discard;
~se de to shirk

descendencia [desθen'denθja] *nf*
(*origen*) origin, descent; (*hijos*) offspring

descender [desθen'der] *vt*
(*bajar: escalera*) to go down ▷ *vi* to
descend; (*temperatura, nivel*) to fall,
drop; **~ de** to be descended from

descendiente [desθen'djente] *nmf*
descendant

descenso [des'θenso] *nm* descent;
(*de temperatura*) drop

descifrar [desθi'frar] *vt* to decipher;
(*mensaje*) to decode

descolgar [deskol'ɣar] *vt* (*bajar*)
to take down; (*teléfono*) to pick up;
descolgarse *vr* to let o.s. down

descolorido, -a [deskolo'riðo, a] *adj*
faded; (*pálido*) pale

descompasado, -a
[deskompa'saðo, a] *adj* (*sin
proporción*) out of all proportion;
(*excesivo*) excessive

descomponer [deskompo'ner] *vt*
(*desordenar*) to disarrange, disturb; (*Tec*)
to put out of order; (*dividir*) to break
down (into parts); (*fig*) to provoke;
descomponerse *vr* (*corromperse*) to
rot, decompose; (*LAM Tec*) to break
down

descomposición [deskomposi'θjon]
nf (*de un objeto*) breakdown; (*de fruta
etc*) decomposition; **descomposición
de vientre** (*ESP*) stomach upset,
diarrhoea

descompostura [deskompos'tura]
nf (*MÉX: avería*) breakdown, fault;
(*LAM: diarrea*) diarrhoea

descomprimir [deskompri'mir]
(*Internet*) to unzip

descompuesto, -a
[deskom'pwesto, a] *adj* (*corrompido*)
decomposed; (*roto*) broken

desconcertado, -a
[deskonθer'taðo, a] *adj* disconcerted,
bewildered

desconcertar [deskonθer'tar] *vt*

(*confundir*) to baffle; (*incomodar*) to
upset, put out; **desconcertarse** *vr*
(*turbarse*) to be upset

desconchado, -a [deskon'tʃaðo, a]
adj (*pintura*) peeling

desconcierto *etc* [deskon'θjerto] *vb*
V **desconcertar** ▷ *nm* (*gen*) disorder;
(*desorientación*) uncertainty; (*inquietud*)
uneasiness

desconectar [deskonek'tar] *vt* to
disconnect

desconfianza [deskon'fjanθa] *nf*
distrust

desconfiar [deskon'fjar] *vi* to be
distrustful; **~ de** to distrust, suspect

descongelar [deskonxe'lar] *vt* to
defrost; (*Com, Pol*) to unfreeze

descongestionar
[deskonxestjo'nar] *vt* (*cabeza, tráfico*)
to clear

desconocer [deskono'θer] *vt*
(*ignorar*) not to know, be ignorant of

desconocido, -a [deskono'θiðo, a]
adj unknown ▷ *nm/f* stranger

desconocimiento *nm falta de
conocimientos*, ignorance

desconsiderado, -a
[deskonsiðe'raðo, a] *adj*
inconsiderate; (*insensible*) thoughtless

desconsuelo *etc* [deskon'swelo] *vb*
V **desconsolar** ▷ *nm* (*tristeza*) distress;
(*desesperación*) despair

descontado, -a [deskon'taðo, a]
adj: **dar por ~ (que)** to take (it) for
granted (that)

descontar [deskon'tar] *vt* (*deducir*)
to take away, deduct; (*rebajar*) to
discount

descontento, -a [deskon'tento, a]
adj dissatisfied ▷ *nm* dissatisfaction,
discontent

descorchar [deskor'tʃar] *vt* to
uncork

descorrer [desko'rrer] *vt* (*cortinas,
cerrojo*) to draw back

descortés [deskor'tes] *adj* (*mal
educado*) discourteous; (*grosero*) rude

descoser [desko'ser] vt to unstitch; **descoserse** vr to come apart (at the seams)

descosido, -a [desko'siðo, a] adj (Costura) unstitched

descreído, -a [deskre'iðo, a] adj (incrédulo) incredulous; (falto de fe) unbelieving

descremado, -a [deskre'maðo, a] adj skimmed

describir [deskri'ßir] vt to describe; **descripción** [deskrip'θjon] nf description

descrito [des'krito] pp de **describir**

descuartizar [deskwarti'θar] vt (animal) to cut up

descubierto, -a [desku'ßjerto, a] pp de **descubrir** ▷ adj uncovered, bare; (persona) bareheaded ▷ nm (bancario) overdraft; **al ~** in the open

descubrimiento [deskußri'mjento] nm (hallazgo) discovery; (revelación) revelation

descubrir [desku'ßrir] vt to discover, find; (inaugurar) to unveil; (vislumbrar) to detect; (revelar) to reveal, show; (destapar) to uncover; **descubrirse** vr to reveal o.s.; (quitarse sombrero) to take off one's hat; (confesar) to confess

descuento etc [des'kwento] vb V **descontar** ▷ nm discount

descuidado, -a [deskwi'ðaðo, a] adj (sin cuidado) careless; (desordenado) untidy; (olvidadizo) forgetful; (dejado) neglected; (desprevenido) unprepared

descuidar [deskwi'ðar] vt (dejar) to neglect; (olvidar) to overlook; **descuidarse** vr (distraerse) to be careless; (abandonarse) to let o.s. go; (desprevenirse) to drop one's guard; **¡descuida!** don't worry!; **descuido** nm (dejadez) carelessness; (olvido) negligence

○ PALABRA CLAVE

desde ['desðe] prep 1 (lugar) from;

desde Burgos hasta mi casa hay 30 km it's 30 km from Burgos to my house

2 (posición): **hablaba desde el balcón** she was speaking from the balcony

3 (tiempo: + adv, n): **desde ahora** from now on; **desde la boda** since the wedding; **desde niño** since I etc was a child; **desde 3 años atrás** since 3 years ago

4 (tiempo: + vb, fecha) since; for; **nos conocemos desde 1992/desde hace 20 años** we've known each other since 1992/for 20 years; **no le veo desde 1997/desde hace 5 años** I haven't seen him since 1997/for 5 years

5 (gama): **desde los más lujosos hasta los más económicos** from the most luxurious to the most reasonably priced

6: **desde luego (que no)** of course (not)

▷ conj: **desde que: desde que recuerdo** for as long as I can remember; **desde que llegó no ha salido** he hasn't been out since he arrived

desdén [des'ðen] nm scorn

desdeñar [desðe'nar] vt (despreciar) to scorn

desdicha [des'ðitʃa] nf (desgracia) misfortune; (infelicidad) unhappiness; **desdichado, -a** adj (sin suerte) unlucky; (infeliz) unhappy

desear [dese'ar] vt to want, desire, wish for

desechar [dese'tʃar] vt (basura) to throw out o away; (ideas) to reject, discard; **desechos** nmpl rubbish sg, waste sg

desembalar [desemba'lar] vt to unpack

desembarazar [desembara'θar] vt (desocupar) to clear; (desenredar) to free; **desembarazarse** vr: **~se de** to free o.s. of, get rid of

desembarcar [desembar'kar] vt (mercancías etc) to unload ▷ vi to disembark

desembocadura [desemboka'ðura]
nf (de río) mouth; (de calle) opening

desembocar [desembo'kar] vi (río)
to flow into; (fig) to result in

desembolso [desem'bolso] nm
payment

desembrollar [desembro'Aar]
vt (madeja) to unravel; (asunto,
malentendido) to sort out

desemejanza [deseme'xanθa] nf
dissimilarity

desempaquetar [desempake'tar]
vt (regalo) to unwrap; (mercancía) to
unpack

desempate [desem'pate] nm (Fútbol)
replay, play-off; (Tenis) tie-break(er)

desempeñar [desempe'ɲar] vt
(cargo) to hold; (papel) to perform; (lo
empeñado) to redeem; **~ un papel** (fig)
to play (a role)

desempleado, -a [desemple'aðo, a]
nm/f unemployed person; **desempleo**
nm unemployment

desencadenar [desenkaðe'nar]
vt to unchain; (ira) to unleash;
desencadenarse vr to break loose;
(tormenta) to burst; (guerra) to break out

desencajar [desenka'xar] vt (hueso)
to dislocate; (mecanismo, pieza) to
disconnect, disengage

desencanto [desen'kanto] nm
disillusionment

desenchufar [desentʃu'far] vt to
unplug

desenfadado, -a [desenfa'ðaðo,
a] adj (desenvuelto) uninhibited;
(descarado) forward; **desenfado** nm
(libertad) freedom; (comportamiento)
free and easy manner; (descaro)
forwardness

desenfocado, -a [desenfo'kaðo, a]
adj (Foto) out of focus

desenfreno [desen'freno] nm
wildness; (de las pasiones) lack of
self-control

desenganchar [desengan'tʃar] vt
(gen) to unhook; (Ferro) to uncouple

desengañar [desenga'ɲar] vt to
disillusion; **desengañarse** vr to
become disillusioned; **desengaño**
nm disillusionment; (decepción)
disappointment

desenlace [desen'laθe] nm outcome

desenmascarar [desenmaska'rar]
vt to unmask

desenredar [desenre'ðar] vt (pelo) to
untangle; (problema) to sort out

desenroscar [desenros'kar] vt to
unscrew

desentenderse [desenten'derse]
vr: **~ de** to pretend not to know about;
(apartarse) to have nothing to do with

desenterrar [desente'rrar] vt to
exhume; (tesoro, fig) to unearth, dig up

desentonar [desento'nar] vi (Mús)
to sing (o play) out of tune; (color)
to clash

desentrañar [desentra'ɲar] vt
(misterio) to unravel

desenvoltura [desenβol'tura]
nf ease

desenvolver [desenβol'βer] vt
(paquete) to unwrap; (fig) to develop;
desenvolverse vr (desarrollarse) to
unfold, develop; (arreglárselas) to cope

deseo [de'seo] nm desire, wish;
deseoso, -a adj: **estar deseoso de** to
be anxious to

desequilibrado, -a [desekili'βraðo,
a] adj unbalanced

desertar [deser'tar] vi to desert

desértico, -a [de'sertiko, a] adj
desert cpd

desesperación [desespera'θjon]
nf (impaciencia) desperation, despair;
(irritación) fury

desesperar [desespe'rar] vt to
drive to despair; (exasperar) to drive
to distraction ▷ vi: **~ de** to despair of;
desesperarse vr to despair, lose hope

desestabilizar [desestaβili'θar] vt
to destabilize

desestimar [desesti'mar] vt
(menospreciar) to have a low opinion of;
(rechazar) to reject

desfachatez [desfatʃa'teθ] nf
(insolencia) impudence; (descaro)
rudeness

desfalco [des'falko] nm
embezzlement

desfallecer [desfaʎe'θer] vi
(perder las fuerzas) to become weak;
(desvanecerse) to faint

desfasado, -a [desfa'saðo, a] adj
(anticuado) old-fashioned; **desfase** nm
(diferencia) gap

desfavorable [desfaβo'raβle] adj
unfavourable

desfigurar [desfiɣu'rar] vt (cara) to
disfigure; (cuerpo) to deform

desfiladero [desfila'ðero] nm gorge

desfilar [desfi'lar] vi to parade;
desfile nm procession; **desfile de
modelos** fashion show

desgana [des'ɣana] nf (falta de
apetito) loss of appetite; (apatía)
unwillingness; **desganado, -a**
adj: **estar desganado** (sin apetito) to
have no appetite; (sin entusiasmo) to
have lost interest

desgarrar [desɣa'rrar] vt to tear
(up); (fig) to shatter; **desgarro** nm (en
tela) tear; (aflicción) grief

desgastar [desɣas'tar] vt (deteriorar)
to wear away o down; (estropear) to
spoil; **desgastarse** vr to get worn out;
desgaste nm wear (and tear)

desglosar [desɣlo'sar] vt (factura) to
break down

desgracia [des'ɣraθja] nf
misfortune; (accidente) accident;
(vergüenza) disgrace; (contratiempo)
setback; **por ~** unfortunately;
desgraciado, -a [desɣra'θjaðo, a]
adj (sin suerte) unlucky, unfortunate;
(miserable) wretched; (infeliz) miserable

desgravar [desɣra'βar] vt (impuestos)
to reduce the tax o duty on

desguace [des'ɣwaθe] (ESP) nm
junkyard

deshabitado, -a [desaβi'taðo, a] adj
uninhabited

deshacer [desa'θer] vt (casa) to

break up; (Tec) to take apart; (enemigo)
to defeat; (diluir) to melt; (contrato) to
break; (intriga) to solve; **deshacerse**
vr (disolverse) to melt; (despedazarse) to
come apart o undone; **~se de** to get rid
of; **~se en lágrimas** to burst into tears

deshecho, -a [des'etʃo, a]
adj undone; (roto) smashed;
(persona): **estar ~** to be shattered

desheredar [desere'ðar] vt to
disinherit

deshidratar [desiðra'tar] vt to
dehydrate

deshielo [des'jelo] nm thaw

deshonesto, -a [deso'nesto, a] adj
indecent

deshonra [des'onra] nf (deshonor)
dishonour; (vergüenza) shame

deshora [des'ora]: **a ~** adv at the
wrong time

deshuesadero [deswesa'ðero] (MÉX)
nm junkyard

deshuesar [deswe'sar] vt (carne) to
bone; (fruta) to stone

desierto, -a [de'sjerto, a] adj (casa,
calle, negocio) deserted ▷ nm desert

designar [desiɣ'nar] vt (nombrar) to
designate; (indicar) to fix

desigual [desi'ɣwal] adj (terreno)
uneven; (lucha etc) unequal

desilusión [desilu'sjon] nf
disillusionment; (decepción)
disappointment; **desilusionar**
vt to disillusion; to disappoint;
desilusionarse vr to become
disillusioned

desinfectar [desinfek'tar] vt to
disinfect

desinflar [desin'flar] vt to deflate

desintegración [desinteɣra'θjon]
nf disintegration

desinterés [desinte'res] nm
(desgana) lack of interest; (altruismo)
unselfishness

desintoxicarse [desintoksi'karse]
vr (drogadicto) to undergo
detoxification

desistir [desis'tir] vi (renunciar) to

stop, desist

desleal [desle'al] *adj* (*infiel*) disloyal;
(*Com: competencia*) unfair; **deslealtad**
nf disloyalty

desligar [desli'ɣar] *vt* (*desatar*) to
untie, undo; (*separar*) to separate;
desligarse *vr* (*de un compromiso*) to
extricate o.s.

desliz [des'liθ] *nm* (*fig*) lapse; **deslizar**
vt to slip, slide

deslumbrar [deslum'brar] *vt* to
dazzle

desmadrarse [desma'ðrarse]
(*fam*) *vr* (*descontrolarse*) to run wild;
(*divertirse*) to let one's hair down;
desmadre (*fam*) *nm* (*desorganización*)
chaos; (*jaleo*) commotion

desmán [des'man] *nm* (*exceso*)
outrage; (*abuso de poder*) abuse

desmantelar [desmante'lar] *vt*
(*deshacer*) to dismantle; (*casa*) to strip

desmaquillador [desmakiʎa'ðor]
nm make-up remover

desmayar [desma'jar] *vi* to lose
heart; **desmayarse** *vr* (*Med*) to
faint; **desmayo** *nm* (*Med: acto*) faint;
(: *estado*) unconsciousness

desmemoriado, -a
[desmemo'rjaðo, a] *adj* forgetful

desmentir [desmen'tir] *vt*
(*contradecir*) to contradict; (*refutar*)
to deny

desmenuzar [desmenu'θar] *vt*
(*deshacer*) to crumble; (*carne*) to chop;
(*examinar*) to examine closely

desmesurado, -a [desmesu'raðo, a]
adj disproportionate

desmontable [desmon'taβle]
adj (*que se quita: pieza*) detachable;
(*plegable*) collapsible, folding

desmontar [desmon'tar] *vt*
(*deshacer*) to dismantle; (*tierra*) to level
▷ *vi* to dismount

desmoralizar [desmorali'θar] *vt* to
demoralize

desmoronar [desmoro'nar] *vt* to
wear away, erode; **desmoronarse** *vr*
(*edificio, dique*) to collapse; (*economía*)

to decline

desnatado, -a [desna'taðo, a] *adj*
skimmed

desnivel [desni'βel] *nm* (*de terreno*)
unevenness

desnudar [desnu'ðar] *vt* (*desvestir*) to
undress; (*despojar*) to strip; **desnudarse**
vr (*desvestirse*) to get undressed;
desnudo, -a *adj* naked ▷ *nm/f* nude;
desnudo de devoid o bereft of

desnutrición [desnutri'θjon] *nf*
malnutrition; **desnutrido, -a** *adj*
undernourished

desobedecer [desoβeðe'θer] *vt*,
vi to disobey; **desobediencia** *nf*
disobedience

desocupado, -a [desoku'paðo,
a] *adj* at leisure; (*desempleado*)
unemployed; (*deshabitado*) empty,
vacant

desodorante [desoðo'rante] *nm*
deodorant

desolación [desola'θjon] *nf* (*de lugar*)
desolation; (*fig*) grief

desolar [deso'lar] *vt* to ruin, lay
waste

desorbitado, -a [desorβi'taðo,
a] *adj* (*excesivo: ambición*) boundless;
(*deseos*) excessive; (: *precio*) exorbitant

desorden [des'orðen] *nm* confusion;
(*político*) disorder, unrest

desorganización
[desorɣaniθa'θjon] *nf* (*de persona*)
disorganization; (*en empresa, oficina*)
disorder, chaos

desorientar [desorjen'tar] *vt*
(*extraviar*) to mislead; (*confundir,
desconcertar*) to confuse; **desorientarse**
vr (*perderse*) to lose one's way

despabilado, -a [despaβi'laðo,
a] *adj* (*despierto*) wide-awake; (*fig*)
alert, sharp

despachar [despa'tʃar] *vt* (*negocio*) to
do, complete; (*enviar*) to dispatch;
(*vender*) to sell, deal in; (*billete*) to issue;
(*mandar ir*) to send away

despacho [des'patʃo] *nm* (*oficina*)
office; (*de paquetes*) dispatch; (*venta*)

sale; (comunicación) message; **~ de billetes** o **boletos** (LAM) booking office

despacio [des'paθjo] adv slowly

desparpajo [despar'paxo] nm self-confidence; (pey) nerve

desparramar [desparra'mar] vt (esparcir) to scatter; (líquido) to spill

despecho [des'petʃo] nm spite

despectivo, -a [despek'tiβo, a] adj (despreciativo) derogatory; (Ling) pejorative

despedida [despe'ðiða] nf (adiós) farewell; (de obrero) sacking

despedir [despe'ðir] vt (visita) to see off, show out; (empleado) to dismiss; (inquilino) to evict; (objeto) to hurl; (olor etc) to give out o off; **despedirse** vr: **~se de** to say goodbye to

despegar [despe'xar] vt to unstick ▷ vi (avión) to take off; **despegarse** vr to come loose, come unstuck; **despego** nm detachment

despegue etc [des'peɣe] vb V **despegar** ▷ nm takeoff

despeinado, -a [despei'naðo, a] adj dishevelled, unkempt

despejado, -a [despe'xaðo, a] adj (lugar) clear, free; (cielo) clear; (persona) wide-awake, bright

despejar [despe'xar] vt (gen) to clear; (misterio) to clear up ▷ vi (el tiempo) to clear; **despejarse** vr (tiempo, cielo) to clear (up); (misterio) to become clearer; (cabeza) to clear

despensa [des'pensa] nf larder

despeñarse [despe'ɲarse] vr to hurl o.s. down; (coche) to tumble over

desperdicio [desper'ðiθjo] nm (despilfarro) squandering; **desperdicios** nmpl (basura) rubbish sg (BRIT), garbage sg (US); (residuos) waste sg

desperezarse [despere'θarse] vr to stretch

desperfecto [desper'fekto] nm (deterioro) slight damage; (defecto) flaw, imperfection

despertador [desperta'ðor] nm alarm clock

despertar [desper'tar] nm awakening ▷ vt (persona) to wake up; (recuerdos) to revive; (sentimiento) to arouse ▷ vi to awaken, wake up; **despertarse** vr to awaken, wake up

despido etc [des'piðo] vb V **despedir** ▷ nm dismissal, sacking

despierto, -a etc [des'pjerto, a] vb V **despertar** ▷ adj awake; (fig) sharp, alert

despilfarro [despil'farro] nm (derroche) squandering; (lujo desmedido) extravagance

despistar [despis'tar] vt to throw off the track o scent; (confundir) to mislead, confuse; **despistarse** vr to take the wrong road; (confundirse) to become confused

despiste [des'piste] nm absent-mindedness; **un ~** a mistake o slip

desplazamiento [desplaθa'mjento] nm displacement

desplazar [despla'θar] vt to move; (Náut) to displace; (Inform) to scroll; (fig) to oust; **desplazarse** vr (persona) to travel

desplegar [desple'xar] vt (tela, papel) to unfold, open out; (bandera) to unfurl; **despliegue** etc [des'pleɣe] vb V **desplegar** ▷ nm display

desplomarse [desplo'marse] vr (edificio, gobierno, persona) to collapse

desplumar [desplu'mar] vt (ave) to pluck; (fam: estafar) to fleece

despoblado, -a [despo'βlaðo, a] adj (sin habitantes) uninhabited

despojar [despo'xar] vt (alguien de sus bienes) to divest of, deprive of; (casa) to strip, leave bare; (alguien: de su cargo) to strip of

despojo [des'poxo] nm (acto) plundering; (objetos) plunder, loot; **despojos** nmpl (de ave, res) offal sg

desposados, -a [despo'saðo, a] adj, nm/f newly-wed

despreciar [despre'θjar] vt (desdeñar) to despise, scorn; (afrentar) to slight; **desprecio** nm scorn, contempt; slight

desprender [despren'der] vt
(broche) to unfasten; (olor) to give off;
desprenderse vr (botón: caerse) to fall
off; (broche) to come unfastened; (olor,
perfume) to be given off; **~se de algo
que ...** to draw from sth that ...

desprendimiento
[desprendi'mjento] nm (gen)
loosening; (generosidad)
disinterestedness; (de tierra, rocas)
landslide; **desprendimiento de retina**
detachment of the retina

despreocupado, -a [despreoku'paðo, a] adj (sin
preocupación) unworried, nonchalant;
(negligente) careless

despreocuparse [despreoku'parse]
vr not to worry; **~ de** to have no
interest in

desprestigiar [despresti'xjar] vt
(criticar) to run down; (desacreditar) to
discredit

desprevenido, -a [despreβe'niðo,
a] adj (no preparado) unprepared,
unready

desproporcionado, -a
[desproporθjo'naðo, a] adj
disproportionate, out of proportion

desprovisto, -a [despro'βisto, a]
adj: **~ de** devoid of

después [des'pwes] adv afterwards,
later; (próximo paso) next; **~ de comer**
after lunch; **un año ~** a year later; **~ se
debatió el tema** next the matter was
discussed; **~ de corregido el texto**
after the text had been corrected; **~ de
todo** after all

desquiciado, -a [deski'θjaðo, a]
adj deranged

destacar [desta'kar] vt to
emphasize, point up; (Mil) to detach,
detail ▷ vi (resaltarse) to stand
out; (persona) to be outstanding o
exceptional; **destacarse** vr to stand
out; to be outstanding o exceptional

destajo [des'taxo] nm: **trabajar a ~** to
do piecework

destapar [desta'par] vt (botella)

to open; (cacerola) to take the lid off;
(descubrir) to uncover; **destaparse** vr
(revelarse) to reveal one's true character

destartalado, -a [destarta'laðo,
a] adj (desordenado) untidy; (ruinoso)
tumbledown

destello [des'teʎo] nm (de estrella)
twinkle; (de faro) signal light

destemplado, -a [destem'plaðo,
a] adj (Mús) out of tune; (voz) harsh; (Med)
out of sorts; (tiempo) unpleasant, nasty

desteñir [deste'ɲir] vt to fade ▷ vi to
fade; **desteñirse** vr to fade; **esta tela
no destiñe** this fabric will not run

desternillarse [desterni'ʎarse] vr: **~
de risa** to split one's sides laughing

desterrar [deste'rrar] vt (exiliar) to
exile; (fig) to banish, dismiss

destiempo [des'tjempo]: **a ~** adv
out of turn

destierra etc [des'tjerra] vb V
desterrar ▷ nm exile

destilar [desti'lar] vt to distil;
destilería nf distillery

destinar [desti'nar] vt (funcionario)
to appoint, assign; (fondos): **~ (a)** to set
aside o for

destinatario, -a [destina'tarjo, a]
nm/f addressee

destino [des'tino] nm (suerte)
destiny; (de avión, viajero) destination;
con ~ a Londres (barco) (bound) for
London; (avión, carta) to London

destituir [destitu'ir] vt to dismiss

destornillador [destorniʎa'ðor] nm
screwdriver

destornillar [destorni'ʎar] vt
(tornillo) to unscrew; **destornillarse** vr
to unscrew

destreza [des'treθa] nf (habilidad)
skill; (maña) dexterity

destrozar [destro'θar] vt (romper) to
smash, break (up); (estropear) to ruin;
(nervios) to shatter

destrozo [des'troθo] nm (acción)
destruction; (desastre) smashing;
destrozos nmpl (pedazos) pieces;
(daños) havoc sg

destrucción [destruk'θjon] nf
destruction

destruir [destru'ir] vt to destroy

desuso [des'uso] nm disuse; **caer en
~** to become obsolete

desvalijar [desβali'xar] vt (persona)
to rob; (casa, tienda) to burgle; (coche)
to break into

desván [des'βan] nm attic

desvanecer [desβane'θer] vt
(disipar) to dispel; (borrar) to blur;
desvanecerse vr (humo etc) to vanish,
disappear; (color) to fade; (recuerdo,
sonido) to fade away; (Med) to pass out;
(duda) to be dispelled

desvariar [desβa'rjar] vi (enfermo) to
be delirious

desvelar [desβe'lar] vt to keep
awake; **desvelarse** vr (no poder dormir)
to stay awake; (preocuparse) to be
vigilant o watchful

desventaja [desβen'taxa] nf
disadvantage

desvergonzado, -a [desβerɣon'θaðo, a] adj shameless

desvestir [desβes'tir] vt to undress;
desvestirse vr to undress

desviación [desβja'θjon] nf
deviation; (Auto) diversion, detour

desviar [des'βjar] vt to turn aside;
(río) to alter the course of; (navío)
to divert, re-route; (conversación) to
sidetrack; **desviarse** vr (apartarse del
camino) to turn aside; (: barco) to go
off course

desvío etc [des'βio] vb V **desviar**
▷ nm (desviación) detour, diversion; (fig)
indifference

desvivirse [desβi'βirse] vr: **~ por**
(anhelar) to long for, crave for; (hacer lo
posible por) to do one's utmost for

detallar [deta'ʎar] vt to detail

detalle [de'taʎe] nm detail; (gesto)
gesture, token; **al ~** in detail; (Com)
retail

detallista [deta'ʎista] nmf (Com)
retailer

detective [detek'tiβe] nmf detective;

detective privado private detective

detención [deten'θjon] nf (arresto)
arrest; (prisión) detention

detener [dete'ner] vt (gen) to
stop; (Jur) to arrest; (objeto) to keep;
detenerse vr to stop; (demorarse): **~se**
en to delay over, linger over

detenidamente [deteniða'mente]
adv (minuciosamente) carefully;
(extensamente) at great length

detenido, -a [dete'niðo, a] adj
(arrestado) under arrest ▷ nm/f person
under arrest, prisoner

detenimiento [deteni'mjento]
nm: **con ~** thoroughly; (observar,
considerar) carefully

detergente [deter'xente] nm
detergent

deteriorar [deterjo'rar] vt (plazo)
spoil, damage; **deteriorarse** vr
to deteriorate; **deterioro** nm
deterioration

determinación [determina'θjon]
nf (empeño) determination; (decisión)
decision; **determinado, -a** adj
specific

determinar [determi'nar] vt (plazo)
to fix; (precio) to settle; **determinarse**
vr to decide

detestar [detes'tar] vt to detest

detractor, a [detrak'tor, a] nm/f
slanderer, libeller

detrás [de'tras] adv (tb: **por ~**)
behind; (atrás) at the back; **~ de** behind

detrimento [detri'mento] nm: **en ~
de** to the detriment of

deuda ['deuða] nf debt; **deuda
exterior/pública** foreign/national
debt

devaluación [deβalwa'θjon] nf
devaluation

devastar [deβas'tar] vt (destruir) to
devastate

deveras [de'βeras] (MÉX) nf inv: **un
amigo de (a) ~** a true o real friend

devoción [deβo'θjon] nf devotion

devolución [deβolu'θjon] nf (reenvío)
return, sending back; (reembolso)

repayment; (Jur) devolution

devolver [deβol'βer] vt to return; (lo extraviado, lo prestado) to give back; (carta al correo) to send back; (Com) to repay, refund ▷ vi (vomitar) to be sick

devorar [deβo'rar] vt to devour

devoto, -a [de'βoto, a] adj devout ▷ nm/f admirer

devuelta etc vb V **devolver**

devuelto pp de **devolver**

devuelva etc vb V **devolver**

di etc vb V **dar; decir**

día ['dia] nm day; **¿qué ~ es?** what's the date?; **estar/poner al ~** to be/keep up to date; **el ~ de hoy/de mañana** today/tomorrow; **al ~ siguiente** (on) the following day; **vivir al ~** to live from hand to mouth; **de ~** by day, in daylight; **en pleno ~** in full daylight; **Día de la Independencia** Independence Day; **Día de los Muertos** (MÉX) All Souls' Day; **Día de Reyes** Epiphany; **día feriado** (LAM) holiday; **día festivo** (ESP) holiday; **día lectivo** teaching day; **día libre** day off

diabetes [dja'βetes] nf diabetes

diablo [dja'βlo] nm devil; **diablura** nf prank

diadema [dja'ðema] nf tiara

diafragma [dja'fraxma] nm diaphragm

diagnóstico [djax'nostiko] nm = **diagnosis**

diagonal [djaxo'nal] adj diagonal

diagrama [dja'xrama] nm diagram

dial [djal] nm dial

dialecto [dja'lekto] nm dialect

dialogar [djalo'xar] vi: **~ con** (Pol) to hold talks with

diálogo ['djaloxo] nm dialogue

diamante [dja'mante] nm diamond

diana ['djana] nf (Mil) reveille; (de blanco) centre, bull's-eye

diapositiva [djaposi'tiβa] nf (Foto) slide, transparency

diario, -a ['djarjo, a] adj daily ▷ nm newspaper; **a ~** daily; **de ~** everyday

diarrea [dja'rrea] nf diarrhoea

dibujar [diβu'xar] vt to draw;

sketch; **dibujo** nm drawing; **dibujos animados** cartoons

diccionario [dikθjo'narjo] nm dictionary

dice etc vb V **decir**

dicho, -a ['ditʃo, a] pp de **decir** ▷ adj: **en ~s países** in the aforementioned countries ▷ nm saying

dichoso, -a [di'tʃoso, a] adj happy

diciembre [di'θjembre] nm December

dictado [dik'taðo] nm dictation

dictador [dikta'ðor] nm dictator; **dictadura** nf dictatorship

dictar [dik'tar] vt (carta) to dictate; (Jur: sentencia) to pronounce; (decreto) to issue; (LAM: clase) to give

didáctico, -a [di'ðaktiko, a] adj educational

diecinueve [djeθi'nweβe] num nineteen

dieciocho [djeθi'otʃo] num eighteen

dieciséis [djeθi'seis] num sixteen

diecisiete [djeθi'sjete] num seventeen

diente ['djente] nm (Anat, Tec) tooth; (Zool) fang; (: de elefante) tusk; (de ajo) clove

diera etc vb V **dar**

diesel ['disel] adj: **motor ~** diesel engine

diestro, -a ['djestro, a] adj (derecho) right; (hábil) skilful

dieta ['djeta] nf diet; **estar a ~** to be on a diet

diez [djeθ] num ten

diferencia [dife'renθja] nf difference; **a ~ de** unlike; **diferenciar** vt to differentiate between ▷ vi to differ; **diferenciarse** vr to differ, be different; (distinguirse) to distinguish o.s.

diferente [dife'rente] adj different

diferido [dife'riðo] nm: **en ~** (TV etc) recorded

difícil [di'fiθil] adj difficult

dificultad [difikul'taθ] nf difficulty;

dificultar [difikul'tar] vt (*complicar*) to complicate, make difficult; (*estorbar*) to obstruct

difundir [difun'dir] vt (*calor, luz*) to diffuse; (*Radio, TV*) to broadcast; **~ una noticia** to spread a piece of news; **difundirse** vr to spread (out)

difunto, -a [di'funto, a] adj dead, deceased ▷ nm/f deceased (person)

difusión [difu'sjon] nf (*Radio, TV*) broadcasting

diga etc vb V **decir**

digerir [dixe'rir] vt to digest; (*fig*) to absorb; **digestión** nf digestion; **digestivo, -a** adj digestive

digital [dixi'tal] adj digital

dignarse [dix'narse] vr to deign to

dignidad [dixni'ðað] nf dignity

digno, -a [di'xno, a] adj worthy

digo etc vb V **decir**

dije etc vb V **decir**

dilatar [dila'tar] vt (*cuerpo*) to dilate; (*prolongar*) to prolong

dilema [di'lema] nm dilemma

diluir [dilu'ir] vt to dilute

diluvio [di'luβjo] nm deluge, flood

dimensión [dimen'sjon] nf dimension

diminuto, -a [dimi'nuto, a] adj tiny, diminutive

dimitir [dimi'tir] vi to resign

dimos vb V **dar**

Dinamarca [dina'marka] nf Denmark

dinámico, -a [di'namiko, a] adj dynamic

dinamita [dina'mita] nf dynamite

dínamo [di'namo] nf dynamo

dineral [dine'ral] nm large sum of money, fortune

dinero [di'nero] nm money; **dinero en efectivo** o **metálico** cash; **dinero suelto** (loose) change

dio vb V **dar**

dios [djos] nm god; **¡D~ mío!** (oh,) my God!; **¡por D~!** for heaven's sake!; **diosa** ['djosa] nf goddess

diploma [di'ploma] nm diploma

diplomacia [diplo'maθja] nf diplomacy; (*fig*) tact

diplomado, -a [diplo'maðo, a] adj qualified

diplomático, -a [diplo'matiko, a] adj diplomatic ▷ nm/f diplomat

diputación [diputa'θjon] nf (tb: **~ provincial**) = county council

diputado, -a [dipu'taðo, a] nm/f delegate; (*Pol*) = member of parliament (BRIT) = representative (US)

dique ['dike] nm dyke

diré etc vb V **decir**

dirección [direk'θjon] nf direction; (*señas*) address; (*Auto*) steering; (*gerencia*) management; (*Pol*) leadership; **dirección única/prohibida** one-way street/no entry

direccional [direkθjo'nal] nf (MÉX) (*Auto*) indicator

directa [di'rekta] nf (*Auto*) top gear

directiva [direk'tiβa] nf (tb: **junta ~**) board of directors

directo, -a [di'rekto, a] adj direct; (*Radio, TV*) live; **transmitir en ~** to broadcast live

director, a [direk'tor, a] adj leading ▷ nm/f director; (*Escol*) head(teacher) (BRIT), principal (US); (*gerente*) manager/ess; (*Prensa*) editor; **director de cine** film director; **director general** managing director

directorio [direk'torjo] nm (MÉX) (*telefónico*) phone book

dirigente [diri'xente] nmf (*Pol*) leader

dirigir [diri'xir] vt to direct; (*carta*) to address; (*obra de teatro, film*) to direct; (*Mús*) to conduct; (*negocio*) to manage; **dirigirse** vr: **~se a** to go towards, make one's way towards; (*hablar con*) to speak to

dirija etc vb V **dirigir**

disciplina [disθi'plina] nf discipline

discípulo, -a [dis'θipulo, a] nm/f disciple

Discman® ['diskman] nm

Discman®

disco ['disko] nm disc; (Deporte) discus; (Tel) dial; (Auto: semáforo) light; (Mús) record; **disco compacto de larga duración** compact disc/long-playing record; **disco de freno** brake disc; **disco flexible/duro** o **rígido** (Inform) floppy/hard disk

disconforme [diskon'forme] adj differing; **estar ~ (con)** to be in disagreement (with)

discordia [dis'korðja] nf discord

discoteca [disko'teka] nf disco(theque)

discreción [diskre'θjon] nf discretion; (reserva) prudence; **comer a ~** to eat as much as one wishes

discreto, -a [dis'kreto, a] adj discreet

discriminación [diskrimina'θjon] nf discrimination

disculpa [dis'kulpa] nf excuse; (pedir perdón) apology; **pedir ~s a/por** to apologize to/for; **disculpar** vt to excuse, pardon; **disculparse** vr to excuse o.s.; to apologize

discurso [dis'kurso] nm speech

discusión [disku'sjon] nf (diálogo) discussion; (riña) argument

discutir [disku'tir] vt (debatir) to discuss; (pelear) to argue about; (contradecir) to argue against ⊳ vi (debatir) to discuss; (pelearse) to argue

disecar [dise'kar] vt (conservar: animal) to stuff; (: planta) to dry

diseñar [dise'ɲar] vt, vi to design

diseño [di'seɲo] nm design

disfraz [dis'fraθ] nm (máscara) disguise; (excusa) pretext; **disfrazar** vt to disguise; **disfrazarse** vr: **disfrazarse de** to disguise o.s. as

disfrutar [disfru'tar] vt to enjoy ⊳ vi to enjoy o.s.; **~ de** to enjoy, possess

disgustar [disɣus'tar] vt (no gustar) to displease; (contrariar, enojar) to annoy, upset; **disgustarse** vr (enfadarse) to get upset; (dos personas)

to fall out

No confundir **disgustar** con la palabra inglesa **disgust**.

disgusto [dis'ɣusto] nm (contrariedad) annoyance; (tristeza) grief; (riña) quarrel

disimular [disimu'lar] vt (ocultar) to hide, conceal ⊳ vi to dissemble

diskette [dis'ket] nm (Inform) diskette, floppy disk

dislocarse [dislo'karse] vr (articulación) to sprain, dislocate

disminución [disminu'θjon] nf decrease, reduction

disminuido, -a [disminu'iðo, a] nm/f: **~ mental/físico** mentally/physically handicapped person

disminuir [disminu'ir] vt to decrease, diminish

disolver [disol'βer] vt (gen) to dissolve; **disolverse** vr to dissolve; (Com) to go into liquidation

disparar [dispa'rar] vt, vi to shoot, fire

disparate [dispa'rate] nm (tontería) foolish thing; (error) blunder; **decir ~s** to talk nonsense

disparo [dis'paro] nm shot

dispersar [disper'sar] vt to disperse; **dispersarse** vr to scatter

disponer [dispo'ner] vt (arreglar) to arrange; (ordenar) to put in order; (preparar) to prepare, get ready ⊳ vi: **~ de** to have, own; **disponerse** vr: **~se a** o **para hacer** to prepare to do

disponible [dispo'niβle] adj available

disposición [disposi'θjon] nf arrangement, disposition; (voluntad) willingness; (Inform) layout; **a su ~** at your service

dispositivo [disposi'tiβo] nm device, mechanism

dispuesto, -a [dis'pwesto, a] pp de **disponer** ⊳ adj (arreglado) arranged; (preparado) disposed

disputar [dispu'tar] vt (carrera) to compete in

disquete [dis'kete] nm floppy disk, diskette

distancia [dis'tanθja] nf distance; **distanciar** [distan'θjar] vt to space out; **distanciarse** vr to become estranged; **distante** [dis'tante] adj distant

diste vb V **dar**

disteis vb V **dar**

distinción [distin'θjon] nf distinction; (elegancia) elegance; (honor) honour

distinguido, -a [distin'giðo, a] adj distinguished

distinguir [distin'gir] vt to distinguish; (escoger) to single out; **distinguirse** vr to be distinguished

distintivo [distin'tiβo] nm badge; (fig) characteristic

distinto, -a [dis'tinto, a] adj different; (claro) clear

distracción [distrak'θjon] nf distraction; (pasatiempo) hobby, pastime; (olvido) absent-mindedness, distraction

distraer [distra'er] vt (atención) to distract; (divertir) to amuse; (fondos) to embezzle; **distraerse** vr (entretenerse) to amuse o.s.; (perder la concentración) to allow one's attention to wander

distraído, -a [distra'iðo, a] adj (gen) absent-minded; (entretenido) amusing

distribuidor, a [distriβui'ðor, a] nm/f distributor; **distribuidora** nf (Com) dealer, agent; (Cine) distributor

distribuir [distriβu'ir] vt to distribute

distrito [dis'trito] nm (sector, territorio) region; (barrio) district; **Distrito Federal** (MÉX) Federal District; **distrito postal** postal district

disturbio [dis'turβjo] nm disturbance; (desorden) riot

disuadir [diswa'ðir] vt to dissuade

disuelto [di'swelto] pp de **disolver**

DIU nm abr (= dispositivo intrauterino) IUD

diurno, -a ['djurno, a] adj day cpd

divagar [diβa'ɣar] vi (desviarse) to digress

diván [di'βan] nm divan

diversidad [diβersi'ðað] nf diversity, variety

diversión [diβer'sjon] nf (gen) entertainment; (actividad) hobby, pastime

diverso, -a [di'βerso, a] adj diverse; **~s libros** several books; **diversos** nmpl sundries

divertido, -a [diβer'tiðo, a] adj (chiste) amusing; (fiesta etc) enjoyable

divertir [diβer'tir] vt (entretener, recrear) to amuse; **divertirse** vr (pasarlo bien) to have a good time; (distraerse) to amuse o.s.

dividendos [diβi'ðendos] nmpl (Com) dividends

dividir [diβi'ðir] vt (gen) to divide; (distribuir) to distribute, share out

divierta etc vb V **divertir**

divino, -a [di'βino, a] adj divine

divirtiendo etc vb V **divertir**

divisa [di'βisa] nf (emblema) emblem, badge; **divisas** nfpl foreign exchange sg

divisar [diβi'sar] vt to make out, distinguish

división [diβi'sjon] nf (gen) division; (de partido) split; (de país) partition

divorciar [diβor'θjar] vt to divorce; **divorciarse** vr to get divorced; **divorcio** nm divorce

divulgar [diβul'ɣar] vt (ideas) to spread; (secreto) to divulge

DNI (ESP) nm abr (= Documento Nacional de Identidad) national identity card

● **DNI**
●
● The **Documento Nacional de**
● **Identidad** is a Spanish ID card
● which must be carried at all times
● and produced on request for the
● police. It contains the holder's
● photo, fingerprints and personal
● details. It is also known as the **DNI**
● or "carnet de identidad".

Dña. abr (= doña) Mrs

do [do] nm (Mús) do, C

dobladillo [doβla'ðiʎo] nm (de vestido) hem; (de pantalón: vuelta) turn-up (BRIT), cuff (US)

doblar [do'βlar] vt to double; (papel) to fold; (caño) to bend; (la esquina) to turn, go round; (film) to dub ▷ vi to turn; (campana) to toll; **doblarse** vr (plegarse) to fold (up), crease; (encorvarse) to bend; **~ a la derecha/izquierda** to turn right/left

doble ['doβle] adj double; (de dos aspectos) dual; (fig) two-faced ▷ nm double ▷ nmf (Teatro) double, stand-in; **dobles** nmpl (Deporte) doubles sg; **con ~ sentido** with a double meaning

doce ['doθe] num twelve; **docena** nf dozen

docente [do'θente] adj: **centro/personal ~** teaching establishment/staff

dócil ['doθil] adj (pasivo) docile; (obediente) obedient

doctor, a [dok'tor, a] nm/f doctor

doctorado [dokto'raðo] nm doctorate

doctrina [dok'trina] nf doctrine, teaching

documentación [dokumenta'θjon] nf documentation, papers pl

documental [dokumen'tal] adj, nm documentary

documento [doku'mento] nm (certificado) document; **documento adjunto** (Inform) attachment; **documento nacional de identidad** identity card

dólar ['dolar] nm dollar

doler [do'ler] vt, vi to hurt; (fig) to grieve; **dolerse** vr (de su situación) to grieve, feel sorry; (de las desgracias ajenas) to sympathize; **me duele el brazo** my arm hurts

dolor [do'lor] nm pain; (fig) grief, sorrow; **dolor de cabeza/estómago/muelas** headache/stomachache/toothache

domar [do'mar] vt to tame

domesticar [domesti'kar] vt = **domar**

doméstico, -a [do'mestiko, a] adj (vida, servicio) home; (tareas) household; (animal) tame, pet

domicilio [domi'θiljo] nm home; **servicio a ~** home delivery service; **sin ~ fijo** of no fixed abode; **domicilio particular** private residence

dominante [domi'nante] adj dominant; (persona) domineering

dominar [domi'nar] vt (gen) to dominate; (idiomas) to be fluent in ▷ vi to dominate, prevail

domingo [do'miŋgo] nm Sunday; **Domingo de Ramos/Resurrección** Palm/Easter Sunday

dominio [do'minjo] nm (tierras) domain; (autoridad) power, authority; (de las pasiones) grip, hold; (de idiomas) command

don [don] nm (talento) gift; **~ Juan Gómez** Mr Juan Gómez, Juan Gómez Esq (BRIT)

- **DON/DOÑA**

- The term **don/doña** often
- abbreviated to **D./Dña** is placed
- before the first name as a mark
- of respect to an older or more
- senior person – eg Don Diego,
- Doña Inés. Although becoming
- rarer in Spain it is still used
- with names and surnames on
- official documents and formal
- correspondence – eg "Sr. D. Pedro
- Rodríguez Hernández", "Sra. Dña.
- Inés Rodríguez Hernández".

dona ['dona] (MÉX) nf doughnut, donut (US)

donar [do'nar] vt to donate

donativo [dona'tiβo] nm donation

donde ['donde] adv where ▷ prep: **el coche está allí ~ el farol** the car is over there by the lamppost o where the lamppost is; **en ~** where, in which

dónde ['donde] *adv* where?; **¿a ~ vas?** where are you going (to)?; **¿de ~ vienes?** where have you been?; **¿por ~?** where?, whereabouts?

dondequiera [donde'kjera] *adv* anywhere; **por ~** everywhere, all over the place ▷ *conj*: **~ que** wherever

donut® [do'nut] (ESP) *nm* doughnut, donut (us)

doña ['doɲa] *nf*: **~ Alicia** Alicia; **~ Victoria Benito** Mrs Victoria Benito

dorado, -a [do'raðo, a] *adj* (color) golden; (Tec) gilt

dormir [dor'mir] *vt*: **~ la siesta** to have an afternoon nap ▷ *vi* to sleep; **dormirse** *vr* to fall asleep

dormitorio [dormi'torjo] *nm* bedroom

dorsal [dor'sal] *nm* (Deporte) number

dorso ['dorso] *nm* (de mano) back; (de hoja) other side

dos [dos] *num* two

dosis ['dosis] *nf inv* dose, dosage

dotado, -a [do'taðo, a] *adj* gifted; **~ de** endowed with

dotar [do'tar] *vt* to endow; **dote** *nf* dowry; **dotes** *nfpl* (talentos) gifts

doy [doj] *vb* V **dar**

drama ['drama] *nm* drama; **dramaturgo** [drama'turɣo] *nm* dramatist, playwright

drástico, -a ['drastiko, a] *adj* drastic

drenaje [dre'naxe] *nm* drainage

droga ['droɣa] *nf* drug; **drogadicto, -a** [droɣa'ðikto, a] *nm/f* drug addict

drogarse [dro'ɣarse] *vr* to take drugs

droguería [droɣe'ria] *nf* hardware shop (BRIT) o store (us)

ducha ['dutʃa] *nf* (baño) shower; (Med) douche; **ducharse** *vr* to take a shower

duda ['duða] *nf* doubt; **no cabe ~** there is no doubt about it; **dudar** *vt, vi* to doubt; **dudoso, -a** [du'ðoso, a] *adj* (incierto) hesitant; (sospechoso) doubtful

duela etc *vb* V **doler**

duelo ['dwelo] *vb* V **doler** ▷ *nm* (combate) duel; (luto) mourning

duende ['dwende] *nm* imp, goblin

dueño, -a ['dweɲo, a] *nm/f* (propietario) owner; (de pensión, taberna) landlord/lady; (empresario) employer

duermo etc *vb* V **dormir**

dulce ['dulθe] *adj* sweet ▷ *adv* gently, softly ▷ *nm* sweet

dulcería [dulθe'ria] (LAM) *nf* confectioner's (shop)

dulzura [dul'θura] *nf* sweetness; (ternura) gentleness

dúo ['duo] *nm* duet

duplicar [dupli'kar] *vt* (hacer el doble de) to duplicate

duque ['duke] *nm* duke; **duquesa** *nf* duchess

durable [dura'βle] *adj* durable

duración [dura'θjon] *nf* (de película, disco etc) length; (de pila etc) life; (curso: de acontecimientos etc) duration

duradero, -a [dura'ðero, a] *adj* (tela etc) hard-wearing; (fe, paz) lasting

durante [du'rante] *prep* during

durar [du'rar] *vi* to last; (recuerdo) to remain

durazno [du'raθno] (LAM) *nm* (fruta) peach; (árbol) peach tree

durex ['dureks] (MÉX, ARG) *nm* (tira adhesiva) Sellotape® (BRIT), Scotch tape® (us)

dureza [du'reθa] *nf* (calidad) hardness

duro, -a ['duro, a] *adj* hard; (carácter) tough ▷ *adv* hard ▷ *nm* (moneda) five-peseta coin o piece

DVD *nm abr* (= *disco de vídeo digital*) DVD

e

E *abr* (=*este*) E

e [e] *conj* and

ébano ['eβano] *nm* ebony

ebrio, -a ['eβrjo, a] *adj* drunk

ebullición [eβuʎi'θjon] *nf* boiling

echar [e'tʃar] *vt* to throw; (*agua, vino*)
to pour (out); (*empleado: despedir*) to
fire, sack; (*hojas*) to sprout; (*cartas*) to
post; (*humo*) to emit, give out ▷ *vi*: ~
a correr to run off; ~ **una mirada** to
give a look; ~ **sangre** to bleed; **echarse**
vr to lie down; ~ **llave a** to lock (up); ~
abajo (*gobierno*) to overthrow; (*edificio*)
to demolish; ~ **mano a** to lay hands on;
~ **una mano a algn** (*ayudar*) to give sb
a hand; ~ **de menos** to miss; ~**se atrás**
(*fig*) to back out

eclesiástico, -a [ekle'sjastiko, a]
adj ecclesiastical

eco ['eko] *nm* echo; **tener** ~ to
catch on

ecología [ekolo'ɣia] *nf* ecology;
ecológico, -a *adj* (*producto,
método*) environmentally-friendly;
(*agricultura*) organic; **ecologista** *adj*

ecological, environmental ▷ *nmf*
environmentalist

economía [ekono'mia] *nf* (*sistema*)
economy; (*carrera*) economics

económico, -a [eko'nomiko, a] *adj*
(*barato*) cheap, economical; (*ahorrativo*)
thrifty; (*Com: año etc*) financial;
(: *situación*) economic

economista [ekono'mista] *nmf*
economist

Ecuador [ekwa'ðor] *nm* Ecuador;
ecuador *nm* (*Geo*) equator

ecuatoriano, -a [ekwato'rjano, a]
adj, nm/f Ecuadorian

ecuestre [e'kwestre] *adj* equestrian

edad [e'ðað] *nf* age; **¿qué ~ tienes?**
how old are you?; **tiene ocho años de**
~ he's eight (years old); **de ~ mediana/
avanzada** middle-aged/advanced in
years; **la E~ Media** the Middle Ages

edición [eði'θjon] *nf* (*acto*)
publication; (*ejemplar*) edition

edificar [eðifi'kar] *vt, vi* to build

edificio [eði'fiθjo] *nm* building; (*fig*)
edifice, structure

Edimburgo [eðim'burxo] *nm*
Edinburgh

editar [eði'tar] *vt* (*publicar*) to publish;
(*preparar textos*) to edit

editor, a [eði'tor, a] *nm/f* (*que
publica*) publisher; (*redactor*) editor
▷ *adj* publishing *cpd*; **editorial** *adj*
editorial ▷ *nm* leading article,
editorial; **casa editorial** publisher

edredón [eðre'ðon] *nm* duvet

educación [eðuka'θjon] *nf*
education; (*crianza*) upbringing;
(*modales*) (good) manners *pl*

educado, -a [eðu'kaðo, a] *adj*: **bien/
mal** ~ well/badly behaved

educar [eðu'kar] *vt* to educate; (*criar*)
to bring up; (*voz*) to train

EE. UU. *nmpl abr* (= *Estados Unidos*)
US(A)

efectivamente [efectiβa'mente]
adv (*como respuesta*) exactly, precisely;
(*verdaderamente*) really; (*de hecho*) in fact

efectivo, -a [efek'tiβo, a] *adj*

effective; (*real*) actual, real ▷ *nm*: **pagar en** ~ to pay (in) cash; **hacer** ~ **un cheque** to cash a cheque

efecto [e'fekto] *nm* effect, result; **efectos** *nmpl* (*efectos personales*) effects; (*bienes*) goods; (*Com*) assets; **en** ~ in fact; (*respuesta*) exactly, indeed; **efecto invernadero**greenhouse effect; **efectos especiales/ secundarios/sonoros**special/side/ sound effects

efectuar [efek'twar] *vt* to carry out; (*viaje*) to make

eficacia [efi'kaθja] *nf* (*de persona*) efficiency; (*de medicamento etc*) effectiveness

eficaz [efi'kaθ] *adj* (*persona*) efficient; (*acción*) effective

eficiente [efi'θjente] *adj* efficient

egipcio, -a [e'xipθjo, a] *adj, nm/f* Egyptian

Egipto [e'xipto] *nm* Egypt

egoísmo [exo'ismo] *nm* egoism

egoísta [exo'ista] *adj* egoistical, selfish ▷ *nmf* egoist

Eire ['eire] *nm* Eire

ej. *abr* (= *ejemplo*) eg

eje ['exe] *nm* (*Geo, Mat*) axis; (*de rueda*) axle; (*de máquina*) shaft, spindle

ejecución [exeku'θjon] *nf* execution; (*cumplimiento*) fulfilment; (*Mús*) performance; (*Jur: embargo de deudor*) attachment

ejecutar [exeku'tar] *vt* to execute, carry out; (*matar*) to execute; (*cumplir*) to fulfil; (*Mús*) to perform; (*Jur: embargar*) to attach, distrain (on)

ejecutivo, -a [exeku'tiβo, a] *adj* executive; **el (poder)** ~ the executive (power)

ejemplar [exem'plar] *adj* exemplary ▷ *nm* example; (*Zool*) specimen; (*de libro*) copy; (*de periódico*) number, issue

ejemplo [e'xemplo] *nm* example; **por** ~ for example

ejercer [exer'θer] *vt* to exercise; (*influencia*) to exert; (*un oficio*) to practise ▷ *vi* (*practicar*): ~ **(de)** to

practise (as)

ejercicio [exer'θiθjo] *nm* exercise; (*período*) tenure; **hacer** ~ to take exercise; **ejercicio comercial**financial year

ejército [e'xerθito] *nm* army; **entrar en el** ~ to join the army, join up; **ejército del aire/de tierra**Air Force/Army

ejote [e'xote] (*MÉX*) *nm* green bean

○ **PALABRA CLAVE**

el [el] (*f* **la**, *pl* **los, las**, *neutro* **lo**) *art def* **1** the: **el libro/la mesa/los estudiantes** the book/table/students

2 (*con n abstracto: no se traduce*): **el amor/la juventud** love/youth

3 (*posesión: se traduce a menudo por un posesivo*): **romperse el brazo** to break one's arm; **levantó la mano** he put his hand up; **se puso el sombrero** she put her hat on

4 (*valor descriptivo*): **tener la boca grande/los ojos azules** to have a big mouth/blue eyes

5 (*con días*) on; **me iré el viernes** I'll leave on Friday; **los domingos suelo ir a nadar** on Sundays I generally go swimming

6 (*lo +adj*): **lo difícil/caro** what is difficult/expensive; (*cuán*): **no se da cuenta de lo pesado que es** he doesn't realise how boring he is

▷ *pron demos* **1** **mi libro y el de usted** my book and yours; **las de Pepe son mejores** Pepe's are better; **no la(s) blanca(s) sino la(s) gris(es)** not the white one(s) but the grey one(s)

2 lo de: lo de ayer what happened yesterday; **lo de las facturas** that business about the invoices

▷ *pron relativo* **1** (*indef*): **el que: el (los) que quiera(n) que se vaya(n)** anyone who wants to can leave; **llévese el que más le guste** take the one you like best

2 (*def*): **el que: el que compré ayer** the one I bought yesterday; **los que se van**

those who leave
3 : lo que: lo que pienso yo/más me gusta what I think/like most
▷ *conj :* **el que: el que lo diga** the fact that he says so; **el que sea tan vago me molesta** his being so lazy bothers me
▷ *excl :* **¡el susto que me diste!** what a fright you gave me!
▷ *pron personal* **1** (*persona: m*) him; (: *f*) her; (: *pl*) them; **lo/las veo** I can see him/them
2 (*animal, cosa: sg*) it; (: *pl*) them; **lo** (*o* **la**) **veo** I can see it; **los** (*o* **las**) **veo** I can see them
3 (*como sustituto de frase*): **lo: no lo sabía** I didn't know; **ya lo entiendo** I understand now

él [el] *pron* (*persona*) he; (*cosa*) it; (*después de prep: persona*) him; (: *cosa*) it; **de ~** his

elaborar [elaβo'rar] *vt* (*producto*) to make, manufacture; (*preparar*) to prepare; (*madera, metal etc*) to work; (*proyecto etc*) to work on o out

elástico, -a [e'lastiko, a] *adj* elastic; (*flexible*) flexible ▶ *nm* elastic; (*un elástico*) elastic band

elección [elek'θjon] *nf* election; (*selección*) choice, selection; **elecciones generales** general election *sg*

electorado [elekto'raðo] *nm* electorate, voters *pl*

electricidad [elektriθi'ðað] *nf* electricity

electricista [elektri'θista] *nmf* electrician

eléctrico, -a [e'lektriko, a] *adj* electric

electro... [elektro] *prefijo*
electro...: electrocardiograma *nm* electrocardiogram; **electrocutar** *vt* to electrocute; **electrodo** *nm* electrode; **electrodomésticos** *nmpl* (electrical) household appliances

electrónica [elek'tronika] *nf* electronics *sg*

electrónico, -a [elek'troniko, a] *adj* electronic

electrotren [elektro'tren] *nm* express electric train

elefante [ele'fante] *nm* elephant

elegancia [ele'ɣanθja] *nf* elegance, grace; (*estilo*) stylishness

elegante [ele'ɣante] *adj* elegant, graceful; (*estiloso*) stylish, fashionable

elegir [ele'xir] *vt* (*escoger*) to choose, select; (*optar*) to opt for; (*presidente*) to elect

elemental [elemen'tal] *adj* (*claro, obvio*) elementary; (*fundamental*) elemental, fundamental

elemento [ele'mento] *nm* element; (*fig*) ingredient; **elementos** *nmpl* elements, rudiments

elevación [eleβa'θjon] *nf* elevation; (*acto*) raising, lifting; (*de precios*) rise; (*Geo etc*) height, altitude

elevado [ele'βaðo] *adj* high

elevar [ele'βar] *vt* to raise, lift (up); (*precio*) to put up; **elevarse** *vr* (*edificio*) to rise; (*precios*) to go up

eligiendo *etc vb* **V elegir**

elija *etc vb* **V elegir**

eliminar [elimi'nar] *vt* to eliminate, remove

eliminatoria [elimina'torja] *nf* heat, preliminary (round)

élite ['elite] *nf* elite

ella ['eʎa] *pron* (*persona*) she; (*cosa*) it; (*después de prep: persona*) her; (: *cosa*) it; **de ~** hers

ellas ['eʎas] *pron* (*personas y cosas*) they; (*después de prep*) them; **de ~** theirs

ello ['eʎo] *pron* it

ellos ['eʎos] *pron* they; (*después de prep*) them; **de ~** theirs

elogiar [elo'xjar] *vt* to praise; **elogio** *nm* praise

elote [e'lote] (*MÉX*) *nm* corn on the cob

eludir [elu'ðir] *vt* to avoid

email [i'mel] *nm* email; (*dirección*) email address; **mandar un ~ a algn** to email sb, send sb an email

embajada [emba'xaða] *nf* embassy

embajador, a [embaxa'ðor, a] *nm/f*
ambassador/ambassadress

embalar [emba'lar] *vt* to parcel,
wrap (up); **embalarse** *vr* to go fast

embalse [em'balse] *nm* (*presa*) dam;
(*lago*) reservoir

embarazada [embara'θaða] *adj*
pregnant ▷ *nf* pregnant woman
▌ No confundir **embarazada** con la
▌ palabra inglesa *embarrassed*.

embarazo [emba'raθo] *nm* (*de mujer*)
pregnancy; (*impedimento*) obstacle,
obstruction; (*timidez*) embarrassment;
embarazoso, -a *adj* awkward,
embarrassing

embarcación [embarka'θjon] *nf*
(*barco*) boat, craft; (*acto*) embarkation,
boarding

embarcadero [embarka'ðero] *nm*
pier, landing stage

embarcar [embar'kar] *vt*
(*cargamento*) to ship, stow; (*persona*) to
embark, put on board; **embarcarse** *vr*
to embark, go on board

embargar [embar'ɣar] *vt* (*Jur*) to
seize, impound

embargo [em'barɣo] *nm* (*Jur*)
seizure; (*Com, Pol*) embargo

embargue *etc vb* V **embargar**

embarque *etc* [em'barke] *vb* V
embarcar ▷ *nm* shipment, loading

embellecer [embeʎe'θer] *vt* to
embellish, beautify

embestida [embes'tiða] *nf* attack,
onslaught; (*carga*) charge

embestir [embes'tir] *vt* to attack,
assault; to charge, attack ▷ *vi* to
attack

emblema [em'blema] *nm* emblem

embobado, -a [embo'βaðo, a] *adj*
(*atontado*) stunned, bewildered

embolia [em'bolja] *nf* (*Med*) clot

émbolo ['embolo] *nm* (*Auto*) piston

emborrachar [emborra'tʃar]
vt to make drunk, intoxicate;
emborracharse *vr* to get drunk

emboscada [embos'kaða] *nf* ambush

embotar [embo'tar] *vt* to blunt, dull

embotellamiento
[emboteʎa'mjento] *nm* (*Auto*)
traffic jam

embotellar [embote'ʎar] *vt* to bottle

embrague [em'braɣe] *nm* (*tb:* **pedal
de ~**) clutch

embrión [em'brjon] *nm* embryo

embrollo [em'broʎo] *nm* (*enredo*)
muddle, confusion; (*aprieto*) fix, jam

embrujado, -a [embru'xado, a] *adj*
bewitched; **casa embrujada** haunted
house

embrutecer [embrute'θer] *vt*
(*atontar*) to stupefy

embudo [em'buðo] *nm* funnel

embuste [em'buste] *nm* (*mentira*)
lie; **embustero, -a** *adj* lying, deceitful
▷ *nm/f* (*mentiroso*) liar

embutido [embu'tiðo] *nm* (*Culin*)
sausage; (*Tec*) inlay

emergencia [emer'xenθja] *nf*
emergency; (*surgimiento*) emergence

emerger [emer'xer] *vi* to emerge,
appear

emigración [emiɣra'θjon] *nf*
emigration; (*de pájaros*) migration

emigrar [emi'ɣrar] *vi* (*personas*) to
emigrate; (*pájaros*) to migrate

eminente [emi'nente] *adj* eminent,
distinguished; (*elevado*) high

emisión [emi'sjon] *nf* (*acto*)
emission; (*Com etc*) issue; (*Radio,
TV*: *acto*) broadcasting; (*: programa*)
broadcast, programme (*BRIT*), program
(*US*)

emisora [emi'sora] *nf* radio o
broadcasting station

emitir [emi'tir] *vt* (*olor etc*) to emit,
give off; (*moneda etc*) to issue; (*opinión*)
to express; (*Radio*) to broadcast

emoción [emo'θjon] *nf* emotion;
(*excitación*) excitement; (*sentimiento*)
feeling

emocionante [emoθjo'nante] *adj*
(*excitante*) exciting, thrilling

emocionar [emoθjo'nar] *vt* (*excitar*)
to excite, thrill; (*conmover*) to move,
touch; (*impresionar*) to impress

emoticón [emoti'kon], **emoticono** [emoti'kono] nm smiley

emotivo, -a [emo'tiβo, a] adj emotional

empacho [em'patʃo] nm (Med) indigestion; (fig) embarrassment

empalagoso, -a [empala'ɣoso, a] adj cloying; (fig) tiresome

empalmar [empal'mar] vt to join, connect ▷ vi (dos caminos) to meet, join; **empalme** nm joint, connection; (de trenes) connection

empanada [empa'naða] nf pie, pasty

empañarse [empa'ɲarse] vr (cristales etc) to steam up

empapar [empa'par] vt (mojar) to soak, saturate; (absorber) to soak up, absorb; **empaparse** vr: **~se de** to soak up

empapelar [empape'lar] vt (paredes) to paper

empaquetar [empake'tar] vt to pack, parcel up

empastar [empas'tar] vt (embadurnar) to paste; (diente) to fill

empaste [em'paste] nm (de diente) filling

empatar [empa'tar] vi to draw, tie; **~n a dos** they drew two-all; **empate** nm draw, tie

empecé etc vb V **empezar**

empedernido, -a [empeðer'niðo, a] adj hard, heartless; (fumador) inveterate

empeine [em'peine] nm (de pie, zapato) instep

empeñado, -a [empe'ɲaðo, a] adj (persona) determined; (objeto) pawned

empeñar [empe'ɲar] vt (objeto) to pawn, pledge; (persona) to compel; **empeñarse** vr (endeudarse) to get into debt; **~se en** to be set on, be determined to

empeño [em'peɲo] nm (determinación, insistencia) determination, insistence; **casa de ~s** pawnshop

empeorar [empeo'rar] vt to make worse, worsen ▷ vi to get worse, deteriorate

empezar [empe'θar] vt, vi to begin, start

empiece etc vb V **empezar**

empiezo etc vb V **empezar**

emplasto [em'plasto] nm (Med) plaster

emplazar [empla'θar] vt (ubicar) to site, place, locate; (Jur) to summons; (convocar) to summon

empleado, -a [emple'aðo, a] nm/f (gen) employee; (de banco etc) clerk

emplear [emple'ar] vt (usar) to use, employ; (dar trabajo a) to employ; **emplearse** vr (conseguir trabajo) to be employed; (ocuparse) to occupy o.s.

empleo [em'pleo] nm (puesto) job; (puestos: colectivamente) employment; (uso) use, employment

empollar [empo'ʎar] (ESP: fam) vt, vi to swot (up); **empollón, -ona** (ESP: fam) nm/f swot

emporio [em'porjo] (LAM) nm (gran almacén) department store

empotrado, -a [empo'traðo, a] adj (armario etc) built-in

emprendedor, a [emprende'ðor, a] adj enterprising

emprender [empren'der] vt (empezar) to begin, embark on; (acometer) to tackle, take on

empresa [em'presa] nf (de espíritu etc) enterprise; (Com) company, firm; **empresariales** nfpl business studies; **empresario, -a** nm/f (Com) businessman(-woman)

empujar [empu'xar] vt to push, shove

empujón [empu'xon] nm push, shove

empuñar [empu'ɲar] vt (asir) to grasp, take (firm) hold of

○ **PALABRA CLAVE**

en [en] prep 1 (posición) in; (: sobre) on;

está en el cajón it's in the drawer; **en Argentina/La Paz** in Argentina/La Paz; **en la oficina/el colegio** at the office/school; **está en el suelo/quinto piso** it's on the floor/the fifth floor 2 *(dirección)* into; **entró en el aula** she went into the classroom; **meter algo en el bolso** to put sth in one's bag 3 *(tiempo)* in; on; **en 1605/3 semanas/invierno** in 1605/3 weeks/winter; **en (el mes de) enero** in (the month of) January; **en aquella ocasión/época** on that occasion/that time 4 *(precio)* for; **lo vendió en 20 dólares** he sold it for 20 dollars 5 *(diferencia)* by; **reducir/aumentar en una tercera parte/un 20 por ciento** to reduce/increase by a third/20 per cent 6 *(manera)*: **en avión/autobús** by plane/bus; **escrito en inglés** written in English 7 *(después de vb que indica gastar etc)* on; **han cobrado demasiado en dietas** they've charged too much to expenses; **se le va la mitad del sueldo en comida** he spends half his salary on food 8 *(tema, ocupación)*: **experto en la materia** expert on the subject; **trabaja en la construcción** he works in the building industry 9 *(adj + en + infin)*: **lento en reaccionar** slow to react

enaguas [e'naɣwas] *nfpl* petticoat sg, underskirt sg

enajenación [enaxena'θjon] *nf (Psico: tb)*: **~ mental** mental derangement

enamorado, -a [enamo'raðo, a] *adj* in love ▷ *nm/f* lover; **estar ~ (de)** to be in love (with)

enamorar [enamo'rar] *vt* to win the love of; **enamorarse** *vr*: **~se de algn** to fall in love with sb

enano, -a [e'nano, a] *adj* tiny ▷ *nm/f* dwarf

encabezamiento [enkaβeθa'mjento] *nm (de carta)* heading; *(de periódico)* headline

encabezar [enkaβe'θar] *vt (movimiento, revolución)* to lead, head; *(lista)* to head, be at the top of; *(carta)* to put a heading to

encadenar [enkaðe'nar] *vt* to chain (together); *(poner grilletes a)* to shackle

encajar [enka'xar] *vt (ajustar)*: **~ (en)** to fit (into); *(fam: golpe)* to take ▷ *vi* to fit (well); *(fig: corresponder a)* to match

encaje [en'kaxe] *nm (labor)* lace

encallar [enka'ʎar] *vi (Náut)* to run aground

encaminar [enkami'nar] *vt* to direct, send

encantado, -a [enkan'taðo, a] *adj (hechizado)* bewitched; *(muy contento)* delighted; **¡~!** how do you do, pleased to meet you

encantador, a [enkanta'ðor, a] *adj* charming, lovely ▷ *nm/f* magician, enchanter/enchantress

encantar [enkan'tar] *vt (agradar)* to charm, delight; *(hechizar)* to bewitch, cast a spell on; **me encanta eso** I love that; **encanto** *nm (hechizo)* spell, charm; *(fig)* charm, delight

encarcelar [enkarθe'lar] *vt* to imprison, jail

encarecer [enkare'θer] *vt* to put up the price of; **encarecerse** *vr* to get dearer

encargado, -a [enkar'xaðo, a] *adj* in charge ▷ *nm/f* agent, representative; *(responsable)* person in charge

encargar [enkar'xar] *vt* to entrust; *(recomendar)* to urge, recommend; **encargarse** *vr*: **~se de** to look after, take charge of; **~ algo a algn** to put sb in charge of sth; **~ a algn que haga algo** to ask sb to do sth

encargo [en'karxo] *nm (tarea)* assignment, job; *(responsabilidad)* responsibility; *(Com)* order

encariñarse [enkari'narse] *vr*: **~ con**

to grow fond of, get attached to
encarnación [enkarna'θjon] *nf*
incarnation, embodiment
encarrilar [enkarri'lar] *vt* (*tren*) to
put back on the rails; (*fig*) to correct,
put on the right track
encasillar [enkasi'λar] *vt* (*fig*) to
pigeonhole; (*actor*) to typecast
encendedor [enθende'ðor] *nm*
lighter
encender [enθen'der] *vt* (*con
fuego*) to light; (*luz, radio*) to put on,
switch on; (*avivar: pasión*) to inflame;
encenderse *vr* to catch fire; (*excitarse*)
to get excited; (*de cólera*) to flare up; (*el
rostro*) to blush
encendido [enθen'diðo] *nm* (*Auto*)
ignition
encerado [enθe'raðo] *nm* (*Escol*)
blackboard
encerrar [enθe'rrar] *vt* (*confinar*) to
shut in, shut up; (*comprender, incluir*) to
include, contain
encharcado, -a [entʃar'kaðo, a] *adj*
(*terreno*) flooded
encharcarse [entʃar'karse] *vr* to
get flooded
enchufado, -a [entʃu'faðo, a] (*fam*)
nm/f well-connected person
enchufar [entʃu'far] *vt* (*Elec*) to
plug in; (*Tec*) to connect, fit together;
enchufe *nm* (*Elec: clavija*) plug; (*: toma*)
socket; (*de dos tubos*) joint, connection;
(*fam: influencia*) contact, connection;
(*: puesto*) cushy job
encía [en'θia] *nf* gum
encienda *etc vb* V **encender**
encierro *etc* [en'θjerro] *vb* V **encerrar**
▷ *nm* shutting in, shutting up;
(*calabozo*) prison
encima [en'θima] *adv* (*sobre*) above,
over; (*además*) besides; **~ de** (*en*) on,
on top of; (*sobre*) above, over; (*además
de*) besides, on top of; **por ~ de** over;
¡**llevas dinero ~?** have you (got) any
money on you?; **se me vino ~** it took
me by surprise
encina [en'θina] *nf* holm oak

encinta [en'θinta] *adj* pregnant
enclenque [en'klenke] *adj* weak,
sickly
encoger [enko'xer] *vt* to shrink,
contract; **encogerse** *vr* to shrink,
contract; (*fig*) to cringe; **~se de
hombros** to shrug one's shoulders
encomendar [enkomen'dar] *vt* to
entrust, commend; **encomendarse**
vr: **~se a** to put one's trust in
encomienda *etc* [enko'mjenda]
vb V **encomendar** ▷ *nf* (*encargo*)
charge, commission; (*elogio*) tribute;
encomienda postal (*LAM*) package
encontrar [enkon'trar] *vt* (*hallar*)
to find; (*inesperadamente*) to meet, run
into; **encontrarse** *vr* to meet (each
other); (*situarse*) to be (situated); **~se
con** to meet; **~se bien (de salud)** to
feel well
encrucijada [enkruθi'xaða] *nf*
crossroads *sg*
encuadernación
[enkwaðerna'θjon] *nf* binding
encuadrar [enkwa'ðrar] *vt* (*retrato*)
to frame; (*ajustar*) to fit, insert;
(*contener*) to contain
encubrir [enku'βrir] *vt* (*ocultar*) to
hide, conceal; (*criminal*) to harbour,
shelter
encuentro *etc* [en'kwentro] *vb* V
encontrar ▷ *nm* (*de personas*) meeting;
(*Auto etc*) collision, crash; (*Deporte*)
match, game; (*Mil*) encounter
encuerado, -a (*MÉX*) [enkwe'raðo,
a] *adj* nude, naked
encuesta [en'kwesta] *nf* inquiry,
investigation; (*sondeo*) (public)
opinion poll
encumbrar [enkum'brar] *vt*
(*persona*) to exalt
endeble [en'deβle] *adj* (*persona*)
weak; (*argumento, excusa, persona*) weak
endemoniado, -a [endemo'njaðo,
a] *adj* possessed (of the devil);
(*travieso*) devilish
enderezar [endere'θar] *vt* (*poner
derecho*) to straighten (out);

(: *verticalmente*) to set upright; (*situación*) to straighten o sort out; (*dirigir*) to direct; **enderezarse** *vr* (*persona sentada*) to straighten up

endeudarse [endeu'ðarse] *vr* to get into debt

endiablado, -a [endja'βlaðo, a] *adj* devilish, diabolical; (*travieso*) mischievous

endilgar [endil'ɣar] (*fam*) *vt*: **~le algo a algn** to lumber sb with sth

endiñar [endi'ɲar] (*ESP: fam*) *vt* (*bofetón*) to land, belt

endosar [endo'sar] *vt* (*cheque etc*) to endorse

endulzar [endul'θar] *vt* to sweeten; (*suavizar*) to soften

endurecer [endure'θer] *vt* to harden; **endurecerse** *vr* to harden, grow hard

enema [e'nema] *nm* (*Med*) enema

enemigo, -a [ene'miɣo, a] *adj* enemy, hostile ▷ *nm/f* enemy

enemistad [enemis'tað] *nf* enmity

enemistar [enemis'tar] *vt* to make enemies of, cause a rift between; **enemistarse** *vr* to become enemies; (*amigos*) to fall out

energía [ener'xia] *nf* (*vigor*) energy, drive; (*empuje*) push; (*Tec, Elec*) energy, power; **energía eólica** wind power; **energía solar** solar energy o power

enérgico, -a [e'nerxiko, a] *adj* (*gen*) energetic; (*voz, modales*) forceful

energúmeno, -a [ener'xumeno, a] (*fam*) *nm/f* (*fig*) madman(-woman)

enero [e'nero] *nm* January

enfadado, -a [enfa'ðaðo, a] *adj* angry, annoyed

enfadar [enfa'ðar] *vt* to anger, annoy; **enfadarse** *vr* to get angry o annoyed

enfado [en'faðo] *nm* (*enojo*) anger, annoyance; (*disgusto*) trouble, bother

énfasis ['enfasis] *nm* emphasis, stress

enfático, -a [en'fatiko, a] *adj* emphatic

enfermar [enfer'mar] *vt* to make ill ▷ *vi* to fall ill, be taken ill

enfermedad [enferme'ðað] *nf* illness; **enfermedad venérea** venereal disease

enfermera [enfer'mera] *nf* nurse

enfermería [enferme'ria] *nf* infirmary; (*de colegio etc*) sick bay

enfermero [enfer'mero] *nm* (male) nurse

enfermizo, -a [enfer'miθo, a] *adj* (*persona*) sickly, unhealthy; (*fig*) unhealthy

enfermo, -a [en'fermo, a] *adj* ill, sick ▷ *nm/f* invalid, sick person; (*en hospital*) patient; **caer** o **ponerse ~** to fall ill

enfocar [enfo'kar] *vt* (*foto etc*) to focus; (*problema etc*) to approach

enfoque *etc* [en'foke] *vb* V **enfocar** ▷ *nm* focus

enfrentar [enfren'tar] *vt* (*peligro*) to face (up to), confront; (*oponer*) to bring face to face; **enfrentarse** *vr* (*dos personas*) to face o confront each other; (*Deporte: dos equipos*) to meet; **~se a** o **con** to face up to, confront

enfrente [en'frente] *adv* opposite; **la casa de ~** the house opposite, the house across the street; **~ de** opposite, facing

enfriamiento [enfria'mjento] *nm* chilling, refrigeration; (*Med*) cold, chill

enfriar [enfri'ar] *vt* (*alimentos*) to cool, chill; (*algo caliente*) to cool down; **enfriarse** *vr* to cool down; (*Med*) to catch a chill; (*amistad*) to cool

enfurecer [enfure'θer] *vt* to enrage, madden; **enfurecerse** *vr* to become furious, fly into a rage; (*mar*) to get rough

enganchar [engan'tʃar] *vt* to hook; (*dos vagones*) to hitch up; (*Tec*) to couple, connect; (*Mil*) to recruit; **engancharse** *vr* (*Mil*) to enlist, join up

enganche [en'gantʃe] *nm* hook; (*ESP Tec*) coupling, connection; (*acto*) hooking (up); (*Mil*) recruitment, enlistment; (MÉX: depósito) deposit

engañar [enga'ɲar] vt to deceive;
(estafar) to cheat, swindle; **engañarse**
vr (equivocarse) to be wrong; (disimular
la verdad) to deceive o.s.

engaño [en'gaɲo] nm deceit;
(estafa) trick, swindle; (error) mistake,
misunderstanding; (ilusión) delusion;
engañoso, -a adj (tramposo)
crooked; (mentiroso) dishonest,
deceitful; (aspecto) deceptive; (consejo)
misleading

engatusar [engatu'sar] (fam) vt
to coax

engendro [en'xendro] nm (Bio)
foetus; (fig) monstrosity

englobar [englo'βar] vt to include,
comprise

engordar [engor'ðar] vt to fatten
▷ vi to get fat, put on weight

engorroso, -a [engo'rroso, a] adj
bothersome, trying

engranaje [engra'naxe] nm (Auto)
gear

engrasar [engra'sar] vt (Tec: poner
grasa) to grease; (: lubricar) to lubricate,
oil; (manchar) to make greasy

engreído, -a [engre'iðo, a] adj vain,
conceited

enhebrar [ene'βrar] vt to thread

enhorabuena [enora'βwena]
excl ¡~! congratulations! ▷ nf: **dar la ~
a** to congratulate

enigma [e'niɣma] nm enigma;
(problema) puzzle; (misterio) mystery

enjambre [en'xambre] nm swarm

enjaular [enxau'lar] vt (to put in a)
cage; (fam) to jail, lock up

enjuagar [enxwa'ɣar] vt (ropa) to
rinse (out)

enjuague etc [en'xwaɣe] vb V
enjuagar ▷ nm (Med) mouthwash; (de
ropa) rinse, rinsing

enjugar [enxu'ɣar] vt to wipe (off);
(lágrimas) to dry; (déficit) to wipe out

enlace [en'laθe] nm link, connection;
(relación) relationship; (tb: ~
matrimonial) marriage; (de carretera,

trenes) connection; **enlace sindical**
shop steward

enlatado, -a [enla'taðo, a] adj
(alimentos, productos) tinned, canned

enlazar [enla'θar] vt (unir con lazos) to
bind together; (atar) to tie; (conectar) to
link, connect; (LAM: caballo) to lasso

enloquecer [enloke'θer] vt to drive
mad ▷ vi to go mad

enmarañar [enmara'ɲar] vt
(enredar) to tangle (up), entangle;
(complicar) to complicate; (confundir)
to confuse

enmarcar [enmar'kar] vt (cuadro)
to frame

enmascarar [enmaska'rar] vt to
mask; **enmascararse** vr to put on
a mask

enmendar [enmen'dar] vt to
emend, correct; (constitución etc) to
amend; (comportamiento) to reform;
enmendarse vr to reform, mend
one's ways; **enmienda** nf correction;
amendment; reform

enmudecer [enmuðe'θer] vi (perder
el habla) to fall silent; (guardar silencio)
to remain silent

ennoblecer [ennoβle'θer] vt to
ennoble

enojado, -a [eno'xaðo, a] (LAM)
adj angry

enojar [eno'xar] vt (encolerizar) to
anger; (disgustar) to annoy, upset;
enojarse vr to get angry; to get
annoyed

enojo [e'noxo] nm (cólera) anger;
(irritación) annoyance

enorme [e'norme] adj enormous,
huge; (fig) monstrous

enredadera [enreða'ðera] nf (Bot)
creeper, climbing plant

enredar [enre'ðar] vt (cables,
hilos etc) to tangle (up), entangle;
(situación) to complicate, confuse;
(meter cizaña) to sow discord among
o between; (implicar) to embroil,
implicate; **enredarse** vr to get
entangled, get tangled (up); (situación)

to get complicated; (*persona*) to get embroiled; (LAM: *fam*) to meddle

enredo [en'reðo] *nm* (*maraña*) tangle; (*confusión*) mix-up, confusion; (*intriga*) intrigue

enriquecer [enrike'θer] *vt* to make rich, enrich; **enriquecerse** *vr* to get rich

enrojecer [enroxe'θer] *vt* to redden ▷ *vi* (*persona*) to blush; **enrojecerse** *vr* to blush

enrollar [enro'ʎar] *vt* to roll (up), wind (up)

ensalada [ensa'laða] *nf* salad; **ensaladilla (rusa)** *nf* Russian salad

ensanchar [ensan'tʃar] *vt* (*hacer más ancho*) to widen; (*agrandar*) to enlarge, expand; (*Costura*) to let out; **ensancharse** *vr* to get wider, expand

ensayar [ensa'jar] *vt* to test, try (out); (*Teatro*) to rehearse

ensayo [en'sajo] *nm* test, trial; (*Quím*) experiment; (*Teatro*) rehearsal; (*Deporte*) try; (*Escol, Literatura*) essay

enseguida [ense'ɣiða] *adv* at once, right away

ensenada [ense'naða] *nf* inlet, cove

enseñanza [ense'nanθa] *nf* (*educación*) education; (*acción*) teaching; (*doctrina*) teaching, doctrine; **enseñanza (de) primaria/secundaria** elementary/secondary education

enseñar [ense'nar] *vt* (*educar*) to teach; (*mostrar, señalar*) to show

enseres [en'seres] *nmpl* belongings

ensuciar [ensu'θjar] *vt* (*manchar*) to dirty, soil; (*fig*) to defile; **ensuciarse** *vr* to get dirty; (*bebé*) to dirty one's nappy

entablar [enta'βlar] *vt* (*recubrir*) to board (up); (*Ajedrez, Damas*) to set up; (*conversación*) to strike up; (*Jur*) to file ▷ *vi* to draw

ente ['ente] *nm* (*organización*) body, organization; (*fam*: *persona*) odd character

entender [enten'der] *vt* (*comprender*) to understand; (*darse cuenta*) to realize ▷ *vi* to understand; (*creer*) to think,

believe; **entenderse** *vr* (*comprenderse*) to be understood; (*ponerse de acuerdo*) to agree, reach an agreement; **~ de** to know a lot about; **~ algo de** to know a little about; **~ en** to deal with, have to do with; **~ mal** to misunderstand; **~se con algn** (*llevarse bien*) to get on o along with sb; **~se mal** (*dos personas*) to get on badly

entendido, -a [enten'diðo, a] *adj* (*comprendido*) understood; (*hábil*) skilled; (*inteligente*) knowledgeable ▷ *nm/f* (*experto*) expert ▷ *excl* agreed!; **entendimiento** *nm* (*comprensión*) understanding; (*inteligencia*) mind, intellect; (*juicio*) judgement

enterado, -a [ente'raðo, a] *adj* well-informed; **estar ~ de** to know about, be aware of

enteramente [entera'mente] *adv* entirely, completely

enterar [ente'rar] *vt* (*informar*) to inform, tell; **enterarse** *vr* to find out, get to know

enterito [ente'rito] (RPL) *nm* boiler suit (BRIT), overalls (US)

entero, -a [en'tero, a] *adj* (*total*) whole, entire; (*fig*: *honesto*) honest; (: *firme*) firm, resolute ▷ *nm* (Com: *punto*) point

enterrar [ente'rrar] *vt* to bury

entidad [enti'ðað] *nf* (*empresa*) firm, company; (*organismo*) body; (*sociedad*) society; (*Filosofía*) entity

entiendo *etc vb* V **entender**

entierro [en'tjerro] *nm* (*acción*) burial; (*funeral*) funeral

entonación [entona'θjon] *nf* (*Ling*) intonation

entonar [ento'nar] *vt* (*canción*) to intone; (*colores*) to tone; (*Med*) to tone up ▷ *vi* to be in tune

entonces [en'tonθes] *adv* then, at that time; **desde ~** since then; **en aquel ~** at that time; **(pues) ~** and so

entornar [entor'nar] *vt* (*puerta, ventana*) to half-close, leave ajar; (*los ojos*) to screw up

entorno [en'torno] nm setting, environment; **~ de redes** (Inform) network environment

entorpecer [entorpe'θer] vt (entendimiento) to dull; (impedir) to obstruct, hamper; (: tránsito) to slow down, delay

entrada [en'traða] nf (acción) entry, access; (sitio) entrance, way in; (Inform) input; (Com) receipts pl, takings pl; (Culin) starter; (Deporte) innings sg; (Teatro) house, audience; (billete) ticket; **~s y salidas** (Com) income and expenditure; **de ~** from the outset; **entrada de aire** (Tec) air intake o inlet

entrado, -a [en'traðo, a] adj: **~ en años** elderly; **una vez ~ el verano** in the summer(time), when summer comes

entramparse [entram'parse] vr to get into debt

entrante [en'trante] adj next, coming; **mes/año ~** next month/year; **entrantes** nmpl starters

entraña [en'traɲa] nf (fig: centro) heart, core; (raíz) root; **entrañas** nfpl (Anat) entrails; (fig) heart sg; **entrañable** adj close, intimate; **entrañar** vt to entail

entrar [en'trar] vt (introducir) to bring in; (Inform) to input ▷ vi (meterse) to go in, come in, enter; (comenzar): **~ diciendo** to begin by saying; **hacer ~** to show in; **me entró sed/sueño** I started to feel thirsty/sleepy; **no me entra** I can't get the hang of it

entre ['entre] prep (dos) between; (más de dos) among(st)

entreabrir [entrea'ßrir] vt to half-open, open halfway

entrecejo [entre'θexo] nm: **fruncir el ~** to frown

entredicho [entre'ðitʃo] nm (Jur) injunction; **poner en ~** to cast doubt on; **estar en ~** to be in doubt

entrega [en'treɣa] nf (de mercancías) delivery; (de novela etc) instalment; **entregar** [entre'ɣar] vt (dar) to hand

(over), deliver; **entregarse** vr (rendirse) to surrender, give in, submit; (dedicarse) to devote o.s.

entremeses [entre'meses] nmpl hors d'œuvres

entremeter [entreme'ter] vt to insert, put in; **entremeterse** vr to meddle, interfere; **entremetido, -a** adj meddling, interfering

entremezclar [entremeθ'klar] vt to intermingle; **entremezclarse** vr to intermingle

entrenador, a [entrena'ðor, a] nm/f trainer, coach

entrenarse [entre'narse] vr to train

entrepierna [entre'pjerna] nf crotch

entresuelo [entre'swelo] nm mezzanine

entretanto [entre'tanto] adv meanwhile, meantime

entretecho [entre'tetʃo] (cs) nm attic

entretejer [entrete'xer] vt to interweave

entretener [entrete'ner] vt (divertir) to entertain, amuse; (detener) to hold up, delay; **entretenerse** vr (divertirse) to amuse o.s.; (retrasarse) to delay, linger; **entretenido, -a** adj entertaining, amusing

entretenimiento nm entertainment, amusement

entrever [entre'ßer] vt to glimpse, catch a glimpse of

entrevista [entre'ßista] nf interview; **entrevistar** vt to interview; **entrevistarse** vr to have an interview

entristecer [entriste'θer] vt to sadden, grieve; **entristecerse** vr to grow sad

entrometerse [entrome'terse] vr: **~ (en)** to interfere (in o with)

entumecer [entume'θer] vt to numb, benumb; **entumecerse** vr (por el frío) to go o become numb

enturbiar [entur'ßjar] vt (el agua)

to make cloudy; (fig) to confuse; **enturbiarse** vr (oscurecerse) to become cloudy; (fig) to get confused, become obscure

entusiasmar [entusjas'mar] vt to excite, fill with enthusiasm; (gustar mucho) to delight; **entusiasmarse** vr: **~se con o por** to get enthusiastic or excited about

entusiasmo [entu'sjasmo] nm enthusiasm; (excitación) excitement

entusiasta [entu'sjasta] adj enthusiastic ▷nmf enthusiast

enumerar [enume'rar] vt to enumerate

envainar [embai'nar] vt to sheathe

envalentonar [embalento'nar] vt to give courage to; **envalentonarse** vr (pey: jactarse) to boast, brag

envasar [emba'sar] vt (empaquetar) to pack, wrap; (enfrascar) to bottle; (enlatar) to can; (embolsar) to pocket

envase [em'base] nm (en paquete) packing, wrapping; (en botella) bottling; (en lata) canning; (recipiente) container; (paquete) package; (botella) bottle; (lata) tin (BRIT), can

envejecer [embexe'θer] vt to make old, age ▷vi (volverse viejo) to grow old; (parecer viejo) to age

envenenar [embene'nar] vt to poison; (fig) to embitter

envergadura [emberɣa'ðura] nf (fig) scope, compass

enviar [em'bjar] vt to send; **~ un mensaje a algn** (por movil) to text sb, to send sb a text message

enviciarse [embi'θjarse] vr: **~ (con)** to get addicted to

envidia [em'biðja] nf envy; **tener ~ a** to envy, be jealous of; **envidiar** vt to envy

envío [em'bio] nm (acción) sending; (de mercancías) consignment; (de dinero) remittance

enviudar [embju'ðar] vi to be widowed

envoltura [embol'tura] nf (cobertura) cover; (embalaje) wrapper, wrapping; **envoltorio** nm package

envolver [embol'βer] vt to wrap (up); (cubrir) to cover; (enemigo) to surround; (implicar) to involve, implicate

envuelto [em'bwelto] pp de **envolver**

enyesar [enje'sar] vt (pared) to plaster; (Med) to put in plaster

enzarzarse [enθar'θarse] vr: **~ en** (pelea) to get mixed up in; (disputa) to get involved in

épica ['epika] nf epic

epidemia [epi'ðemja] nf epidemic

epilepsia [epi'lepsja] nf epilepsy

episodio [epi'soðjo] nm episode

época ['epoka] nf period, time; (Hist) age, epoch; **hacer ~** to be epoch-making

equilibrar [ekili'βrar] vt to balance; **equilibrio** nm balance, equilibrium; **mantener/perder el equilibrio** to keep/lose one's balance; **equilibrista** nmf (funámbulo) tightrope walker; (acróbata) acrobat

equipaje [eki'paxe] nm luggage; (avíos): **hacer el ~** to pack; **equipaje de mano** hand luggage

equipar [eki'par] vt (proveer) to equip

equipararse [ekipa'rarse] vr: **~ con** to be on a level with

equipo [e'kipo] nm (conjunto de cosas) equipment; (Deporte) team; (de obreros) shift; **~ de música/de hi-fi** music centre

equis ['ekis] nf inv (the letter) X

equitación [ekita'θjon] nf horse riding

equivalente [ekiβa'lente] adj, nm equivalent

equivaler [ekiβa'ler] vi to be equivalent o equal

equivocación [ekiβoka'θjon] nf mistake, error

equivocado, -a [ekiβo'kaðo, a] adj wrong, mistaken

equivocarse [ekiβo'karse] vr to be wrong, make a mistake; **~ de camino**

to take the wrong road

era ['era] *vb* V **ser** ▷ *nf* era, age

erais *vb* V **ser**

éramos *vb* V **ser**

eran *vb* V **ser**

eras *vb* V **ser**

erección [erek'θjon] *nf* erection

eres *vb* V **ser**

erigir [eri'xir] *vt* to erect, build;
erigirse *vr*: **~se en** to set o.s. up as

erizo [e'riθo] *nm* (*Zool*) hedgehog;
erizo de mar sea-urchin

ermita [er'mita] *nf* hermitage;
ermitaño, -a [ermi'taɲo, a] *nm/f*
hermit

erosión [ero'sjon] *nf* erosion

erosionar [erosjo'nar] *vt* to erode

erótico, -a [e'rotiko, a] *adj* erotic;
erotismo *nm* eroticism

errante [e'rrante] *adj* wandering,
errant

erróneo, -a [e'rroneo, a] *adj*
(*equivocado*) wrong, mistaken

error [e'rror] *nm* error, mistake;
(*Inform*) bug; **error de imprenta**
misprint

eructar [eruk'tar] *vt* to belch, burp

erudito, -a [eru'ðito, a] *adj* erudite,
learned

erupción [erup'θjon] *nf* eruption;
(*Med*) rash

es *vb* V **ser**

esa ['esa] (*pl* **~s**) *adj* demos V **ese**

ésa ['esa] (*pl* **~s**) *pron* V **ése**

esbelto, -a [es'βelto, a] *adj* slim,
slender

esbozo [es'βoθo] *nm* sketch, outline

escabeche [eska'βetʃe] *nm* brine; (*de
aceitunas etc*) pickle; **en ~** pickled

escabullirse [eskaβu'ʎirse] *vr* to slip
away, to clear out

escafandra [eska'fandra] *nf* (*buzo*)
diving suit; (*escafandra espacial*)
space suit

escala [es'kala] *nf* (*proporción, Mús*)
scale; (*de mano*) ladder; (*Aviac*) stopover;
hacer ~ en to stop or call in at

escalafón [eskala'fon] *nm* (*escala de*
**salarios*) salary scale, wage scale

escalar [eska'lar] *vt* to climb, scale

escalera [eska'lera] *nf* stairs *pl*,
staircase; (*escala*) ladder; (*Naipes*) run;
escalera de caracol spiral staircase;
escalera de incendios fire escape;
escalera mecánica escalator

escalfar [eskal'far] *vt* (*huevos*) to
poach

escalinata [eskali'nata] *nf* staircase

escalofriante [eskalo'frjante] *adj*
chilling

escalofrío [eskalo'frio] *nm* (*Med*)
chill; **escalofríos** *nmpl* (*fig*) shivers

escalón [eska'lon] *nm* step, stair; (*de
escalera*) rung

escalope [eska'lope] *nm* (*Culin*)
escalope

escama [es'kama] *nf* (*de pez,
serpiente*) scale; (*de jabón*) flake; (*fig*)
resentment

escampar [eskam'par] *vb impers* to
stop raining

escandalizar [eskandali'θar] *vt* to
scandalize, shock; **escandalizarse**
vr to be shocked; (*ofenderse*) to be
offended

escándalo [es'kandalo] *nm* scandal;
(*alboroto, tumulto*) row, uproar;
escandaloso, -a *adj* scandalous,
shocking

escandinavo, -a [eskandi'naβo, a]
adj, nm/f Scandinavian

escanear [eskane'ar] *vt* to scan

escaño [es'kaɲo] *nm* bench; (*Pol*) seat

escapar [eska'par] *vi* (*gen*) to escape,
run away; (*Deporte*) to break away;
escaparse *vr* to escape, get away;
(*agua, gas*) to leak (out)

escaparate [eskapa'rate] *nm* shop
window; **ir de ~s** to go window-
shopping

escape [es'kape] *nm* (*de agua, gas*)
leak; (*de motor*) exhaust

escarabajo [eskara'βaxo] *nm* beetle

escaramuza [eskara'muθa] *nf*
skirmish

escarbar [eskar'βar] *vt* (*tierra*) to

scratch

escarceos [eskar'θeos] nmpl: **en mis ~ con la política ...** in my dealings with politics ...; **escarceos amorosos** love affairs

escarcha [es'kartʃa] nf frost; **escarchado, -a** [eskar'tʃaðo, a] adj (Culin: fruta) crystallized

escarlatina [eskarla'tina] nf scarlet fever

escarmentar [eskarmen'tar] vt to punish severely ▷ vi to learn one's lesson

escarmiento etc [eskar'mjento] vb V **escarmentar** ▷ nm (ejemplo) lesson; (castigo) punishment

escarola [eska'rola] nf endive

escarpado, -a [eskar'paðo, a] adj (pendiente) sheer, steep; (rocas) craggy

escasear [eskase'ar] vi to be scarce

escasez [eska'seθ] nf (falta) shortage, scarcity; (pobreza) poverty

escaso, -a [es'kaso, a] adj (poco) scarce; (raro) rare; (ralo) thin, sparse; (limitado) limited

escatimar [eskati'mar] vt to skimp (on), be sparing with

escayola [eska'jola] nf plaster

escena [es'θena] nf scene; **escenario** [esθe'narjo] nm (Teatro) stage; (Cine) set; (fig) scene

> No confundir **escenario** con la palabra inglesa scenery.

escenografía nf set design

escéptico, -a [es'θeptiko, a] adj sceptical ▷ nm/f sceptic

esclarecer [esklare'θer] vt (misterio, problema) to shed light on

esclavitud [esklaβi'tuð] nf slavery

esclavizar [esklaβi'θar] vt to enslave

esclavo, -a [es'klaβo, a] nm/f slave

escoba [es'koβa] nf broom; **escobilla** nf brush

escocer [esko'θer] vi to burn, sting; **escocerse** vr to chafe, get chafed

escocés, -esa [esko'θes, esa] adj Scottish ▷ nm/f Scotsman(-woman), Scot

Escocia [es'koθja] nf Scotland

escoger [esko'xer] vt to choose, pick, select; **escogido, -a** adj chosen, selected

escolar [esko'lar] adj school cpd ▷ nm schoolboy(-girl), pupil

escollo [es'koλo] nm (obstáculo) pitfall

escolta [es'kolta] nf escort; **escoltar** vt to escort

escombros [es'kombros] nmpl (basura) rubbish sg; (restos) debris sg

esconder [eskon'der] vt to hide, conceal; **esconderse** vr to hide; **escondidas** (LAM) nfpl: **a escondidas** secretly; **escondite** nm hiding place; (ESP: juego) hide-and-seek; **escondrijo** nm hiding place, hideout

escopeta [esko'peta] nf shotgun

escoria [es'korja] nf (de alto horno) slag; (fig) scum, dregs pl

Escorpio [es'korpjo] nm Scorpio

escorpión [eskor'pjon] nm scorpion

escotado, -a [esko'taðo, a] adj low-cut

escote [es'kote] nm (de vestido) low neck; **pagar a ~** to share the expenses

escotilla [esko'tiλa] nf (Náut) hatch(way)

escozor [esko'θor] nm (dolor) sting(ing)

escribible [eskri'βiβle] adj writable

escribir [eskri'βir] vt, vi to write; **~ a máquina** to type; **¿cómo se escribe?** how do you spell it?

escrito, -a [es'krito, a] pp de **escribir** ▷ nm (documento) document; (manuscrito) text, manuscript; **por ~** in writing

escritor, a [eskri'tor, a] nm/f writer

escritorio [eskri'torjo] nm desk

escritura [eskri'tura] nf (acción) writing; (caligrafía) (hand)writing; (Jur: documento) deed

escrúpulo [es'krupulo] nm scruple; (minuciosidad) scrupulousness; **escrupuloso, -a** adj scrupulous

escrutinio [eskru'tinjo] nm (examen atento) scrutiny; (Pol: recuento de votos) count(ing)

escuadra [es'kwaðra] nf (Mil etc)
squad; (Náut) squadron; (flota: de coches
etc) fleet; **escuadrilla** nf (de aviones)
squadron; (LAM: de obreros) gang

escuadrón [eskwa'ðron] nm
squadron

escuálido, -a [es'kwaliðo, a] adj
skinny, scraggy; (sucio) squalid

escuchar [esku'tʃar] vt to listen to
▷ vi to listen

escudo [es'kuðo] nm shield

escuela [es'kwela] nf school; **escuela
de artes y oficios** (ESP) ≈ technical
college; **escuela de choferes** (LAM),
driving school; **escuela de manejo**
(MÉX) driving school

escueto, -a [es'kweto, a] adj plain;
(estilo) simple

escuincle, -a [es'kwinkle, a]
(MÉX: fam) nm/f kid

esculpir [eskul'pir] vt to sculpt;
(grabar) to engrave; (tallar) to carve;
escultor, a nm/f sculptor(-tress);
escultura nf sculpture

escupidera [eskupi'ðera] nf
spittoon

escupir [esku'pir] vt, vi to spit (out)

escurreplatos [eskurre'platos]
(ESP) nm inv draining board (BRIT),
drainboard (US)

escurridero [eskurri'ðero] (LAM) nm
draining board (BRIT), drainboard (US)

escurridizo, -a [eskurri'ðiθo, a]
adj slippery

escurridor [eskurri'ðor] nm
colander

escurrir [esku'rrir] vt (ropa) to wring
out; (verduras, platos) to drain ▷ vi
(líquidos) to drip; **escurrirse** vr (secarse)
to drain; (resbalarse) to slip, slide;
(escaparse) to slip away

ese ['ese] (f **esa**, pl **esos, esas**) adj
demos (sg) that; (pl) those

ése ['ese] (f **ésa**, pl **ésos, ésas**) pron
(sg) that (one); (pl) those (ones); **~ ...
éste ...** the former ... the latter ...; **no
me vengas con ésas** don't give me any

more of that nonsense

esencia [e'senθja] nf essence;
esencial adj essential

esfera [es'fera] nf sphere; (de reloj)
face; **esférico, -a** adj spherical

esforzarse [esfor'θarse] vr to exert
o.s., make an effort

esfuerzo etc [es'fwerθo] vb V
esforzarse ▷ nm effort

esfumarse [esfu'marse] vr (apoyo,
esperanzas) to fade away

esgrima [es'ɣrima] nf fencing

esguince [es'ɣinθe] nm (Med) sprain

eslabón [esla'ßon] nm link

eslip [ez'lip] nm pants pl (BRIT),
briefs pl

eslovaco, -a [eslo'ßako, a] adj, nm/f
Slovak, Slovakian ▷ nm (Ling) Slovak,
Slovakian

Eslovaquia [eslo'ßakja] nf Slovakia

esmalte [es'malte] nm enamel;
esmalte de uñas nail varnish or polish

esmeralda [esme'ralda] nf emerald

esmerarse [esme'rarse] vr (aplicarse)
to take great pains, exercise great care;
(afanarse) to work hard

esmero [es'mero] nm (great) care

esnob [es'nob] (pl **~s**) adj (persona)
snobbish ▷ nmf snob

eso ['eso] pron that, that thing o
matter; **~ de su coche** that business
about his car; **~ de ir al cine** all that
about going to the cinema; **a ~ de
las cinco** at about five o'clock; **en ~**
thereupon, at that point; **~ es** that's
it; **¡~ sí que es vida!** now that is really
living!; **por ~ te lo dije** that's why I told
you; **y ~ que llovía** in spite of the fact
it was raining

esos adj demos V **ese**

ésos pron V **ese**

espabilar etc [espaßi'lar] = **despabilar**
etc

espacial [espa'θjal] adj (del espacio)
space cpd

espaciar [espa'θjar] vt to space (out)

espacio [es'paθjo] nm space; (Mús)
interval; (Radio, TV) programme (BRIT),

program (us); **el ~ space; espacio aéreo/exterior** air/outer space; **espacioso, -a** adj spacious, roomy

espada [es'paða] nf sword; **espadas** nfpl (Naipes) spades

espaguetis [espa'ɣetis] nmpl spaghetti sg

espalda [es'palda] nf (gen) back; **espaldas** nfpl (hombros) shoulders; **a ~s de algn** behind sb's back; **estar de ~s** to have one's back turned; **tenderse de ~s** to lie (down) on one's back; **volver la ~ a algn** to cold-shoulder sb

espantajo [espan'taxo] nm = **espantapájaros**

espantapájaros [espanta'paxaros] nm inv scarecrow

espantar [espan'tar] vt (asustar) to frighten, scare; (ahuyentar) to frighten off; (asombrar) to horrify, appal; **espantarse** vr to get frightened o scared; to be appalled

espanto [es'panto] nm (susto) fright; (terror) terror; (asombro) astonishment; **espantoso, -a** adj frightening; terrifying; astonishing

España [es'paɲa] nf Spain; **español, a** adj Spanish ▷ nm/f Spaniard ▷ nm (Ling) Spanish

esparadrapo [espara'ðrapo] nm (sticking) plaster (BRIT), adhesive tape (us)

esparcir [espar'θir] vt to spread; (diseminar) to scatter; **esparcirse** vr to spread (out), to scatter; (divertirse) to enjoy o.s.

espárrago [es'parraxo] nm asparagus

esparto [es'parto] nm esparto (grass)

espasmo [es'pasmo] nm spasm

espátula [es'patula] nf spatula

especia [es'peθja] nf spice

especial [espe'θjal] adj special; **especialidad** nf speciality (BRIT), specialty (us)

especie [es'peθje] nf (Bio) species; (clase) kind, sort; **en ~** in kind

especificar [espeθifi'kar] vt to

specify; **específico, -a** adj specific

espécimen [es'peθimen] (pl **especímenes**) nm specimen

espectáculo [espek'takulo] nm (gen) spectacle; (Teatro etc) show

espectador, a [espekta'ðor, a] nm/f spectator

especular [espeku'lar] vt, vi to speculate

espejismo [espe'xismo] nm mirage

espejo [es'pexo] nm mirror; (espejo) **retrovisor** rear-view mirror

espeluznante [espeluθ'nante] adj horrifying, hair-raising

espera [es'pera] nf (pausa, intervalo) wait; (Jur: plazo) respite; **en ~ de** waiting for; (con expectativa) expecting

esperanza [espe'ranθa] nf (confianza) hope; (expectativa) expectation; **hay pocas ~s de que venga** there is little prospect of his coming; **esperanza de vida** life expectancy

esperar [espe'rar] vt (aguardar) to wait for; (tener expectativa de) to expect; (desear) to hope for ▷ vi to wait; to expect; to hope; **hacer ~ a algn** to keep sb waiting; **~ un bebé** to be expecting (a baby)

esperma [es'perma] nf sperm

espeso, -a [es'peso, a] adj thick; **espesor** nm thickness

espía [es'pia] nm/f spy; **espiar** vt (observar) to spy on

espiga [es'piɣa] nf (Bot: de trigo etc) ear

espigón [espi'ɣon] nm (Bot) ear; (Náut) breakwater

espina [es'pina] nf thorn; (de pez) bone; **espina dorsal** (Anat) spine

espinaca [espi'naka] nf spinach

espinazo [espi'naθo] nm spine, backbone

espinilla [espi'niʎa] nf (Anat: tibia) shin(bone); (grano) blackhead

espinoso, -a [es'pinoso, a] adj (planta) thorny, prickly; (asunto) difficult

espionaje [espjo'naxe] nm spying, espionage

espiral [espi'ral] adj, nf spiral

espirar [espi'rar] vt to breathe out, exhale

espiritista [espiri'tista] adj, nmf spiritualist

espíritu [es'piritu] nm spirit; **Espíritu Santo** Holy Ghost o Spirit; **espiritual** adj spiritual

espléndido, -a [es'plendiðo, a] adj (magnífico) magnificent, splendid; (generoso) generous

esplendor [esplen'dor] nm splendour

espolvorear [espolβore'ar] vt to dust, sprinkle

esponja [es'ponxa] nf sponge; (fig) sponger; **esponjoso, -a** adj spongy

espontaneidad [espontanei'ðað] nf spontaneity; **espontáneo, -a** adj spontaneous

esposa [es'posa] nf wife; **esposas** nfpl handcuffs; **esposar** vt to handcuff

esposo [es'poso] nm husband

espray [es'prai] nm spray

espuela [es'pwela] nf spur

espuma [es'puma] nf foam; (de cerveza) froth, head; (de jabón) lather; **espuma de afeitar** shaving foam; **espumadera** nf (utensilio) skimmer; **espumoso, -a** adj frothy, foamy; (vino) sparkling

esqueleto [eske'leto] nm skeleton

esquema [es'kema] nm (diagrama) diagram; (dibujo) plan; (Filosofía) schema

esquí [es'ki] (pl **-s**) nm (objeto) ski; (Deporte) skiing; **esquí acuático** waterskiing; **esquiar** vi to ski

esquilar [eski'lar] vt to shear

esquimal [eski'mal] adj, nmf Eskimo

esquina [es'kina] nf corner; **esquinazo** [eski'naðo] nm: **dar esquinazo a algn** to give sb the slip

esquirol [eski'rol] (ESP) nm strikebreaker, scab

esquivar [eski'βar] vt to avoid

esta [‘esta] adj demos V **este²**

está vb V **estar**

ésta pron V **éste**

estabilidad [estaβili'ðað] nf stability; **estable** adj stable

establecer [estaβle'θer] vt to establish; **establecerse** vr to establish o.s.; (echar raíces) to settle (down); **establecimiento** nm establishment

establo [es'taβlo] nm (Agr) stable

estaca [es'taka] nf stake, post; (de tienda de campaña) peg

estacada [esta'kaða] nf (cerca) fence, fencing; (palenque) stockade

estación [esta'θjon] nf station; (del año) season; **estación balnearia** seaside resort; **estación de autobuses** bus station; **estación de servicio** service station

estacionamiento [estaθjona'mjento] nm (Auto) parking; (Mil) stationing

estacionar [estaθjo'nar] vt (Auto) to park; (Mil) to station

estadía [esta'ðia] (LAM) nf stay

estadio [es'taðjo] nm (fase) stage, phase; (Deporte) stadium

estadista [esta'ðista] nm (Pol) statesman; (Mat) statistician

estadística [esta'ðistika] nf figure, statistic; (ciencia) statistics sg

estado [es'taðo] nm (Pol: condición) state; **estar en ~** to be pregnant; **estado civil** marital status; **estado de ánimo** state of mind; **estado de cuenta** bank statement; **estado de sitio** state of siege; **estado mayor** staff; **Estados Unidos** United States (of America)

estadounidense [estaðouni'ðense] adj United States cpd, American ▷ nmf American

estafa [es'tafa] nf swindle, trick; **estafar** vt to swindle, defraud

estáis vb V **estar**

estallar [esta'ʎar] vi to burst; (bomba)

to explode, go off; (epidemia, guerra, rebelión) to break out; ~ **en llanto** to burst into tears; **estallido** nm explosion; (fig) outbreak

estampa [es'tampa] nf print, engraving; **estampado, -a** [estam'paðo, a] adj printed ▷ nm (impresión: acción) printing; (: efecto) print; (marca) stamping

estampar [estam'par] vt (imprimir) to print; (marcar) to stamp; (metal) to engrave; (poner sello en) to stamp; (fig) to stamp, imprint

estampida [estam'piða] nf stampede

estampido [estam'piðo] nm bang, report

estampilla [estam'piʎa] (LAM) nf (postage) stamp

están vb V **estar**

estancado, -a [estan'kaðo, a] adj stagnant

estancar [estan'kar] vt (aguas) to hold up, hold back; (Com) to monopolize; (fig) to block, hold up; **estancarse** vr to stagnate

estancia [es'tanθja] nf (ESP, MÉX: permanencia) stay; (sala) room; (RPL: de ganado) farm, ranch; **estanciero** (RPL) nm farmer, rancher

estanco, -a [es'tanko, a] adj watertight ▷ nm tobacconist's (shop), cigar store (US)

○ **ESTANCO**
○
○ Cigarettes, tobacco, postage
○ stamps and official forms are all
○ sold under state monopoly in
○ shops called **estancos**. Although
○ tobacco products can also be
○ bought in bars and quioscos they
○ are generally more expensive.

estándar [es'tandar] adj, nm standard

estandarte [estan'darte] nm banner, standard

estanque [es'tanke] nm (lago) pool, pond; (Agr) reservoir

estanquero, -a [estan'kero, a] nm/f tobacconist

estante [es'tante] nm (armario) rack, stand; (biblioteca) bookcase; (anaquel) shelf; **estantería** nf shelving, shelves pl

○ **PALABRA CLAVE**

estar [es'tar] vi **1** (posición) to be; **está en la plaza** it's in the square; **¿está Juan?** is Juan in?; **estamos a 30 km de Junín** we're 30 kms from Junín

2 (+ adj: estado) to be; **estar enfermo** to be ill; **está muy elegante** he's looking very smart; **¿cómo estás?** how are you keeping?

3 (+ gerundio) to be; **estoy leyendo** I'm reading

4 (uso pasivo): **está condenado a muerte** he's been condemned to death; **está envasado en ...** it's packed in ...

5 (con fechas): **¿a cuántos estamos?** what's the date today?; **estamos a 5 de mayo** it's the 5th of May

6 (locuciones): **¿estamos?** (¿de acuerdo?) okay?; (¿listo?) ready?

7. estar de: estar de vacaciones/ viaje to be on holiday/away on a trip; **está de camarero** he's working as a waiter

8: estar para: está para salir he's about to leave; **no estoy para bromas** I'm not in the mood for jokes

9: estar por (propuesta etc) to be in favour of; (persona etc) to support, side with; **está por limpiar** it still has to be cleaned

10: estar sin: estar sin dinero to have no money; **está sin terminar** it isn't finished yet

estarse vr: **se estuvo en la cama toda la tarde** he stayed in bed all afternoon

estas ['estas] adj demos V **este²**

éstas pron V **éste**

estatal [esta'tal] adj state cpd

estático, -a [es'tatiko, a] adj static

estatua [es'tatwa] nf statue

estatura [esta'tura] nf stature, height

este¹ ['este] nm east

este² ['este] (**esta**, pl **estos, estas**) adj demos (sg) this; (pl) these

esté etc vb V **estar**

éste ['este] (**ésta**, pl **éstos, éstas**) pron (sg) this (one); (pl) these (ones); **ése ... ~ ...** the former ... the latter ...

estén etc vb V **estar**

estepa [es'tepa] nf (Geo) steppe

estera [es'tera] nf mat(ting)

estéreo [es'tereo] adj inv, nm stereo; **estereotipo** nm stereotype

estéril [es'teril] adj sterile, barren; (fig) vain, futile; **esterilizar** vt to sterilize

esterlina [ester'lina] adj: **libra~** pound sterling

estés etc vb V **estar**

estética [es'tetika] nf aesthetics

estético, -a [es'tetiko, a] adj aesthetic

estiércol [es'tjerkol] nm dung, manure

estigma [es'tiɣma] nm stigma

estilo [es'tilo] nm style; (Tec) stylus; (Natación) stroke; **algo por el ~** something along those lines

estima [es'tima] nf esteem, respect; **estimación** [estima'θjon] nf (evaluación) estimation; (aprecio, afecto) esteem, regard; **estimado, a** adj esteemed; **E~ señor** Dear Sir

estimar [esti'mar] vt (evaluar) to estimate; (valorar) to value; (apreciar) to esteem, respect; (pensar, considerar) to think, reckon

estimulante [estimu'lante] adj stimulating ▷ nm stimulant

estimular [estimu'lar] vt to stimulate; (excitar) to excite

estímulo [es'timulo] nm stimulus; (ánimo) encouragement

estirar [esti'rar] vt to stretch; (dinero, suma etc) to stretch out; **estirarse** vr to stretch

estirón [esti'ron] nm pull, tug; (crecimiento) spurt, sudden growth; **dar o pegar un ~** (fam: niño) to shoot up (inf)

estirpe [es'tirpe] nf stock, lineage

estival [esti'βal] adj summer cpd

esto ['esto] pron this, this thing o matter; **~ de la boda** this business about the wedding

Estocolmo [esto'kolmo] nm Stockholm

estofado [esto'faðo] nm stew

estómago [es'tomaxo] nm stomach; **tener ~** to be thick-skinned

estorbar [estor'βar] vt to hinder, obstruct; (molestar) to bother, disturb ▷ vi to be in the way; **estorbo** nm (molestia) bother, nuisance; (obstáculo) hindrance, obstacle

estornudar [estornu'ðar] vi to sneeze

estos ['estos] adj demos V **este²**

éstos pron V **éste**

estoy vb V **estar**

estrado [es'traðo] nm platform

estrafalario, -a [estrafa'larjo, a] adj odd, eccentric

estrago [es'traxo] nm ruin, destruction; **hacer ~s en** to wreak havoc among

estragón [estra'ɣon] nm tarragon

estrambótico, -a [estram'botiko, a] adj (persona) eccentric; (peinado, ropa) outlandish

estrangular [estrangu'lar] vt (persona) to strangle; (Med) to strangulate

estratagema [estrata'xema] nf (Mil) stratagem; (astucia) cunning

estrategia [estra'texja] nf strategy; **estratégico, -a** adj strategic

estrato [es'trato] nm stratum, layer

estrechar [estre'tʃar] vt (reducir) to narrow; (Costura) to take in; (abrazar) to hug, embrace; **estrecharse** vr (reducirse) to narrow, grow narrow;

(*abrazarse*) to embrace; **~ la mano** to shake hands

estrechez [estre'tʃeθ] nf narrowness; (*de ropa*) tightness; **estrecheces** nfpl (*dificultades económicas*) financial difficulties

estrecho, -a [es'tretʃo, a] adj narrow; (*apretado*) tight; (*íntimo*) close, intimate; (*miserable*) mean ▸ nm strait; **~ de miras** narrow-minded

estrella [es'treʎa] nf star; **estrella de mar** (*Zool*) starfish; **estrella fugaz** shooting star

estrellar [estre'ʎar] vt (*hacer añicos*) to smash (to pieces); (*huevos*) to fry; **estrellarse** vr to smash; (*chocarse*) to crash; (*fracasar*) to fail

estremecer [estreme'θer] vt to shake; **estremecerse** vr to shake, tremble

estrenar [estre'nar] vt (*vestido*) to wear for the first time; (*casa*) to move into; (*película, obra de teatro*) to première; **estrenarse** vr (*persona*) to make one's début; **estreno** nm (*Cine etc*) première

estreñido, -a [estre'niðo, a] adj constipated

estreñimiento [estreni'mjento] nm constipation

estrepitoso, -a [estrepi'toso, a] adj noisy; (*fiesta*) rowdy

estrés [es'tres] nm stress

estría [es'tria] nf groove

estribar [estri'βar] vi: **~ en** to lie on

estribillo [estri'βiʎo] nm (*Literatura*) refrain; (*Mús*) chorus

estribo [es'triβo] nm (*de jinete*) stirrup; (*de coche, tren*) step; (*de puente*) support; (*Geo*) spur; **perder los ~s** to fly off the handle

estribor [estri'βor] nm (*Náut*) starboard

estricto, -a [es'trikto, a] adj (*riguroso*) strict; (*severo*) severe

estridente [estri'ðente] adj (*color*) loud; (*voz*) raucous

estropajo [estro'paxo] nm scourer

estropear [estrope'ar] vt to spoil; (*dañar*) to damage; **estropearse** vr (*objeto*) to get damaged; (*persona, piel*) to be ruined

estructura [estruk'tura] nf structure

estrujar [estru'xar] vt (*apretar*) to squeeze; (*aplastar*) to crush; (*fig*) to drain, bleed

estuario [es'twarjo] nm estuary

estuche [es'tutʃe] nm box, case

estudiante [estu'ðjante] nmf student; **estudiantil** adj student cpd

estudiar [estu'ðjar] vt to study

estudio [es'tuðjo] nm study; (*Cine, Arte, Radio*) studio; **estudios** nmpl studies; (*erudición*) learning sg; **estudioso, -a** adj studious

estufa [es'tufa] nf heater, fire

estupefaciente [estupefa'θjente] nm drug, narcotic

estupefacto, -a [estupe'fakto, a] adj speechless, thunderstruck

estupendo, -a [estu'pendo, a] adj wonderful, terrific; (*fam*) great; **¡~!** that's great! fantastic!

estupidez [estupi'ðeθ] nf (*torpeza*) stupidity; (*acto*) stupid thing (to do)

estúpido, -a [es'tupiðo, a] adj stupid, silly

estuve etc vb V **estar**

ETA ['eta] (ESP) nf abr (= Euskadi ta Askatasuna) ETA

etapa [e'tapa] nf (*de viaje*) stage; (*Deporte*) leg; (*parada*) stopping place; (*fase*) stage, phase

etarra [e'tarra] nmf member of ETA

etc. abr (= etcétera) etc

etcétera [et'θetera] adv etcetera

eternidad [eterni'ðað] nf eternity; **eterno, -a** adj eternal, everlasting

ética ['etika] nf ethics pl

ético, -a ['etiko, a] adj ethical

etiqueta [eti'keta] nf (*modales*) etiquette; (*rótulo*) label, tag

Eucaristía [eukaris'tia] nf Eucharist

euforia [eu'forja] nf euphoria

euro ['euro] nm (*moneda*) euro

eurodiputado, -a [eurodiputaðo, a] nm/f Euro MP, MEP

Europa [eu'ropa] nf Europe; **europeo, -a** adj, nm/f European

Euskadi [eus'kaði] nm the Basque Country o Provinces pl

euskera [eus'kera] nm (Ling) Basque

evacuación [eβakwa'θjon] nf evacuation

evacuar [eβa'kwar] vt to evacuate

evadir [eβa'ðir] vt to evade, avoid; **evadirse** vr to escape

evaluar [eβa'lwar] vt to evaluate

evangelio [eβan'xeljo] nm gospel

evaporar [eβapo'rar] vt to evaporate; **evaporarse** vr to vanish

evasión [eβa'sjon] nf escape, flight; (fig) evasion; **evasión de capitales** flight of capital

evasiva [eβa'siβa] nf (pretexto) excuse

evento [e'βento] nm event

eventual [eβen'twal] adj possible, conditional (upon circumstances); (trabajador) casual, temporary

☐ No confundir **eventual** con la palabra inglesa eventual.

evidencia [eβi'ðenθja] nf evidence, proof

evidente [eβi'ðente] adj obvious, clear, evident

evitar [eβi'tar] vt (evadir) to avoid; (impedir) to prevent; **~ hacer algo** to avoid doing sth

evocar [eβo'kar] vt to evoke, call forth

evolución [eβolu'θjon] nf (desarrollo) evolution, development; (cambio) change; (Mil) manoeuvre; **evolucionar** vi to evolve; to manoeuvre

ex [eks] adj ex-; **el ~ ministro** the former minister, the ex-minister

exactitud [eksakti'tuð] nf exactness; (precisión) accuracy; (puntualidad) punctuality; **exacto, -a** adj exact; accurate; punctual; **¡exacto!** exactly!

exageración [eksaxera'θjon] nf exaggeration

exagerar [eksaxe'rar] vt, vi to exaggerate

exaltar [eksal'tar] vt to exalt, glorify; **exaltarse** vr (excitarse) to get excited o worked up

examen [ek'samen] nm examination; **examen de conducir** driving test; **examen de ingreso** entrance examination

examinar [eksami'nar] vt to examine; **examinarse** vr to be examined, take an examination

excavadora [ekskaβa'ðora] nf excavator

excavar [ekska'βar] vt to excavate

excedencia [eksθe'ðenθja] nf: **estar en ~** to be on leave; **pedir** o **solicitar la ~** to ask for leave

excedente [eksθe'ðente] adj, nm excess, surplus

exceder [eksθe'ðer] vt to exceed, surpass; **excederse** vr (extralimitarse) to go too far

excelencia [eksθe'lenθja] nf excellence; **su E~** his Excellency; **excelente** adj excellent

excéntrico, -a [eks'θentriko, a] adj, nm/f eccentric

excepción [eksθep'θjon] nf exception; **a ~ de** with the exception of, except for; **excepcional** adj exceptional

excepto [eks'θepto] adv excepting, except (for)

exceptuar [eksθep'twar] vt to except, exclude

excesivo, -a [eksθe'siβo, a] adj excessive

exceso [eks'θeso] nm (gen) excess; (Com) surplus; **exceso de equipaje/peso** excess luggage/weight; **exceso de velocidad** speeding

excitado, -a [eksθi'taðo, a] adj excited; (emociones) aroused

excitar [eksθi'tar] vt to excite; (incitar) to urge; **excitarse** vr to get excited

exclamación [eksklama'θjon] nf

exclamation

exclamar [ekskla'mar] vi to exclaim

excluir [eksklu'ir] vt to exclude; (dejar fuera) to shut out; (descartar) to reject

exclusiva [eksklu'siβa] nf (Prensa) exclusive, scoop; (Com) sole right

exclusivo, -a [eksklu'siβo, a] adj exclusive; **derecho ~** sole o exclusive right

Excmo. abr = **excelentísimo**

excomulgar [ekskomul'ɣar] vt (Rel) to excommunicate

excomunión [ekskomu'njon] nf excommunication

excursión [ekskur'sjon] nf excursion, outing; **excursionista** nmf (turista) sightseer

excusa [eks'kusa] nf excuse; (disculpa) apology; **excusar** [eksku'sar] vt to excuse

exhaustivo, -a [eksaus'tiβo, a] adj (análisis) thorough; (estudio) exhaustive

exhausto, -a [ek'sausto, a] adj exhausted

exhibición [eksiβi'θjon] nf exhibition, display, show

exhibir [eksi'βir] vt to exhibit, display, show

exigencia [eksi'xenθja] nf demand, requirement; **exigente** [eksi'xente] adj demanding

exigir [eksi'xir] vt (gen) to demand, require; **~ el pago** to demand payment

exiliado, -a [eksi'ljaðo, a] adj exiled ▷ nm/f exile

exilio [ek'siljo] nm exile

eximir [eksi'mir] vt to exempt

existencia [eksis'tenθja] nf existence; **existencias** nfpl stock(s) pl

existir [eksis'tir] vi to exist, be

éxito ['eksito] nm (triunfo) success; (Mús etc) hit; **tener ~** to be successful

    No confunda **éxito** con la palabra inglesa exit.

exorbitante [eksorβi'tante] adj (precio) exorbitant; (cantidad) excessive

exótico, -a [ek'sotiko, a] adj exotic

expandir [ekspan'dir] vt to expand

expansión [ekspan'sjon] nf expansion

expansivo, -a [ekspan'siβo, a] adj: **onda expansiva** shock wave

expatriarse [ekspa'trjarse] vr to emigrate; (Pol) to go into exile

expectativa [ekspekta'tiβa] nf (espera) expectation; (perspectiva) prospect

expedición [ekspeði'θjon] nf (excursión) expedition

expediente [ekspe'ðjente] nm expedient; (Jur: procedimiento) action, proceedings pl; (: papeles) dossier, file, record

expedir [ekspe'ðir] vt (despachar) to send, forward; (pasaporte) to issue

expensas [eks'pensas] nfpl: **a ~ de** at the expense of

experiencia [ekspe'rjenθja] nf experience

experimentado, -a [eksperimen'taðo, a] adj experienced

experimentar [eksperimen'tar] vt (en laboratorio) to experiment with; (probar) to test, try out; (notar, observar) to experience; (deterioro, pérdida) to suffer; **experimento** nm experiment

experto, -a [eks'perto, a] adj expert, skilled ▷ nm/f expert

expirar [ekspi'rar] vi to expire

explanada [ekspla'naða] nf (llano) plain

explayarse [ekspla'jarse] vr (en discurso) to speak at length; **~ con algn** to confide in sb

explicación [eksplika'θjon] nf explanation

explicar [ekspli'kar] vt to explain; **explicarse** vr to explain (o.s.)

explícito, -a [eks'pliθito, a] adj explicit

explique etc vb V **explicar**

explorador, a [eksplora'ðor, a] nm/f (pionero) explorer; (Mil) scout ▷ nm (Med) probe; (Tec)(radar) scanner

explorar [eksplo'rar] vt to explore; (Med) to probe; (radar) to scan

explosión [eksplo'sjon] nf
explosion; **explosivo, -a** adj explosive

explotación [eksplota'θjon] nf
exploitation; (de planta etc) running

explotar [eksplo'tar] vt to exploit to
run, operate ▷ vi to explode

exponer [ekspo'ner] vt to expose;
(cuadro) to display; (vida) to risk;
(idea) to explain; **exponerse** vr: **~se
a (hacer) algo** to run the risk of
(doing) sth

exportación [eksporta'θjon] nf
(acción) export; (mercancías) exports pl

exportar [ekspor'tar] vt to export

exposición [eksposi'θjon] nf (gen)
exposure; (de arte) show, exhibition;
(explicación) explanation; (declaración)
account, statement

expresamente [ekspresa'mente]
adv (decir) clearly; (a propósito) expressly

expresar [ekspre'sar] vt to express;
expresión nf expression

expresivo, -a [ekspre'siβo, a] adj
(persona, gesto, palabras) expressive;
(cariñoso) affectionate

expreso, -a [eks'preso, a] pp de
expresar ▷ adj (explícito) express;
(claro) specific, clear; (tren) fast
▷ adv: **enviar ~** to send by express
(delivery)

express [eks'pres] (LAM) adv: **enviar
algo ~** to send sth special delivery

exprimidor [eksprimi'ðor] nm
squeezer

exprimir [ekspri'mir] vt (fruta) to
squeeze; (zumo) to squeeze out

expuesto, -a [eks'pwesto, a] pp de
exponer ▷ adj exposed; (cuadro etc) on
show, on display

expulsar [ekspul'sar] vt (echar) to
eject, throw out; (alumno) to expel;
(despedir) to sack, fire; (Deporte) to
send off; **expulsión** nf expulsion;
sending-off

exquisito, -a [ekski'sito, a] adj
exquisite; (comida) delicious

éxtasis ['ekstasis] nm ecstasy

extender [eksten'der] vt to extend;

(los brazos) to stretch out, hold out;
(mapa, tela) to spread (out), open (out);
(mantequilla) to spread; (certificado)
to issue; (cheque, recibo) to make out;
(documento) to draw up; **extenderse**
vr (gen) to extend; (persona: en el suelo)
to stretch out; (epidemia) to spread;
extendido, -a adj (abierto) spread out,
open; (brazos) outstretched; (costumbre)
widespread

extensión [eksten'sjon] nf (de
terreno, mar) expanse, stretch;
(de tiempo) length, duration; (Tel)
extension; **en toda la ~ de la palabra**
in every sense of the word

extenso, -a [eks'tenso, a] adj
extensive

exterior [ekste'rjor] adj (de fuera)
external; (afuera) outside, exterior;
(apariencia) outward; (deuda, relaciones)
foreign ▷ nm (gen) exterior, outside;
(aspecto) outward appearance;
(Deporte) wing(er); (países extranjeros)
abroad; **en el ~** abroad; **al ~** outwardly,
on the surface

exterminar [ekstermi'nar] vt to
exterminate

externo, -a [eks'terno, a] adj
(exterior) external, outside; (superficial)
outward ▷ nm/f day pupil

extinguir [ekstin'gir] vt (fuego) to
extinguish, put out; (raza, población) to
wipe out; **extinguirse** vr (fuego) to go
out; (Bio) to die out, become extinct

extintor [ekstin'tor] nm (fire)
extinguisher

extirpar [ekstir'par] vt (Med) to
remove (surgically)

extra ['ekstra] adj inv (tiempo) extra;
(chocolate, vino) good-quality ▷ nmf
extra ▷ nm extra; (bono) bonus

extracción [ekstrak'θjon] nf
extraction; (en lotería) draw

extracto [eks'trakto] nm extract

extradición [ekstraði'θjon] nf
extradition

extraer [ekstra'er] vt to extract,
take out

extraescolar [ekstraesko'lar] *adj*: **actividad ~** extracurricular activity

extranjero, -a [ekstran'xero, a] *adj* foreign ▷ *nm/f* foreigner ▷ *nm* foreign countries *pl*; **en el ~** abroad

No confundir **extranjero** con la palabra inglesa *stranger*.

extrañar [ekstra'ɲar] *vt* (*sorprender*) to find strange o odd; (*echar de menos*) to miss; **extrañarse** *vr* (*sorprenderse*) to be amazed, be surprised; **me extraña** I'm surprised

extraño, -a [eks'traɲo, a] *adj* (*extranjero*) foreign; (*raro, sorprendente*) strange, odd

extraordinario, -a [ekstraorði'narjo, a] *adj* extraordinary; (*edición, número*) special ▷ *nm* (*de periódico*) special edition; **horas extraordinarias** overtime *sg*

extrarradio [ekstra'rraðjo] *nm* suburbs

extravagante [ekstraβa'ɣante] *adj* (*excéntrico*) eccentric; (*estrafalario*) outlandish

extraviado, -a [ekstra'βjaðo, a] *adj* lost, missing

extraviar [ekstra'βjar] *vt* (*persona: desorientar*) to mislead, misdirect; (*perder*) to lose, misplace; **extraviarse** *vr* to lose one's way, get lost

extremar [ekstre'mar] *vt* to carry to extremes

extremaunción [ekstremaun'θjon] *nf* extreme unction

extremidad [ekstremi'ðað] *nf* (*punta*) extremity; **extremidades** *nfpl* (Anat) extremities

extremo, -a [eks'tremo, a] *adj* extreme; (*último*) last ▷ *nm* end; (*límite, grado sumo*) extreme; **en último ~** as a last resort

extrovertido, -a [ekstroβer'tiðo, a] *adj, nm/f* extrovert

exuberante [eksuβe'rante] *adj* exuberant; (*fig*) luxuriant, lush

eyacular [ejaku'lar] *vt, vi* to

ejaculate

o lose one's way, get lost

extremar [ekstre'mar] *vt* to carry to extremes

extremaunción [ekstremaun'θjon] *nf* extreme unction

extremidad [ekstremi'ðað] *nf* (*punta*) extremity; **extremidades** *nfpl* (Anat) extremities

extremo, -a [eks'tremo, a] *adj* extreme; (*último*) last ▷ *nm* end; (*límite, grado sumo*) extreme; **en último ~** as a last resort

extrovertido, -a [ekstroβer'tiðo, a] *adj, nm/f* extrovert

exuberante [eksuβe'rante] *adj* exuberant; (*fig*) luxuriant, lush

eyacular [ejaku'lar] *vt, vi* to ejaculate

f

fa [fa] nm (Mús) fa, F

fabada [fa'βaða] nf bean and sausage stew

fábrica ['faβrika] nf factory; **marca de ~** trademark; **precio de ~** factory price

No confundir **fábrica** con la palabra inglesa *fabric*.

fabricación [faβrika'θjon] nf (manufactura) manufacture; (producción) production; **de ~ casera** home-made; **fabricación en serie** mass production

fabricante [faβri'kante] nmf manufacturer

fabricar [faβri'kar] vt (manufacturar) to manufacture, make; (construir) to build; (cuento) to fabricate, devise

fábula ['faβula] nf (cuento) fable; (chisme) rumour; (mentira) fib

fabuloso, -a [faβu'loso, a] adj (oportunidad, tiempo) fabulous, great

facción [fak'θjon] nf (Pol) faction; **facciones** nfpl (de rostro) features

faceta [fa'θeta] nf facet

facha ['fatʃa] (fam) nf (aspecto) look; (cara) face

fachada [fa'tʃaða] nf (Arq) façade, front

fácil ['faθil] adj (simple) easy; (probable) likely

facilidad [faθili'ðað] nf (capacidad) ease; (sencillez) simplicity; (de palabra) fluency; **facilidades** nfpl facilities; **facilidades de pago** credit facilities

facilitar [faθili'tar] vt (hacer fácil) to make easy; (proporcionar) to provide

factor [fak'tor] nm factor

factura [fak'tura] nf (cuenta) bill; **facturación** nf (de equipaje) check-in; **facturar** vt (Com) to invoice, charge for; (equipaje) to check in

facultad [fakul'tað] nf (aptitud, Escol etc) faculty; (poder) power

faena [fa'ena] nf (trabajo) work; (quehacer) task, job

faisán [fai'san] nm pheasant

faja ['faxa] nf (para la cintura) sash; (de mujer) corset; (de tierra) strip

fajo ['faxo] nm (de papeles) bundle; (de billetes) wad

falda ['falda] nf (prenda de vestir) skirt; **falda pantalón** culottes pl, split skirt

falla ['faʎa] nf (defecto) fault, flaw; **falla humana** (LAM) human error

fallar [fa'ʎar] vt (Jur) to pronounce sentence on ▷vi (memoria) to fail; (motor) to miss

Fallas ['faʎas] nfpl Valencian celebration of the feast of St Joseph

---

FALLAS

In the week of 19 March (the feast of San José), Valencia honours its patron saint with a spectacular fiesta called **Las Fallas**. The **Fallas** are huge papier-mâché, cardboard and wooden sculptures which are built by competing teams throughout the year. They depict politicians and well-known public figures and are thrown onto

● bonfires and set alight once a jury has judged them – only the best sculpture escapes the flames.

fallecer [faʎeˈθer] vi to pass away, die; **fallecimiento** nm decease, demise

fallido, -a [faˈʎiðo, a] adj (gen) frustrated, unsuccessful

fallo [ˈfaʎo] nm (Jur) verdict, ruling; (fracaso) failure; **fallo cardíaco** heart failure; **fallo humano** (ESP) human error

falsificar [falsifiˈkar] vt (firma etc) to forge; (moneda) to counterfeit

falso, -a [ˈfalso, a] adj false; (documento, moneda etc) fake; **en ~** falsely

falta [ˈfalta] nf (defecto) fault, flaw; (privación) lack, want; (ausencia) absence; (carencia) shortage; (equivocación) mistake; (Deporte) foul; **echar en ~** to miss; **hacer ~ hacer algo** to be necessary to do sth; **me hace ~ una pluma** I need a pen; **falta de educación** bad manners pl; **falta de ortografía** spelling mistake

faltar [falˈtar] vi (escasear) to be lacking, be wanting; (ausentarse) to be absent, be missing; **faltan 2 horas para llegar** there are 2 hours to go till arrival; **~ al respeto a algn** to be disrespectful to sb; **¡no faltaba más!** (no hay de qué) don't mention it!

fama [ˈfama] nf (renombre) fame; (reputación) reputation

familia [faˈmilja] nf family; **familia numerosa** large family; **familia política** in-laws pl

familiar [famiˈljar] adj (relativo a la familia) family cpd; (conocido, informal) familiar ▷ nm relative, relation

famoso, -a [faˈmoso, a] adj (renombrado) famous

fan [fan] (pl **-s**) nmf fan

fanático, -a [faˈnatiko, a] adj fanatical ▷ nm/f fanatic; (Cine, Deporte) fan

fanfarrón, -ona [fanfaˈrron, ona] adj boastful

fango [ˈfaŋgo] nm mud

fantasía [fantaˈsia] nf fantasy, imagination; **joyas de ~** imitation jewellery sg

fantasma [fanˈtasma] nm (espectro) ghost, apparition; (fanfarrón) show-off

fantástico, -a [fanˈtastiko, a] adj fantastic

farmacéutico, -a [farmaˈθeutiko, a] adj pharmaceutical ▷ nm/f chemist (BRIT), pharmacist

farmacia [farˈmaθja] nf chemist's (shop) (BRIT), pharmacy; **farmacia de guardia** all-night chemist

fármaco [ˈfarmako] nm drug

faro [ˈfaro] nm (Náut: torre) lighthouse; (Auto) headlamp; **faros antiniebla** fog lamps; **faros delanteros/traseros** headlights/rear lights

farol [faˈrol] nm lantern, lamp

farola [faˈrola] nf street lamp (BRIT) o light (US)

farra [ˈfarra] nf (LAM: fam) party; **ir de ~** to go on a binge

farsa [ˈfarsa] nf (gen) farce

farsante [farˈsante] nmf fraud, fake

fascículo [fasˈθikulo] nm (de revista) part, instalment

fascinar [fasθiˈnar] vt (gen) to fascinate

fascismo [fasˈθismo] nm fascism; **fascista** adj, nmf fascist

fase [ˈfase] nf phase

fashion [ˈfaʃon] adj (fam) trendy

fastidiar [fastiˈðjar] vt (molestar) to annoy, bother; (estropear) to spoil; **fastidiarse** vr: **¡que se fastidie!** (fam) he'll just have to put up with it

fastidio [fasˈtiðjo] nm (molestia) annoyance; **fastidioso, -a** adj (molesto) annoying

fatal [faˈtal] adj (gen) fatal; (desgraciado) ill-fated; (fam: malo, pésimo) awful; **fatalidad** nf (destino) fate; (mala suerte) misfortune

fatiga [fa'tixa] *nf* (*cansancio*) fatigue, weariness

fatigar [fati'ɣar] *vt* to tire, weary

fatigoso, -a [fati'ɣoso, a] *adj* (*cansador*) tiring

fauna ['fauna] *nf* fauna

favor [fa'βor] *nm* favour; **estar a ~ de** to be in favour of; **haga el ~ de ...** would you be so good as to ...; kindly ...; **por ~** please; **favorable** *adj* favourable

favorecer [faβore'θer] *vt* to favour; (*vestido etc*) to become, flatter; **este peinado le favorece** this hairstyle suits him

favorito, -a [faβo'rito, a] *adj, nm/f* favourite

fax [faks] *nm inv* fax; **mandar por ~** to fax

fe [fe] *nf* (*Rel*) faith; (*documento*) certificate; **actuar con buena/mala ~** to act in good/bad faith

febrero [fe'βrero] *nm* February

fecha ['fetʃa] *nf* date; **con ~ adelantada** postdated; **en ~ próxima** soon; **hasta la ~** to date, so far; **poner ~** to date; **fecha de caducidad** (*de producto alimenticio*) sell-by date; (*de contrato etc*) expiry date; **fecha de nacimiento** date of birth; **fecha límite** *o* **tope** deadline

fecundo, -a [fe'kundo, a] *adj* (*fértil*) fertile; (*fig*) prolific; (*productivo*) productive

federación [feðera'θjon] *nf* federation

felicidad [feliθi'ðað] *nf* happiness; **¡~es!** (*deseos*) best wishes, congratulations!; (*en cumpleaños*) happy birthday!

felicitación [feliθita'θjon] *nf* (*tarjeta*) greeting(s) card

felicitar [feliθi'tar] *vt* to congratulate

feliz [fe'liθ] *adj* happy

felpudo [fel'puðo] *nm* doormat

femenino, -a [feme'nino, a] *adj, nm* feminine

feminista [femi'nista] *adj, nmf* feminist

fenómeno [fe'nomeno] *nm* phenomenon; (*fig*) freak, accident ▷ *adj* great ▷ *excl* great!; marvellous!

fenomenal *adj* **=fenómeno**

feo, -a ['feo, a] *adj* (*gen*) ugly; (*desagradable*) bad, nasty

féretro ['feretro] *nm* (*ataúd*) coffin; (*sarcófago*) bier

feria ['ferja] *nf* (*gen*) fair; (*descanso*) holiday, rest day; (*MÉX: cambio*) small *o* loose change; (*cs: mercado*) village market

feriado [fe'rjaðo] (*LAM*) *nm* holiday

fermentar [fermen'tar] *vi* to ferment

feroz [fe'roθ] *adj* (*cruel*) cruel; (*salvaje*) fierce

férreo, -a ['ferreo, a] *adj* iron

ferretería [ferrete'ria] *nf* (*tienda*) ironmonger's (shop) (*BRIT*), hardware store (*us*); **ferretero** [ferre'tero] *nm* ironmonger

ferrocarril [ferroka'rril] *nm* railway

ferroviario, -a [ferro'βjarjo, a] *adj* rail *cpd*

ferry ['ferri] (*pl* **~s** *o* **ferries**) *nm* ferry

fértil ['fertil] *adj* (*productivo*) fertile; (*rico*) rich; **fertilidad** *nf* (*gen*) fertility; (*productividad*) fruitfulness

fervor [fer'βor] *nm* fervour

festejar [feste'xar] *vt* (*celebrar*) to celebrate

festejo [fes'texo] *nm* celebration; **festejos** *nmpl* (*fiestas*) festivals

festín [fes'tin] *nm* feast, banquet

festival [festi'βal] *nm* festival

festividad [festiβi'ðað] *nf* festivity

festivo, -a [fes'tiβo, a] *adj* (*de fiesta*) festive; (*Cine, Literatura*) humorous; **día ~** holiday

feto ['feto] *nm* foetus

fiable ['fjaβle] *adj* (*persona*) trustworthy; (*máquina*) reliable

fiambre ['fjambre] *nm* cold meat

fiambrera [fjam'brera] *nf* (*para almuerzo*) lunch box

fianza ['fjanθa] *nf* surety;

(Jur): **libertad bajo ~** release on bail

fiar [fi'ar] vt (salir garante de) to guarantee; (vender a crédito) to sell on credit ▷ vi to trust; **fiarse** vr to trust (in), rely on; **~ a** (secreto) to confide (to); **~se de algn** to rely on sb

fibra ['fiβra] nf fibre; **fibra óptica** optical fibre

ficción [fik'θjon] nf fiction

ficha ['fitʃa] nf (Tel) token; (en juegos) counter, marker; (tarjeta) (index) card; **fichaje** nm (Deporte) signing; **fichar** vt (archivar) to file, index; (Deporte) to sign; **estar fichado** to have a record; **fichero** nm box file; (Inform) file

ficticio, -a [fik'tiθjo, a] adj (imaginario) fictitious; (falso) fabricated

fidelidad [fiðeli'ðað] nf (lealtad) fidelity, loyalty; **alta ~** high fidelity, hi-fi

fideos [fi'ðeos] nmpl noodles

fiebre ['fjeβre] nf (Med) fever; (fig) fever, excitement; **tener ~** to have a temperature; **fiebre aftosa** foot-and-mouth disease

fiel [fjel] adj (leal) faithful, loyal; (fiable) reliable; (exacto) accurate, faithful ▷ nm: **los ~es** the faithful

fieltro ['fjeltro] nm felt

fiera ['fjera] nf (animal feroz) wild animal o beast; (fig) dragon; V tb **fiero**

fiero, -a ['fjero, a] adj (cruel) cruel; (feroz) fierce; (duro) harsh

fierro ['fjerro] nm (LAM) (hierro) iron; (de pueblo)

fiesta ['fjesta] nf party; (de pueblo) festival; (vacaciones: tb: **~s**) holiday sg; **fiesta mayor** annual festival; **fiesta patria** (LAM) independence day

FIESTAS

Fiestas can be official public holidays or holidays set by each autonomous region, many of which coincide with religious festivals. There are also many **fiestas** all over Spain for a local patron saint or the Virgin Mary.

These often last several days and can include religious processions, carnival parades, bullfights and dancing.

figura [fi'ɣura] nf (gen) figure; (forma, imagen) shape, form; (Naipes) face card

figurar [fixu'rar] vt (representar) to represent; (fingir) to figure ▷ vi to figure; **figurarse** vr (imaginarse) to imagine; (suponer) to suppose

fijador [fixa'ðor] nm (Foto etc) fixative; (de pelo) gel

fijar [fi'xar] vt (gen) to fix; (estampilla) to affix, stick (on); **fijarse** vr: **~se en** to notice

fijo, -a ['fixo, a] adj (gen) fixed; (firme) firm; (permanente) permanent ▷ adv: **mirar ~** to stare

fila ['fila] nf row; (Mil) rank; **ponerse en ~** to line up, get into line; **fila india** single file

filatelia [fila'telja] nf philately, stamp collecting

filete [fi'lete] nm (de carne) fillet steak; (de pescado) fillet

filiación [filja'θjon] nf (Pol) affiliation

filial [fi'ljal] adj filial ▷ nf subsidiary

Filipinas [fili'pinas] nfpl: **las (Islas) ~** the Philippines; **filipino, -a** adj, nm/f Philippine

filmar [fil'mar] vt to film, shoot

filo ['filo] nm (gen) edge; **sacar ~ a** to sharpen; **al ~ del mediodía** at midday; **de doble ~** double-edged

filología [filolo'xia] nf philology; **filología inglesa** (Univ) English Studies

filón [fi'lon] nm (Minería) vein, lode; (fig) goldmine

filosofía [filoso'fia] nf philosophy; **filósofo, -a** nm/f philosopher

filtrar [fil'trar] vt, vi to filter, strain; **filtrarse** vr to filter; **filtro** nm (Tec, utensilio) filter

fin [fin] nm (remate) end; (objetivo) aim, purpose; **al ~ y al cabo** when all's said and done; **a ~ de** in order to; **por ~**

finally; **en ~** in short; **fin de semana** weekend

final [fi'nal] *adj* final ▷ *nm* end, conclusion ▷ *nf* final; **al ~** in the end; **a ~es de** at the end of; **finalidad** *nf* (*propósito*) purpose, intention; **finalista** *nmf* finalist; **finalizar** *vt* to end, finish; (*Inform*) to log out o off ▷ *vi* to end, come to an end

financiar [finan'θjar] *vt* to finance; **financiero, -a** *adj* financial ▷ *nm/f* financier

finca ['finka] *nf* (*casa de campo*) country house; (*ESP: bien inmueble*) property, land; (*LAM: granja*) farm

finde ['finde] *nm abr* (*fam: fin de semana*) weekend

fingir [fin'xir] *vt* (*simular*) to simulate, feign ▷ *vi* (*aparentar*) to pretend

finlandés, -esa [finlan'des, esa] *adj* Finnish ▷ *nm/f* Finn ▷ *nm* (*Ling*) Finnish

Finlandia [fin'landja] *nf* Finland

fino, -a ['fino, a] *adj* fine; (*delgado*) slender; (*de buenas maneras*) polite, refined; (*jerez*) fino, dry

firma ['firma] *nf* signature; (*Com*) firm, company

firmamento [firma'mento] *nm* firmament

firmar [fir'mar] *vt* to sign

firme ['firme] *adj* firm; (*estable*) stable; (*sólido*) solid; (*constante*) steady; (*decidido*) resolute ▷ *nm* road (surface); **firmeza** *nf* firmness; (*constancia*) steadiness; (*solidez*) solidity

fiscal [fis'kal] *adj* fiscal ▷ *nmf* public prosecutor; **año ~** tax o fiscal year

fisgonear [fisɣone'ar] *vt* to poke one's nose into ▷ *vi* to pry, spy

física ['fisika] *nf* physics *sg*; *V tb* **físico**

físico, -a ['fisiko, a] *adj* physical ▷ *nm* physique ▷ *nm/f* physicist

fisura [fi'sura] *nf* crack; (*Med*) fracture

flác(c)ido, -a ['fla(k)θiðo, a] *adj* flabby

flaco, -a ['flako, a] *adj* (*muy delgado*) skinny, thin; (*débil*) weak, feeble

flagrante [fla'ɣrante] *adj* flagrant

flama ['flama] (*MÉX*) *nf* flame; **flamable** (*MÉX*) *adj* flammable

flamante [fla'mante] (*fam*) *adj* brilliant; (*nuevo*) brand-new

flamenco, -a [fla'menko, a] *adj* (*de Flandes*) Flemish; (*baile, música*) flamenco ▷ *nm* (*baile, música*) flamenco; (*Zool*) flamingo

flamingo [fla'mingo] (*MÉX*) *nm* flamingo

flan [flan] *nm* creme caramel

▌ No confundir **flan** con la palabra inglesa *flan*.

flash [flaʃ] (*pl ~ o ~es*) *nm* (*Foto*) flash

flauta ['flauta] *nf* (*Mús*) flute

flecha ['fletʃa] *nf* arrow

flechazo [fle'tʃaθo] *nm* love at first sight

fleco ['fleko] *nm* fringe

flema ['flema] *nm* phlegm

flequillo [fle'kiʎo] *nm* (*pelo*) fringe

flexible [flek'siβle] *adj* flexible

flexión [flek'sjon] *nf* press-up

flexo ['flekso] *nm* adjustable table-lamp

flirtear [flirte'ar] *vi* to flirt

flojera [flo'xera] (*LAM: fam*) *nf*: **me da ~** I can't be bothered

flojo, -a ['floxo, a] *adj* (*gen*) loose; (*sin fuerzas*) limp; (*débil*) weak

flor [flor] *nf* flower; **a ~ de** on the surface of; **flora** *nf* flora; **florecer** *vi* (*Bot*) to flower, bloom; (*fig*) to flourish; **florería** (*LAM*) *nf* florist's (shop); **florero** *nm* vase; **floristería** *nf* florist's (shop)

flota ['flota] *nf* fleet

flotador [flota'ðor] *nm* (*gen*) float; (*para nadar*) rubber ring

flotar [flo'tar] *vi* (*gen*) to float; **flote** *nm*: **a flote** afloat; **salir a flote** (*fig*) to get back on one's feet

fluidez [flui'ðeθ] *nf* fluidity; (*fig*) fluency

fluido, -a ['fluiðo, a] *adj, nm* fluid

fluir [flu'ir] *vi* to flow

flujo ['fluxo] *nm* flow; **flujo y reflujo**

ebb and flow

flúor ['fluor] nm fluoride

fluorescente [flwores'θente] adj fluorescent ▷ nm fluorescent light

fluvial [fluβi'al] adj (navegación, cuenca) fluvial, river cpd

fobia ['foβja] nf phobia; **fobia a las alturas** fear of heights

foca ['foka] nf seal

foco ['foko] nm focus; (Elec) floodlight; (Méx: bombilla) (light) bulb

fofo, -a ['fofo, a] adj soft, spongy; (carnes) flabby

fogata [fo'ɣata] nf bonfire

fogón [fo'ɣon] nm (de cocina) ring, burner

folio ['foljo] nm folio, page

follaje [fo'ʎaxe] nm foliage

folleto [fo'ʎeto] nm (Pol) pamphlet

follón [fo'ʎon] (ESP: fam) nm (lío) mess; (conmoción) fuss; **armar un ~** to kick up a row

fomentar [fomen'tar] vt (Med) to foment

fonda ['fonda] nf inn

fondo ['fondo] nm (de mar) bottom; (de coche, sala) back; (Arte etc) background; (reserva) fund; **fondos** nmpl (Com) funds, resources; **una investigación a ~** a thorough investigation; **en el ~** at bottom, deep down

fonobuzón [fonoβu'θon] nm voice mail

fontanería [fontane'ria] nf plumbing; **fontanero, -a** nm/f plumber

footing ['futin] nm jogging; **hacer ~** to jog, go jogging

forastero, -a [foras'tero, a] nm/f stranger

forcejear [forθexe'ar] vi (luchar) to struggle

forense [fo'rense] nmf pathologist

forma ['forma] nf (figura) form, shape; (Med) fitness; (método) way, means; **las ~s** the conventions; **estar en ~** to be fit; **de ~ que ...** so that ...; **de**

todas ~s in any case

formación [forma'θjon] nf (gen) formation; (educación) education; **formación profesional** vocational training

formal [for'mal] adj (gen) formal; (fig: serio) serious; (: de fiar) reliable; **formalidad** nf formality; seriousness; **formalizar** vt (Jur) to formalize; (situación) to put in order, regularize; **formalizarse** vr (situación) to be put in order, be regularized

formar [for'mar] vt (componer) to form, shape; (constituir) to make up, constitute; (Escol) to train, educate; **formarse** vr (Escol) to be trained, educated; (cobrar forma) to form, take form; (desarrollarse) to develop

formatear [formate'ar] vt to format

formato [for'mato] nm format

formidable [formi'ðaβle] adj (temible) formidable; (estupendo) tremendous

fórmula ['formula] nf formula

formulario [formu'larjo] nm form

fornido, -a [for'niðo, a] adj well-built

foro ['foro] nm (Pol, Inform etc) forum

forrar [fo'rrar] vt (abrigo) to line; (libro) to cover; **forro** nm (de cuaderno) cover; (Costura) lining; (de sillón) upholstery; **forro polar** fleece

fortalecer [fortale'θer] vt to strengthen

fortaleza [forta'leθa] nf (Mil) fortress, stronghold; (fuerza) strength; (determinación) resolution

fortuito, -a [for'twito, a] adj accidental

fortuna [for'tuna] nf (suerte) fortune, (good) luck; (riqueza) fortune, wealth

forzar [for'θar] vt (puerta) to force (open); (compeler) to compel

forzoso, -a [for'θoso, a] adj necessary

fosa ['fosa] nf (sepultura) grave; (en tierra) pit; **fosas nasales** nostrils

fósforo ['fosforo] nm (Quím)

phosphorus; (cerilla) match

fósil ['fosil] nm fossil

foso ['foso] nm ditch; (Teatro) pit; (Auto) inspection pit

foto ['foto] nf photo, snap(shot); **sacar una ~** to take a photo o picture; **foto (de) carné** passport(-size) photo

fotocopia [foto'kopja] nf photocopy; **fotocopiadora** nf photocopier; **fotocopiar** vt to photocopy

fotografía [fotoɣra'fia] nf (Arte) photography; (una fotografía) photograph; **fotografiar** vt to photograph

fotógrafo, -a [fo'toɣrafo, a] nm/f photographer

fotomatón [fotoma'ton] nm photo booth

FP (ESP) nf abr (= Formación Profesional) vocational courses for 14- to 18-year-olds

fracasar [fraka'sar] vi (gen) to fail

fracaso [fra'kaso] nm failure

fracción [frak'θjon] nf fraction

fractura [frak'tura] nf fracture, break

fragancia [fra'ɣanθja] nf (olor) fragrance, perfume

frágil ['fraxil] adj (débil) fragile; (Com) breakable

fragmento [fraɣ'mento] nm (pedazo) fragment

fraile ['fraile] nm (Rel) friar; (: monje) monk

frambuesa [fram'bwesa] nf raspberry

francés, -esa [fran'θes, esa] adj French ▷ nm/f Frenchman(-woman) ▷ nm (Ling) French

Francia ['franθja] nf France

franco, -a ['franko, a] adj (cándido) frank, open; (Com: exento) free ▷ nm (moneda) franc

francotirador, a [frankotira'ðor, a] nm/f sniper

franela [fra'nela] nf flannel

franja ['franxa] nf fringe

franquear [franke'ar] vt (camino) to clear; (carta, paquete postal) to frank,

stamp; (obstáculo) to overcome

franqueo [fran'keo] nm postage

franqueza [fran'keθa] nf (candor) frankness

frasco ['frasko] nm bottle, flask

frase ['frase] nf sentence; **frase hecha** set phrase; (pey) stock phrase

fraterno, -a [fra'terno, a] adj brotherly, fraternal

fraude ['frauðe] nm (cualidad) dishonesty; (acto) fraud

frazada [fra'saða] (LAM) nf blanket

frecuencia [fre'kwenθja] nf frequency; **con ~** frequently, often

frecuentar [frekwen'tar] vt to frequent

frecuente [fre'kwente] adj (gen) frequent

fregadero [freɣa'ðero] nm (kitchen) sink

fregar [fre'ɣar] vt (frotar) to scrub; (platos) to wash (up); (LAM: fam: fastidiar) to annoy; (: malograr) to screw up

fregona [fre'ɣona] nf mop

freir [fre'ir] vt to fry

frenar [fre'nar] vt to brake; (fig) to check

frenazo [fre'naθo] nm: **dar un ~** to brake sharply

frenesí [frene'si] nm frenzy

freno ['freno] nm (Tec, Auto) brake; (de cabalgadura) bit; (fig) check; **freno de mano** handbrake

frente ['frente] nm (Arq, Pol) front; (de objeto) front part ▷ nf forehead, brow; **~ a** in front of; (en situación opuesta de) opposite; **al ~ de** (fig) at the head of; **chocar de ~** to crash head-on; **hacer ~ a** to face up to

fresa ['fresa] nf (ESP) strawberry

fresco, -a ['fresko, a] adj (nuevo) fresh; (frío) cool; (descarado) cheeky ▷ nm (aire) fresh air; (Arte) fresco; (LAM: jugo) fruit drink ▷ nm/f (fam: descaro) cheek, nerve: **ser un ~** to have a nerve; **tomar el ~** to get some fresh air; **frescura** nf freshness; (descaro) cheek, nerve

frialdad [frial'dað] nf (gen) coldness;

(*indiferencia*) indifference

frigidez [frixi'ðeθ] nf frigidity

frigo ['frixo] nm fridge

frigorífico [friɣo'rifiko] nm refrigerator

frijol [fri'xol] nm kidney bean

frío, -a etc ['frio, a] vb V **freír** ▷ adj cold; (*indiferente*) indifferent ▷ nm cold; (*indiferencia*) indifference; **hace ~** it's cold; **tener ~** to be cold

frito, -a ['frito, a] adj fried; **me trae ~ ese hombre** I'm sick and tired of that man; **fritos** nmpl fried food

frívolo, -a ['friβolo, a] adj frivolous

frontal [fron'tal] adj frontal; **choque ~** head-on collision

frontera [fron'tera] nf frontier; **fronterizo, -a** adj frontier cpd; (*contiguo*) bordering

frontón [fron'ton] nm (*Deporte: cancha*) pelota court; (*: juego*) pelota

frotar [fro'tar] vt to rub; **frotarse** vr: **~se las manos** to rub one's hands

fructífero, -a [fruk'tifero, a] adj fruitful

fruncir [frun'θir] vt to pucker; (*Costura*) to pleat; **~ el ceño** to knit one's brow

frustrar [frus'trar] vt to frustrate

fruta ['fruta] nf fruit; **frutería** nf fruit shop; **frutero, -a** adj fruit cpd ▷ nm/f fruiterer ▷ nm fruit bowl

frutilla [fru'tiʎa] (cs) nf strawberry

fruto ['fruto] nm fruit; (*fig: resultado*) result; (*: beneficio*) benefit; **frutos secos** nuts and dried fruit pl

fucsia ['fuksja] nf fuchsia

fue [fwe] vb V **ser; ir**

fuego ['fweɣo] nm (gen) fire; **a ~ lento** on a low heat; **¿tienes ~?** have you (got) a light?; **fuego amigo** friendly fire; **fuegos artificiales** fireworks

fuente ['fwente] nf fountain; (*manantial, fig*) spring; (*origen*) source; (*plato*) large dish

fuera ['fwera] vb V **ser; ir** ▷ adv out(side); (*en otra parte*) away; (*excepto, salvo*) except, save ▷ prep: **~ de** outside;

(*fig*) besides; **~ de sí** beside o.s.; **por ~** (on the) outside

fuera-borda [fwera'βorða] nm speedboat

fuerte ['fwerte] adj strong; (*golpe*) hard; (*ruido*) loud; (*comida*) rich; (*lluvia*) heavy; (*dolor*) intense ▷ adv strongly; hard; loud(ly); **ser ~ en** to be good at

fuerza etc ['fwerθa] vb V **forzar** ▷ nf (*fortaleza*) strength; (*Tec, Elec*) power; (*coacción*) force; (*Mil, Pol*) force; **a ~ de** by dint of; **cobrar ~s** to recover one's strength; **tener ~s para** to have the strength to; **a la ~** forcibly, by force; **por ~** of necessity; **fuerza de voluntad** willpower; **fuerzas aéreas** air force sg; **fuerzas armadas** armed forces

fuga ['fuɣa] nf (*huida*) flight, escape; (*de gases etc*) leak

fugarse [fu'ɣarse] vr to flee, escape

fugaz [fu'ɣaθ] adj fleeting

fugitivo, -a [fuxi'tiβo, a] adj, nm/f fugitive

fui [fwi] vb V **ser; ir**

fulano, -a [fu'lano, a] nm/f so-and-so, what's-his-name/what's-her-name

fulminante [fulmi'nante] adj (*fig: mirada*) fierce; (*Med: enfermedad, ataque*) sudden; (*fam: éxito, golpe*) sudden

fumador, a [fuma'ðor, a] nm/f smoker

fumar [fu'mar] vt, vi to smoke; **~ en pipa** to smoke a pipe

función [fun'θjon] nf function; (*en trabajo*) duties pl; (*espectáculo*) show; **entrar en funciones** to take up one's duties

funcionar [funθjo'nar] vi (gen) to function; (*máquina*) to work; **"no funciona"** "out of order"

funcionario, -a [funθjo'narjo, a] nm/f civil servant

funda ['funda] nf (gen) cover; (*de almohada*) pillowcase

fundación [funda'θjon] nf foundation

fundamental [fundamen'tal] adj

fundamental, basic
fundamento [funda'mento] *nm*
(*base*) foundation
fundar [fun'dar] *vt* to found;
fundarse *vr*: **~se en** to be founded on
fundición [fundiθ'θjon] *nf* fusing;
(*fábrica*) foundry
fundir [fun'dir] *vt* (*gen*) to fuse;
(*metal*) to smelt, melt down; (*nieve
etc*) to melt; (*Com*) to merge; (*estatua*)
to cast; **fundirse** *vr* (*colores etc*) to
merge, blend; (*unirse*) to fuse together;
(*Elec*: *fusible, lámpara etc*) to fuse, blow;
(*nieve etc*) to melt
fúnebre ['funeβre] *adj* funeral *cpd*,
funereal
funeral [fune'ral] *nm* funeral;
funeraria *nf* undertaker's
funicular [funiku'lar] *nm* (*tren*)
funicular; (*teleférico*) cable car
furgón [fur'ɣon] *nm* wagon;
furgoneta *nf* (*Auto, Com*) (transit) van
(BRIT), pick-up (truck) (US)
furia ['furja] *nf* (*ira*) fury; (*violencia*)
violence; **furioso, -a** *adj* (*iracundo*)
furious; (*violento*) violent
furtivo, -a [fur'tiβo, a] *adj* furtive
▷ *nm* poacher
fusible [fu'siβle] *nm* fuse
fusil [fu'sil] *nm* rifle; **fusilar** *vt* to
shoot
fusión [fu'sjon] *nf* (*gen*) melting;
(*unión*) fusion; (*Com*) merger
fútbol ['futβol] *nm* football (BRIT),
soccer (US); **fútbol americano**
American football (BRIT), football
(US); **fútbol sala** indoor football (BRIT)
o soccer (US); **futbolín** *nm* table
football; **futbolista** *nmf* footballer
futuro, -a [fu'turo, a] *adj, nm* future

g

gabardina [gaβar'ðina] *nf* raincoat,
gabardine
gabinete [gaβi'nete] *nm* (*Pol*)
cabinet; (*estudio*) study; (*de abogados
etc*) office
gachas ['gatʃas] *nfpl* porridge *sg*
gafas ['gafas] *nfpl* glasses; **gafas de
sol** sunglasses
gafe ['gafe] (*ESP*) *nmf* jinx
gaita ['gaita] *nf* bagpipes *pl*
gajes ['gaxes] *nmpl*: **~ del oficio**
occupational hazards
gajo ['gaxo] *nm* (*de naranja*) segment
gala ['gala] *nf* (*traje de etiqueta*) full
dress; **galas** *nfpl* (*ropa*) finery *sg*; **estar
de ~** to be in one's best clothes; **hacer
~ de** to display
galápago [ga'lapaxo] *nm* (*Zool*)
turtle
galardón [galar'ðon] *nm* award,
prize
galaxia [ga'laksja] *nf* galaxy
galera [ga'lera] *nf* (*nave*) galley; (*carro*)
wagon; (*Imprenta*) galley
galería [gale'ria] *nf* (*gen*) gallery;

(balcón) veranda(h); (pasillo) corridor; **galería comercial** shopping mall

Gales ['ɣales] nm (tb: **País de ~**) Wales; **galés, -esa** adj Welsh ▷ nm/f Welshman(-woman) ▷ nm (Ling) Welsh

galgo, -a ['ɣalɣo, a] nm/f greyhound

gallego, -a [ɣa'ʎeɣo, a] adj, nm/f Galician

galleta [ɣa'ʎeta] nf biscuit (BRIT), cookie (US)

gallina [ɣa'ʎina] nf hen ▷ nmf (fam: cobarde) chicken; **gallinero** nm henhouse; (Teatro) top gallery

gallo [ɣa'ʎo] nm cock, rooster

galopar [ɣalo'par] vi to gallop

gama ['ɣama] nf (fig) range

gamba ['ɣamba] nf prawn (BRIT), shrimp (US)

gamberro, -a [ɣam'berro, a] (ESP) nm/f hooligan, lout

gamuza [ɣa'muθa] nf chamois

gana ['ɣana] nf (deseo) desire, wish; (apetito) appetite; (voluntad) will; (añoranza) longing; **de buena ~** willingly; **de mala ~** reluctantly; **me da ~s de** I feel like, I want to; **no me da la ~** I don't feel like it; **tener ~s de** to feel like

ganadería [ɣanaðe'ria] nf (ganado) livestock; (ganado vacuno) cattle pl; (cría, comercio) cattle raising

ganadero, -a [ɣana'ðero, a] (ESP) nm/f (hacendado) rancher

ganado [ɣa'naðo] nm livestock; **ganado porcino** pigs pl

ganador, a [ɣana'ðor, a] adj winning ▷ nm/f winner

ganancia [ɣa'nanθja] nf (lo ganado) gain; (aumento) increase; (beneficio) profit; **ganancias** nfpl (ingresos) earnings; (beneficios) profit sg, winnings

ganar [ɣa'nar] vt (obtener) to get, obtain; (sacar ventaja) to gain; (salario etc) to earn; (Deporte, premio) to win; (derrotar a) to beat; (alcanzar) to reach ▷ vi (Deporte) to win; **ganarse** vr: **~se**

la vida to earn one's living

ganchillo [ɣan't̮ʃiʎo] nm crochet

gancho ['ɣant̮ʃo] nm (gen) hook; (colgador) hanger

gandul, a [ɣan'dul, a] adj, nm/f good-for-nothing, layabout

ganga ['ɣanga] nf bargain

gangrena [ɣan'grena] nf gangrene

ganso, -a ['ɣanso, a] nm/f (Zool) goose; (fam) idiot

ganzúa [ɣan'θua] nf skeleton key

garabato [ɣara'βato] nm (escritura) scrawl, scribble

garaje [ɣa'raxe] nm garage; **garajista** [ɣara'xista] nmf mechanic

garantía [ɣaran'tia] nf guarantee

garantizar [ɣaranti'θar] vt to guarantee

garbanzo [ɣar'βanθo] nm chickpea (BRIT), garbanzo (US)

garfio ['ɣarfjo] nm grappling iron

garganta [ɣar'ɣanta] nf (Anat) throat; (de botella) neck; **gargantilla** nf necklace

gárgaras ['ɣarɣaras] nfpl: **hacer ~** to gargle

gargarear [ɣarxare'ar] (LAM) vi to gargle

garita [ɣa'rita] nf cabin, hut; (Mil) sentry box

garra ['ɣarra] nf (de gato, Tec) claw; (de ave) talon; (fam: mano) hand, paw

garrafa [ɣa'rrafa] nf carafe, decanter

garrapata [ɣarra'pata] nf tick

gas [ɣas] nm gas; **gases lacrimógenos** tear gas sg

gasa ['ɣasa] nf gauze

gaseosa [ɣase'osa] nf lemonade

gaseoso, -a [ɣase'oso, a] adj gassy, fizzy

gasoil [ɣa'soil] nm diesel (oil)

gasóleo [ɣa'soleo] nm = **gasoil**

gasolina [ɣaso'lina] nf petrol (BRIT), gas(oline) (US); **gasolinera** nf petrol (BRIT) o gas (US) station

gastado, -a [ɣas'taðo, a] adj (dinero) spent; (ropa) worn out; (usado: frase etc) trite

gastar [gas'tar] vt (dinero, tiempo) to spend; (fuerzas) to use up; (desperdiciar) to waste; (llevar) to wear; **gastarse** vr to wear out; (estropearse) to wear out; ~ **en** to spend on; ~ **bromas** to crack jokes; **¿qué número gastas?** what size (shoe) do you take?

gasto ['gasto] nm (desembolso) expenditure, spending; (consumo, uso) use; **gastos** nmpl (desembolsos) expenses; (cargos) charges, costs

gastronomía [gastrono'mia] nf gastronomy

gatear [gate'ar] vi (andar a gatas) to go on all fours

gatillo [ga'tiʎo] nm (de arma de fuego) trigger; (de dentista) forceps

gato, -a ['gato, a] nm/f cat ▷ nm (Tec) jack; **andar a gatas** to go on all fours

gaucho ['gautʃo] nm gaucho

○ GAUCHO
○
○ **Gauchos** are the herdsmen or
○ riders of the Southern Cone plains.
○ Although popularly associated
○ with Argentine folklore, **gauchos**
○ belong equally to the cattle-
○ raising areas of Southern Brazil
○ and Uruguay. **Gauchos'** traditions
○ and clothing reflect their mixed
○ ancestry and cultural roots. Their
○ baggy trousers are Arabic in
○ origin, while the horse and guitar
○ are inherited from the Spanish
○ conquistadors; the poncho, maté
○ and **boleadoras** (strips of leather
○ weighted at either end with
○ stones) form part of the Indian
○ tradition.

gaviota [ga'βjota] nf seagull
gay [ge] adj inv, nm gay, homosexual
gazpacho [gaθ'patʃo] nm gazpacho
gel [xel] nm: ~ **de baño/ducha** bath/shower gel
gelatina [xela'tina] nf jelly; (polvos etc) gelatine

gema ['xema] nf gem
gemelo, -a [xe'melo, a] adj, nm/f twin; **gemelos** nmpl (de camisa) cufflinks; (prismáticos) field glasses, binoculars

gemido [xe'miðo] nm (quejido) moan, groan; (aullido) howl

Géminis ['xeminis] nm Gemini

gemir [xe'mir] vi (quejarse) to moan, groan; (aullar) to howl

generación [xenera'θjon] nf generation

general [xene'ral] adj general ▷ nm general; **por lo** o **en** ~ in general; **Generalitat** nf Catalan parliament; **generalizar** vt to generalize; **generalizarse** vr to become generalized, spread

generar [xene'rar] vt to generate

género ['xenero] nm (clase) kind, sort; (tipo) type; (Bio) genus; (Ling) gender; (Com) material; **género humano** human race

generosidad [xenerosi'ðað] nf generosity; **generoso, -a** adj generous

genial [xe'njal] adj inspired; (idea) brilliant; (estupendo) wonderful

genio ['xenjo] nm (carácter) nature, disposition; (humor) temper; (facultad creadora) genius; **de mal** ~ bad-tempered

genital [xeni'tal] adj genital; **genitales** nmpl genitals

genoma [xe'noma] nm genome

gente ['xente] nf (personas) people pl; (parientes) relatives pl

gentil [xen'til] adj (elegante) graceful; (encantador) charming
 No confundir **gentil** con la palabra inglesa *gentle*.

genuino, -a [xe'nwino, a] adj genuine

geografía [xeoɤra'fia] nf geography
geología [xeolo'xia] nf geology
geometría [xeome'tria] nf geometry
gerente [xe'rente] nmf (supervisor)

manager; (*jefe*) director

geriatría [xeria'tria] nf (*Med*)
geriatrics sg

germen ['xermen] nm germ

gesticular [xestiku'lar] vi to
gesticulate; (*hacer muecas*) to grimace;
gesticulación nf gesticulation;
(*mueca*) grimace

gestión [xes'tjon] nf management;
(*diligencia, acción*) negotiation

gesto ['xesto] nm (*mueca*) grimace;
(*ademán*) gesture

Gibraltar [xiβral'tar] nm Gibraltar;
gibraltareño, -a adj, nm/f
Gibraltarian

gigante [xi'ɣante] adj, nmf giant;
gigantesco, -a adj gigantic

gilipollas [xili'poʎas] (*fam*) adj inv
daft ▷ nmf inv wally

gimnasia [xim'nasja] nf gymnastics
pl; **gimnasio** nm gymnasium;
gimnasta nmf gymnast; **gimnástica**
[xim'nastika] nf inv gymnastics sg

ginebra [xi'neβra] nf gin

ginecólogo, -a [xine'koloɣo, a]
nm/f gynaecologist

gira ['xira] nf tour, trip

girar [xi'rar] vt (*dar la vuelta*) to
turn (around); (: *rápidamente*) to spin;
(*Com: giro postal*) to draw; (: *letra de
cambio*) to issue ▷ vi to turn (round);
(*rápido*) to spin

girasol [xira'sol] nm sunflower

giratorio, -a [xira'torjo, a] adj
revolving

giro ['xiro] nm (*movimiento*) turn,
revolution; (*Ling*) expression; (*Com*)
draft; **giro bancario/postal** bank
draft/money order

gis [xis] (*MÉX*) nm chalk

gitano, -a [xi'tano, a] adj, nm/f
gypsy

glacial [gla'θjal] adj icy, freezing

glaciar [gla'θjar] nm glacier

glándula ['glandula] nf gland

global [glo'βal] adj global;
globalización nf globalization

globo ['gloβo] nm (*esfera*) globe,

sphere; (*aerostato, juguete*) balloon

glóbulo ['gloβulo] nm globule; (*Anat*)
corpuscle

gloria ['glorja] nf glory

glorieta [glo'rjeta] nf (*de jardín*)
bower, arbour; (*plazoleta*) roundabout
(*BRIT*), traffic circle (*US*)

glorioso, -a [glo'rjoso, a] adj
glorious

glotón, -ona [glo'ton, ona] adj
gluttonous, greedy ▷ nm/f glutton

glucosa [glu'kosa] nf glucose

gobernador, a [goβerna'ðor, a]
adj governing ▷ nm/f governor;
gobernante adj governing

gobernar [goβer'nar] vt (*dirigir*) to
guide, direct; (*Pol*) to rule, govern ▷ vi
to govern; (*Náut*) to steer

gobierno etc [go'βjerno] vb V
gobernar ▷ nm (*Pol*) government;
(*dirección*) guidance, direction; (*Náut*)
steering

goce etc ['goθe] vb V **gozar** ▷ nm
enjoyment

gol [gol] nm goal

golf [golf] nm golf

golfa ['golfa] (*fam!*) nf (*mujer*) slut,
whore

golfo ['golfo, a] nm (*Geo*) gulf
▷ nm/f (*fam: niño*) urchin; (*gamberro*)
lout

golondrina [golon'drina] nf
swallow

golosina [golo'sina] nf (*dulce*) sweet;
goloso, -a adj sweet-toothed

golpe ['golpe] nm blow; (*de puño*)
punch; (*de mano*) smack; (*de remo*)
stroke; (*fig: choque*) clash; **no dar~** to
be bone idle; **de un~** with one blow;
de~ suddenly; **golpe (de estado)** coup
(d'état); **golpear** vt, vi to strike, knock;
(*asestar*) to beat; (*de puño*) to punch;
(*golpetear*) to tap

goma ['goma] nf (*caucho*) rubber;
(*elástico*) elastic; (*una goma*) elastic
band; **goma de borrar** eraser, rubber
(*BRIT*); **goma espuma** foam rubber

gomina [go'mina] nf hair gel

gomita [go'mita] (RPL) nf rubber band

gordo, -a ['gorðo, a] adj (gen) fat; (fam) enormous; **el (premio) ~** (en lotería) first prize

gorila [go'rila] nm gorilla

gorra ['gorra] nf cap; (de bebé) bonnet; (militar) bearskin; **entrar de ~** (fam) to gatecrash; **ir de ~** to sponge

gorrión [go'rrjon] nm sparrow

gorro ['gorro] nm (gen) cap; (de bebé, mujer) bonnet

gorrón, -ona [go'rron, ona] nm/f scrounger; **gorronear** (fam) vi to scrounge

gota ['gota] nf (gen) drop; (de sudor) bead; (Med) gout; **gotear** vi to drip; (lloviznar) to drizzle; (gotera) nf leak

gozar [go'θar] vi to enjoy o.s.; **~ de** (disfrutar) to enjoy; (poseer) to possess

gr. abr (= gramo, gramos) g

grabación [graβa'θjon] nf recording

grabado [gra'βaðo] nm print, engraving

grabadora [graβa'ðora] nf tape-recorder; **grabadora de CD/DVD** CD/DVD writer

grabar [gra'βar] vt to engrave; (discos, cintas) to record

gracia ['graθja] nf (encanto) grace, gracefulness; (humor) humour, wit; **¡(muchas) ~s!** thanks (very much!); **~s a** thanks to; **dar las ~s a algn por algo** to thank sb for sth; **tener ~** (chiste etc) to be funny; **no me hace ~** I am not keen; **gracioso, -a** adj (divertido) funny, amusing; (cómico) comical ▷ nm/f (Teatro) comic character

grada ['graða] nf (de escalera) step; (de anfiteatro) tier, row; **gradas** nfpl (Deporte: de estadio) terraces

grado ['graðo] nm degree; (de aceite, vino) grade; (grada) step; (Mil) rank; **de buen ~** willingly; **grado centígrado/Fahrenheit** degree centigrade/Fahrenheit

graduación [graðwa'θjon] nf (del alcohol) proof, strength; (Escol)

graduation; (Mil) rank

gradual [gra'ðwal] adj gradual

graduar [gra'ðwar] vt (gen) to graduate; (Mil) to commission; **graduarse** vr to graduate; **~se la vista** to have one's eyes tested

gráfica ['grafika] nf graph

gráfico, -a ['grafiko, a] adj graphic ▷ nm diagram; **gráficos** nmpl (Inform) graphics

grajo ['graxo] nm rook

gramática [gra'matika] nf grammar

gramo ['gramo] nm gramme (BRIT), gram (US)

gran [gran] adj V **grande**

grana ['grana] nf (color, tela) scarlet

granada [gra'naða] nf pomegranate; (Mil) grenade

granate [gra'nate] adj deep red

Gran Bretaña [gran bre'taɲa] nf Great Britain

grande ['grande] (antes de nmsg **gran**) adj (de tamaño) big, large; (alto) tall; (distinguido) great; (impresionante) grand ▷ nm grandee

granel [gra'nel]: **a ~** adv (Com) in bulk

granero [gra'nero] nm granary, barn

granito [gra'nito] nm (Agr) small grain; (roca) granite

granizado [grani'θaðo] nm iced drink

granizar [grani'θar] vi to hail; **granizo** nm hail

granja ['granxa] nf (gen) farm; **granjero, -a** nm/f farmer

grano ['grano] nm grain; (semilla) seed; (de café) bean; (Med) pimple, spot

granuja [gra'nuxa] nmf rogue; (golfillo) urchin

grapa ['grapa] nf staple; (Tec) clamp; **grapadora** nf stapler

grasa ['grasa] nf (gen) grease; (de cocinar) fat, lard; (sebo) suet; (mugre) filth; **grasiento, -a** adj (de aceite) oily; **graso, -a** adj (leche, queso, carne) fatty; (pelo, piel) greasy

gratinar [grati'nar] vt to cook au gratin

gratis ['gratis] adv free

grato, -a ['grato, a] adj (agradable) pleasant, agreeable

gratuito, -a [gra'twito, a] adj (gratis) free; (sin razón) gratuitous

grave ['graβe] adj heavy; (serio) grave, serious; **gravedad** nf gravity

Grecia ['greθja] nf Greece

gremio ['gremjo] nm trade, industry

griego, -a ['grjeɣo, a] adj, nm/f Greek

grieta ['grjeta] nf crack

grifo ['grifo] (ESP) nm tap (BRIT), faucet (US)

grillo ['griʎo] nm (Zool) cricket

gripa ['gripa] (MÉX) nf flu, influenza

gripe ['gripe] nf flu, influenza; **gripe aviar** bird flu

gris [gris] adj (color) grey

gritar [gri'tar] vt, vi to shout, yell; **grito** nm shout, yell; (de horror) scream

grosella [gro'seʎa] nf (red)currant

grosero, -a [gro'sero, a] adj (poco cortés) rude, bad-mannered; (ordinario) vulgar, crude

grosor [gro'sor] nm thickness

grúa ['grua] nf (Tec) crane; (de petróleo) derrick

grueso, -a ['grweso, a] adj thick; (persona) stout ▷ nm bulk; **el ~ de** the bulk of

grulla ['gruʎa] nf crane

grumo ['grumo] nm clot, lump

gruñido [gru'ɲiðo] nm grunt; (de persona) grumble

gruñir [gru'ɲir] vi (animal) to growl; (persona) to grumble

grupo ['grupo] nm group; (Tec) unit, set; **grupo de presión** pressure group; **grupo sanguíneo** blood group

gruta ['gruta] nf grotto

guacho, -a ['gwatʃo, a] (cs) nm/f homeless child

guajolote [gwaxo'lote] (MÉX) nm turkey

guante ['gwante] nm glove; **guantes de goma** rubber gloves; **guantera** nf glove compartment

guapo, -a ['gwapo, a] adj good-looking, attractive; (elegante) smart

guarda ['gwarða] nm/f (persona) guard, keeper ▷ nf (acto) guarding; (custodia) custody; **guarda jurado** (armed) security guard; **guardabarros** nm inv mudguard (BRIT), fender (US); **guardabosques** nm inv gamekeeper; **guardacostas** nm inv coastguard vessel ▷ nm/f guardian, protector; **guardaespaldas** nm/f inv bodyguard; **guardameta** nm goalkeeper; **guardar** vt (gen) to keep; (vigilar) to guard, watch over; (dinero: ahorrar) to save; **guardarse** vr (preservarse) to protect o.s.; (evitar) to avoid; **guardar cama** to stay in bed; **guardarropa** (armario) wardrobe; (en establecimiento público) cloakroom

guardería [gwarðe'ria] nf nursery

guardia ['gwarðja] nf (Mil) guard; (cuidado) care, custody ▷ nm/f guard; (policía) policeman(-woman); **estar de ~** to be on guard; **montar ~** to mount guard; **Guardia Civil** Civil Guard

guardián, -ana [gwar'ðjan, ana] nm/f (gen) guardian, keeper

guarida [gwa'riða] nf (de animal) den, lair; (refugio) refuge

guarnición [gwarni'θjon] nf (de vestimenta) trimming; (de piedra) mount; (Culin) garnish; (arneses) harness; (Mil) garrison

guarro, -a ['gwarro, a] nm/f pig

guasa ['gwasa] nf joke; **guasón, -ona** adj (bromista) joking ▷ nm/f wit; joker

Guatemala [gwate'mala] nf Guatemala

guay [gwai] (fam) adj super, great

güero, -a ['gwero, a] (MÉX) adj blond(e)

guerra ['gerra] nf war; **dar ~** to annoy; **guerra civil** civil war; **guerra fría** cold war; **guerrero, -a** adj fighting; (carácter) warlike ▷ nm/f warrior

guerrilla [ge'rriʎa] nf guerrilla warfare; (tropas) guerrilla band o group

guía etc ['gia] vb V **guiar** ▷ nm/f

(persona) guide; (nf: libro) guidebook;
guía telefónica telephone directory;
guía turística tourist guide

guiar [gi'ar] vt to guide, direct; (Auto)
to steer; **guiarse** vr: **~se por** to be
guided by

guinda ['ginda] nf morello cherry

guindilla [gin'diʎa] nf chilli pepper

guiñar [gi'nar] vt to wink

guión [gi'on] nm (Ling) hyphen,
dash; (Cine) script; **guionista** nmf
scriptwriter

guiri ['giri] (ESP: fam, pey) nmf
foreigner

guirnalda [gir'nalda] nf garland

guisado [gi'saðo] nm stew

guisante [gi'sante] nm pea

guisar [gi'sar] vt, vi to cook; **guiso**
nm cooked dish

guitarra [gi'tarra] nf guitar

gula ['gula] nf gluttony, greed

gusano [gu'sano] nm worm; (lombriz)
earthworm

gustar [gus'tar] vt to taste, sample
▷ vi to please, be pleasing; **~ de algo** to
like o enjoy sth; **me gustan las uvas** I
like grapes; **le gusta nadar** she likes o
enjoys swimming

gusto ['gusto] nm (sentido, sabor)
taste; (placer) pleasure; **tiene ~ a
menta** it tastes of mint; **tener buen
~** to have good taste; **coger el o
tomar ~ a algo** to take a liking to sth;
sentirse a ~ to feel at ease; **mucho ~
(en conocerle)** pleased to meet you;
el ~ es mío the pleasure is mine; **con ~**
willingly, gladly

h

ha vb V **haber**

haba ['aβa] nf bean

Habana [a'βana] nf: **la ~** Havana

habano [a'βano] nm Havana cigar

habéis vb V **haber**

○ PALABRA CLAVE

haber [a'βer] vb aux **1** (tiempos
compuestos) to have; **había comido** I
had eaten; **antes/después de haberlo
visto** before seeing/after seeing o
having seen it

2: **¡haberlo dicho antes!** you should
have said so before!

3: **haber de: he de hacerlo** I have to
do it; **ha de llegar mañana** it should
arrive tomorrow

▷ vb impers **1** (existencia: sg) there is;
(: pl) there are; **hay un hermano/dos
hermanos** there is one brother/there
are two brothers; **¿cuánto hay de
aquí a Sucre?** how far is it from here
to Sucre?

2 (obligación): **hay que hacer algo**

something must be done; **hay que apuntarlo para acordarse** you have to write it down to remember

7: **¡hay que ver!** well I never!

4: **¡no hay de o por** (LAM) **qué!** don't mention it!, not at all!

5: **¿qué hay?** (¿qué pasa?) what's up?, what's the matter?; (¿qué tal?) how's it going?

▷ vt: **he aquí unas sugerencias** here are some suggestions; **no hay cintas blancas pero sí las hay rojas** there aren't any white ribbons but there are some red ones

▷ *nm* (en cuenta) credit side; **haberes** *nmpl* assets; **¿cuánto tengo en el haber?** how much do I have in my account?; **tiene varias novelas en su haber** he has several novels to his credit

haberse *vr*: **habérselas con algn** to have it out with sb

habichuela [aβi'tʃwela] *nf* kidney bean

hábil ['aβil] *adj* (listo) clever, smart; (capaz) fit, capable; (experto) expert; **día ~** working day; **habilidad** *nf* skill, ability

habitación [aβita'θjon] *nf* (cuarto) room; (Bio: morada) habitat; **habitación doble** o **de matrimonio** double room; **habitación individual** o **sencilla** single room

habitante [aβi'tante] *nmf* inhabitant

habitar [aβi'tar] *vt* (residir en) to inhabit; (ocupar) to occupy ▷ *vi* to live

hábito ['aβito] *nm* habit

habitual [aβi'twal] *adj* usual

habituar [aβi'twar] *vt* to accustom; **habituarse** vr: **~se a** to get used to

habla ['aβla] *nf* (capacidad de hablar) speech; (idioma) language; (dialecto) dialect; **perder el ~** to become speechless; **de ~ francesa** French-speaking; **estar al ~** to be in contact; (Tel) to be on the line; **¡González al ~!** (Tel) González speaking!

hablador, a [aβla'ðor, a] *adj*

talkative ▷ *nm/f* chatterbox

habladuría [aβlaðu'ria] *nf* rumour; **habladurías** *nfpl* gossip *sg*

hablante [a'βlante] *adj* speaking ▷ *nmf* speaker

hablar [a'βlar] *vt* to speak, talk ▷ *vi* to speak; **hablarse** *vr* to speak to each other; **~ con** to speak to; **~ de** to speak of o about; **¡ni ~!** it's out of the question!; **"se habla inglés"** "English spoken here"

habré *etc* [a'βre] *vb* V **haber**

hacendado [aθen'daðo] (LAM) *nm* rancher, farmer

hacendoso, -a [aθen'doso, a] *adj* industrious

🔘 **PALABRA CLAVE**

hacer [a'θer] *vt* **1** (fabricar, producir) to make; (construir) to build; **hacer una película/un ruido** to make a film/noise; **el guisado lo hice yo** I made o cooked the stew

2 (ejecutar: trabajo etc) to do; **hacer la colada** to do the washing; **hacer la comida** to do the cooking; **¿qué haces?** what are you doing?; **hacer el malo** o **el papel del malo** (Teatro) to play the villain

3 (estudios, algunos deportes) to do; **hacer español/económicas** to do o study Spanish/economics; **hacer yoga/gimnasia** to do yoga/go to gym

4 (transformar, incidir en): **esto lo hará más difícil** this will make it more difficult; **salir te hará sentir mejor** going out will make you feel better

5 (cálculo): **2 y 2 hacen 4** 2 and 2 make 4; **éste hace 100** this one makes 100

6 (+ sub): **esto hará que ganemos** this will make us win; **harás que no quiera venir** you'll stop him wanting to come

7 (como quitado de vb) to do; **él bebió y yo hice lo mismo** he drank and I did likewise

8 no hace más que criticar all he does is criticize

▷ vb semi-aux (directo): **hacer +infin: les hice venir** I made o had them come; **hacer trabajar a los demás** to get others to work

▷ vi 1 **haz como que no lo sabes** act as if you don't know

2 (ser apropiado): **si os hace** if it's alright with you

3 **hacer de: hacer de Otelo** to play Othello

▷ vb impers 1 **hace calor/frío** it's hot/cold; V tb **bueno, sol, tiempo**

2 (tiempo): **hace 3 años** 3 years ago; **hace un mes que voy/no voy** I've been going/I haven't been for a month

3 **¿cómo has hecho para llegar tan rápido?** how did you manage to get here so quickly?

hacerse vr 1 (volverse) to become; **se hicieron amigos** they became friends

2 (acostumbrarse): **hacerse a** to get used to

3 **se hace con huevos y leche** it's made out of eggs and milk; **eso no se hace** that's not done

4 (obtener): **hacerse de** o **con algo** to get hold of sth

5 (fingirse): **hacerse el sueco** to turn a deaf ear

hacha ['atʃa] nf axe; (antorcha) torch
hachís [a'tʃis] nm hashish
hacia ['aθja] prep (en dirección de) towards; (cerca de) near; (actitud) towards; **~ adelante/atrás** forwards/backwards; **~ arriba/abajo** up(wards)/down(wards); **~ mediodía/las cinco** about noon/five
hacienda [a'θjenda] nf (propiedad) property; (finca) farm; (LAM: rancho) ranch; **(Ministerio de) H~** Exchequer (BRIT), Treasury Department (US); **hacienda pública** public finance
hada ['aða] nf fairy
hago etc vb V **hacer**
Haití [ai'ti] nm Haiti
halagar [ala'ɣar] vt to flatter
halago [a'laɣo] nm flattery

halcón [al'kon] nm falcon, hawk
hallar [a'ʎar] vt (gen) to find; (descubrir) to discover; (toparse con) to run into; **hallarse** vr to be (situated)
halterofilia [altero'filja] nf weightlifting
hamaca [a'maka] nf hammock
hambre ['ambre] nf hunger; (plaga) famine; (deseo) longing; **tener ~** to be hungry; **¡me muero de ~!** I'm starving!; **hambriento, -a** adj hungry, starving
hamburguesa [ambur'ɣesa] nf hamburger; **hamburguesería** nf burger bar
hámster ['amster] nm hamster
han vb V **haber**
harapos [a'rapos] nmpl rags
haré vb V **hacer**
harina [a'rina] nf flour; **harina de maíz** cornflour (BRIT), cornstarch (US); **harina de trigo** wheat flour
hartar [ar'tar] vt to satiate, glut; (fig) to tire, sicken; **hartarse** vr (de comida) to fill o.s.; (cansarse): **~se (de)** to get fed up (with); **harto, -a** adj (lleno) full; (cansado) fed up ▷ adv (bastante) enough; (muy) very; **estar harto de hacer algo/de algn** to be fed up of doing sth/with sb
has vb V **haber**
hasta ['asta] adv even ▷ prep (alcanzando a) as far as; up to; down to; (de tiempo: a tal hora) until, till; (antes de) before ▷ conj: **~ que** ... until; **~ luego/el sábado** see you soon/on Saturday; **~ ahora** (al despedirse) see you in a minute; **~ pronto** see you soon
hay vb V **haber**
Haya ['aja] nf: **la ~** The Hague
haya etc ['aja] vb V **haber** ▷ nf beech tree
haz [aθ] vb V **hacer** ▷ nm (de luz) beam
hazaña [a'θaɲa] nf feat, exploit
hazmerreír [aθmerre'ir] nm inv laughing stock
he vb V **haber**
hebilla [e'βiʎa] nf buckle, clasp

hebra ['eβra] *nf* thread; *(Bot: fibra)* fibre, grain

hebreo, -a [e'βreo, a] *adj, nm/f* Hebrew ▷ *nm (Ling)* Hebrew

hechizar [etʃi'θar] *vt* to cast a spell on, bewitch

hechizo [e'tʃiθo] *nm* witchcraft, magic; *(acto de magia)* spell, charm

hecho, -a ['etʃo, a] *pp de* **hacer** ▷ *adj (carne)* done; *(Costura)* ready-to-wear ▷ *nm* deed, act; *(dato)* fact; *(cuestión)* matter; *(suceso)* event ▷ *excl* agreed!, done!; **de ~ es que** ... the fact is that ...; **¡bien ~!** well done!

hechura [e'tʃura] *nf (forma)* form, shape; *(de persona)* build

hectárea [ek'tarea] *nf* hectare

helada [e'laða] *nf* frost

heladera [ela'ðera] (LAM) *nf (refrigerador)* refrigerator

helado, -a [e'laðo, a] *adj* frozen; *(glacial)* icy; *(fig)* chilly, cold ▷ *nm* ice cream

helar [e'lar] *vt* to freeze, ice (up); *(dejar atónito)* to amaze; *(desalentar)* to discourage ▷ *vi* to freeze; **helarse** *vr* to freeze

helecho [e'letʃo] *nm* fern

hélice ['eliθe] *nf (Tec)* propeller

helicóptero [eli'koptero] *nm* helicopter

hembra ['embra] *nf (Bot, Zool)* female; *(mujer)* woman; *(Tec)* nut

hemorragia [emo'rraxja] *nf* haemorrhage

hemorroides [emo'rroiðes] *nfpl* haemorrhoids, piles

hemos *vb* V **haber**

heno ['eno] *nm* hay

heredar [ere'ðar] *vt* to inherit; **heredero, -a** *nm/f* heir(ess)

hereje [e'rexe] *nmf* heretic

herencia [e'renθja] *nf* inheritance

herida [e'riða] *nf* wound, injury; V *tb* **herido**

herido, -a [e'riðo, a] *adj* injured, wounded ▷ *nm/f* casualty

herir [e'rir] *vt* to wound, injure; *(fig)* to offend

hermanación [ermana'θjon] *nf (of towns)* twinning

hermanado [erma'naðo] *adj (town)* twinned

hermanastro, -a [erma'nastro, a] *nm/f* stepbrother/sister

hermandad [erman'dað] *nf* brotherhood

hermano, -a [er'mano, a] *nm/f* brother/sister; **hermano(-a) gemelo(-a)**, twin brother/sister; **hermano(-a) político(-a)**, brother-in-law/sister-in-law

hermético, -a [er'metiko, a] *adj* hermetic; *(fig)* watertight

hermoso, -a [er'moso, a] *adj* beautiful, lovely; *(estupendo)* splendid; *(guapo)* handsome; **hermosura** *nf* beauty

hernia ['ernja] *nf* hernia; **hernia discal** slipped disc

héroe ['eroe] *nm* hero

heroína [ero'ina] *nf (mujer)* heroine; *(droga)* heroin

herradura [erra'ðura] *nf* horseshoe

herramienta [erra'mjenta] *nf* tool

herrero [e'rrero] *nm* blacksmith

hervidero [erβi'ðero] *nm (fig)* swarm; *(Pol etc)* hotbed

hervir [er'βir] *vi* to boil; *(burbujear)* to bubble; **~ a fuego lento** to simmer; **hervor** *nm* boiling; *(fig)* ardour, fervour

heterosexual [eterosek'swal] *adj* heterosexual

hice *etc vb* V **hacer**

hidratante [iðra'tante] *adj*: **crema ~** moisturizing cream, moisturizer; **hidratar** *vt (piel)* to moisturize; **hidrato** *nm* hydrate; **hidratos de carbono** carbohydrates

hidráulico, -a [i'ðrauliko, a] *adj* hydraulic

hidro... [iðro] *prefijo* hydro..., water-...; **hidrodeslizador** *nm* hovercraft; **hidroeléctrico, -a**

adj hydroelectric; **hidrógeno** *nm* hydrogen

hiedra ['jeðra] *nf* ivy

hiel [jel] *nf* gall, bile; *(fig)* bitterness

hiela *etc vb* V **helar**

hielo ['jelo] *nm (gen)* ice; *(escarcha)* frost; *(fig)* coldness, reserve

hiena ['jena] *nf* hyena

hierba ['jerβa] *nf (pasto)* grass; *(Culin, Med: planta)* herb; **mala ~** weed; *(fig)* evil influence; **hierbabuena** *nf* mint

hierro ['jerro] *nm (metal)* iron; *(objeto)* iron object

hígado ['iɣaðo] *nm* liver

higiene [i'xjene] *nf* hygiene; **higiénico, -a** *adj* hygienic

higo ['iɣo] *nm* fig; **higo seco** dried fig; **higuera** *nf* fig tree

hijastro, -a [i'xastro, a] *nm/f* stepson/daughter

hijo, -a ['ixo, a] *nm/f* son/daughter, child; **hijos** *nmpl* children, sons and daughters; **hijo adoptivo** adopted child; **hijo de papá/mamá** daddy's/ mummy's boy; **hijo de puta** (fam!) bastard (!), son of a bitch (!); **hijo/a político/a** son-/daughter-in-law; **hijo único** only child

hilera [i'lera] *nf* row, file

hilo ['ilo] *nm* thread; *(Bot)* fibre; *(metal)* wire; *(de agua)* trickle, thin stream

hilvanar [ilβa'nar] *vt (Costura)* to tack (BRIT), baste (US); *(fig)* to do hurriedly

himno ['imno] *nm* hymn; **himno nacional** national anthem

hincapié [inka'pje] *nm*: **hacer ~ en** to emphasize

hincar [in'kar] *vt* to drive (in), thrust (in)

hincha ['intʃa] (fam) *nmf* fan

hinchado, -a [in'tʃaðo, a] *adj (gen)* swollen; *(persona)* pompous

hinchar [in'tʃar] *vt (gen)* to swell; *(inflar)* to blow up, inflate; *(fig)* to exaggerate; **hincharse** *vr (inflarse)* to swell up; *(fam: de comer)* to stuff o.s.; **hinchazón** *nf (Med)* swelling; *(altivez)*

arrogance

hinojo [i'noxo] *nm* fennel

hipermercado [ipermer'kaðo] *nm* hypermarket, superstore

hípico, -a ['ipiko, a] *adj* horse *cpd*

hipnotismo [ipno'tismo] *nm* hypnotism; **hipnotizar** *vt* to hypnotize

hipo ['ipo] *nm* hiccups *pl*

hipocresía [ipokre'sia] *nf* hypocrisy; **hipócrita** *adj* hypocritical ▷ *nmf* hypocrite

hipódromo [i'poðromo] *nm* racetrack

hipopótamo [ipo'potamo] *nm* hippopotamus

hipoteca [ipo'teka] *nf* mortgage

hipótesis [i'potesis] *nf inv* hypothesis

hispánico, -a [is'paniko, a] *adj* Hispanic

hispano, -a [is'pano, a] *adj* Hispanic, Spanish, Hispano- ▷ *nm/f* Spaniard; **Hispanoamérica** *nf* Latin America; **hispanoamericano, -a** *adj, nm/f* Latin American

histeria [is'terja] *nf* hysteria

historia [is'torja] *nf* history; *(cuento)* story, tale; **historias** *nfpl (chismes)* gossip *sg*; **dejarse de ~s** to come to the point; **pasar a la ~** to go down in history; **historiador, a** *nm/f* historian; **historial** *nm (profesional)* curriculum vitae, C.V.; *(Med)* case history; **histórico, -a** *adj* historical; *(memorable)* historic

historieta [isto'rjeta] *nf* tale, anecdote, *(xokei)* comic strip

hito ['ito] *nm (fig)* landmark

hizo *vb* V **hacer**

hocico [o'θiko] *nm* snout

hockey ['xokei] *nm* hockey; **hockey sobre hielo/patines** ice/roller hockey

hogar [o'ɣar] *nm* fireplace, hearth; *(casa)* home; *(vida familiar)* home life; **hogareño, -a** *adj* home *cpd*; *(persona)* home-loving

hoguera [o'ɣera] *nf (gen)* bonfire

hoja ['oxa] nf (gen) leaf; (de flor) petal; (de papel) sheet; (página) page; **hoja de afeitar** (LAM) razor blade; **hoja electrónica** o **de cálculo** spreadsheet; **hoja informativa** leaflet, handout

hojalata [oxa'lata] nf tin(plate)

hojaldre [o'xaldre] nm (Culin) puff pastry

hojear [oxe'ar] vt to leaf through, turn the pages of

hojuela [o'xwela] (MÉX) nf flake

hola ['ola] excl hello!

holá [o'la] (RPL) excl hello!

Holanda [o'landa] nf Holland; **holandés, -esa** adj Dutch ▷ nm/f Dutchman(-woman) ▷ nm (Ling) Dutch

holgado, -a [ol'ɣaðo, a] adj (ropa) loose, baggy; (rico) comfortable

holgar [ol'ɣar] vi (descansar) to rest; (sobrar) to be superfluous

holgazán, -ana [olɣa'θan, ana] adj idle, lazy ▷ nm/f loafer

hollín [o'ʎin] nm soot

hombre [o'mbre] nm (gen) man; (raza humana): **el ~** man(kind) ▷ excl: **¡sí ~!** (claro) of course!; (para énfasis) man, old boy; **hombre de negocios** businessman; **hombre de pro** honest man; **hombre-rana** frogman

hombrera [om'brera] nf shoulder strap

hombro [o'mbro] nm shoulder

homenaje [ome'naxe] nm (gen) homage; (tributo) tribute

homicida [omi'θiða] adj homicidal ▷ nmf murderer; **homicidio** nm murder, homicide

homologar [omolo'ðar] vt (Com: productos, tamaños) to standardize

homólogo, -a [o'moloɣo, a] nm/f: **su** etc ~ his etc counterpart o opposite number

homosexual [omosek'swal] adj, nmf homosexual

honda ['onda] (CS) nf catapult

hondo, -a ['ondo, a] adj deep; **lo ~** the depth(s) pl, the bottom; **hondonada** nf hollow, depression; (cañón) ravine

Honduras [on'duras] nf Honduras

hondureño, -a [ondu'reɲo, a] adj, nm/f Honduran

honestidad [onesti'ðað] nf purity, chastity; (decencia) decency; **honesto, -a** adj chaste; decent; honest; (justo) just

hongo ['ongo] nm (Bot: gen) fungus; (: comestible) mushroom; (: venenoso) toadstool

honor [o'nor] nm (gen) honour; **en ~ a la verdad** to be fair; **honorable** adj honourable

honorario, -a [ono'rarjo, a] adj honorary; **honorarios** nmpl fees

honra ['onra] nf (gen) honour; (renombre) good name; **honradez** nf honesty; (de persona) integrity; **honrado, -a** adj honest, upright; **honrar** [on'rar] vt to honour

hora ['ora] nf (una hora) hour; (tiempo) time; **¿qué ~ es?** what time is it?; **¿a qué ~?** at what time?; **media ~** half an hour; **a la ~ de recreo** at playtime; **a primera ~** first thing (in the morning); **a última ~** at the last moment; **a altas ~s** in the small hours; **¡a buena ~!** about time too!; **pedir ~** to make an appointment; **dar la ~** to strike the hour; **horas de oficina/trabajo** office/working hours; **horas de visita** visiting times; **horas extras** o **extraordinarias** overtime sg; **horas pico** (LAM) rush o peak hours; **horas punta** (ESP) rush hours

horario, -a [o'rarjo, a] adj hourly, hour cpd ▷ nm timetable; **horario comercial** business hours pl

horca ['orka] nf gallows sg

horcajadas [orka'xaðas]: **a ~** adv astride

horchata [or'tʃata] nf cold drink made from tiger nuts and water, tiger nut milk

horizontal [oriθon'tal] adj

horizontal

horizonte [oriˈθonte] *nm* horizon

horma [ˈorma] *nf* mould

hormiga [orˈmiɣa] *nf* ant; **hormigas** *nfpl* (*Med*) pins and needles

hormigón [ormiˈɣon] *nm* concrete; **hormigón armado/pretensado** reinforced/prestressed concrete; **hormigonera** *nf* cement mixer

hormigueo [ormiˈɣeo] *nm* (*comezón*) itch

hormona [orˈmona] *nf* hormone

hornillo [orˈniʎo] *nm* (*cocina*) portable stove; **hornillo de gas** gas ring

horno [ˈorno] *nm* (*Culin*) oven; (*Tec*) furnace; **alto ~** blast furnace

horóscopo [oˈroskopo] *nm* horoscope

horquilla [orˈkiʎa] *nf* hairpin; (*Agr*) pitchfork

horrendo, -a [oˈrrendo, a] *adj* horrendous, frightful

horrible [oˈrriβle] *adj* horrible, dreadful

horripilante [orripiˈlante] *adj* hair-raising, horrifying

horror [oˈrror] *nm* horror, dread; (*atrocidad*) atrocity; **¡qué ~!** how awful!; **horrorizar** *vt* to horrify, frighten; **horrorizarse** *vr* to be horrified; **horroroso, -a** *adj* horrifying, ghastly

hortaliza [ortaˈliθa] *nf* vegetable

hortelano, -a [orteˈlano, a] *nm/f* (market) gardener

hortera [orˈtera] (*fam*) *adj* tacky

hospedar [ospeˈðar] *vt* to put up; **hospedarse** *vr* to stay, lodge

hospital [ospiˈtal] *nm* hospital

hospitalario, -a [ospitaˈlarjo, a] *adj* (*acogedor*) hospitable; **hospitalidad** *nf* hospitality

hostal [osˈtal] *nm* small hotel

hostelería [osteleˈria] *nf* hotel business o trade

hostia [ˈostja] *nf* (*Rel*) host, consecrated wafer; (*fam!: golpe*) whack, punch ▷ *excl* (*fam!*) **¡~(s)!** damn!

hostil [osˈtil] *adj* hostile

hotdog [otˈdoɡ] (*LAM*) *nm* hot dog

hotel [oˈtel] *nm* hotel; **hotelero, -a** *adj* hotel *cpd* ▷ *nm/f* hotelier

● **HOTEL**

● In Spain you can choose from
● the following categories of
● accommodation, in descending
● order of quality and price: **hotel**
● (from 5 stars to 1), **hostal**, **pensión**,
● **casa de huéspedes**, **fonda**. The
● State also runs luxury hotels called
● **paradores**, which are usually sited
● in places of particular historical
● interest and are often historic
● buildings themselves.

hoy [oi] *adv* (*este día*) today; (*la actualidad*) now(adays) ▷ *nm* present time; **~ (en) día** now(adays)

hoyo [ˈojo] *nm* hole, pit

hoz [oθ] *nf* sickle

hube *etc* *vb* V **haber**

hucha [ˈutʃa] *nf* money box

hueco, -a [ˈweko, a] *adj* (*vacío*) hollow, empty; (*resonante*) booming ▷ *nm* hollow, cavity

huelga *etc* [ˈwelɣa] *vb* V **holgar** ▷ *nf* strike; **declararse en ~** to go on strike, come out on strike; **huelga de hambre** hunger strike; **huelga general** general strike

huelguista [welˈɣista] *nmf* striker

huella [ˈweʎa] *nf* (*pisada*) tread; (*marca del paso*) footprint, footstep; (: *de animal, máquina*) track; **huella dactilar** fingerprint

huelo *etc* *vb* V **oler**

huérfano, -a [ˈwerfano, a] *adj* orphan(ed) ▷ *nm/f* orphan

huerta [ˈwerta] *nf* market garden; (*en Murcia y Valencia*) irrigated region

huerto [ˈwerto] *nm* kitchen garden; (*de árboles frutales*) orchard

hueso [ˈweso] *nm* (*Anat*) bone; (*de fruta*) stone

huésped ['wespeð] nmf guest

hueva ['weβa] nf roe

huevera [we'βera] nf eggcup

huevo ['weβo] nm egg; **huevo a la copa** (cs) soft-boiled egg; **huevo duro/escalfado** hard-boiled/poached egg; **huevo estrellado** (LAM) fried egg; **huevo frito** (ESP) fried egg; **huevo pasado por agua** soft-boiled egg; **huevos revueltos** scrambled eggs; **huevo tibio** (MÉX) soft-boiled egg

huida [u'iða] nf escape, flight

huir [u'ir] vi (escapar) to flee, escape; (evitar) to avoid

hule ['ule] nm oilskin; (MÉX: goma) rubber

hulera [u'lera] nf (MÉX) catapult

humanidad [umani'ðað] nf (género humano) man(kind); (cualidad) humanity

humanitario, -a [umani'tarjo, a] adj humanitarian

humano, -a [u'mano, a] adj (gen) human; (humanitario) humane ▷ nm human; **ser ~** human being

humareda [uma'reða] nf cloud of smoke

humedad [ume'ðað] nf (de clima) humidity; (de pared etc) dampness; **a prueba de ~** damp-proof; **humedecer** vt to moisten, wet; **humedecerse** vr to get wet

húmedo, -a ['umeðo, a] adj (mojado) damp, wet; (tiempo etc) humid

humilde [u'milde] adj humble, modest

humillación [umiʎa'θjon] nf humiliation; **humillante** adj humiliating

humillar [umi'ʎar] vt to humiliate

humo ['umo] nm (de fuego) smoke; (gas nocivo) fumes pl; (vapor) steam, vapour; **humos** nmpl (fig) conceit sg

humor [u'mor] nm (disposición) mood, temper; (lo que divierte) humour; **de buen/mal ~** in a good/bad mood; **humorista** nmf comic; **humorístico, -a** adj funny, humorous

hundimiento [undi'mjento] nm (gen) sinking; (colapso) collapse

hundir [un'dir] vt to sink; (edificio, plan) to ruin, destroy; **hundirse** vr to sink, collapse

húngaro, -a ['ungaro, a] adj, nm/f Hungarian

Hungría [un'gria] nf Hungary

huracán [ura'kan] nm hurricane

huraño, -a [u'raɲo, a] adj (antisocial) unsociable

hurgar [ur'ɣar] vt to poke, jab; (remover) to stir (up); **hurgarse** vr: **~se (las narices)** to pick one's nose

hurón, -ona [u'ron, ona] nm (Zool) ferret

hurtadillas [urta'ðiʎas] : **a ~** adv stealthily, on the sly

hurtar [ur'tar] vt to steal; **hurto** nm theft, stealing

husmear [usme'ar] vt (oler) to sniff out, scent; (fam) to pry into

huyo etc vb V **huir**

i

iba etc vb V **ir**

ibérico, -a [i'βeriko, a] adj Iberian

iberoamericano, -a
[iβeroameri'kano, a] adj, nm/f Latin
American

Ibiza [i'βiθa] nf Ibiza

iceberg [iθe'βer] nm iceberg

icono [i'kono] nm ikon, icon

ida [i'ða] nf going, departure; **~ y
vuelta** round trip, return

idea [i'ðea] nf idea; **no tengo la
menor ~** I haven't a clue

ideal [iðe'al] adj, nm ideal; **idealista**
nmf idealist; **idealizar** vt to idealize

ídem ['iðem] pron ditto

idéntico, -a [i'ðentiko, a] adj
identical

identidad [iðenti'ðað] nf identity

identificación [iðentifika'θjon] nf
identification

identificar [iðentifi'kar] vt to
identify; **identificarse** vr: **~se con** to
identify with

ideología [iðeolo'xia] nf ideology

idilio [i'ðiljo] nm love-affair

idioma [i'ðjoma] nm (gen) language
■ No confundir **idioma** con la palabra
inglesa idiom.

idiota [i'ðjota] adj idiotic ▷ nmf idiot

ídolo ['iðolo] nm (tb fig) idol

idóneo, -a [i'ðoneo, a] adj suitable

iglesia [i'ɣlesja] nf church

ignorante [iɣno'rante] adj ignorant,
uninformed ▷ nmf ignoramus

ignorar [iɣno'rar] vt not to know, be
ignorant of; (no hacer caso a) to ignore

igual [i'ɣwal] adj (gen) equal; (similar)
like, similar; (mismo) (the) same;
(constante) constant; (temperatura)
even ▷ nm equal; **~ que** like, the same
as; **me da ~ es** I don't care; **son ~es**
they're the same; **al ~ que** (prep, conj)
like, just like

igualar [iɣwa'lar] vt (gen) to equalize,
make equal; (allanar, nivelar) to level
(off), even (out); **igualarse** vr (platos de
balanza) to balance out

igualdad [iɣwal'dað] nf equality;
(similaridad) sameness; (uniformidad)
uniformity

igualmente [iɣwal'mente] adv
equally; (también) also, likewise ▷ excl
the same to you!

ilegal [ile'ɣal] adj illegal

ilegítimo, -a [ile'xitimo, a] adj
illegitimate

ileso, -a [i'leso, a] adj unhurt

ilimitado, -a [ilimi'taðo, a] adj
unlimited

iluminación [ilumina'θjon] nf
illumination; (alumbrado) lighting

iluminar [ilumi'nar] vt to
illuminate, light (up); (fig) to enlighten

ilusión [ilu'sjon] nf illusion; (quimera)
delusion; (esperanza) hope; **hacerse
ilusiones** to build up one's hopes;
ilusionado, -a adj excited; **ilusionar**
vi: **le ilusiona ir de vacaciones** he's
looking forward to going on holiday;
ilusionarse vr: ilusionarse (con) to
get excited (about)

iluso, -a [i'luso, a] adj easily
deceived ▷ nm/f dreamer

ilustración [ilustra'θjon] *nf* illustration; (*saber*) learning, erudition; **la l~** the Enlightenment; **ilustrado, -a** *adj* illustrated; learned

ilustrar [ilus'trar] *vt* to illustrate; (*instruir*) to instruct; (*explicar*) to explain, make clear

ilustre [i'lustre] *adj* famous, illustrious

imagen [i'maxen] *nf* (*gen*) image; (*dibujo*) picture

imaginación [imaxina'θjon] *nf* imagination

imaginar [imaxi'nar] *vt* (*gen*) to imagine; (*idear*) to think up; (*suponer*) to suppose; **imaginarse** *vr* to imagine; **imaginario, -a** *adj* imaginary; **imaginativo, -a** *adj* imaginative

imán [i'man] *nm* magnet

imbécil [im'beθil] *nmf* imbecile, idiot

imitación [imita'θjon] *nf* imitation; **de ~** imitation *cpd*

imitar [imi'tar] *vt* to imitate; (*parodiar, remedar*) to mimic, ape

impaciente [impa'θjente] *adj* impatient; (*nervioso*) anxious

impacto [im'pakto] *nm* impact

impar [im'par] *adj* odd

imparcial [impar'θjal] *adj* impartial, fair

impecable [impe'kaβle] *adj* impeccable

impedimento [impeði'mento] *nm* impediment, obstacle

impedir [impe'ðir] *vt* (*obstruir*) to impede, obstruct; (*estorbar*) to prevent; **~ a algn hacer** o **que algn haga algo** to prevent sb (from) doing sth, stop sb doing sth

imperativo, -a [impera'tiβo, a] *adj* (*urgente, Ling*) imperative

imperdible [imper'ðiβle] *nm* safety pin

imperdonable [imperðo'naβle] *adj* unforgivable, inexcusable

imperfecto, -a [imper'fekto, a] *adj* imperfect

imperio [im'perjo] *nm* empire;

(*autoridad*) rule, authority; (*fig*) pride, haughtiness

impermeable [imperme'aβle] *adj* waterproof ▷ *nm* raincoat, mac (*BRIT*)

impersonal [imperso'nal] *adj* impersonal

impertinente [imperti'nente] *adj* impertinent

ímpetu ['impetu] *nm* (*impulso*) impetus, impulse; (*impetuosidad*) impetuosity; (*violencia*) violence

implantar [implan'tar] *vt* to introduce

implemento [imple'mento] (*LAM*) *nm* tool, implement

implicar [impli'kar] *vt* to involve; (*entrañar*) to imply

implícito, -a [im'pliθito, a] *adj* (*tácito*) implicit; (*sobreentendido*) implied

imponente [impo'nente] *adj* (*impresionante*) impressive, imposing; (*solemne*) grand

imponer [impo'ner] *vt* (*gen*) to impose; (*exigir*) to exact; **imponerse** *vr* to assert o.s.; (*prevalecer*) to prevail; **imponible** *adj* (*Com*) taxable

impopular [impopu'lar] *adj* unpopular

importación [importa'θjon] *nf* (*acto*) importing; (*mercancías*) imports *pl*

importancia [impor'tanθja] *nf* importance; (*valor*) value, significance; (*extensión*) size, magnitude; **no tiene** - it's nothing; **importante** *adj* important; valuable, significant

importar [impor'tar] *vt* (*del extranjero*) to import; (*costar*) to amount to ▷ *vi* to be important, matter; **me importa un rábano** I couldn't care less; **no importa** it doesn't matter; **¿le importa que fume?** do you mind if I smoke?

importe [im'porte] *nm* (*total*) amount; (*valor*) value

imposible [impo'siβle] *adj* (*gen*) impossible; (*insoportable*) unbearable, intolerable

imposición [imposi'θjon] nf
imposition; (Com: impuesto) tax;
(: inversión) deposit

impostor, a [impos'tor, a] nm/f
impostor

impotencia [impo'tenθja] nf
impotence; **impotente** adj impotent

impreciso, -a [impre'θiso, a] adj
imprecise, vague

impregnar [impreɣ'nar] vt to
impregnate; **impregnarse** vr to
become impregnated

imprenta [im'prenta] nf (acto)
printing; (aparato) press; (casa)
printer's; (letra) print

imprescindible [impresθin'diβle]
adj essential, vital

impresión [impre'sjon] nf (gen)
impression; (Imprenta) printing;
(edición) edition; (Foto) print; (marca)
imprint; **impresión digital** fingerprint

impresionante [impresjo'nante]
adj impressive; (tremendo) tremendous;
(maravilloso) great, marvellous

impresionar [impresjo'nar] vt
(conmover) to move; (afectar) to impress,
strike; (película fotográfica) to expose;
impresionarse vr to be impressed;
(conmoverse) to be moved

impreso, -a [im'preso, a] pp de
imprimir ▷ adj printed; **impresos**
nmpl printed matter; **impresora** nf
printer

imprevisto, -a [impre'βisto, a]
adj (gen) unforeseen; (inesperado)
unexpected

imprimir [impri'mir] vt to imprint,
impress, stamp; (textos) to print;
(Inform) to output, print out

improbable [impro'βaβle] adj
improbable; (inverosímil) unlikely

impropio, -a [im'propjo, a] adj
improper

improvisado, -a [improβi'saðo, a]
adj improvised

improvisar [improβi'sar] vt to
improvise

improviso, -a [impro'βiso, a] adj: **de**
~ unexpectedly, suddenly

imprudencia [impru'ðenθja] nf
imprudence; (indiscreción) indiscretion;
(descuido) carelessness; **imprudente**
adj unwise, imprudent; (indiscreto)
indiscreet

impuesto, -a [im'pwesto, a] adj
imposed ▷ nm tax; **impuesto al valor**
agregado o **añadido** (LAM) value added
tax (BRIT) ≈ sales tax (US); **impuesto**
sobre el valor añadido (ESP) value
added tax (BRIT) ≈ sales tax (US)

impulsar [impul'sar] vt to drive;
(promover) to promote, stimulate

impulsivo, -a [impul'siβo, a] adj
impulsive; **impulso** nm impulse;
(fuerza, empuje) thrust, drive;
(fig: sentimiento) urge, impulse

impureza [impu'reθa] nf impurity;
impuro, -a adj impure

inaccesible [inakθe'siβle] adj
inaccessible

inaceptable [inaθep'taβle] adj
unacceptable

inactivo, -a [inak'tiβo, a] adj
inactive

inadecuado, -a [inaðe'kwaðo, a]
adj (insuficiente) inadequate; (inapto)
unsuitable

inadvertido, -a [inaðβer'tiðo, a]
adj (no visto) unnoticed

inaguantable [inaɣwan'taβle] adj
unbearable

inanimado, -a [inani'maðo, a] adj
inanimate

inaudito, -a [inau'ðito, a] adj
unheard-of

inauguración [inauɣura'θjon] nf
inauguration; opening

inaugurar [inauɣu'rar] vt to
inaugurate; (exposición) to open

inca ['inka] nmf Inca

incalculable [inkalku'laβle] adj
incalculable

incandescente [inkandes'θente]
adj incandescent

incansable [inkan'saβle] adj

tireless, untiring

incapacidad [inkapaθi'ðað]
nf incapacity; (incompetencia)
incompetence; **incapacidad física/
mental** physical/mental disability

incapacitar [inkapaθi'tar] vt
(inhabilitar) to incapacitate, render
unfit; (descalificar) to disqualify

incapaz [inka'paθ] adj incapable

incautarse [inkau'tarse] vr: ~ **de** to
seize, confiscate

incauto, -a [in'kauto, a] adj
(imprudente) incautious, unwary

incendiar [inθen'djar] vt to set
fire to; (fig) to inflame; **incendiarse**
vr to catch fire; **incendiario, -a** adj
incendiary

incendio [in'θendjo] nm fire

incentivo [inθen'tiβo] nm incentive

incertidumbre [inθerti'ðumbre] nf
(inseguridad) uncertainty; (duda) doubt

incesante [inθe'sante] adj incessant

incesto [in'θesto] nm incest

incidencia [inθi'ðenθja] nf (Mat)
incidence

incidente [inθi'ðente] nm incident

incidir [inθi'ðir] vi (influir) to
influence; (afectar) to affect

incienso [in'θjenso] nm incense

incierto, -a [in'θjerto, a] adj
uncertain

incineración [inθinera'θjon] nf
incineration; (de cadáveres) cremation

incinerar [inθine'rar] vt to burn;
(cadáveres) to cremate

incisión [inθi'sjon] nf incision

incisivo, -a [inθi'siβo, a] adj sharp,
cutting; (fig) incisive

incitar [inθi'tar] vt to incite, rouse

inclemencia [inkle'menθja] nf
(severidad) harshness, severity; (del
tiempo) inclemency

inclinación [inklina'θjon] nf (gen)
inclination; (de tierras) slope, incline;
(de cabeza) nod, bow; (fig) leaning, bent

inclinar [inkli'nar] vt to incline;
(cabeza) to nod, bow ▷ vi to lean, slope;
inclinarse vr to bow; (encorvarse) to

stoop; **~se a** (parecerse a) to take after,
resemble; **~se ante** to bow down
to; **me inclino a pensar que ...** I'm
inclined to think that ...

incluir [inklu'ir] vt to include;
(incorporar) to incorporate; (meter) to
enclose

inclusive [inklu'siβe] adv inclusive
▷ prep including

incluso [in'kluso] adv even

incógnita [in'koɣnita] nf (Mat)
unknown quantity

incógnito [in'koɣnito] nm: **de ~**
incognito

incoherente [inkoe'rente] adj
incoherent

incoloro, -a [inko'loro, a] adj
colourless

incomodar [inkomo'ðar] vt to
inconvenience; (molestar) to bother,
trouble; (fastidiar) to annoy

incomodidad [inkomoði'ðað]
nf inconvenience; (fastidio, enojo)
annoyance; (de vivienda) discomfort

incómodo, -a [in'komoðo, a] adj
(incomfortable) uncomfortable; (molesto)
annoying; (inconveniente) inconvenient

incomparable [inkompa'raβle] adj
incomparable

incompatible [inkompa'tiβle] adj
incompatible

incompetente [inkompe'tente] adj
incompetent

incompleto, -a [inkom'pleto, a] adj
incomplete, unfinished

incomprensible [inkompren'siβle]
adj incomprehensible

incomunicado, -a [inkomuni'kaðo,
a] adj (aislado) cut off, isolated;
(confinado) in solitary confinement

incondicional [inkondiθjo'nal] adj
unconditional; (apoyo) wholehearted;
(partidario) staunch

inconfundible [inkonfun'diβle] adj
unmistakable

incongruente [inkoŋ'grwente] adj
incongruous

inconsciente [inkons'θjente] adj

unconscious; thoughtless

inconsecuente [inkonse'kwente]
adj inconsistent

inconstante [inkons'tante] *adj*
inconstant

incontable [inkon'taβle] *adj*
countless, innumerable

inconveniencia [inkombe'njenθja]
nf unsuitability, inappropriateness;
(*descortesía*) impoliteness;
inconveniente *adj* unsuitable;
impolite ▷ *nm* obstacle; (*desventaja*)
disadvantage; **el inconveniente es
que ...** the trouble is that ...

incordiar [inkor'ðjar] (*fam*) *vt* to
bug, annoy

incorporar [inkorpo'rar] *vt* to
incorporate; **incorporarse** *vr* to sit
up; **-se a** to join

incorrecto, -a [inko'rrekto,
a] *adj* (*gen*) incorrect, wrong;
(*comportamiento*) bad-mannered

incorregible [inkorre'xiβle] *adj*
incorrigible

incrédulo, -a [in'kreðulo, a] *adj*
incredulous, unbelieving; sceptical

increíble [inkre'iβle] *adj* incredible

incremento [inkre'mento] *nm*
increment; (*aumento*) rise, increase

increpar [inkre'par] *vt* to reprimand

incruento, -a [in'krwento, a] *adj*
bloodless

incrustar [inkrus'tar] *vt* to incrust;
(*piedras: en joya*) to inlay

incubar [inku'βar] *vt* to incubate

inculcar [inkul'kar] *vt* to inculcate

inculto, -a [in'kulto, a] *adj* (*persona*)
uneducated; (*grosero*) uncouth ▷ *nm/f*
ignoramus

incumplimiento
[inkumpli'mjento] *nm* non-
fulfilment; **incumplimiento de
contrato** breach of contract

incurrir [inku'rrir] *vi*: **~ en** to incur;
(*crimen*) to commit

indagar [inda'ɣar] *vt* to investigate;
to search; (*averiguar*) to ascertain

indecente [inde'θente] *adj* indecent,

improper; (*lascivo*) obscene

indeciso, -a [inde'θiso, a] *adj* (*por
decidir*) undecided; (*vacilante*) hesitant

indefenso, -a [inde'fenso, a] *adj*
defenceless

indefinido, -a [inde'finiðo, a] *adj*
indefinite; (*vago*) vague, undefined

indemne [in'demne] *adj* (*objeto*)
undamaged; (*persona*) unharmed,
unhurt

indemnizar [indemni'θar] *vt* to
indemnify; (*compensar*) to compensate

independencia [indepen'denθja] *nf*
independence

independiente [indepen'djente]
adj (*libre*) independent; (*autónomo*)
self-sufficient

indeterminado, -a
[indetermi'naðo, a] *adj* indefinite;
(*desconocido*) indeterminate

India ['indja] *nf*: **la ~** India

indicación [indika'θjon] *nf*
indication; (*señal*) sign; (*sugerencia*)
suggestion, hint

indicado, -a [indi'kaðo, a] *adj*
(*momento, método*) right; (*tratamiento*)
appropriate; (*solución*) likely

indicador [indika'ðor] *nm* indicator;
(*Tec*) gauge, meter

indicar [indi'kar] *vt* (*mostrar*) to
indicate, show; (*termómetro etc*) to
read, register; (*señalar*) to point to

índice ['indiθe] *nm* index; (*catálogo*)
catalogue; (*Anat*) index finger,
forefinger; **índice de materias** table
of contents

indicio [in'diθjo] *nm* indication, sign;
(*en pesquisa etc*) clue

indiferencia [indife'renθja]
nf indifference; (*apatía*) apathy;
indiferente *adj* indifferent

indígena [in'dixena] *adj* indigenous,
native ▷ *nmf* native

indigestión [indixes'tjon] *nf*
indigestion

indigesto, -a [indi'xesto, a] *adj*
(*alimento*) indigestible; (*fig*) turgid

indignación [indiɣna'θjon] *nf*

indignation

indignar [indiɣ'nar] vt to anger, make indignant; **indignarse** vr: **~se por** to get indignant about

indigno, -a [in'diɣno, a] adj (despreciable) low, contemptible; (inmerecido) unworthy

indio, -a ['indjo, a] adj, nm/f Indian

indirecta [indi'rekta] nf insinuation, innuendo; (sugerencia) hint

indirecto, -a [indi'rekto, a] adj indirect

indiscreción [indiskre'θjon] nf (imprudencia) indiscretion; (irreflexión) tactlessness; (acto) gaffe, faux pas

indiscreto, -a [indis'kreto, a] adj indiscreet

indiscutible [indisku'tiβle] adj indisputable, unquestionable

indispensable [indispen'saβle] adj indispensable, essential

indispuesto, -a [indis'pwesto, a] adj (enfermo) unwell, indisposed

indistinto, -a [indis'tinto, a] adj indistinct; (vago) vague

individual [indiβi'ðwal] adj individual; (habitación) single ▷ nm (Deporte) singles sg

individuo, -a [indi'βiðwo, a] adj, nm individual

índole ['indole] nf (naturaleza) nature; (clase) sort, kind

inducir [indu'θir] vt to induce; (inferir) to infer; (persuadir) to persuade

indudable [indu'ðaβle] adj undoubted; (incuestionable) unquestionable

indultar [indul'tar] vt (perdonar) to pardon, reprieve; (librar de pago) to exempt; **indulto** nm pardon; exemption

industria [in'dustrja] nf industry; (habilidad) skill; **industrial** adj industrial ▷ nm industrialist

inédito, -a [in'eðito, a] adj (texto) unpublished; (nuevo) new

ineficaz [inefi'kaθ] adj (inútil) ineffective; (ineficiente) inefficient

ineludible [inelu'ðiβle] adj inescapable, unavoidable

ineptitud [inepti'tuð] nf ineptitude, incompetence; **inepto, -a** adj inept, incompetent

inequívoco, -a [ine'kiβoko, a] adj unequivocal; (inconfundible) unmistakable

inercia [in'erθja] nf inertia; (pasividad) passivity

inerte [in'erte] adj inert; (inmóvil) motionless

inesperado, -a [inespe'raðo, a] adj unexpected, unforeseen

inestable [ines'taβle] adj unstable

inevitable [ineβi'taβle] adj inevitable

inexacto, -a [inek'sakto, a] adj inaccurate; (falso) untrue

inexperto, -a [inek'sperto, a] adj (novato) inexperienced

infalible [infa'liβle] adj infallible; (plan) foolproof

infame [in'fame] adj infamous; (horrible) dreadful; **infamia** nf infamy; (deshonra) disgrace

infancia [in'fanθja] nf infancy, childhood

infantería [infante'ria] nf infantry

infantil [infan'til] adj (pueril, aniñado) infantile; (cándido) childlike; (literatura, ropa etc) children's

infarto [in'farto] nm (tb: **~ de miocardio**) heart attack

infatigable [infati'ɣaβle] adj tireless, untiring

infección [infek'θjon] nf infection; **infeccioso, -a** adj infectious

infectar [infek'tar] vt to infect; **infectarse** vr to become infected

infeliz [infe'liθ] adj unhappy, wretched ▷ nmf wretch

inferior [infe'rjor] adj inferior; (situación) lower ▷ nmf inferior, subordinate

inferir [infe'rir] vt (deducir) to infer, deduce; (causar) to cause

infidelidad [infiðeli'ðað] nf (gen)

infidelity, unfaithfulness

infiel [in'fjel] *adj* unfaithful, disloyal; (*erróneo*) inaccurate ▷ *nmf* infidel, unbeliever

infierno [in'fjerno] *nm* hell

infiltrarse [infil'trarse] *vr*: **~ en** to infiltrate in(to); (*persona*) to work one's way in(to)

ínfimo, -a ['infimo, a] *adj* (*más bajo*) lowest; (*despreciable*) vile, mean

infinidad [infini'ðað] *nf* infinity; (*abundancia*) great quantity

infinito, -a [infi'nito, a] *adj*, *nm* infinite

inflación [infla'θjon] *nf* (*hinchazón*) swelling; (*monetaria*) inflation; (*fig*) conceit

inflamable [infla'maβle] *adj* flammable

inflamar [infla'mar] *vt* (*Med*: *fig*) to inflame; **inflamarse** *vr* to catch fire; to become inflamed

inflar [in'flar] *vt* (*hinchar*) to inflate, blow up; (*fig*) to exaggerate; **inflarse** *vr* to swell (up); (*fig*) to get conceited

inflexible [inflek'siβle] *adj* inflexible; (*fig*) unbending

influencia [influ'enθja] *nf* influence

influir [influ'ir] *vt* to influence

influjo [in'fluxo] *nm* influence

influya *etc* *vb* V **influir**

influyente [influ'jente] *adj* influential

información [informa'θjon] *nf* information; (*noticias*) news *sg*; (*Jur*) inquiry; **I~** (*oficina*) Information Office; (*mostrador*) Information Desk; (*Tel*) Directory Enquiries

informal [infor'mal] *adj* (*gen*) informal

informar [infor'mar] *vt* (*gen*) to inform; (*revelar*) to reveal, make known ▷ *vi* (*Jur*) to plead; (*denunciar*) to inform; (*dar cuenta de*) to report on; **informarse** *vr* to find out; **~se de** to inquire into

informática [infor'matika] *nf* computer science, information technology

informe [in'forme] *adj* shapeless ▷ *nm* report

infracción [infrak'θjon] *nf* infraction, infringement

infravalorar [infrabalo'rar] *vt* to undervalue, underestimate

infringir [infrin'xir] *vt* to infringe, contravene

infundado, -a [infun'daðo, a] *adj* groundless, unfounded

infundir [infun'dir] *vt* to infuse, instil

infusión [infu'sjon] *nf* infusion; **infusión de manzanilla** camomile tea

ingeniería [inxenje'ria] *nf* engineering; **ingeniería genética** genetic engineering; **ingeniero, -a** *nm/f* engineer; **ingeniero civil** o **de caminos** civil engineer

ingenio [in'xenjo] *nm* (*talento*) talent; (*agudeza*) wit; (*habilidad*) ingenuity, inventiveness; **ingenio azucarero** (*LAM*) sugar refinery; **ingenioso, -a** [inxe'njoso, a] *adj* ingenious, clever; (*divertido*) witty; **ingenuo, -a** *adj* ingenuous

ingerir [inxe'rir] *vt* to ingest; (*tragar*) to swallow; (*consumir*) to consume

Inglaterra [ingla'terra] *nf* England

ingle ['ingle] *nf* groin

inglés, -esa [in'gles, esa] *adj* English ▷ *nm/f* Englishman(-woman) ▷ *nm* (*Ling*) English

ingrato, -a [in'grato, a] *adj* (*gen*) ungrateful

ingrediente [ingre'ðjente] *nm* ingredient

ingresar [ingre'sar] *vt* (*dinero*) to deposit ▷ *vi* to come in; **~ en el hospital** to go into hospital

ingreso [in'greso] *nm* (*entrada*) entry; (*en hospital etc*) admission; **ingresos** *nmpl* (*dinero*) income *sg*; (*Com*) takings *pl*

inhabitable [inaβi'taβle] *adj* uninhabitable

inhalar [ina'lar] *vt* to inhale

inhibir [ini'βir] *vt* to inhibit

inhóspito, -a [i'nospito, a] *adj*
(*región, paisaje*) inhospitable

inhumano, -a [inu'mano, a] *adj*
inhuman

inicial [ini'θjal] *adj, nf* initial

iniciar [ini'θjar] *vt* (*persona*) to
initiate; (*empezar*) to begin, commence;
(*conversación*) to start up

iniciativa [iniθja'tiβa] *nf* initiative;
iniciativa privada private enterprise

ininterrumpido, -a
[ininterrum'piðo, a] *adj*
uninterrupted

injertar [inxer'tar] *vt* to graft;
injerto *nm* graft

injuria [in'xurja] *nf* (*agravio, ofensa*)
offence; (*insulto*) insult

> No confundir **injuria** con la palabra
> inglesa *injury*.

injusticia [inxus'tiθja] *nf* injustice

injusto, -a [in'xusto, a] *adj* unjust,
unfair

inmadurez [inmaðu'reθ] *nf*
immaturity

inmediaciones [inmeðja'θjones]
nfpl neighbourhood sg, environs

inmediato, -a [inme'ðjato,
a] *adj* immediate; (*contiguo*)
adjoining; (*rápido*) prompt; (*próximo*)
neighbouring, next; **de ~** immediately

inmejorable [inmexo'raβle] *adj*
unsurpassable; (*precio*) unbeatable

inmenso, -a [in'menso, a] *adj*
immense, huge

inmigración [inmiɣra'θjon] *nf*
immigration

inmobiliaria [inmoβi'ljarja] *nf*
estate agency

inmolar [inmo'lar] *vt* to immolate,
sacrifice

inmoral [inmo'ral] *adj* immoral

inmortal [inmor'tal] *adj* immortal;
inmortalizar *vt* to immortalize

inmóvil [in'moβil] *adj* immobile

inmueble [in'mweβle] *adj*: **bienes
~s** real estate, landed property ▷ *nm*
property

inmundo, -a [in'mundo, a] *adj*

filthy

inmune [in'mune] *adj*: **~ (a)** (*Med*)
immune (to)

inmunidad [inmuni'ðað] *nf*
immunity

inmutarse [inmu'tarse] *vr* to turn
pale; **no se inmutó** he didn't turn a hair

innato, -a [in'nato, a] *adj* innate

innecesario, -a [inneθe'sarjo, a] *adj*
unnecessary

innovación [innoβa'θjon] *nf*
innovation

innovar [inno'βar] *vt* to introduce

inocencia [ino'θenθja] *nf* innocence

inocentada [inoθen'taða] *nf*
practical joke

inocente [ino'θente] *adj* (*ingenuo*)
naive, innocent; (*inculpable*) innocent;
(*sin malicia*) harmless ▷ *nmf* simpleton;
el día de los (Santos) l~s ≈ April
Fool's Day

> **DÍA DE LOS (SANTOS)**
> **INOCENTES**
>
> The 28th December, el **día de los
> (Santos) Inocentes**, is when
> the Church commemorates the
> story of Herod's slaughter of the
> innocent children of Judaea.
> On this day Spaniards play
> **inocentadas** (practical jokes) on
> each other, much like our April
> Fool's Day pranks.

inodoro [ino'ðoro] *nm* toilet,
lavatory (*BRIT*)

inofensivo, -a [inofen'siβo, a] *adj*
inoffensive, harmless

inolvidable [inolβi'ðaβle] *adj*
unforgettable

inoportuno, -a [inopor'tuno, a] *adj*
untimely; (*molesto*) inconvenient

inoxidable [inoksi'ðaβle] *adj*: **acero
~** stainless steel

inquietar [inkje'tar] *vt* to worry,
trouble; **inquietarse** *vr* to worry,
get upset; **inquieto, -a** *adj* anxious,

worried; **inquietud** nf anxiety, worry
inquilino, -a [iŋki'lino, a] nm/f
tenant
insaciable [insa'θjaβle] adj
insatiable
inscribir [inskri'βir] vt to inscribe; ~
a algn en (lista) to put sb on; (censo) to
register sb on
inscripción [inskrip'θjon] nf
inscription; (Escol etc) enrolment; (en
censo) registration
insecticida [insekti'θiða] nm
insecticide
insecto [in'sekto] nm insect
inseguridad [inseɣuri'ðað] nf
insecurity; **inseguridad ciudadana**
lack of safety in the streets
inseguro, -a [inse'ɣuro, a] adj
insecure; (inconstante) unsteady;
(incierto) uncertain
insensato, -a [insen'sato, a] adj
foolish, stupid
insensible [insen'siβle] adj
(gen) insensitive; (movimiento)
imperceptible; (sin sentido) numb
insertar [inser'tar] vt to insert
inservible [inser'βiβle] adj useless
insignia [in'siɣnja] nf (señal
distintiva) badge; (estandarte) flag
insignificante [insiɣnifi'kante] adj
insignificant
insinuar [insi'nwar] vt to insinuate,
imply
insípido, -a [in'sipiðo, a] adj insipid
insistir [insis'tir] vi to insist; ~ **en
algo** to insist on sth; (enfatizar) to
stress sth
insolación [insola'θjon] nf (Med)
sunstroke
insolente [inso'lente] adj insolent
insólito, -a [in'solito, a] adj unusual
insoluble [inso'luβle] adj insoluble
insomnio [in'somnjo] nm insomnia
insonorizado [insonori'θaðo, a]
adj (cuarto etc) soundproof
insoportable [insopor'taβle] adj
unbearable
inspección [inspek'θjon] nf

inspection, check; **inspeccionar**
vt (examinar) to inspect, examine;
(controlar) to check
inspector, a [inspek'tor, a] nm/f
inspector
inspiración [inspira'θjon] nf
inspiration
inspirar [inspi'rar] vt to inspire;
(Med) to inhale; **inspirarse** vr: **~se en**
to be inspired by
instalación [instala'θjon] nf (equipo)
fittings pl, equipment; **instalación
eléctrica** wiring
instalar [insta'lar] vt (establecer)
to install; (erguir) to set up, erect;
instalarse vr to establish o.s.; (en una
vivienda) to move into
instancia [ins'tanθja] nf (Jur)
petition; (ruego) request; **en última ~**
as a last resort
instantáneo, -a [instan'taneo,
a] adj instantaneous; **café ~** instant
coffee
instante [ins'tante] nm instant,
moment; **al ~** right now
instar [ins'tar] vt to press, urge
instaurar [instau'rar] vt (costumbre)
to establish; (normas, sistema) to bring
in, introduce; (gobierno) to instal
instigar [insti'ɣar] vt to instigate
instinto [ins'tinto] nm instinct; **por
~** instinctively
institución [institu'θjon] nf
institution, establishment
instituir [institu'ir] vt to establish;
(fundar) to found; **instituto** nm (gen)
institute; (Esp Escol) = comprehensive
(BRIT) o high (US) school
institutriz [institu'triθ] nf
governess
instrucción [instruk'θjon] nf
instruction
instructor [instruk'tor] nm
instructor
instruir [instru'ir] vt (gen) to
instruct; (enseñar) to teach, educate
instrumento [instru'mento] nm
(gen) instrument; (herramienta) tool,

implement

insubordinarse [insuβorði'narse] vr to rebel

insuficiente [insufi'θjente] adj (gen) insufficient; (Escol: calificación) unsatisfactory

insular [insu'lar] adj insular

insultar [insul'tar] vt to insult; **insulto** nm insult

insuperable [insupe'raβle] adj (excelente) unsurpassable; (problema etc) insurmountable

insurrección [insurrek'θjon] nf insurrection, rebellion

intachable [inta'tʃaβle] adj irreproachable

intacto, -a [in'takto, a] adj intact

integral [inte'γral] adj integral; (completo) complete; pan ~ wholemeal (BRIT) o wholewheat (US) bread

integrar [inte'γrar] vt to make up, compose; (Mat: fig) to integrate

integridad [inteγri'ðað] nf wholeness; (carácter) integrity; **íntegro, -a** adj whole, entire; (honrado) honest

intelectual [intelek'twal] adj, nmf intellectual

inteligencia [inteli'xenθja] nf (ingenio) ability; **inteligente** adj intelligent

intemperie [intem'perje] nf: **a la ~** out in the open, exposed to the elements

intención [inten'θjon] nf (gen) intention, purpose; **con segundas intenciones** maliciously; **con ~** deliberately

intencionado, -a [intenθjo'naðo, a] adj deliberate; **mal ~** ill-disposed, hostile

intensidad [intensi'ðað] nf (gen) intensity; (Elec, Tec) strength; **llover con ~** to rain hard

intenso, -a [in'tenso, a] adj intense; (sentimiento) profound, deep

intentar [inten'tar] vt (tratar) to try, attempt; **intento** nm attempt

interactivo, -a [interak'tiβo, a] adj (Inform) interactive

intercalar [interka'lar] vt to insert

intercambio [inter'kambjo] nm exchange, swap

interceder [interθe'ðer] vi to intercede

interceptar [interθep'tar] vt to intercept

interés [inte'res] nm (gen) interest; (parte) share, part; (pey) self-interest; **intereses creados** vested interests

interesado, -a [intere'saðo, a] adj interested; (prejuiciado) prejudiced; (pey) mercenary, self-seeking

interesante [intere'sante] adj interesting

interesar [intere'sar] vt, vi to interest, be of interest to; **interesarse** vr: **~se en o por** to take an interest in

interferir [interfe'rir] vt to interfere with; (Tel) to jam ▷ vi to interfere

interfón [inter'fon] (MÉX) nm entry phone

interino, -a [inte'rino, a] adj temporary ▷ nm/f temporary holder of a post; (Med) locum; (Escol) supply teacher

interior [inte'rjor] adj inner, inside; (Com) domestic, internal ▷ nm interior, inside; (fig) soul, mind; **Ministerio del I~** ≈ Home Office (BRIT); Department of the Interior (US); **interiorista** (ESP) nmf interior designer

interjección [interxek'θjon] nf interjection

interlocutor, a [interloku'tor, a] nm/f speaker

intermedio, -a [inter'meðjo, a] adj intermediate ▷ nm interval

interminable [intermi'naβle] adj endless

intermitente [intermi'tente] adj intermittent ▷ nm (Auto) indicator

internacional [internaθjo'nal] adj international

internado [inter'naðo] nm boarding

school

internar [inter'nar] vt to intern; (en un manicomio) to commit; **internarse** vr (penetrar) to penetrate

internauta [inter'nauta] nmf web surfer, Internet user

Internet, internet [inter'net] nm o f Internet

interno, -a [in'terno, a] adj internal, interior; (Pol etc) domestic ▷ nm/f (alumno) boarder

interponer [interpo'ner] vt to interpose, put in; **interponerse** vr to intervene

interpretación [interpreta'θjon] nf interpretation

interpretar [interpre'tar] vt to interpret; (Teatro, Mús) to perform, play; **intérprete** nmf (Ling) interpreter, translator; (Mús, Teatro) performer, artist(e)

interrogación [interroxa'θjon] nf interrogation; (Ling: tb: **signo de ~**) question mark

interrogar [interro'xar] vt to interrogate, question

interrumpir [interrum'pir] vt to interrupt

interrupción [interrup'θjon] nf interruption

interruptor [interrup'tor] nm (Elec) switch

intersección [intersek'θjon] nf intersection

interurbano, -a [interur'βano, a] adj: **llamada interurbana** long-distance call

intervalo [inter'βalo] nm interval; (descanso) break

intervenir [interβe'nir] vt (controlar) to control, supervise; (Med) to operate on ▷ vi (participar) to take part, participate; (mediar) to intervene

interventor, a [interβen'tor, a] nm/f inspector; (Com) auditor

intestino [intes'tino] nm (Med) intestine

intimar [inti'mar] vi to become

friendly

intimidad [intimi'ðað] nf intimacy; (familiaridad) familiarity; (vida privada) private life; (Jur) privacy

íntimo, -a ['intimo, a] adj intimate

intolerable [intole'raβle] adj intolerable, unbearable

intoxicación [intoksika'θjon] nf poisoning; **intoxicación alimenticia** food poisoning

intranet [intra'net] nf intranet

intranquilo, -a [intran'kilo, a] adj worried

intransitable [intransi'taβle] adj impassable

intrépido, -a [in'trepiðo, a] adj intrepid

intriga [in'trixa] nf intrigue; (plan) plot; **intrigar** vt, vi to intrigue

intrínseco, -a [in'trinseko, a] adj intrinsic

introducción [introðuk'θjon] nf introduction

introducir [introðu'θir] vt (gen) to introduce; (moneda etc) to insert; (Inform) to input, enter

intromisión [intromi'sjon] nf interference, meddling

introvertido, -a [introβer'tiðo, a] adj, nm/f introvert

intruso, -a [in'truso, a] adj intrusive ▷ nm/f intruder

intuición [intwi'θjon] nf intuition

inundación [inunda'θjon] nf flood(ing); **inundar** vt to flood; (fig) to swamp, inundate

inusitado, -a [inusi'taðo, a] adj unusual, rare

inútil [in'util] adj useless; (esfuerzo) vain, fruitless

inutilizar [inutili'θar] vt to make o render useless

invadir [imba'ðir] vt to invade

inválido, -a [im'baliðo, a] adj invalid ▷ nm/f invalid

invasión [imba'sjon] nf invasion

invasor, a [imba'sor, a] adj invading ▷ nm/f invader

invención [imben'θjon] *nf* invention

inventar [imben'tar] *vt* to invent

inventario [imben'tarjo] *nm* inventory

invento [im'bento] *nm* invention

inventor, a [imben'tor, a] *nm/f* inventor

invernadero [imberna'ðero] *nm* greenhouse

inverosímil [imbero'simil] *adj* implausible

inversión [imber'sjon] *nf* (Com) investment

inverso, -a [im'berso, a] *adj* inverse, opposite; **en el orden ~** in reverse order; **a la inversa** inversely, the other way round

inversor, a [imber'sor, a] *nm/f* (Com) investor

invertir [imber'tir] *vt* (Com) to invest; (volcar) to turn upside down; (tiempo etc) to spend

investigación [imbestiɣa'θjon] *nf* investigation; (Escol) research; **investigación y desarrollo** research and development

investigar [imbesti'ɣar] *vt* to investigate; (Escol) to do research into

invierno [im'bjerno] *nm* winter

invisible [imbi'siβle] *adj* invisible

invitación [imbita'θjon] *nf* invitation

invitado, -a [imbi'taðo, a] *nm/f* guest

invitar [imbi'tar] *vt* to invite; (incitar) to entice; (pagar) to buy, pay for

invocar [imbo'kar] *vt* to invoke, call on

involucrar [imbolu'krar] *vt*: **~ en** to involve in; **involucrarse** *vr* (persona): **~se en** to get mixed up in

involuntario, -a [imbolun'tarjo, a] *adj* (movimiento, gesto) involuntary; (error) unintentional

inyección [injek'θjon] *nf* injection

inyectar [injek'tar] *vt* to inject

iPod® ['ipoð] (*pl* **~s**) *nm* iPod®

○ **PALABRA CLAVE**

ir [ir] *vi* 1 to go; (*a pie*) to walk; (*viajar*) to travel; **ir caminando** to walk; **fui en tren** I went o travelled by train; **¡(ahora) voy!** (I'm just) coming!

2: **ir (a) por: ir (a) por el médico** to fetch the doctor

3 (*progresar: persona, cosa*) to go; **el trabajo va muy bien** work is going very well; **¿cómo te va?** how are things going?; **me va muy bien** I'm getting on very well; **le fue fatal** it went awfully badly for him

4 (*funcionar*) **el coche no va muy bien** the car isn't running very well

5: **te va estupendamente ese color** that colour suits you fantastically well

6 (*locuciones*): **¿vino? – ¡que va!** did he come? – of course not!; **vamos, no llores** come on, don't cry; **¡vaya coche!** what a car!, that's some car!

7: **no vaya a ser: tienes que correr, no vaya a ser que pierdas el tren** you'll have to run so as not to miss the train

8 (*+ pp*): **iba vestido muy bien** he was very well dressed

9: **ni me** etc **va ni me** etc **viene** I etc don't care

▷ *vb aux* 1 **ir a: voy/iba a hacerlo hoy** I am/was going to do it today

2 (*+ gerundio*): **iba anocheciendo** it was getting dark; **todo se me iba aclarando** everything was gradually becoming clearer to me

3 (*+ pp: = pasivo*): **van vendidos 300 ejemplares** 300 copies have been sold so far

irse *vr* 1: **¿por dónde se va al zoológico?** which is the way to the zoo?

2 (*marcharse*) to leave; **ya se habrán ido** they must already have left o gone

ira ['ira] *nf* anger, rage

Irak [i'rak] nm = **Iraq**

Irán [i'ran] nm Iran; **iraní** adj, nmf
Iranian

Iraq [i'rak] nm Iraq; **iraquí** adj,
nmf Iraqi

iris ['iris] nm inv (tb: **arco ~**) rainbow;
(Anat) iris

Irlanda [ir'landa] nf Ireland;
Irlanda del Norte Northern Ireland;
irlandés, -esa adj Irish ▷ nm/f
Irishman(-woman); **los irlandeses**
the Irish

ironía [iro'nia] nf irony; **irónico, -a**
adj ironic(al)

IRPF nm abr (= Impuesto sobre la Renta
de las Personas Físicas) (personal)
income tax

irreal [irre'al] adj unreal

irregular [irreɣu'lar] adj (gen)
irregular; (situación) abnormal

irremediable [irreme'ðjaβle] adj
irremediable; (vicio) incurable

irreparable [irrepa'raβle] adj (daños)
irreparable; (pérdida) irrecoverable

irrespetuoso, -a [irrespe'twoso, a]
adj disrespectful

irresponsable [irrespon'saβle] adj
irresponsible

irreversible [irreβer'sible] adj
irreversible

irrigar [irri'ɣar] vt to irrigate

irrisorio, -a [irri'sorjo, a] adj
derisory, ridiculous

irritar [irri'tar] vt to irritate, annoy

irrupción [irrup'θjon] nf irruption;
(invasión) invasion

isla ['isla] nf island

Islam [is'lam] nm Islam; **las
enseñanzas del ~** the teachings of
Islam; **islámico, -a** adj Islamic

islandés, -esa [islan'des, esa] adj
Icelandic ▷ nm/f Icelander

Islandia [is'landja] nf Iceland

isleño, -a [is'leɲo, a] adj island cpd
▷ nm/f islander

Israel [isra'el] nm Israel; **israelí** adj,
nmf Israeli

istmo ['istmo] nm isthmus

Italia [i'talja] nf Italy; **italiano, -a** adj,
nm/f Italian

itinerario [itine'rarjo] nm itinerary,
route

ITV (ESP) nf abr (= inspección técnica
de vehículos) roadworthiness test, ≈
MOT (BRIT)

IVA ['iβa] nm abr (= impuesto sobre el
valor añadido) VAT

izar [i'θar] vt to hoist

izdo, -a abr (= izquierdo, a) l

izquierda [iθ'kjerda] nf left; (Pol) left
(wing); **a la ~** (estar) on the left; (torcer
etc) (to the) left

izquierdo, -a [iθ'kjerðo, a] adj left

J

jabalí [xaβa'li] *nm* wild boar

jabalina [xaβa'lina] *nf* javelin

jabón [xa'βon] *nm* soap

jaca ['xaka] *nf* pony

jacal [xa'kal] (MÉX) *nm* shack

jacinto [xa'θinto] *nm* hyacinth

jactarse [xak'tarse] *vr* to boast, brag

jadear [xaðe'ar] *vi* to pant, gasp for breath

jaguar [xa'ɣwar] *nm* jaguar

jaiba ['xaiβa] (LAM) *nf* crab

jalar [xa'lar] (LAM) *vt* to pull

jalea [xa'lea] *nf* jelly

jaleo [xa'leo] *nm* racket, uproar; **armar un ~** to kick up a racket

jalón [xa'lon] (LAM) *nm* tug

jamás [xa'mas] *adv* never

jamón [xa'mon] *nm* ham; **jamón dulce** *o* **de York** cooked ham; **jamón serrano** cured ham

Japón [xa'pon] *nm* Japan; **japonés, -esa** *adj, nm/f* Japanese ▷ *nm* (Ling) Japanese

jaque ['xake] *nm* (*Ajedrez*) check; **jaque mate** checkmate

jaqueca [xa'keka] *nf* (very bad) headache, migraine

jarabe [xa'raβe] *nm* syrup

jardín [xar'ðin] *nm* garden; **jardín infantil** *o* **de infancia** nursery (school); **jardinería** *nf* gardening; **jardinero, -a** *nm/f* gardener

jardinaje [xarði'naxe] *nm* gardening

jarra ['xarra] *nf* jar; (*jarro*) jug

jarro ['xarro] *nm* jug

jarrón [xa'rron] *nm* vase

jaula ['xaula] *nf* cage

jauría [xau'ria] *nf* pack of hounds

jazmín [xaθ'min] *nm* jasmine

J.C. *abr* (=*Jesucristo*) J.C.

jeans [jins, dʒins] (LAM) *nmpl* jeans, denims; **unos ~** a pair of jeans

jefatura [xefa'tura] *nf* (*tb:* **~ de policía**) police headquarters *sg*

jefe, -a ['xefe, a] *nm/f* (*gen*) chief, head; (*patrón*) boss; **jefe de cocina** chef; **jefe de estación** stationmaster; **jefe de Estado** head of state; **jefe de estudios** (*Escol*) director of studies; **jefe de gobierno** head of government

jengibre [xen'xiβre] *nm* ginger

jeque ['xeke] *nm* sheik

jerárquico, -a [xe'rarkiko, a] *adj* hierarchic(al)

jerez [xe'reθ] *nm* sherry

jerga ['xerxa] *nf* jargon

jeringa [xe'ringa] *nf* syringe; (LAM: *molestia*) annoyance, bother; **jeringuilla** *nf* syringe

jeroglífico [xero'xlifiko] *nm* hieroglyphic

jersey [xer'sei] (*pl* **~s**) *nm* jersey, pullover, jumper

Jerusalén [xerusa'len] *n* Jerusalem

Jesucristo [xesu'kristo] *nm* Jesus Christ

jesuita [xe'swita] *adj, nm* Jesuit

Jesús [xe'sus] *nm* Jesus; **¡~!** good heavens!; (*al estornudar*) bless you!

jinete [xi'nete] *nmf* horseman(-woman), rider

jipijapa [xipi'xapa] (LAM) *nm* straw hat

jirafa ['xi'rafa] nf giraffe

jirón [xi'ron] nm rag, shred

jitomate [xito'mate] (MÉX) nm tomato

joder [xo'ðer] (fam!) vt, vi to fuck (!)

jogging ['joχin] (RPL) nm tracksuit (BRIT), sweat suit (US)

jornada [xor'naða] nf (viaje de un día) day's journey; (camino o viaje entero) journey; (día de trabajo) working day

jornal [xor'nal] nm (day's) wage; **jornalero, -a** nm/f (day) labourer

joroba [xo'roβa] nf hump, hunched back; **jorobado, -a** adj hunchbacked ▷ nm/f hunchback

jota ['xota] nf (the letter) J; (danza) Aragonese dance; **no saber ni ~** to have no idea

joven ['xoβen] (pl **jóvenes**) adj young ▷ nm young man, youth ▷ nf young woman, girl

joya ['xoja] nf jewel, gem; (fig: persona) gem; **joyas de fantasía** costume o imitation jewellery; **joyería** nf (joyas) jewellery; (tienda) jeweller's (shop); **joyero** nm (persona) jeweller; (caja) jewel case

juanete [xwa'nete] nm (del pie) bunion

jubilación [xuβila'θjon] nf (retiro) retirement

jubilado, -a [xuβi'laðo, a] adj retired ▷ nm/f pensioner (BRIT), senior citizen

jubilar [xuβi'lar] vt to pension off, retire; (fam) to discard; **jubilarse** vr to retire

júbilo ['xuβilo] nm joy, rejoicing; **jubiloso, -a** adj jubilant

judía [xu'ðia] (ESP) nf (Culin) bean; **judía blanca/verde** haricot/French bean; V tb **judío**

judicial [xuði'θjal] adj judicial

judío, -a [xu'ðio, a] adj Jewish ▷ nm/f Jew(ess)

judo ['juðo] nm judo

juego etc ['xwexo] vb V **jugar** ▷ nm (gen) play; (pasatiempo, partido) game; (en casino) gambling; (conjunto) set;

fuera de ~ (Deporte: persona) offside; (: pelota) out of play; **juego de mesa** board game; **juego de palabras** pun, play on words; **Juegos Olímpicos** Olympic Games

juerga ['xwerxa] (ESP: fam) nf binge; (fiesta) party; **ir de ~** to go out on a binge

jueves ['xweβes] nm inv Thursday

juez [xweθ] nmf judge; **juez de instrucción** examining magistrate; **juez de línea** linesman; **juez de salida** starter

jugada [xu'xaða] nf play; **buena ~** good move o shot o stroke etc

jugador, a [xuxa'ðor, a] nm/f player; (en casino) gambler

jugar [xu'xar] vt, vi to play; (en casino) to gamble; (apostar) to bet; **~ al fútbol** to play football

juglar [xu'xlar] nm minstrel

jugo ['xuxo] nm (Bot) juice; (fig) essence, substance; **jugo de naranja** (LAM) orange juice; **jugoso, -a** adj juicy; (fig) substantial, important

juguete [xu'xete] nm toy; **juguetear** vi to play; **juguetería** nf toyshop

juguetón, -ona [xuxe'ton, ona] adj playful

juicio ['xwiθjo] nm judgement; (razón) sanity, reason; (opinión) opinion

julio ['xuljo] nm July

jumper etc ['dʒumper] (LAM) nm pinafore dress (BRIT), jumper (US)

junco ['xunko] nm rush, reed

jungla ['xunɡla] nf jungle

junio ['xunjo] nm June

junta ['xunta] nf (asamblea) meeting, assembly; (comité, consejo) council, committee; (Com, Finanzas) board; (Tec) joint; **junta directiva** board of directors

juntar [xun'tar] vt to join, unite; (maquinaria) to assemble, put together; (dinero) to collect; **juntarse** vr to join, meet; (reunirse: personas) to meet, assemble; (arrimarse) to approach, draw closer; **~se con algn** to join sb

junto, -a ['xunto, a] *adj* joined; (*unido*) united; (*anexo*) near, close; (*contiguo, próximo*) next, adjacent ▷ *adv*: **todo ~** all at once; **~s** together; **~ a** near (to), next to; **~ con** (together) with

jurado [xu'raðo] *nm* (Jur: *individuo*) juror; (: *grupo*) jury; (*de concurso*: *grupo*) panel (of judges); (: *individuo*) member of a panel

juramento [xura'mento] *nm* oath; (*maldición*) oath, curse; **prestar ~** to take the oath; **tomar ~ a** to swear in, administer the oath to

jurar [xu'rar] *vt, vi* to swear; **~ en falso** to commit perjury; **tenérsela jurada a algn** to have it in for sb

jurídico, -a [xu'riðiko, a] *adj* legal

jurisdicción [xurisðik'θjon] *nf* (*poder, autoridad*) jurisdiction; (*territorio*) district

justamente [xusta'mente] *adv* justly, fairly; (*precisamente*) just, exactly

justicia [xus'tiθja] *nf* justice; (*equidad*) fairness, justice

justificación [xustifika'θjon] *nf* justification; **justificar** *vt* to justify

justo, -a ['xusto, a] *adj* (*equitativo*) just, fair, right; (*preciso*) exact, correct; (*ajustado*) tight ▷ *adv* (*precisamente*) exactly, precisely; (LAM: *apenas a tiempo*) just in time

juvenil [xuβe'nil] *adj* youthful

juventud [xuβen'tuð] *nf* (*adolescencia*) youth; (*jóvenes*) young people *pl*

juzgado [xuθ'yaðo] *nm* tribunal; (Jur) court

juzgar [xuθ'yar] *vt* to judge; **a ~ por ...** to judge by ..., judging by ...

k

kárate ['karate] *nm* karate

kg *abr* (= *kilogramo*) kg

kilo ['kilo] *nm* kilo; **kilogramo** *nm* kilogramme; **kilometraje** *nm* distance in kilometres ≈ mileage; **kilómetro** *nm* kilometre; **kilovatio** *nm* kilowatt

kiosco ['kjosko] *nm* = **quiosco**

kleenex® [kli'neks] *nm* paper handkerchief, tissue

Kosovo [ko'soβo] *nm* Kosovo

km *abr* (= *kilómetro*) km

kv *abr* (= *kilovatio*) kw

l abr (= litro) l

la [la] art def the ▷ pron her; (Ud.) you; (cosa) it ▷ nm (Mús) la; **~ del sombrero rojo** the girl in the red hat; V tb **el**

laberinto [laβeˈrinto] nm labyrinth

labio [ˈlaβjo] nm lip

labor [laˈβor] nf labour; (Agr) farm work; (tarea) job, task; (Costura) needlework; **labores domésticas o del hogar** household chores; **laborable** adj (Agr) workable; **día laborable** working day; **laboral** adj (accidente) at work; (jornada) working

laboratorio [laβoraˈtorjo] nm laboratory

laborista [laβoˈrista] adj: **Partido L~** Labour Party

labrador, a [laβraˈðor, a] adj farming cpd ▷ nm/f farmer

labranza [laˈβranθa] nf (Agr) cultivation

labrar [laˈβrar] vt (gen) to work; (madera etc) to carve; (fig) to cause, bring about

laca [ˈlaka] nf lacquer

lacio, -a [ˈlaθjo, a] adj (pelo) straight

lacón [laˈkon] nm shoulder of pork

lactancia [lakˈtanθja] nf lactation

lácteo, -a [ˈlakteo, a] adj: **productos ~s** dairy products

ladear [laðeˈar] vt to tip, tilt ▷ vi to tilt; **ladearse** vr to lean

ladera [laˈðera] nf slope

lado [ˈlaðo] nm (gen) side; (fig) protection; (Mil) flank; **al ~ de** beside; **poner de ~** to put on its side; **poner a un ~** to put aside; **por todos ~s** on all sides, all round (BRIT)

ladrar [laˈðrar] vi to bark; **ladrido** nm bark, barking

ladrillo [laˈðriʎo] nm (gen) brick; (azulejo) tile

ladrón, -ona [laˈðron, ona] nm/f thief

lagartija [lavarˈtixa] nf (Zool) (small) lizard

lagarto [laˈvarto] nm (Zool) lizard

lago [ˈlavo] nm lake

lágrima [ˈlavrima] nf tear

laguna [laˈvuna] nf (lago) lagoon; (hueco) gap

lamentable [lamenˈtaβle] adj lamentable, regrettable; (miserable) pitiful

lamentar [lamenˈtar] vt (sentir) to regret; (deplorar) to lament; **lamentarse** vr to lament; **lo lamento mucho** I'm very sorry

lamer [laˈmer] vt to lick

lámina [ˈlamina] nf (plancha delgada) sheet; (para estampar, estampa) plate

lámpara [ˈlampara] nf lamp; **lámpara de alcohol/gas** spirit/gas lamp; **lámpara de pie** standard lamp

lana [ˈlana] nf wool

lancha [ˈlantʃa] nf launch; **lancha motora** motorboat, speedboat

langosta [lanˈgosta] nf (crustáceo) lobster; (: de río) crayfish; **langostino** nm Dublin Bay prawn

lanza [ˈlanθa] nf (arma) lance, spear

lanzamiento [lanθaˈmjento] nm (gen) throwing; (Náut, Com) launch, launching; **lanzamiento de peso** putting the shot

lanzar [lan'θar] vt (gen) to throw; (Deporte: pelota) to bowl; (Náut, Com) to launch; (Jur) to evict; **lanzarse** vr to throw o.s.

lapa ['lapa] nf limpet

lapicero [lapi'θero] (CAM) nm (bolígrafo) ballpoint pen, Biro®

lápida ['lapiða] nf stone; **lápida mortuoria** headstone

lápiz ['lapiθ] nm pencil; **lápiz de color** coloured pencil; **lápiz de labios** lipstick; **lápiz de ojos** eyebrow pencil

largar [lar'ɣar] vt (soltar) to release; (aflojar) to loosen; (lanzar) to launch; (fam) to let fly; (velas) to unfurl; (LAM: lanzar) to throw; **largarse** vr (fam) to beat it; **~se a** (cs: empezar) to start to

largo, -a ['larɣo, a] adj (longitud) long; (tiempo) lengthy; (fig) generous ▷ nm length; (Mús) largo; **dos años ~s** two long years; **tiene 9 metros de ~** it is 9 metres long; **a la larga** in the long run; **a lo ~ de** along; (tiempo) all through, throughout

⚠ No confundir **largo** con la palabra inglesa *large*.

largometraje nm feature film

laringe [la'rinxe] nf larynx; **laringitis** nf laryngitis

las [las] art def the ▷ pron them; **~ que cantan** the ones o women o girls who sing; V tb **el**

lasaña [la'saɲa] nf lasagne, lasagna

láser ['laser] nm laser

lástima ['lastima] nf (pena) pity; **dar ~** to be pitiful; **es una ~ que ...** it's a pity that ...; **¡qué ~!** what a pity!; **está hecha una ~** she looks pitiful

lastimar [lasti'mar] vt (herir) to wound; (ofender) to offend; **lastimarse** vr to hurt o.s.

lata ['lata] nf (metal) tin; (caja) tin (BRIT), can; (fam) nuisance; **en ~** tinned (BRIT), canned; **dar la ~** to be a nuisance

latente [la'tente] adj latent

lateral [late'ral] adj side cpd, lateral ▷ nm (Teatro) wings

latido [la'tiðo] nm (de corazón) beat

latifundio [lati'fundjo] nm large estate

latigazo [lati'ɣaθo] nm (golpe) lash; (sonido) crack

látigo ['latiɣo] nm whip

latín [la'tin] nm Latin

latino, -a [la'tino, a] adj Latin; **latinoamericano, -a** adj, nm/f Latin-American

latir [la'tir] vi (corazón, pulso) to beat

latitud [lati'tuð] nf (Geo) latitude

latón [la'ton] nm brass

laurel [lau'rel] nm (Bot) laurel; (Culin) bay

lava ['laβa] nf lava

lavabo [la'βaβo] nm (pila) washbasin; (tb: **~s**) toilet

lavado [la'βaðo] nm washing; (de ropa) laundry; (Arte) wash; **lavado de cerebro** brainwashing; **lavado en seco** dry-cleaning

lavadora [laβa'ðora] nf washing machine

lavanda [la'βanda] nf lavender

lavandería [laβande'ria] nf laundry; (automática) launderette

lavaplatos [laβa'platos] nm inv dishwasher

lavar [la'βar] vt to wash; (borrar) to wipe away; **lavarse** vr to wash o.s.; **~se las manos** to wash one's hands; **~se los dientes** to brush one's teeth; **~ y marcar** (pelo) to shampoo and set; **~ en seco** to dry-clean; **~ los platos** to wash the dishes

lavarropas [laβa'rropas] (RPL) nm inv washing machine

lavavajillas [laβaβa'xiʎas] nm inv dishwasher

laxante [lak'sante] nm laxative

lazarillo [laθa'riʎo] nm (tb: **perro ~**) guide dog

lazo ['laθo] nm knot; (lazada) bow; (para animales) lasso; (trampa) snare;

(vínculo) tie

le [le] pron (directo) him (o her); (: usted) you; (indirecto) to him (o her o it); (: usted) to you

leal [le'al] adj loyal; **lealtad** nf loyalty

lección [lek'θjon] nf lesson

leche ['letʃe] nf milk; **tiene mala ~** (fam!) he's a swine (fam!); **leche condensada** condensed milk; **leche desnatada** skimmed milk

lechería [letʃe'ria] nf dairy

lecho ['letʃo] nm (cama: de río) bed; (Geo) layer

lechón [le'tʃon] nm sucking (BRIT) o suckling (US) pig

lechoso, -a [le'tʃoso, a] adj milky

lechuga [le'tʃuɣa] nf lettuce

lechuza [le'tʃuθa] nf owl

lector, a [lek'tor, a] nm/f reader
▷ nm: **- de discos compactos** CD player

lectura [lek'tura] nf reading

leer [le'er] vt to read

legado [le'ɣaðo] nm (don) bequest; (herencia) legacy; (enviado) legate

legajo [le'ɣaxo] nm file

legal [le'ɣal] adj (gen) legal; (persona) trustworthy; **legalizar** [leɣali'θar] vt to legalize; (documento) to authenticate

legaña [le'ɣaɲa] nf sleep (in eyes)

legión [le'xjon] nf legion; **legionario, -a** adj legionary ▷ nm legionnaire

legislación [lexisla'θjon] nf legislation

legislar [lexis'lar] vi to legislate

legislatura [lexisla'tura] nf (Pol) period of office

legítimo, -a [le'xitimo, a] adj (genuino) authentic; (legal) legitimate

legua ['leɣwa] nf league

legumbres [le'ɣumbres] nfpl pulses

leído, -a [le'iðo, a] adj well-read

lejanía [lexa'nia] nf distance; **lejano, -a** adj far-off; (en el tiempo) distant; (fig) remote

lejía [le'xia] nf bleach

lejos ['lexos] adv far, far away; **a lo ~** in the distance; **de o desde ~** from afar;

~ de far from

lema ['lema] nm motto; (Pol) slogan

lencería [lenθe'ria] nf linen, drapery

lengua ['lenɣwa] nf tongue; (Ling) language; **morderse la ~** to hold one's tongue

lenguado [len'ɣwaðo] nm sole

lenguaje [len'ɣwaxe] nm language; **lenguaje de programación** program(m)ing language

lengüeta [len'ɣweta] nf (Anat) epiglottis; (zapatos) tongue; (Mús) reed

lente ['lente] nf lens; (lupa) magnifying glass; **lentes** nfpl lenses ▷ nmpl (LAM: gafas) glasses; **lentes bifocales/de sol** (LAM) bifocals/ sunglasses; **lentes de contacto** contact lenses

lenteja [len'texa] nf lentil; **lentejuela** nf sequin

lentilla [len'tiλa] nf contact lens

lentitud [lenti'tuð] nf slowness; **con ~** slowly

lento, -a ['lento, a] adj slow

leña ['leɲa] nf firewood; **leñador, a** nm/f woodcutter

leño ['leɲo] nm (trozo de árbol) log; (madero) timber; (fig) blockhead

Leo ['leo] nm Leo

león [le'on] nm lion; **león marino** sea lion

leopardo [leo'parðo] nm leopard

leotardos [leo'tarðos] nmpl tights

lepra ['lepra] nf leprosy; **leproso, -a** nm/f leper

les [les] pron (directo) them; (: ustedes) you; (indirecto) to them; (: ustedes) to you

lesbiana [les'βjana] adj, nf lesbian

lesión [le'sjon] nf wound, lesion; (Deporte) injury; **lesionado, -a** adj injured ▷ nm/f injured person

letal [le'tal] adj lethal

letanía [leta'nia] nf litany

letra ['letra] nf letter; (escritura) handwriting; (Mús) lyrics pl; **letra de cambio** bill of exchange; **letra de imprenta** print; **letrado, -a** adj learned ▷ nm/f lawyer; **letrero** nm (cartel) sign; (etiqueta) label

letrina [le'trina] nf latrine

leucemia [leu'θemja] nf leukaemia

levadura [leßa'ðura] nf (para el pan) yeast; (de cerveza) brewer's yeast

levantar [leßan'tar] vt (gen) to raise; (del suelo) to pick up; (hacia arriba) to lift (up); (plan) to make, draw up; (mesa) to clear; (campamento) to strike; (fig) to cheer up, hearten; **levantarse** vr to get up; (enderezarse) to straighten up; (rebelarse) to rebel; **~ el ánimo** to cheer up

levante [le'ßante] nm east coast; **el L-** region of Spain extending from Castellón to Murcia

levar [le'ßar] vt to weigh

leve [leße] adj light; (fig) trivial

levita [le'ßita] nf frock coat

léxico ['leksiko] nm (vocabulario) vocabulary

ley [lei] nf (gen) law; (metal) standard

leyenda [le'jenda] nf legend

leyó etc vb ▷ **leer**

liar [li'ar] vt to tie (up); (unir) to bind; (envolver) to wrap (up); (enredar) to confuse; (cigarrillo) to roll; **liarse** vr (fam) to get involved; **~se a palos** to get involved in a fight

Líbano ['lißano] nm: **el ~** the Lebanon

libélula [li'ßelula] nf dragonfly

liberación [lißera'θjon] nf liberation; (de la cárcel) release

liberal [liße'ral] adj, nm/f liberal

liberar [liße'rar] vt to liberate

libertad [lißer'tað] nf liberty, freedom; **libertad bajo fianza** bail; **libertad bajo palabra** parole; **libertad condicional** probation; **libertad de culto/de prensa/de comercio** freedom of worship/of the press/of trade

libertar [lißer'tar] vt (preso) to set free; (de una obligación) to release; (eximir) to exempt

libertino, -a [lißer'tino, a] adj permissive ▷ nm/f permissive person

libra ['lißra] nf pound; **L- (Astrología)** Libra; **libra esterlina** pound sterling

libramiento [lißra'mjento] (MÉX) nm ring road (BRIT), beltway (US)

librar [li'ßrar] vt (de peligro) to save; (batalla) to wage, fight; (de impuestos) to exempt; (cheque) to make out; (Jur) to exempt; **librarse** vr: **~se de** to escape from, free o.s. from

libre ['lißre] adj free; (lugar) unoccupied; (asiento) vacant; (de deudas) free of debts; **~ de impuestos** free of tax; **tiro ~** free kick; **los 100 metros ~s** the 100 metres free-style (race); **al aire ~** in the open air

librería [liße'ria] nf (tienda) bookshop

> No confundir **librería** con la palabra inglesa library.

librero, -a nm/f bookseller

libreta [li'ßreta] nf notebook

libro ['lißro] nm book; **libro de bolsillo** paperback; **libro de texto** textbook; **libro electrónico** e-book

Lic. abr = **licenciado, a**

licencia [li'θenθja] nf (gen) licence; (permiso) permission; **licencia de caza** game licence; **licencia por enfermedad** (MÉX, RPL) sick leave; **licenciado, -a** adj licensed ▷ nm/f graduate; **licenciar** vt (empleado) to dismiss; (permitir) to permit, allow; (soldado) to discharge; (estudiante) to confer a degree upon; **licenciarse** vr: **licenciarse en Derecho** to graduate in law

licenciatura [liθenθja'tura] nf (título) degree; (estudios) degree course

lícito, -a [li'θito, a] adj (legal) lawful; (justo) fair, just; (permisible) permissible

licor [li'kor] nm spirits pl (BRIT), liquor (US); (de frutas etc) liqueur

licuadora [likwa'ðora] nf blender

líder ['liðer] nm/f leader; **liderato** nm leadership; **liderazgo** nm leadership

lidia ['liðja] nf bullfighting; (una lidia) bullfight; **toros de ~** fighting bulls; **lidiar** vt, vi to fight

liebre ['ljeβre] nf hare

lienzo ['ljenθo] nm linen; (Arte) canvas; (Arq) wall

liga ['liɣa] nf (de medias) garter, suspender; (LAM: goma) rubber band; (confederación) league

ligadura [liɣa'ðura] nf bond, tie; (Med, Mús) ligature

ligamento [liɣa'mento] nm ligament

ligar [li'ɣar] vt (atar) to tie; (unir) to join; (Med) to bind up; (Mús) to slur ▷ vi to mix, blend; (fam: **(él) liga mucho** he pulls a lot of women; **ligarse** vr to commit o.s.

ligero, -a [li'xero, a] adj (de peso) light; (tela) thin; (rápido) swift, quick; (ágil) agile, nimble; (de importancia) slight; (de carácter) flippant, superficial ▷ adv: **a la ligera** superficially

liguero [li'ɣero] nm suspender (BRIT) o garter (US) belt

lija ['lixa] nf (Zool) dogfish; (tb: **papel de ~**) sandpaper

lila ['lila] nf lilac

lima ['lima] nf file; (Bot) lime; **lima de uñas** nailfile; **limar** vt to file

limitación [limita'θjon] nf limitation, limit

limitar [limi'tar] vt to limit; (reducir) to reduce, cut down ▷ vi: **~ con** to border on; **limitarse** vr: **~se a** to limit o.s. to

límite ['limite] nm (gen) limit; (fin) end; (frontera) border; **límite de velocidad** speed limit

limítrofe [li'mitrofe] adj neighbouring

limón [li'mon] nm lemon ▷ adj: **amarillo ~** lemon-yellow; **limonada** nf lemonade

limosna [li'mosna] nf alms pl; **vivir de ~** to live on charity

limpiador, a [limpja'ðor] (MÉX) nm = **limpiaparabrisas**

limpiaparabrisas [limpjapara'βrisas] nm inv windscreen (BRIT) o windshield (US) wiper

limpiar [lim'pjar] vt to clean; (con trapo) to wipe; (quitar) to wipe away; (zapatos) to shine, polish; (Inform) to debug; (fig) to clean up

limpieza [lim'pjeθa] nf (estado) cleanliness; (acto) cleaning; (: de las calles) cleansing; (: de zapatos) polishing; (habilidad) skill; (fig: Policía) clean-up; (pureza) purity; (Mil): **operación de ~** mopping-up operation; **limpieza en seco** dry cleaning

limpio, -a ['limpjo, a] adj clean; (moralmente) pure; (Com) clear, net; (fam) honest ▷ adv: **jugar ~** to play fair; **pasar a** (ESP) **o en** (LAM) **~** to make a clean copy of

lince ['linθe] nm lynx

linchar [lin'tʃar] vt to lynch

lindar [lin'dar] vi to adjoin; **~ con** to border on

lindo, -a ['lindo, a] adj pretty, lovely ▷ adv: **nos divertimos de lo ~** we had a marvellous time; **canta muy ~** (LAM) he sings beautifully

línea ['linea] nf (gen) line; **en ~** (Inform) on line; **línea aérea** airline; **línea de meta** goal line; (en carrera) finishing line; **línea discontinua** (Auto) broken line; **línea recta** straight line

lingote [lin'ɡote] nm ingot

lingüista [lin'ɡwista] nmf linguist; **lingüística** nf linguistics sg

lino ['lino] nm linen; (Bot) flax

linterna [lin'terna] nf torch (BRIT), flashlight (US)

lío ['lio] nm bundle; (fam) fuss; (desorden) muddle, mess; **armar un ~** to make a fuss

liquen ['liken] nm lichen

liquidación [likiða'θjon] nf liquidation; **venta de ~** clearance sale

liquidar [liki'ðar] vt (mercancías) to liquidate; (deudas) to pay off; (empresa) to wind up

líquido, -a ['likiðo, a] adj liquid; (ganancia) net ▷ nm liquid; **líquido imponible** net taxable income

lira ['lira] nf (Mús) lyre; (moneda) lira

lírico, -a [ˈliriko, a] *adj* lyrical

lirio [ˈlirjo] *nm* (Bot) iris

lirón [liˈron] *nm* (Zool) dormouse; (fig) sleepyhead

Lisboa [lisˈβoa] *n* Lisbon

lisiar [liˈsjar] *vt* to maim

liso, -a [ˈliso, a] *adj* (terreno) flat; (cabello) straight; (superficie) even; (tela) plain

lista [ˈlista] *nf* list; (de alumnos) school register; (de libros) catalogue; (de platos) menu; (de precios) price list; **pasar ~** to call the roll; **tela de ~** striped material; **lista de espera** waiting list; **lista de precios** price list; **listín** *nm* (tb: **listín telefónico o de teléfonos**) telephone directory

listo, -a [ˈlisto, a] *adj* (perspicaz) smart, clever; (preparado) ready

listón [lisˈton] *nm* (de madera, metal) strip

litera [liˈtera] *nf* (en barco, tren) berth; (en dormitorio) bunk, bunk bed

literal [liteˈral] *adj* literal

literario, -a [liteˈrarjo, a] *adj* literary

literato, -a [liteˈrato, a] *adj* literary ▷ *nm/f* writer

literatura [literaˈtura] *nf* literature

litigio [liˈtixjo] *nm* (Jur) lawsuit; (fig) **en ~ con** in dispute with

litografía [litograˈfia] *nf* lithography; (una litografía) lithograph

litoral [litoˈral] *adj* coastal ▷ *nm* coast, seaboard

litro [ˈlitro] *nm* litre

lívido, -a [ˈliβiðo, a] *adj* livid

llaga [ˈʎaɣa] *nf* wound

llama [ˈʎama] *nf* flame; (Zool) llama

llamada [ʎaˈmaða] *nf* call; **llamada a cobro revertido** reverse-charge (BRIT) o collect (US) call; **llamada al orden** call to order; **llamada de atención** warning; **llamada local** (LAM) local call; **llamada metropolitana** (ESP) local call; **llamada por cobrar** (MÉX) reverse-charge (BRIT) o collect (US) call

llamamiento [ʎamaˈmjento] *nm* call

llamar [ʎaˈmar] *vt* to call; (atención) to attract ▷ *vi* (por teléfono) to telephone; (a la puerta) to knock o (ring); (por señas) to beckon; (Mil) to call up; **llamarse** *vr* to be called, be named; **¿cómo se llama (usted)?** what's your name?

llamativo, -a [ʎamaˈtiβo, a] *adj* showy; (color) loud

llano, -a [ˈʎano, a] *adj* (superficie) flat; (persona) straightforward; (estilo) clear ▷ *nm* plain, flat ground

llanta [ˈʎanta] *nf* (ESP) (wheel) rim; **llanta (de goma)** (LAM: neumático) tyre; (: cámara) inner (tube); **llanta de repuesto** (LAM) spare tyre

llanto [ˈʎanto] *nm* weeping

llanura [ʎaˈnura] *nf* plain

llave [ˈʎaβe] *nf* key; (del agua) tap; (Mecánica) spanner; (de la luz) switch; (Mús) key; **echar la ~** to lock up; **llave de contacto** (ESP Auto) ignition key; **llave de encendido** (LAM Auto) ignition key; **llave de paso** stopcock; **llave inglesa** monkey wrench; **llave maestra** master key; **llavero** *nm* keyring

llegada [ʎeˈɣaða] *nf* arrival

llegar [ʎeˈɣar] *vi* to arrive; (alcanzar) to reach; (bastar) to be enough; **llegarse** *vr*: **~se a** to approach; **~ a** to manage to, succeed in; **~ a saber** to find out; **~ a ser** to become; **~ a las manos de** to come into the hands of

llenar [ʎeˈnar] *vt* to fill; (espacio) to cover; (formulario) to fill in o up; (fig) to heap

lleno, -a [ˈʎeno, a] *adj* full, filled; (repleto) full up ▷ *nm* (Teatro) full house; **dar de ~ contra un muro** to hit a wall head-on

llevadero, -a [ʎeβaˈðero, a] *adj* bearable, tolerable

llevar [ʎeˈβar] *vt* to take; (ropa) to wear; (cargar) to carry; (quitar) to take away; (en coche) to drive; (transportar) to transport; (traer: dinero) to carry; (conducir) to lead; (Mat) to carry ▷ *vi* (suj: camino etc): **~ a** to lead to; **llevarse**

vr to carry off, take away; **llevamos dos días aquí** we have been here for two days; **él me lleva 2 años** he's 2 years older than me; **~ los libros** (Com) to keep the books; **~se bien** to get on well (together)

llorar [ʎo'rar] *vt, vi* to cry, weep; **~ de risa** to cry with laughter

llorón, -ona [ʎo'ron, ona] *adj* tearful ▷ *nm/f* cry-baby

lloroso, -a [ʎo'roso, a] *adj* (*gen*) weeping, tearful; (*triste*) sad, sorrowful

llover [ʎo'βer] *vi* to rain

llovizna [ʎo'βiθna] *nf* drizzle; **lloviznar** *vi* to drizzle

llueve *etc vb V* **llover**

lluvia [ʎuβja] *nf* rain; **lluvia radioactiva** (radioactive) fallout; **lluvioso, -a** *adj* rainy

lo [lo] *art def*: **~ bel-** the beautiful, what is beautiful, that which is beautiful ▷ *pron* (*persona*) him; (*cosa*) it; **~ que sea** whatever; *V tb* **el**

loable [lo'aβle] *adj* praiseworthy

lobo ['loβo] *nm* wolf; **lobo de mar** (*fig*) sea dog

lóbulo ['loβulo] *nm* lobe

local [lo'kal] *adj* local ▷ *nm* place, site; (*oficinas*) premises *pl*; **localidad** *nf* (*barrio*) locality; (*lugar*) location; (*Teatro*) seat, ticket; **localizar** *vt* (*ubicar*) to locate, find; (*restringir*) to localize; (*situar*) to place

loción [lo'θjon] *nf* lotion

loco, -a ['loko, a] *adj* mad ▷ *nm/f* lunatic, mad person; **estar ~ con** *o* **por algo/por algn** to be mad about sth/sb

locomotora [lokomo'tora] *nf* engine, locomotive

locuaz [lo'kwaθ] *adj* loquacious

locución [loku'θjon] *nf* expression

locura [lo'kura] *nf* madness; (*acto*) crazy act

locutor, -a [loku'tor, a] *nm/f* (*Radio*) announcer; (*comentarista*) commentator; (*TV*) newsreader

locutorio [loku'torjo] *nm* (*en telefónica*) telephone booth

lodo ['loðo] *nm* mud

lógica ['loxika] *nf* logic

lógico, -a ['loxiko, a] *adj* logical

login [loxin] *nm* login

logística [lo'xistika] *nf* logistics *sg*

logotipo [loɣo'tipo] *nm* logo

logrado, -a [lo'ɣraðo, a] *adj* (*interpretación, reproducción*) polished, excellent

lograr [lo'ɣrar] *vt* to achieve; (*obtener*) to get, obtain; **~ hacer** to manage to do; **~ que algn venga** to manage to get sb to come

logro ['loɣro] *nm* achievement, success

lóker ['loker] (LAM) *nm* locker

loma ['loma] *nf* hillock (BRIT), small hill

lombriz [lom'briθ] *nf* worm

lomo ['lomo] *nm* (*de animal*) back; (Culin: *de cerdo*) pork loin; (: *de vaca*) rib steak; (*de libro*) spine

lona ['lona] *nf* canvas

loncha ['lontʃa] *nf* = **lonja**

lonchería [lontʃe'ria] (LAM) *nf* snack bar, diner (us)

Londres ['londres] *n* London

longaniza [longa'niθa] *nf* pork sausage

longitud [lonxi'tuð] *nf* length; (*Geo*) longitude; **tener 3 metros de ~** to be 3 metres long; **longitud de onda** wavelength

lonja ['lonxa] *nf* slice; (*de tocino*) rasher; **lonja de pescado** fish market

loro ['loro] *nm* parrot

los [los] *art def* **the** ▷ *pron* them; (*ustedes*) you; **mis libros y ~ tuyos** my books and yours; *V tb* **el**

losa ['losa] *nf* stone

lote ['lote] *nm* portion; (*Com*) lot

lotería [lote'ria] *nf* lottery; (*juego*) lotto

● **LOTERÍA**

●
● Millions of pounds are spent
● on lotteries each year in Spain,
● two of which are state-run: the

Lotería Primitiva and the Lotería Nacional, with money raised going directly to the government. One of the most famous lotteries is run by the wealthy and influential society for the blind, "la ONCE".

loza ['loθa] nf crockery

lubina [lu'βina] nf sea bass

lubricante [luβri'kante] nm lubricant

lubricar [luβri'kar] vt to lubricate

lucha ['lutʃa] nf fight, struggle; **lucha de clases** class struggle; **lucha libre** wrestling; **luchar** vi to fight

lúcido, -a [lu'θiðo, a] adj (persona) lucid; (mente) logical; (idea) crystal-clear

luciérnaga [lu'θjernaɣa] nf glow-worm

lucir [lu'θir] vt to illuminate, light (up); (ostentar) to show off ▷ vi (brillar) to shine; **lucirse** vr (irónico) to make a fool of o.s.

lucro ['lukro] nm profit, gain

lúdico, -a ['luðiko, a] adj (aspecto, actividad) play cpd

luego ['lweɣo] adv (después) next; (más tarde) later, afterwards

lugar [lu'ɣar] nm place; (sitio) spot; **en primer ~** in the first place, firstly; **en ~ de** instead of; **hacer ~** to make room; **fuera de ~** out of place; **sin ~ a dudas** without doubt, undoubtedly; **dar ~ a** to give rise to; **tener ~** to take place; **yo en su ~** if I were him; **lugar común** commonplace

lúgubre ['luɣuβre] adj mournful

lujo ['luxo] nm luxury; (fig) profusion, abundance; **de ~** luxury cpd, de luxe; **lujoso, -a** adj luxurious

lujuria [lu'xurja] nf lust

lumbre ['lumbre] nf fire; (para cigarrillo) light

luminoso, -a [lumi'noso, a] adj luminous, shining

luna ['luna] nf moon; (de un espejo) glass; (de gafas) lens; (fig) crescent; **estar en la ~** to have one's head in the clouds; **luna de miel** honeymoon; **luna llena/nueva** full/new moon

lunar [lu'nar] adj lunar ▷ nm (Anat) mole; **tela de ~es** spotted material

lunes ['lunes] nm inv Monday

lupa ['lupa] nf magnifying glass

lustre ['lustre] nm polish; (fig) lustre; **dar ~ a** to polish

luto ['luto] nm mourning; **llevar el o vestirse de ~** to be in mourning

Luxemburgo [luksem'burɣo] nm Luxembourg

luz [luθ] (pl **luces**) nf light; **dar a ~ un niño** to give birth to a child; **sacar a la ~** to bring to light; **dar o encender** (esp) o **prender** (lam)/**apagar la ~** to switch the light on/off; **tener pocas luces** to be dim o stupid; **traje de luces** bullfighter's costume; **luces de tráfico** traffic lights; **luz de freno** brake light; **luz roja/verde** red/green light

m

nature, character; **una ~** a piece of wood

madrastra [ma'ðrastra] nf stepmother

madre ['maðre] adj mother cpd ▷ nf mother; (de vino etc) dregs pl; **madre política/soltera** mother-in-law/unmarried mother

Madrid [ma'ðrið] n Madrid

madriguera [maðri'ɣera] nf burrow

madrileño, -a [maðri'leɲo, a] adj of o from Madrid ▷ nm/f native of Madrid

madrina [ma'ðrina] nf godmother; (Arq) prop, shore; (Tec) brace; (de boda) bridesmaid

madrugada [maðru'ɣaða] nf early morning; (alba) dawn, daybreak

madrugador, a [maðruɣa'ðor, a] adj early-rising

madrugar [maðru'ɣar] vi to get up early; (fig) to get ahead

madurar [maðu'rar] vt, vi (fruta) to ripen; (fig) to mature; **madurez** nf ripeness; maturity; **maduro, -a** adj ripe; mature

maestra [ma'estra] nf V **maestro**

maestría [maes'tria] nf mastery; (habilidad) skill, expertise

maestro, -a [ma'estro, a] adj masterly; (principal) main ▷ nm/f master/mistress; (profesor) teacher ▷ nm (autoridad) authority; (Mús) maestro; (experto) master; **maestro albañil** master mason

magdalena [maɣða'lena] nf fairy cake

magia ['maxja] nf magic; **mágico, -a** adj magic(al) ▷ nm/f magician

magisterio [maxis'terjo] nm (enseñanza) teaching; (profesión) teaching profession; (maestros) teachers pl

magistrado [maxis'traðo] nm magistrate

magistral [maxis'tral] adj magisterial; (fig) masterly

magnate [maɣ'nate] nm magnate, tycoon

m abr (= metro) m; (= minuto) m

macana [ma'kana] (MÉX) nf truncheon (BRIT), billy club (US)

macarrones [maka'rrones] nmpl macaroni sg

macedonia [maθe'ðonja] nf (tb: **~ de frutas**) fruit salad

maceta [ma'θeta] nf (de flores) pot of flowers; (para plantas) flowerpot

machacar [matʃa'kar] vt to crush, pound ▷ vi (insistir) to go on, keep on

machete [ma'tʃete] nm machete, (large) knife

machetear [matʃete'ar] (MÉX) vt to swot (BRIT), grind away (US)

machismo [ma'tʃismo] nm male chauvinism; **machista** adj, nm sexist

macho ['matʃo] adj male; (fig) virile ▷ nm male; (fig) he-man

macizo, -a [ma'θiθo, a] adj (grande) massive; (fuerte, sólido) solid ▷ nm mass, chunk

madeja [ma'ðexa] nf (de lana) skein, hank; (de pelo) mass, mop

madera [ma'ðera] nf wood; (fig)

magnético, -a [maɣ'netiko, a] *adj*
magnetic

magnetofón [maɣneto'fon] *nm*
tape recorder

magnetófono [maɣne'tofono] *nm* =
magnetofón

magnífico, -a [maɣ'nifiko, a] *adj*
splendid, magnificent

magnitud [maɣni'tuð] *nf*
magnitude

mago, -a ['maɣo, a] *nm/f* magician;
los Reyes M~s the Three Wise Men

magro, -a ['maɣro, a] *adj* (*carne*) lean

mahonesa [mao'nesa] *nf*
mayonnaise

maître ['metre] *nm* head waiter

maíz [ma'iθ] *nm* maize (BRIT), corn
(US); sweet corn

majestad [maxes'tað] *nf* majesty

majo, -a ['maxo, a] *adj* nice; (*guapo*)
attractive, good-looking; (*elegante*)
smart

mal [mal] *adv* badly; (*equivocadamente*)
wrongly ▷ *adj* = **malo** ▷ *nm* evil;
(*desgracia*) misfortune; (*daño*) harm,
damage; (*Med*) illness; **~ que bien**
rightly or wrongly; **ir de ~ en peor** to
get worse and worse

malabarista [malaβa'rista] *nmf*
juggler

malaria [ma'larja] *nf* malaria

malcriado, -a [mal'krjaðo, a] *adj*
spoiled

maldad [mal'dað] *nf* evil,
wickedness

maldecir [malde'θir] *vt* to curse

maldición [maldi'θjon] *nf* curse

maldito, -a [mal'dito, a] *adj*
(*condenado*) damned; (*perverso*) wicked;
¡~ sea! damn it!

malecón [male'kon] (LAM) *nm* sea
front, promenade

maleducado, -a [maleðu'kaðo, a]
adj bad-mannered, rude

malentendido [malenten'diðo] *nm*
misunderstanding

malestar [males'tar] *nm* (*gen*)
discomfort; (*fig: inquietud*) uneasiness;

(*Pol*) unrest

maleta [ma'leta] *nf* case, suitcase;
(*Auto*) boot (BRIT), trunk (US); **hacer las
~s** to pack; **maletero** *nm* (*Auto*) boot
(BRIT), trunk (US); **maletín** *nm* small
case, bag

maleza [ma'leθa] *nf* (*malas hierbas*)
weeds *pl*; (*arbustos*) thicket

malgastar [malɣas'tar] *vt* (*tiempo*,
dinero) to waste; (*salud*) to ruin

malhechor, -a [male'tʃor, a] *nm/f*
delinquent

malhumorado, -a [malumo'raðo,
a] *adj* bad-tempered

malicia [ma'liθja] *nf* (*maldad*)
wickedness; (*astucia*) slyness, guile;
(*mala intención*) malice, spite; (*carácter
travieso*) mischievousness

maligno, -a [ma'liɣno, a] *adj* evil;
(*malévolo*) malicious; (*Med*) malignant

malla ['maʎa] *nf* mesh; (*de baño*)
swimsuit; (*de ballet, gimnasia*) leotard;
mallas *nfpl* tights; **malla de alambre**
wire mesh

Mallorca [ma'ʎorka] *nf* Majorca

malo, -a ['malo, a] *adj* bad, false
▷ *nm/f* villain; **estar ~** to be ill

malograr [malo'ɣrar] *vt* to spoil;
(*plan*) to upset; (*ocasión*) to waste

malparado, -a [malpa'raðo, a]
adj: **salir ~** to come off badly

malpensado, -a [malpen'saðo, a]
adj nasty

malteada [malte'aða] (LAM) *nf*
milkshake

maltratar [maltra'tar] *vt* to ill-treat,
mistreat

malvado, -a [mal'βaðo, a] *adj* evil,
villainous

Malvinas [mal'βinas] *nfpl* (tb: **Islas
~**) Falklands, Falkland Islands

mama ['mama] *nf* (*de animal*) teat; (*de
mujer*) breast

mamá [ma'ma] (*pl* **~s**) (*fam*) *nf* mum,
mummy

mamar [ma'mar] *vi, vt* to suck

mamarracho [mama'rratʃo] *nm*
sight, mess

mameluco [mameˈluko] (RPL) nm
dungarees pl (BRIT), overalls pl (US)

mamífero [maˈmifero] nm mammal

mampara [mamˈpara] nf (entre
habitaciones) partition; (biombo) screen

mampostería [mamposteˈria] nf
masonry

manada [maˈnaða] nf (Zool) herd;
(: de leones) pride; (: de lobos) pack

manantial [mananˈtjal] nm spring

mancha [ˈmantʃa] nf stain, mark;
(Zool) patch; **manchar** vt (gen) to
stain, mark; (ensuciar) to soil, dirty

manchego, -a [manˈtʃeɣo, a] adj of
o from La Mancha

manco, -a [ˈmanko, a] adj (de un
brazo) one-armed; (de una mano) one-
handed; (fig) defective, faulty

mancuernas [manˈkwernas] (MÉX)
nfpl cufflinks

mandado [manˈdaðo] (LAM) nm
errand

mandamiento [mandaˈmjento]
nm (orden) order, command; (Rel)
commandment

mandar [manˈdar] vt (ordenar) to
order; (dirigir) to lead, command;
(enviar) to send; (pedir) to order, ask for
▷ vi to be in charge; (pey) to be bossy;
¿mande? (MÉX: ¿cómo dice?) pardon?,
excuse me?; **~ hacer un traje** to have
a suit made

mandarina [mandaˈrina] (ESP) nf
tangerine, mandarin (orange)

mandato [manˈdato] nm (orden)
order; (Pol: período) term of office;
(: territorio) mandate

mandíbula [manˈdiβula] nf jaw

mandil [manˈdil] nm apron

mando [ˈmando] nm (Mil) command;
(de país) rule; (el primer lugar) lead; (Pol)
term of office; (Tec) control; **~ a la
izquierda** left-hand drive; **mando a
distancia** remote control

mandón, -ona [manˈdon, ona] adj
bossy, domineering

manejar [maneˈxar] vt to manage;
(máquina) to work, operate; (caballo

etc) to handle; (casa) to run, manage;
(LAM: coche) to drive; **manejarse**
vr (comportarse) to act, behave;
(arreglárselas) to manage; **manejo**
nm (de bicicleta) handling; (de negocio)
management, running; (LAM Auto)
driving; (facilidad de trato) ease,
confidence; **manejos** nmpl (intrigas)
intrigues

manera [maˈnera] nf way, manner,
fashion; **maneras** nfpl (modales)
manners; **su ~ de ser** the way he
is; (aire) his manner; **de ninguna
~** no way, by no means; **de otra ~**
otherwise; **de todas ~s** at any rate; **no
hay ~ de persuadirle** there's no way of
convincing him

manga [ˈmanga] nf (de camisa) sleeve;
(de riego) hose

mango [ˈmango] nm handle; (Bot)
mango

manguera [manˈgera] nf hose

maní [maˈni] (LAM) nm peanut

manía [maˈnia] nf (Med) mania;
(fig: moda) rage, craze; (disgusto) dislike;
(malicia) spite; **coger ~ a algn** to take a
dislike to sb; **tener ~ a algn** to dislike
sb; **maníaco, -a** adj maniac(al) ▷ nm/f
maniac

maniático, -a [maˈnjatiko, a] adj
maniac(al) ▷ nm/f maniac

manicomio [maniˈkomjo] nm
mental hospital (BRIT), insane asylum
(US)

manifestación [manifestaˈθjon] nf
(declaración) statement, declaration;
(de emoción) show, display; (Pol: desfile
demonstration; (: concentración) mass
meeting

manifestar [manifesˈtar] vt to
show, manifest; (declarar) to state,
declare; **manifiesto, -a** adj clear,
manifest ▷ nm manifesto

manillar [maniˈʎar] nm handlebars pl

maniobra [maˈnjoβra] nf
manoeuvre; **maniobras** nfpl (Mil)
manoeuvres; **maniobrar** vt to
manoeuvre

manipulación [manipula'θjon] nf
manipulation

manipular [manipu'lar] vt to
manipulate; (manejar) to handle

maniquí [mani'ki] nm dummy
▷ nmf model

manivela [mani'βela] nf crank

manjar [man'xar] nm (tasty) dish

mano ['mano] nf hand; (Zool) foot,
paw; (de pintura) coat; (serie) lot, series;
a ~ by hand; **a ~ derecha/izquierda**
on the right(-hand side)/left(-hand
side); **de primera ~** (at) first hand; **de
segunda ~** (at) second hand; **robo a ~
armada** armed robbery; **estrechar la
~ a algn** to shake sb's hand; **mano de
obra** labour, manpower; **manos libres**
adj inv (teléfono, dispositivo) hands-free
▷ nm inv hands-free kit

manojo [ma'noxo] nm handful,
bunch; (de llaves) bunch

manopla [ma'nopla] nf mitten

manosear [manose'ar] vt (tocar)
to handle, touch; (desordenar) to mess
up, rumple; (insistir en) to overwork;
(LAM: acariciar) to caress, fondle

manotazo [mano'taθo] nm slap,
smack

mansalva [man'salβa]: **a ~** adv
indiscriminately

mansión [man'sjon] nf mansion

manso, -a ['manso, a] adj gentle,
mild; (animal) tame

manta ['manta] (ESP) nf blanket

manteca [man'teka] nf fat;
(cs: mantequilla) butter; **manteca de
cerdo** lard

mantecado [mante'kaðo] (ESP) nm
Christmas sweet made from flour, almonds
and lard

mantel [man'tel] nm tablecloth

mantendré etc vb V **mantener**

mantener [mante'ner] vt to
support, maintain; (alimentar) to
sustain; (conservar) to keep; (Tec) to
maintain, service; **mantenerse** vr
(seguir de pie) to be still standing;
(no ceder) to hold one's ground;

(subsistir) to sustain o.s., keep going;
mantenimiento nm maintenance;
sustenance; (sustento) support

mantequilla [mante'kiʎa] nf butter

mantilla [man'tiʎa] nf mantilla;
mantillas nfpl (de bebé) baby clothes

manto ['manto] nm (capa) cloak; (de
ceremonia) robe, gown

mantuve etc vb V **mantener**

manual [ma'nwal] adj manual ▷ nm
manual, handbook

manuscrito, -a [manus'krito, a] adj
handwritten ▷ nm manuscript

manutención [manuten'θjon] nf
maintenance; (sustento) support

manzana [man'θana] nf apple; (Arq)
block (of houses)

manzanilla [manθa'niʎa] nf (planta)
camomile; (infusión) camomile tea

manzano [man'θano] nm apple tree

maña ['maɲa] nf (gen) skill, dexterity;
(pey) guile; (destreza) trick, knack

mañana [ma'ɲana] adv tomorrow
▷ nm future ▷ nf morning; **de o por
la ~** in the morning; **¡hasta ~!** see you
tomorrow!; **por la ~** tomorrow morning

mapa ['mapa] nm map

maple ['maple] (LAM) nm maple

maqueta [ma'keta] nf (scale) model

maquiladora [makila'ðora] (MÉX) nf
(Com) bonded assembly plant

maquillaje [maki'ʎaxe] nm make-
up; (acto) making up

maquillar [maki'ʎar] vt to make
up; **maquillarse** vr to put on (some)
make-up

máquina ['makina] nf machine;
(de tren) locomotive, engine; (Foto)
camera; (fig) machinery; **escrito a
~** typewritten; **máquina de afeitar**
electric razor; **máquina de coser**
sewing machine; **máquina de escribir**
typewriter; **máquina fotográfica**
camera

maquinaria [maki'narja] nf
(máquinas) machinery; (mecanismo)
mechanism, works pl

maquinilla [maki'niʎa] (ESP) nf

m

(tb: ~ **de afeitar**) razor

maquinista [maki'nista] nmf (de tren) engine driver; (Tec) operator; (Náut) engineer

mar [mar] nm of sea; ~ **adentro** out at sea; **en alta** ~ on the high seas; **la** ~ **de** (fam) lots of; **el Mar Negro/Báltico** the Black/Baltic Sea

maraña [ma'raɲa] nf (maleza) thicket; (confusión) tangle

maravilla [mara'βiʎa] nf marvel, wonder; (Bot) marigold; **maravillar** vt to astonish, amaze; **maravillarse** vr to be astonished, be amazed; **maravilloso, -a** adj wonderful, marvellous

marca ['marka] nf (gen) mark; (sello) stamp; (Com) make, brand; **de** ~ excellent, outstanding; **marca de fábrica** trademark; **marca registrada** registered trademark

marcado, -a [mar'kaðo, a] adj marked, strong

marcador [marka'ðor] nm (Deporte) scoreboard; (: persona) scorer

marcapasos [marka'pasos] nm inv pacemaker

marcar [mar'kar] vt (gen) to mark; (número de teléfono) to dial; (gol) to score; (números) to record, keep a tally of; (pelo) to set ▷ vi (Deporte) to score; (Tel) to dial

marcha ['martʃa] nf march; (Tec) running, working; (Auto) gear; (velocidad) speed; (fig) progress; (dirección) course; **poner en ~** to put into gear; (fig) to set in motion, get going; **dar ~ atrás** to reverse, put into reverse; **estar en ~** to be under way, be in motion

marchar [mar'tʃar] vi (ir) to go; (funcionar) to work, go; **marcharse** vr to go (away), leave

marchitar [martʃi'tar] vt to wither, dry up; **marchitarse** vr (Bot) to wither, (fig) to fade away; **marchito, -a** adj withered, faded; (fig) in decline

marciano, -a [mar'θjano, a] adj,

nm/f Martian

marco ['marko] nm frame; (moneda) mark; (fig) framework

marea [ma'rea] nf tide; **marea negra** oil slick

marear [mare'ar] vt (fig) to annoy, upset; (Med): ~ **a algn** to make sb feel sick; **marearse** vr (tener náuseas) to feel sick; (desvanecerse) to feel faint; (aturdirse) to feel dizzy; (fam: emborracharse) to get tipsy

maremoto [mare'moto] nm tidal wave

mareo [ma'reo] nm (náusea) sick feeling; (en viaje) travel sickness; (aturdimiento) dizziness; (fam: lata) nuisance

marfil [mar'fil] nm ivory

margarina [marɣa'rina] nf margarine

margarita [marɣa'rita] nf (Bot) daisy; (Tip) daisywheel

margen ['marxen] nm (borde) edge, border; (fig) margin, space ▷ nf (de río etc) bank; **dar ~ para** to give an opportunity for; **mantenerse al ~** to keep out (of things)

marginar [marxi'nar] vt (socialmente) to marginalize, ostracize

mariachi [ma'rjatʃi] nm (persona) mariachi musician; (grupo) mariachi band

MARIACHI

Mariachi music is the musical style most characteristic of Mexico. From the state of Jalisco in the 19th century, this music spread rapidly throughout the country, until each region had its own particular style of the Mariachi "sound". A Mariachi band can be made up of several singers, up to eight violins, two trumpets, guitars, a "vihuela" (an old form of guitar), and a harp. The dance associated with this music is called the "zapateado".

marica [ma'rika] (fam) nm
sissy

maricón [mari'kon] (fam) nm
queer

marido [ma'riðo] nm husband

marihuana [mari'wana] nf
marijuana, cannabis

marina [ma'rina] nf navy; **marina
mercante** merchant navy

marinero, -a [mari'nero, a] adj sea
cpd ▷ nm sailor, seaman

marino, -a [ma'rino, a] adj sea cpd,
marine ▷ nm sailor

marioneta [marjo'neta] nf
puppet

mariposa [mari'posa] nf
butterfly

mariquita [mari'kita] nf ladybird
(BRIT), ladybug (US)

marisco [ma'risko] (ESP) nm shellfish
inv, seafood; **mariscos** (LAM) =
marisco

marítimo, -a [ma'ritimo, a] adj sea
cpd, maritime

mármol ['marmol] nm marble

marqués, -esa [mar'kes, esa] nm/f
marquis/marchioness

marrón [ma'rron] adj brown

marroquí [marro'ki] adj, nmf
Moroccan ▷ nm Morocco (leather)

Marruecos [ma'rrwekos] nm
Morocco

martes ['martes] nm inv Tuesday; ~ **y
trece** ≈ Friday 13th

- **MARTES Y TRECE**
-
- According to Spanish superstition
- Tuesday is an unlucky day, even
- more so if it falls on the 13th of
- the month.

martillo [mar'tiʎo] nm hammer

mártir ['martir] nmf martyr;
martirio nm martyrdom; (fig) torture,
torment

marxismo [mark'sismo] nm
Marxism

marzo ['marθo] nm March

○ **PALABRA CLAVE**

más [mas] adj, adv **1**: **más (que** o **de)**
(comparr) more (than), ...+ er (than); **más
grande/inteligente** bigger/
more intelligent; **trabaja más (que
yo)** he works more (than me); V tb **cada**
2 (superl): **el más** the most, ...+ est; **el
más grande/inteligente (de)** the
biggest/most intelligent (in)
3 (negativo): **no tengo más dinero** I
haven't got any more money; **no viene
más por aquí** he doesn't come round
here any more
4 (adicional): **no le veo más solución
que ...** I see no other solution than to
...; **¿quién más?** anybody else?
5 (+ adj: valor intensivo): **¡qué perro
más sucio!** what a filthy dog!; **¡es más
tonto!** he's so stupid!
6 (locuciones): **más o menos** more or
less; **los más** most people; **es más**
furthermore; **más bien** rather;
¡qué más da! what does it matter!;
V tb **no**
7: **por más: por más que te esfuerces**
no matter how hard you try; **por más
que quisiera ...** much as I should
like to ...
8: **de más: veo que aquí estoy de más**
I can see I'm not needed here; **tenemos
uno de más** we've got one extra
▷ prep: **2 más 2 son 4** 2 and 2 are 4
▷ nm inv: **este trabajo tiene sus más
y sus menos** this job's got its good
points and its bad points

mas [mas] conj but

masa ['masa] nf (mezcla) dough;
(volumen) volume, mass; (Física) mass;
en ~ en masse; **las ~s** (Pol) the masses

masacre [ma'sakre] nf massacre

masaje [ma'saxe] nm massage

máscara ['maskara] nf mask;
máscara antigás/de oxígeno
gas/oxygen mask; **mascarilla** nf (de

belleza, Med) mask
masculino, -a [masku'lino, a] *adj*
masculine; *(Bio)* male
masía [ma'sia] *nf* farmhouse
masivo, -a [ma'siβo, a] *adj* mass *cpd*
masoquista [maso'kista] *nmf*
masochist
máster ['master] *(ESP) nm* master
masticar [masti'kar] *vt* to chew
mástil ['mastil] *nm (de navío)* mast;
(de guitarra) neck
mastín [mas'tin] *nm* mastiff
masturbarse [mastur'βarse] *vr* to
masturbate
mata ['mata] *nf (arbusto)* bush, shrub;
(de hierba) tuft
matadero [mata'ðero] *nm*
slaughterhouse, abattoir
matador, a [mata'ðor, a] *adj* killing
▷ *nm/f* killer ▷ *nm (Taur)* matador,
bullfighter
matamoscas [mata'moskas] *nm inv*
(pala) fly swat
matanza [ma'tanθa] *nf* slaughter
matar [ma'tar] *vt, vi* to kill; **matarse**
vr (suicidarse) to kill o.s., commit
suicide; *(morir)* to be o get killed; **~ el
hambre** to stave off hunger
matasellos [mata'seλos] *nm inv*
postmark
mate ['mate] *adj* matt ▷ *nm (en
ajedrez)* (check)mate; *(LAM: hierba)*
maté; *(: vasija)* gourd
matemáticas [mate'matikas] *nfpl*
mathematics; **matemático, -a** *adj*
mathematical ▷ *nm/f* mathematician
materia [ma'terja] *nf (gen)* matter;
(Tec) material; *(Escol)* subject; **en ~
de** on the subject of; **materia prima**
raw material; **material** *adj* material
▷ *nm* material; *(Tec)* equipment;
materialista *adj* materialist(ic);
materialmente *adv* materially; *(fig)*
absolutely
maternal [mater'nal] *adj* motherly,
maternal
maternidad [materni'ðað] *nf*
motherhood, maternity; **materno, -a**

adj maternal; *(lengua)* mother *cpd*
matinal [mati'nal] *adj* morning *cpd*
matiz [ma'tiθ] *nm* shade; **matizar** *vt*
(variar) to vary; *(Arte)* to blend; **matizar
de** to tinge with
matón [ma'ton] *nm* bully
matorral [mato'rral] *nm* thicket
matrícula [ma'trikula] *nf (registro)*
register; *(Auto)* registration number;
(: placa) number plate; **matrícula de
honor** *(Univ)* top marks in a subject at
university with the right to free registration
the following year; **matricular** *vt* to
register, enrol
matrimonio [matri'monjo] *nm*
(pareja) (married) couple; *(unión)*
marriage
matriz [ma'triθ] *nf (Anat)* womb;
(Tec) mould
matrona [ma'trona] *nf (persona de
edad)* matron; *(comadrona)* midwife
matufia [ma'tufja] *(RPL: fam) nf*
put-up job
maullar [mau'λar] *vi* to mew, miaow
maxilar [maksi'lar] *nm* jaw(bone)
máxima ['maksima] *nf* maxim
máximo, -a ['maksimo, a] *adj*
maximum; *(más alto)* highest; *(más
grande)* greatest ▷ *nm* maximum;
como ~ at most
mayo ['majo] *nm* May
mayonesa [majo'nesa] *nf*
mayonnaise
mayor [ma'jor] *adj* main, chief;
(adulto) adult; *(de edad avanzada)*
elderly; *(Mús)* major; *(compar: de
tamaño)* bigger; *(: de edad)* older;
(superl: de tamaño) biggest; *(: de edad)*
oldest ▷ *nm (adulto)* adult; **mayores**
nmpl (antepasados) ancestors; **al por ~**
wholesale; **mayor de edad** adult
mayoral [majo'ral] *nm* foreman
mayordomo [major'ðomo] *nm*
butler
mayoría [majo'ria] *nf* majority,
greater part
mayorista [majo'rista] *nmf*
wholesaler

mayoritario, -a [majori'tarjo, a] *adj* majority *cpd*

mayúscula [ma'juskula] *nf* capital letter

mazapán [maθa'pan] *nm* marzipan

mazo ['maθo] *nm* (*martillo*) mallet; (*de flores*) bunch; (*Deporte*) bat

me [me] *pron* (*directo*) me; (*indirecto*) (to) me; (*reflexivo*) (to) myself; **¡dá-lo!** give it to me!

mear [me'ar] (*fam*) *vi* to pee, piss (*!*)

mecánica [me'kanika] *nf* (*Escol*) mechanics *sg*; (*mecanismo*) mechanism; *V tb* **mecánico**

mecánico, -a [me'kaniko, a] *adj* mechanical ▷ *nm/f* mechanic

mecanismo [meka'nismo] *nm* mechanism; (*marcha*) gear

mecanografía [mekanoɣra'fia] *nf* typewriting; **mecanógrafo, -a** *nm/f* typist

mecate [me'kate] (*MÉX, CAM*) *nm* rope

mecedora [meθe'ðora] *nf* rocking chair

mecer [me'θer] *vt* (*cuna*) to rock; **mecerse** *vr* to rock; (*rama*) to sway

mecha ['metʃa] *nf* (*de vela*) wick; (*de bomba*) fuse

mechero [me'tʃero] *nm* (*cigarette*) lighter

mechón [me'tʃon] *nm* (*gen*) tuft; (*de pelo*) lock

medalla [me'ðaʎa] *nf* medal

media ['meðja] *nf* stocking; (*LAM: calcetín*) sock; (*promedio*) average; **medias** [me'ðjas] *nfpl* (*ropa interior*) tights

mediado, -a [me'ðjaðo, a] *adj* half-full; (*trabajo*) half-completed; **a ~s de** in the middle of, halfway through

mediano, -a [me'ðjano, a] *adj* (*regular*) medium, average; (*mediocre*) mediocre

medianoche [meðja'notʃe] *nf* midnight

mediante [me'ðjante] *adv* by (means of), through

mediar [me'ðjar] *vi* (*interceder*) to mediate, intervene

medicamento [meðika'mento] *nm* medicine, drug

medicina [meði'θina] *nf* medicine

médico, -a ['meðiko, a] *adj* medical ▷ *nm/f* doctor

medida [me'ðiða] *nf* measure; (*medición*) measurement; (*prudencia*) moderation, prudence; **en cierta/gran ~** up to a point/to a great extent; **un traje a la ~** a made-to-measure suit; **~ de cuello** collar size; **a ~ de** in proportion to; (*de acuerdo con*) in keeping with; **a ~ que** (*conforme*) as; **medidor** (*LAM*) *nm* meter

medio, -a ['meðjo, a] *adj* half (a); (*punto*) middle; (*promedio*) average ▷ *adv* half ▷ *nm* (*centro*) middle, centre; (*promedio*) average; (*método*) means, way; (*ambiente*) environment; **medios** *nmpl* means, resources; **~ litro** half a litre; **las tres y media** half past three; **a ~ terminar** half finished; **pagar a medias** to share the cost; **medio ambiente** environment; **medio de transporte** means of transport; **Medio Oriente** Middle East; **medios de comunicación** media; **medioambiental** (*política, efectos*) environmental

mediocre [me'ðjokre] *adj* mediocre

mediodía [meðjo'ðia] *nm* midday, noon

medir [me'ðir] *vt, vi* (*gen*) to measure

meditar [meði'tar] *vt* to ponder, think over, meditate on; (*planear*) to think out

mediterráneo, -a [meðite'rraneo, a] *adj* Mediterranean ▷ *nm*: **el M~** the Mediterranean

médula ['meðula] *nf* (*Anat*) marrow; **médula espinal** spinal cord

medusa [me'ðusa] (*ESP*) *nf* jellyfish

megáfono [me'ɣafono] *nm* megaphone

megapíxel [meɣa'piksel] (*pl* **megapixels** *or* **-es**) *nm* megapixel

mejicano, -a [mexi'kano, a] *adj,
nm/f* Mexican

Méjico ['mexiko] *nm* Mexico

mejilla [me'xiʎa] *nf* cheek

mejillón [mexi'ʎon] *nm* mussel

mejor [me'xor] *adj, adv* (*compar*)
better; (*superl*) best; **a lo ~** probably;
(*quizá*) maybe; **~ dicho** rather; **tanto ~**
so much the better

mejora [me'xora] *nf* improvement;
mejorar *vt* to improve, make better
▷ *vi* to improve, get better; **mejorarse**
vr to improve, get better

melancólico, -a [melan'koliko, a]
adj (*triste*) sad, melancholy; (*soñador*)
dreamy

melena [me'lena] *nf* (*de persona*) long
hair; (*Zool*) mane

mellizo, -a [me'ʎiθo, a] *adj, nm/f*
twin

melocotón [meloko'ton] (ESP) *nm*
peach

melodía [melo'ðia] *nf* melody, tune

melodrama [melo'ðrama] *nm*
melodrama; **melodramático, -a** *adj*
melodramatic

melón [me'lon] *nm* melon

membrete [mem'brete] *nm*
letterhead

membrillo [mem'briʎo] *nm* quince;
(carne de) ~ quince jelly

memoria [me'morja] *nf* (*gen*)
memory; **memorias** *nfpl* (*de autor*)
memoirs; **memorizar** *vt* to memorize

menaje [me'naxe] *nm* (*tb: **artículos
de ~***) household items

mencionar [menθjo'nar] *vt* to
mention

mendigo, -a [men'dixo, a] *nm/f*
beggar

menear [mene'ar] *vt* to move;
menearse *vr* to shake; (*balancearse*)
to sway; (*moverse*) to move; (*fig*) to get
a move on

menestra [me'nestra] *nf* (*tb: **~ de
verduras***) vegetable stew

menopausia [meno'pausja] *nf*
menopause

menor [me'nor] *adj* (*más
pequeño: compar*) smaller; (*: superl*)
smallest; (*más joven: compar*) younger;
(*: superl*) youngest; (*Mús*) minor ▷ *nmf*
(*joven*) young person, juvenile; **no
tengo la ~ idea** I haven't the faintest
idea; **al por ~** retail; **menor de edad**
person under age

Menorca [me'norka] *nf* Minorca

○ PALABRA CLAVE

menos [menos] *adj* **1: menos
(que** o **de)** (*compar: cantidad*) less
(than); (*: número*) fewer (than);
con menos entusiasmo with less
enthusiasm; **menos gente** fewer
people; *V tb* **cada**

2 (*superl*): **es el que menos culpa tiene**
he is the least to blame

▷ *adv* **1** (*compar*): **menos (que** o **de)** less
(than); **me gusta menos que el otro** I
like it less than the other one

2 (*superl*): **es el menos listo (de su
clase)** he's the least bright in his class;
**de todas ellas es la que menos me
agrada** out of all of them she's the one
I like least

3 (*locuciones*): **no quiero verle y menos
visitarle** I don't want to see him, let
alone visit him; **tenemos siete de
menos** we're seven short; **(por) lo
menos** at (the very) least; **¡menos mal!**
thank goodness!

▷ *prep* except; (*cifras*) minus; **todos
menos él** everyone except (for) him;
5 menos 2 5 minus 2; **las 7 menos 10**
(*hora*) 10 to 7

▷ *conj*: **a menos que: a menos que
venga mañana** unless he comes
tomorrow

menospreciar [menospre'θjar] *vt*
to underrate, undervalue; (*despreciar*)
to scorn, despise

mensaje [men'saxe] *nm* message;
enviar un ~ a algn (*por móvil*) to text
sb, send sb a text message; **mensaje**

de texto text message **mensaje electrónico** email; **mensajero, -a** *nm/f* messenger

menso, -a ['menso, a] (*MÉX: fam*) *adj* stupid

menstruación [menstrwa'θjon] *nf* menstruation

mensual [men'swal] *adj* monthly; **100 euros ~es** 100 euros a month; **mensualidad** *nf* (*salario*) monthly salary; (*Com*) monthly payment, monthly instalment

menta ['menta] *nf* mint

mental [men'tal] *adj* mental; **mentalidad** *nf* mentality; **mentalizar** *vt* (*sensibilizar*) to make aware; (*convencer*) to convince; (*padres*) to prepare (mentally); **mentalizarse** *vr* (*concienciarse*) to become aware; **mentalizarse (de)** to get used to the idea (of); **mentalizarse de que ...** (*convencerse*) to get it into one's head that ...

mente ['mente] *nf* mind

mentir [men'tir] *vi* to lie

mentira [men'tira] *nf* (*una mentira*) lie; (*acto*) lying; (*invención*) fiction; **parece mentira que ...** it seems incredible that ..., I can't believe that ...; **mentiroso, -a** [menti'roso, a] *adj* lying ▷ *nm/f* liar

menú [me'nu] (*pl* **~s**) *nm* menu; **menú del día** set menu; **menú turístico** tourist menu

menudencias [menu'ðenθjas] (*LAM*) *nfpl* giblets

menudo, -a [me'nuðo, a] *adj* (*pequeño*) small, tiny; (*sin importancia*) petty, insignificant; **¡~ negocio!** (*fam*) some deal!; **a ~** often, frequently

meñique [me'ɲike] *nm* little finger

mercadillo [merka'ðiʎo] (*ESP*) *nm* flea market

mercado [mer'kaðo] *nm* market; **mercado de pulgas** (*LAM*) flea market

mercancía [merkan'θia] *nf* commodity; **mercancías** *nfpl* goods, merchandise *sg*

mercenario, -a [merθe'narjo, a] *adj, nm* mercenary

mercería [merθe'ria] *nf* haberdashery (*BRIT*), notions *pl* (*US*); (*tienda*) haberdasher's (*BRIT*), notions store (*US*)

mercurio [mer'kurjo] *nm* mercury

merecer [mere'θer] *vt* to deserve, merit ▷ *vi* to be deserving, be worthy; **merece la pena** it's worthwhile; **merecido, -a** *adj* (well) deserved; **llevar su merecido** to get one's deserts

merendar [meren'dar] *vt* to have for tea ▷ *vi* to have tea; (*en el campo*) to have a picnic; **merendero** *nm* open-air café

merengue [me'renge] *nm* meringue

meridiano [meri'ðjano] *nm* (*Geo*) meridian

merienda [me'rjenda] *nf* (light) tea, afternoon snack; (*de campo*) picnic

mérito ['merito] *nm* merit; (*valor*) worth, value

merluza [mer'luθa] *nf* hake

mermelada [merme'laða] *nf* jam

mero, -a ['mero, a] *adj* mere; (*MÉX, CAM: fam*) very

merodear [meroðe'ar] *vi*: **~ por** to prowl about

mes [mes] *nm* month

mesa ['mesa] *nf* table; (*de trabajo*) desk; (*Geo*) plateau; **poner/quitar la ~** to lay/clear the table; **mesa electoral** officials in charge of a polling station; **mesa redonda** (*reunión*) round table; **mesero, -a** (*LAM*) *nm/f* waiter/waitress

meseta [me'seta] *nf* (*Geo*) plateau, tableland

mesilla [me'siʎa] *nf* (*tb*: **~ de noche**) bedside table

mesón [me'son] *nm* inn

mestizo, -a [mes'tiθo, a] *adj* half-caste, of mixed race ▷ *nm/f* half-caste

meta ['meta] *nf* goal; (*de carrera*) finish

metabolismo [metaβo'lismo] *nm* metabolism

metáfora [me'tafora] *nf* metaphor

metal [me'tal] *nm* (*materia*) metal; (*Mús*) brass; **metálico, -a** *adj* metallic; (*de metal*) metal ▷ *nm* (*dinero contante*) cash

meteorología [meteoroˈloˈxia] *nf* meteorology

meter [me'ter] *vt* (*colocar*) to put, place; (*introducir*) to put in, insert; (*involucrar*) to involve; (*causar*) to make, cause; **meterse** *vr*: **~se en** to go into, enter; (*fig*) to interfere in, meddle in; **~se a** to start; **~se a escritor** to become a writer; **~se con uno** to provoke sb, pick a quarrel with sb

meticuloso, -a [metiku'loso, a] *adj* meticulous, thorough

metódico, -a [me'toðiko, a] *adj* methodical

método ['metoðo] *nm* method

metralleta [metra'ʎeta] *nf* sub-machine-gun

métrico, -a ['metriko, a] *adj* metric

metro ['metro] *nm* metre; (*tren*) underground (*BRIT*), subway (*US*)

metrosexual [metrosek'swal] *adj, nm* metrosexual

mexicano, -a [mexi'kano, a] *adj, nm/f* Mexican

México ['mexiko] *nm* Mexico; **Ciudad de ~** Mexico City

mezcla [ˈmeθkla] *nf* mixture; **mezcladora** (*MÉX*) *nf* (*tb*: **mezcladora de cemento**) cement mixer; **mezclar** *vt* to mix (up); **mezclarse** *vr* to mix, mingle; **mezclarse en** to get mixed up in, get involved in

mezquino, -a [meθ'kino, a] *adj* mean

mezquita [meθ'kita] *nf* mosque

mg. *abr* (= *miligramo*) mg

mi [mi] *adj pos* my ▷ *nm* (*Mús*) E

mí [mi] *pron* me; myself

mía *pron* V **mío**

michelín [mitʃe'lin] (*fam*) *nm* (*de grasa*) spare tyre

microbio [mi'kroβjo] *nm* microbe

micrófono [mi'krofono] *nm*

microphone

microondas [mikro'ondas] *nm inv* (*tb*: **horno ~**) microwave (oven)

microscopio [mikro'skopjo] *nm* microscope

miedo ['mjeðo] *nm* fear; (*nerviosismo*) apprehension, nervousness; **tener ~ to** be afraid; **de ~** wonderful, marvellous; **hace un frío de ~** (*fam*) it's terribly cold; **miedoso, -a** *adj* fearful, timid

miel [mjel] *nf* honey

miembro ['mjembro] *nm* limb; (*socio*) member; **miembro viril** penis

mientras ['mjentras] *conj* while; (*duración*) as long as ▷ *adv* meanwhile; **~ tanto** meanwhile

miércoles ['mjerkoles] *nm inv* Wednesday

mierda ['mjerða] (*fam!*) *nf* shit (!)

miga ['miɣa] *nf* crumb; (*fig*: *meollo*) essence; **hacer buenas ~s** (*fam*) to get on well

mil [mil] *num* thousand; **dos ~ libras** two thousand pounds

milagro [mi'laɣro] *nm* miracle; **milagroso, -a** *adj* miraculous

milésima [mi'lesima] *nf* (*de segundo*) thousandth

mili ['mili] (*ESP*: *fam*) *nf*: **hacer la ~** to do one's military service

milímetro [mi'limetro] *nm* millimetre

militante [mili'tante] *adj* militant

militar [mili'tar] *adj* military ▷ *nmf* soldier ▷ *vi* (*Mil*) to serve; (*en un partido*) to be a member

milla ['miʎa] *nf* mile

millar [mi'ʎar] *nm* thousand

millón [mi'ʎon] *num* million; **millonario, -a** *nm/f* millionaire

milusos [mi'lusos] (*MÉX*) *nm inv* odd-job man

mimar [mi'mar] *vt* to spoil, pamper

mimbre ['mimbre] *nm* wicker

mímica ['mimika] *nf* (*para comunicarse*) sign language; (*imitación*) mimicry

mimo ['mimo] *nm* (*caricia*) caress; (*de*

niño) spoiling; (*Teatro*) mime; (: *actor*) mime artist

mina ['mina] *nf* mine

mineral [mine'ral] *adj* mineral ▷ *nm* (*Geo*) mineral; (*mena*) ore

minero, -a [mi'nero, a] *adj* mining *cpd* ▷ *nm/f* miner

miniatura [minja'tura] *adj inv, nf* miniature

minidisco [mini'disko] *nm* MiniDisc®

minifalda [mini'falda] *nf* miniskirt

mínimo, -a ['minimo, a] *adj, nm* minimum

minino, -a [mi'nino, a] (*fam*) *nm/f* puss, pussy

ministerio [minis'terjo] *nm* Ministry; **Ministerio de Hacienda/de Asuntos Exteriores** Treasury (BRIT), Treasury Department (US)/Foreign Office (BRIT), State Department (US)

ministro, -a [mi'nistro, a] *nm/f* minister

minoría [mino'ria] *nf* minority

minúscula [mi'nuskula] *nf* small letter

minúsculo, -a [mi'nuskulo, a] *adj* tiny, minute

minusválido, -a [minus'βaliðo, a] *adj* (physically) handicapped ▷ *nm/f* (physically) handicapped person

minuta [mi'nuta] *nf* (*de comida*) menu

minutero [minu'tero] *nm* minute hand

minuto [mi'nuto] *nm* minute

mío, -a ['mio, a] *pron*: **el ~/la mía** mine; **un amigo ~** a friend of mine; **lo ~** what is mine

miope [mi'ope] *adj* short-sighted

mira ['mira] *nf* (*de arma*) sight(s) (*pl*); (*fig*) aim, intention

mirada [mi'raða] *nf* look, glance; (*expresión*) look, expression; **clavar la ~ en** to stare at; **echar una ~ a** to glance at

mirado, -a [mi'raðo, a] *adj* (*sensato*) sensible; (*considerado*) considerate;

bien/mal ~ (*estimado*) well/not well thought of; **bien ~ ...** all things considered ...

mirador [mira'ðor] *nm* viewpoint, vantage point

mirar [mi'rar] *vt* to look at; (*observar*) to watch; (*considerar*) to consider, think over; (*vigilar, cuidar*) to watch, look after ▷ *vi* to look; (*Arq*) to face; **mirarse** *vr* (*dos personas*) to look at each other; **~ bien/mal** to think highly of/have a poor opinion of; **~se al espejo** to look at o.s. in the mirror

mirilla [mi'riʎa] *nf* spyhole, peephole

mirlo ['mirlo] *nm* blackbird

misa ['misa] *nf* mass

miserable [mise'raβle] *adj* (*avaro*) mean, stingy; (*nimio*) miserable, paltry; (*lugar*) squalid; (*fam*) vile, despicable ▷ *nmf* (*malvado*) rogue

miseria [mi'serja] *nf* (*pobreza*) poverty; (*tacañería*) meanness, stinginess; (*condiciones*) squalor; **una ~ a** pittance

misericordia [miseri'korðja] *nf* (*compasión*) compassion, pity; (*piedad*) mercy

misil [mi'sil] *nm* missile

misión [mi'sjon] *nf* mission; **misionero, -a** *nm/f* missionary

mismo, -a ['mismo, a] *adj* (*semejante*) same; (*después de pron*) -self; (*para énfasis*) very ▷ *adv*: **aquí/hoy ~** right here/this very day; **ahora ~** right now ▷ *conj*: **lo ~ que** just like o as; **el ~ traje** the same suit; **en ese ~ momento** at that very moment; **vino el ~ ministro** the minister himself came; **yo ~ lo vi** I saw it myself; **lo ~** the same (thing); **da lo ~** it's all the same; **quedamos en las mismas** we're no further forward; **por lo ~** for the same reason

misterio [mis'terjo] *nm* mystery; **misterioso, -a** *adj* mysterious

mitad [mi'tað] *nf* (*medio*) half; (*centro*) middle; **a ~ de precio** (at) half-price; **en o a ~ del camino** halfway along the road; **cortar por la ~** to cut through the middle

mitin ['mitin] (*pl* **mítines**) *nm* meeting

mito ['mito] *nm* myth

mixto, -a ['miksto, a] *adj* mixed

ml. *abr* (= *mililitro*) ml

mm. *abr* (= *milímetro*) mm

mobiliario [moβi'ljarjo] *nm* furniture

mochila [mo'tʃila] *nf* rucksack (BRIT), back-pack

moco ['moko] *nm* mucus; **mocos** *nmpl* (*fam*) snot; **limpiarse los ~s de la nariz** (*fam*) to wipe one's nose

moda ['moða] *nf* fashion; (*estilo*) style; **a la o de ~** in fashion, fashionable; **pasado de ~** out of fashion

modales [mo'ðales] *nmpl* manners

modelar [moðe'lar] *vt* to model

modelo [mo'ðelo] *adj inv, nmf* model

módem ['moðem] *nm* (*Inform*) modem

moderado, -a [moðe'raðo, a] *adj* moderate

moderar [moðe'rar] *vt* to moderate; (*violencia*) to restrain, control; (*velocidad*) to reduce; **moderarse** *vr* to restrain o.s., control o.s.

modernizar [moðerni'θar] *vt* to modernize

moderno, -a [mo'ðerno, a] *adj* modern; (*actual*) present-day

modestia [mo'ðestja] *nf* modesty; **modesto, -a** *adj* modest

modificar [moðifi'kar] *vt* to modify

modisto, -a [mo'ðisto, a] *nm/f* (*diseñador*) couturier, designer; (*que confecciona*) dressmaker

modo ['moðo] *nm* way, manner; (*Mús*) mode; **modos** *nmpl* manners; **de ningún ~** in no way; **de todos ~s** at any rate; **modo de empleo** directions *pl* (for use)

mofarse [mo'farse] *vr*: **~ de** to mock, scoff at

mofle ['mofle] (*MÉX, CAM*) *nm* silencer (BRIT), muffler (US)

mogollón [moɣoˈʎon] (*ESP: fam*) *adv* a hell of a lot

moho ['moo] *nm* mould, mildew; (*en metal*) rust

mojar [mo'xar] *vt* to wet; (*humedecer*) to damp(en), moisten; (*calar*) to soak; **mojarse** *vr* to get wet

molcajete [molka'xete] (*MÉX*) *nm* mortar

molde ['molde] *nm* mould; (*Costura*) pattern; (*fig*) model; **moldeado** *nm* soft perm; **moldear** *vt* to mould

mole ['mole] *nf* mass, bulk; (*edificio*) pile

moler [mo'ler] *vt* to grind, crush

molestar [moles'tar] *vt* to bother; (*fastidiar*) to annoy; (*incomodar*) to inconvenience, put out ▷ *vi* to be a nuisance; **molestarse** *vr* to bother; (*incomodarse*) to go to trouble; (*ofenderse*) to take offence; **¿(no) te molesta si ...?** do you mind if ...?

▌ No confundir **molestar** con la palabra inglesa *molest*.

molestia [mo'lestja] *nf* bother, trouble; (*incomodidad*) inconvenience; (*Med*) discomfort; **es una ~** it's a nuisance; **molesto, -a** *adj* (*que fastidia*) annoying; (*incómodo*) inconvenient; (*inquieto*) uncomfortable, ill at ease; (*enfadado*) annoyed

molido, -a [mo'liðo, a] *adj*: **estar ~** (*fig*) to be exhausted o dead beat

molinillo [moli'niʎo] *nm* hand mill; **molinillo de café** coffee grinder

molino [mo'lino] *nm* (*edificio*) mill; (*máquina*) grinder

momentáneo, -a [momen'taneo, a] *adj* momentary

momento [mo'mento] *nm* moment; **de ~** at o for the moment

momia ['momja] *nf* mummy

monarca [mo'narka] *nmf* monarch, ruler; **monarquía** *nf* monarchy

monasterio [monas'terjo] *nm* monastery

mondar [mon'dar] *vt* to peel; **mondarse** *vr* (*ESP*): **~se de risa** (*fam*)

mondongo [mon'dongo] (LAM) nm tripe

moneda [mo'neða] nf (tipo de dinero) currency, money; (pieza) coin; **una ~ de 2 euros** a 2 euro piece; **monedero** nm purse

monitor, a [moni'tor, a] nm/f instructor, coach ▷ nm (TV) set; (Inform) monitor

monja ['monxa] nf nun

monje ['monxe] nm monk

mono, -a ['mono, a] adj (bonito) lovely, pretty; (gracioso) nice, charming ▷ nm/f monkey, ape ▷ nm dungarees pl; (overoles) overalls pl

monopatín [monopa'tin] nm skateboard

monopolio [mono'poljo] nm monopoly; **monopolizar** vt to monopolize

monótono, -a [mo'notono, a] adj monotonous

monstruo ['monstrwo] nm monster ▷ adj inv fantastic; **monstruoso, -a** adj monstrous

montaje [mon'taxe] nm assembly; (Teatro) décor; (Cine) montage

montaña [mon'taɲa] nf (monte) mountain; (sierra) mountains pl, mountainous area; **montaña rusa** roller coaster; **montañero, -a** nm/f mountaineer; **montañismo** nm mountaineering

montar [mon'tar] vt (subir a) to mount, get on; (Tec) to assemble, put together; (negocio) to set up; (arma) to cock; (colocar) to lift on to; (Culin) to beat ▷ vi to mount, get on; (sobresalir) to overlap; **~ en bicicleta** to ride a bicycle; **~ en cólera** to get angry; **~ a caballo** to ride, go horseriding

monte ['monte] nm (montaña) mountain; (bosque) woodland; (área sin cultivar) wild area, wild country; **monte de piedad** pawnshop

montón [mon'ton] nm heap, pile; (fig) **un ~ de** heaps of, lots of

monumento [monu'mento] nm monument

moño ['moɲo] nm bun

moqueta [mo'keta] nf fitted carpet

mora ['mora] nf blackberry; V tb **moro**

morado, -a [mo'raðo, a] adj purple, violet ▷ nm bruise

moral [mo'ral] adj moral ▷ nf (ética) ethics pl; (moralidad) morals pl, morality; (ánimo) morale

moraleja [mora'lexa] nf moral

morboso, -a [mor'βoso, a] adj morbid

morcilla [mor'θiʎa] nf blood sausage = black pudding (BRIT)

mordaza [mor'ðaθa] nf (para la boca) gag; (Tec) clamp

morder [mor'ðer] vt to bite; (fig: consumir) to eat away, eat into; **mordisco** nm bite

moreno, -a [mo'reno, a] adj (color) (dark) brown; (de tez) dark; (de pelo moreno) dark-haired; (negro) black

morfina [mor'fina] nf morphine

moribundo, -a [mori'βundo, a] adj dying

morir [mo'rir] vi to die; (fuego) to die down; (luz) to go out; **morirse** vr to die; (fig) to be dying; **murió en un accidente** he was killed in an accident; **~se por algo** to be dying for sth

moro, -a ['moro, a] adj Moorish ▷ nm/f Moor

moroso, -a [mo'roso, a] nm/f bad debtor, defaulter

morralla [mo'raʎa] (MÉX) nf (cambio) small o loose change

morro ['moro] nm (Zool) snout, nose; (Auto, Aviac) nose

morsa ['morsa] nf walrus

mortadela [morta'ðela] nf mortadella

mortal [mor'tal] adj mortal; (golpe) deadly; **mortalidad** nf mortality

mortero [mor'tero] nm mortar

mosca ['moska] nf fly

Moscú [mos'ku] n Moscow

mosquearse [moske'arse] (fam) vr (enojarse) to get cross; (ofenderse) to take offence

mosquitero [moski'tero] nm mosquito net

mosquito [mos'kito] nm mosquito

mostaza [mos'taθa] nf mustard

mosto ['mosto] nm (unfermented) grape juice

mostrador [mostra'ðor] nm (de tienda) counter; (de café) bar

mostrar [mos'trar] vt to show; (exhibir) to display, exhibit; (explicar) to explain; **mostrarse** vr: **~se amable** to be kind; to prove to be kind; **no se muestra muy inteligente** he doesn't seem (to be) very intelligent

mota ['mota] nf speck, tiny piece; (en diseño) dot

mote ['mote] nm nickname

motín [mo'tin] nm (del pueblo) revolt, rising; (del ejército) mutiny

motivar [moti'βar] vt (causar) to cause, motivate; (explicar) to explain, justify; **motivo** nm motive, reason

moto ['moto] (fam) nf = **motocicleta**

motocicleta [motoθi'kleta] nf motorbike (BRIT), motorcycle

motociclista [motoθik'lista] nmf motorcyclist, biker

motoneta [moto'neta] (cs) nf scooter

motor [mo'tor] nm motor, engine; **motor a chorro o de reacción/de explosión** jet engine/internal combustion engine

motora [mo'tora] nf motorboat

movedizo, -a adj V **arena**

mover [mo'βer] vt to move; (cabeza) to shake; (accionar) to drive; (fig) to cause, provoke; **moverse** vr to move; (fig) to get a move on

móvil ['moβil] adj mobile; (pieza de máquina) moving; (mueble) movable ▷ nm (motivo) motive; (teléfono)

mobile; (us) cellphone

movimiento [moβi'mjento] nm movement; (Tec) motion; (actividad) activity

mozo, -a ['moθo, a] adj (joven) young ▷ nm/f youth, young man/girl; (cs: mesero) waiter/waitress

MP3 nm MP3; **reproductor (de) ~** MP3 player

mucama [mu'kama] (RPL) nf maid

muchacho, -a [mu'tʃatʃo, a] nm/f (niño) boy/girl; (criado) servant; (criada) maid

muchedumbre [mutʃe'ðumbre] nf crowd

○ **PALABRA CLAVE**

mucho, -a ['mutʃo, a] adj 1 (cantidad) a lot of, much; (número) lots of, a lot of, many; **mucho dinero** a lot of money; **hace mucho calor** it's very hot; **muchas amigas** lots o a lot of friends 2 (sg: grande) **ésta es mucha casa para él** this house is much too big for him
▷ pron: **tengo mucho que hacer** I've got a lot to do; **muchos dicen que ...** a lot of people say that ...; V tb **tener**
▷ adv 1 **me gusta mucho** I like it a lot; **lo siento mucho** I'm very sorry; **come mucho** he eats a lot; **¿te vas a quedar mucho?** are you going to be staying long?
2 (respuesta) very; **¿estás cansado? – ¡mucho!** are you tired? – very!
3 (locuciones): **como mucho** at (the most); **con mucho: el mejor con mucho** by far the best; **ni mucho menos: no es rico ni mucho menos** he's far from being rich
4: **por mucho que: por mucho que lo creas** no matter how o however much you believe her

muda ['muða] nf change of clothes

mudanza [mu'ðanθa] nf (de casa) move

mudar [mu'ðar] vt to change; (Zool) to shed ▷ vi to change; **mudarse** vr (ropa) to change; **~se de casa** to move house

mudo, -a ['muðo, a] adj dumb; (callado, Cine) silent

mueble ['mweβle] nm piece of furniture; **muebles** nmpl furniture sg

mueca ['mweka] nf face, grimace; **hacer ~s a** to make faces at

muela ['mwela] nf back tooth; **muela del juicio** wisdom tooth

muelle ['mweʎe] nm spring; (Náut) wharf; (malecón) pier

muero etc vb V **morir**

muerte ['mwerte] nf death; (homicidio) murder; **dar ~ a** to kill

muerto, -a ['mwerto, a] pp de **morir** ▷ adj dead ▷ nm/f dead man/woman; (difunto) deceased; (cadáver) corpse; **estar ~ de cansancio** to be dead tired; **Día de los Muertos** (MÉX) All Souls' Day

> **DÍA DE LOS MUERTOS**
>
> All Souls' Day (or "Day of the Dead")
> in Mexico coincides with All
> Saints' Day, which is celebrated
> in the Catholic countries of Latin
> America on November 1st and
> 2nd. All Souls' Day is actually
> a celebration which begins
> in the evening of October 31st
> and continues until November
> 2nd. It is a combination of the
> Catholic tradition of honouring
> the Christian saints and martyrs,
> and the ancient Mexican or Aztec
> traditions, in which death was not
> something sinister. For this reason
> all the dead are honoured by
> bringing offerings of food, flowers
> and candles to the cemetery.

muestra ['mwestra] nf (señal) indication, sign; (demostración) demonstration; (prueba) proof; (estadística) sample; (modelo) model,

pattern; (testimonio) token

muestro etc vb V **mostrar**

muevo etc vb V **mover**

mugir [mu'xir] vi (vaca) to moo

mugre ['muɣre] nf dirt, filth

mujer [mu'xer] nf woman; (esposa) wife; **mujeriego** nm womanizer

mula ['mula] nf mule

muleta [mu'leta] nf (para andar) crutch; (Taur) stick with red cape attached

multa ['multa] nf fine; **poner una ~ a** to fine; **multar** vt to fine

multicines [multi'θines] nmpl multiscreen cinema sg

multinacional [multinaθjo'nal] nf multinational

múltiple ['multiple] adj multiple; (pl) many, numerous

multiplicar [multipli'kar] vt (Mat) to multiply; (fig) to increase; **multiplicarse** vr (Bio) to multiply; (fig) to be everywhere at once

multitud [multi'tuð] nf (muchedumbre) crowd; **~ de** lots of

mundial [mun'djal] adj world-wide, universal; (guerra, récord) world cpd

mundo ['mundo] nm world; **todo el ~** everybody; **tener ~** to be experienced, know one's way around

munición [muni'θjon] nf ammunition

municipal [muniθi'pal] adj municipal, local

municipio [muni'θipjo] nm (ayuntamiento) town council, corporation; (territorio administrativo) town, municipality

muñeca [mu'ɲeka] nf (Anat) wrist; (juguete) doll

muñeco [mu'ɲeko] nm (figura) figure; (marioneta) puppet; (fig) puppet, pawn

mural [mu'ral] adj mural, wall cpd ▷ nm mural

muralla [mu'raʎa] nf (city) wall(s) (pl)

murciélago [mur'θjelaɣo] nm bat

murmullo [mur'muʎo] nm

murmur(ing); (*cuchicheo*) whispering
murmurar [murmu'rar] *vi* to
murmur, whisper; (*cotillear*) to gossip
muro ['muro] *nm* wall
muscular [musku'lar] *adj* muscular
músculo ['muskulo] *nm* muscle
museo [mu'seo] *nm* museum; **museo
de arte** art gallery
musgo ['musxo] *nm* moss
música ['musika] *nf* music; V *tb*
músico
músico, -a ['musiko, a] *adj* musical
▷ *nm/f* musician
muslo ['muslo] *nm* thigh
musulmán, -ana [musul'man,
ana] *nm/f* Moslem
mutación [muta'θjon] *nf* (*Bio*)
mutation; (*cambio*) (sudden) change
mutilar [muti'lar] *vt* to mutilate; (*a
una persona*) to maim
mutuo, -a ['mutwo, a] *adj* mutual
muy [mwi] *adv* very; (*demasiado*) too;
M~ Señor mío Dear Sir; **~ de noche**
very late at night; **eso es ~ de él** that's
just like him

N *abr* (= *norte*) N
nabo ['naβo] *nm* turnip
nacer [na'θer] *vi* to be born; (*de huevo*)
to hatch; (*vegetal*) to sprout; (*río*) to
rise; **nací en Barcelona** I was born
in Barcelona; **nacido, -a** *adj* born;
recién nacido newborn; **nacimiento**
nm birth; (*de Navidad*) Nativity; (*de
río*) source
nación [na'θjon] *nf* nation; **nacional**
adj national; **nacionalismo** *nm*
nationalism
nacionalidad [naθjonali'ðað] *nf*
nationality
nada ['naða] *pron* nothing ▷ *adv*
not at all, in no way; **no decir ~** to say
nothing, not to say anything; **~ más**
nothing else; **de ~** don't mention it
nadador, a [naða'ðor, a] *nm/f*
swimmer
nadar [na'ðar] *vi* to swim
nadie ['naðje] *pron* nobody, no-one;
~ habló nobody spoke; **no había ~**
there was nobody there, there wasn't
anybody there

nado ['naðo] **a nado**: adv: **pasar a ~** to swim across

nafta ['nafta] (RPL) nf petrol (BRIT), gas (US)

naipe ['naipe] nm (playing) card; **naipes** nmpl cards

nalgas ['nalɣas] nfpl buttocks

nalguear [nalɣe'ar] (MÉX, CAM) vt to spank

nana ['nana] (ESP) nf lullaby

naranja [na'ranxa] adj inv, nf orange; **media ~** (fam) better half; **naranjada** nf orangeade; **naranjo** nm orange tree

narciso [nar'θiso] nm narcissus

narcótico, -a [nar'kotiko, a] adj, nm narcotic; **narcotizar** vt to drug; **narcotráfico** nm drug trafficking o running

nariz [na'riθ] nf nose; **nariz chata/ respingona** snub/turned-up nose

narración [narra'θjon] nf narration

narrar [na'rrar] vt to narrate, recount; **narrativa** nf narrative

nata ['nata] nf cream; **nata montada** whipped cream

natación [nata'θjon] nf swimming

natal [na'tal] adj: **ciudad ~** home town; **natalidad** nf birth rate

natillas [na'tiʎas] nfpl custard sg

nativo, -a [na'tiβo, a] adj, nm/f native

natural [natu'ral] adj natural; (fruta etc) fresh ▷ nmf native ▷ nm (disposición) nature

naturaleza [natura'leθa] nf nature; (género) nature, kind; **naturaleza muerta** still life

naturalmente [natural'mente] adv (de modo natural) in a natural way; **¡~!** of course!

naufragar [naufra'ɣar] vi to sink; **naufragio** nm shipwreck

nauseabundo, -a [nausea'βundo, a] adj nauseating, sickening

náuseas ['nauseas] nfpl nausea sg; **me da ~** it makes me feel sick

náutico, -a [na'utiko, a] adj nautical

navaja [na'βaxa] nf knife; (de barbero, peluquero) razor

naval [na'βal] adj naval

Navarra [na'βarra] n Navarre

nave ['naβe] nf (barco) ship, vessel; (Arq) nave; **nave espacial** spaceship; **nave industrial** factory premises pl

navegador [naβeɣa'ðor] nm (Inform) browser

navegante [naβeɣa'nte] nmf navigator

navegar [naβe'ɣar] vi (barco) to sail; (avión) to fly; **~ por Internet** to surf the Net

Navidad [naβi'ðað] nf Christmas; **Navidades** nfpl Christmas time; **¡Feliz ~!** Merry Christmas!; **navideño, -a** adj Christmas cpd

nazca etc vb V **nacer**

nazi ['naθi] adj, nmf Nazi

NE abr (= nor(d)este) NE

neblina [ne'βlina] nf mist

necesario, -a [neθe'sarjo, a] adj necessary

neceser [neθe'ser] nm toilet bag; (bolsa grande) holdall

necesidad [neθesi'ðað] nf need; (lo inevitable) necessity; (miseria) poverty; **en caso de ~** in case of need o emergency; **hacer sus ~es** to relieve o.s.

necesitado, -a [neθesi'taðo, a] adj needy, poor; **~ de** in need of

necesitar [neθesi'tar] vt to need, require

necio, -a ['neθjo, a] adj foolish

nectarina [nekta'rina] nf nectarine

nefasto, -a [ne'fasto, a] adj ill-fated, unlucky

negación [neɣa'θjon] nf negation; (rechazo) refusal, denial

negar [ne'ɣar] vt (renegar, rechazar) to refuse; (prohibir) to deny; (desmentir) to deny; **negarse** vr: **~se a** to refuse to

negativa [neɣa'tiβa] nf negative; (rechazo) refusal, denial

negativo, -a [neɣa'tiβo, a] adj, nm

negative

negligente [neɣliˈxente] *adj*
negligent

negociación [neɣoθjaˈθjon] *nf*
negotiation

negociante [neɣoˈθjante] *nmf*
businessman/woman

negociar [neɣoˈθjar] *vt, vi* to
negotiate; **~ en** to deal o trade in

negocio [neˈɣoθjo] *nm* (Com)
business; (*asunto*) affair, business;
(*operación comercial*) deal, transaction;
(*lugar*) place of business; **los ~s**
business *sg*; **hacer ~** to do business

negra [ˈneɣra] *nf* (Mús) crotchet; V
tb **negro**

negro, -a [ˈneɣro, a] *adj* black;
(*suerte*) awful ▷ *nm* black ▷ *nm/f* black
man/woman

nene, -a [ˈnene, a] *nm/f* baby,
small child

neón [neˈon] *nm*: **luces/lámpara de ~**
neon lights/lamp

neoyorquino, -a [neojorˈkino, a]
adj (of) New York

nervio [ˈnerβjo] *nm* nerve;
nerviosismo *nm* nervousness, nerves
pl; **nervioso, -a** *adj* nervous

neto, -a [ˈneto, a] *adj* net

neumático, -a [neuˈmatiko, a] *adj*
pneumatic ▷ *nm* (ESP) tyre (BRIT),
tire (US); **neumático de recambio**
spare tyre

neurólogo, -a [neuˈroloɣo, a] *nm/f*
neurologist

neurona [neuˈrona] *nf* nerve cell

neutral [neuˈtral] *adj* neutral;
neutralizar *vt* to neutralize;
(*contrarrestar*) to counteract

neutro, -a [ˈneutro, a] *adj* (Bio,
Ling) neuter

neutrón [neuˈtron] *nm* neutron

nevada [neˈβaða] *nf* snowstorm;
(*caída de nieve*) snowfall

nevar [neˈβar] *vi* to snow

nevera [neˈβera] *nf* (ESP) refrigerator
(BRIT), icebox (US)

nevería [neβeˈria] *nf* (MÉX) ice-cream

parlour

nexo [ˈnekso] *nm* link, connection

ni [ni] *conj* nor, neither; (*tb*: **~ siquiera**)
not ... even; **~ aunque** not even
if; **~ blanco ~ negro** neither white
nor black

Nicaragua [nikaˈraɣwa] *nf*
Nicaragua; **nicaragüense** *adj, nmf*
Nicaraguan

nicho [ˈnitʃo] *nm* niche

nicotina [nikoˈtina] *nf* nicotine

nido [ˈniðo] *nm* nest

niebla [ˈnjeβla] *nf* fog; (*neblina*) mist

niego *etc vb* V **negar**

nieto, -a [ˈnjeto, a] *nm/f* grandson/
daughter; **nietos** *nmpl* grandchildren

nieve *etc* [ˈnjeβe] *vb* V **nevar** ▷ *nf*
snow; (MÉX: *helado*) ice cream

NIF *nm abr* (= Número de Identificación
Fiscal) personal identification number used
for financial and tax purposes

ninfa [ˈninfa] *nf* nymph

ningún *adj* V **ninguno**

ninguno, -a [ninˈɣuno, a] (*adj*
ningún) no *pron* (*nadie*) nobody; (*ni
uno*) none, not one; (*ni uno ni otro*)
neither; **de ninguna manera** by no
means, not at all

niña [ˈniɲa] *nf* (Anat) pupil; V *tb* **niño**

niñera [niˈɲera] *nf* nursemaid, nanny

niñez [niˈɲeθ] *nf* childhood; (*infancia*)
infancy

niño, -a [ˈniɲo, a] *adj* (*joven*) young;
(*inmaduro*) immature ▷ *nm/f* child,
boy/girl

nipón, -ona [niˈpon, ona] *adj, nm/f*
Japanese

níquel [ˈnikel] *nm* nickel

níspero [ˈnispero] *nm* medlar

nítido, -a [ˈnitiðo, a] *adj* clear; sharp

nitrato [niˈtrato] *nm* nitrate

nitrógeno [niˈtroxeno] *nm* nitrogen

nivel [niˈβel] *nm* (Geo) level; (*norma*)
level, standard; (*altura*) height; **nivel
de aceite** oil level; **nivel de aire** spirit
level; **nivel de vida** standard of living;
nivelar *vt* to level out; (*fig*) to even up;
(Com) to balance

no [no] *adv* no; not; (*con verbo*) not
▷ *excl* no!; **~ tengo nada** I don't have
anything, I have nothing; **~ es el mío**
it's not mine; **ahora ~** not now; **¿~ lo
sabes?** don't you know?; **~ mucho** not
much; **~ bien termine, lo entregaré** as
soon as I finish, I'll hand it over; **~ más:
ayer ~ más** just yesterday; **¡pase ~
más!** come in!; **¡a que ~ lo sabes!** I bet
you don't know!; **¡cómo ~!** of course!;
la ~ intervención non-intervention

noble ['noβle] *adj, nmf* noble; **nobleza**
nf nobility

noche ['notʃe] *nf* night, night-time;
(*la tarde*) evening; **de ~, por la ~** at
night; **es de ~** it's dark; **Noche de San
Juan** *see note*

○ **NOCHE DE SAN JUAN**
○
○ The **Noche de San Juan** on the
○ 24th June is a **fiesta** coinciding
○ with the summer solstice and
○ which has taken the place of
○ other ancient pagan festivals.
○ Traditionally fire plays a major
○ part in these festivities with
○ celebrations and dancing taking
○ place around bonfires in towns
○ and villages across the country.

nochebuena [notʃe'βwena] *nf*
Christmas Eve

○ **NOCHEBUENA**
○
○ Traditional Christmas
○ celebrations in Spanish-speaking
○ countries mainly take place
○ on the night of **Nochebuena**,
○ Christmas Eve. Families gather
○ together for a large meal and the
○ more religiously inclined attend
○ Midnight Mass. While presents are
○ traditionally given by **los Reyes
○ Magos** on the 6th January, more
○ and more people are exchanging
○ gifts on Christmas Eve.

nochevieja [notʃe'βjexa] *nf* New
Year's Eve

nocivo, -a [no'θiβo, a] *adj* harmful

noctámbulo, -a [nok'tambulo, a]
nm/f sleepwalker

nocturno, -a [nok'turno, a] *adj* (*de
la noche*) nocturnal, night *cpd*; (*de la
tarde*) evening *cpd* ▷ *nm* nocturne

nogal [no'ɣal] *nm* walnut tree

nómada ['nomaða] *adj* nomadic
▷ *nmf* nomad

nombrar [nom'brar] *vt* (*designar*)
to name; (*mencionar*) to mention; (*dar
puesto a*) to appoint

nombre ['nombre] *nm* name;
(*sustantivo*) noun; **~ y apellidos** name
in full; **poner ~ a** to call, name; **nombre
común/propio** common/proper
noun; **nombre de pila/de soltera**
Christian/maiden name

nómina ['nomina] *nf* (*lista*) payroll;
(*hoja*) payslip

nominal [nomi'nal] *adj* nominal

nominar [nomi'nar] *vt* to nominate

nominativo, -a [nomina'tiβo, a]
adj (Com): **cheque ~ a X** cheque made
out to X

nordeste [nor'ðeste] *adj* north-east,
north-eastern, north-easterly ▷ *nm*
north-east

nórdico, -a ['norðiko, a] *adj* Nordic

noreste [no'reste] *adj, nm* = **nordeste**

noria ['norja] *nf* (Agr) waterwheel; (*de
carnaval*) big (BRIT) o Ferris (US) wheel

norma ['norma] *nf* rule (of thumb)

normal [nor'mal] *adj* (*corriente*)
normal; (*habitual*) usual, natural;
normalizarse *vr* to return to normal;
normalmente *adv* normally

normativa [norma'tiβa] *nf* (set of)
rules *pl*, regulations *pl*

noroeste [noro'este] *adj* north-west,
north-western, north-westerly ▷ *nm*
north-west

norte ['norte] *adj* north, northern,
northerly ▷ *nm* north; (*fig*) guide

norteamericano, -a
[norteameri'kano, a] *adj, nm/f*

(North) American

Noruega [noˈrweɣa] nf Norway

noruego, -a [noˈrweɣo, a] adj, nm/f
Norwegian

nos [nos] pron (directo) us; (indirecto)
us; to us; for us; (reflexivo) (to)
ourselves; (recíproco) (to) each other; **levantamos a las 7** we get up at 7

nosotros, -as [noˈsotros, as] pron
(sujeto) we; (después de prep) us

nostalgia [nosˈtalxja] nf nostalgia

nota [ˈnota] nf note; (Escol) mark

notable [noˈtaβle] adj notable; (Escol)
outstanding

notar [noˈtar] vt to notice;
notarse vr to be obvious; **se nota que
...** one observes that ...

notario [noˈtarjo] nm notary

noticia [noˈtiθja] nf (información)
piece of news; **las ~s** the news sg;
tener ~s de algn to hear from sb
▷ No confundir **noticia** con la palabra
inglesa notice.

noticiero [notiˈθjero] (LAM) nm news
bulletin

notificar [notifiˈkar] vt to notify,
inform

notorio, -a [noˈtorjo, a] adj (público)
well-known; (evidente) obvious

novato, -a [noˈβato, a] adj
inexperienced ▷ nm/f beginner,
novice

novecientos, -as [noβeˈθjentos, as]
num nine hundred

novedad [noβeˈðað] nf (calidad de
nuevo) newness; (noticia) piece of news;
(cambio) change, (new) development

novel [noˈβel] adj new; (inexperto)
inexperienced ▷ nmf beginner

novela [noˈβela] nf novel

noveno, -a [noˈβeno, a] adj ninth

noventa [noˈβenta] num ninety

novia [ˈnoβja] nf V **novio**

noviazgo [noˈβjaθɣo] nm
engagement

novicio, -a [noˈβiθjo, a] nm/f novice

noviembre [noˈβjembre] nm
November

novillada [noβiˈʎaða] nf (Taur)
bullfight with young bulls; **novillero**
nm novice bullfighter; **novillo** nm young
bull, bullock; **hacer novillos** (fam) to
play truant

novio, -a [ˈnoβjo, a] nm/f boyfriend/
girlfriend; (prometido) fiancé/fiancée;
(recién casado) bridegroom/bride; **los
~s** the newly-weds

nube [ˈnuβe] nf cloud

nublado, -a [nuˈβlaðo, a] adj
cloudy; **nublarse** vr to grow dark

nubosidad [nuβosiˈðað] nf
cloudiness; **había mucha ~** it was
very cloudy

nuboso [nuˈβoso] adj cloudy

nuca [ˈnuka] nf nape of the neck

nuclear [nukleˈar] adj nuclear

núcleo [ˈnukleo] nm (centro) core;
(Física) nucleus; **núcleo urbano** city
centre

nudillo [nuˈðiʎo] nm knuckle

nudista [nuˈðista] adj nudist

nudo [ˈnuðo] nm knot; (de carreteras)
junction

nuera [ˈnwera] nf daughter-in-law

nuestro, -a [ˈnwestro, a] adj pos
our ▷ pron ours; **~ padre** our father;
un amigo ~ a friend of ours; **es el ~**
it's ours

Nueva York [-ˈjork] n New York

Nueva Zelanda [-θeˈlanda] nf New
Zealand

nueve [ˈnweβe] num nine

nuevo, -a [ˈnweβo, a] adj (gen) new;
de ~ again

nuez [nweθ] nf walnut; (Anat) Adam's
apple; **nuez moscada** nutmeg

nulo, -a [ˈnulo, a] adj (inepto, torpe)
useless; (inválido) (null and) void;
(Deporte) drawn, tied

núm. abr (=número) no.

numerar [numeˈrar] vt to number

número [ˈnumero] nm (gen) number;
(tamaño: de zapato) size; (ejemplar: de
diario) number, issue; **sin ~** numberless,
unnumbered; **número atrasado** back
number; **número de matrícula/**

teléfono registration/telephone number; **número impar/par** odd/even number; **número romano** Roman numeral

numeroso, -a [nume'roso, a] adj numerous

nunca ['nunka] adv (jamás) never; **~ lo pensé** I never thought it; **no viene ~ he** never comes; **~ más** never again; **más que ~** more than ever

nupcias ['nupθjas] nfpl wedding sg, nuptials

nutria ['nutrja] nf otter

nutrición [nutri'θjon] nf nutrition

nutrir [nu'trir] vt (alimentar) to nourish; (dar de comer) to feed; (fig) to strengthen; **nutritivo, -a** adj nourishing, nutritious

nylon [ni'lon] nm nylon

ñango, -a ['ŋaŋgo, a] (MÉX) adj puny

ñapa ['ŋapa] (LAM) nf extra

ñata ['ŋata] (LAM: fam) nf nose; V tb **ñato**

ñato, -a ['ŋato, a] (LAM) adj snub-nosed

ñoñería [ŋoŋe'ria] nf insipidness

ñoño, -a ['ŋoŋo, a] adj (fam: tonto) silly, stupid; (soso) insipid; (persona) spineless; (ESP: película, novela) sentimental

ñ

O

O *abr* (= *oeste*) W

o [o] *conj* or; **o ... o** either ... or

oasis [o'asis] *nm inv* oasis

obcecarse [oβθe'karse] *vr* to get o become stubborn

obedecer [oβeðe'θer] *vt* to obey; **obediente** *adj* obedient

obertura [oβer'tura] *nf* overture

obeso, -a [o'βeso, a] *adj* obese

obispo [o'βispo] *nm* bishop

obituario [oβi'twarjo] (LAM) *nm* obituary

objetar [oβxe'tar] *vt, vi* to object

objetivo, -a [oβxe'tiβo, a] *adj, nm* objective

objeto [oβ'xeto] *nm* (*cosa*) object; (*fin*) aim

objetor, a [oβxe'tor, a] *nm/f* objector

obligación [oβliɣa'θjon] *nf* obligation; (*Com*) bond

obligar [oβli'ɣar] *vt* to force; **obligarse** *vr* to bind o.s.; **obligatorio, -a** *adj* compulsory, obligatory

oboe [o'βoe] *nm* oboe

obra ['oβra] *nf* work; (*Arq*) construction, building; (*Teatro*) play; **por ~ de** thanks to (the efforts of); **obra maestra** masterpiece; **obras públicas** public works; **obrar** *vt* to work; (*tener efecto*) to have an effect on ▷ *vi* to act, behave; (*tener efecto*) to have an effect; **la carta obra en su poder** the letter is in his/her possession

obrero, -a [o'βrero, a] *adj* (*clase*) working; (*movimiento*) labour *cpd* ▷ *nm/f* (*gen*) worker; (*sin oficio*) labourer

obsceno, -a [oβs'θeno, a] *adj* obscene

obscu... = oscu...

obsequiar [oβse'kjar] *vt* (*ofrecer*) to present with; (*agasajar*) to make a fuss of, lavish attention on; **obsequio** *nm* (*regalo*) gift; (*cortesía*) courtesy, attention

observación [oβserβa'θjon] *nf* observation; (*reflexión*) remark

observador, a [oβserβa'ðor, a] *nm/f* observer

observar [oβser'βar] *vt* to observe; (*anotar*) to notice; **observarse** *vr* to keep to, observe

obsesión [oβse'sjon] *nf* obsession; **obsesivo, -a** *adj* obsessive

obstáculo [oβs'takulo] *nm* obstacle; (*impedimento*) hindrance, drawback

obstante [oβs'tante]: **no ~** *adv* nevertheless

obstinado, -a [oβsti'naðo, a] *adj* obstinate, stubborn

obstinarse [oβsti'narse] *vr* to be obstinate; **~ en** to persist in

obstruir [oβstru'ir] *vt* to obstruct

obtener [oβte'ner] *vt* (*gen*) to obtain; (*premio*) to win

obturador [oβtura'ðor] *nm* (*Foto*) shutter

obvio, -a ['oββjo, a] *adj* obvious

oca ['oka] *nf* (*animal*) goose; (*juego*) ≈ snakes and ladders

ocasión [oka'sjon] *nf* (*oportunidad*) opportunity, chance; (*momento*) occasion, time; (*causa*) cause; **de ~**

secondhand; **ocasionar** vt to cause
ocaso [o'kaso] nm (fig) decline
occidente [okθi'ðente] nm west
OCDE nf abr (= Organización de
Cooperación y Desarrollo Económico)
OECD
océano [o'θeano] nm ocean; **Océano
índico** Indian Ocean
ochenta [o'tʃenta] num eighty
ocho ['otʃo] num eight; **dentro de ~
días** within a week
ocio ['oθjo] nm (tiempo) leisure; (pey)
idleness
octavilla [okta'viʎa] nf leaflet,
pamphlet
octavo, -a [ok'taβo, a] adj eighth
octubre [ok'tuβre] nm October
oculista [oku'lista] nmf oculist
ocultar [okul'tar] vt (esconder) to
hide; (callar) to conceal; **oculto, -a** adj
hidden; (fig) secret
ocupación [okupa'θjon] nf
occupation
ocupado, -a [oku'paðo, a] adj
(persona) busy; (plaza) occupied, taken;
(teléfono) engaged; **ocupar** vt (gen) to
occupy; **ocuparse** vr: **ocuparse de
o en** (gen) to concern o.s. with; (cuidar)
to look after
ocurrencia [oku'rrenθja] nf (idea)
bright idea
ocurrir [oku'rrir] vi to happen;
ocurrirse vr: **se me ocurrió que ...** it
occurred to me that ...
odiar [o'ðjar] vt to hate; **odio** nm
hate, hatred; **odioso, -a** adj (gen)
hateful; (malo) nasty
odontólogo, -a [oðon'toloxo, a]
nm/f dentist, dental surgeon
oeste [o'este] nm west; **una película
del ~** a western
ofender [ofen'der] vt (agraviar) to
offend; (insultar) to insult; **ofenderse**
vr to take offence; **ofensa** nf offence;
ofensiva nf offensive; **ofensivo, -a**
adj offensive
oferta [o'ferta] nf offer; (propuesta)
proposal; **la ~ y la demanda** supply

and demand; **artículos en ~** goods
on offer
oficial [ofi'θjal] adj official ⊳ nm
(Mil) officer
oficina [ofi'θina] nf office; **oficina
de correos** post office; **oficina de
información** information bureau;
oficina de turismo tourist office;
oficinista nmf clerk
oficio [o'fiθjo] nm (profesión)
profession; (puesto) post; (Rel) service;
ser del ~ to be an old hand; **tener
mucho ~** to have a lot of experience;
oficio de difuntos funeral service
ofimática [ofi'matika] nf office
automation
ofrecer [ofre'θer] vt (dar) to offer;
(proponer) to propose; **ofrecerse**
vr (persona) to offer o.s., volunteer;
(situación) to present itself; **¿qué se le
ofrece?, ¿se le ofrece algo?** what can I
do for you, can I get you anything?
ofrecimiento [ofreθi'mjento]
nm offer
oftalmólogo, -a [oftal'moloxo, a]
nm/f ophthalmologist
oída [o'iða] nf: **de ~s** by hearsay
oído [o'iðo] nm (Anat) ear; (sentido)
hearing
oigo etc vb V **oír**
oír [o'ir] vt (gen) to hear; (atender a)
to listen to; **¡oiga!** listen!; **~ misa** to
attend mass
OIT nf abr (= Organización Internacional
del Trabajo) ILO
ojal [o'xal] nm buttonhole
ojalá [oxa'la] excl if only (it were so)!,
some hope! ⊳ conj if only ...!, would
that ...!; **~ (que) venga hoy** I hope he
comes today
ojeada [oxe'aða] nf glance
ojera [o'xera] nf: **tener ~s** to have bags
under one's eyes
ojo ['oxo] nm eye; (de puente) span;
(de cerradura) keyhole ⊳ excl careful!;
tener ~ para to have an eye for; **ojo de
buey** porthole
okey ['okei] (LAM) excl O.K.

okupa [o'kupa] (*ESP: fam*) *nmf* squatter

ola ['ola] *nf* wave

olé [o'le] *excl* bravo!, olé!

oleada [ole'aða] *nf* big wave, swell; (*fig*) wave

oleaje [ole'axe] *nm* swell

óleo ['oleo] *nm* oil; **oleoducto** *nm* (oil) pipeline

oler [o'ler] *vt* (*gen*) to smell; (*inquirir*) to pry into; (*fig: sospechar*) to sniff out ▷ *vi* to smell; **~ a** to smell of

olfatear [olfate'ar] *vt* to smell; (*inquirir*) to pry into; **olfato** *nm* sense of smell

olimpiada [olim'piaða] *nf*: **las O~s** the Olympics; **olímpico, -a** [o'limpiko, a] *adj* Olympic

oliva [o'liβa] *nf* (*aceituna*) olive; **aceite de ~** olive oil; **olivo** *nm* olive tree

olla ['oʎa] *nf* pan; (*comida*) stew; **olla exprés o a presión** (*ESP*) pressure cooker; **olla podrida** type of Spanish stew

olmo ['olmo] *nm* elm (tree)

olor [o'lor] *nm* smell; **oloroso, -a** *adj* scented

olvidar [olβi'ðar] *vt* to forget; (*omitir*) to omit; **olvidarse** *vr* (*fig*) to forget o.s.; **se me olvidó** I forgot

olvido [ol'βiðo] *nm* oblivion; (*despiste*) forgetfulness

ombligo [om'bliɣo] *nm* navel

omelette [ome'lete] (*LAM*) *nf* omelet(te)

omisión [omi'sjon] *nf* (*abstención*) omission; (*descuido*) neglect

omiso, -a [o'miso, a] *adj*: **hacer caso ~** to ignore, pass over

omitir [omi'tir] *vt* to omit

omnipotente [omnipo'tente] *adj* omnipotent

omóplato [o'moplato] *nm* shoulder blade

OMS *nf abr* (= *Organización Mundial de la Salud*) WHO

once ['onθe] *num* eleven; **onces** (*CS*) *nfpl* tea break *sg*

onda ['onda] *nf* wave; **onda corta/larga/media** short/long/medium wave; **ondear** *vt*, *vi* to wave; (*tener ondas*) to wave; (*agua*) to ripple

ondulación [ondula'θjon] *nf* undulation; **ondulado, -a** *adj* wavy

ONG *nf abr* (= *organización no gubernamental*) NGO

ONU ['onu] *nf abr* (= *Organización de las Naciones Unidas*) UNO

opaco, -a [o'pako, a] *adj* opaque

opción [op'θjon] *nf* (*gen*) option; (*derecho*) right, option

OPEP ['opep] *nf abr* (= *Organización de Países Exportadores de Petróleo*) OPEC

ópera ['opera] *nf* opera; **ópera bufa** o **cómica** comic opera

operación [opera'θjon] *nf* (*gen*) operation; (*Com*) transaction, deal

operador, a [opera'ðor, a] *nm/f* operator; (*Cine: de proyección*) projectionist; (*: de rodaje*) cameraman

operar [ope'rar] *vt* (*producir*) to produce, bring about; (*Med*) to operate on ▷ *vi* (*Com*) to operate; deal; **operarse** *vr* to occur; (*Med*) to have an operation

opereta [ope'reta] *nf* operetta

opinar [opi'nar] *vt* to think ▷ *vi* to give one's opinion; **opinión** *nf* (*creencia*) belief; (*criterio*) opinion

opio ['opjo] *nm* opium

oponer [opo'ner] *vt* (*resistencia*) to put up, offer; **oponerse** *vr* (*objetar*) to object; (*estar frente a frente*) to be opposed; (*dos personas*) to oppose each other; **~ A a B** to set A against B; **me opongo a pensar que ...** I refuse to believe o think that ...

oportunidad [oportuni'ðað] *nf* (*ocasión*) opportunity; (*posibilidad*) chance

oportuno, -a [opor'tuno, a] *adj* (*en su tiempo*) opportune, timely; (*respuesta*) suitable; **en el momento ~** at the right moment

oposición [oposi'θjon] *nf* opposition; **oposiciones** *nfpl* (*Escol*) public examinations

opositor, a [oposi'tor, a] nm/f (adversario) opponent; (candidato): ~ **(a)** candidate (for)

opresión [opre'sjon] nf oppression; **opresor, a** nm/f oppressor

oprimir [opri'mir] vt to squeeze; (fig) to oppress

optar [op'tar] vi (elegir) to choose; ~ **por** to opt for; **optativo, -a** adj optional

óptico, -a ['optiko, a] adj optic(al) ▷ nm/f optician; **óptica** nf optician's (shop); **desde esta óptica** from this point of view

optimismo [opti'mismo] nm optimism; **optimista** nmf optimist

opuesto, -a [o'pwesto, a] adj (contrario) opposite; (antagónico) opposing

oración [ora'θjon] nf (Rel) prayer; (Ling) sentence

orador, a [ora'ðor, a] nm/f (conferenciante) speaker, orator

oral [o'ral] adj oral

orangután [orangu'tan] nm orangutan

orar [o'rar] vi to pray

oratoria [ora'torja] nf oratory

órbita ['orβita] nf orbit

orden ['orðen] nm (gen) order ▷ nf (gen) order; (Inform) command; **en ~ de prioridad** in order of priority; **orden del día** agenda

ordenado, -a [orðe'naðo, a] adj (metódico) methodical; (arreglado) orderly

ordenador [orðena'ðor] nm computer; **ordenador central** mainframe computer

ordenar [orðe'nar] vt (mandar) to order; (poner orden) to put in order, arrange; **ordenarse** vr (Rel) to be ordained

ordeñar [orðe'nar] vt to milk

ordinario, -a [orði'narjo, a] adj (común) ordinary, usual; (vulgar) vulgar, common

orégano [o'reɣano] nm oregano

oreja [o'rexa] nf ear; (Mecánica) lug, flange

orfanato [orfa'nato] nm orphanage

orfebrería [orfeβre'ria] nf gold/ silver work

orgánico, -a [or'ɣaniko, a] adj organic

organismo [orɣa'nismo] nm (Bio) organism; (Pol) organization

organización [orɣaniθa'θjon] nf organization; **organizar** vt to organize

órgano ['orɣano] nm organ

orgasmo [or'ɣasmo] nm orgasm

orgía [or'xia] nf orgy

orgullo [or'ɣuʎo] nm pride; **orgulloso, -a** adj (gen) proud; (altanero) haughty

orientación [orjenta'θjon] nf (posición) position; (dirección) direction

oriental [orjen'tal] adj eastern; (del Extremo Oriente) oriental

orientar [orjen'tar] vt (situar) to orientate; (señalar) to point; (dirigir) to direct; (guiar) to guide; **orientarse** vr to get one's bearings

oriente [o'rjente] nm east; **el O-Medio** the Middle East; **el Próximo/ Extremo O-** the Near/Far East

origen [o'rixen] nm origin

original [orixi'nal] adj (nuevo) original; (extraño) odd, strange; **originalidad** nf originality

originar [orixi'nar] vt to start, cause; **originarse** vr to originate; **originario, -a** adj original; **originario de** native of

orilla [o'riʎa] nf (borde) border; (de río) bank; (de bosque, tela) edge; (de mar) shore

orina [o'rina] nf urine; **orinal** nm (chamber) pot; **orinar** vi to urinate; **orinarse** vr to wet o.s.

oro ['oro] nm gold; **oros** nmpl (Naipes) hearts

orquesta [or'kesta] nf orchestra; **orquesta sinfónica** symphony orchestra

orquídea [orˈkiðea] nf orchid
ortiga [orˈtiɣa] nf nettle
ortodoxo, -a [ortoˈðokso, a] adj orthodox
ortografía [ortoɣraˈfia] nf spelling
ortopedia [ortoˈpeðja] nf orthopaedics sg; **ortopédico, -a** adj orthopaedic
oruga [oˈruxa] nf caterpillar
orzuelo [orˈθwelo] nm stye
os [os] pron (gen) you; (a vosotros) to you
osa [ˈosa] nf (she-)bear; **Osa Mayor/ Menor** Great/Little Bear
osadía [osaˈðia] nf daring
osar [oˈsar] vi to dare
oscilación [osθilaˈθjon] nf (movimiento) oscillation; (fluctuación) fluctuation
oscilar [osθiˈlar] vi to oscillate; to fluctuate
oscurecer [oskureˈθer] vt to darken ▷ vi to grow dark; **oscurecerse** vr to grow o get dark
oscuridad [oskuriˈðað] nf obscurity; (tinieblas) darkness
oscuro, -a [osˈkuro, a] adj dark; (fig) obscure; **a oscuras** in the dark
óseo, -a [ˈoseo, a] adj bone; (del hueso) bony
oso [ˈoso] nm bear; **oso de peluche** teddy bear; **oso hormiguero** anteater
ostentar [ostenˈtar] vt (gen) to show; (pey) to flaunt, show off; (poseer) to have, possess
ostión [osˈtjon] (MÉX) nm = **ostra**
ostra [ˈostra] nf oyster
OTAN [ˈotan] nf abr (= Organización del Tratado del Atlántico Norte) NATO
otitis [oˈtitis] nf earache
otoñal [otoˈɲal] adj autumnal
otoño [oˈtoɲo] nm autumn
otorgar [otorˈxar] vt (conceder) to concede; (dar) to grant
otorrino, -a [otoˈrrino, a], **otorrinolaringólogo, -a** [otorrinolarinˈɣoloɣo, a] nm/f ear,

nose and throat specialist

○ **PALABRA CLAVE**

otro, -a [ˈotro, a] adj 1 (distinto: sg) another; (: pl) other; **con otros amigos** with other o different friends
2 (adicional): **tráigame otro café (más), por favor** can I have another coffee please; **otros diez días más** another ten days
▷ pron 1 **el otro** the other one; **(los) otros** (them) others; **de otro** somebody else's; **que lo haga otro** let somebody else do it
2 (recíproco): **se odian (la) una a (la) otra** they hate one another o each other
3: **otro tanto: comer otro tanto** to eat the same o as much again; **recibió una decena de telegramas y otras tantas llamadas** he got about ten telegrams and as many calls

ovación [oβaˈθjon] nf ovation
oval [oˈβal] adj oval; **ovalado, -a** adj oval; **óvalo** nm oval
ovario [oˈβarjo] nm ovary
oveja [oˈβexa] nf sheep
overol [oβeˈrol] (LAM) nm overalls pl
ovillo [oˈβiʎo] nm (de lana) ball of wool
OVNI [ˈoβni] nm abr (= objeto volante no identificado) UFO
ovulación [oβulaˈθjon] nf ovulation; **óvulo** nm ovum
oxidación [oksiðaˈθjon] nf rusting
oxidar [oksiˈðar] vt to rust; **oxidarse** vr to go rusty
óxido [ˈoksiðo] nm oxide
oxigenado, -a [oksixeˈnaðo, a] adj (Quím) oxygenated; (pelo) bleached
oxígeno [okˈsixeno] nm oxygen
oyente [oˈjente] nm/f listener
oyes etc vb V **oír**
ozono [oˈθono] nm ozone

p

(fam): **un éxito ~** a tremendous
success; **padres** nmpl parents; **padre
político**father-in-law

padrino [pa'ðrino] nm (Rel)
godfather; (tb: **~ de boda**) best man;
(fig) sponsor, patron; **padrinos** nmpl
godparents

padrón [pa'ðron] nm (censo) census,
roll

padrote [pa'ðrote] (MÉX: fam) nm
pimp

paella [pa'eʎa] nf paella, dish of rice
with meat, shellfish etc

paga ['paxa] nf (pago) payment;
(sueldo) pay, wages pl

pagano, -a [pa'ɣano, a] adj, nm/f
pagan, heathen

pagar [pa'ɣar] vt to pay; (las compras,
crimen) to pay for; (fig: favor) to repay
▷ vi to pay; **~ al contado/a plazos** to
pay (in) cash/in instalments

pagaré [paxa're] nm I.O.U.

página ['paxina] nf page; **página de
inicio**(Inform) home page; **página web**
(Inform) web page

pago ['paxo] nm (dinero) payment; **en
~ de** in return for; **pago anticipado/a
cuenta/contra reembolso/en
especie**advance payment/payment
on account/cash on delivery/payment
in kind

pág(s). abr (= página(s)) p(p).

pagueetc vb V **pagar**

país [pa'is] nm (gen) country;
(región) land; **los P~es Bajos** the Low
Countries; **el P~ Vasco** the Basque
Country

paisaje [pai'saxe] nm landscape,
scenery

paisano, -a [pai'sano, a] adj of the
same country ▷ nm/f (compatriota)
fellow countryman/woman; **vestir de
~** (soldado) to be in civvies; (guardia) to
be in plain clothes

paja ['paxa] nf straw; (fig) rubbish
(BRIT), trash (US)

pajarita [paxa'rita] nf (corbata)
bow tie

pabellón [paβe'ʎon] nm bell tent;
(Arq) pavilion; (de hospital etc) block,
section; (bandera) flag

pacer [pa'θer] vi to graze

paciencia [pa'θjenθja] nf patience

paciente [pa'θjente] adj, nmf patient

pacificación [paθifika'θjon] nf
pacification

pacífico, -a [pa'θifiko, a] adj
(persona) peaceable; (existencia)
peaceful; **el (Océano) P~** the Pacific
(Ocean)

pacifista [paθi'fista] nmf pacifist

pacotilla [pako'tiʎa] nf: **de ~** (actor,
escritor) third-rate

pactar [pak'tar] vt to agree to o on
▷ vi to come to an agreement

pacto ['pakto] nm (tratado) pact;
(acuerdo) agreement

padecer [paðe'θer] vt (sufrir) to
suffer; (soportar) to endure, put up with;
padecimiento nm suffering

padrastro [pa'ðrastro] nm
stepfather

padre ['paðre] nm father ▷ adj

pájaro ['paxaro] nm bird; **pájaro carpintero** woodpecker

pajita [pa'xita] nf (drinking) straw

pala ['pala] nf spade, shovel; (raqueta etc) bat; (: de tenis) racquet; (Culin) slice; **pala mecánica** power shovel

palabra [pa'laβra] nf word; (facultad) (power of) speech; (derecho de hablar) right to speak; **tomar la ~** (en mitin) to take the floor

palabrota [pala'brota] nf swearword

palacio [pa'laθjo] nm palace; (mansión) mansion, large house; **palacio de justicia** courthouse; **palacio municipal** town o city hall

paladar [pala'ðar] nm palate; **paladear** vt to taste

palanca [pa'lanka] nf lever; (fig) pull, influence

palangana [palan'gana] nf washbasin

palco ['palko] nm box

Palestina [pales'tina] nf Palestine; **palestino, -a** nm/f Palestinian

paleta [pa'leta] nf (de pintor) palette; (de albañil) trowel; (de ping-pong) bat; (MÉX, CAM: helado) ice lolly (BRIT), Popsicle® (US)

palidecer [paliðe'θer] vi to turn pale; **palidez** nf paleness; **pálido, -a** adj pale

palillo [pa'liʎo] nm (mondadientes) toothpick; (para comer) chopstick

palito [pa'lito] nm (RPL) (de helado) ice lolly (BRIT), Popsicle® (US)

paliza [pa'liθa] nf beating, thrashing

palma ['palma] nf (Anat) palm; (árbol) palm tree; **batir o dar ~s** to clap, applaud; **palmada** nf slap; **palmadas** nfpl clapping sg, applause sg

palmar [pal'mar] (fam) vi (tb: **~la**) to die, kick the bucket

palmear [palme'ar] vi to clap

palmera [pal'mera] nf (Bot) palm tree

palmo ['palmo] nm (medida) span; (fig) small amount; **~ a ~** inch by inch

palo ['palo] nm stick; (poste) post; (de tienda de campaña) pole; (mango) handle, shaft; (golpe) blow, hit; (de golf) club; (de béisbol) bat; (Náut) mast; (Naipes) suit

paloma [pa'loma] nf dove, pigeon

palomitas [palo'mitas] nfpl popcorn sg

palpar [pal'par] vt to touch, feel

palpitar [palpi'tar] vi to palpitate; (latir) to beat

palta ['palta] nf (CS) avocado

paludismo [palu'ðismo] nm malaria

pamela [pa'mela] nf picture hat, sun hat

pampa ['pampa] nf (AM) pampas, prairie

pan [pan] nm bread; (una barra) loaf; **pan integral** wholemeal (BRIT) o wholewheat (US) bread; **pan rallado** breadcrumbs pl; **pan tostado** (MÉX: tostada) toast

pana ['pana] nf corduroy

panadería [panaðe'ria] nf baker's (shop); **panadero, -a** nm/f baker

Panamá [pana'ma] nm Panama; **panameño, -a** adj Panamanian

pancarta [pan'karta] nf placard, banner

panceta [pan'θeta] nf (ESP, RPL) bacon

pancho ['pantʃo] nm (RPL) hot dog

pancito [pan'θito] nm (bread) roll

panda ['panda] nm (Zool) panda

pandereta [pande'reta] nf tambourine

pandilla [pan'diʎa] nf set, group; (de criminales) gang; (pey: camarilla) clique

panecillo [pane'θiʎo] (ESP) nm (bread) roll

panel [pa'nel] nm panel; **panel solar** solar panel

panfleto [pan'fleto] nm pamphlet

pánico [pa'niko] nm panic

panorama [pano'rama] nm panorama; (vista) view

panqueque [pan'keke] nm (LAM) pancake

pantalla [pan'taʎa] nf (de cine) screen; (de lámpara) lampshade

pantalón [panta'lon] nm trousers;
  pantalones nmpl trousers;
  pantalones cortes shorts
pantano [pan'tano] nm (ciénaga)
  marsh, swamp; (depósito: de agua)
  reservoir; (fig) jam, difficulty
panteón [pante'on] nm (monumento)
  pantheon
pantera [pan'tera] nf panther
pantimedias [panti'meðjas] (MÉX)
  nfpl = **pantis**
pantis ['pantis] nmpl tights (BRIT),
  pantyhose (US)
pantomima [panto'mima] nf
  pantomime
pantorrilla [panto'rriʎa] nf calf
  (of the leg)
pants [pants] (MÉX) nmpl tracksuit
  (BRIT), sweat suit (US)
pantufla [pan'tufla] nf slipper
panty(s) ['panti(s)] nm(pl) tights
  (BRIT), pantyhose (US)
panza ['panθa] nf belly, paunch
pañal [pa'nal] nm nappy (BRIT),
  diaper (US); **pañales** nmpl (fig) early
  stages, infancy sg
paño ['pano] nm (tela) cloth; (pedazo
  de tela) (piece of) cloth; (trapo) duster, rag;
  paños menores underclothes
pañuelo [pa'nwelo] nm
  handkerchief, hanky; (fam: para la
  cabeza) (head)scarf
papa ['papa] nm: **el P~** the Pope ⊳ nf
  (LAM: patata) potato; **papas fritas** (LAM)
  French fries, chips (BRIT); (de bolsa)
  crisps (BRIT), potato chips (US)
papá [pa'pa] nm dad (fam), pa (US)
papada [pa'paða] nf double chin
papagayo [papa'xajo] nm parrot
papalote [papa'lote] (MÉX, CAM)
  nm kite
papanatas [papa'natas] (fam) nm
  inv simpleton
papaya [pa'paja] nf papaya
papear [pape'ar] (fam) vt, vi to scoff
papel [pa'pel] nm paper; (hoja de
  papel) sheet of paper; (Teatro: fig) role;
  papel de aluminio aluminium (BRIT)

o aluminum (US) foil; **papel de arroz/
envolver/fumar/ice/wrapping/**
cigarette paper; **papel de estaño** o
plata tinfoil; **papel de lija** sandpaper;
papel higiénico toilet paper; **papel
moneda** paper money; **papel pintado**
wallpaper; **papel secante** blotting
paper
papeleo [pape'leo] nm red tape
papelera [pape'lera] nf wastepaper
basket; (en la calle) litter bin; **papelera
(de reciclaje)** (Inform) wastebasket
papelería [papele'ria] nf stationer's
(shop)
papeleta [pape'leta] (ESP) nf (Pol)
ballot paper
paperas [pa'peras] nfpl mumps sg
papilla [pa'piʎa] nf (de bebé) baby
food
paquete [pa'kete] nm (de cigarrillos
etc) packet; (Correos etc) parcel
par [par] adj (igual) like, equal; (Mat)
even ⊳ nm equal; (de guantes) pair; (de
veces) couple; (Pol) peer; (Golf, Com) par;
abrir b ~ en ~ to open wide
para ['para] prep for; **no es ~ comer**
it's not for eating; **decir ~ sí** to say to
o.s.; **¿~ qué lo quieres?** what do you
want it for?; **se casaron ~ separarse
otra vez** they married only to separate
again; **lo tendré ~ mañana** I'll have
it (for) tomorrow; **ir ~ casa** to go
home, head for home; **~ profesor es
muy estúpido** he's very stupid for a
teacher; **¿quién es usted ~ gritar así?**
who are you to shout like that?; **tengo
bastante ~ vivir** I have enough to live
on; V tb **con**
parabién [para'βjen] nm
congratulations pl
parábola [pa'raβola] nf parable;
(Mat) parabola; **parabólica** nf
(tb: **antena parabólica**) satellite dish
parabrisas [para'βrisas] nm inv
windscreen (BRIT), windshield (US)
paracaídas [paraka'iðas] nm
inv parachute; **paracaidista** nmf
parachutist; (Mil) paratrooper

P

parachoques [para'tʃokes] nm inv (Auto) bumper; (Mecánica etc) shock absorber

parada [pa'raða] nf stop; (acto) stopping; (de industria) shutdown, stoppage; (lugar) stopping place; **parada de autobús** bus stop; **parada de taxis** taxi stand o rank (BRIT)

paradero [para'ðero] nm stopping-place; (situación) whereabouts

parado, -a [pa'raðo, a] adj (persona) motionless, standing still; (fábrica) closed, at a standstill; (coche) stopped; (LAM: de pie) standing (up); (ESP: sin empleo) unemployed, idle

paradoja [para'ðoxa] nf paradox

parador [para'ðor] nm parador, state-run hotel

paragolpes [para'golpes] (RPL) nm inv (Auto) bumper, fender (US)

paraguas [pa'raxwas] nm inv umbrella

Paraguay [para'xwai] nm Paraguay; **paraguayo, -a** adj, nm/f Paraguayan

paraíso [para'iso] nm paradise, heaven

paraje [pa'raxe] nm place, spot

paralelo, -a [para'lelo, a] adj parallel

parálisis [pa'ralisis] nf inv paralysis; **paralítico, -a** adj, nm/f paralytic

paralizar [parali'θar] vt to paralyse; **paralizarse** vr to become paralysed; (fig) to come to a standstill

páramo ['paramo] nm bleak plateau

paranoico, -a [para'noiko, a] nm/f paranoiac

parapente [para'pente] nm (deporte) paragliding; (aparato) paraglider

parapléjico, -a [para'plexiko, a] adj, nm/f paraplegic

parar [pa'rar] vt to stop; (golpe) to ward off ▷ vi to stop; **pararse** vr to stop; (LAM: ponerse de pie) to stand up; **ha parado de llover** it has stopped raining; **van a ir a ~ a comisaría** they're going to end up in the police station; **~se en** to pay attention to

pararrayos [para'rrajos] nm inv lightning conductor

parásito [pa'rasito, a] nm/f parasite

parasol [para'sol] nm parasol, sunshade

parcela [par'θela] nf plot, piece of ground

parche ['partʃe] nm (gen) patch

parchís [par'tʃis] nm ludo

parcial [par'θjal] adj (pago) part-; (eclipse) partial; (Jur) prejudiced, biased; (Pol) partisan

parecer [pare'θer] nm (opinión) opinion, view; (aspecto) looks ▷ vi (tener apariencia) to seem, look; (asemejarse) to look o seem like; (aparecer, llegar) to appear; **parecerse** vr to look alike, resemble each other; **al ~** apparently; **según parece** evidently, apparently; **~se a** to look like, resemble; **me parece que** I think (that), it seems to me that

parecido, -a [pare'θiðo, a] adj similar ▷ nm similarity, likeness, resemblance; **bien ~** good-looking, nice-looking

pared [pa'reð] nf wall

pareja [pa'rexa] nf (par) pair; (dos personas) couple; (otro: de un par) other one (of a pair); (persona) partner

parentesco [paren'tesko] nm relationship

paréntesis [pa'rentesis] nm inv parenthesis; (en escrito) bracket

parezco etc vb V **parecer**

pariente [pa'rjente] nmf relative, relation

> ⚠ No confundir **pariente** con la palabra inglesa parent.

parir [pa'rir] vt to give birth to ▷ vi (mujer) to give birth, have a baby

París [pa'ris] n Paris

parka ['parka] (LAM) nf anorak

parking ['parkin] nm car park (BRIT), parking lot (US)

parlamentar [parlamen'tar] vi to parley

parlamentario, -a [parlamen'tarjo, a] *adj* parliamentary ▷ *nm/f* member of parliament

parlamento [parla'mento] *nm* parliament

parlanchín, -ina [parlan'tʃin, ina] *adj* indiscreet ▷ *nm/f* chatterbox

parlar [par'lar] *vi* to chatter (away)

paro ['paro] *nm* (*huelga*) stoppage (of work), strike; (*Esp: desempleo*) unemployment; (*: subsidio*) unemployment benefit; **estar en ~** (*Esp*) to be unemployed; **paro cardíaco** cardiac arrest

parodia [pa'roðja] *nf* parody; **parodiar** *vt* to parody

parpadear [parpaðe'ar] *vi* (*ojos*) to blink; (*luz*) to flicker

párpado ['parpaðo] *nm* eyelid

parque ['parke] *nm* (*lugar verde*) park; (*MÉX: munición*) ammunition; **parque de atracciones** fairground; **parque de bomberos** (*Esp*) fire station; **parque infantil/temático/zoológico** playground/theme park/zoo

parqué [par'ke] *nm* parquet (flooring)

parquímetro [par'kimetro] *nm* parking meter

parra ['parra] *nf* (grape)vine

párrafo ['parrafo] *nm* paragraph; **echar un ~** (*fam*) to have a chat

parranda [pa'rranda] *nf* (*fam*) spree, binge

parrilla [pa'rriʎa] *nf* (*Culin*) grill; (*de coche*) grille; **(carne a la) ~** barbecue; **parrillada** *nf* barbecue

párroco ['parroko] *nm* parish priest

parroquia [pa'rrokja] *nf* parish; (*iglesia*) parish church; (*Com*) clientele, customers (*pl*); **parroquiano, -a** *nm/f* parishioner; (*Com*) client, customer

parte ['parte] *nm* message; (*informe*) report ▷ *nf* part; (*lado, cara*) side; (*de reparto*) share; (*Jur*) party; **en alguna ~ de Europa** somewhere in Europe; **en o por todas ~s** everywhere; **en gran ~** to a large extent; **la mayor ~**

de los españoles most Spaniards; **de un tiempo a esta ~** for some time past; **de ~ de algn** on sb's behalf; **¿de ~ de quién?** (*Tel*) who is speaking?; **por ~ de** on the part of; **yo por mí ~** I for my part; **por otra ~** on the other hand; **dar ~** to inform; **tomar ~** to take part; **parte meteorológico** weather forecast o report

participación [partiθipa'θjon] *nf* (*acto*) participation, taking part; (*parte, Com*) share; (*de lotería*) shared prize; (*aviso*) notice, notification

participante [partiθi'pante] *nmf* participant

participar [partiθi'par] *vt* to notify, inform ▷ *vi* to take part, participate

partícipe [par'tiθipe] *nmf* participant

particular [partiku'lar] *adj* (*especial*) particular, special; (*individual, personal*) private, personal ▷ *nm* (*punto, asunto*) particular, point; (*individuo*) individual; **tiene coche ~** he has a car of his own

partida [par'tiða] *nf* (*salida*) departure; (*Com*) entry, item; (*juego*) game; (*grupo de personas*) band, group; **mala ~** dirty trick; **partida de nacimiento/matrimonio/defunción** (*Esp*) birth/marriage/death certificate

partidario, -a [parti'ðarjo, a] *adj* partisan ▷ *nm/f* supporter, follower

partido [par'tiðo] *nm* (*Pol*) party; (*Deporte*) game, match; **sacar ~ de** to profit o benefit from; **tomar ~** to take sides

partir [par'tir] *vt* (*dividir*) to split, divide; (*compartir, distribuir*) to share (out), distribute; (*romper*) to break open, split open; (*rebanada*) to cut (off) ▷ *vi* (*ponerse en camino*) to set off o out; (*comenzar*) to start (off o out); **partirse** *vr* to crack o split o break (in two *etc*); **a ~ de** (starting) from

partitura [parti'tura] *nf* (*Mús*) score

parto ['parto] *nm* birth; (*fig*) product, creation; **estar de ~** to be in labour

parvulario [parβu'larjo] (*Esp*) *nm*

nursery school, kindergarten

pasa ['pasa] *nf* raisin; **pasa de Corinto** currant

pasacintas [pasa'θintas] (LAM) *nm* cassette player

pasada [pasa'saða] *nf* passing, passage; **de ~** in passing, incidentally; **una mala ~** a dirty trick

pasadizo [pasa'ðiθo] *nm* (*pasillo*) passage, corridor; (*callejuela*) alley

pasado, -a [pasa'saðo, a] *adj* (*malo: comida, fruta*) bad; (*muy cocido*) overdone; (*anticuado*) out of date ▷ *nm* past; **~ mañana** the day after tomorrow; **el mes ~** last month

pasador [pasa'ðor] *nm* (*cerrojo*) bolt; (*de pelo*) hair slide; (*horquilla*) grip

pasaje [pa'saxe] *nm* passage; (*pago de viaje*) fare; (*los pasajeros*) passengers *pl*; (*pasillo*) passageway

pasajero, -a [pasa'xero, a] *adj* passing; (*situación, estado*) temporary; (*amor, enfermedad*) brief ▷ *nm/f* passenger

pasamontañas [pasamon'taɲas] *nm inv* balaclava helmet

pasaporte [pasa'porte] *nm* passport

pasar [pa'sar] *vt* to pass; (*tiempo*) to spend; (*desgracias*) to suffer, endure; (*noticia*) to give, pass on; (*río*) to cross; (*barrera*) to pass through; (*falta*) to overlook, tolerate; (*contrincante*) to surpass, do better than; (*coche*) to overtake; (*Cine*) to show; (*enfermedad*) to give, infect with; **~ la aspiradora** to do the vacuuming, to hoover o do the hoovering ▷ *vi* (*gen*) to pass; (*terminarse*) to be over; (*ocurrir*) to happen; **pasarse** *vr* (*flores*) to fade; (*comida*) to go bad o off; (*fig*) to overdo it, go too far; **~ de** to go beyond, exceed; **~ por** (LAM) to fetch; **~lo bien/mal** to have a good/bad time; **¡pase!** come in!; **hacer ~** to show in; **lo que pasa es que ...** the thing is ...; **~se al enemigo** to go over to the enemy; **se me pasó** I forgot; **no se le pasa nada** he misses nothing; **pase lo que pase**

come what may; **¿qué pasa?** what's going on?, what's up?; **¿qué te pasa?** what's wrong?

pasarela [pasa'rela] *nf* footbridge; (*en barco*) gangway

pasatiempo [pasa'tjempo] *nm* pastime, hobby

Pascua [pa'skwa] *nf* (*en Semana Santa*) Easter; **Pascuas** *nfpl* Christmas (time); **¡felices ~s!** Merry Christmas!

pase ['pase] *nm* pass; (*Cine*) performance, showing

pasear [pase'ar] *vt* to take for a walk; (*exhibir*) to parade, show off ▷ *vi* to walk, go for a walk; **pasearse** *vr* to walk, go for a walk; **~ en coche** to go for a drive; **paseo** *nm* (*avenida*) avenue; (*distancia corta*) walk, stroll; **dar un o ir de paseo** to go for a walk; **paseo marítimo** (ESP) promenade

pasillo [pa'siʎo] *nm* passage, corridor

pasión [pa'sjon] *nf* passion

pasivo, -a [pa'siβo, a] *adj* passive; (*inactivo*) inactive ▷ *nm* (*Com*) liabilities *pl*, debts *pl*

pasmoso, -a [pas'moso, a] *adj* amazing, astonishing

paso, -a [ˈpaso, a] *adj* dried ▷ *nm* step; (*modo de andar*) walk; (*huella*) footprint; (*rapidez*) speed, pace, rate; (*camino accesible*) way through, passage; (*cruce*) crossing; (*pasaje*) passing, passage; (*Geo*) pass; (*estrecho*) strait; **a ese ~** (*fig*) at that rate; **salir al ~ de o a** to waylay; **estar de ~** to be passing through; **prohibido el ~** no entry; **ceda el ~** give way; **paso a nivel** (*Ferro*) level-crossing; **paso (de) cebra** (ESP) zebra crossing; **paso de peatones** pedestrian crossing; **paso elevado** flyover

pasota [pa'sota] (ESP: *fam*) *adj, nmf* **~** dropout; **ser un ~** to be a bit of a dropout; **(ser) indiferente** not to care about anything

pasta ['pasta] *nf* paste; (*Culin: masa*) dough; (: *de bizcochos etc*) pastry; (*fam*) dough; **pastas** *nfpl* (*bizcochos*) pastries, small cakes; (*fideos, espaguetis etc*) pasta; **pasta dentífrica** o **de dientes** toothpaste

pastar [pas'tar] *vt, vi* to graze

pastel [pas'tel] *nm* (*dulce*) cake; (*Arte*) pastel; **pastel de carne** meat pie; **pastelería** *nf* cake shop

pastilla [pas'tiʎa] *nf* (*de jabón, chocolate*) bar; (*píldora*) tablet, pill

pasto ['pasto] *nm* (*hierba*) grass; (*lugar*) pasture, field; **pastor, a** [pas'tor, a] *nm/f* shepherd/ess ⊳ *nm* (*Rel*) clergyman, pastor; **pastor alemán** Alsatian

pata ['pata] *nf* (*pierna*) leg; (*pie*) foot; (*de muebles*) leg; **~s arriba** upside down; **metedura de ~** (*fam*) gaffe; **meter la ~** (*fam*) to put one's foot in it; **tener buena/mala ~** to be lucky/unlucky; **pata de cabra** (*Tec*) crowbar; **patada** *nf* kick; (*en el suelo*) stamp

patata [pa'tata] *nf* potato; **patatas fritas** chips, French fries; (*de bolsa*) crisps

paté [pa'te] *nm* pâté

patente [pa'tente] *adj* obvious, evident; (*Com*) patent ⊳ *nf* patent

paternal [pater'nal] *adj* fatherly, paternal; **paterno, -a** *adj* paternal

patético, -a [pa'tetiko, a] *adj* pathetic, moving

patilla [pa'tiʎa] *nf* (*de gafas*) side(piece); **patillas** *nfpl* sideburns

patín [pa'tin] *nm* skate; (*de trineo*) runner; **patín de ruedas** roller skate; **patinaje** *nm* skating; **patinar** *vi* to skate; (*resbalarse*) to skid, slip; (*fam*) to slip up, blunder

patineta [pati'neta] *nf* (*MÉX: patinete*) scooter; (*cs: monopatín*) skateboard

patinete [pati'nete] *nm* scooter

patio ['patjo] *nm* (*de casa*) patio, courtyard; **patio de recreo** playground

pato ['pato] *nm* duck; **pagar el ~** (*fam*) to take the blame, carry the can

patoso, -a [pa'toso, a] (*fam*) *adj* clumsy

patotero [pato'tero] (*cs*) *nm*

hooligan, lout

patraña [pa'traɲa] *nf* story, fib

patria ['patrja] *nf* native land, mother country

patrimonio [patri'monjo] *nm* inheritance; (*fig*) heritage

patriota [pa'trjota] *nmf* patriot

patrocinar [patroθi'nar] *vt* to sponsor

patrón, -ona [pa'tron, ona] *nm/f* (*jefe*) boss, chief, master(mistress); (*propietario*) landlord/lady; (*Rel*) patron saint ⊳ *nm* (*Tec, Costura*) pattern

patronato [patro'nato] *nm* sponsorship; (*acto*) patronage; (*fundación benéfica*) trust, foundation

patrulla [pa'truʎa] *nf* patrol

pausa ['pausa] *nf* pause, break

pauta ['pauta] *nf* line, guide line

pava ['paβa] (*RPL*) *nf* kettle

pavimento [paβi'mento] *nm* (*de losa*) pavement, paving

pavo ['paβo] *nm* turkey; **pavo real** peacock

payaso, -a [pa'jaso, a] *nm/f* clown

payo, -a [ˈpajo, a] *nm/f* non-gipsy

paz [paθ] *nf* peace; (*tranquilidad*) peacefulness, tranquillity; **hacer las paces** to make peace; (*fig*) to make up; **¡déjame en ~!** leave me alone!

PC *nm* PC, personal computer

P.D. *abr* (= *posdata*) P.S., p.s.

peaje [pe'axe] *nm* toll

peatón [pea'ton] *nm* pedestrian; **peatonal** *adj* pedestrian

peca ['peka] *nf* freckle

pecado [pe'kaðo] *nm* sin; **pecador, a** *adj* sinful ⊳ *nm/f* sinner

pecaminoso, -a [pekami'noso, a] *adj* sinful

pecar [pe'kar] *vi* (*Rel*) to sin; **peca de generoso** he is generous to a fault

pecera [pe'θera] *nf* fish tank; (*redonda*) goldfish bowl

pecho ['petʃo] *nm* (*Anat*) chest; (*de mujer*) breast; **dar el ~** to breast-feed; **tomar algo a ~** to take sth to heart

pechuga [pe'tʃuɣa] *nf* breast

peculiar [pe'kuljar] adj special, peculiar; (característico) typical, characteristic

pedal [pe'ðal] nm pedal; **pedalear** vi to pedal

pédalo ['pedalo] nm pedalo, pedal boat

pedante [pe'ðante] adj pedantic ▷ nmf pedant

pedazo [pe'ðaθo] nm piece, bit; **hacerse ~s** to smash, shatter

pediatra [pe'ðjatra] nmf paediatrician

pedido [pe'ðiðo] nm (Com) order; (petición) request

pedir [pe'ðir] vt to ask for, request; (comida, Com: mandar) to order; (necesitar) to need, demand, require ▷ vi to ask; **me pidió que cerrara la puerta** he asked me to shut the door; **¿cuánto piden por el coche?** how much are they asking for the car?

pedo ['peðo] (fam!) nm fart

pega ['peɣa] nf snag; **poner ~s (a)** to complain (about)

pegadizo, -a [peɣa'ðiθo, a] adj (Mús) catchy

pegajoso, -a [peɣa'xoso, a] adj sticky, adhesive

pegamento [peɣa'mento] nm gum, glue

pegar [pe'ɣar] vt (papel, sellos) to stick (on); (cartel) to stick up; (coser) to sew (on); (unir: partes) to join, fix together; (Comput) to paste; (Med) to give, infect with; (dar: golpe) to give, deal ▷ vi (adherirse) to stick, adhere; (ir juntos: colores) to match, go together; (golpear) to hit; (quemar: el sol) to strike hot, burn; **pegarse** vr (gen) to stick; (dos personas) to hit each other, fight; (fam): **~ un grito** to let out a yell; **~ un salto** to jump (with fright); **~ en** to touch; **~se un tiro** to shoot o.s.; **~ fuego** to catch fire

pegatina [peɣa'tina] nf sticker

pegote [pe'ɣote] (fam) nm eyesore, sight

peinado [pei'naðo] nm hairstyle

peinar [pei'nar] vt to comb; (hacer estilo) to style; **peinarse** vr to comb one's hair

peine ['peine] nm comb; **peineta** nf ornamental comb

p.ej. abr (= por ejemplo) e.g.

Pekín [pe'kin] n Pekin(g)

pelado, -a [pe'laðo, a] adj (fruta, patata etc) peeled; (cabeza) shorn; (campo, fig) bare; (fam: sin dinero) broke

pelar [pe'lar] vt (fruta, patatas etc) to peel; (cortar el pelo a) to cut the hair of; (quitar la piel: animal) to skin; **pelarse** vr (la piel) to peel; **voy a ~me** I'm going to get my hair cut

peldaño [pel'daɲo] nm step

pelea [pe'lea] nf (lucha) fight; (discusión) quarrel, row; **peleado, -a** [pele'aðo, a] adj: **estar peleado (con algn)** to have fallen out (with sb); **pelear** [pe'lear] vi to fight; **pelearse** vr to fight; (reñirse) to fall out, quarrel

pelela [pe'lela] (cs) nf potty

peletería [pelete'ria] nf furrier's, fur shop

pelícano [pe'likano] nm pelican

película [pe'likula] nf film; (cobertura ligera) thin covering; (Foto: rollo) roll o reel of film; **película de dibujos (animados)/del oeste** cartoon/western

peligro [pe'liɣro] nm danger; (riesgo) risk; **correr ~ de** to run the risk of; **peligroso, -a** adj dangerous; risky

pelirrojo, -a [peli'rroxo, a] adj red-haired, red-headed ▷ nm/f redhead

pellejo [pe'ʎexo] nm (de animal) skin, hide

pellizcar [peʎiθ'kar] vt to pinch, nip

pelma ['pelma] (Esp: fam) nmf pain (in the neck)

pelmazo [pel'maθo] (fam) nm = **pelma**

pelo ['pelo] nm (cabellos) hair; (de barba, bigote) whisker; (de animal: pellejo) hair, fur, coat; **venir al ~** to be exactly what one needs; **un**

hombre de ~ en pecho a brave man; **por los ~s** by the skin of one's teeth; **no tener ~s en la lengua** to be outspoken, not to mince one's words; **con ~ s y señales** in minute detail; **tomar el ~ a algn** to pull sb's leg

pelota [pe'lota] nf ball; **en ~** stark naked; **hacer la ~ (a algn)** (ESP: fam) to creep (to sb); **pelota vasca** pelota

pelotón [pelo'ton] nm (Mil) squad, detachment

peluca [pe'luka] nf wig

peluche [pe'lutʃe] nm: **oso/muñeco de ~** teddy bear/soft toy

peludo, -a [pe'luðo, a] adj hairy, shaggy

peluquería [peluke'ria] nf hairdresser's; **peluquero, -a** nm/f hairdresser

pelusa [pe'lusa] nf (Bot) down; (en tela) fluff

pena ['pena] nf (congoja) grief, sadness; (remordimiento) regret; (dificultad) trouble; (dolor) pain; (Jur) sentence; **merecer o valer la ~** to be worthwhile; **a duras ~s** with great difficulty; **¡qué ~!** what a shame!; **pena capital** capital punishment; **pena de muerte** death penalty

penal [pe'nal] adj penal ▷ nm (cárcel) prison

penalidad [penali'ðað] nf (problema, dificultad) trouble, hardship; (Jur) penalty, punishment; **penalidades** nfpl trouble sg, hardship sg

penalti [pe'nalti] nm = **penalty**

penalty [pe'nalti] nm (pl ~s o **penalties**) nm penalty (kick)

pendiente [pen'djente] adj pending, unsettled ▷ nm earring ▷ nf hill, slope

pene ['pene] nm penis

penetrante [pene'trante] adj (herida) deep; (persona, arma) sharp; (sonido) penetrating, piercing; (mirada) searching; (viento, ironía) biting

penetrar [pene'trar] vt to penetrate, pierce; (entender) to grasp ▷ vi to penetrate, go in; (entrar) to enter, go in;

(líquido) to soak in; (fig) to pierce

penicilina [peniθi'lina] nf penicillin

península [pe'ninsula] nf peninsula; **peninsular** adj peninsular

penique [pe'nike] nm penny

penitencia [peni'tenθja] nf penance

penoso, -a [pe'noso, a] adj (lamentable) distressing; (difícil) arduous, difficult

pensador, a [pensa'ðor, a] nm/f thinker

pensamiento [pensa'mjento] nm thought; (mente) mind; (idea) idea

pensar [pen'sar] vt to think; (considerar) to think over, think out; (proponerse) to intend, plan; (imaginarse) to think up, invent ▷ vi to think; **~ en** to aim at, aspire to; **pensativo, -a** adj thoughtful, pensive

pensión [pen'sjon] nf (casa) boarding o guest house; (dinero) pension; (cama y comida) board and lodging; **media ~** half-board; **pensión completa** full board; **pensionista** nmf (jubilado) (old-age) pensioner; (huésped) lodger

penúltimo, -a [pe'nultimo, a] adj penultimate, last but one

penumbra [pe'numbra] nf half-light

peña ['pena] nf (roca) rock; (cuesta) cliff, crag; (grupo) group, circle; (LAM: club) folk club

peñasco [pe'nasko] nm large rock, boulder

peñón [pe'non] nm wall of rock; **el P~** the Rock (of Gibraltar)

peón [pe'on] nm labourer; (LAM Agr) farm labourer, farmhand; (Ajedrez) pawn

peonza [pe'onθa] nf spinning top

peor [pe'or] adj (comparativo) worse; (superlativo) worst ▷ adv worse; worst; **de mal en ~** from bad to worse

pepinillo [pepi'niλo] nm gherkin

pepino [pe'pino] nm cucumber; **(no) me importa un ~** I don't care one bit

pepita [pe'pita] nf (Bot) pip; (Minería) nugget

pepito [pe'pito] (ESP) nm (tb: **~ de**

ternera) steak sandwich

pequeño, -a [pe'keɲo, a] adj small, little

pera ['pera] nf pear; **peral** nm pear tree

percance [per'kanθe] nm setback, misfortune

percatarse [perka'tarse] vr: **~ de** to notice, take note of

percebe [per'θeβe] nm barnacle

percepción [perθep'θjon] nf (vista) perception; (idea) notion, idea

percha ['pertʃa] nf (coat)hanger; (ganchos) coat hooks pl; (de ave) perch

percibir [perθi'βir] vt to perceive, notice; (Com) to earn, get

percusión [perku'sjon] nf percussion

perdedor, -a [perðe'ðor, a] adj losing ▷ nm/f loser

perder [per'ðer] vt (gen) to lose; (tiempo, palabras) to waste; (oportunidad) to lose, miss; (tren) to miss ▷ vi to lose; **perderse** vr (extraviarse) to get lost; (desaparecer) to disappear, be lost to view; (arruinarse) to be ruined; **echar a ~** (comida) to spoil, ruin; (oportunidad) to waste

pérdida ['perðiða] nf loss; (de tiempo) waste; **pérdidas** nfpl (Com) losses

perdido, -a [per'ðiðo, a] adj lost

perdiz [per'ðiθ] nf partridge

perdón [per'ðon] nm (disculpa) pardon, forgiveness; (clemencia) mercy; **¡~!** sorry!, I beg your pardon!; **perdonar** vt to pardon, forgive; (la vida) to spare; (excusar) to exempt, excuse; **¡perdone (usted)!** sorry!, I beg your pardon!

perecedero, -a [pereθe'ðero, a] adj perishable

perecer [pere'θer] vi to perish, die

peregrinación [pereɣrina'θjon] nf (Rel) pilgrimage

peregrino, -a [pere'ɣrino, a] adj (idea) strange, absurd ▷ nm/f pilgrim

perejil [pere'xil] nm parsley

perenne [pe'renne] adj everlasting, perennial

pereza [pe'reθa] nf laziness, idleness; **perezoso, -a** adj lazy, idle

perfección [perfek'θjon] nf perfection; **perfeccionar** vt to perfect; (mejorar) to improve; (acabar) to complete, finish

perfecto, -a [per'fekto, a] adj perfect; (total) complete

perfil [per'fil] nm profile; (contorno) silhouette, outline; (Arq) (cross) section; **perfiles** nmpl features

perforación [perfora'θjon] nf perforation; (con taladro) drilling; **perforadora** nf punch

perforar [perfo'rar] vt to perforate; (agujero) to drill, bore; (papel) to punch a hole in ▷ vi to drill, bore

perfume [per'fume] nm perfume, scent

periferia [peri'ferja] nf periphery; (de ciudad) outskirts pl

periférico [peri'feriko] (LAM) nm ring road (BRIT), beltway (US)

perilla [pe'riʎa] nf (barba) goatee; (LAM: de puerta) doorknob, door handle

perímetro [pe'rimetro] nm perimeter

periódico, -a [pe'rjoðiko, a] adj periodic(al) ▷ nm newspaper

periodismo [perjo'ðismo] nm journalism; **periodista** nmf journalist

periodo [pe'rjoðo] nm period

período [pe'rioðo] nm = **periodo**

periquito [peri'kito] nm budgerigar, budgie

perito, -a [pe'rito, a] adj (experto) expert; (diestro) skilled, skilful ▷ nm/f expert; skilled worker; (técnico) technician

perjudicar [perxuði'kar] vt (gen) to damage, harm; **perjudicial** adj damaging, harmful; (en detrimento) detrimental; **perjuicio** nm damage, harm

perjurar [perxu'rar] vi to commit perjury

perla ['perla] nf pearl; **me viene de ~s** it suits me fine

permanecer [permane'θer] vi
(quedarse) to stay, remain; (seguir) to
continue to stay

permanente [perma'nente] adj
permanent, constant ▷ nf perm

permiso [per'miso] nm permission;
(licencia) permit, licence; **con ~** excuse
me; **estar de ~** (Mil) to be on leave;
permiso de conducir driving licence
(BRIT), driver's license (US); **permiso
por enfermedad** (LAM) sick leave

permitir [permi'tir] vt to permit,
allow

pernera [per'nera] nf trouser leg

pero ['pero] conj but; (aún) yet ▷ nm
(defecto) flaw, defect; (reparo) objection

perpendicular [perpendiku'lar] adj
perpendicular

perpetuo, -a [per'petwo, a] adj
perpetual

perplejo, -a [per'plexo, a] adj
perplexed, bewildered

perra ['perra] nf (Zool) bitch; **estar sin
una ~** (ESP: fam) to be flat broke

perrera [pe'rrera] nf kennel

perrito [pe'rrito] nm (tb: **~ caliente**)
hot dog

perro ['perro] nm dog

persa ['persa] adj, nmf Persian

persecución [perseku'θjon] nf
pursuit, chase; (Rel, Pol) persecution

perseguir [perse'xir] vt to pursue,
hunt; (cortejar) to chase after; (molestar)
to pester, annoy; (Rel, Pol) to persecute

persiana [per'sjana] nf (Venetian)
blind

persistente [persis'tente] adj
persistent

persistir [persis'tir] vi to persist

persona [per'sona] nf person;
persona mayor elderly person

personaje [perso'naxe] nm
important person, celebrity; (Teatro
etc) character

personal [perso'nal] adj (particular)
personal; (para una persona) single, for
one person ▷ nm personnel, staff;
personalidad nf personality

personarse [perso'narse] vr to
appear in person

personificar [personifi'kar] vt to
personify

perspectiva [perspek'tiβa] nf
perspective; (vista, panorama) view,
panorama; (posibilidad futura) outlook,
prospect

persuadir [perswa'ðir] vt (gen) to
persuade; (convencer) to convince;
persuadirse vr to become convinced;
persuasión nf persuasion

pertenecer [pertene'θer] vi to
belong; (fig) to concern; **perteneciente**
adj: **perteneciente a** belonging
to; **pertenencia** nf ownership;
pertenencias nfpl (bienes)
possessions, property sg

pertenezca etc vb V **pertenecer**

pértiga ['pertixa] nf: **salto de ~**
pole vault

pertinente [perti'nente] adj
relevant, pertinent; (apropiado)
appropriate; **~ a** concerning, relevant
to

perturbación [perturβa'θjon]
nf (Pol) disturbance; (Med) upset,
disturbance

Perú [pe'ru] nm Peru; **peruano, -a**
adj, nm/f Peruvian

perversión [perβer'sjon] nf
perversion; **perverso, -a** adj perverse;
(depravado) depraved

pervertido, -a [perβer'tiðo, a] adj
perverted ▷ nm/f pervert

pervertir [perβer'tir] vt to pervert,
corrupt

pesa ['pesa] nf weight; (Deporte) shot

pesadez [pesa'ðeθ] nf (peso)
heaviness; (lentitud) slowness;
(aburrimiento) tediousness

pesadilla [pesa'ðiʎa] nf nightmare,
bad dream

pesado, -a [pe'saðo, a] adj heavy;
(lento) slow; (difícil, duro) tough, hard;
(aburrido) boring, tedious; (tiempo)
sultry

pésame ['pesame] nm expression of

condolence, message of sympathy; **dar el ~** to express one's condolences

pesar [pe'sar] vt to weigh ▷ vi to weigh; (ser pesado) to weigh a lot, be heavy; (fig: opinión) to carry weight; **no pesa mucho** it's not very heavy ▷ nm (arrepentimiento) regret; (pena) grief, sorrow; **a ~ de** o **pese a (que)** in spite of, despite

pesca ['peska] nf (acto) fishing; (lo pescado) catch; **ir de ~** to go fishing

pescadería [peskaðe'ria] nf fish shop, fishmonger's (BRIT)

pescadilla [peska'ðiʎa] nf whiting

pescado [pes'kaðo] nm fish

pescador, a [peska'ðor, a] nm/f fisherman/woman

pescar [pes'kar] vt (tomar) to catch; (intentar tomar) to fish for; (conseguir: trabajo) to manage to get ▷ vi to fish, go fishing

pesebre [pe'seβre] nm manger

peseta [pe'seta] nf (Hist) peseta

pesimista [pesi'mista] adj pessimistic ▷ nmf pessimist

pésimo, -a ['pesimo, a] adj awful, dreadful

peso ['peso] nm weight; (balanza) scales pl; (moneda) peso; **vender al ~** to sell by weight; **peso bruto/neto** gross/net weight; **peso pesado/pluma** heavyweight/featherweight

pesquero, -a [pes'kero, a] adj fishing cpd

pestaña [pes'taɲa] nf (Anat) eyelash; (borde) rim

peste ['peste] nf plague; (mal olor) stink, stench

pesticida [pesti'θiða] nm pesticide

pestillo [pes'tiʎo] nm (cerrojo) bolt; (picaporte) door handle

petaca [pe'taka] nf (de cigarros) cigarette case; (de pipa) tobacco pouch; (MÉX: maleta) suitcase

pétalo ['petalo] nm petal

petardo [pe'tarðo] nm firework, firecracker

petición [peti'θjon] nf (pedido) request, plea; (memorial) petition; (Jur) plea

peto ['peto] (ESP) nm dungarees pl, overalls pl (US)

petróleo [pe'troleo] nm oil, petroleum; **petrolero, -a** adj petroleum cpd ▷ nm (oil) tanker

peyorativo, -a [pejora'tiβo, a] adj pejorative

pez [peθ] nm fish; **pez dorado/de colores** goldfish; **pez espada** swordfish

pezón [pe'θon] nm teat, nipple

pezuña [pe'θuɲa] nf hoof

pianista [pja'nista] nmf pianist

piano ['pjano] nm piano

piar [pjar] vi to cheep

pibe, -a ['piβe, a] (RPL) nm/f boy/girl

picadero [pika'ðero] nm riding school

picadillo [pika'ðiʎo] nm mince, minced meat

picado, -a [pi'kaðo, a] adj pricked, punctured; (Culin) minced, chopped; (mar) choppy; (diente) bad; (tabaco) cut; (enfadado) cross

picador [pika'ðor] nm (Taur) picador; (minero) faceworker

picadura [pika'ðura] nf (pinchazo) puncture; (de abeja) sting; (de mosquito) bite; (tabaco picado) cut tobacco

picante [pi'kante] adj hot; (comentario) racy, spicy

picaporte [pika'porte] nm (manija) doorhandle; (pestillo) latch

picar [pi'kar] vt (agujerear, perforar) to prick, puncture; (abeja) to sting; (mosquito, serpiente) to bite; (Culin) to mince, chop; (incitar) to incite, goad; (dañar, irritar) to annoy, bother; (quemar: lengua) to burn, sting ▷ vi (pez) to bite, take the bait; (sol) to burn, scorch; (abeja, Med) to sting; (mosquito) to bite; **picarse** vr (agriarse) to turn sour, go off; (ofenderse) to take offence

picardía [pikar'ðia] nf villainy; (astucia) slyness, craftiness; (una picardía) dirty trick; (palabra) rude/bad word o expression

pícaro, -a ['pikaro, a] adj (malicioso) villainous; (travieso) mischievous ▷ nm (astuto) crafty sort; (sinvergüenza) rascal, scoundrel

pichi ['pitʃi] (ESP) nm pinafore dress (BRIT), jumper (US)

pichón [pi'tʃon] nm young pigeon

pico ['piko] nm (de ave) beak; (punta) sharp point; (Tec) pick, pickaxe; (Geo) peak, summit; **y** ~ and a bit; **las seis y ~** six and a bit

picor [pi'kor] nm itch

picoso, -a [pi'koso, a] (MÉX) adj (comida) hot

picudo, -a [pi'kuðo, a] adj pointed, with a point

pidió etc vb V **pedir**

pido etc vb V **pedir**

pie [pje] (pl ~s) nm foot; (fig: motivo) motive, basis; (: fundamento) foothold; **ir a ~** to go on foot, walk; **estar de ~** to be standing (up); **ponerse de ~** to stand up; **de ~s a cabeza** from top to bottom; **al ~ de la letra** (citar) literally, verbatim; (copiar) exactly, word for word; **en ~ de guerra** on a war footing; **dar a ~ a** to give cause for; **hacer ~** (en el agua) to touch (the) bottom

piedad [pje'ðað] nf (lástima) pity, compassion; (clemencia) mercy; (devoción) piety, devotion

piedra ['pjeðra] nf stone; (roca) rock; (de mechero) flint; (Meteorología) hailstone; **piedra preciosa** precious stone

piel [pjel] nf (Anat) skin; (Zool) skin, hide, fur; (cuero) leather; (Bot) skin, peel

pienso etc vb V **pensar**

pierdo etc vb V **perder**

pierna ['pjerna] nf leg

pieza ['pjeθa] nf piece; (habitación) room; **pieza de recambio o repuesto** spare (part)

pigmeo, -a [piɣ'meo, a] adj, nm/f pigmy

pijama [pi'xama] nm pyjamas pl (BRIT), pajamas pl (US)

pila ['pila] nf (Elec) battery; (montón) heap, pile; (lavabo) sink

píldora ['pildora] nf pill; **la ~ (anticonceptiva)** the (contraceptive) pill

pileta [pi'leta] (RPL) nf (fregadero) (kitchen) sink; (piscina) swimming pool

pillar [pi'ʎar] vt (saquear) to pillage, plunder; (fam: coger) to catch; (: agarrar) to grasp, seize; (: entender) to grasp, catch on to; **pillarse** vr: **~se un dedo con la puerta** to catch one's finger in the door

pillo, -a ['piʎo, a] adj villainous; (astuto) sly, crafty ▷ nm/f rascal, rogue, scoundrel

piloto [pi'loto] nm pilot; (de aparato) (pilot) light; (Auto: luz) tail o rear light; (: conductor) driver; **piloto automático** automatic pilot

pimentón [pimen'ton] nm paprika

pimienta [pi'mjenta] nf pepper

pimiento [pi'mjento] nm pepper, pimiento

pin [pin] (pl ~s) nm badge

pinacoteca [pinako'teka] nf art gallery

pinar [pi'nar] nm pine forest (BRIT), pine grove (US)

pincel [pin'θel] nm paintbrush

pinchadiscos [pintʃa'ðiskos] (ESP) nmf inv disc-jockey, DJ

pinchar [pin'tʃar] vt (perforar) to prick, pierce; (neumático) to puncture; (fig) to prod; (Inform) to click

pinchazo [pin'tʃaθo] nm (perforación) prick; (de neumático) puncture; (fig) prod

pincho ['pintʃo] nm savoury (snack); **pincho de tortilla** small slice of omelette; **pincho moruno** shish kebab

ping-pong ['pin'pon] nm table tennis

pingüino [pin'gwino] nm penguin

pino ['pino] nm pine (tree)

pinta ['pinta] nf spot; (de líquidos) spot, drop; (aspecto) appearance, look(s) (pl); **pintado, -a** adj spotted; (de colores) colourful; **pintadas** nfpl graffiti sg

pintalabios [pinta'laβjos] (ESP) nm
inv lipstick

pintar [pin'tar] vt to paint ▷ vi to
paint; (fam) to count, be important;
pintarse vr to put on make-up

pintor, a [pin'tor, a] nm/f painter

pintoresco, -a [pinto'resko, a] adj
picturesque

pintura [pin'tura] nf painting;
pintura al óleo oil painting

pinza ['pinθa] nf (Zool) claw; (para
colgar ropa) clothes peg; (Tec) pincers
pl; **pinzas** nfpl (para depilar etc)
tweezers pl

piña ['pina] nf (de pino) pine cone;
(fruta) pineapple; (fig) group

piñata [pi'nata] nf container hung up
at parties to be beaten with sticks until
sweets or presents fall out

● **PIÑATA**

● **Piñata** is a very popular party
● game in Mexico. The **piñata** itself
● is a hollow figure made of papier
● maché, or, traditionally, from
● adobe, in the shape of an object,
● a star, a person or an animal. It is
● filled with either sweets and toys,
● or fruit and yam beans. The game
● consists of hanging the **piñata**
● from the ceiling, and beating it
● with a stick, blindfolded, until it
● breaks and the presents fall out.

piñón [pi'non] nm (fruto) pine nut;
(Tec) pinion

pío, -a ['pio, a] adj (devoto) pious,
devout; (misericordioso) merciful

piojo ['pjoxo] nm louse

pipa ['pipa] nf pipe; **pipas** nfpl (Bot)
(edible) sunflower seeds

pipí [pi'pi] (fam) nm: **hacer ~** to have
a wee (-wee) (BRIT), to go (wee-
wee) (US)

pique ['pike] nm (resentimiento)
pique, resentment; (rivalidad)

rivalry, competition; **irse a ~** to sink;
(esperanza, familia) to be ruined

piqueta [pi'keta] nf pick(axe)

piquete [pi'kete] nm (Mil) squad,
party; (de obreros) picket; (MÉX: de
insecto) bite; **piquetear** (LAM) vt to
picket

pirado, -a [pi'raðo, a] (fam) adj
round the bend ▷ nm/f nutter

piragua [pi'raxwa] nf canoe;
piragüismo nm canoeing

pirámide [pi'ramiðe] nf pyramid

pirata [pi'rata] adj, nm/f pirate; **pirata
informático** hacker

Pirineo(s) [piri'neo(s)] nm(pl)
Pyrenees pl

pirómano, -a [pi'romano, a] nm/f
(Med, Jur) arsonist

piropo [pi'ropo] nm compliment,
(piece of) flattery

pirueta [pi'rweta] nf pirouette

piruleta [piru'leta] (ESP) nf lollipop

pis [pis] (fam) nm pee, piss; **hacer ~** to
have a pee; (para niños) to wee-wee

pisada [pi'saða] nf (paso) footstep;
(huella) footprint

pisar [pi'sar] vt (caminar sobre) to walk
on, tread on; (apretar con el pie) to press;
(fig) to trample on, walk all over ▷ vi to
tread, step, walk

piscina [pis'θina] nf swimming pool

Piscis ['pisθis] nm Pisces

piso ['piso] nm (suelo, planta)
floor; (ESP: apartamento) flat (BRIT),
apartment; **primer ~** (ESP) first floor;
(LAM: planta baja) ground floor

pisotear [pisote'ar] vt to trample (on
o underfoot)

pista ['pista] nf track, trail; (indicio)
clue; **pista de aterrizaje** runway; **pista
de baile** dance floor; **pista de hielo** ice
rink; **pista de tenis** tennis court

pistola [pis'tola] nf pistol; (Tec)
spray-gun

pistón [pis'ton] nm (Tec) piston;
(Mús) key

pitar [pi'tar] vt (silbato) to blow;
(rechiflar) to whistle at, boo ▷ vi to

whistle; (Auto) to sound o toot one's horn; (LAM: fumar) to smoke

pitillo [pi'tiʎo] nm cigarette

pito ['pito] nm whistle; (de coche) horn

pitón [pi'ton] nm (Zool) python

pitonisa [pito'nisa] nf fortune-teller

pitorreo [pito'rreo] nm joke; **estar de ~** to be joking

píxel ['piksel] (pl **pixels** or **~es**) nm pixel

piyama [pi'jama] (LAM) nm pyjamas pl (BRIT), pajamas pl (US)

pizarra [pi'θarra] nf (piedra) slate; (ESP: encerado) blackboard; **pizarra blanca** whiteboard; **pizarra interactiva** interactive whiteboard

pizarrón [piθa'rron] (LAM) nm blackboard

pizca ['piθka] nf pinch, spot; (fig) spot, speck; **ni ~** not a bit

placa ['plaka] nf plate; (distintivo) badge, insignia; **placa de matrícula** (LAM) number plate

placard [pla'kar] (RPL) nm cupboard

placer [pla'θer] nm pleasure ▷ vt to please

plaga ['plaxa] nf pest; (Med) plague; (abundancia) abundance

plagio [plaxjo] nm plagiarism

plan [plan] nm (esquema, proyecto) plan; (idea, intento) idea, intention; **tener ~** (fam) to have a date; **tener un ~** (fam) to have an affair; **en ~ económico** (fam) on the cheap; **vamos en ~ de turismo** we're going as tourists; **si te pones en ese ~ ...** if that's your attitude ...

plana ['plana] nf sheet (of paper), page; (Tec) trowel; **en primera ~** on the front page

plancha ['plantʃa] nf (para planchar) iron; (rótulo) plate, sheet; (Náut) gangway; **a la ~** (Culin) grilled; **planchar** vt to iron ▷ vi to do the ironing

planear [plane'ar] vt to plan ▷ vi to glide

planeta [pla'neta] nm planet

plano, -a ['plano, a] adj flat, level, even ▷ nm (Mat, Tec) plane; (Foto) shot; (Arq) plan; (Geo) map; (de ciudad) map, street plan; **primer ~** close-up

planta ['planta] nf (Bot, Tec) plant; (Anat) sole of the foot, foot; (piso) floor; (LAM: personal) staff; **planta baja** ground floor

plantar [plan'tar] vt (Bot) to plant; (levantar) to erect, set up; **plantarse** vr to stand firm; **~ a algn en la calle** to throw sb out; **dejar plantado a algn** (fam) to stand sb up

plantear [plante'ar] vt (problema) to pose; (dificultad) to raise

plantilla [plan'tiʎa] nf (de zapato) insole; (ESP: personal) personnel; **ser de ~** (ESP) to be on the staff

plantón [plan'ton] nm (Mil) guard, sentry; (fam) long wait; **dar (un) ~ a algn** to stand sb up

plasta ['plasta] (ESP: fam) adj inv boring ▷ nmf bore

plástico, -a ['plastiko, a] adj plastic ▷ nm plastic

Plastilina® [plasti'lina] nf Plasticine®

plata ['plata] nf (metal) silver; (cosas hechas de plata) silverware; (cs: dinero) cash, dough

plataforma [plata'forma] nf platform; **plataforma de lanzamiento/perforación** launch(ing) pad/drilling rig

plátano ['platano] nm (fruta) banana; (árbol) plane tree; banana tree

platea [pla'tea] nf (Teatro) pit

plática ['platika] nf talk, chat; **platicar** vi to talk, chat

platillo [pla'tiʎo] nm saucer; **platillos** nmpl (Mús) cymbals; **platillo volante** flying saucer

platino [pla'tino] nm platinum; **platinos** nmpl (Auto) contact points

plato ['plato] nm plate, dish; (parte de comida) course; (comida) dish; **primer ~** first course; **plato combinado** set main course (served on one plate); **plato**

P

playa | 214

fuerte main course
playa ['plaja] *nf* beach; *(costa)*
seaside; **playa de estacionamiento**
(cs) car park *(BRIT)*, parking lot *(us)*
playera [pla'jera] *nf (MÉX: camiseta)*
T-shirt; **playeras** *nfpl (zapatos)* canvas
shoes
plaza ['plaθa] *nf* square; *(mercado)*
market(place); *(sitio)* room, space; *(de
vehículo)* seat, place; *(colocación)* post,
job; **plaza de toros** bullring
plazo ['plaθo] *nm (lapso de tiempo)*
time, period; *(fecha de vencimiento)*
expiry date; *(pago parcial)* instalment;
a corto/largo ~ short-/long-term;
comprar algo a ~s to buy sth on hire
purchase *(BRIT)* o on time *(us)*
plazoleta [plaθo'leta] *nf* small
square
plebeyo, -a [ple'βejo, a] *adj*
plebeian; *(pey)* coarse, common
plegable [ple'γaβle] *adj* collapsible;
(silla) folding
pleito ['pleito] *nm (Jur)* lawsuit, case;
(fig) dispute, feud
plenitud [pleni'tuð] *nf* plenitude,
fullness; *(abundancia)* abundance
pleno, -a ['pleno, a] *adj* full;
(completo) complete ▷ *nm* plenum; **en
~ día** in broad daylight; **en ~ verano**
at the height of summer; **en plena cara**
full in the face
pliego *etc* ['pljeγo] *vb* V **plegar**
▷ *nm (hoja)* sheet (of paper); *(carta)*
sealed letter/document; **pliego de
condiciones** details *pl*, specifications
pl
pliegue *etc* ['pljeγe] *vb* V **plegar**
fold, crease; *(de vestido)* pleat
plomería [plome'ria] *nf (LAM)*
plumbing; **plomero** *(LAM)* *nm* plumber
plomo ['plomo] *nm (metal)* lead; *(Elec)*
fuse; **sin ~** unleaded
pluma ['pluma] *nf* feather; *(para
escribir)*: **~ (estilográfica)** ink pen; **~
fuente** *(LAM)* fountain pen
plumero [plu'mero] *nm (para el polvo)*
feather duster

plumón [plu'mon] *nm (de ave)* down
plural [plu'ral] *adj* plural
pluriempleo [plurjem'pleo] *nm*
having more than one job
plus [plus] *nm* bonus
población [poβla'θjon] *nf*
population; *(pueblo, ciudad)* town, city
poblado, -a [po'βlaðo, a] *adj*
inhabited ▷ *nm (aldea)* village; *(pueblo)*
(small) town; **densamente ~** densely
populated
poblador, a [poβla'ðor, a] *nm/f*
settler, colonist
pobre ['poβre] *adj* poor ▷ *nmf* poor
person; **pobreza** *nf* poverty
pocilga [po'θilxa] *nf* pigsty

○ **PALABRA CLAVE**

poco, -a ['poko, a] *adj* **1** *(sg)* little,
not much; **poco tiempo** little o not
much time; **de poco interés** of little
interest, not very interesting; **poca
cosa** not much
2 *(pl)* few, not many; **unos pocos** a
few, some; **pocos niños comen lo que
les conviene** few children eat what
they should
▷ *adv* **1** little, not much; **cuesta poco** it
doesn't cost much
2 *(+ adj: negativo, antónimo)*: **poco
amable/inteligente** not very nice/
intelligent
3: **por poco me caigo** I almost fell
4: **a poco: a poco de haberse casado**
shortly after getting married
5: **poco a poco** little by little
▷ *nm* a little, a bit; **un poco triste/de
dinero** a little sad/money

podar [po'ðar] *vt* to prune
podcast ['poðkast] *nm* podcast;
podcastear [poðkaste'ar] *vi* to
podcast

○ **PALABRA CLAVE**

poder [po'ðer] *vi* **1** *(tener capacidad)*

can, be able to; **no puedo hacerlo** I can't do it, I'm unable to do it **2** (*tener permiso*) can, may, be allowed to; **¿se puede?** may I (*o* we)?; **puedes irte ahora** you may go now; **no se puede fumar en este hospital** smoking is not allowed in this hospital **3** (*tener posibilidad*) may, might, could; **puede llegar mañana** he may *o* might arrive tomorrow; **pudiste haberte hecho daño** you might *o* could have hurt yourself; **¡podías habérmelo dicho antes!** you might have told me before! **4**: **puede ser** perhaps; **puede ser que lo sepa Tomás** Tomás may *o* might know **5**: **¡no puedo más!** I've had enough!; **es tonto a más no poder** he's as stupid as they come **6**: **poder con: no puedo con este crío** this kid's too much for me ⊳ *nm* power; **detentar** *o* **ocupar** *o* **estar en el poder** to be in power; **poder adquisitivo/ejecutivo/ legislativo** purchasing/executive/ legislative power; **poder judicial** judiciary

poderoso, -a [poðeˈroso, a] *adj* (*político, país*) powerful

podio [ˈpoðjo] *nm* (*Deporte*) podium

podium [ˈpoðjum] = **podio**

podrido, -a [poˈðriðo, a] *adj* rotten, bad; (*fig*) rotten, corrupt

podrir [poˈðrir] = **pudrir**

poema [poˈema] *nm* poem

poesía [poeˈsia] *nf* poetry

poeta [poˈeta] *nmf* poet; **poético, -a** *adj* poetic(al)

poetisa [poeˈtisa] *nf* (*woman*) poet

póker [ˈpoker] *nm* poker

polaco, -a [poˈlako, a] *adj* Polish ⊳ *nm/f* Pole

polar [poˈlar] *adj* polar

polea [poˈlea] *nf* pulley

polémica [poˈlemika] *nf* polemics

sg; (*una polémica*) controversy, polemic

polen [ˈpolen] *nm* pollen

policía [poliˈθia] *nmf* policeman/ woman ⊳ *nf* police; **policíaco, -a** *adj* police *cpd*; **novela policíaca** detective story; **policial** *adj* police *cpd*

polideportivo [poliðeporˈtiβo] *nm* sports centre *o* complex

polígono [poˈliɣono] *nm* (*Mat*) polygon; **polígono industrial**(ESP) industrial estate

polilla [poˈliʎa] *nf* moth

polio [ˈpoljo] *nf* polio

política [poˈlitika] *nf* politics *sg*; (*económica, agraria etc*) policy; V tb **político**

político, -a [poˈlitiko, a] *adj* political; (*discreto*) tactful; (*de familia*) ...-in-law ⊳ *nm/f* politician; **padre ~** father-in-law

póliza [ˈpoliθa] *nf* certificate, voucher; (*impuesto*) tax stamp; **póliza de seguro(s)** insurance policy

polizón [poliˈθon] *nm* stowaway

pollera [poˈʎera] (cs) *nf* skirt

pollo [ˈpoʎo] *nm* chicken

polo [ˈpolo] *nm* (*Geo, Elec*) pole; (*helado*) ice lolly (BRIT), Popsicle® (us); (*Deporte*) polo; (*suéter*) polo-neck; **polo Norte/Sur** North/South Pole

Polonia [poˈlonja] *nf* Poland

poltrona [polˈtrona] *nf* easy chair

polución [poluˈθjon] *nf* pollution

polvera [polˈβera] *nf* powder compact

polvo [ˈpolβo] *nm* dust; (*Quím, Culin, Med*) powder; **polvos** *nmpl* (*maquillaje*) powder *sg*; **en ~** powdered; **quitar el ~** to dust; **estar hecho ~** (*fam*) to be worn out *o* exhausted; **polvos de talco** talcum powder *sg*

pólvora [ˈpolβora] *nf* gunpowder

polvoriento, -a [polβoˈrjento, a] *adj* (*superficie*) dusty; (*sustancia*) powdery

pomada [poˈmaða] *nf* cream, ointment

pomelo [po'melo] nm grapefruit

pómez ['pomeθ] nf: **piedra ~** pumice stone

pomo ['pomo] nm doorknob

pompa ['pompa] nf (burbuja) bubble; (bomba) pump; (esplendor) pomp, splendour

pómulo ['pomulo] nm cheekbone

pon [pon] vb V **poner**

ponchadura [pontʃa'ðura] (MÉX) nf puncture (BRIT), flat (US); **ponchar** (MÉX) vt (llanta) to puncture

ponche ['pontʃe] nm punch

poncho ['pontʃo] nm poncho

pondré etc vb V **poner**

🔘 **PALABRA CLAVE**

poner [po'ner] vt 1 (colocar) to put; (telegrama) to send; (obra de teatro) to put on; (película) to show; **ponlo más fuerte** turn it up; **¿qué ponen en el Excelsior?** what's on at the Excelsior?

2 (tienda) to open; (instalar: gas etc) to put in; (radio, TV) to switch to turn on

3 (suponer): **pongamos que...** let's suppose that...

4 (contribuir): **el gobierno ha puesto otro millón** the government has contributed another million

5 (Tel): **póngame con el Sr. López** can you put me through to Mr. López?

6: **poner de: le han puesto de director general** they've appointed him general manager

7 (+ adj) to make; **me estás poniendo nerviosa** you're making me nervous

8 (dar nombre): **al hijo le pusieron Diego** they called their son Diego

▷ vi (gallina) to lay

ponerse vr 1 (colocarse): **se puso a mi lado** he came and stood beside me; **tú ponte en esa silla** you go and sit on that chair; **ponerse en camino** to set off

2 (vestido, cosméticos) to put on; **¿por qué no te pones el vestido nuevo?**

why don't you put on o wear your new dress?

3 (+ adj) to turn; to get, become; **se puso muy serio** he got very serious; **después de lavarla la tela se puso azul** after washing it the material turned blue

4: **ponerse a: se puso a llorar** he started to cry; **tienes que ponerte a estudiar** you must get down to studying

---

pongo etc vb V **poner**

poniente [po'njente] nm (occidente) west; (viento) west wind

pontífice [pon'tifiθe] nm pope, pontiff

pop [pop] adj inv, nm (Mus) pop

popa ['popa] nf stern

popote [po'pote] (MÉX) nm straw

popular [popu'lar] adj popular; (cultura) of the people, folk cpd; **popularidad** nf popularity

---

🔘 **PALABRA CLAVE**

por [por] prep 1 (objetivo) for: **luchar por la patria** to fight for one's country

2 (+ infin): **por no llegar tarde** so as not to arrive late; **por citar unos ejemplos** to give a few examples

3 (causa) out of, because of; **por escasez de fondos** through o for lack of funds

4 (tiempo): **por la mañana/noche** in the morning/at night; **se queda por una semana** she's staying (for) a week

5 (lugar): **pasar por Madrid** to pass through Madrid; **ir a Guayaquil por Quito** to go to Guayaquil via Quito; **caminar por la calle** to walk along the street; **¿Hay un banco por aquí?** Is there a bank near here?; V tb **todo**

6 (cambio, precio): **te doy uno nuevo por el que tienes** I'll give you a new one (in return) for the one you've got

7 (valor distributivo): **6 euros por**

hora/cabeza 6 euros an o per hour/a o per head

8 (modo, medio) by; **por correo/avión** by post/air; **entrar por la entrada principal** to go in through the main entrance

9 : **10 por 10 son 100** 10 times 10 is 100

10 (en lugar de): **vino él por su jefe** he came instead of his boss

11 : **por mí que revienten** as far as I'm concerned they can drop dead

12 : **¿por qué?** why?; **¿por qué no?** why not?

porcelana [porθe'lana] nf porcelain; (china) china

porcentaje [porθen'taxe] nm percentage

porción [por'θjon] nf (parte) portion, share; (cantidad) quantity, amount

porfiar [por'fjar] vi to persist, insist; (disputar) to argue stubbornly

pormenor [porme'nor] nm detail, particular

pornografía [pornoɣra'fia] nf pornography

poro ['poro] nm pore

pororó [poro'ro] (RPL) nm popcorn

poroso, -a [po'roso, a] adj porous

poroto [po'roto] (CS) nm bean

porque ['porke] conj (a causa de) because; (ya que) since; (con el fin de) so that, in order that

porqué [por'ke] nm reason, cause

porquería [porke'ria] nf (suciedad) filth, dirt; (acción) dirty trick; (objeto) small thing, trifle; (fig) rubbish

porra ['porra] (ESP) nf (arma) stick, club

porrazo [po'rraθo] nm blow, bump

porro ['porro] (fam) nm (droga) joint (fam)

porrón [po'rron] nm glass wine jar with a long spout

portaaviones [porta'(a)βjones] nm inv aircraft carrier

portada [por'taða] nf (de revista) cover

portador, a [porta'ðor, a] nm/f carrier, bearer; (Com) bearer, payee

portaequipajes [portaeki'paxes] nm inv (Auto: maletero) boot; (: baca) luggage rack

portafolio [porta'foljo] (LAM) nm briefcase

portal [por'tal] nm (entrada) vestibule, hall; (portada) porch, doorway; (puerta de entrada) main door; (Internet) portal; **portales** nmpl (LAM) arcade sg

portamaletas [portama'letas] nm inv (Auto: maletero) boot; (: baca) roof rack

portamonedas [portamo'neðas] nm inv purse

portarse [por'tarse] vr to behave, conduct o.s.

portátil [por'tatil] adj portable; **(ordenador) portátil** laptop computer

portavoz [porta'βoθ] nmf spokesman/woman

portazo [por'taθo] nm: **dar un ~ to** slam the door

porte ['porte] nm (Com) transport; (precio) transport charges pl

portentoso, -a [porten'toso, a] adj marvellous, extraordinary

porteño, -a [por'teɲo, a] adj of o from Buenos Aires

portería [porte'ria] nf (oficina) porter's office; (Deporte) goal

portero, -a [por'tero, a] nm/f porter; (conserje) caretaker; (ujier) doorman; (Deporte) goalkeeper; **portero automático** (ESP) entry phone

pórtico [por'tiko] nm (patio) portico, porch; (fig) gateway; (arcada) arcade

portorriqueño, -a [portorri'keɲo, a] adj Puerto Rican

Portugal [portu'ɣal] nm Portugal; **portugués, -esa** adj, nm/f Portuguese ▷ nm (Ling) Portuguese

porvenir [porβe'nir] nm future

pos [pos] prep: **en ~ de** after, in pursuit of

posaderas [posa'ðeras] nfpl

backside sg, buttocks

posar [po'sar] vt (en el suelo) to lay down, put down; (la mano) to place, put gently ▷ vi (modelo) to sit, pose; **posarse** vr to settle; (pájaro) to perch; (avión) to land, come down

posavasos [posa'basos] nm inv coaster; (para cerveza) beermat

posdata [pos'ðata] nf postscript

pose ['pose] nf pose

poseedor, a [posee'ðor, a] nm/f owner, possessor; (de récord, puesto) holder

poseer [pose'er] vt to possess, own; (ventaja) to enjoy; (récord, puesto) to hold

posesivo, -a [pose'siβo, a] adj possessive

posibilidad [posiβili'ðað] nf possibility; (oportunidad) chance; **posibilitar** vt to make possible; (hacer realizable) to make feasible

posible [po'siβle] adj possible; (realizable) feasible; **de ser ~** if possible; **en lo ~** as far as possible

posición [posi'θjon] nf position; (rango social) status

positivo, -a [posi'tiβo, a] adj positive

poso ['poso] nm sediment; (heces) dregs pl

posponer [pospo'ner] vt (relegar) to put behind/below; (aplazar) to postpone

posta ['posta] nf: **a ~** deliberately, on purpose

postal [pos'tal] adj postal ▷ nf postcard

poste ['poste] nm (de telégrafos etc) post, pole; (columna) pillar

póster ['poster] (pl **-es, -s**) nm poster

posterior [poste'rjor] adj back, rear; (siguiente) following, subsequent; (más tarde) later

postgrado [post'graðo] nm = **posgrado**

postizo, -a [pos'tiθo, a] adj false, artificial ▷ nm hairpiece

postre ['postre] nm sweet, dessert

póstumo, -a ['postumo, a] adj posthumous

postura [pos'tura] nf (del cuerpo) posture, position; (fig) attitude, position

potable [po'taβle] adj drinkable; **agua ~** drinking water

potaje [po'taxe] nm thick vegetable soup

potencia [po'tenθja] nf power; **potencial** [poten'θjal] adj, nm potential

potente [po'tente] adj powerful

potro, -a ['potro, a] nm/f (Zool) colt/ filly ▷ nm (de gimnasia) vaulting horse

pozo ['poθo] nm well; (de río) deep pool; (de mina) shaft

PP (ESP) nm abr = **Partido Popular**

práctica ['praktika] nf practice; (método) method; (arte, capacidad) skill; **en la ~** in practice

practicable [prakti'kaβle] adj practicable; (camino) passable

practicante [prakti'kante] nmf (Med: ayudante de doctor) medical assistant; (: enfermero) nurse; (quien practica algo) practitioner ▷ adj practising

practicar [prakti'kar] vt to practise; (Deporte) to play; (realizar) to carry out, perform

práctico, -a ['praktiko, a] adj practical; (instruido: persona) skilled, expert

practique etc vb V **practicar**

pradera [pra'ðera] nf meadow; (us etc) prairie

prado ['praðo] nm (campo) meadow, field; (pastizal) pasture

Praga ['praxa] n Prague

pragmático, -a [prax'matiko, a] adj pragmatic

precario, -a [pre'karjo, a] adj precarious

precaución [prekau'θjon] nf (medida preventiva) preventive measure, precaution; (prudencia) caution, wariness

precedente [preθe'ðente] adj preceding; (anterior) former ▷ nm precedent

preceder [preθe'ðer] vt, vi to precede, go before, come before

precepto [pre'θepto] nm precept

precinto [pre'θinto] nm (tb: ~ de garantía) seal

precio ['preθjo] nm price; (costo) cost; (valor) value, worth; (de viaje) fare; **precio al contado/de coste/de oportunidad** cash/cost/bargain price; **precio al por menor** retail price; **precio de ocasión** bargain price; **precio de venta al público** retail price; **precio tope** top price

preciosidad [preθjosi'ðað] nf (valor) (high) value, (great) worth; (encanto) charm; (cosa bonita) beautiful thing; **es una ~** it's lovely, it's really beautiful

precioso, -a [pre'θjoso, a] adj precious; (de mucho valor) valuable; (fam) lovely, beautiful

precipicio [preθi'piθjo] nm cliff, precipice; (fig) abyss

precipitación [preθipita'θjon] nf haste; (lluvia) rainfall

precipitado, -a [preθipi'taðo, a] adj (conducta) hasty, rash; (salida) hasty, sudden

precipitar [preθipi'tar] vt (arrojar) to hurl down, throw; (apresurar) to hasten; (acelerar) to speed up, accelerate; **precipitarse** vr to throw o.s.; (apresurarse) to rush; (actuar sin pensar) to act rashly

precisamente [preθisa'mente] adv precisely; (exactamente) precisely, exactly

precisar [preθi'sar] vt (necesitar) to need, require; (fijar) to determine exactly, fix; (especificar) to specify

precisión [preθi'sjon] nf (exactitud) precision

preciso, -a [pre'θiso, a] adj (exacto) precise; (necesario) necessary, essential

preconcebido, -a [prekonθe'βiðo,

a] adj preconceived

precoz [pre'koθ] adj (persona) precocious; (calvicie etc) premature

predecir [preðe'θir] vt to predict, forecast

predestinado, -a [preðesti'naðo, a] adj predestined

predicar [preði'kar] vt, vi to preach

predicción [preðik'θjon] nf prediction

predilecto, -a [preði'lekto, a] adj favourite

predisposición [preðisposi'θjon] nf inclination; prejudice, bias

predominar [preðomi'nar] vt to dominate ▷ vi to predominate; (prevalecer) to prevail; **predominio** nm predominance; prevalence

preescolar [pre(e)sko'lar] adj preschool

prefabricado, -a [prefaβri'kaðo, a] adj prefabricated

prefacio [pre'faθjo] nm preface

preferencia [prefe'renθja] nf preference; **de ~** preferably, for preference

preferible [prefe'riβle] adj preferable

preferido, -a [prefe'riðo, a] adj, nm/f favourite, favorite (us)

preferir [prefe'rir] vt to prefer

prefiero etc vb V **preferir**

prefijo [pre'fixo] nm (Tel) (dialling) code

pregunta [pre'ɣunta] nf question; **hacer una ~** to ask a question; **preguntas frecuentes** FAQs, frequently asked questions

preguntar [preɣun'tar] vt to ask; (cuestionar) to question ▷ vi to ask; **preguntarse** vr to wonder; **preguntar por algn** to ask for sb; **preguntón, -ona** [preɣun'ton, ona] adj inquisitive

prehistórico, -a [preis'toriko, a] adj prehistoric

prejuicio [pre'xwiθjo] nm (acto) prejudgement; (idea preconcebida) preconception; (parcialidad) prejudice, bias

preludio [pre'luðjo] *nm* prelude

prematuro, -a [prema'turo, a] *adj* premature

premeditar [premeði'tar] *vt* to premeditate

premiar [pre'mjar] *vt* to reward; (*en un concurso*) to give a prize to

premio ['premjo] *nm* reward; prize; (*Com*) premium

prenatal [prena'tal] *adj* antenatal, prenatal

prenda ['prenda] *nf* (*ropa*) garment, article of clothing; (*garantía*) pledge; **prendas** *nfpl* (*talentos*) talents, gifts

prender [pren'der] *vt* (*captar*) to catch, capture; (*detener*) to arrest; (*Costura*) to pin, attach; (*sujetar*) to fasten ▷ *vi* to catch; (*arraigar*) to take root; **prenderse** *vr* (*encenderse*) to catch fire

prendido, -a [pren'diðo, a] (*LAM*) *adj* (*luz etc*) on

prensa ['prensa] *nf* press; **la ~** the press

preñado, -a [pre'ɲaðo, a] *adj* pregnant; **~ de** pregnant with, full of

preocupación [preokupa'θjon] *nf* worry, concern; (*ansiedad*) anxiety

preocupado, -a [preoku'paðo, a] *adj* worried, concerned; (*ansioso*) anxious

preocupar [preoku'par] *vt* to worry; **preocuparse** *vr* to worry; **~se de algo** (*hacerse cargo*) to take care of sth

preparación [prepara'θjon] *nf* (*acto*) preparation; (*estado*) readiness; (*entrenamiento*) training

preparado, -a [prepa'raðo, a] *adj* (*dispuesto*) prepared; (*Culin*) ready (to serve) ▷ *nm* preparation

preparar [prepa'rar] *vt* (*disponer*) to prepare, get ready; (*Tec: tratar*) to prepare, process; (*entrenar*) to teach, train; **prepararse** *vr*: **~se a** o **para** to prepare to o for; to get ready to o for; **preparativo, -a** *adj* preparatory, preliminary; **preparativos** *nmpl*

preparations; **preparatoria** (*MÉX*) *nf* sixth-form college (*BRIT*), senior high school (*US*)

presa ['presa] *nf* (*cosa apresada*) catch; (*víctima*) victim; (*de animal*) prey; (*de agua*) dam

presagiar [presa'xjar] *vt* to presage, forebode; **presagio** *nm* omen

prescindir [presθin'dir] *vi*: **~ de** (*privarse de*) to do o go without; (*descartar*) to dispense with

prescribir [preskri'βir] *vt* to prescribe

presencia [pre'senθja] *nf* presence; **presenciar** *vt* to be present at; (*asistir a*) to attend; (*ver*) to see, witness

presentación [presenta'θjon] *nf* presentation; (*introducción*) introduction

presentador, a [presenta'ðor, a] *nm/f* presenter, compère

presentar [presen'tar] *vt* to present; (*ofrecer*) to offer; (*mostrar*) to show, display; (*a una persona*) to introduce; **presentarse** *vr* (*llegar inesperadamente*) to appear, turn up; (*ofrecerse: como candidato*) to run, stand; (*aparecer*) to show, appear; (*solicitar empleo*) to apply

presente [pre'sente] *adj* present ▷ *nm* present; **hacer ~** to state, declare; **tener ~** to remember, bear in mind

presentimiento [presenti'mjento] *nm* premonition, presentiment

presentir [presen'tir] *vt* to have a premonition of

preservación [preserβa'θjon] *nf* protection, preservation

preservar [preser'βar] *vt* to protect, preserve; **preservativo** *nm* sheath, condom

presidencia [presi'ðenθja] *nf* presidency; (*de comité*) chairmanship

presidente [presi'ðente] *nmf* president; (*de comité*) chairman/woman

presidir [presi'ðir] *vt* (*dirigir*) to preside at, preside over; (: *comité*) to take the chair at; (*dominar*) to dominate, rule ▷ vi to preside; to take the chair

presión [pre'sjon] nf pressure; **presión atmosférica** atmospheric o air pressure; **presionar** vt to press; (fig) to press, put pressure on ▷ vi: **presionar para** to press for

preso, -a ['preso, a] nm/f prisoner; **tomar o llevar ~ a algn** to arrest sb, take sb prisoner

prestación [presta'θjon] nf service; (subsidio) benefit; **prestaciones** nfpl (Tec, Auto) performance features

prestado, -a [pres'taðo, a] adj on loan; **pedir ~** to borrow

prestamista [presta'mista] nmf moneylender

préstamo ['prestamo] nm loan; **préstamo hipotecario** mortgage

prestar [pres'tar] vt to lend, loan; (atención) to pay; (ayuda) to give

prestigio [pres'tixjo] nm prestige; **prestigioso, -a** adj (honorable) prestigious; (famoso, renombrado) renowned, famous

presumido, -a [presu'miðo, a] adj (persona) vain

presumir [presu'mir] vt to presume ▷ vi (tener aires) to be conceited; **presunto, -a** adj (supuesto) supposed, presumed; (así llamado) so-called; **presuntuoso, -a** adj conceited, presumptuous

presupuesto [presu'pwesto] pp de **presuponer** ▷ nm (Finanzas) budget; (estimación: de costo) estimate

pretencioso, -a [preten'θjoso, a] adj pretentious

pretender [preten'der] vt (intentar) to try to, seek to; (reivindicar) to claim; (buscar) to seek, try for; (cortejar) to woo, court; **~ que** to expect that

> No confundir **pretender** con la palabra inglesa pretend.

pretendiente nmf (amante) suitor; (al trono) pretender; **pretensión** nf (aspiración) aspiration; (reivindicación) claim; (orgullo) pretension

pretexto [pre'teksto] nm pretext; (excusa) excuse

prevención [preβen'θjon] nf prevention; (precaución) precaution

prevenido, -a [preβe'niðo, a] adj prepared, ready; (cauteloso) cautious

prevenir [preβe'nir] vt (impedir) to prevent; (predisponer) to prejudice, bias; (avisar) to warn; (preparar) to prepare, get ready; **prevenirse** vr to get ready, prepare; **~se contra** to take precautions against; **preventivo, -a** adj preventive, precautionary

prever [pre'βer] vt to foresee

previo, -a ['preβjo, a] adj (anterior) previous; (preliminar) preliminary ▷ prep: **~ acuerdo de los otros** subject to the agreement of the others

previsión [preβi'sjon] nf (perspicacia) foresight; (predicción) forecast; **previsto, -a** adj anticipated, forecast

prima ['prima] nf (Com) bonus; (de seguro) premium; V tb **primo**

primario, -a [pri'marjo, a] adj primary

primavera [prima'βera] nf spring(-time)

primera [pri'mera] nf (Auto) first gear; (Ferro: tb: **~ clase**) first class; **de ~** (fam) first-class, first-rate

Primer Ministro [pri'mer-] nm Prime Minister

primero, -a [pri'mero, a] (adj **primer**) first; (principal) prime adv first; (más bien) sooner, rather; **primera plana** front page

primitivo, -a [primi'tiβo, a] adj primitive; (original) original

primo, -a ['primo, a] adj prime ▷ nm/f cousin; (fam) fool, idiot; **materias primas** raw materials; **primo hermano** first cousin

primogénito, -a [primo'xenito, a] adj first-born

primoroso, -a [primo'roso, a] adj exquisite, delicate

princesa [prin'θesa] nf princess

principal [prinθi'pal] adj principal,

main ▷ nm (jefe) chief, principal
príncipe ['prinθipe] nm prince
principiante [prinθi'pjante] nmf
beginner
principio [prin'θipjo] nm (comienzo)
beginning, start; (origen) origin;
(primera etapa) rudiment, basic idea;
(moral) principle; **desde el ~** from the
first; **en un ~** at first; **a ~s de** at the
beginning of
pringue ['pringe] nm (grasa) grease,
fat, dripping
prioridad [priori'ðað] nf priority
prisa ['prisa] nf (apresuramiento) hurry,
haste; (rapidez) speed; (urgencia) (sense
of) urgency; **a o de ~** quickly; **correr
~** to be urgent; **darse ~** to hurry up;
tener ~ to be in a hurry
prisión [pri'sjon] nf (cárcel) prison;
(período de cárcel) imprisonment;
prisionero, -a nm/f prisoner
prismáticos [pris'matikos] nmpl
binoculars
privado, -a [pri'βaðo, a] adj private
privar [pri'βar] vt to deprive;
privativo, -a adj exclusive
privilegiar [priβile'xjar] vt to grant
a privilege to; (favorecer) to favour
privilegio [priβi'lexjo] nm privilege;
(concesión) concession
pro [pro] nm o f profit, advantage
▷ prep: **asociación ~ ciegos**
association for the blind ▷ prefijo: **~
americano** pro-American; **en ~ de** on
behalf of, for; **los ~s y los contras** the
pros and cons
proa ['proa] nf bow, prow; **de ~** bow
cpd, fore
probabilidad [proβaβili'ðað] nf
probability, likelihood; (oportunidad,
posibilidad) chance, prospect; **probable**
adj probable, likely
probador [proβa'ðor] nm (en tienda)
fitting room
probar [pro'βar] vt (demostrar) to
prove; (someter a prueba) to test, try out;
(ropa) to try on; (comida) to taste ▷ vi to
try; **~se un traje** to try on a suit

probeta [pro'βeta] nf test tube
problema [pro'βlema] nm problem
procedente [proθe'ðente] adj
(razonable) reasonable; (conforme a
derecho) proper, fitting; **~ de** coming
from, originating in
proceder [proθe'ðer] vi (avanzar) to
proceed; (actuar) to act; (ser correcto)
to be right (and proper), be fitting
▷ nm (comportamiento) behaviour,
conduct; **~ de** to come from, originate
in; **procedimiento** nm procedure;
(proceso) process; (método) means pl,
method
procesador [proθesa'ðor] nm
processor; **procesador de textos** word
processor
procesar [proθe'sar] vt to try, put
on trial
procesión [proθe'sjon] nf procession
proceso [pro'θeso] nm process;
(Jur) trial
proclamar [prokla'mar] vt to
proclaim
procrear [prokre'ar] vt, vi to
procreate
procurador, a [prokura'ðor, a] nm/f
attorney
procurar [proku'rar] vt (intentar)
to try, endeavour; (conseguir) to get,
obtain; (asegurar) to secure; (producir)
to produce
prodigio [pro'ðixjo] nm prodigy;
(milagro) wonder, marvel; **prodigioso,
-a** adj prodigious, marvellous
pródigo, -a ['proðixo, a] adj: **hijo ~**
prodigal son
producción [proðuk'θjon] nf
(gen) production; (producto) output;
producción en serie mass production
producir [proðu'θir] vt to produce;
(causar) to cause, bring about;
producirse vr (cambio) to come about;
(accidente) to take place; (problema etc)
to arise; (hacerse) to be produced, be
made; (estallar) to break out
productividad [proðuktiβi'ðað]
nf productivity; **productivo, -a** adj

productive; (*provechoso*) profitable
producto [pro'ðukto] *nm* product
productor, a [proðuk'tor, a] *adj*
productive, producing ▷ *nm/f* producer
proeza [pro'eθa] *nf* exploit, feat
profano, -a [pro'fano, a] *adj* profane
▷ *nm/f* layman/woman
profecía [profe'θia] *nf* prophecy
profesión [profe'sjon] *nf* profession;
(*en formulario*) occupation; **profesional**
adj professional
profesor, a [profe'sor, a] *nm/f*
teacher; **profesorado** *nm* teaching
profession
profeta [pro'feta] *nmf* prophet
prófugo, -a ['profuxo, a] *nm/f*
fugitive; (*Mil: desertor*) deserter
profundidad [profundi'ðað] *nf*
depth; **profundizar** *vi*: **profundizar**
en to go deeply into; **profundo, -a** *adj*
deep; (*misterio, pensador*) profound
progenitor [proxeni'tor] *nm*
ancestor; **progenitores** *nmpl* (*padres*)
parents
programa [pro'xrama] *nm*
programme (BRIT), program (US);
programa de estudios curriculum,
syllabus; **programación** *nf*
programming; **programador, a**
nm/f programmer; **programar** *vt* to
program
progresar [proxre'sar] *vi* to
progress, make progress; **progresista**
adj, nmf progressive; **progresivo,**
-a *adj* progressive; (*gradual*) gradual;
(*continuo*) continuous; **progreso** *nm*
progress
prohibición [proiβi'θjon] *nf*
prohibition, ban
prohibir [proi'βir] *vt* to prohibit, ban,
forbid; **prohibido o se prohibe fumar**
no smoking; **"prohibido el paso"**
"no entry"
prójimo, -a ['proximo, a] *nm/f*
fellow man; (*vecino*) neighbour
prólogo ['proloxo] *nm* prologue
prolongar [prolon'xar] *vt* to extend;
(*reunión etc*) to prolong; (*calle, tubo*)

to extend
promedio [pro'meðjo] *nm* average;
(*de distancia*) middle, mid-point
promesa [pro'mesa] *nf* promise
prometer [prome'ter] *vt* to promise
▷ *vi* to show promise; **prometerse** *vr*
(*novios*) to get engaged; **prometido,**
-a *adj* promised; engaged ▷ *nm/f*
fiancé/fiancée
prominente [promi'nente] *adj*
prominent
promoción [promo'θjon] *nf*
promotion
promotor [promo'tor] *nm* promoter;
(*instigador*) instigator
promover [promo'βer] *vt* to
promote; (*causar*) to cause; (*instigar*) to
instigate, stir up
promulgar [promul'xar] *vt* to
promulgate; (*anunciar*) to proclaim
pronombre [pro'nombre] *nm*
pronoun
pronosticar [pronosti'kar] *vt* to
predict, foretell, forecast; **pronóstico**
nm prediction, forecast; **pronóstico**
del tiempo weather forecast
pronto, -a ['pronto, a] *adj* (*rápido*)
prompt, quick; (*preparado*) ready ▷ *adv*
quickly, promptly; (*en seguida*) at once,
right away; (*dentro de poco*) soon;
(*temprano*) early ▷ *nm*: **tiene unos**
~s muy malos he gets ratty all of a
sudden (*inf*); **de ~** suddenly; **por lo ~**
meanwhile, for the present
pronunciación [pronunθja'θjon] *nf*
pronunciation
pronunciar [pronun'θjar] *vt* to
pronounce; (*discurso*) to make, deliver;
pronunciarse *vr* to revolt, rebel;
(*declararse*) to declare o.s.
propagación [propaxa'θjon] *nf*
propagation
propaganda [propa'xanda] *nf* (*Pol*)
propaganda; (*Com*) advertising
propenso, -a [pro'penso, a] *adj*
inclined to; **ser ~ a** to be inclined to,
have a tendency to
propicio, -a [pro'piθjo, a] *adj*

favourable, propitious

propiedad [propje'ðað] nf property; (posesión) possession, ownership; **propiedad particular** private property

propietario, -a [propje'tarjo, a] nm/f owner, proprietor

propina [pro'pina] nf tip

propio, -a ['propjo, a] adj own, of one's own; (característico) characteristic, typical; (debido) proper; (mismo) selfsame, very; **el ~ ministro** the minister himself; **¿tienes casa propia?** have you a house of your own?

proponer [propo'ner] vt to propose, put forward; (problema) to pose; **proponerse** vr to propose, intend

proporción [propor'θjon] nf proportion; (Mat) ratio; **proporciones** nfpl (dimensiones) dimensions; (fig) size sg; **proporcionado, -a** adj proportionate (regular) medium, middling; (justo) just right; **proporcionar** vt (dar) to give, supply, provide

proposición [proposi'θjon] nf proposition; (propuesta) proposal

propósito [pro'posito] nm purpose; (intento) aim, intention ▷ adv: **a ~** by the way, incidentally; (a posta) on purpose, deliberately; **a ~ de** about, with regard to

propuesta [pro'pwesta] vb V **proponer** ▷ nf proposal

propulsar [propul'sar] vt to drive, propel; (fig) to promote, encourage; **propulsión** nf propulsion; **propulsión a chorro o por reacción** jet propulsion

prórroga ['prorroxa] nf extension; (Jur) stay; (Com) deferment; (Deporte) extra time; **prorrogar** vt (período) to extend; (decisión) to defer, postpone

prosa ['prosa] nf prose

proseguir [prose'xir] vt to continue, carry on ▷ vi to continue, go on

prospecto [pros'pekto] nm prospectus

prosperar [prospe'rar] vi to prosper, thrive, flourish; **prosperidad** nf prosperity; (éxito) success; **próspero,**

-a adj prosperous, flourishing; (que tiene éxito) successful

prostíbulo [pros'tiβulo] nm brothel (BRIT), house of prostitution (US)

prostitución [prostitu'θjon] nf prostitution

prostituir [prosti'twir] vt to prostitute; **prostituirse** vr to prostitute o.s., become a prostitute

prostituta [prosti'tuta] nf prostitute

protagonista [protaɣo'nista] nmf protagonist

protección [protek'θjon] nf protection

protector, a [protek'tor, a] adj protective, protecting ▷ nm/f protector

proteger [prote'xer] vt to protect; **protegido, -a** nm/f protégé/protégée

proteína [prote'ina] nf protein

protesta [pro'testa] nf protest; (declaración) protestation

protestante [protes'tante] adj Protestant

protestar [protes'tar] vt to protest, declare ▷ vi to protest

protocolo [proto'kolo] nm protocol

prototipo [proto'tipo] nm prototype

provecho [pro'βetʃo] nm advantage, benefit; (Finanzas) profit; **¡buen ~!** bon appétit!; **en ~ de** to the benefit of; **sacar ~ de** to benefit from, profit by

provenir [proβe'nir] vi: **~ de** to come o stem from

proverbio [pro'βerβjo] nm proverb

providencia [proβi'ðenθja] nf providence

provincia [pro'βinθja] nf province

provisión [proβi'sjon] nf provision; (abastecimiento) provision, supply; (medida) measure, step

provisional [proβisjo'nal] adj provisional

provocar [proβo'kar] vt to provoke; (alentar) to tempt, invite; (causar) to bring about, lead to; (promover) to promote; (estimular) to rouse, stimulate; **¿te provoca un café?** (CAM) would you like a coffee?; **provocativo,**

-a *adj* provocative

proxeneta [prokse'neta] *nm* pimp

próximamente [proksima'mente] *adv* shortly, soon

proximidad [proksimi'ðað] *nf* closeness, proximity; (*cercanía*) -a *adj* near, close; (*vecino*) neighbouring; (*siguiente*) next

proyectar [projek'tar] *vt* (*objeto*) to hurl, throw; (*luz*) to cast, shed; (*Cine*) to screen, show; (*planear*) to plan

proyectil [projek'til] *nm* projectile, missile

proyecto [pro'jekto] *nm* plan; (*estimación de costo*) detailed estimate

proyector [projek'tor] *nm* (*Cine*) projector

prudencia [pru'ðenθja] *nf* (*sabiduría*) wisdom; (*cuidado*) care; **prudente** *adj* sensible, wise; (*conductor*) careful

prueba *etc* ['prweßa] *vb* V **probar** ⊳ *nf* proof; (*ensayo*) test, trial; (*degustación*) tasting, sampling; (*de ropa*) fitting; **a ~** on trial; **a ~ de** proof against; **a ~ de agua/fuego** waterproof/fireproof; **someter a ~** to put to the test

psico... [siko] *prefijo* psycho...; **psicología** *nf* psychology; **psicológico, -a** *adj* psychological; **psicólogo, -a** *nm/f* psychologist; **psicópata** *nmf* psychopath; **psicosis** *nf inv* psychosis

psiquiatra [si'kjatra] *nmf* psychiatrist; **psiquiátrico, -a** *adj* psychiatric

PSOE [pe'soe] (*ESP*) *nm abr* = **Partido Socialista Obrero Español**

púa ['pua] *nf* (*Bot, Zool*) prickle, spine; (*para guitarra*) plectrum (*BRIT*), pick (*US*); **alambre de ~** barbed wire

pubertad [pußer'tað] *nf* puberty

publicación [pußlika'θjon] *nf* publication

publicar [pußli'kar] *vt* (*editar*) to publish; (*hacer público*) to publicize; (*divulgar*) to make public, divulge

publicidad [pußliθi'ðað] *nf* publicity; (*Com: propaganda*)

advertising; **publicitario, -a** *adj* publicity *cpd*; advertising *cpd*

público, -a ['pußliko, a] *adj* public ⊳ *nm* public; (*Teatro etc*) audience

puchero [pu'tʃero] *nm* (*Culin: guiso*) stew; (*: olla*) cooking pot; **hacer ~s** to pout

pucho ['putʃo] (*cs: fam*) *nm* cigarette, fag (*BRIT*)

pude *etc* *vb* V **poder**

pudiente [pu'ðjente] *adj* (*rico*) wealthy, well-to-do

pudiera *etc* *vb* V **poder**

pudor [pu'ðor] *nm* modesty

pudrir [pu'ðrir] *vt* to rot; **pudrirse** *vr* to rot, decay

pueblo ['pweßlo] *nm* people; (*nación*) nation; (*aldea*) village

puedo *etc* *vb* V **poder**

puente ['pwente] *nm* bridge; **hacer ~** (*fam*) to take extra days off work between 2 public holidays; to take a long weekend; **puente aéreo** shuttle service; **puente colgante** suspension bridge; **puente levadizo** drawbridge

● **HACER PUENTE**
●
● When a public holiday in Spain
● falls on a Tuesday or Thursday it is
● common practice for employers
● to make the Monday or Friday
● a holiday as well and to give
● everyone a four-day weekend. This
● is known as **hacer puente**. When
● a named public holiday such as the
● **Día de la Constitución** falls on a
● Tuesday or Thursday, people refer
● to the whole holiday period as e.g.
● the **puente de la Constitución**.

puerco, -a ['pwerko, a] *nm/f* pig/ sow ⊳ *adj* (*sucio*) dirty, filthy; (*obsceno*) disgusting; **puerco espín** porcupine

pueril [pwe'ril] *adj* childish

puerro ['pwerro] *nm* leek

puerta ['pwerta] *nf* door; (*de jardín*) gate; (*portal*) doorway; (*fig*) gateway (*portería*) goal; **a la ~** at the door; **a ~ cerrada** behind closed doors; **puerta giratoria** revolving door

puerto ['pwerto] *nm* port; (*paso*) pass; (*fig*) haven, refuge

Puerto Rico ['pwerto'riko] *nm* Puerto Rico; **puertorriqueño, -a** *adj, nm/f* Puerto Rican

pues [pwes] *adv* (*entonces*) then; (*bueno*) well, well then; (*así que*) so ▷ *conj* (*ya que*) since; **¡~ sí!** yes!, certainly!

puesta ['pwesta] *nf* (*apuesta*) bet, stake; **puesta al día** updating; **puesta a punto** fine tuning; **puesta de sol** sunset; **puesta en marcha** start

puesto, -a ['pwesto, a] *pp de* **poner**
▷ *adj*: **tener algo ~** to have sth on, be wearing sth ▷ *nm* (*lugar, posición*) place; (*trabajo*) post, job; (*Com*) stall
▷ *conj*: **~ que** since, as

púgil ['puxil] *nm* boxer

pulga ['pulɣa] *nf* flea

pulgada [pul'ɣaða] *nf* inch

pulgar [pul'ɣar] *nm* thumb

pulir [pu'lir] *vt* to polish; (*alisar*) to smooth; (*fig*) to polish up, touch up

pulmón [pul'mon] *nm* lung; **pulmonía** *nf* pneumonia

pulpa ['pulpa] *nf* pulp; (*de fruta*) flesh, soft part

pulpería [pulpe'ria] (*LAM*) *nf* (*tienda*) small grocery store

púlpito ['pulpito] *nm* pulpit

pulpo ['pulpo] *nm* octopus

pulque ['pulke] *nm* pulque

> **PULQUE**
>
> **Pulque** is a thick, white, alcoholic drink which is very popular in Mexico. In ancient times it was considered sacred by the Aztecs. It is produced by fermenting the juice of the **maguey**, a Mexican cactus similar to the agave. It can be drunk by itself or mixed with fruit or vegetable juice.

pulsación [pulsa'θjon] *nf* beat; **pulsaciones** pulse rate

pulsar [pul'sar] *vt* (*tecla*) to touch, tap; (*Mús*) to play; (*botón*) to press, push ▷ *vi* to pulsate; (*latir*) to beat, throb

pulsera [pul'sera] *nf* bracelet

pulso ['pulso] *nm* (*Anat*) pulse; (*fuerza*) strength; (*firmeza*) steadiness, steady hand

pulverizador [pulβeriθa'ðor] *nm* spray, spray gun

pulverizar [pulβeri'θar] *vt* to pulverize; (*líquido*) to spray

puna ['puna] (*CAM*) *nf* mountain sickness

punta ['punta] *nf* point, tip; (*extremo*) end; (*fig*) touch, trace; **horas ~** peak *o* rush hours; **sacar ~ a** to sharpen

puntada [pun'taða] *nf* (*Costura*) stitch

puntal [pun'tal] *nm* prop, support

puntapié [punta'pje] *nm* kick

puntería [punte'ria] *nf* (*de arma*) aim, aiming; (*destreza*) marksmanship

puntero, -a [pun'tero, a] *adj* leading
▷ *nm* (*palo*) pointer

puntiagudo, -a [puntja'ɣuðo, a] *adj* sharp, pointed

puntilla [pun'tiʎa] *nf* (*encaje*) lace edging *o* trim; **(andar) de ~s** (to walk) on tiptoe

punto ['punto] *nm* (*gen*) point; (*señal diminuta*) spot, dot; (*Costura, Med*) stitch; (*lugar*) spot, place; (*momento*) point, moment; **a ~** ready; **estar a ~ de** to be on the point of *o* about to; **en ~** on the dot; **hasta cierto ~** to some extent; **hacer ~** (*ESP: tejer*) to knit; **dos ~s** (*Ling*) colon; **punto de interrogación** question mark; **punto de vista** point of view, viewpoint; **punto final** full stop (*BRIT*), period (*US*); **punto muerto** dead center; (*Auto*) neutral (*gear*); **punto y aparte** (*en dictado*) full stop, new paragraph; **punto y coma** semicolon

puntocom [punto'kom] *adj inv, nf inv* dotcom

puntuación [puntwa'θjon] nf punctuation; (*puntos: en examen*) mark(s) (pl); (*Deporte*) score

puntual [pun'twal] adj (*a tiempo*) punctual; (*exacto*) exact, accurate; **puntualidad** nf punctuality; exactness, accuracy

puntuar [pun'twar] vi (*Deporte*) to score, count

punzante [pun'θante] adj (*dolor*) shooting, sharp; (*herramienta*) sharp

puñado [pu'naðo] nm handful

puñal [pu'nal] nm dagger; **puñalada** nf stab

puñetazo [pune'taθo] nm punch

puño ['puno] nm (*Anat*) fist; (*cantidad*) fistful, handful; (*Costura*) cuff; (*de herramienta*) handle

pupila [pu'pila] nf pupil

pupitre [pu'pitre] nm desk

puré [pu're] nm purée; (*sopa*) (thick) soup; **puré de papas** (LAM) mashed potatoes; **puré de patatas** (ESP) mashed potatoes

purga ['purva] nf purge; **purgante** adj, nm purgative

purgatorio [purva'torjo] nm purgatory

purificar [purifi'kar] vt to purify; (*refinar*) to refine

puritano, -a [puri'tano, a] adj (*actitud*) puritanical; (*iglesia, tradición*) puritan ▷ nm/f puritan

puro, -a ['puro, a] adj pure; (*verdad*) simple, plain ▷ nm cigar

púrpura ['purpura] nf purple

pus [pus] nm pus

puse etc vb V **poder**

pusiera etc vb V **poder**

puta ['puta] (fam!) nf whore, prostitute

putrefacción [putrefak'θjon] nf rotting, putrefaction

PVP nm abr (= *precio de venta al público*) RRP

pyme, PYME ['pime] nf abr (= *Pequeña y Mediana Empresa*) SME

q

PALABRA CLAVE

que [ke] conj 1 (*con oración subordinada: muchas veces no se traduce*) that; **dijo que vendría** he said (that) he would come; **espero que lo encuentres** I hope (that) you find it; V tb **el**

2 (*en oración independiente*): **¡que entre!** send him in; **¡que aproveche!** enjoy your meal!; **¡que se mejore tu padre!** I hope your father gets better

3 (*enfático*): **¿me quieres? - ¡que sí!** do you love me? - of course!

4 (*consecutivo: muchas veces no se traduce*) that; **es tan grande que no lo puedo levantar** it's so big (that) I can't lift it

5 (*comparaciones*) than; **yo que tú/él** if I were you/him; V tb **más, menos, mismo**

6 (*valor disyuntivo*): **que le guste o no** whether he likes it or not; **que venga o que no venga** whether he comes or not

7 (*porque*): **no puedo, que tengo que quedarme en casa** I can't, I've got to stay in
▷ *pron* **1** (*cosa*) that, which; (+ *prep*) which; **el sombrero que te compraste** the hat (that o which) you bought; **la cama en que dormí** the bed (that o which) I slept in
2 (*persona: suj*) that, who; (: *objeto*) that, whom; **el amigo que me acompañó al museo** the friend that o who went to the museum with me; **la chica que invité** the girl (the whom) I invited

qué [ke] *adj* what?, which? ▷ *pron* what?; **¡~ divertido!** how funny!; **¿~ edad tienes?** how old are you?; **¿de ~ me hablas?** what are you saying to me?; **¿~ tal?** how are you?, how are things?; **¿~ hay (de nuevo)?** what's new?

quebrado, -a [ke'βraðo, a] *adj* (*roto*) broken ▷ *nm/f* bankrupt ▷ *nm* (*Mat*) fraction

quebrantar [keβran'tar] *vt* (*infringir*) to violate, transgress

quebrar [ke'βrar] *vt* to break, smash ▷ *vi* to go bankrupt

quedar [ke'ðar] *vi* to stay, remain; (*encontrarse: sitio*) to be; (*haber aún*) to remain, to be left; **quedarse** *vr* to remain, stay (behind); **~se (con) algo** to keep sth; **~ en** (*acordar*) to agree on/to; **~ en nada** to come to nothing; **~ por hacer** to be still to be done; **~ ciego/mudo** to be left blind/dumb; **no te queda bien ese vestido** that dress doesn't suit you; **eso queda muy lejos** that's a long way (away); **quedamos a las seis** we agreed to meet at six

quedo, -a [ke'ðo, a] *adj* still ▷ *adv* softly, gently

quehacer [kea'θer] *nm* task, job; **quehaceres (domésticos)** *nmpl* household chores

queja ['kexa] *nf* complaint; **quejarse** *vr* (*enfermo*) to moan, groan; (*protestar*) to complain; **quejarse de que** to

complain (about the fact) that;
quejido *nm* moan

quemado, -a [ke'maðo, a] *adj* burnt

quemadura [kema'ðura] *nf* burn, scald

quemar [ke'mar] *vt* to burn; (*fig: malgastar*) to burn up, squander ▷ *vi* to be burning hot; **quemarse** *vr* (*consumirse*) to burn (up); (*del sol*) to get sunburnt

quemarropa [kema'rropa]: **a ~** *adv* point-blank

quepo *etc vb V* **caber**

querella [ke'reʎa] *nf* (*Jur*) charge; (*disputa*) dispute

○ **PALABRA CLAVE**

querer [ke'rer] *vt* **1** (*desear*) to want; **quiero más dinero** I want more money; **quisiera o querría un té** I'd like a tea; **sin querer** unintentionally; **quiero ayudar/que vayas** I want to help/you to go
2 (*preguntas: para pedir algo*): **¿quiere abrir la ventana?** could you open the window?; **¿quieres echarme una mano?** can you give me a hand?
3 (*amar*) to love; (*tener cariño a*) to be fond of; **te quiere mucho** he/she loves you; **quiere mucho a sus hijos** he's very fond of his children
4 **le pedí que me dejara ir pero no quiso** I asked him to let me go but he refused

querido, -a [ke'riðo, a] *adj* dear ▷ *nm/f* darling; (*amante*) lover

queso ['keso] *nm* cheese; **queso crema** (*LAM*) cream cheese; **queso de untar** (*ESP*) cream cheese; **queso manchego** *sheep's milk cheese made in La Mancha*; **queso rallado** grated cheese

quicio ['kiθjo] *nm* hinge; **sacar a algn de ~** to get on sb's nerves

quiebra ['kjeβra] *nf* break, split; (*Com*) bankruptcy; (*Econ*) slump

quiebro ['kjeβro] *nm* (*del cuerpo*)

swerve

quien [kjen] *pron* who; **hay ~ piensa que** there are those who think that; **no hay ~ lo haga** no-one will do it

quién [kjen] *pron* who, whom; **¿~ es?** who's there?

quienquiera [kjen'kjera] (*pl* **quienesquiera**) *pron* whoever

quiero *etc vb* V **querer**

quieto, -a ['kjeto, a] *adj* still; (*carácter*) placid

> No confundir *quieto* con la palabra inglesa *quiet*.

quietud *nf* stillness

quilate [ki'late] *nm* carat

químico, -a ['kimiko, a] *adj* chemical ▷ *nm/f* chemist ▷ *nf* chemistry

quincalla [kin'kaʎa] *nf* hardware, ironmongery (BRIT)

quince ['kinθe] *num* fifteen; **~ días** a fortnight; **quinceañero, -a** *nm/f* teenager; **quincena** *nf* fortnight; (*pago*) fortnightly pay; **quincenal** *adj* fortnightly

quiniela [ki'njela] *nf* football pools *pl*; **quinielas** *nfpl* (*impreso*) pools coupon *sg*

quinientos, -as [ki'njentos, as] *adj, num* five hundred

quinto, -a ['kinto, a] *adj* fifth ▷ *nf* country house; (*Mil*) call-up, draft

quiosco ['kjosko] *nm* (*de música*) bandstand; (*de periódicos*) news stand

quirófano [ki'rofano] *nm* operating theatre

quirúrgico, -a [ki'rurxiko, a] *adj* surgical

quise *etc vb* V **querer**

quisiera *etc vb* V **querer**

quisquilloso, -a [kiski'ʎoso, a] *adj* (*susceptible*) touchy; (*meticuloso*) pernickety

quiste ['kiste] *nm* cyst

quitaesmalte [kitaes'malte] *nm* nail-polish remover

quitamanchas [kita'mantʃas] *nm inv* stain remover

quitanieves [kita'njeβes] *nm inv* snowplough (BRIT), snowplow (US)

quitar [ki'tar] *vt* to remove, take away; (*ropa*) to take off; (*dolor*) to relieve; **¡quita de ahí!** get away!; **quitarse** *vr* to withdraw; (*ropa*) to take off; **se quitó el sombrero** he took off his hat

Quito ['kito] *n* Quito

quizá(s) [ki'θa(s)] *adv* perhaps, maybe

r

rábano ['raβano] nm radish; **me importa un ~** I don't give a damn

rabia ['raβja] nf (Med) rabies sg; (ira) fury, rage; **rabiar** vi to have rabies; to rage, be furious; **rabiar por algo** to long for sth

rabieta [ra'βjeta] nf tantrum, fit of temper

rabino [ra'βino] nm rabbi

rabioso, -a [ra'βjoso, a] adj rabid; (fig) furious

rabo ['raβo] nm tail

racha ['ratʃa] nf gust of wind; **buena/mala ~** spell of good/bad luck

racial [ra'θjal] adj racial, race cpd

racimo [ra'θimo] nm bunch

ración [ra'θjon] nf portion; **raciones** nfpl rations

racional [raθjo'nal] adj (razonable) reasonable; (lógico) rational

racionar [raθjo'nar] vt to ration (out)

racismo [ra'θismo] nm racism; **racista** adj, nmf racist

radar [ra'ðar] nm radar

radiador [raðja'ðor] nm radiator

radiante [ra'ðjante] adj radiant

radical [raði'kal] adj, nmf radical

radicar [raði'kar] vi: **~ en** (dificultad, problema) to lie in; (solución) to consist in

radio ['raðjo] nf radio; (aparato) radio (set) ▷ nm (Mat) radius; (Quím) radium; **radioactividad** nf radioactivity; **radioactivo, -a** adj radioactive; **radiografía** nf X-ray; **radioterapia** nf radiotherapy; **radioyente** nmf listener

ráfaga ['rafaɣa] nf gust; (de luz) flash; (de tiros) burst

raíz [ra'iθ] nf root; **a ~ de** as a result of; **raíz cuadrada** square root

raja ['raxa] nf (de melón etc) slice; (grieta) crack; **rajar** vt to split; (fam) to slash; **rajarse** vr to split, crack; **rajarse de** to back out of

rajatabla [raxa'taβla]: **a ~** adv (estrictamente) strictly, to the letter

rallador [raʎa'ðor] nm grater

rallar [ra'ʎar] vt to grate

rama ['rama] nf branch; **ramaje** nm branches pl, foliage; **ramal** nm (de cuerda) strand; (Ferro) branch line (BRIT); (Auto) branch (road) (BRIT)

rambla ['rambla] nf (avenida) avenue

ramo ['ramo] nm branch; (sección) department, section

rampa ['rampa] nf ramp; **rampa de acceso** entrance ramp

rana ['rana] nf frog; **salto de ~** leapfrog

ranchero [ran'tʃero] nm (MÉX) (hacendado) rancher; smallholder

rancho ['rantʃo] nm (grande) ranch; (pequeño) small farm

rancio, -a ['ranθjo, a] adj (comestibles) rancid; (vino) aged, mellow; (fig) ancient

rango ['rango] nm rank, standing

ranura [ra'nura] nf groove; (de teléfono etc) slot

rapar [ra'par] vt to shave; (los cabellos) to crop

rapaz [ra'paθ] (nf **-a**) nmf young

boy/girl ⊳ *adj* (*Zool*) predatory
rape ['rape] *nm* (*pez*) monkfish; **al ~ cropped**
rapé [ra'pe] *nm* snuff
rapidez [rapi'ðeθ] *nf* speed, rapidity; **rápido, -a** *adj* fast, quick ⊳ *adv* quickly ⊳ *nm* (*Ferro*) express; **rápidos** *nmpl* rapids
rapiña [ra'piɲa] *nm* robbery; **ave de ~** bird of prey
raptar [rap'tar] *vt* to kidnap; **rapto** *nm* kidnapping; (*impulso*) sudden impulse; (*éxtasis*) ecstasy, rapture
raqueta [ra'keta] *nf* racquet
raquítico, -a [ra'kitiko, a] *adj* stunted; (*fig*) poor, inadequate
rareza [ra'reθa] *nf* rarity; (*fig*) eccentricity
raro, -a ['raro, a] *adj* (*poco común*) rare; (*extraño*) odd, strange; (*excepcional*) remarkable
ras [ras] *nm*: **a ~** level with; **a ~ de tierra** at ground level
rasar [ra'sar] *vt* (*igualar*) to level
rascacielos [raska'θjelos] *nm inv* skyscraper
rascar [ras'kar] *vt* (*con las uñas etc*) to scratch; (*raspar*) to scrape; **rascarse** *vr* to scratch (o.s.)
rasgar [ras'ɣar] *vt* to tear, rip (up)
rasgo ['rasɣo] *nm* (*con pluma*) stroke; **rasgos** *nmpl* (*facciones*) features, characteristics; **a grandes ~s** in outline, broadly
rasguño [ras'ɣuɲo] *nm* scratch
raso, -a ['raso, a] *adj* (*liso*) flat, level; (*a baja altura*) very low ⊳ *nm* satin; **cielo ~** clear sky
raspadura [raspa'ðura] *nf* (*acto*) scrape, scraping; (*marca*) scratch; **raspaduras** *nfpl* (*de papel etc*) scrapings
raspar [ras'par] *vt* to scrape; (*arañar*) to scratch; (*limar*) to file
rastra ['rastra] *nf* (*Agr*) rake; **a ~s** by dragging; (*fig*) unwillingly
rastrear [rastre'ar] *vt* (*seguir*) to track
rastrero, -a [ras'trero, a] *adj* (*Bot*,

Zool) creeping; (*fig*) despicable, mean
rastrillo [ras'triʎo] *nm* rake
rastro ['rastro] *nm* (*Agr*) rake; (*pista*) track, trail; (*vestigio*) trace; **el R~** (*ESP*) the Madrid fleamarket
rasurado [rasu'raðo] (*MÉX*) *nm* shaving; **rasuradora** [rasura'ðora] *nf* electric shaver; **rasurar** [rasu'rar] (*MÉX*) *vt* to shave; **rasurarse** *vr* to shave
rata ['rata] *nf* rat
ratear [rate'ar] *vt* (*robar*) to steal
ratero, -a [ra'tero, a] *adj* light-fingered ⊳ *nm/f* (*carterista*) pickpocket; (*ladrón*) petty thief
rato ['rato] *nm* while, short time; **a ~s** from time to time; **hay para ~** there's still a long way to go; **al poco ~** soon afterwards; **pasar el ~** to kill time; **pasar un buen/mal ~** to have a good/rough time; **en mis ~s libres** in my spare time
ratón [ra'ton] *nm* mouse; **ratonera** *nf* mousetrap
raudal [rau'ðal] *nm* torrent; **a ~es** in abundance
raya ['raja] *nf* line; (*marca*) scratch; (*en tela*) stripe; (*de pelo*) parting; (*límite*) boundary; (*pez*) ray; (*puntuación*) dash; **a ~s** striped; **pasarse de la ~** to go too far; **tener a ~** to keep in check; **rayar** *vt* to line; to scratch; (*subrayar*) to underline ⊳ *vi*: **rayar en o con** to border on
rayo ['rajo] *nm* (*del sol*) ray, beam; (*de luz*) shaft; (*en una tormenta*) (flash of) lightning; **rayos X** X-rays
raza ['raθa] *nf* race; **raza humana** human race
razón [ra'θon] *nf* reason; (*justicia*) right, justice; (*razonamiento*) reasoning; (*motivo*) reason, motive; (*Mat*) ratio; **a ~ de 10 cada día** at the rate of 10 a day; **en ~ de** with regard to; **dar ~ a algn** to agree that sb is right; **tener ~** to be right; **razón de ser** raison d'être; **razón directa/inversa** direct/inverse proportion; **razonable**

adj reasonable; (*justo, moderado*) fair; **razonamiento** nm (*juicio*) judg(e)ment; (*argumento*) reasoning; **razonar** vt, vi to reason, argue

re [re] nm (*Mús*) D

reacción [reak'θjon] nf reaction; **avión a ~** jet plane; **reacción en cadena** chain reaction; **reaccionar** vi to react

reacio, -a [re'aθjo, a] adj stubborn

reactivar [reakti'βar] vt to revitalize

reactor [reak'tor] nm reactor

real [re'al] adj real; (*del rey, fig*) royal

realidad [reali'ðað] nf reality, fact; (*verdad*) truth

realista [rea'lista] nmf realist

realización [realiθa'θjon] nf fulfilment

realizador, a [realiθa'ðor, a] nm/f film-maker

realizar [reali'θar] vt (*objetivo*) to achieve; (*plan*) to carry out; (*viaje*) to make, undertake; **realizarse** vr to come about, come true

realmente [real'mente] adv really, actually

realzar [real'θar] vt to enhance; (*acentuar*) to highlight

reanimar [reani'mar] vt to revive; (*alentar*) to encourage; **reanimarse** vr to revive

reanudar [reanu'ðar] vt (*renovar*) to renew; (*historia, viaje*) to resume

reaparición [reapari'θjon] nf reappearance

rearme [re'arme] nm rearmament

rebaja [re'βaxa] nf (*Com*) reduction; (*: descuento*) discount; **rebajas** nfpl (*Com*) sale; **rebajar** vt (*bajar*) to lower; (*reducir*) to reduce; (*disminuir*) to lessen; (*humillar*) to humble

rebanada [reβa'naða] nf slice

rebañar [reβa'nar] vt (*comida*) to scrape up; (*plato*) to scrape clean

rebaño [re'βaɲo] nm herd; (*de ovejas*) flock

rebatir [reβa'tir] vt to refute

rebeca [re'βeka] nf cardigan

rebelarse [reβe'larse] vr to rebel, revolt

rebelde [re'βelde] adj rebellious; (*niño*) unruly ▷ nmf rebel; **rebeldía** nf rebelliousness; (*desobediencia*) disobedience

rebelión [reβe'ljon] nf rebellion

reblandecer [reβlande'θer] vt to soften

rebobinar [reβoβi'nar] vt (*cinta, película de vídeo*) to rewind

rebosante [reβo'sante] adj overflowing

rebosar [reβo'sar] vi (*líquido, recipiente*) to overflow; (*abundar*) to abound, be plentiful

rebotar [reβo'tar] vt to bounce; (*rechazar*) to repel ▷ vi (*pelota*) to bounce; (*bala*) to ricochet; **rebote** nm rebound; **de rebote** on the rebound

rebozado, -a [reβo'θaðo, a] adj fried in batter o breadcrumbs

rebozar [reβo'θar] vt to wrap up; (*Culin*) to fry in batter o breadcrumbs

rebuscado, -a [reβus'kaðo, a] adj (*amanerado*) affected; (*palabra*) recherché; (*idea*) far-fetched

rebuscar [reβus'kar] vi: **~ (en/por)** to search carefully (in/for)

recado [re'kaðo] nm (*mensaje*) message; (*encargo*) errand; **tomar un ~** (*Tel*) to take a message

recaer [reka'er] vi to relapse; **~ en** to fall to o on; (*criminal etc*) to fall back into, relapse into; **recaída** nf relapse

recalcar [rekal'kar] vt (*fig*) to stress, emphasize

recalentar [rekalen'tar] vt (*volver a calentar*) to reheat; (*calentar demasiado*) to overheat

recámara [re'kamara] (*MÉX*) nf bedroom

recambio [re'kambjo] nm spare; (*de pluma*) refill

recapacitar [rekapaθi'tar] vi to reflect

recargado, -a [rekar'γaðo, a] adj overloaded

recargar [rekar'ɣar] vt to overload; (batería) to recharge; **~ el saldo de** (Tel) to top up; **recargo** nm surcharge; (aumento) increase

recatado, -a [reka'taðo, a] adj (modesto) modest, demure; (prudente) cautious

recaudación [rekauða'θjon] nf (acción) collection; (cantidad) takings pl; (en deporte) gate; **recaudador, a** nm/f tax collector

recelar [reθe'lar] vt: **~ que ...** (sospechar) to suspect that ...; (temer) to fear that ... ▷ vi: **~ de** to distrust; **recelo** nm distrust, suspicion

recepción [reθep'θjon] nf reception; **recepcionista** nmf receptionist

receptor, a [reθep'tor, a] nm/f recipient ▷ nm (Tel) receiver

recesión [reθe'sjon] nf (Com) recession

receta [re'θeta] nf (Culin) recipe; (Med) prescription

No confundir **receta** con la palabra inglesa receipt.

rechazar [retʃa'θar] vt to reject; (oferta) to turn down; (ataque) to repel

rechazo [re'tʃaθo] nm rejection

rechinar [retʃi'nar] vi to creak; (dientes) to grind

rechistar [retʃis'tar] vi: **sin ~** without a murmur

rechoncho, -a [re'tʃontʃo, a] (fam) adj thickset (BRIT), heavy-set (US)

rechupete [retʃu'pete]: **de ~** adj (comida) delicious, scrumptious

recibidor [reθiβi'ðor] nm entrance hall

recibimiento [reθiβi'mjento] nm reception, welcome

recibir [reθi'βir] vt to receive; (dar la bienvenida) to welcome ▷ vi to entertain; **recibo** nm receipt

reciclable [reθi'klaβle] adj recyclable

reciclar [reθi'klar] vt to recycle

recién [re'θjen] adv recently, newly; **los ~ casados** the newly-weds; **el ~ llegado** the newcomer; **el ~ nacido** the

newborn child

reciente [re'θjente] adj recent; (fresco) fresh

recinto [re'θinto] nm enclosure; (área) area, place

recio, -a ['reθjo, a] adj strong, tough; (voz) loud ▷ adv hard, loud(ly)

recipiente [reθi'pjente] nm receptacle

recíproco, -a [re'θiproko, a] adj reciprocal

recital [reθi'tal] nm (Mús) recital; (Literatura) reading

recitar [reθi'tar] vt to recite

reclamación [reklama'θjon] nf claim, demand; (queja) complaint; **libro de reclamaciones** complaints book

reclamar [rekla'mar] vt to claim, demand ▷ vi: **~ contra** to complain about; **reclamo** nm (anuncio) advertisement; (tentación) attraction

reclinar [rekli'nar] vt to recline, lean; **reclinarse** vr to lean back

reclusión [reklu'sjon] nf (prisión) prison; (refugio) seclusion

recluta [re'kluta] nmf recruit ▷ nf recruitment; **reclutar** vt (datos) to collect; (dinero) to collect up; **reclutamiento** nm recruitment

recobrar [reko'βrar] vt (salud) to recover; (rescatar) to get back; **recobrarse** vr to recover

recodo [re'koðo] nm (de río, camino) bend

recogedor [rekoxe'ðor] nm dustpan

recoger [reko'xer] vt to collect; (Agr) to harvest; (levantar) to pick up; (juntar) to gather; (pasar a buscar) to come for, get; (dar asilo) to give shelter to; (faldas) to gather up; (pelo) to put up; **recogerse** vr (retirarse) to retire; **recogido, -a** adj (lugar) quiet, secluded; (pequeño) small ▷ nf (Correos) collection; (Agr) harvest

recolección [rekolek'θjon] nf (Agr) harvesting; (colecta) collection

recomendación [rekomenda'θjon] nf (sugerencia) suggestion, recommendation; (*referencia*) reference

recomendar [rekomen'dar] *vt* to suggest, recommend; (*confiar*) to entrust

recompensa [rekom'pensa] *nf* reward, recompense; **recompensar** *vt* to reward, recompense

reconciliación [rekonθilja'θjon] *nf* reconciliation

reconciliar [rekonθi'ljar] *vt* to reconcile; **reconciliarse** *vr* to become reconciled

recóndito, -a [re'kondito, a] *adj* (*lugar*) hidden, secret

reconocer [rekono'θer] *vt* to recognize; (*registrar*) to search; (*Med*) to examine; **reconocido, -a** *adj* recognized; (*agradecido*) grateful; **reconocimiento** *nm* recognition; search; examination; gratitude; (*confesión*) admission

reconquista [rekon'kista] *nf* reconquest; **la R~** the Reconquest (of Spain)

reconstituyente [rekonstitu'jente] *nm* tonic

reconstruir [rekonstru'ir] *vt* to reconstruct

reconversión [rekonβer'sjon] *nf* (*reestructuración*) restructuring; **reconversión industrial** industrial rationalization

recopilación [rekopila'θjon] *nf* (*resumen*) summary; (*compilación*) compilation; **recopilar** *vt* to compile

récord ['rekorð] (*pl* **-s**) *adj inv*, *nm* record

recordar [rekor'ðar] *vt* (*acordarse de*) to remember; (*acordar a otro*) to remind ▷ *vi* to remember

No confundir **recordar** con la palabra inglesa **record**.

recorrer [reko'rrer] *vt* (*país*) to cross, travel through; (*distancia*) to cover; (*registrar*) to search; (*repasar*) to look over; **recorrido** *nm* run, journey; **tren de largo recorrido** main-line train

recortar [rekor'tar] *vt* to cut out;

recorte *nm* (*acción, de prensa*) cutting; (*de telas, chapas*) trimming; **recorte presupuestario** budget cut

recostar [rekos'tar] *vt* to lean; **recostarse** *vr* to lie down

recoveco [reko'βeko] *nm* (*de camino, río etc*) bend; (*en casa*) cubby hole

recreación [rekrea'θjon] *nf* recreation

recrear [rekre'ar] *vt* (*entretener*) to entertain; (*volver a crear*) to recreate; **recreativo, -a** *adj* recreational; **recreo** *nm* recreation; (*Escol*) break, playtime

recriminar [rekrimi'nar] *vt* to reproach ▷ *vi* to recriminate; **recriminarse** *vr* to reproach each other

recrudecer [rekruðe'θer] *vt*, *vi* to worsen; **recrudecerse** *vr* to worsen

recta ['rekta] *nf* straight line

rectángulo, -a [rek'tangulo, a] *adj* rectangular ▷ *nm* rectangle

rectificar [rektifi'kar] *vt* to rectify; (*volverse recto*) to straighten ▷ *vi* to correct o.s.

rectitud [rekti'tuð] *nf* straightness

recto, -a ['rekto, a] *adj* straight; (*persona*) honest, upright; **siga todo ~** go straight on ▷ *nm* rectum

rector, a [rek'tor, a] *adj* governing

recuadro [re'kwaðro] *nm* box; (*Tip*) inset

recubrir [reku'βrir] *vt*: **~ (con)** (*pintura, crema*) to cover (with)

recuento [re'kwento] *nm* inventory; **hacer el ~ de** to count o reckon up

recuerdo [re'kwerðo] *nm* souvenir; **recuerdos** *nmpl* (*memorias*) memories; **¡~s a tu madre!** give my regards to your mother!

recular [reku'lar] *vi* to back down

recuperación [rekupera'θjon] *nf* recovery

recuperar [rekupe'rar] *vt* to recover; (*tiempo*) to make up; **recuperarse** *vr* to recuperate

recurrir [reku'rrir] *vi* (*Jur*) to appeal;

~ a to resort to; (*persona*) to turn to; **recurso** *nm* resort; (*medios*) means *pl*, resources *pl*; (*Jur*) appeal

red [reð] *nf* net, mesh; (*Ferro etc*) network; (*trampa*) trap; **la R~** (*Internet*) the Net

redacción [reðak'θjon] *nf* (*acción*) editing; (*personal*) editorial staff; (*Escol*) essay, composition

redactar [reðak'tar] *vt* to draw up, draft; (*periódico*) to edit

redactor, a [reðak'tor, a] *nm/f* editor

redada [re'ðaða] *nf* (*de policía*) raid, round-up

rededor [reðe'ðor] *nm*: **al o en ~** around, round about

redoblar [reðo'βlar] *vt* to redouble ▷ *vi* (*tambor*) to roll

redoma [re'ðoma] *nf*: **a la ~** around, round about

redondear [reðonde'ar] *vt* to round, round off

redondel [reðon'del] *nm* (*círculo*) circle; (*Taur*) bullring, arena

redondo, -a [re'ðondo, a] *adj* (*circular*) round; (*completo*) complete

reducción [reðuk'θjon] *nf* reduction

reducido, -a [reðu'θiðo, a] *adj* reduced; (*limitado*) limited; (*pequeño*) small

reducir [reðu'θir] *vt* to reduce; to limit; **reducirse** *vr* to diminish

redundancia [reðun'danθja] *nf* redundancy

reembolsar [re(e)mbol'sar] *vt* (*persona*) to reimburse; (*dinero*) to repay, pay back; (*depósito*) to refund; **reembolso** *nm* reimbursement; refund

reemplazar [re(e)mpla'θar] *vt* to replace; **reemplazo** *nm* replacement; **de reemplazo** (*Mil*) reserve

reencuentro [re(e)n'kwentro] *nm* reunion

reescribible [reeskri'βiβle] *adj* rewritable

refacción [refak'θjon] (*MÉX*) *nf*

spare (part)

referencia [refe'renθja] *nf* reference; **con ~ a** with reference to

referéndum [refe'rendum] (*pl* **~s**) *nm* referendum

referente [refe'rente] *adj*: **~ a** concerning, relating to

réferi ['referi] (*LAM*) *nmf* referee

referir [refe'rir] *vt* (*contar*) to tell, recount; (*relacionar*) to refer, relate; **referirse** *vr*: **~se a** to refer to

refilón [refi'lon]: **de ~** *adv* obliquely

refinado, -a [refi'naðo, a] *adj* refined

refinar [refi'nar] *vt* to refine; **refinería** *nf* refinery

reflejar [refle'xar] *vt* to reflect; **reflejo, -a** *adj* reflected; (*movimiento*) reflex ▷ *nm* reflection; (*Anat*) reflex

reflexión [reflek'sjon] *nf* reflection; **reflexionar** *vt* to reflect on ▷ *vi* to reflect; (*detenerse*) to pause (to think)

reflexivo, -a [reflek'siβo, a] *adj* thoughtful; (*Ling*) reflexive

reforma [re'forma] *nf* reform; (*Arq etc*) repair; **reforma agraria** agrarian reform

reformar [refor'mar] *vt* to reform; (*modificar*) to change, alter; (*Arq*) to repair; **reformarse** *vr* to mend one's ways

reformatorio [reforma'torjo] *nm* reformatory

reforzar [refor'θar] *vt* to strengthen; (*Arq*) to reinforce; (*fig*) to encourage

refractario, -a [refrak'tarjo, a] *adj* (*Tec*) heat-resistant

refrán [re'fran] *nm* proverb, saying

refregar [refre'ɣar] *vt* to scrub

refrescante [refres'kante] *adj* refreshing, cooling

refrescar [refres'kar] *vt* to refresh ▷ *vi* to cool down; **refrescarse** *vr* to get cooler; (*tomar aire fresco*) to go out for a breath of fresh air; (*beber*) to have a drink

refresco [re'fresko] *nm* soft drink, cool drink; **"~s"** "refreshments"

refriega [re'frjeɣa] nf scuffle, brawl
refrigeración [refrixera'θjon] nf refrigeration; (de sala) air-conditioning
refrigerador [refrixera'ðor] nm refrigerator (BRIT), icebox (US)
refrigerar [refrixe'rar] vt to refrigerate; (sala) to air-condition
refuerzo [re'fwerθo] nm reinforcement; (Tec) support
refugiado, -a [refu'xjaðo, a] nm/f refugee
refugiarse [refu'xjarse] vr to take refuge, shelter
refugio [re'fuxjo] nm refuge; (protección) shelter
refunfuñar [refunfu'ɲar] vi to grunt, growl; (quejarse) to grumble
regadera [reɣa'ðera] nf watering can
regadío [reɣa'ðio] nm irrigated land
regalado, -a [reɣa'laðo, a] adj comfortable, luxurious; (gratis) free, for nothing
regalar [reɣa'lar] vt (dar) to give (as a present); (entregar) to give away; (mimar) to pamper, make a fuss of
regaliz [reɣa'liθ] nm liquorice
regalo [re'ɣalo] nm (obsequio) gift, present; (gusto) pleasure
regañadientes [reɣaɲa'ðjentes]: **a ~** adv reluctantly
regañar [reɣa'ɲar] vt to scold ▷ vi to grumble; **regañón, -ona** adj nagging
regar [re'ɣar] vt to water, irrigate; (fig) to scatter, sprinkle
regatear [reɣate'ar] vt (Com) to bargain over; (escatimar) to be mean with ▷ vi to bargain, haggle; (Deporte) to dribble; **regateo** nm bargaining; dribbling; (del cuerpo) swerve, dodge
regazo [re'ɣaθo] nm lap
regenerar [rexene'rar] vt to regenerate
régimen ['reximen] nm (pl **regímenes**) nm regime; (Med) diet
regimiento [rexi'mjento] nm regiment
regio, -a ['rexjo, a] adj royal, regal; (fig: suntuoso) splendid; (cs: fam) great,

terrific
región [re'xjon] nf region
regir [re'xir] vt to govern, rule; (dirigir) to manage, run ▷ vi to apply, be in force
registrar [rexis'trar] vt (buscar) to search; (: en cajón) to look through; (inspeccionar) to inspect; (anotar) to register, record; (Inform) to log; **registrarse** vr to register; (ocurrir) to happen
registro [re'xistro] nm (acto) registration; (Mús, libro) register; (inspección) inspection, search; **registro civil** registry office
regla ['reɣla] nf (ley) rule, regulation; (de medir) ruler, rule; (Med: período) period; **en ~** in order
reglamentación [reɣlamenta'θjon] nf (acto) regulation; (lista) rules pl
reglamentar [reɣlamen'tar] vt to regulate; **reglamentario, -a** adj statutory; **reglamento** nm rules pl, regulations pl
regocijarse [reɣoθi'xarse] vr (alegrarse) to rejoice; **regocijo** nm joy, happiness
regrabadora [reɣraβa'ðora] nf rewriter; **regrabadora de DVD** DVD rewriter
regresar [reɣre'sar] vi to come back, go back, return; **regreso** nm return
reguero [re'ɣero] nm (de sangre etc) trickle; (de humo) trail
regulador [reɣula'ðor] nm regulator; (de radio etc) knob, control
regular [reɣu'lar] adj regular; (normal) normal, usual; (común) ordinary; (organizado) regular, orderly; (mediano) average; (fam) not bad, so-so ▷ adv so-so, alright ▷ vt (controlar) to control, regulate; (Tec) to adjust; **por lo ~** as a rule; **regularidad** nf regularity; **regularizar** vt to regularize
rehabilitación [reaβilita'θjon] nf rehabilitation; (Arq) restoration
rehabilitar [reaβili'tar] vt to rehabilitate; (Arq) to restore; (reintegrar)

to reinstate

rehacer [rea'θer] vt (reparar) to mend, repair; (volver a hacer) to redo, repeat; **rehacerse** vr (Med) to recover

rehén [re'en] nm hostage

rehuir [reu'ir] vt to avoid, shun

rehusar [reu'sar] vt, vi to refuse

reina ['reina] nf queen; **reinado** nm reign

reinar [rei'nar] vi to reign

reincidir [reinθi'ðir] vi to relapse

reincorporarse [reinkorpo'rarse] vr: **~ a** to rejoin

reino ['reino] nm kingdom; **reino animal/vegetal** animal/plant kingdom; **el Reino Unido** the United Kingdom

reintegrar [reinte'γrar] vt (reconstituir) to reconstruct; (persona) to reinstate; (dinero) to refund, pay back; **reintegrarse** vr: **~se a** to return to

reír [re'ir] vi, **reírse** vr to laugh; **~se de** to laugh at

reiterar [reite'rar] vt to reiterate

reivindicación [reiβindika'θjon] nf (demanda) claim, demand; (justificación) vindication

reivindicar [reiβindi'kar] vt to claim

reja ['rexa] nf (de ventana) grille, bars pl; (en la calle) grating

rejilla [re'xiʎa] nf grating, grille; (muebles) wickerwork; (de ventilación) vent; (de coche etc) luggage rack

rejoneador [rexonea'ðor] nm mounted bullfighter

rejuvenecer [rexuβene'θer] vt, vi to rejuvenate

relación [rela'θjon] nf relation, relationship; (Mat) ratio; (narración) report; **con ~ a, en ~ con** in relation to; **relaciones públicas** public relations; **relacionar** vt to relate, connect; **relacionarse** vr to be connected, be linked

relajación [relaxa'θjon] nf relaxation

relajar [rela'xar] vt to relax; **relajarse** vr to relax

relamerse [rela'merse] vr to lick one's lips

relámpago [re'lampaγo] nm flash of lightning; **visita ~** lightning visit

relatar [rela'tar] vt to tell, relate

relativo, -a [rela'tiβo, a] adj relative; **en lo ~** concerning

relato [re'lato] nm (narración) story, tale

relegar [rele'γar] vt to relegate

relevante [rele'βante] adj eminent, outstanding

relevar [rele'βar] vt (sustituir) to relieve; **relevarse** vr to relay; **~ a algn de un cargo** to relieve sb of his post

relevo [re'leβo] nm relief; **carrera de ~s** relay race

relieve [re'ljeβe] nm (Arte, Tec) relief; (fig) prominence, importance; **bajo ~** bas-relief

religión [reli'xjon] nf religion; **religioso, -a** adj religious ▷ nm/f monk/nun

relinchar [relin'tʃar] vi to neigh

reliquia [re'likja] nf relic; **reliquia de familia** heirloom

rellano [re'ʎano] nm (Arq) landing

rellenar [reʎe'nar] vt (llenar) to fill up; (Culin) to stuff; (Costura) to pad; **relleno, -a** adj full up; stuffed ▷ nm stuffing; (de tapicería) padding

reloj [re'lo(x)] nm clock; **poner el ~ (en hora)** to set one's watch (o the clock); **reloj (de pulsera)** wristwatch; **reloj despertador** alarm (clock); **reloj digital** digital watch; **relojero, -a** nm/f clockmaker; watchmaker

reluciente [relu'θjente] adj brilliant, shining

relucir [relu'θir] vi to shine; (fig) to excel

remachar [rema'tʃar] vt to rivet; (fig) to hammer home, drive home; **remache** nm rivet

remangar [reman'gar] vt to roll up

remanso [re'manso] nm pool

remar [re'mar] vi to row

rematado, -a [rema'taðo, a] adj

complete, utter

rematar [rema'tar] vt to finish off; (Com) to sell off cheap ▷ vi to end, finish off; (Deporte) to shoot

remate [re'mate] nm end, finish; (punta) tip; (Deporte) shot; (Arq) top; **de** o **para ~** to crown it all (BRIT), to top it off

remedar [reme'ðar] vt to imitate

remediar [reme'ðjar] vt to remedy; (subsanar) to make good, repair; (evitar) to avoid

remedio [re'meðjo] nm remedy; (alivio) relief, help; (Jur) recourse, remedy; **poner ~ a** to correct, stop; **no tener más ~** to have no alternative; **¡qué ~!** there's no choice!; **sin ~** hopeless

remendar [remen'dar] vt to repair; (con parche) to patch

remiendo [re'mjendo] nm mend; (con parche) patch; (cosido) darn

remilgado, -a [remil'xaðo, a] adj prim; (afectado) affected

remiso, -a [re'miso, a] adj slack, slow

remite [re'mite] nm (en sobre) name and address of sender

remitir [remi'tir] vt to remit, send ▷ vi to slacken; (en carta): **remite: X** sender: X; **remitente** nmf sender

remo ['remo] nm (de barco) oar; (Deporte) rowing

remojar [remo'xar] vt to steep, soak; (galleta etc) to dip, dunk

remojo [re'moxo] nm: **dejar la ropa en ~** to leave clothes to soak

remolacha [remo'latʃa] nf beet, beetroot

remolcador [remolka'ðor] nm (Náut) tug; (Auto) breakdown lorry

remolcar [remol'kar] vt to tow

remolino [remo'lino] nm eddy; (de agua) whirlpool; (de viento) whirlwind; (de gente) crowd

remolque [re'molke] nm tow, towing; (cuerda) towrope; **llevar a ~** to tow

remontar [remon'tar] vt to mend; **remontarse** vr to soar; **~se a** (Com) to amount to; **~ el vuelo** to soar

remorder [remor'ðer] vt to distress, disturb; **~le la conciencia a algn** to have a guilty conscience; **remordimiento** nm remorse

remoto, -a [re'moto, a] adj remote

remover [remo'ßer] vt to stir; (tierra) to turn over; (objetos) to move around

remuneración [remunera'θjon] nf remuneration

remunerar [remune'rar] vt to remunerate; (premiar) to reward

renacer [rena'θer] vi to be reborn; (fig) to revive; **renacimiento** nm rebirth; **el Renacimiento** the Renaissance

renacuajo [rena'kwaxo] nm (Zool) tadpole

renal [re'nal] adj renal, kidney cpd

rencilla [ren'θiʎa] nf quarrel

rencor [ren'kor] nm rancour, bitterness; **rencoroso, -a** adj spiteful

rendición [rendi'θjon] nf surrender

rendido, -a [ren'diðo, a] adj (sumiso) submissive; (cansado) worn-out, exhausted

rendija [ren'dixa] nf (hendedura) crack, cleft

rendimiento [rendi'mjento] nm (producción) output; (Tec, Com) efficiency

rendir [ren'dir] vt (vencer) to defeat; (producir) to produce; (dar beneficio) to yield; (agotar) to exhaust ▷ vi to pay; **rendirse** vr (someterse) to surrender; (cansarse) to wear o.s. out; **~ homenaje** o **culto a** to pay homage to

renegar [rene'xar] vi (renunciar) to renounce; (blasfemar) to blaspheme; (quejarse) to complain

RENFE ['renfe] nf abr (= Red Nacional de los Ferrocarriles Españoles)

renglón [ren'glon] nm (línea) line; (Com) item, article; **a ~ seguido** immediately after

renombre [re'nombre] nm renown

renovación [renoβa'θjon] nf (de contrato) renewal; (Arq) renovation

renovar [reno'βar] vt to renew; (Arq) to renovate

renta ['renta] nf (ingresos) income; (beneficio) profit; (alquiler) rent; **renta vitalicia** annuity; **rentable** adj profitable

renuncia [re'nunθja] nf resignation; **renunciar** [renun'θjar] vt to renounce; (tabaco, alcohol etc): **renunciar a** to give up; (oferta, oportunidad) to turn down; (puesto) to resign ▷ vi to resign

reñido, -a [re'niðo, a] adj (batalla) bitter, hard-fought; **estar ~ con algn** to be on bad terms with sb

reñir [re'nir] vt (regañar) to scold ▷ vi (estar peleado) to quarrel, fall out; (combatir) to fight

reo ['reo] nmf culprit, offender; (acusado) accused, defendant

reojo [re'oxo]: **de ~** adv out of the corner of one's eye

reparación [repara'θjon] nf (acto) mending, repairing; (Tec) repair; (fig) amends pl, reparation

reparador, a [repara'ðor] adj refreshing; (comida) fortifying ▷ nm repairer

reparar [repa'rar] vt to repair; (fig) to make amends for; (observar) to observe ▷ vi: **en** (darse cuenta de) to notice; (prestar atención a) to pay attention to

reparo [re'paro] nm (advertencia) observation; (duda) doubt; (dificultad) difficulty; **poner ~s (a)** to raise objections (to)

repartidor, a [reparti'ðor, a] nm/f distributor

repartir [repar'tir] vt to distribute, share out; (Correos) to deliver; **reparto** nm distribution; delivery; (Teatro, Cine) cast; (CAM: urbanización) housing estate (BRIT), real estate development (US)

repasar [repa'sar] vt (Escol) to revise; (Mecánica) to check, overhaul; (Costura) to mend; **repaso** nm revision

overhaul, checkup; mending

repecho [re'petʃo] nm steep incline

repelente [repe'lente] adj repellent, repulsive

repeler [repe'ler] vt to repel

repente [re'pente]: **de ~** suddenly

repentino, -a [repen'tino, a] adj sudden

repercusión [reperku'sjon] nf repercussion

repercutir [reperku'tir] vi (objeto) to rebound; (sonido) to echo; **~ en** (fig) to have repercussions on

repertorio [reper'torjo] nm list; (Teatro) repertoire

repetición [repeti'θjon] nf repetition

repetir [repe'tir] vt to repeat; (plato) to have a second helping of ▷ vi to repeat; (sabor) to come back; **repetirse** vr (volver sobre un tema) to repeat o.s.

repetitivo, -a [repeti'tiβo, a] adj repetitive, repetitious

repique [re'pike] nm pealing, ringing; **repiqueteo** nm pealing; (de tambor) drumming

repisa [re'pisa] nf ledge, shelf; (de ventana) windowsill; **la ~ de la chimenea** the mantelpiece

repito etc vb V **repetir**

replantearse [replante'arse] vr: **~ un problema** to reconsider a problem

repleto, -a [re'pleto, a] adj replete, full up

réplica ['replika] nf answer; (Arte) replica

replicar [repli'kar] vi to answer; (objetar) to argue, answer back

repliegue [re'pljexe] nm (Mil) withdrawal

repoblación [repoβla'θjon] nf repopulation; (de río) restocking; **repoblación forestal** reafforestation

repoblar [repo'βlar] vt to repopulate; (con árboles) to reafforest

repollito [repo'ʎito] (cs) nm: **~s de Bruselas** (Brussels) sprouts

repollo [re'poʎo] nm cabbage

reponer [repo'ner] vt to replace, put back; (Teatro) to revive; **reponerse** vr to recover; ~ **que** ... to reply that ...

reportaje [repor'taxe] nm report, article

reportero, -a [repor'tero, a] nm/f reporter

reposacabezas [reposaka'βeθas] nm inv headrest

reposar [repo'sar] vi to rest, repose

reposera [repo'sera] (RPL) nf deck chair

reposición [reposi'θjon] nf replacement; (Cine) remake

reposo [re'poso] nm rest

repostar [repos'tar] vt to replenish; (Auto) to fill up (with petrol (BRIT) o gasoline (US))

repostería [reposte'ria] nf confectioner's (shop)

represa [re'presa] nf dam; (lago artificial) lake, pool

represalia [repre'salja] nf reprisal

representación [representa'θjon] nf representation; (Teatro) performance; **representante** nmf representative; performer

representar [represen'tar] vt to represent; (Teatro) to perform; (edad) to look; **representarse** vr to imagine; **representativo, -a** adj representative

represión [repre'sjon] nf repression

reprimenda [repri'menda] nf reprimand, rebuke

reprimir [repri'mir] vt to repress

reprobar [repro'βar] vt to censure, reprove

reprochar [repro'tʃar] vt to reproach; **reproche** nm reproach

reproducción [reproðuk'θjon] nf reproduction

reproducir [reproðu'θir] vt to reproduce; **reproducirse** vr to breed; (situación) to recur

reproductor, a [reproðuk'tor, a] adj reproductive ▷ nm player; **reproductor de CD** CD player

reptil [rep'til] nm reptile

república [re'puβlika] nf republic; **República Dominicana** Dominican Republic; **republicano, -a** adj, nm republican

repudiar [repu'ðjar] vt to repudiate; (fe) to renounce

repuesto [re'pwesto] nm (pieza de recambio) spare (part); (abastecimiento) supply; **rueda de** ~ spare wheel

repugnancia [repuɣ'nanθja] nf repugnance; **repugnante** adj repugnant, repulsive

repugnar [repuɣ'nar] vt to disgust

repulsa [re'pulsa] nf rebuff

repulsión [repul'sjon] nf repulsion, aversion; **repulsivo, -a** adj repulsive

reputación [reputa'θjon] nf reputation

requerir [reke'rir] vt (pedir) to ask, request; (exigir) to require; (llamar) to send for, summon

requesón [reke'son] nm cottage cheese

requete... [re'kete] prefijo extremely

réquiem ['rekjem] (pl ~s) nm requiem

requisito [reki'sito] nm requirement, requisite

res [res] nf beast, animal

resaca [re'saka] nf (de mar) undertow, undercurrent; (fam) hangover

resaltar [resal'tar] vi to project, stick out; (fig) to stand out

resarcir [resar'θir] vt to compensate; **resarcirse** vr to make up for

resbaladero [resβala'ðero] (MÉX) nm slide

resbaladizo, -a [resβala'ðiθo, a] adj slippery

resbalar [resβa'lar] vi to slip, slide; (fig) to slip (up); **resbalarse** vr to slip, slide; to slip (up); **resbalón** nm (acción) slip

rescatar [reska'tar] vt (salvar) to save, rescue; (objeto) to get back, recover; (cautivos) to ransom

rescate [res'kate] nm rescue; (de objeto) recovery; **pagar un** ~ to pay a ransom

rescindir [resθin'dir] vt to rescind

rescisión [resθi'sjon] nf cancellation

resecar [rese'kar] vt to dry thoroughly; (Med) to cut out, remove; **resecarse** vr to dry up

reseco, -a [re'seko, a] adj very dry; (fig) skinny

resentido, -a [resen'tiðo, a] adj resentful

resentimiento [resenti'mjento] nm resentment, bitterness

resentirse [resen'tirse] vr (debilitarse: persona) to suffer; **~ de** (consecuencias) to feel the effects of; **~ de** (o por) **algo** to resent sth, be bitter about sth

reseña [re'seɲa] nf (cuenta) account; (informe) report; (Literatura) review

reseñar [rese'ɲar] vt to describe; (Literatura) to review

reserva [re'serβa] nf reserve; (reservación) reservation

reservación [reserβa'θjon] nf reservation

reservado, -a [reser'βaðo, a] adj reserved; (retraído) cold, distant ▷ nm private room

reservar [reser'βar] vt (guardar) to keep; (habitación, entrada) to reserve; **reservarse** vr to save o.s.; (callar) to keep to o.s.

resfriado [resfri'aðo] nm cold; **resfriarse** vr to cool; (Med) to catch a cold

resguardar [resɣwar'ðar] vt to protect, shield; **resguardarse** vr: **~se de** to guard against; **resguardo** nm defence; (vale) voucher; (recibo) receipt, slip

residencia [resi'ðenθja] nf residence; **residencia de ancianos** residential home, old people's home; **residencia universitaria** hall of residence; **residencial** nf (urbanización) housing estate

residente [resi'ðente] adj, nmf resident

residir [resi'ðir] vi to reside, live; **~ en** to reside in, lie in

residuo [re'siðwo] nm residue

resignación [resiɣna'θjon] nf resignation; **resignarse** vr: **resignarse a o con** to resign o.s. to, be resigned to

resina [re'sina] nf resin

resistencia [resis'tenθja] nf (dureza) endurance, strength; (oposición, Elec) resistance; **resistente** adj strong, hardy; resistant

resistir [resis'tir] vt (soportar) to bear; (oponerse a) to resist, oppose; (aguantar) to put up with ▷ vi to resist; (aguantar) to last, endure; **resistirse** vr: **~se a** to refuse to, resist

resoluto, -a [reso'luto, a] adj resolute

resolver [resol'βer] vt to resolve; (solucionar) to solve, resolve; (decidir) to decide, settle; **resolverse** vr to make up one's mind

resonar [reso'nar] vi to ring, echo

resoplar [reso'plar] vi to snort; **resoplido** nm heavy breathing

resorte [re'sorte] nm spring; (fig) lever

resortera [resor'tera] (MÉX) nf catapult

respaldar [respal'ðar] vt to back (up), support; **respaldarse** vr to lean back; **~se con o en** (fig) to take one's stand on; **respaldo** nm (de sillón) back; (fig) support, backing

respectivo, -a [respek'tiβo, a] adj respective; **en lo ~ a** with regard to

respecto [res'pekto] nm: **al ~** on this matter; **con ~ a, de** with regard to, in relation to

respetable [respe'taβle] adj respectable

respetar [respe'tar] vt to respect; **respeto** nm respect; (acatamiento) deference; **respetos** nmpl respects; **respetuoso, -a** adj respectful

respingo [res'piŋgo] nm start, jump

respiración [respira'θjon] nf breathing; (Med) respiration;

(ventilación) ventilation; **respiración asistida** artificial respiration (by machine)

respirar [respi'rar] vi to breathe; **respiratorio, -a** adj respiratory; **respiro** nm breathing; (fig: descanso) respite

resplandecer [resplande'θer] vi to shine; **resplandeciente** adj resplendent, shining; **resplandor** nm brilliance, brightness; (de luz, fuego) blaze

responder [respon'der] vt to answer ▷ vi to answer; (fig) to respond; (pey) to answer back; **~ de o por** to answer for; **respondón, -ona** adj cheeky

responsabilidad [responsaβili'ðað] nf responsibility

responsabilizarse [responsaβili'θarse] vr to make o.s. responsible, take charge

responsable [respon'saβle] adj responsible

respuesta [res'pwesta] nf answer, reply

resquebrajar [reskeβra'xar] vt to crack, split; **resquebrajarse** vr to crack, split

resquicio [res'kiθjo] nm chink; (hendedura) crack

resta [resta] nf (Mat) remainder

restablecer [restaβle'θer] vt to re-establish, restore; **restablecerse** vr to recover

restante [res'tante] adj remaining; **lo ~** the remainder

restar [res'tar] vt (Mat) to subtract; (fig) to take away ▷ vi to remain, be left

restauración [restaura'θjon] nf restoration

restaurante [restau'rante] nm restaurant

restaurar [restau'rar] vt to restore

restituir [restitu'ir] vt (devolver) to return, give back; (rehabilitar) to restore

resto [resto] nm (residuo) rest, remainder; (apuesta) stake; **restos** nmpl remains

restorán [resto'ran] nm (Lam) restaurant

restregar [restre'xar] vt to scrub, rub

restricción [restrik'θjon] nf restriction

restringir [restrin'xir] vt to restrict, limit

resucitar [resuθi'tar] vt, vi to resuscitate, revive

resuelto, -a [re'swelto, a] pp de **resolver** ▷ adj resolute, determined

resultado [resul'taðo] nm result; (conclusión) outcome; **resultante** adj resulting, resultant

resultar [resul'tar] vi (ser) to be; (llegar a ser) to turn out to be; (salir bien) to turn out well; (Com) to amount to; **~ de** to stem from; **me resulta difícil hacerlo** it's difficult for me to do it

resumen [re'sumen] (pl **resúmenes**) nm summary, résumé; **en ~** in short

resumir [resu'mir] vt to sum up; (cortar) to abridge, cut down; (condensar) to summarize

No confundir **resumir** con la palabra inglesa resume.

resurgir [resur'xir] vi (reaparecer) to reappear

resurrección [resurre(k)'θjon] nf resurrection

retablo [re'taβlo] nm altarpiece

retaguardia [reta'ɣwarðja] nf rearguard

retahíla [reta'ila] nf series, string

retal [re'tal] nm remnant

retar [re'tar] vt to challenge; (desafiar) to defy, dare

retazo [re'taθo] nm snippet (BRIT), fragment

retención [reten'θjon] nf (tráfico) hold-up; **retención fiscal** deduction for tax purposes

retener [rete'ner] vt (intereses) to withhold

reticente [reti'θente] adj (tono) insinuating; (postura) reluctant; **ser ~ a hacer algo** to be reluctant o unwilling to do sth

retina [re'tina] nf retina

retintín [retin'tin] nm jangle, jingle

retirada [reti'raða] nf (Mil, refugio) retreat; (de dinero) withdrawal; (de embajador) recall; **retirado, -a** (de lugar) remote; (vida) quiet; (jubilado) retired

retirar [reti'rar] vt to withdraw; (quitar) to remove; (jubilar) to retire, pension off; **retirarse** vr to retreat, withdraw; to retire; (acostarse) to retire, go to bed; **retiro** nm retreat; (pago) pension

reto ['reto] nm dare, challenge

retocar [reto'kar] vt (fotografía) to touch up, retouch

retoño [re'toɲo] nm sprout, shoot; (fig) offspring, child

retoque [re'toke] nm retouching

retorcer [retor'θer] vt to twist; (manos, lavado) to wring; **retorcerse** vr to become twisted; (mover el cuerpo) to writhe

retorcido, -a [retor'θiðo, a] adj (persona) devious

retorcijón [retorθi'xon] (LAM) nm (tb: ~ **de tripas**) stomach cramp

retórica [re'torika] nf rhetoric; (pey) affectedness

retorno [re'torno] nm return

retortijón [retorti'xon] (ESP) nm (tb: ~ **de tripas**) stomach cramp

retozar [reto'θar] vi (juguetear) to frolic, romp; (saltar) to gambol

retracción [retrak'θjon] nf retraction

retraerse [retra'erse] vr to retreat, withdraw; **retraído, -a** adj shy, retiring; **retraimiento** nm retirement; (timidez) shyness

retransmisión [retransmi'sjon] nf repeat (broadcast)

retransmitir [retransmi'tir] vt (mensaje) to relay; (TV etc) to repeat, retransmit; (: en vivo) to broadcast live

retrasado, -a [retra'saðo, a] adj late; (Med) mentally retarded; (país etc) backward, underdeveloped

retrasar [retra'sar] vt (demorar) to postpone, put off; (retardar) to slow down ▷vi (atrasarse) to be late; (reloj) to be slow; (producción) to fall (off); (quedarse atrás) to lag behind; **retrasarse** vr to be late; to be slow; to fall (off); to lag behind

retraso [re'traso] nm (demora) delay; (lentitud) slowness; (tardanza) lateness; (atraso) backwardness; **retrasos** nmpl (Finanzas) arrears; **llegar con ~** to arrive late; **retraso mental** mental deficiency

retratar [retra'tar] vt (Arte) to paint the portrait of; (fotografía) to photograph; (fig) to depict, describe; **retrato** nm portrait; (fig) likeness; **retrato-robot** (ESP) nm Identikit®

retrete [re'trete] nm toilet

retribuir [retri'βwir] vt (recompensar) to reward; (pagar) to pay

retro... ['retro] prefijo retro...

retroceder [retroθe'ðer] vi (echarse atrás) to move back(wards); (fig) to back down

retroceso [retro'θeso] nm backward movement; (Med) relapse; (fig) backing down

retrospectivo, -a [retrospek'tiβo, a] adj retrospective

retrovisor [retroβi'sor] nm (tb: **espejo ~**) rear-view mirror

retumbar [retum'bar] vi to echo, resound

reúma [re'uma], **reuma** ['reuma] nm rheumatism

reunión [reu'njon] nf (asamblea) meeting; (fiesta) party

reunir [reu'nir] vt (juntar) to reunite, join (together); (recoger) to gather (together); (personas) to get together; (cualidades) to combine; **reunirse** vr (personas: en reunión) to meet, gather

revalidar [reβali'ðar] vt (ratificar) to confirm, ratify

revalorizar [reβalori'θar] vt to revalue, reassess

revancha [re'βantʃa] nf revenge

revelación [reβela'θjon] nf revelation

revelado [reβe'laðo] nm developing

revelar [reβe'lar] vt to reveal; (Foto) to develop

reventa [re'βenta] nf (de entradas: para concierto) touting

reventar [reβen'tar] vt to burst, explode

reventón [reβen'ton] nm (Auto) blow-out (BRIT), flat (US)

reverencia [reβe'renθja] nf reverence; **reverenciar** vt to revere

reverendo, -a [reβe'rendo, a] adj reverend

reverente [reβe'rente] adj reverent

reversa [re'βersa] nf (MÉX, CAM) reverse (gear)

reversible [reβer'siβle] adj (prenda) reversible

reverso [re'βerso] nm back, other side; (de moneda) reverse

revertir [reβer'tir] vi to revert

revés [re'βes] nm back, wrong side; (fig) reverse, setback; (Deporte) backhand; **al ~** the wrong way round; (de arriba abajo) upside down; (ropa) inside out; **volver algo del ~** to turn sth round; (ropa) to turn sth inside out

revisar [reβi'sar] vt (examinar) to check; (texto etc) to revise; **revisión** nf revision; **revisión salarial** wage review

revisor, a [reβi'sor, a] nm/f inspector; (Ferro) ticket collector

revista [re'βista] nf magazine, review; (Teatro) revue; (inspección) inspection; **pasar ~ a** to review, inspect; **revista del corazón** magazine featuring celebrity gossip and real-life romance stories

revivir [reβi'βir] vi to revive

revolcarse [reβol'karse] vr to roll about

revoltijo [reβol'tixo] nm mess, jumble

revoltoso, -a [reβol'toso, a] adj (travieso) naughty, unruly

revolución [reβolu'θjon] nf revolution; **revolucionario, -a** adj, nm/f revolutionary

revolver [reβol'βer] vt (desordenar) to disturb, mess up; (mover) to move about ▷ vi: **~ en** to go through, rummage (about) in; **revolverse** vr (volver contra) to turn on o against

revólver [re'βolβer] nm revolver

revuelo [re'βwelo] nm fluttering; (fig) commotion

revuelta [re'βwelta] nf (motín) revolt; (agitación) commotion

revuelto, -a [re'βwelto, a] pp de **revolver** ▷ adj (mezclado) mixed-up, in disorder

rey [rei] nm king; **Día de R~es** Twelfth Night; **los R~es Magos** the Three Wise Men, the Magi

- **REYES MAGOS**
-
- On the night before the 6th
- January (the Epiphany), children
- go to bed expecting **los Reyes**
- **Magos** (the Three Wise Men) to
- bring them presents. Twelfth
- Night processions, known as
- **cabalgatas**, take place that
- evening when 3 people dressed
- as **los Reyes Magos** arrive in the
- town by land or sea to the delight
- of the children.

reyerta [re'jerta] nf quarrel, brawl

rezagado, -a [reθa'γaðo, a] nm/f straggler

rezar [re'θar] vi to pray; **~ con** (fam) to concern, have to do with; **rezo** nm prayer

rezumar [reθu'mar] vt to ooze

ría ['ria] nf estuary

riada [ri'aða] nf flood

ribera [ri'βera] nf (de río) bank; (: área) riverside

ribete [ri'βete] nm (de vestido) border; (fig) addition

ricino [ri'θino] nm: **aceite de ~** castor oil

rico, -a ['riko, a] *adj* rich; *(adinerado)* wealthy, rich; *(lujoso)* luxurious; *(comida)* delicious; *(niño)* lovely, cute ⊳ *nm/f* rich person

ridiculez [riðiku'leθ] *nf* absurdity

ridiculizar [riðikuli'θar] *vt* to ridicule

ridículo, -a [ri'ðikulo, a] *adj* ridiculous; **hacer el ~** to make a fool of o.s.; **poner a algn en ~** to make a fool of sb

riego ['rjeɣo] *nm (aspersión)* watering; *(irrigación)* irrigation; **riego sanguíneo** blood flow o circulation

riel [rjel] *nm* rail

rienda ['rjenda] *nf* rein; **dar ~ suelta a** to give free rein to

riesgo ['rjesɣo] *nm* risk; **correr el ~ de** to run the risk of

rifa ['rifa] *nf (lotería)* raffle; **rifar** *vt* to raffle

rifle ['rifle] *nm* rifle

rigidez [rixi'ðeθ] *nf* rigidity, stiffness; *(fig)* strictness; **rígido, -a** *adj* rigid, stiff; *(severo)* strict, inflexible

rigor [ri'ɣor] *nm* strictness, rigour; *(inclemencia)* harshness; **de ~** de rigueur, essential; **riguroso, -a** *adj* rigorous; harsh; *(severo)* severe

rimar [ri'mar] *vi* to rhyme

rimbombante [rimbom'bante] *adj* pompous

rímel ['rimel] *nm* mascara

rímmel ['rimel] *nm* = **rímel**

rin [rin] *(MÉX) nm* (wheel) rim

rincón [rin'kon] *nm* corner *(inside)*

rinoceronte [rinoθe'ronte] *nm* rhinoceros

riña ['riɲa] *nf (disputa)* argument; *(pelea)* brawl

riñón [ri'ɲon] *nm* kidney

río *etc* ['rio] *vb* V **reír** ⊳ *nm* river; *(fig)* torrent, stream; **río abajo/arriba** downstream/upstream; **Río de la Plata** River Plate

rioja [ri'oxa] *nf (vino)* rioja (wine)

rioplatense [riopla'tense] *adj* of o from the River Plate

riqueza [ri'keθa] *nf* wealth, riches *pl*;

(cualidad) richness

risa ['risa] *nf* laughter; *(una risa)* laugh; **¡qué ~!** what a laugh!

risco ['risko] *nm* crag, cliff

ristra ['ristra] *nf* string

risueño, -a [ri'sweɲo, a] *adj (sonriente)* smiling; *(contento)* cheerful

ritmo ['ritmo] *nm* rhythm; **a ~ lento** slowly; **trabajar a ~ lento** to go slow; **ritmo cardíaco** heart rate

rito ['rito] *nm* rite

ritual [ri'twal] *adj, nm* ritual

rival [ri'βal] *adj, nmf* rival; **rivalidad** *nf* rivalry; **rivalizar** *vi*: **rivalizar con** to rival, vie with

rizado, -a [ri'θaðo, a] *adj* curly ⊳ *nm* curls *pl*

rizar [ri'θar] *vt* to curl; **rizarse** *vr (pelo)* to curl; *(agua)* to ripple; **rizo** *nm* curl; ripple

RNE *nf abr* = **Radio Nacional de España**

robar [ro'βar] *vt* to rob; *(objeto)* to steal; *(casa etc)* to break into; *(Naipes)* to draw

roble ['roβle] *nm* oak; **robledal**, **robledo** *nm* oakwood

robo ['roβo] *nm* robbery, theft

robot [ro'βot] *nm* robot; **robot (de cocina)** *(ESP)* food processor

robustecer [roβuste'θer] *vt* to strengthen

robusto, -a [ro'βusto, a] *adj* robust, strong

roca ['roka] *nf* rock

roce ['roθe] *nm (caricia)* brush; *(Tec)* friction; *(en la piel)* graze; **tener ~ con** to be in close contact with

rociar [ro'θjar] *vt* to spray

rocín [ro'θin] *nm* nag, hack

rocío [ro'θio] *nm* dew

rocola [ro'kola] *(LAM) nf* jukebox

rocoso, -a [ro'koso, a] *adj* rocky

rodaballo [roða'βaʎo] *nm* turbot

rodaja [ro'ðaxa] *nf* slice

rodaje [ro'ðaxe] *nm (Cine)* shooting, filming; *(Auto)*: **en ~** running in

rodar [ro'ðar] *vt (vehículo)* to wheel (along); *(escalera)* to roll down; *(viajar)*

por) to travel (over) ▷ *vi* to roll; (*coche*)
to go, run; (*Cine*) to shoot, film
rodear [roðe'ar] *vt* to surround ▷ *vi*
to go round; **rodearse** *vr*: **~se de
amigos** to surround o.s. with friends
rodeo [ro'ðeo] *nm* (*ruta indirecta*)
detour; (*evasión*) evasion; (*Deporte*)
rodeo; **hablar sin ~s** to come to the
point, speak plainly
rodilla [ro'ðiʎa] *nf* knee; **de ~s**
kneeling; **ponerse de ~s** to kneel (down)
rodillo [ro'ðiʎo] *nm* roller; (*Culin*)
rolling-pin
roedor, a [roe'ðor, a] *adj* gnawing
▷ *nm* rodent
roer [ro'er] *vt* (*masticar*) to gnaw;
(*corroer, fig*) to corrode
rogar [ro'ɣar] *vt, vi* (*pedir*) to ask for;
(*suplicar*) to beg, plead; **se ruega no
fumar** please do not smoke
rojizo, -a [ro'xiθo, a] *adj* reddish
rojo, -a ['roxo, a] *adj* red; **al ~
vivo** red-hot
rol [rol] *nm* list, roll; (*papel*) role
rollito [ro'ʎito] *nm* (*tb*: **~ de
primavera**) spring roll
rollizo, -a [ro'ʎiθo, a] *adj* (*objeto*)
cylindrical; (*persona*) plump
rollo ['roʎo] *nm* roll; (*de cuerda*) coil;
(*madera*) log; (*ESP: fam*) bore; **¡qué ~!**
(*ESP: fam*) what a carry-on!
Roma ['roma] *nf* Rome
romance [ro'manθe] *nm* (*amoroso*)
romance; (*Literatura*) ballad
romano, -a [ro'mano, a] *adj, nm/f*
Roman; **a la romana** in batter
romanticismo [romanti'θismo] *nm*
romanticism
romántico, -a [ro'mantiko, a] *adj*
romantic
rombo ['rombo] *nm* (*Geom*) rhombus
romería [rome'ria] *nf* (*Rel*)
pilgrimage; (*excursión*) trip, outing

● **ROMERÍA**

Originally a pilgrimage to a shrine
or church to express devotion to

the Virgin Mary or a local Saint,
the **romería** has also become a
rural festival which accompanies
the pilgrimage. People come from
all over to attend, bringing their
own food and drink, and spend the
day in celebration.

romero, -a [ro'mero, a] *nm/f* pilgrim
▷ *nm* rosemary
romo, -a ['romo, a] *adj* blunt;
(*fig*) dull
rompecabezas [rompeka'βeθas]
nm inv riddle, puzzle; (*juego*) jigsaw
(puzzle)
rompehuelgas [rompe'welɣas]
(*LAM*) *nm inv* strikebreaker, scab
rompeolas [rompe'olas] *nm inv*
breakwater
romper [rom'per] *vt* to break; (*hacer
pedazos*) to smash; (*papel, tela etc*)
to tear, rip ▷ *vi* (*olas*) to break; (*sol,
diente*) to break through; **romperse**
vr to break; **~ un contrato** to break
a contract; **~ a** (*empezar a*) to start
(suddenly) to; **~ a llorar** to burst into
tears; **~ con algn** to fall out with sb
ron [ron] *nm* rum
roncar [ron'kar] *vi* to snore
ronco, -a ['ronko, a] *adj* (*afónico*)
hoarse; (*áspero*) raucous
ronda ['ronda] *nf* (*gen*) round;
(*patrulla*) patrol; **rondar** *vt* to patrol
▷ *vi* to patrol; (*fig*) to prowl round
ronquido [ron'kiðo] *nm* snore,
snoring
ronronear [ronrone'ar] *vi* to purr
roña ['rona] *nf* (*Veterinaria*) mange;
(*mugre*) dirt, grime; (*óxido*) rust
roñoso, -a [ro'noso, a] *adj*
(*mugriento*) filthy; (*tacaño*) mean
ropa ['ropa] *nf* clothes *pl*, clothing;
ropa blanca linen; **ropa de cama** bed
linen; **ropa de color** coloureds *pl*; **ropa
interior** underwear; **ropa sucia** dirty
washing; **ropaje** *nm* gown, robes *pl*
ropero [ro'pero] *nm* linen cupboard;
(*guardarropa*) wardrobe

rosa ['rosa] *adj* pink ▷ *nf* rose
rosado, -a [ro'saðo, a] *adj* pink ▷ *nm* rosé
rosal [ro'sal] *nm* rosebush
rosario [ro'sarjo] *nm* (Rel) rosary; **rezar el ~** to say the rosary
rosca ['roska] *nf* (de tornillo) thread; (de humo) coil, spiral; (pan, postre) ring-shaped roll/pastry
rosetón [rose'ton] *nm* rosette; (Arq) rose window
rosquilla [ros'kiʎa] *nf* doughnut-shaped fritter
rostro ['rostro] *nm* (cara) face
rotativo, -a [rota'tiβo, a] *adj* rotary
roto, -a ['roto, a] *pp de* **romper** ▷ *adj* broken
rotonda [ro'tonda] *nf* roundabout
rótula ['rotula] *nf* kneecap; (Tec) ball-and-socket joint
rotulador [rotula'ðor] *nm* felt-tip pen
rótulo ['rotulo] *nm* heading; title; label; (letrero) sign
rotundamente [rotunda'mente] *adv* (negar) flatly; (responder, afirmar) emphatically; **rotundo, -a** *adj* round; (enfático) emphatic
rotura [ro'tura] *nf* (acto) breaking; (Med) fracture
rozadura [roθa'ðura] *nf* abrasion, graze
rozar [ro'θar] *vt* (frotar) to rub; (arañar) to scratch; (tocar ligeramente) to shave, touch lightly; **rozarse** *vr* to rub (together); **~se con** (fam) to rub shoulders with
rte. *abr* (= remite, remitente) sender
RTVE *nf abr* = **Radiotelevisión Española**
rubí [ru'βi] *nm* ruby; (de reloj) jewel
rubio, -a ['ruβjo, a] *adj* fair-haired, blond(e) ▷ *nm/f* blond/blonde; **tabaco ~** Virginia tobacco
rubor [ru'βor] *nm* (sonrojo) blush; (timidez) bashfulness; **ruborizarse** *vr* to blush
rúbrica ['ruβrika] *nf* (de la firma)

flourish; **rubricar** *vt* (firmar) to sign with a flourish; (concluir) to sign and seal
rudimentario, -a [ruðimen'tarjo, a] *adj* rudimentary
rudo, -a ['ruðo, a] *adj* (sin pulir) unpolished; (grosero) coarse; (violento) violent; (sencillo) simple
rueda ['rweða] *nf* wheel; (círculo) ring, circle; (rodaja) slice, round; **rueda de auxilio** (RPL) spare tyre; **rueda delantera/trasera/de repuesto** front/back/spare wheel; **rueda de prensa** press conference; **rueda gigante** (LAM) big (BRIT) o Ferris (US) wheel
ruedo ['rweðo] *nm* (círculo) circle; (Taur) arena, bullring
ruego *etc* ['rwexo] *vb* V **rogar** ▷ *nm* request
rugby ['ruxβi] *nm* rugby
rugido [ru'xiðo] *nm* roar
rugir [ru'xir] *vi* to roar
rugoso, -a [ru'xoso, a] *adj* (arrugado) wrinkled; (áspero) rough; (desigual) ridged
ruido ['rwiðo] *nm* noise; (sonido) sound; (alboroto) racket, row; (escándalo) commotion, rumpus; **ruidoso, -a** *adj* noisy, loud; (fig) sensational
ruin [rwin] *adj* contemptible, mean
ruina ['rwina] *nf* ruin; (colapso) collapse; (de persona) ruin, downfall
ruinoso, -a [rwi'noso, a] *adj* ruinous; (destartalado) dilapidated, tumbledown; (Com) disastrous
ruiseñor [rwise'ɲor] *nm* nightingale
rulero [ru'lero] *nm* (RPL) roller
ruleta [ru'leta] *nf* roulette
rulo ['rulo] *nm* (para el pelo) curler
Rumanía [ruma'nia] *nf* Rumania
rumba ['rumba] *nf* rumba
rumbo ['rumbo] *nm* (ruta) route, direction; (ángulo de dirección) course, bearing; (fig) course of events; **ir con ~ a** to be heading for
rumiante [ru'mjante] *nm* ruminant

r

rumiar [ru'mjar] vt to chew; (fig) to chew over ▷ vi to chew the cud
rumor [ru'mor] nm (ruido sordo) low sound; (murmuración) murmur, buzz; **rumorearse** vr: **se rumorea que ...** it is rumoured that ...
rupestre [ru'pestre] adj rock cpd
ruptura [rup'tura] nf rupture
rural [ru'ral] adj rural
Rusia ['rusja] nf Russia; **ruso, -a** adj, nm/f Russian
rústico, -a ['rustiko, a] adj rustic; (ordinario) coarse, uncouth ▷ nm/f yokel
ruta ['ruta] nf route
rutina [ru'tina] nf routine

S

S abr (= santo, a) St; (= sur) S
s. abr (= siglo) C.; (= siguiente) foll
S.A. abr (= Sociedad Anónima) Ltd. (BRIT), Inc. (US)
sábado ['saβaðo] nm Saturday
sábana ['saβana] nf sheet
sabañón [saβa'non] nm chilblain
saber [sa'βer] vt to know; (llegar a conocer) to find out, learn; (tener capacidad de) to know how to ▷ vi: ~ **a** to taste of, taste like ▷ nm knowledge, learning; **a ~** namely; **¿sabes conducir/nadar?** can you drive/swim?; **¿sabes francés?** do you speak French?; ~ **de memoria** to know by heart; **hacer ~ algo a algn** to inform sb of sth, let sb know sth
sabiduría [saβiðu'ria] nf (conocimientos) wisdom; (instrucción) learning
sabiendas [sa'βjendas]: **a ~** adv knowingly
sabio, -a ['saβjo, a] adj (docto) learned; (prudente) wise, sensible
sabor [sa'βor] nm taste, flavour;

saborear [saβore'ar] vt to taste, savour; (fig) to relish

sabotaje [saβo'taxe] nm sabotage

sabré etc vb V saber

sabroso, -a [sa'βroso, a] adj tasty; (fig: fam) racy, salty

sacacorchos [saka'kortʃos] nm inv corkscrew

sacapuntas [saka'puntas] nm inv pencil sharpener

sacar [sa'kar] vt to take out; (fig: extraer) to get (out); (quitar) to remove, get out; (hacer salir) to bring out; (conclusión) to draw; (novela etc) to publish, bring out; (ropa) to take off; (obra) to make; (premio) to receive; (entradas) to get; (Tenis) to serve; ~ adelante (niño) to bring up; (negocio) to carry on, go on with; ~ a algn a bailar to get sb up to dance; ~ una foto to take a photo; ~ la lengua to stick out one's tongue; ~ buenas/malas notas to get good/bad marks

sacarina [saka'rina] nf saccharin(e)

sacerdote [saθer'ðote] nm priest

saciar [sa'θjar] vt (hambre, sed) to satisfy; saciarse vr (de comida) to get full up

saco ['sako] nm bag; (grande) sack; (su contenido) bagful; (LAM: chaqueta) jacket; saco de dormir sleeping bag

sacramento [sakra'mento] nm sacrament

sacrificar [sakrifi'kar] vt to sacrifice; sacrificio nm sacrifice

sacristía [sakris'tia] nf sacristy

sacudida [saku'ðiða] nf (agitación) shake, shaking; (sacudimiento) jolt, bump; sacudida eléctrica electric shock

sacudir [saku'ðir] vt to shake; (golpear) to hit

Sagitario [saxi'tarjo] nm Sagittarius

sagrado, -a [sa'ɣraðo, a] adj sacred, holy

Sáhara ['saara] nm: el ~ the Sahara (desert)

sal [sal] vb V salir ⊳ nf salt; sales de

baño bath salts

sala ['sala] nf room; (tb: ~ de estar) living room; (Teatro) house, auditorium; (de hospital) ward; sala de espera waiting room; sala de estar living room; sala de fiestas dance hall

salado, -a [sa'laðo, a] adj salty; (fig) witty, amusing; agua salada salt water

salar [sa'lar] vt to salt, add salt to

salariado [sala'rjaðo] adj (empleado) salaried

salario [sa'larjo] nm wage, pay

salchicha [sal'tʃitʃa] nf (pork) sausage; salchichón nm (salami-type) sausage

saldo ['saldo] nm (pago) settlement; (de una cuenta) balance; (lo restante) remnant(s) (pl), remainder; (de móvil) credit; saldos nmpl (en tienda) sale

saldré etc vb V salir

salero [sa'lero] nm salt cellar

salgo etc vb V salir

salida [sa'liða] nf (puerta abierta) exit, way out; (acto) leaving, going out; (de tren, Aviac) departure; (Tec) output, production; (fig) way out; (Com) opening; (Geo, válvula) outlet; (de gas) leak; calle sin ~ cul-de-sac; salida de baño (RPL) bathrobe; salida de emergencia/incendios emergency exit/fire escape

⊙ PALABRA CLAVE

salir [sa'lir] vi (partir: tb: salir de) to leave; Juan ha salido Juan is out; salió de la cocina he came out of the kitchen

2 (aparecer) to appear; (disco, libro) to come out; anoche salió en la tele she appeared o was on TV last night; salió en todos los periódicos it was in all the papers

3 (resultar): la muchacha nos salió muy trabajadora the girl turned out to be a very hard worker; la comida te ha salido exquisita the food was

delicious; **sale muy caro** it's very expensive

4: salirle a uno algo: la entrevista que hice me salió bien/mal the interview I did went o turned out well/badly

5: salir adelante: no sé como haré para salir adelante I don't know how I'll get by

salirse vr (líquido) to spill; (animal) to escape

saliva [sa'liβa] nf saliva

salmo ['salmo] nm psalm

salmón [sal'mon] nm salmon

salmonete [salmo'nete] nm red mullet

salón [sa'lon] nm (de casa) living room, lounge; (muebles) lounge suite; **salón de actos** assembly hall; **salón de baile** dance hall; **salón de belleza** beauty parlour

salpicadera [salpika'ðera] (MÉX) nf mudguard (BRIT), fender (US)

salpicadero [salpika'ðero] nm (Auto) dashboard

salpicar [salpi'kar] vt (rociar) to sprinkle, spatter; (esparcir) to scatter

salpicón [salpi'kon] nm (tb: ~ **de marisco**) seafood salad

salsa ['salsa] nf sauce; (con carne asada) gravy; (fig) spice

saltamontes [salta'montes] nm inv grasshopper

saltar [sal'tar] vt to jump (over), leap (over); (dejar de lado) to skip, miss out ▷ vi to jump, leap; (pelota) to bounce; (al aire) to fly up; (quebrarse) to break; (al agua) to dive; (fig) to explode, blow up

salto ['salto] nm jump, leap; (al agua) dive; **salto de agua** waterfall; **salto de altura/longitud** high/long jump

salud [sa'luð] nf health; **¡(a su) ~!** cheers!, good health!; **saludable** adj (de buena salud) healthy; (provechoso) good, beneficial

saludar [salu'ðar] vt to greet; (Mil) to salute; **saludo** nm greeting;

"saludos" (en carta) "best wishes", "regards"

salvación [salβa'θjon] nf salvation; (rescate) rescue

salvado [sal'βaðo] nm bran

salvaje [sal'βaxe] adj wild; (tribu) savage

salvamanteles [salβaman'teles] nm inv table mat

salvamento [salβa'mento] nm rescue

salvapantallas [salβapan'taʎas] nm inv screen saver

salvar [sal'βar] vt (rescatar) to save, rescue; (resolver) to overcome, resolve; (cubrir distancias) to cover, travel; (hacer excepción) to except, exclude; (barco) to salvage

salvavidas [salβa'βiðas] adj inv: **bote/chaleco ~** lifeboat/life jacket

salvo, -a ['salβo, a] adj safe ▷ adv except (for), save; **a ~** out of danger; **~ que** unless

san [san] adj saint; **S~ Juan** St John

sanar [sa'nar] vt (herida) to heal; (persona) to cure ▷ vi (persona) to get well, recover; (herida) to heal

sanatorio [sana'torjo] nm sanatorium

sanción [san'θjon] nf sanction

sancochado, -a [sanko'tʃado, a] (MÉX) adj (Culin) underdone, rare

sandalia [san'dalja] nf sandal

sandía [san'dia] nf watermelon

sandwich ['sandwitʃ] (pl **-s, -es**) nm sandwich

sanfermines [sanfer'mines] nmpl festivities in celebration of San Fermín (Pamplona)

● **SANFERMINES**
●
●
● The **Sanfermines** is a week-long
● festival in Pamplona made famous
● by Ernest Hemingway. From the
● 7th July, the feast of "San Fermín",
● crowds of mainly young people
● take to the streets drinking,

singing and dancing. Early in the morning bulls are released along the narrow streets leading to the bullring, and young men risk serious injury to show their bravery by running out in front of them, a custom which is also typical of many Spanish villages.

sangrar [san'grar] *vt, vi* to bleed; **sangre** *nf* blood

sangría [san'gria] *nf* sangria, sweetened drink of red wine with fruit

sangriento, -a [san'grjento, a] *adj* bloody

sanguíneo, -a [san'gineo, a] *adj* blood *cpd*

sanidad [sani'ðað] *nf* (*tb*: **~ pública**) public health

San Isidro [sani'siðro] *nm patron saint of Madrid*

● SAN ISIDRO

San Isidro is the patron saint of Madrid, and gives his name to the week-long festivities which take place around the 15th May. Originally an 18th-century trade fair, the **San Isidro** celebrations now include music, dance, a famous **romería**, theatre and bullfighting.

sanitario, -a [sani'tarjo, a] *adj* health *cpd*; **sanitarios** *nmpl* toilets (BRIT), washroom (US)

sano, -a ['sano, a] *adj* healthy; (*sin daños*) sound; (*comida*) wholesome; (*entero*) whole, intact; **~ y salvo** safe and sound

No confundir **sano** con la palabra inglesa *sane*.

Santiago [san'tjaɣo] *nm*: **~ (de Chile)** Santiago

santiamén [santja'men] *nm*: **en un ~** in no time at all

santidad [santi'ðað] *nf* holiness,

sanctity

santiguarse [santi'ɣwarse] *vr* to make the sign of the cross

santo, -a ['santo, a] *adj* holy; (*fig*) wonderful, miraculous ▷ *nm/f* saint ▷ *nm* saint's day; **~ y seña** password

santuario [san'twarjo] *nm* sanctuary, shrine

sapo ['sapo] *nm* toad

saque ['sake] *nm* (*Tenis*) service, serve; (*Fútbol*) throw-in; **saque de esquina** corner (kick)

saquear [sake'ar] *vt* (*Mil*) to sack; (*robar*) to loot, plunder; (*fig*) to ransack

sarampión [saram'pjon] *nm* measles *sg*

sarcástico, -a [sar'kastiko, a] *adj* sarcastic

sardina [sar'ðina] *nf* sardine

sargento [sar'xento] *nm* sergeant

sarmiento [sar'mjento] *nm* (*Bot*) vine shoot

sarna ['sarna] *nf* itch; (*Med*) scabies

sarpullido [sarpu'ʎiðo] *nm* (*Med*) rash

sarro ['sarro] *nm* (*en dientes*) tartar, plaque

sartén [sar'ten] *nf* frying pan

sastre ['sastre] *nm* tailor; **sastrería** *nf* (*arte*) tailoring; (*tienda*) tailor's (shop)

Satanás [sata'nas] *nm* Satan

satélite [sa'telite] *nm* satellite

sátira ['satira] *nf* satire

satisfacción [satisfak'θjon] *nf* satisfaction

satisfacer [satisfa'θer] *vt* to satisfy; (*gastos*) to meet; (*pérdida*) to make good; **satisfacerse** *vr* to satisfy o.s., be satisfied; (*vengarse*) to take revenge; **satisfecho, -a** *adj* satisfied; (*contento*) content(ed), happy; (*tb*: **satisfecho de sí mismo**) self-satisfied, smug

saturar [satu'rar] *vt* to saturate; **saturarse** *vr* (*mercado, aeropuerto*) to reach saturation point

sauce ['sauθe] *nm* willow; **sauce llorón** weeping willow

sauna ['sauna] nf sauna

savia ['saβja] nf sap

saxofón [sakso'fon] nm saxophone

sazonar [saθo'nar] vt to ripen; (Culin) to flavour, season

scooter [e'skuter] (ESP) nm scooter

Scotch® [skotʃ] (LAM) nm Sellotape® (BRIT), Scotch tape® (US)

SE abr (= sudeste) SE

○ PALABRA CLAVE

se [se] pron 1 (reflexivo: sg: m) himself; (: f) herself; (: pl) themselves; (: cosa) itself; (: de Vd) yourself; (: de Vds) yourselves; **se está preparando** she's preparing herself

2 (con complemento indirecto) to him; to her; to them; to it; to you; **a usted se lo dije ayer** I told you yesterday; **se compró un sombrero** he bought himself a hat; **se rompió la pierna** he broke his leg

3 (uso recíproco) each other, one another; **se miraron (el uno al otro)** they looked at each other o one another

4 (en oraciones pasivas): **se han vendido muchos libros** a lot of books have been sold

5 (impers): **se dice que ...** people say that ..., it is said that ...; **allí se come muy bien** the food there is very good, you can eat very well there

sé etc [se] vb V **saber; ser**

sea etc vb V **ser**

sebo ['seβo] nm fat, grease

secador [seka'ðor] nm: ~ **de pelo** hair-dryer

secadora [seka'ðora] nf tumble dryer

secar [se'kar] vt to dry; **secarse** vr to dry (off); (río, planta) to dry up

sección [sek'θjon] nf section

seco, -a ['seko, a] adj dry; (carácter) cold; (respuesta) sharp, curt; **parar en ~** to stop dead; **decir algo a secas** to say sth curtly

secretaría [sekreta'ria] nf secretariat

secretario, -a [sekre'tarjo, a] nm/f secretary

secreto, -a [se'kreto, a] adj secret; (persona) secretive ▷ nm secret; (calidad) secrecy

secta ['sekta] nf sect

sector [sek'tor] nm sector

secuela [se'kwela] nf consequence

secuencia [se'kwenθja] nf sequence

secuestrar [sekwes'trar] vt to kidnap; (bienes) to seize, confiscate; **secuestro** nm kidnapping; seizure, confiscation

secundario, -a [sekun'darjo, a] adj secondary

sed [seð] nf thirst; **tener ~** to be thirsty

seda ['seða] nf silk

sedal [se'ðal] nm fishing line

sedán [se'ðan] (LAM) nm saloon (BRIT), sedan (US)

sedante [se'ðante] nm sedative

sede ['seðe] nf (de gobierno) seat; (de compañía) headquarters pl; **Santa S~** Holy See

sedentario, -a [seðen'tarjo, a] adj sedentary

sediento, -a [se'ðjento, a] adj thirsty

sedimento [seði'mento] nm sediment

seducción [seðuk'θjon] nf seduction

seducir [seðu'θir] vt to seduce; (cautivar) to charm, fascinate; (atraer) to attract; **seductor, a** adj seductive; charming, fascinating; attractive ▷ nm/f seducer

segar [se'ɣar] vt (mies) to reap, cut; (hierba) to mow, cut

seglar [se'ɣlar] adj secular, lay

seguida [se'ɣiða] nf: **en ~** at once, right away

seguido, -a [se'ɣiðo, a] adj (continuo) continuous, unbroken; (recto) straight ▷ adv (directo) straight (on); (después) after; (LAM: a menudo) often; **~s**

consecutive, successive; **5 días ~s** 5 days running, 5 days in a row

seguir [se'ɣir] vt to follow; (venir después) to follow on, come after; (proseguir) to continue; (perseguir) to chase, pursue ▷ vi (gen) to follow; (continuar) to continue, carry o go on; **seguirse** vr to follow; **sigo sin comprender** I still don't understand; **sigue lloviendo** it's still raining

según [se'ɣun] prep according to ▷ adv: **¿irás? - ~** are you going? – it all depends ▷ conj as; **~ caminamos** while we walk

segundo, -a [se'ɣundo, a] adj second ▷ nm second ▷ nf second meaning; **de segunda mano** second-hand; **segunda** (Auto) second class; **segunda (marcha)** (Auto) second (gear)

seguramente [seɣura'mente] adv surely; (con certeza) for sure, with certainty

seguridad [seɣuri'ðað] nf safety; (del estado, de casa etc) security; (certidumbre) certainty; (confianza) confidence; (estabilidad) stability; **seguridad social** social security

seguro, -a [se'ɣuro, a] adj (cierto) sure, certain; (fiel) trustworthy; (libre de peligro) safe; (bien defendido, firme) secure ▷ adv for sure, certainly ▷ nm (Com) insurance; **seguro contra terceros/a todo riesgo** third party/comprehensive insurance; **seguros sociales** social security sg

seis [seis] num six

seísmo [se'ismo] nm tremor, earthquake

selección [selek'θjon] nf selection; **seleccionar** vt to pick, choose, select

selectividad [selektiβi'ðað] (ESP) nf university entrance examination

selecto, -a [se'lekto, a] adj select, choice; (escogido) selected

sellar [se'ʎar] vt (documento oficial) to seal; (pasaporte, visado) to stamp

sello ['seʎo] nm stamp; (precinto) seal

selva ['selβa] nf (bosque) forest, woods pl; (jungla) jungle

semáforo [se'maforo] nm (Auto) traffic lights pl; (Ferro) signal

semana [se'mana] nf week; **entre ~** during the week; **Semana Santa** Holy Week; **semanal** adj weekly; **semanario** nm weekly magazine

○ **SEMANA SANTA**
○
○ In Spain celebrations for **Semana**
○ **Santa** (Holy Week) are often
○ spectacular. "Viernes Santo",
○ "Sábado Santo" and "Domingo de
○ Resurrección" (Good Friday, Holy
○ Saturday, Easter Sunday) are all
○ national public holidays, with
○ additional days being given as
○ local holidays. There are fabulous
○ **procesiones** all over the country,
○ with members of "cofradías"
○ (brotherhoods) dressing in hooded
○ robes and parading their "pasos"
○ (religious floats and sculptures)
○ through the streets. Seville has
○ the most famous Holy Week
○ processions.

sembrar [sem'brar] vt to sow; (objetos) to sprinkle, scatter about; (noticias etc) to spread

semejante [seme'xante] adj (parecido) similar ▷ nm fellow man, fellow creature; **~s** alike, similar; **nunca hizo cosa ~** he never did any such thing; **semejanza** nf similarity, resemblance

semejar [seme'xar] vi to seem like, resemble; **semejarse** vr to look alike, be similar

semen ['semen] nm semen

semestral [semes'tral] adj half-yearly, bi-annual

semicírculo [semi'θirkulo] nm semicircle

semidesnatado, -a [semiðesna'taðo, a] adj semi-skimmed

semifinal [semifiˈnal] nf semifinal

semilla [seˈmiʎa] nf seed

seminario [semiˈnarjo] nm (Rel) seminary; (Escol) seminar

sémola [ˈsemola] nf semolina

senado [seˈnaðo] nm senate; **senador, a** nm/f senator

sencillez [senθiˈʎeθ] nf simplicity; (de persona) naturalness; **sencillo, -a** adj simple; natural, unaffected

senda [ˈsenda] nf path, track

senderismo [sendeˈrismo] nm hiking

sendero [senˈdero] nm path, track

sendos, -as [ˈsendos, as] adj pl: **les dio ~ golpes** he hit both of them

senil [seˈnil] adj senile

seno [ˈseno] nm (Anat) bosom, bust; (fig) bosom; **~s** breasts

sensación [sensaˈθjon] nf sensation; (sentido) sense; (sentimiento) feeling; **sensacional** adj sensational

sensato, -a [senˈsato, a] adj sensible

sensible [senˈsible] adj sensitive; (apreciable) perceptible, appreciable; (pérdida) considerable

▮ No confundir **sensible** con la palabra inglesa *sensible*.

sensiblero, -a adj sentimental

sensitivo, -a [sensiˈtiβo, a] adj sense cpd

sensorial [sensoˈrjal] adj sensory

sensual [senˈswal] adj sensual

sentada [senˈtaða] nf sitting; (protesta) sit-in

sentado, -a [senˈtaðo, a] adj: **estar ~** to sit, be sitting (down); **dar por ~** to take for granted, assume

sentar [senˈtar] vt to sit, seat; (fig) to establish ▷ vi (vestido) to suit; (alimento): **~ bien/mal a** to agree/ disagree with; **sentarse** vr (persona) to sit, sit down; (los depósitos) to settle

sentencia [senˈtenθja] nf (máxima) maxim, saying; (Jur) sentence; **sentenciar** vt to sentence

sentido, -a [senˈtiðo, a] adj (pérdida)

regrettable; (carácter) sensitive ▷ nm sense; (sentimiento) feeling; (significado) sense, meaning; (dirección) direction; **mi más ~ pésame** my deepest sympathy; **tener ~** to make sense; **sentido común** common sense; **sentido del humor** sense of humour; **sentido único** one-way (street)

sentimental [sentimenˈtal] adj sentimental; **vida ~** love life

sentimiento [sentiˈmjento] nm feeling

sentir [senˈtir] vt to feel; (percibir) to perceive, sense; (lamentar) to regret, be sorry for ▷ vi (tener la sensación) to feel; (lamentarse) to feel sorry ▷ nm opinion, judgement; **~se bien/mal** to feel well/ill; **lo siento** I'm sorry

seña [ˈseɲa] nf sign; (Mil) password; **señas** nfpl (dirección) address sg; **señas personales** personal description sg

señal [seˈɲal] nf sign; (síntoma) symptom; (Ferro, Tel) signal; (marca) mark; (Com) deposit; **en ~ de** as a token o sign of; **señalar** vt to mark; (indicar) to point out, indicate

señor [seˈɲor] nm (hombre) man; (caballero) gentleman; (dueño) owner, master; (trato: antes de nombre propio) Mr; (: hablando directamente) sir; **muy ~ mío** Dear Sir; **el ~ alcalde/presidente** the mayor/president

señora [seˈɲora] nf (dama) lady; (trato: antes de nombre propio) Mrs; (: hablando directamente) madam; (esposa) wife; **Nuestra S~** Our Lady

señorita [seɲoˈrita] nf (con nombre y/o apellido) Miss; (mujer joven) young lady

señorito [seɲoˈrito] nm young gentleman; (pey) rich kid

sepa etc vb V **saber**

separación [separaˈθjon] nf separation; (división) division; (hueco) gap

separar [sepaˈrar] vt to divide; **separarse** vr (parte) to come away; (partes) to come apart;

(*persona*) to leave, go away; (*matrimonio*) to separate; **separatismo** *nm* separatism

sepia ['sepja] *nf* cuttlefish

septentrional [septentrjo'nal] *adj* northern

se(p)tiembre [sep'tjembre] *nm* September

séptimo, -a ['septimo, a] *adj, nm* seventh

sepulcral [sepul'kral] *adj* (*fig: silencio, atmósfera*) deadly; **sepulcro** *nm* tomb, grave

sepultar [sepul'tar] *vt* to bury; **sepultura** *nf* (*acto*) burial; (*tumba*) grave, tomb

sequía [se'kia] *nf* drought

séquito ['sekito] *nm* (*de rey etc*) retinue; (*seguidores*) followers *pl*

○ **PALABRA CLAVE**

ser [ser] *vi* 1 (*descripción*) to be; **es médica/muy alta** she's a doctor/very tall; **la familia es de Cuzco** his (*o* her *etc*) family is from Cuzco; **soy Ana** (*Tel*) Ana speaking *o* here

2 (*propiedad*): **es de Joaquín** it's Joaquín's, it belongs to Joaquín

3 (*horas, fechas, números*): **es la una** it's one o'clock; **son las seis y media** it's half-past six; **es el 1 de junio** it's the first of June; **somos/son seis** there are six of us/them

4 (*en oraciones pasivas*): **ha sido descubierto ya** it's already been discovered

5: **es de esperar que ...** it is to be hoped *o* I *etc* hope that ...

6 (*locuciones con sub*): **o sea** that is to say; **sea él sea su hermana** either him or his sister

7: **a no ser por él ...** but for him ...

8: **a no ser que: a no ser que tenga uno u** unless he's got one already ▷ *nm* being; **ser humano** human being

sereno, -a [se'reno, a] *adj* (*persona*) calm, unruffled; (*el tiempo*) fine, settled; (*ambiente*) calm, peaceful ▷ *nm* night watchman

serial [ser'jal] *nm* serial

serie ['serje] *nf* series; (*cadena*) sequence, succession; **fuera de ~** out of order; (*fig*) special, out of the ordinary; **fabricación en ~** mass production

seriedad [serje'ðað] *nf* seriousness; (*formalidad*) reliability; **serio, -a** *adj* serious; reliable, dependable, grave, serious; **en serio** *adv* seriously

serigrafía [seriɣra'fia] *nf* silk-screen printing

sermón [ser'mon] *nm* (*Rel*) sermon

seropositivo, -a [seroposi'tiβo] *adj* HIV positive

serpentear [serpente'ar] *vi* to wriggle; (*camino, río*) to wind, snake

serpentina [serpen'tina] *nf* streamer

serpiente [ser'pjente] *nf* snake; **serpiente de cascabel** rattlesnake

serranía [serra'nia] *nf* mountainous area

serrar [se'rrar] *vt* = **aserrar**

serrín [se'rrin] *nm* sawdust

serrucho [se'rrutʃo] *nm* saw

service ['serβis] (*RPL*) *nm* (*Auto*) service

servicio [ser'βiθjo] *nm* service; (*LAM Auto*) service; **servicios** *nmpl* (*ESP*) toilet(s); **servicio incluido** service charge included; **servicio militar** military service

servidumbre [serβi'ðumbre] *nf* (*sujeción*) servitude; (*criados*) servants *pl*, staff

servil [ser'βil] *adj* servile

servilleta [serβi'ʎeta] *nf* serviette, napkin

servir [ser'βir] *vt* to serve ▷ *vi* to serve; (*tener utilidad*) to be of use, be useful; **servirse** *vr* to serve o.s.; **~se de algo** to make use of sth, use sth; **sírvase pasar** please come in

sesenta [se'senta] num sixty

sesión [se'sjon] nf (Pol) session, sitting; (Cine) showing

seso ['seso] nm brain; **sesudo, -a** adj sensible, wise

seta ['seta] nf mushroom; **seta venenosa** toadstool

setecientos, -as [sete'θjentos, as] adj, num seven hundred

setenta [se'tenta] num seventy

seto ['seto] nm hedge

severo, -a [se'βero, a] adj severe

Sevilla [se'βiʎa] n Seville; **sevillano, -a** adj of o from Seville ▷ nm/f native o inhabitant of Seville

sexo ['sekso] nm sex

sexto, -a ['seksto, a] adj, nm sixth

sexual [sek'swal] adj sexual; **vida ~** sex life

si [si] conj if ▷ nm (Mús) B; **me pregunto ~ ...** I wonder if o whether ...

sí [si] adv yes ▷ nm consent ▷ pron (uso impersonal) oneself; (sg: m) himself; (: f) herself; (: de cosa) itself; (de usted) yourself; (pl) themselves; (de ustedes) yourselves; (recíproco) each other; **él no quiere pero yo ~** he doesn't want to but I do; **ella ~ vendrá** she will certainly come, she is sure to come; **claro que ~** of course; **creo que ~** I think so

siamés, -esa [sja'mes, esa] adj, nm/f Siamese

SIDA ['siða] nm abr (= Síndrome de Inmunodeficiencia Adquirida) AIDS

siderúrgico, -a [siðe'rurxiko, a] adj iron and steel cpd

sidra ['siðra] nf cider

siembra ['sjembra] nf sowing

siempre ['sjempre] adv always; (todo el tiempo) all the time; **~ que** (cada vez) whenever; (dado que) provided that; **como ~** as usual; **para ~** for ever

sien [sjen] nf temple

siento etc vb V **sentar; sentir**

sierra ['sjerra] nf (Tec) saw; (cadena de montañas) mountain range

siervo, -a ['sjerβo, a] nm/f slave

siesta ['sjesta] nf siesta, nap; **echar la ~** to have an afternoon nap o a siesta

siete ['sjete] num seven

sifón [si'fon] nm syphon

sigla ['sixla] nf abbreviation; acronym

siglo ['sixlo] nm century; (fig) age

significado [sixnifi'kaðo] nm (de palabra etc) meaning

significar [sixnifi'kar] vt to mean, signify; (notificar) to make known, express

significativo, -a [sixnifika'tiβo, a] adj significant

signo ['sixno] nm sign; **signo de admiración** o **exclamación** exclamation mark; **signo de interrogación** question mark

sigo etc vb V **seguir**

siguiente [si'xjente] adj next, following

siguió etc vb V **seguir**

sílaba ['silaβa] nf syllable

silbar [sil'βar] vt, vi to whistle; **silbato** nm whistle; **silbido** nm whistle, whistling

silenciador [silenθja'ðor] nm silencer

silenciar [silen'θjar] vt (persona) to silence; (escándalo) to hush up; **silencio** nm silence, quiet; **silencioso, -a** adj silent, quiet

silla ['siʎa] nf (asiento) chair; (tb: ~ **de montar**) saddle; **silla de ruedas** wheelchair

sillón [si'ʎon] nm armchair, easy chair

silueta [si'lweta] nf silhouette; (de edificio) outline; (figura) figure

silvestre [sil'βestre] adj wild

simbólico, -a [sim'boliko, a] adj symbolic(al)

simbolizar [simboli'θar] vt to symbolize

símbolo ['simbolo] nm symbol

similar [simi'lar] adj similar

simio ['simjo] nm ape

simpatía [simpa'tia] nf liking; (afecto) affection; (amabilidad) kindness;

simpático, -a adj nice, pleasant; kind ◼ No confundir **simpático** con la palabra inglesa *sympathetic*.

simpatizante [simpati'θante] nmf sympathizer

simpatizar [simpati'θar] vi: **~ con** to get on well with

simple ['simple] adj simple; (elemental) simple, easy; (mero) mere; (puro) pure, sheer ▷ nm simpleton; **simpleza** nf simpleness; (necedad) silly thing; **simplificar** vt to simplify

simposio [sim'posjo] nm symposium

simular [simu'lar] vt to simulate

simultáneo, -a [simul'taneo, a] adj simultaneous

sin [sin] prep without; **la ropa está ~ lavar** the clothes are unwashed; **~ que** without; **~ embargo** however, still

sinagoga [sina'ɣoɣa] nf synagogue

sinceridad [sinθeri'ðað] nf sincerity; **sincero, -a** adj sincere

sincronizar [sinkroni'θar] vt to synchronize

sindical [sindi'kal] adj union cpd, trade-union cpd; **sindicalista** adj, nmf trade unionist

sindicato [sindi'kato] nm (de trabajadores) trade(s) union; (de negociantes) syndicate

síndrome ['sindrome] nm (Med) syndrome; **síndrome de abstinencia** (Med) withdrawal symptoms; **síndrome de de la clase turista** (Med) economy-class syndrome

sinfín [sin'fin] nm: **un ~ de** a great many, no end of

sinfonía [sinfo'nia] nf symphony

singular [singu'lar] adj singular; (fig) outstanding, exceptional; (raro) peculiar, odd

siniestro, -a [si'njestro, a] adj sinister ▷ nm (accidente) accident

sinnúmero [sin'numero] nm = **sinfín**

sino [sino] nm fate, destiny ▷ conj (pero) but; (salvo) except, save

sinónimo, -a [si'nonimo, a] adj

synonymous ▷ nm synonym

síntesis ['sintesis] nf synthesis; **sintético, -a** adj synthetic

sintió vb V **sentir**

síntoma ['sintoma] nm symptom

sintonía [sinto'nia] nf (Radio, Mús: de programa) tuning; **sintonizar** vt (Radio: emisora) to tune (in)

sinvergüenza [simber'ɣwenθa] nmf rogue, scoundrel; **¡es un ~!** he's got a nerve!

siquiera [si'kjera] conj even if, even though ▷ adv at least; **ni ~** not even

Siria ['sirja] nf Syria

sirviente, -a [sir'βjente, a] nm/f servant

sirvo etc vb V **servir**

sistema [sis'tema] nm system; (método) method; **sistema educativo** education system; **sistemático, -a** adj systematic

SISTEMA EDUCATIVO

The reform of the Spanish **sistema educativo** (education system) begun in the early 90s has replaced the courses EGB, BUP and COU with the following: "Primaria" a compulsory 6 years; "Secundaria" a compulsory 4 years and "Bachillerato" an optional 2-year secondary school course, essential for those wishing to go on to higher education.

sitiar [si'tjar] vt to besiege, lay siege to

sitio ['sitjo] nm (lugar) place; (espacio) room, space; (Mil) siege; **sitio de taxis** (MÉX: parada) taxi stand o rank (BRIT); **sitio web** (Inform) website

situación [sitwa'θjon] nf situation, position; (estatus) position, standing

situado, -a [si'tua'ðo] adj situated, placed

situar [si'twar] vt to place, put; (edificio) to locate, situate

slip [slip] *nm* pants *pl*, briefs *pl*

smoking ['smokin, es'mokin] (*pl* **-s**) *nm* dinner jacket (BRIT), tuxedo (US)
■ No confundir **smoking** con la palabra inglesa *smoking*.

SMS *nm* (*mensaje*) text message, SMS message

snob [es'nob] = **esnob**

SO *abr* (= *suroeste*) SW

sobaco [so'βako] *nm* armpit

sobar [so'βar] *vt* (*ropa*) to rumple; (*comida*) to play around with

soberanía [soβera'nia] *nf* sovereignty; **soberano, -a** *adj* sovereign; (*fig*) supreme ▷ *nm/f* sovereign

soberbia [so'βerβja] *nf* pride; haughtiness, arrogance; magnificence

soberbio, -a [so'βerβjo, a] *adj* (*orgulloso*) proud; (*altivo*) arrogant; (*estupendo*) magnificent, superb

sobornar [soβor'nar] *vt* to bribe; **soborno** *nm* bribe

sobra ['soβra] *nf* excess, surplus; **sobras** *nfpl* left-overs, scraps; **de ~** surplus, extra; **tengo de ~** I've more than enough; **sobrado, -a** *adj* (*más que suficiente*) more than enough; (*superfluo*) excessive; **sobrante** *adj* remaining, extra ▷ *nm* surplus, remainder

sobrar [so'βrar] *vt* to exceed, surpass ▷ *vi* (*tener de más*) to be more than enough; (*quedar*) to remain, be left (over)

sobrasada [soβra'saða] *nf* pork sausage spread

sobre ['soβre] *prep* (*gen*) on; (*encima*) on (top of); (*por encima de, arriba de*) over, above; (*más que*) more than; (*además*) in addition to, besides; (*alrededor de*) about ▷ *nm* envelope; **~ todo** above all

sobrecama [soβre'kama] *nf* bedspread

sobrecargar [soβrekar'ɣar] *vt* (*camión*) to overload; (*Com*) to surcharge

sobredosis [soβre'ðosis] *nf inv* overdose

sobreentender [soβre(e)nten'der] *vt* to deduce, infer; **sobreentenderse** *vr*: **se sobreentiende que ...** it is implied that ...

sobrehumano, -a [soβreu'mano, a] *adj* superhuman

sobrellevar [soβreʎe'βar] *vt* to bear, endure

sobremesa [soβre'mesa] *nf*: **durante la ~** after dinner

sobrenatural [soβrenatu'ral] *adj* supernatural

sobrenombre [soβre'nombre] *nm* nickname

sobrepasar [soβrepa'sar] *vt* to exceed, surpass

sobreponerse [soβrepo'nerse] *vr*: **~ a** to overcome

sobresaliente [soβresa'ljente] *adj* outstanding, excellent

sobresalir [soβresa'lir] *vi* to project, jut out; (*fig*) to stand out, excel

sobresaltar [soβresal'tar] *vt* (*asustar*) to scare, frighten; (*sobrecoger*) to startle; **sobresalto** *nm* (*movimiento*) start; (*susto*) scare; (*turbación*) sudden shock

sobretodo [soβre'toðo] *nm* overcoat

sobrevenir [soβreβe'nir] *vi* (*ocurrir*) to happen (unexpectedly); (*resultar*) to follow, ensue

sobrevivir [soβreβi'βir] *vi* to survive

sobrevolar [soβreβo'lar] *vt* to fly over

sobriedad [soβrje'ðað] *nf* sobriety, soberness; (*moderación*) moderation, restraint

sobrino, -a [so'βrino, a] *nm/f* nephew/niece

sobrio, -a [so'βrjo, a] *adj* sober; (*moderado*) moderate, restrained

socarrón, -ona [soka'rron, ona] *adj* (*sarcástico*) sarcastic, ironic(al)

socavón [soka'βon] *nm* (*hoyo*) hole

sociable [so'θjaβle] *adj* (*persona*) sociable, friendly; (*animal*) social

social [so'θjal] adj social; (Com) company cpd

socialdemócrata [soθjalde'mokrata] nmf social democrat

socialista [soθja'lista] adj, nm socialist

socializar [soθjali'θar] vt to socialize

sociedad [soθje'ðað] nf society; (Com) company; **sociedad anónima** limited company; **sociedad de consumo** consumer society

socio, -a ['soθjo, a] nm/f (miembro) member; (Com) partner

sociología [soθjolo'xia] nf sociology; **sociólogo, -a** nm/f sociologist

socorrer [soko'rrer] vt to help; **socorrista** nmf first aider; (en piscina, playa) lifeguard; **socorro** nm (ayuda) help, aid; (Mil) relief; **¡socorro!** help!

soda ['soða] nf (sosa) soda; (bebida) soda (water)

sofá [so'fa] (pl **-s**) nm sofa, settee; **sofá-cama** nm studio couch; sofa bed

sofocar [sofo'kar] vt to suffocate; (apagar) to smother, put out; **sofocarse** vr to suffocate; (fig) to blush, feel embarrassed; **sofoco** nm suffocation; embarrassment

sofreír [sofre'ir] vt (Culin) to fry lightly

software ['sofwer] nm (Inform) software

soga ['soxa] nf rope

sois etc vb V **ser**

soja ['soxa] nf soya

sol [sol] nm sun; (luz) sunshine, sunlight; (Mús) G; **hace ~** it's sunny

solamente [sola'mente] adv only, just

solapa [so'lapa] nf (de chaqueta) lapel; (de libro) jacket

solapado, -a [sola'paðo, a] adj (intenciones) underhand; (gestos, movimiento) sly

solar [so'lar] adj solar, sun cpd; (terreno) plot (of ground)

soldado [sol'daðo] nm soldier; **soldado raso** private

soldador [solda'ðor] nm soldering iron; (persona) welder

soldar [sol'dar] vt to solder, weld

soleado, -a [sole'aðo, a] adj sunny

soledad [sole'ðað] nf solitude; (estado infeliz) loneliness

solemne [so'lemne] adj solemn

soler [so'ler] vi to be in the habit of, be accustomed to; **suele salir a las ocho** she usually goes out at eight o'clock

solfeo [sol'feo] nm solfa

solicitar [soliθi'tar] vt (permiso) to ask for, seek; (puesto) to apply for; (votos) to canvass for; (atención) to attract

solícito, -a [so'liθito, a] adj (diligente) diligent; (cuidadoso) careful; **solicitud** nf (calidad) great care; (petición) request; (a un puesto) application

solidaridad [soliðari'ðað] nf solidarity; **solidario, -a** adj (participación) joint, common; (compromiso) mutually binding

sólido, -a ['soliðo, a] adj solid

soliloquio [soli'lokjo] nm soliloquy

solista [so'lista] nmf soloist

solitario, -a [soli'tarjo, a] adj (persona) lonely, solitary; (lugar) lonely, desolate ▷ nm/f (recluso) recluse; (en la sociedad) loner ▷ nm solitaire

sollozar [soλo'θar] vi to sob; **sollozo** nm sob

solo, -a ['solo, a] adj (único) single, sole; (sin compañía) alone; (solitario) lonely; **hay una sola dificultad** there is just one difficulty; **a solas** alone, by oneself

sólo ['solo] adv only, just

solomillo [solo'miλo] nm sirloin

soltar [sol'tar] vt (dejar ir) to let go of; (desprender) to unfasten, loosen; (librar) to release, set free; (risa etc) to let out

soltero, -a [sol'tero, a] adj single, unmarried ▷ nm/f bachelor/single woman; **solterón, -ona** nm/f old bachelor/spinster

soltura [sol'tura] nf looseness,

slackness; (de los miembros) agility,
ease of movement; (en el hablar)
fluency, ease

soluble [so'luβle] adj (Quím) soluble;
(problema) solvable; **~ en agua** soluble
in water

solución [solu'θjon] nf solution;
solucionar vt (problema) to solve;
(asunto) to settle, resolve

solventar [solβen'tar] vt (pagar)
to settle, pay; (resolver) to resolve;
solvente adj (Econ: empresa, persona)
solvent

sombra ['sombra] nf shadow;
(como protección) shade; **sombras** nfpl
(oscuridad) darkness sg, shadows; **tener
buena/mala ~** to be lucky/unlucky

sombrero [som'brero] nm hat

sombrilla [som'briʎa] nf parasol,
sunshade

sombrío, -a [som'brio, a] adj
(oscuro) dark; (triste) sombre, sad;
(persona) gloomy

someter [some'ter] vt (país) to
conquer; (persona) to subject to one's
will; (informe) to present, submit;
someterse vr to give in, yield, submit;
~ a to subject to

somier [so'mjer] (pl **-s**) n spring
mattress

somnífero [som'nifero] nm sleeping
pill

somos vb V **ser**

son [son] vb V **ser** ▷ nm sound

sonaja [so'naxa] (MÉX) nf = **sonajero**

sonajero [sona'xero] nm (baby's)
rattle

sonambulismo [sonambu'lismo]
nm sleepwalking; **sonámbulo, -a**
nm/f sleepwalker

sonar [so'nar] vt to ring ▷ vi to
sound; (hacer ruido) to make a noise;
(pronunciarse) to be sounded, be
pronounced; (ser conocido) to sound
familiar; (campana) to ring; (reloj) to
strike, chime; **sonarse** vr: **~se (las
narices)** to blow one's nose; **me suena
ese nombre** that name rings a bell

sonda ['sonda] nf (Náut) sounding;
(Tec) bore, drill; (Med) probe

sondear [sonde'ar] vt to sound; to
bore (into), drill; to probe, sound; (fig)
to sound out; **sondeo** nm sounding,
boring, drilling; (fig) poll, enquiry

sonido [so'niðo] nm sound

sonoro, -a [so'noro, a] adj sonorous;
(resonante) loud, resonant

sonreír [sonre'ir] vi to smile; **sonreírse**
vr to smile; **sonriente** adj
smiling; **sonrisa** nf smile

sonrojarse [sonro'xarse] vr to blush,
go red; **sonrojo** nm blush

soñador, a [soɲa'ðor, a] nm/f
dreamer

soñar [so'ɲar] vt, vi to dream; **~ con**
to dream about o of

soñoliento, -a [soɲo'ljento, a] adj
sleepy, drowsy

sopa ['sopa] nf soup

soplar [so'plar] vt (polvo) to blow
away, blow off; (inflar) to blow up; (vela)
to blow out ▷ vi to blow; **soplo** nm
blow, puff; (de viento) puff, gust

soplón, -ona [so'plon, ona] (fam)
nm/f (niño) telltale; (de policía) grass
(fam)

soporífero [sopo'rifero] nm sleeping
pill

soportable [sopor'taβle] adj
bearable

soportar [sopor'tar] vt to bear, carry;
(fig) to bear, put up with

⬛ No confundir **soportar** con la
palabra inglesa **support**.

soporte nm support; (fig) pillar,
support

soprano [so'prano] nf soprano

sorber [sor'βer] vt (chupar) to sip;
(absorber) to soak up, absorb

sorbete [sor'βete] nm iced fruit drink

sorbo ['sorβo] nm (trago: grande) gulp,
swallow; (: pequeño) sip

sordera [sor'ðera] nf deafness

sórdido, -a ['sorðiðo, a] adj dirty,
squalid

sordo, -a ['sorðo, a] adj (persona) deaf

▷ nm/f deaf person; **sordomudo, -a** adj deaf and dumb

sorna ['sorna] nf sarcastic tone

soroche [so'rotʃe] (CAM) nm mountain sickness

sorprendente [sorpren'dente] adj surprising

sorprender [sorpren'der] vt to surprise; **sorpresa** nf surprise

sortear [sorte'ar] vt to draw lots for; (rifar) to raffle; (dificultad) to avoid; **sorteo** nm (en lotería) draw; (rifa) raffle

sortija [sor'tixa] nf ring; (rizo) ringlet, curl

sosegado, -a [sose'ɣaðo, a] adj quiet, calm

sosiego [so'sjeɣo] nm quiet(ness), calm(ness)

soso, -a ['soso, a] adj (Culin) tasteless; (aburrido) dull, uninteresting

sospecha [sos'petʃa] nf suspicion; **sospechar** vt to suspect; **sospechoso, -a** adj suspicious; (testimonio, opinión) suspect ▷ nm/f suspect

sostén [sos'ten] nm (apoyo) support; (sujetador) bra; (alimentación) sustenance, food

sostener [soste'ner] vt to support; (mantener) to keep up, maintain; (alimentar) to sustain, keep going; **sostenerse** vr to support o.s.; (seguir) to continue, remain; **sostenido, -a** adj continuous, sustained; (prolongado) prolonged

sotana [so'tana] nf (Rel) cassock

sótano ['sotano] nm basement

soy [soi] vb V **ser**

soya ['soja] (LAM) nf soya (BRIT), soy (US)

Sr. abr (=Señor) Mr

Sra. abr (=Señora) Mrs

Sras. abr (=Señoras) Mrs

Sres. abr (=Señores) Messrs

Srta. abr (=Señorita) Miss

Sta. abr (=Santa) St

Sto. abr (=Santo) St

su [su] pron (de él) his; (de ella) her; (de una cosa) its; (de ellos, ellas) their; (de usted, ustedes) your

suave ['swaβe] adj gentle; (superficie) smooth; (trabajo) easy; (música, voz) soft, sweet; **suavidad** nf gentleness; smoothness; softness, sweetness; **suavizante** nm (de ropa) softener; (del pelo) conditioner; **suavizar** vt to soften; (quitar la aspereza) to smooth (out)

subasta [su'βasta] nf auction; **subastar** vt to auction (off)

subcampeón, -ona [suβkampe'on, ona] nm/f runner-up

subconsciente [suβkon'sθjente] adj, nm subconscious

subdesarrollado, -a [suβðesarro'ʎaðo, a] adj underdeveloped

subdesarrollo [suβðesa'rroʎo] nm underdevelopment

subdirector, a [suβðirek'tor, a] nm/f assistant director

súbdito, -a ['suβðito, a] nm/f subject

subestimar [suβesti'mar] vt to underestimate, underrate

subida [su'βiða] nf (de montaña etc) ascent, climb; (de precio) rise, increase; (pendiente) slope, hill

subir [su'βir] vt (objeto) to raise, lift up; (cuesta, calle) to go up; (colina, montaña) to climb; (precio) to raise, put up ▷ vi to go up, come up; (a un coche) to get in; (a un autobús, tren o avión) to get on, board; (precio) to rise, go up; (río, marea) to rise; **subirse** vr to get up, climb

súbito, -a ['suβito, a] adj (repentino) sudden; (imprevisto) unexpected

subjetivo, -a [suβxe'tiβo, a] adj subjective

sublevar [suβle'βar] vt to rouse to revolt; **sublevarse** vr to revolt, rise

sublime [su'βlime] adj sublime

submarinismo [suβmari'nismo] nm scuba diving

submarino, -a [suβma'rino, a] adj

underwater ▷ nm submarine

subnormal [suβ'nor'mal] adj subnormal ▷ nmf subnormal person

subordinado, -a [suβorði'naðo, a] adj, nm/f subordinate

subrayar [suβra'jar] vt to underline

subsanar [suβsa'nar] vt to rectify

subsidio [suβ'siðjo] nm (ayuda) aid, financial help; (subvención) subsidy, grant; (de enfermedad, paro etc) benefit, allowance

subsistencia [suβsis'tenθja] nf subsistence

subsistir [suβsis'tir] vi to subsist; (sobrevivir) to survive, endure

subte ['suβte] (RPL) nm underground (BRIT), subway (US)

subterráneo, -a [suβte'rraneo, a] adj underground, subterranean ▷ nm underpass, underground passage

subtitulado [suβtitu'laðo] adj subtitled

subtítulo [suβ'titulo] nm (Cine) subtitle

suburbio [su'βurβjo] nm (barrio) slum quarter

subvención [suββen'θjon] nf (Econ) subsidy, grant; **subvencionar** vt to subsidize

sucedáneo, -a [suθe'ðaneo, a] adj substitute ▷ nm substitute (food)

suceder [suθe'ðer] vt, vi to happen; (seguir) to succeed, follow; **lo que sucede es que ...** the fact is that ...; **sucesión** nf succession; (serie) sequence, series

sucesivamente [suθesiβa'mente] adv: **y así ~** and so on

sucesivo, -a [suθe'siβo, a] adj successive, following; **en lo ~** in future, from now on

suceso [su'θeso] nm (hecho) event, happening; (incidente) incident

▌No confundir **suceso** con la palabra inglesa **success**.

suciedad [suθje'ðað] nf (estado) dirtiness; (mugre) dirt, filth

sucio, -a [su'θjo, a] adj dirty

suculento, -a [suku'lento, a] adj succulent

sucumbir [sukum'bir] vi to succumb

sucursal [sukur'sal] nf branch (office)

sudadera [suða'ðera] nf sweatshirt

Sudáfrica [suð'afrika] nf South Africa

Sudamérica [suða'merika] nf South America; **sudamericano, -a** adj, nm/f South American

sudar [su'ðar] vt, vi to sweat

sudeste [su'ðeste] nm south-east

sudoeste [suðo'este] nm south-west

sudoku [su'ðoku] nm sudoku

sudor [su'ðor] nm sweat; **sudoroso, -a** adj sweaty, sweating

Suecia [su'eθja] nf Sweden; **sueco, -a** adj Swedish ▷ nm/f Swede

suegro, -a [su'eɣro, a] nm/f father-/mother-in-law

suela ['swela] nf sole

sueldo ['sweldo] nm pay, wage(s) (pl)

suele etc vb V **soler**

suelo ['swelo] nm (tierra) ground; (de casa) floor

suelto, -a ['swelto, a] adj loose; (libre) free; (separado) detached; (ágil) quick, agile ▷ nm (loose) change, small change

sueñito [swe'ɲito] (LAM) nm nap

sueño etc ['sweɲo] vb V **soñar** ▷ nm sleep; (somnolencia) sleepiness, drowsiness; (lo soñado, fig) dream; **tener ~** to be sleepy

suero ['swero] nm (Med) serum; (de leche) whey

suerte ['swerte] nf (fortuna) luck; (azar) chance; (destino) fate, destiny; (especie) sort, kind; **tener ~** to be lucky

suéter ['sweter] nm sweater

suficiente [sufi'θjente] adj enough, sufficient ▷ nm (Escol) pass

sufragio [su'fraxjo] nm (voto) vote; (derecho de voto) suffrage

sufrido, -a [su'friðo, a] adj (persona) tough; (paciente) long-suffering, patient

sufrimiento [sufri'mjento] nm
(dolor) suffering
sufrir [su'frir] vt (padecer) to suffer;
(soportar) to bear, put up with; (apoyar)
to hold up, support ▷ vi to suffer
sugerencia [suxe'renθja] nf
suggestion
sugerir [suxe'rir] vt to suggest;
(sutilmente) to hint
sugestión [suxes'tjon] nf
suggestion; (sutil) hint; **sugestionar**
vt to influence
sugestivo, -a [suxes'tiβo, a] adj
stimulating; (fascinante) fascinating
suicida [sui'θiða] adj suicidal ▷ nmf
suicidal person; (muerto) suicide,
person who has committed suicide;
suicidarse vr to commit suicide, kill
o.s.; **suicidio** nm suicide
Suiza ['swiθa] nf Switzerland; **suizo,
-a** adj, nm/f Swiss
sujeción [suxe'θjon] nf subjection
sujetador [suxeta'ðor] nm (sostén)
bra
sujetar [suxe'tar] vt (fijar) to fasten;
(detener) to hold down; **sujetarse** vr to
subject o.s.; **sujeto, -a** adj fastened,
secure ▷ nm subject; (individuo)
individual; **sujeto a** subject to
suma ['suma] nf (cantidad) total,
sum; (de dinero) sum; (acto) adding (up),
addition; **en ~** in short
sumar [su'mar] vt to add (up) ▷ vi
to add up
sumergir [sumer'xir] vt to
submerge; (hundir) to sink
suministrar [sumini'strar] vt to
supply, provide; **suministro** nm
supply; (acto) supplying, providing
sumir [su'mir] vt to sink, submerge;
(fig) to plunge
sumiso, -a [su'miso, a] adj
submissive, docile
sumo, -a ['sumo, a] adj great,
extreme; (autoridad) highest, supreme
suntuoso, -a [sun'twoso, a] adj

sumptuous, magnificent
supe etc vb V **saber**
super... [super] prefijo super..., over...
superbueno, -a [super'bweno, a]
adj great, fantastic
súper ['super] nf (gasolina) four-star
(petrol)
superar [supe'rar] vt (sobreponerse
a) to overcome; (rebasar) to surpass,
do better than; (pasar) to go beyond;
superarse vr to excel o.s.
superficial [superfi'θjal] adj
superficial; (medida) surface cpd, of
the surface
superficie [super'fiθje] nf surface;
(área) area
superfluo, -a [su'perflwo, a] adj
superfluous
superior [supe'rjor] adj (piso, clase)
upper; (temperatura, número, nivel)
higher; (mejor: calidad, producto)
superior, better ▷ nmf superior;
superioridad nf superiority
supermercado [supermer'kaðo] nm
supermarket
superponer [superpo'ner] vt to
superimpose
superstición [supersti'θjon] nf
superstition; **supersticioso, -a** adj
superstitious
supervisar [superβi'sar] vt to
supervise
supervivencia [superβi'βenθja]
nf survival
superviviente [superβi'βjente] adj
surviving
supiera etc vb V **saber**
suplantar [suplan'tar] vt to
supplant
suplementario, -a
[suplemen'tarjo, a] adj
supplementary
suplemento [suple'mento] nm
supplement
suplente [su'plente] adj, nm
substitute
supletorio, -a [suple'torjo, a] adj
supplementary ▷ nm supplement;

teléfono ~ extension

súplica ['suplika] *nf* request; (*Jur*) petition

suplicar [supli'kar] *vt* (*cosa*) to beg (for), plead for; (*persona*) to beg, plead with

suplicio [su'pliθjo] *nm* torture

suplir [su'plir] *vt* (*compensar*) to make good, make up for; (*reemplazar*) to replace, substitute ▷ *vi*: **~ a** to take the place of, substitute for

supo *etc vb* V **saber**

suponer [supo'ner] *vt* to suppose; **suposición** *nf* supposition

supremír [supri'mir] *vt* to suppress; (*derecho, costumbre*) to abolish; (*palabra etc*) to delete; (*restricción*) to cancel, lift

supuesto, -a [su'pwesto, a] *pp de* **suponer** ▷ *adj* (*hipotético*) supposed ▷ *nm* assumption, hypothesis; **~ que** since; **por ~** of course

sur [sur] *nm* south

suramericano, -a [surameri'kano, a] *adj* South American ▷ *nm/f* South American

surcar [sur'kar] *vt* to plough; **surco** *nm* (*en metal, disco*) groove; (*Agr*) furrow

surfear [surfe'ar] *vt*: **~ el Internet** to surf the internet

surgir [sur'xir] *vi* to arise, emerge; (*dificultad*) to come up, crop up

suroeste [suro'este] *nm* south-west

surtido, -a [sur'tiðo, a] *adj* mixed, assorted ▷ *nm* (*selección*) selection, assortment; (*abastecimiento*) supply, stock; **surtidor** *nm* (*tb*: **surtidor de gasolina**) petrol pump (BRIT), gas pump (US)

surtir [sur'tir] *vt* to supply, provide ▷ *vi* to spout, spurt

susceptible [susθep'tiβle] *adj* susceptible; (*sensible*) sensitive; **~ de** capable of

suscitar [susθi'tar] *vt* to cause, provoke; (*interés, sospechas*) to arouse

suscribir [suskri'βir] *vt* (*firmar*) to sign; (*respaldar*) to subscribe to, endorse; **suscribirse** *vr* to subscribe;

suscripción *nf* subscription

susodicho, -a [suso'ðitʃo, a] *adj* above-mentioned

suspender [suspen'der] *vt* (*objeto*) to hang (up), suspend; (*trabajo*) to stop, suspend; (*Escol*) to fail; (*interrumpir*) to adjourn; (*atrasar*) to postpone

suspense [sus'pense] *nm* suspense; **película/novela de ~** thriller

suspensión [suspen'sjon] *nf* suspension; (*fig*) stoppage, suspense

suspenso, -a [sus'penso, a] *adj* hanging, suspended; (*ESP Escol*) failed ▷ *nm* (*ESP Escol*) **película o novela de ~** (LAM) thriller; **quedar o estar en ~** to be pending

suspicaz [suspi'kaθ] *adj* suspicious, distrustful

suspirar [suspi'rar] *vi* to sigh; **suspiro** *nm* sigh

sustancia [sus'tanθja] *nf* substance

sustento [sus'tento] *nm* support; (*alimento*) sustenance, food

sustituir [sustitu'ir] *vt* to substitute, replace; **sustituto, -a** *nm/f* substitute, replacement

susto ['susto] *nm* fright, scare

sustraer [sustra'er] *vt* to remove, take away; (*Mat*) to subtract

susurrar [susu'rrar] *vi* to whisper; **susurro** *nm* whisper

sutil [su'til] *adj* (*aroma, diferencia*) subtle; (*tenue*) thin; (*inteligencia, persona*) sharp

suyo, -a ['sujo, a] (*con artículo o después del verbo ser*) *adj* (*de él*) his; (*de ella*) hers; (*de ellos, ellas*) theirs; (*de Ud, Uds*) yours; **un amigo ~** a friend of his (o hers o theirs o yours)

t

Tabacalera [taβaka'lera] nf *Spanish state tobacco monopoly*

tabaco [ta'βako] nm tobacco; (ESP: fam) cigarettes pl

tabaquería [tabake'ria] (LAM) nf tobacconist's (shop) (BRIT), smoke shop (US); **tabaquero, -a** (LAM) nm/f tobacconist

taberna [ta'βerna] nf bar, pub (BRIT)

tabique [ta'βike] nm partition (wall)

tabla ['taβla] nf (de madera) plank; (estante) shelf; (de vestido) pleat; (Arte) panel; **tablas** nfpl: **estar** o **quedar** **en ~s** to draw; **tablado** nm (plataforma) platform; (Teatro) stage

tablao [ta'βlao] nm (tb: **~ flamenco**) flamenco show

tablero [ta'βlero] nm (de madera) plank, board; (de ajedrez, damas) board; **tablero de mandos** (LAM Auto) dashboard

tableta [ta'βleta] nf (Med) tablet; (de chocolate) bar

tablón [ta'βlon] nm (de suelo) plank; (de techo) beam; **tablón de anuncios** notice (BRIT) o bulletin (US) board

tabú [ta'βu] nm taboo

taburete [taβu'rete] nm stool

tacaño, -a [ta'kaɲo, a] adj mean

tacha ['tatʃa] nf flaw; (Tec) stud; **tachar** vt (borrar) to cross out; **tachar de** to accuse of

tacho ['tatʃo] (cs) nm (balde) bucket; **tacho de la basura** rubbish bin (BRIT), trash can (US)

taco ['tako] nm (Billar) cue; (de billetes) book; (cs: de zapato) heel; (tarugo) peg; (palabrota) swear word

tacón [ta'kon] nm heel; **de ~ alto** high-heeled

táctica ['taktika] nf tactics pl

táctico, -a ['taktiko, a] adj tactical

tacto ['takto] nm touch; (fig) tact

tajada [ta'xaða] nf slice

tajante [ta'xante] adj sharp

tajo ['taxo] nm (corte) cut; (Geo) cleft

tal [tal] adj such ▷ pron (persona) someone, such a one; (cosa) something, such a thing ▷ adv: **~ como** (igual) just as; ▷ conj: **con ~ de que** provided that; **~ cual** (como es) just as it is; **~ vez** perhaps; **~ como** such as; **~ para cual** (dos iguales) two of a kind; **¿qué ~?** how are things?; **¿qué ~ te gusta?** how do you like it?

taladrar [tala'ðrar] vt to drill; **taladro** nm drill

talante [ta'lante] nm (humor) mood; (voluntad) will, willingness

talar [ta'lar] vt to fell, cut down; (devastar) to devastate

talco ['talko] nm (polvos) talcum powder

talento [ta'lento] nm talent; (capacidad) ability

TALGO ['talɣo] (ESP) nm abr (= tren articulado ligero Goicoechea-Oriol) ≈ HST (BRIT)

talismán [talis'man] nm talisman

talla ['taʎa] nf (estatura, fig, Med) height, stature; (palo) measuring rod; (Arte) carving; (medida) size

tallar [ta'ʎar] vt (madera) to carve;

(metal etc) to engrave; *(medir)* to measure

tallarines [taʎa'rrines] *nmpl* noodles

talle ['taʎe] *nm (Anat)* waist; *(fig)* appearance

taller [ta'ʎer] *nm (Tec)* workshop; *(de artista)* studio

tallo ['taʎo] *nm (de planta)* stem; *(de hierba)* blade; *(brote)* shoot

talón [ta'lon] *nm (Anat)* heel; *(Com)* counterfoil; *(cheque)* cheque *(BRIT)*, check *(US)*

talonario [talo'narjo] *nm (de cheques)* chequebook *(BRIT)*, checkbook *(US)*; *(de recibos)* receipt book

tamaño, -a [ta'maɲo, a] *adj (tan grande)* such a big; *(tan pequeño)* such a small ▷ *nm* size; **de ~ natural** full-size

tamarindo [tama'rindo] *nm* tamarind

tambalearse [tambale'arse] *vr (persona)* to stagger; *(vehículo)* to sway

también [tam'bjen] *adv (igualmente)* also, too, as well; *(además)* besides

tambor [tam'bor] *nm* drum; *(Anat)* eardrum; **tambor del freno** brake drum

Támesis ['tamesis] *nm* Thames

tamizar [tami'θar] *vt* to sieve

tampoco [tam'poko] *adv* nor, neither; **yo ~ lo compré** I didn't buy it either

tampón [tam'pon] *nm* tampon

tan [tan] *adv* so; **~ es así que ...** so much so that ...

tanda ['tanda] *nf (gen)* series; *(turno)* shift

tangente [tan'xente] *nf* tangent

tangerina [tanxe'rina] *(LAM)* *nf* tangerine

tangible [tan'xiβle] *adj* tangible

tanque ['tanke] *nm (cisterna, Mil)* tank; *(Auto)* tanker

tantear [tante'ar] *vt (calcular)* to reckon (up); *(medir)* to take the measure of; *(probar)* to test, try out; *(tomar la medida: persona)* to take the measurements of; *(situación)* to sound out ▷ *vi (Deporte)* to score; **tanteo** *nm (cálculo)*

(rough) calculation; *(prueba)* test, trial; *(Deporte)* scoring

tanto, -a ['tanto, a] *adj (cantidad)* so much, as much ▷ *adv (cantidad)* so much, as much; *(tiempo)* so long, as long ▷ *conj:* **en ~ que** while ▷ *nm (suma)* certain amount; *(proporción)* so much; *(punto)* point; *(gol)* goal; **un ~ perezoso** somewhat lazy ▷ *pron:* **cada uno paga ~** each one pays so much; **~s** so many, as many; **20 y ~s** 20-odd; **hasta ~ (que)** until such time as; **~ tú como yo** both you and I; **~ como eso** as much as that; **~ más ... cuanto que** all the more ... because; **~ mejor/peor** so much the better/the worse; **~ si viene como si va** whether he comes or whether he goes; **~ es así que** so much so that; **por (lo) ~** therefore; **entre ~** meanwhile; **estar al ~** to be up to date; **me he vuelto ronco de o con ~ hablar** I have become hoarse with so much talking; **a ~s de agosto** on such and such a day in August

tapa ['tapa] *nf (de caja, olla)* lid; *(de botella)* top; *(de libro)* cover; *(comida)* snack

tapadera [tapa'ðera] *nf* lid, cover

tapar [ta'par] *vt (cubrir)* to cover; *(envolver)* to wrap o cover up; *(la vista)* to obstruct; *(persona, falta)* to conceal; *(MÉX, CAM: diente)* to fill; **taparse** *vr* to wrap o.s. up

taparrabo [tapa'rraβo] *nm* loincloth

tapete [ta'pete] *nm* table cover

tapia ['tapja] *nf (garden)* wall

tapicería [tapiθe'ria] *nf* tapestry; *(para muebles)* upholstery; *(tienda)* upholsterer's *(shop)*

tapiz [ta'piθ] *nm (alfombra)* carpet; *(tela tejida)* tapestry; **tapizar** *vt (muebles)* to upholster

tapón [ta'pon] *nm (de botella)* top; *(de lavabo)* plug; **tapón de rosca** screw-top

taquigrafía [takiɣra'fia] *nf* shorthand; **taquígrafo, -a** *nm/f* shorthand writer, stenographer

taquilla [ta'kiʎa] *nf (donde se*

compra) booking office; (suma recogida) takings pl

tarántula [ta'rantula] nf tarantula

tararear [tarare'ar] vi to hum

tardar [tar'ðar] vi (tomar tiempo) to take a long time; (llegar tarde) to be late; (demorar) to delay; **¿tarda mucho el tren?** does the train take (very) long; **a más ~** at the latest; **no tardes en venir** come soon

tarde ['tarðe] adv late ▷ nf (de día) afternoon; (al anochecer) evening; **de ~ en ~** from time to time; **¡buenas ~s!** good afternoon!; **a o por la ~** in the afternoon; in the evening

tardío, -a [tar'ðio, a] adj (retrasado) late; (lento) slow to arrive

tarea [ta'rea] nf task; (faena) chore; (Escol) homework

tarifa [ta'rifa] nf (lista de precios) price list; (precio) tariff

tarima [ta'rima] nf (plataforma) platform

tarjeta [tar'xeta] nf card; **tarjeta de crédito/de Navidad/postal/ telefónica** credit card/Christmas card/postcard/phonecard; **tarjeta de embarque** boarding pass; **tarjeta de memoria** memory card; **tarjeta prepago** top-up card; **tarjeta SIM** SIM card

tarro ['tarro] nm jar, pot

tarta ['tarta] nf (pastel) cake; (de base dura) tart

tartamudear [tartamuðe'ar] vi to stammer; **tartamudo, -a** adj stammering ▷ nm/f stammerer

tártaro, -a ['tartaro, a] adj: **salsa tártara** tartar(e) sauce

tasa ['tasa] nf (precio) (fixed) price, rate; (valoración) valuation; (medida, norma) measure, standard; **tasa de cambio/interés** exchange/interest rate; **tasas de aeropuerto** airport tax; **tasas universitarias** university fees

tasar [ta'sar] vt (arreglar el precio) to fix a price for; (valorar) to value, assess

tasca ['taska] (fam) nf pub

tatarabuelo, -a [tatara'βwelo, a] nm/f great-great-grandfather/mother

tatuaje [ta'twaxe] nm (dibujo) tattoo; (acto) tattooing

tatuar [ta'twar] vt to tattoo

taurino, -a [tau'rino, a] adj bullfighting cpd

Tauro ['tauro] nm Taurus

tauromaquia [tauro'makja] nf tauromachy, (art of) bullfighting

taxi ['taksi] nm taxi; **taxista** [tak'sista] nmf taxi driver

taza ['taθa] nf cup; (de retrete) bowl; **~ para café** coffee cup; **taza de café** cup of coffee; **tazón** nm (taza grande) mug, large cup; (de fuente) basin

te [te] pron (complemento de objeto) you; (complemento indirecto) (to) you; (reflexivo) to yourself; **¿~ duele mucho el brazo?** does your arm hurt a lot?; **~ equivocas** you're wrong; **¡cálma~!** calm down!

té [te] nm tea

teatral [tea'tral] adj theatre cpd; (fig) theatrical

teatro [te'atro] nm theatre; (Literatura) plays pl, drama

tebeo [te'βeo] nm comic

techo ['tetʃo] nm (externo) roof; (interno) ceiling; **techo corredizo** sunroof

tecla ['tekla] nf key; **teclado** nm keyboard; **teclear** vi (Mús) to strum; (con los dedos) to tap ▷ vt (Inform) to key in

técnica ['teknika] nf technique; (tecnología) technology; V tb **técnico**

técnico, -a ['tekniko, a] adj technical ▷ nm/f technician; (experto) expert

tecnología [teknolo'xia] nf technology; **tecnológico, -a** adj technological

tecolote [teko'lote] (MÉX) nm owl

tedioso, -a [te'ðjoso, a] adj boring, tedious

teja ['texa] nf tile; (Bot) lime (tree); **tejado** nm (flat) roof

tejanos [te'xanos] nmpl (vaqueros) jeans

tejemaneje [texema'nexe] nm (lío)
fuss; (intriga) intrigue

tejer [te'xer] vt to weave; (hacer punto)
to knit; (fig) to fabricate; **tejido** nm
(tela) material, fabric; (telaraña) web;
(Anat) tissue

tel [tel] abr (= teléfono) tel

tela ['tela] nf (tejido) material;
(telaraña) web; (en líquido) skin; **telar**
nm (máquina) loom

telaraña [tela'raɲa] nf cobweb

tele ['tele] (fam) nf telly (BRIT), tube (US)

tele... ['tele] prefijo tele...; **telebasura**
nf trash TV; **telecomunicación** nf
telecommunication; **telediario** nm
television news; **teledirigido, -a** adj
remote-controlled

teleférico [tele'feriko] nm (de esquí)
ski-lift

telefonear [telefone'ar] vi to
telephone

telefónico, -a [tele'foniko, a] adj
telephone cpd

telefonillo [telefo'niʎo] nm (de
puerta) intercom

telefonista [telefo'nista] nmf
telephonist

teléfono [te'lefono] nm (tele)phone;
estar hablando al ~ to be on the
phone; **llamar a algn por ~** to ring sb
(up) o phone sb (up); **teléfono celular**
(LAM) mobile phone; **teléfono con
cámara** camera phone; **teléfono
inalámbrico** cordless phone; **teléfono
móvil** (ESP) mobile phone

telégrafo [te'leɣrafo] nm telegraph

telegrama [tele'ɣrama] nm
telegram

tele: **telenovela** nf soap (opera);
teleobjetivo nm telephoto lens;
telepatía nf telepathy; **telepático,
-a** adj telepathic; **telerrealidad** nf
reality TV; **telescopio** nm telescope;
telesilla nm chairlift; **telespectador,
a** nm/f viewer; **telesquí** nm ski-lift;
teletarjeta nf phonecard; **teletexto**
nm teletext; **teletipo** nm teletype;
teletrabajador, a nm/f teleworker;

teletrabajo nm teleworking;
televentas nfpl telesales

televidente [teleβi'ðente] nmf
viewer

televisar [teleβi'sar] vt to televise

televisión [teleβi'sjon] nf of television;
televisión digital digital television

televisor [teleβi'sor] nm television
set

télex ['teleks] nm inv telex

telón [te'lon] nm curtain; **telón de
acero** (Pol) iron curtain; **telón de
fondo** backcloth, background

tema ['tema] nm (asunto) subject,
topic; (Mús) theme; **temático, -a** adj
thematic

temblar [tem'blar] vi to shake,
tremble; (por frío) to shiver; **temblor**
nm trembling; (de tierra) earthquake;
tembloroso, -a adj trembling

temer [te'mer] vt to fear ▷ vi to be
afraid; **temo que llegue tarde** I am
afraid he may be late

temible [te'miβle] adj fearsome

temor [te'mor] nm (miedo) fear; (duda)
suspicion

témpano ['tempano] nm (tb: ~ de
hielo) ice-floe

temperamento [tempera'mento]
nm temperament

temperatura [tempera'tura] nf
temperature

tempestad [tempes'taθ] nf storm

templado, -a [tem'plaðo, a] adj
(moderado) moderate; (frugal) frugal;
(agua) lukewarm; (clima) mild;
(Mús) well-tuned; **templanza** nf
moderation; mildness

templar [tem'plar] vt (moderar) to
moderate; (furia) to restrain; (calor) to
reduce; (afinar) to tune (up); (acero) to
temper; (tuerca) to tighten up; **temple**
nm (ajuste) tempering; (afinación)
tuning; (pintura) tempera

templo ['templo] nm (iglesia) church;
(pagano etc) temple

temporada [tempo'raða] nf time,
period; (estación) season

temporal [tempo'ral] *adj (no permanente)* temporary ▷ *nm* storm

temprano, -a [tem'prano, a] *adj* early; *(demasiado pronto)* too soon, too early

ten *vb* V **tener**

tenaces [te'naθes] *adj pl* V **tenaz**

tenaz [te'naθ] *adj (material)* tough; *(persona)* tenacious; *(creencia, resistencia)* stubborn

tenaza(s) [te'naθa(s)] *nf(pl)* (Med) forceps; *(Tec)* pliers; *(Zool)* pincers

tendedero [tende'ðero] *nm (para ropa)* drying place; *(cuerda)* clothes line

tendencia [ten'denθja] *nf* tendency; **tener ~ a** to tend to, have a tendency to

tender [ten'der] *vt (extender)* to spread out; *(colgar)* to hang out; *(vía férrea, cable)* to lay; *(estirar)* to stretch ▷ *vi*: **~ a** to tend to, have a tendency towards; **tenderse** *vr* to lie down; **~ la cama/mesa** (LAM) to make the bed/lay (BRIT) o set (US) the table

tenderete [tende'rete] *nm (puesto)* stall; *(exposición)* display of goods

tendero, -a [ten'dero, a] *nm/f* shopkeeper

tendón [ten'don] *nm* tendon

tendré *etc vb* V **tener**

tenebroso, -a [tene'βroso, a] *adj (oscuro)* dark; *(fig)* gloomy

tenedor [tene'ðor] *nm (Culin)* fork

tenencia [te'nenθja] *nf (de casa)* tenancy; *(de oficio)* tenure; *(de propiedad)* possession

○ PALABRA CLAVE

tener [te'ner] *vt* **1** *(poseer, gen)* to have; *(en la mano)* to hold; **¿tienes un boli?** have you got a pen?; **va a tener un niño** she's going to have a baby; **¡ten** (o **tenga**)!, **¡aquí tienes** (o **tiene**)! here you are!

2 *(edad, medidas)* to be: **tiene 7 años** she's 7 (years old); **tiene 15 cm de largo** it's 15 cm long; V **calor; hambre** etc

3 *(considerar)*: **lo tengo por brillante** I

consider him to be brilliant; **tener en mucho a algn** to think very highly of sb

4 (+ *pp*: *= pretérito*): **tengo terminada ya la mitad del trabajo** I've done half the work already

5: **tener que hacer algo** to have to do sth; **tengo que acabar este trabajo hoy** I have to finish this job today

6: **¿qué tienes, estás enfermo?** what's the matter with you, are you ill?

tenerse *vr* **1 tenerse en pie** to stand up

2 tenerse por to think o.s.

tengo *etc vb* V **tener**

tenia ['tenja] *nf* tapeworm

teniente [te'njente] *nm (rango)* lieutenant; *(ayudante)* deputy

tenis ['tenis] *nm* tennis; **tenis de mesa** table tennis; **tenista** *nmf* tennis player

tenor [te'nor] *nm (sentido)* meaning; *(Mús)* tenor; **a ~ de** on the lines of

tensar [ten'sar] *vt* to tighten; *(arco)* to draw

tensión [ten'sjon] *nf* tension; *(Tec)* stress; **tener la ~ alta** to have high blood pressure; **tensión arterial** blood pressure

tenso, -a ['tenso, a] *adj* tense

tentación [tenta'θjon] *nf* temptation

tentáculo [ten'takulo] *nm* tentacle

tentador, a [tenta'ðor, a] *adj* tempting

tentar [ten'tar] *vt (seducir)* to tempt; *(atraer)* to attract

tentempié [tentem'pje] *nm* snack

tenue ['tenwe] *adj (delgado)* thin, slender; *(neblina)* light; *(lazo, vínculo)* slight

teñir [te'nir] *vt* to dye; *(fig)* to tinge; **teñirse** *vr* to dye; **~se el pelo** to dye one's hair

teología [teolo'xia] *nf* theology

teoría [teo'ria] *nf* theory; **en ~** in theory; **teórico, a** *adj* theoretic(al) ▷ *nm/f* theoretician, theorist; **teorizar**

vi to theorize

terapéutico, -a [tera'peutiko, a] adj therapeutic

terapia [te'rapja] nf therapy

tercer adj V **tercero**

tercermundista [terθermun'dista] adj Third World cpd

tercero, -a [ter'θero, a] (delante de nmsg: **tercer**) adj third ⊳ nm (Jur) third party

terceto [ter'θeto] nm trio

terciar [ter'θjar] vi (participar) to take part; (hacer de árbitro) to mediate; **terciario, -a** adj tertiary

tercio [ter'θjo] nm third

terciopelo [terθjo'pelo] nm velvet

terco, -a ['terko, a] adj obstinate

tergal® [ter'xal] nm type of polyester

tergiversar [terxiβer'sar] vt to distort

termal [ter'mal] adj thermal

termas ['termas] nfpl hot springs

térmico, -a ['termiko, a] adj thermal

terminal [termi'nal] adj, nm, nf terminal

terminante [termi'nante] adj (final) final, definitive; (tajante) categorical; **terminantemente** adv: **terminantemente prohibido** strictly forbidden

terminar [termi'nar] vt (completar) to complete, finish; (concluir) to end ⊳ vi (llegar a su fin) to end; (parar) to stop; (acabar) to finish; **terminarse** vr to come to an end; **por hacer algo** to end up (by) doing sth

término ['termino] nm end, conclusion; (parada) terminus; (límite) boundary; **en último ~** (a fin de cuentas) in the last analysis; (como último recurso) as a last resort; **término medio** average; (fig) middle way

termómetro [ter'mometro] nm thermometer

termo(s)® ['termo(s)] nm Thermos®

termostato [termo'stato] nm thermostat

ternero, -a [ter'nero, a] nm/f (animal) calf ⊳ nf (carne) veal, beef

ternura [ter'nura] nf (trato) tenderness; (palabra) endearment; (cariño) fondness

terrado [te'rraðo] nm terrace

terraplén [terra'plen] nm embankment

terrateniente [terrate'njente] nmf landowner

terraza [te'rraθa] nf (balcón) balcony; (tejado) (flat) roof; (Agr) terrace

terremoto [terre'moto] nm earthquake

terrenal [terre'nal] adj earthly

terreno [te'rreno] nm (tierra) land; (parcela) plot; (suelo) soil; (fig) field; **un ~** a piece of land

terrestre [te'rrestre] adj terrestrial; (ruta) land cpd

terrible [te'rriβle] adj terrible, awful

territorio [terri'torjo] nm territory

terrón [te'rron] nm (de azúcar) lump; (de tierra) clod, lump

terror [te'rror] nm terror; **terrorífico, -a** adj terrifying; **terrorista** adj, nmf terrorist; **terrorista suicida** suicide bomber

terso, -a ['terso, a] adj (liso) smooth; (pulido) polished

tertulia [ter'tulja] nf (reunión informal) social gathering; (grupo) group, circle

tesis ['tesis] nf inv thesis

tesón [te'son] nm (firmeza) firmness; (tenacidad) tenacity

tesorero, -a [teso'rero, a] nm/f treasurer

tesoro [te'soro] nm treasure; (Com, Pol) treasury

testamento [testa'mento] nm will

testarudo, -a [testa'ruðo, a] adj stubborn

testículo [tes'tikulo] nm testicle

testificar [testifi'kar] vt to testify; (fig) to indicate ⊳ vi to give evidence

testigo [tes'tiɣo] nmf witness; **testigo de cargo/descargo** witness for the prosecution/defence; **testigo ocular** eye witness

testimonio [testi'monjo] nm testimony

teta ['teta] nf (de biberón) teat; (Anat: fam) breast

tétanos ['tetanos] nm tetanus

tetera [te'tera] nf teapot

tétrico, -a ['tetriko, a] adj gloomy, dismal

textear [tekste'ar] vt to text

textil [teks'til] adj textile

texto ['teksto] nm text; **textual** adj textual

textura [teks'tura] nf (de tejido) texture

tez [teθ] nf (cutis) complexion

ti [ti] pron you; (reflexivo) yourself

tía ['tia] nf (pariente) aunt; (fam) chick, bird

tibio, -a ['tiβjo, a] adj lukewarm

tiburón [tiβu'ron] nm shark

tic [tik] nm (ruido) click; (de reloj) tick; (Med): **~ nervioso** nervous tic

tictac [tik'tak] nm (de reloj) tick tock

tiempo ['tjempo] nm time; (época, período) age, period; (Meteorología) weather; (Ling) tense; (Deporte) half; **a ~** in time; **a uno al mismo ~** at the same time; **al poco ~** very soon (after); **se quedó poco ~** he didn't stay very long; **hace poco ~** not long ago; **mucho ~** a long time; **de ~ en ~** from time to time; **hace buen/mal ~** the weather's fine/bad; **estar a ~** to be in time; **hace ~** some time ago; **hacer ~** to while away the time; **motor de 2 ~s** two-stroke engine; **primer ~** first half

tienda ['tjenda] nf shop, store; **tienda de abarrotes** (MÉX, CAM) grocer's (BRIT), grocery store (US); **tienda de alimentación** o **comestibles** grocer's (BRIT), grocery store (US); **tienda de campaña** tent

tienes etc vb V **tener**

tienta etc vb V **tentar** ▷ nf: **andar a ~s** to grope one's way along

tiento etc vb V **tentar** ▷ nm

(tacto) touch; (precaución) wariness

tierno, -a ['tjerno, a] adj (blando) tender; (fresco) fresh; (amable) sweet

tierra ['tjerra] nf earth; (suelo) soil; (mundo) earth, world; (país) country, land; **~ adentro** inland

tieso, -a ['tjeso, a] adj (rígido) rigid; (duro) stiff; (fam: orgulloso) conceited

tiesto ['tjesto] nm flowerpot

tifón [ti'fon] nm typhoon

tifus ['tifus] nm typhus

tigre ['tiɣre] nm tiger

tijera [ti'xera] nf scissors pl; (Zool) claw; **tijeras** nfpl scissors; (para plantas) shears

tila ['tila] nf lime blossom tea

tildar [til'dar] vt: **~ de** to brand as

tilde ['tilde] nf (Tip) tilde

tilín [ti'lin] nm tinkle

timar [ti'mar] vt (estafar) to swindle

timbal [tim'bal] nm small drum

timbre ['timbre] nm (sello) stamp; (campanilla) bell; (tono) timbre; (Com) stamp duty

timidez [timi'ðeθ] nf shyness; **tímido, -a** adj shy

timo ['timo] nm swindle

timón [ti'mon] nm helm, rudder; **timonel** nm helmsman

tímpano ['timpano] nm (Anat) eardrum; (Mús) small drum

tina ['tina] nf tub; (baño) bath(tub); **tinaja** nf large jar

tinieblas [ti'njeβlas] nfpl darkness sg; (sombras) shadows

tino ['tino] nm (habilidad) skill; (juicio) insight

tinta ['tinta] nf ink; (Tec) dye; (Arte) colour

tinte ['tinte] nm dye

tintero [tin'tero] nm inkwell

tinto ['tinto] nm red wine

tintorería [tintore'ria] nf dry cleaner's

tío ['tio] nm (pariente) uncle; (fam: individuo) bloke (BRIT), guy

tiovivo [tio'βiβo] nm merry-go-round

típico, -a ['tipiko, a] *adj* typical

tipo ['tipo] *nm* (*clase*) type, kind; (*hombre*) fellow; (*Anat: de hombre*) build; (: *de mujer*) figure; (*Imprenta*) type; **tipo bancario/de descuento/de interés/ de cambio** bank/discount/interest/ exchange rate

tipografía [tipoɣra'fia] *nf* printing *cpd*

tíquet ['tiket] (*pl* **-s**) *nm* ticket; (*en tienda*) cash slip

tiquismiquis [tikis'mikis] *nm inv* fussy person ▷ *nmpl* (*querellas*) squabbling *sg*; (*escrúpulos*) silly scruples

tira ['tira] *nf* strip; (*fig*) abundance; **tira y afloja** give and take

tirabuzón [tiraβu'θon] *nm* (*rizo*) curl

tirachinas [tira'tʃinas] *nm inv* catapult

tirada [ti'raða] *nf* (*acto*) cast, throw; (*serie*) series; (*Tip*) printing, edition; **de una ~** at one go

tirado, -a [ti'raðo, a] *adj* (*barato*) dirt-cheap; (*fam: fácil*) very easy

tirador [tira'ðor] *nm* (*mango*) handle

tirano, -a [ti'rano, a] *adj* tyrannical ▷ *nm/f* tyrant

tirante [ti'rante] *adj* (*cuerda etc*) tight, taut; (*relaciones*) strained ▷ *nm* (*Arq*) brace; (*Tec*) stay; **tirantes** *nmpl* (*de pantalón*) braces (BRIT), suspenders (US); **tirantez** *nf* tightness; (*fig*) tension

tirar [ti'rar] *vt* to throw; (*dejar caer*) to drop; (*volcar*) to upset; (*derribar*) to knock down o over; (*desechar*) to throw out o away; (*dinero*) to squander; (*imprimir*) to print ▷ *vi* (*disparar*) to shoot; (*de la puerta etc*) to pull; (*fam: andar*) to go; (*tender a, buscar realizar*) to tend to; (*Deporte*) to shoot; **tirarse** *vr* to throw o.s.; **~ abajo** to bring down, destroy; **tira más a su padre** he takes more after his father; **ir tirando** to manage

tirita [ti'rita] *nf* (sticking) plaster (BRIT), Bandaid® (US)

tiritar [tiri'tar] *vi* to shiver

tiro ['tiro] *nm* (*lanzamiento*) throw; (*disparo*) shot; (*Deporte*) shot; (*Golf, Tenis*) drive; (*alcance*) range; **caballo de ~** cart-horse; **tiro al blanco** target practice

tirón [ti'ron] *nm* (*sacudida*) pull, tug; **de un ~** in one go, all at once

tiroteo [tiro'teo] *nm* exchange of shots, shooting

tisis ['tisis] *nf inv* consumption, tuberculosis

títere ['titere] *nm* puppet

titubear [tituβe'ar] *vi* to stagger; to stammer; (*fig*) to hesitate; **titubeo** *nm* staggering; stammering; hesitation

titulado, -a [titu'laðo, a] *adj* (*libro*) entitled; (*persona*) titled

titular [titu'lar] *adj* titular ▷ *nmf* holder ▷ *nm* headline ▷ *vt* to title; **titularse** *vr* to be entitled

título *nm* title; (*de diario*) headline; (*certificado*) professional qualification; (*universitario*) (university) degree; **a título de** in the capacity of

tiza ['tiθa] *nf* chalk

toalla [to'aʎa] *nf* towel

tobillo [to'βiʎo] *nm* ankle

tobogán [toβo'ɣan] *nm* (*montaña rusa*) roller-coaster; (*de niños*) chute, slide

tocadiscos [toka'ðiskos] *nm inv* record player

tocado, -a [to'kaðo, a] *adj* (*fam*) touched ▷ *nm* headdress

tocador [toka'ðor] *nm* (*mueble*) dressing table; (*cuarto*) boudoir; (*fam*) ladies' toilet (BRIT) o room (US)

tocar [to'kar] *vt* to touch; (*Mús*) to play; (*referirse a*) to allude to; (*timbre*) to ring ▷ *vi* (*a la puerta*) to knock (on o at the door); (*ser de turno*) to fall to, be the turn of; (*ser hora*) to be due; **tocarse** *vr* (*cubrirse la cabeza*) to cover one's head; (*tener contacto*) to touch (each other); **por lo que a mí me toca** as far as I am concerned; **te toca a ti** it's your turn

tocayo, -a [to'kajo, a] *nm/f* namesake

tocino [to'θino] nm bacon

todavía [toða'βia] adv (aun) even; (aún) still, yet; **~ más** yet more; **~ no** not yet

○ **PALABRA CLAVE**

todo, -a [ˈtoðo, a] adj 1 (con artículo sg) all; **toda la carne** all the meat; **toda la noche** all night, the whole night; **todo el libro** the whole book; **toda una botella** a whole bottle; **todo lo contrario** quite the opposite; **está toda sucia** she's all dirty; **por todo el país** throughout the whole country

2 (con artículo pl) all; every; **todos los libros** all the books; **todas las noches** every night; **todos los que quieran salir** all those who want to leave

▷ pron 1 everything, all; **todos** everyone, everybody; **lo sabemos todo** we know everything; **todos querían más tiempo** everybody o everyone wanted more time; **nos marchamos todos** all of us left

2: **con todo: con todo él me sigue gustando** even so I still like him ▷ adv all; **vaya todo seguido** keep straight on o ahead

▷ nm: **como un todo** as a whole; **del todo: no me agrada del todo** I don't entirely like it

todopoderoso, -a [toðopoðeˈroso, a] adj all powerful; (Rel) almighty

todoterreno [toðoteˈrreno] sm inv four-wheel drive, SUV (ESP US)

toga [ˈtoɣa] nf toga; (Escol) gown

Tokio [ˈtokjo] n Tokyo

toldo [ˈtoldo] nm (para el sol) sunshade (BRIT), parasol; (tienda) marquee

tolerancia [toleˈranθja] nf tolerance; **tolerante** adj (sociedad) liberal; (persona) open-minded

tolerar [toleˈrar] vt to tolerate; (resistir) to endure

toma [ˈtoma] nf (acto) taking; (Med) dose; **toma de corriente** socket; **toma de tierra** earth (wire); **tomacorriente** (LAM) nm socket

tomar [toˈmar] vt to take; (aspecto) to take on; (beber) to drink ▷ vi to take; (LAM: beber) to drink; **tomarse** vr to take; **~se por** to consider o.s. to be; **~ a bien/mal** to take well/badly; **~ en serio** to take seriously; **~ el pelo a algn** to pull sb's leg; **~la con algn** to pick a quarrel with sb; **¡tome!** here you are!; **~ el sol** to sunbathe

tomate [toˈmate] nm tomato

tomillo [toˈmiʎo] nm thyme

tomo [ˈtomo] nm (libro) volume

ton [ton] abr = **tonelada** ▷ nm: **sin ~ ni son** without rhyme or reason

tonalidad [tonaliˈðað] nf tone

tonel [toˈnel] nm barrel

tonelada [toneˈlaða] nf ton; **tonelaje** nm tonnage

tónica [ˈtonika] nf (Mús) tonic; (fig) keynote

tónico, -a [ˈtoniko, a] adj tonic ▷ nm (Med) tonic

tono [ˈtono] nm tone; **fuera de ~** inappropriate; **tono de llamada** ringtone

tontería [tonteˈria] nf (estupidez) foolishness; (cosa) stupid thing; (acto) foolish act; **tonterías** nfpl (disparates) rubbish sg, nonsense sg

tonto, -a [ˈtonto, a] adj stupid, silly ▷ nm/f fool

topar [toˈpar] vi: **~ contra** o **en** to run into; **~ con** to run up against

tope [ˈtope] adj maximum ▷ nm (fin) end; (límite) limit; (Ferro) buffer; (Auto) bumper; **al ~** end to end

tópico, -a [ˈtopiko, a] adj topical ▷ nm platitude

topo [ˈtopo] nm (Zool) mole; (fig) blunderer

toque etc [ˈtoke] vb V **tocar** ▷ nm touch; (Mús) beat; (de campana) peal; **dar un ~ a** to warn; **toque de queda** curfew

toqué etc vb V **tocar**

toquetear [toke'teaɾ] vt to finger

toquilla [to'kiʎa] nf (pañuelo) headscarf; (chal) shawl

tórax ['toɾaks] nm thorax

torbellino [toɾβe'ʎino] nm whirlwind; (fig) whirl

torcedura [toɾθe'ðuɾa] nf twist; (Med) sprain

torcer [toɾ'θeɾ] vt to twist; (la esquina) to turn; (Med) to sprain ▷ vi (desviar) to turn off; **torcerse** vr (ladearse) to bend; (desviarse) to go astray; (fracasar) to go wrong; **torcido, -a** adj twisted; (fig) crooked ▷ nm curl

tordo, -a ['toɾðo, a] adj dappled ▷ nm thrush

torear [tore'aɾ] vt (fig: evadir) to avoid; (jugar con) to tease ▷ vi to fight bulls; **toreo** nm bullfighting; **torero, -a** nm/f bullfighter

tormenta [toɾ'menta] nf storm; (fig: confusión) turmoil

tormento [toɾ'mento] nm torture; (fig) anguish

tornar [toɾ'naɾ] vt (devolver) to return, give back; (transformar) to transform ▷ vi to go back

tornasolado, -a [toɾnaso'laðo, a] adj (brillante) iridescent; (reluciente) shimmering

torneo [toɾ'neo] nm tournament

tornillo [toɾ'niʎo] nm screw

torniquete [toɾni'kete] nm (Med) tourniquet

torno ['toɾno] nm (Tec) winch; (tambor) drum; **en ~ (a)** round, about

toro ['toɾo] nm bull; (fam) he-man; **los ~s** bullfighting

toronja [to'ɾonxa] nf grapefruit

torpe ['toɾpe] adj (poco hábil) clumsy, awkward; (necio) dim; (lento) slow

torpedo [toɾ'peðo] nm torpedo

torpeza [toɾ'peθa] nf (falta de agilidad) clumsiness; (lentitud) slowness; (error) mistake

torre ['toɾe] nf tower; (de petróleo) derrick

torrefacto, -a [tore'facto, a] adj roasted

torrente [to'rrente] nm torrent

torrija [to'rrixa] nf French toast

torsión [toɾ'sjon] nf twisting

torso ['toɾso] nm torso

torta ['toɾta] nf cake; (fam) slap

tortícolis [toɾ'tikolis] nm inv stiff neck

tortilla [toɾ'tiʎa] nf omelette; (LAM: de maíz) maize pancake; **tortilla de papas** (LAM) potato omelette; **tortilla de patatas** (ESP) potato omelette; **tortilla francesa** (ESP) plain omelette

tórtola ['toɾtola] nf turtledove

tortuga [toɾ'tuɣa] nf tortoise

tortuoso, -a [toɾ'twoso, a] adj winding

tortura [toɾ'tuɾa] nf torture; **torturar** vt to torture

tos [tos] nf cough; **tos ferina** whooping cough

toser [to'seɾ] vi to cough

tostada [tos'taða] nf piece of toast; **tostado, -a** adj toasted; (por el sol) dark brown; (piel) tanned

tostador [tosta'ðoɾ] (ESP) nm toaster; **tostadora** (LAM) nf = **tostador**

tostar [tos'taɾ] vt to toast; (café) to roast; (persona) to tan; **tostarse** vr to get brown

total [to'tal] adj total ▷ adv in short; (al fin y al cabo) when all is said and done ▷ nm total; **en ~** in all; **~ que ...** to make (us) a long story short ...

totalidad [totali'ðað] nf whole

totalitario, -a [totali'taɾjo, a] adj totalitarian

tóxico, -a ['toksiko, a] adj toxic ▷ nm poison; **toxicómano, -a** nm/f drug addict

toxina [to'ksina] nf toxin

tozudo, -a [to'θuðo, a] adj obstinate

trabajador, a [traβaxa'ðoɾ, a] adj hard-working ▷ nm/f worker; **trabajador autónomo** o **por cuenta propia** self-employed person

trabajar [traβa'xar] vt to work; (Agr) to till; (empeñarse en) to work at; (convencer) to persuade ▷ vi to work; (esforzarse) to strive; **trabajo** nm work; (tarea) task; (Pol) labour; (fig) effort; **tomarse el trabajo de** to take the trouble to; **trabajo a destajo** piecework; **trabajo en equipo** teamwork; **trabajos por turnos** shift work; **trabajos forzados** hard labour sg

trabalenguas [traβa'lengwas] nm inv tongue twister

tracción [trak'θjon] nf traction; **tracción delantera/trasera** front-wheel/rear-wheel drive

tractor [trak'tor] nm tractor

tradición [traði'θjon] nf tradition; **tradicional** adj traditional

traducción [traðuk'θjon] nf translation

traducir [traðu'θir] vt to translate; **traductor, a** nm/f translator

traer [tra'er] vt to bring; (llevar) to carry; (llevar puesto) to wear; (incluir) to carry; (causar) to cause; **traerse algo** to be up to sth

traficar [trafi'kar] vi to trade

tráfico ['trafiko] nm (Com) trade; (Auto) traffic

tragaluz [traɣa'luθ] nm skylight

tragamonedas [traɣamo'neðas] (LAM) nf inv slot machine

tragaperras [traɣa'perras] (ESP) nf inv slot machine

tragar [tra'ɣar] vt to swallow; (devorar) to devour, bolt down; **tragarse** vr to swallow

tragedia [tra'xeðja] nf tragedy; **trágico, -a** adj tragic

trago ['traɣo] nm (líquido) drink; (bocado) gulp; (fam: de bebida) swig; (desgracia) blow; **echar un ~** to have a drink

traición [trai'θjon] nf treachery; (Jur) treason; (una traición) act of treachery; **traicionar** vt to betray

traidor, a [trai'ðor, a] adj

treacherous ▷ nm/f traitor

traigo etc vb V **traer**

traje ['traxe] vb V **traer** ▷ nm (de hombre) suit; (de mujer) dress; (vestido típico) costume; **traje de baño/chaqueta** swimsuit/suit; **traje de etiqueta** dress suit; **traje de luces** bullfighter's costume

trajera etc vb V **traer**

trajín [tra'xin] nm (fam: movimiento) bustle; **trajinar** vi (moverse) to bustle about

trama ['trama] nf (intriga) plot; (de tejido) weft (BRIT), woof (US); **tramar** vt to plot; (Tec) to weave

tramitar [trami'tar] vt (asunto) to transact; (negociar) to negotiate

trámite ['tramite] nm (paso) step; (Jur) transaction; **trámites** nmpl (burocracia) procedure sg; (Jur) proceedings

tramo ['tramo] nm (de tierra) plot; (de escalera) flight; (de vía) section

trampa ['trampa] nf trap; (en el suelo) trapdoor; (truco) trick; (engaño) fiddle; **trampear** vt, vi to cheat

trampolín [trampo'lin] nm (de piscina etc) diving board

tramposo, -a [tram'poso, a] adj crooked, cheating ▷ nm/f crook, cheat

tranca ['tranka] nf (palo) stick; (de puerta, ventana) bar; **trancar** vt to bar

trance ['tranθe] nm (momento difícil) difficult moment o juncture; (estado hipnotizado) trance

tranquilidad [trankili'ðað] nf (calma) calmness, stillness; (paz) peacefulness

tranquilizar [trankili'θar] vt (calmar) to calm (down); (asegurar) to reassure; **tranquilizarse** vr to calm down; **tranquilo, -a** adj (calmado) calm; (apacible) peaceful; (mar) calm; (mente) untroubled

transacción [transak'θjon] nf transaction

transbordador [transβorða'ðor] nm ferry

transbordo [trans'βorðo] nm
transfer; **hacer ~** to change (trains etc)

transcurrir [transku'rrir] vi (tiempo)
to pass; (hecho) to take place

transcurso [trans'kurso] nm: **~ del
tiempo** lapse of time

transeúnte [transe'unte] nmf
passer-by

transferencia [transfe'renθja] nf
transference; (Com) transfer

transferir [transfe'rir] vt to transfer

transformación [transforma'θjon]
nf transformation

transformador [transforma'ðor]
nm (Elec) transformer

transformar [transfor'mar] vt to
transform; (convertir) to convert

transfusión [transfu'sjon] nf
transfusion

transgénico, -a [trans'xeniko, a]
adj genetically modified, GM

transición [transi'θjon] nf transition

transigir [transi'xir] vi to
compromise, make concessions

transitar [transi'tar] vi to go (from
place to place); **tránsito** nm transit;
(Auto) traffic; **transitorio, -a** adj
transitory

transmisión [transmi'sjon] nf (Tec)
transmission; (transferencia) transfer;
transmisión exterior/en directo
outside/live broadcast

transmitir [transmi'tir] vt to
transmit; (Radio, TV) to broadcast

transparencia [transpa'renθja]
nf transparency; (claridad) clearness,
clarity; (foto) slide

transparentar [transparen'tar]
vt to reveal ▷ vi to be transparent;
transparente adj transparent;
(claro) clear

transpirar [transpi'rar] vi to perspire

transportar [transpor'tar] vt to
transport; (llevar) to carry; **transporte**
nm transport; (Com) haulage

transversal [transβer'sal] adj
transverse, cross

tranvía [tram'bia] nm tram

trapeador [trapea'ðor] (LAM) nm
mop; **trapear** (LAM) vt to mop

trapecio [tra'peθjo] nm trapeze;
trapecista nmf trapeze artist

trapero, -a [tra'pero, a] nm/f
ragman

trapicheo [trapi'tʃeo] (fam) nm
scheme, fiddle

trapo ['trapo] nm (tela) rag; (de
cocina) cloth

tráquea ['trakea] nf windpipe

traqueteo [trake'teo] nm rattling

tras [tras] prep (detrás) behind;
(después) after

trasatlántico [trasat'lantiko] nm
(barco) (cabin) cruiser

trascendencia [trasθen'denθja] nf
(importancia) importance; (Filosofía)
transcendence

trascendental [trasθenden'tal] adj
important; (Filosofía) transcendental

trasero, -a [tra'sero, a] adj back,
rear ▷ nm (Anat) bottom

trasfondo [tras'fondo] nm
background

trasgredir [trasɣre'ðir] vt to
contravene

trashumante [trasu'mante] adj
(animales) migrating

trasladar [trasla'ðar] vt to move;
(persona) to transfer; (postergar) to
postpone; (copiar) to copy; **trasladarse**
vr (mudarse) to move; **traslado** nm
move; (mudanza) move, removal

traslucir [traslu'θir] vt to show

trasluz [tras'luθ] nm reflected light;
al ~ against or up to the light

trasnochador, a [trasnotʃa'ðor, a]
nm/f night owl

trasnochar [trasno'tʃar] vi (acostarse
tarde) to stay up late

traspapelar [traspape'lar] vt
(documento, carta) to mislay, misplace

traspasar [traspa'sar] vt (suj: bala
etc) to pierce, go through; (propiedad)
to sell, transfer; (calle) to cross over;
(límites) to go beyond; (ley) to break;
traspaso nm (venta) transfer, sale

traspatio [tras'patjo] (LAM) nm
backyard

traspié [tras'pje] nm (tropezón) trip;
(error) blunder

trasplantar [trasplan'tar] vt to
transplant

traste ['traste] nm (Mús) fret; **dar al ~
con algo** to ruin sth

trastero [tras'tero] nm storage room

trastienda [tras'tjenda] nf back
of shop

trasto ['trasto] (pey) nm (cosa) piece of
junk; (persona) dead loss

trastornado, -a [trastor'naðo, a]
adj (loco) mad, crazy

trastornar [trastor'nar] vt
(fig: planes) to disrupt; (: nervios) to
shatter; (: persona) to drive crazy;
trastornarse vr (volverse loco) to go
mad o crazy; **trastorno** nm (acto)
overturning; (confusión) confusion

tratable [tra'taβle] adj friendly

tratado [tra'taðo] nm (Pol) treaty;
(Com) agreement

tratamiento [trata'mjento] nm
treatment; **tratamiento de textos**
(Inform) word processing cpd

tratar [tra'tar] vt (ocuparse de) to
treat; (manejar, Tec) to handle; (Med) to
treat; (dirigirse a: persona) to address
▷ vi: **~ de** (hablar sobre) to deal with,
be about; (intentar) to try to; **tratarse**
vr to treat each other; **~ con** (Com) to
trade in; (negociar) to negotiate with;
(tener contactos) to have dealings with;
¿de qué se trata? what's it about?;
trato nm dealings pl; (relaciones)
relationship; (comportamiento) manner;
(Com) agreement

trauma ['trauma] nm trauma

través [tra'βes] nm (fig) reverse; **al ~**
across, crossways; **a ~ de** across; (sobre)
over; (por) through

travesaño [traβe'saɲo] nm (Arq)
crossbeam; (Deporte) crossbar

travesía [traβe'sia] nf (calle) cross-
street; (Náut) crossing

travesura [traβe'sura] nf (broma)

prank; (ingenio) wit

travieso, -a [tra'βjeso, a] adj (niño)
naughty

trayecto [tra'jekto] nm (ruta) road,
way; (viaje) journey; (tramo) stretch;
trayectoria nf trajectory; (fig) path

traza ['traθa] nf (aspecto) looks pl;
(señal) sign; **trazado, -a** adj: **bien
trazado** shapely, well-formed ▷ nm
(Arq) plan, design; (fig) outline

trazar [tra'θar] vt (Arq) to plan; (Arte)
to sketch; (fig) to trace; (plan) to draw
up; **trazo** nm (línea) line; (bosquejo)
sketch

trébol ['treβol] nm (Bot) clover

trece ['treθe] num thirteen

trecho ['tretʃo] nm (distancia)
distance; (tiempo) while

tregua ['trexwa] nf (Mil) truce; (fig)
respite

treinta ['treinta] num thirty

tremendo, -a [tre'mendo, a] adj
(terrible) terrible; (imponente: cosa)
imposing; (fam: fabuloso) tremendous

tren [tren] nm train; **tren de
aterrizaje** undercarriage; **tren de
cercanías** suburban train

trenca ['trenka] nf duffel coat

trenza ['trenθa] nf (de pelo) plait
(BRIT), braid (US)

trepadora [trepa'ðora] nf (Bot)
climber

trepar [tre'par] vt, vi to climb

tres [tres] num three

tresillo [tre'siʎo] nm three-piece
suite; (Mús) triplet

treta ['treta] nf trick

triángulo [tri'angulo] nm triangle

tribu ['triβu] nf tribe

tribuna [tri'βuna] nf (plataforma)
platform; (Deporte) (grand)stand

tribunal [triβu'nal] nm (Jur) court;
(comisión, fig) tribunal; **~ popular** jury

tributo [tri'βuto] nm (Com) tax

trigal [tri'xal] nm wheat field

trigo ['trixo] nm wheat

trigueño, -a [tri'xeɲo, a] adj (pelo)
corn-coloured

trillar [tri'ʎar] vt (Agr) to thresh

trimestral [trimes'tral] adj quarterly; (Escol) termly

trimestre [tri'mestre] nm (Escol) term

trinar [tri'nar] vi (pájaros) to sing; (rabiar) to fume, be angry

trinchar [trin'tʃar] vt to carve

trinchera [trin'tʃera] nf (fosa) trench

trineo [tri'neo] nm sledge

trinidad [trini'ðað] nf trio; (Rel): **la T~** the Trinity

tripa ['tripa] nf (Anat) intestine; (fam: tb: **~s**) insides pl

triple ['triple] adj triple

triplicado, -a [tripli'kaðo, a] adj: **por ~** in triplicate

tripulación [tripula'θjon] nf crew

tripulante [tripu'lante] nmf crewman/woman

tripular [tripu'lar] vt (barco) to man; (Auto) to drive

triquiñuela [triki'nwela] nf trick

tris [tris] nm inv crack

triste ['triste] adj sad; (lamentable) sorry, miserable; **tristeza** nf (aflicción) sadness; (melancolía) melancholy

triturar [tritu'rar] vt (moler) to grind; (mascar) to chew

triunfar [trjun'far] vi (tener éxito) to triumph; (ganar) to win; **triunfo** nm triumph

trivial [tri'βjal] adj trivial

triza ['triθa] nf: **hacer ~s** to smash to bits; (papel) to tear to shreds

trocear [troθe'ar] vt (carne, manzana) to cut up, cut into pieces

trocha ['trotʃa] nf short cut

trofeo [tro'feo] nm (premio) trophy; (éxito) success

tromba ['tromba] nf downpour

trombón [trom'bon] nm trombone

trombosis [trom'bosis] nf inv thrombosis

trompa ['trompa] nf horn; (trompo) humming top; (hocico) snout; (fam): **cogerse una ~** to get tight

trompazo [trom'paθo] nm bump, bang

trompeta [trom'peta] nf trumpet; (clarín) bugle

trompicón [trompi'kon]: **a trompicones** adv in fits and starts

trompo ['trompo] nm spinning top

trompón [trom'pon] nm bump

tronar [tro'nar] vt (MÉX, CAM: fusilar) to shoot; (MÉX: examen) to flunk ▷ vi to thunder; (fig) to rage

tronchar [tron'tʃar] vt (árbol) to chop down; (fig: vida) to cut short; (: esperanza) to blight; (persona) to tire out; **troncharse** vr to fall down

tronco ['tronko] nm (de árbol, Anat) trunk

trono ['trono] nm throne

tropa ['tropa] nf (Mil) troop; (soldados) soldiers pl

tropezar [trope'θar] vi to trip, stumble; (error) to slip up; **~ con** to run into; (topar con) to bump into; **tropezón** nm trip; (fig) blunder

tropical [tropi'kal] adj tropical

trópico ['tropiko] nm tropic

tropiezo [tro'pjeθo] vb V **tropezar** ▷ nm (error) slip, blunder; (desgracia) misfortune; (obstáculo) snag

trotamundos [trota'mundos] nm inv globetrotter

trotar [tro'tar] vi to trot; **trote** nm trot; (fam) travelling; **de mucho trote** hard-wearing

trozar [tro'θar] (LAM) vt to cut up, cut into pieces

trozo ['troθo] nm bit, piece

trucha ['trutʃa] nf trout

truco ['truko] nm (habilidad) knack; (engaño) trick

trueno ['trweno] nm thunder; (estampido) bang

trueque etc ['trweke] vb V **trocar** ▷ nm exchange; (Com) barter

trufa ['trufa] nf (Bot) truffle

truhán, -ana [tru'an, ana] nm/f rogue

truncar [trun'kar] vt (cortar) to truncate; (fig: la vida etc) to cut short; (: el desarrollo) to stunt

tu [tu] *adj* your

tú [tu] *pron* you

tubérculo [tu'βerkulo] *nm* (Bot) tuber

tuberculosis [tuβerku'losis] *nf inv* tuberculosis

tubería [tuβe'ria] *nf* pipes *pl*; (*conducto*) pipeline

tubo ['tuβo] *nm* tube, pipe; **tubo de ensayo** test tube; **tubo de escape** exhaust (pipe)

tuerca ['twerka] *nf* nut

tuerto, -a ['twerto, a] *adj* blind in one eye ▷ *nm/f* one-eyed person

tuerza *etc vb* V **torcer**

tuétano ['twetano] *nm* marrow; (*Bot*) pith

tufo ['tufo] *nm* (*hedor*) stench

tul [tul] *nm* tulle

tulipán [tuli'pan] *nm* tulip

tullido, -a [tu'ʎido, a] *adj* crippled

tumba ['tumba] *nf* (*sepultura*) tomb

tumbar [tum'bar] *vt* to knock down; **tumbarse** *vr* (*echarse*) to lie down; (*extenderse*) to stretch out

tumbo ['tumbo] *nm*: **dar ~s** to stagger

tumbona [tum'bona] *nf* (*butaca*) easy chair; (*de playa*) deckchair (BRIT), beach chair (US)

tumor [tu'mor] *nm* tumour

tumulto [tu'multo] *nm* turmoil

tuna ['tuna] *nf* (*Mús*) student music group; V *tb* **tuno**

○ **TUNA**

○ A **tuna** is a musical group made
○ up of university students or
○ former students who dress up
○ in costumes from the "Edad de
○ Oro", the Spanish Golden Age.
○ These groups go through the
○ town playing their guitars, lutes
○ and tambourines and serenade
○ the young ladies in the halls of
○ residence or make impromptu
○ appearances at weddings or
○ parties singing traditional
○ Spanish songs for a few coins.

tunante [tu'nante] *nmf* rascal

tunear [tune'ar] *vt* (*Auto*) to style, mod (*inf*)

túnel ['tunel] *nm* tunnel

tuning ['tunin] *nm* (*Auto*) car styling, modding (*inf*)

tuno, -a ['tuno, a] *nm/f* (*fam*) rogue ▷ *nm* member of student music group

tupido, -a [tu'piðo, a] *adj* (*denso*) dense; (*tela*) close-woven

turbante [tur'βante] *nm* turban

turbar [tur'βar] *vt* (*molestar*) to disturb; (*incomodar*) to upset

turbina [tur'βina] *nf* turbine

turbio, -a ['turβjo, a] *adj* cloudy; (*tema etc*) confused

turbulencia [turβu'lenθja] *nf* turbulence; (*fig*) restlessness

turbulento, -a *adj* turbulent; (*fig: intranquilo*) restless; (*: ruidoso*) noisy

turco, -a ['turko, a] *adj* Turkish ▷ *nm/f* Turk

turismo [tu'rismo] *nm* tourism; (*coche*) car; **turista** *nmf* tourist; **turístico, -a** *adj* tourist *cpd*

turnar [tur'nar] *vi* to take (it in) turns; **turnarse** *vr* to take (it in) turns; **turno** *nm* (*de trabajo*) shift; (*en juegos etc*) turn

turquesa [tur'kesa] *nf* turquoise

Turquía [tur'kia] *nf* Turkey

turrón [tu'rron] *nm* (*dulce*) nougat

tutear [tute'ar] *vt* to address as familiar "tú"; **tutearse** *vr* to be on familiar terms

tutela [tu'tela] *nf* (*legal*) guardianship; **tutelar** *adj* tutelary ▷ *vt* to protect

tutor, a [tu'tor, a] *nm/f* (*legal*) guardian; (*Escol*) tutor

tuve *etc vb* V **tener**

tuviera *etc vb* V **tener**

tuyo, -a [a 'tujo, a] *adj* yours, of yours ▷ *pron* yours; **un amigo ~** a friend of yours; **los ~s** (*fam*) your relations of family

TV *nf abr* (= televisión) TV

TVE *nf abr* = **Televisión Española**

u

u [u] *nf* (letter)

u [u] *conj* or

ubicar [uβi'kar] *vt* to place, situate; (LAM: *encontrar*) to find; **ubicarse** *vr* (LAM: *encontrarse*) to lie, be located

ubre ['uβre] *nf* udder

UCI *nf abr* (= *Unidad de Cuidados Intensivos*) ICU

Ud(s) *abr* = **usted(es)**

UE *nf abr* (= *Unión Europea*) EU

ufanarse [ufa'narse] *vr* to boast; **ufano, -a** *adj* (*arrogante*) arrogant; (*presumido*) conceited

UGT (ESP) *nf abr* = **Unión General de Trabajadores**

úlcera ['ulθera] *nf* ulcer

ulterior [ulte'rjor] *adj* (*más allá*) farther, further; (*subsecuente, siguiente*) subsequent

últimamente ['ultimamente] *adv* (*recientemente*) lately, recently

ultimar [ulti'mar] *vt* to finish; (*finalizar*) to finalize; (LAM: *matar*) to kill

ultimátum [ulti'matum] (*pl* **-s**) *nm* ultimatum

último, -a ['ultimo, a] *adj* last; (*más*

reciente*) latest, most recent; (*más bajo*) bottom; (*más alto*) top; **en las últimas** on one's last legs; **por ~** finally

ultra ['ultra] *adj* ultra ▷ *nmf* extreme right-winger

ultraje [ul'traxe] *nm* outrage; insult

ultramar [ultra'mar] *nm*: **de** o **en ~** abroad, overseas

ultramarinos [ultrama'rinos] *nmpl* groceries; **tienda de ~** grocer's (shop)

ultranza [ul'tranθa]: **a ~** *adv* (*a todo trance*) at all costs; (*completo*) outright

umbral [um'bral] *nm* (*gen*) threshold

○ PALABRA CLAVE

un, una [un, 'una] *art indef* a; (*antes de vocal*) an; **una mujer/naranja** a woman/an orange
▷ *adj*: **unos** (*o* **unas**): **hay unos regalos para ti** there are some presents for you; **hay unas cervezas en la nevera** there are some beers in the fridge

unánime [u'nanime] *adj* unanimous; **unanimidad** *nf* unanimity

undécimo, -a [un'deθimo, a] *adj* eleventh

ungir [un'xir] *vt* to anoint

ungüento [un'gwento] *nm* ointment

único, -a ['uniko, a] *adj* only, sole; (*sin par*) unique

unidad [uni'ðað] *nf* unity; (Com, Tec etc) unit

unido, -a [u'niðo, a] *adj* joined, linked; (*fig*) united

unificar [unifi'kar] *vt* to unite, unify

uniformar [unifor'mar] *vt* to make uniform, level up; (*persona*) to put into uniform

uniforme [uni'forme] *adj* uniform, equal; (*superficie*) even ▷ *nm* uniform

unilateral [unilate'ral] *adj* unilateral

unión [u'njon] *nf* union; (*acto*) uniting, joining; (*unidad*) unity; (Tec) joint; **Unión Europea** European Union

unir [u'nir] *vt* (*juntar*) to join, unite;

(*atar*) to tie, fasten; (*combinar*) to combine; **unirse** vr to join together, unite; (*empresas*) to merge

unísono [u'nisono] nm: **al ~** in unison

universal [uniβer'sal] adj universal; (*mundial*) world cpd

universidad [uniβersi'ðað] nf university

universitario, -a [uniβersi'tarjo, a] adj university cpd ▷ nm/f (*profesor*) lecturer; (*estudiante*) (university) student; (*graduado*) graduate

universo [uni'βerso] nm universe

○ **PALABRA CLAVE**

uno, -a ['uno, a] adj one; **unos pocos** a few; **unos cien** about a hundred
▷ pron 1 one; **quiero sólo uno** I want one; **uno de ellos** one of them
2 (*alguien*) someone, somebody; **conozco a uno que se te parece** I know somebody o someone who looks like you; **uno mismo** oneself; **unos querían quedarse** some (people) wanted to stay
3 **(los) unos ... (los) otros ...** some ... others
▷ nf one; **es la una** it's one o'clock
▷ nm (number) one

untar [un'tar] vt (*mantequilla*) to spread; (*engrasar*) to grease, oil

uña ['uɲa] nf (Anat) nail; (*garra*) claw; (*casco*) hoof; (*arrancaclavos*) claw

uranio [u'ranjo] nm uranium

urbanización [urβaniθa'θjon] nf (*barrio, colonia*) housing estate

urbanizar [urβani'θar] vt (*zona*) to develop, urbanize

urbano, -a [ur'βano, a] adj (*de ciudad*) urban; (*cortés*) courteous, polite

urbe ['urβe] nf large city

urdir [ur'ðir] vt to warp; (*complot*) to plot, contrive

urgencia [ur'xenθja] nf urgency; (*prisa*) haste, rush; (*emergencia*) emergency; **servicios de ~** emergency

services; **"U~s"** "Casualty"; **urgente** adj urgent

urgir [ur'xir] vi to be urgent; **me urge** I'm in a hurry for it

urinario, -a [uri'narjo, a] adj urinary ▷ nm urinal

urna ['urna] nf urn; (Pol) ballot box

urraca [u'rraka] nf magpie

URSS [urs] nf (Hist): **la URSS** the USSR

Uruguay [uru'ɣwai] nm (tb: **el ~**) Uruguay; **uruguayo, -a** [uru'ɣwajo, a] adj, nm/f Uruguayan

usado, -a [u'saðo, a] adj used; (*de segunda mano*) secondhand

usar [u'sar] vt to use; (*ropa*) to wear; (*tener costumbre*) to be in the habit of; **usarse** vr to be used; **uso** nm use; (*costumbre*) usage, custom; (*moda*) fashion; **al uso** in keeping with custom; **al uso de** in the style of; **de uso externo** (Med) for external use

usted [us'teð] pron (sg) you sg; (pl): **~es** you pl

usual [u'swal] adj usual

usuario, -a [u'swarjo, a] nm/f user

usura [u'sura] nf usury; **usurero, -a** nm/f usurer

usurpar [usur'par] vt to usurp

utensilio [uten'siljo] nm tool; (Culin) utensil

útero ['utero] nm uterus, womb

útil ['util] adj useful ▷ nm tool; **utilidad** nf usefulness; (Com) profit; **utilizar** vt to use, utilize

utopía [uto'pia] nf Utopia; **utópico, -a** adj Utopian

uva ['uβa] nf grape

○ **LAS UVAS**

● In Spain **Las uvas** play a big part on
● New Year's Eve (**Nochevieja**), when
● on the stroke of midnight people
● gather at home, in restaurants or
● in the **plaza mayor** and eat a grape
● for each stroke of the clock of the
● **Puerta del Sol** in Madrid. It is said
● to bring luck for the following year.

V

v abr (=voltio) v

va vb V **ir**

vaca ['baka] nf (animal) cow; **carne de –** beef

vacaciones [baka'θjones] nfpl holidays

vacante [ba'kante] adj vacant, empty ▷ nf vacancy

vaciar [ba'θjar] vt to empty out; (ahuecar) to hollow out; (moldear) to cast; **vaciarse** vr to empty

vacilar [baθi'lar] vi to be unsteady; (al hablar) to falter; (dudar) to hesitate, waver; (memoria) to fail

vacío, -a [ba'θio, a] adj empty; (puesto) vacant; (desocupado) idle; (vano) vain ▷ nm emptiness; (Física) vacuum; (un vacío) (empty) space

vacuna [ba'kuna] nf vaccine; **vacunar** vt to vaccinate

vacuno, -a [ba'kuno, a] adj cow cpd; **ganado –** cattle

vadear [baðe'ar] vt (río) to ford; **vado** nm ford; **'vado permanente'** 'keep clear'

vagabundo, -a [baɣa'βundo, a] adj wandering ▷ nm tramp

vagancia [ba'ɣanθja] nf (pereza) idleness, laziness

vagar [ba'ɣar] vi to wander; (no hacer nada) to idle

vagina [ba'xina] nf vagina

vago, -a ['baɣo, a] adj vague; (perezoso) lazy ▷ nm/f (vagabundo) tramp; (flojo) lazybones sg, idler

vagón [ba'ɣon] nm (Ferro: de pasajeros) carriage; (: de mercancías) wagon

vaho ['bao] nm (vapor) vapour, steam; (respiración) breath

vaina ['baina] nf sheath

vainilla [bai'niʎa] nf vanilla

vais vb V **ir**

vaivén [bai'βen] nm to-and-fro movement; (de tránsito) coming and going; **vaivenes** nmpl (fig) ups and downs

vajilla [ba'xiʎa] nf crockery, dishes pl; (juego) service, set

valdré etc vb V **valer**

vale ['bale] nm voucher; (recibo) receipt; (pagaré) IOU

valedero, -a [bale'ðero, a] adj valid

valenciano, -a [balen'θjano, a] adj Valencian

valentía [balen'tia] nf courage, bravery

valer [ba'ler] vt to be worth; (Mat) to equal; (costar) to cost ▷ vi (ser válido) to be useful; (ser válido) to be valid; **valerse** vr to take care of oneself; **-se de** to make use of, take advantage of; **- la pena** to be worthwhile; **¿vale?** (ESP) OK?; **más vale que nos vayamos** we'd better go; **¡eso sí que no me vale!** (MÉX: fam: no importar) I couldn't care less about that

valeroso, -a [bale'roso, a] adj brave, valiant

valgo etc vb V **valer**

valía [ba'lia] nf worth, value

validar [bali'ðar] vt to validate; **validez** nf validity; **válido, -a** adj valid

valiente [ba'ljente] adj brave, valiant ▷ nm hero

valija [ba'lixa] (cs) nf (suit)case

valioso, -a [ba'ljoso, a] adj valuable

valla ['baʎa] nf fence; (Deporte) hurdle; **valla publicitaria** hoarding; **vallar** vt to fence in

valle ['baʎe] nm valley

valor [ba'lor] nm value, worth; (precio) price; (valentía) valour, courage; (importancia) importance; **valores** nmpl (Com) securities; **valorar** vt to value

vals [bals] nm inv waltz

válvula ['balβula] nf valve

vamos vb V **ir**

vampiro, -resa [bam'piro, 'resa] nm/f vampire

van vb V **ir**

vanguardia [ban'gwardja] nf vanguard; (Arte etc) avant-garde

vanidad [bani'ðað] nf vanity; **vanidoso, -a** adj vain, conceited

vano, -a ['bano, a] adj vain

vapor [ba'por] nm vapour; (vaho) steam; **al ~** (Culin) steamed; **vapor de agua** water vapour; **vaporizador** nm atomizer; **vaporizar** vt to vaporize; **vaporoso, -a** adj vaporous

vaquero, -a [ba'kero, a] adj cattle cpd ▷ nm cowboy; **vaqueros** nmpl (pantalones) jeans

vaquilla [ba'kiʎa] nf (Zool) heifer

vara ['bara] nf stick; (Tec) rod

variable [ba'rjaβle] adj, nf variable

variación [barja'θjon] nf variation

variar [bar'jar] vt to vary; (modificar) to modify; (cambiar de posición) to switch around ▷ vi to vary

varicela [bari'θela] nf chickenpox

varices [ba'riθes] nfpl varicose veins

variedad [barje'ðað] nf variety

varilla [ba'riʎa] nf stick; (Bot) twig; (Tec) rod; (de rueda) spoke

vario, -a ['barjo, a] adj varied; **~s** various, several

varita [ba'rita] nf (tb: ~ **mágica**) magic wand

varón [ba'ron] nm male, man; **varonil** adj manly, virile

Varsovia [bar'soβja] n Warsaw

vas vb V **ir**

vasco, -a ['basko, a] adj, nm/f Basque; **vascongado, -a** [baskoŋ'gaðo, a] adj Basque; **las Vascongadas** the Basque Country

vaselina [base'lina] nf Vaseline®

vasija [ba'sixa] nf container, vessel

vaso ['baso] nm glass, tumbler; (Anat) vessel

  No confundir **vaso** con la palabra inglesa **vase**.

vástago ['bastaxo] nm (Bot) shoot; (Tec) rod; (fig) offspring

vasto, -a ['basto, a] adj vast, huge

Vaticano [bati'kano] nm: **el ~** the Vatican

vatio ['batjo] nm (Elec) watt

vaya etc vb V **ir**

Vd(s) abr = **usted(es)**

ve [be] vb V **ir**; **ver**

vecindad [beθin'dað] nf neighbourhood; (habitantes) residents pl

vecindario [beθin'darjo] nm neighbourhood; residents pl

vecino, -a [be'θino, a] adj neighbouring ▷ nm/f neighbour; (residente) resident

veda ['beða] nf prohibition; **vedar** [be'ðar] vt (prohibir) to ban, prohibit; (impedir) to stop, prevent

vegetación [bexeta'θjon] nf vegetation

vegetal [bexe'tal] adj, nm vegetable

vegetariano, -a [bexeta'rjano, a] adj, nm/f vegetarian

vehículo [be'ikulo] nm vehicle; (Med) carrier

veía etc vb V **ver**

veinte ['beinte] num twenty

vejar [be'xar] vt (irritar) to annoy, vex; (humillar) to humiliate

vejez [be'xeθ] nf old age

vejiga [be'xiɣa] nf (Anat) bladder

vela ['bela] nf (de cera) candle; (Náut)

sail; (insomnio) sleeplessness; (vigilia) vigil; (Mil) sentry duty; **estar a dos -s** (fam: sin dinero) to be skint

velado, -a [be'laðo, a] adj veiled; (sonido) muffled; (Foto) blurred ▷ nf soirée

velar [be'lar] vt (vigilar) to keep watch over ▷ vi to stay awake; **~ por** to watch over, look after

velatorio [bela'torjo] nm (funeral) wake

velero [be'lero] nm (Náut) sailing ship; (Aviac) glider

veleta [be'leta] nf weather vane

veliz [be'lis] (MÉX) nm (suit)case

vello ['beʎo] nm down, fuzz

velo ['belo] nm veil

velocidad [beloθi'ðað] nf speed; (Tec, Auto) gear

velocímetro [belo'θimetro] nm speedometer

velorio [be'lorjo] (LAM) nm (funeral) wake

veloz [be'loθ] adj fast

ven vb V **venir**

vena ['bena] nf vein

venado [be'naðo] nm deer

vencedor, -a [benθe'ðor, a] adj victorious ▷ nm/f victor, winner

vencer [ben'θer] vt (dominar) to defeat, beat; (derrotar) to vanquish; (superar, controlar) to overcome, master ▷ vi (triunfar) to win (through), triumph; (plazo) to expire; **vencido, -a** adj (derrotado) defeated, beaten; (Com) due ▷ adv: **pagar vencido** to pay in arrears

venda ['benda] nf bandage; **vendaje** nm bandage, dressing; **vendar** vt to bandage; **vendar los ojos** to blindfold

vendaval [benda'βal] nm (viento) gale

vendedor, a [bende'ðor, a] nm/f seller

vender [ben'der] vt to sell; **venderse** vr (estar a la venta) to be on sale; **~ al contado/al por mayor/al por menor** to sell for cash/wholesale/retail; **"se**

vende" "for sale"

vendimia [ben'dimja] nf grape harvest

vendré etc vb V **venir**

veneno [be'neno] nm poison; (de serpiente) venom; **venenoso, -a** adj poisonous; venomous

venerable [bene'raβle] adj venerable; **venerar** vt (respetar) to revere; (adorar) to worship

venéreo, -a [be'nereo, a] adj: **enfermedad venérea** venereal disease

venezolano, -a [beneθo'lano, a] adj Venezuelan

Venezuela [bene'θwela] nf Venezuela

venganza [ben'ganθa] nf vengeance, revenge; **vengar** vt to avenge; **vengarse** vr to take revenge; **vengativo, -a** adj (persona) vindictive

vengo etc vb V **venir**

venia ['benja] nf (perdón) pardon; (permiso) consent

venial [be'njal] adj venial

venida [be'niða] nf (llegada) arrival; (regreso) return

venidero, -a [beni'ðero, a] adj coming, future

venir [be'nir] vi to come; (llegar) to arrive; (ocurrir) to happen; (fig): **~ de** to stem from; **~ bien/mal** to be suitable/unsuitable; **el año que viene** next year; **~se abajo** to collapse

venta ['benta] nf (Com) sale; **"en ~"** "for sale"; **estar a la o en ~** to be (up) for sale o on the market; **venta a domicilio** door-to-door selling; **venta a plazos** hire purchase; **venta al contado/al por mayor/al por menor** cash sale/wholesale/retail

ventaja [ben'taxa] nf advantage; **ventajoso, -a** adj advantageous

ventana [ben'tana] nf window; **ventanilla** nf (de taquilla) window (of booking office etc)

ventilación [bentila'θjon] nf ventilation; (corriente) draught

ventilador [bentila'ðor] nm fan
ventilar [benti'lar] vt to ventilate; *(para secar)* to put out to dry; *(asunto)* to air, discuss
ventisca [ben'tiska] nf blizzard
ventrílocuo, -a [ben'trilokwo, a] nm/f ventriloquist
ventura [ben'tura] nf *(felicidad)* happiness; *(buena suerte)* luck; *(destino)* fortune; **a la (buena)** ~ at random; **venturoso, -a** adj happy; *(afortunado)* lucky, fortunate
veo etc vb V **ver**
ver [ber] vt to see; *(mirar)* to look at, watch; *(entender)* to understand; *(investigar)* to look into ▷ vi to see; to understand; **verse** vr *(encontrarse)* to meet; *(dejarse ver)* to be seen; *(hallarse: en un apuro)* to find o.s., be; **(vamos) a** ~ let's see; **no tener nada que** ~ **con** to have nothing to do with; **a mi modo de** ~ as I see it; **ya ~emos** we'll see
vera ['bera] nf edge, verge; *(de río)* bank
veraneante [berane'ante] nm/f holidaymaker, *(summer)* vacationer (US)
veranear [berane'ar] vi to spend the summer; **veraneo** nm summer holiday; **veraniego, -a** adj summer cpd
verano [be'rano] nm summer
veras ['beras] nfpl truth sg; **de** ~ really, truly
verbal [ber'βal] adj verbal
verbena [ber'βena] nf *(baile)* open-air dance
verbo ['berβo] nm verb
verdad [ber'ðað] nf truth; *(fiabilidad)* reliability; **de** ~ real, proper; **a decir** ~ to tell the truth; **verdadero, -a** adj *(veraz)* true, truthful; *(fiable)* reliable; *(fig)* real
verde ['berðe] adj green; *(chiste)* blue, dirty ▷ nm green; **viejo** ~ dirty old man; **verdear** vi to turn green; **verdor** nm greenness

verdugo [ber'ðuxo] nm executioner
verdulero, -a [berðu'lero, a] nm/f greengrocer
verduras [ber'ðuras] nfpl *(Culin)* greens
vereda [be'reða] nf path; *(cs: acera)* pavement *(BRIT)*, sidewalk *(US)*
veredicto [bere'ðikto] nm verdict
vergonzoso, -a [berɣon'θoso, a] adj shameful; *(tímido)* timid, bashful
vergüenza [ber'xwenθa] nf shame, sense of shame; *(timidez)* bashfulness; *(pudor)* modesty; **me da** ~ I'm ashamed
verídico, -a [be'riðiko, a] adj true, truthful
verificar [berifi'kar] vt to check; *(corroborar)* to verify; *(llevar a cabo)* to carry out; **verificarse** vr *(predicción)* to prove to be true
verja ['berxa] nf *(cancela)* iron gate; *(valla)* iron railings pl; *(de ventana)* grille
vermut [ber'mut] *(pl* ~s*)* nm vermouth
verosímil [bero'simil] adj likely, probable; *(relato)* credible
verruga [be'rruxa] nf wart
versátil [ber'satil] adj versatile
versión [ber'sjon] nf version
verso ['berso] nm verse; **un** ~ a line of poetry
vértebra ['berteβra] nf vertebra
verter [ber'ter] vt *(líquido: adrede)* to empty, pour (out); *(: sin querer)* to spill; *(basura)* to dump ▷ vi to flow
vertical [berti'kal] adj vertical
vértice ['bertiθe] nm vertex, apex
vertidos [ber'tiðos] nmpl waste sg
vertiente [ber'tjente] nf slope; *(fig)* aspect
vértigo ['bertixo] nm vertigo; *(mareo)* dizziness
vesícula [be'sikula] nf blister
vespino® [bes'pino] nm o nf moped
vestíbulo [bes'tiβulo] nm hall; *(de teatro)* foyer
vestido [bes'tiðo] nm *(ropa)* clothes pl, clothing; *(de mujer)* dress, frock ▷ pp de **vestir**; ~ **de azul/marinero** dressed

in blue;/as a sailor

vestidor [besti'ðor] (*MÉX*) *nm* (*Deporte*) changing (*BRIT*) o locker (*us*) room

vestimenta [besti'menta] *nf* clothing

vestir [bes'tir] *vt* (*poner: ropa*) to put on; (*llevar: ropa*) to wear; (*proveer de ropa a*) to clothe; (*sastre*) to make clothes for ▷ *vi* to dress; (*verse bien*) to look good; **vestirse** *vr* to get dressed, dress o.s.

vestuario [bes'twarjo] *nm* clothes *pl*, wardrobe; (*Teatro: cuarto*) dressing room; (*Deporte*) changing (*BRIT*) o locker (*us*) room

vetar [be'tar] *vt* to veto

veterano, -a [bete'rano, a] *adj, nm* veteran

veterinaria [beteri'narja] *nf* veterinary science; *V tb* **veterinario**

veterinario, -a [beteri'narjo, a] *nm/f* vet(erinary surgeon)

veto ['beto] *nm* veto

vez [beθ] *nf* time; (*turno*) turn; **a la ~ que** at the same time as; **a su ~** in its turn; **otra ~** again; **una ~** once; **de una ~** in one go; **de una ~ para siempre** once and for all; **en ~ de** instead of; **a o algunas veces** sometimes; **una y otra ~** repeatedly; **de ~ en cuando** from time to time; **7 veces 9** 7 times 9; **hacer las veces de** to stand in for; **tal ~** perhaps

vía ['bia] *nf* track, route; (*Ferro*) line; (*fig*) way; (*Anat*) passage, tube ▷ *prep* via, by way of; **por ~ judicial** by legal means; **en ~s de** in the process of; **vía aérea** airway; **Vía Láctea** Milky Way; **vía pública** public road o thoroughfare

viable ['bjaβle] *adj* (*solución, plan, alternativa*) feasible

viaducto [bja'ðukto] *nm* viaduct

viajante [bja'xante] *nm* commercial traveller

viajar [bja'xar] *vi* to travel; **viaje** *nm* journey; (*gira*) tour; (*Náut*) voyage; **estar de viaje** to be on a trip; **viaje de ida y vuelta** round trip; **viaje**

de novios honeymoon; **viajero, -a** *adj* travelling; (*Zool*) migratory ▷ *nm/f* (*quien viaja*) traveller; (*pasajero*) passenger

víbora ['biβora] *nf* (*Zool*) viper; (: (*MÉX: venenoso*) poisonous snake

vibración [biβra'θjon] *nf* vibration

vibrar [bi'βrar] *vt, vi* to vibrate

vicepresidente [biθepresi'ðente] *nmf* vice-president

viceversa [biθe'βersa] *adv* vice versa

vicio ['biθjo] *nm* vice; (*mala costumbre*) bad habit; **vicioso, -a** *adj* (*muy malo*) vicious; (*corrompido*) depraved ▷ *nm/f* depraved person

víctima ['biktima] *nf* victim

victoria [bik'torja] *nf* victory; **victorioso, -a** *adj* victorious

vid [bið] *nf* vine

vida ['biða] *nf* (*gen*) life; (*duración*) lifetime; **de por ~** for life; **en la o mi ~ never**; **estar con ~** to be still alive; **ganarse la ~** to earn one's living

video ['biðeo] *nm* video ▷ *adj inv*: **película de ~** video film; **videocámara** *nf* camcorder; **videocasete** *nm* video cassette; **videotape; videoclub** *nm* video club; **videojuego** *nm* video game; **videollamada** *nf* video call; **videoteléfono** *nm* videophone

vidrio ['biðrjo] *nm* glass

vieira ['bjeira] *nf* scallop

viejo, -a ['bjexo, a] *adj* old ▷ *nm/f* old man/woman; **hacerse ~** to get old

Viena ['bjena] *n* Vienna

vienes *etc vb V* **venir**

vienés, -esa [bje'nes, esa] *adj* Viennese

viento ['bjento] *nm* wind; **hacer ~** to be windy

vientre ['bjentre] *nm* belly; (*matriz*) womb

viernes ['bjernes] *nm inv* Friday; **Viernes Santo** Good Friday

Vietnam [bjet'nam] *nm* Vietnam; **vietnamita** *adj* Vietnamese

viga ['biɣa] *nf* beam, rafter; (*de metal*)

girder

vigencia [bi'xenθja] nf validity; **estar en ~** to be in force; **vigente** adj valid, in force; (imperante) prevailing

vigésimo, -a [bi'xesimo, a] adj twentieth

vigía [bi'xia] nm look-out

vigilancia [bixi'lanθja] nf: **tener a algn bajo ~** to keep watch on sb

vigilar [bixi'lar] vt to watch over ▷ vi (gen) to be vigilant; (hacer guardia) to keep watch; **~ por** to take care of

vigilia [vi'xilja] nf wakefulness, being awake; (Rel) fast

vigor [bi'ɣor] nm vigour, vitality; **en ~** in force; **entrar/poner en ~** to come/put into effect; **vigoroso, -a** adj vigorous

VIH nm abr (= virus de la inmunodeficiencia humana) HIV; **VIH negativo/positivo** HIV-negative/-positive

vil [bil] adj vile, low

villa ['biʎa] nf (casa) villa; (pueblo) small town; (municipalidad) municipality

villancico [biʎan'θiko] nm (Christmas) carol

vilo ['bilo]: **en ~** adv in the air, suspended; (fig) on tenterhooks, in suspense

vinagre [bi'naɣre] nm vinegar

vinagreta [bina'ɣreta] nf vinaigrette, French dressing

vinculación [binkula'θjon] nf (lazo) link, bond; (acción) linking

vincular [binku'lar] vt to link, bind; **vínculo** nm link, bond

vine etc vb V **venir**

vinicultor, a [binikul'tor] nm/f wine grower

vinicultura [binikul'tura] nf wine growing

viniera etc vb V **venir**

vino ['bino] vb V **venir** ▷ nm wine; **vino blanco/tinto** white/red wine

viña ['biɲa] nf vineyard; **viñedo** nm vineyard

viola ['bjola] nf viola

violación [bjola'θjon] nf violation; (sexual) rape

violar [bjo'lar] vt to violate; (sexualmente) to rape

violencia [bjo'lenθja] nf violence, force; (incomodidad) embarrassment; (acto injusto) unjust act; **violentar** vt to force; (casa) to break into; (agredir) to assault; (violar) to violate; **violento, -a** adj violent; (furioso) furious; (situación) embarrassing; (acto) forced, unnatural

violeta [bjo'leta] nf violet

violín [bjo'lin] nm violin

violón [bjo'lon] nm double bass

virar [bi'rar] vi to change direction

virgen ['birxen] adj, nf virgin

Virgo ['birɣo] nm Virgo

viril [bi'ril] adj virile; **en ~ de** by virtue of; **virilidad** nf virility

virtud [bir'tuð] nf virtue; **en ~ de** by virtue of; **virtuoso, -a** adj virtuous ▷ nm/f virtuoso

viruela [bi'rwela] nf smallpox

virulento, -a [biru'lento, a] adj virulent

virus ['birus] nm inv virus

visa ['bisa] (LAM) nf = **visado**

visado [bi'saðo] (ESP) nm visa

víscera ['bisθera] nf (Anat, Zool) gut, bowel; **vísceras** nfpl entrails

visceral [bisθe'ral] adj (odio) intense; **reacción ~** gut reaction

visera [bi'sera] nf visor

visibilidad [bisiβili'ðað] nf visibility; **visible** adj visible; (fig) obvious

visillos [bi'siʎos] nmpl lace curtains

visión [bi'sjon] nf (Anat) vision, (eye)sight; (fantasía) vision, fantasy

visita [bi'sita] nf call, visit; (persona) visitor; **hacer una ~** to pay a visit; **visitar** [bisi'tar] vt to visit, call on

visitante [bisi'tante] adj visiting ▷ nmf visitor

visón [bi'son] nm mink

visor [bi'sor] nm (Foto) viewfinder

víspera ['bispera] nf: **la ~ de ...** the day before ...

vista ['bista] nf sight, vision; (capacidad de ver) (eye)sight; (mirada) look(s) (pl); **a primera ~** at first glance; **hacer la ~ gorda** to turn a blind eye; **volver la ~** to look back; **está a la ~ que** it's obvious that; **en ~ de** in view of; **en ~ de que** in view of the fact that; **¡hasta la ~!** so long!, see you!; **con ~s a** with a view to; **vistazo** nm glance; **dar o echar un vistazo a** to glance at

visto, -a ['bisto, a] pp de **ver** ▷ vb V tb **vestir** ▷ adj seen; (considerado) considered ▷ nm: **~ bueno** approval; **por lo ~** apparently; **está ~ que** it's clear that; **está bien/mal ~** it's acceptable/unacceptable; **~ que** since, considering that

vistoso, -a [bis'toso, a] adj colourful

visual [bi'swal] adj visual

vital [bi'tal] adj life cpd, living cpd; (fig) vital; (persona) lively, vivacious; **vitalicio, -a** adj for life; **vitalidad** nf (de persona, negocio) energy; (de ciudad) liveliness

vitamina [bita'mina] nf vitamin

vitorear [bitore'ar] vt to cheer, acclaim

vitrina [bi'trina] nf show case; (LAM: escaparate) shop window

viudo, -a ['bjuðo, a] adj nm/f widower/widow

viva ['biβa] excl hurrah!; **¡~ el rey!** long live the king!

vivaracho, -a [biβa'ratʃo, a] adj jaunty, lively; (ojos) bright, twinkling

vivaz [bi'βaθ] adj lively

víveres ['biβeres] nmpl provisions

vivero [bi'βero] nm (para plantas) nursery; (para peces) fish farm; (fig) hotbed

viveza [bi'βeθa] nf liveliness; (agudeza: mental) sharpness

vivienda [bi'βjenda] nf housing; (una vivienda) house; (piso) flat (BRIT), apartment (us)

viviente [bi'βjente] adj living

vivir [bi'βir] vt, vi to live ▷ nm life, living

vivo, -a ['biβo, a] adj living, alive; (fig: descripción) vivid; (persona: astuto) smart, clever; **en ~** (transmisión etc) live

vocablo [bo'kaβlo] nm (palabra) word; (término) term

vocabulario [bokaβu'larjo] nm vocabulary

vocación [boka'θjon] nf vocation; **vocacional** (LAM) nf ≈ technical college

vocal [bo'kal] adj vocal ▷ nf vowel; **vocalizar** vt to vocalize

vocero [bo'θero] (LAM) nmf spokesman/woman

voces ['boθes] pl de **voz**

vodka ['boðka] nf o m vodka

vol abr = **volumen**

volado [bo'laðo] (MÉX) adv in a rush, hastily

volador, a [bola'ðor, a] adj flying

volandas [bo'landas]: **en ~** adv in the air

volante [bo'lante] adj flying ▷ nm (de coche) steering wheel; (de reloj) balance

volar [bo'lar] vt (edificio) to blow up ▷ vi to fly

volátil [bo'latil] adj volatile

volcán [bol'kan] nm volcano; **volcánico, -a** adj volcanic

volcar [bol'kar] vt to upset, overturn; (tumbar, derribar) to knock over; (vaciar) to empty out ▷ vi to overturn; **volcarse** vr to tip over

voleibol [bolei'βol] nm volleyball

volqué etc vb V **volcar**

voltaje [bol'taxe] nm voltage

voltear [bolte'ar] vt to turn over; (volcar) to turn upside down

voltereta [bolte'reta] nf somersault

voltio ['boltjo] nm volt

voluble [bo'luβle] adj fickle

volumen [bo'lumen] (pl **volúmenes**) nm volume; **voluminoso, -a** adj voluminous; (enorme) massive

voluntad [bolun'tað] nf will; (resolución) willpower; (deseo) desire, wish

voluntario, -a [bolun'tarjo, a] *adj*
voluntary ▷ *nm/f* volunteer

volver [bol'βer] *vt* (*gen*) to turn; (*dar
vuelta a*) to turn (over); (*voltear*) to turn
round, turn upside down; (*poner al
revés*) to turn inside out; (*devolver*) to
return ▷ *vi* to return, go back, come
back; **volverse** *vr* to turn round; **~ la
espalda** to turn one's back; **~ triste** *etc*
a algn to make so sad *etc*; **~ a hacer**
to do again; **~ en sí** to come to; **~se
insoportable/muy caro** to get o
become unbearable/very expensive;
~se loco to go mad

vomitar [bomi'tar] *vt, vi* to vomit;
vómito *nm* vomit

voraz [bo'raθ] *adj* voracious

vos [bos] (*LAM*) *pron* you

vosotros, -as [bo'sotros, as] (*ESP*)
pron you; (*reflexivo*): **entre/para ~**
among/for yourselves

votación [bota'θjon] *nf* (*acto*) voting;
(*voto*) vote

votar [bo'tar] *vi* to vote; **voto** *nm*
vote; (*promesa*) vow; **votos** *nmpl*
(good) wishes

voy *vb* V **ir**

voz [boθ] *nf* voice; (*grito*) shout;
(*rumor*) rumour; (*Ling*) word; **dar voces**
to shout, yell; **de viva ~** verbally; **en ~
alta** aloud; **en ~ baja** in a low voice, in
a whisper; **voz de mando** command

vuelco ['bwelko] *vb* V **volcar** ▷ *nm*
spill, overturning

vuelo ['bwelo] *vb* V **volar** ▷ *nm*
flight; (*encaje*) lace, frill; **coger al ~** to
catch in flight; **vuelo chárter/regular**
charter/scheduled flight; **vuelo libre**
(*Deporte*) hang-gliding

vuelque *etc* *vb* V **volcar**

vuelta ['bwelta] *nf* (*gen*) turn; (*curva*)
bend, curve; (*regreso*) return; (*revolución*)
revolution; (*de circuito*) lap; (*de papel,
tela*) reverse; (*cambio*) change; **a la ~**
on one's return; **a la ~ (de la esquina)**
round the corner; **a ~ de correo** by
return of post; **dar ~s** (*cabeza*) to spin;
dar(se) la ~ (*volverse*) to turn round;

dar ~s a una idea to turn over an idea
(in one's head); **estar de ~** to be back;
dar una ~ to go for a walk; (*en coche*) to
go for a drive; **vuelta ciclista** (*Deporte*)
(cycle) tour

vuelto ['bwelto] *pp de* **volver**

vuelvo *etc* *vb* V **volver**

vuestro, -a ['bwestro, a] *adj pos*
your; **un amigo ~** a friend of yours
▷ *pron*: **el ~/la vuestra, los ~s/las
vuestras** yours

vulgar [bul'ɣar] *adj* (*ordinario*)
vulgar; (*común*) common; **vulgaridad**
nf commonness; (*acto*) vulgarity;
(*expresión*) coarse expression

vulnerable [bulne'raβle] *adj*
vulnerable

vulnerar [bulne'rar] *vt* (*ley, acuerdo*)
to violate, breach; (*derechos, intimidad*)
to violate; (*reputación*) to damage

W X

walkie-talkie [walki-'talki] (*pl* **~s**) *nm* walkie-talkie

Walkman® ['walkman] *nm* Walkman®

wáter ['bater] *nm* (*taza*) toilet; (*LAM*: *lugar*) toilet (*BRIT*), rest room (*US*)

web [web] *nm o f* (*página*) website; (*red*) (World Wide) Web; **webcam** *nf* webcam; **webmaster** *nmf* webmaster; **website** *nm* website

western ['western] (*pl* **~s**) *nm* western

whisky ['wiski] *nm* whisky, whiskey

wifi [waɪfaɪ] *nm* Wi-Fi

windsurf ['winsurf] *nm* windsurfing; **hacer ~** to go windsurfing

xenofobia [kseno'foβja] *nf* xenophobia

xilófono [ksi'lofono] *nm* xylophone

xocoyote, -a [ksoko'yote, a] (*MÉX*) *nm/f* baby of the family, youngest child

yogur(t) [joˈɣur(t)] *nm* yoghurt
yuca [ˈjuka] *nf* (*alimento*) cassava, manioc root
Yugoslavia [juɣosˈlaβja] *nf* (*Hist*) Yugoslavia
yugular [juɣuˈlar] *adj* jugular
yunque [ˈjunke] *nm* anvil
yuyo [ˈjujo] (*RPL*) *nm* (*mala hierba*) weed

y [i] *conj* and; (*tiempo*) **la una y cinco** five past one
ya [ja] *adv* (*gen*) already; (*ahora*) now; (*en seguida*) at once; (*pronto*) soon ▷ *excl* all right! ▷ *conj* (*ahora que*) now that; **~ lo sé** I know; **~ que ...** since; **¡~ está bien!** that's (quite) enough!; **¡~ voy!** coming!
yacaré [jakaˈre] (*cs*) *nm* cayman
yacer [jaˈθer] *vi* to lie
yacimiento [jaθiˈmjento] *nm* (*de mineral*) deposit; (*arqueológico*) site
yanqui [ˈjanki] *adj, nmf* Yankee
yate [ˈjate] *nm* yacht
yazco *etc vb V* **yacer**
yedra [ˈjeðra] *nf* ivy
yegua [ˈjeɣwa] *nf* mare
yema [ˈjema] *nf* (*del huevo*) yolk; (*Bot*) leaf bud; (*fig*) best part; **yema del dedo** fingertip
yerno [ˈjerno] *nm* son-in-law
yeso [ˈjeso] *nm* plaster
yo [jo] *pron* I; **soy ~** it's me
yodo [ˈjoðo] *nm* iodine
yoga [ˈjoɣa] *nm* yoga

Z

zafar [θa'far] vt (soltar) to untie; (superficie) to clear; **zafarse** vr (escaparse) to escape; (Tec) to slip off

zafiro [θa'firo] nm sapphire

zaga [θaxa] nf: **a la ~** behind

zaguán [θa'xwan] nm hallway

zalamero, -a [θala'mero, a] adj flattering; (cobista) suave

zamarra [θa'marra] nf (chaqueta) sheepskin jacket

zambullirse [θambu'ʎirse] vr to dive

zampar [θam'par] vt to gobble down

zanahoria [θana'orja] nf carrot

zancadilla [θanka'ðiʎa] nf trip

zanco [θanko] nm stilt

zanja [θanxa] nf ditch; **zanjar** vt (resolver) to resolve

zapata [θa'pata] nf (Mecánica) shoe

zapatería [θapate'ria] nf (oficio) shoemaking; (tienda) shoe shop; (fábrica) shoe factory; **zapatero, -a** nm/f shoemaker

zapatilla [θapa'tiʎa] nf slipper; **zapatilla de deporte** training shoe

zapato [θa'pato] nm shoe

zapping ['θapin] nm channel-hopping; **hacer ~** to channel-hop

zar [θar] nm tsar, czar

zarandear [θarande'ar] (fam) vt to shake vigorously

zarpa [θarpa] nf (garra) claw

zarpar [θar'par] vi to weigh anchor

zarza [θarθa] nf (Bot) bramble; **zarzamora** nf blackberry

zarzuela [θar'θwela] nf Spanish light opera

zigzag [θix'θax] nm zigzag

zinc [θink] nm zinc

zíper ['θiper] (MÉX, CAM) nm zip (fastener) (BRIT), zipper (US)

zócalo ['θokalo] nm (Arq) plinth, base; (de pared) skirting board (BRIT), baseboard (US); (MÉX: plaza) main o public square

zoclo ['θoklo] nm (MÉX) nm skirting board (BRIT), baseboard (US)

zodíaco [θo'ðiako] nm zodiac

zona [θona] nf zone; **zona fronteriza** border area; **zona roja** (LAM) red-light district

zonzo, -a (LAM: fam) ['θonθo, a] adj silly ▷ nm/f fool

zoo ['θoo] nm zoo

zoología [θoolo'xia] nf zoology; **zoológico, -a** adj zoological ▷ nm (tb: **parque zoológico**) zoo; **zoólogo, -a** nm/f zoologist

zoom [θum] nm zoom lens

zopilote [θopi'lote] (MÉX, CAM) nm buzzard

zoquete [θo'kete] nm (fam) blockhead

zorro, -a ['θorro, a] adj crafty ▷ nm/f fox/vixen

zozobrar [θoθo'βrar] vi (hundirse) to capsize; (fig) to fail

zueco ['θweko] nm clog

zumbar [θum'bar] vt (golpear) to hit ▷ vi to buzz; **zumbido** nm buzzing

zumo ['θumo] nm juice

zurcir [θur'θir] vt (coser) to darn

zurdo, -a ['θurðo, a] adj left-handed

zurrar [θu'rrar] (fam) vt to wallop

Phrasefinder

Guía del viajero

TOPICS | TEMAS

TOPICS | TEMAS

Hello!	¡Buenos días!
Good evening!	¡Buenas tardes!
Good night!	¡Buenas noches!
Goodbye!	¡Adiós!
What's your name?	¿Cómo se llama usted?
My name is ...	Me llamo ...
This is ...	Le presento a ...
my wife.	*mi mujer.*
my husband.	*mi marido.*
my partner.	*mi pareja.*
Where are you from?	¿De dónde es usted?
I come from ...	Soy de ...
How are you?	¿Cómo está usted?
Fine, thanks.	Bien, gracias.
And you?	¿Y usted?
Do you speak English?	¿Habla usted inglés?
I don't understand Spanish.	No entiendo el español.
Thanks very much!	¡Muchas gracias!

Asking the Way — ¿Cómo ir hasta ...?

Where is the nearest ...?	¿Dónde está el/la ... más próximo(-a)?
How do I get to ...?	¿Cómo voy hasta el/la ...?
Is it far?	¿Está muy lejos?
How far is it to there?	¿Qué distancia hay hasta allí?
Is this the right way to ...?	¿Es éste el camino correcto para ir al/a la/a ...?
I'm lost.	Me he perdido.
Can you show me on the map?	¿Me lo puede señalar en el mapa?
You have to turn round.	Tiene que dar la vuelta.
Go straight on.	Siga todo recto.
Turn left/right.	Tuerza a la izquierda/ a la derecha.
Take the second street on the left/right.	Tome la segunda calle a la izquierda/a la derecha.

Car Hire — Alquiler de coches

I want to hire ...	Quisiera alquilar ...
a car.	un coche.
a moped.	una motocicleta.
a motorbike.	una moto.
How much is it for ...?	¿Cuánto cuesta por ...?
one day	un día
a week	una semana
I'd like a child seat for a ... -year-old child.	Quisiera un asiento infantil para un niño de ... años.
What do I do if I have an accident/if I break down?	¿Qué debo hacer en caso de accidente/de avería?

Breakdowns	Averías
My car has broken down.	Tengo una avería.
Where is the next garage?	¿Dónde está el taller más próximo?
The exhaust	*El escape*
The gearbox	*El cambio*
... is broken.	... está roto.
The brakes	*Los frenos*
The headlights	*Las luces*
The windscreen wipers	*Los limpiaparabrisas*
... are not working.	... no funcionan.
The battery is flat.	La batería está descargada.
The car won't start.	El motor no arranca.
The engine is overheating.	El motor se recalienta.
I have a flat tyre.	He tenido un pinchazo.
Can you repair it?	¿Puede repararlo?
When will the car be ready?	¿Cuándo estará listo el coche?

Parking	Aparcamiento
Can I park here?	¿Puedo aparcar aquí?
Do I need to buy a (car-parking) ticket?	¿Tengo que sacar un ticket de estacionamiento?
Where is the ticket machine?	¿Dónde está el expendedor de tickets de estacionamiento?
The ticket machine isn't working.	El expendedor de tickets de estacionamiento no funciona.

Petrol Station	Gasolinera
Where is the nearest petrol station?	¿Dónde está la gasolinera más próxima?
Fill it up, please.	Lleno, por favor.

30 euros' worth of ..., please.	30 euros de ...
diesel.	*diesel.*
(unleaded) economy petrol	*gasolina normal.*
premium unleaded	*súper.*
Pump number ... please.	Número ..., por favor.
Please check ...	Por favor, compruebe ...
the tyre pressure.	*la presión de los neumáticos.*
the oil.	*el aceite.*
the water.	*el agua.*

Accident	Accidentes
Please call ...	Por favor, llame ...
the police.	*a la policía.*
the emergency doctor.	*al médico de urgencia.*
Here are my insurance details.	Éstos son los datos de mi seguro.
Give me your insurance details, please.	Por favor, deme los datos de su seguro.
Can you be a witness for me?	¿Puede ser usted mi testigo?
You were driving too fast.	Usted conducía muy rápido.
It wasn't your right of way.	Usted no tenía preferencia.

Travelling by Car	Viajando en coche
What's the best route to ...?	¿Cuál es el mejor camino para ir a ...?
I'd like a motorway tax sticker ...	Quisiera un indicativo de pago de peaje ...
for a week.	*para una semana.*
for a year.	*para un año.*
Do you have a road map of this area?	¿Tiene un mapa de carreteras de esta zona?

Cycling	En bicicleta
Where is the cycle path to ...?	¿Dónde está el carril-bici para ir a ...?
Can I keep my bike here?	¿Puedo dejar aquí mi bicicleta?
My bike has been stolen.	Me han robado la bicicleta.
Where is the nearest bike repair shop?	¿Dónde hay por aquí un taller de bicicletas?
The brake isn't/the gears aren't working.	El freno/el cambio de marchas no funciona.
The chain is broken.	La cadena se ha roto.
I've got a flat tyre.	He tenido un pinchazo.
I need a puncture repair kit.	Necesito una caja de parches.

Train	Ferrocarril
A single to ..., please.	Un billete sencillo para ..., por favor.
I would like to travel first/second class.	Me gustaría viajar en primera/segunda clase.
Two returns to ..., please.	Dos billetes de ida y vuelta para ..., por favor.
Is there a reduction ...?	¿Hay descuento ...?
for students	*para estudiantes*
for pensioners	*para pensionistas*
for children	*para niños*
with this pass	*con este carnet*

I'd like to reserve a seat on the train to ... please.	Una reserva para el tren que va a ..., por favor.
Non smoking/smoking, please.	No fumadores/fumadores, por favor.
I want to book a couchette/a berth to ...	Quisiera reservar una litera/coche-cama para ...
When is the next train to ...?	¿Cuándo sale el próximo tren para ...?
Is there a supplement to pay?	¿Tengo que pagar suplemento?
Do I need to change?	¿Hay que hacer transbordo?
Where do I change?	¿Dónde tengo que hacer transbordo?
Is this the train for ...?	¿Es éste el tren que va a ...?
Excuse me, that's my seat.	Perdone, éste es mi asiento.
I have a reservation.	Tengo una reserva.
Is this seat free?	¿Está libre este asiento?
Please let me know when we get to ...	¿Por favor, avíseme cuando lleguemos a ...?
Where is the buffet car?	¿Dónde está el coche restaurante?
Where is coach number ...?	¿Cuál es el vagón número ...?

Ferry / Transbordador

Is there a ferry to ...?	¿Sale algún transbordador para ...?
When is the next ferry to ...?	¿Cuándo sale el próximo transbordador para ...?
How much is it for a car/camper with ... people?	¿Cuánto cuesta transportar el coche/coche caravana con ... personas?

How long does the crossing take?	¿Cuánto dura la travesía?
Where is ...?	¿Dónde está ...?
the restaurant	*el restaurante*
the bar	*el bar*
the duty-free shop	*la tienda de duty-free*
Where is cabin number ...?	¿Dónde está la cabina número ...?
Do you have anything for seasickness?	¿Tienen algo para el mareo?

Plane | Avión

Where is the luggage for the flight from ...?	¿Dónde está el equipaje procedente de...?
Where is ...?	¿Dónde está ...?
the taxi rank	*la parada de taxis*
the bus stop	*la parada del bus*
the information office	*la oficina de información*
My luggage hasn't arrived.	Mi equipaje no ha llegado.
Can you page ...?	¿Puede llamar por el altavoz a ...?
Where do I check in for the flight to ...?	¿Dónde hay que facturar para el vuelo a ...?
Which gate for the flight to ...?	¿Cuál es la puerta de embarque del vuelo para ...?
When is the latest I can check in?	¿Hasta qué hora como máximo se puede facturar?
When does boarding begin?	¿Cuándo es el embarque?
Window/aisle, please.	Ventanilla/pasillo, por favor.
I've lost my boarding pass/ my ticket.	He perdido la tarjeta de embarque/el billete.

Local Public Transport	**Transporte público de cercanías**
How do I get to ...?	¿Cómo se llega al/a la/hasta ...?
Where is the nearest ...?	¿Dónde está la próxima ...?
bus stop	*parada del bus*
underground station	*estación de metro*
Where is the bus station?	¿Dónde está la estación de autobuses?
A ticket to ..., please.	Un billete a ..., por favor.
Is there a reduction ...?	¿Hay descuento ...?
for students	*para estudiantes*
for pensioners	*para pensionistas*
for children	*para niños*
for the unemployed	*para desempleados*
with this card	*con este carnet*
How does the (ticket) machine work?	¿Cómo funciona la máquina (de billetes)?
Please tell me when to get off.	¿Puede decirme cuándo tengo que bajar?
What is the next stop?	¿Cuál es la próxima parada?
Can I get past, please?	¿Me deja pasar?
Taxi	**Taxi**
Where can I get a taxi?	¿Dónde puedo coger un taxi?
Call me a taxi, please.	¿Puede llamar a un taxi?
To the airport/station, please.	Al aeropuerto/a la estación, por favor.
To this address, please.	A esta dirección, por favor.
I'm in a hurry.	Tengo mucha prisa.
How much is it?	¿Cuánto cuesta el trayecto?
I need a receipt.	Necesito un recibo.
Keep the change.	Quédese con el cambio.
Stop here, please.	Pare aquí, por favor.

Camping | Camping

Is there a campsite here?	¿Hay un camping por aquí?
We'd like a site for ...	Quisiéramos un lugar para ...
a tent.	una tienda de campaña.
a caravan.	una caravana.
We'd like to stay one night/... nights.	Queremos quedarnos una noche/... noches.
How much is it per night?	¿Cuánto es por noche?
Where are ...?	¿Dónde están ...?
the toilets	los lavabos
the showers	las duchas
Where is ...?	¿Dónde está ...?
the site office	la oficina de administración
Can we camp/park here overnight?	¿Podemos acampar/aparcar aquí esta noche?

Self-Catering | Vivienda para las vacaciones

Where do we get the key for the apartment/house?	¿Dónde nos dan la llave para el piso/la casa?
Do we have to pay extra for electricity/gas?	¿Hay que pagar aparte la luz/el gas?
How does the heating work?	¿Cómo funciona la calefacción?
Whom do I contact if there are any problems?	¿Con quién debo hablar si hubiera algún problema?
We need ...	Necesitamos ...
a second key.	otra copia de la llave.
more sheets.	más sábanas.
The gas has run out.	Ya no queda gas.
There is no electricity.	No hay corriente.
Do we have to clean the apartment/the house before we leave?	¿Hay que limpiar el piso/la casa antes de marcharnos?

Hotel	Hotel
Do you have a ... for tonight?	¿Tienen una ... para esta noche?
single room	*habitación individual*
double room	*habitación doble*
with bath	con baño
with shower	con ducha
I want to stay for one night/ ... nights.	Quisiera pasar una noche/ ... noches.
I booked a room in the name of ...	Tengo reservada una habitación a nombre de ...
I'd like another room.	Quisiera otra habitación.
What time is breakfast?	¿Cuándo sirven el desayuno?
Can I have breakfast in my room?	¿Podrían traerme el desayuno a la habitación?
Where is ...?	¿Dónde está ...?
the gym	*el gimnasio*
I'd like an alarm call for tomorrow morning at ...	Por favor, despiértenme mañana a las ...
I'd like to get these things washed/cleaned.	¿Puede lavarme/limpiarme esto?
Please bring me ...	Por favor, tráigame ...
... doesn't work.	... no funciona.
Room number ...	Número de habitación ...
Are there any messages for me?	¿Hay mensajes para mí?

SHOPPING	DE COMPRAS
I'd like ...	Quisiera ...
Do you have ...?	¿Tienen ...?
Do you have this ...?	¿Lo tiene ...?
in another size	*en otra talla*
in another colour	*en otro color*
I take size ...	Mi talla es la ...
I'm a size 5$^1/_2$.	Calzo un cuarenta.
I'll take it.	Me lo quedo.
Do you have anything else?	¿Tienen alguna otra cosa distinta?
That's too expensive.	Es demasiado caro.
I'm just looking.	Sólo estaba mirando.
Do you take credit cards?	¿Aceptan tarjetas de crédito?

Food Shopping	Alimentos
Where is the nearest ...?	¿Dónde hay por aquí cerca ...?
supermarket	*un supermercado*
baker's	*una panadería*
butcher's	*una carnicería*
Where is the market?	¿Dónde está el mercado?
When is the market on?	¿Cuándo hay mercado?
a kilo/pound of ...	un kilo/medio kilo de ...
200 grams of ...	doscientos gramos de ...
... slices of ...	... lonchas de ...
a litre of ...	un litro de ...
a bottle/packet of ...	una botella/un paquete de ...

Post Office	Correos
Where is the nearest post office?	¿Dónde queda la oficina de Correos más cercana?
When does the post office open?	¿Cuándo abre Correos?
Where can I buy stamps?	¿Dónde puedo comprar sellos?

I'd like ... stamps for postcards/letters to Britain/the United States.	Quisiera ... sellos para postales/cartas a Gran Bretaña/Estados Unidos.
I'd like to post/send ...	Quisiera entregar ...
this letter.	*esta carta.*
this parcel.	*este paquete.*
By airmail/express mail/ registered mail.	Por avión/por correo urgente/ certificado.
Is there any mail for me?	¿Tengo correo?
Where is the nearest postbox?	¿Dónde hay un buzón de correos por aquí cerca?

Photos and Videos | Vídeo y fotografía

A colour film/slide film, please.	Un carrete en color/un carrete para diapositivas, por favor.
With twenty-four/thirty-six exposures.	De veinticuatro/treinta y seis fotos.
Can I have batteries for this camera, please?	Quisiera pilas para esta cámara, por favor.
The camera is sticking.	La cámara se atasca.
Can you develop this film, please?	Quisiera revelar este carrete.
I'd like the photos ...	Las fotos las quiero ...
matt.	*en mate.*
glossy.	*en brillo.*
ten by fifteen centimetres.	*en formato de diez por quince.*
When will the photos be ready?	¿Cuándo puedo pasar a recoger las fotos?
How much do the photos cost?	¿Cuánto cuesta el revelado?
Could you take a photo of us, please?	¿Podría sacarnos una foto?

Sightseeing | Visitas turísticas

Where is the tourist office?	¿Dónde está la oficina de turismo?
Do you have any leaflets about ...?	¿Tienen folletos sobre ...?
Are there any sightseeing tours of the town?	¿Se organizan visitas por la ciudad?
When is ... open?	¿Cuándo está abierto(-a) ...?
the museum	*el museo*
the church	*la iglesia*
the castle	*el palacio*
How much does it cost to get in?	¿Cuánto cuesta la entrada?
Are there any reductions ...?	¿Hay descuento ...?
for students	*para estudiantes*
for children	*para niños*
for pensioners	*para pensionistas*
for the unemployed	*para desempleados*
Is there a guided tour in English?	¿Hay alguna visita guiada en inglés?
Can I take photos here?	¿Puedo sacar fotos?
Can I film here?	¿Puedo filmar?

Entertainment | Ocio

What is there to do here?	¿Qué se puede hacer por aquí?
Where can we ...?	¿Dónde se puede ...?
go dancing	*bailar*
hear live music	*escuchar música en directo*
Where is there ...?	¿Dónde hay ... ?
a nice bar	*un buen bar*
a good club	*una buena discoteca*
What's on tonight ...?	¿Qué dan esta noche ...?

at the cinema	*en el cine*
at the theatre	*en el teatro*
at the opera	*en la ópera*
at the concert hall	*en la sala de conciertos*
Where can I buy tickets for …?	¿Dónde puedo comprar entradas para …?
the theatre	*el teatro*
the concert	*el concierto*
the opera	*la ópera*
the ballet	*el ballet*
How much is it to get in?	¿Cuánto cuesta la entrada?
I'd like a ticket/… tickets for …	Quisiera una entrada/… entradas para …
Are there any reductions for …?	¿Hay descuento para …?
children	*niños*
pensioners	*pensionistas*
students	*estudiantes*
the unemployed	*desempleados*

At the Beach	En la playa
How deep is the water?	¿Qué profundidad tiene el agua?
Is it safe to swim here?	¿Se puede nadar aquí sin peligro?
Is there a lifeguard?	¿Hay socorrista?
Where can you …?	¿Dónde se puede … por aquí?
go surfing	*hacer surf*
go waterskiing	*practicar esquí acuático*
go diving	*bucear*
go paragliding	*hacer parapente*

I'd like to hire ...	Quisiera alquilar ...
a deckchair.	*una tumbona.*
a sunshade.	*una sombrilla.*
a surfboard.	*una tabla de surf.*
a jet-ski.	*una moto acuática.*
a rowing boat.	*un bote de remos.*
a pedal boat.	*un patín a pedales.*

Sport | Deporte

Where can we ...?	¿Dónde se puede ...?
play tennis/golf	*jugar a tenis/golf*
go swimming	*ir a nadar*
go riding	*montar a caballo*
go fishing	*ir a pescar*
How much is it per hour?	¿Cuánto cuesta la hora?
Where can I book a court?	¿Dónde puedo reservar una pista?
Where can I hire rackets?	¿Dónde puedo alquilar raquetas de tenis?
Where can I hire a rowing boat/a pedal boat?	¿Dónde puedo alquilar un bote de remos/ un patín a pedales?
Do you need a fishing permit?	¿Se necesita un permiso de pesca?

Skiing | Esquí

Where can I hire skiing equipment?	¿Dónde puedo alquilar un equipo de esquí?
I'd like to hire ...	Quisiera alquilar ...
downhill skis.	*unos esquís (de descenso).*
cross-country skis.	*unos esquís de fondo.*
ski boots.	*unas botas de esquí.*
ski poles.	*unos bastones de esquí.*

Can you tighten my bindings, please?	¿Podría ajustarme la fijación, por favor?
Where can I buy a ski pass?	¿Dónde puedo comprar el forfait?
I'd like a ski pass ...	Quisiera un forfait ...
for a day.	*para un día.*
for five days.	*para cinco días.*
for a week.	*para una semana.*
How much is a ski pass?	¿Cuánto cuesta el forfait?
When does the first/ last chair-lift leave?	¿Cuándo sale el primer/ el último telesilla?
Do you have a map of the ski runs?	¿Tiene un mapa de las pistas?
Where are the beginners' slopes?	¿Dónde están las pistas para principiantes?
How difficult is this slope?	¿Cuál es la dificultad de esta pista?
Is there a ski school?	¿Hay una escuela de esquí?
Where is the nearest mountain rescue service post?	¿Dónde se encuentra la unidad más próxima de servicio de salvamento?
Where is the nearest mountain hut?	¿Dónde se encuentra el refugio más próximo?
What's the weather forecast?	¿Cuál es el pronóstico del tiempo?
What is the snow like?	¿Cómo es el estado de la nieve?
Is there a danger of avalanches?	¿Hay peligro de aludes?

A table for ... people, please.	Una mesa para ... personas, por favor.
The ... please.	Por favor, ...
menu	*la carta.*
wine list	*la carta de vinos.*
What do you recommend?	¿Qué me recomienda?
Do you have ...?	¿Sirven ...?
any vegetarian dishes	*platos vegetarianos*
children's portions	*raciones para niños*
Does that contain ...?	¿Tiene esto ...?
peanuts	*cacahuetes*
alcohol	*alcohol*
Can you bring (more) ... please?	Por favor, traiga (más) ...
I'll have ...	Para mí ...
The bill, please.	La cuenta, por favor.
All together, please.	Cóbrelo todo junto.
Separate bills, please.	Haga cuentas separadas, por favor.
Keep the change.	Quédese con el cambio.
I didn't order this.	Yo no he pedido esto.
The bill is wrong.	La cuenta está mal.
The food is cold/too salty.	La comida está fría/ demasiado salada.

Where can I make a phone call?	¿Dónde puedo hacer una llamada por aquí cerca?
Where is the nearest card phone?	¿Dónde hay un teléfono de tarjetas cerca de aquí?
Where is the nearest coin box?	¿Dónde hay un teléfono de monedas cerca de aquí?
I'd like a twenty-five euro phone card.	Quisiera una tarjeta de teléfono de veinticinco euros.
I'd like some coins for the phone, please.	Necesito monedas para llamar por teléfono.
I'd like to make a reverse charge call.	Quisiera hacer una llamada a cobro revertido.
Hello.	Hola.
This is ...	Soy ...
Who's speaking, please?	¿Con quién hablo?
Can I speak to Mr/Ms ..., please?	¿Puedo hablar con el señor/ la señora ...?
Extension ..., please.	Por favor, póngame con el número ...
I'll phone back later.	Volveré a llamar más tarde.
Can you text me your answer?	¿Puede contestarme con mensaje de móvil?
Where can I charge my mobile phone?	¿Dónde puedo cargar la batería del móvil?
I need a new battery.	Necesito una batería nueva.
Where can I buy a top-up card?	¿Dónde venden tarjetas para móviles?
I can't get a network.	No hay cobertura.

Passport/Customs | Pasaporte/Aduana

Here is ...	Aquí tiene ...
my passport.	*mi pasaporte.*
my identity card.	*mi documento de identidad.*
my driving licence.	*mi permiso de conducir.*
my green card.	*mi carta verde.*
Here are my vehicle documents.	Aquí tiene la documentación de mi vehículo.
The children are on this passport.	Los niños están incluidos en este pasaporte.
Do I have to pay duty on this?	¿Tengo que declararlo?
This is ...	Esto es ...
a present.	*un regalo.*
a sample.	*una muestra.*
This is for my own personal use.	Es para consumo propio.
I'm on my way to ...	Estoy de paso para ir a ...

At the Bank | En el banco

Where can I change money?	¿Dónde puedo cambiar dinero?
Is there a bank/bureau de change here?	¿Hay por aquí un banco/una casa de cambio?
When is the bank/bureau de change open?	¿Cuándo está abierto el banco/abierta la casa de cambio?
I'd like ... euros.	Quisiera ... euros.
I'd like to cash these traveller's cheques/eurocheques.	Quisiera cobrar estos cheques de viaje/eurocheques.

What's the commission?	¿Cuánto cobran de comisión?
Can I use my credit card to get cash?	¿Puedo sacar dinero en efectivo con mi tarjeta de crédito?
Where is the nearest cash machine?	¿Dónde hay por aquí un cajero automático?
The cash machine swallowed my card.	El cajero automático no me ha devuelto la tarjeta.
Can you give me some change, please.	Deme cambio en monedas, por favor.

Repairs — Reparaciones

Where can I get this repaired?	¿Dónde pueden repararme esto?
Can you repair ...?	¿Puede reparar ...?
these shoes	*estos zapatos*
this watch	*este reloj*
this jacket	*esta chaqueta*
Is it worth repairing?	¿Vale la pena repararlo?
How much will the repairs cost?	¿Cuánto cuesta la reparación?
Where can I have my shoes reheeled?	¿Dónde me pueden poner tacones nuevos?
When will it be ready?	¿Cuándo estará listo?
Can you do it straight away?	¿Puede hacerlo ahora mismo?

Emergency Services	Servicios de urgencia
Help!	¡Socorro!
Fire!	¡Fuego!
Please call ...	Por favor, llame a ...
the emergency doctor.	un médico de urgencia.
the fire brigade.	los bomberos.
the police.	la policía.
I need to make an urgent phone call.	Tengo que hacer una llamada urgente.
I need an interpreter.	Necesito un intérprete.
Where is the police station?	¿Dónde está la comisaría?
Where is the nearest hospital?	¿Dónde está el hospital más cercano?
I want to report a theft.	Quisiera denunciar un robo.
... has been stolen.	Han robado ...
There's been an accident.	Ha habido un accidente.
There are ... people injured.	Hay ... heridos.
My location is ...	Estoy en ...
I've been ...	Me han ...
robbed.	robado.
attacked.	atracado.
raped.	violado.
I'd like to phone my embassy.	Quisiera hablar con mi embajada.

Pharmacy | Farmacia

Where is the nearest pharmacy?	¿Dónde hay por aquí una farmacia?
Which pharmacy provides emergency service?	¿Qué farmacia está de guardia?
I'd like something for ...	Quisiera algo para ...
diarrhoea.	*la diarrea.*
a temperature.	*la fiebre.*
travel sickness.	*el mareo.*
a headache.	*el dolor de cabeza.*
a cold.	*el resfriado.*
I'd like ...	Quisiera ...
plasters.	*tiritas.*
a bandage.	*un vendaje.*
some paracetamol.	*paracetamol.*
I can't take ...	Soy alérgico(-a) a la ...
aspirin.	*aspirina.*
penicillin.	*penicilina.*
Is is safe to give to children?	¿Pueden tomarlo los niños?
How should I take it?	¿Cómo tengo que tomarlo?

At the Doctor's | En la consulta médica

I need a doctor.	Necesito que me atienda un médico.
Where is casualty?	¿Dónde está Urgencias?
I have a pain here.	Me duele aquí.
I feel ...	Tengo ...
hot.	*mucho calor.*
cold.	*frío.*
I feel sick.	Me siento mal.
I feel dizzy.	Tengo mareos.

I'm allergic to ...	Tengo alergia a ...
I am ...	Yo ...
pregnant.	*estoy embarazada.*
diabetic.	*soy diabético(-a).*
HIV-positive.	*soy seropositivo(-a).*
I'm on this medication.	Estoy tomando este medicamento.
My blood group is ...	Mi grupo sanguíneo es ...

At the Hospital	En el hospital
Which ward is ... in?	¿En qué unidad está ...?
When are visiting hours?	¿Cuándo son las horas de visita?
I'd like to speak to ...	Quisiera hablar con ...
a doctor.	*un médico.*
a nurse.	*una enfermera.*
When will I be discharged?	¿Cuándo me van a dar de alta?

At the Dentist's	En el dentista
I need a dentist.	Tengo que ir al dentista.
This tooth hurts.	Me duele este diente.
One of my fillings has fallen out.	Se me ha caído un empaste.
I have an abscess.	Tengo un absceso.
I want/don't want an injection for the pain.	Quiero/no quiero que me ponga una inyección para calmar el dolor.
Can you repair my dentures?	¿Me puede reparar la dentadura?
I need a receipt for the insurance.	Necesito un recibo para mi seguro.

Business Travel

I'd like to arrange a meeting with ...	Quisiera concertar hora para una reunión con ...
I have an appointment with Mr/Ms ...	Tengo una cita con el señor/la señora ...
Here is my card.	Aquí tiene mi tarjeta.
I work for ...	Trabajo para ...
How do I get to ...?	¿Cómo se llega ...?
your office	*a su despacho*
I need an interpreter.	Necesito un intérprete.
Can you copy that for me, please?	Por favor, hágame una copia de eso.
May I use ...?	¿Puedo usar ...?
your phone	*su teléfono*
your computer	*su ordenador*

Disabled Travellers

Minusválidos

Is it possible to visit ... with a wheelchair?	¿La visita a ... es posible también para personas en silla de ruedas?
Where is the wheelchair-accessible entrance?	¿Por dónde se puede entrar con la silla de ruedas?
Is your hotel accessible to wheelchairs?	¿Tiene su hotel acceso para minusválidos?
I need a room ...	Necesito una habitación ...
on the ground floor.	*en la planta baja.*
with wheelchair access.	*con acceso para minusuálidos.*
Do you have a lift for wheelchairs?	¿Tienen ascensor para minusválidos?
Do you have wheelchairs?	¿Tienen sillas de ruedas?

Where is the disabled toilet?	¿Dónde está el lavabo para minusválidos?
Can you help me get on/ off please?	¿Podría ayudarme a subir/ bajar, por favor?
A tyre has burst.	Se ha reventado un neumático.
The battery is flat.	La batería está descargada.
The wheels lock.	Las ruedas se bloquean.

Travelling with children | Viajando con niños

Are children allowed in too?	¿Pueden entrar niños?
Is there a reduction for children?	¿Hay descuento para niños?
Do you have children's portions?	¿Sirven raciones para niños?
Do you have ...?	¿Tienen ...?
a high chair	*una sillita*
a cot	*una cama infantil*
a child's seat	*un asiento infantil*
a baby's changing table	*una mesa para cambiar al bebé*
Where can I change the baby?	¿Dónde puedo cambiar al bebé?
Where can I breast-feed the baby?	¿Dónde puedo dar el pecho al niño?
Can you warm this up, please?	¿Puede calentarlo, por favor?
What is there for children to do?	¿Qué pueden hacer aquí los niños?
Is there a child-minding service?	¿Hay aquí un servicio de guardería?
My son/daughter is ill.	Mi hijo/mi hija está enfermo(-a).

bangers and mash salchichas con puré de patatas, cebolla frita y salsa hecha con jugo de carne asada

banoffee pie tarta rellena de plátano, caramelo y nata

BLT (sandwich) sándwich de bacón, lechuga, tomate y mayonesa

butternut squash variedad de calabaza de color amarillo y sabor dulce, que a menudo se sirve asada

Caesar salad ensalada César

chocolate brownie brownie: pastelito de chocolate y nueces

chowder guiso de pescado

chicken Kiev pollo a la Kiev

chicken nuggets croquetas de pollo

club sandwich sándwich caliente de tres pisos; normalmente relleno de carne, queso, lechuga, tomate y cebollas

cottage pie pastel de carne picada y verduras, cubierto con puré de patatas y queso

English breakfast desayuno inglés: huevos, bacón, salchichas, alubias cocidas, pan frito y champiñones

filo pastry masa de hojaldre

haggis plato escocés a base de hígado y corazón de cordero, avena y otros condimentos, hervidos en una bolsa formada por el estómago del animal

hash browns trocitos de patata sofritos con cebolla, que a menudo se sirven con el desayuno

hotpot estofado de carne, verdura y patatas

Irish stew estofado irlandés, a base de cordero, patatas y cebolla

monkfish rape

oatcake galleta de avellana

pavlova pastel de merengue con frutas y nata

ploughman's lunch almuerzo de pub a base de pan, queso y encurtidos

purée puré

Quorn® proteína vegetal usada como sustituto de carne

Savoy cabbage col rizada

sea bass lubina

Scotch broth sopa de carne, cebada y verduras

Scotch egg huevo duro envuelto en carne de salchicha y rebozado

spare ribs costillas de cerdo

spring roll rollito de primavera

Stilton Stilton: queso azul inglés

sundae sundae: helado con jarabe, nueces y nata

Thousand Island dressing salsa rosa

toad in the hole salchichas horneadas en una masa de huevos, leche y harina

Waldorf salad ensalada Waldorf: manzanas troceadas, apio, nueces y mayonesa

Welsh rarebit tostada cubierta con queso derretido y huevo

Yorkshire pudding buñuelo, a veces relleno de verduras, que se sirve acompañando al rosbif

adobo, ... en marinated

ajillo, ... al with garlic

arroz negro black rice (with squid in its own ink)

asadillo roasted sliced red peppers in olive oil and garlic

bandeja de quesos cheese platter

brasa, ... a la barbecued

buñuelos type of fritter. Savoury ones are filled with cheese, ham, mussels or prawns. Sweet ones can be filled with fruit

caldereta stew/casserole

cazuela de fideos bean, meat and noodle stew

chilindrón, ... al sauce made with pepper, tomato, fried onions and meat pork or lamb

chistorra spicy sausage from Navarra

chorizo spicy red sausage

chuletón large steak

churros fried batter sticks sprinkled with sugar, usually eaten with thick hot chocolate.

crema catalana similar to crème brûlée

cuajada cream-based dessert like junket, served with honey or sugar

dulces cakes and pastries

empanadilla pasty/small pie filled with meat or fish

empanado breadcrumbed and fried

ensalada de la casa lettuce, tomato and onion salad (may include tuna)

fritura de pescado fried assortment of fish

gazpacho traditional cold tomato soup of southern Spain. Basic ingredients are water, tomatoes, garlic, fresh bread-crumbs, salt, vinegar and olive oil

horno, ...al baked (in oven)

ibéricos traditional Spanish gourmet products; a surtido de ibéricos means assorted products such as cured ham, cheese, chorizo and salchichón

jamón serrano dark red cured ham

leche frita very thick custard dipped into an egg and breadcrumb mixture, fried and served hot

mariscada mixed shellfish

medallón thick steak (medallion)

mollejas sweetbreads

moros y cristianos rice, black beans and onions with garlic sausage

paella Paella varies from region to region but usually consists of rice, chicken, shellfish, vegetables, garlic and saffron. Paella Valenciana contains rabbit, chicken and sometimes eel

parrilla, ... a la grilled

patatas bravas fried diced potatoes mixed with a garlic, oil and vinegar dressing and flavoured with tomatoes and red chilli peppers

pepitoria de pavo/pollo turkey/chicken fricassée

pimientos morrones sweet red peppers

pote thick soup with beans and sausage which has many regional variations

puchero hotpot made from meat or fish

revuelto scrambled eggs often cooked with another ingredient

romesco sauce made traditionally with olive oil, red pepper and bread. Other ingredients are often added, such as almonds and garlic

salsa verde garlic, olive oil and parsley sauce

sofrito basic sauce made with slowly fried onions, garlic and tomato

tapas Bar snacks. A larger portion of tapas is called a ración. A pincho is a tapa on a cocktail stick.

tortilla (española) traditional potato and onion omelette, often served as a tapa

zarzuela de mariscos mixed seafood with wine and saffron

A [eɪ] n (Mus) la m

○ **KEYWORD**

a [ə] (before vowel or silent h: an) indef art
1 un(a); **a book** un libro; **an apple**
una manzana; **she's a doctor** (ella)
es médica
2 (instead of the number "one") un(a); **a
year ago** hace un año; **a hundred/
thousand** etc **pounds** cien/mil etc
libras
3 (in expressing ratios, prices etc): **3 a
day/week** 3 al día/a la semana; **10 km
an hour** 10 km por hora; **£5 a person** £5
por persona; **30p a kilo** 30p el kilo

A2 (BRIT: Scol) n segunda parte de los
"A levels"

A.A. n abbr (BRIT: = Automobile
Association) ≈ RACE m (SP); (= Alcoholics
Anonymous) Alcohólicos Anónimos

A.A.A. (US) n abbr (= American
Automobile Association) ≈ RACE m (SP)

aback [ə'bæk] adv: **to be taken ~**

quedar desconcertado
abandon [ə'bændən] vt abandonar;
(give up) renunciar a
abattoir ['æbətwɑː*] (BRIT) n
matadero
abbey ['æbɪ] n abadía
abbreviation [əbriːvɪ'eɪʃən] n (short
form) abreviatura
abdomen ['æbdəmən] n abdomen m
abduct [æb'dʌkt] vt raptar,
secuestrar
abide [ə'baɪd] vt: **I can't ~ it/him**
no lo/le puedo ver; **abide by** vt fus
atenerse a
ability [ə'bɪlɪtɪ] n habilidad f,
capacidad f; (talent) talento
able ['eɪbl] adj capaz; (skilled) hábil; **to
be ~ to do sth** poder hacer algo
abnormal [æb'nɔːməl] adj anormal
aboard [ə'bɔːd] adv a bordo ▷ prep
a bordo de
abolish [ə'bɔlɪʃ] vt suprimir, abolir
abolition [æbəu'lɪʃən] n supresión
f, abolición f
abort [ə'bɔːt] vt, vi abortar; **abortion**
[ə'bɔːʃən] n aborto; **to have an
abortion** abortar, hacerse abortar

○ **KEYWORD**

about [ə'baut] adv 1 (approximately)
más o menos, aproximadamente;
about a hundred/thousand etc
unos(unas) cien/mil etc; **it takes
about 10 hours** se tarda unas or más
o menos 10 horas; **at about 2 o'clock**
sobre las dos; **I've just about finished**
casi he terminado
2 (referring to place) por todas partes;
to leave things lying about dejar las
cosas (tiradas) por ahí; **to run about**
correr por todas partes; **to walk about**
pasearse, ir y venir
3: **to be about to do sth** estar a punto
de hacer algo
▷ prep 1 (relating to) de, sobre, acerca
de; **a book about London** un libro
sobre or acerca de Londres; **what is it**

about? ¿de qué se trata?; **we talked about it** hablamos de eso or ello; **what** or **how about doing this?** ¿qué tal si hacemos esto?

2 (referring to place) por; **to walk about the town** caminar por la ciudad

above [əˈbʌv] adv encima, por encima de, arriba ▷ prep encima de; (greater than: in number) más de; (: in rank) superior a; **mentioned ~** susodicho; **~ all** sobre todo

abroad [əˈbrɔːd] adv (to be) en el extranjero; (to go) al extranjero

abrupt [əˈbrʌpt] adj (sudden) brusco; (curt) áspero

abscess [ˈæbsɪs] n absceso

absence [ˈæbsəns] n ausencia

absent [ˈæbsənt] adj ausente; **absent-minded** adj distraído

absolute [ˈæbsəluːt] adj absoluto; **absolutely** [-ˈluːtlɪ] adv (totally) totalmente; (certainly!) ¡por supuesto (que sí)!

absorb [əbˈzɔːb] vt absorber; **to be ~ed in a book** estar absorto en un libro; **absorbent cotton** (us) n algodón m hidrófilo; **absorbing** adj absorbente

abstain [əbˈsteɪn] vi: **to ~ (from)** abstenerse de

abstract [ˈæbstrækt] adj abstracto

absurd [əbˈsəːd] adj absurdo

abundance [əˈbʌndəns] n abundancia

abundant [əˈbʌndənt] adj abundante

abuse [n əˈbjuːs, vb əˈbjuːz] (insults) insultos mpl, injurias fpl; (ill-treatment) malos tratos mpl; (misuse) abuso m ▷ vt insultar; maltratar; abusar de; **abusive** adj ofensivo

abysmal [əˈbɪzməl] adj pésimo; (failure) garrafal; (ignorance) supino

academic [ækəˈdemɪk] adj académico, universitario; (pej: issue) puramente teórico ▷ n estudioso/a, profesor(a) m/f universitario/a; **academic year** n (Univ) año m

académico; (Scol) año m escolar

academy [əˈkædəmɪ] n (learned body) academia; (school) instituto, colegio; **~ of music** conservatorio

accelerate [ækˈseləreɪt] vt, vi acelerar; **acceleration** [æksələˈreɪʃən] n aceleración f; **accelerator** (BRIT) n acelerador m

accent [ˈæksənt] n acento; (fig) énfasis m

accept [əkˈsept] vt aceptar; (responsibility, blame) admitir; **acceptable** adj aceptable; **acceptance** n aceptación f

access [ˈækses] n acceso; **to have ~ to** tener libre acceso a; **accessible** [-ˈsesəbl] adj (place, person) accesible; (knowledge etc) asequible

accessory [ækˈsesərɪ] n accesorio; (Law): **~ to** cómplice de

accident [ˈæksɪdənt] n accidente m; (chance event) casualidad f; **by ~** (unintentionally) sin querer; (by chance) por casualidad; **accidental** [-ˈdentl] adj accidental, fortuito; **accidentally** [-ˈdentəlɪ] adv sin querer; por casualidad; **Accident and Emergency Department** n (BRIT) Urgencias fpl; **accident insurance** n seguro contra accidentes

acclaim [əˈkleɪm] vt aclamar, aplaudir ▷ n aclamación f, aplausos mpl

accommodate [əˈkɒmədeɪt] vt (person) alojar, hospedar; (: car, hotel etc) tener cabida para; (oblige, help) complacer

accommodation [əkɒməˈdeɪʃən] (us **accommodations**) n alojamiento

accompaniment [əˈkʌmpənɪmənt] n acompañamiento

accompany [əˈkʌmpənɪ] vt acompañar

accomplice [əˈkʌmplɪs] n cómplice mf

accomplish [əˈkʌmplɪʃ] vt (finish) concluir; (achieve) lograr; **accomplishment** n (skill: gen pl) talento; (*completion*) realización f

accord [əˈkɔːd] n acuerdo
▷ vt conceder; **of his own ~**
espontáneamente; **accordance**
n: **in accordance with** de acuerdo
con; **according** ▷ **according to** prep
según; (*in accordance with*) conforme
a; **accordingly** adv (*appropriately*)
de acuerdo con esto; (*as a result*) en
consecuencia

account [əˈkaunt] n (*Comm*)
cuenta; (*report*) informe m; **accounts**
npl (*Comm*) cuentas fpl; **of no ~** de
ninguna importancia; **on ~** a cuenta;
on no ~ bajo ningún concepto; **on ~**
of a causa de, por motivo de; **to take**
into ~, take ~ of tener en cuenta;
account for vt fus (*explain*) explicar;
(*represent*) representar; **accountable**
adj: **accountable (to)** responsable
(ante); **accountant** n contable mf,
contador(a) m/f; **account number** n
(*at bank etc*) número de cuenta

accumulate [əˈkjuːmjuleɪt] vt
acumular ▷ vi acumularse

accuracy [ˈækjurəsɪ] n (*of total*)
exactitud f; (*of description etc*)
precisión f

accurate [ˈækjurɪt] adj (*total*) exacto;
(*description*) preciso; (*person*) cuidadoso;
(*device*) de precisión; **accurately** adv
con precisión

accusation [ækjuˈzeɪʃən] n
acusación f

accuse [əˈkjuːz] vt: **to ~ sb (of sth)**
acusar a algn (de algo); **accused** n
(*Law*) acusado/a

accustomed [əˈkʌstəmd] adj: **~ to**
acostumbrado a

ace [eɪs] n as m

ache [eɪk] n dolor m ▷ vi doler; **my**
head ~s me duele la cabeza

achieve [əˈtʃiːv] vt (*aim, result*)
alcanzar; (*success*) lograr, conseguir;
achievement n (*completion*)
realización f; (*success*) éxito

acid [ˈæsɪd] adj ácido; (*taste*) agrio ▷ n
(*Chem, inf: LSD*) ácido

acknowledge [əkˈnɔlɪdʒ] vt
(*letter: also:* **~ receipt of**) acusar recibo
de; (*fact, situation, person*) reconocer;
acknowledgement n acuse m de
recibo

acne [ˈæknɪ] n acné m

acorn [ˈeɪkɔːn] n bellota

acoustic [əˈkuːstɪk] adj acústico

acquaintance [əˈkweɪntəns] n
(*person*) conocido/a; (*with person,*
subject) conocimiento

acquire [əˈkwaɪəʳ] vt adquirir;
acquisition [ækwɪˈzɪʃən] n
adquisición f

acquit [əˈkwɪt] vt absolver, exculpar;
to ~ o.s. well salir con éxito

acre [ˈeɪkəʳ] n acre m

acronym [ˈækrənɪm] n siglas fpl

across [əˈkrɔs] prep (*on the other side*
of) al otro lado de, del otro lado de;
(*crosswise*) a través de ▷ adv de un lado
a otro, de una parte a otra; a través, al
través; (*measurement*) **the road is 10m**
~ la carretera tiene 10m de ancho; **to**
run/swim ~ atravesar corriendo/
nadando; **~ from** enfrente de

acrylic [əˈkrɪlɪk] adj acrílico ▷ n
acrílica

act [ækt] n acto, acción f; (*of play*)
acto; (*in music hall etc*) número;
(*Law*) decreto, ley f ▷ vi (*behave*)
comportarse; (*have effect: drug,*
chemical) hacer efecto; (*Theatre*) actuar;
(*pretend*) fingir; (*take action*) obrar ▷ vt
(*part*) hacer el papel de; **in the ~ of: to**
catch sb in the ~ of ... pillar a algn en
el momento de ...; **to ~ as** actuar
or hacer de; **act up** (*inf*) vi (*person*)
portarse mal; **acting** adj suplente
▷ n (*activity*) actuación f; (*profession*)
profesión f de actor

action [ˈækʃən] n acción f, acto;
(*Mil*) acción f, batalla; (*Law*) proceso,
demanda; **out of ~** (*person*) fuera de
combate; (*thing*) estropeado; **to take ~**
tomar medidas; **action replay** n (*TV*)
repetición f

activate [ˈæktɪveɪt] vt activar

active ['æktɪv] adj activo, enérgico; (volcano) en actividad; **actively** adv (participate) activamente; (discourage, dislike) enérgicamente

activist ['æktɪvɪst] n activista m/f

activity [-'tɪvɪtɪ] n actividad f; **activity holiday** n vacaciones con actividades organizadas

actor ['æktə*] n actor m, actriz f

actress ['æktrɪs] n actriz f

actual ['æktjuəl] adj verdadero, real; (emphatic only) propiamente dicho

  Be careful not to translate **actual** by the Spanish word actual.

actually ['æktjuəlɪ] adv realmente, en realidad; (even) incluso

  Be careful not to translate **actually** by the Spanish word actualmente.

acupuncture ['ækjupʌŋktʃə*] n acupuntura

acute [ə'kjuːt] adj agudo

ad [æd] n abbr = **advertisement**

A.D. adv abbr (= anno Domini) DC

adamant ['ædəmənt] adj firme, inflexible

adapt [ə'dæpt] vt adaptar ▷ vi: to ~ (to) adaptarse (a), ajustarse (a); **adapter** (us **adaptor**) n (Elec) adaptador m; (for several plugs) ladrón m

add [æd] vt añadir, agregar; **add up** vt (figures) sumar ▷ vi (fig): **it doesn't add up** no tiene sentido; **add up to** vt fus (Math) sumar, ascender a; (fig: mean) querer decir, venir a ser

addict ['ædɪkt] n adicto/a; (enthusiast) entusiasta mf; **addicted** [ə'dɪktɪd] adj: **to be addicted to** ser adicto a, ser fanático de; **addiction** [ə'dɪkʃən] n (to drugs etc) adicción f; **addictive** [ə'dɪktɪv] adj que causa adicción

addition [ə'dɪʃən] n (adding up) adición f; (thing added) añadidura, añadido; **in ~** además, por añadidura; **in ~ to** además de; **additional** adj adicional

additive ['ædɪtɪv] n aditivo

address [ə'drɛs] n dirección f, señas

fpl; (speech) discurso ▷ vt (letter) dirigir; (speak to) dirigirse a, dirigir la palabra a; (problem) tratar; **address book** n agenda de direcciones

adequate ['ædɪkwɪt] adj (satisfactory) adecuado; (enough) suficiente

adhere [əd'hɪə*] vi: to ~ to (stick to) pegarse a; (fig: abide by) observar; (: belief etc) ser partidario de

adhesive [əd'hiːzɪv] n adhesivo; **adhesive tape** n (BRIT) cinta adhesiva; (us Med) esparadrapo

adjacent [ə'dʒeɪsənt] adj: ~ to contiguo a, inmediato a

adjective ['ædʒɛktɪv] n adjetivo

adjoining [ə'dʒɔɪnɪŋ] adj contiguo, vecino

adjourn [ə'dʒəːn] vt aplazar ▷ vi suspenderse

adjust [ə'dʒʌst] vt (change) modificar; (clothing) arreglar; (machine) ajustar ▷ vi: to ~ (to) adaptarse (a); **adjustable** adj ajustable; **adjustment** n adaptación f; (to machine, prices) ajuste m

administer [əd'mɪnɪstə*] vt administrar; **administration** [-'treɪʃən] n (management) administración f; (government) gobierno; **administrative** [-trətɪv] adj administrativo

administrator [əd'mɪnɪstreɪtə*] n administrador/a m/f

admiral ['ædmərəl] n almirante m

admiration [ædmə'reɪʃən] n admiración f

admire [əd'maɪə*] vt admirar; **admirer** n (fan) admirador/a m/f

admission [əd'mɪʃən] n (to university, club) ingreso; (entry fee) entrada; (confession) confesión f

admit [əd'mɪt] vt (confess) confesar; (permit to enter) dejar entrar, dar entrada a; (to club, organization) admitir; (accept: defeat) reconocer; **to be ~ted to hospital** ingresar en el hospital; **admit to** vt fus confesar culpable de; **admittance** n entrada; **admittedly** adv es cierto que

adolescent [ædəʊˈlesnt] adj, n adolescente mf

adopt [əˈdɒpt] vt adoptar; **adopted** adj adoptivo; **adoption** [əˈdɒpʃən] n adopción f

adore [əˈdɔːʳ] vt adorar

adorn [əˈdɔːn] vt adornar

Adriatic [eɪdrɪˈætɪk] n: **the ~ (Sea)** el (Mar) Adriático

adrift [əˈdrɪft] adv a la deriva

ADSL abbr (= asymmetrical digital subscriber line) ADSL m

adult [ˈædʌlt] n adulto/a ▷ adj (grown-up) adulto; (for adults) para adultos; **adult education** n educación f para adultos

adultery [əˈdʌltərɪ] n adulterio

advance [ədˈvɑːns] n (progress) adelanto, progreso; (money) anticipo, préstamo; (Mil) avance m ▷ adj: **~ booking** venta anticipada; **~ notice**, **~ warning** previo aviso ▷ vt (money) anticipar; (theory, idea) proponer (para la discusión) ▷ vi avanzar, adelantarse; **to make ~s (to sb)** hacer proposiciones (a algn); **in ~** por adelantado; **advanced** adj avanzado; (Scol: studies) adelantado

advantage [ədˈvɑːntɪdʒ] n (also Tennis) ventaja; **to take ~ of** (person) aprovecharse de; (opportunity) aprovechar

advent [ˈædvənt] n advenimiento; **A~** Adviento

adventure [ədˈventʃəʳ] n aventura; **adventurous** [-tʃərəs] adj atrevido; aventurero

adverb [ˈædvɜːb] n adverbio

adversary [ˈædvəsərɪ] n adversario, contrario

adverse [ˈædvɜːs] adj adverso, contrario

advert [ˈædvɜːt] (BRIT) n abbr = **advertisement**

advertise [ˈædvətaɪz] vi anunciar, hacer publicidad; **to ~ for** buscar por

medio de anuncios ▷ vt anunciar; **advertisement** [ədˈvɜːtɪsmənt] n (Comm) anuncio; **advertiser** n anunciante mf; **advertising** n publicidad f, anuncios mpl; (industry) industria publicitaria

advice [ədˈvaɪs] n consejo, consejos mpl; (notification) aviso; **a piece of ~** un consejo; **to take legal ~** consultar con un abogado

advisable [ədˈvaɪzəbl] adj aconsejable, conveniente

advise [ədˈvaɪz] vt aconsejar; (inform): **to ~ sb of sth** informar a algn de algo; **to ~ sb against sth/doing sth** desaconsejar a algn/aconsejar a algn que no haga algo; **adviser**, **advisor** n consejero/a; (consultant) asesor/a m/f; **advisory** adj consultivo

advocate [vb ˈædvəkeɪt, n -kɪt] vt abogar por ▷ n (lawyer) abogado/a; (supporter): **~ of** defensor/a m/f de

Aegean [iːˈdʒiːən] n: **the ~ (Sea)** el (Mar) Egeo

aerial [ˈɛərɪəl] n antena ▷ adj aéreo

aerobics [ɛəˈrəʊbɪks] n aerobic m

aeroplane [ˈɛərəpleɪn] (BRIT) n avión m

aerosol [ˈɛərəsɒl] n aerosol m

affair [əˈfɛəʳ] n asunto; (also: **love ~**) aventura (amorosa)

affect [əˈfɛkt] vt (influence) afectar, influir en; (afflict, concern) afectar; (move) conmover; **affected** adj afectado; **affection** n afecto, cariño; **affectionate** adj afectuoso, cariñoso

afflict [əˈflɪkt] vt afligir

affluent [ˈæfluənt] adj (wealthy) acomodado; **the ~ society** la sociedad opulenta

afford [əˈfɔːd] vt (provide) proporcionar; **can we ~ (to buy) it?** ¿tenemos bastante dinero para comprarlo?; **affordable** adj asequible

Afghanistan [æfˈgænɪstæn] n Afganistán m

afraid [əˈfreɪd] adj: **to be ~ of** (person) tener miedo a; (thing) tener miedo de;

to be ~ to tener miedo de, temer; **I am ~ that** me temo que; **I am ~ not/so** lo siento, pero no/es así

Africa ['æfrɪkə] n África; **African** adj, n africano/a m/f; **African-American** adj, n afroamericano/a

after ['ɑːftə*] prep (time) después de; (place, order) detrás de, tras ▷ adv después ▷ conj después (de) que; **what/who are you ~?** ¿qué/a quién busca usted?; **~ having done/he left** después de haber hecho/después de que se marchó; **to name sb ~ sb** llamar a algn por algn; **it's twenty ~ eight** (us) son las ocho y veinte; **to ask ~ sb** preguntar por algn; **~ all** después de todo, al fin y al cabo; **~ you!** ¡pase usted!; **after-effects** npl consecuencias fpl, efectos mpl; **aftermath** n consecuencias fpl, resultados mpl; **afternoon** n tarde f; **after-shave (lotion)** n aftershave m; **aftersun (lotion/cream)** n loción f/crema para después del sol, aftersun m; **afterwards** (us **afterward**) adv después, más tarde

again [ə'gɛn] adv otra vez, de nuevo; **to do sth ~** volver a hacer algo; **~ and ~** una y otra vez

against [ə'gɛnst] prep (in opposition to) en contra de; (leaning on, touching) contra, junto a

age [eɪdʒ] n edad f; (period) época ▷ vi envejecer(se) ▷ vt envejecer; **she is 20 years of ~** tiene 20 años; **to come of ~** llegar a la mayoría de edad; **it's been ~s since I saw you** hace siglos que no te veo; **~d 10** de 10 años de edad; **age group** n: **to be in the same age group** tener la misma edad; **age limit** n edad f mínima (or máxima)

agency ['eɪdʒənsɪ] n agencia

agenda [ə'dʒɛndə] n orden m del día

> Be careful not to translate **agenda** by the Spanish word *agenda*.

agent ['eɪdʒənt] n agente mf: (Comm: holding concession) representante mf, delegado/a; (Chem,

fig) agente m

aggravate ['ægrəveɪt] vt (situation) agravar; (person) irritar

aggression [ə'grɛʃən] n agresión f

aggressive [ə'grɛsɪv] adj (belligerent) agresivo; (assertive) enérgico

agile ['ædʒaɪl] adj ágil

agitated ['ædʒɪteɪtɪd] adj agitado

AGM n abbr (= annual general meeting) asamblea anual

ago [ə'gəʊ] adv: **2 days ~** hace 2 días; **not long ~** hace poco; **how long ~?** ¿hace cuánto tiempo?

agony ['ægənɪ] n (pain) dolor m agudo; (distress) angustia; **to be in ~** retorcerse de dolor

agree [ə'griː] vt (price, date) acordar, quedar en ▷ vi (have same opinion): **to ~ (with/that)** estar de acuerdo (con/que); (correspond) coincidir, concordar; (consent) acceder; **to ~ with** (person) estar de acuerdo con, ponerse de acuerdo con; (: food) sentar bien a; (Ling) concordar con; **to ~ to sth/to do sth** consentir en algo/aceptar hacer algo; **to ~ that** (admit) estar de acuerdo en que; **agreeable** adj (sensation) agradable; (person) simpático; (willing) de acuerdo, conforme; **agreed** adj (time, place) convenido; **agreement** n acuerdo; (contract) contrato; **in agreement** de acuerdo, conforme

agricultural [ægrɪ'kʌltʃərəl] adj agrícola

agriculture ['ægrɪkʌltʃə*] n agricultura

ahead [ə'hɛd] adv (in front) delante; (into the future): **she had no time to think ~** no tenía tiempo de hacer planes para el futuro; **~ of** delante de; (in advance of) antes de; **~ of time** antes de la hora; **go right** or **straight ~** (direction) siga adelante; (permission) hazlo or hágalo

aid [eɪd] n ayuda, auxilio; (device) aparato ▷ vt ayudar, auxiliar; **in ~ of** a beneficio de

aide [eɪd] n (person, also Mil) ayudante

mf

AIDS [eidz] n abbr (= acquired immune deficiency syndrome) SIDA m

ailing ['eiliŋ] adj (person, economy) enfermizo

ailment ['eilmənt] n enfermedad f, achaque m

aim [eim] vt (gun, camera) apuntar; (missile, remark) dirigir; (blow) asestar ▷ vi (also: **take ~**) apuntar ▷ n (in shooting: skill) puntería; (objective) propósito, meta; **to ~ at** (with weapon) apuntar a; (objective) aspirar a, pretender; **to ~ to do** tener la intención de hacer

ain't [eint] (inf) (= am not; aren't; isn't

air [eə*] n aire m; (appearance) aspecto ▷ vt (room) ventilar; (clothes, ideas) airear ▷ cpd aéreo; **to throw sth into the ~** (ball etc) lanzar algo al aire; **by ~** (travel) en avión; **to be on the ~** (Radio, TV) estar en antena; **airbag** n airbag m inv; **airbed** (BRIT) n colchón m neumático; **airborne** adj (in the air) en el aire; **as soon as the plane was airborne** tan pronto como el avión estuvo en el aire; **air-conditioned** adj climatizado; **air conditioning** n aire acondicionado m; **aircraft** n inv avión m; **airfield** n campo de aviación; **Air Force** n fuerzas fpl aéreas, aviación f; **air hostess** (BRIT) n azafata; **airing cupboard** (BRIT) n armario m para oreo; **airlift** n puente m aéreo; **airline** n línea aérea; **airliner** n avión m de pasajeros; **airmail** n: **by airmail** por avión; **airplane** (US) n avión m; **airport** n aeropuerto; **air raid** n ataque m aéreo; **airsick** adj: **to be airsick** marearse (en avión); **airspace** n espacio aéreo; **airstrip** n pista de aterrizaje; **air terminal** n terminal f; **airtight** adj hermético; **air-traffic controller** n controlador m/f aéreo/a; **airy** adj (room) bien ventilado; (fig: manner) desenfadado

aisle [ail] n (of church) nave f; (of theatre, supermarket) pasillo m; **aisle seat**

n (on plane) asiento de pasillo

ajar [ə'dʒɑː*] adj entreabierto

à la carte [æləˈkɑːt] adv a la carta

alarm [ə'lɑːm] n (in shop, bank) alarma; (anxiety) inquietud f ▷ vt asustar, inquietar; **alarm call** n (in hotel etc) alarma; **alarm clock** n despertador m; **alarmed** adj (person) alarmado, asustado; (house, car etc) con alarma; **alarming** adj alarmante

Albania [æl'beiniə] n Albania

albeit [ɔːl'biːit] conj aunque

album ['ælbəm] n álbum m; (L.P.) elepé m

alcohol ['ælkəhɔl] n alcohol m; **alcohol-free** adj sin alcohol; **alcoholic** [-'hɔlik] adj, n alcohólico/a m/f

alcove ['ælkəuv] n nicho, hueco

ale [eil] n cerveza

alert [ə'lɜːt] adj (attentive) atento; (to danger, opportunity) alerta ▷ n alerta m, alarma ▷ vt poner sobre aviso; **to be on the ~** (also Mil) estar alerta or sobre aviso

algebra ['ældʒibrə] n álgebra

Algeria [æl'dʒiəriə] n Argelia

alias ['eiliəs] adv alias, conocido por ▷ n (of criminal) apodo; (of writer) seudónimo

alibi ['ælibai] n coartada

alien ['eiliən] n (foreigner) extranjero/a; (extraterrestrial) extraterrestre mf ▷ adj: **to ~** ajeno a; **alienate** vt enajenar, alejar

alight [ə'lait] adj ardiendo; (eyes) brillante ▷ vi (person) apearse, bajar; (bird) posarse

align [ə'lain] vt alinear

alike [ə'laik] adj semejantes, iguales ▷ adv igualmente, del mismo modo; **to look ~** parecerse

alive [ə'laiv] adj vivo; (lively) alegre

○ **KEYWORD**

all [ɔːl] adj (sg) todo/a; (pl) todos/as; **all day** todo el día; **all night** toda la noche; **all men** todos los hombres;

all five came vinieron los cinco; **all the books** todos los libros; **all his life** toda su vida

▷ *pron* **1** todo; **I ate it all, I ate all of it** me lo comí todo; **all of us went** fuimos todos; **all the boys went** fueron todos los chicos; **is that all?** ¿eso es todo?, ¿algo más?; *(in shop)* ¿algo más?, ¿alguna cosa más?

2 *(in phrases)*: **above all** sobre todo; por encima de todo; **after all** después de todo; **at all: not at all** *(in answer to question)* en absoluto; *(in answer to thanks)* de nada; **I'm not at all tired** no estoy nada cansado/a; **anything at all will do** cualquier cosa viene bien; **all in all** a fin de cuentas

▷ *adv*: **all alone** completamente solo/a; **it's not as hard as all that** no es tan difícil como lo pintas; **all the more/the better** tanto más/mejor; **all but** casi; **the score is 2 all** están empatados a 2

Allah ['ælə] *n* Alá *m*
allegation [ælɪ'geɪʃən] *n* alegato
alleged [ə'ledʒd] *adj* supuesto, presunto; **allegedly** *adv* supuestamente, según se afirma
allegiance [ə'liːdʒəns] *n* lealtad *f*
allergic [ə'lɜːdʒɪk] *adj*: **~ to** alérgico a
allergy ['ælədʒɪ] *n* alergia
alleviate [ə'liːvɪeɪt] *vt* aliviar
alley ['ælɪ] *n* callejuela
alliance [ə'laɪəns] *n* alianza
allied ['ælaɪd] *adj* aliado
alligator ['ælɪgeɪtə*] *n* (Zool) caimán *m*
all-in (BRIT) ['ɔːlɪn] *adj, adv* (charge) todo incluido
allocate ['æləkeɪt] *vt* (money etc) asignar
allot [ə'lɒt] *vt* asignar
all-out ['ɔːlaut] *adj* (effort etc) supremo
allow [ə'lau] *vt* permitir, dejar; (a claim) admitir; (sum, time etc)

dar, conceder; (concede): **to ~ that** reconocer que; **to ~ sb to do** permitir a algn hacer; **he's ~ed to ...** se le permite ...; **allow for** *vt fus* tener en cuenta;
allowance *n* subvención *f*; (welfare payment) subsidio, pensión *f*; (pocket money) dinero de bolsillo; (tax allowance) desgravación *f*; **to make allowances for** (person) disculpar a; (thing) tener en cuenta
all right *adv* bien; (as answer) ¡conforme!, ¡está bien!
ally ['ælaɪ] *n* aliado/a ▷ *vt*: **to ~ o.s. with** aliarse con
almighty [ɔːl'maɪtɪ] *adj* todopoderoso; (row etc) imponente
almond ['ɑːmənd] *n* almendra
almost ['ɔːlməust] *adv* casi
alone [ə'ləun] *adj, adv* solo; **to leave sb ~** dejar a algn en paz; **to leave sth ~** no tocar algo, dejar algo sin tocar; **let ~ ...** y mucho menos ...
along [ə'lɒŋ] *prep* a lo largo de, por ▷ *adv*: **is he coming ~ with us?** ¿viene con nosotros?; **he was limping ~** iba cojeando; **~ with** junto con; **all ~** (all the time) desde el principio; **alongside** *prep* al lado de ▷ *adv*: al lado
aloof [ə'luːf] *adj* reservado ▷ *adv*: **to stand ~** mantenerse apartado
aloud [ə'laud] *adv* en voz alta
alphabet ['ælfəbet] *n* alfabeto
Alps [ælps] *npl*: **the ~** los Alpes
already [ɔːl'redɪ] *adv* ya
alright [ɔːl'raɪt] (BRIT) *adv* = **all right**
also ['ɔːlsəu] *adv* también, además
altar ['ɔltə*] *n* altar *m*
alter ['ɔltə*] *vt* cambiar, modificar ▷ *vi* cambiar; **alteration** [ɔltə'reɪʃən] *n* cambio; (to clothes) arreglo; (to building) arreglos *mpl*
alternate [ɔl'tɜːnɪt, *vb* 'ɔltəneɪt] *adj* (actions etc) alternativo; (events) alterno; (us)= **alternative** (con); **to ~ (with)** alternar (con); **on ~ days** un día sí y otro no
alternative [ɔl'tɜːnətɪv] *adj* alternativo ▷ *n* alternativa; **~**

medicine medicina alternativa; **alternatively** adv: **alternatively one could ...** por otra parte se podría ...

although [ɔːl'ðəu] conj aunque

altitude ['æltɪtjuːd] n altura

altogether [ɔːltə'geðə*] adv completamente, del todo; (on the whole) en total, en conjunto

aluminium [ælju'mɪnɪəm] (BRIT), **aluminum** [ə'luːmɪnəm] (US) n aluminio

always ['ɔːlweɪz] adv siempre

Alzheimer's (disease) ['æltshaɪməz-] n enfermedad f de Alzheimer

am [æm] vb see **be**

amalgamate [ə'mælgəmeɪt] vi amalgamarse ▷ vt amalgamar, unir

amass [ə'mæs] vt amontonar, acumular

amateur ['æmətə*] n aficionado/a, amateur mf

amaze [ə'meɪz] vt asombrar, pasmar; **to be ~d (at)** quedar pasmado (de); **amazed** adj asombrado; **amazement** n asombro, sorpresa; **amazing** adj extraordinario; (fantastic) increíble

Amazon ['æməzən] n (Geo) Amazonas m

ambassador [æm'bæsədə*] n embajador(a) m/f

amber ['æmbə*] n ámbar m; **at ~** (BRIT Aut) en el amarillo

ambiguous [æm'bɪgjuəs] adj ambiguo

ambition [æm'bɪʃən] n ambición f; **ambitious** [-ʃəs] adj ambicioso

ambulance ['æmbjuləns] n ambulancia

ambush ['æmbuʃ] n emboscada ▷ vt tender una emboscada a

amen [ɑː'mɛn] excl amén

amend [ə'mɛnd] vt enmendar; **to make ~s** dar cumplida satisfacción; **amendment** n enmienda

amenities [ə'miːnɪtɪz] npl comodidades fpl

America [ə'mɛrɪkə] n (USA)

Estados mpl Unidos; **American** adj, n norteamericano/a; estadounidense mf; **American football** n (BRIT) fútbol m americano

amicable ['æmɪkəbl] adj amistoso, amigable

amid(st) [ə'mɪd(st)] prep entre, en medio de

ammunition [æmju'nɪʃən] n municiones fpl

amnesty ['æmnɪstɪ] n amnistía

among(st) [ə'mʌŋ(st)] prep entre, en medio de

amount [ə'maunt] n (gen) cantidad f; (of bill etc) suma, importe m ▷ vi: **to ~ to** sumar; (be same as) equivaler a, significar

amp(ère) ['æmp(ɛə*)] n amperio

ample ['æmpl] adj (large) grande; (abundant) abundante; (enough) bastante, suficiente

amplifier ['æmplɪfaɪə*] n amplificador m

amputate ['æmpjuteɪt] vt amputar

Amtrak ['æmtræk] (US) n empresa nacional de ferrocarriles de los EEUU

amuse [ə'mjuːz] vt divertir; (distract) distraer, entretener; **amusement** n diversión f; (pastime) pasatiempo; (laughter) risa; **amusement arcade** n salón m de juegos; **amusement park** n parque m de atracciones

amusing [ə'mjuːzɪŋ] adj divertido

an [æn] indef art see **a**

anaemia [ə'niːmɪə] (US **anemia**) n anemia

anaemic [ə'niːmɪk] (US **anemic**) adj anémico; (fig) insípido

anaesthetic [ænɪs'θɛtɪk] (US **anesthetic**) n anestesia

analog(ue) ['ænələg] adj (computer, watch) analógico

analogy [ə'nælədʒɪ] n analogía

analyse ['ænəlaɪz] (US **analyze**) vt analizar; **analysis** [ə'næləsɪs] (pl **analyses**) n análisis m inv; **analyst** [-lɪst] n (political analyst, psychoanalyst) analista mf

analyze ['ænəlaɪz] (us) vt = **analyse**

anarchy ['ænəkɪ] n anarquía, desorden m

anatomy [ə'nætəmɪ] n anatomía

ancestor ['ænsɪstə*] n antepasado

anchor ['æŋkə*] n ancla, áncora ▷ vi (also: **to drop ~**) anclar ▷ vt anclar; **to weigh ~** levar anclas

anchovy ['æntʃəvɪ] n anchoa

ancient ['eɪnʃənt] adj antiguo

and [ænd] conj y; (before i-, hi- + consonant) e; **men ~ women** hombres y mujeres; **father ~ son** padre e hijo; **trees ~ grass** árboles y hierba; **~ so on** etcétera, y así sucesivamente; **try ~ come** procura venir; **he talked ~ talked** habló sin parar; **better ~ better** cada vez mejor

Andes ['ændiːz] npl: **the ~** los Andes

Andorra [æn'dɔːrə] n Andorra

anemia etc [ə'niːmɪə] (us) = **anaemia** etc

anesthetic [ænɪs'θetɪk] (us) = **anaesthetic**

angel ['eɪndʒəl] n ángel m

anger ['æŋgə*] n cólera

angina [æn'dʒaɪnə] n angina (del pecho)

angle ['æŋgl] n ángulo; **from their ~** desde su punto de vista

angler ['æŋglə*] n pescador(a) m/f (de caña)

Anglican ['æŋglɪkən] adj, n anglicano/a m/f

angling ['æŋglɪŋ] n pesca con caña

angrily ['æŋgrɪlɪ] adv coléricamente, airadamente

angry ['æŋgrɪ] adj enfadado, airado; (wound) inflamado; **to be ~ with sb/at sth** estar enfadado con algn/por algo; **to get ~** enfadarse, enojarse

anguish ['æŋgwɪʃ] n (physical) tormentos mpl; (mental) angustia

animal ['ænɪməl] n animal m; (pej: person) bestia ▷ adj animal

animated ['ænɪmeɪtɪd] adj animado

animation [ænɪ'meɪʃən] n animación f

aniseed ['ænɪsiːd] n anís m

ankle ['æŋkl] n tobillo

annex [n 'æneks, vb ə'neks] n (BRIT: also: **-e:** building) edificio anexo ▷ vt (territory) anexionar

anniversary [ænɪ'vɜːsərɪ] n aniversario

announce [ə'naʊns] vt anunciar; **announcement** n anuncio; (official) declaración f; **announcer** n (Radio) locutor(a) m/f; (TV) presentador(a) m/f

annoy [ə'nɔɪ] vt molestar, fastidiar; **don't get ~ed!** ¡no se enfade!; **annoying** adj molesto, fastidioso; (person) pesado

annual ['ænjuəl] adj anual ▷ n (Bot) anual m; (book) anuario; **annually** adv anualmente, cada año

annum ['ænəm] n see **per**

anonymous [ə'nɒnɪməs] adj anónimo

anorak ['ænəræk] n anorak m

anorexia [ænə'reksɪə] n (Med: also: **~ nervosa**) anorexia

anorexic [ænə'reksɪk] adj, n anoréxico/a m/f

another [ə'nʌðə*] adj (one more, a different one) otro ▷ pron otro; see **one**

answer ['ɑːnsə*] n contestación f, respuesta; (to problem) solución f ▷ vi contestar, responder ▷ vt (reply to) contestar a, responder a; (problem) resolver; (prayer) escuchar; **in ~ to your letter** contestando o en contestación a su carta; **to ~ the phone** contestar o coger el teléfono; **to ~ the bell** o **the door** acudir a la puerta; **answer back** vi replicar, ser respondón/ona; **answerphone** n (esp BRIT) contestador m (automático)

ant [ænt] n hormiga

Antarctic [ænt'ɑːktɪk] n: **the ~** el Antártico

antelope ['æntɪləup] n antílope m

antenatal ['æntɪ'neɪtl] adj antenatal, prenatal

antenna [æn'tenə, pl -niː] (pl **antennae**) n antena

anthem ['ænθəm] n: **national ~** himno nacional

anthology [æn'θɒlədʒɪ] n antología

anthrax ['ænθræks] n ántrax m

anthropology [ænθrə'pɒlədʒɪ] n antropología

anti [æntɪ] prefix anti; **antibiotic** [-baɪ'ɒtɪk] n antibiótico; **antibody** ['æntɪbɒdɪ] n anticuerpo

anticipate [æn'tɪsɪpeɪt] vt prever; (expect) esperar, contar con; (look forward to) esperar con ilusión; (do first) anticiparse a, adelantarse a; **anticipation** [-'peɪʃən] n (expectation) previsión f; (eagerness) ilusión f, expectación f

anticlimax [æntɪ'klaɪmæks] n decepción f

anticlockwise [æntɪ'klɒkwaɪz] (BRIT) adv en dirección contraria a la de las agujas del reloj

antics ['æntɪks] npl gracias fpl

anti: antidote ['æntɪdəʊt] n antídoto; **antifreeze** ['æntɪfriːz] n anticongelante m; **antihistamine** [-'hɪstəmiːn] n antihistamínico; **antiperspirant** ['æntɪpə:spɪrənt] n antitranspirante m

antique [æn'tiːk] n antigüedad f
▷ adj antiguo; **antique shop** n tienda de antigüedades

antiseptic [æntɪ'septɪk] adj, n antiséptico

antisocial [æntɪ'səʊʃəl] adj antisocial

antivirus [æntɪ'vaɪərəs] adj (program, software) antivirus inv

antlers ['æntləz] npl cuernas fpl, cornamenta sg

anxiety [æŋ'zaɪətɪ] n inquietud f; (Med) ansiedad f; **~ to do** deseo de hacer

anxious ['æŋkʃəs] adj inquieto, preocupado; (worrying) preocupante; (keen): **to be ~ to do** tener muchas

ganas de hacer

○ KEYWORD

any ['enɪ] adj 1 (in questions etc) algún/alguna; **have you any butter/children?** ¿tienes mantequilla/hijos?; **if there are any tickets left** si quedan billetes, si queda algún billete

2 (with negative): **I haven't any money/books** no tengo dinero/libros

3 (no matter which) cualquier; **any excuse will do** valdrá or servirá cualquier excusa; **choose any book you like** escoge el libro que quieras

4 (in phrases): **in any case** de todas formas, en cualquier caso; **any day now** cualquier día (de estos); **at any moment** en cualquier momento, de un momento a otro; **at any rate** en todo caso; **any time:** come (at) any time ven cuando quieras; **he might come (at) any time** podría llegar de un momento a otro

▷ pron 1 (in questions etc): **have you got any?** ¿tienes alguno(s)/a(s)?; **can any of you sing?** ¿sabe cantar alguno de vosotros/ustedes?

2 (with negative): **I haven't any (of them)** no tengo ninguno

3 (no matter which one(s)): **take any of those books (you like)** toma el libro que quieras de ésos

▷ adv 1 (in questions etc): **do you want any more soup/sandwiches?** ¿quieres más sopa/bocadillos?; **are you feeling any better?** ¿te sientes algo mejor?

2 (with negative): **I can't hear him any more** ya no le oigo; **don't wait any longer** no esperes más

any: anybody pron cualquiera; (in interrogative sentences) alguien; (in negative sentences): **I don't see anybody** no veo a nadie; **if anybody should phone ...** si llama alguien

...;**anyhow** adv (at any rate) de todos modos, de todas formas; (haphazard): **do it anyhow you like** hazlo como quieras; **she leaves things just anyhow** deja las cosas como quiera or de cualquier modo; **I shall go anyhow** de todos modos iré; **anyone** pron = **anybody**; **anything** pron (in questions etc) algo, alguna cosa; (with negative) nada; **can you see anything?** ¿ves algo?; **if anything happens to me** ... si algo me ocurre ...; (no matter what): **you can say anything you like** puedes decir lo que quieras; **anything will do** vale todo or cualquier cosa; **he'll want anything** come de todo or lo que sea; **anytime** adv (at any moment) en cualquier momento, de un momento a otro; (whenever) no importa cuándo, cuando quiera; **anyway** adv (at any rate) de todos modos, de todas formas; **I shall go anyway** iré de todos modos; (besides): **anyway, I couldn't come even if I wanted to** además, no podría venir aunque quisiera; **why are you phoning, anyway?** ¿entonces, por qué llamas? ¿por qué llamas, pues?; **anywhere** adv (in questions etc): **can you see him anywhere?** ¿le ves por algún lado?; **are you going anywhere?** ¿vas a algún sitio?; (with negative): **I can't see him anywhere** no le veo por ninguna parte; **anywhere in the world** (no matter where) en cualquier parte (del mundo); **put the books down anywhere** deja los libros donde quieras

apart [ə'pɑːt] adv (aside) aparte; (situation): **~ (from)** separado (de); (movement): **to pull ~** separar; **10 miles ~** separados por 10 millas; **to take ~** desmontar; **~ from** prep aparte de

apartment [ə'pɑːtmənt] n (US) piso (SP), departamento (LAM), apartamento; (room) cuarto; **apartment building** (US) n edificio de apartamentos

apathy ['æpəθɪ] n apatía,

indiferencia

ape [eɪp] n mono ▷ vt imitar, remedar

aperitif [ə'perɪtɪf] n aperitivo

aperture ['æpətʃʊə*] n rendija, resquicio; (Phot) abertura

APEX ['eɪpeks] n abbr (= Advanced Purchase Excursion Fare) tarifa f APEX

apologize [ə'pɒlədʒaɪz] vi: **to ~ (for sth to sb)** disculparse (con algn de algo)

apology [ə'pɒlədʒɪ] n disculpa, excusa

> Be careful not to translate **apology** by the Spanish word apología.

apostrophe [ə'pɒstrəfɪ] n apóstrofo

appal [ə'pɔːl] (US **appall**) vt horrorizar, espantar; **appalling** adj espantoso; (awful) pésimo

apparatus [æpə'reɪtəs] n (equipment) equipo; (organization) aparato; (in gymnasium) aparatos mpl

apparent [ə'pærənt] adj aparente; (obvious) evidente; **apparently** adv por lo visto, al parecer

appeal [ə'piːl] vi (Law) apelar ▷ n (Law) apelación f; (request) llamamiento; (plea) petición f; (charm) atractivo; **to ~ for** reclamar; **to ~ to** (be attractive to) atraer; **it doesn't ~ to me** no me atrae, no me llama la atención; **appealing** adj (attractive) atractivo

appear [ə'pɪə*] vi aparecer, presentarse; (Law) comparecer; (publication) salir (a luz), publicarse; (seem) parecer; **to ~ on TV/in "Hamlet"** salir por la tele/hacer un papel en "Hamlet"; **it would ~ that** parecería que; **appearance** n aparición f; (look) apariencia, aspecto

appendices [ə'pendɪsiːz] npl of **appendix**

appendicitis [əpendɪ'saɪtɪs] n apendicitis f

appendix [ə'pendɪks] (pl **appendices**) n apéndice m

appetite ['æpɪtaɪt] n apetito; (fig) deseo, anhelo

appetizer [ˈæpɪtaɪzə*] n (drink)
aperitivo; (food) tapas fpl (SP)

applaud [əˈplɔːd] vt, vi aplaudir

applause [əˈplɔːz] n aplausos mpl

apple [ˈæpl] n manzana; **apple pie**
n pastel m de manzana, pay m de
manzana (LAM)

appliance [əˈplaɪəns] n aparato

applicable [əˈplɪkəbl] adj
(relevant): **to be ~ (to)** referirse (a)

applicant [ˈæplɪkənt] n candidato/
a; solicitante mf

application [æplɪˈkeɪʃən] n
aplicación f; (for a job etc) solicitud
f, petición f; **application form** n
solicitud f

apply [əˈplaɪ] vt (paint etc) poner;
(law etc: put into practice) poner en
vigor ▷ vi: **to ~ to** (be applicable)
ser aplicable a; **to ~ for**
(permit, grant, job) solicitar; **to ~ o.s. to**
aplicarse a, dedicarse a

appoint [əˈpɔɪnt] vt (to post)
nombrar a

Be careful not to translate **appoint**
by the Spanish word apuntar.

appointment n (with client) cita;
(act) nombramiento; (post) puesto;
(at hairdresser etc): **to have an
appointment** tener hora; **to make
an appointment (with sb)** citarse
(con algn)

appraisal [əˈpreɪzl] n valoración f

appreciate [əˈpriːʃɪeɪt] vt apreciar,
tener en mucho; (be grateful for)
agradecer; (be aware) comprender
▷ vi (Comm) aumentar(se) en valor;
appreciation [-ˈeɪʃən] n apreciación
f, (gratitude) reconocimiento,
agradecimiento; (Comm) aumento
en valor

apprehension [æprɪˈhenʃən] n
(fear) aprensión f

apprehensive [æprɪˈhensɪv] adj
aprensivo

apprentice [əˈprentɪs] n aprendiz(a)
m/f

approach [əˈprəʊtʃ] vi acercarse

▷ vt acercarse a; (ask, apply to) dirigirse
a; (situation, problem) abordar ▷ n
acercamiento; (access) acceso; (to
problem, situation): **~ (to)** actitud f
(ante)

appropriate [adj əˈprəʊprɪɪt, vb
əˈprəʊprɪeɪt] adj apropiado,
conveniente ▷ vt (take) apropiarse de

approval [əˈpruːvəl] n aprobación
f, visto bueno; (permission)
consentimiento; **on ~** (Comm) a prueba

approve [əˈpruːv] vt aprobar;
approve of vt fus (thing) aprobar; (person): **they don't approve of her**
(ella) no les parece bien

approximate [əˈprɒksɪmɪt] adj
aproximado; **approximately** adv
aproximadamente, más o menos

Apr. abbr (= April) abr

apricot [ˈeɪprɪkɒt] n albaricoque m,
chabacano (MEX), damasco (RPL)

April [ˈeɪprəl] n abril m; **April Fools'
Day** n el primero de abril, ≈ día m de
los Inocentes (28 December)

apron [ˈeɪprən] n delantal m

apt [æpt] adj acertado, apropiado;
(likely): **~ to do** propenso a hacer

aquarium [əˈkwɛərɪəm] n acuario

Aquarius [əˈkwɛərɪəs] n Acuario

Arab [ˈærəb] adj, n árabe mf

Arabia [əˈreɪbɪə] n Arabia; **Arabian**
adj árabe; **Arabic** [ˈærəbɪk] adj árabe;
(numerals) arábigo ▷ n árabe m

arbitrary [ˈɑːbɪtrərɪ] adj arbitrario

arbitration [ɑːbɪˈtreɪʃən] n
arbitraje m

arc [ɑːk] n arco

arcade [ɑːˈkeɪd] n (round a square)
soportales mpl; (shopping mall) galería
comercial

arch [ɑːtʃ] n arco; (of foot) arco del pie
▷ vt arquear

archaeology [ɑːkɪˈɒlədʒɪ] (US
archeology) n arqueología

archbishop [ɑːtʃˈbɪʃəp] n arzobispo

archeology [ɑːkɪˈɒlədʒɪ] (US) =
archaeology

architect [ˈɑːkɪtekt] n arquitecto/a;

architectural [ɑːkɪˈtɛktʃərəl] *adj*
arquitectónico; **architecture** *n*
arquitectura

archive [ˈɑːkaɪv] *n (often pl: also
Comput)* archivo

Arctic [ˈɑːktɪk] *adj* ártico ▷ *n:* **the
~** el Ártico

are [ɑː*] *vb see* **be**

area [ˈɛərɪə] *n* área, región *f; (part of
place)* zona; *(Math etc)* área; *(surface
f; in room: e.g. dining area)* parte *f; (of
knowledge, experience)* campo; **area
code** *(us) (Tel)* prefijo

arena [əˈriːnə] *n* estadio; *(of circus)*
pista

aren't [ɑːnt] = **are not**

Argentina [ɑːdʒənˈtiːnə] *n*
Argentina; **Argentinian** [-ˈtɪnɪən] *adj,
n* argentino/a *m/f*

arguably [ˈɑːɡjuəblɪ] *adv*
posiblemente

argue [ˈɑːɡjuː] *vi (quarrel)* discutir,
pelearse; *(reason)* razonar, argumentar;
to ~ that sostener que

argument [ˈɑːɡjumənt] *n* discusión
f, pelea; *(reasons)* argumento

Aries [ˈɛərɪz] *n* Aries *m*

arise [əˈraɪz] *(pt* **arose***, pp* **arisen***) vi*
surgir, presentarse

arithmetic [əˈrɪθmətɪk] *n*
aritmética

arm [ɑːm] *n* brazo ▷ *vt* armar;
arms *npl* armas *fpl;* **~ in ~** cogidos del
brazo; **armchair** [ˈɑːmtʃɛə*] *n* sillón
m, butaca

armed [ɑːmd] *adj* armado; **armed
robbery** *n* robo a mano armada

armour [ˈɑːmə*] *(us* **armor***) n*
armadura; *(Mil: tanks)* blindaje *m*

armpit [ˈɑːmpɪt] *n* sobaco, axila

armrest [ˈɑːmrɛst] *n* apoyabrazos
m inv

army [ˈɑːmɪ] *n* ejército; *(fig)*
multitud *f*

A road *n (BRIT)* = carretera *f* nacional

aroma [əˈrəumə] *n* aroma *m,*
fragancia; **aromatherapy** *n*
aromaterapia

arose [əˈrəuz] *pt of* **arise**

around [əˈraund] *adv* alrededor;
(in the area) **there is no one else ~**
no hay nadie más por aquí ▷ *prep*
alrededor de

arouse [əˈrauz] *vt* despertar; *(anger)*
provocar

arrange [əˈreɪndʒ] *vt* arreglar,
ordenar; *(organize)* organizar; **to
~ to do sth** quedar en hacer algo;
arrangement *n* arreglo; *(agreement)*
acuerdo; **arrangements** *npl
(preparations)* preparativos *mpl*

array [əˈreɪ] *n:* **~ of** *(things)* serie *f* de;
(people) conjunto de

arrears [əˈrɪəz] *npl* atrasos *mpl;* **to be
in ~ with one's rent** estar retrasado en
el pago del alquiler

arrest [əˈrɛst] *vt* detener; *(sb's
attention)* llamar ▷ *n* detención *f;*
under ~ detenido

arrival [əˈraɪvl] *n* llegada; **new ~**
recién llegado/a; *(baby)* recién nacido

arrive [əˈraɪv] *vi* llegar; *(baby)* nacer;
arrive at *vt fus (decision, solution)*
llegar a

arrogance [ˈærəɡəns] *n* arrogancia,
prepotencia (*LAM*)

arrogant [ˈærəɡənt] *adj* arrogante

arrow [ˈærəu] *n* flecha

arse [ɑːs] *(BRIT: infl!)* *n* culo, trasero

arson [ˈɑːsn] *n* incendio premeditado

art [ɑːt] *n* arte *m; (skill)* destreza; **art
college** *n* escuela *f* de Bellas Artes

artery [ˈɑːtərɪ] *n* arteria

art gallery *n* pinacoteca; *(saleroom)*
galería de arte

arthritis [ɑːˈθraɪtɪs] *n* artritis *f*

artichoke [ˈɑːtɪtʃəuk] *n* alcachofa;
Jerusalem ~ aguaturma

article [ˈɑːtɪkl] *n* artículo

articulate *[adj* ɑːˈtɪkjulɪt, *vb*
ɑːˈtɪkjuleɪt] *adj* claro, bien expresado
▷ *vt* expresar

artificial [ɑːtɪˈfɪʃəl] *adj* artificial;
(affected) afectado

artist [ˈɑːtɪst] *n* artista *mf; (Mus)*
intérprete *mf;* **artistic** [ɑːˈtɪstɪk] *adj*

artístico
art school n escuela de bellas artes

⭕ **KEYWORD**

as [æz] conj **1** (referring to time)
cuando, mientras; a medida que; **as
the years went by** con el paso de los
años; **he came in as I was leaving**
entró cuando me marchaba; **as
from tomorrow** desde o a partir de
mañana
2 (in comparisons): **as big as** tan grande
como; **twice as big as** el doble de
grande que; **as much money/many
books as** tanto dinero/tantos libros
como; **as soon as** en cuanto
3 (since, because) como, ya que; **he left
early as he had to be home by 10** se
fue temprano ya que tenía que estar en
casa a las 10
4 (referring to manner, way): **do as you
wish** haz lo que quieras; **as she said**
como dijo; **he gave it to me as a
present** me lo dio de regalo
5 (in the capacity of): **he works as
a barman** trabaja de barman; **as
chairman of the company, he ...**
como presidente de la compañía ...
6 (concerning): **as for or to that** por o en
lo que respecta a eso
7: **as if or though** como si; **he looked
as if he was ill** parecía como si
estuviera enfermo, tenía aspecto de
enfermo; see also **long; such; well**

a.s.a.p. abbr (= as soon as possible)
cuanto antes
asbestos [æz'bɛstəs] n asbesto,
amianto
ascent [ə'sɛnt] n subida; (slope)
cuesta, pendiente f
ash [æʃ] n ceniza; (tree) fresno
ashamed [ə'ʃeɪmd] adj avergonzado,
apenado; (LAM): **to be ~ of** avergonzarse
de
ashore [ə'ʃɔː*] adv en tierra; (swim
etc) a tierra

ashtray ['æʃtreɪ] n cenicero
Ash Wednesday n miércoles m
de Ceniza
Asia ['eɪʒə] n Asia; **Asian** adj, n
asiático/a m/f
aside [ə'saɪd] adv a un lado ▷ n
aparte m
ask [ɑːsk] vt (question) preguntar;
(invite) invitar; **to ~ sb sth/to do sth**
preguntar algo a algn/pedir a algn que
haga algo; **to ~ sb about sth** preguntar
algo a algn; **to ~ (sb) a question** hacer
una pregunta (a algn); **to ~ sb out to
dinner** invitar a cenar a algn; **ask for** vt
fus pedir; (trouble) buscar
asleep [ə'sliːp] adj dormido; **to fall ~**
dormirse, quedarse dormido
asparagus [əs'pærəgəs] n (plant)
espárrago; (food) espárragos mpl
aspect ['æspɛkt] n aspecto,
apariencia; (direction in which a building
etc faces) orientación f
aspirations [æspə'reɪʃənz] npl
aspiraciones fpl; (ambition) ambición f
aspire [əs'paɪə*] vi: **to ~ to** aspirar a,
ambicionar
aspirin ['æsprɪn] n aspirina
ass [æs] n asno, burro; (inf: idiot)
imbécil mf; (us: inf!) culo, trasero
assassin [ə'sæsɪn] n asesino/a;
assassinate vt asesinar
assault [ə'sɔːlt] n asalto; (Law)
agresión f ▷vt asaltar, atacar;
(sexually) violar
assemble [ə'sɛmbl] vt reunir, juntar;
(Tech) montar ▷vi reunirse, juntarse
assembly [ə'sɛmblɪ] n reunión f,
asamblea; (parliament) parlamento;
(construction) montaje m
assert [ə'sɜːt] vt afirmar; (authority)
hacer valer; **assertion** [-ʃən] n
afirmación f
assess [ə'sɛs] vt valorar, calcular;
(tax, damages) fijar; (for tax) gravar;
assessment n valoración f; (for tax)
gravamen m
asset ['æsɛt] n ventaja; **assets**
npl (Comm) activo; (property, funds)

fondos *mpl*

assign [əˈsaɪn] *vt:* **to ~ (to)** (*date*) fijar (para); (*task*) asignar (a); (*resources*) destinar (a); **assignment** *n* tarea

assist [əˈsɪst] *vt* ayudar; **assistance** *n* ayuda, auxilio; **assistant** *n* ayudante *mf;* (*BRIT: also:* **shop assistant**) dependiente/a *m/f*

associate [*adj, n* əˈsəʊʃɪt, *vb* əˈsəʊʃɪeɪt] *adj* asociado ▷ *n* (*at work*) colega *mf* ▷ *vt* asociar; (*ideas*) relacionar ▷ *vi:* **to ~ with sb** tratar con algn

association [əsəʊsɪˈeɪʃən] *n* asociación *f*

assorted [əˈsɔːtɪd] *adj* surtido, variado

assortment [əˈsɔːtmənt] *n* (*of shapes, colours*) surtido; (*of books*) colección *f;* (*of people*) mezcla

assume [əˈsjuːm] *vt* suponer; (*responsibilities*) asumir; (*attitude*) adoptar, tomar

assumption [əˈsʌmpʃən] *n* suposición *f,* presunción *f;* (*of power etc*) toma

assurance [əˈʃʊərəns] *n* garantía, promesa; (*confidence*) confianza, aplomo; (*insurance*) seguro

assure [əˈʃʊə*] *vt* asegurar

asterisk [ˈæstərɪsk] *n* asterisco

asthma [ˈæsmə] *n* asma

astonish [əˈstɒnɪʃ] *vt* asombrar, pasmar; **astonished** *adj* estupefacto, pasmado; **to be astonished (at)** asombrarse (de); **astonishing** *adj* asombroso, pasmoso; **I find it astonishing that ...** me asombra or pasma que ...; **astonishment** *n* asombro, sorpresa

astound [əˈstaʊnd] *vt* asombrar, pasmar

astray [əˈstreɪ] *adv:* **to go ~** extraviarse; **to lead ~** (*morally*) llevar por mal camino

astrology [æsˈtrɒlədʒɪ] *n* astrología

astronaut [ˈæstrənɔːt] *n* astronauta *mf*

astronomer [əsˈtrɒnəmə*] *n* astrónomo/a

astronomical [æstrəˈnɒmɪkəl] *adj* astronómico

astronomy [əsˈtrɒnəmɪ] *n* astronomía

astute [əsˈtjuːt] *adj* astuto

asylum [əˈsaɪləm] *n* (*refuge*) asilo; (*mental hospital*) manicomio

○ **KEYWORD**

at [æt] *prep* **1** (*referring to position*) en; (*direction*) a; **at the top** en lo alto; **at home/school** en casa/la escuela; **to look at sth/sb** mirar algo/a algn

2 (*referring to time*): **at 4 o'clock** a las 4; **at night** por la noche; **at Christmas** en Navidad; **at times** a veces

3 (*referring to rates, speed etc*): **at £1 a kilo** a una libra el kilo; **two at a time** de dos en dos; **at 50 km/h** a 50 km/h

4 (*referring to manner*): **at a stroke** de un golpe; **at peace** en paz

5 (*referring to activity*): **to be at work** estar trabajando; (*in the office etc*) estar en el trabajo; **to play at cowboys** jugar a los vaqueros; **to be good at sth** ser bueno en algo

6 (*referring to cause*): **shocked/ surprised/annoyed at sth** asombrado/sorprendido/fastidiado por algo; **I went at his suggestion** fui a instancias suyas

7 (*symbol*) arroba

ate [eɪt] *pt of* **eat**

atheist [ˈeɪθiːɪst] *n* ateo/a

Athens [ˈæθɪnz] *n* Atenas

athlete [ˈæθliːt] *n* atleta *mf*

athletic [æθˈlɛtɪk] *adj* atlético; **athletics** *n* atletismo

Atlantic [ətˈlæntɪk] *adj* atlántico ▷ *n:* **the ~ (Ocean)** el (Océano) Atlántico

atlas [ˈætləs] *n* atlas *m inv*

A.T.M. *n abbr* (= *automated teller telling*

machine) cajero automático

atmosphere ['ætməsfɪə*] *n* atmósfera; *(of place)* ambiente *m*

atom ['ætəm] *n* átomo; **atomic** [ə'tɔmɪk] *adj* atómico; **atom(ic) bomb** *n* bomba atómica

A to Z® *n* (*map*) callejero

atrocity [ə'trɔsɪtɪ] *n* atrocidad *f*

attach [ə'tætʃ] *vt* (*fasten*) atar; (*join*) unir, sujetar; (*document, email, letter*) adjuntar; (*importance etc*) dar, conceder; **to be ~ed to sb/sth** (*to like*) tener cariño a algn/algo; **attachment** *n* (*tool*) accesorio; (*Comput*) archivo, documento adjunto; (*love*): **attachment (to)** apego (a)

attack [ə'tæk] *vt* (*Mil*) atacar; (*criminal*) agredir, asaltar; (*criticize*) criticar; (*task*) emprender ▷ *n* ataque *m*, asalto; (*on sb's life*) atentado; (*fig: criticism*) crítica; (*of illness*) ataque *m*; **heart ~** infarto (de miocardio); **attacker** *n* agresor(a) *m/f*, asaltante *mf*

attain [ə'teɪn] *vt* (*also*: **~ to**) alcanzar; (*achieve*) lograr, conseguir

attempt [ə'tempt] *n* tentativa, intento; (*attack*) atentado ▷ *vt* intentar

attend [ə'tend] *vt* asistir a; (*patient*) atender; **attend to** *vt fus* ocuparse de; (*customer, patient*) atender a; **attendance** *n* asistencia, presencia; (*people present*) concurrencia; **attendant** *n* ayudante *mf*; (*in garage etc*) encargado/a ▷ *adj* (*dangers*) concomitante

attention [ə'tenʃən] *n* atención *f*; (*care*) atenciones *fpl* ▷ *excl* (*Mil*) ¡firme(s)!; **for the ~ of ...** (*Admin*) atención ...

attic ['ætɪk] *n* desván *m*

attitude ['ætɪtjuːd] *n* actitud *f*; (*disposition*) disposición *f*

attorney [ə'tɜːnɪ] *n* (*lawyer*) abogado/a; **Attorney General** *n* (*BRIT*) ≈ Presidente *m* del Consejo del Poder Judicial (*SP*); (*US*) ≈ ministro

de Justicia

attract [ə'trækt] *vt* atraer; (*sb's attention*) llamar; **attraction** [ə'trækʃən] *n* encanto; (*gen pl: amusements*) diversiones *fpl*; (*Physics*) atracción *f*; (*fig: towards sb, sth*) atractivo; **attractive** *adj* guapo; (*interesting*) atrayente

attribute [*n* 'ætrɪbjuːt, *vb* ə'trɪbjuːt] *n* atributo ▷ *vt*: **to ~ sth to** atribuir algo a

aubergine ['əʊbəʒiːn] (*BRIT*) *n* berenjena; (*colour*) morado

auburn ['ɔːbən] *adj* color castaño rojizo

auction ['ɔːkʃən] *n* (*also*: **sale by ~**) subasta ▷ *vt* subastar

audible ['ɔːdɪbl] *adj* audible, que se puede oír

audience ['ɔːdɪəns] *n* público; (*Radio*) radioescuchas *mpl*; (*TV*) telespectadores *mpl*; (*interview*) audiencia

audit ['ɔːdɪt] *vt* revisar, intervenir

audition [ɔː'dɪʃən] *n* audición *f*

auditor ['ɔːdɪtə*] *n* interventor/a *m/f*, censor/a *m/f* de cuentas

auditorium [ɔːdɪ'tɔːrɪəm] *n* auditorio

Aug. *abbr* (= *August*) ag

August ['ɔːgəst] *n* agosto

aunt [ɑːnt] *n* tía; **auntie**, **aunty** *n diminutive of* **aunt**

au pair ['əʊ'peə*] *n* (*also*: **~ girl**) (*chica*) au pair *f*

aura ['ɔːrə] *n* aura; (*atmosphere*) ambiente *m*

austerity [ɔ'stɛrɪtɪ] *n* austeridad *f*

Australia [ɔs'treɪlɪə] *n* Australia; **Australian** *adj*, *n* australiano/a *m/f*

Austria ['ɔstrɪə] *n* Austria; **Austrian** *adj*, *n* austríaco/a *m/f*

authentic [ɔː'θεntɪk] *adj* auténtico

author ['ɔːθə*] *n* autor(a) *m/f*

authority [ɔː'θɔrɪtɪ] *n* autoridad *f*; (*official permission*) autorización *f*; **the authorities** *npl* las autoridades

authorize ['ɔːθəraɪz] *vt* autorizar

auto [ˈɔːtəʊ] (US) n coche m (SP), carro (LAM), automóvil m

auto-: autobiography [ɔːtəbaɪˈɒgrəfɪ] n autobiografía; **autograph** [ˈɔːtəgrɑːf] n autógrafo ▷ vt (photo etc) dedicar; (programme) firmar; **automatic** [ɔːtəˈmætɪk] adj automático ▷ n (gun) pistola automática; (car) coche m automático; **automatically** adv automáticamente; **automobile** [ˈɔːtəməbiːl] (US) n coche m (SP), carro (LAM), automóvil m; **autonomous** [ɔːˈtɒnəməs] adj autónomo; **autonomy** [ɔːˈtɒnəmɪ] n autonomía

autumn [ˈɔːtəm] n otoño

auxiliary [ɔːgˈzɪlɪərɪ] adj, n auxiliar mf

avail [əˈveɪl] vt: to ~ o.s. of aprovechar(se) de ▷ n: to no ~ en vano, sin resultado

availability [əveɪləˈbɪlɪtɪ] n disponibilidad f

available [əˈveɪləbl] adj disponible; (unoccupied) libre; (person: unattached) soltero y sin compromiso

avalanche [ˈævəlɑːnʃ] n alud m, avalancha

Ave. abbr = **avenue**

avenue [ˈævənjuː] n avenida; (fig) camino

average [ˈævərɪdʒ] n promedio, término medio ▷ adj medio, de término medio; (ordinary) regular, corriente ▷ vt sacar un promedio de; **on ~** por regla general

avert [əˈvɜːt] vt prevenir; (blow) desviar; (one's eyes) apartar

avid [ˈævɪd] adj ávido

avocado [ævəˈkɑːdəʊ] n (also BRIT: ~ **pear**) aguacate m, palta (SC)

avoid [əˈvɔɪd] vt evitar, eludir

await [əˈweɪt] vt esperar, aguardar

awake [əˈweɪk] (pt **awoke** or **awaked**) adj despierto ▷ vt despertar ▷ vi despertarse; **to be ~** estar despierto

award [əˈwɔːd] n premio;

(Law: damages) indemnización f ▷ vt otorgar, conceder; (Law: damages) adjudicar

aware [əˈweə*] adj: ~ **(of)** consciente (de); **to become ~ of/that** (realize) darse cuenta de/de que; (learn) enterarse de/de que; **awareness** n conciencia; (knowledge) conocimiento

away [əˈweɪ] adv fuera; (movement): **she went ~** se marchó; **far ~** lejos; **two kilometres ~** a dos kilómetros de distancia; **two hours ~ by car** a dos horas en coche; **the holiday was two weeks ~** faltaban dos semanas para las vacaciones; **he's ~ for a week** estará ausente una semana; **to take ~ (from)** quitar a; (subtract) substraer (de); **to work/pedal ~** seguir trabajando/pedaleando; **to fade ~** (colour) desvanecerse; (sound) apagarse

awe [ɔː] n admiración f respetuosa; **awesome** [ˈɔːsəm] (US) adj (excellent) formidable

awful [ˈɔːfəl] adj horroroso; (quantity): **an ~ lot (of)** cantidad (de); **awfully** adv (very) terriblemente

awkward [ˈɔːkwəd] adj desmañado, torpe; (shape) incómodo; (embarrassing) delicado, difícil

awoke [əˈwəʊk] pt of **awake**

awoken [əˈwəʊkən] pp of **awake**

axe [æks] (US **ax**) n hacha ▷ vt (project) cortar; (jobs) reducir

axle [ˈæksl] n eje m, árbol m

ay(e) [aɪ] excl sí

azalea [əˈzeɪlɪə] n azalea

b

B [biː] n (Mus) si m

B.A. abbr = **Bachelor of Arts**

baby ['beɪbɪ] n bebé mf; (us: inf: darling) mi amor; **baby carriage** (us) n cochecito; **baby-sit** vi hacer de canguro; **baby-sitter** n canguro/a; **baby wipe** n toallita húmeda (para bebés)

bachelor ['bætʃələ*] n soltero; **B~ of Arts/Science** licenciado/a en Filosofía y Letras/Ciencias

back [bæk] n (of person) espalda; (of animal) lomo; (of hand) dorso; (as opposed to front) parte f de atrás; (of chair) respaldo; (of page) reverso; (of book) final m; (Football) defensa m; (of crowd): **the ones at the ~** los del fondo ▷ vt (candidate: also: **~ up**) respaldar, apoyar; (horse: at races) apostar a; (car) dar marcha atrás a or con ▷ vi (car etc) ir (or salir or entrar) marcha atrás ▷ adj (payment, rent) atrasado; (seats, wheels) de atrás ▷ adv (not forward) (hacia) atrás; (returned): **he's ~** está de vuelta, ha vuelto; **he ran ~** volvió corriendo;

(restitution): **throw the ball ~** devuelve la pelota; **can I have it ~?** ¿me lo devuelve?; (again): **he called ~** llamó de nuevo; **back down** vi echarse atrás; **back out** vi (of promise) volverse atrás; **back up** vt (person) apoyar, respaldar; (theory) defender; (Comput) hacer una copia preventiva or de reserva; **backache** n dolor m de espalda; **backbencher** (BRIT) n miembro del parlamento sin cargo relevante; **backbone** n columna vertebral; **back door** n puerta f trasera; **backfire** vi (Aut) petardear; (plans) fallar, salir mal; **backgammon** n backgammon m; **background** n fondo m; (of events) antecedentes mpl; (basic knowledge) bases fpl; (experience) conocimientos mpl, educación f; **family background** origen m, antecedentes mpl; **backing** n (fig) apoyo, respaldo; **backlog** n: **backlog of work** trabajo atrasado; **backpack** n mochila; **backpacker** n mochilero/a; **backslash** n pleca, barra inversa; **backstage** adv entre bastidores; **backstroke** n espalda; **backup** adj suplementario; ▷ n (support) apoyo; (also: **backup file**) copia preventiva or de reserva; **backward** adj (movement) atrasado; **backwards** adv hacia atrás; (read a list) al revés; (fall) de espaldas; **backyard** n traspatio

bacon ['beɪkən] n tocino, beicon m

bacteria [bæk'tɪərɪə] npl bacterias fpl

bad [bæd] adj malo; (mistake, accident) grave; (food) podrido, pasado; **his ~ leg** su pierna lisiada; **to go ~** (food) pasarse

badge [bædʒ] n insignia; (policeman's) chapa, placa

badger ['bædʒə*] n tejón m

badly ['bædlɪ] adv mal; **to reflect ~ on sb** influir negativamente en la reputación de algn; **~ wounded** gravemente herido; **he needs it ~** le hace gran falta; **to be ~ off (for money)** andar mal de dinero

bad-mannered ['bæd'mænəd] adj

mal educado
badminton ['bædmɪntən] n
bádminton m
bad-tempered ['bæd'tempəd] adj
de mal genio or carácter; (*temporarily*)
de mal humor
bag [bæg] n bolsa; (*handbag*) bolso;
(*satchel*) mochila; (*case*) maleta; **~s**
of (*inf*) un montón de; **baggage** n
equipaje m; **baggage allowance** n
límite m de equipaje; **baggage**
reclaim n recogida de equipajes;
baggy adj amplio; **bagpipes** npl
gaita
bail [beɪl] n fianza ▷ vt
(*prisoner: gen: grant bail to*) poner en
libertad bajo fianza; (*boat: also: ~ out*)
achicar; **on ~** (*prisoner*) bajo fianza; **to**
~ sb out obtener la libertad de algn
bajo fianza
bait [beɪt] n cebo ▷ vt poner cebo en;
(*tease*) tomar el pelo a
bake [beɪk] vt cocer (al horno) ▷ vi
cocerse; **baked beans** npl judías fpl
en salsa de tomate; **baked potato** n
patata al horno; **baker** n panadero;
bakery n panadería; (*for cakes*)
pastelería; **baking** n (*act*) amasar m;
(*batch*) hornada; **baking powder** n
levadura (en polvo)
balance ['bæləns] n equilibrio;
(*Comm: sum*) balance m; (*remainder*)
resto; (*scales*) balanza ▷ vt equilibrar;
(*budget*) nivelar; (*account*) saldar;
(*make equal*) equilibrar; **~ of trade/**
payments balanza de comercio/
pagos; **balanced** adj (*personality, diet*)
equilibrado; (*report*) objetivo; **balance**
sheet n balance m
balcony ['bælkənɪ] n (*open*) balcón m;
(*closed*) galería; (*in theatre*) anfiteatro
bald [bɔːld] adj calvo; (*tyre*) liso
Balearics [bælɪ'ærɪks] npl: **the ~** las
Baleares
ball [bɔːl] n pelota; (*football*) balón m;
(*of wool, string*) ovillo; (*dance*) baile m; **to**
play ~ (*fig*) cooperar
ballerina [bælə'riːnə] n bailarina

ballet ['bæleɪ] n ballet m; **ballet**
dancer n bailarín/ina m/f
balloon [bə'luːn] n globo
ballot ['bælət] n votación f
ballpoint (pen) ['bɔːlpɔɪnt-] n
bolígrafo
ballroom ['bɔːlrum] n salón m
de baile
Baltic ['bɔːltɪk] n: **the ~ (Sea)** el (Mar)
Báltico
bamboo [bæm'buː] n bambú m
ban [bæn] n prohibición f,
proscripción f ▷ vt prohibir, proscribir
banana [bə'nɑːnə] n plátano, banana
(LAM), banano (CAM)
band [bænd] n grupo; (*strip*) faja, tira;
(*stripe*) lista; (*Mus: jazz*) orquesta; (: *rock*)
grupo; (*Mil*) banda
bandage ['bændɪdʒ] n venda,
vendaje m ▷ vt vendar
Band-Aid® ['bændeɪd] (*us*) n tirita
bandit ['bændɪt] n bandido
bang [bæŋ] n (*of gun, exhaust*)
estallido, detonación f; (*of door*)
portazo; (*blow*) golpe m ▷ vt (*door*)
cerrar de golpe; (*one's head*) golpear ▷ vi
estallar; (*door*) cerrar de golpe
Bangladesh [bɑːŋglə'deʃ] n
Bangladesh m
bangle ['bæŋgl] n brazalete m,
ajorca
bangs [bæŋz] (*us*) npl flequillo
banish ['bænɪʃ] vt desterrar
banister(s) ['bænɪstə(z)] n(pl)
barandilla, pasamanos m inv
banjo ['bændʒəu] (*pl* **~es** or **~s**) n
banjo
bank [bæŋk] n (*Comm*) banco; (*of river,*
lake) ribera, orilla; (*of earth*) terraplén
m ▷ vi (*Aviat*) ladearse; **bank on** vt fus
contar con; **bank account** n cuenta
de banco; **bank balance** n saldo;
bank card n tarjeta bancaria; **bank**
charges npl comisión fsg; **banker** n
banquero; **bank holiday** n (*BRIT*) día
festivo or de fiesta; **banking** n banca;
bank manager n director(a) m/f
(de sucursal) de banco; **banknote**

billete m de banco

El término **bank holiday** se aplica en el Reino Unido a todo día festivo oficial en el que cierran bancos y comercios. Los más importantes son en Navidad, Semana Santa, finales de mayo y finales de agosto y, al contrario que en los países de tradición católica, no coinciden necesariamente con una celebración religiosa.

bankrupt ['bæŋkrʌpt] *adj* quebrado, insolvente; **to go ~** hacer bancarrota; **to be ~** estar en quiebra; **bankruptcy** *n* quiebra

bank statement *n* balance *m* or detalle *m* de cuenta

banner ['bænə*] *n* pancarta

bannister(s) ['bænɪstə(z)] *n(pl)* = **banister(s)**

banquet ['bæŋkwɪt] *n* banquete *m*

baptism ['bæptɪzəm] *n* bautismo; *(act)* bautizo

baptize [bæp'taɪz] *vt* bautizar

bar [bɑ:*] *n (pub)* bar *m*; *(counter)* mostrador *m*; *(rod)* barra; *(of window, cage)* reja; *(of soap)* pastilla; *(of chocolate)* tableta; *(fig: hindrance)* obstáculo; *(prohibition)* proscripción *f*; *(Mus)* barra ▷ *vt (road)* obstruir; *(person)* excluir; *(activity)* prohibir; **the B~** *(Law)* la abogacía; **behind ~s** entre rejas; **~ none** sin excepción

barbaric [bɑ:'bærɪk] *adj* bárbaro

barbecue ['bɑ:bɪkju:] *n* barbacoa

barbed wire ['bɑ:bd-] *n* alambre *m* de púas

barber ['bɑ:bə*] *n* peluquero, barbero; **barber's (shop)** *(US* **barber (shop))** *n* peluquería

bar code *n* código de barras

bare [bɛə*] *adj* desnudo; *(trees)* sin hojas; *(necessities etc)* básico ▷ *vt* desnudar; *(teeth)* enseñar; **barefoot**

adj, adv descalzo; **barely** *adv* apenas

bargain ['bɑ:gɪn] *n* pacto, negocio; *(good buy)* ganga ▷ *vi* negociar; *(haggle)* regatear; **into the ~** además, por añadidura; **bargain for** *vt fus*: **he got more than he bargained for** le resultó peor de lo que esperaba

barge [bɑ:dʒ] *n* barcaza; **barge in** *vi* irrumpir; *(interrupt: conversation)* interrumpir

bark [bɑ:k] *n (of tree)* corteza; *(of dog)* ladrido ▷ *vi* ladrar

barley ['bɑ:lɪ] *n* cebada

barmaid ['bɑ:meɪd] *n* camarera

barman ['bɑ:mən] *(irreg)* *n* camarero, barman *m*

barn [bɑ:n] *n* granero

barometer [bə'rɒmɪtə*] *n* barómetro

baron ['bærən] *n* barón *m*; *(press baron etc)* magnate *m*; **baroness** *n* baronesa

barracks ['bærəks] *npl* cuartel *m*

barrage ['bærɑ:ʒ] *n (Mil)* descarga, bombardeo; *(dam)* presa; *(of criticism)* lluvia, aluvión *m*

barrel ['bærəl] *n* barril *m*; *(of gun)* cañón *m*

barren ['bærən] *adj* estéril

barrette [bə'rɛt] *(US)* *n* pasador *m* *(LAM, SP)*, broche *m* *(MEX)*

barricade [bærɪ'keɪd] *n* barricada

barrier ['bærɪə*] *n* barrera

barring ['bɑ:rɪŋ] *prep* excepto, salvo

barrister ['bærɪstə*] *(BRIT)* *n* abogado/a

barrow ['bærəʊ] *n (cart)* carretilla *(de mano)*

bartender ['bɑ:tɛndə*] *(US)* *n* camarero, barman *m*

base [beɪs] *n* base *f* ▷ *vt*: **to ~ sth on** basar or fundar algo en ▷ *adj* bajo, infame

baseball ['beɪsbɔ:l] *n* béisbol *m*; **baseball cap** *n* gorra *f* de béisbol

basement ['beɪsmənt] *n* sótano

bases¹ ['beɪsi:z] *npl of* **basis**

bases² ['beɪsɪz] *npl of* **base**

bash [bæʃ] *(inf)* *vt* golpear

basic ['beɪsɪk] adj básico; **basically** adv fundamentalmente, en el fondo; (simply) sencillamente; **basics** npl: **the basics** los fundamentos

basil ['bæzl] n albahaca

basin ['beɪsn] n cuenco, tazón m; (Geo) cuenca; (also: **wash~**) lavabo

basis ['beɪsɪs] (pl **bases**) n base f; **on a part-time/trial ~** a tiempo parcial/a prueba

basket ['bɑ:skɪt] n cesta, cesto; canasta; **basketball** n baloncesto

bass [beɪs] n (Mus: instrument) bajo; (double bass) contrabajo; (singer) bajo

bastard ['bɑ:stəd] n bastardo; (inf!) hijo de puta (!)

bat [bæt] n (Zool) murciélago; (for ball games) palo; (BRIT: for table tennis) pala ▷ vt: **he didn't ~ an eyelid** no pestañeó

batch [bætʃ] n (of bread) hornada; (of letters etc) lote m

bath [bɑ:θ, pl bɑ:ðz] n (action) baño; (bathtub) bañera (SP), tina (LAM), bañadera (RPL) ▷ vt bañar; **to have a ~** bañarse, tomar un baño; see also **baths**

bathe [beɪð] vi bañarse ▷ vt (wound) lavar

bathing ['beɪðɪŋ] n el bañarse; **bathing costume** (US **bathing suit**) n traje m de baño

bath: bathrobe (man's) batín m; (woman's) bata; **bathroom** n (cuarto de) baño; **baths** [bɑ:ðz] npl (also: **swimming baths**) piscina; **bath towel** n toalla de baño; **bathtub** n bañera

baton ['bætən] n (Mus) batuta; (Athletics) testigo; (weapon) porra

batter ['bætə*] vt azotar; (rain etc) azotar ▷ n masa (para rebozar); **battered** adj (hat, pan) estropeado

battery ['bætərɪ] n (Aut) batería (of torch) pila; **battery farming** n cría intensiva

battle ['bætl] n batalla; (fig) lucha ▷ vi luchar; **battlefield** n campo m de batalla

bay [beɪ] n (Geo) bahía; **B~ of Biscay**

= mar Cantábrico; **to hold sb at ~** mantener a algn a raya

bazaar [bə'zɑ:*] n bazar m; (fete) venta con fines benéficos

B. & B. n abbr = **bed and breakfast**; (place) pensión f; (terms) cama y desayuno

BBC n abbr (= British Broadcasting Corporation) cadena de radio y televisión estatal británica

B.C. adv abbr (= before Christ) a. de C.

○ **KEYWORD**

be [bi:] (pt **was, were**, pp **been**) aux vb **1** (with present participle: forming continuous tenses): **what are you doing?** ¿qué estás haciendo?, ¿qué haces?; **they're coming tomorrow** vienen mañana; **I've been waiting for you for hours** llevo horas esperándote

2 (with pp: forming passives) ser (but often replaced by active or reflexive constructions); **to be murdered** ser asesinado; **the box had been opened** habían abierto la caja; **the thief was nowhere to be seen** no se veía al ladrón por ninguna parte

3 (in tag questions): **it was fun, wasn't it?** fue divertido, ¿no? or ¿verdad?; **he's good-looking, isn't he?** es guapo, ¿no te parece?; **she's back again, is she?** entonces, ¿ha vuelto?

4 (+to +infin): **the house is to be sold** (necessity) hay que vender la casa; (future) van a vender la casa; **he's not to open it** no tiene que abrirlo ▷ vb +complement **1** (with n or num complement, but see also 3, 4, 5 and impers vb below) ser; **he's a doctor** es médico; **2 and 2 are 4** 2 y 2 son 4

2 (with adj complement: expressing permanent or inherent quality) ser; (: expressing state seen as temporary or reversible) estar; **I'm English** soy inglés/esa; **she's tall/pretty** es alta/bonita; **he's young** es joven; **be careful/good/quiet** ten cuidado/

pórtate bien/cállate; **I'm tired** estoy cansado/a; **it's dirty** está sucio/a
3 (of health) estar; **how are you?** ¿cómo estás?; **he's very ill** está muy enfermo; **I'm better now** ya estoy mejor
4 (of age) tener; **how old are you?** ¿cuántos años tienes?; **I'm sixteen (years old)** tengo dieciséis años
5 (cost) costar; ser; **how much was the meal?** ¿cuánto fue or costó la comida?; **that'll be £5.75, please** son £5.75, por favor; **this shirt is £17** esta camisa cuesta £17
▷ vi **1** (exist, occur etc) existir, haber; **the best singer that ever was** el mejor cantante que existió jamás; **is there a God?** ¿hay un Dios?, ¿existe Dios?; **be that as it may** sea como sea; **so be it** así sea
2 (referring to place) estar; **I won't be here tomorrow** no estaré aquí mañana
3 (referring to movement): **where have you been?** ¿dónde has estado?
▷ impers vb **1** (referring to time): **it's 5 o'clock** son las 5; **it's the 28th of April** estamos a 28 de abril
2 (referring to distance): **it's 10 km to the village** el pueblo está a 10 km
3 (referring to the weather): **it's too hot/cold** hace demasiado calor/frío; **it's windy today** hace viento hoy
4 (emphatic): **it's me** soy yo; **it was Maria who paid the bill** fue María la que pagó la cuenta

beach [biːtʃ] n playa ▷ vt varar
beacon ['biːkən] n (lighthouse) faro; (marker) guía
bead [biːd] n cuenta; (of sweat etc) gota; **beads** npl (necklace) collar m
beak [biːk] n pico
beam [biːm] n (Arch) viga, travesaño; (of light) rayo, haz m de luz ▷ vi brillar; (smile) sonreír
bean [biːn] n judía; **runner/broad ~** habichuela/haba; **coffee ~** grano de café; **beansprouts** npl brotes

mpl de soja
bear [beəʳ] (pt **bore**, pp **borne**) n oso
▷ vt (weight etc) llevar; (cost) pagar; (responsibility) tener; (endure) soportar, aguantar; (children) parir, tener; (fruit) dar ▷ vi: **to ~ right/left** torcer a la derecha/izquierda
beard [bɪəd] n barba
bearer ['beərəʳ] n portador(a) m/f
bearing ['beərɪŋ] n porte m, comportamiento; (connection) relación f
beast [biːst] n bestia; (inf) bruto, salvaje m
beat [biːt] (pt ~, pp **beaten**) n (of heart) latido; (Mus) ritmo, compás m; (of policeman) ronda ▷ vt pegar, golpear; (eggs) batir; (defeat: opponent) vencer, derrotar; (: record) sobrepasar ▷ vi (heart) latir; (drum) redoblar; (rain, wind) azotar; **off the ~en track** aislado; **to ~ it** (inf) largarse; **beat up** vt (attack) dar una paliza a; **beating** n paliza
beautiful ['bjuːtɪful] adj precioso, hermoso, bello; **beautifully** adv maravillosamente
beauty ['bjuːtɪ] n belleza; **beauty parlour** (us **beauty parlor**) n salón m de belleza; **beauty salon** n salón m de belleza; **beauty spot** n (Tourism) lugar m pintoresco
beaver ['biːvəʳ] n castor m
became [bɪ'keɪm] pt of **become**
because [bɪ'kɔz] conj porque; **~ of** debido a, a causa de
beckon ['bekən] vt (also: **~ to**) llamar con señas
become [bɪ'kʌm] (pt **became**, pp **~**) vt (suit) favorecer, sentar bien a ▷ vi (+ n) hacerse, llegar a ser; (+ adj) ponerse, volverse; **to ~ fat** engordar
bed [bed] n cama; (of flowers) macizo; (of coal, clay) capa; (of river) lecho; (of sea) fondo; **to go to ~** acostarse; **bed and breakfast** n (place) pensión f; (terms) cama y desayuno; **bedclothes** npl ropa de cama; **bedding** n ropa de cama; **bed linen** n (BRIT) ropa f

de cama

bed: **bedroom** n dormitorio; **bedside** n: **at the bedside of** a la cabecera de; **bedside lamp** n lámpara de noche; **bedside table** n mesilla de noche; **bedsit(ter)** (BRIT) n cuarto de alquiler; **bedspread** n cubrecama m, colcha; **bedtime** n hora de acostarse

bee [biː] n abeja

beech [biːtʃ] n haya

beef [biːf] n carne f de vaca; **roast ~** rosbif m; **beefburger** n hamburguesa; **Beefeater** n alabardero de la Torre de Londres

been [biːn] pp of **be**

beer [bɪə*] n cerveza; **beer garden** n (BRIT) terraza f de verano, jardín m (de un bar)

beet [biːt] (US) n (also: **red ~**) remolacha

beetle ['biːtl] n escarabajo

beetroot ['biːtruːt] (BRIT) n remolacha

before [bɪ'fɔː*] prep (of time) antes de; (of space) delante de ▷ conj antes (de) que ▷ adv antes, anteriormente; delante, adelante; **~ going** antes de marcharse; **~ she goes** antes de que se vaya; **the week ~** la semana anterior; **I've never seen it ~** no lo he visto nunca; **beforehand** adv de antemano, con anticipación

beg [beg] vi pedir limosna ▷ vt pedir, rogar; (entreat) suplicar; **to ~ sb to do sth** rogar a algn que haga algo; see also **pardon**

began [bɪ'gæn] pt of **begin**

beggar ['begə*] n mendigo/a

begin [bɪ'gɪn] (pt **began**, pp **begun**) vt, vi empezar, comenzar; **to ~ doing** or **to do sth** empezar a hacer algo; **beginner** n principiante mf; **beginning** n principio, comienzo

begun [bɪ'gʌn] pp of **begin**

behalf [bɪ'hɑːf] n: **on ~ of** en nombre de, por; (for benefit of) en beneficio de; **on my/his ~** por mí/él

behave [bɪ'heɪv] vi (person) portarse, comportarse; (well: also: **~ o.s.**) portarse bien; **behaviour** (US **behavior**) n comportamiento, conducta

behind [bɪ'haɪnd] prep detrás de; (supporting): **to be ~ sb** apoyar a algn ▷ adv detrás, por detrás, atrás ▷ n trasero; **to be ~ (schedule)** ir retrasado; **~ the scenes** (fig) entre bastidores

beige [beɪʒ] adj color beige

Beijing ['beɪ'dʒɪŋ] n Pekín m

being ['biːɪŋ] n ser m; (existence): **in ~** existente; **to come into ~** aparecer

belated [bɪ'leɪtɪd] adj atrasado, tardío

belch [beltʃ] vi eructar ▷ vt (gen: belch out: smoke etc) arrojar

Belgian ['beldʒən] adj, n belga mf

Belgium ['beldʒəm] n Bélgica

belief [bɪ'liːf] n opinión f; (faith) fe f

believe [bɪ'liːv] vt, vi creer; **to ~ in** creer en; **believer** n partidario/a, (Rel) creyente mf, fiel mf

bell [bel] n campana; (small) campanilla; (on door) timbre m

bellboy ['belbɔɪ] (BRIT) n botones m inv

bellhop ['belhɔp] (US) n = **bellboy**

bellow ['beləʊ] vi bramar; (person) rugir

bell pepper n (esp US) pimiento, pimentón m (LAM)

belly ['belɪ] n barriga, panza; **belly button** (inf) n ombligo

belong [bɪ'lɔŋ] vi: **to ~ to** pertenecer

a; (club etc) ser socio de; **this book ~s here** este libro va aquí; **belongings** npl pertenencias fpl

beloved [bɪˈlʌvɪd] adj querido/a

below [bɪˈləu] prep bajo, debajo de; (less than) inferior a ▷ adv abajo, (por) debajo; **see ~** véase más abajo

belt [belt] n cinturón m; (Tech) correa, cinta ▷ vt (thrash) pegar con correa; **beltway** (us) n (Aut) carretera de circunvalación

bemused [bɪˈmjuːzd] adj perplejo

bench [bentʃ] n banco; (BRIT Pol): **the Government/Opposition ~es** (los asientos de) los miembros del Gobierno/de la Oposición; **the B~** (Law: judges) magistratura

bend [bend] (pt, pp bent) vt doblar ▷ vi inclinarse ▷ n (BRIT: in road, river) curva; (in pipe) codo; **bend down** vi inclinarse, doblarse; **bend over** vi inclinarse

beneath [bɪˈniːθ] prep bajo, debajo de; (unworthy) indigno de ▷ adv abajo, (por) debajo

beneficial [benɪˈfɪʃəl] adj beneficioso

benefit [ˈbenɪfɪt] n beneficio; (allowance of money) subsidio ▷ vt beneficiar ▷ vi: **he'll ~ from it** le sacará provecho

benign [bɪˈnaɪn] adj benigno; (smile) afable

bent [bent] pt, pp of bend ▷ n inclinación f ▷ adj: **to be ~ on** estar empeñado en

bereaved [bɪˈriːvd] npl: **the ~** los íntimos de una persona afligidos por su muerte

beret [ˈbereɪ] n boina

Berlin [bəːˈlɪn] n Berlín

Bermuda [bəːˈmjuːdə] n las Bermudas

berry [ˈberɪ] n baya

berth [bəːθ] n (in bed) litera; (cabin) camarote m; (for ship) amarradero ▷ vi atracar, amarrar

beside [bɪˈsaɪd] prep junto a, al lado de; **to be ~ o.s. with anger** estar fuera

de sí; **that's ~ the point** eso no tiene nada que ver; **besides** adv además ▷ prep además de

best [best] adj (el/la) mejor ▷ adv (lo) mejor; **the ~ part of** (quantity) la mayor parte de; **at ~** en el mejor de los casos; **to make the ~ of sth** sacar el mejor partido de algo; **to do one's ~** hacer todo lo posible; **to the ~ of my knowledge** que yo sepa; **to the ~ of my ability** como mejor puedo; **best-before date** n fecha de consumo preferente; **best man** (irreg) n padrino de boda; **bestseller** n éxito de librería, bestseller m

bet [bet] (pt, pp ~ or ~ted) n apuesta ▷ vt: **to ~ money on** apostar dinero por ▷ vi apostar; **to ~ sb sth** apostar algo a algn

betray [bɪˈtreɪ] vt traicionar; (trust) faltar a

better [ˈbetə*] adj, adv mejor ▷ vt superar ▷ n: **to get the ~ of sb** quedar por encima de algn; **you had ~ do it** más vale que lo hagas; **he thought ~ of it** cambió de parecer; **to get ~** (Med) mejorar(se)

betting [ˈbetɪŋ] n juego, el apostar; **betting shop** (BRIT) n agencia de apuestas

between [bɪˈtwiːn] prep entre ▷ adv (time) mientras tanto; (place) en medio

beverage [ˈbevərɪdʒ] n bebida

beware [bɪˈwɛə*] vi: **to ~ (of)** tener cuidado (con); **"~ of the dog"** "perro peligroso"

bewildered [bɪˈwɪldəd] adj aturdido, perplejo

beyond [bɪˈjɔnd] prep más allá de; (past: understanding) fuera de; (after: date) después de, más allá de; (above) superior a ▷ adv (in space) más allá; (in time) posteriormente; **~ doubt** fuera de toda duda; **~ repair** irreparable

bias [ˈbaɪəs] n (prejudice) prejuicio, pasión f; (preference) predisposición f; **bias(s)ed** adj parcial

bib [bɪb] *n* babero

Bible ['baɪbl] *n* Biblia

bicarbonate of soda [baɪ'kɑːbənɪt-] *n* bicarbonato sódico

biceps ['baɪsɛps] *n* bíceps *m*

bicycle ['baɪsɪkl] *n* bicicleta; **bicycle pump** *n* bomba de bicicleta

bid [bɪd] (*pt* **bade** *or* ~, *pp* **bidden** *or* ~) *n* oferta, postura; (*in tender*) licitación *f*; (*attempt*) tentativa, conato ▷ *vi* hacer una oferta ▷ *vt* (*offer*) ofrecer; **to ~ sb good day** dar a algn los buenos días; **bidder** *n*: **the highest bidder** el mejor postor

bidet ['biːdeɪ] *n* bidet *m*

big [bɪg] *adj* grande; (*brother, sister*) mayor; **bigheaded** *adj* engreído; **big toe** *n* dedo gordo (del pie)

bike [baɪk] *n* bici *f*; **bike lane** *n* carril-bici *m*

bikini [bɪ'kiːnɪ] *n* bikini *m*

bilateral [baɪ'lætərəl] *adj* (*agreement*) bilateral

bilingual [baɪ'lɪŋgwəl] *adj* bilingüe

bill [bɪl] *n* cuenta; (*invoice*) factura; (*Pol*) proyecto de ley; (*us: banknote*) billete *m*; (*of bird*) pico; (*of show*) programa *m*; **"post no ~s"** prohibido fijar carteles; **to fit** *or* **fill the ~** (*fig*) cumplir con los requisitos; **billboard** (*us*) *n* cartelera; **billfold** ['bɪlfəʊld] (*us*) *n* cartera

billiards ['bɪljədz] *n* billar *m*

billion ['bɪljən] *n* (*BRIT*) billón *m* (*millón de millones*); (*us*) mil millones *mpl*

bin [bɪn] *n* (*for rubbish*) cubo *or* bote *m* (*MEX*) or tacho (*SC*) de la basura; (*container*) recipiente *m*

bind [baɪnd] (*pt, pp* **bound**) *vt* atar; (*book*) encuadernar; (*oblige*) obligar ▷ *n* (*inf: nuisance*) lata

binge [bɪndʒ] (*inf*) *n*: **to go on a ~** ir de juerga

bingo ['bɪŋgəʊ] *n* bingo *m*

binoculars [bɪ'nɔkjuləz] *npl* prismáticos *mpl*

bio... [baɪə] *prefix*: **biochemistry** *n*

bioquímica; **biodegradable** [baɪəʊdɪ'greɪdəbl] *adj* biodegradable; **biography** [baɪ'ɔgrəfɪ] *n* biografía; **biological** *adj* biológico; **biology** [baɪ'ɔlədʒɪ] *n* biología; **biometric** [baɪə'mɛtrɪk] *adj* biométrico

birch [bəːtʃ] *n* (*tree*) abedul *m*

bird [bəːd] *n* ave *f*, pájaro; (*BRIT: inf: girl*) chica; **bird flu** *n* gripe *f* aviar; **bird of prey** *n* ave *f* de presa; **birdwatching** *n*: **he likes to go birdwatching on Sundays** los domingos le gusta ir a ver pájaros

Biro® ['baɪrəʊ] *n* boli *m*

birth [bəːθ] *n* nacimiento; **to give ~ to** parir, dar a luz; **birth certificate** *n* partida de nacimiento; **birth control** *n* (*policy*) control *m* de natalidad; (*methods*) métodos *mpl* anticonceptivos; **birthday** *n* cumpleaños *m inv* ▷ *cpd* (*cake, card etc*) de cumpleaños; **birthmark** *n* antojo, marca de nacimiento; **birthplace** *n* lugar *m* de nacimiento

biscuit ['bɪskɪt] (*BRIT*) *n* galleta

bishop ['bɪʃəp] *n* obispo; (*Chess*) alfil *m*

bistro ['biːstrəʊ] *n* café-bar *m*

bit [bɪt] *pt of* **bite** *n* trozo, pedazo, pedacito; (*Comput*) bit *m*, bitio; (*for horse*) freno, bocado; **a ~ of** un poco de; **a ~ mad** un poco loco; **~ by ~** poco a poco

bitch [bɪtʃ] *n* perra; (*inf!: woman*) zorra (*!*)

bite [baɪt] (*pt* **bit**, *pp* **bitten**) *vt, vi* morder; (*insect etc*) picar ▷ *n* (*insect bite*) picadura; (*mouthful*) bocado; **to ~ one's nails** comerse las uñas; **let's have a ~ (to eat)** (*inf*) vamos a comer algo

bitten ['bɪtn] *pp of* **bite**

bitter ['bɪtə*] *adj* amargo; (*wind*) cortante, penetrante; (*battle*) encarnizado ▷ *n* (*BRIT: beer*) cerveza típica británica a base de lúpulos

bizarre [bɪ'zɑː*] *adj* raro, extraño

black [blæk] *adj* negro; (*tea, coffee*) solo ▷ *n* color *m* negro; (*person*): **B~**

negro/a ▷ vt (BRIT Industry) boicotear;
to give sb a ~ eye ponerle a algn
el ojo morado; **~ and blue** (bruised)
amoratado; **to be in the ~** (bank
account) estar en números negros;
black out vi (faint) desmayarse;
blackberry n zarzamora; **blackbird**
n mirlo; **blackboard** n pizarra; **black
coffee** n café m solo; **blackcurrant**
n grosella negra; **black ice** n hielo
invisible en la carretera; **blackmail**
n chantaje m ▷ vt chantajear; **black
market** n mercado negro; **blackout**
n (Mil) oscurecimiento; (power cut)
apagón m; (TV, Radio) interrupción f de
programas; (fainting) desvanecimiento;
black pepper n pimienta f negra;
black pudding n morcilla; **Black Sea**
n: **the Black Sea** el Mar Negro
bladder ['blædə*] n vejiga
blade [bleid] n hoja; (of propeller)
paleta; **a ~ of grass** una brizna de
hierba
blame [bleim] n culpa ▷ vt: **to ~ sb
for sth** echar a algn la culpa de algo; **to
be to ~ (for)** tener la culpa de (de)
bland [blænd] adj (music, taste) soso
blank [blæŋk] adj en blanco; (look) sin
expresión ▷ n (of memory): **my mind is
a ~** no puedo recordar nada; (on form)
blanco, espacio en blanco; (cartridge)
cartucho sin bala or de fogueo
blanket ['blæŋkit] n manta (SP),
cobija (LAM); (of snow) capa; (of fog)
manto
blast [blɑːst] n (of wind) ráfaga, soplo;
(of explosive) explosión f ▷ vt (blow
up) volar
blatant ['bleitənt] adj descarado
blaze [bleiz] n (fire) fuego; (fig: of
colour) despliegue m; (: of glory)
esplendor m ▷ vi arder en llamas; (fig)
brillar ▷ vt: **to ~ a trail** (fig) abrir (un)
camino; **in a ~ of publicity** con gran
publicidad
blazer ['bleizə*] n chaqueta de uniforme
de colegial o de socio de club
bleach [bliːtʃ] n (also: **household ~**)

lejía ▷ vt blanquear; **bleachers** n
npl (Sport) gradas fpl al sol
bleak [bliːk] adj (countryside) desierto;
(prospect) poco prometedor(a);
(weather) crudo; (smile) triste
bled [bled] pt, pp of **bleed**
bleed [bliːd] (pt, pp bled) vt, vi
sangrar; **my nose is ~ing** me está
sangrando la nariz
blemish ['blemiʃ] n marca, mancha;
(on reputation) tacha
blend [blend] n mezcla ▷ vt mezclar;
(colours etc) combinar, mezclar ▷ vi
(colours etc: also: **~ in**) combinarse,
mezclarse; **blender** n (Culin) batidora
bless [bles] (pt, pp **~ed** or **blest**) vt
bendecir; **~ you!** (after sneeze) ¡Jesús!;
blessing n (approval) aprobación f;
(godsend) don m del cielo, bendición f;
(advantage) beneficio, ventaja
blew [bluː] pt of **blow**
blight [blait] vt (hopes etc) frustrar,
arruinar
blind [blaind] adj ciego; (fig): **~ (to)**
ciego (a) ▷ n (for window) persiana ▷ vt
cegar; (dazzle) deslumbrar; (deceive): **to
~ sb to** ... cegar a algn a ...; **the blind**
npl los ciegos; **blind alley** n callejón
m sin salida; **blindfold** n venda ▷ adv
con los ojos vendados ▷ vt vendar
los ojos a
blink [bliŋk] vi parpadear, pestañear;
(light) oscilar
bliss [blis] n felicidad f
blister ['blistə*] n ampolla ▷ vi
(paint) ampollarse
blizzard ['blizəd] n ventisca
bloated ['bləutid] adj hinchado;
(person: full) ahíto
blob [blob] n (drop) gota; (indistinct
object) bulto
block [blok] n bloque m; (in pipes)
obstáculo; (of buildings) manzana
(SP), cuadra (LAM) ▷ vt obstruir,
cerrar; (progress) estorbar; **~ of flats**
(BRIT) bloque m de pisos; **mental ~**
bloqueo mental; **block up** vt tapar,
obstruir; (pipe) atascar; **blockade**

[-'keɪd] n bloqueo ▷ vt bloquear;
blockage n estorbo, obstrucción f;
blockbuster n (BRIT: book) bestseller m;
(film) éxito de público; **block capitals**
npl mayúsculas fpl; **block letters** npl
mayúsculas fpl

blog [blɔg] n blog m

bloke [bləʊk] n (BRIT: inf) tipo, tío

blond(e) [blɔnd] adj, n rubio/a m/f

blood [blʌd] n sangre f; **blood donor**
n donante m f de sangre; **blood group**
n grupo sanguíneo; **blood poisoning**
n envenenamiento de la sangre; **blood
pressure** n presión f sanguínea;
bloodshed n derramamiento de
sangre; **bloodshot** adj inyectado en
sangre; **bloodstream** n corriente
f sanguínea; **blood test** n análisis
m inv de sangre; **blood transfusion**
n transfusión f de sangre; **blood
type** n grupo sanguíneo; **blood
vessel** n vaso sanguíneo; **bloody**
adj sangriento; (nose etc) lleno de
sangre; (BRIT: infl): **this bloody ...**
este condenado o puñetero ... (!)
▷ adv: **bloody strong/good** (BRIT: infl)
terriblemente fuerte/bueno

bloom [blu:m] n flor f ▷ vi florecer

blossom ['blɔsəm] n flor f ▷ vi
florecer

blot [blɔt] n borrón m; (fig) mancha
▷ vt (stain) manchar

blouse [blauz] n blusa

blow [bləʊ] (pt blew, pp blown) n
golpe m; (with sword) espadazo ▷ vi
soplar; (dust, sand etc) volar; (fuse)
fundirse ▷ vt (wind) llevarse; (fuse)
quemar; (instrument) tocar; **to ~ one's
nose** sonarse; **blow away** vt llevarse,
arrancar; **blow out** vi apagarse; **blow
up** vi estallar ▷ vt volar; (tyre) inflar;
(Phot) ampliar; **blow-dry** n moldeado
(con secador)

blown [bləʊn] pp of **blow**

blue [blu:] adj azul; (depressed)
deprimido; ~ **film/joke** película/chiste
m verde; **out of the ~** (fig) de repente;
bluebell n campanilla, campánula

azul; **blueberry** n arándano; **blue
cheese** n queso azul; **blues** npl: **the
blues** (Mus) el blues; **to have the blues**
estar triste; **bluetit** n herrerillo m
(común)

bluff [blʌf] vi tirarse un farol, farolear
▷ n farol m; **to call sb's ~** coger a algn
la palabra

blunder ['blʌndə*] n patinazo,
metedura de pata ▷ vi cometer un
error, meter la pata

blunt [blʌnt] adj (pencil) despuntado;
(knife) desafilado, romo; (person) franco,
directo

blur [blə:*] n (shape): **to become
a ~** hacerse borroso ▷ vt (vision)
enturbiar; (distinction) borrar; **blurred**
adj borroso

blush [blʌʃ] vi ruborizarse, ponerse
colorado ▷ n rubor m; **blusher** n
colorete m

board [bɔ:d] n (cardboard) cartón m;
(wooden) tabla, tablero; (on wall) tablón
m; (for chess etc) tablero; (committee)
junta, consejo; (in firm) mesa o junta
directiva; (Naut, Aviat): **on ~** a bordo
▷ vt (ship) embarcarse en; (train) subir
a; **full ~** (BRIT) pensión completa; **half
~** (BRIT) media pensión; **to go by the ~**
(fig) ser abandonado o olvidado; **board
game** n juego de tablero; **boarding
card** (BRIT) n tarjeta de embarque;
boarding pass (US) n = **boarding
card**; **boarding school** n internado;
board room n sala de juntas

boast [bəʊst] vi: **to ~ (about o of)**
alardear (de)

boat [bəʊt] n barco, buque m; (small)
barca, bote m

bob [bɔb] vi (also: ~ **up and down**)
menearse, balancearse

bobby pin ['bɔbɪ-] (US) n horquilla

body ['bɔdɪ] n cuerpo; (corpse) cadáver
m; (of car) caja, carrocería; (fig: group)
grupo; (: organization) organismo;
body-building n culturismo;
bodyguard n guardaespaldas m inv;
bodywork n carrocería

bog [bɒg] n pantano, ciénaga ▷vt: **to get ~ged down** (fig) empantanarse, atascarse

bogus ['bəugəs] adj falso, fraudulento

boil [bɔɪl] vt (water) hervir; (eggs) pasar por agua, cocer ▷vi hervir; (fig: with anger) estar furioso; (: with heat) asfixiarse ▷n (Med) furúnculo, divieso; **to come to the ~, to come to a ~** (us) comenzar a hervir; **to bring to** (fig) reducirse a; **boil over** ▷vi salirse, rebosar; (anger etc) llegar al colmo; **boiled egg** n (soft) huevo tibio (MEX) or pasado por agua or a la copa (SC); (hard) huevo duro; **boiled potatoes** npl patatas fpl (SP) or papas fpl (LAM) cocidas; **boiler** n caldera; **boiling** ['bɔɪlɪŋ] adj: **I'm boiling (hot)** (inf) estoy asado; **boiling point** n punto de ebullición

bold [bəuld] adj valiente, audaz; (pej) descarado; (colour) llamativo

Bolivia [bə'lɪvɪə] n Bolivia; **Bolivian** adj, n boliviano/a m/f

bollard ['bɒləd] (BRIT) n (Aut) poste m

bolt [bəult] n (lock) cerrojo; (with nut) perno, tornillo ▷adv: **~ upright** rígido, erguido ▷vt (door) echar el cerrojo a; (also: **~ together**) sujetar con tornillos; (food) engullir ▷vi fugarse; (horse) desbocarse

bomb [bɒm] n bomba ▷vt bombardear; **bombard** [bɒm'bɑːd] vt bombardear; (fig) asediar; **bomber** n (Aviat) bombardero; **bomb scare** n amenaza de bomba

bond [bɒnd] n (promise) fianza; (Finance) bono; (link) vínculo, lazo; (Comm): **in ~** en depósito bajo fianza; **bonds** npl (chains) cadenas fpl

bone [bəun] n hueso; (of fish) espina ▷vt deshuesar; quitar las espinas a

bonfire ['bɒnfaɪə⁺] n hoguera, fogata

bonnet ['bɒnɪt] n gorra; (BRIT: of car) capó m

bonus ['bəunəs] n (payment) paga extraordinaria, plus m; (fig) bendición f

boo [buː] excl ¡uh! ▷vt abuchear,

rechiflar

book [buk] n libro; (of tickets) taco; (of stamps etc) librito ▷vt (seat, room) sacar; (seat, room) reservar; (Comm) cuentas fpl, contabilidad f; **book in** vi (at hotel) registrarse; **book up** vt: **to be booked up** (hotel) estar completo; **bookcase** n librería, estante m para libros; **booking** n reserva; **booking office** n (BRIT Rail) despacho de billetes (SP) or boletos (LAM); (Theatre) taquilla (SP), boletería (LAM); **bookkeeping** n contabilidad f; **booklet** n folleto; **bookmaker** n corredor m de apuestas; **bookmark** n (also Comput) marcador; **bookseller** n librero; **bookshelf** n estante m (para libros); **bookshop, book store** n librería

boom [buːm] n (noise) trueno, estampido; (in prices etc) alza rápida; (Econ, in population) boom m ▷vi (cannon) hacer gran estruendo, retumbar; (Econ) estar en alza

boost [buːst] n estímulo, empuje m ▷vt estimular, empujar

boot [buːt] n bota; (BRIT: of car) maleta, maletero ▷n (Comput) arrancar; **to ~** (in addition) además, por añadidura

booth [buːð] n (telephone booth, voting booth) cabina

booze [buːz] (inf) n bebida

border ['bɔːdə⁺] n borde m, margen m; (of a country) frontera; (for flowers) arriate m ▷vt (road) bordear; (another country: also: **~ on**) lindar con; **borderline** n: **on the borderline** en el límite

bore [bɔː⁺] pt of **bear** ▷n (hole) hacer un agujero en; (well) perforar; (person) aburrir ▷n (person) pelmazo, pesado; (of gun) calibre m; **bored** adj aburrido; **he's bored to tears** or **to death** or **stiff** está aburrido como una ostra, está muerto de aburrimiento; **boredom** n aburrimiento

boring ['bɔːrɪŋ] adj aburrido

born [bɔːn] adj: **to be ~** nacer; **I was ~**

in 1960 nací en 1960

borne [bɔːn] *pp of* **bear**

borough ['bʌrə] *n* municipio

borrow ['bɒrəu] *vt*: **to ~ sth (from sb)** tomar algo prestado (a algn)

Bosnia (-Herzegovina)
['bɒznıə(ˌhɜːzə'gəuvıːnə)] *n*
Bosnia(-Herzegovina); **Bosnian**
['bɒznıən] *adj, n* bosnio/a

bosom ['buzəm] *n* pecho

boss [bɒs] *n* jefe *m* ▷ *vt* (*also*: **~ about or around**) mangonear; **bossy** *adj* mandón/ona

both [bəuθ] *adj, pron* ambos/as, los dos(las dos); **~ of us went, we ~ went** fuimos los dos, ambos fuimos ▷ *adv*: **~ A and B** tanto A como B

bother ['bɒðə*] *vt* (*worry*) preocupar; (*disturb*) molestar, fastidiar ▷ *vi* (*also*: **~ o.s.**) molestarse ▷ *n* (*trouble*) dificultad *f*; (*nuisance*) molestia, lata; **to ~ doing** tomarse la molestia de hacer

bottle ['bɒtl] *n* botella; (*small*) frasco; (*baby's*) biberón *m* ▷ *vt* embotellar; **bottle bank** *n* contenedor *m* de vidrio; **bottle-opener** *n* abrebotellas *m inv*

bottom ['bɒtəm] *n* (*of box, sea*) fondo; (*buttocks*) trasero, culo; (*of page*) pie *m*; (*of list*) final *m*; (*of class*) último/a ▷ *adj* (*lowest*) más bajo; (*last*) último

bought [bɔːt] *pt, pp of* **buy**

boulder ['bəuldə*] *n* canto rodado

bounce [bauns] *vi* (*ball*) (re)botar; (*cheque*) ser rechazado ▷ *vt* hacer (re)botar ▷ *n* (*rebound*) (re)bote *m*; **bouncer** (*inf*) *n* gorila *m* (*que echa a los alborotadores de un bar, club etc*)

bound [baund] *pt, pp of* **bind** ▷ *n* (*leap*) salto; (*gen pl*: *limit*) límite *m* ▷ *vi* (*leap*) saltar ▷ *vt* (*border*) rodear ▷ *adj*: **~ by** rodeado de; **to be ~ to do sth** (*obliged*) tener el deber de hacer algo; **he's ~ to come** es seguro que vendrá; **out of ~s** prohibido el paso; **~ for** con destino a

boundary ['baundrı] *n* límite *m*

bouquet ['bukeı] *n* (*of flowers*) ramo

bourbon ['buəbən] (*us*) *n* (*also*: **~**

whiskey) whisky *m* americano, bourbon *m*

bout [baut] *n* (*of malaria etc*) ataque *m*; (*of activity*) período; (*Boxing etc*) combate *m*, encuentro

boutique [buːˈtiːk] *n* boutique *f*, tienda *f* de ropa

bow¹ [bəu] *n* (*knot*) lazo; (*weapon, Mus*) arco

bow² [bau] *n* (*of the head*) reverencia; (*Naut*: *also*: **~s**) proa ▷ *vi* inclinarse, hacer una reverencia

bowels [bauəlz] *npl* intestinos *mpl*, vientre *m*; (*fig*) entrañas *fpl*

bowl [bəul] *n* tazón *m*, cuenco; (*ball*) bola ▷ *vi* (*Cricket*) arrojar la pelota; *see also* **bowls**; **bowler** *n* (*Cricket*) lanzador *m* (*de la pelota*); (*BRIT*: *also*: **bowler hat**) hongo, bombín *m*; **bowling** *n* (*game*) bochas *fpl*, bolos *mpl*; **bowling alley** *n* bolera; **bowling green** *n* pista para bochas; **bowls** *n* juego de las bochas, bolos *mpl*

bow tie ['bəu'taı] *n* corbata de lazo, pajarita

box [bɒks] *n* (*also*: **cardboard ~**) caja, cajón *m*; (*Theatre*) palco ▷ *vt* encajonar ▷ *vi* (*Sport*) boxear; **boxer** ['bɒksə*] *n* (*person*) boxeador *m*; **boxer shorts** ['bɒksəʃɔːts] *pl n* bóxers; **a pair of boxer shorts** unos bóxers; **boxing** ['bɒksıŋ] *n* (*Sport*) boxeo; **Boxing Day** (*BRIT*) *n* día en que se dan los aguinaldos, 26 de diciembre; **boxing gloves** *npl* guantes *mpl* de boxeo; **boxing ring** *n* ring *m*, cuadrilátero; **box office** *n* taquilla (*SP*), boletería (*LAM*)

boy [bɔı] *n* (*young*) niño *m*; (*older*) muchacho, chico; (*son*) hijo; **boy band** *n* boy band *m* (*grupo musical de chicos*)

boycott ['bɔıkɒt] *n* boicot *m* ▷ *vt* boicotear

boyfriend ['bɔıfrɛnd] *n* novio

bra [brɑː] *n* sostén *m*, sujetador *m*

brace [breıs] *n* (*BRIT*: *also*: **~s** *on teeth*) corrector *m*, aparato; (*tool*) berbiquí *m* ▷ *vt* (*knees, shoulders*) tensionar; **braces** *npl* (*BRIT*) tirantes *mpl*; **to ~ o.s.** (*fig*) prepararse

bracelet ['breɪslɪt] n pulsera, brazalete m

bracket ['brækɪt] n (Tech) soporte m, puntal m; (group) clase f, categoría; (also: **brace ~**) soporte m, abrazadera; (also: **round ~**) paréntesis m inv; (also: **square ~**) corchete m ▷ vt (word etc) poner entre paréntesis

brag [bræg] vi jactarse

braid [breɪd] n (trimming) galón m; (of hair) trenza

brain [breɪn] n cerebro; **brains** npl sesos mpl; **she's got ~s** es muy lista

braise [breɪz] vt cocer a fuego lento

brake [breɪk] n (on vehicle) freno ▷ vi frenar; **brake light** n luz f de frenado

bran [bræn] n salvado

branch [brɑːntʃ] n rama; (Comm) sucursal f; **branch off** vi: **a small road branches off to the right** hay una carretera pequeña que sale hacia la derecha; **branch out** vi (fig) extenderse

brand [brænd] n marca; (fig: type) tipo ▷ vt (cattle) marcar con hierro candente; **brand name** n marca; **brand-new** adj flamante, completamente nuevo

brandy ['brændɪ] n coñac m

brash [bræʃ] adj (forward) descarado

brass [brɑːs] n latón m; **the ~** (Mus) los cobres; **brass band** n banda de metal

brat [bræt] (pej) n mocoso/a

brave [breɪv] adj valiente, valeroso ▷ vt (face up to) desafiar; **bravery** n valor m, valentía

brawl [brɔːl] n pelea, reyerta

Brazil [brə'zɪl] n (el) Brasil; **Brazilian** adj, n brasileño/a m/f

breach [briːtʃ] vt abrir brecha en ▷ n (gap) brecha; (breaking): **~ of contract** infracción f de contrato; **~ of the peace** perturbación f del órden público

bread [bred] n pan m; **breadbin** n panera; **breadbox** (us) n panera; **breadcrumbs** npl migajas fpl; (Culin) pan rallado

breadth [bretθ] n anchura; (fig) amplitud f

break [breɪk] (pt **broke**, pp **broken**) vt romper; (promise) faltar a; (law) violar, infringir; (record) batir ▷ vi romperse, quebrarse; (storm) estallar; (weather) cambiar; (dawn) despuntar; (news etc) darse a conocer ▷ n (gap) abertura; (fracture) fractura; (time) intervalo; (: at school) (período de) recreo; (chance) oportunidad f; **to ~ the news to sb** comunicar la noticia a algn; **break down** vt (figures, data) analizar, descomponer ▷ vi (machine) estropearse; (Aut) averiarse; (person) romper a llorar; (talks) fracasar; **break in** vt (horse etc) domar ▷ vi (burglar) forzar una entrada; (interrupt) interrumpir; **break into** vt fus (house) forzar; **break off** vi (speaker) pararse, detenerse; (branch) partir; **break out** vi estallar; (prisoner) escaparse; **to break out in spots** salirle a algn granos; **break up** vi (ship) hacerse pedazos; (crowd, meeting) disolverse; (marriage) deshacerse; (Scol) terminar (el curso); (line) cortarse ▷ vt (rocks etc) partir; (journey) partir; (fight etc) acabar con; **the line's** or **you're breaking up** se corta; **breakdown** n (Aut) avería; (in communications) interrupción f; (Med: also: **nervous breakdown**) colapso, crisis f nerviosa; (of marriage, talks) fracaso; (of statistics) análisis m inv; **breakdown truck**, **breakdown van** n (camión m) grúa

breakfast ['brekfəst] n desayuno

break: break-in n robo con allanamiento de morada; **breakthrough** n (also fig) avance m

breast [brest] n (of woman) pecho, seno; (chest) pecho; (of bird) pechuga; **breast-feed** (pt, pp **breast-fed**) vt, vi amamantar, criar a los pechos; **breaststroke** n braza (de pecho)

breath [breθ] n aliento, respiración f; **to take a deep ~** respirar hondo; **out of ~** sin aliento, sofocado

Breathalyser ['brɛθəlaɪzə*] (BRIT)
n alcoholímetro

breathe [briːð] vt, vi respirar;
breathe in vt, vi aspirar; **breathe
out** vt, vi espirar; **breathing** n
respiración f

breath: breathless adj sin aliento,
jadeante; **breathtaking** adj
imponente, pasmoso; **breath test** n
prueba de la alcoholemia

bred [brɛd] pt, pp de **breed**

breed [briːd] (pt, pp **bred**) vt criar ▷ vi
reproducirse, procrear ▷ n (Zool) raza,
casta; (type) tipo

breeze [briːz] n brisa

breezy ['briːzɪ] adj de mucho viento,
ventoso; (person) despreocupado

brew [bruː] vt (tea) hacer; (beer)
elaborar ▷ vi (fig: trouble) prepararse;
(storm) amenazar; **brewery** n fábrica
de cerveza, cervecería f

bribe [braɪb] n soborno ▷ vt
sobornar, cohechar; **bribery** n
soborno, cohecho

bric-a-brac ['brɪkəbræk] n inv
baratijas fpl

brick [brɪk] n ladrillo; **bricklayer** n
albañil m

bride [braɪd] n novia; **bridegroom** n
novio; **bridesmaid** n dama de honor

bridge [brɪdʒ] n puente m; (Naut)
puente m de mando; (of nose) caballete
m; (Cards) bridge m ▷ vt (fig): **to ~ a gap**
llenar un vacío

bridle ['braɪdl] n brida, freno

brief [briːf] adj breve, corto ▷ n (Law)
escrito; (task) cometido, encargo
▷ vt informar; **briefs** npl (for men)
calzoncillos mpl; (for women) bragas fpl;
briefcase n cartera (SP), portafolio
(LAM); **briefing** n (Press) informe m;
briefly adv (glance) fugazmente; (say)
en pocas palabras

brigadier [brɪgə'dɪə*] n general m
de brigada

bright [braɪt] adj brillante; (room)
luminoso; (day) de sol; (person: clever)
listo, inteligente; (: lively) alegre;

(colour) vivo; (future) prometedor(a)

brilliant ['brɪljənt] adj brillante; (inf)
fenomenal

brim [brɪm] n borde m; (of hat) ala

brine [braɪn] n (Culin) salmuera

bring [brɪŋ] (pt, pp **brought**) vt (thing,
person: with you) traer; (: to sb) llevar,
conducir; (trouble, satisfaction) causar;
bring about vt ocasionar, producir;
bring back vt volver a traer; (return)
devolver; **bring down** vt (government,
plane) derribar; (price) rebajar; **bring
in** vt (harvest) recoger; (person) hacer
entrar or pasar; (object) traer; (Pol: bill,
law) presentar; (produce: income)
producir, rendir; **bring on** vt (illness,
attack) producir, causar; (player,
substitute) sacar (de la reserva), hacer
salir; **bring out** vt sacar; (book etc)
publicar; (meaning) subrayar; **bring
up** vt subir; (person) educar, criar;
(question) sacar a colación; (food: vomit)
devolver, vomitar

brink [brɪŋk] n borde m

brisk [brɪsk] adj (abrupt: tone) brusco;
(person) enérgico, vigoroso; (pace)
rápido; (trade) activo

bristle ['brɪsl] n cerda ▷ vi: **to ~ in
anger** temblar de rabia

Brit [brɪt] n abbr (inf: = British person)
británico/a

Britain ['brɪtən] n (also: **Great ~**)
Gran Bretaña

British ['brɪtɪʃ] adj británico
▷ npl: **the ~** los británicos; **British Isles**
npl: **the British Isles** las Islas Británicas

Briton ['brɪtən] n británico/a

brittle ['brɪtl] adj quebradizo, frágil

broad [brɔːd] adj ancho; (range)
amplio; (smile) abierto; (general: outlines
etc) general; (accent) cerrado; in **~
daylight** en pleno día; **broadband** n
banda ancha; **broad bean** n haba;
broadcast (pt, pp **~**) n emisión f
▷ vt (Radio) emitir; (TV) transmitir
▷ vi emitir; transmitir; **broaden** vt
ampliar ▷ vi ensancharse; **to broaden
one's mind** hacer más tolerante a

algn; **broadly** adv en general; **broad-minded** adj tolerante, liberal

broccoli ['brɒkəlɪ] n brécol m

brochure ['brəʊʃjʊə*] n folleto

broil [brɔɪl] vt (Culin) asar a la parrilla

broiler ['brɔɪlə*] n (grill) parrilla

broke [brəʊk] pt of **break** ▷ adj (inf) pelado, sin blanca

broken ['brəʊkən] pp of **break** ▷ adj roto; (machine: also: ~ **down**) averiado; ~ **leg** pierna rota; **in ~ English** en un inglés imperfecto

broker ['brəʊkə*] n agente mf, bolsista mf; (insurance broker) agente de seguros

bronchitis [brɒŋ'kaɪtɪs] n bronquitis f

bronze [brɒnz] n bronce m

brooch [brəʊtʃ] n prendedor m, broche m

brood [bru:d] n camada, cría ▷ vi (person) dejarse obsesionar

broom [brum] n escoba; (Bot) retama

Bros. abbr (= Brothers) Hnos

broth [brɒθ] n caldo

brothel ['brɒθl] n burdel m

brother ['brʌðə*] n hermano; **brother-in-law** n cuñado

brought [brɔːt] pt, pp of **bring**

brow [braʊ] n (forehead) frente m; (eyebrow) ceja; (of hill) cumbre f

brown [braʊn] adj (colour) marrón m; (hair) castaño; (tanned) bronceado, moreno ▷ n (colour) marrón m ▷ vt (Culin) dorar; **brown bread** n pan integral

Brownie ['braʊnɪ] n niña exploradora

brown rice n arroz m integral

brown sugar n azúcar m terciado

browse [braʊz] vi (through book) hojear; (in shop) mirar; **browser** n (Comput) navegador m

bruise [bru:z] n cardenal m (sp), moretón m ▷ vt magullar

brunette [bru:'net] n morena

brush [brʌʃ] n cepillo; (for painting, shaving etc) brocha; (artist's) pincel m;

(with police etc) roce m ▷ vt (sweep) barrer; (groom) cepillar; (also: ~ **against**) rozar al pasar

Brussels ['brʌslz] n Bruselas

Brussels sprout n col f de Bruselas

brutal ['bru:tl] adj brutal

B.Sc. abbr (= Bachelor of Science) licenciado en Ciencias

BSE n abbr (= bovine spongiform encephalopathy) encefalopatía f espongiforme bovina

bubble ['bʌbl] n burbuja ▷ vi burbujear, borbotar; **bubble bath** n espuma para el baño; **bubble gum** n chicle m de globo; **bubblejet printer** ['bʌbldʒet-] n impresora de inyección por burbujas

buck [bʌk] n (rabbit) conejo macho; (deer) gamo; (us: inf) dólar m ▷ vi corcovear; **to pass the ~ (to sb)** echar (a algn) el muerto

bucket ['bʌkɪt] n cubo, balde m

buckle ['bʌkl] n hebilla ▷ vt abrochar con hebilla ▷ vi combarse

bud [bʌd] n (of plant) brote m, yema; (of flower) capullo ▷ vi brotar, echar brotes

Buddhism ['bʊdɪzm] n Budismo

Buddhist ['bʊdɪst] adj, n budista m/f

buddy ['bʌdɪ] n (us) compañero, compinche m

budge [bʌdʒ] vt mover; (fig) hacer ceder ▷ vi moverse, ceder

budgerigar ['bʌdʒərɪgɑ:*] n periquito

budget ['bʌdʒɪt] n presupuesto ▷ vi: **to ~ for sth** presupuestar algo

budgie ['bʌdʒɪ] n = **budgerigar**

buff [bʌf] adj (colour) color de ante ▷ n (inf: enthusiast) entusiasta mf

buffalo ['bʌfələʊ] (pl ~ or ~es) n (BRIT) búfalo; (us: bison) bisonte m

buffer ['bʌfə*] n (Comput) memoria intermedia; (Rail) tope m

buffet¹ ['bʌfɪt] vt golpear

buffet² ['bʊfeɪ] n (BRIT: in station) bar m, cafetería; (food) buffet m; **buffet car** (BRIT) n (Rail) coche-comedor m

bug [bʌg] n (esp us: insect) bicho, sabandija; (Comput) error m; (germ) microbio, bacilo; (spy device) micrófono oculto ▷ vt (inf: annoy) fastidiar; (room) poner micrófono oculto en

buggy ['bʌgɪ] n cochecito de niño

build [bɪld] (pt, pp **built**) n (of person) tipo ▷ vt construir, edificar; **build up** ▷ vt (morale, forces, production) acrecentar; (stocks) acumular; **builder** n (contractor) contratista m/f; (structure) construcción f; **building** n (trade) construcción f; (structure) edificio; **building site** n obra; **building society** (BRIT) n sociedad f inmobiliaria

built [bɪlt] pt, pp of **build**; **built-in** adj (cupboard) empotrado; (device) interior, incorporado; **built-up** adj (area) urbanizado

bulb [bʌlb] n (Bot) bulbo; (Elec) bombilla, foco (MEX), bujía (CAM), bombita (RPL)

Bulgaria [bʌl'gɛərɪə] n Bulgaria; **Bulgarian** adj, n búlgaro/a m/f

bulge [bʌldʒ] n bulto, protuberancia ▷ vi bombearse, pandearse; (pocket etc): **to ~ (with)** estar lleno de

bulimia [bə'lɪmɪə] n bulimia

bulimic [bjuː'lɪmɪk] adj, n bulímico/a m/f

bulk [bʌlk] n masa, mole f; **in ~** (Comm) a granel; **the ~ of** la mayor parte de; **bulky** adj voluminoso, abultado

bull [bul] n toro; (male elephant, whale) macho

bulldozer ['buldəuzə*] n bulldozer m

bullet ['bulɪt] n bala

bulletin ['bulɪtɪn] n anuncio, parte m; (journal) boletín m; **bulletin board** n (us) tablón m de anuncios; (Comput) tablero de noticias

bullfight ['bulfaɪt] n corrida de toros; **bullfighter** n torero; **bullfighting** n los toros, el toreo

bully ['bulɪ] n valentón m, matón m ▷ vt intimidar, tiranizar

bum [bʌm] n (inf: backside) culo; (esp us: tramp) vagabundo

bumblebee ['bʌmblbiː] n abejorro

bump [bʌmp] n (blow) tope m, choque m; (jolt) sacudida; (on road etc) bache m; (on head etc) chichón m ▷ vt (strike) chocar contra; **bump into** vt fus chocar contra, tropezar con; (person) topar con; **bumper** n (Aut) parachoques m inv ▷ adj: **bumper crop** or **harvest** cosecha abundante; **bumpy** adj (road) lleno de baches

bun [bʌn] n (BRIT: cake) pastel m; (us: bread) bollo; (of hair) moño

bunch [bʌntʃ] n (of flowers) ramo; (of keys) manojo; (of bananas) piña; (of people) grupo; (pej) pandilla; **bunches** npl (in hair) coletas fpl

bundle ['bʌndl] n bulto, fardo; (of sticks) haz m; (of papers) legajo ▷ vt (also: **~ up**) atar, envolver; **to ~ sth/sb into** meter algo/a algn precipitadamente en

bungalow ['bʌŋgələu] n bungalow m, chalé m

bungee jumping ['bʌndʒiː'dʒʌmpɪŋ] n puenting m, banyi m

bunion ['bʌnjən] n juanete m

bunk [bʌŋk] n litera; **bunk beds** npl literas fpl

bunker ['bʌŋkə*] n (coal store) carbonera; (Mil) refugio; (Golf) bunker m

bunny ['bʌnɪ] n (inf: also: **~ rabbit**) conejito

buoy [bɔɪ] n boya; **buoyant** adj (ship) capaz de flotar; (economy) boyante; (person) optimista

burden ['bəːdn] n carga ▷ vt cargar

bureau [bjuə'rəu] (pl **-x**) n (BRIT: writing desk) escritorio, buró m; (us: chest of drawers) cómoda; (office) oficina, agencia

bureaucracy [bjuə'rɔkrəsɪ] n burocracia

bureaucrat ['bjuərəkræt] n burócrata m/f

bureau de change [-də'ʒɑ̃ʒ] (pl **bureaux de change**) n caja f de cambio

bureaux ['bjuərəuz] npl of **bureau**

burger ['bɜːgə*] n hamburguesa

burglar ['bɜːglə*] n ladrón/ona m/f;
burglar alarm n alarma f antirrobo;
burglary n robo con allanamiento,
robo de una casa

burial ['bɛrɪəl] n entierro

burn [bɜːn] (pt, pp **~ed** or **~t**) vt
quemar; (house) incendiar ▷ vi
quemarse, arder; incendiarse; (sting)
escocer ▷ n quemadura; **burn down**
vt incendiar; **burn out** vt (writer
etc): **to burn o.s. out** agotarse;
burning adj (building etc) en llamas;
(hot: sand etc) abrasador(a); (ambition)
ardiente

Burns' Night [bɜːnz-] n ver recuadro

● BURNS' NIGHT

Cada veinticinco de enero los
escoceses celebran la llamada
Burns' Night (noche de Burns),
en honor al poeta escocés Robert
Burns (1759-1796). Es tradición
hacer una cena en la que, al son
de la música de la gaita escocesa,
se sirve "haggis", plato tradicional
de asadura de cordero cocida
en el estómago del animal,
acompañado de nabos y puré de
patatas. Durante la misma se
recitan poemas del autor y varios
discursos conmemorativos de
carácter festivo.

burnt [bɜːnt] pt, pp of **burn**

burp [bɜːp] (inf) n eructo ▷ vi eructar

burrow ['bʌrəu] n madriguera ▷ vi
hacer una madriguera; (rummage)
hurgar

burst [bɜːst] (pt, pp **~**) vt reventar;
(river: banks etc) romper ▷ vi
reventarse; (tyre) pincharse ▷ n (of
gunfire) ráfaga; (also: **~ pipe**) reventón
m; **a ~ of energy/speed/enthusiasm**
una explosión de energía/un
ímpetu de velocidad/un arranque
de entusiasmo; **to ~ into flames**

estallar en llamas; **to ~ into tears**
deshacerse en lágrimas; **to ~ out
laughing** soltar la carcajada; **to ~
open** abrirse de golpe; **to be ~ing with**
(container) estar lleno a rebosar de;
(: person) reventar por or de; **burst into**
vt fus (room etc) irrumpir en

bury ['bɛrɪ] vt enterrar; (body)
enterrar, sepultar

bus [bʌs] (pl **~es**) n autobús m; **bus
conductor** n cobrador(a) m/f

bush [buʃ] n arbusto; (scrub land)
monte m; **to beat about the ~**
andar(se) con rodeos

business ['bɪznɪs] n (matter) asunto;
(trading) comercio, negocios mpl; (firm)
empresa, casa; (occupation) oficio;
to be away on ~ estar en viaje de
negocios; **it's my ~ to ...** me toca or
corresponde ...; **it's none of my ~** yo no
tengo nada que ver; **he means ~** habla
en serio; **business class** n (Aer) clase f
preferente; **businesslike** adj eficiente;
businessman (irreg) n hombre m de
negocios; **business trip** n viaje m de
negocios; **businesswoman** (irreg) n
mujer f de negocios

busker ['bʌskə*] (BRIT) n músico/a
ambulante

bus: bus pass n bonobús; **bus shelter**
n parada cubierta; **bus station** n
estación f de autobuses; **bus-stop** n
parada de autobús

bust [bʌst] n (Anat) pecho; (sculpture)
busto ▷ adj (inf: broken) roto,
estropeado; **to go ~** quebrar

bustling ['bʌslɪŋ] adj (town)
animado, bullicioso

busy ['bɪzɪ] adj ocupado, atareado;
(shop, street) concurrido, animado;
(Tel: line) comunicando ▷ vt: **to ~ o.s.
with** ocuparse en; **busy signal** (US) n
(Tel) señal f de comunicando

○ KEYWORD

but [bʌt] conj 1 pero; **he's not very
bright, but he's hard-working** no es

muy inteligente, pero es trabajador
2 (*in direct contradiction*) sino; **he's not English but French** no es inglés sino francés; **he didn't sing but he shouted** no cantó sino que gritó
3 (*showing disagreement, surprise etc*): **but that's far too expensive!** ¡pero eso es carísimo!; **but it does work!** ¡(pero) sí que funciona!
▷ *prep* (*apart from, except*) menos, salvo; **we've had nothing but trouble** no hemos tenido más que problemas; **no-one but him can do it** nadie más que él puede hacerlo; **who but a lunatic would do such a thing?** ¿sólo un loco haría una cosa así?; **but for you/your help** si no fuera por ti/tu ayuda; **anything but that** cualquier cosa menos eso
▷ *adv* (*just, only*): **she's but a child** no es más que una niña; **had I but known** si lo hubiera sabido; **I can but try** al menos lo puedo intentar; **it's all but finished** está casi acabado

butcher ['butʃə*] *n* carnicero ▷ *vt* hacer una carnicería con; (*cattle etc*) matar; **butcher's (shop)** *n* carnicería
butler ['bʌtlə*] *n* mayordomo
butt [bʌt] *n* (*barrel*) tonel *m*; (*of gun*) culata; (*of cigarette*) colilla; (BRIT: *target*) blanco ▷ *vt* dar cabezadas contra, top(et)ar
butter ['bʌtə*] *n* mantequilla ▷ *vt* untar con mantequilla; **buttercup** *n* botón *m* de oro
butterfly ['bʌtəflaɪ] *n* mariposa; (*Swimming: also*: ~ **stroke**) braza de mariposa
buttocks ['bʌtəks] *npl* nalgas *fpl*
button ['bʌtn] *n* botón *m*; (*us*) placa, chapa ▷ *vt* (*also*: ~ **up**) abotonar, abrochar ▷ *vi* abrocharse
buy [baɪ] (*pt, pp* **bought**) *vt* comprar ▷ *n* compra; **to ~ sb sth/sth from sb** comprarle algo a algn; **to ~ sb a drink** invitar a algn a tomar algo; **buy out** *vt*

(*partner*) comprar la parte de; **buy up** *vt* (*property*) acaparar; (*stock*) comprar todas las existencias de; **buyer** *n* comprador(a) *m/f*
buzz [bʌz] *n* zumbido; (*inf: phone call*) llamada (por teléfono) ▷ *vi* zumbar; **buzzer** *n* timbre *m*

○ **KEYWORD**

by [baɪ] *prep* **1** (*referring to cause, agent*) por; de; **killed by lightning** muerto por un relámpago; **a painting by Picasso** un cuadro de Picasso
2 (*referring to method, manner, means*): **by bus/car/train** en autobús/coche/ tren; **to pay by cheque** pagar con un cheque; **by moonlight/candlelight** a la luz de la luna/una vela; **by saving hard he ...** ahorrando ...
3 (*via, through*) por; **we came by Dover** vinimos por Dover
4 (*close to, past*): **the house by the river** la casa junto al río; **she rushed by me** pasó a mi lado como una exhalación; **I go by the post office every day** paso por delante de Correos todos los días
5 (*time: not later than*) para; (: *during*): **by daylight** de día; **by 4 o'clock** para las cuatro; **by this time tomorrow** mañana a estas horas; **by the time I got here it was too late** cuando llegué ya era demasiado tarde
6 (*amount*): **by the metre/kilo** por metro/kilo; **paid by the hour** pagado por hora
7 (*Math, measure*): **to divide/multiply by 3** dividir/multiplicar por 3; **a room 3 metres by 4** una habitación de 3 metros por 4; **it's broader by a metre** es un metro más ancho
8 (*according to*) según, de acuerdo con; **it's 3 o'clock by my watch** según mi reloj, son las tres; **it's all right by me** por mí, está bien
9: (**all**) **by oneself** *etc* todo solo; **he did it (all) by himself** lo hizo él solo;

**he was standing (all) by himself in a
corner** estaba de pie solo en un rincón
10: by the way a propósito, por cierto;
this wasn't my idea, by the way
pues, no fue idea mía
▷ *adv* 1 *see* **go; pass** *etc*
2: by and by finalmente; **they'll come
back by and by** acabarán volviendo;
by and large en líneas generales, en
general

bye(-bye) [ˈbaɪˈbaɪ)] *excl* adiós,
hasta luego
by-election (BRIT) *n* elección *f* parcial
bypass [ˈbaɪpɑːs] *n* carretera de
circunvalación; (*Med*) (operación *f* de)
by-pass *f* ▷ *vt* evitar
byte [baɪt] *n* (*Comput*) byte *m*, octeto

C [siː] *n* (*Mus*) do *m*
cab [kæb] *n* taxi *m*; (*of truck*) cabina
cabaret [ˈkæbəreɪ] *n* cabaret *m*
cabbage [ˈkæbɪdʒ] *n* col *f*, berza
cabin [ˈkæbɪn] *n* cabaña; (*on ship*)
camarote *m*; (*on plane*) cabina; **cabin
crew** *n* tripulación *f* de cabina
cabinet [ˈkæbɪnɪt] *n* (*Pol*) consejo
de ministros; (*furniture*) armario; (*also:
display* ~) vitrina; **cabinet minister** *n*
ministro/a (del gabinete)
cable [ˈkeɪbl] *n* cable *m* ▷ *vt*
cablegrafiar; **cable car** *n* teleférico;
cable television *n* televisión *f* por
cable
cactus [ˈkæktəs] *n* (*pl* **cacti**) cacto
café [ˈkæfeɪ] *n* café *m*
cafeteria [kæfɪˈtɪərɪə] *n* cafetería
caffein(e) [ˈkæfiːn] *n* cafeína
cage [keɪdʒ] *n* jaula
cagoule [kəˈguːl] *n* chubasquero
cake [keɪk] *n* (*Culin: large*) tarta;
(: *small*) pastel *m*; (*of soap*) pastilla
calcium [ˈkælsɪəm] *n* calcio
calculate [ˈkælkjuleɪt] *vt* calcular;

calculation [-ˈleɪʃən] n cálculo, cómputo; (estimate) cálculo

calculator n calculadora

calendar [ˈkæləndə*] n calendario

calf [kɑːf] (pl **calves**) n (of cow) ternero, becerro; (of other animals) cría; (also: **~skin**) piel f de becerro; (Anat) pantorrilla

calibre [ˈkælɪbə*] (US **caliber**) n calibre m

call [kɔːl] vt llamar; (meeting) convocar ▷ vi (shout) llamar; (Tel) llamar (por teléfono); (visit: also: **~ in, ~ round**) hacer una visita ▷ n llamada; (of bird) canto; **to be ~ed** llamarse; **on ~** (on duty) de guardia; **call back** vi (return) volver; (Tel) volver a llamar; **call for** vt fus (demand) pedir, exigir; (fetch) pasar a recoger; **call in** vi (doctor, expert, police) llamar; **call off** vt (cancel: meeting, race) cancelar; (: deal) anular; (: strike) desconvocar; **call on** vt fus (visit) visitar; (turn to) acudir a; **call out** vi gritar; **call up** vt (Mil) llamar al servicio militar; (Tel) llamar; **callbox** (BRIT) n cabina telefónica; **call centre** (US **call center**) n centro de atención al cliente; **caller** n visita; (Tel) usuario/a

callous [ˈkæləs] adj insensible, cruel

calm [kɑːm] adj tranquilo; (sea) liso, en calma ▷ n calma, tranquilidad f ▷ vt calmar, tranquilizar; **calm down** vi calmarse, tranquilizarse ▷ vt calmar, tranquilizar; **calmly** [ˈkɑːmlɪ] adv tranquilamente, con calma

Calor gas® [ˈkælə*-] n butano

calorie [ˈkælərɪ] n caloría

calves [kɑːvz] npl of **calf**

camcorder [ˈkæmkɔːdə*] n videocámara

came [keɪm] pt of **come**

camel [ˈkæməl] n camello

camera [ˈkæmərə] n máquina fotográfica; (Cinema, TV) cámara; **in ~** (Law) a puerta cerrada; **cameraman** (irreg) n cámara m; **camera phone** n teléfono con cámara

camouflage [ˈkæməflɑːʒ] n camuflaje m ▷ vt camuflar

camp [kæmp] n campamento, camping m; (Mil) campamento; (for prisoners) campo; (fig: faction) bando ▷ vi acampar ▷ adj afectado, afeminado

campaign [kæmˈpeɪn] n (Mil, Pol etc) campaña ▷ vi hacer campaña; **campaigner** n: **campaigner for** defensor(a) m/f de

camp: campbed (BRIT) n cama de campaña; **camper** n campista mf; (vehicle) caravana; **campground** (US) n camping m, campamento; **camping** n camping m; **to go camping** hacer camping; **campsite** n camping m

campus [ˈkæmpəs] n ciudad f universitaria

can¹ [kæn] n (of oil, water) bidón m; (tin) lata, bote m ▷ vt enlatar

○ **KEYWORD**

can² [kæn] (negative **cannot, can't**, conditional and pt **could**) aux vb 1 (be able to) poder; **you can do it if you try** puedes hacerlo si lo intentas; **I can't see you** no te veo

2 (know how to) saber: **I can swim/play tennis/drive** sé nadar/jugar al tenis/conducir; **can you speak French?** ¿hablas o sabes hablar francés?

3 (may) poder: **can I use your phone?** ¿me dejas o puedo usar tu teléfono?

4 (expressing disbelief, puzzlement etc): **it can't be true!** ¡no puede ser (verdad)!; **what CAN he want?** ¿qué querrá?

5 (expressing possibility, suggestion etc): **he could be in the library** podría estar en la biblioteca; **she could have been delayed** pudo haberse retrasado

Canada [ˈkænədə] n (el) Canadá; **Canadian** [kəˈneɪdɪən] adj, n canadiense mf

canal [kəˈnæl] n canal m

canary [kəˈnɛərɪ] n canario

Canary Islands [kəˈnɛərɪˈaɪləndz]

npl: **the ~** las (Islas) Canarias

cancel ['kænsəl] *vt* cancelar; *(train)* suprimir; *(cross out)* tachar, borrar; **cancellation** [-'leɪʃən] *n* cancelación *f*; supresión *f*

Cancer ['kænsə*] *n (Astrology)* Cáncer *m*

cancer ['kænsə*] *n* cáncer *m*

candidate ['kændɪdeɪt] *n* candidato/a

candle ['kændl] *n* vela; *(in church)* cirio; **candlestick** *n (single)* candelero; *(low)* palmatoria; *(bigger, ornate)* candelabro

candy ['kændɪ] *n* azúcar *m* cande; *(us)* caramelo; **candy bar** *(us) n* barrita *(dulce)*; **candyfloss** *(BRIT) n* algodón *m (azucarado)*

cane [keɪn] *n (Bot)* caña; *(stick)* vara, palmeta; *(for furniture)* mimbre *f* ▷ *vt (BRIT: Scol)* castigar *(con vara)*

cannabis ['kænəbɪs] *n* marijuana

canned [kænd] *adj* en lata, de lata

cannon ['kænən] *(pl ~ or ~s) n* cañón *m*

cannot ['kænɔt] = **can not**

canoe [kə'nu:] *n* canoa; *(Sport)* piragua; **canoeing** *n* piragüismo

canon ['kænən] *n (clergyman)* canónigo; *(standard)* canon *m*

can-opener ['kænəupnə*] *n* abrelatas *m inv*

can't [kænt] = **can not**

canteen [kæn'ti:n] *n (eating place)* cantina; *(BRIT: of cutlery)* juego

canter ['kæntə*] *vi* ir a medio galope

canvas ['kænvəs] *n (material)* lona; *(painting)* lienzo; *(Naut)* velas *fpl*

canvass ['kænvəs] *vi* **to ~ for** solicitar votos por ▷ *vt (Comm)* sondear

canyon ['kænjən] *n* cañón *m*

cap [kæp] *n (hat)* gorra; *(of pen)* capuchón *m*; *(of bottle)* tapa, tapón *m*; *(contraceptive)* diafragma *m*; *(for toy gun)* cápsula ▷ *vt (outdo)* superar; *(limit)*

recortar

capability [keɪpə'bɪlɪtɪ] *n* capacidad *f*

capable ['keɪpəbl] *adj* capaz

capacity [kə'pæsɪtɪ] *n* capacidad *f*; *(position)* calidad *f*

cape [keɪp] *n* capa; *(Geo)* cabo

caper ['keɪpə*] *n (Culin: gen pl)* alcaparra; *(prank)* broma

capital ['kæpɪtl] *n (also: ~ city)* capital *f*; *(money)* capital *m*; *(also: ~ letter)* mayúscula; **capitalism** *n* capitalismo; **capitalist** *adj*, *n* capitalista *mf*; **capital punishment** *n* pena de muerte

Capitol ['kæpɪtl] *n ver recuadro*

Capricorn ['kæprɪkɔ:n] *n* Capricornio

capsize [kæp'saɪz] *vt* volcar, hacer zozobrar ▷ *vi* volcarse, zozobrar

capsule ['kæpsju:l] *n* cápsula

captain ['kæptɪn] *n* capitán *m*

caption ['kæpʃən] *n (heading)* título; *(to picture)* leyenda

captivity [kæp'tɪvɪtɪ] *n* cautiverio

capture ['kæptʃə*] *vt* prender, apresar; *(animal, Comput)* capturar; *(place)* tomar; *(attention)* captar, llamar ▷ *n* apresamiento; captura; toma; *(data capture)* formulación *f* de datos

car [ka:*] *n* coche *m*, carro *(LAM)*, automóvil *m*; *(us Rail)* vagón *m*

carafe [kə'ræf] *n* jarra

caramel ['kærəməl] *n* caramelo

carat ['kærət] *n* quilate *m*

caravan ['kærəvæn] (BRIT) n caravana, ruló f; (in desert) caravana; **caravan site** (BRIT) n camping m para caravanas

carbohydrate [kɑːbəʊ'haɪdreɪt] n hidrato de carbono; (food) fécula

carbon ['kɑːbən] n carbono; **carbon dioxide** n dióxido de carbono, anhídrido carbónico; **carbon footprint** n huella de carbono; **carbon monoxide** n monóxido de carbono

car boot sale n mercadillo organizado en un aparcamiento, en el que se exponen las mercancías en el maletero del coche

carburettor [kɑːbjʊ'rɛtə*] (US **carburetor**) n carburador m

card [kɑːd] n (material) cartulina; (index card etc) ficha; (playing card) carta, naipe m; (visiting card, greetings card etc) tarjeta; **cardboard** n cartón m; **card game** n juego de naipes o cartas

cardigan ['kɑːdɪgən] n rebeca

cardinal ['kɑːdɪnl] adj cardinal; (importance, principal) esencial ▷ n cardenal m

cardphone ['kɑːdfəʊn] n cabina que funciona con tarjetas telefónicas

care [kɛə*] n cuidado; (worry) inquietud f; (charge) cargo, custodia ▷ vi: **to ~ about** (person, animal) tener cariño a; (thing, idea) preocuparse por; **~ of** en casa de, al cuidado de; **in sb's ~** a cargo de algn; **to take ~** cuidarse de, tener cuidado de; **to take ~ of** cuidar; (problem etc) ocuparse de; **I don't ~** no me importa; **I couldn't ~ less** eso me trae sin cuidado; **care for** vt fus cuidar a; (like) querer

career [kə'rɪə*] n profesión f; (in work, school) carrera ▷ vi (also: **~ along**) correr a toda velocidad

care: **carefree** adj despreocupado; **careful** adj cuidadoso; (cautious) cauteloso; **(be) careful!** ¡tenga cuidado!; **carefully** adv con cuidado; **caregiver** (US) n (professional) enfermero/a m/f; (unpaid) persona que

cuida a un pariente o vecino; **careless** adj descuidado; (heedless) poco atento; **carelessness** n descuido, falta de atención; **carer** ['kɛərə*] n (professional) enfermero/a m/f; (unpaid) persona que cuida a un pariente o vecino; **caretaker** n portero/a, conserje mf

car-ferry ['kɑːfɛrɪ] n transbordador m para coches

cargo ['kɑːgəʊ] (pl **-es**) n cargamento, carga

car hire n alquiler m de automóviles

Caribbean [kærɪ'biːən] n: **the ~ (Sea)** el (Mar) Caribe

caring ['kɛərɪŋ] adj humanitario; (behaviour) afectuoso

carnation [kɑː'neɪʃən] n clavel m

carnival ['kɑːnɪvəl] n carnaval m; (US: funfair) parque m de atracciones

carol ['kærəl] n: **(Christmas) ~** villancico

carousel [kærə'sɛl] (US) n tiovivo, caballitos mpl

car park (BRIT) n aparcamiento, parking m

carpenter ['kɑːpɪntə*] n carpintero/a

carpet ['kɑːpɪt] n alfombra; (fitted) moqueta ▷ vt alfombrar

car rental (US) n alquiler m de coches

carriage ['kærɪdʒ] n (BRIT Rail) vagón m; (horse-drawn) coche m; (of goods) transporte m; (: cost) porte m, flete m; **carriageway** (BRIT) n (part of road) calzada

carrier ['kærɪə*] n (transport company) transportista, empresa de transportes; (Med) portador/a m/f; **carrier bag** (BRIT) n bolsa de papel o plástico

carrot ['kærət] n zanahoria

carry ['kærɪ] vt (person) llevar; (transport) transportar; (involve: responsibilities etc) entrañar, implicar; (Med) ser portador de ▷ vi (sound) oírse; **to get carried away** (fig) entusiasmarse; **carry on** vi (continue) seguir (adelante), continuar ▷ vt proseguir, continuar; **carry out** vt (orders) cumplir; (investigation) llevar a cabo, realizar

cart [kɑːt] n carro, carreta ⊳vt (inf: transport) acarrear

carton ['kɑːtən] n (box) caja (de cartón); (of milk etc) bote m; (of yogurt) tarrina

cartoon [kɑːˈtuːn] n (Press) caricatura; (comic strip) tira cómica; (film) dibujos mpl animados

cartridge ['kɑːtrɪdʒ] n (for gun) cartucho; (of pen) recambio

carve [kɑːv] vt (meat) trinchar; (wood, stone) cincelar, esculpir; (initials etc) grabar; **carving** n (object) escultura; (design) talla; (art) tallado

car wash n lavado de coches

case [keɪs] n (container) caja; (Med) caso; (for jewels etc) estuche m; (Law) causa, proceso; (BRIT: also: **suit**-) maleta; **in** ~ **of** en caso de; **in any** ~ en todo caso; **just in** ~ por si acaso

cash [kæʃ] n dinero en efectivo, dinero contante ⊳vt cobrar, hacer efectivo; **to pay (in)** ~ pagar al contado; ~ **on delivery** cóbrese al entregar; **cashback** n (discount) devolución f; (at supermarket etc) retirada de dinero en efectivo de un establecimiento donde se ha pagado con tarjeta; también dinero retirado; **cash card** n tarjeta f dinero; **cash desk** (BRIT) n caja; **cash dispenser** n cajero automático

cashew [kæˈʃuː] n (also: ~ **nut**) anacardo

cashier [kæˈʃɪə*] n cajero/a

cashmere ['kæʃmɪə*] n cachemira

cash point n cajero automático

cash register n caja

casino [kəˈsiːnəu] n casino

casket ['kɑːskɪt] n cofre m, estuche m; (US: coffin) ataúd m

casserole ['kæsərəul] n (food, pot) cazuela

cassette [kæˈsɛt] n casete f; **cassette player, cassette recorder** n casete m

cast [kɑːst] (pt, pp ~) vt (throw) echar, arrojar, lanzar; (glance, eyes) dirigir;

(Theatre): **to ~ sb as Othello** dar a algn el papel de Otelo ⊳vi (Fishing) lanzar ⊳n (Theatre) reparto; (also: **plaster** ~) vaciado; **to ~ one's vote** votar; **to ~ doubt on** suscitar dudas acerca de; **cast off** vi (Naut) desamarrar; (Knitting) cerrar (los puntos)

castanets [kæstəˈnɛts] npl castañuelas fpl

caster sugar ['kɑːstə*-] (BRIT) n azúcar m extrafino

Castile [kæsˈtiːl] n Castilla; **Castilian** adj, n castellano/a m/f

cast-iron ['kɑːstaɪən] adj (lit) (hecho) de hierro fundido; (fig: case) irrebatible

castle ['kɑːsl] n castillo; (Chess) torre f

casual ['kæʒjul] adj fortuito; (irregular: work etc) eventual, temporero; (unconcerned) despreocupado; (clothes) informal

> Be careful not to translate **casual** by the Spanish word casual.

casualty ['kæʒjultɪ] n víctima, herido/a; (dead) muerto/a; (Med: department) urgencias fpl

cat [kæt] n gato; (big cat) felino

Catalan ['kætəlæn] adj, n catalán/ana m/f

catalogue ['kætəlɔg] (us **catalog**) n catálogo ⊳vt catalogar

Catalonia [kætəˈləunɪə] n Cataluña

catalytic converter [kætəˈlɪtɪkkənˈvəːtə*] n catalizador m

cataract ['kætərækt] n (Med) cataratas fpl

catarrh [kəˈtɑː*] n catarro

catastrophe [kəˈtæstrəfɪ] n catástrofe f

catch [kætʃ] (pt, pp **caught**) vt coger (SP), agarrar (LAM); (arrest) detener; (grasp) asir; (breath) contener; (surprise: person) sorprender; (attract: attention) captar; (hear) oír; (Med) contagiarse de, coger; (also: ~ **up**) alcanzar ⊳vi (fire) encenderse; (in branches etc) enredarse ⊳n (fish etc) pesca; (act of catching) cogida; (hidden problem) dificultad f; (game)

pilla-pilla; (of lock) pestillo, cerradura;
to ~ fire encenderse; **to ~ sight of**
divisar; **catch up** vi (fig) ponerse al
día; **catching** ['kætʃɪŋ] adj (Med)
contagioso

category ['kætɪgərɪ] n categoría,
clase f

cater ['keɪtə*] vi: **to ~ for** (BRIT)
abastecer a; (needs) atender a;
(Comm: parties etc) proveer comida a

caterpillar ['kætəpɪlə*] n oruga,
gusano

cathedral [kə'θiːdrəl] n catedral f

Catholic ['kæθəlɪk] adj, n (Rel)
católico/a m/f

Catseye® ['kæts'aɪ] (BRIT) n (Aut)
catafoto

cattle ['kætl] npl ganado

catwalk ['kætwɔːk] n pasarela

caught [kɔːt] pt, pp of **catch**

cauliflower ['kɔlɪflauə*] n coliflor f

cause [kɔːz] n causa, motivo, razón f;
(principle: also Pol) causa ▷ vt causar

caution ['kɔːʃən] n cautela,
prudencia; (warning) advertencia,
amonestación f ▷ vt amonestar;
cautious adj cauteloso, prudente,
precavido

cave [keɪv] n cueva, caverna; **cave in**
vi (roof etc) derrumbarse, hundirse

caviar(e) ['kævɪɑː*] n caviar m

cavity ['kævɪtɪ] n hueco, cavidad f

cc abbr (= cubic centimetres) c.c.; (= carbon
copy) copia hecha con papel del carbón

CCTV n abbr (= closed-circuit television)
circuito cerrado de televisión

CD n abbr (= compact disc) CD m; (player)
(reproductor m de) CD; **CD player** n
reproductor m de CD; **CD-ROM**
[siːdiː'rɔm] n abbr (= CD-ROM); **CD
writer** n grabadora de CD

cease [siːs] vt, vi cesar; **ceasefire** n
alto m el fuego

cedar ['siːdə*] n cedro

ceilidh ['keɪlɪ] n baile con música y
danzas tradicionales escocesas o irlandesas

ceiling ['siːlɪŋ] n techo; (fig) límite m

celebrate ['selɪbreɪt] vt celebrar ▷ vi

divertirse; **celebration** [-'breɪʃən] n
fiesta, celebración f

celebrity [sɪ'lebrɪtɪ] n celebridad f

celery ['selərɪ] n apio

cell [sel] n celda; (Biol) célula; (Elec)
elemento

cellar ['selə*] n sótano; (for wine)
bodega

cello ['tʃeləu] n violoncelo

Cellophane® ['seləfeɪn] n celofán m

cellphone ['selfəʊn] n móvil

Celsius ['selsɪəs] adj centígrado

Celtic ['keltɪk] adj celta

cement [sə'ment] n cemento

cemetery ['semɪtrɪ] n cementerio

censor ['sensə*] n censor m ▷ vt (cut)
censurar; **censorship** n censura

census ['sensəs] n censo

cent [sent] n (unit of dollar) centavo,
céntimo; (unit of euro) céntimo; see
also **per**

centenary [sen'tiːnərɪ] n
centenario

centennial [sen'tenɪəl] (US) n
centenario

center ['sentə*] (US) = **centre**

centi... [sentɪ] prefix: **centigrade**
adj centígrado; **centimetre** (US
centimeter) n centímetro; **centipede**
['sentɪpiːd] n ciempiés m inv

central ['sentrəl] adj central; (of
house etc) céntrico; **Central America**
n Centroamérica; **central heating**
n calefacción f central; **central
reservation** n (BRIT Aut) mediana

centre ['sentə*] (US **center**) n centro;
(fig) núcleo ▷ vt centrar; **centre-
forward** n (Sport) delantero centro;
centre-half n (Sport) medio centro

century ['sentjurɪ] n siglo; **20th ~**
siglo veinte

CEO n abbr = **chief executive officer**

ceramic [sɪ'ræmɪk] adj cerámico

cereal ['siːrɪəl] n cereal m

ceremony ['serɪmənɪ] n ceremonia;
to stand on ~ hacer ceremonias, estar
de cumplido

certain ['sɜːtən] adj seguro;

(person): **a ~ Mr Smith** un tal Sr. Smith;
(particular, some) cierto; **for ~ a** ciencia
cierta; **certainly** adv (undoubtedly)
ciertamente; (of course) desde luego,
por supuesto; **certainty** n certeza,
certidumbre f, seguridad f; (inevitability)
certeza

certificate [sə'tɪfɪkɪt] n certificado
certify ['sɜːtɪfaɪ] vt certificar; (award
diploma to) conceder un diploma a;
(declare insane) declarar loco

cf. abbr (= compare) cfr

CFC n abbr (= chlorofluorocarbon) CFC m

chain [tʃeɪn] n cadena; (of mountains)
cordillera; (of events) sucesión f ▷ vt
(also: **~ up**) encadenar; **chain-smoke** vi
fumar un cigarrillo tras otro

chair [tʃeə*] n silla; (armchair) sillón
m, butaca f; (of university) cátedra f;
(of meeting etc) presidencia ▷ vt
(meeting) presidir; **chairlift** n telesilla;
chairman (irreg) n presidente m;
chairperson n presidente/a m/f;
chairwoman (irreg) n presidenta

chalet ['ʃæleɪ] n chalet m (de madera)

chalk [tʃɔːk] n (Geo) creta; (for writing)
tiza, gis m (MEX); **chalkboard** (US) n
pizarrón (LAM), pizarra (SP)

challenge ['tʃælɪndʒ] n desafío, reto
▷ vt desafiar, retar; (statement, right)
poner en duda; **to ~ sb to do sth** retar a
algn a que haga algo; **challenging** adj
exigente; (tone) de desafío

chamber ['tʃeɪmbə*] n cámara,
sala; (Pol) cámara; (BRIT Law: gen pl)
despacho; **~ of commerce** cámara de
comercio; **chambermaid** n camarera

champagne [ʃæm'peɪn] n
champaña m, champán m

champion ['tʃæmpɪən] n campeón/
ona m/f; (of cause) defensor/a m/f;
championship n campeonato

chance [tʃɑːns] n (opportunity)
ocasión f, oportunidad f; (likelihood)
posibilidad f; (risk) riesgo ▷ vt
arriesgar, probar ▷ adj fortuito,
casual; **to ~ it** arriesgarse, intentarlo;
to take a ~ arriesgarse; **by ~** por

casualidad

chancellor ['tʃɑːnsələ*] n canciller
m; **Chancellor of the Exchequer** (BRIT)
n Ministro de Hacienda

chandelier [ʃændə'lɪə*] n araña
(de luces)

change [tʃeɪndʒ] vt cambiar;
(replace) cambiar, reemplazar; (gear,
clothes, job) cambiar de; (transform)
transformar ▷ vi cambiar(se); (change
trains) hacer transbordo; (traffic lights)
cambiar de color; (be transformed): **to
~ into** transformarse en ▷ n
cambio; (alteration) modificación f;
(transformation) transformación f; (of
clothes) muda; (coins) suelto, sencillo;
(money returned) vuelta; **to ~ gear** (Aut)
cambiar de marcha; **to ~ one's mind**
cambiar de opinión o idea; **for a ~** para
variar; **change over** vi (from sth to sth)
cambiar; (players etc) cambiar(se) ▷ vt
cambiar; **changeable** adj (weather)
cambiable; **change machine** n
máquina de cambio; **changing room**
(BRIT) n vestuario

channel ['tʃænl] n (TV) canal m;
(of river) cauce m; (groove) conducto;
(fig: medium) medio ▷ vt (river etc)
encauzar; **the (English) C~** el Canal
(de la Mancha); **the C~ Islands** las Islas
Normandas; **Channel Tunnel** the
Channel Tunnel el túnel del Canal de la
Mancha, el Eurotúnel

chant [tʃɑːnt] n (of crowd) gritos mpl;
(Rel) canto ▷ vt (slogan, word) repetir
a gritos

chaos ['keɪɒs] n caos m

chaotic [keɪ'ɒtɪk] adj caótico

chap [tʃæp] (BRIT: inf) n (man) tío, tipo

chapel ['tʃæpəl] n capilla

chapped [tʃæpt] adj agrietado

chapter ['tʃæptə*] n capítulo

character ['kærɪktə*] n carácter m,
naturaleza, índole f; (moral strength,
personality) carácter; (in novel, film)
personaje m; **characteristic** [-'rɪstɪk]
adj característico ▷ n característica;
characterize ['kærɪktəraɪz] vt

caracterizar

charcoal ['tʃɑːkəʊl] n carbón m vegetal; (Art) carboncillo

charge [tʃɑːdʒ] n (Law) cargo, acusación f; (cost) precio, coste m; (responsibility) responsabilidad f; (Law): to ~ (with) acusar (de); (battery) cargar; (price) pedir; (customer) cobrar ▷ vi precipitarse; (Mil) cargar, atacar; **charge card** n tarjeta de cuenta; **charger** n (also: **battery charger**) cargador m (de baterías)

charismatic [kærɪzˈmætɪk] adj carismático

charity ['tʃærɪtɪ] n caridad f; (organization) sociedad f benéfica; (money, gifts) limosnas fpl; **charity shop** n (BRIT) tienda de artículos de segunda mano que dedica su recaudación a causas benéficas

charm [tʃɑːm] n encanto, atractivo; (talisman) hechizo; (on bracelet) dije m ▷ vt encantar; **charming** adj encantador/a

chart [tʃɑːt] n (diagram) cuadro; (graph) gráfica f; (map) carta de navegación ▷ vt (course) trazar; (progress) seguir; **charts** npl (Top 40): **the ~s** n los 40 principales (SP)

charter ['tʃɑːtə*] vt (plane) alquilar; (ship) fletar ▷ n (document) carta; (of university, company) estatutos mpl; **chartered accountant**(BRIT) n contable m/f diplomado/a; **charter flight** n vuelo chárter

chase [tʃeɪs] vt (pursue) perseguir; (also: ~ **away**) ahuyentar ▷ n persecución f

chat [tʃæt] vi (also: **have a ~**) charlar; (on Internet) chatear ▷ n charla; **chat up** vt (inf: girl) ligar con, enrollarse con; **chat room** n (Internet) chat m, canal m de charla; **chat show**(BRIT) n programa m de entrevistas

chatter ['tʃætə*] vi (person) charlar; (teeth) castañetear ▷ n (of birds) parloteo; (of people) charla, cháchara

chauffeur ['ʃəʊfə*] n chófer m

chauvinist ['ʃəʊvɪnɪst] n (male chauvinist) machista m; (nationalist) chovinista mf

cheap [tʃiːp] adj barato; (joke) de mal gusto; (poor quality) de mala calidad ▷ adv barato; **cheap day return** n billete de ida y vuelta el mismo día; **cheaply** adv barato, a bajo precio

cheat [tʃiːt] vi hacer trampa ▷ vt: to ~ **sb (out of sth)** estafar (algo) a algn ▷ n (person) tramposo/a; **cheat on** vt fus engañar

Chechnya ['tʃəʊvɪnɪst] n Chechenia

check [tʃek] vt (examine) controlar; (facts) comprobar; (halt) parar, detener; (restrain) refrenar, restringir ▷ n (inspection) control m, inspección f; (curb) freno; (us: bill) nota, cuenta; (us)= **cheque**; (pattern: gen pl) cuadro; **check in** vi (at hotel) firmar el registro; (at airport) facturar el equipaje ▷ vt (luggage) facturar; **check off** vt (esp us: check) comprobar; (cross off) tachar; **check out** vi (of hotel) marcharse; **check up** vi: to **check up on sth** comprobar algo; to **check up on sb** investigar a algn; **checkbook**(us)= **chequebook**; **checked** adj a cuadros; **checkers**(us) n juego de damas; **check-in** n (also: **check-in desk**: at airport) mostrador m de facturación; **checking account**(us) n cuenta corriente; **checklist** n lista (de control); **checkmate** n jaque m mate; **checkout** n (in supermarket) caja; **checkpoint** n (punto de) control m; **checkroom** (us) n consigna; **checkup** n (Med) reconocimiento general

cheddar ['tʃedə*] n (also: ~ **cheese**) queso m cheddar

cheek [tʃiːk] n mejilla; (impudence) descaro; **what a ~!** ¡qué cara!; **cheekbone** n pómulo; **cheeky** adj fresco, descarado

cheer [tʃɪə*] vi vitorear, aplaudir; (gladden) alegrar, animar ▷ vi dar vivas ▷ n viva m; **cheer up** vi animarse ▷ vt alegrar, animar; **cheerful** adj alegre

cheerio [tʃɪərɪ'əʊ] (BRIT) excl ¡hasta luego!

cheerleader ['tʃɪəliːdə*] n animador(a) m/f

cheese [tʃiːz] n queso; **cheeseburger** n hamburguesa con queso; **cheesecake** n pastel m de queso

chef [ʃɛf] n jefe/a m/f de cocina

chemical ['kɛmɪkəl] adj químico ▷ n producto químico

chemist ['kɛmɪst] n (BRIT: pharmacist) farmacéutico/a; (scientist) químico/a; **chemistry** n química; **chemist's (shop)** (BRIT) n farmacia

cheque [tʃɛk] (US **check**) n cheque m; **chequebook** n talonario de cheques (SP), chequera (LAM); **cheque card** n tarjeta de cheque

cherry ['tʃɛrɪ] n cereza; (also: **~ tree**) cerezo

chess [tʃɛs] n ajedrez m

chest [tʃɛst] n (Anat) pecho; (box) cofre m, cajón m

chestnut ['tʃɛsnʌt] n castaña; (also: **~ tree**) castaño

chest of drawers n cómoda

chew [tʃuː] vt mascar, masticar; **chewing gum** n chicle m

chic [ʃiːk] adj elegante

chick [tʃɪk] n pollito, polluelo; (inf: girl) chica

chicken ['tʃɪkɪn] n gallina, pollo; (food) pollo; (inf: coward) gallina mf; **chicken out** (inf) vi rajarse; **chickenpox** n varicela

chickpea ['tʃɪkpiː] n garbanzo

chief [tʃiːf] n jefe/a m/f ▷ adj principal; **chief executive (officer)** n director(a) m/f general; **chiefly** adv principalmente

child [tʃaɪld] (pl **~ren**) n niño/a; (offspring) hijo/a; **child abuse** n (with violence) malos tratos mpl a niños; (sexual) abuso m sexual de niños; **child benefit** n (BRIT) subsidio por cada hijo pequeño; **childbirth** n parto; **child-care** n cuidado de los niños; **childhood** n niñez f, infancia; **childish**

adj pueril, aniñado; **child minder** (BRIT) n madre f de día; **children** ['tʃɪldrən] npl of **child**

Chile ['tʃɪlɪ] n Chile m; **Chilean** adj, n chileno/a m/f

chill [tʃɪl] n frío; (Med) resfriado ▷ vt enfriar; (Culin) congelar; **chill out** vi (esp us: inf) tranquilizarse

chil(l)i ['tʃɪlɪ] (BRIT) n chile m, ají m (SC)

chilly ['tʃɪlɪ] adj frío

chimney ['tʃɪmnɪ] n chimenea

chimpanzee [tʃɪmpæn'ziː] n chimpancé m

chin [tʃɪn] n mentón m, barbilla

China ['tʃaɪnə] n China

china ['tʃaɪnə] n porcelana; (crockery) loza

Chinese [tʃaɪ'niːz] adj chino ▷ n inv chino/a m/f; (Ling) chino

chip [tʃɪp] n (gen pl: Culin: BRIT) patata (SP) or papa (LAM) frita; (: us: also: **potato ~**) patata or papa frita; (of wood) astilla; (of glass, stone) lasca; (at poker) ficha; (Comput) chip m ▷ vt (cup, plate) desconchar; **chip shop** n pescadería (donde se vende principalmente pescado rebozado y patatas fritas)

chiropodist [kɪ'rɔpədɪst] (BRIT) n pedicuro/a, callista m/f

chisel ['tʃɪzl] n (for wood) escoplo; (for stone) cincel m

chives [tʃaɪvz] npl cebollinos mpl

chlorine ['klɔːriːn] n cloro

choc-ice ['tʃɔkaɪs] n (BRIT) helado m cubierto de chocolate

chocolate ['tʃɔklɪt] n chocolate m; (sweet) bombón m

choice [tʃɔɪs] n elección f, selección f; (option) opción f; (preference) preferencia ▷ adj escogido

choir ['kwaɪə*] n coro

choke [tʃəʊk] vi ahogarse; (on food) atragantarse ▷ vt estrangular, ahogar; (block): **to be ~d with** estar atascado de ▷ n (Aut) estárter m

cholesterol [kə'lɛstərʊl] n colesterol m

choose [tʃuːz] (pt **chose**, pp **chosen**)

vt escoger, elegir; (team) seleccionar; **to ~ to do sth** optar por hacer algo

chop [tʃɔp] vt (wood) cortar, tajar; (Culin: also: ~ **up**) picar ▸ n (Culin) chuleta; **chop down** vt (tree) talar; **chop off** vt cortar (de un tajo); **chopsticks** ['tʃɔpstiks] npl palillos mpl

chord [kɔːd] n (Mus) acorde m

chore [tʃɔː*] n faena, tarea; (routine task) trabajo rutinario

chorus ['kɔːrəs] n coro; (repeated part of song) estribillo

chose [tʃəuz] pt of **choose**

chosen ['tʃəuzn] pp of **choose**

Christ [kraist] n Cristo

christen ['krisn] vt bautizar; **christening** n bautizo

Christian ['kristiən] adj, n cristiano/a m/f; **Christianity** [-'æniti] n cristianismo; **Christian name** n nombre m de pila

Christmas ['krisməs] n Navidad f; **Merry ~!** ¡Felices Pascuas!; **Christmas card** n crismas m inv, tarjeta de Navidad; **Christmas carol** n villancico m; **Christmas Day** n día m de Navidad; **Christmas Eve** n Nochebuena; **Christmas pudding** n (esp BRIT) pudin m de Navidad; **Christmas tree** n árbol m de Navidad

chrome [krəum] n cromo

chronic ['krɔnik] adj crónico

chrysanthemum [kri'sænθəməm] n crisantemo

chubby ['tʃʌbi] adj regordete

chuck [tʃʌk] (inf) vt lanzar, arrojar; (BRIT: also: ~ **up**) abandonar; **chuck out** vt (person) echar (fuera); (rubbish etc) tirar

chuckle ['tʃʌkl] vi reírse entre dientes

chum [tʃʌm] n compañero/a

chunk [tʃʌŋk] n pedazo, trozo

church [tʃɜːtʃ] n iglesia; **churchyard** n cementerio

churn [tʃɜːn] n (for butter) mantequera; (for milk) lechera

chute [ʃuːt] n (also: **rubbish ~**)

vertedero; (for coal etc) rampa de caída

chutney ['tʃʌtni] n condimento a base de frutas de la India

CIA (US) n abbr (= Central Intelligence Agency) CIA f

CID (BRIT) n abbr (= Criminal Investigation Department) ≈ B.I.C. f (SP)

cider ['saidə*] n sidra

cigar [si'gɑː*] n puro

cigarette [sigə'ret] n cigarrillo; **cigarette lighter** n mechero

cinema ['sinəmə] n cine m

cinnamon ['sinəmən] n canela

circle ['sɜːkl] n círculo; (in theatre) anfiteatro ▸ vi dar vueltas ▸ vt (surround) rodear, cercar; (move round) dar la vuelta a

circuit ['sɜːkit] n circuito; (tour) gira; (track) pista; (lap) vuelta

circular ['sɜːkjulə*] adj circular ▸ n circular f

circulate ['sɜːkjuleit] vi circular; (person: at party etc) hablar con los invitados ▸ vt poner en circulación; **circulation** [-'leiʃən] n circulación f; (of newspaper) tirada

circumstances ['sɜːkəmstənsiz] npl circunstancias fpl; (financial condition) situación f económica

circus ['sɜːkəs] n circo

cite [sait] vt citar

citizen ['sitizn] n (Pol) ciudadano/a; (of city) vecino/a, habitante mf; **citizenship** n ciudadanía; (BRIT: Scol) civismo

citrus fruits ['sitrəs-] npl agrios mpl

city ['siti] n ciudad f; **the C~** centro financiero de Londres; **city centre** (BRIT) n centro de la ciudad; **city technology college** n centro de formación profesional (centro de enseñanza secundaria que da especial importancia a la ciencia y tecnología)

civic ['sivik] adj cívico; (authorities) municipal

civil ['sivl] adj civil; (polite) atento, cortés; **civilian** [si'viliən] adj civil (no military) ▸ n civil mf, paisano/a

civilization [sɪvɪlaɪˈzeɪʃən] n
civilización f
civilized [ˈsɪvɪlaɪzd] adj civilizado
civil: civil law n derecho civil; **civil
rights** npl derechos mpl civiles; **civil
servant** n funcionario m/a del Estado;
Civil Service n administración f
pública; **civil war** n guerra civil
CJD n abbr (= Creutzfeldt-Jakob disease)
enfermedad de Creutzfeldt-Jakob
claim [kleɪm] vt exigir, reclamar;
(rights etc) reivindicar; (assert)
pretender ▷ vi (for insurance) reclamar
▷ n reclamación f; pretensión f; **claim
form** n solicitud f
clam [klæm] n almeja
clamp [klæmp] n abrazadera,
grapa ▷ vt (two things together) cerrar
fuertemente; (one thing on another)
afianzar (con abrazadera); (Aut: wheel)
poner el cepo a
clan [klæn] n clan m
clap [klæp] vi aplaudir
claret [ˈklærət] n burdeos m inv
clarify [ˈklærɪfaɪ] vt aclarar
clarinet [klærɪˈnɛt] n clarinete m
clarity [ˈklærɪtɪ] n claridad f
clash [klæʃ] n enfrentamiento,
choque m; desacuerdo; estruendo ▷ vi
(fight) enfrentarse; (beliefs) chocar;
(disagree) estar en desacuerdo; (colours)
desentonar; (two events) coincidir
clasp [klɑːsp] n (hold) apretón m; (of
necklace, bag) cierre m ▷ vt apretar;
abrazar
class [klɑːs] n clase f ▷ vt clasificar
classic [ˈklæsɪk] adj, n clásico;
classical adj clásico
classification [klæsɪfɪˈkeɪʃən] n
clasificación f
classify [ˈklæsɪfaɪ] vt clasificar
classmate [ˈklɑːsmeɪt] n
compañero/a de clase
classroom [ˈklɑːsrum] n aula;
classroom assistant n profesor(a)
m/f de apoyo
classy [ˈklɑːsɪ] adj (inf) elegante,
con estilo

clatter [ˈklætə*] n estrépito ▷ vi
hacer ruido or estrépito
clause [klɔːz] n cláusula; (Ling)
oración f
claustrophobic [klɔːstrəˈfəubɪk]
adj claustrofóbico; **I feel ~** me entra
claustrofobia
claw [klɔː] n (of cat) uña; (of bird of
prey) garra; (of lobster) pinza
clay [kleɪ] n arcilla
clean [kliːn] adj limpio; (record,
reputation) bueno, intachable; (joke)
decente ▷ vt limpiar; (hands etc) lavar;
clean up vt limpiar, asear; **cleaner**
n (person) asistenta; (substance)
producto para la limpieza; **cleaner's** n
tintorería; **cleaning** n limpieza
cleanser [ˈklɛnzə*] n (for face) crema
limpiadora
clear [klɪə*] adj claro; (road, way)
libre; (conscience) limpio, tranquilo;
(skin) terso; (sky) despejado ▷ vt
(space) despejar, limpiar; (Law: suspect)
absolver; (obstacle) salvar, saltar por
encima de; (cheque) aceptar ▷ vi (fog
etc) despejarse ▷ adv: **~ of** a distancia
de; **to ~ the table** recoger or levantar
la mesa; **clear away** vt (things, clothes
etc) quitar (de en medio); (dishes)
retirar; **clear up** vt limpiar; (mystery)
aclarar, resolver; **clearance** n (removal)
despeje m; (permission) acreditación f;
clear-cut adj bien definido, nítido;
clearing n (in wood) claro; **clearly**
adv claramente; (evidently) sin duda;
clearway (BRIT) n carretera donde no
se puede parar
clench [klɛntʃ] vt apretar, cerrar
clergy [ˈklɜːdʒɪ] n clero
clerk [klɑːk, (us) klɜːrk] n (BRIT)
oficinista mf; (us) dependiente m/f
clever [ˈklɛvə*] adj (intelligent)
inteligente, listo; (skilful) hábil; (device,
arrangement) ingenioso
cliché [ˈkliːʃeɪ] n cliché m, frase f
hecha
click [klɪk] vt (tongue) chasquear;
(heels) taconear ▷ vi (Comput) hacer

clic; to ~ **on an icon** hacer clic en un icono

client ['klaɪənt] n cliente m/f

cliff [klɪf] n acantilado

climate ['klaɪmɪt] n clima m; **climate change** n cambio climático

climax ['klaɪmæks] n (of battle, career) apogeo; (of film, book) punto culminante; (sexual) orgasmo

climb [klaɪm] vi subir; (plant) trepar; (move with effort): **to ~ over a wall/into a car** trepar a una tapia/subir a un coche ▷ vt (stairs) subir; (tree) trepar a; (mountain) escalar ▷ n subida; **climb down** vi (fig) volverse atrás; **climber** n alpinista mf (SP, MEX), andinista mf (LAM); **climbing** n alpinismo (SP, MEX), andinismo (LAM)

clinch [klɪntʃ] vt (deal) cerrar; (argument) remachar

cling [klɪŋ] (pt, pp **clung**) vi: **to ~ to** agarrarse a; (clothes) pegarse a

Clingfilm® ['klɪŋfɪlm] n plástico adherente

clinic ['klɪnɪk] n clínica

clip [klɪp] n (for hair) horquilla; (also: **paper ~**) sujetapapeles m inv, clip m; (TV, Cinema) fragmento ▷ vt (cut) cortar; (also: **~ together**) unir; **clipping** n (newspaper) recorte m

cloak [kləʊk] n capa, manto ▷ vt (fig) encubrir, disimular; **cloakroom** n guardarropa; (BRIT: WC) lavabo (SP), aseos mpl (SP), baño (LAM)

clock [klɒk] n reloj m; **clock in or on** vi (with card) fichar, picar; (start work) entrar a trabajar; **clock off or out** vi (with card) fichar or picar la salida; (leave work) salir del trabajar; **clockwise** adv en el sentido de las agujas del reloj; **clockwork** n aparato de relojería ▷ adj (toy) de cuerda

clog [klɒg] n zueco, chanclo ▷ vt atascar ▷ vi (also: **~ up**) atascarse

clone [kləʊn] n clon m ▷ vt clonar

close¹ [kləʊs] adj (near): **~ (to)** cerca (de); (friend) íntimo; (connection) estrecho; (examination) detallado,

minucioso; (weather) bochornoso ▷ adv cerca; **~ by, ~ at hand** muy cerca; **to have a ~ shave** (fig) escaparse por un pelo

close² [kləʊz] vt (shut) cerrar; (end) concluir, terminar ▷ vi (shop etc) cerrarse; (end) concluirse, terminarse ▷ n (end) fin m, final m, conclusión f; **close down** vi cerrarse definitivamente; **closed** adj (shop etc) cerrado

closely ['kləʊslɪ] adv (study) con detalle; (watch) de cerca; (resemble) estrechamente

closet ['klɒzɪt] n armario

close-up ['kləʊsʌp] n primer plano

closing time n hora de cierre

closure ['kləʊʒə*] n cierre m

clot [klɒt] n (gen) coágulo; (inf: idiot) imbécil m/f ▷ vi (blood) coagularse

cloth [klɒθ] n (material) tela, paño; (rag) trapo

clothes [kləʊðz] npl ropa; **clothes line** n cuerda (para tender la ropa); **clothes peg** (us **clothes pin**) n pinza

clothing ['kləʊðɪŋ] n = **clothes**

cloud [klaʊd] n nube f; **cloud over** vi (also fig) nublarse; **cloudy** adj nublado, nubloso; (liquid) turbio

clove [kləʊv] n clavo; **~ of garlic** diente m de ajo

clown [klaʊn] n payaso ▷ vi (also: **~ about, ~ around**) hacer el payaso

club [klʌb] n (society) club m; (weapon) porra, cachiporra; (also: **golf ~**) palo ▷ vt aporrear ▷ vi: **to ~ together** (for gift) comprar entre todos; **clubs** npl (Cards) tréboles mpl; **club class** n (Aviat) clase f preferente

clue [kluː] n pista; (in crosswords) indicación f; **I haven't a ~** no tengo ni idea

clump [klʌmp] n (of trees) grupo

clumsy ['klʌmzɪ] adj (person) torpe, desmañado; (tool) difícil de manejar; (movement) desgarbado

clung [klʌŋ] pt, pp of **cling**

cluster ['klʌstə*] n grupo ▷ vi

agruparse, apiñarse

clutch [klʌtʃ] n (Aut) embrague m; (grasp): **-es** garras fpl ▷ vt asir; agarrar

cm abbr (= centimetre) cm

Co. abbr = **county; company**

c/o abbr (= care of) c/a, a/c

coach [kəʊtʃ] n autocar m (SP), coche m de línea; (horse-drawn) coche m; (of train) vagón m, coche m; (Sport) entrenador(a) m/f, instructor(a) m/f; (tutor) profesor(a) m/f particular ▷ vt (Sport) entrenar; (student) preparar, enseñar; **coach station** n estación f de autobuses etc; **coach trip** n excursión f en autocar

coal [kəʊl] n carbón m

coalition [kəʊəˈlɪʃən] n coalición f

coarse [kɔːs] adj basto, burdo; (vulgar) grosero, ordinario

coast [kəʊst] n costa, litoral m ▷ vi (Aut) ir en punto muerto; **coastal** adj costero, costanero; **coastguard** n guardacostas m inv; **coastline** n litoral m

coat [kəʊt] n abrigo; (of animal) pelaje m, lana; (of paint) mano f, capa ▷ vt cubrir, revestir; **coat hanger** n percha (SP), gancho (LAM); **coating** n capa, baño

coax [kəʊks] vt engatusar

cob [kɒb] n see **corn**

cobbled [ˈkɒbld] adj: **~ street** calle f empedrada, calle f adoquinada

cobweb [ˈkɒbwɛb] n telaraña

cocaine [kəˈkeɪn] n cocaína

cock [kɒk] n (rooster) gallo; (male bird) macho ▷ vt (gun) amartillar; **cockerel** n gallito

cockney [ˈkɒknɪ] n habitante m de ciertos barrios de Londres

cockpit [ˈkɒkpɪt] n cabina

cockroach [ˈkɒkrəʊtʃ] n cucaracha

cocktail [ˈkɒkteɪl] n coctel m, cóctel m

cocoa [ˈkəʊkəʊ] n cacao; (drink) chocolate m

coconut [ˈkəʊkənʌt] n coco

cod [kɒd] n bacalao

C.O.D. abbr (= cash on delivery) C.A.E.

code [kəʊd] n código; (cipher) clave f; (dialling code) prefijo; (post code) código postal

coeducational [kəʊɛdjuˈkeɪʃənl] adj mixto

coffee [ˈkɒfɪ] n café m; **coffee bar** (BRIT) n cafetería; **coffee bean** n grano de café; **coffee break** n descanso (para tomar café); **coffee maker** n máquina de hacer café, cafetera; **coffeepot** n cafetera; **coffee shop** n café m; **coffee table** n mesita (para servir el café)

coffin [ˈkɒfɪn] n ataúd m

cog [kɒg] n (wheel) rueda dentada; (tooth) diente m

coherent [kəʊˈhɪərənt] adj coherente

coil [kɔɪl] n rollo; (Elec) bobina, carrete m; (contraceptive) espiral f ▷ vt enrollar

coin [kɔɪn] n moneda ▷ vt (word) inventar, idear

coincide [kəʊɪnˈsaɪd] vi coincidir; (agree) estar de acuerdo; **coincidence** [kəʊˈɪnsɪdəns] n casualidad f

Coke® [kəʊk] n Coca-Cola®

coke [kəʊk] n (coal) coque m

colander [ˈkɒləndə*] n colador m, escurridor m

cold [kəʊld] adj frío ▷ n frío; (Med) resfriado; **it's** ~ hace frío; **to be** ~ (person) tener frío; **to catch (a)** ~ resfriarse, acatarrarse; **in** ~ **blood** a sangre fría; **cold sore** n herpes mpl or fpl

coleslaw [ˈkəʊlslɔː] n especie de ensalada de col

colic [ˈkɒlɪk] n cólico

collaborate [kəˈlæbəreɪt] vi colaborar

collapse [kəˈlæps] vi hundirse, derrumbarse; (Med) sufrir un colapso ▷ n hundimiento, derrumbamiento; (Med) colapso

collar [ˈkɒlə*] n (of coat, shirt) cuello; (of dog etc) collar; **collarbone** n clavícula

colleague ['kɔliːg] n colega mf; (at work) compañero/a

collect [kə'lɛkt] vt (litter, mail etc) recoger; (as a hobby) coleccionar; (BRIT: call and pick up) recoger; (debts, subscriptions etc) recaudar ▷ vi reunirse; (dust) acumularse; **to call ~** (US Tel) llamar a cobro revertido; **collection** [kə'lɛkʃən] n colección f; (of mail, for charity) recogida f; **collective** [kə'lɛktɪv] adj colectivo; **collector** n coleccionista mf

college ['kɔlɪdʒ] n colegio mayor; (of agriculture, technology) escuela universitaria

collide [kə'laɪd] vi chocar

collision [kə'lɪʒən] n choque m

cologne [kə'ləun] n (also: **eau de ~**) (agua de) colonia

Colombia [kə'lɔmbɪə] n Colombia; **Colombian** adj, n colombiano/a

colon ['kəulən] n (sign) dos puntos; (Med) colon m

colonel ['kəːnl] n coronel m

colonial [kə'ləunɪəl] adj colonial

colony ['kɔlənɪ] n colonia

colour etc ['kʌlə*] (US **color** etc) n color m ▷ vt color(e)ar; (dye) teñir; (fig: account) adornar; (: judgement) distorsionar ▷ vi (blush) sonrojarse; **colour in** vt colorear; **colour-blind** adj daltónico; **coloured** adj de color; (photo) en color; **colour film** n película en color; **colourful** adj lleno de color; (story) fantástico; (person) excéntrico; **colouring** n (complexion) tez f; (in food) colorante m; **colour television** n televisión f en color

column ['kɔləm] n columna

coma ['kəumə] n coma m

comb [kəum] n peine m; (ornamental) peineta ▷ vt (hair) peinar; (area) registrar a fondo

combat ['kɔmbæt] n combate m ▷ vt combatir

combination [kɔmbɪ'neɪʃən] n combinación f

combine [vb kəm'baɪn, n 'kɔmbaɪn]

vt combinar; (qualities) reunir ▷ vi combinarse ▷ n (Econ) cartel m

○ **KEYWORD**

come [kʌm] (pt **came**, pp **come**) vi
1 (movement towards) venir; **to come running** venir corriendo
2 (arrive) llegar; **he's come here to work** ha venido aquí para trabajar; **to come home** volver a casa
3 (reach): **to come to** llegar a; **the bill came to £40** la cuenta ascendía a cuarenta libras
4 (occur): **an idea came to me** se me ocurrió una idea
5 (be, become): **to come loose/undone** etc aflojarse/desabrocharse/desatarse etc; **I've come to like him** por fin ha llegado a gustarme

come across vt fus (person) topar con; (thing) dar con

come along vi (BRIT: progress) ir

come back vi (return) volver

come down vi (price) bajar; (tree, building) ser derribado

come from vt fus (place, source) ser de

come in vi (visitor) entrar; (train, report) llegar; (fashion) ponerse de moda; (on deal etc) entrar

come off vi (button) soltarse, desprenderse; (attempt) salir bien

come on vi (pupil) progresar; (work, project) desarrollarse; (lights, electricity) volver; **come on!** ¡vamos!

come out vi (fact) salir a la luz; (book, sun) salir; (stain) quitarse

come round vi (after faint, operation) volver en sí

come to vi (wake) volver en sí

come up vi (sun) salir; (problem) surgir; (event) aproximarse; (in conversation) mencionarse

come up with vt fus (idea) sugerir; (money) conseguir

comeback ['kʌmbæk] n: **to make a ~**

(*Theatre*) volver a las tablas

comedian [kə'miːdiən] n humorista mf

comedy ['kɒmɪdɪ] n comedia; (*humour*) comicidad f

comet ['kɒmɪt] n cometa m

comfort ['kʌmfət] n bienestar m; (*relief*) alivio ▷ vt consolar; **comfortable** adj cómodo; (*financially*) acomodado; (*easy*) fácil; **comfort station** (*us*) n servicios mpl

comic ['kɒmɪk] adj (*also*: **-al**) cómico ▷ n (*comedian*) cómico; (*brit: for children*) tebeo; (*brit: for adults*) comic m; **comic book** (*us*) n libro m de cómics; **comic strip** n tira cómica

comma ['kɒmə] n coma

command [kə'maːnd] n orden f, mandato; (*Mil: authority*) mando; (*mastery*) dominio ▷ vt (*troops*) mandar; (*give orders to*): **to ~ sb to do** mandar or ordenar a algn hacer; **commander** n (*Mil*) comandante m, jefe/a m/f

commemorate [kə'mɛməreɪt] vt conmemorar

commence [kə'mɛns] vt, vi comenzar, empezar; **commencement** (*us*) n (*Univ*) (ceremonia de) graduación f

commend [kə'mɛnd] vt elogiar, alabar; (*recommend*) recomendar

comment ['kɒmɛnt] n comentario ▷ vi: **to ~ on** hacer comentarios sobre; **"no ~"** (*written*) "sin comentarios"; (*spoken*) "no tengo nada que decir"; **commentary** ['kɒməntərɪ] n comentario; **commentator** ['kɒmənteɪtəʳ] n comentarista mf

commerce ['kɒməːs] n comercio

commercial [kə'məːʃəl] adj comercial ▷ n (*TV, Radio*) anuncio; **commercial break** n intermedio para publicidad

commission [kə'mɪʃən] n (*committee, fee*) comisión f ▷ vt (*work of art*) encargar; **out of ~** fuera de servicio; **commissioner** n (*Police*)

comisario de policía

commit [kə'mɪt] vt (*act*) cometer; (*resources*) dedicar; (*to sb's care*) entregar; **to ~ o.s. (to do)** comprometerse (a hacer); **to ~ suicide** suicidarse; **commitment** n compromiso; (*to ideology etc*) entrega

committee [kə'mɪtɪ] n comité m

commodity [kə'mɒdɪtɪ] n mercancía

common ['kɒmən] adj común; (*pej*) ordinario ▷ n campo común; **commonly** adv comúnmente; **commonplace** adj de lo más común; **Commons** (*brit*) npl (*Pol*): **the Commons** (la Cámara de) los Comunes; **common sense** n: sentido común; **Commonwealth** n: **the Commonwealth** la Commonwealth

communal ['kɒmjuːnl] adj (*property*) comunal; (*kitchen*) común

commune [n 'kɒmjuːn, vb kə'mjuːn] n (*group*) comuna ▷ vi: **to ~ with** comulgar or conversar con

communicate [kə'mjuːnɪkeɪt] vt comunicar ▷ vi: **to ~ (with)** comunicarse (con); (*in writing*) estar en contacto (con)

communication [kəmjuːnɪ'keɪʃən] n comunicación f

communion [kə'mjuːnɪən] n (*also*: **Holy ~**) comunión f

communism ['kɒmjunɪzəm] n comunismo; **communist** adj, n comunista mf

community [kə'mjuːnɪtɪ] n comunidad f; (*large group*) colectividad f; **community centre** (*us* **community center**) n centro social; **community service** n trabajo m comunitario (*prestado en lugar de cumplir una pena de prisión*)

commute [kə'mjuːt] vi viajar a diario de la casa al trabajo ▷ vt conmutar; **commuter** n persona que viaja a diario de la casa al trabajo

compact [adj kəm'pækt, n 'kɒmpækt] adj compacto ▷ n (*also*: **powder ~**)

polvera; **compact disc** n compact disc m; **compact disc player** n reproductor m de disco compacto, compact disc m

companion [kəm'pænɪən] n compañero/a

company ['kʌmpənɪ] n compañía; (Comm) sociedad f, compañía; **to keep sb ~** acompañar a algn; **company car** n coche m de la empresa; **company director** n director/a m/f de empresa

comparable ['kɒmpərəbl] adj comparable

comparative [kəm'pærətɪv] adj relativo; (study) comparativo; **comparatively** adv (relatively) relativamente

compare [kəm'pɛə*] vt: **to ~ sth/sb with** or **to** comparar algo/a algn con ▷ vi: **to ~ (with)** comparar(se) (con); **comparison** [-'pærɪsn] n comparación f

compartment [kəm'pɑ:tmənt] n (also: Rail) compartim(i)ento

compass ['kʌmpəs] n brújula; **compasses** npl (Math) compás m

compassion [kəm'pæʃən] n compasión f

compatible [kəm'pætɪbl] adj compatible

compel [kəm'pɛl] vt obligar; **compelling** adj (fig: argument) convincente

compensate ['kɒmpənseɪt] vt compensar ▷ vi: **to ~ for** compensar; **compensation** [-'seɪʃən] n (for loss) indemnización f

compete [kəm'pi:t] vi (take part) tomar parte, concurrir; (vie with): **to ~ with** competir con, hacer competencia a

competent ['kɒmpɪtənt] adj competente, capaz

competition [kɒmpɪ'tɪʃə n] n (contest) concurso; (rivalry) competencia

competitive [kəm'petɪtɪv] adj (Econ, Sport) competitivo

competitor [kəm'petɪtə*] n (rival) competidor(a) m/f; (participant) concursante mf

complacent [kəm'pleɪsənt] adj autocomplaciente

complain [kəm'pleɪn] vi quejarse; (Comm) reclamar; **complaint** n queja; reclamación f; (Med) enfermedad f

complement [n 'kɒmplɪmənt, vb 'kɒmplɪment] n complemento; (esp of ship's crew) dotación f ▷ vt (enhance) complementar; **complementary** [kɒmplɪ'mentərɪ] adj complementario

complete [kəm'pli:t] adj (full) completo; (finished) acabado ▷ vt (fulfil) completar; (finish) acabar; (a form) llenar; **completely** adv completamente; **completion** [-'pli:ʃən] n terminación f; (of contract) realización f

complex ['kɒmpleks] adj, n complejo

complexion [kəm'plekʃən] n (of face) tez f, cutis m

compliance [kəm'plaɪəns] n (submission) sumisión f; (agreement) conformidad f; **in ~ with** de acuerdo con

complicate ['kɒmplɪkeɪt] vt complicar; **complicated** adj complicado; **complication** [-'keɪʃən] n complicación f

compliment [n 'kɒmplɪmənt] n (formal) cumplido ▷ vt felicitar; **complimentary** [-'mentərɪ] adj lisonjero; (free) de favor

comply [kəm'plaɪ] vi: **to ~ with** cumplir con

component [kəm'pəunənt] adj componente ▷ n (Tech) pieza

compose [kəm'pəuz] vt: **to be ~d of** componerse de; (music etc) componer; **to ~ o.s.** tranquilizarse; **composer** n (Mus) compositor/a m/f; **composition** [kɒmpə'zɪʃən] n composición f

composure [kəm'pəuʒə*] n serenidad f, calma

compound ['kɒmpaund] n (Chem)

compuesto; (Ling) palabra compuesta; (enclosure) recinto ▷ adj compuesto; (fracture) complicado

comprehension [-ˈhenʃən] n comprensión f

comprehensive [kɒmprɪˈhensɪv] adj exhaustivo; (Insurance) contra todo riesgo; **comprehensive (school)** n centro estatal de enseñanza secundaria ≈ Instituto Nacional de Bachillerato (SP)

compress [vb kəmˈpres, n ˈkɒmpres] vt comprimir; (information) condensar ▷ n (Med) compresa

comprise [kəmˈpraɪz] vt (also: **be ~d of**) comprender, constar de; (constitute) constituir

compromise [ˈkɒmprəmaɪz] n (agreement) arreglo ▷ vt comprometer ▷ vi transigir

compulsive [kəmˈpʌlsɪv] adj compulsivo; (viewing, reading) obligado

compulsory [kəmˈpʌlsərɪ] adj obligatorio

computer [kəmˈpjuːtə*] n ordenador m, computador m, computadora; **computer game** n juego para ordenador; **computer-generated** adj realizado por ordenador, creado por ordenador; **computerize** vt (data) computerizar; (system) informatizar; **we're computerized now** ya nos hemos informatizado; **computer programmer** n programador(a) m/f; **computer programming** n programación f; **computer science** n informática; **computer studies** npl informática fsg, computación fsg (LAM); **computing** [kəmˈpjuːtɪŋ] n (activity, science) informática

con [kɒn] vt (deceive) engañar; (cheat) estafar ▷ n estafa

conceal [kənˈsiːl] vt ocultar

concede [kənˈsiːd] vt (point, argument) reconocer; (territory) ceder; **to ~ (defeat)** darse por vencido; **to ~ that** admitir que

conceited [kənˈsiːtɪd] adj presumido

conceive [kənˈsiːv] vt, vi concebir

concentrate [ˈkɒnsəntreɪt] vi concentrarse ▷ vt concentrar

concentration [kɒnsənˈtreɪʃən] n concentración f

concept [ˈkɒnsept] n concepto

concern [kənˈsɜːn] n (matter) asunto; (Comm) empresa; (anxiety) preocupación f ▷ vt (worry) preocupar; (involve) afectar; (relate to) tener que ver con; **to be ~ed (about)** interesarse (por), preocuparse (por); **concerning** prep sobre, acerca de

concert [ˈkɒnsət] n concierto; **concert hall** n sala de conciertos

concerto [kənˈtʃɜːtəu] n concierto

concession [kənˈseʃən] n concesión f; **tax ~** privilegio fiscal

concise [kənˈsaɪs] adj conciso

conclude [kənˈkluːd] vt concluir; (treaty etc) firmar; (agreement) llegar a; (decide) llegar a la conclusión de; **conclusion** [-ˈkluːʒən] n conclusión f; firma

concrete [ˈkɒnkriːt] n hormigón m ▷ adj de hormigón; (fig) concreto

concussion [kənˈkʌʃən] n conmoción f cerebral

condemn [kənˈdem] vt condenar; (building) declarar en ruina

condensation [kɒndenˈseɪʃən] n condensación f

condense [kənˈdens] vi condensarse ▷ vt condensar, abreviar

condition [kənˈdɪʃən] n condición f, estado; (requirement) condición f ▷ vt (de) que; **on ~ that** a condición (de) que; **conditional** [kənˈdɪʃənl] adj condicional; **conditioner** n suavizante m

condo [ˈkɒndəu] (US) n (inf) = **condominium**

condom [ˈkɒndəm] n condón m

condominium [kɒndəˈmɪnɪəm] (US) n (building) bloque m de pisos o apartamentos (propiedad de quienes lo habitan), condominio (LAM); (apartment) piso o apartamento (en propiedad),

condominio (LAM)
condone [kən'dəʊn] vt condonar
conduct [n 'kɒndʌkt, vb kən'dʌkt]
n conducta, comportamiento ▷ vt
(lead) conducir; (manage) llevar a
cabo, dirigir; (Mus) dirigir; (us: on train)
comportarse; **conducted tour** (BRIT)
n visita acompañada; **conductor** n
(of orchestra) director m; (us: on train)
revisor(a) m/f; (on bus) cobrador m;
(Elec) conductor m
cone [kəʊn] n cono; (pine cone)
piña; (on road) pivote m; (for ice-cream)
cucurucho
confectionery [kən'fekʃənrɪ] n
dulces mpl
confer [kən'fɜː*] vt: **to ~ sth on**
otorgar algo a ▷ vi conferenciar
conference ['kɒnfərns] n (meeting)
reunión f; (convention) congreso
confess [kən'fes] vt confesar ▷ vi
admitir; **confession** [-'feʃən] n
confesión f
confide [kən'faɪd] vi: **to ~ in** confiar
en
confidence ['kɒnfɪdns] n (also: self-
~) confianza; (secret) confidencia; **in ~**
(speak, write) en confianza; **confident**
adj seguro de sí mismo; **confidential**
[kɒnfɪ'denʃəl] adj confidencial
confine [kən'faɪn] vt (limit) limitar;
(shut up) encerrar; **confined** adj (space)
reducido
confirm [kən'fɜːm] vt confirmar;
confirmation [kɒnfə'meɪʃən] n
confirmación f
confiscate ['kɒnfɪskeɪt] vt confiscar
conflict [n 'kɒnflɪkt, vb kən'flɪkt] n
conflicto ▷ vi (opinions) chocar
conform [kən'fɔːm] vi conformarse;
to ~ to ajustarse a
confront [kən'frʌnt] vt (problems)
hacer frente a; (enemy, danger)
enfrentarse con; **confrontation**
[kɒnfrən'teɪʃən] n enfrentamiento
confuse [kən'fjuːz] vt (perplex)
aturdir, desconcertar; (mix up)

confundir; (complicate) complicar;
confused adj confuso; (person)
perplejo; **confusing** adj confuso
confusion [-'fjuːʒən] n confusión f
congestion [kən'dʒestʃən] n
congestión f
congratulate [kən'grætjuleɪt]
vt: **to ~ sb (on)** felicitar a algn (por);
congratulations [-'leɪʃənz] npl
felicitaciones fpl; **congratulations!**
¡enhorabuena!
congregation [-'geɪʃən] n (of a
church) feligreses mpl
congress ['kɒngres] n congreso;
(us): **C~** Congreso; **congressman**
(irreg: us) n miembro del Congreso;
congresswoman (irreg: us) n
diputada, miembro del Congreso
conifer ['kɒnɪfə*] n conífera
conjugate ['kɒndʒugeɪt] vt conjugar
conjugation [kɒndʒə'geɪʃən] n
conjugación f
conjunction [kən'dʒʌŋkʃən] n
conjunción f; **in ~ with** junto con
conjure ['kʌndʒə*] vi hacer juegos
de manos
connect [kə'nekt] vt juntar, unir;
(Elec) conectar; (Tel: subscriber) poner;
(: caller) poner al habla; (fig) relacionar,
asociar ▷ vi: **to ~ with** (train) enlazar
con; **to be ~ed with** (associated) estar
relacionado con; **connecting flight** n
vuelo m de enlace; **connection**
[-ʃən] n juntura, unión f; (Elec)
conexión f; (Rail) enlace m; (Tel)
comunicación f; (fig) relación f
conquer ['kɒŋkə*] vt (territory)
conquistar; (enemy, feelings) vencer
conquest ['kɒŋkwest] n conquista
cons [kɒnz] npl see **convenience**;
pro; mod
conscience ['kɒnʃəns] n conciencia
conscientious [kɒnʃɪ'enʃəs] adj
concienzudo; (objection) de conciencia
conscious ['kɒnʃəs] adj (deliberate)
deliberado; (awake, aware) consciente;
consciousness n conciencia; (Med)
conocimiento

consecutive [kənˈsɛkjʊtɪv] adj
consecutivo; **on 3 ~ occasions** en 3
ocasiones consecutivas

consensus [kənˈsɛnsəs] n consenso

consent [kənˈsɛnt] n
consentimiento ▷ vi: **to ~ (to)**
consentir (en)

consequence [ˈkɒnsɪkwəns]
n consecuencia; (significance)
importancia

consequently [ˈkɒnsɪkwəntlɪ] adv
por consiguiente

conservation [kɒnsəˈveɪʃən] n
conservación f

conservative [kənˈsɜːvətɪv]
adj conservador(a); (estimate etc)
cauteloso; **Conservative** (BRIT) adj, n
(Pol) conservador(a) m/f

conservatory [kənˈsɜːvətrɪ] n
invernadero; (Mus) conservatorio

consider [kənˈsɪdə*] vt considerar;
(take into account) tener en cuenta;
(study) estudiar, examinar; **to ~
doing sth** pensar en (la posibilidad
de) hacer algo; **considerable** adj
considerable; **considerably** adv
notablemente; **considerate** adj
considerado; **consideration** [kənsɪdəˈreɪʃə
n] n consideración f; (factor) factor
m; **to give sth further consideration**
estudiar algo más a fondo;
considering prep teniendo en cuenta

consignment [kənˈsaɪnmənt] n
envío

consist [kənˈsɪst] vi: **to ~ of** consistir
en

consistency [kənˈsɪstənsɪ]
n (of argument etc) coherencia,
consecuencia; (thickness) consistencia

consistent [kənˈsɪstənt] adj (person)
consecuente; (argument etc) coherente

consolation [kɒnsəˈleɪʃən] n
consuelo

console¹ [kənˈsəul] vt consolar

console² [ˈkɒnsəul] n consola

consonant [ˈkɒnsənənt] n
consonante f

conspicuous [kənˈspɪkjuəs] adj

(visible) visible

conspiracy [kənˈspɪrəsɪ] n conjura,
complot m

constable [ˈkʌnstəbl] (BRIT) n policía
mf; **chief ~** = jefe m de policía

constant [ˈkɒnstənt] adj constante;
constantly adv constantemente

constipated [ˈkɒnstɪpeɪtəd] adj
estreñido

> Be careful not to translate
> **constipated** by the Spanish word
> **constipado**.

constipation [kɒnstɪˈpeɪʃən] n
estreñimiento

constituency [kənˈstɪtjuənsɪ] n
(Pol: area) distrito electoral; (: electors)
electorado

constitute [ˈkɒnstɪtjuːt] vt
constituir

constitution [kɒnstɪˈtjuːʃən] n
constitución f

constraint [kənˈstreɪnt] n
obligación f; (limit) restricción f

construct [kənˈstrʌkt] vt construir;
construction [-ʃən] n construcción f;
constructive adj constructivo

consul [ˈkɒnsl] n cónsul mf;
consulate [ˈkɒnsjulɪt] n consulado

consult [kənˈsʌlt] vt consultar;
consultant n (BRIT Med) especialista
mf; (other specialist) asesor(a)
m/f; **consultation** [kɒnsəlˈteɪʃən] n
consulta; **consulting room** (BRIT) n
consultorio

consume [kənˈsjuːm] vt (eat)
comerse; (drink) beberse; (fire etc,
Comm) consumir; **consumer** n
consumidor(a) m/f

consumption [kənˈsʌmpʃən] n
consumo

cont. abbr (= continued) sigue

contact [ˈkɒntækt] n contacto;
(person) contacto; (: pej) enchufe m ▷ vt
ponerse en contacto con; **contact
lenses** npl lentes fpl de contacto

contagious [kənˈteɪdʒəs] adj
contagioso

contain [kənˈteɪn] vt contener;

to ~ o.s. contenerse; **container** n recipiente m; (for shipping etc) contenedor m

contaminate [kən'tæmɪneɪt] vt contaminar

cont'd abbr (= continued) sigue

contemplate ['kɔntəmpleɪt] vt contemplar; (reflect upon) considerar

contemporary [kən'tempərərɪ] adj, n contemporáneo/a m/f

contempt [kən'tempt] n desprecio; **~ of court** (Law) desacato (a los tribunales)

contend [kən'tend] vt (argue) afirmar ▷ vi: **to ~ with/for** luchar contra/por

content [adj, vb kən'tent, n 'kɔntent] adj (happy) contento; (satisfied) satisfecho ▷ vt contentar; satisfacer ▷ n contenido; **contents** npl contenido; **(table of) ~s** índice m de materias; **contented** adj contento; satisfecho

contest [n 'kɔntest, vb kən'test] n lucha; (competition) concurso ▷ vt (dispute) impugnar; (Pol) presentarse como candidato/a en

> Be careful not to translate **contest** by the Spanish word contestar.

contestant [kən'testənt] n concursante mf; (in fight) contendiente mf

context ['kɔntekst] n contexto

continent ['kɔntɪnənt] n continente m; **the C~** (BRIT) el continente europeo; **continental** [-'nentl] adj continental; **continental breakfast** n desayuno estilo europeo; **continental quilt** (BRIT) n edredón m

continual [kən'tɪnjuəl] adj continuo; **continually** adv constantemente

continue [kən'tɪnjuː] vi, vt seguir, continuar

continuity [kɔntɪ'njuɪtɪ] n (also Cine) continuidad f

continuous [kən'tɪnjuəs] adj continuo; **continuous assessment** n (BRIT) evaluación f continua;

continuously adv continuamente

contour ['kɔntuə*] n contorno; (also: **~ line**) curva de nivel

contraception [kɔntrə'sepʃən] n contracepción f

contraceptive [kɔntrə'septɪv] adj, n anticonceptivo

contract [n 'kɔntrækt, vb kən'trækt] n contrato ▷ vi (Comm): **to ~ to do sth** comprometerse por contrato a hacer algo; (become smaller) contraerse, encogerse ▷ vt contraer; **contractor** n contratista mf

contradict [kɔntrə'dɪkt] vt contradecir; **contradiction** [-ʃən] n contradicción f

contrary[1] ['kɔntrərɪ] adj contrario ▷ n lo contrario; **on the ~** al contrario, **unless you hear to the ~** a no ser que le digan lo contrario

contrary[2] [kən'treərɪ] adj (perverse) terco

contrast [n 'kɔntrɑːst, vt kən'trɑːst] n contraste m ▷ vt comparar; **in ~ to** en contraste con

contribute [kən'trɪbjuːt] vi contribuir ▷ vt: **to ~ £10/an article to** contribuir con 10 libras/un artículo a; **to ~ to** (charity) donar a; (newspaper) escribir para; (discussion) intervenir en; **contribution** [kɔntrɪ'bjuːʃən] n (donation) donativo; (BRIT: for social security) cotización f; (to debate) intervención f; (to journal) colaboración f; **contributor** n (to newspaper) colaborador(a) m/f

control [kən'trəul] vt controlar; (process etc) dirigir; (machinery) manejar; (temper) dominar; (disease) contener ▷ n control m; **controls** npl (of vehicle) instrumentos mpl de mando; (of radio) controles mpl; (governmental) medidas fpl de control; **under ~** bajo control; **to be in ~ of** tener el mando de; **the car went out of ~** se perdió el control del coche; **control tower** n (Aviat) torre f de control

controversial [kɔntrə'vəːʃl] adj

polémico

controversy ['kɒntrəvɜːsɪ] n
polémica

convenience [kən'viːnɪəns] n
(easiness) comodidad f; (suitability)
idoneidad f; (advantage) ventaja f; **at
your ~** cuando le sea conveniente;
all modern ~s, all mod cons (BRIT)
todo confort

convenient [kən'viːnɪənt] adj
(useful) útil; (place, time) conveniente

convent ['kɒnvənt] n convento

convention [kən'venʃən] n
convención f; (meeting) asamblea;
(agreement) convenio; **conventional**
adj convencional

conversation [kɒnvə'seɪʃən] n
conversación f

conversely [-'vɜːslɪ] adv a la inversa

conversion [kən'vɜːʃən] n
conversión f

convert [vb kən'vɜːt, n 'kɒnvɜːt] vt
(Rel, Comm) convertir; (alter): **to ~ sth
into/to** transformar algo en/convertir
algo a ▷ n converso/a; **convertible**
adj convertible ▷ n descapotable m

convey [kən'veɪ] vt llevar; (thanks)
comunicar; (idea) expresar; **conveyor
belt** n cinta transportadora

convict [vb kən'vɪkt, n 'kɒnvɪkt] vt
(find guilty) declarar culpable a ▷ n
presidiario/a; **conviction** [-ʃən] n
(belief, certainty) convicción f

convince [kən'vɪns] vt convencer;
convinced adj: **convinced of/that**
convencido de de/que; **convincing** adj
convincente

convoy ['kɒnvɔɪ] n convoy m

cook [kʊk] vt (stew etc) guisar; (meal)
preparar ▷ vi cocer; (person) cocinar
▷ n cocinero/a; **cook book** n libro de
cocina; **cooker** n cocina; **cookery** n
cocina; **cookery book** (BRIT) n = **cook
book**; **cookie** n (US) n galleta; **cooking**
n cocina

cool [kuːl] adj fresco; (not afraid)
tranquilo; (unfriendly) frío ▷ vt enfriar
▷ vi enfriarse; **cool down** vi enfriarse;

(fig: person, situation) calmarse; **cool
off** vi (become calmer) apaciguarse,
apaciguarse; (lose enthusiasm) perder
(el) interés, enfriarse

cop [kɒp] (inf) n poli mf (SP), tira
mf (MEX)

cope [kəʊp] vi: **to ~ with** (problem)
hacer frente a

copper ['kɒpə*] n (metal) cobre m;
(BRIT: inf) poli mf, tira mf (MEX)

copy ['kɒpɪ] n (of book etc)
ejemplar m ▷ vt copiar; **copyright** n
derechos mpl de autor

coral ['kɒrəl] n coral m

cord [kɔːd] n cuerda; (Elec) cable
m; (fabric) pana; **cords** npl (trousers)
pantalones mpl de pana; **cordless** adj
sin hilos

corduroy ['kɔːdərɔɪ] n pana

core [kɔː*] n centro, núcleo; (of fruit)
corazón m; (of problem) meollo ▷ vt
quitar el corazón de

coriander [kɒrɪ'ændə*] n culantro

cork [kɔːk] n corcho; (tree) alcornoque
m; **corkscrew** n sacacorchos m inv

corn [kɔːn] n (BRIT: cereal crop) trigo;
(US: maize) maíz m; (on foot) callo; **~ on
the cob** (Culin) mazorca, elote m (MEX),
choclo (SC)

corned beef [kɔːnd-] n carne f
acecinada (en lata)

corner ['kɔːnə*] n (outside) esquina;
(inside) rincón m; (in road) curva;
(Football) córner m; (Boxing) esquina
▷ vt (trap) arrinconar; (Comm) acaparar
▷ vi (in car) tomar las curvas; **corner
shop** (BRIT) tienda de la esquina

cornflakes ['kɔːnfleɪks] npl copos
mpl de maíz, cornflakes mpl

cornflour ['kɔːnflaʊə*] (BRIT) n
harina de maíz

cornstarch ['kɔːnstɑːtʃ] (US) n =
cornflour

Cornwall ['kɔːnwəl] n Cornualles m

coronary ['kɒrənərɪ] n (also: ~
thrombosis) infarto

coronation [kɒrə'neɪʃən] n
coronación f

coroner [ˈkɔrənəʳ] n juez mf de
instrucción

corporal [ˈkɔ:pərl] n cabo ▷ adj: **~
punishment** castigo corporal

corporate [ˈkɔ:pərit] adj (action,
ownership) colectivo; (finance, image)
corporativo

corporation [kɔ:pəˈreɪʃən] n
(of town) ayuntamiento; (Comm)
corporación f

corps [kɔ:ʳ, pl kɔ:z] n inv cuerpo;
diplomatic ~ cuerpo diplomático;
press ~ gabinete m de prensa

corpse [kɔ:ps] n cadáver m

correct [kəˈrɛkt] adj justo, exacto;
(proper) correcto ▷ vt corregir; (exam)
corregir, calificar; **correction**
[-ʃən] n corrección f; (instance)
rectificación f

correspond [kɔrɪsˈpɒnd] vi
(write): **to ~ (with)** escribirse (con); (be
equivalent to): **to ~ (to)** corresponder
(a); (be in accordance): **to ~ (with)**
corresponder (con); **correspondence**
n correspondencia; **correspondent**
n corresponsal mf; **corresponding** adj
correspondiente

corridor [ˈkɔrɪdɔ:ʳ] n pasillo

corrode [kəˈrəud] vt corroer ▷ vi
corroerse

corrupt [kəˈrʌpt] adj (person)
corrupto; (Comput) corrompido
▷ vt corromper; (Comput) degradar;
corruption n corrupción f; (of data)
alteración f

Corsica [ˈkɔ:sɪkə] n Córcega

cosmetic [kɒzˈmetɪk] adj, n
cosmético; **cosmetic surgery** n
cirugía f estética

cosmopolitan [kɒzməˈpɒlɪtn] adj
cosmopolita

cost [kɔst] (pt, pp **~**) n (price) precio
▷ vi costar, valer ▷ vt preparar el
presupuesto de; **how much does it ~?**
¿cuánto cuesta?; **to ~ sb time/effort**
costarle a algn tiempo/esfuerzo; **it ~
him his life** le costó la vida; **at all ~s**
cueste lo que cueste; **costs** npl (Comm)

costes mpl; (Law) costas fpl

co-star [ˈkəustɑ:ʳ] n coprotagonista
mf

Costa Rica [ˈkɔstəˈri:kə] n
Costa Rica; **Costa Rican** adj, n
costarriqueño/a

costly [ˈkɔstlɪ] adj costoso

cost of living n costo or coste m (Sp)
de la vida

costume [ˈkɔstju:m] n traje m;
(BRIT: also: **swimming ~**) traje de baño

cosy [ˈkəuzɪ] (us **cozy**) adj (person)
cómodo; (room) acogedor(a)

cot [kɔt] n (BRIT: child's) cuna;
(us: campbed) cama de campaña

cottage [ˈkɔtɪdʒ] n casita de campo;
(rustic) barraca; **cottage cheese** n
requesón m

cotton [ˈkɔtn] n algodón m; (thread)
hilo; **cotton on** vi (inf): **to cotton on
(to sth)** caer en la cuenta (de algo);
cotton bud n (BRIT) bastoncillo m
de algodón; **cotton candy** (us) n
algodón m (azucarado); **cotton wool**
(BRIT) n algodón m (hidrófilo)

couch [kautʃ] n sofá m; (doctor's etc)
diván m

cough [kɔf] vi toser ▷ n tos f; **cough
mixture** n jarabe m para la tos

could [kud] pt of **can²**; **couldn't** =
could not

council [ˈkaunsl] n consejo; **city** or
town ~ consejo municipal; **council
estate** (BRIT) n urbanización de
viviendas municipales de alquiler; **council
house** (BRIT) n vivienda municipal de
alquiler; **councillor** (us **councilor**) n
concejal(a) m/f; **council tax** n (BRIT)
contribución f municipal (dependiente
del valor de la vivienda)

counsel [ˈkaunsl] n (advice) consejo;
(lawyer) abogado/a ▷ vt aconsejar;
counselling (us **counseling**) n (Psych)
asistencia f psicológica; **counsellor** (us
counselor) n consejero/a, abogado/a

count [kaunt] vt contar; (include)
incluir ▷ vi contar ▷ n cuenta;
(of votes) escrutinio; (level) nivel m;

(*nobleman*) conde *m*; **count in** (*inf*) *vt*: **to count sb in on sth** contar con algn para algo; **count on** *vt fus* contar con; **countdown** *n* cuenta atrás

counter ['kaʊntə*] *n* (*in shop*) mostrador *m*; (*in games*) ficha ▷ *vt* contrarrestar ▷ *adv*: **to run ~ to** ser contrario a, ir en contra de; **counter clockwise** (*us*) *adv* en sentido contrario al de las agujas del reloj

counterfeit ['kaʊntəfɪt] *n* falsificación *f*, simulación *f* ▷ *vt* falsificar ▷ *adj* falso, falsificado

counterpart ['kaʊntəpɑːt] *n* homólogo/a

countess ['kaʊntɪs] *n* condesa

countless ['kaʊntlɪs] *adj* innumerable

country ['kʌntrɪ] *n* país *m*; (*native land*) patria *f*; (*as opposed to town*) campo; (*region*) región *f*, tierra; **country and western** (*music*) *n* música country; **country house** *n* casa de campo; **countryside** *n* campo

county ['kaʊntɪ] *n* condado

coup [kuː] (*pl* **~s**) *n* (*also*: **~ d'état**) golpe *m* (de estado); (*achievement*) éxito

couple ['kʌpl] *n* (*of things*) par *m*; (*of people*) pareja; (*married couple*) matrimonio; **a ~ of** un par de

coupon ['kuːpɔn] *n* cupón *m*; (*voucher*) valé *m*

courage ['kʌrɪdʒ] *n* valor *m*, valentía; **courageous** [kə'reɪdʒəs] *adj* valiente

courgette [kuə'ʒet] (*BRIT*) *n* calabacín *m*, calabacita (*MEX*)

courier ['kʊrɪə*] *n* mensajero/a; (*for tourists*) guía *mf* (de turismo)

course [kɔːs] *n* (*direction*) dirección *f*; (*of river, Scol*) curso; (*process*) transcurso; (*Med*): **~ of treatment** tratamiento; (*of ship*) rumbo; (*part of meal*) plato; (*Golf*) campo; **~ desde** luego, naturalmente; **of ~!** ¡claro!

court [kɔːt] *n* (*royal*) corte *f*; (*Law*) tribunal *m*, juzgado; (*Tennis etc*) pista, cancha ▷ *vt* (*woman*) cortejar a **to take to ~** demandar

courtesy ['kəːtəsɪ] *n* cortesía; **(by) ~ of** por cortesía de; **courtesy bus, courtesy coach** *n* autobús *m* gratuito

court: court-house *n* palacio de justicia; **courtroom** ['kɔːtruːm] *n* sala de justicia; **courtyard** ['kɔːtjɑːd] *n* patio

cousin ['kʌzn] *n* primo/a; **first ~** primo/a carnal, primo/a hermano/a

cover ['kʌvə*] *vt* cubrir; (*feelings, mistake*) ocultar; (*with lid*) tapar; (*book etc*) forrar; (*distance*) recorrer; (*include*) abarcar; (*protect: also: Insurance*) cubrir; (*Press*) investigar; (*discuss*) tratar ▷ *n* cubierta; (*lid*) tapa; (*for chair etc*) funda; (*envelope*) sobre *m*; (*for book*) forro; (*of magazine*) portada; (*shelter*) abrigo; (*Insurance*) cobertura; (*of spy*) cobertura; **covers** *npl* (*on bed*) sábanas, mantas; **to take ~** (*shelter*) protegerse, resguardarse; **under ~** (*indoors*) bajo techo; **under ~ of darkness** al amparo de la oscuridad; **under separate ~** (*Comm*) por separado; **cover up** *vi*: **to cover up for sb** encubrir a algn; **coverage** *n* (*TV, Press*) cobertura; **cover charge** *n* precio del cubierto; **cover-up** *n* encubrimiento

cow [kaʊ] *n* vaca; (*infl: woman*) bruja ▷ *vt* intimidar

coward ['kaʊəd] *n* cobarde *mf*; **cowardly** *adj* cobarde

cowboy ['kaʊbɔɪ] *n* vaquero

cozy ['kəʊzɪ] (*us*) *adj* = **cosy**

crab [kræb] *n* cangrejo

crack [kræk] *n* grieta; (*noise*) crujido; (*drug*) crack *m* ▷ *vt* agrietar, romper; (*nut*) cascar; (*solve: problem*) resolver; (*code*) descifrar; (*whip etc*) chasquear; (*knuckles*) crujir; (*joke*) contar ▷ *adj* (*expert*) de primera; **crack down on** *vt fus* adoptar fuertes medidas contra; **cracked** *adj* (*cup, window*) rajado; (*wall*) resquebrajado; **cracker** *n* (*biscuit*) cráquer *m*; (*Christmas cracker*) petardo sorpresa

crackle ['krækl] *vi* crepitar

cradle ['kreɪdl] *n* cuna

craft [krɑːft] n (skill) arte m; (trade) oficio; (cunning) astucia; (boat: pl inv) barco; (plane: pl inv) avión m; **craftsman** (irreg) n artesano m; **craftsmanship** n (quality) destreza

cram [kræm] vt (fill): **to ~ sth with** llenar algo (a reventar) de; (put): **to ~ sth into** meter algo a la fuerza en ▷ vi (for exams) empollar

cramp [kræmp] n (Med) calambre m; **cramped** adj apretado, estrecho

cranberry ['krænbərɪ] n arándano agrio

crane [kreɪn] n (Tech) grúa; (bird) grulla

crap [kræp] n (infl) mierda (!)

crash [kræʃ] n (noise) estrépito; (of cars etc) choque m; (of plane) accidente m de aviación; (Comm) quiebra ▷ vt (car, plane) estrellar ▷ vi (car, plane) estrellarse; (two cars) chocar; (Comm) quebrar; **crash course** n curso acelerado; **crash helmet** n casco (protector)

crate [kreɪt] n cajón m de embalaje; (for bottles) caja

crave [kreɪv] vt, vi: **to ~ (for)** ansiar, anhelar

crawl [krɔːl] vi (drag o.s.) arrastrarse; (child) andar a gatas, gatear; (vehicle) avanzar (lentamente) ▷ n (Swimming) crol m

crayfish ['kreɪfɪʃ] n inv (freshwater) cangrejo de río; (saltwater) cigala

crayon ['kreɪən] n lápiz m de color

craze [kreɪz] n (fashion) moda

crazy ['kreɪzɪ] adj (person) loco; (idea) disparatado; (inf: keen): **~ about sb/sth** loco por algo/algn

creak [kriːk] vi (floorboard) crujir; (hinge etc) chirriar, rechinar

cream [kriːm] n (of milk) nata, crema; (lotion) crema; (fig) flor f y nata ▷ adj (colour) color crema; **cream cheese** n queso blanco; **creamy** adj cremoso

crease [kriːs] n (fold) pliegue m; (in trousers) raya; (wrinkle) arruga ▷ vt (wrinkle) arrugar ▷ vi (wrinkle up) arrugarse

create [kriːˈeɪt] vt crear; **creation** [-ʃən] n creación f; **creative** adj creativo; **creator** n creador(a) m/f

creature ['kriːtʃə*] n (animal) animal m, bicho; (person) criatura

crèche [krɛʃ] n guardería (infantil)

credentials [krɪˈdɛnʃlz] npl (references) referencias fpl; (identity papers) documentos mpl de identidad

credibility [krɛdɪˈbɪlɪtɪ] n credibilidad f

credible ['krɛdɪbl] adj creíble; (trustworthy) digno de confianza

credit ['krɛdɪt] n crédito; (merit) honor m, mérito ▷ vt (Comm) abonar; (believe: also: **give ~ to**) creer, prestar fe a ▷ adj crediticio; **credits** npl (Cinema) fichas fpl técnicas; **to be in ~** (fig) tener saldo a favor; **to ~ sb with** (fig) reconocer el mérito de; **credit card** n tarjeta de crédito; **credit crunch** n crisis f crediticia

creek [kriːk] n cala, ensenada; (us) riachuelo

creep [kriːp] (pt, pp **crept**) vi arrastrarse

cremate [krɪˈmeɪt] vt incinerar

crematorium [krɛməˈtɔːrɪəm] (pl **crematoria**) n crematorio

crept [krɛpt] pt, pp of **creep**

crescent ['krɛsnt] n media luna; (street) calle f (en forma de semicírculo)

cress [krɛs] n berro

crest [krɛst] n (of bird) cresta; (of hill) cima, cumbre f; (of coat of arms) blasón m

crew [kruː] n (of ship etc) tripulación f; (TV, Cinema) equipo; **crew-neck** n cuello a la caja

crib [krɪb] n cuna ▷ vt (inf) plagiar

cricket ['krɪkɪt] n (insect) grillo; (game) críquet m; **cricketer** n jugador(a) m/f de críquet

crime [kraɪm] n (no pl: illegal activities) crimen m; (illegal action) delito

criminal ['krɪmɪnl] n criminal mf, delincuente mf ▷ adj criminal; (illegal) delictivo; (law) penal

crimson ['krɪmzn] adj carmesí

cringe [krɪndʒ] vi agacharse, encogerse

cripple ['krɪpl] n lisiado/a, cojo/a ▷ vt lisiar, mutilar

crisis ['kraɪsɪs] (pl **crises**) n crisis f inv

crisp [krɪsp] adj fresco; (vegetables etc) crujiente; (manner) seco; **crispy** adj crujiente

criterion [kraɪ'tɪərɪən] (pl **criteria**) n criterio

critic ['krɪtɪk] n crítico/a; **critical** adj crítico; (illness) grave; **criticism** ['krɪtɪsɪzm] n crítica; **criticize** ['krɪtɪsaɪz] vt criticar

Croat ['krəʊæt] adj, n = **Croatian**

Croatia [krəʊ'eɪʃə] n Croacia; **Croatian** adj, n croata m/f ▷ n (Ling) croata m

crockery ['krɒkərɪ] n loza, vajilla

crocodile ['krɒkədaɪl] n cocodrilo

crocus ['krəʊkəs] n croco, crocus m

croissant ['krwæsɒ̃] n croissant m, medialuna (esp LAM)

crook [krʊk] n ladrón/ona m/f; (of shepherd) cayado; **crooked** ['krʊkɪd] adj torcido; (dishonest) nada honrado

crop [krɒp] n (produce) cultivo; (amount produced) cosecha; (riding crop) látigo de montar ▷ vt cortar, recortar; **crop up** vi surgir, presentarse

cross [krɒs] n cruz f; (hybrid) cruce m ▷ vt (street etc) cruzar, atravesar ▷ adj de mal humor, enojado; **cross off** vt tachar; **cross out** vt tachar; **cross over** vi cruzar; **cross-Channel ferry** ['krɒs'tʃænl-] n transbordador m que cruza el Canal de la Mancha; **crosscountry (race)** n carrera a campo traviesa, cross m; **crossing** n (sea passage) travesía; (also: **pedestrian crossing**) paso para peatones; **crossing guard** (us) n persona encargada de ayudar a los niños a cruzar la calle; **crossroads** n cruce m, encrucijada; **crosswalk** (us) n paso de peatones; **crossword** n crucigrama m

crotch [krɒtʃ] n (Anat, of garment) entrepierna

crouch [kraʊtʃ] vi agacharse, acurrucarse

crouton ['kru:tɒn] n cubito de pan frito

crow [krəʊ] n (bird) cuervo; (of cock) canto, cacareo ▷ vi (cock) cantar

crowd [kraʊd] n muchedumbre f, multitud f ▷ vt (fill) llenar ▷ vi (gather): **to ~ round** reunirse en torno a; (cram): **to ~ in** entrar en tropel; **crowded** adj (full) atestado; (densely populated) superpoblado

crown [kraʊn] n corona; (of head) coronilla; (for tooth) funda; (of hill) cumbre f ▷ vt coronar; (fig) completar, rematar; **crown jewels** npl joyas fpl reales

crucial ['kru:ʃl] adj decisivo

crucifix ['kru:sɪfɪks] n crucifijo

crude [kru:d] adj (materials) bruto; (fig: basic) tosco; (: vulgar) ordinario; **crude (oil)** n (petróleo) crudo

cruel ['kruəl] adj cruel; **cruelty** n crueldad f

cruise [kru:z] n crucero ▷ vi (ship) hacer un crucero; (car) ir a velocidad de crucero

crumb [krʌm] n miga, migaja

crumble ['krʌmbl] vt desmenuzar ▷ vi (building, also fig) desmoronarse

crumpet ['krʌmpɪt] n ≈ bollo para tostar

crumple ['krʌmpl] vt (paper) estrujar; (material) arrugar

crunch [krʌntʃ] vt (with teeth) mascar; (underfoot) hacer crujir ▷ n (fig) hora or momento de la verdad; **crunchy** adj crujiente

crush [krʌʃ] n (crowd) aglomeración f; (infatuation): **to have a ~ on sb** estar loco por algn; (drink): **lemon ~** limonada ▷ vt aplastar; (paper) estrujar; (cloth) arrugar; (fruit) exprimir; (opposition) aplastar; (hopes) destruir

crust [krʌst] n corteza; (of snow, ice) costra; **crusty** adj (bread) crujiente;

(person) de mal carácter

crutch [krʌtʃ] n muleta

cry [kraɪ] vi llorar ▷ n (shriek) chillido; (shout) grito; **cry out** vi (call out, shout) lanzar un grito, echar un grito ▷ vt gritar

crystal ['krɪstl] n cristal m

cub [kʌb] n cachorro; (also: **~ scout**) niño explorador

Cuba ['kjuːbə] n Cuba; **Cuban** adj, n cubano/a m/f

cube [kjuːb] n cubo ▷ vt (Math) cubicar

cubicle ['kjuːbɪkl] n (at pool) caseta; (for bed) cubículo

cuckoo ['kuːkuː] n cuco

cucumber ['kjuːkʌmbə*] n pepino

cuddle ['kʌdl] vt abrazar ▷ vi abrazarse

cue [kjuː] n (snooker cue) taco; (Theatre etc) señal f

cuff [kʌf] n (of sleeve) puño; (US: of trousers) vuelta; (blow) bofetada ▷ **off the ~** adv de improviso; **cufflinks** npl gemelos mpl

cuisine [kwɪˈziːn] n cocina

cul-de-sac ['kʌldəsæk] n callejón m sin salida

cull [kʌl] vt (idea) sacar ▷ n (of animals) matanza selectiva

culminate ['kʌlmɪneɪt] vi: **to ~ in** terminar en

culprit ['kʌlprɪt] n culpable mf

cult [kʌlt] n culto

cultivate ['kʌltɪveɪt] vt cultivar

cultural ['kʌltʃərəl] adj cultural

culture ['kʌltʃə*] n (also fig) cultura; (Biol) cultivo

cumin ['kʌmɪn] n (spice) comino

cunning ['kʌnɪŋ] n astucia ▷ adj astuto

cup [kʌp] n taza; (as prize) copa

cupboard ['kʌbəd] n armario; (in kitchen) alacena

cup final n (Football) final f de copa

curator [kjuəˈreɪtə*] n director(a) m/f

curb [kəːb] vt refrenar; (person)

reprimir ▷ n freno; (US) bordillo

curdle ['kəːdl] vi cuajarse

cure [kjuə*] vt curar ▷ n cura, curación f; (fig: solution) remedio

curfew ['kəːfjuː] n toque m de queda

curiosity [kjuərɪˈɔsɪtɪ] n curiosidad f

curious ['kjuərɪəs] adj curioso; (person: interested): **to be ~** sentir curiosidad

curl [kəːl] n rizo ▷ vt (hair) rizar ▷ vi rizarse; **curl up** vi (person) hacerse un ovillo; **curler** n rulo; **curly** adj rizado

currant ['kʌrnt] n pasa (de Corinto); (blackcurrant, redcurrant) grosella

currency ['kʌrnsɪ] n moneda; **to gain ~** (fig) difundirse

current ['kʌrnt] n corriente f ▷ adj (accepted) corriente; (present) actual; **current account** (BRIT) n cuenta corriente; **current affairs** npl noticias fpl de actualidad; **currently** adv actualmente

curriculum [kəˈrɪkjuləm] (pl **~s** or **curricula**) n plan m de estudios; **curriculum vitae** n currículum m

curry ['kʌrɪ] n curry m ▷ vt: **to ~ favour with** buscar favores con; **curry powder** n curry m en polvo

curse [kəːs] vi soltar tacos ▷ vt maldecir ▷ n maldición f; (swearword) palabrota, taco

cursor ['kəːsə*] n (Comput) cursor m

curt [kəːt] adj corto, seco

curtain ['kəːtn] n cortina; (Theatre) telón m

curve [kəːv] n curva ▷ vi (road) hacer una curva; (line etc) curvarse; **curved** adj curvo

cushion ['kuʃən] n cojín m; (of air) colchón m ▷ vt (shock) amortiguar

custard ['kʌstəd] n natillas fpl

custody ['kʌstədɪ] n custodia; **to take into ~** detener

custom ['kʌstəm] n costumbre f; (Comm) clientela

customer ['kʌstəmə*] n cliente m/f

customized ['kʌstəmaɪzd] adj (car etc) hecho a encargo

customs ['kʌstəmz] *npl* aduana;
customs officer *n* aduanero/a

cut [kʌt] (*pt, pp* ~) *vt* cortar; (*price*)
rebajar; (*text, programme*) acortar;
(*reduce*) reducir ▷ *vi* cortar ▷ *n* (*of
garment*) corte *m*; (*in skin*) cortadura;
(*in salary etc*) rebaja; (*in spending*)
reducción *f*, recorte *m*; (*slice of meat*)
tajada; **to ~ a tooth** echar un diente;
to ~ and paste (*Comput*) cortar y pegar;
cut back *vt* (*plants*) podar; (*production,
expenditure*) reducir; **cut down** *vt*
(*tree*) derribar; (*reduce*) reducir; **cut
off** *vt* cortar; (*person, place*) aislar;
(*Tel*) desconectar; **cut out** *vt* (*shape*)
recortar; (*stop: activity etc*) dejar;
(*remove*) quitar; **cut up** *vt* cortar (en
pedazos); **cutback** *n* reducción *f*

cute [kjuːt] *adj* mono

cutlery ['kʌtləri] *n* cubiertos *mpl*

cutlet ['kʌtlɪt] *n* chuleta; (*nut etc
cutlet*) plato vegetariano hecho con nueces
y verdura en forma de chuleta

cut-price ['kʌt'praɪs] (*BRIT*) *adj* a
precio reducido

cut-rate ['kʌt'reɪt] (*us*) *adj* =
cut-price

cutting ['kʌtɪŋ] *adj* (*remark*) mordaz
▷ *n* (*BRIT: from newspaper*) recorte *m*;
(*from plant*) esqueje *m*

CV *n abbr* = **curriculum vitae**

cwt *abbr* = **hundredweight(s)**

cybercafé ['saɪbəkæfeɪ] *n* cibercafé
m

cyberspace ['saɪbəspeɪs] *n*
ciberespacio

cycle ['saɪkl] *n* ciclo; (*bicycle*) bicicleta
▷ *vi* ir en bicicleta; **cycle hire** *n*
alquiler *m* de bicicletas; **cycle lane** *n*
carril-bici *m*; **cycle path** *n* carril-bici
m; **cycling** *n* ciclismo; **cyclist** *n*
ciclista *mf*

cyclone ['saɪkləun] *n* ciclón *m*

cylinder ['sɪlɪndə*] *n* cilindro; (*of gas*)
bombona

cymbal ['sɪmbl] *n* címbalo, platillo

cynical ['sɪnɪkl] *adj* cínico

Cypriot ['sɪprɪət] *adj, n* chipriota *m/f*

Cyprus ['saɪprəs] *n* Chipre *f*

cyst [sɪst] *n* quiste *m*; **cystitis**
[-'taɪtɪs] *n* cistitis *f*

czar [zɑː*] *n* zar *m*

Czech [tʃɛk] *adj, n* checo/a *m/f*; **Czech
Republic** *n*: **the Czech Republic** la
República Checa

d

D [di:] n (Mus) re m

dab [dæb] vt (eyes, wound) tocar (ligeramente); (paint, cream) poner un poco de

dad [dæd] n = **daddy**

daddy ['dædɪ] n papá m

daffodil ['dæfədɪl] n narciso

daft [dɑ:ft] adj tonto

dagger ['dægə*] n puñal m, daga

daily ['deɪlɪ] adj diario, cotidiano ▷ adv todos los días, cada día

dairy ['dɛərɪ] n (shop) lechería; (on farm) vaquería; **dairy produce** n productos mpl lácteos

daisy ['deɪzɪ] n margarita

dam [dæm] n presa ▷ vt construir una presa sobre, represar

damage ['dæmɪdʒ] n lesión f; daño; (dents etc) desperfectos mpl; (fig) perjuicio ▷ vt dañar, perjudicar; (spoil, break) estropear; **damages** npl (Law) daños mpl y perjuicios

damn [dæm] vt condenar; (curse) maldecir ▷ n (inf): **I don't give a ~** me importa un pito ▷ adj (inf also: **~ed**)

maldito; **~ (it)!** ¡maldito sea!

damp [dæmp] adj húmedo, mojado ▷ n humedad f ▷ vt (also: **~en**: cloth, rag) mojar; (: enthusiasm) enfriar

dance [dɑ:ns] n baile m ▷ vi bailar; **dance floor** n pista f de baile; **dancer** n bailador(a) m/f; (professional) bailarín/ina m/f; **dancing** n baile m

dandelion ['dændɪlaɪən] n diente m de león

dandruff ['dændrəf] n caspa

Dane [deɪn] n danés/esa m/f

danger ['deɪndʒə*] n peligro; (risk) riesgo; **~! (on sign)** ¡peligro de muerte!; **to be in ~** correr riesgo de; **dangerous** adj peligroso

dangle ['dæŋgl] vt colgar ▷ vi pender, colgar

Danish ['deɪnɪʃ] adj danés/esa ▷ n (Ling) danés m

dare [dɛə*] vt: **to ~ sb to do** desafiar a algn a hacer ▷ vi: **to ~ (to) do sth** atreverse a hacer algo; **I ~ say** (I suppose) puede ser (que); **daring** adj atrevido, osado ▷ n atrevimiento, osadía

dark [dɑ:k] adj oscuro; (hair, complexion) moreno ▷ n: **in the ~** a oscuras; **to be in the ~ about** (fig) no saber nada de; **after ~** después del anochecer; **darken** vt (colour) hacer más oscuro ▷ vi oscurecerse; **darkness** n oscuridad f; **darkroom** n cuarto oscuro

darling ['dɑːlɪŋ] adj, n querido/a m/f

dart [dɑːt] n dardo; (in sewing) sisa ▷ vi precipitarse; **dartboard** n diana; **darts** n (game) dardos mpl

dash [dæʃ] n (small quantity: of liquid) gota, chorrito; (sign) raya ▷ vt (throw) tirar; (hopes) defraudar ▷ vi precipitarse, ir de prisa; **dashboard** n (Aut) salpicadero

data ['deɪtə] npl datos mpl; **database** n base f de datos; **data processing** n proceso de datos

date [deɪt] n (day) fecha; (with

friend) cita; (fruit) dátil m ▷ vt fechar; (person) salir con; **~ of birth** fecha de nacimiento; **to ~** adv hasta la fecha; **dated** adj anticuado

daughter ['dɔ:tə*] n hija; **daughter-in-law** n nuera, hija política

daunting ['dɔ:ntɪŋ] adj desalentador/a

dawn [dɔ:n] n alba, amanecer m; (fig) nacimiento ▷ vi (day) amanecer; (fig): **it ~ed on him that ...** cayó en la cuenta de que ...

day [deɪ] n día m; (working day) jornada; (heyday) tiempos mpl, días mpl; **the ~ before** el día anterior; **the ~ after** el día siguiente; **the ~ after tomorrow** pasado mañana; **the ~ before yesterday** anteayer; **the following ~** el día siguiente; **by ~** de día; **day-care centre** ['deɪkeə-] n centro de día; (for children) guardería infantil; **daydream** vi soñar despierto; **daylight** n luz f (del día); **day return** (BRIT) n billete m de ida y vuelta (en un día); **daytime** n día m; **day-to-day** adj cotidiano; **day trip** n excursión f (de un día)

dazed [deɪzd] adj aturdido

dazzle ['dæzl] vt deslumbrar; **dazzling** adj (light, smile) deslumbrante; (colour) fuerte

DC abbr (= direct current) C.C.

dead [ded] adj muerto; (limb) dormido; (telephone) cortado; (battery) agotado ▷ adv (completely) totalmente; (exactly) exactamente; **to shoot sb ~** matar a algn a tiros; **~ tired** muerto (de cansancio); **to stop ~** parar en seco; **dead end** n callejón m sin salida; **deadline** n fecha (or hora) tope; **deadly** adj mortal, fatal; **Dead Sea** n: **the Dead Sea** el Mar Muerto

deaf [def] adj sordo; **deafen** vt ensordecer; **deafening** adj ensordecedor/a

deal [di:l] (pt, pp ~t) n (agreement) pacto, convenio; (business deal) trato ▷ vt dar; (card) repartir; **a great ~ (of)** bastante, mucho; **deal with**

vt fus (people) tratar con; (problem) ocuparse de; (subject) tratar de; **dealer** n comerciante m/f; (Cards) mano f; **dealings** npl (Comm) transacciones fpl; (relations) relaciones fpl

dealt [delt] pt, pp of **deal**

dean [di:n] n (Rel) deán m; (Scol: BRIT) decano; (: us) decano; rector m

dear [dɪə*] adj querido; (expensive) caro ▷ n: **my ~** mi querido/a ▷ excl: **~ me!** ¡Dios mío!; **D~ Sir/Madam** (in letter) Muy Señor Mío, Estimado Señor/Estimada Señora; **D~ Mr/Mrs X** Estimado/a Señor(a) X; **dearly** adv (love) mucho; (pay) caro

death [deθ] n muerte f; **death penalty** n pena de muerte; **death sentence** n condena a muerte

debate [dɪ'beɪt] n debate m ▷ vt discutir

debit ['debɪt] n debe m ▷ vt: **to ~ a sum to sb** or **to sb's account** cargar una suma en cuenta a algn; **debit card** n tarjeta f de débito

debris ['debri:] n escombros mpl

debt [det] n deuda; **to be in ~** tener deudas

debug [di:'bʌg] vt (Comput) limpiar

debut ['deɪbju:] n presentación f

Dec. abbr (= December) dic.

decade ['dekeɪd] n decenio, década

decaffeinated [dɪ'kæfɪneɪtɪd] adj descafeinado

decay [dɪ'keɪ] n (of building) desmoronamiento; (of tooth) caries f inv ▷ vi (rot) pudrirse

deceased [dɪ'si:st] n: **the ~** el(la) difunto/a

deceit [dɪ'si:t] n engaño; **deceive** [dɪ'si:v] vt engañar

December [dɪ'sembə*] n diciembre m

decency ['di:sənsɪ] n decencia

decent ['di:sənt] adj (proper) decente; (person: kind) amable, bueno

deception [dɪ'sepʃən] n engaño

> Be careful not to translate **deception** by the Spanish word **decepción**.

deceptive [dɪ'septɪv] adj engañoso

decide [dɪˈsaɪd] vt (person) decidir; (question, argument) resolver ▷ vi decidir; **to ~ to do/that** decidir hacer/que; **to ~ on sth** decidirse por algo

decimal [ˈdesɪml] adj decimal ▷ n decimal m

decision [dɪˈsɪʒən] n decisión f

decisive [dɪˈsaɪsɪv] adj decisivo; (person) decidido

deck [dek] n (Naut) cubierta; (of bus) piso; (record player) platina; (of cards) baraja; **deckchair** n tumbona

declaration [deklaˈreɪʃən] n declaración f

declare [dɪˈkleə*] vt declarar

decline [dɪˈklaɪn] n disminución f, descenso ▷ vt rehusar ▷ vi (person, business) decaer; (strength) disminuir

decorate [ˈdekəreɪt] vt (adorn): **to ~ (with)** adornar (de), decorar (de); (paint) pintar; (paper) empapelar; **decoration** [-ˈreɪʃən] n adorno; (act) decoración f; (medal) condecoración f; **decorator** n (workman) pintor m (decorador)

decrease [n ˈdiːkriːs, vb diˈkriːs] n: **~ (in)** disminución f (de) ▷ vt disminuir, reducir ▷ vi reducirse

decree [dɪˈkriː] n decreto

dedicate [ˈdedɪkeɪt] vt dedicar; **dedicated** adj dedicado; (Comput) especializado; **dedicated word processor** procesador m de textos especializado or dedicado; **dedication** [-ˈkeɪʃən] n (devotion) dedicación f; (in book) dedicatoria

deduce [dɪˈdjuːs] vt deducir

deduct [dɪˈdʌkt] vt restar; descontar; **deduction** [dɪˈdʌkʃən] n (amount deducted) descuento; (conclusion) deducción f, conclusión f

deed [diːd] n hecho, acto; (feat) hazaña; (Law) escritura

deem [diːm] vt (formal) juzgar, considerar

deep [diːp] adj (water) de profundidad; (voice) bajo; (breath) profundo; (colour) intenso ▷ adv: **the spectators stood 20 ~** los espectadores se formaron de 20 en fondo; **to be 4 metres ~** tener 4 metros de profundidad; **deep-fry** vt freír en aceite abundante; **deeply** adv (breathe) a pleno pulmón; (interested, moved, grateful) profundamente, hondamente

deer [dɪə*] n inv ciervo

default [dɪˈfɔːlt] n: **by ~** (win) por incomparecencia ▷ adj (Comput) por defecto

defeat [dɪˈfiːt] n derrota ▷ vt derrotar, vencer

defect [n ˈdiːfekt, vb dɪˈfekt] n defecto ▷ vi: **to ~ to the enemy** pasarse al enemigo; **defective** [dɪˈfektɪv] adj defectuoso

defence [dɪˈfens] (us **defense**) n defensa

defend [dɪˈfend] vt defender; **defendant** n acusado/a; (in civil case) demandado/a; **defender** n defensor(a) m/f; (Sport) defensa mf

defense [dɪˈfens] (us) = **defence**

defensive [dɪˈfensɪv] adj defensivo ▷ n: **on the ~** a la defensiva

defer [dɪˈfɜː*] vt aplazar

defiance [dɪˈfaɪəns] n desafío; **in ~ of** en contra de; **defiant** [dɪˈfaɪənt] adj (challenging) desafiante, retador/a

deficiency [dɪˈfɪʃənsɪ] n (lack) falta; (defect) defecto; **deficient** [dɪˈfɪʃənt] adj deficiente

deficit [ˈdefɪsɪt] n déficit m

define [dɪˈfaɪn] vt (word etc) definir; (limits etc) determinar

definite [ˈdefɪnɪt] adj (fixed) determinado; (obvious) claro; (certain) indudable; **he was ~ about it** no dejó lugar a dudas (sobre ello); **definitely** adv desde luego, por supuesto

definition [defɪˈnɪʃən] n definición f; (clearness) nitidez f

deflate [diːˈfleɪt] vt desinflar

deflect [dɪˈflekt] vt desviar

defraud [dɪˈfrɔːd] vt: **to ~ sb of sth** estafar algo a algn

defrost [diːˈfrɒst] vt descongelar

defuse [diːˈfjuːz] vt desactivar; (situation) calmar

defy [dɪˈfaɪ] vt (resist) oponerse a; (challenge) desafiar; (fig): **it defies description** resulta imposible describirlo

degree [dɪˈgriː] n grado; (Scol) título; **to have a ~ in maths** tener una licenciatura en matemáticas; **by ~s** (gradually) poco a poco, por etapas; **to some ~** hasta cierto punto

dehydrated [diːhaɪˈdreɪtɪd] adj deshidratado; (milk) en polvo

de-icer [diːˈaɪsə*] n descongelador m

delay [dɪˈleɪ] vt demorar, aplazar; (person) entretener; (train) retrasar ▷ vi tardar ▷ n demora, retraso; **to be ~ed** retrasarse; **without ~** en seguida, sin tardar

delegate [n ˈdɛlɪgɪt, vb ˈdɛlɪgeɪt] n delegado/a ▷ vt (person) delegar en; (task) delegar

delete [dɪˈliːt] vt suprimir, tachar

deli [ˈdɛlɪ] n = **delicatessen**

deliberate [adj dɪˈlɪbərɪt, vb dɪˈlɪbəreɪt] adj (intentional) intencionado; (slow) pausado, lento ▷ vi deliberar; **deliberately** adv (on purpose) a propósito

delicacy [ˈdɛlɪkəsɪ] n delicadeza; (choice food) manjar m

delicate [ˈdɛlɪkɪt] adj delicado; (fragile) frágil

delicatessen [dɛlɪkəˈtɛsn] n ultramarinos mpl finos

delicious [dɪˈlɪʃəs] adj delicioso

delight [dɪˈlaɪt] n (feeling) placer m, deleite m; (person, experience etc) encanto, delicia ▷ vt encantar, deleitar; **to take ~ in** deleitarse en; **delighted** adj: **delighted (at or with/to do)** encantado (con/de hacer); **delightful** adj encantador(a), delicioso

delinquent [dɪˈlɪŋkwənt] adj, n delincuente mf

deliver [dɪˈlɪvə*] vt (distribute) repartir; (hand over) entregar; (message) comunicar; (speech) pronunciar; (Med) asistir al parto de; **delivery** n reparto; entrega; (of speaker) modo de expresarse; (Med) parto, alumbramiento; **to take delivery of** recibir

delusion [dɪˈluːʒən] n ilusión f, engaño

de luxe [dəˈlʌks] adj de lujo

delve [dɛlv] vi: **to ~ into** hurgar en

demand [dɪˈmɑːnd] vt (gen) exigir; (rights) reclamar ▷ n (claim) reclamación f; (Econ) demanda; **to be in ~** ser muy solicitado; **on ~** a solicitud; **demanding** adj (boss) exigente; (work) absorbente

demise [dɪˈmaɪz] n (death) fallecimiento

demo [ˈdɛməʊ] (inf) n abbr = **demonstration** manifestación f

democracy [dɪˈmɒkrəsɪ] n democracia; **democrat** [ˈdɛməkræt] n demócrata mf; **democratic** [dɛməˈkrætɪk] adj democrático; (us) demócrata

demolish [dɪˈmɒlɪʃ] vt derribar, demoler; (fig: argument) destruir

demolition [dɛməˈlɪʃən] n derribo, demolición f

demon [ˈdiːmən] n (evil spirit) demonio

demonstrate [ˈdɛmənstreɪt] vt demostrar; (skill, appliance) mostrar ▷ vi manifestarse; **demonstration** [-ˈstreɪʃən] n (Pol) manifestación f; (proof, exhibition) demostración f; **demonstrator** n (Pol) manifestante mf; (Comm) demostrador(a) m/f; vendedor(a) m/f

demote [dɪˈməʊt] vt degradar

den [dɛn] n (of animal) guarida; (room) habitación f

denial [dɪˈnaɪəl] n (refusal) negativa; (of report etc) negación f

denim [ˈdɛnɪm] n tela vaquera; **denims** npl vaqueros mpl

Denmark [ˈdɛnmɑːk] n Dinamarca

denomination [dɪnɒmɪˈneɪʃən] n
valor m; (Rel) confesión f

denounce [dɪˈnauns] vt denunciar

dense [dɛns] adj (crowd) denso; (thick)
espeso; (: foliage etc) tupido; (inf: stupid)
torpe

density [ˈdɛnsɪtɪ] n densidad f
▷**single/double-~ disk** n (Comput)
disco de densidad sencilla/de doble
densidad

dent [dɛnt] n abolladura ▷ vt
(also: **make a ~ in**) abollar

dental [ˈdɛntl] adj dental; **dental
floss** [-flɒs] n seda dental; **dental
surgery** n clínica f dental, consultorio
m dental

dentist [ˈdɛntɪst] n dentista mf

dentures [ˈdɛntʃəz] npl dentadura
(postiza)

deny [dɪˈnaɪ] vt negar; (charge)
rechazar

deodorant [diːˈəudərənt] n
desodorante m

depart [dɪˈpɑːt] vi irse, marcharse;
(train) salir; **to ~ from** (fig: differ from)
apartarse de

department [dɪˈpɑːtmənt] n
(Comm) sección f; (Scol) departamento;
(Pol) ministerio; **department store** n
gran almacén m

departure [dɪˈpɑːtʃə*] n partida, ida;
(of train) salida; (of employee) marcha;
a new ~ un nuevo rumbo; **departure
lounge** n (at airport) sala de embarque

depend [dɪˈpɛnd] vi: **to ~ on** depender
de; (rely on) contar con; **it ~s** depende,
según; **~ing on the result** según el
resultado; **dependant** n dependiente
mf; **dependent** adj: **to be dependent
on** depender de ▷ n = **dependant**

depict [dɪˈpɪkt] vt (in picture) pintar;
(describe) representar

deport [dɪˈpɔːt] vt deportar

deposit [dɪˈpɒzɪt] n (Comm); (Chem)
sedimento; (of ore, oil) yacimiento ▷ vt
(gen) depositar; **deposit account** (BRIT)
n cuenta de ahorros

depot [ˈdɛpəu] n (storehouse)

depósito; (for vehicles) parque m; (US)
estación f

depreciate [dɪˈpriːʃɪeɪt] vi
depreciarse, perder valor

depress [dɪˈprɛs] vt deprimir; (wages
etc) hacer bajar; (press down) apretar;
depressed adj deprimido; **depressing**
adj deprimente; **depression**
[dɪˈprɛʃən] n depresión f

deprive [dɪˈpraɪv] vt: **to ~ sb of** privar
a algn de; **deprived** adj necesitado

dept. abbr (= department) dto

depth [dɛpθ] n profundidad f; (of
cupboard) fondo; **to be in the ~s of
despair** sentir la mayor desesperación;
to be out of one's ~ (in water) no hacer
pie; (fig) sentirse totalmente perdido

deputy [ˈdɛpjutɪ] adj: **~ head**
subdirector(a) m/f ▷ n sustituto/a,
suplente mf; (US Pol) diputado/a;
(US: also: **~ sheriff**) agente m del sheriff

derail [dɪˈreɪl] vt: **to be ~ed**
descarrilarse

derelict [ˈdɛrɪlɪkt] adj abandonado

derive [dɪˈraɪv] vt (benefit etc) obtener
▷ vi: **to ~ from** derivarse de

descend [dɪˈsɛnd] vt, vi descender,
bajar; **to ~ from** descender de; **to
~ to** rebajarse a; **descendant** n
descendiente mf

descent [dɪˈsɛnt] n descenso; (origin)
descendencia

describe [dɪsˈkraɪb] vt describir;
description [-ˈkrɪpʃən] n descripción
f; (sort) clase f, género

desert [n ˈdɛzət, vb dɪˈzəːt] n desierto
▷ vt abandonar ▷ vi (Mil) desertar;
deserted [dɪˈzəːtɪd] adj desierto

deserve [dɪˈzəːv] vt merecer, ser
digno de

design [dɪˈzaɪn] n (sketch) bosquejo;
(layout, shape) diseño; (pattern) dibujo;
(intention) intención f ▷ vt diseñar;
design and technology (BRIT: Scol) n
= dibujo y tecnología

designate [vb ˈdɛzɪgneɪt, adj
ˈdɛzɪgnɪt] vt (appoint) nombrar;
(destine) designar ▷ adj designado

designer [dɪˈzaɪnə*] n diseñador(a) m/f; (fashion designer) modisto/a, diseñador(a) m/f de moda

desirable [dɪˈzaɪərəbl] adj (proper) deseable; (attractive) atractivo

desire [dɪˈzaɪə*] n deseo ⊳ vt desear

desk [dɛsk] n (in office) escritorio; (for pupil) pupitre m; (in hotel, at airport) recepción f; (BRIT: in shop, restaurant) caja; **desk-top publishing** [ˈdɛsktɒp-] n autoedición f

despair [dɪsˈpɛə*] n desesperación f ⊳ vi: **to ~ of** perder la esperanza de

despatch [dɪsˈpætʃ] n, vt = **dispatch**

desperate [ˈdɛspərɪt] adj desesperado; (fugitive) peligroso; **to be ~ for sth/to do** necesitar urgentemente algo/hacer; **desperately** adv desesperadamente; (very) terriblemente, gravemente

desperation [dɛspəˈreɪʃən] n desesperación f; **in (sheer) ~** (absolutamente) desesperado

despise [dɪsˈpaɪz] vt despreciar

despite [dɪsˈpaɪt] prep a pesar de, pese a

dessert [dɪˈzəːt] n postre m; **dessertspoon** n cuchara (de postre)

destination [dɛstɪˈneɪʃən] n destino

destined [ˈdɛstɪnd] adj: **~ for London** con destino a Londres

destiny [ˈdɛstɪnɪ] n destino

destroy [dɪsˈtrɔɪ] vt destruir; (animal) sacrificar

destruction [dɪsˈtrʌkʃən] n destrucción f

destructive [dɪsˈtrʌktɪv] adj destructivo, destructor(a)

detach [dɪˈtætʃ] vt separar; (unstick) despegar; **detached** adj (attitude) objetivo, imparcial; **detached house** n ≈ chalé m, ≈ chalet m

detail [ˈdiːteɪl] n detalle m; (no pl; in picture etc) detalles mpl; (trifle) pequeñez f ⊳ vt detallar; (Mil) destacar; **in ~** detalladamente; **detailed** adj detallado

detain [dɪˈteɪn] vt retener; (in captivity) detener

detect [dɪˈtɛkt] vt descubrir; (Med, Police) identificar; (Mil, Radar, Tech) detectar; **detection** [dɪˈtɛkʃən] n descubrimiento; identificación f; **detective** n detective mf; **detective story** n novela policíaca

detention [dɪˈtɛnʃən] n detención f, arresto; (Scol) castigo

deter [dɪˈtəː*] vt (dissuade) disuadir

detergent [dɪˈtəːdʒənt] n detergente m

deteriorate [dɪˈtɪərɪəreɪt] vi deteriorarse

determination [dɪtəːmɪˈneɪʃən] n resolución f

determine [dɪˈtəːmɪn] vt determinar; **determined** adj (person) resuelto, decidido; **determined to do** resuelto a hacer

deterrent [dɪˈtɛrənt] n (Mil) fuerza de disuasión

detest [dɪˈtɛst] vt aborrecer

detour [ˈdiːtuə*] n (gen, us Aut) desviación f

detract [dɪˈtrækt] vt: **to ~ from** quitar mérito a, desvirtuar

detrimental [dɛtrɪˈmɛntl] adj: **~ (to)** perjudicial (a)

devastating [ˈdɛvəsteɪtɪŋ] adj devastador(a); (fig) arrollador(a)

develop [dɪˈvɛləp] vt desarrollar; (Phot) revelar; (disease) coger; (habit) adquirir; (fault) empezar a tener ⊳ vi desarrollarse; (advance) progresar; (facts, symptoms) aparecer; **developing country** n país m en (vías de) desarrollo; **development** n desarrollo; (advance) progreso; (of affair, case) desenvolvimiento; (of land) urbanización f

device [dɪˈvaɪs] n (apparatus) aparato, mecanismo

devil [ˈdɛvl] n diablo, demonio

devious [ˈdiːvɪəs] adj taimado

devise [dɪˈvaɪz] vt idear, inventar

devote [dɪˈvəut] vt: **to ~ sth to** dedicar algo a; **devoted** adj (loyal) leal, fiel; **to be devoted to sb** querer con devoción a algn; **the book is devoted to politics** el libro trata de la política; **devotion** n dedicación f; (Rel) devoción f

devour [dɪˈvauə*] vt devorar

devout [dɪˈvaut] adj devoto

dew [djuː] n rocío

diabetes [daɪəˈbiːtiːz] n diabetes f

diabetic [daɪəˈbetɪk] adj, n diabético/a m/f

diagnose [ˈdaɪəgnəuz] vt diagnosticar

diagnosis [daɪəgˈnəusɪs] (pl **-ses**) n diagnóstico

diagonal [daɪˈægənl] adj, n diagonal f

diagram [ˈdaɪəgræm] n diagrama m, esquema m

dial [ˈdaɪəl] n esfera (SP), cara (LAM); (on radio etc) dial m; (of phone) disco ▷ vt (number) marcar

dialect [ˈdaɪəlekt] n dialecto

dialling code [ˈdaɪəlɪn-] n prefijo

dialling tone (us **dial tone**) n (BRIT) señal f or tono de marcar

dialogue [ˈdaɪəlɒg] (us **dialog**) n diálogo

diameter [daɪˈæmɪtə*] n diámetro

diamond [ˈdaɪəmənd] n diamante m; (shape) rombo; **diamonds** npl (Cards) diamantes mpl

diaper [ˈdaɪəpə*] (us) n pañal m

diarrhoea [daɪəˈriːə] (us **diarrhea**) n diarrea

diary [ˈdaɪərɪ] n (daily account) diario; (book) agenda

dice [daɪs] n inv dados mpl ▷ vt (Culin) cortar en cuadritos

dictate [dɪkˈteɪt] vt dictar; (conditions) imponer; **dictation** [-ˈteɪʃən] n dictado; (giving of orders) órdenes fpl

dictator [dɪkˈteɪtə*] n dictador m

dictionary [ˈdɪkʃənrɪ] n diccionario

did [dɪd] pt of **do**

didn't [ˈdɪdənt] = **did not**

die [daɪ] vi morir; (fig: fade)

desvanecerse, desaparecer; **to be dying for sth/to do sth** morirse por algo/de ganas de hacer algo; **die down** vi apagarse; (wind) amainar; **die out** vi desaparecer

diesel [ˈdiːzəl] n vehículo con motor Diesel

diet [ˈdaɪət] n dieta; (restricted food) régimen m ▷ vi (also: **be on a ~**) estar a dieta, hacer régimen

differ [ˈdɪfə*] vi: **to ~ (from)** (be different) ser distinto (a), diferenciarse (de); (disagree) discrepar (de); **difference** n diferencia; (disagreement) desacuerdo; **different** adj diferente, distinto; **differentiate** [-ˈrenʃɪeɪt] vi: **to differentiate (between)** distinguir (entre); **differently** adv de otro modo, en forma distinta

difficult [ˈdɪfɪkəlt] adj difícil; **difficulty** n dificultad f

dig [dɪg] (pt, pp **dug**) vt (hole, ground) cavar ▷ n (prod) empujón m; (archaeological) excavación f; (remark) indirecta; **to ~ one's nails into** clavar las uñas en; **dig up** vt (information) desenterrar; (plant) desarraigar

digest [vb daɪˈdʒest, n ˈdaɪdʒest] vt (food) digerir; (facts) asimilar ▷ n resumen m; **digestion** [dɪˈdʒestʃən] n digestión f

digit [ˈdɪdʒɪt] n (number) dígito; (finger) dedo; **digital** adj digital; **digital camera** n cámara digital; **digital TV** n televisión f digital

dignified [ˈdɪgnɪfaɪd] adj grave, solemne

dignity [ˈdɪgnɪtɪ] n dignidad f

digs [dɪgz] (BRIT: inf) npl pensión f, alojamiento

dilemma [daɪˈlemə] n dilema m

dill [dɪl] n eneldo

dilute [daɪˈluːt] vt diluir

dim [dɪm] adj (light) débil; (outline) indistinto; (room) oscuro; (inf: stupid) lerdo ▷ vt (light) bajar

dime [daɪm] (us) n moneda de diez centavos

dimension [dɪˈmɛnʃən] n dimensión f

diminish [dɪˈmɪnɪʃ] vt, vi disminuir

din [dɪn] n estruendo, estrépito

dine [daɪn] vi cenar; **diner** n (person) comensal mf

dinghy [ˈdɪŋɡɪ] n bote m; (also: **rubber ~**) lancha (neumática)

dingy [ˈdɪndʒɪ] adj (room) sombrío; (colour) sucio

dining car [ˈdaɪnɪŋ-] n (Rail) coche-comedor m

dining room [ˈdaɪnɪŋ-] n comedor m

dining table n mesa f de comedor

dinner [ˈdɪnə*] n (evening meal) cena; (lunch) comida; (public) cena, banquete m; **dinner jacket** n smoking m; **dinner party** n cena; **dinner time** n (evening) hora de cenar; (midday) hora de comer

dinosaur [ˈdaɪnəsɔː*] n dinosaurio m

dip [dɪp] n (slope) pendiente m; (in sea) baño; (Culin) salsa ▷ vt (in water) mojar; (ladle etc) meter; (BRIT Aut): **to ~ one's lights** poner luces de cruce ▷ vi (road etc) descender, bajar

diploma [dɪˈpləʊmə] n diploma m

diplomacy [dɪˈpləʊməsɪ] n diplomacia

diplomat [ˈdɪpləmæt] n diplomático/a; **diplomatic** [dɪpləˈmætɪk] adj diplomático

dipstick [ˈdɪpstɪk] (BRIT) n (Aut) varilla de nivel (del aceite)

dire [daɪə*] adj calamitoso

direct [daɪˈrɛkt] adj directo; (challenge) claro; (person) franco ▷ vt dirigir; (order): **to ~ sb to do sth** mandar a algn hacer algo ▷ adv derecho; **can you ~ me to ...?** ¿puede indicarme dónde está ...?; **direct debit** (BRIT) n domiciliación f bancaria de recibos

direction [dɪˈrɛkʃən] n dirección f; **sense of ~** sentido de la dirección; **directions** npl (instructions) instrucciones fpl; **~s for use** modo de empleo

directly [dɪˈrɛktlɪ] adv (in straight line)

directamente; (at once) en seguida

director [dɪˈrɛktə*] n director(a) m/f

directory [dɪˈrɛktərɪ] n (Tel) guía (telefónica); (Comput) directorio; **directory enquiries** (US **directory assistance**) n (service) de información f

dirt [dəːt] n suciedad f; (earth) tierra; **dirty** adj sucio; (joke) verde, colorado (MEX) ▷ vt ensuciar; (stain) manchar

disability [dɪsəˈbɪlɪtɪ] n incapacidad f

disabled [dɪsˈeɪbld] adj: **to be physically ~** ser minusválido/a; **to be mentally ~** ser deficiente mental

disadvantage [dɪsədˈvɑːntɪdʒ] n desventaja, inconveniente m

disagree [dɪsəˈɡriː] vi (differ) discrepar; **to ~ (with)** no estar de acuerdo (con); **disagreeable** adj desagradable; (person) antipático; **disagreement** n desacuerdo

disappear [dɪsəˈpɪə*] vi desaparecer; **disappearance** n desaparición f

disappoint [dɪsəˈpɔɪnt] vt decepcionar, defraudar; **disappointed** adj decepcionado; **disappointing** adj decepcionante; **disappointment** n decepción f

disapproval [dɪsəˈpruːvəl] n desaprobación f

disapprove [dɪsəˈpruːv] vi: **to ~ of** ver mal

disarm [dɪsˈɑːm] vt desarmar; **disarmament** [dɪsˈɑːməmənt] n desarme m

disaster [dɪˈzɑːstə*] n desastre m; **disastrous** [dɪˈzɑːstrəs] adj desastroso

disbelief [dɪsbəˈliːf] n incredulidad f

disc [dɪsk] n disco; (Comput) = **disk**

discard [dɪsˈkɑːd] vt (old things) tirar; (fig) descartar

discharge [vb dɪsˈtʃɑːdʒ, n ˈdɪstʃɑːdʒ] vt (task, duty) cumplir; (waste) verter; (patient) dar de alta; (employee) despedir; (soldier) licenciar; (defendant) poner en libertad ▷ n (Elec) descarga; (*Med*) supuración *f*; (*dismissal*) despedida; (*of duty*) desempeño *f*; (*of debt*) pago, descargo

discipline ['dɪsɪplɪn] *n* disciplina ▷ *vt* disciplinar; (*punish*) castigar

disc jockey *n* pinchadiscos *mf inv*

disclose [dɪs'kləʊz] *vt* revelar

disco ['dɪskəʊ] *n abbr* discoteca

discoloured [dɪs'kʌləd], (*us* **discolored**) *adj* descolorido

discomfort [dɪs'kʌmfət] *n* incomodidad *f*; (*unease*) inquietud *f*; (*physical*) malestar *m*

disconnect [dɪskə'nekt] *vt* separar; (*Elec etc*) desconectar

discontent [dɪskən'tent] *n* descontento

discontinue [dɪskən'tɪnjuː] *vt* interrumpir; (*payments*) suspender; **"~d"** (*Comm*) "ya no se fabrica"

discount [*n* 'dɪskaunt, *vb* dɪs'kaunt] *n* descuento ▷ *vt* descontar

discourage [dɪs'kʌrɪdʒ] *vt* desalentar; (*advise against*): **to ~ sb from doing** disuadir a algn de hacer

discover [dɪs'kʌvə*] *vt* descubrir; (*error*) darse cuenta de; **discovery** *n* descubrimiento

discredit [dɪs'kredɪt] *vt* desacreditar

discreet [dɪ'skriːt] *adj* (*tactful*) discreto; (*careful*) prudente

discrepancy [dɪs'krepənsɪ] *n* diferencia

discretion [dɪ'skreʃən] *n* (*tact*) discreción *f*; **at the ~ of** a criterio de

discriminate [dɪs'krɪmɪneɪt] *vi*: **to ~ between** distinguir entre; **to ~ against** discriminar contra; **discrimination** [-'neɪʃən] *n* (*discernment*) perspicacia; (*bias*) discriminación *f*

discuss [dɪs'kʌs] *vt* discutir; (*a theme*) tratar; **discussion** [dɪs'kʌʃən] *n* discusión *f*

disease [dɪ'ziːz] *n* enfermedad *f*

disembark [dɪsɪm'bɑːk] *vt*, *vi* desembarcar

disgrace [dɪs'greɪs] *n* ignominia;

(*shame*) vergüenza, escándalo ▷ *vt* deshonrar; **disgraceful** *adj* vergonzoso

disgruntled [dɪs'grʌntld] *adj* disgustado, descontento

disguise [dɪs'gaɪz] *n* disfraz *m* ▷ *vt* disfrazar; **in ~** disfrazado

disgust [dɪs'gʌst] *n* repugnancia ▷ *vt* repugnar, dar asco a

> Be careful not to translate **disgust** by the Spanish word *disgustar*.

disgusted [dɪs'gʌstɪd] *adj* indignado

> Be careful not to translate **disgusted** by the Spanish word *disgustado*.

disgusting [dɪs'gʌstɪŋ] *adj* repugnante, asqueroso; (*behaviour etc*) vergonzoso

dish [dɪʃ] *n* (*gen*) plato; **to do the ~es** fregar los platos; **dishcloth** *n* estropajo

dishonest [dɪs'ɔnɪst] *adj* (*person*) poco honrado, tramposo; (*means*) fraudulento

dishtowel ['dɪʃtauəl] (*us*) *n* estropajo

dishwasher ['dɪʃwɔʃə*] *n* lavaplatos *m inv*

disillusion [dɪsɪ'luːʒən] *vt* desilusionar

disinfectant [dɪsɪn'fektənt] *n* desinfectante *m*

disintegrate [dɪs'ɪntɪɡreɪt] *vi* disgregarse, desintegrarse

disk [dɪsk] *n* (*esp us*) = **disc**; (*Comput*) disco, disquete *m*; **single-/double-sided** = disco de una cara/dos caras; **disk drive** *n* disco drive *m*; **diskette** *n* = **disk**

dislike [dɪs'laɪk] *n* antipatía, aversión *f* ▷ *vt* tener antipatía a

dislocate ['dɪsləkeɪt] *vt* dislocar

disloyal [dɪs'lɔɪəl] *adj* desleal

dismal ['dɪzml] *adj* (*gloomy*) deprimente, triste; (*very bad*) malísimo, fatal

dismantle [dɪs'mæntl] *vt* desmontar, desarmar

dismay [dɪsˈmeɪ] n consternación f
▷ vt consternar

dismiss [dɪsˈmɪs] vt (worker)
despedir; (pupils) dejar marchar;
(soldiers) dar permiso para irse; (idea,
Law) rechazar; (possibility) descartar;
dismissal n despido

disobedient [dɪsəˈbiːdɪənt] adj
desobediente

disobey [dɪsəˈbeɪ] vt desobedecer

disorder [dɪsˈɔːdəʳ] n desorden m;
(rioting) disturbios mpl; (Med) trastorno

disorganized [dɪsˈɔːɡənaɪzd] adj
desorganizado

disown [dɪsˈəʊn] vt (action) renegar
de; (person) negar cualquier tipo de
relación con

dispatch [dɪsˈpætʃ] vt enviar ▷ n
(sending) envío; (Press) informe m; (Mil)
parte m

dispel [dɪsˈpel] vt disipar

dispense [dɪsˈpens] vt (medicines)
preparar; **dispense with** vt fus
prescindir de; **dispenser** n (container)
distribuidor m automático

disperse [dɪsˈpɜːs] vt dispersar ▷ vi
dispersarse

display [dɪsˈpleɪ] n (in shop window)
escaparate m; (exhibition) exposición
f; (Comput) visualización f; (of feeling)
manifestación f ▷ vt exponer;
manifestar; (ostentatiously) lucir

displease [dɪsˈpliːz] vt (offend)
ofender; (annoy) fastidiar

disposable [dɪsˈpəʊzəbl] adj
desechable; (income) disponible

disposal [dɪsˈpəʊzl] n (of rubbish)
destrucción f; **at one's ~** a su
disposición

dispose [dɪsˈpəʊz] vi: **to ~ of**
(unwanted goods) deshacerse de;
(problem etc) resolver; **disposition**
[dɪspəˈzɪʃən] n (nature)
temperamento; (inclination)
propensión f

disproportionate [dɪsprəˈpɔːʃənət]
adj desproporcionado

dispute [dɪsˈpjuːt] n disputa; (also:

industrial ~) conflicto (laboral) ▷ vt
(argue) disputar, discutir; (question)
cuestionar

disqualify [dɪsˈkwɒlɪfaɪ] vt (Sport)
desclasificar; **to ~ sb for sth/from
doing sth** incapacitar a algn para
algo/hacer algo

disregard [dɪsrɪˈɡɑːd] vt (ignore) no
hacer caso de

disrupt [dɪsˈrʌpt] vt (plans)
desbaratar, trastornar; (conversation)
interrumpir; **disruption**
[dɪsˈrʌpʃən] n trastorno,
desbaratamiento; interrupción f

dissatisfaction [dɪssætɪsˈfækʃən] n
disgusto, descontento

dissatisfied [dɪsˈsætɪsfaɪd] adj
insatisfecho

dissect [dɪˈsekt] vt disecar

dissent [dɪˈsent] n disensión f

dissertation [dɪsəˈteɪʃən] n tesina

dissolve [dɪˈzɒlv] vt disolver
▷ vi disolverse; **to ~ in(to) tears**
deshacerse en lágrimas

distance [ˈdɪstəns] n distancia; **in
the ~** a lo lejos

distant [ˈdɪstənt] adj lejano; (manner)
reservado, frío

distil [dɪsˈtɪl] (us **distill**) vt destilar;
distillery n destilería

distinct [dɪsˈtɪŋkt] adj (different)
distinto; (clear) claro; (unmistakeable)
inequívoco; **as ~ from** a diferencia
de; **distinction** [dɪsˈtɪŋkʃən] n
distinción f; (honour) honor m; (in
exam) sobresaliente m; **distinctive** adj
distintivo

distinguish [dɪsˈtɪŋɡwɪʃ] vt
distinguir; **to ~ o.s.** destacarse;
distinguished adj (eminent)
distinguido

distort [dɪsˈtɔːt] vt distorsionar;
(shape, image) deformar

distract [dɪsˈtrækt] vt distraer;
distracted adj distraído; **distraction**
[dɪsˈtrækʃən] n distracción f;
(confusion) aturdimiento

distraught [dɪsˈtrɔːt] adj loco de

inquietud
distress [dɪs'trɛs] n (anguish)
angustia, aflicción f ▷ vt afligir;
distressing adj angustioso; doloroso
distribute [dɪs'trɪbjuːt] vt distribuir;
(share out) repartir; **distribution**
[-'bjuːʃən] n distribución f, reparto m;
distributor n (Aut) distribuidor m;
(Comm) distribuidora f
district ['dɪstrɪkt] n (of country)
zona, región f; (of town) barrio; (Admin)
distrito; **district attorney** (US) n
fiscal mf
distrust [dɪs'trʌst] n desconfianza
▷ vt desconfiar de
disturb [dɪs'təːb] vt (person: bother,
interrupt) molestar; (: upset)
perturbar, inquietar; (disorganize)
alterar; **disturbance** n (upheaval)
perturbación f; (political etc: gen
pl) disturbio; (of mind) trastorno;
disturbed adj (worried, upset)
preocupado, angustiado; **emotionally
disturbed** trastornado; (childhood)
inseguro; **disturbing** adj inquietante,
perturbador(a)
ditch [dɪtʃ] n zanja; (irrigation ditch)
acequia f ▷ vi (inf: partner) deshacerse
de; (: plan, car etc) abandonar
ditto ['dɪtəu] adv ídem, lo mismo
dive [daɪv] n (from board) salto;
(underwater) buceo; (of submarine)
sumersión f ▷ vi (swimmer: into water)
saltar; (: under water) zambullirse,
bucear; (fish, submarine) sumergirse;
(bird) lanzarse en picado; **to ~ into** (bag
etc) meter la mano en; (place) meterse
de prisa en; **diver** n (underwater) buzo
diverse [daɪ'vəːs] adj diversos/as,
varios/as
diversion [daɪ'vəːʃən] n (BRIT Aut)
desviación f; (distraction, Mil) diversión
f; (of funds) distracción f
diversity [daɪ'vəːsɪtɪ] n diversidad f
divert [daɪ'vəːt] vt (turn aside) desviar
divide [dɪ'vaɪd] vt dividir; (separate)
separar ▷ vi dividirse; (road)
bifurcarse; **divided highway** (US) n

carretera de doble calzada
divine [dɪ'vaɪn] adj (also fig) divino
diving ['daɪvɪŋ] n (Sport) salto;
(underwater) buceo; **diving board** n
trampolín m
division [dɪ'vɪʒən] n división f;
(sharing out) reparto; (disagreement)
diferencias fpl; (Comm) sección f
divorce [dɪ'vɔːs] n divorcio
▷ vt divorciarse de; **divorced** adj
divorciado/a; **divorcee** [-'siː] n
divorciado/a
D.I.Y. (BRIT) adj, n abbr = **do-it-
yourself**
dizzy ['dɪzɪ] adj (spell) de mareo; **to
feel ~** marearse
DJ n abbr = **disc jockey**
DNA n abbr (= deoxyribonucleic acid)
ADN m

○ **KEYWORD**

do [duː] (pt **did**, pp **done**) n (inf: party
etc): **we're having a little do on
Saturday** damos una fiestecita el
sábado; **it was rather a grand do** fue
un acontecimiento a lo grande
▷ aux vb 1 (in negative constructions: not
translated): **I don't understand** no
entiendo
2 (to form questions: not translated):
didn't you know? ¿no lo sabías?; **what
do you think?** ¿qué opinas?
3 (for emphasis, in polite expressions):
**people do make mistakes
sometimes** sí que se cometen errores
a veces; **she does seem rather late**
a mí también me parece que se ha
retrasado; **do sit down/help yourself**
siéntate/sírvete por favor; **do take
care!** ¡ten cuidado!, ¡te pido!)
4 (used to avoid repeating vb): **she sings
better than I do** canta mejor que yo;
do you agree? – yes, I do/no, I don't
¿estás de acuerdo? – sí (lo estoy)/no
(lo estoy); **she lives in Glasgow – so
do I** vive en Glasgow – yo también; **he
didn't like it and neither did we** no

le gustó y a nosotros tampoco; **who made this mess? – I did** ¿quién hizo esta chapuza? – yo; **he asked me to help him and I did** me pidió que le ayudara y lo hice

5 (*in question tags*): **you like him, don't you?** te gusta, ¿verdad? or ¿no?; **I don't know him, do I?** creo que no le conozco

▷ *vt* **1** (*gen, carry out, perform etc*): **what are you doing tonight?** ¿qué haces esta noche?; **what can I do for you?** ¿en qué puedo servirle?; **to do the washing-up/cooking** fregar los platos/cocinar; **to do one's teeth/hair/nails** lavarse los dientes/arreglarse el pelo/arreglarse las uñas **2** (*Aut etc*): **the car was doing 100** el coche iba a 100; **we've done 200 km already** ya hemos hecho 200 km; **he can do 100 in that car** puede ir a 100 en ese coche

▷ *vi* **1** (*act, behave*) hacer; **do as I do** haz como yo

2 (*get on, fare*): **he's doing well/badly at school** va bien/mal en la escuela; **the firm is doing well** la empresa anda or va bien; **how do you do?** mucho gusto; (*less formal*) ¿qué tal?

3 (*suit*): **will it do?** ¿sirve?, ¿está or va bien?

4 (*be sufficient*) bastar; **will £10 do?** ¿será bastante con £10?; **that'll do** así está bien; **that'll do!** (*in annoyance*) ¡ya está bien!, ¡basta ya!; **to make do (with)** arreglárselas (con)

do up *vt* (*laces*) atar; (*zip, dress, shirt*) abrochar; (*renovate: room, house*) renovar

do with *vt fus* (*need*): **I could do with a drink/some help** no me vendría mal un trago/un poco de ayuda; (*be connected*) tener que ver con; **what has it got to do with you?** ¿qué tiene que ver contigo?

do without *vi* pasar sin; **if you're late for tea then you'll do without** si llegas tarde tendrás que quedarte

sin cenar

▷ *vt fus* pasar sin; **I can do without a car** puedo pasar sin coche

dock [dɔk] *n* (*Naut*) muelle *m*; (*Law*) banquillo (de los acusados) ▷ *vi* (*enter dock*) atracar (la) muelle; (*Space*) acoplarse; **docks** *npl* (*Naut*) muelles *mpl*, puerto *sg*

doctor ['dɔktə*] *n* médico/a; (*Ph. D. etc*) doctor(a) *m/f* ▷ *vt* (*drink etc*) adulterar; **Doctor of Philosophy** *n* Doctor en Filosofía y Letras

document ['dɔkjumənt] *n* documento; **documentary** [-'mentəri] *adj* documental ▷ *n* documental *m*; **documentation** [-men'teiʃən] *n* documentación *f*

dodge [dɔdʒ] *n* (*fig*) truco ▷ *vt* evadir; (*blow*) esquivar

dodgy ['dɔdʒi] *adj* (*inf: uncertain*) dudoso; (*suspicious*) sospechoso; (*risky*) arriesgado

does [dʌz] *vb see* **do**

doesn't ['dʌznt] = **does not**

dog [dɔg] *n* perro ▷ *vt* seguir los pasos de; (*bad luck*) perseguir; **doggy bag** ['dɔgi-] *n* bolsa para llevarse las sobras de la comida

do-it-yourself ['du:itjɔ:'self] *n* bricolaje *m*

dole [dəul] *n* (*BRIT*) *n* (*payment*) subsidio de paro; **on the ~** parado

doll [dɔl] *n* muñeca; (*us: inf: woman*) muñeca, gachí *f*

dollar ['dɔlə*] *n* dólar *m*

dolphin ['dɔlfin] *n* delfín *m*

dome [dəum] *n* (*Arch*) cúpula

domestic [də'mestik] *adj* (*animal, duty*) doméstico; (*flight, policy*) nacional; **domestic appliance** *n* aparato *m* doméstico, aparato *m* de uso doméstico

dominant ['dɔminənt] *adj* dominante

dominate ['dɔmineit] *vt* dominar

domino ['dɔminəu] (*pl* **-es**) *n* ficha de dominó; **dominoes** *n* (*game*) dominó

donate [dəˈneɪt] vt donar; **donation**
[dəˈneɪʃən] n donativo

done [dʌn] pp of **do**

donkey [ˈdɔŋkɪ] n burro

donor [ˈdəʊnə*] n donante mf; **donor
card** n carnet m de donante

don't [dəʊnt] = **do not**

doodle [ˈduːdl] vi hacer dibujitos or
garabatos

doom [duːm] n (fate) suerte f ▷ vt: **to
be ~ed to failure** estar condenado
al fracaso

door [dɔː*] n puerta; **doorbell** n
timbre m; **door handle** n tirador m; (of
car) manija; **doorknob** n pomo m de
la puerta, manilla f (LAM); **doorstep** n
peldaño; **doorway** n entrada, puerta

dope [dəʊp] n (inf: illegal drug) droga;
(: person) imbécil mf ▷ vt (horse etc)
drogar

dormitory [ˈdɔːmɪtrɪ] n (BRIT)
dormitorio; (US) colegio mayor

DOS n abbr (= disk operating system)
DOS m

dosage [ˈdəʊsɪdʒ] n dosis f inv

dose [dəʊs] n dosis f inv

dot [dɔt] n punto ▷ vi: **~ted with**
salpicado de; **on the ~** en punto;
dotcom [dɔtˈkɒm] n punto com f inv;
dotted line [ˈdɔtɪd-] n: **to sign on the
dotted line** firmar

double [ˈdʌbl] adj doble ▷ adv
(twice): **to cost ~** costar el doble ▷ n
doble m ▷ vt doblar ▷ vi doblarse;
on the ~, **at the ~** (BRIT) corriendo;
double back vi (person) volver sobre
sus pasos; **double bass** n contrabajo;
double bed n cama de matrimonio;
double-check vt volver a revisar
▷ vi: **I'll double-check** voy a revisarlo
otra vez; **double-click** n (Comput)
hacer doble clic; **double-cross** vt
(trick) engañar; (betray) traicionar;
doubledecker n autobús m de dos
pisos; **double glazing** (BRIT) n doble
acristalamiento; **double room** n
habitación f doble; **doubles** n (Tennis)

juego de dobles; **double yellow lines**
npl (BRIT: Aut) línea doble amarilla de
prohibido aparcar, ≈ línea f sg amarilla
continua

doubt [daʊt] n duda ▷ vt dudar;
(suspect) dudar de; **to ~ that** dudar que;
doubtful adj dudoso; (person): **to be
doubtful about sth** tener dudas sobre
algo; **doubtless** adv sin duda

dough [dəʊ] n masa, pasta;
doughnut (US **donut**) n ≈ rosquilla

dove [dʌv] n paloma

down [daʊn] n (feathers) plumón m,
flojel m ▷ adv (downwards) abajo, hacia
abajo; (on the ground) por o en tierra
▷ prep abajo ▷ vt (inf: drink) beberse;
~ with X! ¡abajo X!; **down-and-out**
n vagabundo/a; **downfall** n caída,
ruina; **downhill** adv: **to go downhill**
(also fig) ir cuesta abajo

Downing Street [ˈdaʊnɪŋ-] n (BRIT)
Downing Street f

down: **download** vt (Comput)
bajar; **downloadable** adj (Comput)
descargable; **downright** adj (nonsense,
lie) manifiesto; (refusal) terminante

Down's syndrome [ˈdaʊnz-] n
síndrome m de Down

down: **downstairs** adv (below) (en el
piso de) abajo; (downwards) escaleras
abajo; **down-to-earth** adj práctico;
downtown adv en el centro de la
ciudad; **down under** adv en Australia
(or Nueva Zelanda); **downward**
[-wəd] adj, adv hacia abajo;
downwards [-wədz] adv hacia abajo

doz. abbr = **dozen**

doze [dəʊz] vi dormitar

dozen [ˈdʌzn] n docena; **a ~ books**
una docena de libros; **~s of** cantidad de

Dr. abbr = **doctor**; **drive**

drab [dræb] adj gris, monótono

draft [drɑːft] n (first copy) borrador m;
(Pol: of bill) anteproyecto; (US: call-up)
quinta ▷ vt (plan) preparar; (write
roughly) hacer un borrador de; see also
draught

drag [dræg] vt arrastrar; (river) dragar;

rastrear ▷ vi (time) pasar despacio; (play, film etc) hacerse pesado ▷ n (inf) lata; (women's clothing): **in ~** vestido de travesti; **to ~ and drop** (Comput) arrastrar y soltar

dragon ['drægən] n dragón m

dragonfly ['drægənflaɪ] n libélula

drain [dreɪn] n desaguadero; (in street) sumidero; (source of loss): **to be a ~ on** consumir, agotar ▷ vt (land, marshes) desaguar; (reservoir) desecar; (vegetables) escurrir ▷ vi escurrirse; **drainage** n (act) desagüe m; (Med, Agr) drenaje m; (sewage) alcantarillado; **drainpipe** n tubo de desagüe

drama ['drɑːmə] n (art) teatro; (play) drama m; (excitement) emoción f; **dramatic** [drə'mætɪk] adj dramático; (sudden, marked) espectacular

drank [dræŋk] pt of **drink**

drape [dreɪp] vt (cloth) colocar; (flag) colgar; **drapes** npl (us) cortinas fpl

drastic ['dræstɪk] adj (measure) severo; (change) radical, drástico

draught [drɑːft] (us **draft**) n (of air) corriente f de aire; (Naut) calado; **on ~** (beer) de barril; **draught beer** n cerveza de barril; **draughts** (BRIT) n (game) juego de damas

draw [drɔː] (pt **drew**, pp **drawn**) vt (picture) dibujar; (cart) tirar de; (curtain) correr; (take out) sacar; (attract) atraer; (money) retirar; (wages) cobrar ▷ vi (Sport) empatar ▷ n (Sport) empate m; (lottery) sorteo; **draw out** vi (lengthen) alargarse ▷ vt sacar; **draw up** vi (stop) pararse ▷ vt (chair) acercar; (document) redactar; **drawback** n inconveniente m, desventaja

drawer [drɔː*] n cajón m

drawing ['drɔːɪŋ] n dibujo; **drawing pin** (BRIT) n chincheta; **drawing room** n salón m

drawn [drɔːn] pp of **draw**

dread [drɛd] n pavor m, terror m ▷ vt temer, tener miedo or pavor a; **dreadful** adj horroroso

dream [driːm] n (pt, pp **~ed** or **~t**)

sueño ▷ vt, vi soñar; **dreamer** n soñador(a) m/f

dreamt [drɛmt] pt, pp of **dream**

dreary ['drɪərɪ] adj monótono

drench [drɛntʃ] vt empapar

dress [drɛs] n vestido; (clothing) ropa ▷ vt vestir; (wound) vendar ▷ vi vestirse; **to get ~ed** vestirse; **dress up** vi vestirse de etiqueta; (in fancy dress) disfrazarse; **dress circle** (BRIT) n principal m; **dresser** n (furniture) aparador m; (: US) cómoda (con espejo); **dressing** n (Med) vendaje m; (Culin) aliño; **dressing gown** (BRIT) n bata; **dressing room** n (Theatre) camarín m; (Sport) vestuario; **dressing table** n tocador m; **dressmaker** n modista, costurera

drew [druː] pt of **draw**

dribble ['drɪbl] vi (baby) babear ▷ vt (ball) regatear

dried [draɪd] adj (fruit) seco; (milk) en polvo

drier ['draɪə*] n = **dryer**

drift [drɪft] n (of current etc) flujo; (of snow) ventisquero; (meaning) significado ▷ vi (boat) ir a la deriva; (sand, snow) amontonarse

drill [drɪl] n (drill bit) broca; (tool for DIY etc) taladro; (of dentist) fresa; (for mining etc) perforadora, barrena; (Mil) instrucción f ▷ vt perforar, taladrar; (troops) enseñar la instrucción a ▷ vi (for oil) perforar

drink [drɪŋk] (pt **drank**, pp **drunk**) n bebida; (sip) trago ▷ vt, vi beber; **to have a ~** tomar algo; tomar una copa or un trago; **a ~ of water** un trago de agua; **drink-driving** n: **to be charged with drink-driving** ser acusado de conducir borracho or en estado de embriaguez; **drinker** n bebedor(a) m/f; **drinking water** n agua potable

drip [drɪp] n (act) goteo; (one drip) gota; (Med) gota a gota m ▷ vi gotear

drive [draɪv] (pt **drove**, pp **driven**) n (journey) viaje m (en coche); (also: **~way**) entrada; (energy) energía, vigor m; (Comput: also: **disk ~**) drive m ▷ vt (car) conducir (SP); manejar (LAM); (nail) clavar; (push) empujar; (Tech: motor) impulsar ▷ vi (Aut: at controls) conducir; (: travel) pasearse en coche; **left-/right-hand ~** conducción f a la izquierda/derecha; **to ~ sb mad** volverle loco a algn; **drive out** vt (force out) expulsar, echar; **drive-in** adj (esp US): **drive-in cinema** autocine m

driven ['drɪvn] pp of **drive**

driver ['draɪvə*] n conductor(a) m/f (SP), chofer m (LAM); (of taxi, bus) chófer mf(SP), chofer mf(LAM); **driver's license** (US) n carnet m de conducir

driveway ['draɪvweɪ] n entrada

driving ['draɪvɪŋ] n conducción (SP), el manejar (LAM); **driving instructor** n profesor(a) m/f de autoescuela (SP), instructor(a) m/f de manejo (LAM); **driving lesson** n clase f de conducir (SP) or manejar (LAM); **driving licence** (BRIT) n licencia de manejo (LAM), carnet m de conducir (SP); **driving test** n examen m de conducir (SP) or manejar (LAM)

drizzle ['drɪzl] n llovizna

droop [dru:p] vi (flower) marchitarse; (shoulders) encorvarse; (head) inclinarse

drop [drɔp] n (of water) gota; (lessening) baja; (fall) caída ▷ vt dejar caer; (voice, eyes, price) bajar; (passenger) dejar; (omit) omitir ▷ vi (object) caer; (wind) amainar; **drop in** vi (inf: visit): **to drop in (on)** pasar por casa (de); **drop off** vi (sleep) dormirse ▷ vt (passenger) dejar; **drop out** vi (withdraw) retirarse

drought [draut] n sequía

drove [drəuv] pt of **drive**

drown [draun] vt ahogar ▷ vi ahogarse

drowsy ['drauzɪ] adj soñoliento; **to be ~** tener sueño

drug [drʌg] n medicamento; (narcotic) droga ▷ vt drogar; **to be on ~s** drogarse; **drug addict** n drogadicto/a; **drug dealer** n traficante mf de drogas; **druggist** (US) n farmacéutico;

drugstore (US) n farmacia

drum [drʌm] n tambor m; (for oil, petrol) bidón m; **drums** npl batería; **drummer** n trombor m

drunk [drʌŋk] pp of **drink** ▷ adj borracho ▷ n (also: **~ard**) borracho/a; **drunken** adj borracho; (laughter, party) de borrachos

dry [draɪ] adj seco; (day) sin lluvia; (climate) árido, seco ▷ vt secar; (tears) enjugarse ▷ vi secarse; **dry off** vi secarse ▷ vt secar; **dry up** vi (river) secarse; **dry-cleaner's** n tintorería; **dry-cleaning** n lavado en seco; **dryer** n (for hair) secador m; (US: for clothes) secadora

DSS n abbr = **Department of Social Security**

D & T (BRIT: Scol) n abbr = (design and technology) = dibujo y tecnología

DTP n abbr = desk-top publishing autoedición f

dual ['djuəl] adj doble; **dual carriageway** (BRIT) n carretera de doble calzada

dubious ['dju:bɪəs] adj indeciso; (reputation, company) sospechoso

duck [dʌk] n pato ▷ vi agacharse

due [dju:] adj (owed): **he is ~ £10** se le deben 10 libras; (expected: event): **the meeting is ~ on Wednesday** la reunión tendrá lugar el miércoles; (: arrival): **the train is ~ at 8am** el tren tiene su llegada para las 8; (proper) debido ▷ n: **to give sb his (or her) ~** ser justo con algn ▷ adv: **~ north** derecho al norte

duel ['djuəl] n duelo

duet [dju:'ɛt] n dúo

dug [dʌg] pt, pp of **dig**

duke [dju:k] n duque m

dull [dʌl] adj (light) débil; (stupid) torpe; (boring) pesado; (sound, pain) sordo; (weather, day) gris ▷ vt (pain, grief) aliviar; (mind, senses) entorpecer

dumb [dʌm] adj mudo; (pej: stupid) estúpido

dummy ['dʌmɪ] n (tailor's dummy)

maniquí m; (mock-up) maqueta; (BRIT: for baby) chupete m ⊳ adj falso, postizo

dump [dʌmp] n (also: **rubbish ~**) basurero, vertedero; (inf: place) cuchitril m ⊳ vt (put down) dejar; (get rid of) deshacerse de; (Comput: data) transferir

dumpling ['dʌmplɪŋ] n bola de masa hervida

dune [djuːn] n duna

dungarees [dʌŋgə'riːz] npl mono

dungeon ['dʌndʒən] n calabozo

duplex ['djuːpleks] n dúplex m

duplicate [n 'djuːplɪkət, vb 'djuːplɪkeɪt] n duplicado ⊳ vt duplicar; (photocopy) fotocopiar; (repeat) repetir; **in ~** por duplicado

durable ['djuərəbl] adj duradero

duration [djuə'reɪʃən] n duración f

during ['djuərɪŋ] prep durante

dusk [dʌsk] n crepúsculo, anochecer m

dust [dʌst] n polvo ⊳ vt quitar el polvo a, desempolvar; (cake etc) **to ~ with** espolvorear de; **dustbin** (BRIT) n cubo or bote m (MEX) or tacho (SC) de la basura; **duster** n paño, trapo; **dustman** (BRIT: irreg) n basurero; **dustpan** n cogedor m; **dusty** adj polvoriento

Dutch [dʌtʃ] adj holandés/esa ⊳ n (Ling) holandés m; **the Dutch** npl los holandeses; **to go ~** (inf) pagar cada uno lo suyo; **Dutchman** (irreg) n holandés m; **Dutchwoman** (irreg) n holandésa

duty ['djuːtɪ] n deber m; (tax) derechos mpl de aduana; **on ~** de servicio; (at night etc) de guardia; **off ~** libre (de servicio); **duty-free** adj libre de impuestos

duvet ['duːveɪ] (BRIT) n edredón m

DVD n abbr (= digital versatile or video disc) DVD m; **DVD player** n lector m de DVD; **DVD writer** n grabadora de DVD

dwarf [dwɔːf] (pl **dwarves**) n enano/a ⊳ vt empequeñecer

dwell [dwel] (pt, pp **dwelt**) vi morar; **dwell on** vt fus explayarse en

dwelt [dwelt] pt, pp of **dwell**

dye [daɪ] n tinte m ⊳ vt teñir

dying ['daɪɪŋ] adj moribundo

dynamic [daɪ'næmɪk] adj dinámico

dynamite ['daɪnəmaɪt] n dinamita

dyslexia [dɪs'leksɪə] n dislexia

dyslexic [dɪs'leksɪk] adj, n disléxico/a m/f

e

E [iː] n (Mus) mi m

E111 n abbr (= form E111) impreso E111

each [iːtʃ] adj cada inv ▷ pron cada uno; **~ other** el uno al otro; **they hate ~ other** se odian (entre ellos or mutuamente); **they have 2 books ~** tienen 2 libros por persona

eager ['iːgə*] adj (keen) entusiasmado; **to be ~ to do sth** tener muchas ganas de hacer algo, impacientarse por hacer algo; **to be ~ for** tener muchas ganas de

eagle ['iːgl] n águila

ear [ɪə*] n oreja; oído; (of corn) espiga; **earache** n dolor m de oídos; **eardrum** n tímpano

earl [əːl] n conde m

earlier ['əːlɪə*] adj anterior ▷ adv antes

early ['əːlɪ] adv temprano; (before time) con tiempo, con anticipación ▷ adj temprano; (settlers etc) primitivo; (death, departure) prematuro; (reply) pronto; **to have an ~ night** acostarse temprano; **in the ~** or **in the**

spring/19th century a principios de primavera/del siglo diecinueve; **early retirement** n jubilación f anticipada

earmark ['ɪəmɑːk] vt: **to ~ (for)** reservar (para), destinar (a)

earn [əːn] vt (salary) percibir; (interest) devengar; (praise) merecerse

earnest ['əːnɪst] adj (wish) fervoroso; (person) serio, formal; **in ~** en serio

earnings ['əːnɪŋz] npl (personal) sueldo, ingresos mpl; (company) ganancias fpl

ear: earphones npl auriculares mpl; **earplugs** npl tapones mpl para los oídos; **earring** n pendiente m, arete m

earth [əːθ] n tierra; (BRIT Elec) cable m de toma de tierra ▷ vt (BRIT Elec) conectar a tierra; **earthquake** n terremoto

ease [iːz] n facilidad f; (comfort) comodidad f ▷ vt (lessen: problem) mitigar; (: pain) aliviar; (: tension) reducir; **to ~ sth in/out** meter/sacar algo con cuidado; **at ~!** (Mil) ¡descansen!

easily ['iːzɪlɪ] adv fácilmente

east [iːst] n este m ▷ adj del este, oriental; (wind) este ▷ adv al este, hacia el este; **the E~** el Oriente; (Pol) los países del Este; **eastbound** adj en dirección este

Easter ['iːstə*] n Pascua (de Resurrección); **Easter egg** n huevo de Pascua

eastern ['iːstən] adj del este, oriental; (oriental) oriental

Easter Sunday n Domingo de Resurrección

easy ['iːzɪ] adj fácil; (simple) sencillo; (comfortable) holgado, cómodo; (relaxed) tranquilo ▷ adv: **to take it** or **things** ~ (not worry) tomarlo con calma; (rest) descansar; **easy-going** adj acomodadizo

eat [iːt] (pt **ate**, pp **eaten**) vt comer; **eat out** vi comer fuera

eavesdrop ['iːvzdrɔp] vi: **to ~ (on)** escuchar a escondidas

e-book ['iːbuk] n libro electrónico

e-business ['iːbɪznɪs] n (company) negocio electrónico; (commerce) comercio electrónico

EC n abbr (= European Community) CE f

eccentric [ɪk'sentrɪk] adj, n excéntrico/a m/f

echo ['ekəʊ] (pl -es) n eco ▷ vt (sound) repetir ▷ vi resonar, hacer eco

eclipse [ɪ'klɪps] n eclipse m

eco-friendly ['iːkəʊfrendlɪ] adj ecológico

ecological [iːkə'lɒdʒɪkl] adj ecológico

ecology [ɪ'kɒlədʒɪ] n ecología

e-commerce n abbr comercio electrónico

economic [iːkə'nɒmɪk] adj económico; (business etc) rentable

economical adj económico

economics n (Scol) economía ▷ npl (of project etc) rentabilidad f

economist [ɪ'kɒnəmɪst] n economista m/f

economize [ɪ'kɒnəmaɪz] vi economizar, ahorrar

economy [ɪ'kɒnəmɪ] n economía; **economy class** n (Aviat) clase f económica; **economy class syndrome** n síndrome m de la clase turista

ecstasy ['ekstəsɪ] n éxtasis m inv; (drug) éxtasis m inv; **ecstatic** [eks'tætɪk] adj extático

eczema ['eksɪmə] n eczema m

edge [edʒ] n (of knife) filo; (of object) borde m; (of lake) orilla ▷ vt (Sewing) ribetear; **on ~** (fig) = **edgy**; **to ~ away from** alejarse poco a poco de

edgy ['edʒɪ] adj nervioso, inquieto

edible ['edɪbl] adj comestible

Edinburgh ['edɪnbərə] n Edimburgo

edit ['edɪt] vt (be editor of) dirigir; (text, report) corregir, preparar; **edition** [ɪ'dɪʃən] n edición f; **editor** n (of newspaper) director(a) m/f; (of column): **foreign/political editor** encargado de la sección de extranjero/política; (of book) redactor(a) m/f;

editorial [-'tɔːrɪəl] adj editorial ▷ n editorial m

educate ['edjukeɪt] vt (gen) educar; (instruct) instruir; **educated** ['edjukeɪtd] adj culto

education [edju'keɪʃən] n educación f; (schooling) enseñanza; (Scol) pedagogía; **educational** adj (policy etc) educacional; (experience) docente; (toy) educativo

eel [iːl] n anguila

eerie ['ɪərɪ] adj misterioso

effect [ɪ'fekt] n efecto ▷ vt efectuar, llevar a cabo; **to take ~** (law) entrar en vigor o vigencia; (drug) surtir efecto; **in ~** en realidad; **effects** npl (property) efectos mpl; **effective** adj eficaz; (actual) verdadero; **effectively** adv eficazmente; (in reality) efectivamente

efficiency [ɪ'fɪʃənsɪ] n eficiencia; rendimiento

efficient [ɪ'fɪʃənt] adj eficiente; (machine) de buen rendimiento; **efficiently** adv eficientemente, de manera eficiente

effort ['efət] n esfuerzo; **effortless** adj sin ningún esfuerzo; (style) natural

e.g. adv abbr (= exempli gratia) p. ej.

egg [eg] n huevo; **hard-boiled/soft-boiled ~** huevo duro/pasado por agua; **eggcup** n huevera f; **eggplant** (esp us) n berenjena; **eggshell** n cáscara de huevo; **egg white** n clara de huevo; **egg yolk** n yema de huevo

ego ['iːgəʊ] n ego

Egypt ['iːdʒɪpt] n Egipto; **Egyptian** [ɪ'dʒɪpʃən] adj, n egipcio/a m/f

eight [eɪt] num ocho; **eighteen** num diez y ocho, dieciocho; **eighteenth** adj decimoctavo; **the eighteenth floor** la planta dieciocho; **the eighteenth of August** el dieciocho de agosto; **eighth** num octavo; **eightieth** ['eɪtɪɪθ] adj octogésimo

eighty ['eɪtɪ] num ochenta

Eire ['eərə] n Eire m

either ['aɪðə] adj cualquiera de los dos; (both, each) cada ▷ pron: **~ (of**

them) cualquiera (de los dos) ▷ *adv*
tampoco ▷ *conj*: **~ yes or no** o sí o no;
on ~ side en ambos lados; **I don't like ~**
no me gusta ninguno/a de los(las) dos;
no, I don't ~ no, yo tampoco

eject [ɪ'dʒɛkt] *vt* echar, expulsar;
(*tenant*) desahuciar

elaborate [*adj* ɪ'læbərɪt, *vb* ɪ'læbəreɪt]
adj (*complex*) complejo ▷ *vt* (*expand*)
ampliar; (*refine*) refinar ▷ *vi* explicar
con más detalles

elastic [ɪ'læstɪk] *n* elástico ▷ *adj*
elástico; (*fig*) flexible; **elastic band**
(BRIT) *n* gomita

elbow [ˈɛlbəʊ] *n* codo

elder [ˈɛldə*] *adj* mayor ▷ *n* (*tree*)
saúco; (*person*) mayor; **elderly** *adj* de
edad, mayor ▷ *npl*: **the elderly** los
mayores

eldest [ˈɛldɪst] *adj*, *n* el/la mayor

elect [ɪ'lɛkt] *vt* elegir ▷ *adj*: **the**
president ~ el presidente electo; **to**
~ to do optar por hacer; **election**
elección *f*; **electoral** *adj* electoral;
electorate *n* electorado

electric [ɪ'lɛktrɪk] *adj* eléctrico;
electrical *adj* eléctrico; **electric**
blanket *n* manta eléctrica; **electric**
fire *n* estufa eléctrica; **electrician**
[ɪlɛk'trɪʃən] *n* electricista *mf*;
electricity [ɪlɛk'trɪsɪtɪ] *n* electricidad
f; **electric shock** *n* electrochoque
m; **electrify** [ɪ'lɛktrɪfaɪ] *vt* (Rail)
electrificar; (*fig*: *audience*) electrizar

electronic [ɪlɛk'trɒnɪk] *adj*
electrónico; **electronic mail** *n* correo
electrónico; **electronics** *n* electrónica

elegance [ˈɛlɪɡəns] *n* elegancia

elegant [ˈɛlɪɡənt] *adj* elegante

element [ˈɛlɪmənt] *n* elemento; (*of*
kettle etc) resistencia

elementary [ɛlɪ'mɛntərɪ] *adj*
elemental; (*primitive*) rudimentario;
elementary school (US) *n* escuela de
enseñanza primaria

elephant [ˈɛlɪfənt] *n* elefante *m*

elevate [ˈɛlɪveɪt] *vt* (*gen*) elevar; (*in*
rank) ascender

elevator [ˈɛlɪveɪtə*] (US) *n* ascensor
m; (*in warehouse etc*) montacargas *m inv*

eleven [ɪ'lɛvn] *num* once; **eleventh**
num undécimo

eligible [ˈɛlɪdʒəbl] *adj*: **an ~ young**
man/woman un buen partido; **to be ~**
for sth llenar los requisitos para algo

eliminate [ɪ'lɪmɪneɪt] *vt* (*suspect*,
possibility) descartar

elm [ɛlm] *n* olmo

eloquent [ˈɛləkwənt] *adj* elocuente

else [ɛls] *adv*: **something ~** otra
cosa; **somewhere ~** en otra parte;
everywhere ~ en todas partes menos
aquí; **where ~?** ¿dónde más?, ¿en qué
otra parte?; **there was little ~ to do**
apenas quedaba otra cosa que hacer;
nobody ~ spoke no habló nadie más;
elsewhere *adv* (*be*) en otra parte; (*go*)
a otra parte

elusive [ɪ'luːsɪv] *adj* esquivo; (*quality*)
difícil de encontrar

email [ˈiːmeɪl] *n abbr* (= *electronic mail*)
correo electrónico, e-mail *m*; **email**
address *n* dirección *f* electrónica,
email *m*

embankment [ɪm'bæŋkmənt] *n*
terraplén *m*

embargo [ɪm'bɑːɡəʊ] (*pl* **~es**) *n*
(Comm, Naut) embargo; (*prohibition*)
prohibición *f*; **to put an ~ on sth** poner
un embargo a algo

embark [ɪm'bɑːk] *vi* embarcarse ▷ *vt*
embarcar; **to ~ on** (*journey*) emprender;
(*course of action*) lanzarse a

embarrass [ɪm'bærəs] *vt*
avergonzar; (*government etc*) dejar en
mal lugar; **embarrassed** *adj* (*laugh*,
silence) embarazoso

> ▌ Be careful not to translate
> **embarrassed** by the Spanish word
> *embarazada*.

embarrassing *adj* (*situation*)
violento; (*question*) embarazoso;
embarrassment *n* (*shame*)
vergüenza; (*problem*): **to be an**
embarrassment for sb poner en un
aprieto a algn

embassy ['embəsɪ] n embajada

embrace [ɪm'breɪs] vt abrazar, dar un abrazo a; (include) abarcar ▷ vi abrazarse ▷ n abrazo

embroider [ɪm'brɔɪdə*] vt bordar; **embroidery** n bordado

embryo ['embrɪəu] n embrión m

emerald ['emərəld] n esmeralda

emerge [ɪ'mə:dʒ] vi salir; (arise) surgir

emergency [ɪ'mə:dʒənsɪ] n crisis f inv; **in an ~** en caso de urgencia; **state of ~** estado de emergencia; **emergency brake** (us) n freno de mano; **emergency exit** n salida de emergencia; **emergency landing** n aterrizaje m forzoso; **emergency room** (us: Med) n sala f de urgencias; **emergency services** npl (fire, police, ambulance) servicios mpl de urgencia

emigrate ['emɪgreɪt] vi emigrar; **emigration** [emɪ'greɪʃən] n emigración f

eminent ['emɪnənt] adj eminente

emissions [ɪ'mɪʃənz] npl emisión f

emit [ɪ'mɪt] vt emitir; (smoke) arrojar; (smell) despedir; (sound) producir

emoticon [ɪ'məutɪkən] n emoticon n

emotion [ɪ'məuʃən] n emoción f; **emotional** adj (needs) emocional; (person) sentimental; (scene) conmovedor(a), emocionante; (speech) emocionado

emperor ['empərə*] n emperador m

emphasis ['emfəsɪs] (pl **-ses**) n énfasis m inv

emphasize ['emfəsaɪz] vt (word, point) subrayar, recalcar; (feature) hacer resaltar

empire ['empaɪə*] n imperio

employ [ɪm'plɔɪ] vt emplear; **employee** [-'iː] n empleado/a; **employer** n patrón/ona m/f; empresario; **employment** n (work) trabajo; **employment agency** n agencia de colocaciones

empower [ɪm'pauə*] vt: **to ~ sb to do sth** autorizar a algn para hacer algo

empress ['emprɪs] n emperatriz f

emptiness ['emptɪnɪs] n vacío; (of life etc) vaciedad f

empty ['emptɪ] adj vacío; (place) desierto; (house) desocupado; (threat) vano ▷ vt vaciar; (place) dejar vacío ▷ vi vaciarse; (house etc) quedar desocupado; **empty-handed** adj con las manos vacías

EMU n abbr (= European Monetary Union) UME f

emulsion [ɪ'mʌlʃən] n emulsión f; (also: ~ paint) pintura emulsión

enable [ɪ'neɪbl] vt: **to ~ sb to do sth** permitir a algn hacer algo

enamel [ɪ'næməl] n esmalte m; (also: ~ paint) pintura esmaltada

enchanting [ɪn'tʃɑːntɪŋ] adj encantador(a)

encl. abbr (= enclosed) adj

enclose [ɪn'kləuz] vt (land) cercar; (letter etc) adjuntar; **please find ~d** te mandamos adjunto

enclosure [ɪn'kləuʒə*] n cercado, recinto

encore [ɔŋ'kɔː*] excl ¡otra!, ¡bis! ▷ n bis m

encounter [ɪn'kauntə*] n encuentro ▷ vt encontrar, encontrarse con; (difficulty) tropezar con

encourage [ɪn'kʌrɪdʒ] vt alentar, animar; (activity) fomentar; (growth) estimular; **encouragement** n estímulo; (of industry) fomento

encouraging [ɪn'kʌrɪdʒɪŋ] adj alentador(a)

encyclop(a)edia [ensaɪkləu'piːdɪə] n enciclopedia

end [end] n fin m; (of table) extremo; (of street) final m; (Sport) lado ▷ vt terminar, acabar; (also: **bring to an ~**, **put an ~ to**) acabar con ▷ vi terminar, acabar; **in the ~** al fin; **on ~** (object) de punta, de cabeza; **to stand on ~** (hair) erizarse; **for hours on ~** hora tras hora; **end up** vi: **to end up in** terminar en; (place) ir a parar en

endanger [ɪn'deɪndʒə*] vt poner en peligro; **an ~ed species** una especie en

peligro de extinción
endearing [ɪn'dɪərɪŋ] adj simpático, atractivo
endeavour [ɪn'devə*] (US **endeavor**) n esfuerzo; (attempt) tentativa ▷ vi: **to ~ to do** esforzarse por hacer; (try) procurar hacer
ending ['endɪŋ] n (of book) desenlace m; (Ling) terminación f
endless ['endlɪs] adj interminable, inacabable
endorse [ɪn'dɔːs] vt (cheque) endosar; (approve) aprobar; **endorsement** n (on driving licence) nota de inhabilitación
endurance [ɪn'djuərəns] n resistencia
endure [ɪn'djuə*] vt (bear) aguantar, soportar ▷ vi (last) durar
enemy ['enəmɪ] adj, n enemigo/a m/f
energetic [enə'dʒetɪk] adj enérgico
energy ['enədʒɪ] n energía
enforce [ɪn'fɔːs] vt (Law) hacer cumplir
engaged [ɪn'geɪdʒd] adj (BRIT: busy, in use) ocupado; (betrothed) prometido; **to get ~** prometerse; **engaged tone** (BRIT) n (Tel) señal f de comunicando
engagement [ɪn'geɪdʒmənt] n (appointment) compromiso, cita; (booking) contratación f; (to marry) compromiso; (period) noviazgo m; **engagement ring** n anillo de prometida
engaging [ɪn'geɪdʒɪŋ] adj atractivo
engine ['endʒɪn] n (Aut) motor m; (Rail) locomotora
engineer [endʒɪ'nɪə*] n ingeniero; (BRIT: for repairs) mecánico; (on ship, US Rail) maquinista m; **engineering** n ingeniería
England ['ɪŋglənd] n Inglaterra
English ['ɪŋglɪʃ] adj inglés/esa ▷ n (Ling) inglés m; **the English** npl los ingleses mpl; **English Channel** n: **the English Channel** (el Canal de) la Mancha; **Englishman** (irreg) n inglés m; **Englishwoman** (irreg) n inglesa
engrave [ɪn'greɪv] vt grabar

engraving [ɪn'greɪvɪŋ] n grabado
enhance [ɪn'hɑːns] vt (gen) aumentar; (beauty) realzar
enjoy [ɪn'dʒɔɪ] vt (health, fortune) disfrutar de, gozar de; (like) gustarle a algn; **to ~ o.s.** divertirse; **enjoyable** adj agradable; (amusing) divertido; **enjoyment** n (joy) placer m; (activity) diversión f
enlarge [ɪn'lɑːdʒ] vt aumentar; (broaden) extender; (Phot) ampliar ▷ vi: **to ~ on** (subject) tratar con más detalles; **enlargement** n (Phot) ampliación f
enlist [ɪn'lɪst] vt alistar; (support) conseguir ▷ vi alistarse
enormous [ɪ'nɔːməs] adj enorme
enough [ɪ'nʌf] adj: **~ time/books** bastante tiempo/bastantes libros ▷ pron bastante(s) ▷ adv: **big ~** bastante grande; **he has not worked ~** no ha trabajado bastante; **have you got ~?** ¿tiene usted bastante(s)?; **~ to eat** (lo) suficiente de (o lo) bastante para comer; **~!** ¡basta ya!; **that's ~, thanks** con eso basta, gracias; **I've had ~ of him** estoy harto de él; **... which, funnily or oddly ~ ...** ... lo que, por extraño que parezca ...
enquire [ɪn'kwaɪə*] vt, vi = **inquire**
enquiry [ɪn'kwaɪərɪ] n (official investigation) investigación
enrage [ɪn'reɪdʒ] vt enfurecer
enrich [ɪn'rɪtʃ] vt enriquecer
enrol [ɪn'rəʊl] (US **enroll**) vt (members) inscribir; (Scol) matricular ▷ vi inscribirse; matricularse; **enrolment** (US **enrollment**) n inscripción f; matriculación f
en route [ɒn'ruːt] adv durante el viaje
en suite [ɒn'swiːt] adj: **with ~ bathroom** con baño
ensure [ɪn'ʃuə*] vt asegurar
entail [ɪn'teɪl] vt suponer
enter ['entə*] vt (room) entrar en; (club) hacerse socio de; (army) alistarse en; (sb for a competition) inscribir; (write

down) anotar, apuntar; (*Comput*) meter
▷ *vi* entrar

enterprise ['entəpraiz] *n*
empresa; (*spirit*) iniciativa; **free
~ la** libre empresa; **private ~ la**
iniciativa privada; **enterprising** *adj*
emprendedor(a)

entertain [entə'teɪn] *vt* (*amuse*)
divertir; (*invite: guest*) invitar (a casa);
(*idea*) abrigar; **entertainer** *n* artista
mf; **entertaining** *adj* divertido,
entretenido; **entertainment** *n*
(*amusement*) diversión *f*; (*show*)
espectáculo

enthusiasm [ɪn'θuːzɪæzəm] *n*
entusiasmo

enthusiast [ɪn'θuːzɪæst] *n*
entusiasta *mf*; **enthusiastic** [-'æstɪk]
adj entusiasta; **to be enthusiastic
about** entusiasmarse por

entire [ɪn'taɪə*] *adj* entero; **entirely**
adv totalmente

entitle [ɪn'taɪtl] *vt*: **to ~ sb to sth** dar
a algn derecho a algo; **entitled** *adj*
(*book*) titulado; **to be entitled to do**
tener derecho a hacer

entrance [*n* 'entrəns, *vb* ɪn'trɑːns] *n*
entrada ▷ *vt* encantar, hechizar; **to
gain ~ to** (*university etc*) ingresar en;
entrance examination *n* examen
m de ingreso; **entrance fee** *n* cuota;
entrance ramp (*us*) *n* (*Aut*) rampa
de acceso

entrant ['entrənt] *n* (*in race,
competition*) participante *mf*; (*in
examination*) candidato/a

entrepreneur [ɔntrəprə'nɜː] *n*
empresario

entrust [ɪn'trʌst] *vt*: **to ~ sth to sb**
confiar algo a algn

entry ['entrɪ] *n* entrada; (*in
competition*) participación *f*; (*in
register*) apunte *m*; (*in account*) partida;
(*in reference book*) artículo; **"no ~"**
"prohibido el paso"; (*Aut*) "dirección
prohibida"; **entry phone** *n* portero
automático

envelope ['envələup] *n* sobre *m*

envious ['envɪəs] *adj* envidioso; (*look*)
de envidia

environment [ɪn'vaɪərnmənt] *n*
(*surroundings*) entorno; (*natural world*):
the ~ el medio ambiente;
environmental [-'mentl] *adj*
ambiental; medioambiental;
environmentally [-'mentəlɪ]
adv: **environmentally sound/friendly**
ecológico

envisage [ɪn'vɪzɪdʒ] *vt* prever

envoy ['envɔɪ] *n* enviado

envy ['envɪ] *n* envidia ▷ *vt* tener
envidia a; **to ~ sb sth** envidiar algo
a algn

epic ['epɪk] *n* épica ▷ *adj* épico

epidemic [epɪ'demɪk] *n* epidemia

epilepsy ['epɪlepsɪ] *n* epilepsia

epileptic [epɪ'leptɪk] *adj*, *n*
epiléptico/a *m/f*; **epileptic fit**
[ep'leptɪk-] *n* ataque *m* de epilepsia,
acceso *m* epiléptico

episode ['epɪsəud] *n* episodio

equal ['iːkwl] *adj* igual; (*treatment*)
equitativo ▷ *n* igual *mf* ▷ *vt* ser igual
a; (*fig*) igualar; **to be ~ to** (*task*) estar
a la altura de; **equality** [iː'kwɔlɪtɪ]
n igualdad *f*; **equalize** *vi* (*Sport*)
empatar; **equally** *adv* igualmente;
(*share etc*) a partes iguales

equation [ɪ'kweɪʒən] *n* (*Math*)
ecuación *f*

equator [ɪ'kweɪtə*] *n* ecuador *m*

equip [ɪ'kwɪp] *vt* equipar; (*person*)
proveer; **to be well ~ped** estar bien
equipado; **equipment** *n* equipo;
(*tools*) avíos *mpl*

equivalent [ɪ'kwɪvələnt] *adj*: **~ (to)**
equivalente (a) ▷ *n* equivalente *m*

ER *abbr* (*BRIT*: = *Elizabeth Regina*) *la reina
Isabel*; (*us*: *Med*) = **emergency room**

era ['ɪərə] *n* era, época

erase [ɪ'reɪz] *vt* borrar; **eraser** *n*
goma de borrar

erect [ɪ'rekt] *adj* erguido ▷ *vt* erigir,
levantar; (*assemble*) montar; **erection**
[-ʃən] *n* construcción *f*; (*assembly*)
montaje *m*; (*Physiol*) erección *f*

ERM n abbr (= Exchange Rate Mechanism) tipo de cambio europeo

erode [ɪ'rəʊd] vt (Geo) erosionar; (metal) corroer, desgastar; (fig) desgastar

erosion [ɪ'rəʊʒən] n erosión f; desgaste m

erotic [ɪ'rɒtɪk] adj erótico

errand ['ɛrnd] n recado (SP), mandado (LAM)

erratic [ɪ'rætɪk] adj desigual, poco uniforme

error ['ɛrə*] n error m, equivocación f

erupt [ɪ'rʌpt] vi entrar en erupción; (fig) estallar; **eruption** [ɪ'rʌpʃən] n erupción f; (of war) estallido

escalate ['ɛskəleɪt] vi extenderse, intensificarse

escalator ['ɛskəleɪtə*] n escalera móvil

escape [ɪ'skeɪp] n fuga ▷ vi escaparse; (flee) huir, evadirse; (leak) fugarse ▷ vt (responsibility etc) evitar, eludir; (consequences) escapar a; (elude): **his name ~s me** no me sale su nombre; **to ~ from** (place) escaparse de; (person) escaparse a

escort [n 'ɛskɔːt, vb ɪ'skɔːt] n acompañante mf; (Mil) escolta mf ▷ vt acompañar

especially [ɪ'spɛʃlɪ] adv (above all) sobre todo; (particularly) en particular, especialmente

espionage ['ɛspɪənɑːʒ] n espionaje m

essay ['ɛseɪ] n (Literature) ensayo; (Scol: short) redacción f; (: long) trabajo

essence ['ɛsns] n esencia

essential [ɪ'sɛnʃl] adj (necessary) imprescindible; (basic) esencial; **essentially** adv esencialmente; **essentials** npl lo imprescindible, lo esencial

establish [ɪ'stæblɪʃ] vt establecer; (prove) demostrar; (relations) entablar; (reputation) ganarse; **establishment** n establecimiento; **the Establishment**

la clase dirigente

estate [ɪ'steɪt] n (land) finca, hacienda; (inheritance) herencia; (BRIT: also: **housing ~**) urbanización f; **estate agent** (BRIT) n agente mf inmobiliario/a; **estate car** (BRIT) n furgoneta

estimate [n 'ɛstɪmət, vb 'ɛstɪmeɪt] n estimación f, apreciación f; (assessment) tasa, cálculo; (Comm) presupuesto ▷ vt estimar, tasar; calcular

etc abbr (= et cetera) etc

eternal [ɪ'tɜːnl] adj eterno

eternity [ɪ'tɜːnɪtɪ] n eternidad f

ethical ['ɛθɪkl] adj ético; **ethics** ['ɛθɪks] n ética ▷ npl moralidad f

Ethiopia [iːθɪ'əʊpɪə] n Etiopía

ethnic ['ɛθnɪk] adj étnico; **ethnic minority** n minoría étnica

e-ticket ['iːtɪkɪt] n billete m electrónico (SP), boleto electrónico (LAM)

etiquette ['ɛtɪkɛt] n etiqueta

EU n abbr (= European Union) UE f

euro n euro

Europe ['jʊərəp] n Europa; **European** [-'piːən] adj, n europeo/a m/f; **European Community** n Comunidad f Europea; **European Union** n Unión f Europea

Eurostar® ['jʊərəʊstɑː*] n Eurostar® m

evacuate [ɪ'vækjueɪt] vt (people) evacuar; (place) desocupar

evade [ɪ'veɪd] vt evadir, eludir

evaluate [ɪ'væljueɪt] vt evaluar; (value) tasar; (evidence) interpretar

evaporate [ɪ'væpəreɪt] vi evaporarse; (fig) desvanecerse

eve [iːv] n: **on the ~ of** en vísperas de

even ['iːvn] adj (level) llano; (smooth) liso; (speed, temperature) uniforme; (number) par ▷ adv hasta, incluso; (introducing a comparison) aún, todavía; **~ if, ~ though** aunque +subjun; **~ more** aun más; **~ so** aun así; **not ~** ni siquiera; **~ he was there** hasta él estuvo allí; **~ on Sundays** incluso los

domingos; **to get ~ with sb** ajustar
cuentas con algn

evening ['iːvnɪŋ] n tarde f; (late)
noche f; **in the ~** por la tarde; **evening
class** n clase f nocturna; **evening
dress** n (no pl: formal clothes) traje m de
etiqueta; (woman's) traje m de noche

event [ɪ'vɛnt] n suceso,
acontecimiento; (Sport) prueba; **in
the ~ of** en caso de; **eventful** (day)
activo; (day) ajetreado

eventual [ɪ'vɛntʃuəl] adj final

> ▌ Be careful not to translate **eventual**
> by the Spanish word **eventual**.

eventually adv (finally) finalmente; (in
time) con el tiempo

ever ['ɛvə*] adv (at any time) nunca,
jamás; (at all times) siempre; (in
question): **why ~ not?** ¿y por qué no?;
the best ~ lo nunca visto; **have you
~ seen it?** ¿lo ha visto usted alguna
vez?; **better than ~** mejor que nunca; **~
since** adv desde entonces ▷ conj
después de que; **evergreen** n árbol m
de hoja perenne

○ **KEYWORD**

every ['ɛvrɪ] adj 1 (each) cada; **every
one of them** (persons) todos ellos/as;
(objects) cada uno de ellos/as; **every
shop in the town was closed** todas
las tiendas de la ciudad estaban
cerradas

2 (all possible) todo/a; **I gave you every
assistance** te di toda la ayuda posible;
I have every confidence in him tiene
toda mi confianza; **we wish you every
success** te deseamos toda suerte
de éxitos

3 (showing recurrence) todo/a; **every
day/week** todos los días/todas las
semanas; **every other car had been
broken into** habían forzado uno
de cada dos coches; **she visits me
every other/third day** me visita cada
dos/tres días; **every now and then** de
vez en cuando

every: everybody pron = **everyone**;
everyday adj (daily) cotidiano, de
todos los días; (usual) acostumbrado;
everyone pron todos/as, todo el
mundo; **everything** pron todo; **this
shop sells everything** esta tienda
vende de todo; **everywhere** adv: **I've
been looking for you everywhere** te
he estado buscando por todas partes;
everywhere you go you meet ... en
todas partes encuentras ...

evict [ɪ'vɪkt] vt deshauciar

evidence ['ɛvɪdəns] n (proof) prueba;
(of witness) testimonio; (sign) indicios
mpl; **to give ~** prestar declaración, dar
testimonio

evident ['ɛvɪdənt] adj evidente,
manifiesto; **evidently** adv por lo visto

evil ['iːvl] adj malo; (influence) funesto
▷ n mal m

evoke [ɪ'vəuk] vt evocar

evolution [iːvə'luːʃən] n evolución f

evolve [ɪ'vɔlv] vt desarrollar ▷ vi
evolucionar, desarrollarse

ewe [juː] n oveja

ex [ɛks] (inf) n: **my ~** mi ex

ex- [ɛks] prefix ex

exact [ɪg'zækt] adj exacto; (person)
meticuloso ▷ vt: **to ~ sth (from)** exigir
algo (de); **exactly** adv exactamente;
(indicating agreement) exacto

exaggerate [ɪg'zædʒəreɪt] vt, vi
exagerar; **exaggeration** [-'reɪʃən] n
exageración f

exam [ɪg'zæm] n abbr (Scol) =
examination

examination [ɪgzæmɪ'neɪʃən] n
examen m; (Med) reconocimiento

examine [ɪg'zæmɪn] vt examinar;
(inspect) inspeccionar, escudriñar;
(Med) reconocer; **examiner** n
examinador(a) m/f

example [ɪg'zɑːmpl] n ejemplo; **for
~** por ejemplo

exasperated [ɪg'zɑːspəreɪtɪd] adj
exasperado

excavate ['ɛkskəveɪt] vt excavar

exceed [ɪk'siːd] vt (amount) exceder;

(number) pasar de; (speed limit) sobrepasar; (powers) excederse en; (hopes) superar; **exceedingly** adv sumamente, sobremanera
excel [ɪkˈsɛl] vi sobresalir; **to ~ o.s** lucirse
excellence [ˈɛksələns] n excelencia
excellent [ˈɛksələnt] adj excelente
except [ɪkˈsɛpt] prep (also: **~ for, ~ing**) excepto, salvo ▷ vt excluir; **~ if/when** excepto si/cuando; **~ that** salvo que; **exception** [ɪkˈsɛpʃən] n excepción f; **to take exception to** ofenderse por; **exceptional** [ɪkˈsɛpʃənl] adj excepcional; **exceptionally** [ɪkˈsɛpʃənəlɪ] adv excepcionalmente, extraordinariamente
excerpt [ˈɛksəːpt] n extracto
excess [ɪkˈsɛs] n exceso; **excess baggage** n exceso de equipaje; **excessive** adj excesivo
exchange [ɪksˈtʃeɪndʒ] n intercambio; (conversation) diálogo; (also: **telephone ~**) central f (telefónica) ▷ vt: **to ~ (for)** cambiar (por); **exchange rate** n tipo de cambio
excite [ɪkˈsaɪt] vt (stimulate) estimular; (arouse) excitar; **excited** adj: **to get excited** emocionarse; **excitement** n (agitation) excitación f; (exhilaration) emoción f; **exciting** adj emocionante
exclaim [ɪksˈkleɪm] vi exclamar; **exclamation** [ɛkskləˈmeɪʃən] n exclamación f; **exclamation mark** n punto de admiración; **exclamation point** (US) = **exclamation mark**
exclude [ɪksˈkluːd] vt excluir; exceptuar
excluding [ɪksˈkluːdɪŋ] prep: **~ VAT** IVA no incluido
exclusion [ɪksˈkluːʒən] n exclusión f; **to the ~ of** con exclusión de
exclusive [ɪksˈkluːsɪv] adj exclusivo; (club, district) selecto; **~ of tax** excluyendo impuestos; **exclusively** adv únicamente

excruciating [ɪkˈskruːʃɪeɪtɪŋ] adj (pain) agudísimo, atroz; (noise, embarrassment) horrible
excursion [ɪkˈskəːʃən] n (tourist excursion) excursión f
excuse [n ɪkˈskjuːs, vb ɪkˈskjuːz] n disculpa, excusa; (pretext) pretexto ▷ vt (justify) justificar; (forgive) disculpar, perdonar; **to ~ sb from doing sth** dispensar a algn de hacer algo; **~ me!** (attracting attention) ¡por favor!; (apologizing) ¡perdón!; **if you will ~ me** con su permiso
ex-directory [ˈɛksdɪˈrɛktərɪ] (BRIT) adj que no consta en la guía
execute [ˈɛksɪkjuːt] vt (plan) realizar; (order) cumplir; (person) ajusticiar, ejecutar; **execution** [-ˈkjuːʃən] n realización f; cumplimiento; ejecución f
executive [ɪgˈzɛkjutɪv] n (person, committee) ejecutivo; (Pol: committee) poder m ejecutivo ▷ adj ejecutivo
exempt [ɪgˈzɛmpt] adj: **~ from** exento de ▷ vt: **to ~ sb from** eximir a algn de
exercise [ˈɛksəsaɪz] n ejercicio ▷ vt (patience) usar de; (right) valerse de; (dog) llevar de paseo; (mind) preocupar ▷ vi (also: **to take ~**) hacer ejercicio(s); **exercise book** n cuaderno
exert [ɪgˈzəːt] vt ejercer; **to ~ o.s.** esforzarse; **exertion** [-ʃən] n esfuerzo
exhale [ɛksˈheɪl] vt despedir ▷ vi exhalar
exhaust [ɪgˈzɔːst] n (Aut: also: **~ pipe**) escape m; (: fumes) gases mpl de escape ▷ vt agotar; **exhausted** adj agotado; **exhaustion** [ɪgˈzɔːstʃən] n agotamiento; **nervous exhaustion** postración f nerviosa
exhibit [ɪgˈzɪbɪt] n (Art) obra expuesta; (Law) objeto expuesto ▷ vt (show: emotions) manifestar; (: courage, skill) demostrar; (paintings) exponer; **exhibition** [ɛksɪˈbɪʃən] n exposición f; (of talent etc) demostración f
exhilarating [ɪgˈzɪləreɪtɪŋ] adj estimulante, tónico

exile ['eksaɪl] n exilio; (*person*)
exiliado/a ▷ vt desterrar, exiliar

exist [ɪg'zɪst] vi existir; (*live*) vivir;
existence n existencia; **existing** adj
existente, actual

exit ['eksɪt] n salida ▷ vi (*Theatre*)
hacer mutis; (*Comput*) salir (del
sistema)

    Be careful not to translate **exit** by
    the Spanish word *éxito*.

exit ramp (us) n (*Aut*) vía de acceso

exotic [ɪg'zɒtɪk] adj exótico

expand [ɪk'spænd] vt ampliar;
(*number*) aumentar ▷ vi (*population*)
aumentar; (*trade etc*) expandirse; (*gas,
metal*) dilatarse

expansion [ɪk'spænʃən] n (*of
population*) aumento; (*of trade*)
expansión f

expect [ɪk'spekt] vt esperar;
(*require*) contar con; (*suppose*) suponer
▷ vi: **to be ~ing** (*pregnant woman*)
estar embarazada; **expectation**
[ekspek'teɪʃən] n (*hope*) esperanza;
(*belief*) expectativa

expedition [ekspə'dɪʃən] n
expedición f

expel [ɪk'spel] vt arrojar; (*from place*)
expulsar

expenditure [ɪks'pendɪtʃə*] n
gastos mpl, desembolso; consumo

expense [ɪk'spens] n gasto, gastos
mpl; (*high cost*) costa; **expenses** npl
(*Comm*) gastos mpl; **at the ~ of** a costa
de; **expense account** n cuenta de
gastos

expensive [ɪk'spensɪv] adj caro,
costoso

experience [ɪk'spɪərɪəns] n
experiencia ▷ vt experimentar;
(*suffer*) sufrir; **experienced** adj
experimentado

experiment [ɪk'spεrɪmənt] n
experimento ▷ vi hacer experimentos;
experimental [-'mentl] adj
experimental; **the process is still at
the experimental stage** el proceso
está todavía en prueba

expert ['ekspə:t] adj experto, perito
▷ n experto/a, perito/a; (*specialist*)
especialista mf; **expertise** [-'ti:z] n
pericia

expire [ɪk'spaɪə*] vi caducar, vencer;
expiry n vencimiento; **expiry date**
n (*of medicine, food item*) fecha de
caducidad

explain [ɪk'spleɪn] vt explicar;
explanation [eksplə'neɪʃən] n
explicación f

explicit [ɪk'splɪsɪt] adj explícito

explode [ɪk'spləud] vi estallar,
explotar; (*population*) crecer
rápidamente; (*with anger*) reventar

exploit [n 'eksplɔɪt, vb ɪk'splɔɪt] n
hazaña ▷ vt explotar; **exploitation**
[-'teɪʃən] n explotación f

explore [ɪk'splɔː*] vt explorar; (*fig*)
examinar, investigar; **explorer** n
explorador(a) m/f

explosion [ɪk'spləuʒən] n explosión
f; **explosive** [ɪks'pləusɪv] adj, n
explosivo

export [vb ek'spɔːt, n, cpd 'eks-pɔːt]
vt exportar ▷ n (*process*) exportación
f; (*product*) producto de exportación
▷ cpd de exportación; **exporter** n
exportador m

expose [ɪk'spəuz] vt exponer;
(*unmask*) desenmascarar; **exposed**
adj expuesto

exposure [ɪk'spəuʒə*] n exposición
f; (*publicity*) publicidad f; (*Phot: speed*)
velocidad f de obturación; (: *shot*)
fotografía f; **to die from ~** (*Med*) morir
de frío

express [ɪk'spres] adj (*definite*)
expreso, explícito; (ʙʀɪᴛ: *letter etc*)
urgente ▷ n (*train*) rápido ▷ vt
expresar; **expression** [-ʃən] n
expresión f; (*of actor etc*) sentimiento;
expressway (us) n (*urban motorway*)
autopista

exquisite [ek'skwɪzɪt] adj exquisito

extend [ɪk'stend] vt (*visit, street*)
prolongar; (*building*) ampliar;
(*invitation*) ofrecer ▷ vi (*land*)

extenderse; (period of time) prolongarse
extension [ɪk'stenʃən] n extensión
f; (building) ampliación f; (of time)
prolongación f; (Tel: in private house)
línea derivada; (: in office) extensión
f; **extension lead** n alargador m,
alargadera
extensive [ɪk'stensɪv] adj extenso;
(damage) importante; (knowledge)
amplio
extent [ɪk'stent] n (breadth)
extensión f; (scope) alcance m; **to some
~** hasta cierto punto; **to the ~ of ...**
hasta el punto de ...; **to such an ~ that
...** hasta tal punto que ...; **to what ~?**
¿hasta qué punto?
exterior [ek'stɪərɪə*] adj exterior,
externo ▷ n exterior m
external [ek'stənl] adj externo
extinct [ɪk'stɪŋkt] adj (volcano)
extinguido; (race) extinto; **extinction**
n extinción f
extinguish [ɪk'stɪŋgwɪʃ] vt
extinguir, apagar
extra ['ekstrə] adj adicional ▷ adv (in
addition) de más ▷ n (luxury, addition)
extra m; (Cinema, Theatre) extra mf,
comparsa mf
extract [vb ɪk'strækt, n 'ekstrækt] vt
sacar; (tooth) extraer; (money, promise)
obtener ▷ n extracto
extradite ['ekstrədaɪt] vt extraditar
extraordinary [ɪk'strɔ:dnrɪ] adj
extraordinario; (odd) raro
extravagance [ɪk'strævəgəns] n
derroche m, despilfarro; (thing bought)
extravagancia
extravagant [ɪk'strævəgənt]
adj (lavish: person) pródigo, f; (: gift)
(demasiado) caro; (wasteful)
despilfarrador(a)
extreme [ɪk'stri:m] adj extremo,
extremado ▷ n extremo; **extremely**
adv sumamente, extremadamente
extremist [ɪk'stri:mɪst] adj, n
extremista m/f
extrovert ['ekstrəvə:t] n
extrovertido/a

eye [aɪ] n ojo ▷ vt mirar de soslayo,
ojear; **to keep an ~ on** vigilar; **eyeball**
n globo ocular; **eyebrow** n ceja;
eyedrops npl gotas fpl para los ojos,
colirio; **eyelash** n pestaña; **eyelid** n
párpado; **eyeliner** n delineador m (de
ojos); **eyeshadow** n sombreador m de
ojos; **eyesight** n vista; **eye witness** n
testigo mf presencial

f

F [ɛf] n (Mus) fa m

fabric ['fæbrɪk] n tejido, tela
Be careful not to translate **fabric** by the Spanish word **fábrica**.

fabulous ['fæbjuləs] adj fabuloso

face [feɪs] n (Anat) cara, rostro; (of clock) esfera (SP), cara (LAM); (of mountain) cara, ladera; (of building) fachada ▷ vt (direction) estar de cara a; (situation) hacer frente a; (facts) aceptar; **~ down** (person, card) boca abajo; **to lose ~** desprestigiarse; **to make** or **pull a ~** hacer muecas; **in the ~ of** (difficulties etc) ante; **on the ~ of it** a primera vista; **to ~** cara a cara; **face up to** vt fus hacer frente a, arrostrar; **face cloth** (BRIT) n manopla; **face pack** (BRIT) n mascarilla

facial ['feɪʃəl] adj de la cara ▷ n (also: **beauty ~**) tratamiento facial, limpieza

facilitate [fə'sɪlɪteɪt] vt facilitar

facilities [fə'sɪlɪtɪz] npl (buildings) instalaciones fpl; (equipment) servicios mpl; **credit ~** facilidades fpl de crédito

fact [fækt] n hecho; **in ~** en realidad

faction ['fækʃən] n facción f

factor ['fæktə*] n factor m

factory ['fæktərɪ] n fábrica

factual ['fæktjuəl] adj basado en los hechos

faculty ['fækəltɪ] n facultad f; (US: teaching staff) personal m docente

fad [fæd] n novedad f, moda

fade [feɪd] vi desteñirse; (sound, smile) desvanecerse; (light) apagarse; (flower) marchitarse; (hope, memory) perderse; **fade away** vi (sound) apagarse

fag [fæg] (BRIT: inf) n (cigarette) pitillo (SP), cigarro

Fahrenheit ['fɑːrənhaɪt] n Fahrenheit m

fail [feɪl] vt (candidate, test) suspender (SP), reprobar (LAM); (memory etc) fallar a ▷ vi suspender (SP), reprobar (LAM); (be unsuccessful) fracasar; (strength, brakes) fallar; (light) acabarse; **to ~ to do sth** (neglect) dejar de hacer algo; (be unable) no poder hacer algo; **without ~** sin falta; **failing** n falta, defecto ▷ prep a falta de; **failure** ['feɪljə*] n fracaso; (person) fracasado/a; (mechanical etc) fallo

faint [feɪnt] adj débil; (recollection) vago; (mark) apenas visible ▷ n desmayo ▷ vi desmayarse; **to feel ~** estar mareado, marearse; **faintest** adj: **I haven't the faintest idea** no tengo la más remota idea; **faintly** adv débilmente; (vaguely) vagamente

fair [fɛə*] adj justo; (hair, person) rubio; (weather) bueno; (good enough) regular; (considerable) considerable ▷ adv (play) limpio ▷ n feria; (BRIT: funfair) parque m de atracciones; **fairground** n recinto ferial; **fair-haired** adj (person) rubio; **fairly** adv (justly) con justicia; (quite) bastante; **fair trade** n comercio justo; **fairway** n (Golf) calle f

fairy ['fɛərɪ] n hada; **fairy tale** n cuento de hadas

faith [feɪθ] n fe f; (trust) confianza; (sect) religión f; **faithful** adj

(loyal: troops etc) leal; (spouse) fiel;
(account) exacto; **faithfully** adv
fielmente; **yours faithfully** (BRIT: in
letters) le saluda atentamente
fake [feɪk] n (painting etc) falsificación
f; (person) impostor(a) m/f ▷ adj falso
▷ vt fingir; (painting etc) falsificar
falcon ['fɔ:lkən] n halcón m
fall [fɔ:l] (pt **fell**, pp **fallen**) n caída;
(in price etc) descenso; (US) otoño ▷ vi
caer(se); (price) bajar, descender; **falls**
npl (waterfall) cascada, salto de agua;
to ~ flat (on one's face) caerse (boca
abajo); (plan) fracasar; (joke, story) no
hacer gracia; **fall apart** vi deshacerse;
fall down vi (person) caerse; (building,
hopes) derrumbarse; **fall for** vt fus
(trick) dejarse engañar por; (person)
enamorarse de; **fall off** vi caerse;
(diminish) disminuir; **fall out** vi (friends
etc) reñir; (hair, teeth) caerse; **fall over**
vi caer(se); **fall through** vi (plan,
project) fracasar
fallen ['fɔ:lən] pp of **fall**
fallout ['fɔ:laut] n lluvia radioactiva
false [fɔ:ls] adj falso; **under ~
pretences** con engaños; **false alarm**
n falsa alarma; **false teeth** (BRIT) npl
dentadura postiza
fame [feɪm] n fama
familiar [fə'mɪlɪə*] adj conocido,
familiar; (tone) de confianza; **to
be ~ with** (subject) conocer (bien);
familiarize [fə'mɪlɪəraɪz] vt: **to
familiarize o.s. with** familiarizarse
con
family ['fæmɪlɪ] n familia; **family
doctor** n médico/a de cabecera;
family planning n planificación f
familiar
famine ['fæmɪn] n hambre f,
hambruna
famous ['feɪməs] adj famoso, célebre
fan [fæn] n abanico; (Elec) ventilador
m; (of pop star) fan m; (Sport) hincha mf
▷ vt abanicar; (fire, quarrel) avivar
fanatic [fə'nætɪk] n fanático/a
fan belt n correa del ventilador

fan club n club m de fans
fancy ['fænsɪ] n (whim) capricho,
antojo; (imagination) imaginación f
▷ adj (luxury) lujoso, de lujo ▷ vt (feel
like, want) tener ganas de; (imagine)
imaginarse; (think) creer; **to take a ~ to
sb** tomar cariño a algn; **he fancies her**
(inf) le gusta (ella) mucho; **fancy dress**
n disfraz m
fan heater n calefactor m de aire
fantasize ['fæntəsaɪz] vi fantasear,
hacerse ilusiones
fantastic [fæn'tæstɪk] adj (enormous)
enorme; (strange, wonderful) fantástico
fantasy ['fæntəzɪ] n (dream) sueño;
(unreality) fantasía
fanzine ['fænziːn] n fanzine m
FAQs abbr (= frequently asked questions)
preguntas frecuentes
far [fɑ:*] adj (distant) lejano ▷ adv
lejos; (much, greatly) mucho; **~ away, ~
off** (a lo) lejos; **~ better** mucho mejor;
~ from lejos de; **by ~** con mucho; **go as
~ as the farm** vaya hasta la granja; **as
~ as I know** que yo sepa; **how ~?** ¿hasta
dónde?; (fig) ¿hasta qué punto?
farce [fɑ:s] n farsa
fare [fɛə*] n (on trains, buses) precio
(del billete); (in taxi: cost) tarifa; (food)
comida; **half ~** medio pasaje m; **full ~**
pasaje completo
Far East n: **the ~** el Extremo Oriente
farewell [fɛə'wɛl] excl, n adiós m
farm [fɑ:m] n cortijo (SP), hacienda
(LAM), rancho (MEX), estancia (RPL)
▷ vt cultivar; **farmer** n granjero,
hacendado (LAM), ranchero (MEX),
estanciero (RPL); **farmhouse** n granja,
casa del hacendado (LAM), rancho
(MEX), casco de la estancia (RPL);
farming n agricultura; (of crops)
cultivo; (of animals) cría; **farmyard**
n corral m
far-reaching [fɑ:'riːtʃɪŋ] adj (reform,
effect) de gran alcance
fart [fɑ:t] (inf!) vi tirarse un pedo (!)
farther ['fɑ:ðə*] adv más lejos, más
allá ▷ adj más lejano

farthest ['fɑːðɪst] superlative of **far**

fascinate ['fæsɪneɪt] vt fascinar;
fascinated adj fascinado

fascinating ['fæsɪneɪtɪŋ] adj
fascinante

fascination [-'neɪʃən] n fascinación f

fascist ['fæʃɪst] adj, n fascista m/f

fashion ['fæʃən] n moda; (fashion
industry) industria de la moda; (manner)
manera ▷ vt formar; **in ~** a la moda;
out of ~ pasado de moda; **fashionable**
adj de moda; **fashion show** n desfile
m de modelos

fast [fɑːst] adj (speed) rápido; (dye, colour)
resistente; (clock): **to be ~** estar
adelantado ▷ adv rápidamente,
de prisa; (stuck, held) firmemente
▷ n ayuno ▷ vi ayunar; **~ asleep**
profundamente dormido

fasten ['fɑːsn] vt atar, sujetar; (coat,
belt) abrochar ▷ vi atarse; abrocharse

fast food n comida rápida, platos mpl
preparados

fat [fæt] adj gordo; (book) grueso;
(profit) grande, pingüe ▷ n grasa; (on
person) carnes fpl; (lard) manteca

fatal ['feɪtl] adj (mistake) fatal;
(injury) mortal; **fatality** [fə'tælɪtɪ] n
(road death etc) víctima; **fatally** adv
fatalmente; mortalmente

fate [feɪt] n destino; (of person)
suerte f

father ['fɑːðə*] n padre m; **Father
Christmas** n Papá m Noel; **father-in-
law** n suegro

fatigue [fə'tiːɡ] n fatiga, cansancio

fattening ['fætnɪŋ] adj (food) que
hace engordar

fatty ['fætɪ] adj (food) graso ▷ n (inf)
gordito/a, gordinflón/ona m/f

faucet ['fɔːsɪt] (us) n grifo (SP), llave
f, canilla (RPL)

fault [fɔːlt] n (blame) culpa; (defect: in
person, machine) defecto; (Geo) falla
▷ vt criticar; **it's my ~** es culpa mía; **to
find ~ with** criticar, poner peros a; **at ~**
culpable; **faulty** adj defectuoso

fauna ['fɔːnə] n fauna

favour etc ['feɪvə*] (us **favor** etc) n
favor m; (approval) aprobación f ▷ vt
(proposition) estar a favor de, aprobar;
(assist) ser propicio a; **to do sb a ~**
hacer un favor a algn; **to find ~ with sb**
caer en gracia a algn; **in ~ of** a favor de;
favourable adj favorable; **favourite**
['feɪvrɪt] adj, n favorito, preferido

fawn [fɔːn] n cervato ▷ adj (also: **~
coloured**) color de cervato, leonado
▷ vi: **to ~ (up)on** adular

fax [fæks] n (document) fax m;
(machine) telefax m ▷ vt mandar por
telefax

FBI (us) n abbr (= Federal Bureau of
Investigation) ≈ BIC f (SP)

fear [fɪə*] n miedo, temor m ▷ vt
tener miedo de, temer; **for ~ of** por si;
fearful adj temeroso, miedoso; (awful)
terrible; **fearless** adj audaz

feasible ['fiːzəbl] adj factible

feast [fiːst] n banquete m; (Rel: also: **~
day**) fiesta ▷ vi festejar

feat [fiːt] n hazaña

feather ['feðə*] n pluma

feature ['fiːtʃə*] n característica;
(article) artículo de fondo ▷ vt (film)
presentar ▷ vi: **to ~ in** tener un
papel destacado en; **features** npl (of
face) facciones fpl; **feature film** n
largometraje m

Feb. abbr (= February) feb

February ['februərɪ] n febrero

fed [fed] pt, pp of **feed**

federal ['fedərəl] adj federal

federation [fedə'reɪʃən] n
federación f

fed up [fed'ʌp] adj: **to be ~ (with)**
estar harto (de)

fee [fiː] n pago; (professional) derechos
mpl, honorarios mpl; (of club) cuota;
school ~s matrícula

feeble ['fiːbl] adj débil; (joke) flojo

feed [fiːd] (pt, pp **fed**) n comida; (of
animal) pienso; (on printer) dispositivo
de alimentación ▷ vt alimentar;
(BRIT: baby: breastfeed) dar el pecho
a; (animal) dar de comer a; (data,

information); **to ~ into** meter en;
feedback n reacción f, feedback m

feel [fi:l] (pt, pp **felt**) n (sensation)
sensación f; (sense of touch) tacto;
(impression): **to have the ~ of** parecerse
a ▷ vt tocar; (pain etc) sentir; (think,
believe) creer; **to ~ hungry/cold** tener
hambre/frío; **to ~ lonely/better**
sentirse solo/mejor; **I don't ~ well**
no me siento bien; **it ~s soft** es suave
al tacto; **to ~ like** (want) tener ganas
de; **feeling** n (physical) sensación f;
(foreboding) presentimiento; (emotion)
sentimiento

feet [fi:t] npl of **foot**

fell [fɛl] pt of **fall** ▷ vt (tree) talar

fellow ['fɛləu] n tipo, tío (sp);
(comrade) compañero; (of learned
society) socio/a; **fellow citizen** n
conciudadano/a; **fellow countryman**
(irreg) n compatriota m; **fellow men**
npl semejantes mpl; **fellowship** n
compañerismo; (grant) beca

felony ['fɛlənɪ] n crimen m

felt [fɛlt] pt, pp of **feel** ▷ n fieltro;
felt-tip n (also: **felt-tip pen**)
rotulador m

female ['fi:meɪl] n (pej: woman) mujer
f, tía; (Zool) hembra ▷ adj femenino;
hembra

feminine ['fɛmɪnɪn] adj femenino

feminist ['fɛmɪnɪst] n feminista

fence [fɛns] n valla, cerca ▷ vt (also: ~
in) cercar ▷ vi (Sport) hacer esgrima;
fencing n esgrima

fend [fɛnd] vi: **to ~ for o.s.** valerse por
sí mismo; **fend off** vt (attack) rechazar;
(questions) evadir

fender ['fɛndə*] (US) n guardafuego;
(Aut) parachoques m inv

fennel ['fɛnl] n hinojo

ferment [vb fə'mɛnt, n 'fə:mɛnt] vi
fermentar ▷ n ['fə:] agitación f

fern [fə:n] n helecho

ferocious [fə'rəʊʃəs] adj feroz

ferret ['fɛrɪt] n hurón m

ferry ['fɛrɪ] n (small) barca (de pasaje),
balsa; (large: also: **~boat**) transbordador

m, ferry m ▷ vt transportar

fertile ['fə:taɪl] adj fértil; (Biol)
fecundo; **fertilize** ['fə:tɪlaɪz] vt (Biol)
fecundar; (Agr) abonar; **fertilizer** n
abono

festival ['fɛstɪvəl] n (Rel) fiesta; (Art,
Mus) festival m

festive ['fɛstɪv] adj festivo; **the ~
season** (BRIT: Christmas) las Navidades

fetch [fɛtʃ] vt ir a buscar; (sell for)
venderse por

fête [feɪt] n fiesta

fetus ['fi:təs] (US) n =**foetus**

feud [fju:d] n (hostility) enemistad f;
(quarrel) disputa

fever ['fi:və*] n fiebre f; **feverish**
adj febril

few [fju:] adj (not many) pocos ▷ pron
pocos; algunos; **a ~** adj unos pocos,
algunos; **fewer** adj menos; **fewest** adj
los(las) menos

fiancé [fɪ'ɑːŋseɪ] n novio, prometido;
fiancée n novia, prometida

fiasco [fɪ'æskəu] n fiasco

fib [fɪb] n mentirilla

fibre ['faɪbə*] (US **fiber**) n fibra;
fibreglass (US **Fiberglass®**) n fibra
de vidrio

fickle ['fɪkl] adj inconstante

fiction ['fɪkʃən] n ficción f; **fictional**
adj novelesco

fiddle ['fɪdl] n (Mus) violín m;
(cheating) trampa ▷ vt (BRIT: accounts)
falsificar; **fiddle with** vt fus juguetear
con

fidelity [fɪ'dɛlɪtɪ] n fidelidad f

field [fi:ld] n campo; (fig) campo,
esfera; (Sport) campo (SP), cancha (LAM);
field marshal n mariscal m

fierce [fɪəs] adj feroz; (wind, heat)
fuerte; (fighting, enemy) encarnizado

fifteen [fɪf'ti:n] num quince;
fifteenth adj decimoquinto; **the
fifteenth floor** la planta quince;
the fifteenth of August el quince
de agosto

fifth [fɪfθ] num quinto

fiftieth ['fɪftɪɪθ] adj quincuagésimo

fifty ['fɪftɪ] num cincuenta; **fifty-fifty** adj (deal, split) a medias ▷ adv a medias, mitad por mitad

fig [fɪg] n higo

fight [faɪt] (pt, pp **fought**) n (gen) pelea; (Mil) combate m; (struggle) lucha ▷ vt luchar contra; (cancer, alcoholism) combatir; (election) intentar ganar; (emotion) resistir ▷ vi pelear, luchar; **fight back** vi defenderse; (after illness) recuperarse ▷ vt (tears) contener; **fight off** vt (attack, attacker) rechazar; (disease, sleep, urge) luchar contra; **fighting** n combate m, pelea

figure ['fɪgə*] n (Drawing, Geom) figura, dibujo; (number, cipher) cifra; (body, outline) tipo; (personality) figura ▷ vt (esp us) imaginar ▷ vi (appear) figurar; **figure out** vt (work out) resolver

file [faɪl] n (tool) lima; (dossier) expediente m; (folder) carpeta; (Comput) fichero; (row) fila ▷ vt limar; (Law: claim) presentar; (store) archivar; **filing cabinet** n fichero, archivador m

Filipino [fɪlɪ'piːnəʊ] adj filipino ▷ n (person) filipino/a m/f; (Ling) tagalo

fill [fɪl] vt (space): to ~ (with) llenar (de); (vacancy, need) cubrir ▷ n: to eat one's ~ llenarse; **fill in** vt rellenar; **fill out** vt (form, receipt) rellenar; **fill up** vt llenar (hasta el borde) ▷ vi (Aut) poner gasolina

fillet ['fɪlɪt] n filete m; **fillet steak** n filete m de ternera

filling ['fɪlɪŋ] n (Culin) relleno; (for tooth) empaste m; **filling station** n estación f de servicio

film [fɪlm] n película ▷ vt (scene) filmar ▷ vi rodar (una película); **film star** n astro, estrella de cine

filter ['fɪltə*] n filtro ▷ vt filtrar; **filter lane** (BRIT) n carril m de selección

filth [fɪlθ] n suciedad f; **filthy** adj sucio; (language) obsceno

fin [fɪn] n (gen) aleta

final ['faɪnl] adj (last) final, último; (definitive) definitivo, terminante ▷ n

(BRIT Sport) final f; **finals** npl (Scol) examen m final; (US Sport) final f

finale [fɪ'nɑːlɪ] n final m

finalist n (Sport) finalista mf; **finalize** vt concluir, completar; **finally** adv (lastly) por último, finalmente; (eventually) por fin

finance [faɪ'næns] n (money) fondos mpl ▷ vt financiar; **finances** npl finanzas fpl; (personal finances) situación f económica; **financial** [-'nænʃəl] adj financiero; **financial year** n ejercicio (financiero)

find [faɪnd] (pt, pp **found**) vt encontrar, hallar; (come upon) descubrir ▷ n hallazgo; descubrimiento; **to ~ sb guilty** (Law) declarar culpable a algn; **find out** vt averiguar; (truth, secret) descubrir; **to find out about** (subject) informarse sobre; (by chance) enterarse de; **findings** npl (Law) veredicto, fallo; (of report) recomendaciones fpl

fine [faɪn] adj excelente; (thin) fino ▷ adv (well) bien ▷ n (Law) multa ▷ vt (Law) multar; **to be ~** (person) estar bien; (weather) hacer buen tiempo; **fine arts** npl bellas artes fpl

finger ['fɪŋgə*] n dedo ▷ vt (touch) manosear; **little/index ~** (dedo) meñique m/índice m; **fingernail** n uña; **fingerprint** n huella dactilar; **fingertip** n yema del dedo

finish ['fɪnɪʃ] n (end) fin m; (Sport) meta; (polish etc) acabado ▷ vt, vi terminar; **to ~ doing sth** acabar de hacer algo; **to ~ third** llegar el tercero; **finish off** vt acabar, terminar; (kill) acabar con; **finish up** vt acabar, terminar ▷ vi ir a parar, terminar

Finland ['fɪnlənd] n Finlandia

Finn [fɪn] n finlandés/esa m/f; **Finnish** adj finlandés/esa f; (Ling) finlandés m

fir [fə:*] n abeto

fire ['faɪə*] n fuego; (in hearth) lumbre f; (accidental) incendio; (heater) estufa ▷ vt (gun) disparar; (interest) despertar; (inf: dismiss) despedir ▷ vi (shoot) disparar; **on ~** ardiendo, en llamas; **fire alarm** n alarma de incendios; **firearm** n arma de fuego; **fire brigade** (US **fire department**) n (cuerpo de) bomberos mpl; **fire engine** (BRIT) n coche m de bomberos; **fire escape** n escalera de incendios; **fire exit** n salida de incendios; **fire extinguisher** n extintor m (de incendios); **fireman** (irreg) n bombero; **fireplace** n chimenea; **fire station** n parque m de bomberos; **firetruck** (US) n = **fire engine**; **firewall** n (Internet) firewall m; **firewood** n leña; **fireworks** npl fuegos mpl artificiales

firm [fə:m] adj firme; (look, voice) resuelto ▷ n firma, empresa; **firmly** adv firmemente; resueltamente

first [fə:st] adj primero ▷ adv (before others) primero; (when listing reasons etc) en primer lugar, primeramente ▷ n (person: in race) primero/a; (Aut) primera; (BRIT Scol) título de licenciado con calificación de sobresaliente; **at ~** al principio; **~ of all** ante todo; **first aid** n primera ayuda, primeros auxilios mpl; **first-aid kit** n botiquín m; **first-class** adj (excellent) de primera (categoría); (ticket etc) de primera clase; **first-hand** adj de primera mano; **first lady** n (esp US) primera dama; **firstly** adv en primer lugar; **first name** n nombre m (de pila); **first-rate** adj estupendo

fiscal ['fɪskəl] adj fiscal; **fiscal year** n año fiscal, ejercicio

fish [fɪʃ] n inv pez m; (food) pescado ▷ vt, vi pescar; **to go ~ing** ir de pesca; **~ and chips** pescado frito con patatas fritas; **fisherman** (irreg) n pescador m; **fish fingers** (BRIT) npl croquetas fpl de pescado; **fishing** n pesca; **fishing boat** n barca de pesca; **fishing line** n sedal m; **fishing rod** n (BRIT) pescador/a n; **fishmonger's (shop)** (BRIT) n pescadería fpl; **fish sticks** (US) npl = **fish fingers**; **fishy** (inf) adj sospechoso

fist [fɪst] n puño

fit [fɪt] adj (healthy) en (buena) forma; (proper) adecuado, apropiado ▷ vt (clothes) estar o sentar bien a; (install) poner; (equip) proveer, dotar; (facts) cuadrar o corresponder con ▷ vi (clothes) sentar bien; (in space, gap) caber; (facts) coincidir ▷ n (Med) ataque m; **~ to** (ready) a punto de; **~ for** apropiado para; **a ~ of anger/pride** un arranque de cólera/orgullo; **this dress is a good ~** éste vestido me sienta bien; **by ~s and starts** a rachas; **fit in** vi (fig: person) llevarse bien (con todos); **fitness** n (Med) salud f; **fitted** adj (jacket, shirt) entallado; (sheet) de cuatro picos; **fitted carpet** n moqueta; **fitted kitchen** n cocina amueblada; **fitting** adj apropiado n (of dress) prueba; (of piece of equipment) instalación f; **fitting room** n probador m; **fittings** npl instalaciones fpl

five [faɪv] num cinco; **fiver** (inf) n (BRIT) billete m de cinco libras; (US) billete m de cinco dólares

fix [fɪks] vt (secure) fijar, asegurar; (mend) arreglar; (prepare) preparar ▷ n: **to be in a ~** estar en un aprieto; **fix up** vt (meeting) arreglar; **to fix sb up with sth** proveer a algn de algo; **fixed** adj (prices etc) fijo; **fixture** n (Sport) encuentro

fizzy ['fɪzɪ] adj (drink) gaseoso

flag [flæg] n bandera; (stone) losa ▷ vi decaer ▷ vt: **to ~ sb down** hacer señas a algn para que se pare; **flagpole** n asta de bandera

flair [fleə*] n aptitud f especial

flak [flæk] n (Mil) fuego antiaéreo; (inf: criticism) lluvia de críticas

flake [fleɪk] n (of rust, paint) escama; (of snow, soap powder) copo ▷ vi (also: **~ off**) desconcharse

flamboyant [flæm'bɔɪənt] adj (dress) vistoso; (person) extravagante

flame [fleɪm] n llama

flamingo [flə'mɪŋgəʊ] n flamenco

flammable ['flæməbl] adj

inflamable

flan [flæn] (BRIT) n tarta

   Be careful not to translate **flan** by the Spanish word *flan*.

flank [flæŋk] n (*of animal*) ijar m; (*of army*) flanco ▷ vt flanquear

flannel ['flænl] n (BRIT: also: **face ~**) manopla; (*fabric*) franela

flap [flæp] n (*of pocket, envelope*) solapa ▷ vt (*wings, arms*) agitar ▷ vi (*sail, flag*) ondear

flare [flɛə*] n llamarada; (*in skirt etc*) vuelo; **flares** npl (*trousers*) pantalones mpl de campana; **flare up** vi encenderse; (fig: *person*) encolerizarse; (: *revolt*) estallar

flash [flæʃ] n relámpago; (also: **news ~**) noticias fpl de última hora; (Phot) flash m ▷ vt (*light, headlights*) lanzar un destello de; (*news, message*) transmitir; (*smile*) lanzar ▷ vi brillar; (*hazard light etc*) lanzar destellos; **in a ~** = en un instante; **he ~ed by** or **past** pasó como un rayo; **flashback** n (Cinema) flashback m; **flashbulb** n bombilla fusible; **flashlight** n linterna

flask [flɑːsk] n frasco; (also: **vacuum ~**) termo

flat [flæt] adj llano; (*smooth*) liso; (*tyre*) desinflado; (*battery*) descargado; (*beer*) muerto; (*refusal etc*) rotundo; (Mus) desafinado; (*rate*) fijo ▷ n (BRIT: *apartment*) piso (SP), departamento (LAM), apartamento (Aut) pinchazo; (Mus) bemol m; **to work ~ out** trabajar a toda mecha; **flatten** vt (also: **flatten out**) allanar; (*smooth out*) alisar; (*building, plants*) arrasar

flatter ['flætə*] vt adular, lisonjear; **flattering** adj halagüeño; (*dress*) que favorece

flaunt [flɔːnt] vt ostentar, lucir

flavour etc ['fleɪvə*] (us **flavor** etc) n sabor m, gusto ▷ vt sazonar, condimentar; **strawberry-flavoured** con sabor a fresa; **flavouring** n (*in product*) aromatizante m

flaw [flɔː] n defecto; **flawless** adj

impecable

flea [fliː] n pulga; **flea market** n rastro, mercadillo

flee [fliː] (pt, pp **fled**) vt huir de ▷ vi huir, fugarse

fleece [fliːs] n vellón m; (*wool*) lana; (*top*) forro polar ▷ vt (inf) desplumar

fleet [fliːt] n flota; (*of lorries etc*) escuadra

fleeting ['fliːtɪŋ] adj fugaz

Flemish ['flemɪʃ] adj flamenco

flesh [fleʃ] n carne f; (*skin*) piel f; (*of fruit*) pulpa

flew [fluː] pt of **fly**

flex [fleks] n cordón m ▷ vt (*muscles*) tensar; **flexibility** n flexibilidad f; **flexible** adj flexible; **flexitime** (us **flextime**) n horario flexible

flick [flɪk] n capirotazo; chasquido ▷ vt (*with hand*) dar un capirotazo a; (*whip etc*) chasquear; (*switch*) accionar; **flick through** vt fus hojear

flicker ['flɪkə*] vi (*light*) parpadear; (*flame*) vacilar

flies [flaɪz] npl of **fly**

flight [flaɪt] n vuelo; (*escape*) huida, fuga; (also: **~ of steps**) tramo (de escaleras); **flight attendant** n auxiliar mf de vuelo

flimsy ['flɪmzɪ] adj (*thin*) muy ligero; (*building*) endeble; (*excuse*) flojo

flinch [flɪntʃ] vi encogerse; **to ~ from** retroceder ante

fling [flɪŋ] (pt, pp **flung**) vt arrojar

flint [flɪnt] n pedernal m; (*in lighter*) piedra

flip [flɪp] vt dar la vuelta a; (*switch: turn on*) encender; (*turn*) apagar; (*coin*) echar a cara o cruz

flip-flops ['flɪpflɒps] npl (esp BRIT) chancletas fpl

flipper ['flɪpə*] n aleta

flirt [flɜːt] vi coquetear, flirtear ▷ n coqueta

float [fləʊt] n flotador m; (*in procession*) carroza; (*money*) reserva ▷ vi flotar; (*swimmer*) hacer la plancha

flock [flɒk] n (*of sheep*) rebaño; (*of*

birds) bandada ▷ *vi:* **to ~ to** acudir
en tropel a

flood [flʌd] *n* inundación *f;* (*of
letters, imports etc*) avalancha ▷ *vt*
inundar ▷ *vi* (*place*) inundarse;
(*people*): **to ~ into** inundar; **flooding** *n*
inundaciones *fpl;* **floodlight** *n* foco

floor [flɔ:*] *n* suelo; (*storey*) piso; (*of
sea*) fondo ▷ *vt* (*question*) dejar sin
respuesta; (: *blow*) derribar; **ground ~,
first ~** (*us*) planta baja; **first ~, second
~** (*us*) primer piso; **floorboard** *n* tabla;
flooring *n* suelo; (*material*) solería;
floor show *n* cabaret *m*

flop [flɔp] *n* fracaso ▷ *vi* (*fail*)
fracasar; (*fall*) derrumbarse; **floppy** *adj*
flojo ▷ *n* (*Comput: also:* **floppy disk**)
floppy *m*

flora [ˈflɔ:rə] *n* flora

floral [ˈflɔ:rl] *adj* (*pattern*) floreado

florist [ˈflɔrɪst] *n* florista *mf;* **florist's
(shop)** *n* floristería

flotation [fləʊˈteɪʃən] *n* (*of shares*)
emisión *f;* (*of company*) lanzamiento

flour [ˈflaʊə*] *n* harina

flourish [ˈflʌrɪʃ] *vi* florecer ▷ *n*
ademán *m*, movimiento (*ostentoso*)

flow [fləʊ] *n* (*movement*) flujo; (*of
traffic*) circulación *f;* (*tide*) corriente *f*
▷ *vi* (*river, blood*) fluir; (*traffic*) circular

flower [ˈflaʊə*] *n* flor *f* ▷ *vi* florecer;
flower bed *n* macizo; **flowerpot**
n tiesto

flown [fləʊn] *pp of* **fly**

fl. oz. *abbr* (= *fluid ounce*)

flu [flu:] *n:* **to have ~** tener la gripe

fluctuate [ˈflʌktjueɪt] *vi* fluctuar

fluent [ˈflu:ənt] *adj* (*linguist*) que
habla perfectamente; (*speech*)
elocuente; **he speaks ~ French, he's ~
in French** domina el francés

fluff [flʌf] *n* pelusa; **fluffy** *adj* de
pelo suave

fluid [ˈflu:ɪd] *adj* (*movement*) fluido,
líquido; (*situation*) inestable ▷ *n* fluido,
líquido; **fluid ounce** *n* onza líquida

fluke [flu:k] (*inf*) *n* chiripa

flung [flʌŋ] *pt, pp of* **fling**

fluorescent [fluəˈrɛsnt] *adj*
fluorescente

fluoride [ˈfluəraɪd] *n* fluoruro

flurry [ˈflʌrɪ] *n* (*of snow*) temporal *m;* **~
of activity** frenesí *m* de actividad

flush [flʌʃ] *n* rubor *m;* (*fig: of youth
etc*) resplandor *m* ▷ *vt* limpiar con
agua ▷ *vi* ruborizarse ▷ *adj:* **~ with** a
ras de; **to ~ the toilet** hacer funcionar
la cisterna

flute [flu:t] *n* flauta

flutter [ˈflʌtə*] *n* (*of wings*) revoloteo,
aleteo; (*fig*); **a ~ of panic/excitement**
una oleada de pánico/excitación ▷ *vi*
revolotear

fly [flaɪ] (*pt* **flew**, *pp* **flown**) *n* mosca;
(*on trousers: also:* **flies**) bragueta ▷ *vt*
(*plane*) pilot(e)ar; (*cargo*) transportar
(en avión); (*distances*) recorrer en
avión ▷ *vi* volar; (*passengers*) ir en
avión; (*escape*) evadirse; (*flag*) ondear;
fly away, fly off *vi* emprender el
vuelo; **fly-drive** *n:* **fly-drive holiday**
vacaciones que incluyen vuelo y alquiler
de coche; **flying** *n* (*activity*) (el) volar;
(*action*) vuelo ▷ *adj:* **flying visit** visita
relámpago; **with flying colours** con
lucimiento; **flying saucer** *n* platillo
volante; **flyover** (*BRIT*) *n* paso a
desnivel or superior

FM *abbr* (*Radio*) (= *frequency modulation*)
FM

foal [fəʊl] *n* potro

foam [fəʊm] *n* espuma ▷ *vi* hacer
espuma

focus [ˈfəʊkəs] (*pl* **~es**) *n* foco; (*centre*)
centro *m* ▷ *vt* (*field glasses etc*) enfocar
▷ *vi:* **to ~ (on)** enfocar a; (*issue etc*)
centrarse en; **in/out of ~** enfocado/
desenfocado

foetus [ˈfi:təs] (*us* **fetus**) *n* feto

fog [fɔg] *n* niebla; **foggy** *adj:* **it's
foggy** hay niebla, está brumoso;
fog lamp (*us* **fog light**) *n* faro
de niebla

foil [fɔɪl] *vt* frustrar ▷ *n* hoja; (*kitchen
foil*) papel *m* (de) aluminio; (*complement*)
complemento; (*Fencing*) florete *m*

fold [fəuld] n (bend, crease) pliegue m; (Agr) redil m ▷ vt doblar; (arms) cruzar; **fold up** vi plegarse, doblarse; (business) quebrar ▷ vt (map etc) plegar; **folder** n (for papers) carpeta; (Comput) directorio; **folding** adj (chair, bed) plegable

foliage ['fəulɪdʒ] n follaje m

folk [fəuk] npl gente f ▷ adj popular, folklórico; **folks** npl (family) familia sg, parientes mpl; **folklore** ['fəuklɔː'] n folklore m; **folk music** n música folk; **folk song** n canción f popular

follow ['fɒləu] vt seguir ▷ vi seguir; (result) resultar; **to ~ suit** hacer lo mismo; **follow up** vt (letter, offer) responder a; (case) investigar; **follower** n (of person, belief) partidario/a; **following** adj siguiente ▷ n afición f, partidarios mpl; **follow-up** n continuación f

fond [fɒnd] adj (memory, smile etc) cariñoso; (hopes) ilusorio; **to be ~ of** tener cariño a; (pastime, food) ser aficionado a

food [fuːd] n comida; **food mixer** n batidora; **food poisoning** n intoxicación f alimenticia; **food processor** n robot m de cocina; **food stamp** (US) n vale m para comida

fool [fuːl] n tonto/a; (Culin) puré m de frutas con nata ▷ vt engañar ▷ vi (gen) bromear; **fool about, fool around** vi hacer el tonto; **foolish** adj tonto; (careless) imprudente; **foolproof** adj (plan etc) infalible

foot [fut] (pl feet) n pie m; (measure) pie m (= 304 mm); (of animal) pata ▷ vt (bill) pagar; **on ~** a pie; **footage** n (Cinema) imágenes fpl; **foot-and-mouth (disease)** [fʊtənd'mauθ-] n fiebre f aftosa; **football** n balón m; (game: BRIT) fútbol m; (: US) fútbol m americano; **footballer** n (BRIT) = **football player**; **football match** n partido de fútbol; **football player** n (BRIT) futbolista mf; (US) jugador m de fútbol americano; **footbridge** n

puente m para peatones; **foothills** npl estribaciones fpl; **foothold** n pie m firme; **footing** n (fig) posición f; **to lose one's footing** perder el pie; **footnote** n nota (al pie de la página); **footpath** n sendero; **footprint** n huella, pisada; **footstep** n paso; **footwear** n calzado

○ KEYWORD

for [fɔː] prep 1 (indicating destination, intention) para; **the train for London** el tren con destino a or de Londres; **he left for Rome** marchó para Roma; **he went for the paper** fue por el periódico; **is this for me?** ¿es esto para mí?; **it's time for lunch** es la hora de comer

2 (indicating purpose) para; **what's it for?** ¿para qué (es)?; **to pray for peace** rezar por la paz

3 (on behalf of, representing): **the MP for Hove** el diputado por Hove; **he works for the government/a local firm** trabaja para el gobierno/en una empresa local; **I'll ask him for you** se lo pediré por ti; **G for George** G de Gerona

4 (because of) por esta razón; **for fear of being criticized** por temor a ser criticado

5 (with regard to) para; **it's cold for July** hace frío para julio; **he has a gift for languages** tiene don de lenguas

6 (in exchange for) por; **I sold it for £5** lo vendí por £5; **to pay 50 pence for a ticket** pagar 50 peniques por un billete

7 (in favour of): **are you for or against us?** ¿estás con nosotros o contra nosotros?; **I'm all for it** estoy totalmente a favor; **vote for X** vote (a) X

8 (referring to distance): **there are roadworks for 5 km** hay obras en 5 km; **we walked for miles** caminamos kilómetros y kilómetros

9 (referring to time): **he was away for two years** estuvo fuera (durante) dos

años; **it hasn't rained for 3 weeks** no ha llovido durante or en 3 semanas; **I have known her for years** la conozco desde hace años; **can you do it for tomorrow?** ¿lo podrás hacer para mañana?
10 (with infinitive clauses): **it is not for me to decide** la decisión no es cosa mía; **it would be best for you to leave** sería mejor que te fueras; **there is still time for you to do it** todavía te queda tiempo para hacerlo; **for this to be possible ...** para que esto sea posible ...
11 (in spite of) a pesar de; **for all his complaints** a pesar de sus quejas ▷ conj (since, as: rather formal) puesto que

forbid [fə'bɪd] (pt **forbad(e)**, pp **forbidden**) vt prohibir; **to ~ sb to do sth** prohibir a algn hacer algo; **forbidden** pt of **forbid** ▷ adj (food, area) prohibido; (word, subject) tabú

force [fɔːs] n fuerza ▷ vt forzar; (push) meter a la fuerza; **to ~ o.s. to do** hacer un esfuerzo por hacer; **forced** adj forzado; **forceful** adj enérgico

ford [fɔːd] n vado

fore [fɔː*] n: **to come to the ~** empezar a destacar; **forearm** n antebrazo; **forecast** (pt, pp **forecast**) n pronóstico ▷ vt pronosticar; **forecourt** n patio; **forefinger** n (dedo) índice m; **forefront** n: **in the forefront of** en la vanguardia de; **foreground** n primer plano; **forehead** ['fɒrɪd] n frente f

foreign ['fɒrɪn] adj extranjero; (trade) exterior; (object) extraño; **foreign currency** n divisas fpl; **foreigner** n extranjero/a; **foreign exchange** n divisas fpl; **Foreign Office** (BRIT) n Ministerio de Asuntos Exteriores; **Foreign Secretary** (BRIT) n Ministro de Asuntos Exteriores

fore: **foreman** (irreg) n capataz m; (in construction) maestro de obras; **foremost** adj principal ▷ adv: **first**

and foremost ante todo; **forename** n nombre m (de pila)

forensic [fə'rensɪk] adj forense

foresee [fɔː'siː] (pt **foresaw**, pp **foreseen**) vt prever; **foreseeable** adj previsible

forest ['fɒrɪst] n bosque m; **forestry** n silvicultura

forever [fə'rɛvə*] adv para siempre; (endlessly) constantemente

foreword ['fɔːwəːd] n prefacio

forfeit ['fɔːfɪt] vt perder

forgave [fə'geɪv] pt of **forgive**

forge [fɔːdʒ] n herrería ▷ vt (signature, money) falsificar; (metal) forjar; **forger** n falsificador(a) m/f; **forgery** n falsificación f

forget [fə'gɛt] (pt **forgot**, pp **forgotten**) vt olvidar ▷ vi olvidarse; **forgetful** adj despistado

forgive [fə'gɪv] (pt **forgave**, pp **forgiven**) vt perdonar; **to ~ sb for sth** perdonar algo a algn

forgot [fə'gɒt] pt of **forget**

forgotten [fə'gɒtn] pp of **forget**

fork [fɔːk] n (for eating) tenedor m; (for gardening) horca; (of roads) bifurcación f ▷ vi (road) bifurcarse

forlorn [fə'lɔːn] adj (person) triste, melancólico; (place) abandonado; (attempt, hope) desesperado

form [fɔːm] n forma; (document) formulario f ▷ vt formar; (idea) concebir; (habit) adquirir; **in top ~** en plena forma; **to ~ a queue** hacer cola

formal ['fɔːməl] adj (offer, receipt) por escrito; (person etc) correcto; (occasion, dinner) de etiqueta; (dress) correcto; (garden) de estilo) clásico; **formality** [-'mælɪtɪ] n (procedure) trámite m; corrección f; etiqueta

format ['fɔːmæt] n formato ▷ vt (Comput) formatear

formation [fɔː'meɪʃən] n formación f

former ['fɔːmə*] adj anterior; (earlier) antiguo; (ex) ex; **the ~ ... the latter ...** aquél ... éste ...; **formerly** adv antes

formidable ['fɔ:mɪdəbl] *adj* formidable

formula ['fɔ:mjulə] *n* fórmula

fort [fɔ:t] *n* fuerte *m*

forthcoming [fɔ:θ'kʌmɪŋ] *adj* próximo, venidero; (*help, information*) disponible; (*character*) comunicativo

fortieth ['fɔ:tɪɪθ] *adj* cuadragésimo

fortify ['fɔ:tɪfaɪ] *vt* (*city*) fortificar; (*person*) fortalecer

fortnight ['fɔ:tnaɪt] (BRIT) *n* quince días *mpl*, quincena; **fortnightly** *adj* de cada quince días, quincenal ⊳ *adv* cada quince días, quincenalmente

fortress ['fɔ:trɪs] *n* fortaleza

fortunate ['fɔ:tʃənɪt] *adj* afortunado; **it is ~ that ...** (es una) suerte que ...; **fortunately** *adv* afortunadamente

fortune ['fɔ:tʃən] *n* suerte *f*; (*wealth*) fortuna; **fortune-teller** *n* adivino/a *f*

forty ['fɔ:tɪ] *num* cuarenta

forum ['fɔ:rəm] *n* foro

forward ['fɔ:wəd] *adj* (*movement, position*) avanzado; (*front*) delantero; (*in time*) adelantado; (*not shy*) atrevido ⊳ *n* (*Sport*) delantero ⊳ *vt* (*letter*) remitir; (*career*) promocionar; **to move ~ avanzar; forwarding address** *n* destinatario; **forward(s)** *adv* (hacia) adelante; **forward slash** *n* barra diagonal

fossil ['fɔsl] *n* fósil *m*

foster ['fɔstə*] *vt* (*child*) acoger en una familia; fomentar; **foster child** *n* hijo/a adoptivo/a; **foster mother** *n* madre *f* adoptiva

fought [fɔ:t] *pt, pp of* **fight**

foul [faul] *adj* sucio, puerco; (*weather, smell etc*) asqueroso; (*language*) grosero; (*temper*) malísimo ⊳ *n* (*Sport*) falta ⊳ *vt* (*dirty*) ensuciar; **foul play** *n* (*Law*) muerte *f* violenta

found [faund] *pt, pp of* **find** ⊳ *vt* fundar; **foundation** [-'deɪʃən] *n* (*act*) fundación *f*; (*basis*) base *f*; (*also:* **foundation cream**) crema base; **foundations** *npl* (*of building*)

cimientos *mpl*

founder ['faundə*] *n* fundador(a) *m/f* ⊳ *vi* hundirse

fountain ['fauntɪn] *n* fuente *f*; **fountain pen** *n* (pluma) estilográfica (sp), pluma-fuente *f* (LAM)

four [fɔ:*] *num* cuatro; **on all ~s** a gatas; **four-letter word** *n* taco; **four-poster** *n* (*also:* **four-poster bed**) cama de columnas; **fourteen** *num* catorce; **fourteenth** *adj* decimocuarto; **fourth** *num* cuarto; **four-wheel drive** *n* tracción *f* a las cuatro ruedas

fowl [faul] *n* ave *f* (de corral)

fox [fɔks] *n* zorro ⊳ *vt* confundir

foyer ['fɔɪeɪ] *n* vestíbulo

fraction ['frækʃən] *n* fracción *f*

fracture ['fræktʃə*] *n* fractura

fragile ['frædʒaɪl] *adj* frágil

fragment ['frægmənt] *n* fragmento

fragrance ['freɪɡrəns] *n* fragancia

frail [freɪl] *adj* frágil; (*person*) débil

frame [freɪm] *n* (*Tech*) armazón *m*; (*of person*) cuerpo; (*of picture, door etc*) marco; (*of spectacles: also:* **~s**) montura ⊳ *vt* enmarcar; **framework** *n* marco

France [fra:ns] *n* Francia

franchise ['fræntʃaɪz] *n* (*Pol*) derecho de votar, sufragio; (*Comm*) licencia, concesión *f*

frank [fræŋk] *adj* franco ⊳ *vt* (*letter*) franquear; **frankly** *adv* francamente

frantic ['fræntɪk] *adj* (*distraught*) desesperado; (*hectic*) frenético

fraud [frɔ:d] *n* fraude *m*; (*person*) impostor(a) *m/f*

fraught [frɔ:t] *adj*: **~ with** lleno de

fray [freɪ] *vi* deshilacharse

freak [fri:k] *n* (*person*) fenómeno; (*event*) suceso anormal

freckle ['frekl] *n* peca

free [fri:] *adj* libre; (*gratis*) gratuito ⊳ *vt* (*prisoner etc*) poner en libertad; (*jammed object*) soltar; **~ (of charge), for~** gratis; **freedom** *n* libertad *f*; **Freefone®** *n* número gratuito; **free gift** *n* prima; **free kick** *n* tiro libre; **freelance** *adj* independiente

freeze | 394

▷ adv por cuenta propia; **freely** adv libremente; (liberally) generosamente; **Freepost®** n porte m pagado; **free-range** adj (hen, eggs) de granja; **freeway** (us) n autopista; **free will** n libre albedrío; **of one's own free will** por su propia voluntad

freeze [friːz] (pt **froze**, pp **frozen**) vi (weather) helar; (liquid, pipe, person) helarse, congelarse ▷ vt helar; (food, prices, salaries) congelar ▷ n helada; (on arms, wages) congelación f; **freezer** n congelador m, freezer m (sc)

freezing ['friːzɪŋ] adj helado; **three degrees below** = tres grados bajo cero; **freezing point** n punto de congelación

freight [freɪt] n (goods) carga; (money charged) flete m; **freight train** (us) n tren m de mercancías

French [frɛntʃ] adj francés/esa ▷ n (Ling) francés m; **the French** npl los franceses; **French bean** n judía verde; **French bread** n pan m francés; **French dressing** n (Culin) vinagreta; **French fried potatoes**, **French fries** (us) npl patatas fpl (SP) or papas fpl (LAM) fritas; **Frenchman** (irreg) n francés m; **Frenchwoman** (irreg) n francesa; **French stick** n barra de pan; **French window** n puerta de cristal

frenzy ['frɛnzɪ] n frenesí m

○ **KEYWORD**

frequency ['friːkwənsɪ] n frecuencia f

frequent [adj 'friːkwənt, vb frɪ'kwɛnt] adj frecuente ▷ vt frecuentar; **frequently** [-əntlɪ] adv frecuentemente, a menudo

fresh [frɛʃ] adj fresco; (bread) tierno; (new) nuevo; **freshen** vi (wind, air) soplar más recio; **freshen up** vi (person) arreglarse, lavarse; **fresher** (BRIT: inf) n (Univ) estudiante mf de primer año; **freshly** adv (painted, made etc) recién; **freshman** (us: irreg) n = **fresher**; **freshwater** adj (fish) de agua dulce

fret [frɛt] vi inquietarse

Fri abbr (= Friday) vier

friction ['frɪkʃən] n fricción f

Friday ['fraɪdɪ] n viernes m inv

fridge [frɪdʒ] (BRIT) n frigorífico (SP), nevera (SP), refrigerador m (LAM), heladera (RPL)

fried [fraɪd] adj frito

friend [frɛnd] n amigo/a; **friendly** adj simpático; (government) amigo; (place) acogedor(a); (match) amistoso; **friendship** n amistad f

fries [fraɪz] (esp us) npl = **French fried potatoes**

frigate ['frɪgɪt] n fragata f

fright [fraɪt] n (terror) terror m; (scare) susto; **to take** = asustarse; **frighten** vt asustar; **frightened** adj asustado; **frightening** adj espantoso; **frightful** adj espantoso, horrible

frill [frɪl] n volante m

fringe [frɪndʒ] n (BRIT: of hair) flequillo; (on lampshade etc) flecos mpl; (of forest etc) borde m, margen m

Frisbee® ['frɪzbɪ] n frisbee® m

fritter ['frɪtə*] n buñuelo

frivolous ['frɪvələs] adj frívolo

fro [frəʊ] see **to**

frock [frɔk] n vestido

frog [frɔg] n rana; **frogman** (irreg) n hombre-rana m

○ **KEYWORD**

from [frɔm] prep **1** (indicating starting place) de, desde; **where do you come from?** ¿de dónde eres?; **from London to Glasgow** de Londres a Glasgow; **to escape from sth/sb** escaparse de algo/algn

2 (indicating origin etc) de; **a letter/telephone call from my sister** una carta/llamada de mi hermana; **tell him from me that …** dígale de mi parte que …

3 (indicating time): **from one o'clock to** or **until** or **till two** (de)sde la una a or hasta las dos; **from January (on)** a partir de enero

4 (indicating distance) de; **the hotel is**

1 km from the beach el hotel está a 1 km de la playa
5 (indicating price, number etc) de; **prices range from £10 to £50** los precios van desde £10 a or hasta £50; **the interest rate was increased from 9% to 10%** el tipo de interés fue incrementado de un 9% a un 10%
6 (indicating difference) de; **he can't tell red from green** no sabe distinguir el rojo del verde; **to be different from sb/sth** ser diferente a algn/algo
7 (because of, on the basis of): **from what he says** por lo que dice; **weak from hunger** debilitado por el hambre

front [frʌnt] n (foremost part) parte f delantera; (of house) fachada; (of dress) delantero; (promenade: also: **sea ~**) paseo marítimo; (Mil, Pol, Meteorology) frente m; (fig: appearances) apariencias fpl ▷ adj (wheel, leg) delantero; (row, line) primero; **in ~ (of)** delante (de); **front door** n puerta principal; **frontier** ['frʌntɪə*] n frontera; **front page** n primera plana; **front-wheel drive** n tracción f delantera

frost [frɒst] n helada; (also: **hoar~**) escarcha; **frostbite** n congelación f; **frosting** n (esp US: icing) glaseado; **frosty** adj (weather) de helada; (welcome etc) glacial

froth [frɒθ] n espuma

frown [fraun] vi fruncir el ceño

froze [frəuz] pt of **freeze**

frozen ['frəuzn] pp of **freeze**

fruit [fru:t] n inv fruta; fruto; (fig) fruto; resultados mpl; **fruit juice** n zumo (SP) or jugo (LAM) de fruta; **fruit machine** (BRIT) n máquina f tragaperras; **fruit salad** n macedonia (SP) or ensalada (LAM) de frutas

frustrate [frʌs'treɪt] vt frustrar; **frustrated** adj frustrado

fry [fraɪ] (pt, pp **fried**) vt freír; **small ~** gente f menuda; **frying pan** n sartén f

ft. abbr =**foot; feet**

fudge [fʌdʒ] n (Culin) caramelo blando

fuel [fjuəl] n (for heating) combustible m; (coal) carbón m; (wood) leña; (for engine) carburante m; **fuel tank** n depósito (de combustible)

fulfil [ful'fɪl] vt (function) cumplir con; (condition) satisfacer; (wish, desire) realizar

full [ful] adj lleno; (fig) pleno; (complete) completo; (maximum) máximo; (information) detallado; (price) íntegro; (skirt) amplio ▷ adv: **to know ~ well** that saber muy bien; **I'm ~ (up)** no puedo más; **~ employment** pleno empleo; **a ~ two hours** dos horas completas; **at ~ speed** a máxima velocidad; **in ~** (reproduce, quote) íntegramente; **full-length** adj (novel etc) entero; (coat) largo; (portrait) de cuerpo entero; **full moon** n luna llena; **full-scale** adj (attack, war) en gran escala; (model) de tamaño natural; **full stop** n punto; **full-time** adj (work) de tiempo completo ▷ adv: **to work full-time** trabajar a tiempo completo; **fully** adv completamente; (at least) por lo menos

fumble ['fʌmbl] vi: **to ~ with** manejar torpemente

fume [fju:m] vi (rage) estar furioso; **fumes** npl humo, gases mpl

fun [fʌn] n (amusement) diversión f; **to have ~** divertirse; **for ~** en broma; **to make ~ of** burlarse de

function ['fʌŋkʃən] n función f ▷ vi funcionar

fund [fʌnd] n fondo; (reserve) reserva; **funds** npl (money) fondos mpl

fundamental [fʌndə'mentl] adj fundamental

funeral ['fju:nərəl] n (burial) entierro; (ceremony) funerales mpl; **funeral director** n director(a) m/f de pompas fúnebres; **funeral parlour** (BRIT) n funeraria

funfair ['fʌnfeə*] (BRIT) n parque m de atracciones

fungus ['fʌŋgəs] (pl **fungi**) n hongo; (mould) moho

funnel ['fʌnl] n embudo; (of ship) chimenea

funny ['fʌnɪ] adj gracioso, divertido; (strange) curioso, raro

fur [fə:*] n piel f; (BRIT: in kettle etc) sarro; **fur coat** n abrigo de pieles

furious ['fjuərɪəs] adj furioso; (effort) violento

furnish ['fə:nɪʃ] vt amueblar; (supply) suministrar; (information) facilitar; **furnishings** npl muebles mpl

furniture ['fə:nɪtʃə*] n muebles mpl; **piece of ~** mueble m

furry ['fə:rɪ] adj peludo

further ['fə:ðə*] adj (new) nuevo, adicional ▷ adv más lejos; (more) más; (moreover) además ▷ vt promover, adelantar; **further education** n educación f superior; **furthermore** adv además

furthest ['fə:ðɪst] superlative of **far**

fury ['fjuərɪ] n furia

fuse [fju:z] (US **fuze**) n fusible m; (for bomb etc) mecha ▷ vt (metal) fundir; (fig) fusionar ▷ vi fundirse; fusionarse; (BRIT Elec): **to ~ the lights** fundir los plomos; **fuse box** n caja de fusibles

fusion ['fju:ʒən] n fusión f

fuss [fʌs] n (excitement) conmoción f; (trouble) alboroto; **to make a ~** armar un lío or jaleo; **to make a ~ of sb** mimar a algn; **fussy** adj (person) exigente; (too ornate) recargado

future ['fju:tʃə*] adj futuro; (coming) venidero ▷ n futuro; (prospects) porvenir m; **in ~** de ahora en adelante; **futures** npl (Comm) operaciones fpl a término, futuros mpl

fuze [fju:z] (US) = **fuse**

fuzzy ['fʌzɪ] adj (Phot) borroso; (hair) muy rizado

g

G [dʒi:] n (Mus) sol m

g. abbr (= gram(s)) gr.

gadget ['gædʒɪt] n aparato

Gaelic ['geɪlɪk] adj, n (Ling) gaélico

gag [gæg] n (on mouth) mordaza; (joke) chiste m ▷ vt amordazar

gain [geɪn] n: **~ (in)** aumento (de); (profit) ganancia ▷ vt ganar ▷ vi (watch) adelantarse; **to ~ from/by sth** sacar provecho de algo; **to ~ on sb** ganar terreno a algn; **to ~ 3 lbs (in weight)** engordar 3 libras

gal. abbr = **gallon**

gala ['gɑ:lə] n fiesta

galaxy ['gæləksɪ] n galaxia

gale [geɪl] n (wind) vendaval m

gall bladder ['gɔ:l-] n vesícula biliar

gallery ['gælərɪ] n (also: **art ~**: public) pinacoteca; (: private) galería de arte; (for spectators) tribuna

gallon ['gæln] n galón m (BRIT = 4,546 litros, US = 3,785 litros)

gallop ['gæləp] n galope m ▷ vi galopar

gallstone ['gɔ:lstəun] n cálculo

biliario

gamble ['gæmbl] n (risk) riesgo ▷ vt jugar, apostar ▷ vi (take a risk) jugárselas; (bet) apostar; **to ~ on** apostar a; (success etc) contar con; **gambler** n jugador(a) m/f; **gambling** n juego

game [geɪm] n juego; (match) partido; (of cards) partida; (Hunting) caza ▷ adj (willing): **to be ~ for anything** atreverse a todo; **big ~** caza mayor (contest) juegos; (BRIT: Scol) deportes mpl; **games console** [geɪmz-] n consola de juegos; **game show** n programa m concurso m, concurso

gammon ['gæmən] n (bacon) tocino ahumado; (ham) jamón m ahumado

gang [gæŋ] n (of criminals) pandilla; (of friends etc) grupo; (of workmen) brigada

gangster ['gæŋstə*] n gángster m

gap [gæp] n vacío (SP), hueco (LAM); (in trees, traffic) claro; (in time) intervalo; (difference): **~ (between)** diferencia (entre)

gape [geɪp] vi mirar boquiabierto; (shirt etc) abrirse (completamente)

gap year n año sabático (antes de empezar a estudiar en la universidad)

garage ['gæraːʒ] n garaje m; (for repairs) taller m; **garage sale** n venta de objetos usados (en el jardín de una casa particular)

garbage ['gaːbɪdʒ] (US) n basura; (inf: nonsense) tonterías fpl; **garbage can** n cubo o bote m (MEX) o tacho (SC) de la basura; **garbage collector** (US) n basurero/a

garden ['gaːdn] n jardín m; **gardens** npl (park) parque m; **garden centre** (BRIT) n centro de jardinería; **gardener** n jardinero/a; **gardening** n jardinería

garlic ['gaːlɪk] n ajo

garment ['gaːmənt] n prenda (de vestir)

garnish ['gaːnɪʃ] vt (Culin) aderezar

garrison ['gærɪsn] n guarnición f

gas [gæs] n gas m; (fuel) combustible m; (US: gasoline) gasolina ▷ vt asfixiar con gas; **gas cooker** (BRIT) n cocina de gas; **gas cylinder** n bombona de gas; **gas fire** n estufa de gas

gasket ['gæskɪt] n (Aut) junta de culata

gasoline ['gæsəliːn] (US) n gasolina

gasp [gaːsp] n boqueada; (of shock etc) grito sofocado ▷ vi (pant) jadear

gas: gas pedal n (esp US) acelerador m; **gas station** (US) n gasolinera; **gas tank** (US) n (Aut) depósito (de gasolina)

gate [geɪt] n puerta; (iron gate) verja

gateau ['gætəu] (pl **~x**) n tarta

gatecrash ['geɪtkræʃ] (BRIT) vt colarse en

gateway ['geɪtweɪ] n puerta

gather ['gæðə*] vt (flowers, fruit) coger (SP), recoger; (assemble) reunir; (pick up) recoger; (Sewing) fruncir; (understand) entender ▷ vi (assemble) reunirse; **to ~ speed** ganar velocidad; **gathering** n reunión f, asamblea

gauge [geɪdʒ] n (instrument) indicador m ▷ vt medir; (fig) juzgar

gave [geɪv] pt of **give**

gay [geɪ] adj (homosexual) gay; (joyful) alegre; (colour) vivo

gaze [geɪz] n mirada fija ▷ vi: **to ~ at sth** mirar algo fijamente

GB abbr = **Great Britain**

GCSE (BRIT) n abbr (= General Certificate of Secondary Education) examen de reválida que se hace a los 16 años

gear [gɪə*] n equipo, herramientas fpl; (Tech) engranaje m; (Aut) velocidad f, marcha f ▷ vt (fig: adapt): **to ~ sth to** adaptar o ajustar algo a; **top** o **high** (US)/**low ~** cuarta/primera velocidad; **in ~** en marcha; **gear up** vi prepararse; **gear box** n caja de cambios; **gear lever** n palanca de cambio; **gear shift** (US) n = **gear lever**; **gear stick** n (BRIT) palanca de cambios

geese [giːs] npl of **goose**

9

gel [dʒɛl] n gel m
gem [dʒɛm] n piedra preciosa
Gemini ['dʒɛmɪnaɪ] n Géminis m, Gemelos mpl
gender ['dʒɛndə*] n género
gene [dʒiːn] n gen(e) m
general ['dʒɛnərl] n general m ▷ adj general; **in ~** en general; **general anaesthetic** (US **general anesthetic**) n anestesia general; **general election** n elecciones fpl generales; **generalize** vi generalizar; **generally** adv generalmente, en general; **general practitioner** n médico general; **general store** n tienda (que vende de todo) (LAM, SP), almacén m (SC, SP)
generate ['dʒɛnəreɪt] vt (Elec) generar; (jobs, profits) producir
generation [dʒɛnə'reɪʃən] n generación f
generator ['dʒɛnəreɪtə*] n generador m
generosity [dʒɛnə'rɒsɪtɪ] n generosidad f
generous ['dʒɛnərəs] adj generoso
genetic [dʒɪ'nɛtɪk] adj: **~ engineering** ingeniería genética; **~ fingerprinting** identificación f genética; **genetically modified** adj transgénico; **genetics** n genética
genitals ['dʒɛnɪtlz] npl (órganos) genitales mpl
genius ['dʒiːnɪəs] n genio
genome ['giːnəʊm] n genoma m
gent [dʒɛnt] n abbr (BRIT inf) = **gentleman**
gentle ['dʒɛntl] adj amable, dulce; (animal) manso; (breeze, curve etc) suave

▌ Be careful not to translate **gentle** with the Spanish word gentil.

gentleman ['dʒɛntlmən] (irreg) n señor m; (well-bred man) caballero
gently ['dʒɛntlɪ] adv dulcemente; suavemente
gents [dʒɛnts] n aseos mpl (de caballeros)
genuine ['dʒɛnjuɪn] adj auténtico; (person) sincero; **genuinely** adv

sinceramente
geographic(al) [dʒɪə'græfɪk(l)] adj geográfico
geography [dʒɪ'ɒgrəfɪ] n geografía
geology [dʒɪ'ɒlədʒɪ] n geología
geometry [dʒɪ'ɒmətrɪ] n geometría
geranium [dʒɪ'reɪnjəm] n geranio
gerbil ['dʒəːbɪl] n gerbo
geriatric [dʒɛrɪ'ætrɪk] adj, n geriátrico/a m/f
germ [dʒəːm] n (microbe) microbio, bacteria; (seed, fig) germen m
German ['dʒəːmən] adj alemán/ana ▷ n alemán/ana m/f; (Ling) alemán m; **German measles** n rubéola
Germany ['dʒəːmənɪ] n Alemania
gesture ['dʒɛstʃə*] n gesto; (symbol) muestra

○ **KEYWORD**

get [gɛt] (pt, pp **got**, pp **gotten** (US)) vi
1 (become, be) ponerse, volverse; **to get old/tired** envejecer/cansarse; **to get drunk** emborracharse; **to get dirty** ensuciarse; **when do I get paid?** ¿cuándo me pagan or se me paga?; **it's getting late** se está haciendo tarde
2 (go): **to get to/from** llegar a/de; **to get home** llegar a casa
3 (begin) empezar a; **to get to know sb** (llegar a) conocer a algn; **I'm getting to like him** me está empezando a gustar; **let's get going** or **started** ¡vamos ya empezar!
4 (modal aux vb): **you've got to do it** tienes que hacerlo
▷ vt 1: **to get sth done** (finish) terminar algo; (have done) mandar hacer algo; **to get one's hair cut** cortarse el pelo; **to get the car going** or **to go** arrancar el coche; **to get sb to do sth** conseguir or hacer que algn haga algo; **to get sth/sb ready** preparar algo/a algn
2 (obtain: money, permission, results) conseguir; (find: job, flat) encontrar; (fetch: person, doctor) buscar; (object) ir a buscar, traer; **to get sth for sb**

conseguir algo para algn; **get me Mr Jones, please** (*Tel*) póngame (*SP*) or comuníqueme (*LAM*) con el Sr. Jones, por favor; **can I get you a drink?** ¿quieres algo de beber?

3 (*receive: present, letter*) recibir; (*acquire: reputation*) alcanzar; (*: prize*) ganar; **what did you get for your birthday?** ¿qué te regalaron por tu cumpleaños?; **how much did you get for the painting?** ¿cuánto sacaste por el cuadro?

4 (*catch*) coger (*SP*), agarrar (*LAM*); (*hit: target etc*) dar en; **to get sb by the arm/throat** coger or agarrar a algn por el brazo/cuello; **get him!** ¡cógelo! (*SP*), ¡atrápalo! (*LAM*); **the bullet got him in the leg** la bala le dio en la pierna

5 (*take, move*) llevar; **to get sth to sb** hacer llegar algo a algn; **do you think we'll get it through the door?** ¿crees que lo podremos meter por la puerta?

6 (*catch, take: plane, bus etc*) coger (*SP*), tomar (*LAM*); **where do I get the train for Birmingham?** ¿dónde se coge or se toma el tren para Birmingham?

7 (*understand*) entender; (*hear*) oír; **I've got it!** ¡ya lo tengo!, ¡eureka!; **I don't get your meaning** no te entiendo; **I'm sorry, I didn't get your name** lo siento, no cogí tu nombre

8 (*have, possess*) **to have got** tener

get away *vi* marcharse; (*escape*) escaparse

get away with *vt fus* hacer impunemente

get back *vi* (*return*) volver ▷ *vt* recobrar

get in *vi* entrar; (*train*) llegar; (*arrive home*) volver a casa, regresar

get into *vt fus* entrar en; (*vehicle*) subir a; **to get into a rage** enfadarse

get off *vi* (*from train etc*) bajar; (*depart: person, car*) marcharse ▷ *vt* (*remove*) quitar ▷ *vt fus* (*train, bus*) bajar de

get on *vi* (*at exam etc*) **how are you getting on?** ¿cómo te va?; (*agree*) **to**

get on (with) llevarse bien (con) ▷ *vt fus* subir a

get out *vi* salir; (*of vehicle*) bajar ▷ *vt* sacar

get out of *vt fus* salir de; (*duty etc*) escaparse de

get over *vt fus* (*illness*) recobrarse de

get through *vi* (*Tel*) lograr comunicarse

get up *vi* (*rise*) levantarse ▷ *vt fus* subir

getaway ['gɛtəweɪ] *n* fuga

Ghana ['gɑːnə] *n* Ghana

ghastly ['gɑːstlɪ] *adj* horrible

ghetto ['gɛtəu] *n* gueto

ghost [gəust] *n* fantasma *m*

giant ['dʒaɪənt] *n* gigante *mf* ▷ *adj* gigantesco, gigante

gift [gɪft] *n* regalo; (*ability*) talento; **gifted** *adj* dotado; **gift shop** (*us* **gift store**) *n* tienda de regalos; **gift token, gift voucher** *n* vale *m* canjeable por un regalo

gig [gɪg] *n* (*inf: concert*) actuación *f*

gigabyte ['dʒɪgəbaɪt] *n* gigabyte *m*

gigantic [dʒaɪˈgæntɪk] *adj* gigantesco

giggle ['gɪgl] *vi* reírse tontamente

gills [gɪlz] *npl* (*of fish*) branquias *fpl*, agallas *fpl*

gilt [gɪlt] *adj, n* dorado

gimmick ['gɪmɪk] *n* truco

gin [dʒɪn] *n* ginebra

ginger ['dʒɪndʒə*] *n* jengibre *m*

gipsy ['dʒɪpsɪ] *n* = **gypsy**

giraffe [dʒɪˈrɑːf] *n* jirafa

girl [gəːl] *n* (*small*) niña; (*young woman*) chica, joven *f*, muchacha; (*daughter*) hija; **an English ~** una (chica) inglesa; **girl band** *n* grupo musical (*de chicas*); **girlfriend** *n* (*of girl*) amiga; (*of boy*) novia; **Girl Scout** (*us*) *n* = **Girl Guide**

gist [dʒɪst] *n* lo esencial

give [gɪv] (*pt* **gave**, *pp* **given**) *vt* dar; (*deliver*) entregar; (*as gift*) regalar ▷ *vi* (*break*) romperse; (*stretch: fabric*) dar de sí; **to ~ sth to sb**, **~ sth to sb** dar algo a algn; **give away** vt (give free) regalar; (betray) traicionar; (disclose) revelar; **give back** vi devolver; **give in** vi ceder ▷ vt entregar; **give out** vt distribuir; **give up** vi rendirse, darse por vencido ▷ vt renunciar a; **to give up smoking** dejar de fumar; **to give o.s. up** entregarse

given ['gɪvn] pp of **give** ▷ adj (fixed: time, amount) determinado ▷ adj (fixed: time, amount) determinado ▷ conj: **~ (that)** dado (que) ...; **~ the circumstances ...** dadas las circunstancias ...

glacier ['glæsɪə*] n glaciar m
glad [glæd] adj contento; **gladly** ['-lɪ] adv con mucho gusto
glamour ['glæmə*] (US **glamor**) n encanto, atractivo; **glamorous** adj encantador/a, atractivo
glance [glɑːns] n ojeada, mirada ▷ vi: **to ~ at** echar una ojeada a
gland [glænd] n glándula
glare [glɛə*] n (of anger) mirada feroz; (of light) deslumbramiento, brillo; **to be in the ~ of publicity** ser el foco de la atención pública ▷ vi deslumbrar; **to ~ at** mirar con odio a; **glaring** adj (mistake) manifiesto
glass [glɑːs] n vidrio, cristal m; (for drinking) vaso; (: with stem) copa; **glasses** npl (spectacles) gafas fpl
glaze [gleɪz] vt (window) poner cristales a; (pottery) vidriar ▷ n vidriado
gleam [gliːm] vi brillar
glen [glen] n cañada
glide [glaɪd] vi deslizarse; (Aviat: plane) planear; **glider** n (Aviat) planeador m
glimmer ['glɪmə*] n luz f tenue; (of interest) muestra; (of hope) rayo
glimpse [glɪmps] n vislumbre m ▷ vt vislumbrar, entrever
glint [glɪnt] vi centellear
glisten ['glɪsn] vi relucir, brillar
glitter ['glɪtə*] vi relucir, brillar
global ['gləubl] adj mundial; **globalization** n globalización f;

global warming n (re)calentamiento global or de la tierra
globe [gləub] n globo; (model) globo terráqueo
gloom [gluːm] n oscuridad f; (sadness) tristeza; **gloomy** adj (dark) oscuro; (sad) triste; (pessimistic) pesimista
glorious ['glɔːrɪəs] adj glorioso; (weather etc) magnífico
glory ['glɔːrɪ] n gloria
gloss [glɔs] n (shine) brillo; (paint) pintura de aceite
glossary ['glɔsərɪ] n glosario
glossy ['glɔsɪ] adj lustroso; (magazine) de lujo
glove [glʌv] n guante m; **glove compartment** n (Aut) guantera
glow [gləu] vi brillar
glucose ['gluːkəus] n glucosa
glue [gluː] n goma (de pegar), cemento ▷ vt pegar
GM adj abbr (= genetically modified) transgénico
gm abbr (= gram) g
GMO n abbr (= genetically modified organism) organismo transgénico
GMT abbr (= Greenwich Mean Time) GMT
gnaw [nɔː] vt roer
go [gəu] (pt **went**, pp **gone**, pl **~es**) vi ir; (travel) viajar; (depart) irse, marcharse; (work) funcionar, marchar; (be sold) venderse; (time) pasar; (fit, suit): **to ~ with** hacer juego con; (become) ponerse; (break etc) estropearse, romperse ▷ n: **to have a ~ (at)** probar suerte (con); **to be on the ~** no parar; **whose ~ is it?** ¿a quién le toca?; **he's ~ing to do it** va a hacerlo; **to ~ for a walk** ir de paseo; **to ~ dancing** ir a bailar; **how did it ~?** ¿qué tal salió or resultó?, ¿cómo ha ido?; **to ~ round the back** pasar por detrás; **go ahead** vi seguir adelante; **go away** vi irse, marcharse; **go back** vi volver; **go by** vi (time) pasar ▷ vt fus guiarse por; **go down** vi bajar; (ship) hundirse; (sun) ponerse ▷ vt fus bajar; **go for** vt fus (fetch) ir por; (like) gustar; (attack)

atacar; **go in** vi entrar; **go into** vt fus entrar en; (*investigate*) investigar; (*embark on*) dedicarse a; **go off** vi irse, marcharse; (*food*) pasarse; (*explode*) estallar; (*event*) realizarse ▷ vt fus dejar de gustar; **I'm going off him/the idea** ya no me gusta tanto él/la idea; **go on** vi (*continue*) seguir, continuar; (*happen*) pasar, ocurrir; **to go on doing sth** seguir haciendo algo; **go out** vi salir; (*fire, light*) apagarse; **go over** vi (*ship*) zozobrar ▷ vt fus (*check*) revisar; **go past** vi, vt fus pasar; **go round** vi (*circulate: news, rumour*) correr; (*suffice*) alcanzar, bastar; (*revolve*) girar, dar vueltas; (*visit*): **to go round (to sb's)** pasar a ver (a algn); **to go round (by)** (*make a detour*) dar la vuelta (por); **go through** vt fus (*town etc*) atravesar; **go up** vi, vt fus subir; **go with** vt fus (*accompany*) acompañar a; **go without** vt fus pasarse sin

go-ahead ['gəuəhɛd] adj (*person*) dinámico; (*firm*) innovador a ▷ n luz f verde

goal [gəul] n meta; (*score*) gol m; **goalkeeper** n portero; **goal-post** n poste m (de la portería)

goat [gəut] n cabra

gobble ['gɔbl] vt (*also*: **~ down, ~ up**) tragarse, engullir

God [gɔd] n Dios m; **godchild** n ahijado/a; **goddaughter** n ahijada; **goddess** n diosa; **godfather** n padrino; **godmother** n madrina; **godson** n ahijado

goggles ['gɔglz] npl gafas fpl

going ['gəuɪŋ] n (*conditions*) estado del terreno ▷ adj: **the ~ rate** la tarifa corriente or en vigor

gold [gəuld] n oro ▷ adj de oro; **golden** adj (*made of gold*) de oro; (*gold in colour*) dorado; **goldfish** n pez m de colores; **goldmine** n (*also fig*) mina de oro; **gold-plated** adj chapado en oro

golf [gɔlf] n golf m; **golf ball** n (*for game*) pelota de golf; (*on typewriter*) esfera; **golf club** n club m de golf;

(*stick*) palo (de golf); **golf course** n campo de golf; **golfer** n golfista mf

gone [gɔn] pp of **go**

gong [gɔŋ] n gong m

good [gud] adj bueno; (*pleasant*) agradable; (*kind*) bueno, amable; (*well-behaved*) educado ▷ n bien m, provecho; **goods** npl (*Comm*) mercancías fpl; **¡qué bien!**; **to be ~ at** tener aptitud para; **to be ~ for** servir para; **it's ~ for you** te hace bien; **would you be ~ enough to ...?** ¿podría hacerme el favor de ...?; **a ~ deal (of)** mucho; **a ~ many** muchos; **to make ~** reparar; **it's no ~ complaining** no vale la pena de quejarse; **for ~** para siempre, definitivamente; **~ morning/ afternoon!** ¡buenos días/buenas tardes!; **~ evening!** ¡buenas noches!; **~ night!** ¡buenas noches!

goodbye [gud'baɪ] excl ¡adiós!; **to say ~ (to)** (*person*) despedirse (de)

good: Good Friday n Viernes m Santo; **good-looking** adj guapo; **good-natured** adj amable, simpático; **goodness** n (*of person*) bondad f; **for goodness sake!** ¡por Dios!; **goodness gracious!** ¡Dios mío!; **goods train** (*BRIT*) n tren m de mercancías; **goodwill** n buena voluntad f

Google® ['gu:gl] n Google® n ▷ vi hacer búsquedas en Internet ▷ vt buscar información en Internet sobre

goose [gu:s] (*pl* **geese**) n ganso, oca

gooseberry ['guzbərɪ] n grosella espinosa; **to play ~** hacer de carabina

goose bumps, goose pimples npl carne f de gallina

gorge [gɔ:dʒ] n barranco ▷ vr: **to ~ o.s. (on)** atracarse (de)

gorgeous ['gɔ:dʒəs] adj (*thing*) precioso; (*weather*) espléndido; (*person*) guapísimo

gorilla [gə'rɪlə] n gorila m

gosh [gɔʃ] (*inf*) excl ¡cielos!

gospel ['gɔspl] n evangelio

gossip ['gɔsɪp] n (*scandal*)

cotillео, chismes *mpl*; (*chat*) charla; (*scandalmonger*) cotilla *m/f*, chismoso/a ▷ *vi* cotillear; **gossip column** *n* ecos *mpl* de sociedad

got [gɒt] *pt, pp* of **get**

gotten (*us*) [ˈgɒtn] *pp* of **get**

gourmet [ˈguəmeɪ] *n* gastrónomo/a *m/f*

govern [ˈgʌvən] *vt* gobernar; (*influence*) dominar; **government** *n* gobierno; **governor** *n* gobernador(a) *m/f*; (*of school etc*) miembro del consejo; (*of jail*) director(a) *m/f*

gown [gaʊn] *n* traje *m*; (*of teacher, BRIT: of judge*) toga

G.P. *n abbr* = **general practitioner**

grab [græb] *vt* coger (SP), agarrar (LAM), arrebatar ▷ *vi*: **to ~ at** intentar agarrar

grace [greɪs] *n* gracia ▷ *vt* honrar; (*adorn*) adornar; **5 days' ~** un plazo de 5 días; **graceful** *adj* grácil, ágil; (*style, shape*) elegante, gracioso; **gracious** [ˈgreɪʃəs] *adj* amable

grade [greɪd] *n* (*quality*) clase *f*, calidad *f*; (*in hierarchy*) grado; (*Scol: mark*) nota; (*us: school class*) curso ▷ *vt* clasificar; **grade crossing** (*us*) *n* paso a nivel; **grade school** (*us*) *n* escuela primaria

gradient [ˈgreɪdɪənt] *n* pendiente *f*

gradual [ˈgrædjʊəl] *adj* paulatino; **gradually** *adv* paulatinamente

graduate [*n* ˈgrædjuɪt, *vb* ˈgrædjueɪt] *n* (*us: of high school*) graduado/a; (*of university*) licenciado/a ▷ *vi* graduarse; licenciarse; **graduation** [-ˈeɪʃən] *n* (*ceremony*) entrega del título

graffiti [grəˈfiːtɪ] *n* pintadas *fpl*

graft [grɑːft] *n* (*Agr, Med*) injerto; (*BRIT: inf*) trabajo duro; (*bribery*) corrupción *f* ▷ *vt* injertar

grain [greɪn] *n* (*single particle*) grano; (*corn*) granos *mpl*, cereales *mpl*; (*of wood*) fibra

gram [græm] *n* gramo

grammar [ˈgræmə*] *n* gramática; **grammar school** (*BRIT*) *n* ≈ instituto

de segunda enseñanza, liceo (SP)

gramme [græm] *n* = **gram**

gran [græn] (*inf*) *n* (*BRIT*) abuelita

grand [grænd] *adj* magnífico, imponente; (*wonderful*) estupendo; (*gesture etc*) grandioso; **grandad** (*inf*) *n* = **granddad**; **grandchild** (*pl* **grandchildren**) *n* nieto/a *m/f*; **granddad** (*inf*) *n* yayo, abuelito; **granddaughter** *n* nieta; **grandfather** *n* abuelo; **grandma** (*inf*) *n* yaya, abuelita; **grandmother** *n* abuela; **grandpa** (*inf*) *n* = **granddad**; **grandparents** *npl* abuelos *mpl*; **grand piano** *n* piano de cola; **Grand Prix** [ˈgrɑːˈpriː] *n* (*Aut*) gran premio, Grand Prix *m*; **grandson** *n* nieto

granite [ˈgrænɪt] *n* granito

granny [ˈgrænɪ] (*inf*) *n* abuelita, yaya

grant [grɑːnt] *vt* (*concede*) conceder; (*admit*) reconocer ▷ *n* (*Scol*) beca; (*Admin*) subvención *f*; **to take sth/sb for ~ed** dar algo por sentado/no hacer ningún caso a algn

grape [greɪp] *n* uva

grapefruit [ˈgreɪpfruːt] *n* pomelo (SP, SC), toronja (LAM)

graph [grɑːf] *n* gráfica; **graphic** [ˈgræfɪk] *adj* gráfico; **graphics** *n* artes *fpl* gráficas ▷ *npl* (*drawings*) dibujos *mpl*

grasp [grɑːsp] *vt* agarrar, asir; (*understand*) comprender ▷ *n* (*grip*) asimiento; (*understanding*) comprensión *f*

grass [grɑːs] *n* hierba; (*lawn*) césped *m*; **grasshopper** *n* saltamontes *m inv*

grate [greɪt] *n* parrilla de chimenea ▷ *vi*: **to ~ (on)** chirriar (sobre) ▷ *vt* (*Culin*) rallar

grateful [ˈgreɪtful] *adj* agradecido

grater [ˈgreɪtə*] *n* rallador *m*

gratitude [ˈgrætɪtjuːd] *n* agradecimiento

grave [greɪv] *n* tumba ▷ *adj* serio, grave

gravel [ˈgrævl] *n* grava

gravestone [ˈgreɪvstəun] *n* lápida

graveyard ['greɪvjɑːd] n cementerio

gravity ['grævɪtɪ] n gravedad f

gravy ['greɪvɪ] n salsa de carne

gray [greɪ] adj = **grey**

graze [greɪz] vi pacer ▷ vt (touch lightly) rozar; (scrape) raspar ▷ n (Med) abrasión f

grease [griːs] n (fat) grasa; (lubricant) lubricante m ▷ vt engrasar; lubrificar; **greasy** adj grasiento

great [greɪt] adj grande; (inf) magnífico, estupendo; **Great Britain** n Gran Bretaña; **great-grandfather** n bisabuelo; **great-grandmother** n bisabuela; **greatly** adv muy; (with verb) mucho

Greece [griːs] n Grecia

greed [griːd] n (also: **~iness**) codicia, avaricia; (for food) gula; (for power etc) avidez f; **greedy** adj avaro; (for food) glotón/ona

Greek [griːk] adj griego ▷ n griego/a; (Ling) griego

green [griːn] adj (also Pol) verde; (inexperienced) novato ▷ n verde m; (stretch of grass) césped m; (Golf) green m **greens** npl (vegetables) verduras fpl; **green card** n (Aut) carta verde; (us: work permit) permiso de trabajo para los extranjeros en EE. UU.; **greengage** n (ciruela) claudia; **greengrocer** (BRIT) n verdulero/a; **greenhouse** n invernadero; **greenhouse effect** n efecto invernadero

Greenland ['griːnlənd] n Groenlandia

green salad n ensalada f (de lechuga, pepino, pimiento verde, etc)

greet [griːt] vt (welcome) dar la bienvenida a; (receive: news) recibir; **greeting** n (welcome) bienvenida; **greeting(s) card** n tarjeta de felicitación

grew [gruː] pt of **grow**

grey [greɪ] (us **gray**) adj gris; (weather) sombrío; **grey-haired** adj canoso; **greyhound** n galgo

grid [grɪd] n reja; (Elec) red f; **gridlock**

n (traffic jam) retención f

grief [griːf] n dolor m, pena

grievance ['griːvəns] n motivo de queja, agravio

grieve [griːv] vi afligirse, acongojarse ▷ vt dar pena a; **to ~ for** llorar por

grill [grɪl] n (on cooker) parrilla; (also: **mixed ~**) parrillada ▷ vt (BRIT) asar a la parrilla; (inf: question) interrogar

grille [grɪl] n reja; (Aut) rejilla

grim [grɪm] adj (place) sombrío; (situation) triste; (person) ceñudo

grime [graɪm] n mugre f, suciedad f

grin [grɪn] n sonrisa abierta ▷ vi sonreír abiertamente

grind [graɪnd] (pt, pp **ground**) vt (coffee, pepper etc) moler; (us: meat) picar; (make sharp) afilar ▷ n (work) rutina

grip [grɪp] n (hold) asimiento; (control) control m, dominio; (of tyre etc) agarre m; **to have a good/bad ~** agarrarse bien/mal; (handle) asidero; (holdall) maletín m ▷ vt agarrar; (viewer, reader) fascinar; **to get to ~s** with enfrentarse con; **gripping** adj absorbente

grit [grɪt] n gravilla; (courage) valor m ▷ vt (road) poner gravilla en; **to ~ one's teeth** apretar los dientes

grits [grɪts] (us) npl maíz msg a medio moler

groan [grəʊn] n gemido; quejido ▷ vi gemir; quejarse

grocer ['grəʊsə*] n tendero (de ultramarinos (SP)); **groceries** npl comestibles mpl; **grocer's (shop)** n tienda de comestibles or (MEX, CAM) abarrotes, almacén (SC); **grocery** (shop) tienda de ultramarinos

groin [grɔɪn] n ingle f

groom [gruːm] n mozo/a de cuadra; (also: **bride~**) novio ▷ vt (horse) almohazar; (fig): **to ~ sb** preparar a algn para; **well-~ed** de buena presencia

groove [gruːv] n ranura, surco

grope [grəʊp] vi: **to ~ for** buscar a tientas

gross [grəʊs] adj (neglect, injustice) grave; (vulgar: behaviour) grosero;

(: *appearance*) de mal gusto; (*Comm*) bruto; **grossly** *adv* (*greatly*) enormemente

grotesque [grə'tesk] *adj* grotesco

ground [graund] *pt, pp of* **grind** ▷ *n* suelo, tierra; (*Sport*) campo, terreno; (*reason: gen pl*) causa, razón *f*; (*us: also:* **~ wire**) tierra ▷ *vt* (*plane*) mantener en tierra; (*us Elec*) conectar con tierra; **grounds** *npl* (*of coffee etc*) poso; (*gardens etc*) jardines *mpl*, parque *m*; **on the ~** en el suelo; **to the ~** al suelo; **to gain/lose ~** ganar/perder terreno; **ground floor** *n* (*BRIT*) planta baja; **groundsheet** (*BRIT*) *n* tela impermeable; suelo; **groundwork** *n* preparación *f*

group [gru:p] *n* grupo; (*musical*) conjunto ▷ *vt* (*also:* **~ together**) agrupar ▷ *vi* (*also:* **~ together**) agruparse

grouse [graus] *n inv* (*bird*) urogallo ▷ *vi* (*complain*) quejarse

grovel ['grɔvl] *vi* (*fig*): **to ~ before** humillarse ante

grow [grəu] (*pt* **grew**, *pp* **grown**) *vi* crecer; (*increase*) aumentar; (*expand*) desarrollarse; (*become*) volverse; **to ~ rich/weak** enriquecerse/debilitarse ▷ *vt* cultivar; (*hair, beard*) dejar crecer; **grow on** *vt fus*: **that painting is growing on me** ese cuadro me gusta cada vez más; **grow up** *vi* crecer, hacerse hombre/mujer

growl [graul] *vi* gruñir

grown [grəun] *pp of* **grow**; **grown-up** *n* adulto/a, mayor *mf*

growth [grəuθ] *n* crecimiento, desarrollo; (*what has grown*) brote *m*; (*Med*) tumor *m*

grub [grʌb] *n* larva, gusano; (*inf: food*) comida

grubby ['grʌbɪ] *adj* sucio, mugriento

grudge [grʌdʒ] *n* (*motivo de*) rencor *m* ▷ *vt*: **to ~ sb sth** dar algo a algn de mala gana; **to bear sb a ~** guardar rencor a algn

gruelling ['gruəlɪŋ] (*us* **grueling**) *adj*

penoso, duro

gruesome ['gru:səm] *adj* horrible

grumble ['grʌmbl] *vi* refunfuñar, quejarse

grumpy ['grʌmpɪ] *adj* gruñón/ona

grunt [grʌnt] *vi* gruñir

guarantee [gærən'ti:] *n* garantía ▷ *vt* garantizar

guard [ga:d] *n* (*squad*) guardia; (*one man*) guardia *mf*; (*BRIT Rail*) jefe *m* de tren; (*on machine*) dispositivo de seguridad; (*also:* **fire~**) rejilla de protección ▷ *vt* guardar; (*prisoner*) vigilar; **to be on one's ~** estar alerta; **guardian** *n* guardián/ana *m/f*; (*of minor*) tutor/a *m/f*

guerrilla [gə'rɪlə] *n* guerrillero/a

guess [ges] *vi* adivinar; (*us*) suponer ▷ *vt* adivinar; suponer ▷ *n* suposición *f*, conjetura; **to take** o **have a ~** tratar de adivinar

guest [gest] *n* invitado/a; (*in hotel*) huésped *mf*; **guest house** *n* casa de huéspedes, pensión *f*; **guest room** *n* cuarto de huéspedes

guidance ['gaɪdəns] *n* (*advice*) consejos *mpl*

guide [gaɪd] *n* (*person*) guía *mf*; (*book, fig*) guía; (*also:* **Girl ~**) guía ▷ *vt* (*round museum etc*) guiar; (*lead*) conducir; (*direct*) orientar; **guidebook** *n* guía; **guide dog** *n* perro *m* guía; **guided tour** *n* visita *f* con guía; **guidelines** *npl* (*advice*) directrices *fpl*

guild [gɪld] *n* gremio

guilt [gɪlt] *n* culpabilidad *f*; **guilty** *adj* culpable

guinea pig ['gɪnɪ-] *n* cobaya; (*fig*) conejillo de Indias

guitar [gɪ'tɑ:] *n* guitarra; **guitarist** *n* guitarrista *mf*

gulf [gʌlf] *n* golfo; (*abyss*) abismo

gull [gʌl] *n* gaviota

gulp [gʌlp] *vi* tragar saliva ▷ *vt* (*also:* **~ down**) tragarse

gum [gʌm] *n* (*Anat*) encía; (*glue*) goma, cemento; (*sweet*) caramelo de goma; (*also:* **chewing-~**) chicle *m* ▷ *vt* pegar con goma

gun [gʌn] n (small) pistola, revólver m; (shotgun) escopeta; (rifle) fusil m; (cannon) cañón m; **gunfire** n disparos mpl; **gunman** (irreg) n pistolero; **gunpoint** n: **at gunpoint** a mano armada; **gunpowder** n pólvora; **gunshot** n escopetazo

gush [gʌʃ] vi salir a raudales; (person) deshacerse en efusiones

gust [gʌst] n (of wind) ráfaga

gut [gʌt] n intestino; **guts** npl (Anat) tripas fpl; (courage) valor m

gutter ['gʌtə*] n (of roof) canalón m; (in street) cuneta

guy [gaɪ] n (also: **~rope**) cuerda; (inf: man) tío (sp), tipo; (figure) monigote m

Guy Fawkes' Night [gaɪ'fɔːks-] n ver recuadro

gym [dʒɪm] n gimnasio; **gymnasium** n gimnasio m; **gymnast** n gimnasta mf; **gymnastics** n gimnasia; **gym shoes** npl zapatillas fpl (de deporte)

gynaecologist [gaɪnɪ'kɒlədʒɪst] (us **gynecologist**) n ginecólogo/a

gypsy ['dʒɪpsɪ] n gitano/a

h

haberdashery [hæbə'dæʃərɪ] (BRIT) n mercería

habit ['hæbɪt] n hábito, costumbre f; (drug habit) adicción f; (costume) hábito

habitat ['hæbɪtæt] n hábitat m

hack [hæk] vt (cut) cortar; (slice) tajar ▷ n (pej: writer) escritor(a) m/f a sueldo; **hacker** n (Comput) pirata mf informático/a

had [hæd] pt, pp of **have**

haddock ['hædək] (pl ~ or ~s) n especie de merluza

hadn't ['hædnt] = **had not**

hemorrhage ['hemərɪdʒ] (us **hemorrhage**) n hemorragia

haemorrhoids ['hemərɔɪdz] (us **hemorrhoids**) npl hemorroides fpl

haggle ['hægl] vi regatear

Hague [heɪg] n: **The ~** La Haya

hail [heɪl] n granizo; (fig) lluvia ▷ vt saludar; (taxi) llamar a; (acclaim) aclamar ▷ vi granizar; **hailstone** n (piedra de) granizo

hair [heə*] n pelo, cabellos mpl; (one hair) pelo, cabello; (on legs etc) vello;

to do one's ~ arreglarse el pelo; **to have grey ~** tener canas fpl; **hairband** n cinta; **hairbrush** n cepillo (para el pelo); **haircut** n corte m (de pelo); **hairdo** n peinado m; **hairdresser** n peluquero/a; **hairdresser's** n peluquería f; **hair dryer** n secador m de pelo; **hair gel** n fijador; **hair spray** n laca; **hairstyle** n peinado m; **hairy** adj peludo; velludo; (inf: frightening) espeluznante

hake [heɪk] (pl ~ or ~s) n merluza

half [hɑːf] (pl **halves**) n mitad f; (of beer) ≈ caña (SP), media pinta f; (Rail, Bus) billete m de niño ⊳ adj medio ⊳ adv medio, a medias; **two and a ~** dos y media; **~ a dozen** media docena; **~ a pound** media libra; **to cut sth in ~** cortar algo por la mitad; **half board** n (BRIT: in hotel) media pensión; **half-brother** n hermanastro; **half day** n medio día m, media jornada; **half fare** n medio pasaje m; **half-hearted** adj indiferente, poco entusiasta; **half-hour** n media hora; **half-price** adj, adv a mitad de precio; **half term** n (BRIT) (Scol) vacaciones de mediados del trimestre; **half-time** n descanso; **halfway** adv a medio camino; **halfway through** a mitad de

hall [hɔːl] n (for concerts) sala; (entrance way) hall m; vestíbulo

hallmark [ˈhɔːlmɑːk] n sello

hallo [həˈləʊ] excl = **hello**

hall of residence (BRIT) n residencia

Hallowe'en [hæləʊˈiːn] n víspera de Todos los Santos

● HALLOWE'EN

● La tradición anglosajona dice que en la noche del 31 de octubre, **Hallowe'en**, víspera de Todos los Santos, es posible ver a brujas y fantasmas. En este día los niños se disfrazan y van de puerta en puerta llevando un farol hecho con una calabaza en forma de cabeza

humana. Cuando se les abre la puerta gritan "trick or treat", amenazando con gastar una broma a quien no les dé golosinas o algo de calderilla.

hallucination [həluːsɪˈneɪʃən] n alucinación f

hallway [ˈhɔːlweɪ] n vestíbulo

halo [ˈheɪləʊ] n (of saint) halo, aureola

halt [hɔːlt] n (stop) alto, parada ⊳ vt parar; interrumpir ⊳ vi pararse

halve [hɑːv] vt partir por la mitad

halves [hɑːvz] npl of **half**

ham [hæm] n jamón m (cocido)

hamburger [ˈhæmbəːgə*] n hamburguesa

hamlet [ˈhæmlɪt] n aldea

hammer [ˈhæmə*] n martillo ⊳ vt (nail) clavar; (force): **to ~ an idea into sb/a message home** meter una idea en la cabeza a algn/machacar una idea ⊳ vi dar golpes

hammock [ˈhæmək] n hamaca

hamper [ˈhæmpə*] vt estorbar ⊳ n cesto

hamster [ˈhæmstə*] n hámster m

hamstring [ˈhæmstrɪŋ] n (Anat) tendón m de la corva

hand [hænd] n mano f; (of clock) aguja; (writing) letra; (worker) obrero ⊳ vt dar, pasar; **to give or lend sb a ~** echar una mano a algn, ayudar a algn; **at ~** a mano; **in ~** (time) libre; (job etc) entre manos; **on ~** (person, services) a mano, al alcance; **to ~** (information etc) a mano; **on the one ~ ..., on the other ~ ...** por una parte ... por otra (parte) ...; **hand down** vt pasar, bajar; (tradition) transmitir; (heirloom) dejar en herencia; (us: sentence, verdict) imponer; **hand in** vt entregar; **hand out** vt distribuir; **hand over** vt (deliver) entregar; **handbag** n bolso, cartera (LAM), bolsa (MEX); **hand baggage** n = **hand luggage**; **handbook** n manual m; **handbrake** n freno de mano; **handcuffs** npl esposas fpl; **handful**

n puñado

handicap ['hændɪkæp] *n* minusvalía; *(disadvantage)* desventaja; *(Sport)* handicap *m* ▷ *vt* estorbar; **to be mentally ~ped** ser mentalmente *m/f* discapacitado; **to be physically ~ped** ser minusválido,a

handkerchief ['hæŋkətʃif] *n* pañuelo

handle ['hændl] *n (of door etc)* tirador *m*; *(of cup etc)* asa; *(of knife etc)* mango; *(for winding)* manivela ▷ *vt (touch)* tocar; *(deal with)* encargarse de; *(treat: people)* manejar; **"~ with care"** "(manéjese) con cuidado"; **to fly off the ~** perder los estribos; **handlebar(s)** *n(pl)* manillar *m*

hand: hand luggage *n* equipaje *m* de mano; **handmade** *adj* hecho a mano; **handout** *n (money etc)* limosna; *(leaflet)* folleto; **hands-free** *adj (phone)* manos libres *inv*; **hands-free kit** *n* manos libres *m inv*

handsome ['hænsəm] *adj* guapo; *(building)* bello; *(fig: profit)* considerable

handwriting ['hændraɪtɪŋ] *n* letra

handy ['hændɪ] *adj (close at hand)* a la mano; *(tool etc)* práctico; *(skilful)* hábil, diestro

hang [hæŋ] *(pt, pp* **hung)** *vt* colgar; *(criminal: pt, pp* **hanged)** ahorcar ▷ *vi (painting, coat etc)* colgar; *(hair, drapery)* caer; **to get the ~ of sth** *(inf)* lograr dominar algo; **hang about** *or* **around** *vi* haraganear; **hang down** *vi* colgar, pender; **hang on** *vi (wait)* esperar; **hang out** *vt (washing)* tender; colgar ▷ *vi (inf: live)* vivir; *(spend time)* pasar el rato; **to hang out of sth** colgar fuera de algo; **hang round** *vi* = **hang around; hang up** *vi (Tel)* colgar ▷ *vt* colgar

hanger ['hæŋə*] *n* percha

hang-gliding ['-glaɪdɪŋ] *n* vuelo libre

hangover ['hæŋəuvə*] *n (after drinking)* resaca

hankie, hanky ['hæŋkɪ] *n abbr* =

handkerchief

happen ['hæpən] *vi* suceder, ocurrir; *(chance)*: **he ~ed to hear/see** dió la casualidad de que oyó/vió; **as it ~s** da la casualidad de que

happily ['hæpɪlɪ] *adv (luckily)* afortunadamente; *(cheerfully)* alegremente

happiness ['hæpɪnɪs] *n* felicidad *f*; *(cheerfulness)* alegría

happy ['hæpɪ] *adj* feliz; *(cheerful)* alegre; **to be ~ (with)** estar contento (con); **to be ~ (to do)** estar encantado de hacer; **~ birthday!** ¡feliz cumpleaños!

harass ['hærəs] *vt* acosar, hostigar; **harassment** *n* persecución *f*

harbour ['hɑ:bə*] *(US* **harbor)** *n* puerto ▷ *vt (fugitive)* dar abrigo a; *(hope etc)* abrigar

hard [hɑ:d] *adj* duro; *(difficult)* difícil; *(work)* arduo; *(person)* severo; *(fact)* innegable ▷ *adv (work)* mucho, duro; *(think)* profundamente; **to look ~ at** clavar los ojos en; **to try ~** esforzarse; **no ~ feelings!** ¡sin rencor(es)!; **to be ~ of hearing** ser duro de oído; **to be ~ done by** ser tratado injustamente; **hardback** *n* libro en cartoné; **hardboard** *n* aglomerado *m (de madera)*; **hard disk** *n (Comput)* disco duro o rígido; **harden** *vt* endurecer; *(fig)* curtir ▷ *vi* endurecerse; curtirse

hardly ['hɑ:dlɪ] *adv* apenas; **~ ever** casi nunca

hard: hardship *n* privación *f*; **hard shoulder** (BRIT) *n (Aut)* arcén *m*; **hard-up** *(inf) adj (sin dinero)* pelado, sin un centavo (MEX), pato (SC); **hardware** *n* ferretería; *(Comput)* hardware *m*; *(Mil)* armamento; **hardware shop** *(US* **hardware store)** *n* ferretería; **hard-working** *adj* trabajador(a)

hardy ['hɑ:dɪ] *adj* fuerte; *(plant)* resistente

hare [hɛə*] *n* liebre *f*

harm [hɑ:m] *n* daño, mal *m* ▷ *vt (person)* hacer daño a; *(health, interests)* perjudicar; *(thing)* dañar; **out of ~'s**

way a salvo; **harmful** adj dañino; **harmless** adj (person) inofensivo; (joke etc) inocente

harmony ['hɑːmənɪ] n armonía

harness ['hɑːnɪs] n arreos mpl; (for child) arnés m; (safety harness) arnés mpl ▷ vt (horse) enjaezar; (resources) aprovechar

harp [hɑːp] n arpa ▷ vi: **to ~ on (about)** machacar (con)

harsh [hɑːʃ] adj (cruel) duro, cruel; (severe) severo; (sound) áspero; (light) deslumbrador(a)

harvest ['hɑːvɪst] n (harvest time) siega; (of cereals etc) cosecha; (of grapes) vendimia ▷ vt cosechar

has [hæz] vb see **have**

hasn't ['hæznt] = **has not**

hassle ['hæsl] (inf) n lata

haste [heɪst] n prisa; **hasten** ['heɪsn] vt acelerar ▷ vi darse prisa; **hastily** adv de prisa; precipitadamente; **hasty** adj apresurado; (rash) precipitado

hat [hæt] n sombrero

hatch [hætʃ] n (Naut: also: **~way**) escotilla; (also: **service ~**) ventanilla ▷ vi (bird) salir del cascarón ▷ vt incubar; (plot) tramar; **5 eggs have ~ed** han salido 5 pollos

hatchback ['hætʃbæk] n (Aut) tres or cinco puertas m

hate [heɪt] vt odiar, aborrecer ▷ n odio; **hatred** ['heɪtrɪd] n odio

haul [hɔːl] vt tirar ▷ n (of fish) redada; (of stolen goods etc) botín m

haunt [hɔːnt] vt (ghost) aparecerse en; (obsess) obsesionar ▷ n guarida; **haunted** (house) (castle etc) embrujado; (look) de angustia

🔘 **KEYWORD**

have [hæv] (pt, pp **had**) aux vb **1** (gen) haber; **to have arrived/eaten** haber llegado/comido; **having finished** or **when he had finished, he left** cuando hubo acabado, se fue

2 (in tag questions): **you've done it,**

haven't you? lo has hecho, ¿verdad? or ¿no?

3 (in short answers and questions): **I haven't** no; **so I have** pues, es verdad; **we haven't paid - yes we have!** no hemos pagado – ¡sí hemos pagado!; **I've been there before, have you?** he estado allí antes, ¿y tú?

▷ modal aux vb (be obliged): **to have (got) to do sth** tener que hacer algo; **you haven't to tell her** no hay que or no debes decírselo

▷ vt **1** (possess): **to have (got) blue eyes/dark hair** tiene los ojos azules/el pelo negro

2 (referring to meals etc): **to have breakfast/lunch/dinner** desayunar/comer/cenar; **to have a drink/a cigarette** tomar algo/fumar un cigarrillo

3 (receive) recibir; (obtain) obtener; **may I have your address?** ¿puedes darme tu dirección?; **you can have it for £5** te lo puedes quedar por £5; **I must have it by tomorrow** lo necesito para mañana; **to have a baby** tener un niño or bebé

4 (maintain, allow): **I won't have it/this nonsense!** ¡no lo permitiré!/¡no permitiré estas tonterías!; **we can't have that** no podemos permitir eso

5 **to have sth done** hacer or mandar hacer algo; **to have one's hair cut** cortarse el pelo; **to have sb do sth** hacer que algn haga algo

6 (experience, suffer): **to have a cold/flu** tener un resfriado/la gripe; **she had her bag stolen/her arm broken** le robaron el bolso/se rompió un brazo; **to have an operation** operarse

7 (+ noun): **to have a swim/walk/bath/rest** nadar/dar un paseo/darse un baño/descansar; **let's have a look** vamos a ver; **to have a meeting/party** celebrar una reunión/una fiesta; **let me have a try** déjame intentarlo

haven ['heɪvn] n puerto; (fig) refugio

haven't ['hævnt] = **have not**

havoc ['hævək] n estragos mpl

Hawaii [hə'waiːi] n (Islas fpl) Hawai fpl

hawk [hɔːk] n halcón m

hawthorn ['hɔːθɔːn] n espino

hay [heɪ] n heno; **hay fever** n fiebre f del heno; **haystack** n almiar m

hazard ['hæzəd] n peligro ▷vt aventurar; **hazardous** adj peligroso; **hazard warning lights** npl (Aut) señales fpl de emergencia

haze [heɪz] n brumoso

hazel ['heɪzl] n (tree) avellano ▷ adj (eyes) color m de avellano; **hazelnut** n avellana

hazy ['heɪzɪ] adj brumoso; (idea) vago

he [hiː] pron el; **~ who ...** él que ..., quien ...

head [hɛd] n cabeza; (leader) jefe/a m/f; (of school) director(a) m/f ▷vt (list) encabezar; (group) capitanear; (company) dirigir; **~s (or tails)** cara (o cruz); **~ first** de cabeza; **~ over heels** (in love) perdidamente; **to ~ the ball** cabecear (la pelota); **head for** vt fus dirigirse a; (disaster) ir camino de; **head off** vt (threat, danger) evitar; **headache** n dolor m de cabeza; **heading** n título; **headlamp** (BRIT) n = **headlight**; **headlight** n faro; **headline** n titular m; **head office** n oficina central, central f; **headphones** npl auriculares mpl; **headquarters** npl sede f central; (Mil) cuartel m general; **headroom** n (in car) altura interior; (under bridge) (límite m de) altura; **headscarf** n pañuelo; **headset** n cascos mpl; **headteacher** n director(a) (directora); **head waiter** n maître m

heal [hiːl] vt curar ▷vi cicatrizarse

health [hɛlθ] n salud f; **health care** n asistencia sanitaria; **health centre** (BRIT) n ambulatorio, centro médico; **health food** n alimentos mpl orgánicos; **Health Service** (BRIT) n el servicio de salud (la salud) británico, ≈ el Insalud (SP); **healthy** adj sano, saludable

heap [hiːp] n montón m ▷vt: **to ~ (up)** amontonar; **to ~ sth with** llenar algo hasta arriba de; **~s of** un montón de

hear [hɪə*] (pt, pp **~d**) vt (also Law) oír; (news) saber ▷vi oír; **to ~ about** oír hablar de; **to ~ from sb** tener noticias de algn

heard [hɜːd] pt, pp of **hear**

hearing ['hɪərɪŋ] n (sense) oído; (Law) vista; **hearing aid** n audífono

hearse [hɜːs] n coche m fúnebre

heart [hɑːt] n corazón m; (fig) valor m; (of lettuce) cogollo; **hearts** npl (Cards) corazones mpl; **to lose/take ~** descorazonarse/cobrar ánimo; **at ~** en el fondo; **by ~** (learn, know) de memoria; **heart attack** n infarto (de miocardio); **heartbeat** n latido (del corazón); **heartbroken** adj: **she was heartbroken about it** esto le partió el corazón; **heartburn** n acedía; **heart disease** n enfermedad f cardíaca

hearth [hɑːθ] n (fireplace) chimenea

heartless ['hɑːtlɪs] adj despiadado

hearty ['hɑːtɪ] adj (person) campechano; (laugh) sano; (dislike, support) absoluto

heat [hiːt] n calor m; (Sport: also: **qualifying ~**) prueba eliminatoria ▷vt calentar; **heat up** vi calentarse ▷vt calentar; **heated** adj caliente; (fig) acalorado; **heater** n estufa; (in car) calefacción f

heather ['hɛðə*] n brezo

heating ['hiːtɪŋ] n calefacción f

heatwave ['hiːtweɪv] n ola de calor

heaven ['hɛvn] n cielo; (fig) una maravilla; **heavenly** adj celestial; (fig) maravilloso

heavily ['hɛvɪlɪ] adv pesadamente; (drink, smoke) con exceso; (sleep, sigh) profundamente; (depend) mucho

heavy ['hɛvɪ] adj pesado; (work, blow) duro; (sea, rain, meal) fuerte; (drinker, smoker) grande; (responsibility) grave; (schedule) ocupado; (weather) bochornoso

Hebrew ['hi:bru:] *adj, n* (Ling) hebreo
hectare ['hɛktɑ:*] *n* (BRIT) hectárea
hectic ['hɛktɪk] *adj* agitado
he'd [hi:d]= **he would; he had**
hedge [hɛdʒ] *n* seto ▷ *vi* contestar
con evasivas; **to ~ one's bets** (fig)
cubrirse
hedgehog ['hɛdʒhɔg] *n* erizo
heed [hi:d] *vt* (*also:* **take ~**): *pay
attention to*) hacer caso de
heel [hi:l] *n* talón *m*; (of shoe) tacón *m*
▷ *vt* (*shoe*) poner tacón a
hefty ['hɛftɪ] *adj* (*person*) fornido;
(*parcel, profit*) gordo
height [haɪt] *n* (of person) estatura;
(of building) altura; (high ground) cerro;
(altitude) altitud f; (fig: of season): **at the
~ of summer** en los días más calurosos
del verano; (: of power etc) cúspide f;
(: of stupidity etc) colmo; **heighten** *vt*
elevar; (fig) aumentar
heir [ɛə*] *n* heredero; **heiress** *n*
heredera
held [hɛld] *pt, pp of* **hold**
helicopter ['hɛlɪkɔptə*] *n*
helicóptero
hell [hɛl] *n* infierno; **~!** (inf)
¡demonios!
he'll [hi:l]= **he will; he shall**
hello [hə'ləu] *excl* ¡hola!; (*to attract
attention*) ¡oiga!; (*surprise*) ¡caramba!
helmet ['hɛlmɪt] *n* casco
help [hɛlp] *n* ayuda; (cleaner etc)
criada, asistenta ▷ *vt* ayudar; **~!**
¡socorro!; **~ yourself** sírvete; **he
can't ~ it** no es culpa suya; **help out** *vi*
ayudar, echar una mano ▷ *vt*: **to help
sb out** ayudar a algn, echar una mano
a algn; **helper** *n* ayudante *mf*; **helpful**
adj útil; (*person*) servicial; (*advice*)
útil; **helping** *n* ración f; **helpless**
adj (*incapable*) incapaz; (*defenceless*)
indefenso; **helpline** *n* teléfono de
asistencia al público
hem [hɛm] *n* dobladillo ▷ *vt* poner or
coser el dobladillo de
hemisphere ['hɛmɪsfɪə*] *n*
hemisferio

hemorrhage ['hɛmərɪdʒ] (US) *n* =
haemorrhage
hemorrhoids ['hɛmərɔɪdz] (US) *npl* =
haemorrhoids
hen [hɛn] *n* gallina; (female bird)
hembra
hence [hɛns] *adv* (therefore) por lo
tanto; **2 years ~** de aquí a 2 años
hen night, hen party *n* (BRIT)
despedida de soltera
hepatitis [hɛpə'taɪtɪs] *n* hepatitis f
her [hə:*] *pron* (direct) la; (indirect) le;
(stressed, after prep) ella ▷ *adj* su; *see
also* **me; my**
herb [hə:b] *n* hierba; **herbal** *adj* de
hierbas; **herbal tea** *n* infusión f de
hierbas
herd [hə:d] *n* rebaño
here [hɪə*] *adv* aquí; (at this point)
en este punto; **~!** (present) ¡presente!;
~ is/are aquí está/están; **~ she is**
aquí está
hereditary [hɪ'rɛdɪtrɪ] *adj*
hereditario
heritage ['hɛrɪtɪdʒ] *n* patrimonio
hernia ['hə:nɪə] *n* hernia
hero ['hɪərəu] (*pl* **~es**) *n* héroe *m*;
(in book, film) protagonista *m*; **heroic**
[hɪ'rəuɪk] *adj* heroico
heroin ['hɛrəuɪn] *n* heroína
heroine ['hɛrəuɪn] *n* heroína; (in
book, film) protagonista
heron ['hɛrən] *n* garza
herring ['hɛrɪŋ] *n* arenque *m*
hers [hə:z] *pron* (el) suyo/(la) suya) etc;
see also **mine[1]**
herself [hə:'sɛlf] *pron* (reflexive) se;
(emphatic) ella misma; (after prep) sí
(misma); *see also* **oneself**
he's [hi:z]= **he is; he has**
hesitant ['hɛzɪtənt] *adj* vacilante
hesitate ['hɛzɪteɪt] *vi* vacilar; (in
speech) titubear; (be unwilling) resistirse
a; **hesitation** [-'teɪʃən] *n* indecisión f;
titubeo; dudas fpl
heterosexual [hɛtərəu'sɛksjuəl] *adj*
heterosexual
hexagon ['hɛksəgən] *n* hexágono

hey [heɪ] *excl* ¡oye!, ¡oiga!

heyday ['heɪdeɪ] *n*: **the ~ of** el apogeo de

HGV *n abbr* (= **heavy goods vehicle**) vehículo pesado

hi [haɪ] *excl* ¡hola!; (*to attract attention*) ¡oiga!

hibernate ['haɪbəneɪt] *vi* invernar

hiccough ['hɪkʌp] = **hiccup**

hiccup ['hɪkʌp] *vi* hipar

hid [hɪd] *pt of* **hide**

hidden ['hɪdn] *pp of* **hide** ▷ *adj*: **~ agenda** plan *m* encubierto

hide [haɪd] (*pt* hid, *pp* hidden) *n* (*skin*) piel *f* ▷ *vt* esconder, ocultar ▷ *vi*: **to ~ (from sb)** esconderse or ocultarse (de algn)

hideous ['hɪdɪəs] *adj* horrible

hiding ['haɪdɪŋ] *n* (*beating*) paliza; **to be in ~** (*concealed*) estar escondido

hi-fi ['haɪfaɪ] *n* estéreo, hifi *m* ▷ *adj* de alta fidelidad

high [haɪ] *adj* alto; (*speed, number*) grande; (*price*) elevado; (*wind*) fuerte; (*voice*) agudo ▷ *adv* alto, a gran altura; **it is 20 m ~** tiene 20 m de altura; **~ in the air** en las alturas; **highchair** *n* silla alta; **high-class** *adj* (*hotel*) de lujo; (*person*) distinguido, de categoría; (*food*) de alta categoría; **higher education** *n* educación *f* or enseñanza superior; **high heels** *npl* (*heels*) tacones *mpl* altos; (*shoes*) zapatos *mpl* de tacón; **high jump** *n* (*Sport*) salto de altura; **highlands** ['haɪləndz] *npl* tierras *fpl* altas; **the Highlands** (*in Scotland*) las Tierras Altas de Escocia; **highlight** *n* (*fig: of event*) punto culminante ▷ *vt* subrayar; **highlights** *npl* (*in hair*) reflejos *mpl*; **highlighter** *n* rotulador *m*; **highly** *adv* (*paid*) muy bien; (*critical, confidential*) sumamente; (*a lot*): **to speak/think highly of** hablar muy bien de/tener en mucho a; **highness** *n* altura; **Her/His Highness** Su Alteza; **high-rise** *n* (*also*: **high-rise block, high-rise building**) torre *f* de pisos; **high school**

n = Instituto Nacional de Bachillerato (SP); **high season** (BRIT) *n* temporada alta; **high street** (BRIT) *n* calle *f* mayor; **high-tech** (*inf*) *adj* alta-tec (BRIT), de alta tecnología; **highway** *n* carretera; (US) carretera nacional; autopista; **Highway Code** (BRIT) *n* código de la circulación

hijack ['haɪdʒæk] *vt* secuestrar; **hijacker** *n* secuestrador(a) *m/f*

hike [haɪk] *vi* (*go walking*) ir de excursión (a pie) ▷ *n* caminata; **hiker** *n* excursionista *mf*; **hiking** *n* senderismo

hilarious [hɪ'lɛərɪəs] *adj* divertidísimo

hill [hɪl] *n* colina; (*high*) montaña; (*slope*) cuesta; **hillside** *n* ladera; **hill walking** *n* senderismo (de montaña); **hilly** *adj* montañoso

him [hɪm] *pron* (*direct*) le, lo; (*indirect*) le; (*stressed, after prep*) él; *see also* **me**; **himself** *pron* (*reflexive*) se; (*emphatic*) él mismo; (*after prep*) sí (mismo); *see also* **oneself**

hind [haɪnd] *adj* posterior

hinder ['hɪndə*] *vt* estorbar, impedir

hindsight ['haɪndsaɪt] *n*: **with ~** en retrospectiva

Hindu ['hɪnduː] *n* hindú *mf*; **Hinduism** *n* (*Rel*) hinduismo

hinge [hɪndʒ] *n* bisagra, gozne *m* ▷ *vi* (*fig*): **to ~ on** depender de

hint [hɪnt] *n* indirecta; (*advice*) consejo; (*sign*) dejo ▷ *vt*: **to ~ that** insinuar que ▷ *vi*: **to ~ at** hacer alusión a

hip [hɪp] *n* cadera

hippie ['hɪpɪ] *n* hippie *m/f*, jipi *m/f*

hippo ['hɪpəʊ] (*pl* **~s**) *n* hipopótamo

hippopotamus [hɪpə'pɒtəməs] (*pl* **~es** *or* **hippopotami**) *n* hipopótamo

hippy ['hɪpɪ] *n* = **hippie**

hire ['haɪə*] *vt* (BRIT: *car, equipment*) alquilar; (*worker*) contratar ▷ *n* alquiler *m*; **for ~** se alquila; (*taxi*) libre; **hire(d) car** (BRIT) *n* coche *m* de alquiler; **hire purchase** (BRIT) *n* compra a plazos

his [hɪz] *pron* (el) suyo/(la) suya) *etc*
▷ *adj* su; *see also* **mine¹; my**
Hispanic [hɪs'pænɪk] *adj* hispánico
hiss [hɪs] *vi* silbar
historian [hɪ'stɔ:rɪən] *n*
historiador(a) *m/f*
historic(al) [hɪ'stɔrɪk(l)] *adj*
histórico
history ['hɪstərɪ] *n* historia
hit [hɪt] (*pt, pp* ~) *vt* (*strike*) golpear,
pegar; (*reach: target*) alcanzar; (*collide
with: car*) chocar contra; (*fig: affect*)
afectar ▷ *n* golpe *m*; (*success*) éxito;
(*on website*) visita; (*in web search*)
correspondencia; **to ~ it off with
sb** llevarse bien con algn; **hit back**
vi defenderse; (*fig*) devolver golpe
por golpe
hitch [hɪtʃ] *vt* (*fasten*) atar, amarrar;
(*also:* ~ **up**) remangar ▷ *n* (*difficulty*)
dificultad *f*; **to ~ a lift** hacer
autostop
hitch-hike ['hɪtʃhaɪk] *vi* hacer
autostop; **hitch-hiker** *n* autostopista
m/f; **hitch-hiking** *n* autostop *m*
hi-tech [haɪ'tek] *adj* de alta
tecnología
hitman ['hɪtmæn] (*irreg*) *n* asesino
a sueldo
HIV *n abbr* (= human immunodeficiency
virus) VIH *m*; ~**negative/positive**
VIH negativo/positivo
hive [haɪv] *n* colmena
hoard [hɔ:d] *n* (*treasure*) tesoro;
(*stockpile*) provisión *f* ▷ *vt* acumular;
(*goods in short supply*) acaparar
hoarse [hɔ:s] *adj* ronco
hoax [həʊks] *n* trampa
hob [hɒb] *n* quemador *m*
hobble ['hɒbl] *vi* cojear
hobby ['hɒbɪ] *n* pasatiempo, afición
f
hobo ['həʊbəʊ] (*us*) *n* vagabundo
hockey ['hɒkɪ] *n* hockey *m*; **hockey
stick** *n* palo *m* de hockey
hog [hɒg] *n* cerdo, puerco ▷ *vt*
acaparar; **to go the whole ~** poner
toda la carne en el asador

Hogmanay [hɒgmə'neɪ] *n ver
recuadro*

hoist [hɔɪst] *n* (*crane*) grúa ▷ *vt*
levantar, alzar; (*flag, sail*) izar
hold [həʊld] (*pt, pp* **held**) *vt* sostener;
(*contain*) contener; (*have: power,
qualification*) tener; (*keep back*) retener;
(*believe*) sostener; (*consider*) considerar;
(*keep in position*) **to ~ one's head up**
mantener la cabeza alta; (*meeting*)
celebrar ▷ *vi* (*withstand pressure*)
resistir; (*be valid*) valer ▷ *n* (*grasp*)
asimiento; (*fig*) dominio; **~ the line!**
(*Tel*) ¡no cuelgue!; **to ~ one's own** (*fig*)
defenderse; **to catch** *or* **get (a) ~ of**
agarrarse *or* asirse de; **hold back** *vt*
retener; (*secret*) ocultar; **hold on** *vi*
agarrarse bien; (*wait*) esperar; **hold
on!** (*Tel*) ¡espere) un momento!; **hold
out** *vt* ofrecer ▷ *vi* (*resist*) resistir;
hold up *vt* (*raise*) levantar; (*support*)
apoyar; (*delay*) retrasar; (*rob*) asaltar;
holdall (*BRIT*) *n* bolsa; **holder** *n*
(*container*) receptáculo; (*of ticket, record*)
poseedor(a) *m/f*; (*of office, title etc*)
titular *mf*
hole [həʊl] *n* agujero
holiday ['hɒlɪdɪ] *n* vacaciones
fpl; (*public holiday*) (día *m* de) fiesta,
día *m* feriado; **on ~** de vacaciones;
holiday camp *n* (*BRIT: also*: **holiday
centre**) centro de vacaciones; **holiday**

job n (BRIT) trabajillo extra para las vacaciones; **holiday-maker** (BRIT) n turista mf; **holiday resort** n centro turístico

Holland ['hɒlənd] n Holanda

hollow ['hɒləʊ] adj hueco; (claim) vacío; (eyes) hundido; (sound) sordo ▷ n hueco; (in ground) hoyo ▷ vt: to ~ **out** excavar

holly ['hɒlɪ] n acebo

Hollywood ['hɒlɪwʊd] n Hollywood m

holocaust ['hɒləkɔːst] n holocausto

holy ['həʊlɪ] adj santo, sagrado; (water) bendito

home [həʊm] n casa; (country) patria; (institution) asilo ▷ cpd (domestic) casero, de casa; (Econ, Pol) nacional ▷ adv (direction) a casa; (right in: nail etc) a fondo; **at ~** en casa; (in country) en el país; (fig) como pez en el agua; **to go/come ~** ir/volver a casa; **make yourself at ~** ¡estás en tu casa!; **home address** n domicilio; **homeland** n tierra natal; **homeless** adj sin hogar, sin casa; **homely** adj (simple) sencillo; **home-made** adj casero; **home match** n partido en casa; **Home Office** (BRIT) n Ministerio del Interior; **home owner** n propietario/a m/f de una casa; **home page** n página de inicio; **Home Secretary** (BRIT) n Ministro del Interior; **to be homesick** tener morriña, sentir nostalgia; **home town** n ciudad f natal; **homework** n deberes mpl

homicide ['hɒmɪsaɪd] (US) n homicidio

homoeopathic [həʊmɪə'pæθɪk] (US **homeopathic**) adj homeopático

homoeopathy [həʊmɪ'ɒpəθɪ] (US **homeopathy**) n homeopatía

homosexual [hɒməu'sɛksjuəl] adj, n homosexual mf

honest ['ɒnɪst] adj honrado; (sincere) franco, sincero; **honestly** adv honradamente; francamente; **honesty** n honradez f

honey ['hʌnɪ] n miel f; **honeymoon** n luna de miel; **honeysuckle** n madreselva

Hong Kong ['hɒŋ'kɒŋ] n Hong-Kong m

honorary ['ɒnərərɪ] adj (member, president) de honor; (title) honorífico; ~ **degree** doctorado honoris causa

honour ['ɒnə*] (US **honor**) vt honrar; (commitment, promise) cumplir con ▷ n honor m, honra; **to graduate with ~s** = licenciarse con matrícula de honor); **honourable** (US **honorable**) adj honorable; **honours degree** n (Scol) título de licenciado con calificación alta

hood [hud] n capucha; (BRIT Aut) capota; (US Aut) capó m; (of cooker) campana de humos; **hoodie** n (top) jersey m con capucha

hoof [huːf] (pl **hooves**) n pezuña

hook [huk] n gancho; (on dress) corchete m, broche m; (for fishing) anzuelo ▷ vt enganchar; (fish) pescar

hooligan ['huːlɪgən] n gamberro

hoop [huːp] n aro

hooray [huː'reɪ] excl = **hurray**

hoot [huːt] (BRIT) vi (Aut) tocar el pito, pitar; (siren) (hacer) sonar; (owl) ulular

Hoover® ['huːvə*] (BRIT) n aspiradora ▷ vt: **to hoover** pasar la aspiradora por

hooves [huːvz] npl of **hoof**

hop [hɒp] vi saltar, brincar; (on one foot) saltar con un pie

hope [həʊp] vt, vi esperar ▷ n esperanza; **I ~ so/not** espero que sí/no; **hopeful** adj (person) optimista; (situation) prometedor(a); **hopefully** adv con esperanza; (one hopes): **hopefully he will recover** esperamos que se recupere; **hopeless** adj desesperado; (person): **to be hopeless** ser un desastre

hops [hɒps] npl lúpulo

horizon [hə'raɪzn] n horizonte m; **horizontal** [hɒrɪ'zɒntl] adj horizontal

hormone ['hɔːməun] n hormona

horn [hɔːn] n cuerno; (Mus: also:

French ~) trompa; (Aut) pito, claxon m
horoscope ['hɒrəskəup] n horóscopo
horrendous [hɒ'rɛndəs] adj horrendo
horrible ['hɒrɪbl] adj horrible
horrid ['hɒrɪd] adj horrible, horroroso
horrific [hɒ'rɪfɪk] adj (accident)
horroroso; (film) horripilante
horrifying ['hɒrɪfaɪɪŋ] adj horroroso
horror ['hɒrə*] n horror m; **horror
film** n película de horror
hors d'œuvre [ɔː'dəːvrə] n
entremeses mpl
horse [hɔːs] n caballo m; **on horseback**
n: **on horseback** a caballo; **horse
chestnut** n (tree) castaño de Indias;
(nut) castaña de Indias; **horsepower**
n caballo (de fuerza); **horse-racing** n
carreras fpl de caballos; **horseradish** n
rábano picante; **horse riding** n (BRIT)
equitación f
hose [həuz] n manguera; **hosepipe**
n manguera
hospital ['hɒspɪtl] n hospital m
hospitality [hɒspɪ'tælɪtɪ] n
hospitalidad f
host [həust] n anfitrión m; (TV, Radio)
presentador m; (Rel) hostia; (large
number): **a ~ of** multitud de
hostage ['hɒstɪdʒ] n rehén m
hostel ['hɒstl] n hostal m; **(youth)
hostel** n albergue m juvenil
hostess ['həustɪs] n anfitriona;
(BRIT: air hostess) azafata; (TV, Radio)
presentadora
hostile ['hɒstaɪl] adj hostil
hostility [hɒ'stɪlɪtɪ] n hostilidad f
hot [hɒt] adj caliente; (weather)
caluroso, de calor; (as opposed to warm)
muy caliente; (spicy) picante; **to be
~** (person) tener calor; (object) estar
caliente; (weather) hacer calor; **hot dog**
n perro caliente
hotel [həu'tɛl] n hotel m
hotspot ['hɒtspɒt] n (Comput):
wireless hotspot punto m de acceso
inalámbrico
hot-water bottle [hɒt'wɔːtə*-] n
bolsa de agua caliente

hound [haund] vt acosar ▷ n perro
(de caza)
hour ['auə*] n hora; **hourly** adj (de)
cada hora
house [n haus, pl 'hauzɪz, vb hauz] n
(gen, firm) casa; (Pol) cámara; (Theatre)
sala ▷ vt (person) alojar; (collection)
albergar; **on the ~** (fig) la casa invita;
household n familia; (home) casa;
householder n propietario/a; (head of
house) cabeza de familia; **housekeeper**
n ama de llaves; **housekeeping**
n (work) trabajos mpl domésticos;
housewife (irreg) n ama de casa;
house wine n vino m de la casa;
housework n faenas fpl (de la casa)
housing ['hauzɪŋ] n (act)
alojamiento; (houses) viviendas fpl;
**housing development, housing
estate** (BRIT) n urbanización f
hover ['hɒvə*] vi flotar (en el aire);
hovercraft n aerodeslizador m
how [hau] adv (in what way) cómo;
~ are you? ¿cómo estás?; **~ much milk/
many people?** ¿cuánta leche/gente?;
~ much does it cost? ¿cuánto cuesta?;
~ long have you been here? ¿cuánto
hace que estás aquí?; **~ old are you?**
¿cuántos años tienes?; **~ tall is he?**
¿cómo es de alto?; **~ is school?** ¿cómo
(te) va (en) la escuela?; **~ was the film?**
¿qué tal la película?; **~ lovely/awful!**
¡qué bonito/horror!
however [hau'ɛvə*] adv: **~ I do it** lo
haga como lo haga; **~ cold it is** por
mucho frío que haga; **~ did you do it?**
¿cómo lo hiciste? ▷ conj sin embargo,
no obstante
howl [haul] n aullido ▷ vi aullar;
(person) dar alaridos; (wind) ulular
H.P. n abbr = **hire purchase**
h.p. abbr = **horsepower**
HQ n abbr = **headquarters**
hr(s) abbr = **hour(s)**) h
HTML n abbr (= hypertext markup
language) lenguaje m de hipertexto
hubcap ['hʌbkæp] n tapacubos m inv
huddle ['hʌdl] vi: **to ~ together**

acurrucarse

huff [hʌf] n: **in a ~** enojado

hug [hʌɡ] vt abrazar; (thing) apretar con los brazos

huge [hjuːdʒ] adj enorme

hull [hʌl] n (of ship) casco

hum [hʌm] vt tararear, canturrear ▷ vi tararear, canturrear; (insect) zumbar

human ['hjuːmən] adj, n humano

humane [hjuːˈmeɪn] adj humano, humanitario

humanitarian [hjuːmænɪˈtɛərɪən] adj humanitario

humanity [hjuːˈmænɪtɪ] n humanidad f

human rights npl derechos mpl humanos

humble ['hʌmbl] adj humilde

humid ['hjuːmɪd] adj húmedo; **humidity** [-'mɪdɪtɪ] n humedad f

humiliate [hjuːˈmɪlɪeɪt] vt humillar

humiliating [hjuːˈmɪlɪeɪtɪŋ] adj humillante, vergonzoso

humiliation [hjuːmɪlɪˈeɪʃən] n humillación f

hummus ['huməs] n paté de garbanzos

humorous ['hjuːmərəs] adj gracioso, divertido

humour ['hjuːmə*] (US **humor**) n humorismo, sentido del humor; (mood) humor m ▷ vt (person) complacer

hump [hʌmp] n (in ground) montículo; (camel's) giba

hunch [hʌntʃ] n (premonition) presentimiento

hundred ['hʌndrəd] num ciento; (before n) cien; **~s of** centenares de; **hundredth** [-ɪdθ] adj centésimo

hung [hʌŋ] pt, pp of **hang**

Hungarian [hʌŋˈɡɛərɪən] adj, n húngaro/a m/f

Hungary ['hʌŋɡərɪ] n Hungría

hunger ['hʌŋɡə*] n hambre f ▷ vi: **to ~ for** (fig) tener hambre de, anhelar

hungry ['hʌŋɡrɪ] adj: **~ (for)** hambriento (de); **to be ~** tener hambre

hunt [hʌnt] vt (seek) buscar; (Sport) cazar ▷ vi (search): **to ~ (for)** buscar; (Sport) cazar ▷ n búsqueda; caza, cacería; **hunter** n cazador(a) m/f; **hunting** n caza

hurdle ['həːdl] n (Sport) valla; (fig) obstáculo

hurl [həːl] vt lanzar, arrojar

hurrah [huˈrɑː] excl = **hurray**

hurray [huˈreɪ] excl ¡viva!

hurricane ['hʌrɪkən] n huracán m

hurry ['hʌrɪ] n prisa ▷ vt (also: **~ up**: person) dar prisa a; (: work) apresurar, hacer de prisa; **to be in a ~** tener prisa ▷ vi darse prisa, apurarse (LAM)

hurt [həːt] (pt, pp **~**) vt hacer daño a ▷ vi doler ▷ adj lastimado

husband ['hʌzbənd] n marido

hush [hʌʃ] n silencio ▷ vt hacer callar; **~!** ¡chitón!, ¡cállate!

husky ['hʌskɪ] adj ronco ▷ n perro esquimal

hut [hʌt] n cabaña; (shed) cobertizo

hyacinth ['haɪəsɪnθ] n jacinto

hydrangea [haɪˈdreɪnʒə] n hortensia

hydrofoil ['haɪdrəfɔɪl] n aerodeslizador m

hydrogen ['haɪdrədʒən] n hidrógeno

hygiene ['haɪdʒiːn] n higiene f; **hygienic** [-'dʒiːnɪk] adj higiénico

hymn [hɪm] n himno

hype [haɪp] (inf) n bombardeo publicitario

hyperlink ['haɪpəlɪŋk] n hiperlink m

hyphen ['haɪfn] n guión m

hypnotize ['hɪpnətaɪz] vt hipnotizar

hypocrite ['hɪpəkrɪt] n hipócrita mf

hypocritical [hɪpəˈkrɪtɪkl] adj hipócrita

hypothesis [haɪˈpɔθɪsɪs] (pl **hypotheses** [-siːz]) n hipótesis f inv

hysterical [hɪˈstɛrɪkl] adj histérico; (funny) para morirse de risa

hysterics [hɪˈstɛrɪks] npl histeria; **to be in ~** (fig) morirse de risa

they're **ideally suited** hacen una pareja ideal

identical [aɪˈdɛntɪkəl] *adj* idéntico

identification [aɪdɛntɪfɪˈkeɪʃə n] *n* identificación *f*; **(means of) ~** documentos *mpl* personales

identify [aɪˈdɛntɪfaɪ] *vt* identificar

identity [aɪˈdɛntɪtɪ] *n* identidad *f*; **identity card** *n* carnet *m* de identidad; **identity theft** *n* robo de identidad

ideology [aɪdɪˈɒlədʒɪ] *n* ideología

idiom [ˈɪdɪəm] *n* modismo; *(style of speaking)* lenguaje *m*

> Be careful not to translate **idiom** by the Spanish word **idioma**.

idiot [ˈɪdɪət] *n* idiota *mf*

idle [ˈaɪdl] *adj (inactive)* ocioso; *(lazy)* holgazán/ana; *(unemployed)* parado, desocupado; *(machinery etc)* parado; *(talk etc)* frívolo ▷ *vi (machine)* marchar en vacío

idol [ˈaɪdl] *n* ídolo

idyllic [ɪˈdɪlɪk] *adj* idílico

i.e. *abbr* (=that is) esto es

if [ɪf] *conj* si; **~ necessary** si fuera necesario, si hiciese falta; **~ I were you** yo en tu lugar; **~ so/not** de ser así/si no; **~ only I could!** ¡ojalá pudiera!; *see also* **as; even**

ignite [ɪɡˈnaɪt] *vt (set fire to)* encender ▷ *vi* encenderse

ignition [ɪɡˈnɪʃən] *n (Aut: process)* ignición *f*; *(: mechanism)* encendido; **to switch on/off the ~** arrancar/apagar el motor

ignorance [ˈɪɡnərəns] *n* ignorancia

ignorant [ˈɪɡnərənt] *adj* ignorante; **to be ~ of** ignorar

ignore [ɪɡˈnɔː] *vt (person, advice)* no hacer caso de; *(fact)* pasar por alto

I'll [aɪl] = **I will; I shall**

ill [ɪl] *adj* enfermo, malo ▷ *n* mal *m* ▷ *adv* mal; **to be taken ~** ponerse enfermo

illegal [ɪˈliːɡl] *adj* ilegal

illegible [ɪˈlɛdʒɪbl] *adj* ilegible

illegitimate [ɪlɪˈdʒɪtɪmət] *adj*

I [aɪ] *pron* yo

ice [aɪs] *n* hielo; *(ice cream)* helado ▷ *vt (cake)* alcorzar ▷ *vi (also:* **~ over, ~ up)** helarse; **iceberg** *n* iceberg *m*; **ice cream** *n* helado; **ice cube** *n* cubito de hielo; **ice hockey** *n* hockey *m* sobre hielo

Iceland [ˈaɪslənd] *n* Islandia; **Icelander** *n* islandés/esa *m/f*; **Icelandic** [aɪsˈlændɪk] *adj* islandés/ esa ▷ *n (Ling)* islandés *m*

ice: ice lolly (BRIT) *n* polo; **ice rink** *n* pista de hielo; **ice skating** *n* patinaje *m* sobre hielo

icing [ˈaɪsɪŋ] *n (Culin)* alcorza; **icing sugar** (BRIT) *n* azúcar *m* glas(eado)

icon [ˈaɪkɒn] *n* icono

ICT (BRIT: Scol) *n abbr* (= information and communications technology) informática *f*

icy [ˈaɪsɪ] *adj* helado

I'd [aɪd] = **I would; I had**

ID card *n* (identity card) DNI *m*

idea [aɪˈdɪə] *n* idea

ideal [aɪˈdɪəl] *n* ideal *m* ▷ *adj* ideal; **ideally** [-dɪəlɪ] *adv* idealmente;

ilegítimo

ill health n mala salud f; **to be in ~** estar mal de salud

illiterate [ɪˈlɪtərət] adj analfabeto

illness [ˈɪlnɪs] n enfermedad f

illuminate [ɪˈluːmɪneɪt] vt (room, street) iluminar, alumbrar

illusion [ɪˈluːʒən] n ilusión f; (trick) truco

illustrate [ˈɪləstreɪt] vt ilustrar

illustration [ɪləˈstreɪʃən] n (act of illustrating) ilustración f; (example) ejemplo, ilustración f; (in book) lámina

I'm [aɪm] = **I am**

image [ˈɪmɪdʒ] n imagen f

imaginary [ɪˈmædʒɪnərɪ] adj imaginario

imagination [ɪmædʒɪˈneɪʃən] n imaginación f; (inventiveness) inventiva

imaginative [ɪˈmædʒɪnətɪv] adj imaginativo

imagine [ɪˈmædʒɪn] vt imaginarse

imbalance [ɪmˈbæləns] n desequilibrio

imitate [ˈɪmɪteɪt] vt imitar; **imitation** [ɪmɪˈteɪʃən] n imitación f; (copy) copia

immaculate [ɪˈmækjulət] adj inmaculado

immature [ɪməˈtjuə*] adj (person) inmaduro

immediate [ɪˈmiːdɪət] adj inmediato; (pressing) urgente, apremiante; (nearest: family) próximo; (: neighbourhood) inmediato; **immediately** adv (at once) en seguida; (directly) inmediatamente; **immediately next to** muy junto a

immense [ɪˈmens] adj inmenso, enorme; (importance) enorme; **immensely** adv enormemente

immerse [ɪˈmɜːs] vt (submerge) sumergir; **to be ~d in** (fig) estar absorto en

immigrant [ˈɪmɪgrənt] n inmigrante mf; **immigration** [ɪmɪˈgreɪʃən] n inmigración f

imminent [ˈɪmɪnənt] adj inminente

immoral [ɪˈmɔrl] adj inmoral

immortal [ɪˈmɔːtl] adj inmortal

immune [ɪˈmjuːn] adj: **~ (to)** inmune (a); **immune system** n sistema m inmunitario

immunize [ˈɪmjunaɪz] vt inmunizar

impact [ˈɪmpækt] n impacto

impair [ɪmˈpeə*] vt perjudicar

impartial [ɪmˈpɑːʃl] adj imparcial

impatience [ɪmˈpeɪʃəns] n impaciencia

impatient [ɪmˈpeɪʃənt] adj impaciente; **to get** or **grow ~** impacientarse

impeccable [ɪmˈpekəbl] adj impecable

impending [ɪmˈpendɪŋ] adj inminente

imperative [ɪmˈperətɪv] adj (tone) imperioso; (need) imprescindible

imperfect [ɪmˈpɜːfɪkt] adj (goods etc) defectuoso ▷ n (Ling: also: **~ tense**) imperfecto

imperial [ɪmˈpɪərɪəl] adj imperial

impersonal [ɪmˈpɜːsənl] adj impersonal

impersonate [ɪmˈpɜːsəneɪt] vt hacerse pasar por; (Theatre) imitar

impetus [ˈɪmpətəs] n ímpetu m; (fig) impulso

implant [ɪmˈplɑːnt] vt (Med) injertar, implantar; (fig: idea, principle) inculcar

implement [n ˈɪmplɪmənt, vb ˈɪmplɪment] n herramienta f; (for cooking) utensilio ▷ vt (regulation) hacer efectivo; (plan) realizar

implicate [ˈɪmplɪkeɪt] vt (compromise) comprometer; **to ~ sb in sth** comprometer a algn en algo

implication [ɪmplɪˈkeɪʃən] n consecuencia; **by ~** indirectamente

implicit [ɪmˈplɪsɪt] adj implícito; (belief, trust) absoluto

imply [ɪmˈplaɪ] vt (involve) suponer; (hint) dar a entender que

impolite [ɪmpəˈlaɪt] adj mal educado

import [vb ɪmˈpɔːt, n ˈɪmpɔːt] vt
importar ▷ n (Comm) importación
f; (: article) producto importado;
(meaning) significado, sentido

importance [ɪmˈpɔːtəns] n
importancia

important [ɪmˈpɔːtənt] adj
importante; **it's not ~** no importa, no
tiene importancia

importer [ɪmˈpɔːtə*] n
importador(a) m/f

impose [ɪmˈpəuz] vt imponer
▷ vi: **to ~ on sb** abusar de algn;
imposing adj imponente,
impresionante

impossible [ɪmˈpɔsɪbl] adj
imposible; (person) insoportable

impotent [ˈɪmpətənt] adj impotente

impoverished [ɪmˈpɔvərɪʃt] adj
necesitado

impractical [ɪmˈpræktɪkl] adj
(person, plan) poco práctico

impress [ɪmˈpres] vt impresionar;
(mark) estampar; **to ~ sth on sb** hacer
entender algo a algn

impression [ɪmˈpreʃən] n
impresión f; (imitation) imitación f; **to
be under the ~ that** tener la impresión
de que

impressive [ɪmˈpresɪv] adj
impresionante

imprison [ɪmˈprɪzn] vt encarcelar;
imprisonment n encarcelamiento;
(term of imprisonment) cárcel f

improbable [ɪmˈprɔbəbl] adj
improbable, inverosímil

improper [ɪmˈprɔpə*] adj
(unsuitable: conduct etc) incorrecto;
(: activities) deshonesto

improve [ɪmˈpruːv] vt mejorar;
(foreign language) perfeccionar
▷ vi mejorarse; **improvement** n
mejoramiento; perfección f;
progreso

improvise [ˈɪmprəvaɪz] vt, vi
improvisar

impulse [ˈɪmpʌls] n impulso; **to act
on ~** obrar sin reflexión; **impulsive**

[ɪmˈpʌlsɪv] adj irreflexivo

○ **KEYWORD**

in [ɪn] prep **1** (indicating place,
position, with place names) en; **in the
house/garden** en (la) casa/el jardín;
in here/there aquí/ahí or allí dentro;
in London/England en Londres/
Inglaterra

2 (indicating time) en; **in spring** en (la)
primavera; **in the afternoon** por la
tarde; **at 4 o'clock in the afternoon**
a las 4 de la tarde; **I did it in 3 hours/
days** lo hice en 3 horas/días; **I'll see
you in 2 weeks** or **in 2 weeks' time** te
veré dentro de 2 semanas

3 (indicating manner etc) en; **in a loud/
soft voice** en voz alta/baja; **in pencil/
ink** a lápiz/bolígrafo; **the boy in the
blue shirt** el chico de la camisa azul

4 (indicating circumstances): **in the sun/
shade/rain** al sol/a la sombra/bajo la
lluvia; **a change in policy** un cambio
de política

5 (indicating mood, state): **in tears** en
lágrimas, llorando; **in anger/despair**
enfadado/desesperado; **to live in
luxury** vivir lujosamente

6 (with ratios, numbers): **1 in 10
households, 1 household in 10** una
de cada 10 familias; **20 pence in the
pound** 20 peniques por libra; **they
lined up in twos** se alinearon de dos
en dos

7 (referring to people, works) en; entre;
the disease is common in children
la enfermedad es común entre los niños;
in (the works of) Dickens en (las
obras de) Dickens

8 (indicating profession etc): **to be in
teaching** estar en la enseñanza

9 (after superlative) de; **the best pupil
in the class** el(la) mejor alumno/a
de la clase

10 (with present participle): **in saying
this** al decir esto

▷ adv: **to be in** (person: at home) estar en

casa; (at work) estar; (train, ship, plane) haber llegado; (in fashion) estar de moda; **she'll be in later today** llegará más tarde hoy; **to ask sb in** hacer pasar a algn; **to run/limp etc in** entrar corriendo/cojeando etc
▷ n: **the ins and outs** (of proposal, situation etc) los detalles

inability [ɪnəˈbɪlɪtɪ] n: **~ (to do)** incapacidad f (de hacer)

inaccurate [ɪnˈækjʊrət] adj inexacto, incorrecto

inadequate [ɪnˈædɪkwət] adj (income, reply etc) insuficiente; (person) incapaz

inadvertently [ɪnədˈvɜːtntlɪ] adv por descuido

inappropriate [ɪnəˈprəʊprɪət] adj inadecuado; (improper) poco oportuno

inaugurate [ɪˈnɔːgjʊreɪt] vt inaugurar; (president, official) investir

Inc. (US) abbr (= incorporated) S.A.

incapable [ɪnˈkeɪpəbl] adj incapaz

incense [n ˈɪnsens, vb ɪnˈsens] n incienso ▷ vt (anger) indignar, encolerizar

incentive [ɪnˈsentɪv] n incentivo, estímulo

inch [ɪntʃ] n pulgada; **to be within an ~ of** estar a dos dedos de; **he didn't give an ~** no dio concesión alguna

incidence [ˈɪnsɪdns] n (of crime, disease) incidencia

incident [ˈɪnsɪdnt] n incidente m

incidentally [ɪnsɪˈdentəlɪ] adv (by the way) a propósito

inclination [ɪnklɪˈneɪʃən] n (tendency) tendencia, inclinación f; (desire) deseo; (disposition) propensión f

incline [n ˈɪnklaɪn, vb ɪnˈklaɪn] n pendiente m, cuesta ▷ vt (head) poner de lado ▷ vi inclinarse; **to be ~d to** (tend) tener tendencia a, hacer algo

include [ɪnˈkluːd] vt (incorporate) incluir; (in letter) adjuntar; **including** prep incluso, inclusive

inclusion [ɪnˈkluːʒən] n inclusión f

inclusive [ɪnˈkluːsɪv] adj inclusivo; **~ of tax** incluidos los impuestos

income [ˈɪnkʌm] n (earned) ingresos mpl; (from property etc) renta; (from investment etc) rédito; **income support** n (BRIT) ≈ ayuda familiar; **income tax** n impuesto sobre la renta

incoming [ˈɪnkʌmɪŋ] adj (flight, government etc) entrante

incompatible [ɪnkəmˈpætɪbl] adj incompatible

incompetence [ɪnˈkɒmpɪtəns] n incompetencia

incompetent [ɪnˈkɒmpɪtənt] adj incompetente

incomplete [ɪnkəmˈpliːt] adj (partial: achievement etc) incompleto; (unfinished: painting etc) inacabado

inconsistent [ɪnkənˈsɪstənt] adj inconsecuente; (contradictory) incongruente; **~ with** (que) no concuerda con

inconvenience [ɪnkənˈviːnjəns] n inconvenientes mpl; (trouble) molestia, incomodidad f ▷ vt incomodar

inconvenient [ɪnkənˈviːnjənt] adj incómodo, poco práctico; (time, place, visitor) inoportuno

incorporate [ɪnˈkɔːpəreɪt] vt incorporar; (contain) comprender; (add) agregar

incorrect [ɪnkəˈrekt] adj incorrecto

increase [n ˈɪnkriːs, vb ɪnˈkriːs] n aumento ▷ vi aumentar; (grow) crecer; (price) subir ▷ vt aumentar; (price) subir; **increasingly** adv cada vez más, más y más

incredible [ɪnˈkredɪbl] adj increíble; **incredibly** adv increíblemente

incur [ɪnˈkɜː] vt (expenses) incurrir; (loss) sufrir; (anger, disapproval) provocar

indecent [ɪnˈdiːsnt] adj indecente

indeed [ɪnˈdiːd] adv efectivamente, en realidad; (in fact) en efecto; (furthermore) es más; **yes ~!** ¡claro que sí

indefinitely [ɪnˈdɛfɪnɪtlɪ] adv (wait)
indefinidamente

independence [ɪndɪˈpɛndns] n
independencia; **Independence Day**
(US) n Día m de la Independencia

● **INDEPENDENCE DAY**
●
● El cuatro de julio es **Independence
Day**, la fiesta nacional de Estados
Unidos, que se celebra en
conmemoración de la Declaración
de Independencia, escrita por
Thomas Jefferson y aprobada
en 1776. En ella se proclamaba
la independencia total de Gran
Bretaña de las trece colonias
americanas que serían el origen de
los Estados Unidos de América.

independent [ɪndɪˈpɛndənt] adj
independiente; **independent school**
n (BRIT) escuela f privada, colegio m
privado

index [ˈɪndɛks] (pl **-es**) n (in book)
índice m; (: in library etc) catálogo; (pl
indices: ratio, sign) exponente m

India [ˈɪndɪə] n la India; **Indian** adj, n
indio/a; **Red Indian** piel roja mf

indicate [ˈɪndɪkeɪt] vt indicar;
indication [-ˈkeɪʃən] n indicio, señal
f; **indicative** [ɪnˈdɪkətɪv] adj; **to be
indicative of** indicar; **indicator** n
indicador m; (Aut) intermitente m

indices [ˈɪndɪsiːz] npl of **index**

indict [ɪnˈdaɪt] vt acusar; **indictment**
n acusación f

indifference [ɪnˈdɪfrəns] n
indiferencia

indifferent [ɪnˈdɪfrənt] adj
indiferente; (mediocre) regular

indigenous [ɪnˈdɪdʒɪnəs] adj
indígena

indigestion [ɪndɪˈdʒɛstʃən] n
indigestión f

indignant [ɪnˈdɪɡnənt] adj; **to be
~ at sth/with sb** indignarse por

algo/con algn

indirect [ɪndɪˈrɛkt] adj indirecto

indispensable [ɪndɪˈspɛnsəbl] adj
indispensable, imprescindible

individual [ɪndɪˈvɪdjuəl] n individuo
▷ adj individual; (personal) personal;
(particular) particular; **individually** adv
(singly) individualmente

Indonesia [ɪndəˈniːzɪə] n Indonesia

indoor [ˈɪndɔː] adj (swimming pool)
cubierto; (plant) de interior; (sport) bajo
cubierta; **indoors** [ɪnˈdɔːz] adv dentro

induce [ɪnˈdjuːs] vt inducir,
persuadir; (bring about) producir;
(labour) provocar

indulge [ɪnˈdʌldʒ] vt (whim)
satisfacer; (person) complacer; (child)
mimar ▷ vi: **to ~ in** darse el gusto de;
indulgent adj indulgente

industrial [ɪnˈdʌstrɪəl] adj
industrial; **industrial estate** (BRIT) n
polígono (SP) or zona (LAM) industrial;
industrialist n industrial mf;
industrial park (US) n = **industrial
estate**

industry [ˈɪndəstrɪ] n industria;
(diligence) aplicación f

inefficient [ɪnɪˈfɪʃənt] adj ineficaz,
ineficiente

inequality [ɪnɪˈkwɒlɪtɪ] n
desigualdad f

inevitable [ɪnˈɛvɪtəbl] adj inevitable;
inevitably adv inevitablemente

inexpensive [ɪnɪkˈspɛnsɪv] adj
económico

inexperienced [ɪnɪkˈspɪərɪənst] adj
inexperto

inexplicable [ɪnɪkˈsplɪkəbl] adj
inexplicable

infamous [ˈɪnfəməs] adj infame

infant [ˈɪnfənt] n niño/a; (baby) niño/
a pequeño/a, bebé mf; (pej) aniñado

infantry [ˈɪnfəntrɪ] n infantería

infant school (BRIT) n parvulario

infect [ɪnˈfɛkt] vt (wound) infectar;
(food) contaminar; (person, animal)
contagiar; **infection** [ɪnˈfɛkʃən] n
infección f; (fig) contagio; **infectious**

[ɪn'fekfəs] adj (also fig) contagioso

infer [ɪn'fə:*] vt deducir, inferir

inferior [ɪn'fɪərɪə*] adj, n inferior mf

infertile [ɪn'fə:taɪl] adj estéril; (person) infecundo

infertility [ɪnfə:'tɪlɪtɪ] n esterilidad f; infecundidad f

infested [ɪn'festɪd] adj: ~ with plagado de

infinite ['ɪnfɪnɪt] adj infinito; infinitely adv infinitamente

infirmary [ɪn'fə:mərɪ] n hospital m

inflamed [ɪn'fleɪmd] adj: to become ~ inflamarse

inflammation [ɪnflə'meɪʃən] n inflamación f

inflatable [ɪn'fleɪtəbl] adj (ball, boat) inflable

inflate [ɪn'fleɪt] vt (tyre, price etc) inflar; (fig) hinchar; inflation [ɪn'fleɪʃən] n (Econ) inflación f

inflexible [ɪn'fleksəbl] adj (rule) rígido; (person) inflexible

inflict [ɪn'flɪkt] vt: to ~ sth on sb infligir algo en algn

influence ['ɪnfluəns] n influencia ▷ vt influir en, influenciar; under the ~ of alcohol en estado de embriaguez; influential [-'enʃl] adj influyente

influx ['ɪnflʌks] n afluencia

info (inf) ['ɪnfəu] n = information

inform [ɪn'fɔ:m] vt: to ~ sb of sth informar a algn sobre or de algo ▷ vi: to ~ on sb delatar a algn

informal [ɪn'fɔ:məl] adj (manner, tone) familiar; (dress, interview, occasion) informal; (visit, meeting) extraoficial

information [ɪnfə'meɪʃən] n información f; (knowledge) conocimientos mpl; a piece of ~ un dato; information office n información f; information technology n informática

informative [ɪn'fɔ:mətɪv] adj informativo

infra-red [ɪnfrə'red] adj infrarrojo

infrastructure ['ɪnfrəstrʌktʃə*] n (of system etc) infraestructura

infrequent [ɪn'fri:kwənt] adj infrecuente

infuriate [ɪn'fjuərɪeɪt] vt: to become ~d ponerse furioso

infuriating [ɪn'fjuərɪeɪtɪŋ] adj (habit, noise) enloquecedor(a)

ingenious [ɪn'dʒi:njəs] adj ingenioso

ingredient [ɪn'gri:dɪənt] n ingrediente m

inhabit [ɪn'hæbɪt] vt vivir en; inhabitant n habitante mf

inhale [ɪn'heɪl] vt inhalar ▷ vi (breathe in) aspirar; (in smoking) tragar; inhaler n inhalador m

inherent [ɪn'hɪərənt] adj: ~ in or to inherente a

inherit [ɪn'herɪt] vt heredar; inheritance n herencia; (fig) patrimonio

inhibit [ɪn'hɪbɪt] vt inhibir, impedir; inhibition [-'bɪʃən] n cohibición f

initial [ɪ'nɪʃl] adj primero n inicial f ▷ vt firmar con las iniciales; initials npl (as signature) iniciales fpl; (abbreviation) siglas fpl; initially adv al principio

initiate [ɪ'nɪʃɪeɪt] vt iniciar; to ~ proceedings against sb (Law) entablar proceso contra algn

initiative [ɪ'nɪʃətɪv] n iniciativa

inject [ɪn'dʒekt] vt inyectar; to ~ sb with sth inyectar algo a algn; injection [ɪn'dʒekʃən] n inyección f

injure ['ɪndʒə*] vt (hurt) herir, lastimar; (fig: reputation etc) perjudicar; injured adj (person, arm) herido, lastimado; injury n herida, lesión f; (wrong) perjuicio, daño

Be careful not to translate **injury** by the Spanish word *injuria*.

injustice [ɪn'dʒʌstɪs] n injusticia

ink [ɪŋk] n tinta; ink-jet printer ['ɪŋkdʒet-] n impresora de chorro de tinta

inland [adj 'ɪnlənd, adv ɪn'lænd] adj (waterway, port etc) interior ▷ adv tierra adentro; **Inland Revenue** (BRIT) n departamento de impuestos ≈

Hacienda (SP)

in-laws ['ɪnlɔːz] npl suegros mpl

inmate ['ɪnmeɪt] n (in prison) preso/a, presidiario/a; (in asylum) internado/a

inn [ɪn] n posada, mesón m

inner ['ɪnə*] adj (courtyard, calm) interior; (feelings) íntimo; **inner-city** adj (schools, problems) de las zonas céntricas pobres, de los barrios céntricos pobres

inning ['ɪnɪŋ] n (US: Baseball) inning m, entrada; **~s** (Cricket) entrada, turno

innocence ['ɪnəsns] n inocencia

innocent ['ɪnəsnt] adj inocente

innovation [ɪnəu'veɪʃən] n novedad f

innovative ['ɪnəu'veɪtɪv] adj innovador

in-patient ['ɪnpeɪʃənt] n paciente m/f interno/a

input ['ɪnput] n entrada; (of resources) inversión f; (Comput) entrada de datos

inquest ['ɪnkwest] n (coroner's) encuesta judicial

inquire [ɪn'kwaɪə*] vi preguntar ⊳ vt: **to ~ whether** preguntar si; **to ~ about** (person) preguntar por; (fact) informarse de; **inquiry** n pregunta; (investigation) investigación f, pesquisa; **"Inquiries"** "Información"

ins. abbr = **inches**

insane [ɪn'seɪn] adj loco; (Med) demente

insanity [ɪn'sænɪtɪ] n demencia, locura

insect ['ɪnsekt] n insecto; **insect repellent** n loción f contra insectos

insecure [ɪnsɪ'kjuə*] adj inseguro

insecurity [ɪnsɪ'kjuərɪtɪ] n inseguridad f

insensitive [ɪn'sensɪtɪv] adj insensible

insert [vb ɪn'sɜːt, n 'ɪnsɜːt] vt (into sth) introducir ⊳ n encarte m

inside ['ɪn'saɪd] n interior m ⊳ adj interior, interno ⊳ adv (be) (por) dentro; (go) hacia dentro ⊳ prep dentro de; (of time): **~ 10 minutes** en menos

de 10 minutos; **inside lane** n (Aut: in Britain) carril m izquierdo; (: in US, Europe etc) carril m derecho; **inside out** adv (turn) al revés; (know) a fondo

insight ['ɪnsaɪt] n perspicacia

insignificant [ɪnsɪg'nɪfɪknt] adj insignificante

insincere [ɪnsɪn'sɪə*] adj poco sincero

insist [ɪn'sɪst] vi insistir; **to ~ on** insistir en; **to ~ that** insistir en que; (claim) exigir que; **insistent** adj insistente; (noise, action) persistente

insomnia [ɪn'sɔmnɪə] n insomnio

inspect [ɪn'spekt] vt inspeccionar, examinar; (troops) pasar revista a; **inspection** [ɪn'spekʃən] n inspección f, examen m; (of troops) revista; **inspector** n inspector(a) m/f; (BRIT: on buses, trains) revisor(a) m/f

inspiration [ɪnspə'reɪʃən] n inspiración f; **inspire** [ɪn'spaɪə*] vt inspirar; **inspiring** adj inspirador(a)

instability [ɪnstə'bɪlɪtɪ] n inestabilidad f

install [ɪn'stɔːl] (US **instal**) vt instalar; (official) nombrar; **installation** [ɪnstə'leɪʃən] n instalación f

installment [ɪn'stɔːlmənt] (US **installment**) n plazo; (of story) entrega; (of TV serial etc) capítulo; **in ~s** (pay, receive) a plazos

instance ['ɪnstəns] n ejemplo, caso; **for ~** por ejemplo; **in the first ~** en primer lugar

instant ['ɪnstənt] n instante m, momento ⊳ adj inmediato; (coffee etc) instantáneo; **instantly** adv en seguida; **instant messaging** n mensajería instantánea

instead [ɪn'sted] adv en cambio; **~ of** en lugar de, en vez de

instinct ['ɪnstɪŋkt] n instinto; **instinctive** adj instintivo

institute ['ɪnstɪtjuːt] n instituto; (professional body) colegio ⊳ vt (begin) iniciar, empezar; (proceedings) entablar; (system, rule) establecer

institution [ˌɪnstɪˈtjuːʃən] n institución f; (Med: home) asilo; (: asylum) manicomio; (of system etc) establecimiento; (of custom) iniciación f

instruct [ɪnˈstrʌkt] vt: **to ~ sb in sth** instruir a algn en or sobre algo; **to ~ sb to do sth** dar instrucciones a algn de hacer algo; **instruction** [ɪnˈstrʌkʃən] n (teaching) instrucción f; **instructions** npl (orders) órdenes fpl; **instructions (for use)** modo de empleo; **instructor** n instructor(a) m/f

instrument [ˈɪnstrəmənt] n instrumento; **instrumental** [-ˈmentl] adj (Mus) instrumental; **to be instrumental in** ser (el) artífice de

insufficient [ˌɪnsəˈfɪʃənt] adj insuficiente

insulate [ˈɪnsjuleɪt] vt aislar; **insulation** [-ˈleɪʃən] n aislamiento

insulin [ˈɪnsjulɪn] n insulina

insult [n ˈɪnsʌlt, vb ɪnˈsʌlt] n insulto ⊳vt insultar; **insulting** adj insultante

insurance [ɪnˈʃuərəns] n seguro; **fire/life ~** seguro contra incendios/ sobre la vida; **insurance company** n compañía f de seguros; **insurance policy** n póliza f (de seguros)

insure [ɪnˈʃuə*] vt asegurar

intact [ɪnˈtækt] adj íntegro, (unharmed) intacto

intake [ˈɪnteɪk] n (of food) ingestión f; (of air) consumo; (BRIT Scol): **an ~ of 200 a year** 200 matriculados al año

integral [ˈɪntɪɡrəl] adj (whole) íntegro; (part) integrante

integrate [ˈɪntɪɡreɪt] vt integrar ⊳vi integrarse

integrity [ɪnˈtɛɡrɪtɪ] n honradez f, rectitud f

intellect [ˈɪntəlɛkt] n intelecto; **intellectual** [-ˈlɛktjuəl] adj, n intelectual mf

intelligence [ɪnˈtɛlɪdʒəns] n inteligencia

intelligent [ɪnˈtɛlɪdʒənt] adj inteligente

intend [ɪnˈtɛnd] vt (gift etc): **to ~ sth for** destinar algo a; **to ~ to do sth** tener intención de or pensar hacer algo

intense [ɪnˈtɛns] adj intenso

intensify [ɪnˈtɛnsɪfaɪ] vt intensificar; (increase) aumentar

intensity [ɪnˈtɛnsɪtɪ] n (gen) intensidad f

intensive [ɪnˈtɛnsɪv] adj intensivo; **intensive care** n: **to be in intensive care** estar bajo cuidados intensivos; **intensive care unit** n unidad f de vigilancia intensiva

intent [ɪnˈtɛnt] n propósito; (Law) premeditación f ⊳ adj (absorbed) absorto; (attentive) atento; **to all ~s and purposes** prácticamente; **to be ~ on doing sth** estar resuelto a hacer algo

intention [ɪnˈtɛnʃən] n intención f, propósito; **intentional** adj deliberado

interact [ɪntərˈækt] vi influirse mutuamente; **interaction** [ɪntərˈækʃən] n interacción f, acción f recíproca; **interactive** adj (Comput) interactivo

intercept [ɪntəˈsɛpt] vt interceptar; (stop) detener

interchange [ˈɪntətʃeɪndʒ] n intercambio; (on motorway) intersección f

intercourse [ˈɪntəkɔːs] n (sexual) relaciones fpl sexuales

interest [ˈɪntrɪst] n (also Comm) interés m ⊳ vt interesar; **interested** adj interesado; **to be interested in** interesarse por; **interesting** adj interesante; **interest rate** n tipo or tasa de interés

interface [ˈɪntəfeɪs] n (Comput) junción f

interfere [ɪntəˈfɪə*] vi: **to ~ in** entrometerse en; **to ~ with** (hinder) estorbar; (damage) estropear

interference [ɪntəˈfɪərəns] n intromisión f; (Radio, TV) interferencia

interim [ˈɪntərɪm] n: **in the ~** en el ínterin ⊳ adj provisional

interior [ɪn'tɪərɪə*] n interior
m ▷ adj interior; **interior design**
n interiorismo, decoración f de
interiores
intermediate [ɪntə'miːdɪət] adj
intermedio
intermission [ɪntə'mɪʃən] n
intermisión f; (Theatre) descanso
intern [vb ɪn'təːn, n 'ɪntəːn] (US) vt
internar ▷ n interno/a
internal [ɪn'təːnl] adj (layout, pipes,
security) interior; (injury, structure,
memo) internal; **Internal Revenue
Service** (US) n departamento de
impuestos, = Hacienda (sp)
international [ɪntə'næʃənl] adj
internacional ▷ n (BRIT: match) partido
internacional
Internet ['ɪntənet] n: **the ~** Internet
m or f; **Internet café** n cibercafé
m; **Internet Service Provider** n
proveedor m de (acceso a) Internet;
Internet user n internauta mf
interpret [ɪn'təːprɪt] vt interpretar;
(translate) traducir; (understand)
entender ▷ vi hacer de intérprete;
interpretation
n interpretación f; traducción f;
interpreter n intérprete mf
interrogate [ɪn'terəgeɪt] vt
interrogar; **interrogation** [-'geɪʃən] n
interrogatorio
interrogative [ɪntə'rɔgətɪv] adj
interrogativo
interrupt [ɪntə'rʌpt] vt, vi
interrumpir; **interruption** [-'rʌpʃən] n
interrupción f
intersection [ɪntə'sekʃən] n (of
roads) cruce m
interstate ['ɪntəsteɪt] (US) n
carretera interestatal
interval ['ɪntəvl] n intervalo; (BRIT
Theatre, Sport) descanso; (Scol) recreo;
at ~s a ratos, de vez en cuando
intervene [ɪntə'viːn] vi intervenir;
(event) interponerse; (time) transcurrir
interview ['ɪntəvjuː] n entrevista
▷ vt entrevistarse con; **interviewer** n

entrevistador(a) m/f
intimate [adj 'ɪntɪmɪt, vb 'ɪntɪmeɪt]
adj íntimo; (friendship) estrecho;
(knowledge) profundo ▷ vt dar a
entender
intimidate [ɪn'tɪmɪdeɪt] vt
intimidar, amedrentar
intimidating [ɪn'tɪmɪdeɪtɪŋ] adj
amedrentador, intimidante
into ['ɪntuː] prep en; (towards) a;
(inside) hacia el interior de; **~ 3 pieces/
French** en 3 pedazos/al francés
intolerant [ɪn'tɔlərənt] adj: **~ (of)**
intolerante (con or para)
intranet ['ɪntrənet] n intranet f
intransitive [ɪn'trænsɪtɪv] adj
intransitivo
intricate ['ɪntrɪkət] adj (design,
pattern) intrincado
intrigue [ɪn'triːg] n intriga ▷ vt
fascinar; **intriguing** adj fascinante
introduce [ɪntrə'djuːs] vt introducir,
meter; (speaker, TV show etc) presentar;
to ~ sb (to sb) presentar a algn (a
algn); **to ~ sb to** (pastime, technique)
introducir a algn a; **introduction**
[-'dʌkʃən] n introducción f; (of person)
presentación f; **introductory**
[-'dʌktərɪ] adj introductorio; (lesson,
offer) de introducción
intrude [ɪn'truːd] vi (person)
entrometerse; **to ~ on** estorbar;
intruder n intruso/a
intuition [ɪntjuː'ɪʃən] n intuición f
inundate ['ɪnʌndeɪt] vt: **to ~ with**
inundar de
invade [ɪn'veɪd] vt invadir
invalid [n 'ɪnvəlɪd, adj ɪn'vælɪd] n
(Med) minusválido/a ▷ adj (not valid)
inválido, nulo
invaluable [ɪn'væljuəbl] adj
inestimable
invariably [ɪn'vɛərɪəblɪ] adv sin
excepción, siempre; **she is ~ late**
siempre llega tarde
invasion [ɪn'veɪʒən] n invasión f
invent [ɪn'vent] vt inventar;
invention [ɪn'venʃən] n invento;

(lie) ficción f, mentira; **inventor** n inventor(a) m/f

inventory ['ɪnvəntrɪ] n inventario

inverted commas [ɪn'vɜːtɪd-] *(BRIT)* npl comillas fpl

invest [ɪn'vest] vt invertir ▷ vi: **to ~ in** *(company etc)* invertir dinero en; *(fig: sth useful)* comprar

investigate [ɪn'vestɪgeɪt] vt investigar; **investigation** [-'geɪʃən] n investigación f, pesquisa

investigator [ɪn'vestɪgeɪtə*] n investigador(a) m/f; **private ~** investigador(a) m/f privado/a

investment [ɪn'vestmənt] n inversión f

investor [ɪn'vestə*] n inversionista mf

invisible [ɪn'vɪzɪbl] adj invisible

invitation [ɪnvɪ'teɪʃən] n invitación f

invite [ɪn'vaɪt] vt invitar; *(opinions etc)* solicitar, pedir; **inviting** adj atractivo; *(food)* apetitoso

invoice ['ɪnvɔɪs] n factura ▷ vt facturar

involve [ɪn'vɒlv] vt suponer, implicar; tener que ver con; *(concern, affect)* corresponder; **to ~ sb (in sth)** comprometer a algn (con algo); **involved** adj complicado; **to be involved in** *(take part)* tomar parte en; *(be engrossed)* estar muy metido en; **involvement** n participación f; dedicación f

inward ['ɪnwəd] adj *(movement)* interior, interno; *(thought, feeling)* íntimo; **inward(s)** adv hacia dentro

iPod ® ['aɪpɒd] n iPod ® m

IQ n abbr (= *intelligence quotient*) cociente m intelectual

IRA n abbr (= *Irish Republican Army*) IRA m

Iran [ɪ'rɑːn] n Irán m; **Iranian** [ɪ'reɪnɪən] adj, n iraní mf

Iraq [ɪ'rɑːk] n Iraq; **Iraqi** adj, n iraquí mf

Ireland ['aɪələnd] n Irlanda

iris ['aɪrɪs] (pl **~es**) n *(Anat)* iris m;

(Bot) lirio

Irish ['aɪrɪʃ] adj irlandés/esa ▷ npl: **the ~** los irlandeses; **Irishman** *(irreg)* n irlandés m; **Irishwoman** *(irreg)* n irlandésa

iron ['aɪən] n hierro; *(for clothes)* plancha ▷ cpd de hierro ▷ vt *(clothes)* planchar

ironic(al) [aɪ'rɒnɪk(l)] adj irónico; **ironically** adv irónicamente

ironing ['aɪənɪŋ] n *(activity)* planchado; *(clothes: ironed)* ropa planchada; *(: to be ironed)* ropa por planchar; **ironing board** n tabla de planchar

irony ['aɪrənɪ] n ironía

irrational [ɪ'ræʃənl] adj irracional

irregular [ɪ'regjulə*] adj irregular; *(surface)* desigual; *(action, event)* anómalo; *(behaviour)* poco ortodoxo

irrelevant [ɪ'reləvənt] adj fuera de lugar, inoportuno

irresistible [ɪrɪ'zɪstɪbl] adj irresistible

irresponsible [ɪrɪ'spɒnsɪbl] adj *(act)* irresponsable; *(person)* poco serio

irrigation [ɪrɪ'geɪʃən] n riego

irritable ['ɪrɪtəbl] adj *(person)* de mal humor

irritate ['ɪrɪteɪt] vt fastidiar; *(Med)* picar; **irritating** adj fastidioso; **irritation** [-'teɪʃən] n fastidio; enfado; picazón f

IRS *(US)* n abbr = **Internal Revenue Service**

is [ɪz] vb see **be**

ISDN n abbr (= *Integrated Services Digital Network)* RDSI f

Islam ['ɪzlɑːm] n Islam m; **Islamic** [ɪz'læmɪk] adj islámico

island ['aɪlənd] n isla; **islander** n isleño/a

isle [aɪl] n isla

isn't ['ɪznt] = **is not**

isolated ['aɪsəleɪtɪd] adj aislado

isolation [aɪsə'leɪʃən] n aislamiento

ISP n abbr = **Internet Service Provider**

Israel ['ɪzreɪl] n Israel m; **Israeli**

[ɪz'reɪlɪ] *adj, n* israelí *mf*

issue ['ɪsjuː] *n (problem, subject)*
cuestión f; *(outcome)* resultado; *(of
banknotes etc)* emisión f; *(of newspaper
etc)* edición f ▷ *vt (rations, equipment)*
distribuir, repartir; *(orders)* dar;
(certificate, passport) expedir; *(decree)*
promulgar; *(magazine)* publicar;
(cheques) extender; *(banknotes, stamps)*
emitir; **at ~** en cuestión; **to take ~
with sb (over)** estar en desacuerdo
con algn (sobre); **to make an ~ of sth**
hacer una cuestión de algo

IT *n abbr* = **information technology**

○ **KEYWORD**

it [ɪt] *pron* 1 *(specific subject: not generally
translated)* él (ella); *(: direct object)* lo, la;
(: indirect object) le; *(after prep)* él (ella);
(abstract concept) ello; **it's on the table**
está en la mesa; **I can't find it** no lo (or
la) encuentro; **give it to me** dámelo
(or dámela); **I spoke to him about
it** le hablé del asunto; **what did you
learn from it?** ¿qué aprendiste de él (or
ella)?; **did you go to it?** *(party, concert
etc)* ¿fuiste?
2 *(impersonal)*: **it's raining** llueve, está
lloviendo; **it's 6 o'clock/the 10th of
August** son las 6/es el 10 de agosto;
how far is it? – **it's 10 miles/2 hours
on the train** ¿a qué distancia está? – a
10 millas/2 horas en tren; **who is it?**
– **it's me** ¿quién es? – soy yo

Italian [ɪ'tæljən] *adj* italiano ▷ *n*
italiano/a; *(Ling)* italiano
italics [ɪ'tælɪks] *npl* cursiva
Italy ['ɪtəlɪ] *n* Italia
itch [ɪtʃ] *n* picazón f ▷ *vi (part of body)*
picar; **to ~ to do sth** rabiar por hacer
algo; **itchy** *adj*: **my hand is itchy** me
pica la mano
it'd ['ɪtd] = **it would; it had**
item ['aɪtəm] *n* artículo; *(on agenda)*
asunto (a tratar); *(also:* **news ~**) noticia
itinerary [aɪ'tɪnərərɪ] *n* itinerario

it'll ['ɪtl] = **it will; it shall**
its [ɪts] *adj* su; sus *pl*
it's [ɪts] = **it is; it has**
itself [ɪt'sɛlf] *pron (reflexive)* sí mismo/
a; *(emphatic)* él mismo (ella misma)
ITV *n abbr* (BRIT: = *Independent
Television)* cadena de televisión comercial
independiente del Estado
I've [aɪv] = **I have**
ivory ['aɪvərɪ] *n* marfil *m*
ivy ['aɪvɪ] *n (Bot)* hiedra

jab [dʒæb] vt: **to ~ sth into sth** clavar algo en algo ▷ n (inf: Med) pinchazo
jack [dʒæk] n (Aut) gato; (Cards) sota
jacket ['dʒækɪt] n chaqueta, americana (SP), saco (LAM); (of book) sobrecubierta; **jacket potato** n patata asada (con piel)
jackpot ['dʒækpɒt] n premio gordo
Jacuzzi® [dʒə'ku:zɪ] n jacuzzi® m
jagged ['dʒægɪd] adj dentado
jail [dʒeɪl] n cárcel f ▷ vt encarcelar; **jail sentence** n pena f de cárcel
jam [dʒæm] n mermelada; (also: **traffic ~**) embotellamiento; (inf: difficulty) apuro ▷ vt (passage etc) obstruir; (mechanism, drawer etc) atascar; (Radio) interferir ▷ vi atascarse, trabarse; **to ~ sth into sth** meter algo a la fuerza en algo
Jamaica [dʒə'meɪkə] n Jamaica
jammed [dʒæmd] adj atascado
Jan abbr (= January) ene
janitor ['dʒænɪtə*] n (caretaker) portero, conserje m
January ['dʒænjuərɪ] n enero

Japan [dʒə'pæn] n (el) Japón;
Japanese [dʒæpə'ni:z] adj japonés/esa ▷ n inv japonés/esa m/f; (Ling) japonés m
jar [dʒɑ:*] n tarro, bote m ▷ vi (sound) chirriar; (colours) desentonar
jargon ['dʒɑ:gən] n jerga
javelin ['dʒævlɪn] n jabalina
jaw [dʒɔ:] n mandíbula
jazz [dʒæz] n jazz m
jealous ['dʒeləs] adj celoso; (envious) envidioso; **jealousy** n celos mpl; envidia
jeans [dʒi:nz] npl vaqueros mpl, tejanos mpl
Jello® ['dʒeləu] (US) n gelatina
jelly ['dʒelɪ] n (jam) jalea; (dessert etc) gelatina; **jellyfish** n inv medusa, aguaviva (RPL)
jeopardize ['dʒepədaɪz] vt arriesgar, poner en peligro
jerk [dʒɜ:k] n (jolt) sacudida; (wrench) tirón m; (inf) imbécil mf ▷ vt tirar bruscamente de ▷ vi (vehicle) traquetear
jersey ['dʒɜ:zɪ] n Jersey m
jersey ['dʒɜ:zɪ] n Jersey m; (fabric) (tejido de) punto
Jesus ['dʒi:zəs] n Jesús m
jet [dʒet] n (of gas, liquid) chorro; (Aviat) avión m a reacción; **jet lag** n desorientación f después de un largo vuelo; **jet-ski** vi practicar el motociclismo acuático
jetty ['dʒetɪ] n muelle m, embarcadero
Jew [dʒu:] n judío/a
jewel ['dʒu:əl] n joya; (in watch) rubí m; **jeweller** (US **jeweler**) n joyero/a; **jeweller's (shop)** (US **jewelry store**) n joyería; **jewellery** (US **jewelry**) n joyas fpl, alhajas fpl
Jewish ['dʒu:ɪʃ] adj judío
jigsaw ['dʒɪgsɔ:] n (also: **~ puzzle**) rompecabezas m inv, puzle m
job [dʒɒb] n (task) tarea; (post) empleo; **it's not my ~** no me incumbe a mí; **it's a good ~ that ...** menos mal que

...; **just the ~!** ¡estupendo!; **job centre** (BRIT) n oficina estatal de colocaciones; **jobless** adj sin trabajo

jockey ['dʒɔkɪ] n jockey mf ▷ vi: **to ~ for position** maniobrar para conseguir una posición

jog [dʒɔg] vt empujar (ligeramente) ▷ vi (run) hacer footing; **to ~ sb's memory** refrescar la memoria a algn; **jogging** n footing m

join [dʒɔɪn] vt (things) juntar, unir; (club) hacerse socio de; (Pol: party) afiliarse a; (queue) ponerse en; (meet: people) reunirse con ▷ vi (roads) juntarse; (rivers) confluir ▷ n juntura; **join in** vi tomar parte, participar ▷ vt fus reunarse parte or participar en; **join up** vi reunirse; (Mil) alistarse

joiner ['dʒɔɪnə*] (BRIT) n carpintero/a

joint [dʒɔɪnt] n (Tech) junta, unión f; (Anat) articulación f, (BRIT Culin) pieza de carne (para asar); (inf: place) tugurio; (: of cannabis) porro ▷ adj (common) común; (combined) combinado; **joint account** n (with bank etc) cuenta común; **jointly** adv (gen) en común; (together) conjuntamente

joke [dʒəuk] n chiste m; (also: **practical ~**) broma ▷ vi bromear; **to play a ~ on** gastar una broma a; **joker** n (Cards) comodín m

jolly ['dʒɔlɪ] adj (merry) alegre; (enjoyable) divertido ▷ adv (BRIT: inf) muy, terriblemente

jolt [dʒəult] n (jerk) sacudida; (shock) susto ▷ vt (physically) sacudir; (emotionally) asustar

Jordan ['dʒɔːdən] n (country) Jordania; (river) Jordán m

journal ['dʒəːnl] n (magazine) revista; (diary) periódico, diario; **journalism** n periodismo; **journalist** n periodista mf, reportero/a

journey ['dʒəːnɪ] n viaje m; (distance covered) trayecto

joy [dʒɔɪ] n alegría; **joyrider** n gamberro que roba un coche para dar una vuelta y luego abandonarlo; **joy stick** n

(Aviat) palanca de mando; (Comput) palanca de control

Jr abbr = **junior**

judge [dʒʌdʒ] n juez mf; (fig: expert) perito ▷ vt juzgar; (consider) considerar

judo ['dʒuːdəu] n judo

jug [dʒʌg] n jarra

juggle ['dʒʌgl] vi hacer juegos malabares; **juggler** n malabarista mf

juice [dʒuːs] n zumo (SP), jugo (LAM); **juicy** adj jugoso

Jul abbr (= July) jul

July [dʒuːˈlaɪ] n julio

jumble ['dʒʌmbl] n revoltijo ▷ vt (also: **~ up**) revolver; **jumble sale** (BRIT) n venta de objetos usados con fines benéficos

○
○ JUMBLE SALE
○
○ Los **jumble sales** son unos
○ mercadillos que se organizan con
○ fines benéficos en los locales de
○ un colegio, iglesia u otro centro
○ público. En ellos puede comprarse
○ todo tipo de artículos baratos de
○ segunda mano, sobre todo ropa,
○ juguetes, libros, vajillas o muebles.
○

jumbo ['dʒʌmbəu] n (also: **~ jet**) jumbo

jump [dʒʌmp] vi saltar, dar saltos; (with fear etc) pegar un bote; (increase) aumentar ▷ vt saltar ▷ n salto; aumento; **to ~ the queue** (BRIT) colarse

jumper ['dʒʌmpə*] n (BRIT: pullover) suéter m, jersey m; (us: dress) mandil m

jumper cables (us) npl = **jump leads**

jump leads (BRIT) npl cables mpl puente de batería

Jun. abbr = **junior**

junction ['dʒʌŋkʃən] n (BRIT: of roads) cruce m; (Rail) empalme m

June [dʒuːn] n junio

jungle ['dʒʌŋgl] n selva, jungla

junior ['dʒuːnɪə*] adj (in age) menor, más joven; (brother/sister etc): **seven**

years her ~ siete años menor que ella; *(position)* subalterno ▷ *n* menor *mf*, joven *mf*; **junior high school** (us) *n* centro de educación secundaria; *see also* **high school**; **junior school** (BRIT) *n* escuela primaria

junk [dʒʌŋk] *n (cheap goods)* baratijas *fpl*; *(rubbish)* basura; **junk food** *n* alimentos preparados y envasados de escaso valor nutritivo

junkie ['dʒʌŋkɪ] *(inf)* *n* drogadicto/a, yonqui *mf*

junk mail *n* propaganda de buzón

Jupiter ['dʒuːpɪtə*] *n (Mythology, Astrology)* Júpiter *m*

jurisdiction [dʒuərɪs'dɪkʃən] *n* jurisdicción *f*; **it falls** *or* **comes within/ outside our** ~ es/no es de nuestra competencia

jury ['dʒuərɪ] *n* jurado

just [dʒʌst] *adj* justo ▷ *adv (exactly)* exactamente; *(only)* sólo, solamente; **he's ~ done it/left** acaba de hacerlo/ irse; ~ **right** perfecto; ~ **two o'clock** las dos en punto; **she's ~ as clever as you** (ella) es tan lista como tú; ~ **as well that ...** menos mal que ...; ~ **as he was leaving** en el momento en que se marchaba; ~ **before/enough** justo antes/lo suficiente; ~ **here** aquí mismo; **he ~ missed** ha fallado por poco; ~ **listen to this** escucha esto un momento

justice ['dʒʌstɪs] *n* justicia; *(us: judge)* juez *mf*; **to do ~ to** *(fig)* hacer justicia a

justification [dʒʌstɪfɪ'keɪʃən] *n* justificación *f*

justify ['dʒʌstɪfaɪ] *vt* justificar; *(text)* alinear

jut [dʒʌt] *vi (also:* ~ **out)** sobresalir

juvenile ['dʒuːvənaɪl] *adj (court)* de menores; *(humour, mentality)* infantil ▷ *n* menor *m* de edad

K

K *abbr* (= *one thousand*) mil; (= *kilobyte*) kilobyte *m*, kiloocteto

kangaroo [kæŋgə'ruː] *n* canguro

karaoke [kɑːrə'əʊkɪ] *n* karaoke

karate [kə'rɑːtɪ] *n* karate *m*

kebab [kə'bæb] *n* pincho moruno

keel [kiːl] *n* quilla; **on an even** ~ *(fig)* en equilibrio

keen [kiːn] *adj (interest, desire)* grande, vivo; *(eye, intelligence)* agudo; *(competition)* reñido; *(edge)* afilado; *(eager)* entusiasta; **to be ~ to do** *or* **on doing sth** tener muchas ganas de hacer algo; **to be ~ on sth/sb** interesarse por algo/algn

keep [kiːp] *(pt, pp* **kept)** *vt (preserve, store)* guardar; *(hold back)* quedarse con; *(maintain)* mantener; *(detain)* detener; *(shop)* ser propietario de; *(feed: family etc)* mantener; *(promise)* cumplir; *(chickens, bees etc)* criar; *(accounts)* llevar; *(diary)* escribir; *(prevent)*: **to ~ sb from doing sth** impedir a algn hacer algo ▷ *vi (food)* conservarse; *(remain)* seguir, continuar ▷ *n (of* *castle*) torreón *m*; (*food etc*) comida, subsistencia (*inf*): **for ~s** para siempre; **to ~ doing sth** seguir haciendo algo; **to ~ sb happy** tener a algn contento; **to ~ a place tidy** mantener un lugar limpio; **to ~ sth to o.s.** guardar algo para sí mismo; **to ~ sth (back) from sb** ocultar algo a algn; **to ~ time** (*clock*) mantener la hora exacta; **keep away** *vt*: **to keep sth/sb away from sb** mantener algo/a algn apartado de algn ▷ *vi*: **to keep away (from)** mantenerse apartado (de); **keep back** *vt* (*crowd, tears*) contener; (*money*) quedarse con; (*conceal: information*): **to keep sth back from sb** ocultar algo a algn ▷ *vi* hacerse a un lado; **keep off** *vt* (*dog, person*) mantener a distancia ▷ *vi*: **if the rain keeps off** so no llueve; **keep your hands off!** ¡no toques!; **"keep off the grass"** prohibido pisar el césped"; **keep on** *vi*: **to keep on doing** seguir o continuar haciendo; **to keep on (about sth)** no parar de hablar (de algo); **keep out** *vi* (*stay out*) permanecer fuera; **"keep out"** "prohibida la entrada"; **keep up** *vt* mantener, conservar ▷ *vi* no retrasarse; **to keep up with** (*pace*) ir al paso de; (*level*) mantenerse a la altura de; **keeper** *n* guardián/ana *m/f*; **keeping** *n* (*care*) cuidado; **in keeping with** de acuerdo con

kennel ['kɛnl] *n* perrera; **kennels** *npl* residencia canina

Kenya ['kɛnjə] *n* Kenia

kept [kɛpt] *pt, pp* of **keep**

kerb [kə:b] (*BRIT*) *n* bordillo

kerosene ['kɛrəsiːn] *n* keroseno

ketchup ['kɛtʃəp] *n* salsa de tomate, catsup *m*

kettle ['kɛtl] *n* hervidor *m* de agua

key [kiː] *n* llave *f*; (*Mus*) tono; (*of piano, typewriter*) tecla ▷ *adj* (*issue etc*) clave *inv* ▷ *vt* (*also*: **~ in**) teclear; **keyboard** *n* teclado; **keyhole** *n* ojo (de la cerradura); **keyring** *n* llavero

kg *abbr* (= **kilogram**) kg

khaki ['kɑːkɪ] *n* caqui

kick [kɪk] *vt* dar una patada o un puntapié a; (*inf: habit*) quitarse de ▷ *vi* (*horse*) dar coces ▷ *n* patada; puntapié *m*; (*of animal*) coz *f*; (*thrill*): **he does it for ~s** lo hace por pura diversión; **kick off** *vi* (*Sport*) hacer el saque inicial; **the kick-off is at 10 o'clock** el partido empieza a las diez

kid [kɪd] *n* (*inf: child*) chiquillo/a; (*animal*) cabrito; (*leather*) cabritilla ▷ *vi* (*inf*) bromear

kidnap ['kɪdnæp] *vt* secuestrar; **kidnapping** *n* secuestro

kidney ['kɪdnɪ] *n* riñón *m*; **kidney bean** *n* judía, alubia

kill [kɪl] *vt* matar; (*murder*) asesinar ▷ *n* matanza; **to ~ time** matar el tiempo; **killer** *n* asesino/a; **killing** *n* (*one*) asesinato; (*several*) matanza; **to make a killing** (*fig*) hacer su agosto

kiln [kɪln] *n* horno

kilo ['kiːləʊ] *n* kilo; **kilobyte** *n* (*Comput*) kilobyte *m*, kilocteto; **kilogram(me)** *n* kilo, kilogramo; **kilometre** ['kɪləmiːtə*] (*US* **kilometer**) *n* kilómetro; **kilowatt** *n* kilovatio

kilt [kɪlt] *n* falda escocesa

kin [kɪn] *n see* **next-of-kin**

kind [kaɪnd] *adj* amable, atento ▷ *n* clase *f*, especie *f*; (*species*) género; **in ~** (*Comm*) en especie; **a ~ of** una especie de; **to be two of a ~** ser tal para cual

kindergarten ['kɪndəɡɑːtn] *n* jardín *m* de la infancia

kindly ['kaɪndlɪ] *adj* bondadoso; cariñoso ▷ *adv* bondadosamente, amablemente; **will you ~...** sea usted tan amable de...

kindness ['kaɪndnɪs] *n* (*quality*) bondad *f*, amabilidad *f*; (*act*) favor *m*

king [kɪŋ] *n* rey *m*; **kingdom** *n* reino; **kingfisher** *n* martín *m* pescador; **king-size(d) bed** *n* cama de matrimonio extragrande

kiosk ['kiːɒsk] *n* quiosco; (*BRIT Tel*) cabina

kipper ['kɪpə*] *n* arenque *m* ahumado

kiss [kɪs] n beso ▷ vt besar; **to ~ (each other)** besarse; **kiss of life** n respiración f boca a boca

kit [kɪt] n (equipment) equipo; (tools etc) caja (de) herramientas fpl; (assembly kit) juego de armar

kitchen ['kɪtʃɪn] n cocina

kite [kaɪt] n (toy) cometa

kitten ['kɪtn] n gatito/a

kiwi ['kiːwiː-] n (also: ~ **fruit**) kiwi m

km abbr (= kilometre) km

km/h abbr (= kilometres per hour) km/h

knack [næk] n: **to have the ~ of doing sth** tener el don de hacer algo

knee [niː] n rodilla; **kneecap** n rótula

kneel [niːl] (pt, pp **knelt**) vi (also: ~ **down**) arrodillarse

knelt [nɛlt] pt, pp of **kneel**

knew [njuː] pt of **know**

knickers ['nɪkəz] (BRIT) npl bragas fpl

knife [naɪf] (pl **knives**) n cuchillo ▷ vt acuchillar

knight [naɪt] n caballero; (Chess) caballo

knit [nɪt] vt tejer, tricotar ▷ vi hacer punto, tricotar; (bones) soldarse; **to ~ one's brows** fruncir el ceño; **knitting** n labor f de punto; **knitting needle** n aguja de hacer punto; **knitwear** n prendas fpl de punto

knives [naɪvz] npl of **knife**

knob [nɔb] n (of door) tirador m; (of stick) puño; (on radio, TV) botón m

knock [nɔk] vt (strike) golpear; (bump into) chocar contra; (inf) criticar ▷ n golpe m; (on door) llamada; **to ~ at/on** llamar a ▷ n golpe m; (on door) llamada; **knock down** vt atropellar; **knock off** (inf) vi (finish) salir del trabajo ▷ vt (from price) descontar; (inf: steal) birlar; **knock out** vt dejar sin sentido; (Boxing) poner fuera de combate, dejar K.O.; (in competition) eliminar; **knock over** vt (object) tirar; (person) atropellar; **knockout** n (Boxing) K.O. m, knockout m ▷ cpd (competition etc) eliminatorio

knot [nɔt] n nudo ▷ vt anudar

know [nəu] (pt **knew**, pp **known**)

vt (facts) saber; (be acquainted with) conocer; (recognize) reconocer, conocer; **to ~ how to swim** saber nadar; **to ~ about** or **of sb/sth** saber de algn/algo; **know-all** n sabelotodo mf; **know-how** n conocimientos mpl; **knowing** adj (look) de complicidad; **knowingly** adv (purposely) adrede; (smile, look) con complicidad; **know-it-all** (us) n = **know-all**

knowledge ['nɔlɪdʒ] n conocimiento; (learning) saber m, conocimientos mpl; **knowledgeable** adj entendido

known [nəun] pp of **know** ▷ adj (thief, facts) conocido; (expert) reconocido

knuckle ['nʌkl] n nudillo

koala [kəu'aːlə] n (also: ~ **bear**) koala m

Koran [kɔ'raːn] n Corán m

Korea [kə'riə] n Corea; **Korean** adj, n coreano/a m/f

kosher ['kəuʃə*] adj autorizado por la ley judía

Kosovar ['kɔsəva*], **Kosovan** ['kɔːsəvən] adj kosovar

Kosovo ['kɔsəvəu] n Kosovo

Kremlin ['krɛmlɪn] n: **the ~** el Kremlin

Kuwait [ku'weɪt] n Kuwait m

k

for ~ of por falta de; **to be ~ing** faltar, no haber; **to be ~ing in sth** faltarle a algn algo

lacquer ['lækə*] n laca

lacy ['leɪsɪ] adj (of lace) de encaje; (like lace) como de encaje

lad [læd] n muchacho, chico

ladder ['lædə*] n escalera (de mano); (BRIT: in tights) carrera

ladle ['leɪdl] n cucharón m

lady ['leɪdɪ] n señora; (dignified, graceful) dama; **"ladies and gentlemen ..."** "señoras y caballeros ..."; **young ~** señorita; **the ladies' (room)** los servicios de señoras; **ladybird** (us **ladybug**) n mariquita

lag [læg] n retraso ▷ vi (also: ~ **behind**) retrasarse, quedarse atrás ▷ vt (pipes) revestir

lager ['lɑːgə*] n cerveza (rubia)

lagoon [lə'guːn] n laguna

laid [leɪd] pt, pp of **lay**; **laid back** (inf) adj relajado

lain [leɪn] pp of **lie**

lake [leɪk] n lago

lamb [læm] n cordero; (meat) (carne f de) cordero

lame [leɪm] adj cojo; (excuse) poco convincente

lament [lə'mɛnt] n quejo ▷ vt lamentarse de

lamp [læmp] n lámpara; **lamppost** (BRIT) n (poste m de) farol m; **lampshade** n pantalla

land [lænd] n tierra; (country) país m; (piece of land) terreno; (estate) tierras fpl, finca ▷ vi (from ship) desembarcar; (Aviat) aterrizar; (fig: fall) caer, terminar ▷ vt (passengers, goods) desembarcar; **to ~ sb with sth** (inf) hacer cargar a algn con algo; **landing** n aterrizaje m; (of staircase) rellano; **landing card** n tarjeta de desembarque; **landlady** n (of rented house, pub etc) dueña; **landlord** n propietario; (of pub etc) patrón m; **landmark** n lugar m conocido; **to be a landmark** (fig) marcar un hito histórico; **landowner** n

---

L (BRIT) abbr = **learner driver**

l. abbr (= litre) l

lab [læb] n abbr = **laboratory**

label ['leɪbl] n etiqueta ▷ vt poner etiqueta a

labor etc ['leɪbə*] (US) = **labour** etc

laboratory [lə'bɒrətərɪ] n laboratorio

Labor Day (US) n día m de los trabajadores (primer lunes de septiembre)

labor union (US) n sindicato

labour ['leɪbə*] (US **labor**) n (hard work) trabajo; (labour force) mano f de obra; (Med): **to be in ~** estar de parto ▷ vi: **to ~ (at sth)** trabajar (en algo) ▷ vt: **to ~ a point** insistir en un punto; **L~, the L~ party** (BRIT) el partido laborista, los laboristas mpl; **labourer** n peón m; **farm labourer** peón m; (day labourer) jornalero

lace [leɪs] n encaje m; (of shoe etc) cordón m ▷ vt (shoes: also: ~ **up**) atarse (los zapatos)

lack [læk] n (absence) falta ▷ vt faltarle a algn, carecer de; **through** or

terrateniente *mf*; **landscape** *n* paisaje *m*; **landslide** *n* (Geo) corrimiento de tierras; (fig: Pol) victoria arrolladora

lane [leɪn] *n* (in country) camino; (Aut) carril *m*; (in race) calle *f*

language ['læŋgwɪdʒ] *n* lenguaje *m*; (national tongue) idioma *m*, lengua; **bad ~** palabrotas *fpl*; **language laboratory** *n* laboratorio de idiomas; **language school** *n* academia de idiomas

lantern ['læntn] *n* linterna, farol *m*

lap [læp] *n* (of track) vuelta; (of body) regazo ⊳ *vt* (also: **~ up**) beber a lengüetadas ⊳ *vi* (waves) chapotear; **to sit on sb's ~** sentarse en las rodillas de algn

lapel [lə'pel] *n* solapa

lapse [læps] *n* fallo; (moral) desliz *m*; (of time) intervalo ⊳ *vi* (expire) caducar; (time) pasar, transcurrir; **to ~ into bad habits** caer en malos hábitos

laptop (computer) ['læptɒp-] *n* (ordenador *m*) portátil *m*

lard [lɑːd] *n* manteca (de cerdo)

larder ['lɑːdə*] *n* despensa

large [lɑːdʒ] *adj* grande; **at ~** (free) en libertad; (generally) en general

⬛ Be careful not to translate **large** by the Spanish word *largo*.

largely *adv* (mostly) en su mayor parte; (introducing reason) en gran parte; **large-scale** *adj* (map) en gran escala; (fig) importante

lark [lɑːk] *n* (bird) alondra; (joke) broma

laryngitis [lærɪn'dʒaɪtɪs] *n* laringitis *f*

lasagne [lə'zænjə] *n* lasaña

laser ['leɪzə*] *n* láser *m*; **laser printer** *n* impresora (por) láser

lash [læʃ] *n* latigazo; (also: **eye~**) pestaña ⊳ *vt* azotar; (tie): **to ~ to/ together** atar a/atar; **lash out** *vi*: **to lash out (at sb)** (hit) arremeter (contra algn); **to lash out against sb** lanzar invectivas contra algn

lass [læs] (BRIT) *n* chica

last [lɑːst] *adj* último; (end: of series

etc) final ⊳ *adv* (most recently) la última vez; (finally) por último ⊳ *vi* durar; (continue) continuar, seguir; **~ night** anoche; **~ week** la semana pasada; **at ~** por fin; **~ but one** penúltimo; **lastly** *adv* por último, finalmente; **last-minute** *adj* de última hora

latch [lætʃ] *n* pestillo; **latch onto** *vt fus* (person, group) pegarse a; (idea) agarrarse a

late [leɪt] *adj* (far on: in time, process etc) al final de; (not on time) tarde, atrasado; (dead) fallecido ⊳ *adv* tarde; (behind time, schedule) con retraso; **of ~** últimamente; **~ at night** a última hora de la noche; **in ~ May** hacia fines de mayo; **the ~ Mr X** el difunto Sr X; **latecomer** *n* recién llegado/a; **lately** *adv* últimamente; **later** *adj* (date etc) posterior; (version etc) más reciente ⊳ *adv* más tarde, después; **latest** ['leɪtɪst] *adj* último; **at the latest** a más tardar

lather ['lɑːðə*] *n* espuma (de jabón) ⊳ *vt* enjabonar

Latin ['lætɪn] *n* latín *m* ⊳ *adj* latino; **Latin America** *n* América latina; **Latin American** *adj*, *n* latinoamericano/a *m/f*

latitude ['lætɪtjuːd] *n* latitud *f*; (fig) libertad *f*

latter ['lætə*] *adj* último; (of two) segundo ⊳ *n*: **the ~** el último, éste

laugh [lɑːf] *n* risa ⊳ *vi* reír(se); **(to do sth) for a ~** (hacer algo) en broma; **laugh at** *vt fus* reírse de; **laughter** *n* risa

launch [lɔːntʃ] *n* lanzamiento; (boat) lancha *f*; (ship) botar; (rocket etc) lanzar; (fig) comenzar; **launch into** *vt fus* lanzarse a

launder ['lɔːndə*] *vt* lavar

Launderette® [lɔːn'drɛt] (BRIT) *n* lavandería (automática)

Laundromat® ['lɔːndrəmæt] (US) *n* = **Launderette**

laundry ['lɔːndrɪ] *n* (dirty) ropa sucia; (clean) colada; (room) lavadero

lava ['lɑːvə] n lava

lavatory ['lævətəri] n váter m

lavender ['lævəndə*] n lavanda

lavish ['lævɪʃ] adj (amount) abundante; (person): **~ with** pródigo en ▷ vt: **to ~ sth on sb** colmar a algn de algo

law [lɔː] n ley f; (Scol) derecho; (a rule) regla; (professions connected with law) jurisprudencia; **lawful** adj legítimo, lícito; **lawless** adj (action) criminal

lawn [lɔːn] n césped m; **lawnmower** n cortacésped m

lawsuit ['lɔːsuːt] n pleito

lawyer ['lɔːjə*] n abogado/a; (for sales, wills etc) notario/a

lax [læks] adj laxo

laxative ['læksətɪv] n laxante m

lay [leɪ] (pt, pp **laid**) pt of **lie** ▷ adj laico; (not expert) lego ▷ vt (place) colocar; (eggs, table) poner; (cable) tender; (carpet) extender; **lay down** vt (pen etc) dejar; (rules etc) establecer; **to lay down the law** (pej) imponer las normas; **lay off** vt (workers) despedir; **lay on** vt (meal, facilities) proveer; **lay out** vt (spread out) disponer, exponer; **lay-by** n (BRIT Aut) área de aparcamiento

layer ['leɪə*] n capa

layman ['leɪmən] (irreg) n lego

layout ['leɪaut] n (design) plan m, trazado; (Press) composición f

lazy ['leɪzɪ] adj perezoso, vago; (movement) lento

lb. abbr = **pound** (weight)

lead¹ [liːd] (pt, pp **led**) n (front position) delantera; (clue) pista; (Elec) cable m; (for dog) correa; (Theatre) papel m principal ▷ vt (walk etc in front) ira la cabeza de; (guide): **to ~ sb somewhere** conducir a algn a algún sitio; (be leader) dirigir; (start, guide: activity) protagonizar ▷ vi (Sport) ir primero; **to be in the ~** (Sport) llevar la delantera; (fig) ira la cabeza; **to ~ the way** llevar la delantera; **lead up to** vt fus (events)

conducir a; (in conversation) preparar el terreno para

lead² [lɛd] n (metal) plomo; (in pencil) mina

leader ['liːdə*] n jefe/a m/f, líder mf; (Sport) líder mf; **leadership** n dirección f; (position) mando; (quality) iniciativa

lead-free ['lɛdfriː] adj sin plomo

leading ['liːdɪŋ] adj (main) principal; (first) primero; (front) delantero

lead singer [liːd-] n cantante mf

leaf [liːf] (pl **leaves**) n hoja ▷ vi: **to ~ through** hojear; **to turn over a new ~** reformarse

leaflet ['liːflɪt] n folleto

league [liːg] n sociedad f; (Football) liga; **to be in ~ with** haberse confabulado con

leak [liːk] n (of liquid, gas) escape m, fuga; (in pipe) agujero; (in roof) gotera; (in security) filtración f ▷ vi (shoes, ship) hacer agua; (pipe) tener (un) escape; (roof) gotear; (liquid, gas) escaparse, fugarse; (fig) divulgarse ▷ vt (fig) filtrar

lean [liːn] (pt, pp **~ed** or **~t**) adj (thin) flaco; (meat) magro ▷ vt: **to ~ sth on sth** apoyar algo en algo ▷ vi (slope) inclinarse; **to ~ against** apoyarse contra; **to ~ on** apoyarse en; **lean forward** vi inclinarse hacia adelante; **lean over** vi inclinarse; **leaning** n: **leaning (towards)** inclinación f (hacia)

leant [lɛnt] pt, pp of **lean**

leap [liːp] (pt, pp **~ed** or **~t**) n salto ▷ vi saltar

leapt [lɛpt] pt, pp of **leap**

leap year n año bisiesto

learn [ləːn] (pt, pp **~ed** or **~t**) vt aprender ▷ vi aprender; **to ~ about sth** enterarse de algo; **to ~ to do sth** aprender a hacer algo

learner n (BRIT: also: **learner driver**) principiante mf; **learning** n el saber m, conocimientos mpl

learnt [ləːnt] pp of **learn**

lease [liːs] n arriendo ▷ vt arrendar

leash [liːʃ] n correa

least [liːst] adj: **the ~** (slightest) el menor, el más pequeño; (smallest amount of) mínimo ▷ adv (+ vb) menos; (+ adj): **the ~ expensive** el (la) menos costoso/a; **the ~ possible effort** el menor esfuerzo posible; **at ~** por lo menos, al menos; **you could at ~ have written** por lo menos podías haber escrito; **not in the ~** en absoluto

leather ['leðə*] n cuero

leave [liːv] (pt, pp **left**) vt dejar; (go away from) abandonar; (place etc: permanently) salir de ▷ vi irse; (train etc) salir ▷ n permiso; **to ~ sth to sb** (money etc) legar algo a algn; (responsibility etc) encargar de algo a algn; **to be left** quedar, sobrar; **there's some milk left over** sobra or queda algo de leche; **on ~** de permiso; **leave behind** vt (on purpose) dejar; (accidentally) dejarse; **leave out** vt omitir

leaves [liːvz] npl of **leaf**

Lebanon ['lebənən] n: **the ~** el Líbano

lecture ['lektʃə*] n conferencia; (Scol) clase ▷ vi dar una clase ▷ vt (scold): **to ~ sb on** or **about sth** echar una reprimenda a algn por algo; **to give a ~ on** dar una conferencia sobre; **lecture hall** n sala de conferencias; **lecturer** n conferenciante mf; (Brit: at university) profesor(a) m/f; **lecture theatre** n = **lecture hall**

led [led] pt, pp of **lead**[1]

ledge [ledʒ] n repisa; (of window) alféizar m; (of mountain) saliente m

leek [liːk] n puerro

left [left] pt, pp of **leave** ▷ adj izquierdo; (remaining): **there are two ~** quedan dos ▷ n izquierda ▷ adv a la izquierda; **on** or **to the ~** a la izquierda; **the L~** (Pol) la izquierda; **left-hand** adj: **the left-hand side** la izquierda; **left-hand drive** adj: **a left-hand drive car** un coche con el volante a la izquierda; **left-handed** adj zurdo; **left-luggage locker** n (Brit) consigna f automática; **left-luggage**

(office) (Brit) n consigna; **left-overs** npl sobras fpl; **left-wing** adj (Pol) de izquierdas, izquierdista

leg [leg] n pierna; (of animal, chair) pata; (trouser leg) pernera; (Culin: of lamb) pierna; (: of chicken) pata; (of journey) etapa

legacy ['legəsi] n herencia

legal ['liːgl] adj (permitted by law) lícito; (of law) legal; **legal holiday** (US) n fiesta oficial; **legalize** vt legalizar; **legally** adv legalmente

legend ['ledʒənd] n (also fig: person) leyenda; **legendary** ['-əri] adj legendario

leggings ['legiŋz] npl mallas fpl, leggins mpl

legible ['ledʒəbl] adj legible

legislation [ledʒɪs'leɪʃən] n legislación f

legislative ['ledʒɪslətɪv] adj legislativo

legitimate [lɪ'dʒɪtɪmət] adj legítimo

leisure ['leʒə*] n ocio, tiempo libre; **at ~** con tranquilidad; **leisure centre** (Brit) n centro de recreo; **leisurely** adj sin prisa; lento

lemon ['lemən] n limón m; **lemonade** n (fizzy) gaseosa; **lemon tea** n té m con limón

lend [lend] (pt, pp **lent**) vt: **to ~ sth to sb** prestar algo a algn

length [leŋθ] n (size) largo, longitud f; (distance): **the ~ of** todo lo largo de; (of swimming pool, cloth) largo; (of wood, string) trozo; (amount of time) duración f; **at ~** (at last) por fin, finalmente; (lengthily) largamente; **lengthen** vt alargar ▷ vi alargarse; **lengthways** adv a lo largo; **lengthy** adj largo, extenso

lens [lenz] n (of spectacles) lente f; (of camera) objetivo

Lent [lent] n Cuaresma

lent [lent] pt, pp of **lend**

lentil ['lentl] n lenteja

Leo ['liːəu] n Leo

leopard ['lepəd] n leopardo

leotard ['li:əta:d] n mallas fpl

leprosy ['leprəsɪ] n lepra

lesbian ['lezbɪən] n lesbiana

less [les] adj (in size, degree etc) menor; (in quality) menos ▷ pron, adv menos ▷ prep: ~ **tax/10% discount** menos impuestos/el 10 por ciento de descuento; ~ **than half** menos de la mitad; ~ **than ever** menos que nunca; ~ **and** ~ cada vez menos; **the** ~ **he works** ... cuanto menos trabaja …; **lessen** vi disminuir, reducirse ▷ vt disminuir, reducir; **lesser** ['lesə*] adj menor; **to a lesser extent** en menor grado

lesson ['lesn] n clase f; (warning) lección f

let [let] (pt, pp ~) vt (allow) dejar, permitir; (BRIT: lease) alquilar; **to** ~ **sb do sth** dejar que algn haga algo; **to** ~ **sb know sth** comunicar algo a algn; ~**'s go** ¡vamos!; ~ **him come** que venga; **"to** ~**"** "se alquila"; **let down** vt (tyre) desinflar; (disappoint) defraudar; **let in** vt dejar entrar; (visitor etc) hacer pasar; **let off** vt (culprit) dejar escapar; (gun) disparar; (bomb) accionar; (firework) hacer estallar; **let out** vt dejar salir; (sound) soltar

lethal ['li:θl] adj (weapon) mortífero; (poison, wound) mortal

letter ['letə*] n (of alphabet) letra; (correspondence) carta; **letterbox** (BRIT) n buzón m

lettuce ['letɪs] n lechuga

leukaemia [lu:'ki:mɪə] (US **leukemia**) n leucemia

level ['levl] adj (flat) llano ▷ adv: **to draw** ~ **with** llegar a la altura de ▷ n nivel m; (height) altura ▷ vt nivelar; allanar; (destroy: building) derribar; (: forest) arrasar; **to be** ~ **with** estar a nivel de; **A** ~**s** (BRIT) = exámenes mpl de bachillerato superior, B.U.P.; **AS** ~ (BRIT) asignatura aprobada entre los "GCSEs" y los "A levels"; **on the** ~ (fig: honest) serio; **level crossing** (BRIT) n paso a nivel

lever ['li:və*] n (also fig) palanca ▷ vt: **to** ~ **up** levantar con palanca; **leverage** n (using bar etc) apalancamiento; (fig: influence) influencia

levy ['levɪ] n impuesto ▷ vt exigir, recaudar

liability [laɪə'bɪlɪtɪ] n (pej: person, thing) estorbo, lastre m; (Jur: responsibility) responsabilidad f

liable ['laɪəbl] adj (subject): ~ **to** sujeto a; (responsible): ~ **for** responsable de; (likely): ~ **to do** propenso a hacer

liaise [lɪ'eɪz] vi: **to** ~ **with** enlazar con

liar ['laɪə*] n mentiroso/a

liberal ['lɪbərəl] adj liberal; (offer, amount etc) generoso; **Liberal Democrat** (BRIT) n demócrata m/f liberal

liberate ['lɪbəreɪt] vt (people: from poverty etc) librar; (prisoner) libertar; (country) liberar

liberation [lɪbə'reɪʃən] n liberación f

liberty ['lɪbətɪ] n libertad f; **to be a** ~ (criminal) estar en libertad; **to be at** ~ **to do** estar libre para hacer; **to take the** ~ **of doing sth** tomarse la libertad de hacer algo

Libra ['li:brə] n Libra

librarian [laɪ'brɛərɪən] n bibliotecario/a

library ['laɪbrərɪ] n biblioteca

   Be careful not to translate **library** by the Spanish word librería.

Libya ['lɪbɪə] n Libia

lice [laɪs] npl of **louse**

licence ['laɪsəns] (US **license**) n licencia; (permit) permiso; (also: **driving** ~) carnet m de conducir (SP), licencia de manejo (LAM)

license ['laɪsəns] n (US) = **licence** ▷ vt autorizar, dar permiso a; **licensed** adj (for alcohol) autorizado para vender bebidas alcohólicas; (car) matriculado; **license plate** (US) n placa (de matrícula); **licensing hours** (BRIT) npl horas durante las cuales se permite la venta y consumo de alcohol (en un bar etc)

lick [lɪk] vt lamer; (inf: defeat) dar una paliza a; **to ~ one's lips** relamerse

lid [lɪd] n (of box, case) tapa; (of pan) tapadera

lie [laɪ] (pt **lay**, pp **lain**) vi (rest) estar echado, estar acostado; (of object: be situated) estar, encontrarse; (tell lies: pt, pp **lied**) mentir ▷ n mentira; **to ~ low** (fig) mantenerse a escondidas; **lie about** or **around** vi (things) estar tirado; (BRIT: people) estar tumbado; **lie down** vi echarse, tumbarse

Liechtenstein ['lɪktənstaɪn] n Liechtenstein m

lie-in ['laɪɪn] (BRIT) n: **to have a ~** quedarse en la cama

lieutenant [lefˈtenənt, US luːˈtenənt] n (Mil) teniente mf

life [laɪf] (pl **lives**) n vida; **to come to ~** animarse; **life assurance** (BRIT) n seguro de vida; **lifeboat** n lancha de socorro; **lifeguard** n vigilante mf, socorrista mf; **life insurance** n = **life assurance**; **life jacket** n chaleco salvavidas; **lifelike** adj (model etc): (realistic) realista; **life preserver** (US) n cinturón m/chaleco salvavidas; **life sentence** n cadena perpetua; **lifestyle** n estilo de vida; **lifetime** n (of person) vida; (of thing) período de vida

lift [lɪft] vt levantar; (end: ban, rule) levantar, suprimir ▷ vi (fog) disiparse ▷ n (BRIT: machine) ascensor m; **to give sb a ~** (BRIT) llevar a algn en el coche; **lift up** vt levantar; **lift-off** n despegue m

light [laɪt] (pt, pp **~ed** or **lit**) n luz f; (lamp) luz f, lámpara; (Aut) faro; (for cigarette etc): **have you got a ~?** ¿tienes fuego? ▷ vt (candle, cigarette, fire) encender (SP), prender (LAM); (room) alumbrar ▷ adj (colour) claro; (not heavy, also fig) ligero; (room) con mucha luz; (gentle, graceful) ágil; **lights** npl (traffic lights) semáforos mpl; **to come to ~** salir a luz; **in the ~ of** (new evidence etc) a la luz de; **light up** vi

(smoke) encender un cigarrillo; (face) iluminarse ▷ vt (illuminate) iluminar, alumbrar; (set fire to) encender; **light bulb** n bombilla (SP), foco (MEX), bujía (CAM), bombita (RPL); **lighten** vt (make less heavy) aligerar; **lighter** n (also: **cigarette lighter**) encendedor m, mechero (SP); **light-hearted** adj (person) alegre; (remark etc) divertido; **lighthouse** n faro; **lighting** n (system) alumbrado; **lightly** adv ligeramente; (not seriously) con poca seriedad; **to get off lightly** ser castigado con poca severidad

lightning ['laɪtnɪŋ] n relámpago, rayo

lightweight ['laɪtweɪt] adj (suit) ligero ▷ n (Boxing) peso ligero

like [laɪk] vt gustarle a algn ▷ prep como ▷ adj parecido, semejante ▷ n: **and the ~** y otros por el estilo; **his ~s and dislikes** sus gustos y aversiones; **I would ~, I'd ~** me gustaría; (for purchase) quisiera; **would you ~ a coffee?** ¿te apetece un café?; **I ~ swimming** me gusta nadar; **she ~s apples** le gustan las manzanas; **to be or look ~ sb/sth** parecerse a algn/algo; **what does it look/taste/sound ~?** ¿cómo es/a qué sabe/cómo suena?; **that's just ~ him** es muy de él, es característico de él; **do it ~ this** hazlo así; **it is nothing ~ ...** no tiene parecido alguno con ...; **likeable** adj simpático, agradable

likelihood ['laɪklɪhʊd] n probabilidad f

likely ['laɪklɪ] adj probable; **he's ~ to leave** es probable que se vaya; **not ~!** ¡ni hablar!

likewise ['laɪkwaɪz] adv igualmente; **to do ~** hacer lo mismo

liking ['laɪkɪŋ] n: ~ (**for**) (person) cariño (a); (thing) afición (a); **to be to sb's ~** ser del gusto de algn

lilac ['laɪlək] n (tree) lila; (flower) lila

Lilo® ['laɪləʊ] n colchoneta inflable

lily ['lɪlɪ] n lirio, azucena; **~ of the**

valley lirio de los valles

limb [lɪm] n miembro m

limbo ['lɪmbəʊ] n: **to be in ~** (fig) quedar a la expectativa

lime [laɪm] n (tree) limero; (fruit) lima; (Geo) cal f

limelight ['laɪmlaɪt] n: **to be in the ~** (fig) ser el centro de atención

limestone ['laɪmstəʊn] n piedra caliza

limit ['lɪmɪt] n límite m ⊳ vt limitar; **limited** adj limitado; **to be limited to** limitarse a

limousine ['lɪməziːn] n limusina

limp [lɪmp] n: **to have a ~** tener cojera ⊳ vi cojear ⊳ adj flojo; (material) fláccido

line [laɪn] n línea; (rope) cuerda; (for fishing) sedal m; (wire) hilo; (row, series) fila, hilera; (of writing) línea, renglón m, línea; (of song) verso; (on face) arruga; (Rail) vía ⊳ vt (road etc) llenar; (Sewing) forrar; **to ~ the streets** llenar las aceras; **in ~ with** alineado con; (according to) de acuerdo con; **line up** vi hacer cola ⊳ vt alinear; (prepare) preparar; organizar

linear ['lɪnɪə*] adj lineal

linen ['lɪnɪn] n ropa blanca; (cloth) lino

liner ['laɪnə*] n vapor m de línea, transatlántico; (for bin) bolsa (de basura)

line-up ['laɪnʌp] n (US: queue) cola; (Sport) alineación f

linger ['lɪŋɡə*] vi retrasarse, tardar en marcharse; (smell, tradition) persistir

lingerie ['lænʒəriː] n lencería

linguist ['lɪŋɡwɪst] n lingüista mf; **linguistic** adj lingüístico

lining ['laɪnɪŋ] n forro; (Anat) (membrana) mucosa

link [lɪŋk] n (of a chain) eslabón m; (relationship) relación f, vínculo; (Internet) link m, enlace m ⊳ vt vincular, unir; (associate) **to ~ with** or **to** relacionar con; **links** npl (Golf) campo de golf; **link up** vt acoplar ⊳ vi conectarse

lion ['laɪən] n león m; **lioness** n leona

lip [lɪp] n labio; **lipread** vi leer los labios; **lip salve** n crema protectora para labios; **lipstick** n lápiz m de labios, carmín m

liqueur [lɪ'kjʊə*] n licor m

liquid ['lɪkwɪd] adj, n líquido; **liquidizer** [-aɪzə*] n licuadora

liquor ['lɪkə*] n licor m, bebidas fpl alcohólicas; **liquor store** (US) n bodega, tienda de vinos y bebidas alcohólicas

Lisbon ['lɪzbən] n Lisboa

lisp [lɪsp] n ceceo ⊳ vi cecear

list [lɪst] n lista ⊳ vt (mention) enumerar; (put on a list) poner en una lista

listen ['lɪsn] vi escuchar, oír; **to ~ to sb/sth** escuchar a algn/algo; **listener** n oyente mf; (Radio) radioyente mf

lit [lɪt] pt, pp of **light**

liter ['liːtə*] (US) n = **litre**

literacy ['lɪtərəsɪ] n capacidad f de leer y escribir

literal ['lɪtərl] adj literal; **literally** adv literalmente

literary ['lɪtərərɪ] adj literario

literate ['lɪtərət] adj que sabe leer y escribir; (educated) culto

literature ['lɪtərɪtʃə*] n literatura; (brochures etc) folletos mpl

litre ['liːtə*] (us **liter**) n litro

litter ['lɪtə*] n (rubbish) basura; (young animals) camada, cría; **litter bin** (BRIT) n papelera; **littered** adj: **littered with** (scattered) lleno de

little ['lɪtl] adj (small) pequeño; (not much) poco ⊳ adv poco; **a ~** un poco (de); **~ house/bird** casita/pajarito; **a ~ bit** un poquito; **~ by ~** poco a poco; **little finger** n dedo meñique

live¹ [laɪv] adj (animal) vivo; (wire) conectado; (broadcast) en directo; (shell) cargado

live² [lɪv] vi vivir; **live together** vi vivir juntos; **live up to** vt fus (fulfil) cumplir con

livelihood ['laɪvlɪhʊd] n sustento

lively ['laɪvlɪ] adj vivo;

(*interesting: place, book etc*) animado

liven up ['laɪvn-] *vt* animar ▷ *vi* animarse

liver ['lɪvə*] *n* hígado

lives [laɪvz] *npl of* **life**

livestock ['laɪvstɔk] *n* ganado

living ['lɪvɪŋ] *adj* (*alive*) vivo ▷ *n*: **to earn** *or* **make a ~** ganarse la vida; **living room** *n* sala (de estar)

lizard ['lɪzəd] *n* lagarto; (*small*) lagartija

load [ləʊd] *n* carga; (*weight*) peso ▷ *vt* (*Comput*) cargar; (*also*: **~ up**): **to ~ (with)** cargar (con *or* de); **a ~ of rubbish** (*inf*) tonterías *fpl*; **a ~ of**, **~s of** (*fig*) (gran) cantidad de, montones de; **loaded** *adj* (*vehicle*): **to be loaded with** estar cargado de

loaf [ləʊf] (*pl* **loaves**) *n* (barra de) pan *m*

loan [ləʊn] *n* préstamo ▷ *vt* prestar; **on ~** prestado

loathe [ləʊð] *vt* aborrecer; (*person*) odiar

loaves [ləʊvz] *npl of* **loaf**

lobby ['lɔbɪ] *n* vestíbulo, sala de espera; (*Pol: pressure group*) grupo de presión ▷ *vt* presionar

lobster ['lɔbstə*] *n* langosta

local ['ləʊkl] *adj* local ▷ *n* (*pub*) bar *m*; **the locals** *npl* los vecinos, los del lugar; **local anaesthetic** *n* (*Med*) anestesia local; **local authority** *n* municipio, ayuntamiento (*SP*); **local government** *n* gobierno municipal; **locally** [-kəlɪ] *adv* en la vecindad; por aquí

locate [ləʊ'keɪt] *vt* (*find*) localizar; (*situate*): **to be ~d in** estar situado en

location [ləʊ'keɪʃən] *n* situación *f*; **on ~** (*Cinema*) en exteriores

loch [lɔx] *n* lago

lock [lɔk] *n* (*of door, box*) cerradura; (*of canal*) esclusa; (*of hair*) mechón *m* ▷ *vt* (*with key*) cerrar (con llave) ▷ *vi* (*door etc*) cerrarse (con llave); (*wheels*) trabarse; **lock in** *vt* encerrar; **lock out** *vt* (*person*) cerrar la puerta a; **lock up** *vt* (*criminal*) meter en la cárcel; (*mental*

patient) encerrar; (*house*) cerrar (con llave) ▷ *vi* echar la llave

locker ['lɔkə*] *n* casillero; **locker-room** *n* (*US*) (*Sport*) vestuario

locksmith ['lɔksmɪθ] *n* cerrajero/a

locomotive [ləʊkə'məʊtɪv] *n* locomotora

lodge [lɔdʒ] *n* casita (del guarda) ▷ *vi* (*person*): **to ~ (with)** alojarse (en casa de); (*bullet, bone*) incrustarse ▷ *vt* presentar; **lodger** *n* huésped *mf*

lodging ['lɔdʒɪŋ] *n* alojamiento, hospedaje *m*

loft [lɔft] *n* desván *m*

log [lɔg] *n* (*of wood*) leño, tronco; (*written account*) diario ▷ *vt* anotar; **log in, log on** *vi* (*Comput*) entrar en el sistema, hacer un login; **log off, log out** *vi* (*Comput*) salir del sistema

logic ['lɔdʒɪk] *n* lógica; **logical** *adj* lógico

login ['lɔgɪn] *n* (*Comput*) login *m*

lollipop ['lɔlɪpɔp] *n* pirulí *m*; **lollipop man/lady** (*BRIT: irreg*) *n* persona encargada de ayudar a los niños a cruzar la calle

lolly ['lɔlɪ] *n* (*inf: ice cream*) polo; (*: lollipop*) piruleta; (*: money*) guita

London ['lʌndən] *n* Londres; **Londoner** *n* londinense *mf*

lone [ləʊn] *adj* solitario

loneliness ['ləʊnlɪnɪs] *n* soledad *f*; aislamiento

lonely ['ləʊnlɪ] *adj* (*situation*) solitario; (*person*) solo; (*place*) aislado

long [lɔŋ] *adj* largo ▷ *adv* mucho tiempo, largamente ▷ *vi*: **to ~ for sth** anhelar algo; **so** *or* **as ~ as** mientras, con tal que; **don't be ~!** ¡no tardes!, ¡vuelve pronto!; **how ~ is the street?** ¿cuánto tiene la calle de largo?; **how ~ is the lesson?** ¿cuánto dura la clase?; **6 metres ~** que mide 6 metros, de 6 metros de largo; **6 months ~** que dura 6 meses, de 6 meses de duración; **all night ~** toda la noche; **he no ~er comes** ya no viene; **I can't stand it any ~er** ya no lo aguanto más; **~ before**

mucho antes; **before ~** (+ *future*) dentro de poco; (+ *past*) poco tiempo después; **at ~ last** al fin, por fin; **long-distance** *adj* de larga distancia; (*race*) de larga distancia; (*call*) interurbano; **long-haul** *adj* (*flight*) de larga distancia; **longing** *n* anhelo, ansia; (*nostalgia*) nostalgia ▷ *adj* anhelante

longitude ['lɒŋɡɪtjuːd] *n* longitud *f*

long: **long jump** *n* salto de longitud; **long-life** *adj* (*batteries*) de larga duración; (*milk*) uperizado; **long-sighted** (BRIT) *adj* présbita; **long-standing** *adj* de mucho tiempo; **long-term** *adj* a largo plazo

loo [luː] (BRIT: *inf*) *n* wáter *m*

look [lʊk] *vi* mirar; (*seem*) parecer; (*building etc*): **to ~ south/on to the sea** dar al sur/al mar ▷ *n* (*gen*): **to have a ~** mirar; (*glance*) mirada; (*appearance*) aire *m*, aspecto; **looks** *npl* (*good looks*) belleza; **~ (here)!** (*expressing annoyance etc*) ¡oye!; **~!** (*expressing surprise*) ¡mira!; **look after** *vt fus* (*care for*) cuidar a; (*deal with*) encargarse de; **look around** *vi* echar una mirada alrededor; **look at** *vt fus* mirar; (*read quickly*) echar un vistazo a; **look back** *vi* mirar hacia atrás; **look down on** *vt fus* (*fig*) despreciar, mirar con desprecio; **look for** *vt fus* buscar; **look forward to** *vt fus* esperar con ilusión; (*in letters*): **we look forward to hearing from you** quedamos a la espera de sus gratas noticias; **look into** *vt* investigar; **look out** *vi* (*beware*): **to look out (for)** tener cuidado (de); **look out for** *vt fus* (*seek*) buscar; (*await*) esperar; **look round** *vi* volver la cabeza; **look through** *vt fus* (*examine*) examinar; **look up** *vi* mirar hacia arriba; (*improve*) mejorar ▷ *vt* (*word*) buscar; **look up to** *vt fus* admirar; **lookout** *n* (*tower etc*) puesto de observación; (*person*) vigía *mf*; **to be on the lookout for sth** estar al acecho de algo

loom [luːm] *vi*: **~ (up)** (*threaten*) surgir, amenazar; (*event: approach*) aproximarse

loony ['luːnɪ] (*inf*) *n*, *adj* loco/a *m/f*

loop [luːp] *n* lazo ▷ *vt*: **to ~ sth round sth** pasar algo alrededor de algo; **loophole** *n* escapatoria

loose [luːs] *adj* suelto; (*clothes*) ancho; (*morals, discipline*) relajado; **to be on the ~** estar en libertad; **to be at a ~ end** or **at ~ ends** (US) no saber qué hacer; **loosely** *adv* libremente, aproximadamente; **loosen** *vt* aflojar

loot [luːt] *n* botín *m* ▷ *vt* saquear

lop-sided ['lɒp'saɪdɪd] *adj* torcido

lord [lɔːd] *n* señor *m*; **L~ Smith** Lord Smith; **the L~** el Señor; **my ~** (*to bishop*) Ilustrísima; (*to noble etc*) Señor; **good L~!** ¡Dios mío!; **Lords** *npl* (BRIT: *Pol*): **the (House of) Lords** la Cámara de los Lores

lorry ['lɒrɪ] (BRIT) *n* camión *m*; **lorry driver** (BRIT) *n* camionero/a

lose [luːz] (*pt*, *pp* **lost**) *vt* perder ▷ *vi* perder, ser vencido; **to ~ (time)** (*clock*) atrasarse; **lose out** *vi* salir perdiendo; **loser** *n* perdedor(a) *m/f*

loss [lɒs] *n* pérdida; **the L~** el Señor; **my ~** (*Mil*) grandes pérdidas; **to be at a ~** no saber qué hacer; **to make a ~** sufrir pérdidas

lost [lɒst] *pt*, *pp* de **lose** ▷ *adj* perdido; **lost property** (US **lost and found**) *n* objetos *mpl* perdidos

lot [lɒt] *n* (*group: of things*) grupo; (*at auctions*) lote *m*; **the ~** el todo, todos; **a ~** (*large number: of books etc*) muchos; (*a great deal*) muchísimo, bastante; **a ~ of**, **~s of** mucho(s) (*pl*); **I read a ~** leo bastante; **to draw ~s (for sth)** echar suertes (para decidir algo)

lotion ['ləʊʃən] *n* loción *f*

lottery ['lɒtərɪ] *n* lotería

loud [laʊd] *adj* (*voice, sound*) fuerte; (*laugh, shout*) estrepitoso; (*condemnation etc*) enérgico; (*gaudy*) chillón/ona ▷ *adv* (*speak etc*) fuerte; **out ~** en voz alta; **loudly** *adv* (*noisily*) fuerte; (*aloud*) en voz alta; **loudspeaker** *n* altavoz *m*

lounge [laʊndʒ] *n* salón *m*, sala (de

estar); (at airport etc) sala; (BRIT: also: **~-bar**) salón-bar m ▷ vi (also: **~ about** or **around**) reposar, holgazanear

louse [laus] (pl **lice**) n piojo

lousy ['lauzi] (inf) adj (bad quality) malísimo, asqueroso; (ill) fatal

love [lʌv] n (romantic, sexual) amor m; (kind, caring) cariño ▷ vt amar, querer; (thing, activity) encantarle a algn; "**~ from Anne**" (on letter) "un abrazo (de) Anne"; **to ~ to do** encantarle a algn hacer; **to be/fall in ~ with** estar enamorado/enamorarse de; **to make ~** hacer el amor; **for the ~ of** por amor de; **"15 ~"** (Tennis) "15 a cero"; **I ~ you** te quiero; **I ~ paella** me encanta la paella; **love affair** n aventura sentimental; **love life** n vida sentimental

lovely ['lʌvli] adj (delightful) encantador(a); (beautiful) precioso

lover ['lʌvə*] n amante mf; (in love) enamorado; (amateur): **a ~ of** un(a) aficionado/a or un(a) amante de

loving ['lʌvɪŋ] adj amoroso, cariñoso; (action) tierno

low [ləu] adj, adv bajo ▷ n (Meteorology) área de baja presión; **to be ~ on** (supplies etc) andar mal de; **to feel ~** sentirse deprimido; **to turn (down)** bajar; **low-alcohol** adj de bajo contenido en alcohol; **low-calorie** adj bajo en calorías

lower ['ləuə*] adj más bajo; (less important) menos importante ▷ vt bajar; (reduce) reducir ▷ vr: **to ~ o.s. to** (fig) rebajarse a

low-fat adj (milk, yoghurt) desnatado; (diet) bajo en calorías

loyal ['lɔɪəl] adj leal; **loyalty** n lealtad f; **loyalty card** n tarjeta cliente

L.P. n abbr (= long-playing record) elepé m

L-plates ['ɛl-] (BRIT) npl placas fpl de aprendiz de conductor

● **L-PLATES**

● En el Reino Unido las personas
● que están aprendiendo a conducir
● deben llevar en la parte delantera
● y trasera de su vehículo unas
● placas blancas con una L en rojo
● conocidas como **L-Plates** (de
● **learner**). No es necesario que
● asistan a clases teóricas sino que,
● desde el principio, se le entrega
● un carnet de conducir provisional
● ("provisional driving licence")
● para que realicen sus prácticas,
● aunque no pueden circular por
● las autopistas y deben ir siempre
● acompañadas por un conductor
● con carnet definitivo ("full driving
● licence").

Lt abbr (= lieutenant) Tte.

Ltd abbr (= limited company) S.A.

luck [lʌk] n suerte f; **bad ~** mala suerte; **good ~!** ¡que tengas suerte!, ¡suerte!; **bad** or **hard** or **tough ~!** ¡qué pena!; **luckily** adv afortunadamente; **lucky** adj afortunado; (at cards etc) con suerte; (object) que trae suerte

lucrative ['lu:krətɪv] adj lucrativo

ludicrous ['lu:dɪkrəs] adj absurdo

luggage ['lʌgɪdʒ] n equipaje m; **luggage rack** n (on car) baca, portaequipajes m inv

lukewarm [lu:kwɔ:m] adj tibio

lull [lʌl] n tregua ▷ vt: **to ~ sb to sleep** arrullar a algn; **to ~ sb into a false sense of security** dar a algn una falsa sensación de seguridad

lullaby ['lʌləbaɪ] n nana

lumber ['lʌmbə*] n (junk) trastos mpl viejos; (wood) maderos mpl

luminous ['lu:mɪnəs] adj luminoso

lump [lʌmp] n terrón m; (fragment) trozo; (swelling) bulto ▷ vt (also: **~ together**) juntar; **lump sum** n suma global; **lumpy** adj (sauce) lleno de grumos; (mattress) lleno de bultos

lunatic ['lu:nətɪk] adj loco

lunch [lʌntʃ] n almuerzo, comida ▷ vi almorzar; **lunch break**, **lunch hour** n hora del almuerzo; **lunch time** n hora de comer

lung [lʌŋ] n pulmón m
lure [luə*] n (attraction) atracción f
▷ vt tentar
lurk [lə:k] vi (person, animal) estar al
acecho; (fig) acechar
lush [lʌʃ] adj exuberante
lust [lʌst] n lujuria; (greed) codicia
Luxembourg ['lʌksəmbə:g] n
Luxemburgo
luxurious [lʌg'zjuərɪəs] adj lujoso
luxury ['lʌkʃərɪ] n lujo ▷ cpd de lujo
Lycra ® ['laɪkrə] n licra®
lying ['laɪɪŋ] n mentiras fpl ▷ adj
mentiroso
lyrics ['lɪrɪks] npl (of song) letra

m. abbr = metre; mile; million
M.A. abbr = Master of Arts
ma (inf) [mɑ:] n mamá
mac [mæk] (BRIT) n impermeable m
macaroni [mækə'rəunɪ] n
macarrones mpl
Macedonia [mæsɪ'dəunɪə] n
Macedonia; **Macedonian** [-'dəunɪən]
adj macedonio ▷ n macedonio/a;
(Ling) macedonio
machine [mə'ʃi:n] n máquina
▷ vt (dress etc) coser a máquina;
(Tech) hacer a máquina; **machine
gun** n ametralladora; **machinery**
n maquinaria; (fig) mecanismo;
machine washable adj lavable a
máquina
macho ['mætʃəu] adj machista
mackerel ['mækrl] n inv caballa
mackintosh ['mækɪntɔʃ] (BRIT) n
impermeable m
mad [mæd] adj loco; (idea)
disparatado; (angry) furioso; (keen): **to
be ~ about sth** volverle loco a algn algo
Madagascar [mædə'gæskə*] n

Madagascar m

madam ['mædəm] n señora

mad cow disease n encefalopatía
espongiforme bovina

made [meɪd] pt, pp of **make**;
made-to-measure (BRIT) adj hecho
a la medida; **made-up** ['meɪdʌp] adj
(story) ficticio

madly ['mædlɪ] adv locamente

madman ['mædmən] (irreg) n loco

madness ['mædnɪs] n locura

Madrid [mə'drɪd] n Madrid

Mafia ['mæfɪə] n Mafia

mag [mæg] n abbr (BRIT inf) =
magazine

magazine [mægə'ziːn] n revista;
(Radio, TV) programa m magazine

maggot ['mægət] n gusano

magic ['mædʒɪk] n magia ▷ adj
mágico; **magical** adj mágico;
magician [mə'dʒɪʃən] n mago/a;
(conjurer) prestidigitador/a m/f

magistrate ['mædʒɪstreɪt] n juez mf
(municipal)

magnet ['mægnɪt] n imán m;
magnetic [-'nɛtɪk] adj magnético;
(personality) atrayente

magnificent [mæg'nɪfɪsənt] adj
magnífico

magnify ['mægnɪfaɪ] vt (object)
ampliar; (sound) aumentar;
magnifying glass n lupa

magpie ['mægpaɪ] n urraca

mahogany [mə'hɒgənɪ] n caoba

maid [meɪd] n criada; **old ~** (pej)
solterona

maiden name n nombre m de soltera

mail [meɪl] n correo; (letters) cartas
fpl ▷ vt echar al correo; **mailbox** (US)
n buzón m; **mailing list** n lista de
direcciones; **mailman** (US: irreg) n
cartero; **mail-order** n pedido postal

main [meɪn] adj principal, mayor
▷ n (pipe) cañería maestra; (US) red f
eléctrica ▷ the ~s npl (Elect) la red
eléctrica; **in the ~** en general; **main
course** n (Culin) plato principal;
mainland n tierra firme; **mainly**

adv principalmente; **main road** n
carretera; **mainstream** n corriente f
principal; **main street** n calle f mayor

maintain [meɪn'teɪn] vt mantener;
maintenance ['meɪntənəns] n
mantenimiento; (Law) manutención f

maisonette [meɪzə'nɛt] n dúplex m

maize [meɪz] (BRIT) n maíz m,
choclo (SC)

majesty ['mædʒɪstɪ] n majestad f;
(title): **Your M~** Su Majestad

major ['meɪdʒə*] n (Mil) comandante
mf ▷ adj principal; (Mus) mayor

Majorca [mə'jɔːkə] n Mallorca

majority [mə'dʒɒrɪtɪ] n mayoría

make [meɪk] (pt, pp **made**) vt hacer;
(manufacture) fabricar; (mistake)
cometer; (speech) pronunciar; (cause
to be): **to ~ sb sad** poner triste a algn;
(force): **to ~ sb do sth** obligar a algn
a hacer algo; (earn) ganar; (equal): **2
and 2 ~ 4** 2 y 2 son 4 ▷ n marca; **to ~
the bed** hacer la cama; **to ~ a fool
of sb** poner a algn en ridículo; **to ~ a
profit/loss** obtener ganancias/sufrir
pérdidas; **to ~ it** (arrive) llegar; (achieve
sth) tener éxito; **what time do you
~ it?** ¿qué hora tienes? ▷ **to ~ do with**
contentarse con; **make off** vi largarse;
make out vt (decipher) descifrar;
(understand) entender; (see) distinguir;
(cheque) extender; **make up** vt (invent)
inventar; (prepare) hacer; (constitute)
constituir ▷ vi reconciliarse; (with
cosmetics) maquillarse; **make up
for** vt fus compensar; **makeover**
['meɪkəʊvə*] n (by beautician)
sesión f de maquillaje y peluquería;
(change of image) lavado de cara;
maker n fabricante mf; (of film,
programme) autor(a) m/f; **makeshift**
adj improvisado; **make-up** n
maquillaje m

making ['meɪkɪŋ] n (fig): **in the ~** en
vías de formación; **to have the ~s of**
(person) tener madera de

malaria [mə'lɛərɪə] n malaria

Malaysia [mə'leɪzɪə] n Malasia,

Malaysia

male [meɪl] n (Biol) macho ▷ adj (sex, attitude) masculino; (child etc) varón

malicious [mə'lɪʃəs] adj malicioso; rencoroso

malignant [mə'lɪgnənt] adj (Med) maligno

mall [mɔːl] n (also: **shopping ~**) centro comercial

mallet ['mælɪt] n mazo

malnutrition [mælnjuː'trɪʃən] n desnutrición f

malpractice [mæl'præktɪs] n negligencia profesional

malt [mɔːlt] n malta; (whisky) whisky m de malta

Malta ['mɔːltə] n Malta; **Maltese** [-'tiːz] adj, n inv maltés/esa m/f

mammal ['mæml] n mamífero

mammoth ['mæməθ] n mamut m ▷ adj gigantesco

man [mæn] (pl **men**) n hombre m; (mankind) el hombre ▷ vt (Naut) tripular; (Mil) guarnecer; (operate: machine) manejar; **an old ~** un viejo; **~ and wife** marido y mujer

manage ['mænɪdʒ] vi arreglárselas, ir tirando ▷ vt (be in charge of) dirigir; (control: person) manejar; (: ship) gobernar; **manageable** adj manejable; **management** n dirección f; **manager** n director(a) m/f; (of pop star) mánager mf; (Sport) entrenador(a) m/f; **manageress** n directora; entrenadora; **managerial** [-ə'dʒɪərɪəl] adj directivo; **managing director** n director(a) m/f gerente

mandarin ['mændərɪn] n (also: ~ **orange**) mandarina; (person) mandarín m

mandate ['mændeɪt] n mandato

mandatory ['mændətərɪ] adj obligatorio

mane [meɪn] n (of horse) crin f; (of lion) melena

maneuver [mə'nuːvə*] (US) = **manoeuvre**

mangetout [mɒnʒ'tuː] n tirabeque

m

mango ['mæŋgəu] (pl **-es**) n mango

man: manhole n agujero de acceso; **manhood** n edad f viril; (state) virilidad f

mania ['meɪnɪə] n manía; **maniac** ['meɪnɪæk] n maníaco/a; (fig) maniático

manic ['mænɪk] adj frenético

manicure ['mænɪkjuə*] n manicura

manifest ['mænɪfest] vt manifestar, mostrar ▷ adj manifiesto

manifesto [mænɪ'festəu] n manifiesto

manipulate [mə'nɪpjuleɪt] vt manipular

man: mankind [mæn'kaɪnd] n humanidad f, género humano; **manly** adj varonil; **man-made** adj artificial

manner ['mænə*] n manera, modo; (behaviour) conducta, manera de ser; (type): **all ~ of things** toda clase de cosas; **manners** npl (behaviour) modales mpl; **bad ~s** mala educación

manoeuvre [mə'nuːvə*] (US **maneuver**) vt, vi maniobrar ▷ n maniobra

manpower ['mænpauə*] n mano f de obra

mansion ['mænʃən] n palacio, casa grande

manslaughter ['mænslɔːtə*] n homicidio no premeditado

mantelpiece ['mæntlpiːs] n repisa, chimenea

manual ['mænjuəl] adj manual ▷ n manual m

manufacture [mænju'fæktʃə*] vt fabricar ▷ n fabricación f; **manufacturer** n fabricante mf

manure [mə'njuə*] n estiércol m

manuscript ['mænjuskrɪpt] n manuscrito

many ['menɪ] adj, pron muchos/as; **a great ~** muchísimos, un buen número de; **~ a time** muchas veces

map [mæp] n mapa m ▷ to ~ **out** vt proyectar

maple ['meɪpl] n arce m, maple m (LAM)

Mar abbr (= March) mar

mar [ma:*] vt estropear

marathon ['mærəθən] n maratón m

marble ['ma:bl] n mármol m; (toy) canica

March [ma:tʃ] n marzo

march [ma:tʃ] vi (Mil) marchar; (demonstrators) manifestarse ▷ n marcha; (demonstration) manifestación f

mare [meə*] n yegua

margarine [ma:dʒə'ri:n] n margarina

margin ['ma:dʒɪn] n margen m; (Comm: profit margin) margen m de beneficios; marginal adj marginal; marginally adv ligeramente

marigold ['mærɪgəuld] n caléndula

marijuana [mærɪ'wɑ:nə] n marijuana

marina [mə'ri:nə] n puerto deportivo

marinade [mærɪ'neɪd] n adobo

marinate ['mærɪneɪt] vt marinar

marine [mə'ri:n] adj marino ▷ n soldado de marina

marital ['mærɪtl] adj matrimonial; marital status n estado m civil

maritime ['mærɪtaɪm] adj marítimo

marjoram ['ma:dʒərəm] n mejorana

mark [ma:k] n marca, señal f; (in snow, mud etc) huella; (stain) mancha; (BRIT Scol) nota ▷ vt marcar; manchar; (damage: furniture) rayar; (indicate: place etc) señalar; (BRIT Scol) calificar, corregir; to ~ time marcar el paso; (fig) marcar(se) un ritmo; marked adj (obvious) marcado, acusado; marker n (sign) marcador m; (bookmark) señal f (de libro)

market ['ma:kɪt] n mercado ▷ vt (Comm) comercializar; marketing n márketing m; marketplace n mercado; market research n análisis m inv de mercados

marmalade ['ma:məleɪd] n mermelada de naranja

maroon [mə'ru:n] vt: to be ~ed quedar aislado; (fig) quedar abandonado ▷ n (colour) granate m

marquee [ma:'ki:] n entoldado

marriage ['mærɪdʒ] n (relationship, institution) matrimonio; (wedding) boda; (act) casamiento; marriage certificate n partida de casamiento

married ['mærɪd] adj casado; (life, love) conyugal

marrow ['mærəu] n médula; (vegetable) calabacín m

marry ['mærɪ] vt casarse con; (father, priest etc) casar ▷ vi (also: get married) casarse

Mars [ma:z] n Marte m

marsh [ma:ʃ] n pantano; (salt marsh) marisma

marshal ['ma:ʃl] n (Mil) mariscal m; (at sports meeting etc) oficial m; (us: of police, fire department) jefe/a m/f ▷ vt (thoughts etc) ordenar; (soldiers) formar

martyr ['ma:tə*] n mártir m f

marvel ['ma:vl] n maravilla, prodigio ▷ vi: to ~ (at) maravillarse (de); marvellous (us marvelous) adj maravilloso

Marxism ['ma:ksɪzəm] n marxismo

Marxist ['ma:ksɪst] adj, n marxista m f

marzipan ['ma:zɪpæn] n mazapán m

mascara [mæs'ka:rə] n rímel m

mascot ['mæskət] n mascota

masculine ['mæskjulɪn] adj masculino

mash [mæʃ] vt machacar; mashed potato(es) n(pl) puré m de patatas (SP) or papas (LAM)

mask [ma:sk] n máscara ▷ vt (cover): to ~ one's face ocultarse la cara; (hide: feelings) esconder

mason ['meɪsn] n (also: stone~) albañil m; (also: free~) masón m

masonry ['meɪsnrɪ] n (in building) mampostería

mass [mæs] n (people) muchedumbre f; (of air, liquid etc) masa; (of detail, hair etc) gran cantidad f; (Rel) misa ▷ cpd masivo ▷vi reunirse; concentrarse; **the masses** npl las masas; **~es of** (inf) montones de

massacre ['mæsəkə*] n masacre f

massage ['mæsɑːʒ] n masaje m ▷vt dar masaje en

massive ['mæsɪv] adj enorme; (support, changes) masivo

mass media npl medios mpl de comunicación

mass-produce ['mæsprə'djuːs] vt fabricar en serie

mast [mɑːst] n (Naut) mástil m; (Radio etc) torre f

master ['mɑːstə*] n (of servant) amo; (of situation) dueño, maestro; (in primary school) maestro; (in secondary school) profesor m; (title for boys): **M~ X** Señorito X ▷vt dominar; **mastermind** n inteligencia superior ▷vt dirigir, planear; **Master of Arts/Science** n licenciatura superior en Letras/Ciencias; **masterpiece** n obra maestra

masturbate ['mæstəbeɪt] vi masturbarse

mat [mæt] n estera; (also: **door~**) felpudo; (also: **table~**) salvamanteles m inv, posavasos m inv ▷adj = **matt**

match [mætʃ] n cerilla, fósforo; (game) partido; (equal) igual m/f ▷vt (go well with) hacer juego con; (equal) igualar; (correspond to) corresponderse con; (pair: also: **~ up**) casar con ▷vi hacer juego; **to be a good ~** hacer juego; **matchbox** n caja de cerillas; **matching** adj que hace juego

mate [meɪt] n (workmate) colega mf; (inf: friend) amigo; (animal) macho/ hembra; (in merchant navy) segundo de a bordo ▷vi acoplarse, aparearse ▷vt aparear

material [mə'tɪərɪəl] n (substance) materia; (information) material m; (cloth) tela, tejido ▷adj material; (important) esencial; **materials** npl materiales mpl

materialize [mə'tɪərɪəlaɪz] vi

materializarse

maternal [mə'tɜːnl] adj maternal

maternity [mə'tɜːnɪtɪ] n maternidad f; **maternity hospital** n hospital m de maternidad; **maternity leave** n baja por maternidad

math [mæθ] (US) n = **mathematics**

mathematical [mæθə'mætɪkl] adj matemático

mathematician [mæθəmə'tɪʃən] n matemático/a

mathematics [mæθə'mætɪks] n matemáticas fpl

maths [mæθs] (BRIT) n = **mathematics**

matinée ['mætɪneɪ] n sesión f de tarde

matron ['meɪtrən] n enfermera f jefe; (in school) ama de llaves

matt [mæt] adj mate

matter ['mætə*] n cuestión f, asunto; (Physics) sustancia, materia; (reading matter) material m; (Med: pus) pus m ▷vi importar; **matters** npl (affairs) asuntos mpl, temas mpl; **it doesn't ~** no importa; **what's the ~?** ¿qué pasa?; **no ~ what** pase lo que pase; **as a ~ of course** por rutina; **as a ~ of fact** de hecho

mattress ['mætrɪs] n colchón m

mature [mə'tjuə*] adj maduro ▷vi madurar; **mature student** n estudiante de más de 21 años; **maturity** n madurez f

maul [mɔːl] vt magullar

mauve [məuv] adj de color malva (SP) or guinda (LAM)

max abbr = **maximum**

maximize ['mæksɪmaɪz] vt (profits etc) llevar al máximo; (chances) maximizar

maximum ['mæksɪməm] (pl **maxima**) adj máximo ▷n máximo

May [meɪ] n mayo

may [meɪ] (conditional **might**) vi (indicating possibility): **he ~ come** puede que venga; (be allowed to): **~ I smoke?** ¿puedo fumar?; (wishes): **~ God bless**

you! ¡que Dios le bendiga!; **you ~ as
well go** bien puedes irte

maybe ['meɪbɪ] adv quizá(s)

May Day n el primero de Mayo

mayhem ['meɪhem] n caos m total

mayonnaise [meɪə'neɪz] n
mayonesa

mayor [mɛə*] n alcalde m; **mayoress**
n alcaldesa

maze [meɪz] n laberinto

MD n abbr = **managing director**

me [miː] pron (direct) me; (stressed,
after prep) mí; **can you hear ~?** ¿me
oyes?; **he heard ME** ¡me oyó a mí!; **it's
~ soy yo**; **give them to ~** dámelos/las;
with/without ~ conmigo/sin mí

meadow ['medəʊ] n prado, pradera

meagre ['miːgə*] (US **meager**) adj
escaso, pobre

meal [miːl] n comida; (flour) harina;
mealtime n hora de comer

mean [miːn] (pt, pp **~t**) adj (with
money) tacaño; (unkind) mezquino,
malo; (shabby) humilde; (average) medio
▷ vt (signify) querer decir, significar;
(refer to) referirse a; (intend): **to ~ to
do sth** pensar or pretender hacer algo
▷ n medio, término medio; **means**
npl (way) medio, manera; (money)
recursos mpl, medios mpl; **by ~s of**
mediante, por medio de; **by all ~s!**
¡naturalmente!, ¡claro que sí!; **do you ~
it?** ¿lo dices en serio?; **what do you ~?**
¿qué quiere decir?; **to be ~t for sb/sth**
ser para algn/algo

meaning ['miːnɪŋ] n significado,
sentido; (purpose) sentido, propósito;
meaningful adj significativo;
meaningless adj sin sentido

meant [ment] pt, pp of **mean**

meantime ['miːntaɪm] adv (also: **in
the ~**) mientras tanto

meanwhile ['miːnwaɪl] adv =
meantime

measles ['miːzlz] n sarampión m

measure ['meʒə*] vt, vi medir ▷ n
medida; (ruler) regla; **measurement**
['meʒəmənt] n (measure) medida;

(act) medición f; **to take sb's
measurements** tomar las medidas
a algn

meat [miːt] n carne f; **cold ~** fiambre
m; **meatball** n albóndiga

Mecca ['mekə] n La Meca

mechanic [mɪ'kænɪk] n mecánico/
a; **mechanical** adj mecánico

mechanism ['mekənɪzəm] n
mecanismo

medal ['medl] n medalla; **medallist**
(US **medalist**) n (Sport) medallista mf

meddle ['medl] vi: **to ~ in**
entrometerse en; **to ~ with sth**
manosear algo

media ['miːdɪə] npl medios mpl de
comunicación ▷ npl of **medium**

mediaeval [medɪ'iːvl] adj =
medieval

mediate ['miːdɪeɪt] vi mediar

medical ['medɪkl] adj médico ▷ n
reconocimiento médico; **medical
certificate** n certificado m médico

medicated ['medɪkeɪtɪd] adj
medicinal

medication [medɪ'keɪʃən] n
medicación f

medicine ['medsɪn] n medicina;
(drug) medicamento

medieval [medɪ'iːvl] adj medieval

mediocre [miːdɪ'əʊkə*] adj
mediocre

meditate ['medɪteɪt] vi meditar

meditation [medɪ'teɪʃən] n
meditación f

Mediterranean [medɪtə'reɪnɪən]
adj mediterráneo; **the ~ (Sea)** el (Mar)
Mediterráneo

medium ['miːdɪəm] (pl **media**)
adj mediano, regular ▷ n (means)
medio; (pl mediums: person) médium
mf; **medium-sized** adj de tamaño
mediano; (clothes) de (la) talla mediana;
medium wave n onda media

meek [miːk] adj manso, sumiso

meet [miːt] (pt, pp **met**) vt encontrar;
(accidentally) encontrarse con,
tropezar con; (by arrangement) reunirse

con; (for the first time) conocer; (go and fetch) ir a buscar; (opponent) enfrentarse con; (obligations) cumplir; (encounter: problem) hacer frente a; (need) satisfacer ▷ vi encontrarse; (in session) reunirse; (join: objects) unirse; (for the first time) conocerse; **meet up** vi: **to meet up with sb** reunirse con algn; **meet with** vt fus (difficulty) tropezar con; **to meet with success** tener éxito; **meeting** n encuentro m; (arranged) cita, compromiso; (business meeting) reunión f; (Pol) mitin m; **meeting place** n lugar m de reunión or encuentro

megabyte ['mɛɡəbaɪt] n (Comput) megabyte m, megaocteto

megaphone ['mɛɡəfəʊn] n megáfono

megapixel ['mɛɡəpɪksl] n megapíxel m

melancholy ['mɛlənkəlɪ] n melancolía ▷ adj melancólico

melody ['mɛlədɪ] n melodía

melon ['mɛlən] n melón m

melt [mɛlt] vi (metal) fundirse; (snow) derretirse ▷ vt fundir

member ['mɛmbə*] n (gen, Anat) miembro; (of club) socio/a; **Member of Congress** (us) n miembro mf del Congreso; **Member of Parliament** (BRIT) diputado/a m/f, parlamentario/a m/f; **Member of the European Parliament** n diputado/a m/f del Parlamento Europeo, eurodiputado/a m/f; **Member of the Scottish Parliament** (BRIT) diputado/a del Parlamento escocés; **membership** n (members) número de miembros; (state) filiación f; **membership card** n carnet m de socio

memento [mə'mɛntəʊ] n recuerdo

memo ['mɛməʊ] n apunte m, nota

memorable ['mɛmərəbl] adj memorable

memorandum [mɛmə'rændəm] (pl **memoranda**) n apunte m, nota; (official note) acta

memorial [mɪ'mɔːrɪəl] n monumento conmemorativo ▷ adj conmemorativo

memorize ['mɛməraɪz] vt aprender de memoria

memory ['mɛmərɪ] n (also: Comput) memoria; (instance) recuerdo; (of dead person): **in ~ of** a la memoria de; **memory card** n tarjeta de memoria; **memory stick** n barra de memoria

men [mɛn] npl of **man**

menace ['mɛnəs] n amenaza ▷ vt amenazar

mend [mɛnd] vt reparar, arreglar; (darn) zurcir ▷ vi reponerse ▷ n arreglo, reparación f zurcido ▷ n: **to be on the ~** ir mejorando; **to ~ one's ways** enmendarse

meningitis [mɛnɪn'dʒaɪtɪs] n meningitis f

menopause ['mɛnəʊpɔːz] n menopausia

men's room (us) n: **the ~** el servicio de caballeros

menstruation [mɛnstru'eɪʃən] n menstruación f

menswear ['mɛnzwɛə*] n confección f de caballero

mental ['mɛntl] adj mental; **mental hospital** n (hospital m) psiquiátrico; **mentality** [mɛn'tælɪtɪ] n mentalidad f; **mentally** adv: **to be mentally ill** tener una enfermedad mental

menthol ['mɛnθəl] n mentol m

mention ['mɛnʃən] n mención f ▷ vt mencionar; (speak) hablar de; **don't ~ it!** ¡de nada!

menu ['mɛnjuː] n (set menu) menú m; (printed) carta; (Comput) menú m

MEP n abbr = **Member of the European Parliament**

mercenary ['məːsɪnərɪ] adj, n mercenario/a

merchandise ['məːtʃəndaɪz] n mercancías fpl

merchant ['məːtʃənt] n comerciante mf; **merchant navy** (us), **merchant marine** n marina mercante

merciless ['mɜːsɪlɪs] adj despiadado
mercury ['mɜːkjʊrɪ] n mercurio
mercy ['mɜːsɪ] n compasión f; (Rel) misericordia; **at the ~ of** a la merced de
mere [mɪə*] adj simple, mero; **merely** adv simplemente, sólo
merge [mɜːdʒ] vt (join) unir ▷ vi unirse; (Comm) fusionarse; (colours etc) fundirse; **merger** n (Comm) fusión f
meringue [mə'ræŋ] n merengue m
merit ['merɪt] n mérito ▷ vt merecer
mermaid ['mɜːmeɪd] n sirena
merry ['merɪ] adj alegre; **M~ Christmas!** ¡Felices Pascuas!; **merry-go-round** n tiovivo
mesh [meʃ] n malla
mess [mes] n (muddle: of situation) confusión f; (: of room) revoltijo; (dirt) porquería; (Mil) comedor m; **mess about or around** (inf) vi perder el tiempo; (pass the time) entretenerse; **mess up** vt (spoil) estropear; (dirty) ensuciar; **mess with** (inf) vt fus (challenge, confront) meterse con (inf); (interfere with) interferir con
message ['mesɪdʒ] n recado, mensaje m
messenger ['mesɪndʒə*] n mensajero/a
Messrs abbr (on letters) (= Messieurs) Sres
messy ['mesɪ] adj (dirty) sucio; (untidy) desordenado
met [met] pt, pp of **meet**
metabolism [me'tæbəlɪzəm] n metabolismo
metal ['metl] n metal m; **metallic** [-'tælɪk] adj metálico
metaphor ['metəfə*] n metáfora
meteor ['miːtɪə*] n meteoro; **meteorite** [-aɪt] n meteorito
meteorology [miːtɪə'rɒlədʒɪ] n meteorología
meter ['miːtə*] n (instrument) contador m; (us: unit) = **metre** ▷ vt (us Post) franquear
method ['meθəd] n método; **methodical** [mɪ'θɒdɪkl] adj metódico

meths [meθs] n (BRIT) alcohol m metilado or desnaturalizado
meticulous [me'tɪkjʊləs] adj meticuloso
metre ['miːtə*] (US **meter**) n metro
metric ['metrɪk] adj métrico
metro ['metrəʊ] n metro
metropolitan [metrə'pɒlɪtən] adj metropolitano; **the M~ Police** (BRIT) la policía londinense
Mexican ['meksɪkən] adj, n mexicano/a, mejicano/a
Mexico ['meksɪkəʊ] n México, Méjico (SP)
mg abbr (= milligram) mg
mice [maɪs] npl of **mouse**
micro... [maɪkrəʊ] prefix micro...; **microchip** n microplaqueta; **microphone** n micrófono; **microscope** n microscopio; **microwave** n (also: **microwave oven**) horno microondas
mid [mɪd] adj: **in ~ May** a mediados de mayo; **in ~ afternoon** a media tarde; **in ~ air** en el aire; **midday** n mediodía m
middle ['mɪdl] n centro; (half-way point) medio; (waist) cintura ▷ adj de en medio; (course, way) intermedio; **in the ~ of the night** en plena noche; **middle-aged** adj de mediana edad; **Middle Ages** npl: **the Middle Ages** la Edad Media; **middle-class** adj de clase media; **the middle class(es)** clase media; **Middle East** n Oriente m Medio; **middle name** n segundo nombre; **middle school** n (us) colegio para niños de doce a catorce años; (BRIT) colegio para niños de ocho o nueve a doce o trece años
midge [mɪdʒ] n mosquito
midget ['mɪdʒɪt] n enano/a
midnight ['mɪdnaɪt] n medianoche f
midst [mɪdst] n: **in the ~ of** (crowd) en medio de; (situation, action) en mitad de
midsummer [mɪd'sʌmə*] n: **in ~** en pleno verano
midway [mɪd'weɪ] adj, adv: **~ (between)** a medio camino (entre); **~**

m

through a la mitad (de)

midweek [mɪd'wiːk] *adv* entre semana

midwife ['mɪdwaɪf] (*irreg*) *n* comadrona, partera

midwinter [mɪd'wɪntə*] *n*: **in ~** en pleno invierno

might [maɪt] *vb see* **may** ▷ *n* fuerza, poder *m*; **mighty** *adj* fuerte, poderoso

migraine ['miːɡreɪn] *n* jaqueca

migrant ['maɪɡrənt] *n, adj* (*bird*) migratorio; (*worker*) emigrante

migrate [maɪ'ɡreɪt] *vi* emigrar

migration [maɪ'ɡreɪʃən] *n* emigración *f*

mike [maɪk] *n abbr* (= *microphone*) micro

mild [maɪld] *adj* (*person*) apacible; (*climate*) templado; (*slight*) ligero; (*taste*) suave; (*illness*) leve; **mildly** ['-lɪ] *adv* ligeramente; suavemente; **to put it mildly** para no decir más

mile [maɪl] *n* milla; **mileage** *n* número de millas = kilometraje *m*; **mileometer** [maɪ'lɔmɪtə*] *n* = cuentakilómetros *m*inv; **milestone** *n* mojón *m*

military ['mɪlɪtərɪ] *adj* militar

militia [mɪ'lɪʃə] *n* milicia

milk [mɪlk] *n* leche *f* ▷ *vt* (*cow*) ordeñar; (*fig*) chupar; **milk chocolate** *n* chocolate *m* con leche; **milkman** (*irreg*) *n* lechero; **milky** *adj* lechoso

mill [mɪl] *n* (*windmill etc*) molino; (*coffee mill*) molinillo; (*factory*) fábrica ▷ *vt* moler ▷ *vi* (*also*: ~ **about**) arremolinarse

millennium [mɪ'lenɪəm] (*pl* ~**s** or **millennia**) *n* milenio, milenario

milli... ['mɪlɪ] *prefix*: **milligram(me)** *n* miligramo; **millilitre** (*US* **milliliter**) ['mɪlɪliːtə*] *n* mililitro; **millimetre** (*US* **millimeter**) *n* milímetro

million ['mɪljən] *n* millón *m*; **a ~ times** un millón de veces; **millionaire** [-jə'nɛə*] *n* millonario/a; **millionth** [-θ] *adj* millonésimo

milometer [maɪ'lɔmɪtə*] (*BRIT*) *n* =

mileometer

mime [maɪm] *n* mímica; (*actor*) mimo/a ▷ *vt* remedar ▷ *vi* actuar de mimo

mimic ['mɪmɪk] *n* imitador(a) *m/f* ▷ *adj* mímico ▷ *vt* remedar, imitar

min. *abbr* = **minimum; minute(s)**

mince [mɪns] *vt* picar ▷ *n* (*BRIT Culin*) carne *f* picada; **mincemeat** *n* conserva de fruta picada; (*US: meat*) carne *f* picada; **mince pie** *n* empanadilla rellena de fruta picada

mind [maɪnd] *n* mente *f*; (*intellect*) intelecto; (*contrasted with matter*) espíritu *m* ▷ *vt* (*attend to, look after*) ocuparse de, cuidar; (*be careful*) tener cuidado con; (*object to*): **I don't ~ the noise** no me molesta el ruido; **it is on my ~** me preocupa; **to bear sth in ~** tomar o tener algo en cuenta; **to make up one's ~** decidirse; **I don't ~** me es igual; **~ you ...** te advierto que ...; **never ~!** ¡es igual!, ¡no importa!; (*don't worry*) ¡no te preocupes!; **"~ the step"** "cuidado con el escalón"; **mindless** *adj* (*crime*) sin motivo; (*work*) de autómata

mine¹ [maɪn] *pron* el mío/la mía etc; **a friend of ~** un(a) amigo/a mío/mía ▷ *adj*: **this book is ~** este libro es mío

mine² [maɪn] *n* mina ▷ *vt* (*coal*) extraer; (*bomb: beach etc*) minar; **minefield** *n* campo de minas; **miner** *n* minero/a

mineral ['mɪnərəl] *adj* mineral ▷ *n* mineral *m*; **mineral water** *n* agua mineral

mingle ['mɪŋɡl] *vi*: **to ~ with** mezclarse con

miniature ['mɪnətʃə*] *adj* (*en*) miniatura ▷ *n* miniatura

minibar ['mɪnɪbɑː*] *n* minibar *m*

minibus ['mɪnɪbʌs] *n* microbús *m*

minicab ['mɪnɪkæb] *n* taxi *m* (*que sólo puede pedirse por teléfono*)

minimal ['mɪnɪml] *adj* mínimo

minimize ['mɪnɪmaɪz] *vt* minimizar; (*play down*) empequeñecer

minimum ['mɪnɪməm] (*pl* **minima**)

n, adj mínimo

mining ['maɪnɪŋ] *n* explotación f minera

miniskirt ['mɪnɪskəːt] *n* minifalda

minister ['mɪnɪstə*] *n* (BRIT Pol) ministro/a (SP), secretario/a (LAM); (Rel) pastor *m* ▷ *vi*: **to ~ to** atender a

ministry ['mɪnɪstrɪ] *n* (BRIT Pol) ministerio, secretaría (MEX); (Rel) sacerdocio

minor ['maɪnə*] *adj* (repairs, injuries) leve; (poet, planet) menor; (Mus) menor ▷ *n* (Law) menor *m* de edad

Minorca [mɪˈnɔːkə] *n* Menorca

minority [maɪˈnɔrɪtɪ] *n* minoría f

mint [mɪnt] *n* (plant) menta, hierbabuena; (sweet) caramelo de menta ▷ *vt* (coins) acuñar; **the (Royal) M~**, **the (US) M~** la Casa de la Moneda; **in ~ condition** en perfecto estado

minus ['maɪnəs] *n* (also: **~ sign**) signo de menos ▷ *prep* menos; **12 ~ 6 equals 6** 12 menos 6 son 6; **~ 24 °C** menos 24 grados

minute¹ ['mɪnɪt] *n* minuto; (fig) momento; **minutes** *npl* (of meeting) actas *fpl*; **at the last ~** a última hora

minute² [maɪˈnjuːt] *adj* diminuto; (search) minucioso

miracle ['mɪrəkl] *n* milagro

miraculous [mɪˈrækjuləs] *adj* milagroso

mirage ['mɪrɑːʒ] *n* espejismo

mirror ['mɪrə*] *n* espejo; (in car) retrovisor *m*

misbehave [mɪsbɪˈheɪv] *vi* portarse mal

misc. *abbr* = **miscellaneous**

miscarriage ['mɪskærɪdʒ] *n* (Med) aborto; **~ of justice** error *m* judicial

miscellaneous [mɪsɪˈleɪnɪəs] *adj* varios/as, diversos/as

mischief ['mɪstʃɪf] *n* travesuras *fpl*, diabluras *fpl*; (maliciousness) malicia; **mischievous** [-ʃɪvəs] *adj* travieso

misconception [mɪskənˈsepʃən] *n* idea equivocada; equivocación f

misconduct [mɪsˈkɔndʌkt] *n* mala conducta; **professional ~** falta profesional

miser ['maɪzə*] *n* avaro/a

miserable ['mɪzərəbl] *adj* (unhappy) triste, desgraciado; (unpleasant, contemptible) miserable

misery ['mɪzərɪ] *n* tristeza; (wretchedness) miseria, desdicha

misfortune [mɪsˈfɔːtʃən] *n* desgracia

misgiving [mɪsˈgɪvɪŋ] *n* (apprehension) presentimiento; **to have ~s about sth** tener dudas acerca de algo

misguided [mɪsˈgaɪdɪd] *adj* equivocado

mishap ['mɪshæp] *n* desgracia, contratiempo

misinterpret [mɪsɪnˈtəːprɪt] *vt* interpretar mal

misjudge [mɪsˈdʒʌdʒ] *vt* juzgar mal

mislay [mɪsˈleɪ] *vt* extraviar, perder

mislead [mɪsˈliːd] *vt* llevar a conclusiones erróneas; **misleading** *adj* engañoso

misplace [mɪsˈpleɪs] *vt* extraviar

misprint ['mɪsprɪnt] *n* errata, error *m* de imprenta

misrepresent [mɪsreprɪˈzent] *vt* falsificar

Miss [mɪs] *n* Señorita

miss [mɪs] *vt* (train etc) perder; (fail to hit: target) errar; (regret the absence of): **I ~ him** (yo) le echo de menos or a faltar; **you can't ~ it** no tiene pérdida ▷ *vi* fallar ▷ *n* (shot) tiro fallido or perdido; **miss out** (BRIT) *vt* omitir; **miss out on** *vt fus* (fun, party, opportunity) perderse

missile ['mɪsaɪl] *n* (Aviat) misil *m*; (object thrown) proyectil *m*

missing ['mɪsɪŋ] *adj* (pupil) ausente; (thing) perdido; (Mil): **~ in action** desaparecido en combate

mission ['mɪʃən] *n* misión f; (official representation) delegación f; **missionary** *n* misionero/a

misspell [mɪsˈspɛl] (*pt, pp* **misspelt** (BRIT) *or* **~ed**) *vt* escribir mal

mist [mɪst] *n* (*light*) neblina; (*heavy*) niebla; (*at sea*) bruma ▷ *vi* (*eyes: also:* **~ over, ~ up**) llenarse de lágrimas; (BRIT: *windows: also:* **~ over, ~ up**) empañarse

mistake [mɪsˈteɪk] (*vt: irreg*) *n* error *m* ▷ *vt* entender mal; **by ~** por equivocación; **to make a ~** equivocarse; **to ~ A for B** confundir A con B; **mistaken** *pp of* **mistake** ▷ *adj* equivocado; **to be mistaken** equivocarse, engañarse

mister ['mɪstə*] (*inf*) *n* señor *m*; *see* **Mr**

mistletoe ['mɪsltəʊ] *n* muérdago

mistook [mɪsˈtuk] *pt of* **mistake**

mistress ['mɪstrɪs] *n* (*lover*) amante *f*; (*of house*) señora (de la casa); (BRIT: in primary school) maestra; (in secondary school) profesora; (of situation) dueña

mistrust [mɪsˈtrʌst] *vt* desconfiar de

misty ['mɪstɪ] *adj* (*day*) de niebla; (*glasses etc*) empañado

misunderstand [mɪsʌndəˈstænd] (*irreg*) *vt, vi* entender mal; **misunderstanding** *n* malentendido

misunderstood [mɪsʌndəˈstud] *pt, pp of* **misunderstand** ▷ *adj* (*person*) incomprendido

misuse [*n* mɪsˈjuːs, *vb* mɪsˈjuːz] *n* mal uso; (*of power*) abuso; (*of funds*) malversación *f* ▷ *vt* abusar de; malversar

mitt(en) ['mɪt(n)] *n* manopla

mix [mɪks] *vt* mezclar; (*combine*) unir ▷ *vi* mezclarse; (*people*) llevarse bien ▷ *n* mezcla; **mix up** *vt* mezclar; (*confuse*) confundir; **mixed** *adj* mixto; (*feelings etc*) encontrado; **mixed grill** *n* (BRIT) parrillada mixta; **mixed salad** *n* ensalada mixta; **mixed-up** *adj* (*confused*) confuso, revuelto; **mixer** *n* (*for food*) licuadora; (*for drinks*) coctelera; (*person*): **he's a good mixer** tiene don de gentes; **mixture** *n* mezcla; (*also:* **cough mixture**) jarabe

m; **mix-up** *n* confusión *f*

ml *abbr* (= *millilitre(s)*) ml

mm *abbr* (= *millimetre*) mm

moan [məʊn] *n* gemido ▷ *vi* gemir; (*inf: complain*): **to ~ (about)** quejarse (de)

moat [məʊt] *n* foso

mob [mɒb] *n* multitud *f* ▷ *vt* acosar

mobile ['məʊbaɪl] *adj* móvil ▷ *n* móvil *m*; **mobile home** *n* caravana; **mobile phone** *n* teléfono móvil

mobility [məʊˈbɪlɪtɪ] *n* movilidad *f*

mobilize ['məʊbɪlaɪz] *vt* movilizar

mock [mɒk] *vt* (*ridicule*) ridiculizar; (*laugh at*) burlarse de ▷ *adj* fingido; **~ exam** *examen* preparatorio antes de los exámenes oficiales (BRIT: Scol: inf) exámenes *mpl* de prueba; **mockery** *n* burla

mod cons ['mɒdˈkɒnz] *npl* *abbr* (= *modern conveniences*) *see* **convenience**

mode [məʊd] *n* modo

model ['mɒdl] *n* modelo; (*fashion model, artist's model*) modelo *mf* ▷ *adj* modelo ▷ *vt* (*with clay etc*) modelar; (*copy*): **to ~ o.s. on** tomar como modelo a ▷ *vi* ser modelo; **to ~ clothes** pasar modelos, ser modelo

modem ['məʊdæm] *n* modem *m*

moderate [*adj* 'mɒdərət, *vb* 'mɒdəreɪt] *adj* moderado/a ▷ *vi* moderarse, calmarse ▷ *vt* moderar

moderation [mɒdəˈreɪʃən] *n* moderación *f*; **in ~** con moderación

modern ['mɒdən] *adj* moderno; **modernize** *vt* modernizar; **modern languages** *npl* lenguas *fpl* modernas

modest ['mɒdɪst] *adj* modesto; (*small*) módico; **modesty** *n* modestia

modification [mɒdɪfɪˈkeɪʃən] *n* modificación *f*

modify ['mɒdɪfaɪ] *vt* modificar

module ['mɒdjuːl] *n* (*in unit, component, Space*) módulo

mohair ['məʊhɛə*] *n* mohair *m*

Mohammed [məˈhæmɛd] *n* Mahoma *m*

moist [mɔɪst] *adj* húmedo; **moisture** ['mɔɪstʃə*] *n* humedad *f*; **moisturizer** ['mɔɪstʃəraɪz*] *n* crema hidratante

mold *etc* ['məʊld] (US) = **mould**

mole [məʊl] *n* (animal, spy) topo; (spot) lunar *m*

molecule ['mɒlɪkjuːl] *n* molécula

molest [məʊ'lest] *vt* importunar; (assault sexually) abusar sexualmente de

> Be careful not to translate **molest** by the Spanish word molestar.

molten ['məʊltən] *adj* fundido; (lava) líquido

mom [mɒm] (US) *n* = **mum**

moment ['məʊmənt] *n* momento; **at the** ~ de momento, por ahora; **momentarily** ['məʊməntrɪlɪ] *adv* momentáneamente; (US: very soon) de un momento a otro; **momentary** *adj* momentáneo; **momentous** [-'mentəs] *adj* trascendental, importante

momentum [məʊ'mentəm] *n* momento; (fig) ímpetu *m*; **to gather ~** cobrar velocidad; (fig) ganar fuerza

mommy ['mɒmɪ] (US) *n* = **mummy**

Mon *abbr* (= Monday) lun

Monaco ['mɒnəkəʊ] *n* Mónaco

monarch ['mɒnək] *n* monarca *mf*; **monarchy** *n* monarquía

monastery ['mɒnəstərɪ] *n* monasterio

Monday ['mʌndɪ] *n* lunes *m inv*

monetary ['mʌnɪtərɪ] *adj* monetario

money ['mʌnɪ] *n* dinero; (currency) moneda; **to make** ~ ganar dinero; **money belt** *n* riñonera; **money order** *n* giro

mongrel ['mʌŋgrəl] *n* (dog) perro mestizo

monitor ['mɒnɪtə*] *n* (Scol) monitor *m*; (also: **television** ~) receptor *m* de control; (of computer) monitor *m* ▷ *vt* controlar

monk [mʌŋk] *n* monje *m*

monkey ['mʌŋkɪ] *n* mono

monologue ['mɒnəlɒg] *n* monólogo

monopoly [mə'nɒpəlɪ] *n* monopolio

monosodium glutamate [mɒnə'səʊdɪəm'gluːtəmeɪt] *n* glutamato monosódico

monotonous [mə'nɒtənəs] *adj* monótono

monsoon [mɒn'suːn] *n* monzón *m*

monster ['mɒnstə*] *n* monstruo

month [mʌnθ] *n* mes *m*; **monthly** *adj* mensual ▷ *adv* mensualmente

monument ['mɒnjumənt] *n* monumento

mood [muːd] *n* humor *m*; (of crowd, group) clima *m*; **to be in a good/bad ~** estar de buen/mal humor; **moody** *adj* (changeable) de humor variable; (sullen) malhumorado

moon [muːn] *n* luna; **moonlight** *n* luz *f* de la luna

moor [mʊə*] *n* páramo ▷ *vt* (ship) amarrar ▷ *vi* echar las amarras

moose [muːs] *n inv* alce *m*

mop [mɒp] *n* fregona; (of hair) greña, melena ▷ *vt* fregar; **mop up** *vt* limpiar

mope [məʊp] *vi* estar or andar deprimido

moped ['məʊped] *n* ciclomotor *m*

moral ['mɒrl] *adj* moral ▷ *n* moraleja; **morals** *npl* moralidad *f*, moral *f*

morale [mɒ'rɑːl] *n* moral *f*

morality [mə'rælɪtɪ] *n* moralidad *f*

morbid ['mɔːbɪd] *adj* (interest) morboso; (Med) mórbido

O **KEYWORD**

more [mɔː*] *adj* **1** (greater in number etc) más; **more people/work than before** más gente/trabajo que antes

2 (additional) más; **do you want (some) more tea?** ¿quieres más té?; **is there any more wine?** ¿queda vino?; **it'll take a few more weeks** tardará unas semanas más; **it's 2 kms more to the house** faltan 2 kms para la casa; **more time/letters than we expected**

más tiempo del que/más cartas de las
que esperábamos
▷ *pron* (*greater amount, additional
amount*) más; **more than 10** más
de 10; **it cost more than the other
one/than we expected** costó más que
el otro/más de lo que esperábamos;
is there any more? ¿hay más?;
many/much more muchos(as)/
mucho(a) más
▷ *adv* más; **more dangerous/easily
(than)** más peligroso/fácilmente
(que); **more and more expensive**
cada vez más caro; **more or less** más
o menos; **more than ever** más que
nunca

moreover [mɔːˈrəuvə*] *adv* además,
por otra parte
morgue [mɔːg] *n* depósito de
cadáveres
morning [ˈmɔːnɪŋ] *n* mañana; (*early
morning*) madrugada ▷*cpd* matutino,
de la mañana; **in the ~** por la mañana;
7 o'clock in the ~ las 7 de la mañana;
morning sickness *n* náuseas *fpl*
matutinas
Moroccan [məˈrɔkən] *adj, n*
marroquí *m/f*
Morocco [məˈrɔkəu] *n* Marruecos *m*
moron [ˈmɔːrɔn] (*inf*) *n* imbécil *mf*
morphine [ˈmɔːfiːn] *n* morfina
Morse [mɔːs] *n* (*also:* ~ **code**) (código)
Morse
mortal [ˈmɔːtl] *adj, n* mortal *m*
mortar [ˈmɔːtə*] *n* argamasa
mortgage [ˈmɔːgɪdʒ] *n* hipoteca
▷*vt* hipotecar
mortician [mɔːˈtɪʃən] (*us*) *n*
director/a *m/f* de pompas fúnebres
mortified [ˈmɔːtɪfaɪd] *adj*: **I was ~ me**
dio muchísima vergüenza
mortuary [ˈmɔːtjuərɪ] *n* depósito de
cadáveres
mosaic [məuˈzeɪɪk] *n* mosaico
Moslem [ˈmɔzləm] *adj, n* = **Muslim**
mosque [mɔsk] *n* mezquita
mosquito [mɔsˈkiːtəu] (*pl* ~**es**) *n*

mosquito (*sp*), zancudo (*LAM*)
moss [mɔs] *n* musgo
most [məust] *adj* la mayor parte de,
la mayoría de ▷*pron* la mayor parte, la
mayoría ▷*adv* el más; (*very*) muy; **the
~** (*also:* + *adj*) el más; **~ of them** la mayor
parte de ellos; **I saw the ~** yo vi el que
más; **at the (very)** ~ a lo sumo, todo
lo más; **to make the ~ of** aprovechar
(al máximo); **a ~ interesting book** un
libro interesantísimo; **mostly** *adv* en
su mayor parte, principalmente
MOT (*BRIT*) *n abbr* = **Ministry of
Transport**; **the ~ (test)** inspección
(anual) obligatoria de coches y camiones
motel [məuˈtel] *n* motel *m*
moth [mɔθ] *n* mariposa nocturna;
(*clothes moth*) polilla
mother [ˈmʌðə*] *n* madre *f* ▷*adj*
materno *f* (*care for*) cuidar
(como una madre); **motherhood**
n maternidad *f*; **mother-in-law**
n suegra; **mother-of-pearl** *n* nácar *m*;
Mother's Day *n* Día de la Madre;
mother-to-be *n* futura madre *f*;
mother tongue *n* lengua materna
motif [məuˈtiːf] *n* motivo
motion [ˈməuʃən] *n* movimiento;
(*gesture*) ademán *m*, señal *f*; (*at meeting*)
moción *f* ▷*vt, vi*: **to ~ (to) sb to do
sth** hacer señas a algn para que haga
algo; **motionless** *adj* inmóvil; **motion
picture** *n* película
motivate [ˈməutɪveɪt] *vt* motivar
motivation [məutɪˈveɪʃən] *n*
motivación *f*
motive [ˈməutɪv] *n* motivo
motor [ˈməutə*] *n* motor *m*;
(*BRIT: inf: vehicle*) coche *m* (*sp*), carro
(*LAM*), automóvil *m* ▷*adj* motor
(*f: motora or motriz*); **motorbike**
n moto *f*; **motorboat** *n* lancha
motora; **motorcar** (*BRIT*) *n* coche
m, carro, automóvil *m*; **motorcycle**
n motocicleta; **motorcyclist**
n motociclista *mf*; **motoring** (*BRIT*)
n automovilismo; **motorist**
n conductor(a) *m/f*, automovilista *mf*;

motor racing (BRIT) n carreras fpl de coches, automovilismo; **motorway** (BRIT) n autopista

motto ['mɒtəʊ] (pl **-es**) n lema m; (watchword) consigna

mould [məʊld] (US **mold**) n molde m; (mildew) moho ▷ vt moldear; (fig) formar; **mouldy** adj enmohecido

mound [maʊnd] n montón m, montículo

mount [maʊnt] n monte m ▷ vt montar, subir a; (jewel) engarzar; (picture) enmarcar; (exhibition etc) organizar ▷ vi (increase) aumentar; **mount up** vi aumentar

mountain ['maʊntɪn] n montaña ▷ cpd de montaña; **mountain bike** n bicicleta de montaña; **mountaineer** n alpinista mf (SP, MEX), andinista mf (LAM); **mountaineering** n alpinismo m (SP, MEX), andinismo (LAM); **mountainous** adj montañoso; **mountain range** n sierra

mourn [mɔːn] vt llorar, lamentar ▷ vi: **to ~ for** llorar la muerte de; **mourner** n doliente mf; dolorido/a; **mourning** n luto; **in mourning** de luto

mouse [maʊs] (pl **mice**) n (Zool, Comput) ratón m; **mouse mat** n (Comput) alfombrilla

moussaka [mu'sɑːkə] n musaca

mousse [muːs] n (Culin) crema batida; (for hair) espuma (moldeadora)

moustache [məs'tɑːʃ] (US **mustache**) n bigote m

mouth [maʊθ, pl maʊðz] n boca; (of river) desembocadura; **mouthful** n bocado; **mouth organ** n armónica; **mouthpiece** n (of musical instrument) boquilla; (spokesman) portavoz mf; **mouthwash** n enjuague m

move [muːv] n (movement) movimiento; (in game) jugada; (: turn to play) turno; (change: of house) mudanza; (: of job) cambio de trabajo ▷ vt mover; (emotionally) conmover; (Pol: resolution etc) proponer ▷ vi moverse; (traffic)

circular; (also: **~ house**) trasladarse, mudarse; **to ~ sb to do sth** mover a algn a hacer algo; **to get a ~ on** darse prisa; **move back** vi retroceder; **move in** vi (to a house) instalarse; (police, soldiers) intervenir; **move off** vi ponerse en camino; **move on** vi ponerse en camino; **move out** vi (of house) mudarse; **move over** vi apartarse, hacer sitio; **move up** vi (employee) ser ascendido; **movement** n movimiento

movie ['muːvɪ] n película; **to go to the ~s** ir al cine; **movie theater** (US) n cine m

moving ['muːvɪŋ] adj (emotional) conmovedor(a); (that moves) móvil

mow [məʊ] (pt **~ed**, pp **mowed** or **mown**) vt (grass, corn) cortar, segar; **mower** n (also: **lawnmower**) cortacéspedes m inv

Mozambique [məʊzæm'biːk] n Mozambique m

MP n abbr = **Member of Parliament**

MP3 n MP3; **MP3 player** n reproductor m (de) MP3

mpg n abbr = **miles per gallon**

m.p.h. abbr = **miles per hour** (60 m.p.h. = 96 k.p.h.)

Mr ['mɪstə] (US **Mr.**) n: **~ Smith** (el) Sr. Smith

Mrs ['mɪsɪz] (US **Mrs.**) n: **~ Smith** (la) Sra. Smith

Ms [mɪz] (US **Ms.**) n = **Miss** or **Mrs**; **~ Smith** (la) Sr(t)a. Smith

MSP n abbr = **Member of the Scottish Parliament**

Mt abbr (Geo) (= mount) m

much [mʌtʃ] adj mucho ▷ adv mucho; (before pp) muy ▷ n or pron mucho; **how ~ is it?** ¿cuánto es?, ¿cuánto cuesta?; **too ~** demasiado; **it's not ~** no es mucho; **as ~ as** tanto como; **however ~ he tries** por mucho que se esfuerce

muck [mʌk] n suciedad f; **muck up** (inf) vt arruinar, estropear; **mucky** adj (dirty) sucio

mucus ['mju:kəs] n mucosidad f, moco

mud [mʌd] n barro, lodo

muddle ['mʌdl] n desorden m, confusión f; (mix-up) embrollo, lío ▷ vt (also: ~ **up**) embrollar, confundir

muddy ['mʌdɪ] adj fangoso, cubierto de lodo

mudguard ['mʌdgɑːd] n guardabarros m inv

muesli ['mju:zlɪ] n muesli m

muffin ['mʌfɪn] n panecillo dulce

muffled ['mʌfld] (noise etc) amortiguado, apagado

muffler (US) ['mʌflə*] n (Aut) silenciador m

mug [mʌg] n taza grande (sin platillo); (for beer) jarra; (inf: face) jeta ▷ vt (assault) asaltar; **mugger** ['mʌgə*] n atracador(a) m/f; **mugging** n asalto

muggy ['mʌgɪ] adj bochornoso

mule [mju:l] n mula

multicoloured [mʌltɪˈkʌləd] (US), **multicolored** adj multicolor

multimedia ['mʌltɪˈmiːdɪə] adj multimedia

multinational [mʌltɪˈnæʃənl] n multinacional f ▷ adj multinacional

multiple ['mʌltɪpl] adj múltiple ▷ n múltiplo; **multiple choice (test)** n examen m de tipo test; **multiple sclerosis** n esclerosis f múltiple

multiplex cinema ['mʌltɪpleks-] n multicines mpl

multiplication [mʌltɪplɪˈkeɪʃən] n multiplicación f

multiply ['mʌltɪplaɪ] vt multiplicar ▷ vi multiplicarse

multistorey [mʌltɪˈstɔːrɪ] (BRIT) adj de muchos pisos

mum [mʌm] (BRIT: inf) n mamá ▷ adj: **to keep ~** mantener la boca cerrada

mumble ['mʌmbl] vt, vi hablar entre dientes, refunfuñar

mummy ['mʌmɪ] n (BRIT: mother) mamá; (embalmed) momia

mumps [mʌmps] n paperas fpl

munch [mʌntʃ] vt, vi mascar

municipal [mjuːˈnɪsɪpl] adj municipal

mural ['mjuərl] n (pintura) mural m

murder ['mɜːdə*] n asesinato; (in law) homicidio ▷ vt asesinar, matar; **murderer** n asesino

murky ['mɜːkɪ] adj (water) turbio; (street, night) lóbrego

murmur ['mɜːmə*] n murmullo ▷ vt, vi murmurar

muscle ['mʌsl] n músculo; (fig: strength) garra, fuerza; **muscular** ['mʌskjulə*] adj muscular; (person) musculoso

museum [mjuːˈzɪəm] n museo

mushroom ['mʌʃrum] n seta, hongo; (Culin) champiñón m ▷ vi crecer de la noche a la mañana

music ['mju:zɪk] n música; **musical** adj musical; (sound) melodioso; (person) con talento musical ▷ n (show) comedia musical; **musical instrument** n instrumento musical; **musician** [-'zɪʃən] n músico/a

Muslim ['mʌzlɪm] adj, n musulmán/ ana m/f

muslin ['mʌzlɪn] n muselina

mussel ['mʌsl] n mejillón m

must [mʌst] aux vb (obligation): **I ~ do it** debo hacerlo, tengo que hacerlo; (probability): **he ~ be there by now** ya debe (de) estar allí ▷ n: **it's a ~** es imprescindible

mustache ['mʌstæʃ] (US) n = **moustache**

mustard ['mʌstəd] n mostaza

mustn't ['mʌsnt] = **must not**

mute [mju:t] adj, n mudo/a m/f

mutilate ['mju:tɪleɪt] vt mutilar

mutiny ['mju:tɪnɪ] n motín m ▷ vi amotinarse

mutter ['mʌtə*] vt, vi murmurar

mutton ['mʌtn] n carne f de cordero

mutual ['mju:tʃuəl] adj mutuo; (interest) común

muzzle ['mʌzl] n hocico; (for dog) bozal m; (of gun) boca ▷ vt (dog) poner

un bozal a

my [maɪ] *adj* mi(s); **~ house/brother/ sisters** mi casa/mi hermano/mis hermanas; **I've washed ~ hair/cut ~ finger** me he lavado el pelo/cortado un dedo; **is this ~ pen or yours?** ¿es este bolígrafo mío o tuyo?

myself [maɪˈsɛlf] *pron* (*reflexive*) me; (*emphatic*) yo mismo; (*after prep*) mí (mismo); *see also* **oneself**

mysterious [mɪsˈtɪərɪəs] *adj* misterioso

mystery [ˈmɪstərɪ] *n* misterio

mystical [ˈmɪstɪkl] *adj* místico

mystify [ˈmɪstɪfaɪ] *vt* (*perplex*) dejar perplejo

myth [mɪθ] *n* mito; **mythology** [mɪˈθɒlədʒɪ] *n* mitología

n/a *abbr* (= *not applicable*) no interesa

nag [næg] *vt* (*scold*) regañar

nail [neɪl] *n* (*human*) uña; (*metal*) clavo ▷ *vt* clavar; **to ~ sth to sth** clavar algo en algo; **to ~ sb down to doing sth** comprometer a algn a que haga algo; **nailbrush** *n* cepillo para las uñas; **nailfile** *n* lima para las uñas; **nail polish** *n* esmalte *m* or laca para las uñas; **nail polish remover** *n* quitaesmalte *m*; **nail scissors** *npl* tijeras *fpl* para las uñas; **nail varnish** (BRIT) *n* = **nail polish**

naïve [naɪˈiːv] *adj* ingenuo

naked [ˈneɪkɪd] *adj* (*nude*) desnudo; (*flame*) expuesto al aire

name [neɪm] *n* nombre *m*; (*surname*) apellido; (*reputation*) fama, renombre *m* ▷ *vt* (*child*) poner nombre a; (*criminal*) identificar; (*price, date etc*) fijar; **what's your ~?** ¿cómo se llama?; **by ~** de nombre; **in the ~ of** en nombre de; **to give one's ~ and address** dar sus señas; **namely** *adv* a saber

nanny [ˈnænɪ] *n* niñera

nap [næp] n (sleep) sueñecito, siesta
napkin ['næpkɪn] n (also: **table ~**)
  servilleta
nappy ['næpɪ] (BRIT) n pañal m
narcotics npl (illegal drugs)
  estupefacientes mpl, narcóticos mpl
narrative ['nærətɪv] n narrativa
  ▷ adj narrativo
narrator [nə'reɪtə*] n narrador(a)
  m/f
narrow ['nærəʊ] adj estrecho,
  angosto; (fig: majority etc) corto; (: ideas
  etc) estrecho ▷ vi (road) estrecharse;
  (diminish) reducirse; **to have a ~
  escape** escaparse por los pelos;
  narrow down vt (search, investigation,
  possibilities) restringir, limitar; (list)
  reducir; **narrowly** adv (miss) por
  poco; **narrow-minded** adj de miras
  estrechas
nasal ['neɪzl] adj nasal
nasty ['nɑːstɪ] adj (remark) feo;
  (person) antipático; (revolting: taste,
  smell) asqueroso; (wound, disease etc)
  peligroso, grave
nation ['neɪʃən] n nación f
national ['næʃənl] adj, n nacional
  m/f; **national anthem** n himno
  nacional; **national dress** n vestido
  nacional; **National Health Service**
  (BRIT) n servicio nacional de salud
  pública = Insalud m (SP); **National
  Insurance** (BRIT) n seguro social
  nacional; **nationalist** adj, n
  nacionalista mf; **nationality** [-'nælɪtɪ]
  n nacionalidad f; **nationalize** vt
  nacionalizar; **national park** (BRIT) n
  parque m nacional; **National Trust** n
  (BRIT) organización encargada de preservar
  el patrimonio histórico británico
nationwide ['neɪʃənwaɪd] adj en
  escala o a nivel nacional
native ['neɪtɪv] n (local inhabitant)
  natural mf, vecino mf ▷ adj
  (indigenous) indígena; (country) natal;
  (innate) natural, innato; **a ~ of Russia**
  un(a) natural mf de Rusia; **Native
  American** adj, n americano/a

indígena, amerindio/a; **native
speaker** n hablante mf nativo/a
NATO ['neɪtəʊ] n abbr (= North Atlantic
Treaty Organization) OTAN f
natural ['nætʃrəl] adj natural;
  natural gas n gas m natural; **natural
  history** n historia natural; **naturally**
  adv (speak etc) naturalmente; (of course)
  desde luego, por supuesto; **natural
  resources** npl recursos mpl naturales
nature ['neɪtʃə*] n (also: **N~**)
  naturaleza; (group, sort) género, clase f;
  (character) carácter m, genio; **by ~** por
  o de naturaleza; **nature reserve** n
  reserva natural
naughty ['nɔːtɪ] adj (child) travieso
nausea ['nɔːsɪə] n náuseas fpl
naval ['neɪvl] adj naval, de marina
navel ['neɪvl] n ombligo
navigate ['nævɪgeɪt] vt gobernar
  ▷ vi navegar; (Aut) ir de copiloto;
  navigation [-'geɪʃən] n (action)
  navegación f; (science) náutica
navy ['neɪvɪ] n marina de guerra;
  (ships) armada, flota
Nazi ['nɑːtsɪ] n nazi mf
NB abbr (= nota bene) nótese
near [nɪə*] adj (place, relation)
  cercano; (time) próximo ▷ adv cerca
  ▷ prep (also: **~ to**: space) cerca de, junto
  a; (: time) cerca de ▷ vt acercarse a,
  aproximarse a; **nearby** [nɪə'baɪ] adj
  cercano, próximo ▷ adv cerca; **nearly**
  adv casi, por poco; **I nearly fell** por
  poco me caigo; **near-sighted** adj
  miope, corto de vista
neat [niːt] adj (place) ordenado,
  bien cuidado; (person) pulcro; (plan)
  ingenioso; (spirits) solo; **neatly**
  adv (tidily) con esmero; (skilfully)
  ingeniosamente
necessarily ['nɛsɪsrɪlɪ] adv
  necesariamente
necessary ['nɛsɪsrɪ] adj necesario,
  preciso
necessity [nɪ'sɛsɪtɪ] n necesidad f
neck [nɛk] n (of person, garment,
  bottle) cuello; (of animal) pescuezo ▷ vi

(inf) besuquearse; **~ and ~** parejos;

necklace ['nɛklɪs] n collar m; **necktie** ['nɛktaɪ] n corbata

nectarine ['nɛktərɪn] n nectarina

need [niːd] n (lack) escasez f, falta; (necessity) necesidad f; n vt (require) necesitar; **I ~ to do it** tengo que o debo hacerlo; **you don't ~ to go** no hace falta que (te) vayas

needle ['niːdl] n aguja ▷ vt (fig: inf) picar, fastidiar

needless ['niːdlɪs] adj innecesario; **~ to say** huelga decir que

needlework ['niːdlwəːk] n (activity) costura, labor f de aguja

needn't ['niːdnt] = **need not**

needy ['niːdɪ] adj necesitado

negative ['nɛgətɪv] n (Phot) negativo; (Ling) negación f ▷ adj negativo

neglect [nɪ'glɛkt] vt (one's duty) faltar a, no cumplir con; (child) descuidar, desatender ▷ n (of house, garden etc) abandono; (of child) desatención f; (of duty) incumplimiento

negotiate [nɪ'gəʊʃɪeɪt] vt (treaty, loan) negociar; (obstacle) franquear; (bend in road) tomar ▷ vi: **to ~ (with)** negociar (con)

negotiations [nɪgəʊʃɪ'eɪʃənz] npl negociaciones

negotiator [nɪ'gəʊʃɪeɪtə*] n negociador(a) m/f

neighbour ['neɪbə*] (US **neighbor** etc) n vecino/a; **neighbourhood** n (place) vecindad f, barrio; (people) vecindario; **neighbouring** adj vecino

neither ['naɪðə*] adj ni ▷ conj: **I didn't move and ~ did John** no me he movido, ni Juan tampoco ▷ pron ninguno ↔ adv: **~ good nor bad** ni bueno ni malo; **~ is true** ninguno/a de los(las) dos es cierto/a

neon ['niːɔn] n neón m

Nepal [nɪ'pɔːl] n Nepal m

nephew ['nɛvjuː] n sobrino

nerve [nəːv] n (Anat) nervio; (courage) valor m; (impudence) descaro, frescura

(nervousness) nerviosismo msg, nervios mpl; **a fit of ~s** un ataque de nervios

nervous ['nəːvəs] adj (anxious, Anat) nervioso; (timid) tímido, miedoso; **nervous breakdown** n crisis f nerviosa

nest [nɛst] n (of bird) nido; (wasps' nest) avispero n vi anidar

net [nɛt] n (gen) red f; (fabric) tul m ▷ adj (Comm) neto, líquido ▷ vt coger (SP) or agarrar (LAM) con red; (Sport) marcar; **netball** n balonred m

Netherlands ['nɛðələndz] npl: **the ~** los Países Bajos

nett [nɛt] adj = **net**

nettle ['nɛtl] n ortiga

network ['nɛtwəːk] n red f

neurotic [njuə'rɔtɪk] adj neurótico/a

neuter ['njuːtə*] adj (Ling) neutro ▷ vt castrar, capar

neutral ['njuːtrəl] adj (person) neutral; (colour etc, Elec) neutro ▷ n (Aut) punto muerto

never ['nɛvə*] adv nunca, jamás; **I ~ went** no fui nunca; **~ in my life** jamás en la vida; see also **mind**; **never-ending** adj interminable, sin fin; **nevertheless** [nɛvəðə'lɛs] adv sin embargo, no obstante

new [njuː] adj nuevo; (brand new) a estrenar; (recent) reciente; **New Age** n Nueva Era; **newborn** adj recién nacido; **newcomer** ['njuːkʌmə*] n recién venido/a o llegado/a; **newly** adv nuevamente, recién

news [njuːz] n noticias fpl; **a piece of ~** una noticia; **the ~** (Radio, TV) las noticias fpl; **news agency** n agencia de noticias; **newsagent** (BRIT) n vendedor(a) m/f de periódicos; **newscaster** n presentador(a) m/f, locutor(a) m/f; **news dealer** (US) n = **newsagent**; **newsletter** n hoja informativa, boletín m; **newspaper** n periódico, diario; **newsreader** n = **newscaster**

newt [njuːt] n tritón m

New Year n Año Nuevo; **New Year's**

Day n Día m de Año Nuevo; **New Year's Eve** n Nochevieja

New Zealand [njuːˈziːlənd] n Nueva Zelanda; **New Zealander** n neozelandés/esa m/f

next [nɛkst] adj (likeable, room) vecino; (bus stop, meeting) próximo; (following: page etc) siguiente ▷ adv después; **the ~ day** el día siguiente; **~ time** la próxima vez; **~ year** el año próximo or que viene; **~ to** junto a, al lado de; **~ to nothing** casi nada; **please!** ¡el siguiente!; **next door** adv en la casa de al lado ▷ adj vecino, de al lado; **next-of-kin** n pariente m más cercano

NHS n abbr = **National Health Service**

nibble [ˈnɪbl] vt mordisquear, mordiscar

nice [naɪs] adj (likeable) simpático; (kind) amable; (pleasant) agradable; (attractive) bonito, lindo (LAM); **nicely** adv amablemente; bien

niche [niːʃ] n (Arch) nicho, hornacina

nick [nɪk] n (wound) rasguño; (cut, indentation) mella, muesca ▷ vt (inf) birlar, robar; **in the ~ of time** justo a tiempo

nickel [ˈnɪkl] n níquel m; (us) moneda de 5 centavos

nickname [ˈnɪkneɪm] n apodo, mote m ▷ vt apodar

nicotine [ˈnɪkətiːn] n nicotina

niece [niːs] n sobrina

Nigeria [naɪˈdʒɪərɪə] n Nigeria

night [naɪt] n noche f; (evening) tarde f; **the ~ before last** anteanoche; **at ~, by ~** de noche, por la noche; **night club** n cabaret m; **nightdress** (BRIT) n camisón m; **nightie** [ˈnaɪtɪ] n = **nightdress**; **nightlife** n vida nocturna; **nightly** adj de todas las noches ▷ adv todas las noches, cada noche; **nightmare** n pesadilla; **night school** n clase(s) f(pl) nocturna(s); **night shift** n turno nocturno or de noche; **night-time** n noche f

nil [nɪl] (BRIT) n (Sport) cero, nada

nine [naɪn] num nueve; **nineteen** num diecinueve, diez y nueve; **nineteenth** [naɪnˈtiːnθ] adj decimonoveno, decimonono; **ninetieth** [ˈnaɪntɪɪθ] adj nonagésimo; **ninety** num noventa

ninth [naɪnθ] adj noveno

nip [nɪp] vt (pinch) pellizcar; (bite) morder

nipple [ˈnɪpl] n (Anat) pezón m

nitrogen [ˈnaɪtrədʒən] n nitrógeno

🔘 **KEYWORD**

no [nəu] (pl **noes**) adv (opposite of "yes") no; **are you coming? – no (I'm not)** ¿vienes? – no (no voy); **would you like some more? – no thank you** ¿quieres más? – no gracias ▷ adj (not any): **I have no money/time/books** no tengo dinero/tiempo/libros; **no other man would have done it** ningún otro lo hubiera hecho; **"no entry"** "prohibido el paso"; **"no smoking"** "prohibido fumar"
▷ n no m

nobility [nəuˈbɪlɪtɪ] n nobleza

noble [ˈnəubl] adj noble

nobody [ˈnəubədɪ] pron nadie

nod [nɔd] vi saludar con la cabeza; (in agreement) decir que sí con la cabeza; (doze) dar cabezadas ▷ vt: to ~ **one's head** inclinar la cabeza ▷ n inclinación f de cabeza; **nod off** vi dar cabezadas

noise [nɔɪz] n ruido; (din) escándalo, estrépito; **noisy** adj ruidoso; (child) escandaloso

nominal [ˈnɔmɪnl] adj nominal

nominate [ˈnɔmɪneɪt] vt (propose) proponer; (appoint) nombrar; **nomination** [nɔmɪˈneɪʃən] n propuesta; nombramiento; **nominee** [ˈniː] n candidato/a

none [nʌn] pron ninguno/a ▷ adv de ninguna manera; **~ of you** ninguno de vosotros; **I've ~ left** no me queda ninguno/a; **he's ~ the worse for it** no le ha hecho ningún mal

nonetheless [nʌnðə'lɛs] adv sin embargo, no obstante

non-fiction [nɒn'fɪkʃən] n literatura no novelesca

nonsense ['nɒnsəns] n tonterías fpl, disparates fpl; **~!** ¡qué tonterías!

non: **non-smoker** n no fumador(a) m/f; **non-smoking** adj (de) no fumador; **non-stick** adj (pan, surface) antiadherente

noodles ['nu:dlz] npl tallarines mpl

noon [nu:n] n mediodía m

no-one ['nəuwʌn] pron = **nobody**

nor [nɔ:ʳ] conj = **neither** ▷ adv see **neither**

norm [nɔ:m] n norma

normal ['nɔ:ml] adj normal; **normally** adv normalmente

north [nɔ:θ] n norte m ▷ adj del norte, norteño ▷ adv al or hacia el norte; **North America** n América del Norte; **North American** adj, n norteamericano/a m/f; **northbound** ['nɔ:θbaund] adj (traffic) que se dirige al norte; (carriageway) de dirección norte; **north-east** n nor(d)este m; **northeastern** adj del nor(d)este; **northern** ['nɔ:ðən] adj norteño, del norte; **Northern Ireland** n Irlanda del Norte; **North Korea** n Corea del Norte; **North Pole** n Polo Norte; **North Sea** n Mar m del Norte; **north-west** n nor(d)oeste m; **northwestern** [nɔ:θ'wɛstən] adj noroeste, del noroeste

Norway ['nɔ:weɪ] n Noruega; **Norwegian** [-'wi:dʒən] adj noruego/a ▷ n noruego/a; (Ling) noruego

nose [nəuz] n (Anat) nariz f; (Zool) hocico; (sense of smell) olfato ▷ vi: to **~ about** curiosear; **nosebleed** n hemorragia nasal; **nosey** (inf) adj curioso, fisgón/ona

nostalgia [nɒs'tældʒɪə] n nostalgia

nostalgic [nɒs'tældʒɪk] adj nostálgico

nostril ['nɒstrɪl] n ventana de la nariz

nosy ['nəuzɪ] (inf) adj = **nosey**

not [nɒt] adv no; **~ that** ... no es que ...; **it's too late, isn't it?** es demasiado tarde, ¿verdad or no?; **~ yet/now** todavía/ahora no; **why ~?** ¿por qué no?; see also **all; only**

notable ['nəutəbl] adj notable; **notably** adv especialmente

notch [nɒtʃ] n muesca, corte m

note [nəut] n (Mus, record, letter) nota; (banknote) billete m; (tone) tono ▷ vt (observe) notar, observar; (write down) apuntar, anotar; **notebook** n libreta, cuaderno; **noted** ['nəutɪd] adj célebre, conocido; **notepad** n bloc m; **notepaper** n papel m para cartas

nothing ['nʌθɪŋ] n nada; (zero) cero; **he does ~** no hace nada; **~ new** nada nuevo; **~ much** no mucho; **for ~** (free) gratis, sin pago; (in vain) en balde

notice ['nəutɪs] n (announcement) anuncio; (warning) aviso; (dismissal) despido; (resignation) dimisión f; (period of time) plazo ▷ vt (observe) notar, observar; **to bring sth to sb's ~** (attention) llamar la atención de algn sobre algo; **to take ~ of** tomar nota de, prestar atención a; **at short ~** con poca anticipación; **until further ~** hasta nuevo aviso; **to hand in one's ~** dimitir

> Be careful not to translate **notice** by the Spanish word noticia.

noticeable adj evidente, obvio

notify ['nəutɪfaɪ] vt: **to ~ sb (of sth)** comunicar (algo) a algn

notion ['nəuʃən] n idea; (opinion) opinión f; **notions** npl (us) mercería

notorious [nəu'tɔ:rɪəs] adj notorio

notwithstanding [nɒtwɪθ'stændɪŋ] adv no obstante, sin embargo; **~ this** a pesar de esto

nought [nɔ:t] n cero

noun [naun] n nombre m, sustantivo

nourish ['nʌrɪʃ] vt nutrir; (fig) alimentar; **nourishment** n alimento, sustento

Nov. abbr (= November) nov

novel ['nɒvl] n novela ▷ adj (new)

nuevo, original; (*unexpected*) insólito;
novelist *n* novelista *mf*; **novelty** *n*
novedad *f*

November [nəu'vembə*] *n*
noviembre *m*

novice ['nɒvɪs] *n* (*Rel*) novicio/a

now [nau] *adv* (*at the present time*)
ahora; (*these days*) actualmente, hoy
día ▷ *conj*: **~ (that)** ya que, ahora que;
right ~ ahora mismo; **by ~** ya; **just
~** ahora mismo; **~ and then, ~ and
again** de vez en cuando; **from ~ on** de
ahora en adelante; **nowadays** ['nauə
deɪz] *adv* hoy (en) día, actualmente

nowhere ['nəuweə*] *adv* (*direction*)
a ninguna parte; (*location*) en ninguna
parte

nozzle ['nɒzl] *n* boquilla

nr *abbr* (*BRIT*) = **near**

nuclear ['nju:klɪə*] *adj* nuclear

nucleus ['nju:klɪəs] (*pl* **nuclei**) *n*
núcleo

nude [nju:d] *adj*, *n* desnudo/a *m/f*; **in
the ~** desnudo

nudge [nʌdʒ] *vt* dar un codazo a

nudist ['nju:dɪst] *n* nudista *mf*

nudity ['nju:dɪtɪ] *n* desnudez *f*

nuisance ['nju:sns] *n* molestia,
fastidio; (*person*) pesado, latoso; **what
a ~!** ¡qué lata!

numb [nʌm] *adj*: **~ with cold/fear**
entumecido por el frío/paralizado
de miedo

number ['nʌmbə*] *n* número;
(*quantity*) cantidad *f* ▷ *vt* (*pages etc*)
numerar, poner número a; (*amount to*)
sumar, ascender a; **to be ~ed among**
figurar entre; **a ~ of** varios, algunos;
they were ten in ~ eran diez; **number
plate** (*BRIT*) *n* matrícula, placa;
Number Ten (*BRIT*: 10 *Downing
Street*) residencia del primer ministro

numerical [nju:'merɪkl] *adj*
numérico

numerous ['nju:mərəs] *adj*
numeroso

nun [nʌn] *n* monja, religiosa

nurse [nə:s] *n* enfermero/a; (*also*:

~maid) niñera ▷ *vt* (*patient*) cuidar,
atender

nursery ['nə:sərɪ] *n* (*institution*)
guardería infantil; (*room*) cuarto de los
niños; (*for plants*) criadero, semillero;
nursery rhyme *n* canción *f* infantil;
nursery school *n* parvulario, escuela
de párvulos; **nursery slope** (*BRIT*) *n*
(*Ski*) cuesta para principiantes

nursing ['nə:sɪŋ] *n* (*profession*)
profesión *f* de enfermera; (*care*)
asistencia, cuidado; **nursing home** *n*
clínica de reposo

nurture ['nə:tʃə*] *vt* (*child, plant*)
alimentar, nutrir

nut [nʌt] *n* (*Tech*) tuerca; (*Bot*) nuez *f*

nutmeg ['nʌtmeg] *n* nuez *f* moscada

nutrient ['nju:trɪənt] *adj* nutritivo
▷ *n* elemento nutritivo

nutrition [nju:'trɪʃn] *n* nutrición *f*,
alimentación *f*

nutritious [nju:'trɪʃəs] *adj* nutritivo,
alimenticio

nuts [nʌts] (*inf*) *adj* loco

NVQ *n abbr* (*BRIT*) = **National
Vocational Qualification**

nylon ['naɪlɔn] *n* nilón *m* ▷ *adj* de
nilón

O

oath [əʊθ] n juramento; (swear word) palabrota; **on** (BRIT) or **under ~** bajo juramento

oak [əʊk] n roble m ▷ adj de roble

O.A.P. (BRIT) n, abbr = **old-age pensioner**

oar [ɔː*] n remo

oasis [əʊˈeɪsɪs] (pl **oases**) n oasis m inv

oath [əʊθ] n juramento; (swear word) palabrota; **on** (BRIT) or **under ~** bajo juramento

oatmeal [ˈəʊtmiːl] n harina de avena

oats [əʊts] npl avena

obedience [əˈbiːdɪəns] n obediencia

obedient [əˈbiːdɪənt] adj obediente

obese [əʊˈbiːs] adj obeso

obesity [əʊˈbiːsɪtɪ] n obesidad f

obey [əˈbeɪ] vt obedecer; (instructions, regulations) cumplir

obituary [əˈbɪtjʊərɪ] n necrología

object [n ˈɒbdʒɪkt, vb əbˈdʒɛkt] n objeto; (purpose) objeto, propósito; (Ling) complemento ▷ vi: **to ~ to** estar en contra de; (proposal) oponerse a; **to ~ that** objetar que; **expense is no**

~ no importa cuánto cuesta; **I ~!** ¡yo protesto!; **objection** [əbˈdʒɛkʃən] n protesta; **I have no objection to ...** no tengo inconveniente en que ...;

objective adj, n objetivo

obligation [ɒblɪˈgeɪʃən] n obligación f; (debt) deber m; **without ~** sin compromiso

obligatory [əˈblɪgətərɪ] adj obligatorio

oblige [əˈblaɪdʒ] vt (do a favour for) complacer, hacer un favor a; **to ~ sb to do sth** forzar or obligar a algn a hacer algo; **to be ~d to sb for sth** estarle agradecido a algn por algo

oblique [əˈbliːk] adj oblicuo; (allusion) indirecto

obliterate [əˈblɪtəreɪt] vt borrar

oblivious [əˈblɪvɪəs] adj: **~ of** inconsciente de

oblong [ˈɒblɒŋ] adj rectangular ▷ n rectángulo

obnoxious [əbˈnɒkʃəs] adj odioso, detestable; (smell) nauseabundo

oboe [ˈəʊbəʊ] n oboe m

obscene [əbˈsiːn] adj obsceno

obscure [əbˈskjʊə*] adj oscuro ▷ vt oscurecer; (hide: sun) esconder

observant [əbˈzɜːvnt] adj observador(a)

observation [ɒbzəˈveɪʃən] n observación f; (Med) examen m

observatory [əbˈzɜːvətrɪ] n observatorio

observe [əbˈzɜːv] vt observar; (rule) cumplir; **observer** n observador(a) m/f

obsess [əbˈsɛs] vt obsesionar; **obsession** [əbˈsɛʃən] n obsesión f; **obsessive** adj obsesivo; obsesionante

obsolete [ˈɒbsəliːt] adj: **to be ~** estar en desuso

obstacle [ˈɒbstəkl] n obstáculo; (nuisance) obstáculo

obstinate [ˈɒbstɪnɪt] adj terco, porfiado; (determined) obstinado

obstruct [əbˈstrʌkt] vt obstruir; (hinder) estorbar, obstaculizar; **obstruction** [əbˈstrʌkʃən] n (action) obstrucción f; (object) estorbo, obstáculo

obtain [əb'teɪn] vt obtener; (achieve) conseguir

obvious ['ɔbvɪəs] adj obvio, evidente; **obviously** adv evidentemente, naturalmente; **obviously not** por supuesto que no

occasion [ə'keɪʒən] n oportunidad f, ocasión f; (event) acontecimiento; **occasional** adj poco frecuente, ocasional; **occasionally** adv de vez en cuando

occult [ə'kʌlt] adj (gen) oculto

occupant ['ɔkjupənt] n (of house) inquilino/a; (of car) ocupante mf

occupation [ɔkju'peɪʃən] n ocupación f; (job) trabajo; (pastime) ocupaciones fpl

occupy ['ɔkjupaɪ] vt (seat, post, time) ocupar; (house) habitar; **to ~ o.s. in doing** pasar el tiempo haciendo

occur [ə'kɔː*] vi pasar, suceder; **to ~ to sb** ocurrírsele a algn; **occurrence** [ə'kʌrəns] n acontecimiento; (existence) existencia

ocean ['əuʃən] n océano

o'clock [ə'klɔk] adv: **it is 5 ~** son las 5

Oct. abbr (= October) oct

October [ɔk'təubə*] n octubre m

octopus ['ɔktəpəs] n pulpo

odd [ɔd] adj extraño, raro; (number) impar; (sock, shoe etc) suelto; **60-~** 60 y pico; **at ~ times** de vez en cuando; **to be the ~ one out** estar de más; **oddly** adv curiosamente, extrañamente; see also **enough**; **odds** npl (in betting) puntos mpl de ventaja; **it makes no odds** da lo mismo; **at odds** reñidos/as; **odds and ends** minucias fpl

odometer [ɔ'dɔmɪtə*] (us) n cuentakilómetros m inv

odour ['əudə*] (us **odor**) n olor m; (unpleasant) hedor m

⊙ **KEYWORD**

of [ɔv, əv] prep 1 (gen) de; **a friend of ours** un amigo nuestro; **a boy of 10** un

chico de 10 años; **that was kind of you** eso fue muy amable por o de tu parte

2 (expressing quantity, amount, dates etc) de; **a kilo of flour** un kilo de harina; **there were three of them** había tres; **three of us went** tres de nosotros fuimos; **the 5th of July** el 5 de julio

3 (from, out of) de; **made of wood** (hecho) de madera

off [ɔf] adj, adv (engine) desconectado; (light) apagado; (tap) cerrado; (BRIT: food: bad) pasado, malo; (: milk) cortado; (cancelled) cancelado ▷ prep de; **to be ~** (to leave) irse, marcharse; **to be ~ sick** estar enfermo or de baja; **a day ~** un día libre o sin trabajar; **to have an ~ day** tener un día malo; **he had his coat ~** se había quitado el abrigo; **10% ~** (Comm) (con el) 10% de descuento; **5 km ~ (the road)** a 5 km (de la carretera); **~ the coast** frente a la costa; **I'm ~ meat** (no longer eat/like it) paso de la carne; **on the ~ chance** por si acaso; **~ and on** de vez en cuando

offence [ə'fens] (us **offense**) n (crime) delito; **to take ~ at** ofenderse por

offend [ə'fend] vt (person) ofender; **offender** n delincuente mf

offense [ə'fens] (us) = **offence**

offensive [ə'fensɪv] adj ofensivo; (smell etc) repugnante ▷ n (Mil) ofensiva

offer ['ɔfə*] n oferta, ofrecimiento; (proposal) propuesta ▷ vt ofrecer; (opportunity) facilitar; **"on ~"** (Comm) "en oferta"

offhand [ɔf'hænd] adj informal ▷ adv de improviso

office ['ɔfɪs] n (place) oficina; (room) despacho; (position) carga, oficio; **doctor's ~** (us) consultorio; **to take ~** entrar en funciones; **office block** (us), **office building** n bloque m de oficinas; **office hours** npl horas fpl de oficina; (us Med) horas fpl de consulta

officer ['ɔfɪsə*] n (Mil etc) oficial mf;

(also: **police ~**) agente mf de policía; (of organization) director(a) m/f

office worker n oficinista mf

official [əˈfɪʃl] adj oficial, autorizado ▷ n funcionario/a, oficial mf

off-licence (BRIT) n (shop) bodega tienda de vinos y bebidas alcohólicas; **off-line** adj, adv (Comput) fuera de línea; **off-peak** adj (electricity) fuera de banda económica; (ticket) billete de precio reducido por viajar fuera de las horas punta; **off-putting** (BRIT) adj (person) asqueroso; (remark) desalentador(a); **off-season** adj, adv fuera de temporada

- **OFF-LICENCE**

En el Reino Unido la venta de bebidas alcohólicas está estrictamente regulada y se necesita una licencia especial, con la que cuentan los bares, restaurantes y los establecimientos de **off-licence**, los únicos lugares en donde se pueden adquirir bebidas alcohólicas fuera del local, de donde viene su nombre. También venden bebidas no alcohólicas, tabaco, chocolatinas, patatas fritas, etc. y a menudo forman parte de la cadena nacional.

offset [ˈɔfsɛt] vt contrarrestar, compensar

offshore [ɔfˈʃɔ:*] adj (breeze, island) costera; (fishing) de bajura

offside [ˈɔfsaɪd] adj (Sport) fuera de juego; (Aut: in US) del lado derecho; (: in US, Europe etc) del lado izquierdo

offspring [ˈɔfsprɪŋ] n inv descendencia

often [ˈɔfn] adv a menudo, con frecuencia; **how ~ do you go?** ¿cada cuánto vas?

oh [əu] excl ¡ah!

oil [ɔɪl] n aceite m; (petroleum) petróleo; (for heating) aceite m combustible ▷ vt engrasar; **oil filter** n (Aut) filtro de aceite; **oil painting** n pintura al óleo; **oil refinery** n refinería de petróleo; **oil rig** n torre f de perforación; **oil slick** n marea negra; **oil tanker** n petrolero; (truck) camión m cisterna; **oil well** n pozo (de petróleo); **oily** adj aceitoso; (food) grasiento

ointment [ˈɔɪntmənt] n ungüento

O.K., okay [ˈəuˈkeɪ] excl ¡O.K.!, ¡está bien!, ¡vale! (SP) ▷ adj bien ▷ vt dar el visto bueno a

old [əuld] adj viejo; (former) antiguo; **how ~ are you?** ¿cuántos años tienes?, ¿qué edad tienes?; **he's 10 years ~** tiene 10 años; **~er brother** hermano mayor; **old age** n vejez f; **old-age pension** n (BRIT) jubilación f, pensión f; **old-age pensioner** (BRIT) n jubilado/a; **old-fashioned** adj anticuado, pasado de moda; **old people's home** n (esp BRIT) residencia f de ancianos

olive [ˈɔlɪv] n (fruit) aceituna; (tree) olivo ▷ adj (also: **~-green**) verde oliva; **olive oil** n aceite m de oliva

Olympic [əuˈlɪmpɪk] adj olímpico; **the ~ Games, the ~s** las Olimpiadas

omelet(te) [ˈɔmlɪt] n tortilla francesa (SP), omelette f (LAM)

omen [ˈəumən] n presagio

ominous [ˈɔmɪnəs] adj de mal agüero, amenazador(a)

omit [əuˈmɪt] vt omitir

○ **KEYWORD**

on [ɔn] prep 1 (indicating position) en; sobre; **on the wall** en la pared; **it's on the table** está sobre or en la mesa; **on the left** a la izquierda

2 (indicating means, method, condition etc): **on foot** a pie; **on the train/**

plane (go) en tren/avión; (be) en el tren/el avión; **on the radio/television/telephone** por or en la radio/televisión/al teléfono; **to be on drugs** drogarse; (Med) estar a tratamiento; **to be on holiday/business** estar de vacaciones/en/viaje de negocios

3 (referring to time): **on Friday** el viernes; **on Fridays** los viernes; **on June 20th** el 20 de junio; **a week on Friday** del viernes en una semana; **on arrival** al llegar; **on seeing this** al ver esto

4 (about, concerning) sobre, acerca de; **a book on physics** un libro de or sobre física

▷ **adv 1** (referring to dress): **to have one's coat on** tener or llevar el abrigo puesto; **she put her gloves on** se puso los guantes

2 (referring to covering): **"screw the lid on tightly"** "cerrar bien la tapa"

3 (further, continuously): **to walk etc on** seguir caminando etc

▷ **adj 1** (functioning, in operation: machine, radio, TV, light) encendido/a (SP), prendido/a (LAM); (: tap) abierto/a; (: brakes) echado/a, puesto/a; **is the meeting still on?** (in progress) ¿todavía continúa la reunión?; (not cancelled) ¿va a haber reunión al fin?; **there's a good film on at the cinema** ponen una buena película en el cine

2 **that's not on!** (inf: not possible) ¡eso ni hablar!; (: not acceptable) ¡eso no se hace!

once [wʌns] **adv** una vez; (formerly) antiguamente ▷ **conj** una vez que; **~ he had left/it was done** una vez que se había marchado/se hizo; **at ~** en seguida, inmediatamente; (simultaneously) a la vez; **~ a week** una vez por semana; **~ more** otra vez; **~ and for all** de una vez por todas; **~ upon a time** érase una vez

oncoming [ˈɔnkʌmɪŋ] **adj** (traffic)

que viene de frente

○ **KEYWORD**

one [wʌn] **num** un(o)/una; **one hundred and fifty** ciento cincuenta; **one by one** uno a uno

▷ **adj 1** (sole) único; **the one book which** el único libro que; **the one man who** el único que

2 (same) mismo/a; **they came in the one car** vinieron en un solo coche

▷ **pron 1 this one** éste(ésta); **that one** ése(ésa); (more remote) aquél(aquella); **I've already got (a red) one** ya tengo uno/a rojo/a; **one by one** uno/a por uno/a

2 one another os (SP), se (+el uno al otro, unos a otros etc); **do you two ever see one another?** ¿vosotros dos os veis alguna vez? (SP), ¿se ven ustedes dos alguna vez?; **the boys didn't dare look at one another** los chicos no se atrevieron a mirarse (el uno al otro); **they all kissed one another** se besaron unos a otros

3 (impers): **one never knows** nunca se sabe; **to cut one's finger** cortarse el dedo; **one needs to eat** hay que comer

one-off [BRIT: inf] **n** (event) acontecimiento único

oneself [wʌnˈself] **pron** (reflexive) se; (after prep) sí; (emphatic) uno/a mismo/a; **to hurt ~** hacerse daño; **to keep sth for ~** guardarse algo; **to talk to ~** hablar solo

one: **one-shot** [wʌnˈʃɔt] (US) **n** = **one-off**; **one-sided adj** (argument) parcial; **one-to-one adj** (relationship) de dos; **one-way adj** (street) de sentido único

ongoing [ˈɔngəʊɪŋ] **adj** continuo

onion [ˈʌnjən] **n** cebolla

on-line [ˈɔnlaɪn] **adj, adv** (Comput) en línea

onlooker [ˈɔnlʊkə*] **n** espectador(a) m/f

only ['əunlı] adv solamente, sólo ▷ adj único, solo ▷ conj solamente que, pero; **an ~ child** un hijo único; **not ~ ... but also ~** no sólo ... sino también ...

on-screen [ɒn'skri:n] adj (Comput etc) en pantalla; (romance, kiss) cinematográfico

onset ['ɒnset] n comienzo

onto ['ɒntu] prep = **on to**

onward(s) ['ɒnwəd(z)] adv (move) (hacia) adelante; **from that time ~** desde entonces en adelante

oops [ups] excl (also: **~-a-daisy!**) ¡huy!

ooze [u:z] vi rezumar

opaque [əu'peık] adj opaco

open ['əupn] adj abierto; (car) descubierto; (road, view) despejado; (meeting) público; (admiration) manifiesto ▷ vt abrir ▷ vi abrirse; (book etc: commence) comenzar; **in the ~ (air)** al aire libre; **open up** vt abrir; (blocked road) despejar ▷ vi abrirse, empezar; **open-air** adj al aire libre; **opening** n abertura; (start) comienzo; (opportunity) oportunidad f; **opening hours** npl horario de apertura; **open learning** n enseñanza flexible a tiempo parcial; **openly** adv abiertamente; **open-minded** adj imparcial; **open-necked** adj (shirt) desabrochado; sin corbata; **open-plan** adj; **open-plan office** gran oficina sin particiones; **Open University** (BRIT) ≈ Universidad Nacional de Enseñanza a Distancia, UNED f

○ **OPEN UNIVERSITY**

○ La **Open University**, fundada
○ en 1969, está especializada en
○ impartir cursos a distancia que no
○ exigen una dedicación exclusiva.
○ Cuenta con sus propios materiales
○ de apoyo, entre ellos programas de
○ radio y televisión emitidos por la
○ **BBC** y para conseguir los créditos
○ de la licenciatura es necesaria la

○ presentación de unos trabajos y la
○ asistencia a los cursos de verano.

opera ['ɒpərə] n ópera; **opera house** n teatro de la ópera; **opera singer** n cantante m/f de ópera

operate ['ɒpəreıt] vt (machine) hacer funcionar; (company) dirigir ▷ vi funcionar; **to ~ on sb** (Med) operar a algn

operating room ['ɒpəreıtıŋ-] (US) n quirófano, sala de operaciones

operating theatre (BRIT) n sala de operaciones

operation [ɒpə'reıʃən] n operación f; (of machine) funcionamiento; **to be in ~** estar funcionando or en funcionamiento; **to have an ~** (Med) ser operado; **operational** adj operacional, en buen estado

operative ['ɒpərətıv] adj en vigor

operator ['ɒpəreıtə*] n (of machine) maquinista m/f, operario/a; (Tel) operador(a) m/f, telefonista mf

opinion [ə'pınıən] n opinión f; **in my ~** en mi opinión, a mi juicio; **opinion poll** n encuesta, sondeo

opponent [ə'pəunənt] n adversario/a, contrincante m/f

opportunity [ɒpə'tju:nıtı] n oportunidad f; **to take the ~ of doing** aprovechar la ocasión para hacer

oppose [ə'pəuz] vt oponerse a; **to be ~d to sth** oponerse a algo; **as ~d to** a diferencia de

opposite ['ɒpəzıt] adj opuesto, contrario a; (house etc) de enfrente ▷ adv en frente ▷ prep en frente de, frente a ▷ n lo contrario

opposition [ɒpə'zıʃən] n oposición f

oppress [ə'pres] vt oprimir

opt [ɒpt] vi: **to ~ for** optar por; **to ~ to do** optar por hacer; **opt out** vi: **to opt out of** optar por no hacer

optician [ɒp'tıʃən] n óptico m/f

optimism ['ɒptımızəm] n optimismo

optimist ['ɒptımıst] n optimista mf;

optimistic [-'mɪstɪk] adj optimista
optimum ['ɔptɪməm] adj óptimo
option ['ɔpʃən] n opción f; **optional** adj facultativo, discrecional
or [ɔː*] conj o; (before o, ho) u; (with negative): **he hasn't seen ~ heard anything** no ha visto ni oído nada; **~ else** si no
oral ['ɔːrəl] adj oral ▷ n examen m oral
orange ['ɔrɪndʒ] n (fruit) naranja ▷ adj color naranja; **orange juice** n jugo de naranja, zumo de naranja (SP); **orange squash** n naranjada
orbit ['ɔːbɪt] n órbita ▷ vt, vi orbitar
orchard ['ɔːtʃəd] n huerto
orchestra ['ɔːkɪstrə] n orquesta; (US: seating) platea
orchid ['ɔːkɪd] n orquídea
ordeal [ɔː'diːl] n experiencia horrorosa
order ['ɔːdə*] n orden m; (command) orden f; (good order) buen estado; (Comm) pedido ▷ vt (also: **put in ~**) arreglar, poner en orden; (Comm) pedir; (command) mandar, ordenar; **in ~** en orden; (of document) en regla; **in (working) ~** en funcionamiento; **in ~ to/that** para hacer/que; **on ~** (Comm) pedido; **to be out of ~** estar desordenado; (not working) no funcionar; **to ~ sb to do sth** mandar a algn hacer algo; **order form** n hoja de pedido; **orderly** n (Mil) ordenanza m; (Med) enfermero/a (auxiliar) ▷ adj ordenado
ordinary ['ɔːdnrɪ] adj corriente, normal; (pej) común y corriente; **out of the ~** fuera de lo común
ore [ɔː*] n mineral m
oregano [ɔrɪ'ɡɑːnəu] n orégano
organ ['ɔːɡən] n órgano; **organic** [ɔː'ɡænɪk] adj orgánico; **organism** n organismo
organization [ɔːɡənaɪ'zeɪʃən] n organización f
organize ['ɔːɡənaɪz] vt organizar; **organized** ['ɔːɡənaɪzd] adj organizado; **organizer** n

organizador(a) m/f
orgasm ['ɔːɡæzəm] n orgasmo
orgy ['ɔːdʒɪ] n orgía
oriental [ɔːrɪ'entl] adj oriental
orientation [ɔːrɪen'teɪʃən] n orientación f
origin ['ɔrɪdʒɪn] n origen m
original [ə'rɪdʒɪnl] adj original; (first) primero; (earlier) primitivo ▷ n original m; **originally** adv al principio
originate [ə'rɪdʒɪneɪt] vi: **to ~ from**, **to ~ in** surgir de, tener su origen en
Orkneys ['ɔːknɪz] npl: **the ~** (also: **the Orkney Islands**) las Orcadas
ornament ['ɔːnəmənt] n adorno; (trinket) chuchería; **ornamental** [-'mentl] adj decorativo, de adorno
ornate [ɔː'neɪt] adj muy ornado, vistoso
orphan ['ɔːfn] n huérfano/a
orthodox ['ɔːθədɔks] adj ortodoxo
orthopaedic [ɔːθə'piːdɪk] (US **orthopedic**) adj ortopédico
osteopath ['ɔstɪəpæθ] n osteópata mf
ostrich ['ɔstrɪtʃ] n avestruz m
other ['ʌðə*] adj otro ▷ pron: **the ~ (one)** el/la otro/a ▷ adv: **~ than** aparte de; **otherwise** adv de otra manera ▷ conj (if not) si no
otter ['ɔtə*] n nutria
ouch [autʃ] excl ¡ay!
ought [ɔːt] (pt ~) aux vb: **I ~ to do it** debería hacerlo; **this ~ to have been corrected** esto debiera haberse corregido; **he ~ to win** (probability) debe or debiera ganar
ounce [auns] n onza (28.35g)
our ['auə*] adj nuestro; see also **my**; **ours** pron (el) nuestro/(la) nuestra etc; see also **mine¹**; **ourselves** pron pl (reflexive, after prep) nosotros; (emphatic) nosotros mismos; see also **oneself**
oust [aust] vt desalojar
out [aut] adv fuera, afuera; (not at home) fuera (de casa); (light, fire) apagado; **~ there** allí (fuera); **he's ~** (absent) no está, ha salido; **to be ~ in**

one's calculations equivocarse (en sus cálculos); **to run ~** salir corriendo; **~ loud** en alta voz; **~ of** (outside) fuera de; (because of: anger etc) por; **~ of petrol** sin gasolina; **"~ of order"** "no funciona";

outback n interior m; **outbound** adj (flight) de salida; (flight: not return) de ida; **outbreak** n (of war) comienzo m; (of disease) epidemia; (of violence etc) ola; **outburst** n explosión f, arranque m; **outcast** n paria mf; **outcome** n resultado; **outcry** n protestas fpl; **outdated** adj anticuado, fuera de moda; **outdoor** adj exterior, de aire libre; (clothes) de calle; **outdoors** adv al aire libre

outer ['autə*] adj exterior, externo; **outer space** n espacio exterior

outfit ['autfɪt] n (clothes) conjunto m

out: outgoing adj (character) extrovertido; (retiring: president etc) saliente; **outgoings** (BRIT) npl gastos mpl; **outhouse** n dependencia

outing ['autɪŋ] n excursión f, paseo

out: outlaw n proscrito ▷ vt proscribir; **outlay** n inversión f; **outlet** n salida; (of pipe) desagüe m; (US Elec) toma de corriente; (also: **retail outlet**) punto de venta; **outline** n (shape) contorno, perfil m; (sketch, plan) esbozo ▷ vt (plan etc) esbozar; **in outline** (fig) a grandes rasgos; **outlook** n (fig: prospects) perspectivas fpl; (: for weather) pronóstico; **outnumber** vt superar en número; **out-of-date** adj (passport) caducado; (clothes) pasado de moda; **out-of-doors** adv al aire libre; **out-of-the-way** adj apartado; **out-of-town** adj (shopping centre etc) en las afueras; **outpatient** n paciente mf externo/a; **outpost** n puesto avanzado; **output** n (volumen m de) producción m, rendimiento; (Comput) salida

outrage ['autreɪdʒ] n escándalo; (atrocity) atrocidad f ▷ vt ultrajar; **outrageous** [-'reɪdʒəs] adj monstruoso

outright [adv aut'raɪt, adj 'autraɪt] adv (ask, deny) francamente; (refuse) rotundamente; (win) de manera absoluta; (be killed) en el acto ▷ adj franco; rotundo

outset ['autset] n principio

outside [aut'saɪd] n exterior m ▷ adj exterior, externo ▷ adv fuera ▷ prep fuera de; (beyond) más allá de; **at the ~** (fig) a lo sumo; **outside lane** n (Aut: in Britain) carril m de la derecha; (: in US, Europe etc) carril m de la izquierda; **outside line** n (Tel) línea (exterior); **outsider** n (stranger) extraño, forastero

out: outsize adj (clothes) de talla grande; **outskirts** npl alrededores mpl, afueras fpl; **outspoken** adj muy franco; **outstanding** adj excepcional, destacado; (remaining) pendiente

outward ['autwəd] adj externo; (journey) de ida; **outwards** adv (esp BRIT) = **outward**

outweigh [aut'weɪ] vt pesar más que

oval ['əuvl] adj ovalado ▷ n óvalo

ovary ['əuvərɪ] n ovario

oven ['ʌvn] n horno; **oven glove** n guante m para el horno, manopla para el horno; **ovenproof** adj resistente al horno; **oven-ready** adj listo para el horno

over ['əuvə*] adv por encima, por encima ▷ adj or adv (finished) terminado; (surplus) de sobra ▷ prep (por) encima de; (above) sobre; (on the other side of) al otro lado de; (more than) más de; (during) durante; **~ here** (por) aquí; **~ there** (por) allí or allá; **all ~** (everywhere) por todas partes; **~ and ~ (again)** una y otra vez; **~ and above** además de; **to ask sb ~** invitar a algn a casa; **to bend ~** inclinarse

overall [adj, n 'əuvərɔːl, adv əuvər'ɔːl] adj (length etc) total; (study) de conjunto ▷ adv en conjunto ▷ n (BRIT) guardapolvo; **overalls** npl (boiler suit) mono (SP) or overol m (LAM) (de trabajo)

overboard adv (Naut) por la borda

overcame [əuvəˈkeɪm] *pt of* **overcome**

overcast [ˈəuvəkɑːst] *adj* encapotado

overcharge [əuvəˈtʃɑːdʒ] *vt*: **to ~ sb** cobrar un precio excesivo a algn

overcoat [ˈəuvəkəut] *n* abrigo, sobretodo

overcome [əuvəˈkʌm] *vt* vencer; (difficulty) superar

over: overcrowded *adj* atestado de gente; (city, country) superpoblado; **overdo** (irreg) *vt* exagerar; (overcook) cocer demasiado; **to overdo it** (work etc) pasarse; **overdone** [əuvəˈdʌn] *adj* (vegetables) recocido; (steak) demasiado hecho; **overdose** *n* sobredosis f inv; **overdraft** *n* saldo deudor; **overdrawn** *adj* (account) en descubierto; **overdue** *adj* retrasado; **overestimate** *vt* sobreestimar

overflow [vb əuvəˈfləu, n ˈəuvəfləu] *vi* desbordarse ▷ n (also: **~ pipe**) (cañería de) desagüe m

overgrown [əuvəˈɡrəun] *adj* (garden) invadido por la vegetación

overhaul [vb əuvəˈhɔːl, n ˈəuvəhɔːl] *vt* revisar, repasar ▷ n revisión f

overhead [adv əuvəˈhed, adj, n ˈəuvəhed] *adv* por arriba or encima ▷ adj (cable) aéreo ▷ n (US) = **overheads**; **overhead projector** *n* retroproyector; **overheads** *npl* (expenses) gastos mpl generales

over: overhear (irreg) *vt* oír por casualidad; **overheat** *vi* (engine) recalentarse; **overland** *adj, adv* por tierra; **overlap** [əuvəˈlæp] *vi* traslaparse; **overleaf** *adv* al dorso; **overload** *vt* sobrecargar; **overlook** *vt* (have view of) dar a, tener vistas a; (miss: by mistake) pasar por alto; (excuse) perdonar

overnight [əuvəˈnaɪt] *adv* durante la noche; (fig) de la noche a la mañana ▷ adj de noche; **to stay ~** pasar la noche; **overnight bag** *n* fin m de semana, neceser m de viaje

overpass (US) [ˈəuvəpɑːs] *n* paso superior

overpower [əuvəˈpauə*] *vt* dominar; (fig) embargar; **overpowering** *adj* (heat) agobiante; (smell) penetrante

over: overreact [əuvəriˈækt] *vi* reaccionar de manera exagerada; **overrule** *vt* (decision) anular; (claim) denegar; **overrun** (irreg) *vt* (country) invadir; (time limit) rebasar, exceder

overseas [əuvəˈsiːz] *adv* (abroad: live) en el extranjero; (travel) al extranjero ▷ adj (trade) exterior; (visitor) extranjero

oversee [əuvəˈsiː] (irreg) *vt* supervisar

overshadow [əuvəˈʃædəu] *vt*: **to be ~ed by** estar a la sombra de

oversight [ˈəuvəsaɪt] *n* descuido

oversleep [əuvəˈsliːp] (irreg) *vi* quedarse dormido

overspend [əuvəˈspend] (irreg) *vi* gastar más de la cuenta: **we have overspent by 5 pounds** hemos excedido el presupuesto en 5 libras

overt [əuˈvəːt] *adj* abierto

overtake [əuvəˈteɪk] (irreg) *vt* sobrepasar; (BRIT Aut) adelantar

over: overthrow (irreg) *vt* (government) derrocar; **overtime** *n* horas fpl extraordinarias

overtook [əuvəˈtuk] *pt of* **overtake**

over: overturn *vt* volcar; (fig: plan) desbaratar; (: government) derrocar ▷ vi volcar; **overweight** *adj* demasiado gordo or pesado; **overwhelm** *vt* aplastar; (emotion) sobrecoger; **overwhelming** *adj* (victory, defeat) arrollador(a); (feeling) irresistible

ow [au] *excl* ¡ay!

owe [əu] *vt*: **to ~ sb sth, to ~ sth to sb** deber algo a algn; **owing to** *prep* debido a, por causa de

owl [aul] *n* búho, lechuza

own [əun] *vt* tener, poseer ▷ adj propio; **a room of my ~** una habitación propia; **to get one's ~ back** tomar revancha; **on one's ~** solo, a solas; **own up** *vi* confesar; **owner** *n* dueño/a;

ownership n posesión f
ox [ɔks] (pl **~en**) n buey m
Oxbridge ['ɔksbrɪdʒ] n universidades
de Oxford y Cambridge
oxen ['ɔksən] npl of **ox**
oxygen ['ɔksɪdʒən] n oxígeno
oyster ['ɔɪstə*] n ostra
oz. abbr = **ounce(s)**
ozone ['əʊzəʊn] n ozono; **ozone
friendly** adj que no daña la capa de
ozono; **ozone layer** n capa f de ozono

p

p [piː] abbr = **penny; pence**
P.A. n abbr = **personal assistant;
public address system**
p.a. abbr = **per annum**
pace [peɪs] n paso ▷ vi: **to ~ up and
down** pasearse de un lado a otro; **to
keep ~ with** llevar el mismo paso que;
pacemaker n (Med) regulador m
cardíaco, marcapasos m inv; (Sport: also:
pacesetter) liebre f
Pacific [pə'sɪfɪk] n: **the ~ (Ocean)** el
(Océano) Pacífico
pacifier ['pæsɪfaɪə*] (us) n (dummy)
chupete m
pack [pæk] n (packet) paquete m;
(of hounds) jauría; (of people) manada,
bando; (of cards) baraja; (bundle) fardo;
(us: ~ of cigarettes) paquete m; (back pack)
mochila ▷ vt (fill) llenar; (in suitcase etc)
meter, poner; (cram) atestar; **to
~ (one's bags)** hacerse la maleta; **to
~ sb off** despachar a algn; **pack in** vi
(watch, car) estropearse ▷ vt (inf) dejar;
pack it in! ¡para!, ¡basta ya!; **pack up** vi
(inf: machine) estropearse; (person) irse

▷vt (belongings, clothes) recoger; (goods, presents) empaquetar, envolver
package ['pækɪdʒ] n paquete m; (bulky) bulto m; (also: ~ **deal**) acuerdo global; **package holiday** n vacaciones fpl organizadas; **package tour** n viaje m organizado

packaging ['pækɪdʒɪŋ] n envase m

packed [pækt] adj abarrotado; **packed lunch** n almuerzo m frío

packet ['pækɪt] n paquete m

packing ['pækɪŋ] n embalaje m

pact [pækt] n pacto m

pad [pæd] n (of paper) bloc m; (cushion) cojinete m; (inf: home) casa ▷vt rellenar; **padded** adj (jacket) acolchado; (bra) reforzado

paddle ['pædl] n (oar) canalete m; (us: for table tennis) paleta f ▷vt impulsar con canalete ▷vi (with feet) chapotear; **paddling pool** (BRIT) n estanque m de juegos

paddock ['pædək] n corral m

padlock ['pædlɔk] n candado

paedophile ['piːdəufail] (us **pedophile**) adj de pedófilos ▷n pedófilo/a

page [peɪdʒ] n (of book) página; (of newspaper) plana; (also: ~ **boy**) paje m ▷vt (in hotel etc) llamar por altavoz a

pager ['peɪdʒə*] n (Tel) busca m

paid [peɪd] pt, pp of **pay** ▷adj (work) remunerado; (holiday) pagado; (official etc) a sueldo; **to put ~ to** (BRIT) acabar con

pain [peɪn] n dolor m; **to be in ~** sufrir; **to take ~s to do sth** tomarse grandes molestias en hacer algo; **painful** adj doloroso; (difficult) penoso; (disagreeable) desagradable; **painkiller** n analgésico; **painstaking** ['peɪnzteɪkɪŋ] adj (person) concienzudo, esmerado

paint [peɪnt] n pintura ▷vt pintar; **to ~ the door blue** pintar la puerta de azul; **paintbrush** n (of artist) pincel m; (of decorator) brocha; **painter** n pintor(a) m/f; **painting** n pintura

pair [peə*] n (of shoes, gloves etc) par m; (of people) pareja; **a ~ of scissors** unas tijeras; **a ~ of trousers** unos pantalones, un pantalón

pajamas [pə'dʒɑ:məz] (us) npl pijama m

Pakistan [pɑ:kɪ'stɑ:n] n Paquistán m; **Pakistani** adj, n paquistaní mf

pal [pæl] (inf) n compinche mf, compañero/a

palace ['pæləs] n palacio

pale [peɪl] adj (gen) pálido; (colour) claro ▷n: **to be beyond the ~** pasarse de la raya

Palestine ['pælɪstaɪn] n Palestina; **Palestinian** [-'tɪnɪən] adj, n palestino/a m/f

palm [pɑ:m] n (Anat) palma; (also: ~ **tree**) palmera, palma ▷vt: **to ~ sth off on sb** (inf) encajar algo a algn

pamper ['pæmpə*] vt mimar

pamphlet ['pæmflət] n folleto

pan [pæn] n (also: **sauce~**) cacerola, cazuela, olla; (also: **frying ~**) sartén f

pancake ['pænkeɪk] n crepe f

panda ['pændə] n panda m

pane [peɪn] n cristal m

panel ['pænl] n (of wood etc) panel m; (Radio, TV) panel m de invitados

panhandler ['pænhændlə*] (us) n (inf) mendigo/a

panic ['pænɪk] n terror m pánico ▷vi dejarse llevar por el pánico

panorama [pænə'rɑ:mə] n panorama m

pansy ['pænzɪ] n (Bot) pensamiento; (inf, pej) maricón m

pant [pænt] vi jadear

panther ['pænθə*] n pantera

panties ['pæntɪz] npl bragas fpl, pantis mpl

pantomime ['pæntəmaɪm] (BRIT) n revista musical representada en Navidad, basada en cuentos dehadas

○
○ **PANTOMIME**
○
○ En época navideña se ponen en

- escena en los teatros británicos
- las llamadas **pantomimes**, que
- son versiones libres de cuentos
- tradicionales como Aladino
- o El gato con botas. En ella
- nunca faltan personajes como
- la dama ("dame"), papel que
- siempre interpreta un actor, el
- protagonista joven ("principal
- boy") normalmente interpretado
- por una actriz, y el malvado
- ("villain"). Es un espectáculo
- familiar en el que se anima al
- público a participar y aunque
- va dirigido principalmente a los
- niños, cuenta con grandes dosis de
- humor para adultos.

pants [pænts] *n* (BRIT: *underwear*:
woman's) bragas *fpl*; (: *man's*)
calzoncillos *mpl*; (us: *trousers*)
pantalones *mpl*

paper ['peɪpə*] *n* papel *m*; (*also*:
news~) periódico, diario; (*academic
essay*) ensayo; (*exam*) examen *m* ▷ *adj*
de papel ▷ *vt* empapelar, tapizar (MEX);
papers *npl* (*also*: **identity ~s**) papeles
mpl, documentos *mpl*; **paperback** *n*
libro en rústica; **paper bag** *n* bolsa
de papel; **paper clip** *n* clip *m*; **paper
shop** (BRIT) *n* tienda de periódicos;
paperwork *n* trabajo administrativo

paprika ['pæprɪkə] *n* pimentón *m*

par [pɑ:*] *n* par *f*; (*Golf*) par *m*; **to be on
a ~ with** estar a la par con

paracetamol [pærə'si:təmɔl] (BRIT)
n paracetamol *m*

parachute ['pærəʃu:t] *n* paracaídas
m inv

parade [pə'reɪd] *n* desfile *m* ▷ *vt*
(*show*) hacer alarde de ▷ *vi* desfilar;
(*Mil*) pasar revista

paradise ['pærədaɪs] *n* paraíso

paradox ['pærədɔks] *n* paradoja

paraffin ['pærəfɪn] (BRIT) *n* (*also*: **~
oil**) parafina

paragraph ['pærəgrɑ:f] *n* párrafo

parallel ['pærəlel] *adj* en paralelo;

(*fig*) semejante ▷ *n* (*line*) paralela; (*fig,
Geo*) paralelo

paralysed ['pærəlaɪzd] *adj*
paralizado

paralysis [pə'rælɪsɪs] *n* parálisis *f inv*

paramedic [pærə'medɪk] *n* auxiliar
m/f sanitario/a

paranoid ['pærənɔɪd] *adj* (*person,
feeling*) paranoico

parasite ['pærəsaɪt] *n* parásito/a

parcel ['pɑ:sl] *n* paquete *m* ▷ *vt*
(*also*: **~ up**) empaquetar, embalar

pardon ['pɑ:dn] *n* (*Law*) indulto ▷ *vt*
perdonar; **~ me!, I beg your ~!** (*I'm
sorry!*) ¡perdone usted!; **(I beg your) ~?,
~ me?** (us: *what did you say?*) ¿cómo?

parent ['peərənt] *n* (*mother*) madre
f; (*father*) padre *m*; **parents** *npl* padres
mpl

> Be careful not to translate **parent**
> by the Spanish word *pariente*.

parental [pə'rentl] *adj* paternal/
maternal

Paris ['pærɪs] *n* París

parish ['pærɪʃ] *n* parroquia

Parisian [pə'rɪzɪən] *adj, n* parisiense
mf

park [pɑ:k] *n* parque *m* ▷ *vt* aparcar,
estacionar ▷ *vi* aparcar, estacionarse

parking ['pɑ:kɪŋ] *n* aparcamiento,
estacionamiento; **"no ~"** "prohibido
estacionarse"; **parking lot** (us)
n parking *m*; **parking meter** *n*
parquímetro; **parking ticket** *n* multa
de aparcamiento

parkway ['pɑ:kweɪ] (us) *n* alameda

parliament ['pɑ:ləmənt] *n*
parlamento; (*Spanish*) Cortes *fpl*;
parliamentary [-'mentərɪ] *adj*
parlamentario

- **PARLIAMENT**
-
- El Parlamento británico
- (**Parliament**) tiene como sede
- el palacio de Westminster,
- también llamado "Houses of
- Parliament" y consta de dos

cámaras. La Cámara de los Comunes ("House of Commons"), compuesta por 650 diputados (**Members of Parliament**) elegidos por sufragio universal en su respectiva circunscripción electoral (constituency), se reúne 175 días al año y sus sesiones son moderadas por el Presidente de la Cámara (**Speaker**). La cámara alta es la Cámara de los Lores ("House of Lords") y está formada por miembros que han sido nombrados por el monarca o que han heredado su escaño. Su poder es limitado, aunque actúa como tribunal supremo de apelación, excepto en Escocia.

Parmesan [pɑːmɪˈzæn] n (also: ~ **cheese**) queso parmesano

parole [pəˈrəʊl] n: **on** ~ libre bajo palabra

parrot [ˈpærət] n loro, papagayo

parsley [ˈpɑːslɪ] n perejil m

parsnip [ˈpɑːsnɪp] n chirivía

parson [ˈpɑːsn] n cura m

part [pɑːt] n (gen, Mus) parte f; (bit) trozo; (of machine) pieza; (Theatre etc) papel m; (of serial) entrega; (us: in hair) raya ▷ adv en parte; **partly** ▷ vt separar ▷ vi (people) separarse; (crowd) apartarse; **to take** ~ **in** tomar parte o participar en; **to take sth in good** ~ tomar algo en buena parte; **to take sb's** ~ defender a algn; **for my** ~ por mi parte; **for the most** ~ en su mayor parte; **to** ~ **one's hair** hacerse la raya; **part with** vt fus ceder, entregar; (money) pagar; **part of speech** n parte f de la oración, categoría f gramatical

partial [ˈpɑːʃl] adj parcial; **to be** ~ **to** ser aficionado a

participant [pɑːˈtɪsɪpənt] n (in competition) concursante mf; (in campaign etc) participante mf

participate [pɑːˈtɪsɪpeɪt] vi: **to** ~ **in** participar en

particle [ˈpɑːtɪkl] n partícula; (of dust) grano

particular [pəˈtɪkjʊlə*] adj (special) particular; (concrete) concreto; (given) determinado; (fussy) quisquilloso; (demanding) exigente; **in** ~ en particular; **particularly** adv (in particular) sobre todo; (difficult, good etc) especialmente; **particulars** npl (information) datos mpl; (details) pormenores mpl

parting [ˈpɑːtɪŋ] n (act) separación f; (farewell) despedida; (BRIT: in hair) raya ▷ adj de despedida

partition [pɑːˈtɪʃən] n (Pol) división f; (wall) tabique m

partly [ˈpɑːtlɪ] adv en parte

partner [ˈpɑːtnə*] n (Comm) socio/a; (Sport, at dance) pareja; (spouse) cónyuge mf; (lover) compañero/a; **partnership** n asociación f; (Comm) sociedad f

partridge [ˈpɑːtrɪdʒ] n perdiz f

part-time [ˈpɑːtˈtaɪm] adj, adv a tiempo parcial

party [ˈpɑːtɪ] n (Pol) partido; (celebration) fiesta; (group) grupo; (Law) parte f interesada ▷ cpd (Pol) de partido

pass [pɑːs] vt (time, object) pasar; (place) pasar por; (overtake) rebasar; (exam) aprobar; (approve) aprobar ▷ vi pasar; (Scol) aprobar, ser aprobado ▷ n (permit) permiso; (membership card) carnet m; (in mountains) puerto, desfiladero; (Sport) pase m; (Scol: also: ~ **mark**): **to get a** ~ **in** aprobar en; **to** ~ **sth through sth** pasar algo por algo; **to make a** ~ **at sb** (inf) hacer proposiciones a algn; **pass away** vi fallecer; **pass by** vi pasar ▷ vt (ignore) pasar por alto; **pass on** vt transmitir; **pass out** vi desmayarse; **pass over** vi, vt omitir, pasar por alto; **pass up** vt (opportunity) renunciar a; **passable** adj (road) transitable; (tolerable) pasable

passage [ˈpæsɪdʒ] n (also: ~**way**) pasillo; (act of passing) tránsito; (fare, in book) pasaje m; (by boat) travesía; (Anat) tubo

passenger ['pæsɪndʒə*] n pasajero/a, viajero/a

passer-by [pɑːsə'baɪ] n transeúnte mf

passing place n (Aut) apartadero

passion ['pæʃən] n pasión f; **passionate** adj apasionado; **passion fruit** n fruta de la pasión, granadilla

passive ['pæsɪv] adj (gen, also Ling) pasivo

passport ['pɑːspɔːt] n pasaporte m; **passport control** n control m de pasaporte; **passport office** n oficina de pasaportes

password ['pɑːswɜːd] n contraseña

past [pɑːst] prep (in front of) por delante de; (further than) más allá de; (later than) después de ▷ adj pasado; (president etc) antiguo ▷ n (time) pasado; (of person) antecedentes mpl; **he's ~ forty** tiene más de cuarenta años; **ten/quarter ~ eight** las ocho y diez/cuarto; **for the ~ few/3 days** durante los últimos días/últimos 3 días; **to run ~ sb** pasar a algn corriendo

pasta ['pæstə] n pasta

paste [peɪst] n pasta; (glue) engrudo ▷ vt pegar

pastel ['pæstl] adj pastel; (painting) al pastel

pasteurized ['pæstəraɪzd] adj pasteurizado

pastime ['pɑːstaɪm] n pasatiempo

pastor ['pɑːstə*] n pastor m

past participle [-'pɑːtɪsɪpl] n (Ling) participio m (de) pasado or (de) pretérito or pasivo

pastry ['peɪstrɪ] n (dough) pasta; (cake) pastel m

pasture ['pɑːstʃə*] n pasto

pasty¹ ['pæstɪ] n empanada

pasty² [peɪstɪ] adj (complexion) pálido

pat [pæt] vt dar una palmadita a; (dog etc) acariciar

patch [pætʃ] n (of material,: eye patch) parche m; (mended part) remiendo; (of

land) terreno ▷ vt remendar; **(to go through) a bad ~** (pasar por) una mala racha; **patchy** adj desigual

pâté ['pæteɪ] n paté m

patent ['peɪtnt] n patente f ▷ vt patentar ▷ adj patente, evidente

paternal [pə'tɜːnl] adj paternal; (relation) paterno

paternity leave [pə'tɜːnɪtɪ-] n permiso m por paternidad, licencia por paternidad

path [pɑːθ] n camino, sendero; (trail, track) pista; (of missile) trayectoria

pathetic [pə'θetɪk] adj patético, lastimoso; (very bad) malísimo

pathway ['pɑːθweɪ] n sendero, vereda

patience ['peɪʃns] n paciencia; (BRIT Cards) solitario

patient ['peɪʃnt] n paciente mf ▷ adj paciente, sufrido

patio ['pætɪəʊ] n patio

patriotic [pætrɪ'ɒtɪk] adj patriótico

patrol [pə'trəʊl] n patrulla ▷ vt patrullar por; **patrol car** n coche m patrulla

patron ['peɪtrən] n (in shop) cliente mf; (of charity) patrocinador(a) m/f; **~ of the arts** mecenas m

patronizing ['pætrənaɪzɪŋ] adj condescendiente

pattern ['pætən] n (Sewing) patrón m; (design) dibujo; **patterned** adj (material) estampado

pause [pɔːz] n pausa ▷ vi hacer una pausa

pave [peɪv] vt pavimentar; **to ~ the way for** preparar el terreno para

pavement ['peɪvmənt] (BRIT) n acera, banqueta (MEX), andén m (CAM), vereda (SC)

pavilion [pə'vɪlɪən] n (Sport) caseta

paving ['peɪvɪŋ] n pavimento, enlosado

paw [pɔː] n pata

pawn [pɔːn] n (Chess) peón m; (fig) instrumento ▷ vt empeñar; **pawn broker** n prestamista mf

pay [peɪ] (pt, pp **paid**) n (wage etc) sueldo, salario ▷ vt pagar ▷ vi (be profitable) rendir; **to ~ attention (to)** prestar atención (a); **to ~ sb a visit** hacer una visita a algn; **to ~ one's respects to sb** presentar sus respetos a algn; **pay back** vt (money) reembolsar; (person) pagar; **pay for** vt fus pagar; **pay in** vt ingresar; **pay off** vt saldar ▷ vi (scheme, decision) dar resultado; **pay out** vt (money) gastar, desembolsar; **pay up** vt pagar (de mala gana); **payable** adj: **payable to** pagadero a; **pay day** n día m de paga; **pay envelope** (US) n = **pay packet; payment** n pago; **monthly payment** mensualidad f; **payout** n pago; (in competition) premio en metálico; **pay packet** (BRIT) n sobre m (de paga); **pay phone** n teléfono público; **payroll** n nómina f; **pay slip** n recibo de sueldo; **pay television** n televisión f de pago

PC n abbr = **personal computer**; (BRIT) (= police constable) policía mf ▷ adv abbr = **politically correct**

p.c. abbr = **per cent**

PDA n abbr (= personal digital assistant) agenda electrónica

PE n abbr (= physical education) ed. física

pea [piː] n guisante m (SP), arveja (LAM), chícharo (MEX, CAM)

peace [piːs] n paz f; (calm) paz f, tranquilidad f; **peaceful** adj (gentle) pacífico; (calm) tranquilo, sosegado

peach [piːtʃ] n melocotón m (SP), durazno (LAM)

peacock ['piːkɒk] n pavo real

peak [piːk] n (of mountain) cumbre f, cima; (of cap) visera f; (fig) cumbre f; **peak hours** npl horas f pl punta

peanut ['piːnʌt] n cacahuete m (SP), maní m (LAM), cacahuate m (MEX); **peanut butter** n manteca de cacahuete or maní

pear [pɛə*] n pera

pearl [pɜːl] n perla

peasant ['pɛznt] n campesino/a

peat [piːt] n turba

pebble ['pɛbl] n guijarro

peck [pɛk] vt (also: **~ at**) picotear ▷ n picotazo; (kiss) besito; **peckish** (BRIT: inf) adj: **I feel peckish** tengo ganas de picar algo

peculiar [pɪ'kjuːlɪə*] adj (odd) extraño, raro; (typical) propio, característico; **~ to** propio de

pedal ['pɛdl] n pedal m ▷ vi pedalear

pedalo ['pɛdələʊ] n patín m a pedal

pedestal ['pɛdəstl] n pedestal m

pedestrian [pɪ'dɛstrɪən] n peatón/ ona m/f ▷ adj pedestre; **pedestrian crossing** (BRIT) n paso de peatones; **pedestrianized** adj: **a pedestrianized street** una calle peatonal; **pedestrian precinct** (US **pedestrian zone**) n zona peatonal

pedigree ['pɛdɪgriː] n genealogía; (of animal) raza, pedigrí m ▷ cpd (animal) de raza, de casta

pedophile ['piːdəʊfaɪl] (US) n = **paedophile**

pee [piː] (inf) vi mear

peek [piːk] vi mirar a hurtadillas

peel [piːl] n (of orange, lemon) cáscara; (: removed) peladuras fpl ▷ vt pelar ▷ vi (paint etc) desconcharse; (wallpaper) despegarse, desprenderse; (skin) pelar

peep [piːp] n (BRIT: look) mirada furtiva; (sound) pío ▷ vi (BRIT: look) mirar furtivamente

peer [pɪə*] vi: **to ~ at** esudriñar ▷ n (noble) par m; (equal) igual m; (contemporary) contemporáneo/a

peg [pɛg] n (for coat etc) gancho, colgadero; (BRIT: also: **clothes ~**) pinza

pelican ['pɛlɪkən] n pelícano; **pelican crossing** (BRIT) n (Aut) paso de peatones señalizado

pelt [pɛlt] vt: **to ~ sb with sth** arrojarle algo a algn ▷ vi (rain) llover a cántaros; (inf: run) correr ▷ n pellejo

pelvis ['pɛlvɪs] n pelvis f

pen [pɛn] n (fountain pen) pluma; (ballpoint pen) bolígrafo; (for sheep) redil m

penalty ['penltɪ] n (gen) pena; (fine) multa

pence [pens] npl of **penny**

pencil ['pensl] n lápiz m; **pencil in** vt (appointment) apuntar con carácter provisional; **pencil case** n estuche m; **pencil sharpener** n sacapuntas m inv

pendant ['pendnt] n pendiente m

pending ['pendɪŋ] prep antes de ▷ adj pendiente

penetrate ['penɪtreɪt] vt penetrar

penfriend ['penfrend] (BRIT) n amigo/a por carta

penguin ['peŋgwɪn] n pingüino

penicillin [penɪ'sɪlɪn] n penicilina

peninsula [pə'nɪnsjulə] n península

penis ['pi:nɪs] n pene m

penitentiary [penɪ'tenʃərɪ] (US) n cárcel f, presidio

penknife ['pennaɪf] n navaja

penniless ['penɪlɪs] adj sin dinero

penny ['penɪ] (pl **pennies** or **pence**) (BRIT) n penique m; (US) centavo

penpal ['penpæl] n amigo/a por carta

pension ['penʃən] n (state benefit) jubilación f; **pensioner** (BRIT) n jubilado/a

pentagon ['pentəgən] (US) n: **the P~** (Pol) el Pentágono

○ **PENTAGON**

○ Se conoce como **Pentagon** al edificio de planta pentagonal que alberga las dependencias del Ministerio de Defensa estadounidense ("Department of Defense") en Arlington, Virginia. En lenguaje periodístico se aplica también a la dirección militar del país.

penthouse ['penthaus] n ático de lujo

penultimate [pe'nʌltɪmət] adj penúltimo

people ['pi:pl] npl gente f; (citizens) pueblo, ciudadanos mpl; (Pol): **the ~** el pueblo ▷ n (nation, race) pueblo, nación f; **several ~ came** vinieron varias personas; **~ say that ...** dice la gente que ...

pepper ['pepə*] n (spice) pimienta; (vegetable) pimiento ▷ vt: **to ~ with** (fig) salpicar de; **peppermint** n (sweet) pastilla de menta

per [pə:*] prep por; **~ day/~son** por día/persona; **~ annum** al año

perceive [pə'si:v] vt percibir; (realize) darse cuenta de

per cent n por ciento

percentage [pə'sentɪdʒ] n porcentaje m

perception [pə'sepʃən] n percepción f; (insight) perspicacia; (opinion etc) opinión f

perch [pə:tʃ] n (fish) perca; (for bird) percha ▷ vi: **to ~ (on)** (bird) posarse (en); (person) encaramarse (en)

percussion [pə'kʌʃən] n percusión f

perfect [adj, n 'pə:fɪkt, vb pə'fekt] adj perfecto ▷ n (also: **~ tense**) perfecto ▷ vt perfeccionar; **perfection** [pə'fekʃən] n perfección f; **perfectly** ['pə:fɪktlɪ] adv perfectamente

perform [pə'fɔ:m] vt (carry out) realizar, llevar a cabo; (Theatre) representar; (piece of music) interpretar ▷ vi (well, badly) funcionar; **performance** n (of a play) representación f; (of actor, athlete etc) actuación f; (of car, engine, company) rendimiento; (of economy) resultados mpl; **performer** n (actor) actor m, actriz f

perfume ['pə:fju:m] n perfume m

perhaps [pə'hæps] adv quizá(s), tal vez

perimeter [pə'rɪmɪtə*] n perímetro

period ['pɪərɪəd] n período; (Scol) clase f; (full stop) punto; (Med) regla ▷ adj (costume, furniture) de época; **periodical** [pɪərɪ'ɔdɪkl] n periódico; **periodically** adv de vez en cuando, cada cierto tiempo

perish ['perɪʃ] vi perecer; (decay) echarse a perder

perjury ['pəːdʒərɪ] n (Law) perjurio

perk [pəːk] n extra m

perm [pəːm] n permanente f

permanent ['pəːmənənt] adj permanente; **permanently** adv (lastingly) para siempre, de modo definitivo; (all the time) permanentemente

permission [pə'mɪʃən] n permiso

permit [n 'pəːmɪt, vt pə'mɪt] n permiso, licencia f ▷ vt permitir

perplex [pə'pleks] vt dejar perplejo

persecute ['pəːsɪkjuːt] vt perseguir

persecution [pəːsɪ'kjuːʃən] n persecución f

persevere [pəːsɪ'vɪə*] vi persistir

Persian ['pəːʃən] adj, n persa mf; **the ~ Gulf** el Golfo Pérsico

persist [pə'sɪst] vi: **to ~ (in doing sth)** persistir (en hacer algo); **persistent** adj persistente; (determined) porfiado

person ['pəːsn] n persona; **in ~** en persona; **personal** adj personal; individual; (visit) en persona; **personal assistant** n ayudante mf personal; **personal computer** n ordenador m personal; **personality** [-'nælɪtɪ] n personalidad f; **personally** adv personalmente; (in person) en persona; **to take sth personally** tomarse algo a mal; **personal organizer** n agenda; **personal stereo** n Walkman® m

personnel [pəːsə'nel] n personal m

perspective [pə'spektɪv] n perspectiva

perspiration [pəːspɪ'reɪʃən] n transpiración f

persuade [pə'sweɪd] vt: **to ~ sb to do sth** persuadir a algn para que haga algo

persuasion [pə'sweɪʒən] n persuasión f; (persuasiveness) persuasiva

persuasive [pə'sweɪsɪv] adj persuasivo

perverse [pə'vəːs] adj perverso; (wayward) travieso

pervert [n 'pəːvəːt, vb pə'vəːt] n pervertido/a ▷ vt pervertir; (truth, sb's words) tergiversar

pessimism ['pesɪmɪzəm] n pesimismo

pessimist ['pesɪmɪst] n pesimista mf; **pessimistic** [-'mɪstɪk] adj pesimista

pest [pest] n (insect) insecto nocivo; (fig) lata, molestia

pester ['pestə*] vt molestar, acosar

pesticide ['pestɪsaɪd] n pesticida m

pet [pet] n animal m doméstico ▷ cpd favorito ▷ vt acariciar; **teacher's ~** favorito/a (del profesor); **~ hate** manía

petal ['petl] n pétalo

petite [pə'tiːt] adj chiquita

petition [pə'tɪʃən] n petición f

petrified ['petrɪfaɪd] adj horrorizado

petrol ['petrəl] (BRIT) n gasolina

petroleum [pə'trəuliəm] n petróleo

petrol: petrol pump (BRIT) n (in garage) surtidor m de gasolina; **petrol station** (BRIT) n gasolinera; **petrol tank** (BRIT) n depósito (de gasolina)

petticoat ['petɪkəut] n enaguas fpl

petty ['petɪ] adj (mean) mezquino; (unimportant) insignificante

pew [pjuː] n banco

pewter ['pjuːtə*] n peltre m

phantom ['fæntəm] n fantasma m

pharmacist ['faːməsɪst] n farmacéutico/a

pharmacy ['faːməsɪ] n farmacia

phase [feɪz] n fase f; **phase in** vt introducir progresivamente; **phase out** vt (machinery, product) retirar progresivamente; (job, subsidy) eliminar por etapas

Ph.D. abbr = **Doctor of Philosophy**

pheasant ['feznt] n faisán m

phenomena [fə'nɔmɪnə] npl of **phenomenon**

phenomenal [fɪ'nɔmɪnl] adj fenomenal, extraordinario

phenomenon [fə'nɔmɪnən] (pl **phenomena**) n fenómeno

Philippines ['fɪlɪpiːnz] npl: **the ~** las

Filipinas
philosopher [fɪ'lɔsəfə*] n filósofo/a
philosophical [fɪlə'sɔfɪkl] adj
filosófico
philosophy [fɪ'lɔsəfɪ] n filosofía
phlegm [flɛm] n flema
phobia ['fəubjə] n fobia
phone [fəun] n teléfono ▷ vt
telefonear, llamar por teléfono; **to be
on the ~** tener teléfono; (be calling)
estar hablando por teléfono; **phone
back** vt, vi volver a llamar; **phone up**
vt, vi llamar por teléfono; **phone book**
n guía telefónica; **phone booth** n
cabina telefónica; **phone box** (BRIT) n
= **phone booth**; **phone call** n llamada
(telefónica); **phonecard** n tarjeta;
phone number n número de teléfono
phonetics [fə'nɛtɪks] n fonética
phoney ['fəunɪ] adj falso
photo ['fəutəu] n foto; **photo album**
n álbum m de fotos; **photocopier**
n fotocopiadora; **photocopy** n
fotocopia ▷ vt fotocopiar
photograph ['fəutəgrɑːf]
n fotografía ▷ vt fotografiar;
photographer [fə'tɔgrəfə*] n
fotógrafo; **photography** [fə'tɔgrəfɪ]
n fotografía
phrase [freɪz] n frase f ▷ vt expresar;
phrase book n libro de frases
physical ['fɪzɪkl] adj físico; **physical
education** n educación f física;
physically adv físicamente
physician [fɪ'zɪʃən] n médico/a
physicist ['fɪzɪsɪst] n físico/a
physics ['fɪzɪks] n física
physiotherapist [fɪzɪəu'θerəpɪst] n
fisioterapeuta
physiotherapy [fɪzɪəu'θerəpɪ] n
fisioterapia
physique [fɪ'ziːk] n físico
pianist ['pɪənɪst] n pianista mf
piano [pɪ'ænəu] n piano
pick [pɪk] n (tool: also: **~-axe**) pico,
piqueta ▷ vt (select) elegir, escoger;
(gather) coger (SP), recoger; (remove,
take out) sacar, quitar; (lock) abrir con

ganzúa; **take your ~** escoja lo que
quiera; **the ~ of** lo mejor de; **to ~ one's
nose/teeth** hurgarse las narices/
limpiarse los dientes; **to ~ a quarrel
with sb** meterse con algn; **pick on** vt
fus (person) meterse con; **pick out** vt
escoger; (distinguish) identificar; **pick
up** vi (improve: sales) ir mejor; (: patient)
reponerse; (Finance) recobrarse ▷ vt
recoger; (learn) aprender; (Police: arrest)
detener; (person: for sex) ligar; (Radio)
captar; **to pick up speed** acelerarse; **to
pick o.s. up** levantarse
pickle ['pɪkl] n (also: **~s**: as condiment)
escabeche m; (fig: mess) apuro ▷ vt
encurtir
pickpocket ['pɪkpɔkɪt] n carterista
mf
pick-up ['pɪkʌp] n (also: **~ truck**)
furgoneta, camioneta
picnic ['pɪknɪk] n merienda ▷ vi ir
de merienda; **picnic area** n zona de
picnic; (Aut) área de descanso
picture ['pɪktʃə*] n cuadro; (painting)
pintura; (photograph) fotografía; (TV)
imagen f; (film) película; (fig: description)
descripción f; (: situation) situación
f ▷ vt (imagine) imaginar; **pictures**
npl: **the ~s** (BRIT) el cine; **picture frame**
n marco; **picture messaging** n (envío
de) mensajes con imágenes
picturesque [pɪktʃə'resk] adj
pintoresco
pie [paɪ] n pastel m; (open) tarta;
(small: of meat) empanada
piece [piːs] n pedazo, trozo; (of
cake) trozo; (item) pieza; **a ~ of clothing/
furniture/advice** una prenda (de
vestir)/un mueble/un consejo ▷ vt: **to
~ together** juntar; (Tech) armar; **to
take to ~s** desmontar
pie chart n gráfico de sectores or
tarta
pier [pɪə*] n muelle m, embarcadero
pierce [pɪəs] vt perforar; **pierced**
adj: **I've got pierced ears** tengo los
agujeros hechos en las orejas
pig [pɪg] n cerdo, chancho (LAM);

(*pej: unkind person*) asqueroso; (*: greedy person*) glotón/ona *m/f*
pigeon ['pɪdʒən] *n* paloma; (*as food*) pichón *m*
piggy bank ['pɪgɪ-] *n* hucha (*en forma de cerdito*)
pigsty ['pɪgstaɪ] *n* pocilga
pigtail *n* (*girl's*) trenza
pike [paɪk] *n* (*fish*) lucio
pilchard ['pɪltʃəd] *n* sardina
pile [paɪl] *n* montón *m*; (*of carpet, cloth*) pelo; **pile up** *vi +adv* (*accumulate*) amontonarse, acumularse ▷ *vt +adv* (*put in a heap: books, clothes*) apilar, amontonar; (*accumulate*) acumular; **piles** *npl* (*Med*) almorranas *fpl*, hemorroides *mpl*; **pile-up** *n* (*Aut*) accidente *m* múltiple
pilgrimage ['pɪlgrɪmɪdʒ] *n* peregrinación *f*, romería
pill [pɪl] *n* píldora; **the ~** la píldora
pillar ['pɪlə*] *n* pilar *m*
pillow ['pɪləʊ] *n* almohada; **pillowcase** *n* funda
pilot ['paɪlət] *n* piloto ▷ *cpd* (*scheme etc*) piloto ▷ *vt* pilotar; **pilot light** *n* piloto
pimple ['pɪmpl] *n* grano
PIN *n abbr* (= *personal identification number*) número personal
pin [pɪn] *n* alfiler *m* ▷ *vt* prender (*con alfiler*); **~s and needles** hormigueo; **to ~ sb down** (*fig*) hacer que algn concrete; **to ~ sth on sb** (*fig*) colgarle a algn el sambenito de algo
pinafore ['pɪnəfɔ:*] *n* delantal *m*
pinch [pɪntʃ] *n* (*of salt etc*) pizca ▷ *vt* pellizcar; (*inf: steal*) birlar; **at a ~** en caso de apuro
pine [paɪn] *n* (*also: ~ tree*) pino ▷ *vi*: **to ~** suspirar por
pineapple ['paɪnæpl] *n* piña, ananás *m*
ping [pɪŋ] *n* (*noise*) sonido agudo; **ping-pong®** *n* pingpong®
pink [pɪŋk] *adj* rosado, (*color de*) rosa ▷ *n* (*colour*) rosa; (*Bot*) clavel *m*, clavellina

pinpoint ['pɪnpɔɪnt] *vt* precisar
pint [paɪnt] *n* pinta (*BRIT = 568cc, US = 473cc*); (*BRIT: inf: of beer*) pinta de cerveza ≈ jarra (*SP*)
pioneer [paɪə'nɪə*] *n* pionero/a
pious ['paɪəs] *adj* piadoso, devoto
pip [pɪp] *n* (*seed*) pepita; **the ~s** (*BRIT*) la señal
pipe [paɪp] *n* tubo, caño; (*for smoking*) pipa ▷ *vt* conducir en cañerías; **pipeline** *n* (*for oil*) oleoducto; (*for gas*) gasoducto; **piper** *n* gaitero/a
pirate ['paɪərət] *n* pirata *mf* ▷ *vt* (*cassette, book*) piratear
Pisces ['paɪsiːz] *n* Piscis *m*
piss [pɪs] (*infl*) *vi* mear; **pissed** (*infl*) *adj* (*drunk*) borracho
pistol ['pɪstl] *n* pistola
piston ['pɪstən] *n* pistón *m*, émbolo
pit [pɪt] *n* hoyo; (*also: coal ~*) mina; (*in garage*) foso de inspección; (*also: orchestra ~*) platea ▷ *vt*: **to ~ one's wits against sb** medir fuerzas con algn
pitch [pɪtʃ] *n* (*Mus*) tono; (*BRIT Sport*) campo, terreno; (*fig*) punto; (*tar*) brea ▷ *vt* (*throw*) arrojar, lanzar ▷ *vi* (*fall*) caer(se); **to ~ a tent** montar una tienda (*de campaña*); **pitch-black** *adj* negro como boca de lobo
pitfall ['pɪtfɔːl] *n* riesgo
pith [pɪθ] *n* (*of orange*) médula
pitiful ['pɪtɪful] *adj* (*touching*) lastimoso, conmovedor
pity ['pɪtɪ] *n* compasión *f*, piedad *f* ▷ *vt* compadecer(se de); **what a ~!** ¡qué pena!
pizza ['piːtsə] *n* pizza
placard ['plækɑːd] *n* letrero; (*in march etc*) pancarta
place [pleɪs] *n* lugar *m*, sitio; (*seat*) plaza, asiento; (*post*) puesto; (*home*) casa; **at/to his ~** en/a su casa; (*role: in society etc*) papel *m* ▷ *vt* (*object*) poner, colocar; (*identify*) reconocer; **to take ~** tener lugar; **to be ~d** (*in race, exam*) colocarse; **out of ~** (*not suitable*) fuera de lugar; **in the first ~** en primer lugar; **to change ~s with sb** cambiarse de

sitio con algn; **~ of birth** lugar m de nacimiento; **place mat** n (wooden etc) salvamanteles m inv; (linen etc) mantel m individual; **placement** n (positioning) colocación f; (at work) emplazamiento

placid ['plæsɪd] adj apacible

plague [pleɪg] n plaga; (Med) peste f ▷ vt (fig) acosar, atormentar

plaice [pleɪs] n inv platija

plain [pleɪn] adj (unpatterned) liso; (clear) claro, evidente; (simple) sencillo; (not handsome) poco atractivo ▷ adv claramente ▷ n llano, llanura; **plain chocolate** n chocolate m amargo; **plainly** adv claramente

plaintiff ['pleɪntɪf] n demandante mf

plait [plæt] n trenza

plan [plæn] n (drawing) plano m; (scheme) plan m, proyecto ▷ vt proyectar, planificar ▷ vi hacer proyectos; **to ~ to do** pensar hacer

plane [pleɪn] n (Aviat) avión m; (Math, fig) plano; (also: **~ tree**) plátano; (tool) cepillo

planet ['plænɪt] n planeta m

plank [plæŋk] n tabla

planning ['plænɪŋ] n planificación f; **family ~** planificación familiar

plant [plɑːnt] n (machinery) maquinaria; (factory) fábrica ▷ vt plantar; (field) sembrar; (bomb) colocar

plantation [plæn'teɪʃən] n plantación f; (estate) hacienda

plaque [plæk] n placa

plaster ['plɑːstə*] n (for walls) yeso; (also: **~ of Paris**) yeso mate, escayola (SP); (BRIT: also: **sticking ~**) tirita (SP), curita (LAM) ▷ vt enyesar; (cover): **to ~ with** llenar or cubrir de; **plaster cast** n (Med) escayola; (model, statue) vaciado de yeso

plastic ['plæstɪk] n plástico ▷ adj de plástico; **plastic bag** n bolsa de plástico; **plastic surgery** n cirujía plástica

plate [pleɪt] n (dish) plato; (metal, in book) lámina; (dental plate) placa de

dentadura postiza

plateau ['plætəʊ] (pl **~s** or **~x**) n meseta, altiplanicie f

platform ['plætfɔːm] n (Rail) andén m; (stage, BRIT: on bus) plataforma; (at meeting) tribuna; (Pol) programa m (electoral)

platinum ['plætɪnəm] adj, n platino

platoon [plə'tuːn] n pelotón m

platter ['plætə*] n fuente f

plausible ['plɔːzɪbl] adj verosímil; (person) convincente

play [pleɪ] n (Theatre) obra, comedia ▷ vt (game) jugar; (compete against) jugar contra; (instrument) tocar; (part: in play etc) hacer el papel de; (tape, record) poner ▷ vi jugar; (band) tocar; (tape, record) sonar; **to ~ safe** ir a lo seguro; **play back** vt (tape) poner; **play up** vi (cause trouble to) dar guerra; **player** n jugador/a m/f; (Theatre) actor(actriz) m/f; (Mus) músico/a; **playful** adj juguetón/ona; **playground** n (in school) patio de recreo; (in park) parque m infantil; **playgroup** n jardín m de niños; **playing card** n naipe m, carta; **playing field** n campo de deportes; **playschool** n = **playgroup**; **playtime** n (Scol) recreo; **playwright** n dramaturgo/a

plc abbr (= public limited company) ≈ S.A.

plea [pliː] n súplica, petición f; (Law) alegato, defensa

plead [pliːd] vt (Law): **to ~ sb's case** defender a algn; (give as excuse) poner como pretexto ▷ vi (Law) declararse; (beg): **to ~ with sb** suplicar or rogar a algn

pleasant ['plɛznt] adj agradable

please [pliːz] excl ¡por favor! ▷ vt (give pleasure to) dar gusto a, agradar ▷ vi (think fit): **do as you ~** haz lo que quieras; **~ yourself!** (inf) ¡haz lo que quieras!, ¡como quieras!; **pleased** adj (happy) alegre, contento; **pleased (with)** satisfecho (de); **pleased to meet you** ¡encantado!, ¡tanto gusto!

pleasure ['plɛʒə*] n placer m, gusto;

p

"it's a ~" "el gusto es mío"
pleat [pliːt] *n* pliegue *m*
pledge [pledʒ] *n* (*promise*) promesa, voto ▷*vt* prometer
plentiful ['plentɪfʊl] *adj* copioso, abundante
plenty ['plentɪ] *n*: ~**of** mucho(s)/a(s)
pliers ['plaɪəz] *npl* alicates *mpl*, tenazas *fpl*
plight [plaɪt] *n* situación *f* difícil
plod [plɒd] *vi* caminar con paso pesado; (*fig*) trabajar laboriosamente
plonk [plɒŋk] (*inf*) *n* (BRIT: *wine*) vino peleón ▷*vt*: **to ~ sth down** dejar caer algo
plot [plɒt] *n* (*scheme*) complot *m*, conjura; (*of story, play*) argumento; (*of land*) terreno ▷*vt* (*mark out*) trazar; (*conspire*) tramar, urdir ▷*vi* conspirar
plough [plaʊ] (US **plow**) *n* arado *m* ▷*vt* (*earth*) arar; **to ~ money into** invertir dinero en
plow [plaʊ] (US) = **plough**
ploy [plɔɪ] *n* truco, estratagema
pluck [plʌk] *vt* (*fruit*) coger (SP), recoger (LAM); (*musical instrument*) puntear; (*bird*) desplumar; (*eyebrows*) depilar; **to ~ up courage** hacer de tripas corazón
plug [plʌg] *n* tapón *m*; (*Elec*) enchufe *m*, clavija; (*Aut: also*: **spark(ing) ~**) bujía ▷*vt* (*hole*) tapar; (*inf: advertise*) dar publicidad a; **plug in** *vt* (*Elec*) enchufar; **plughole** *n* desagüe *m*
plum [plʌm] *n* (*fruit*) ciruela
plumber ['plʌmə*] *n* fontanero/a (SP, CAM), plomero/a (LAM)
plumbing ['plʌmɪŋ] *n* (*trade*) fontanería, plomería; (*piping*) cañería
plummet ['plʌmɪt] *vi*: **to ~ (down)** caer a plomo
plump [plʌmp] *adj* rechoncho, rollizo ▷*vi*: **to ~ for** (*inf: choose*) optar por
plunge [plʌndʒ] *vt* sumergir, hundir ▷*vi* (*fall*) caer; (*dive*) saltar; (*person*) arrojarse; **to take the ~** lanzarse
plural ['plʊərl] *adj* plural ▷*n* plural *m*

plus [plʌs] *n* (*also*: ~**sign**) signo más ▷*prep* más, y, además de; **ten/twenty** ~ más de diez/veinte
ply [plaɪ] *vt* (*a trade*) ejercer ▷*vi* (*ship*) ir y venir ▷*n* (*of wool, rope*) cabo; **to ~ sb with drink** insistir en ofrecer a algn muchas copas; **plywood** *n* madera contrachapada
P.M. *n abbr* = **Prime Minister**
p.m. *adv abbr* (= *post meridiem*) de la tarde or noche
PMS *n abbr* (= *premenstrual syndrome*) SPM *m*
PMT *n abbr* (= *premenstrual tension*) SPM *m*
pneumatic drill [njuːˈmætɪk-] *n* martillo neumático
pneumonia [njuːˈməʊnɪə] *n* pulmonía
poach [pəʊtʃ] *vt* (*cook*) escalfar; (*steal*) cazar (or pescar) en vedado ▷*vi* cazar (or pescar) en vedado; **poached** *adj* escalfado
P.O. Box *n abbr* (= *Post Office Box*) apdo., aptdo.
pocket ['pɒkɪt] *n* bolsillo; (*fig: small area*) bolsa ▷*vt* meter en el bolsillo; (*steal*) embolsar; **to be out of ~** (BRIT) salir perdiendo; **pocketbook** (US) *n* cartera; **pocket money** *n* asignación *f*
pod [pɒd] *n* vaina
podcast ['pɒdkɑːst] *n* podcast *m* ▷*vi* podcastear
podiatrist [pɒˈdiːətrɪst] (US) *n* pedicuro/a
podium ['pəʊdɪəm] *n* podio
poem ['pəʊɪm] *n* poema *m*
poet ['pəʊɪt] *n* poeta *m/f*; **poetic** [-'etɪk] *adj* poético; **poetry** *n* poesía
poignant ['pɔɪnjənt] *adj* conmovedor(a)
point [pɔɪnt] *n* punto; (*tip*) punta; (*purpose*) fin *m*, propósito; (*use*) utilidad *f*; (*significant part*) lo significativo; (*moment*) momento; (*Elec*) toma (de corriente); (*also*: **decimal ~**): **2 ~ 3** (**2.3**) dos coma tres (2,3) ▷*vt* señalar; (*gun etc*): **to ~ sth at sb** apuntar algo

a algn ▷ vi: **to ~ at** señalar; **points** npl (Aut) contactos mpl; (Rail) agujas fpl; **to be on the ~ of doing sth** estar a punto de hacer algo; **to make a ~ of** poner empeño en; **to get/miss the ~** comprender/no comprender; **to come to the ~** ir al meollo; **there's no ~ (in doing)** no tiene sentido (hacer); **point out** vt señalar; **point-blank** adv (say, refuse) sin más hablar; (also: **at point-blank range**) a quemarropa; **pointed** adj (shape) puntiagudo, afilado; (remark) intencionado; **pointer** n (needle) aguja, indicador m; **pointless** adj sin sentido; **point of view** n punto de vista

poison ['pɔɪzn] n veneno ▷ vt envenenar; **poisonous** adj venenoso; (fumes etc) tóxico

poke [pəuk] vt (jab with finger, stick etc) empujar; (put): **to ~ sth in(to)** introducir algo en; **poke about or around** vi fisgonear; **poke out** vi (stick out) salir

poker ['pəukə*] n atizador m; (Cards) póker m

Poland ['pəulənd] n Polonia

polar ['pəulə*] adj polar; **polar bear** n oso polar

Pole [pəul] n polaco/a

pole [pəul] n palo; (fixed) poste m; (Geo) polo; **pole bean** n (us) ≈ judía verde; **pole vault** n salto con pértiga

police [pə'li:s] n policía ▷ vt vigilar; **police car** n coche-patrulla m; **police constable** (BRIT) n guardia m, policía m; **police force** n cuerpo de policía; **policeman** (irreg) n policía m, guardia m; **police officer** n policía m, guardia m; **police station** n comisaría; **policewoman** (irreg) n mujer f policía

policy ['pɔlɪsɪ] n política; (also: **insurance ~**) póliza

polio ['pəulɪəu] n polio f

Polish ['pəulɪʃ] adj polaco ▷ n (Ling) polaco

polish ['pɔlɪʃ] n (for shoes) betún m; (for floor) cera (de lustrar); (shine) brillo,

lustre m; (fig: refinement) educación f ▷ vt (shoes) limpiar; (make shiny) pulir, sacar brillo a; **polish off** vt (food) despachar; **polished** adj (fig: person) elegante

polite [pə'laɪt] adj cortés, atento; **politeness** n cortesía

political [pə'lɪtɪkl] adj político; **politically** adv políticamente; **politically correct** políticamente correcto

politician [pɔlɪ'tɪʃən] n político/a

politics ['pɔlɪtɪks] n política

poll [pəul] n (election) votación f; (also: **opinion ~**) sondeo, encuesta ▷ vt encuestar; (votes) obtener

pollen ['pɔlən] n polen m

polling station ['pəulɪŋ-] n centro electoral

pollute [pə'lu:t] vt contaminar

pollution [pə'lu:ʃən] n polución f, contaminación f del medio ambiente

polo ['pəuləu] n (sport) polo; **polo-neck** adj de cuello vuelto ▷ n (sweater) suéter m de cuello vuelto; **polo shirt** n polo, niqui m

polyester [pɔlɪ'estə*] n poliéster m

polystyrene [pɔlɪ'staɪri:n] n poliestireno

polythene ['pɔlɪθi:n] (BRIT) n politeno; **polythene bag** n bolsa de plástico

pomegranate ['pɔmɪgrænɪt] n granada

pompous ['pɔmpəs] adj pomposo

pond [pɔnd] n (natural) charca; (artificial) estanque m

ponder ['pɔndə*] vt meditar

pony ['pəunɪ] n poni m; **ponytail** n coleta; **pony trekking** (BRIT) n excursión f a caballo

poodle ['pu:dl] n caniche m

pool [pu:l] n (natural) charca; (also: **swimming ~**) piscina, alberca (MEX), pileta (RPL); (fig: of light etc) charco; (Sport) chapolín m ▷ vt juntar; **pools** npl quinielas fpl

poor [puə*] adj pobre; (bad) de mala

calidad ▷ *npl*: **the ~** los pobres; **poorly** *adj* mal, enfermo ▷ *adv* mal

pop [pɒp] *n* (*sound*) ruido seco; (*Mus*) (*música*) pop *m*; (*inf*: *father*) papá *m*; (*drink*) gaseosa ▷ *vt* (*put quickly*) meter (de prisa) ▷ *vi* reventar; (*cork*) saltar; **pop in** *vi* entrar un momento; **pop out** *vi* salir un momento; **popcorn** *n* palomitas *fpl*

poplar ['pɒplə*] *n* álamo

popper ['pɒpə*] (*BRIT*) *n* automático

poppy ['pɒpɪ] *n* amapola

Popsicle® ['pɒpsɪkl] (*US*) *n* polo

pop star *n* estrella del pop

popular ['pɒpjulə*] *adj* popular; **popularity** [pɒpju'lærɪtɪ] *n* popularidad *f*

population [pɒpju'leɪʃən] *n* población *f*

pop-up ['pɒpʌp] (*Comput*) *adj* (*menu, window*) emergente ▷ *n* ventana emergente, (*ventana f*) pop-up *f*

porcelain ['pɔːslɪn] *n* porcelana

porch [pɔːtʃ] *n* pórtico, entrada; (*US*) veranda

pore [pɔː*] *n* poro ▷ *vi*: **to ~ over** engolfarse en

pork [pɔːk] *n* carne *f* de cerdo or (*LAM*) chancho; **pork chop** *n* chuleta de cerdo; **pork pie** *n* (*BRIT Culin*) empanada de carne de cerdo

porn [pɔːn] *adj* (*inf*) porno *inv* ▷ *n* porno; **pornographic** [pɔːnə'græfɪk] *adj* pornográfico; **pornography** [pɔː'nɔgrəfɪ] *n* pornografía

porridge ['pɒrɪdʒ] *n* gachas *fpl* de avena

port [pɔːt] *n* puerto; (*Naut*: *left side*) babor *m*; (*wine*) vino de Oporto; **~ of call** puerto de escala

portable ['pɔːtəbl] *adj* portátil

porter ['pɔːtə*] *n* (*for luggage*) maletero; (*doorkeeper*) portero/a, conserje *m/f*

portfolio [pɔːt'fəuliəu] *n* cartera

portion ['pɔːʃən] *n* porción *f*; (*of food*) ración *f*

portrait ['pɔːtreɪt] *n* retrato

portray [pɔː'treɪ] *vt* retratar; (*actor*) representar

Portugal ['pɔːtjugl] *n* Portugal *m*

Portuguese [pɔːtju'giːz] *adj* portugués/esa ▷ *n inv* portugués/esa *m/f*; (*Ling*) portugués *m*

pose [pəuz] *n* postura, actitud *f* ▷ *vi* (*pretend*): **to ~ as** hacerse pasar por ▷ *vt* (*question*) plantear; **to ~ for** posar para

posh [pɒʃ] (*inf*) *adj* elegante, de lujo

position [pə'zɪʃən] *n* posición *f*; (*job*) puesto; (*situation*) situación *f* ▷ *vt* colocar

positive ['pɒzɪtɪv] *adj* positivo; (*certain*) seguro; (*definite*) definitivo; **positively** *adv* (*affirmatively, enthusiastically*) de forma positiva; (*inf*: *really*) absolutamente

possess [pə'zes] *vt* poseer; **possession** [pə'zeʃən] *n* posesión *f*; **possessions** *npl* (*belongings*) pertenencias *fpl*; **possessive** *adj* posesivo

possibility [pɒsɪ'bɪlɪtɪ] *n* posibilidad *f*

possible ['pɒsɪbl] *adj* posible; **as big as ~** lo más grande posible; **possibly** *adv* posiblemente; **I cannot possibly come** me es imposible venir

post [pəust] *n* (*BRIT*: *system*) correos *mpl*; (*BRIT*: *letters, delivery*) correo; (*job, situation*) puesto; (*pole*) poste *m* ▷ *vt* (*BRIT*: *send by post*) echar al correo; (*BRIT*: *appoint*): **to ~ to** enviar a; **postage** *n* porte *m*, franqueo; **postal** *adj* postal, de correos; **postal order** *n* giro postal; **postbox** (*BRIT*) *n* buzón *m*; **postcard** *n* tarjeta postal; **postcode** (*BRIT*) *n* código postal

poster ['pəustə*] *n* cartel *m*

postgraduate ['pəust'grædjuət] *n* posgraduado/a

postman ['pəustmən] (*BRIT*: *irreg*) *n* cartero

postmark ['pəustmɑːk] *n* matasellos *m inv*

post-mortem [-'mɔːtəm] *n* autopsia

post office n (building) (oficina de) correos m; (organization): **the Post Office** Correos m inv (SP), Dirección f General de Correos (LAM)

postpone [pəs'pəun] vt aplazar

posture ['pɒstʃə*] n postura, actitud f

postwoman ['pəustwumən] (BRIT: irreg) n cartera

pot [pɒt] n (for cooking) olla; (teapot) tetera; (coffeepot) cafetera; (for flowers) maceta; (for jam) tarro, pote m; (inf: marijuana) chocolate m ▷ vt (plant) poner en tiesto; **to go to ~** (inf) irse al traste

potato [pə'teɪtəu] (pl **-es**) n patata (SP), papa (LAM); **potato peeler** n pelapatatas m inv

potent ['pəutnt] adj potente, poderoso; (drink) fuerte

potential [pə'tenʃl] adj potencial, posible ▷ n potencial m

pothole ['pɒthəul] n (in road) bache m; (BRIT: underground) gruta

pot plant ['pɒtplɑ:nt] n planta de interior

potter ['pɒtə*] n alfarero/a ▷ vi: **to ~ around** or **about** (BRIT) hacer trabajitos; **pottery** n cerámica; (factory) alfarería

potty ['pɒtɪ] n orinal m de niño

pouch [pautʃ] n (Zool) bolsa; (for tobacco) petaca

poultry ['pəultrɪ] n aves fpl de corral; (meat) pollo

pounce [pauns] vi: **to ~ on** precipitarse sobre

pound [paund] n libra (weight = 453g or 16oz; money = 100 pence) ▷ vt (beat) golpear; (crush) machacar ▷ vi (heart) latir; **pound sterling** n libra esterlina

pour [pɔ:*] vt echar; (tea etc) servir ▷ vi correr, fluir; **to ~ sb a drink** servirle a algn una copa; **pour in** vi (people) entrar en tropel; **pour out** vi salir en tropel ▷ vt (drink) echar, servir; (fig): **to pour out one's feelings** desahogarse; **pouring** adj: **pouring rain** lluvia torrencial

pout [paut] vi hacer pucheros

poverty ['pɒvətɪ] n pobreza, miseria

powder ['paudə*] n polvo; (also: **~**) polvos mpl ▷ vt polvorear; **to ~ one's face** empolvarse la cara; **powdered milk** n leche f en polvo

power ['pauə*] n poder m; (strength) fuerza; (nation, Tech) potencia; (drive) empuje m; (Elec) fuerza, energía ▷ vt impulsar; **to be in ~** (Pol) estar en el poder; **power cut** (BRIT) n apagón m; **power failure** n = **power cut**; **powerful** adj poderoso; (engine) potente; (speech etc) convincente; **powerless** adj: **powerless (to do)** incapaz (de hacer); **power point** n enchufe m; **power station** n central f eléctrica

p.p. abbr (= per procurationem): **p.p. J. Smith** p.p. (por poder de) J. Smith; (= pages) págs

PR n abbr = **public relations**

practical ['præktɪkl] adj práctico; **practical joke** n broma pesada; **practically** adv (almost) casi

practice ['præktɪs] n (habit) costumbre f; (exercise) práctica, ejercicio; (training) adiestramiento; (Med: of profession) práctica, ejercicio; (Med, Law: business) consulta ▷ vt, vi (US) = **practise**; **in ~** (in reality) en la práctica; **out of ~** desentrenado

practise ['præktɪs] (US **practice**) vt (carry out) practicar; (profession) ejercer; (train at) practicar ▷ vi ejercer; (train) practicar; **practising** adj (Christian etc) practicante; (lawyer) en ejercicio

practitioner [præk'tɪʃənə*] n (Med) médico/a

pragmatic [præg'mætɪk] adj pragmático

prairie ['preərɪ] n pampa

praise [preɪz] n alabanza(s) f(pl), elogio(s) m(pl) ▷ vt alabar, elogiar

pram [præm] (BRIT) n cochecito de niño

prank [præŋk] n travesura

prawn [prɔ:n] n gamba; **prawn**

cocktail n cóctel m de gambas

pray [preɪ] vi rezar; **prayer** [prɛə*] n oración f, rezo; (entreaty) ruego, súplica

preach [priːtʃ] vi predicar; **preacher** n predicador(a) m/f

precarious [prɪˈkɛərɪəs] adj precario

precaution [prɪˈkɔːʃən] n precaución f

precede [prɪˈsiːd] vt, vi preceder; **precedent** [ˈprɛsɪdənt] n precedente m; **preceding** [prɪˈsiːdɪŋ] adj anterior

precinct [ˈpriːsɪŋkt] n recinto

precious [ˈprɛʃəs] adj precioso

precise [prɪˈsaɪs] adj preciso, exacto; **precisely** adv precisamente, exactamente

precision [prɪˈsɪʒən] n precisión f

predator [ˈprɛdətə*] n depredador m

predecessor [ˈpriːdɪsɛsə*] n antecesor(a) m/f

predicament [prɪˈdɪkəmənt] n apuro

predict [prɪˈdɪkt] vt pronosticar; **predictable** adj previsible; **prediction** [-ˈdɪkʃən] n predicción f

predominantly [prɪˈdɒmɪnəntlɪ] adv en su mayoría

preface [ˈprɛfəs] n prefacio

prefect [ˈpriːfɛkt] (BRIT) n (in school) monitor(a) m/f

prefer [prɪˈfə:*] vt preferir; **to ~ doing** or **to do** preferir hacer; **preferable** [ˈprɛfrəbl] adj preferible; **preferably** [ˈprɛfrəblɪ] adv de preferencia; **preference** [ˈprɛfrəns] n preferencia; (priority) prioridad f

prefix [ˈpriːfɪks] n prefijo

pregnancy [ˈprɛgnənsɪ] n (of woman) embarazo; (of animal) preñez f

pregnant [ˈprɛgnənt] adj (woman) embarazada; (animal) preñada

prehistoric [ˈpriːhɪsˈtɔrɪk] adj prehistórico

prejudice [ˈprɛdʒudɪs] n prejuicio; **prejudiced** adj (person) predispuesto

preliminary [prɪˈlɪmɪnərɪ] adj preliminar

prelude [ˈprɛljuːd] n preludio

premature [ˈprɛmətʃuə*] adj prematuro

premier [ˈprɛmɪə*] adj primero, principal ▷ n (Pol) primer(a) ministro/a

première [ˈprɛmɪɛə*] n estreno

Premier League [prɛmɪəˈliːg] n primera división

premises [ˈprɛmɪsɪz] npl (of business etc) local m; **on the ~** en el lugar mismo

premium [ˈpriːmɪəm] n premio; (insurance) prima; **to be at a ~** ser muy solicitado

premonition [prɛməˈnɪʃən] n presentimiento

preoccupied [prɪˈɔkjupaɪd] adj ensimismado

prepaid [priːˈpeɪd] adj porte pagado

preparation [prɛpəˈreɪʃən] n preparación f; **preparations** npl preparativos mpl

preparatory school [prɪˈpærətəri-] n escuela preparatoria

prepare [prɪˈpɛə*] vt preparar, disponer; (Culin) preparar ▷ vi: **to ~ for** (action) prepararse or disponerse para; (event) hacer preparativos para; **~d to** dispuesto a; **~d for** listo para

preposition [prɛpəˈzɪʃən] n preposición f

prep school [prɛp-] n = **preparatory school**

prerequisite [priːˈrɛkwɪzɪt] n requisito

preschool [ˈpriːskuːl] adj preescolar

prescribe [prɪˈskraɪb] vt (Med) recetar

prescription [prɪˈskrɪpʃən] n (Med) receta

presence [ˈprɛzns] n presencia; **in sb's ~** en presencia de algn; **~ of mind** aplomo

present [adj, n ˈprɛznt, vb prɪˈzɛnt] adj (in attendance) presente; (current) actual ▷ n (gift) regalo; (actuality): **the ~** la actualidad, el presente ▷ vt (introduce, describe) presentar; (expound) exponer; (give) presentar, dar, ofrecer; (Theatre) representar; **to give sb a ~** regalar algo a algn; **at ~** actualmente; **presentable** [prɪˈzɛntəbl] *adj*: **to make o.s. presentable** arreglarse; **presentation** [ˈ-ˈteɪʃən] *n* presentación *f*; *(of report etc)* exposición *f*; *(formal ceremony)* entrega de un regalo; **present-day** *adj* actual; **presenter** [prɪˈzɛntə*] *n (Radio, TV)* locutor(a) *m/f*; **presently** *adv (soon)* dentro de poco; *(now)* ahora; **present participle** *n* participio (de) presente

preservation [prezəˈveɪʃən] *n* conservación *f*

preservative [prɪˈzəːvətɪv] *n* conservante *m*

preserve [prɪˈzəːv] *vt (keep safe)* preservar, proteger; *(maintain)* mantener; *(food)* conservar ▷ *n (for game)* coto, vedado; *(often pl: jam)* conserva, confitura

preside [prɪˈzaɪd] *vi* presidir

president [ˈprezɪdənt] *n* presidente *m/f*; **presidential** [ˈ-ˈdenʃl] *adj* presidencial

press [pres] *n (newspapers)*: **the P~** la prensa; *(printer's)* imprenta; *(of button)* pulsación *f* ▷ *vt* empujar; *(button etc)* apretar; *(clothes: iron)* planchar; *(put pressure on: person)* presionar; *(insist)*: **to ~ sth on sb** insistir en que algn acepte algo ▷ *vi (squeeze)* apretar; *(pressurize)*: **to ~ for** presionar por; **we are ~ed for time/money** estamos apurados de tiempo/dinero; **press conference** *n* rueda de prensa; **pressing** *adj* apremiante; **press stud** *n (BRIT)* botón *m* de presión; **press-up** *n (BRIT)* plancha

pressure [ˈpreʃə*] *n* presión *f*; **to put ~ on sb** presionar a algn; **pressure cooker** *n* olla a presión; **pressure group** *n* grupo de presión

prestige [presˈtiːʒ] *n* prestigio

prestigious [presˈtɪdʒəs] *adj* prestigioso

presumably [prɪˈzjuːməblɪ] *adv* es de suponer que, cabe presumir que

presume [prɪˈzjuːm] *vt*: **to ~ (that)** presumir (que), suponer (que)

pretence [prɪˈtens] *(US* **pretense)** *n* fingimiento; **under false ~s** con engaños

pretend [prɪˈtend] *vt, vi (feign)* fingir
> Be careful not to translate **pretend** by the Spanish word *pretender*.

pretense [prɪˈtens] *(US) n* = **pretence**

pretentious [prɪˈtenʃəs] *adj* presumido; *(ostentatious)* ostentoso, aparatoso

pretext [ˈpriːtekst] *n* pretexto

pretty [ˈprɪtɪ] *adj* bonito, lindo *(LAM)* ▷ *adv* bastante

prevail [prɪˈveɪl] *vi (gain mastery)* prevalecer; *(be current)* predominar; **prevailing** *adj (dominant)* predominante

prevalent [ˈprevələnt] *adj (widespread)* extendido

prevent [prɪˈvent] *vt*: **to ~ sb from doing sth** impedir a algn hacer algo; **to ~ sth from happening** evitar que ocurra algo; **prevention** [prɪˈvenʃə n] *n* prevención *f*; **preventive** *adj* preventivo

preview [ˈpriːvjuː] *n (of film)* preestreno

previous [ˈpriːviəs] *adj* previo, anterior; **previously** *adv* antes

prey [preɪ] *n* presa ▷ *vi*: **to ~ on** *(feed on)* alimentarse de; **it was ~ing on his mind** le preocupaba, le obsesionaba

price [praɪs] *n* precio ▷ *vt (goods)* fijar el precio de; **priceless** *adj* que no tiene precio; **price list** *n* tarifa

prick [prɪk] *n (sting)* picadura ▷ *vt* pinchar; *(hurt)* picar; **to ~ up one's ears** aguzar el oído

prickly [ˈprɪklɪ] *adj* espinoso; *(fig: person)* enojadizo

pride [praɪd] *n* orgullo; *(pej)* soberbia ▷ *vt*: **to ~ o.s. on** enorgullecerse de

priest [priːst] *n* sacerdote *m*

primarily [ˈpraɪmərɪlɪ] *adv* ante todo

primary [ˈpraɪmərɪ] *adj (first in importance)* principal ▷ *n (US Pol)*

P

elección f primaria; **primary school**
(BRIT) n escuela primaria
prime [praɪm] adj primero, principal;
(excellent) selecto, de primera clase
▷ n: **in the ~ of life** en la flor de la vida
▷ vt (wood: fig) preparar; **~ example**
ejemplo típico; **Prime Minister** n
primer(a) ministro/a
primitive ['prɪmɪtɪv] adj primitivo;
(crude) rudimentario
primrose ['prɪmrəuz] n primavera,
prímula
prince [prɪns] n príncipe m
princess [prɪn'ses] n princesa
principal ['prɪnsɪpl] adj principal,
mayor ▷ n director(a) m/f; **principally**
adv principalmente
principle ['prɪnsɪpl] n principio; **in ~**
en principio; **on ~** por principio
print [prɪnt] n (footprint) huella,
(fingerprint) huella dactilar; (letters)
letra de molde; (fabric) estampado;
(Art) grabado; (Phot) impresión
f ▷ vt imprimir; (cloth) estampar;
(write in capitals) escribir en letras de
molde; **out of ~** agotado; **print out** vt
(Comput) imprimir; **printer** n (person)
impresor/a m/f; (machine) impresora;
printout n (Comput) impresión f
prior ['praɪə*] adj anterior, previo;
(more important) más importante; **~
to** antes de
priority [praɪ'ɔrɪtɪ] n prioridad f; **to
have ~ (over)** tener prioridad (sobre)
prison ['prɪzn] n cárcel f, prisión f
▷ cpd carcelario; **prisoner** n (in prison)
preso/a; (captured person) prisionero/a;
prisoner-of-war n prisionero de
guerra
pristine ['prɪstiːn] adj prístino
privacy ['prɪvəsɪ] n intimidad f
private ['praɪvɪt] adj (personal)
particular; (property, industry, discussion
etc) privado; (person) reservado; (place)
tranquilo ▷ n soldado raso; **"~"** (in
envelope) "confidencial"; (on door)
"prohibido el paso"; **in ~** en privado;
privately adv en privado; (in o.s.)

en secreto; **private property** n
propiedad f privada; **private school** n
colegio particular
privatize ['praɪvɪtaɪz] vt privatizar
privilege ['prɪvɪlɪdʒ] n privilegio;
(prerogative) prerrogativa
prize [praɪz] n premio ▷ adj de
primera clase ▷ vt apreciar, estimar;
prize-giving n distribución f de
premios; **prizewinner** n premiado/a
pro [prəu] n (Sport) profesional mf
▷ prep a favor de; **the ~s and cons** los
pros y los contras
probability [prɔbə'bɪlɪtɪ] n
probabilidad f; **in all ~** con toda
probabilidad
probable ['prɔbəbl] adj probable
probably ['prɔbəblɪ] adv
probablemente
probation [prə'beɪʃən] n: **on ~**
(employee) a prueba; (Law) en libertad
condicional
probe [prəub] n (Med, Space) sonda;
(enquiry) encuesta, investigación f ▷ vt
sondar; (investigate) investigar
problem ['prɔbləm] n problema m
procedure [prə'siːdʒə*] n
procedimiento; (bureaucratic) trámites
mpl
proceed [prə'siːd] vi (do
afterwards): **to ~ to do sth** proceder
a hacer algo; (continue): **to ~ (with)**
continuar or seguir (con); **proceedings**
npl acto(s) (pl); (Law) proceso;
proceeds ['prəusiːdz] npl (money)
ganancias fpl, ingresos mpl
process ['prəuses] n proceso ▷ vt
tratar, elaborar
procession [prə'seʃən] n desfile m;
funeral ~ cortejo fúnebre
proclaim [prə'kleɪm] vt (announce)
anunciar
prod [prɔd] vt empujar ▷ n empujón
m
produce [n 'prɔdjuːs, vt prə'djuːs]
n (Agr) productos mpl agrícolas ▷ vt
producir; (play, film, programme)
presentar; **producer** n productor(a)

m/f; (of film, programme)
director(a) m/f; (of record) productor(a)
m/f

product ['prɒdʌkt] n producto;
production [prə'dʌkʃən] n
producción f; (Theatre) presentación
f; **productive** [prə'dʌktɪv]
adj productivo; **productivity**
[prɒdʌk'tɪvɪtɪ] n productividad f

Prof. [prɒf] abbr (= professor) Prof

profession [prə'feʃən] n profesión
f; **professional** adj profesional ▷ n
profesional m/f; (skilled person) perito

professor [prə'fesə*] n (BRIT)
catedrático/a; (US, CANADA) profesor(a)
m/f

profile ['prəʊfaɪl] n perfil m

profit ['prɒfɪt] n (Comm) ganancia
f ▷ vi: **to ~ by** or **from** aprovechar o sacar
provecho de; **profitable** adj (Econ)
rentable

profound [prə'faʊnd] adj profundo

programme ['prəʊɡræm] (US
program) n programa m ▷ vt
programar; **programmer** (US
programer) n programador(a) m/f;
programming (US **programing**) n
programación f

progress [n 'prəʊɡres, vi prə'ɡres]
n progreso; (development) desarrollo
▷ vi progresar, avanzar; **in ~** en curso;
progressive [-'ɡresɪv] adj progresivo;
(person) progresista

prohibit [prə'hɪbɪt] vt prohibir; **to
~ sb from doing sth** prohibir a algn
hacer algo

project [n 'prɒdʒekt, vb
prə'dʒekt] n proyecto ▷ vt
proyectar ▷ vi (stick out) salir,
sobresalir; **projection**
[prə'dʒekʃən] n proyección f;
(overhang) saliente m; **projector**
[prə'dʒektə*] n proyector m

prolific [prə'lɪfɪk] adj prolífico

prolong [prə'lɒŋ] vt prolongar,
extender

prom [prɒm] n abbr = **promenade**
(US: ball) baile m de gala; **the P~s** ver

recuadro

promenade [prɒmə'nɑːd] n (by sea)
paseo marítimo

prominent ['prɒmɪnənt] adj
(standing out) saliente; (important)
eminente, importante

promiscuous [prə'mɪskjuəs] adj
(sexually) promiscuo

promise ['prɒmɪs] n promesa
▷ vt, vi prometer; **promising** adj
prometedor(a)

promote [prə'məʊt] vt (employee)
ascender; (product, pop star) hacer
propaganda por; (ideas) fomentar;
promotion [-'məʊʃən] n (advertising
campaign) campaña f de promoción; (in
rank) ascenso

prompt [prɒmpt] adj rápido ▷ adv: **at
6 o'clock** a las seis en punto ▷ n
(Comput) aviso ▷ vt (urge) mover,
incitar; (when talking) instar; (Theatre)
apuntar; **to ~ sb to do sth** instar
a algn a hacer algo; **promptly** adv
rápidamente; (exactly) puntualmente

prone [prəʊn] adj (lying) postrado; **~
to** propenso a

prong [prɒŋ] n diente m, punta

pronoun ['prəʊnaʊn] n pronombre

m
pronounce [prə'nauns] vt
pronunciar
pronunciation [prənʌnsɪ'eɪʃən] n
pronunciación f
proof [pruːf] n prueba ▷ adj: **~
against** a prueba de
prop [prɒp] n apoyo; (fig) sostén m
accesorios mpl, at(t)rezzo msg; **prop up**
vt (roof, structure) apuntalar; (economy)
respaldar
propaganda [prɒpə'gændə] n
propaganda
propeller [prə'pelə*] n hélice f
proper ['prɒpə*] adj (suited, right)
propio; (exact) justo; (seemly) correcto,
decente; (authentic) verdadero;
(referring to place): **the village ~**
el pueblo mismo; **properly** adv
(adequately) correctamente; (decently)
decentemente; **proper noun** n
nombre m propio
property ['prɒpətɪ] n propiedad f;
(personal) bienes mpl muebles
prophecy ['prɒfɪsɪ] n profecía f
prophet ['prɒfɪt] n profeta m
proportion [prə'pɔːʃən] n
proporción f; (share) parte f;
proportions npl (size) dimensiones fpl;
proportional adj: **proportional (to)**
en proporción (con)
proposal [prə'pəuzl] n (offer of
marriage) oferta de matrimonio; (plan)
proyecto
propose [prə'pəuz] vt proponer ▷ vi
declararse; **to ~ to do** tener intención
de hacer
proposition [prɒpə'zɪʃən] n
propuesta
proprietor [prə'praɪətə*] n
propietario/a, dueño/a
prose [prəuz] n prosa
prosecute ['prɒsɪkjuːt] vt (Law)
procesar; **prosecution** [-'kjuːʃən]
n proceso, causa; (accusing
side) acusación f; **prosecutor** n
acusador(a) m/f; (also: **public
prosecutor**) fiscal mf

prospect [n 'prɒspekt, vb
prə'spekt] n (possibility) posibilidad
f; (outlook) perspectiva ▷ vi: **to ~
for** buscar; **prospects** npl (for work
etc) perspectivas fpl; **prospective**
[prə'spektɪv] adj futuro
prospectus [prə'spektəs] n
prospecto
prosper ['prɒspə*] vi prosperar;
prosperity [-'sperɪtɪ] n prosperidad f;
prosperous adj próspero
prostitute ['prɒstɪtjuːt] n
prostituta; (male) hombre que se dedica a
la prostitución
protect [prə'tekt] vt proteger;
protection [-'tekʃən] n protección f;
protective adj protector(a)
protein ['prəutiːn] n proteína
protest [n 'prəutest, vb prə'test] n
protesta ▷ vi: **to ~ about** or **at/against**
protestar de/contra ▷ vt (insist): **to ~
(that)** insistir en (que)
Protestant ['prɒtɪstənt] adj, n
protestante mf
protester [prə'testə*] n
manifestante mf
protractor [prə'træktə*] n (Geom)
transportador m
proud [praud] adj orgulloso; (pej)
soberbio, altanero
prove [pruːv] vt probar; (show)
demostrar ▷ vi: **to ~ (to be) correct**
resultar correcto; **to ~ o.s.** probar
su valía
proverb ['prɒvɜːb] n refrán m
provide [prə'vaɪd] vt proporcionar,
dar; **to ~ sb with sth** proveer a algn
de algo; **provide for** vt fus (person)
mantener a; (problem etc) tener en
cuenta; **provided** conj: **provided
(that)** con tal de que, a condición
de que; **providing** [prə'vaɪdɪŋ]
conj: **providing (that)** a condición de
que, con tal de que
province ['prɒvɪns] n provincia; (fig)
esfera; **provincial** [prə'vɪnʃəl] adj
provincial; (pej) provinciano
provision [prə'vɪʒən] n (supplying)

suministro, abastecimiento; (of contract etc) disposición f; **provisions** npl (food) comestibles mpl; **provisional** adj provisional

provocative [prə'vɔkətɪv] adj provocativo

provoke [prə'vəʊk] vt (cause) provocar, incitar; (anger) enojar

prowl [praʊl] vi (also: ~ **about**, ~ **around**) merodear ▷ n: **on the ~** de merodeo

proximity [prɔk'sɪmɪtɪ] n proximidad f

proxy ['prɔksɪ] n: **by ~** por poderes

prudent ['pruːdənt] adj prudente

prune [pruːn] n ciruela pasa ▷ vt podar

pry [praɪ] vi: **to ~ (into)** entrometerse (en)

PS n abbr (= postscript) P.D.

pseudonym ['sjuːdənɪm] n seudónimo

PSHE (BRIT: Scol) n abbr (= personal, social and health education) formación social y sanitaria

psychiatric [saɪkɪ'ætrɪk] adj psiquiátrico

psychiatrist [saɪ'kaɪətrɪst] n psiquiatra mf

psychic ['saɪkɪk] adj (also: **~al**) psíquico

psychoanalysis [saɪkəʊə'nælɪsɪs] n psicoanálisis m inv

psychological [saɪkə'lɔdʒɪkl] adj psicológico

psychologist [saɪ'kɔlədʒɪst] n psicólogo/a

psychology [saɪ'kɔlədʒɪ] n psicología

psychotherapy [saɪkəʊ'θerəpɪ] n psicoterapia

pt abbr = **pint(s)**; **point(s)**

PTO abbr (= please turn over) sigue

pub [pʌb] n abbr (= public house) pub m, bar m

puberty ['pjuːbətɪ] n pubertad f

public ['pʌblɪk] adj público ▷ n: **the ~** el público; **in ~** en público; **to make ~**

hacer público

publication [pʌblɪ'keɪʃən] n publicación f

public: public company n sociedad f anónima; **public convenience** (BRIT) n aseos mpl públicos (SP), sanitarios mpl (LAM); **public holiday** (día m de) fiesta (SP), (día m) feriado (LAM); **public house** (BRIT) n bar m, pub m

publicity [pʌb'lɪsɪtɪ] n publicidad f

publicize ['pʌblɪsaɪz] vt publicitar

public: public limited company n sociedad f anónima (S.A.); **publicly** adv públicamente, en público; **public opinion** n opinión f pública; **public relations** n relaciones fpl públicas; **public school** n (BRIT) escuela privada; (us) instituto; **public transport** n transporte m público

publish ['pʌblɪʃ] vt publicar; **publisher** n (person) editor(a) m/f; (firm) editorial f; **publishing** n (industry) industria del libro

pub lunch n almuerzo que se sirve en un pub; **to go for a ~** almorzar o comer en un pub

pudding ['pʊdɪŋ] n pudín m; (BRIT: dessert) postre m; **black ~** morcilla

puddle ['pʌdl] n charco

Puerto Rico [pweːtəʊ'riːkəʊ] n Puerto Rico

puff [pʌf] n soplo; (of smoke, air) bocanada; (of breathing) resoplido ▷ vt: **to ~ one's pipe** chupar la pipa ▷ vi (pant) jadear; **puff pastry** n hojaldre m

pull [pʊl] n (tug): **to give sth a ~** dar un tirón a algo ▷ vt tirar de; (press: trigger) apretar; (haul) tirar, arrastrar; (curtain) correr ▷ vi tirar; **to ~ to pieces** hacer pedazos; **not to ~ one's punches** no andarse con bromas; **to ~ one's weight** hacer su parte; **to ~ o.s. together** sobreponerse; **to ~ sb's leg** tomar el pelo a algn; **pull apart** vt (break) romper; **pull away** vi (vehicle: move off) salir, arrancar; (draw back) apartarse bruscamente; **pull back** vt (lever etc)

P

tirar hacia sí; (*curtains*) descorrer ▷ vi
(*refrain*) contenerse; (*Mil: withdraw*)
retirarse; **pull down** vt (*building*)
derribar; **pull in** vi (*car etc*) parar
(junto a la acera); (*train*) llegar a la
estación; **pull off** vt (*deal etc*) cerrar;
pull out vi (*car, train etc*) salir ▷ vt
sacar, arrancar; **pull over** vi (*Aut*)
hacerse a un lado; **pull up** vi (*stop*)
parar ▷ vt (*raise*) levantar; (*uproot*)
arrancar, desarraigar
pulley ['pulɪ] n polea
pullover ['puləuvə*] n jersey m,
suéter m
pulp [pʌlp] n (*of fruit*) pulpa
pulpit ['pulpɪt] n púlpito
pulse [pʌls] n (*Anat*) pulso; (*rhythm*)
pulsación f; (*Bot*) legumbre f; **pulses** pl
n legumbres
puma ['pju:mə] n puma m
pump [pʌmp] n bomba; (*shoe*)
zapatilla f ▷ vt sacar con una bomba;
pump up vt inflar
pumpkin ['pʌmpkɪn] n calabaza
pun [pʌn] n juego de palabras
punch [pʌntʃ] n (*blow*) golpe m,
puñetazo; (*tool*) punzón m; (*drink*)
ponche m ▷ vt (*hit*): **to ~ sb/sth** dar
un puñetazo a algn/golpear a algn/algo;
punch-up (*BRIT: inf*) n riña
punctual ['pʌŋktjuəl] adj puntual
punctuation [pʌŋktju'eɪʃən] n
puntuación f
puncture ['pʌŋktʃə*] (*BRIT*) n
pinchazo ▷ vt pinchar
punish ['pʌnɪʃ] vt castigar;
punishment n castigo
punk [pʌŋk] n (*also: ~ rocker*)
punki m/f; (*also: ~ rock*) música punk;
(*us: inf: hoodlum*) rufián m
pup [pʌp] n cachorro
pupil ['pju:pl] n alumno/a; (*of eye*)
pupila
puppet ['pʌpɪt] n títere m
puppy ['pʌpɪ] n cachorro, perrito
purchase ['pəːtʃɪs] n compra ▷ vt
comprar
pure [pjuə*] adj puro; **purely** adv

puramente
purify ['pjuərɪfaɪ] vt purificar,
depurar
purity ['pjuərɪtɪ] n pureza
purple ['pəːpl] adj purpúreo; morado
purpose ['pəːpəs] n propósito; **on ~ a**
propósito, adrede
purr [pəː*] vi ronronear
purse [pəːs] n monedero; (
us: handbag) bolso (*SP*), cartera (*LAM*),
bolsa (*MEX*) ▷ vt fruncir
pursue [pə'sjuː] vt seguir
pursuit [pə'sjuːt] n (*chase*) caza;
(*occupation*) actividad f
pus [pʌs] n pus m
push [puʃ] n empuje m, empujón
m; (*of button*) presión f; (*drive*) empuje
m ▷ vt empujar; (*button*) apretar;
(*promote*) promover ▷ vi empujar;
(*demand*): **to ~ for** luchar por; **push in**
vi colarse; **push off** (*inf*) vi largarse;
push on vi seguir adelante; **push over**
vt (*cause to fall*) hacer caer, derribar;
(*knock over*) volcar; **push through** vt
(*crowd*) abrirse paso a empujones ▷ vt
(*measure*) despachar; **pushchair** (*BRIT*)
n sillita de ruedas; **pusher** n (*drug
pusher*) traficante m/f de drogas; **push-
up** (*us*) n plancha
pussy(-cat) ['pusɪ-] (*inf*) n minino
(*inf*)
put [put] (*pt, pp ~*) vt (*place*) poner,
colocar; (*put into*) meter; (*say*) expresar;
(*a question*) hacer; (*estimate*) estimar;
put aside vt (*lay down: book etc*) dejar
or poner a un lado; (*save*) ahorrar; (*in
shop*) guardar; **put away** vt (*store*)
guardar; **put back** vt (*replace*) devolver
a su lugar; (*postpone*) aplazar; **put by**
vt (*money*) guardar; **put down** vt (*on
ground*) poner en el suelo; (*animal*)
sacrificar; (*in writing*) apuntar; (*revolt
etc*) sofocar; (*attribute*): **to put sth
down to** atribuir algo a; **put forward**
vt (*ideas*) presentar, proponer; **put
in** vt (*complaint*) presentar; (*time*)
dedicar; **put off** vt (*postpone*) aplazar;
(*discourage*) desanimar; **put on** vt

ponerse; (*light etc*) encender; (*play etc*)
presentar; (*gain*): **to put on weight**
engordar; (*brake*) echar; (*record, kettle
etc*) poner; (*assume*) adoptar; **put out**
vt (*fire, light*) apagar; (*rubbish etc*) sacar;
(*cat etc*) echar; (*one's hand*) alargar;
(*inf: person*): **to be put out** alterarse;
put through vt (*Tel*) poner; (*plan etc*)
hacer aprobar; **put together** vt unir,
reunir; (*assemble: furniture*) armar,
montar; (*meal*) preparar; **put up** vt
(*raise*) levantar, alzar; (*hang*) colgar;
(*build*) construir; (*increase*) aumentar;
(*accommodate*) alojar; **put up with** vt
fus aguantar

putt [pʌt] n putt m, golpe m corto;
putting green n green m; minigolf m
puzzle ['pʌzl] n rompecabezas m
inv; (*also:* **crossword ~**) crucigrama
m; (*mystery*) misterio ▷ vt dejar
perplejo, confundir ▷ vi: **to ~ over sth**
devanarse los sesos con algo; **puzzled**
adj perplejo; **puzzling** adj misterioso,
extraño
pyjamas [pɪˈdʒɑːməz] (BRIT) npl
pijama m
pylon ['paɪlən] n torre f de
conducción eléctrica
pyramid ['pɪrəmɪd] n pirámide f

q

quack [kwæk] n graznido; (*pej: doctor*)
curandero/a
quadruple [kwɔˈdruːpl] vt, vi
cuadruplicar
quail [kweɪl] n codorniz f ▷ vi: **to ~ at**
or **before** amedrentarse ante
quaint [kweɪnt] adj extraño;
(*picturesque*) pintoresco
quake [kweɪk] vi temblar ▷ n abbr =
earthquake
qualification [kwɔlɪfɪˈkeɪʃən] n
(*ability*) capacidad f; (*often pl: diploma
etc*) título; (*reservation*) salvedad f
qualified ['kwɔlɪfaɪd] adj
capacitado; (*professionally*) titulado;
(*limited*) limitado
qualify ['kwɔlɪfaɪ] vt (*make competent*)
capacitar; (*modify*) modificar ▷ vi (*in
competition*): **to ~ (for)** calificarse
(para); (*pass examination(s)*): **to ~ (as)**
calificarse (de), graduarse (en); (*be
eligible*): **to ~ (for)** reunir los requisitos
(para)
quality ['kwɔlɪtɪ] n calidad f; (*of
person*) cualidad f

q

qualm [kwɑːm] n escrúpulo

quantify ['kwɒntɪfaɪ] vt cuantificar

quantity ['kwɒntɪtɪ] n cantidad f; **in ~** en grandes cantidades

quarantine ['kwɒrntiːn] n cuarentena

quarrel ['kwɒrl] n riña, pelea ▷ vi reñir, pelearse

quarry ['kwɒrɪ] n cantera

quart [kwɔːt] n ≈ litro

quarter ['kwɔːtə*] n cuarto, cuarta parte f; (us: coin) moneda de 25 centavos; (of year) trimestre m; (district) barrio ▷ vt dividir en cuartos; (Mil: lodge) alojar; **quarters** npl (barracks) cuartel m; (living quarters) alojamiento; **a ~ of an hour** un cuarto de hora; **quarter final** n cuarto de final; **quarterly** adj trimestral ▷ adv cada 3 meses, trimestralmente

quartet(te) [kwɔː'tɛt] n cuarteto

quartz [kwɔːts] n cuarzo

quay [kiː] n (also: **~side**) muelle m

queasy ['kwiːzɪ] adj: **to feel ~** tener náuseas

queen [kwiːn] n reina; (Cards etc) dama

queer [kwɪə*] adj raro, extraño ▷ n (inf: highly offensive) maricón m

quench [kwɛntʃ] vt: **to ~ one's thirst** apagar la sed

query ['kwɪərɪ] n (question) pregunta ▷ vt dudar de

quest [kwɛst] n busca, búsqueda

question ['kwɛstʃən] n pregunta; (doubt) duda; (matter) asunto, cuestión f ▷ vt (doubt) dudar de; (interrogate) interrogar, hacer preguntas a; **beyond ~** fuera de toda duda; **out of the ~** imposible; ni hablar; **questionable** adj dudoso; **question mark** n punto de interrogación; **questionnaire** [-'nɛə*] n cuestionario

queue [kjuː] (BRIT) n cola ▷ vi (also: **~ up**) hacer cola

quiche [kiːʃ] n quiche m

quick [kwɪk] adj rápido; (agile) ágil; (mind) listo ▷ n: **cut to the ~** (fig) herido en lo vivo; **be ~!** ¡date prisa!; **quickly** adv rápidamente, de prisa

quid [kwɪd] (BRIT: inf) n inv libra

quiet ['kwaɪət] adj (voice, music etc) bajo; (person, place) tranquilo; (ceremony) íntimo ▷ n silencio; (calm) tranquilidad f ▷ vt, vi (us) = **quieten**

> Be careful not to translate **quiet** by the Spanish word quieto.

quietly adv tranquilamente; (silently) silenciosamente

quilt [kwɪlt] n edredón m

quirky ['kwɜːkɪ] adj raro, estrafalario

quit [kwɪt] (pt, pp = **or ~ted**) vt dejar, abandonar; (premises) desocupar ▷ vi (give up) renunciar; (resign) dimitir

quite [kwaɪt] adv (rather) bastante; (entirely) completamente; **that's not ~ big enough** no acaba de serlo bastante grande; **~ a few of them** un buen número de ellos; **~ (so)!** ¡así es!, ¡exactamente!

quits [kwɪts] adj: **~ (with)** en paz (con); **let's call it ~** dejémoslo en tablas

quiver ['kwɪvə*] vi estremecerse

quiz [kwɪz] n concurso ▷ vt interrogar

quota ['kwəʊtə] n cuota

quotation [kwəʊ'teɪʃən] n cita; (estimate) presupuesto; **quotation marks** npl comillas fpl

quote [kwəʊt] n cita; (estimate) presupuesto ▷ vt citar; (price) cotizar ▷ vi: **to ~ from** citar de; **quotes** npl (inverted commas) comillas fpl

r

rabbi ['ræbaɪ] n rabino
rabbit ['ræbɪt] n conejo
rabies ['reɪbiːz] n rabia
RAC (BRIT) n abbr (= Royal Automobile Club) ≈ RACE m
rac(c)oon [rəˈkuːn] n mapache m
race [reɪs] n carrera; (species) raza ▷ vt (horse) hacer correr; (engine) acelerar ▷ vi (compete) competir; (run) correr; (pulse) latir a ritmo acelerado; **race car** (US) n = **racing car; racecourse** n hipódromo; **racehorse** n caballo de carreras; **racetrack** n pista; (for cars) autódromo
racial ['reɪʃl] adj racial
racing ['reɪsɪŋ] n carreras fpl; **racing car** (BRIT) n coche m de carreras; **racing driver** (BRIT) n piloto mf de carreras
racism ['reɪsɪzəm] n racismo; **racist** [-sɪst] adj, n racista mf
rack [ræk] n (also: **luggage ~**) rejilla; (shelf) estante m; (also: **roof ~**) baca, portaequipajes m inv; (dish rack) escurreplatos m inv; (clothes rack)

percha ▷ vt atormentar; **to ~ one's brains** devanarse los sesos
racket ['rækɪt] n (for tennis) raqueta; (noise) ruido, estrépito; (swindle) estafa, timo
racquet ['rækɪt] n raqueta
radar ['reɪdɑːʳ] n radar m
radiation [reɪdɪˈeɪʃən] n radiación f
radiator ['reɪdɪeɪtəʳ] n radiador m
radical ['rædɪkl] adj radical
radio ['reɪdɪəu] n radio f; **on the ~** por radio; **radioactive** adj radioactivo; **radio station** n emisora
radish ['rædɪʃ] n rábano
RAF n abbr (= Royal Air Force) las Fuerzas Aéreas Británicas
raffle ['ræfl] n rifa, sorteo
raft [rɑːft] n balsa; (also: **life ~**) balsa salvavidas
rag [ræg] n (piece of cloth) trapo; (torn cloth) harapo; (pej: newspaper) periodicucho; (for charity) actividades estudiantiles benéficas; **rags** npl (torn clothes) harapos mpl
rage [reɪdʒ] n rabia, furor m ▷ vi (person) rabiar, estar furioso; (storm) bramar; **it's all the ~** (very fashionable) está muy de moda
ragged ['rægɪd] adj (edge) desigual, mellado; (appearance) andrajoso, harapiento
raid [reɪd] n (Mil) incursión f; (criminal) asalto; (by police) redada ▷ vt invadir, atacar; asaltar
rail [reɪl] n (on stair) barandilla; pasamanos m inv; (on bridge, balcony) pretil m; (of ship) barandilla; (also: **towel ~**) toallero; **railcard** (BRIT) n tarjeta para obtener descuentos en el tren; **railing(s)** n(pl) vallado; **railroad** (US) n = **railway; railway** (BRIT) n ferrocarril m, vía férrea; **railway line** (BRIT) n línea (de ferrocarril); **railway station** n estación f de ferrocarril
rain [reɪn] n lluvia ▷ vi llover; **in the ~** bajo la lluvia; **it's ~ing** llueve, está lloviendo; **rainbow** n arco iris;

raincoat n impermeable m; **raindrop**
n gota de lluvia; **rainfall** n lluvia;
rainforest n selvas fpl tropicales;
rainy adj lluvioso

raise [reɪz] n aumento ▷ vt levantar;
(increase) aumentar; (improve: morale)
subir; (: standards) mejorar; (doubts)
suscitar; (a question) plantear; (cattle,
family) criar; (crop) cultivar; (army)
reclutar; (loan) obtener; **to ~ one's
voice** alzar la voz

raisin ['reɪzn] n pasa de Corinto

rake [reɪk] n (tool) rastrillo; (person)
libertino ▷ vt (garden) rastrillar

rally ['rælɪ] n (Pol etc) reunión f, mitin
m; (Aut) rallye m; (Tennis) peloteo ▷ vt
reunir ▷ vi recuperarse

RAM [ræm] n abbr (= random access
memory) RAM f

ram [ræm] n carnero; (also: **battering
~**) ariete m ▷ vt (crash into) dar contra,
chocar con; (push: fist etc) empujar
con fuerza

Ramadan [ræmə'dæn] n ramadán m

ramble ['ræmbl] n caminata,
excursión f en el campo ▷ vi (pej: also: **~
on**) divagar; **rambler** n excursionista
mf; (Bot) trepadora; **rambling** adj
(speech) inconexo; (house) laberíntico;
(Bot) trepador(a)

ramp [ræmp] n rampa; **on/off ~** (US
Aut) vía de acceso/salida

rampage [ræm'peɪdʒ] n: **to be
on the ~** desmandarse ▷ vi: **they
went rampaging through the
town** recorrieron la ciudad armando
alboroto

ran [ræn] pt of **run**

ranch [rɑːntʃ] n hacienda, estancia

random ['rændəm] adj fortuito, sin
orden; (Comput, Math) aleatorio ▷ n: **at
~** al azar

rang [ræŋ] pt of **ring**

range [reɪndʒ] n (of mountains)
cadena de montañas, cordillera; (of
missile) alcance m; (of voice) escala;
(series) serie f; (of products) surtido;
(Mil: also: **shooting ~**) campo de tiro;

(also: **kitchen ~**) fogón m ▷ vt (place)
colocar; (arrange) arreglar ▷ vi: **to ~
over** (extend) extenderse por; **to ~ from
... to ...** oscilar entre ... y ...

ranger [reɪndʒə*] n guardabosques
mf inv

rank [ræŋk] n (row) fila; (Mil) rango;
(status) categoría; (BRIT: also: **taxi
~**) parada de taxis ▷ vi: **to ~ among**
figurar entre ▷ adj fétido, rancio; **the ~
and file** (fig) la base

ransom ['rænsəm] n rescate m; **to
hold to ~** (fig) hacer chantaje a

rant [rænt] n vi divagar, desvariar

rap [ræp] vt golpear, dar un golpecito
en ▷ n (music) rap m

rape [reɪp] n violación f; (Bot) colza
▷ vt violar

rapid ['ræpɪd] adj rápido; **rapidly**
adv rápidamente; **rapids** npl (Geo)
rápidos mpl

rapist ['reɪpɪst] n violador m

rapport [ræ'pɔː*] n simpatía

rare [rɛə*] adj raro, poco común;
(Culin: steak) poco hecho; **rarely** adv
pocas veces

rash [ræʃ] adj imprudente,
precipitado ▷ n (Med) sarpullido,
erupción f (cutánea); (of events) serie f

rasher ['ræʃə*] n lonja

raspberry ['rɑːzbərɪ] n frambuesa

rat [ræt] n rata

rate [reɪt] n (ratio) razón f; (price)
precio; (: of hotel etc) tarifa; (of interest)
tipo; (speed) velocidad f ▷ vt (value)
tasar; (estimate) estimar; **rates** npl
(BRIT: property tax) impuesto municipal;
(fees) tarifa; **to ~ sth/sb as** considerar
algo/a algn como

rather ['rɑːðə*] adv: **it's ~ expensive**
es algo caro; (too much) es demasiado
caro; (to some extent) más bien; **there's
~ a lot** hay bastante; **I would** or **I'd ~ go**
preferiría ir; **or ~** mejor dicho

rating ['reɪtɪŋ] n tasación f; (score)
índice m; (of ship) clase f; **ratings** npl
(Radio, TV) niveles mpl de audiencia

ratio ['reɪʃɪəʊ] n razón f; **in the ~ of**

100 to 1a razón de 100 a 1

ration ['ræʃən] n ración f ▷ vt racionar; **rations** npl víveres mpl

rational ['ræʃənl] adj (solution, reasoning) lógico, razonable; (person) cuerdo, sensato

rattle ['rætl] n golpeteo; (of train etc) traqueteo; (for baby) sonaja, sonajero ▷ vi castañetear; (car, bus): **to ~ along** traquetear ▷ vt hacer sonar agitando

rave [reɪv] vi (in anger) encolerizarse; (with enthusiasm) entusiasmarse; (Med) delirar, desvariar ▷ n (inf: party) rave m

raven ['reɪvn] n cuervo

ravine [rə'viːn] n barranco

raw [rɔː] adj crudo; (not processed) bruto; (sore) vivo; (inexperienced) novato, inexperto; **~ materials** materias primas

ray [reɪ] n rayo; **~ of hope** (rayo de esperanza)

razor ['reɪzə*] n (open) navaja; (safety razor) máquina de afeitar; (electric razor) máquina (eléctrica) de afeitar; **razor blade** n hoja de afeitar

Rd abbr = **road**

RE n abbr (BRIT) = **religious education**

re [riː] prep con referencia a

reach [riːtʃ] n alcance m; (of river etc) extensión f entre dos recodos ▷ vt alcanzar, llegar a; (achieve) lograr ▷ vi extenderse; **within ~** al alcance (de la mano); **out of ~** fuera del alcance; **reach out** vt (hand) tender ▷ vi: **to reach out for sth** alargar or tender la mano para tomar algo

react [riː'ækt] vi reaccionar; **reaction** [-'ækʃən] n reacción f; **reactor** [riː'æktə*] n (also: **nuclear reactor**) reactor (nuclear)

read [riːd, pt, pp red] (pt, pp ~) vi leer ▷ vt leer; (understand) entender; (study) estudiar; **read out** vt leer en alta voz; **reader** n lector(a) m/f; (BRIT: at university) profesor(a) m/f adjunto/a

readily ['rɛdɪlɪ] adv (willingly) de buena gana; (easily) fácilmente; (quickly) en seguida

reading ['riːdɪŋ] n lectura; (on instrument) indicación f

ready ['rɛdɪ] adj listo, preparado; (willing) dispuesto; (available) disponible ▷ adv: **~-cooked** listo para comer ▷ n: **at the ~** (Mil) listo para tirar; **to get ~** vi prepararse ▷ vt preparar; **ready-made** adj confeccionado

real [rɪəl] adj verdadero, auténtico; **in ~ terms** en términos reales; **real ale** n cerveza elaborada tradicionalmente; **real estate** n bienes mpl raíces; **realistic** [-'lɪstɪk] adj realista; **reality** [riː'ælɪtɪ] n realidad f; **reality TV** n telerrealidad f

realization [rɪəlaɪ'zeɪʃən] n comprensión f; (fulfilment, Comm) realización f

realize ['rɪəlaɪz] vt (understand) darse cuenta de

really ['rɪəlɪ] adv realmente; (for emphasis) verdaderamente; (actually): **what ~ happened** lo que pasó en realidad; **~?** ¿de veras?; **~!** (annoyance) ¡vamos!, ¡por favor!

realm [rɛlm] n reino; (fig) esfera

realtor ['rɪəltɔː*] (US) n agente mf inmobiliario/a

reappear [riːə'pɪə*] vi reaparecer

rear [rɪə*] adj trasero ▷ n parte f trasera ▷ vt (cattle, family) criar ▷ vi (also: **~ up**: animal) encabritarse

rearrange [riːə'reɪndʒ] vt ordenar or arreglar de nuevo

rear: rear-view mirror n (Aut) (espejo) retrovisor m; **rear-wheel drive** n tracción f trasera

reason ['riːzn] n razón f ▷ vi: **to ~ with sb** tratar de que algn entre en razón; **it stands to ~ that** es lógico que ...; **reasonable** adj razonable; (sensible) sensato; **reasonably** adv razonablemente; **reasoning** n razonamiento, argumentos mpl

reassurance [riːə'ʃuərəns] n consuelo

reassure [riːə'ʃuə*] vt tranquilizar,

alentar; **to ~ sb that ...** tranquilizar a algn asegurando que ...

rebate ['ri:beɪt] n (on tax etc) desgravación f

rebel [n 'rebl, vi rɪ'bel] n rebelde m ▷ vi rebelarse, sublevarse; **rebellion** [rɪ'beljən] n rebelión f, sublevación f; **rebellious** [rɪ'beljəs] adj rebelde; (child) revoltoso

rebuild [ri:'bɪld] vt reconstruir

recall [vb rɪ'kɔːl, n 'ri:kɔl] vt (remember) recordar; (ambassador etc) retirar ▷ n recuerdo; retirada

rec'd abbr (=received) rbdo

receipt [rɪ'si:t] n (document) recibo; (for parcel etc) acuse m de recibo; (act of receiving) recepción f; **receipts** npl (Comm) ingresos mpl

> Be careful not to translate **receipt** by the Spanish word *receta*.

receive [rɪ'si:v] vt recibir; (guest) acoger; (wound) sufrir; **receiver** n (Tel) auricular m; (Radio) receptor m; (of stolen goods) perista m f; (Comm) administrador m jurídico

recent ['ri:snt] adj reciente; **recently** adv recientemente; **recently arrived** recién llegado

reception [rɪ'sepʃən] n recepción f; (welcome) acogida; **reception desk** n recepción f; **receptionist** n recepcionista m f

recession [rɪ'seʃən] n recesión f

recharge [ri:'tʃɑːdʒ] vt (battery) recargar

recipe ['resɪpɪ] n receta; (for disaster, success) fórmula

recipient [rɪ'sɪpɪənt] n recibidor(a) m/f; (of letter) destinatario/a

recital [rɪ'saɪtl] n recital m

recite [rɪ'saɪt] vt (poem) recitar

reckless ['rekləs] adj temerario, imprudente; (driving, driver) peligroso

reckon ['rekən] vt calcular; (consider) considerar; (think): **I ~ that ...** me parece que ...

reclaim [rɪ'kleɪm] vt (land, waste) recuperar; (land: from sea) rescatar;

(demand back) reclamar

recline [rɪ'klaɪn] vi reclinarse

recognition [rekəg'nɪʃən] n reconocimiento; **transformed beyond ~** irreconocible

recognize ['rekəgnaɪz] vt: **to ~ (by/as)** reconocer (por/como)

recollection [rekə'lekʃən] n recuerdo

recommend [rekə'mend] vt recomendar; **recommendation** [rekəmen'deɪʃən] n recomendación f

reconcile ['rekənsaɪl] vt (two people) reconciliar; (two facts) compaginar; **to ~ o.s. to sth** conformarse a algo

reconsider [ri:kən'sɪdə*] vt repensar

reconstruct [ri:kən'strʌkt] vt reconstruir

record [n, adj 'rekɔːd, vt rɪ'kɔːd] n (Mus) disco; (of meeting etc) acta; (register) registro, partida; (file) archivo; (also: **criminal ~**) antecedentes mpl; (written) expediente m; (Sport, Comput) récord m ▷ adj récord, sin precedentes ▷ vt registrar; (Mus: song etc) grabar; **in ~ time** en un tiempo récord; **off the ~** adj no oficial ▷ adv confidencialmente; **recorded delivery** (BRIT) n (Post) entrega con acuse de recibo; **recorder** n (Mus) flauta de pico; **recording** n (Mus) grabación f; **record player** n tocadiscos m inv

recount [rɪ'kaunt] vt contar

recover [rɪ'kʌvə*] vt recuperar ▷ vi (from illness, shock) recuperarse; **recovery** n recuperación f

recreate [ri:krɪ'eɪt] vt recrear

recreation [rekrɪ'eɪʃən] n recreo; **recreational vehicle** (us) n caravan o rulota pequeña; **recreational drug** droga recreativa

recruit [rɪ'kruːt] n recluta m f ▷ vt reclutar; (staff) contratar; **recruitment** n reclutamiento

rectangle ['rektæŋgl] n rectángulo; **rectangular** [-'tæŋgjulə*] adj rectangular

rectify ['rektɪfaɪ] vt rectificar

rector ['rɛktə*] n (Rel) párroco

recur [rɪ'kə:*] vi repetirse; (pain, illness) producirse de nuevo; **recurring** adj (problem) repetido, constante

recyclable [riː'saɪkləbl] adj reciclable

recycle [riː'saɪkl] vt reciclar

recycling [riː'saɪklɪŋ] n reciclaje

red [rɛd] n rojo ▷ adj rojo; (hair) pelirrojo; (wine) tinto; **to be in the ~** (account) estar en números rojos; (business) tener un saldo negativo; **to give sb the ~ carpet treatment** recibir a algn con todos los honores; **Red Cross** n Cruz f Roja; **redcurrant** n grosella roja

redeem [rɪ'diːm] vt redimir; (promises) cumplir; (sth in pawn) desempeñar; (fig, also Rel) rescatar

red: red-haired adj pelirrojo; **redhead** n pelirrojo/a; **red-hot** adj candente; **red light** n: **to go through a red light** (Aut) pasar la luz roja; **red-light district** n barrio chino

red meat n carne f roja

reduce [rɪ'djuːs] vt reducir; **to ~ to tears** hacer llorar a algn; **"~ speed now"** (Aut) "reduzca la velocidad"; **reduced** adj (decreased) reducido, rebajado; **at a reduced price** con rebaja or descuento; **"greatly reduced prices"** "grandes rebajas"; **reduction** [rɪ'dʌkʃən] n reducción f; (of price) rebaja; (discount) descuento; (smaller-scale copy) copia reducida

redundancy [rɪ'dʌndənsɪ] n (dismissal) despido; (unemployment) desempleo

redundant [rɪ'dʌndnt] adj (BRIT: worker) parado, sin trabajo; (detail, object) superfluo; **to be made ~** quedar(se) sin trabajo

reed [riːd] n (Bot) junco, caña; (Mus) lengüeta

reef [riːf] n (at sea) arrecife m

reel [riːl] n carrete m, bobina; (of film) rollo; (dance) baile escocés ▷ vt (also: **~ up**) devanar; (also: **~ in**) sacar ▷ vi

(sway) tambalear(se)

ref [rɛf] (inf) n abbr = **referee**

refectory [rɪ'fɛktərɪ] n comedor m

refer [rɪ'fə:*] vt (send: patient) referir; (: matter) remitir ▷ vi: **to ~ to** (allude to) referirse a, aludir a; (apply to) relacionarse con; (consult) consultar

referee [rɛfə'riː] n árbitro; (BRIT: for job application): **to be a ~ for sb** proporcionar referencias a algn ▷ vt (match) arbitrar en

reference ['rɛfrəns] n referencia; (for job application: letter) carta de recomendación; **with ~ to** (Comm: in letter) me remito a; **reference number** n número de referencia

refill [vt riː'fɪl, n 'riːfɪl] vt rellenar ▷ n repuesto, recambio

refine [rɪ'faɪn] vt refinar; **refined** adj (person) fino; **refinery** n refinería

reflect [rɪ'flɛkt] vt reflejar ▷ vi (think) reflexionar, pensar; **it ~s badly/well on him** le perjudica/le hace honor; **reflection** [-'flɛkʃən] n (act) reflexión f; (image) reflejo; (criticism) crítica; **on reflection** pensándolo bien

reflex ['riːflɛks] adj, n reflejo

reform [rɪ'fɔːm] n reforma ▷ vt reformar

refrain [rɪ'freɪn] vi: **to ~ from doing** abstenerse de hacer ▷ n estribillo

refresh [rɪ'frɛʃ] vt refrescar; **refreshing** adj refrescante; **refreshments** npl refrescos mpl

refrigerator [rɪ'frɪdʒəreɪtə*] n frigorífico (SP), nevera (SP), refrigerador m (LAM), heladera (RPL)

refuel [riː'fjuəl] vi repostar (combustible)

refuge ['rɛfjuːdʒ] n refugio, asilo; **to take ~ in** refugiarse en; **refugee** [rɛfju'dʒiː] n refugiado/a

refund [n 'riːfʌnd, vb rɪ'fʌnd] n reembolso ▷ vt devolver, reembolsar

refurbish [riː'fəːbɪʃ] vt restaurar, renovar

refusal [rɪ'fjuːzəl] n negativa; **to have first ~ on** tener la primera opción a

refuse¹ ['refju:s] n basura

refuse² [rɪ'fju:z] vt rechazar; (invitation) declinar; (permission) denegar ▷ vi: **to ~ to do sth** negarse a hacer algo; (horse) rehusar

regain [rɪ'geɪn] vt recobrar, recuperar

regard [rɪ'gɑːd] n mirada; (esteem) respeto; (attention) consideración f ▷ vt (consider) considerar; **to give one's ~s to** saludar de su parte a; **"with kindest ~s"** "con muchos recuerdos"; **as ~s, with ~ to** con respecto a, en cuanto a; **regarding** prep con respecto a, en cuanto a; **regardless** adv a pesar de todo; **regardless of** sin reparar en

regenerate [rɪ'dʒenəreɪt] vt regenerar

reggae ['regeɪ] n reggae m

regiment ['redʒɪmənt] n regimiento

region ['riːdʒən] n región f; **in the ~ of** (fig) alrededor de; **regional** adj regional

register ['redʒɪstə*] n registro ▷ vt registrar; (birth) declarar; (car) matricular; (letter) certificar; (instrument) marcar, indicar ▷ vi (at hotel) registrarse; (as student) matricularse; (make impression) producir impresión; **registered** adj (letter, parcel) certificado

registrar ['redʒɪstrɑː*] n secretario/a (del registro civil)

registration [redʒɪs'treɪʃən] n (act) declaración f; (Aut: also: **~ number**) matrícula

registry office ['redʒɪstrɪ-] (BRIT) n registro civil; **to get married in a ~** casarse por lo civil

regret [rɪ'gret] n sentimiento, pesar m ▷ vt sentir, lamentar; **regrettable** adj lamentable

regular ['regjulə*] adj regular; (soldier) profesional; (usual) habitual; (: doctor) de cabecera ▷ n (client etc) cliente a/m f habitual; **regularly** adv con regularidad; (often) repetidas veces

regulate ['regjuleɪt] vt controlar;

regulation [-'leɪʃən] n (rule) regla, reglamento

rehabilitation ['riːəbɪlɪ'teɪʃən] n rehabilitación f

rehearsal [rɪ'həːsl] n ensayo

rehearse [rɪ'həːs] vt ensayar

reign [reɪn] n reinado; (fig) predominio ▷ vi reinar; (fig) imperar

reimburse [riːɪm'bəːs] vt reembolsar

rein [reɪn] n (for horse) rienda

reincarnation [riːɪnkaː'neɪʃən] n reencarnación f

reindeer ['reɪndɪə*] n inv reno

reinforce [riːɪn'fɔːs] vt reforzar; **reinforcements** npl (Mil) refuerzos mpl

reinstate [riːɪn'steɪt] vt reintegrar; (tax, law) reinstaurar

reject [n 'riːdʒekt, vb rɪ'dʒekt] n (thing) desecho ▷ vt rechazar; (suggestion) descartar; (coin) expulsar; **rejection** [rɪ'dʒekʃən] n rechazo

rejoice [rɪ'dʒɔɪs] vi: **to ~ at** or **over** regocijarse or alegrarse de

relate [rɪ'leɪt] vt (tell) contar, relatar; (connect) relacionar ▷ vi relacionarse; **related** adj afín; (person) emparentado; **related to** (subject) relacionado con; **relating to** prep referente a

relation [rɪ'leɪʃən] n (person) pariente mf; (link) relación f; **relations** npl (relatives) familiares mpl; **relationship** n relación f; (personal) relaciones fpl; (also: **family relationship**) parentesco

relative ['relətɪv] n pariente mf, familiar mf ▷ adj relativo; **relatively** adv (comparatively) relativamente

relax [rɪ'læks] vi descansar; (unwind) relajarse ▷ vt (one's grip) soltar, aflojar; (control) relajar; (mind, person) descansar; **relaxation** [riːlæk'seɪʃən] n descanso; (of rule, control) relajamiento; (entertainment) diversión f; **relaxed** adj relajado; (tranquil) tranquilo; **relaxing** adj relajante

relay ['riːleɪ] n (race) carrera de relevos

▷vt (Radio, TV) retransmitir

release [rɪˈliːs] n (liberation) liberación f; (from prison) puesta en libertad; (of gas etc) escape m; (of film etc) estreno; (of record) lanzamiento ▷vt (prisoner) poner en libertad; (gas) despedir, arrojar; (from wreckage) soltar; (catch, spring etc) desenganchar; (film) estrenar; (book) publicar; (news) difundir

relegate [ˈrelɪgeɪt] vt relegar; (BRIT Sport): **to be ~d to** bajar a

relent [rɪˈlent] vi ablandarse; **relentless** adj implacable

relevant [ˈreləvənt] adj (fact) pertinente; **~ to** relacionado con

reliable [rɪˈlaɪəbl] adj (person, firm) de confianza, de fiar; (method, machine) seguro; (source) fidedigno

relic [ˈrelɪk] n (Rel) reliquia f; (of the past) vestigio

relief [rɪˈliːf] n (from pain, anxiety) alivio; (help, supplies) socorro, ayuda; (Art, Geo) relieve m

relieve [rɪˈliːv] vt (pain) aliviar; (bring help to) ayudar, socorrer; (take over from) sustituir; (guard) relevar; **to ~ sb of sth** quitar algo a algn; **to ~ o.s.** hacer sus necesidades; **relieved** adj: **to be relieved** sentir un gran alivio

religion [rɪˈlɪdʒən] n religión f

religious [rɪˈlɪdʒəs] adj religioso; **religious education** n educación f religiosa

relish [ˈrelɪʃ] n (Culin) salsa; (enjoyment) entusiasmo ▷vt (food etc) saborear; (enjoy): **to ~ sth** hacerle mucha ilusión a algn algo

relocate [riːləʊˈkeɪt] vt cambiar de lugar, mudar ▷vi mudarse

reluctance [rɪˈlʌktəns] n renuncia f

reluctant [rɪˈlʌktənt] adj renuente; **reluctantly** adv de mala gana

rely on [rɪˈlaɪ-] vt fus depender de; (trust) contar con

remain [rɪˈmeɪn] vi (survive) quedar; (be left) sobrar; (continue) quedar(se), permanecer; **remainder** n resto;

remaining adj que queda(n); (surviving) restante(s); **remains** npl restos mpl

remand [rɪˈmɑːnd] n: on ~ detenido (bajo custodia) ▷vt: **to be ~ed in custody** quedar detenido bajo custodia

remark [rɪˈmɑːk] n comentario ▷vt comentar; **remarkable** adj (outstanding) extraordinario

remarry [riːˈmærɪ] vi volver a casarse

remedy [ˈremədɪ] n remedio ▷vt remediar, curar

remember [rɪˈmembə*] vt recordar, acordarse de; (bear in mind) tener presente; (send greetings to): **~ me to him** dale recuerdos de mi parte; **Remembrance Day** n = día en el que se recuerda a los caídos en las dos guerrasmundiales

REMEMBRANCE DAY

En el Reino Unido el domingo más próximo al 11 de noviembre se conoce como **Remembrance Sunday** o **Remembrance Day**, aniversario de la firma del armisticio de 1918 que puso fin a la Primera Guerra Mundial. Ese día, a las once de la mañana (hora en que se firmó el armisticio), se recuerda a los que murieron en las dos guerras mundiales con dos minutos de silencio ante los monumentos a los caídos. Allí se colocan coronas de amapolas, flor que también se suele llevar prendida en el pecho tras pagar un donativo destinado a los inválidos de guerra.

remind [rɪˈmaɪnd] vt: **to ~ sb to do sth** recordar a algn que haga algo; **to ~ sb of sth** (of fact) recordar algo a algn; **she ~s me of her mother** me recuerda a su madre; **reminder** n notificación f; (memento) recuerdo

reminiscent [remɪˈnɪsnt] *adj*: **to be ~ of sth** recordar algo

remnant [ˈrɛmnənt] *n* resto; (*of cloth*) retal *m*

remorse [rɪˈmɔːs] *n* remordimiento *mpl*

remote [rɪˈməʊt] *adj* (*distant*) lejano; (*person*) distante; **remote control** *n* telecontrol *m*; **remotely** *adv* remotamente; (*slightly*) levemente

removal [rɪˈmuːvəl] *n* (*taking away*) el quitar; (BRIT: *from house*) mudanza; (*from office: dismissal*) destitución *f*; (*Med*) extirpación *f*; **removal man** (*irreg*) *n* (BRIT) mozo de mudanzas; **removal van** (BRIT) *n* camión *m* de mudanzas

remove [rɪˈmuːv] *vt* quitar; (*employee*) destituir; (*name: from list*) tachar, borrar; (*doubt*) disipar; (*abuse*) suprimir, acabar con; (*Med*) extirpar

Renaissance [rɪˈneɪsɑ̃s] *n*: **the ~** el Renacimiento

rename [riːˈneɪm] *vt* poner nuevo nombre a

render [ˈrɛndəʳ] *vt* (*thanks*) dar; (*aid*) proporcionar, prestar; (*make*): **to ~ sth useless** hacer algo inútil

rendezvous [ˈrɒndɪvuː] *n* cita

renew [rɪˈnjuː] *vt* renovar; (*resume*) reanudar; (*loan etc*) prorrogar; **renewable** *adj* (*energy*) renovable

renovate [ˈrɛnəveɪt] *vt* renovar

renowned [rɪˈnaʊnd] *adj* renombrado

rent [rɛnt] *n* (*for house*) arriendo, renta ▷ *vt* alquilar; **rental** *n* (*for television, car*) alquiler *m*

reorganize [riːˈɔːgənaɪz] *vt* reorganizar

rep [rɛp] *n abbr* = **representative**

repair [rɪˈpɛəʳ] *n* reparación *f*, compostura ▷ *vt* reparar, componer; (*shoes*) remendar; **in good/bad ~** en buen/mal estado; **repair kit** *n* caja de herramientas

repay [riːˈpeɪ] *vt* (*money*) devolver, reembolsar; (*person*) pagar; (*debt*)

liquidar; (*sb's efforts*) devolver, corresponder a; **repayment** *n* reembolso, devolución *f*; (*sum of money*) recompensa

repeat [rɪˈpiːt] *n* (*Radio, TV*) reposición *f* ▷ *vt* repetir ▷ *vi* repetirse; **repeatedly** *adv* repetidas veces; **repeat prescription** *n* (BRIT) receta renovada

repellent [rɪˈpɛlənt] *adj* repugnante ▷ *n*: **insect ~** crema or loción *f* antiinsectos

repercussions [riːpəˈkʌʃənz] *npl* consecuencias *fpl*

repetition [rɛpɪˈtɪʃən] *n* repetición *f*

repetitive [rɪˈpɛtɪtɪv] *adj* repetitivo

replace [rɪˈpleɪs] *vt* (*put back*) devolver a su sitio; (*take the place*) reemplazar, sustituir; **replacement** *n* (*act*) reposición *f*; (*thing*) recambio; (*person*) suplente *mf*

replay [ˈriːpleɪ] *n* (*Sport*) desempate *m*; (*of tape, film*) repetición *f*

replica [ˈrɛplɪkə] *n* copia, reproducción *f* (*exacta*)

reply [rɪˈplaɪ] *n* respuesta, contestación *f* ▷ *vi* contestar, responder

report [rɪˈpɔːt] *n* informe *m*; (*Press etc*) reportaje *m*; (BRIT: *also*: **school ~**) boletín *m* escolar; (*of gun*) estallido ▷ *vt* informar de; (*Press etc*) hacer un reportaje sobre; (*notify: accident, culprit*) denunciar ▷ *vi* (*make a report*) presentar un informe; (*present o.s.*): **to ~ (to sb)** presentarse (ante algn); **report card** *n* (US, SCOTTISH) cartilla escolar; **reportedly** *adv* según se dice; **reporter** *n* periodista *mf*

represent [rɛprɪˈzɛnt] *vt* representar; (*Comm*) ser agente de; (*describe*): **to ~ sth as** describir algo como; **representation** [-ˈteɪʃən] *n* representación *f*; **representative** *n* representante *mf*; (US *Pol*) diputado/a *m/f* ▷ *adj* representativo

repress [rɪˈprɛs] *vt* reprimir; **repression** [-ˈprɛʃən] *n* represión *f*

reprimand [ˈrɛprɪmɑːnd] *n*

reprimenda ▷vt reprender

reproduce [ri:prə'dju:s] vt reproducir ▷vi reproducirse; **reproduction** [-'dʌkʃən] n reproducción f

reptile ['reptaɪl] n reptil m

republic [rɪ'pʌblɪk] n república; **republican** adj, n republicano/a m/f

reputable ['repjutəbl] adj (make etc) de renombre

reputation [repju'teɪʃən] n reputación f

request [rɪ'kwest] n petición f; (formal) solicitud f ▷vt: to ~ sth of or from sb solicitar algo a algn; **request stop** (BRIT) n parada discrecional

require [rɪ'kwaɪə*] vt (need: person) necesitar, tener necesidad de; (: thing, situation) exigir; (want) pedir; to ~ sb to do sth pedir a algn que haga algo; **requirement** n requisito; (need) necesidad f

resat [ri:'sæt] pt, pp of **resit**

rescue ['reskju:] n rescate m ▷vt rescatar

research [rɪ'sə:tʃ] n investigaciones fpl ▷vt investigar

resemblance [rɪ'zembləns] n parecido

resemble [rɪ'zembl] vt parecerse a

resent [rɪ'zent] vt tomar a mal; **resentful** adj resentido; **resentment** n resentimiento

reservation [rezə'veɪʃən] n reserva; **reservation desk** (us) n (in hotel) recepción f

reserve [rɪ'zə:v] n reserva; (Sport) suplente mf ▷vt reservar; **reserved** adj reservado

reservoir ['rezəvwɑ:*] n (artificial lake) embalse m, tank; (small) depósito

residence ['rezɪdəns] n (formal: home) domicilio; (length of stay) permanencia; **residence permit** (BRIT) n permiso de permanencia

resident ['rezɪdənt] n (of area) vecino/a; (in hotel) huésped mf ▷adj (population) permanente; (doctor)

residente; residential [-'denʃəl] adj residencial

residue ['rezɪdju:] n resto

resign [rɪ'zaɪn] vt renunciar a ▷vi dimitir; to ~ o.s. to (situation) resignarse a; **resignation** [rezɪg'neɪʃə n] n dimisión f; (state of mind) resignación f

resin ['rezɪn] n resina

resist [rɪ'zɪst] vt resistir, oponerse a; **resistance** n resistencia

resit ['ri:sɪt] (BRIT) (pt, pp **resat**) vt (exam) volver a presentarse a; (subject) recuperar, volver a examinarse de (SP)

resolution [rezə'lu:ʃən] n resolución f

resolve [rɪ'zɔlv] n resolución f ▷vt resolver ▷vi: to ~ to do resolver hacer

resort [rɪ'zɔ:t] n (town) centro turístico; (recourse) recurso ▷vi: to ~ to recurrir a; **in the last** ~ como último recurso

resource [rɪ'sɔ:s] n recurso; **resourceful** adj despabilado, ingenioso

respect [rɪs'pekt] n respeto ▷vt respetar; **respectable** adj respetable; (large: amount) apreciable; (passable) tolerable; **respectful** adj respetuoso; **respective** adj respectivo; **respectively** adv respectivamente

respite ['respaɪt] n respiro

respond [rɪs'pɔnd] vi responder; (react) reaccionar; **response** [-'pɔns] n respuesta; reacción f

responsibility [rɪspɔnsɪ'bɪlɪtɪ] n responsabilidad f

responsible [rɪs'pɔnsɪbl] adj (character) serio, formal; (job) de confianza; (liable): ~ (for) responsable (de); **responsibly** adv con seriedad

responsive [rɪs'pɔnsɪv] adj sensible

rest [rest] n descanso, reposo; (Mus.) pausa, silencio; (support) apoyo; (remainder) resto ▷vi descansar; (be supported): to ~ on descansar sobre ▷vt: to ~ sth on/against apoyar algo en or sobre/contra; **the ~ of them** (people, objects) los demás; **it ~s with him to ...** depende de él que ...

restaurant ['rɛstərɒŋ] n restaurante m; **restaurant car** (BRIT) n (Rail) coche-comedor m

restless ['rɛstlɪs] adj inquieto

restoration [rɛstə'reɪʃən] n restauración f; devolución f

restore [rɪ'stɔː*] vt (building) restaurar; (sth stolen) devolver; (health) restablecer; (to power) volver a poner a

restrain [rɪs'treɪn] vt (feeling) contener, refrenar; (person): **to ~ (from doing)** disuadir (de hacer); **restraint** n (restriction) restricción f; (moderation) moderación f; (of manner) reserva f

restrict [rɪs'trɪkt] vt restringir, limitar; **restriction** [-kʃən] n restricción f, limitación f

rest room (US) n aseos mpl

restructure [riː'strʌktʃə*] vt reestructurar

result [rɪ'zʌlt] n resultado ▷ vi: **to ~ in** terminar en, tener por resultado; **as a ~ of** a consecuencia de

resume [rɪ'zjuːm] vt reanudar ▷ vi comenzar de nuevo

⬛ Be careful not to translate **resume** by the Spanish word resumir.

résumé ['reɪzjuːmeɪ] n resumen m; (US) currículum m

resuscitate [rɪ'sʌsɪteɪt] vt (Med) resucitar

retail ['riːteɪl] adj, adv al por menor; **retailer** n detallista m

retain [rɪ'teɪn] vt (keep) retener, conservar

retaliation [rɪtælɪ'eɪʃən] n represalias fpl

retarded [rɪ'tɑːdɪd] adj retrasado

retire [rɪ'taɪə*] vi (give up work) jubilarse; (withdraw) retirarse; (go to bed) acostarse; **retired** adj (person) jubilado; **retirement** n (giving up work: state) retiro; (: act) jubilación f

retort [rɪ'tɔːt] vi contestar

retreat [rɪ'triːt] n (place) retiro; (Mil)

retirada ▷ vi retirarse

retrieve [rɪ'triːv] vt recobrar; (situation, honour) salvar; (Comput) recuperar; (error) reparar

retrospect ['rɛtrəspɛkt] n: **in ~** retrospectivamente; **retrospective** [-'spɛktɪv] adj retrospectivo; (law) retroactivo

return [rɪ'təːn] n (going or coming back) vuelta, regreso; (of sth stolen etc) devolución f; (Finance: from land, shares) ganancia, ingresos mpl ▷ cpd (journey) de regreso; (BRIT: ticket) de ida y vuelta; (match) de vuelta ▷ vi (person etc: come or go back) volver, regresar; (symptoms etc) reaparecer; (regain): **to ~ to** recuperar ▷ vt devolver; (favour, love etc) corresponder a; (verdict) pronunciar; (Pol: candidate) elegir; **returns** npl (Comm) ingresos mpl; **in ~ (for)** a cambio (de); **by ~ of post** a vuelta de correo; **many happy ~s (of the day)!** ¡feliz cumpleaños!; **return ticket** n (esp BRIT) billete m (SP) or boleto m (LAM) de ida y vuelta, billete m redondo (MEX)

reunion [riː'juːnɪən] n (of family) reunión f; (of two people, school) reencuentro

reunite [riːjuː'naɪt] vt reunir; (reconcile) reconciliar

revamp [riː'væmp] vt renovar

reveal [rɪ'viːl] vt revelar; **revealing** adj revelador(a)

revel ['rɛvl] vi: **to ~ in sth/in doing sth** gozar de algo/con hacer algo

revelation [rɛvə'leɪʃən] n revelación f

revenge [rɪ'vɛndʒ] n venganza; **to take ~ on** vengarse de

revenue ['rɛvənjuː] n ingresos mpl, rentas fpl

Reverend ['rɛvərənd] adj (in titles): **the ~ John Smith** (Anglican) el Reverendo John Smith; (Catholic) el Padre John Smith; (Protestant) el Pastor John Smith

reversal [rɪ'vəːsl] n (of order)

inversión f; (of direction, policy) cambio; (of decision) revocación f

reverse [rɪ'vɜːs] n (opposite) contrario; (back: of cloth) revés m; (: of coin) reverso; (: of paper) dorso; (Aut: also: ~ **gear**) marcha atrás, revés m ▷ adj (order) inverso; (direction) contrario; (process) opuesto ▷ vt (decision, Aut) dar marcha atrás a; (position, function) invertir ▷ vi (Brit Aut) dar marcha atrás; **reverse-charge call** (Brit) n llamada a cobro revertido; **reversing lights** (Brit) npl (Aut) luces fpl de retroceso

revert [rɪ'vɜːt] vi: **to ~ to** volver a

review [rɪ'vjuː] n (magazine, Mil) revista; (of book, film) reseña; (us: examination) repaso, examen m ▷ vt repasar, examinar; (Mil) pasar revista a; (book, film) reseñar

revise [rɪ'vaɪz] vt (manuscript) corregir; (opinion) modificar; (price, procedure) revisar ▷ vi (study) repasar; **revision** [rɪ'vɪʒən] n corrección f; modificación f; (for exam) repaso

revival [rɪ'vaɪvəl] n (recovery) reanimación f; (of interest) renacimiento; (Theatre) reestreno; (of faith) despertar m

revive [rɪ'vaɪv] vt resucitar; (custom) restablecer; (hope) despertar; (play) reestrenar ▷ vi (person) volver en sí; (business) reactivarse

revolt [rɪ'vəult] n rebelión f ▷ vi rebelarse, sublevarse ▷ vt dar asco a, repugnar; **revolting** adj asqueroso, repugnante

revolution [revə'luːʃən] n revolución f; **revolutionary** adj, n revolucionario/a m/f

revolve [rɪ'vɔlv] vi dar vueltas, girar; (life, discussion) girar en torno a; **to ~ (a)round** girar en torno a

revolver [rɪ'vɔlvə*] n revólver m

reward [rɪ'wɔːd] n premio, recompensa ▷ vt: **to ~ (for)** recompensar or premiar (por); **rewarding** adj (fig) valioso

rewind [riː'waɪnd] vt rebobinar

rewritable [riː'raɪtəbl] adj (CD, DVD) reescribible

rewrite [riː'raɪt] (pt **rewrote**, pp **rewritten**) vt reescribir

rheumatism ['ruːmətɪzəm] n reumatismo, reúma m

rhinoceros [raɪ'nɔsərəs] n rinoceronte m

rhubarb ['ruːbɑːb] n ruibarbo

rhyme [raɪm] n rima; (verse) poesía

rhythm ['rɪðm] n ritmo

rib [rɪb] n (Anat) costilla ▷ vt (mock) tomar el pelo a

ribbon ['rɪbən] n cinta; **in ~s** (torn) hecho trizas

rice [raɪs] n arroz m; **rice pudding** n arroz m con leche

rich [rɪtʃ] adj rico; (soil) fértil; (food) pesado; (: sweet) empalagoso; (abundant): **~ in** (minerals etc) rico en

rid [rɪd] (pt, pp **~**) vt: **to ~ sb of sth** librar a algn de algo; **to get ~ of** deshacerse or desembarazarse de

riddle ['rɪdl] n (puzzle) acertijo; (mystery) enigma m, misterio ▷ vt: **to be ~d with** ser lleno o plagado de

ride [raɪd] (pt **rode**, pp **ridden**) n paseo; (distance covered) viaje m, recorrido ▷ vi (as sport) montar; (go somewhere: on horse, bicycle) dar un paseo, pasearse; (travel: on bicycle, motorcycle, bus) viajar ▷ vt (a horse) montar a; (a bicycle, motorcycle) andar en; (distance) recorrer; **to take sb for a ~** (fig) engañar a algn; **rider** n (on horse) jinete m; (on bicycle) ciclista mf; (on motorcycle) motociclista mf

ridge [rɪdʒ] n (of hill) cresta; (of roof) caballete m; (wrinkle) arruga

ridicule ['rɪdɪkjuːl] n irrisión f, burla ▷ vt poner en ridículo, burlarse de; **ridiculous** [-'dɪkjuləs] adj ridículo

riding ['raɪdɪn] n equitación f; **I like ~** me gusta montar a caballo; **riding school** n escuela de equitación

rife [raɪf] adj: **to be ~** ser muy común; **to be ~ with** abundar en

rifle ['raɪfl] n rifle m, fusil m ▷ vt saquear

rift [rɪft] n (in clouds) claro; (fig: disagreement) desavenencia

rig [rɪg] n (also: **oil** ~: at sea) plataforma petrolera ▷ vt (election etc) amañar

right [raɪt] adj (correct) correcto, exacto; (suitable) indicado, debido; (proper) apropiado; (just) justo; (morally good) bueno; (not left) derecho ▷ n bueno; (title, claim) derecho; (not left) derecha ▷ adv bien, correctamente; (not left) a la derecha; (exactly): ~ **now** ahora mismo ▷ vt enderezar; (correct) corregir ▷ excl ¡bueno!, ¡está bien!; **to be** ~ (person) tener razón; (answer) ser correcto; **is that the** ~ **time?** (of clock) ¿es esa la hora buena?; **by** ~**s** en justicia; **on the** ~ a la derecha; **to be in the** ~ tener razón; ~ **away** en seguida; ~ **in the middle** exactamente en el centro; **right angle** n ángulo recto; **rightful** adj legítimo; **right-hand** adj: **right-hand drive** conducción f por la derecha; **the right-hand side** derecha; **right-handed** adj diestro; **rightly** adv correctamente, debidamente; (with reason) con razón; **right of way** n (on path etc) derecho de paso; (Aut) prioridad f; **right-wing** adj (Pol) derechista

rigid ['rɪdʒɪd] adj rígido; (person, ideas) inflexible

rigorous ['rɪgərəs] adj riguroso

rim [rɪm] n borde m; (of spectacles) aro; (of wheel) llanta

rind [raɪnd] n (of bacon) corteza; (of lemon etc) cáscara; (of cheese) costra

ring [rɪŋ] (pt **rang**, pp **rung**) n (of metal) aro; (on finger) anillo; (of people) corro; (of objects) círculo; (gang) banda; (for boxing) cuadrilátero; (of circus) pista; (bull ring) ruedo, plaza; (sound of bell) toque m ▷ vi (telephone) llamar por teléfono; (bell) repicar; (doorbell, phone) sonar; (also: ~ **out**) sonar; (ears) zumbar ▷ vt (Brit Tel) llamar, telefonear; (bell etc) hacer sonar;

(doorbell) tocar; **to give sb a** ~ (Brit Tel) llamar or telefonear a algn; **ring back** (Brit) vt, vi (Tel) devolver la llamada; **ring off** (Brit) vi (Tel) colgar, cortar la comunicación; **ring up** (Brit) vt (Tel) llamar, telefonear; **ringing tone** n (Tel) tono de llamada; **ringleader** n (of gang) cabecilla m; **ring road** n (Brit) carretera periférica or de circunvalación; **ringtone** n (on mobile) tono de llamada

rink [rɪŋk] n (also: **ice** ~) pista de hielo

rinse [rɪns] n aclarado; (dye) tinte m ▷ vt aclarar; (mouth) enjuagar

riot ['raɪət] n motín m, disturbio ▷ vi amotinarse; **to run** ~ desmandarse

rip [rɪp] n rasgón m, rasgadura ▷ vt rasgar, desgarrar ▷ vi rasgarse, desgarrarse; **rip off** vt (inf: cheat) estafar; **rip up** vt hacer pedazos

ripe [raɪp] adj maduro

rip-off ['rɪpɔf] n (inf): **it's a** ~! ¡es una estafa!, ¡es un timo!

ripple ['rɪpl] n onda, rizo; (sound) murmullo ▷ vi rizarse

rise [raɪz] (pt **rose**, pp **risen**) n (slope) cuesta, pendiente f; (hill) altura; (Brit: in wages) aumento; (in prices, temperature) subida; (fig: to power etc) ascenso ▷ vi subir; (waters) crecer; (sun, moon) salir; (person: from bed etc) levantarse; (also: ~ **up**: rebel) sublevarse; (in rank) ascender; **to give** ~ **to** dar lugar or origen a; **to** ~ **to the occasion** ponerse a la altura de las circunstancias; **risen** ['rɪzn] pp of **rise**; **rising** adj (increasing: number) creciente; (: prices) en aumento or alza; (tide) creciente; (sun, moon) naciente

risk [rɪsk] n riesgo, peligro ▷ vt arriesgar; (run the risk of) exponerse a; **to take** or **run the** ~ **of doing** correr el riesgo de hacer; **at** ~ en peligro; **at one's own** ~ bajo su propia responsabilidad; **risky** adj arriesgado, peligroso

rite [raɪt] n rito; **last** ~**s** exequias fpl

ritual ['rɪtjuəl] adj ritual ▷ n ritual

m, rito

rival ['raɪvl] n rival mf; (in business) competidor(a) m/f ▷ adj rival, opuesto ▷vt competir con; **rivalry** n competencia

river ['rɪvə*] n río ▷ cpd (port) de río; (traffic) fluvial; **up/down** ~ río arriba/ abajo; **riverbank** n orilla (del río)

rivet ['rɪvɪt] n roblón m, remache m ▷ vt (fig) captar

road [rəud] n camino; (motorway etc) carretera; (in town) calle f ▷ cpd (accident) de tráfico; **major/minor** ~ carretera principal/secundaria; **roadblock** n barricada; **road map** n mapa m de carreteras; **road rage** n agresividad en la carretera; **road safety** n seguridad f vial; **roadside** n borde m (del camino); **roadsign** n señal f de tráfico; **road tax** n (BRIT) impuesto de rodaje; **roadworks** npl obras fpl

roam [rəum] vi vagar

roar [rɔː*] n rugido m; (of vehicle, storm) estruendo; (of laughter) carcajada ▷ vi rugir; hacer estruendo; **to ~ with laughter** reírse a carcajadas; **to do a ~ing trade** hacer buen negocio

roast [rəust] n carne f asada, asado ▷ vt asar; (coffee) tostar; **roast beef** n rosbif m

rob [rɔb] vt robar; **to ~ sb of sth** robar algo a algn; (fig: deprive) quitar algo a algn; **robber** n ladrón/ona m/f; **robbery** n robo

robe [rəub] n (for ceremony etc) toga; (also: **bath~**) albornoz m

robin ['rɔbɪn] n petirrojo

robot ['rəubɔt] n robot m

robust [rəu'bʌst] adj robusto, fuerte

rock [rɔk] n roca; (boulder) peña, peñasco; (us: small stone) piedrecita; (BRIT: sweet) ≈ pirulí ▷ vt (swing gently: cradle) balancear, mecer; (: child) arrullar; (shake) sacudir ▷ vi mecerse, balancearse; sacudirse; **on the ~s** (drink) con hielo; (marriage etc) en ruinas; **rock and roll** n rocanrol m; **rock climbing** n (Sport) escalada

rocket ['rɔkɪt] n cohete m; **rocking chair** ['rɔkɪŋ-] n mecedora

rocky ['rɔkɪ] adj rocoso

rod [rɔd] n vara, varilla; (also: **fishing ~**) caña

rode [rəud] pt of **ride**

rodent ['rəudnt] n roedor m

rogue [rəug] n pícaro, pillo

role [rəul] n papel m; **role-model** n modelo a imitar

roll [rəul] n rollo; (of bank notes) fajo; (also: **bread ~**) panecillo; (register, list) lista, nómina; (sound of drums etc) redoble m ▷ vt hacer rodar; (also: **~ up**: string) enrollar; (cigarette) liar; (also: **~ out**: pastry) aplanar; (flatten: road, lawn) apisonar ▷vi rodar; (drum) redoblar; (ship) balancearse; **roll over** vi dar una vuelta; **roll up** vi (inf: arrive) aparecer ▷vt (carpet) arrollar; (: sleeves) arremangar; **roller** n rodillo; (: wheel) rueda; (for road) apisonadora; (for hair) rulo; **Rollerblades**® npl patines en línea; **roller coaster** n montaña rusa; **roller skates** npl patines mpl de rueda; **roller-skating** n patinaje sobre ruedas; **to go roller-skating** ir a patinar (sobre ruedas); **rolling pin** n rodillo (de cocina)

ROM [rɔm] n abbr (Comput: = read only memory) ROM f

Roman ['rəumən] (irreg) adj romano/a; **Roman Catholic** (irreg) adj, n católico/a m/f (romano/a)

romance [rə'mæns] n (love affair) amor m; (charm) lo romántico; (novel) novela de amor

Romania etc [ru:'meɪnɪə] n = **Rumania** etc

Roman numeral n número romano

romantic [rə'mæntɪk] adj romántico

Rome [rəum] n Roma

roof [ruːf] (pl ~**s**) n techo; (of house) techo, tejado ▷ vt techar; poner techo a; **the ~ of the mouth** el paladar; **roof rack** n (Aut) baca, portaequipajes m inv

rook [ruk] n (bird) graja; (Chess) torre f

room [ru:m] n cuarto, habitación f; (also: **bed~**) dormitorio, recámara (MEX), pieza (SC); (in school etc) sala; (space, scope) sitio, cabida; **roommate** n compañero/a de cuarto; **room service** n servicio de habitaciones; **roomy** adj espacioso; (garment) amplio

rooster ['ru:stə*] n gallo

root [ru:t] n raíz f ▷ vi arraigarse

rope [rəup] n cuerda; (Naut) cable m ▷ vt (tie) atar o amarrar con (una) cuerda; (climbers: also: ~ **together**) encordarse; (an area: also: ~ **off**) acordonar; **to know the ~s** (fig) conocer los trucos (del oficio)

rose [rəuz] pt of **rise** ▷ n rosa; (shrub) rosal m; (on watering can) roseta

rosé ['rəuzeɪ] n vino rosado

rosemary ['rəuzmərɪ] n romero

rosy ['rəuzɪ] adj rosado, sonrosado; **a ~ future** un futuro prometedor

rot [rɔt] n podredumbre f; (fig: pej) tonterías fpl ▷ vt pudrir ▷ vi pudrirse

rota ['rəutə] n (sistema m de) turnos m

rotate [rəu'teɪt] vt (revolve) hacer girar, dar vueltas a; (jobs) alternar ▷ vi girar, dar vueltas

rotten ['rɔtn] adj podrido; (dishonest) corrompido; (inf: bad) pocho; **to feel ~** (ill) sentirse fatal

rough [rʌf] adj (skin, surface) áspero; (terrain) quebrado; (road) desigual; (voice) bronco; (person, manner) tosco, grosero; (weather) borrascoso; (treatment) brutal; (sea) picado; (town, area) peligroso; (cloth) basto; (plan) preliminar; (guess) aproximado ▷ n (Golf): **in the ~** en las hierbas altas; **to ~ it** vivir sin comodidades; **to sleep ~** (BRIT) pasar la noche al raso; **roughly** adv (handle) torpemente; (make) toscamente; (speak) groseramente; (approximately) aproximadamente

roulette [ru:'let] n ruleta

round [raund] adj redondo ▷ n círculo; (BRIT: of toast) rebanada;

(of policeman) ronda; (of milkman) recorrido; (of doctor) visitas fpl; (game: of cards, in competition) partida; (of ammunition) cartucho; (Boxing) asalto; (of talks) ronda ▷ vt (corner) doblar ▷ prep alrededor de; (surrounding): ~ **his neck/the table** en su cuello/alrededor de la mesa; (in a circular movement): **to move ~ the room/sail ~ the world** dar una vuelta a la habitación/circunnavigar el mundo; (in various directions): **to move ~ a room/house** moverse por toda la habitación/casa; (approximately) alrededor de ▷ adv: **all ~** por todos lados; **the long way ~** por el camino menos directo; **all (the) year ~** durante todo el año; **it's just ~ the corner** (fig) está a la vuelta de la esquina; ~ **the clock** adv las 24 horas; **to go ~ to sb's (house)** ir a casa de algn; **to go ~ the back** pasar por atrás; **enough to go ~** bastante (para todos); **a ~ of applause** una salva de aplausos; **a ~ of drinks/sandwiches** una ronda de bebidas/bocadillos; **round off** vt (speech etc) acabar, poner término a; **round up** vt (cattle) acorralar; (people) reunir; (price) redondear; **roundabout** (BRIT) n (Aut) isleta; (at fair) tiovivo ▷ adj (route, means) indirecto; **round trip** n viaje m de ida y vuelta; **roundup** n rodeo; (of criminals) redada; (of news) resumen m

rouse [rauz] vt (wake up) despertar; (stir up) suscitar

route [ru:t] n ruta, camino; (of bus) recorrido; (of shipping) derrota

routine [ru:'ti:n] adj rutinario ▷ n rutina; (Theatre) número

row¹ [rau] n (line) fila, hilera; (Knitting) pasada ▷ vi (in boat) remar ▷ vt conducir remando; **4 days in a ~** 4 días seguidos

row² [rau] n (racket) escándalo; (dispute) bronca, pelea; (scolding) regaño ▷ vi pelear(se)

rowboat ['rəubəut] (US) = **rowing boat**

rowing ['rəʊɪŋ] n remo; **rowing boat** (BRIT) n bote m de remos

royal ['rɔɪəl] adj real; **royalty** n (royal persons) familia real; (payment to author) derechos mpl de autor

rpm abbr (= revs per minute) r.p.m.

R.S.V.P. abbr (= répondez s'il vous plaît) SRC

Rt. Hon. abbr (BRIT) (= Right Honourable) título honorífico de diputado

rub [rʌb] vt frotar; (scrub) restregar ▷ n: **to give sth a ~** frotar algo; **to ~ sb up o ~ sb the wrong way** (US) entrarle algn por mal ojo; **rub in** vt (ointment) aplicar frotando; **rub off** vi borrarse; **rub out** vt borrar

rubber ['rʌbə*] n (substance) caucho, goma; (BRIT: eraser) goma de borrar; **rubber band** n goma, gomita; **rubber gloves** npl guantes mpl de goma

rubbish ['rʌbɪʃ] (BRIT) n basura; (waste) desperdicios mpl; (fig: pej) tonterías fpl; (junk) pacotilla; **rubbish bin** n cubo o bote m (MEX) or tacho (SC) de la basura; **rubbish dump** (BRIT) n vertedero, basurero

rubble ['rʌbl] n escombros mpl

ruby ['ru:bɪ] n rubí m

rucksack ['rʌksæk] n mochila

rudder ['rʌdə*] n timón m

rude [ru:d] adj (impolite: person) mal educado; (: word, manners) grosero; (crude) crudo; (indecent) indecente

ruffle ['rʌfl] vt (hair) despeinar; (clothes) arrugar; **to get ~d** (fig: person) alterarse

rug [rʌg] n alfombra; (BRIT: blanket) manta

rugby ['rʌgbɪ] n rugby m

rugged ['rʌgɪd] adj (landscape) accidentado; (features) robusto

ruin ['ru:ɪn] n ruina ▷ vt arruinar; (spoil) estropear; **ruins** npl ruinas fpl, restos mpl

rule [ru:l] n (norm) norma, costumbre f; (regulation, ruler) regla; (government) dominio ▷ vt (country, person) gobernar ▷ vi gobernar; (Law) fallar;

as a ~ por regla general; **rule out** vt excluir; **ruler** n (sovereign) soberano; (for measuring) regla; **ruling** adj (party) gobernante; (class) dirigente ▷ n (Law) fallo, decisión f

rum [rʌm] n ron m

Rumania [ru:'meɪnɪə] n Rumanía; **Rumanian** adj rumano/a ▷ n rumano/a m/f; (Ling) rumano

rumble ['rʌmbl] n (noise) ruido sordo ▷ vi retumbar, hacer un ruido sordo; (stomach, pipe) sonar

rumour ['ru:mə*] (US **rumor**) n rumor m ▷ vt: **it is ~ed that ...** se rumorea que ...

rump steak n filete m de lomo

run [rʌn] (pt ran, pp run) n (fast pace): **at a ~** corriendo; (Sport, in tights) carrera; (outing) paseo, excursión f; (distance travelled) trayecto; (series) serie f; (Theatre) temporada; (Ski) pista ▷ vt (operate: business) dirigir; (: competition, course) organizar; (: hotel, house) administrar, llevar; (Comput) ejecutar; (pass: hand) pasar; (Press: feature) publicar ▷ vi correr; (work: machine) funcionar, marchar; (bus, train: operate) circular, ir; (: travel) ir; (continue: play) seguir; (contract) ser válido; (flow: river) fluir; (colours, washing) desteñirse; (in election) ser candidato; **there was a ~ on** (meat, tickets) hubo mucha demanda de; **in the long ~** a la larga; **on the ~** en fuga; **I'll ~ you to the station** te llevaré a la estación (en coche); **to ~ a risk** correr un riesgo; **run after** vt fus (chase) perseguir; (run for) correr tras; **run away** vi huir; **run down** vt (production) ir reduciendo; (factory) ir restringiendo la producción en; (car) atropellar; (criticize) criticar; **to be run down** (person: tired) estar debilitado; **run into** vt fus (meet: person, trouble) tropezar con; (collide with) chocar con; **run off** vt (water) dejar correr; (copies) sacar ▷ vi huir corriendo; **run out** vi (person) salir

corriendo; (liquid) irse; (lease) caducar,
vencer; (money etc) acabarse; **run out
of** vt fus quedarse sin; **run over** vt (Aut)
atropellar ▷ vt fus (revise) repasar; **run
through** vt fus (instructions) repasar;
run up vt (debt) contraer; **to run up
against** (difficulties) tropezar con;
runaway adj (horse) desbocado; (truck)
sin frenos; (child) escapado de casa
rung [rʌŋ] pp of **ring** ▷ n (of ladder)
escalón m, peldaño
runner ['rʌnə*] n (in race: person)
corredor(a) m/f; (: horse) caballo;
(on sledge) patín m; **runner bean**
(BRIT) n = judía verde; **runner-up** n
subcampeón/ona m/f
running ['rʌnɪŋ] n (sport) atletismo;
(of business) administración f ▷ adj
(water, costs) corriente; (commentary)
continuo; **to be in/out of the ~ for sth**
tener/no tener posibilidades de ganar
algo; **6 days ~** 6 días seguidos
runny ['rʌnɪ] adj fluido; (nose, eyes)
gastante
run-up ['rʌnʌp] n: **~ to** (election etc)
período previo a
runway ['rʌnweɪ] n (Aviat) pista de
aterrizaje
rupture ['rʌptʃə*] n (Med) hernia
▷ vt: **to ~ o.s** causarse una hernia
rural ['ruərl] adj rural
rush [rʌʃ] n ímpetu m; (hurry) prisa;
(Comm) demanda repentina; (current)
corriente f fuerte; (of feeling) torrente m;
(Bot) junco ▷ vt apresurar; (work) hacer
de prisa ▷ vi correr, precipitarse; **rush
hour** n horas fpl punta
Russia ['rʌʃə] n Rusia; **Russian** adj
ruso/a ▷ n ruso/a m/f; (Ling) ruso
rust [rʌst] n herrumbre f, moho ▷ vi
oxidarse
rusty ['rʌstɪ] adj oxidado
ruthless ['ruːθlɪs] adj despiadado
RV (us) n abbr = **recreational vehicle**
rye [raɪ] n centeno

S

Sabbath ['sæbəθ] n domingo;
(Jewish) sábado
sabotage ['sæbətɑːʒ] n sabotaje m
▷ vt sabotear
saccharin(e) ['sækərɪn] n sacarina
sachet ['sæʃeɪ] n sobrecito
sack [sæk] n (bag) saco, costal m ▷ vt
(dismiss) despedir; (plunder) saquear; **to
get the ~** ser despedido
sacred ['seɪkrɪd] adj sagrado, santo
sacrifice ['sækrɪfaɪs] n sacrificio
▷ vt sacrificar
sad [sæd] adj (unhappy) triste;
(deplorable) lamentable
saddle ['sædl] n silla (de montar); (of
cycle) sillín m ▷ vt (horse) ensillar; **to
be ~d with sth** (inf) quedar cargado
con algo
sadistic [sə'dɪstɪk] adj sádico
sadly ['sædlɪ] adv lamentablemente;
to be ~ lacking in estar por desgracia
carente de
sadness ['sædnɪs] n tristeza
s.a.e. abbr (= stamped addressed
envelope) sobre con las propias señas de

uno y con sello

safari [sə'fɑ:rɪ] n safari m

safe [seɪf] adj (out of danger) fuera de peligro; (not dangerous, sure) seguro; (unharmed) ileso ▷ n caja de caudales, caja fuerte; **~ and sound** sano y salvo; **(just) to be on the ~ side** para mayor seguridad; **safely** adv seguramente, con seguridad; **to arrive safely** llegar bien; **safe sex** n sexo seguro or sin riesgo

safety ['seɪftɪ] n seguridad f; **safety belt** n cinturón m (de seguridad); **safety pin** n imperdible m, seguro (MEX), alfiler m de gancho (SC)

saffron ['sæfrən] n azafrán m

sag [sæg] vi aflojarse

sage [seɪdʒ] n (herb) salvia; (man) sabio

Sagittarius [sædʒɪ'tɛərɪəs] n Sagitario

Sahara [sə'hɑ:rə] n: **the ~ (Desert)** el (desierto del) Sáhara

said [sɛd] pt, pp of **say**

sail [seɪl] n (on boat) vela; (trip): **to go for a ~** dar un paseo en barco ▷ vt (boat) gobernar ▷ vi (travel: ship) navegar; (Sport) hacer vela; (begin voyage) salir; **they ~ed into Copenhagen** arribaron a Copenhague; **sailboat** (US) n = **sailing boat**; **sailing** n (Sport) vela; **to go sailing** hacer vela; **sailing boat** n barco de vela; **sailor** n marinero, marino

saint [seɪnt] n santo

sake [seɪk] n: **for the ~ of** por

salad ['sæləd] n ensalada; **salad cream** (BRIT) n (especie f de) mayonesa; **salad dressing** n aliño

salami [sə'lɑ:mɪ] n salami m, salchichón m

salary ['sælərɪ] n sueldo

sale [seɪl] n venta; (at reduced prices) liquidación f, saldo; (auction) subasta; **sales** npl (total amount sold) ventas fpl, facturación f; **"for ~"** se vende; **on ~** en venta; **on ~ or return** (goods) venta por reposición; **sales assistant** (US),

sales clerk n dependiente/a m/f; **salesman/woman** (irreg) n (in shop) dependiente/a m/f, **salesperson** (irreg) n vendedor/a m/f, dependiente/a m/f; **sales rep** n representante mf, agente mf comercial

saline ['seɪlaɪn] adj salino

saliva [sə'laɪvə] n saliva

salmon ['sæmən] n inv salmón m

salon ['sælɒn] n (hairdressing salon) peluquería f; (beauty salon) salón m de belleza

saloon [sə'lu:n] n (US) bar m, taberna; (BRIT Aut) coche m (de) turismo; (ship's lounge) cámara, salón m

salt [sɔlt] n sal f ▷ vt salar; (put salt on) poner sal en; **saltwater** adj de agua salada; **salty** adj salado

salute [sə'lu:t] n saludo; (of guns) salva ▷ vt saludar

salvage ['sælvɪdʒ] n (saving) salvamento, recuperación f; (things saved) mpl objetos mpl salvados ▷ vt salvar

Salvation Army [sæl'veɪʃən-] n Ejército de Salvación

same [seɪm] adj mismo ▷ pron: **the ~** el(la) mismo/a, los(las) mismos/as; **the ~ book as** el mismo libro que; **at the ~ time** (at the same moment) al mismo tiempo; (yet) sin embargo; **all or just the ~** sin embargo, aun así; **to do the ~ (as sb)** hacer lo mismo (que algn); **the ~ to you!** ¡igualmente!

sample ['sɑ:mpl] n muestra ▷ vt (food) probar; (wine) catar

sanction ['sæŋkʃən] n aprobación f ▷ vt sancionar; aprobar; **sanctions** npl (Pol) sanciones fpl

sanctuary ['sæŋktjʊərɪ] n santuario; (refuge) asilo, refugio; (for wildlife) reserva

sand [sænd] n arena; (beach) playa ▷ vt (also: **~ down**) lijar

sandal ['sændl] n sandalia

sand: **sandbox** (US) n = **sandpit**; **sandcastle** n castillo de arena; **sand dune** n duna; **sandpaper** n papel m de lija; **sandpit** n (for children) cajón de arena;**sands** npl playa sg de arena;

sandstone ['sændstǝun] n piedra arenisca

sandwich ['sændwɪtʃ] n sandwich m ▷ vt intercalar; **~ed between** apretujado entre; **cheese/ham ~** sandwich de queso/jamón

sandy ['sændɪ] adj arenoso; (colour) rojizo

sane [seɪn] adj cuerdo; (sensible) sensato

> Be careful not to translate **sane** with the Spanish word sano.

sang [sæŋ] pt of **sing**

sanitary towel (US **sanitary napkin**) n paño higiénico, compresa

sanity ['sænɪtɪ] n cordura; (of judgment) sensatez f

sank [sæŋk] pt of **sink**

Santa Claus [sæntǝ'klɔːz] n San Nicolás, Papá Noel

sap [sæp] n (of plants) savia ▷ vt (strength) minar, agotar

sapphire ['sæfaɪǝ*] n zafiro

sarcasm ['sɑːkæzm] n sarcasmo

sarcastic [sɑː'kæstɪk] adj sarcástico

sardine [sɑː'diːn] n sardina

SASE (US) n abbr (= self-addressed stamped envelope) sobre con las propias señas de uno y con sello

Sat. abbr (= Saturday) sáb

sat [sæt] pt, pp of **sit**

satchel ['sætʃl] n (child's) mochila, cartera (SP)

satellite ['sætǝlaɪt] n satélite m; **satellite dish** n antena de televisión por satélite; **satellite television** n televisión f vía satélite

satin ['sætɪn] n raso ▷ adj de raso

satire ['sætaɪǝ*] n sátira

satisfaction [sætɪs'fækʃǝn] n satisfacción f

satisfactory [sætɪs'fæktǝrɪ] adj satisfactorio

satisfied ['sætɪsfaɪd] adj satisfecho; **to be ~ (with sth)** estar satisfecho (de algo)

satisfy ['sætɪsfaɪ] vt satisfacer;

(convince) convencer

Saturday ['sætǝdɪ] n sábado

sauce [sɔːs] n salsa; (sweet) crema; jarabe m;**saucepan** n cacerola, olla

saucer ['sɔːsǝ*] n platillo;**Saudi Arabia** n Arabia Saudí or Saudita

sauna ['sɔːnǝ] n sauna

sausage ['sɔsɪdʒ] n salchicha; **sausage roll** n empanadilla de salchicha

sautéed ['sǝuteɪd] adj salteado

savage ['sævɪdʒ] adj (cruel, fierce) feroz, furioso; (primitive) salvaje ▷ n salvaje mf ▷ vt (attack) embestir

save [seɪv] vt (rescue) salvar, rescatar; (money, time) ahorrar; (put by, keep: seat) guardar; (Comput) salvar (y guardar); (avoid: trouble) evitar; (Sport) parar ▷ vi (also: **~ up**) ahorrar ▷ n (Sport) parada ▷ prep salvo, excepto

savings ['seɪvɪŋz] npl ahorros mpl; **savings account** n cuenta de ahorros; **savings and loan association** (US) n sociedad f de ahorro y préstamo

savoury ['seɪvǝrɪ] (US **savory**) adj sabroso; (dish: not sweet) salado

saw [sɔː] (pt **~ed**, pp **~ed** or **~n**) pt of **see** ▷ n (tool) sierra ▷ vt serrar; **sawdust** n (a)serrín m

sawn [sɔːn] pp of **saw**

saxophone ['sæksǝfǝun] n saxófono

say [seɪ] (pt, pp **said**) vt: **to have one's ~** expresar su opinión ▷ vt decir; **to have a** or **some ~ in sth** tener voz or tener que ver en algo; **to ~ yes/no** decir que sí/no; **could you ~ that again?** ¿podría repetir eso?; **that is to ~** es decir; **that goes without ~ing** ni que decir tiene;**saying** n dicho, refrán m

scab [skæb] n costra; (pej) esquirol m

scaffolding ['skæfǝldɪŋ] n andamio, andamiaje m

scald [skɔːld] n escaldadura ▷ vt escaldar

scale [skeɪl] n (gen, Mus) escala; (of fish) escama; (of salaries, fees etc) escalafón m ▷ vt (mountain) escalar; (tree) trepar; **scales** npl (for *weighing: small*) balanza; (: *large*) báscula; **on a large ~** en gran escala; **~ of charges** tarifa, lista de precios

scallion ['skæljən] (*us*) *n* cebolleta

scallop ['skɔləp] *n* (*Zool*) venera; (*Sewing*) festón *m*

scalp [skælp] *n* cabellera ▷ *vt* escalpar

scalpel ['skælpl] *n* bisturí *m*

scam [skæm] *n* (*inf*) estafa, timo

scampi ['skæmpɪ] *npl* gambas *fpl*

scan [skæn] *vt* (*examine*) escudriñar; (*glance at quickly*) dar un vistazo a; (*TV, Radar*) explorar, registrar ▷ *n* (*Med*): **to have a ~** pasar por el escáner

scandal ['skændl] *n* escándalo; (*gossip*) chismes *mpl*

Scandinavia [skændɪ'neɪvɪə] *n* Escandinavia; **Scandinavian** *adj, n* escandinavo/a *m/f*

scanner ['skænə*] *n* (*Radar, Med*) escáner *m*

scapegoat ['skeɪpgəut] *n* cabeza de turco, chivo expiatorio

scar [skɑ:] *n* cicatriz *f*; (*fig*) señal *f* ▷ *vt* dejar señales en

scarce [skɛəs] *adj* escaso; **to make o.s. ~** (*inf*) esfumarse; **scarcely** *adv* apenas

scare [skɛə*] *n* susto, sobresalto; (*panic*) pánico ▷ *vt* asustar, espantar; **to ~ sb stiff** dar a algn un susto de muerte; **bomb ~** amenaza de bomba; **scarecrow** *n* espantapájaros *m inv*; **scared** *adj*: **to be scared** estar asustado

scarf [skɑ:f] (*pl* **~s** *or* **scarves**) *n* (*long*) bufanda; (*square*) pañuelo

scarlet ['skɑ:lɪt] *adj* escarlata

scarves [skɑ:vz] *npl of* **scarf**

scary ['skɛərɪ] (*inf*) *adj* espeluznante

scatter ['skætə*] *vt* (*spread*) esparcir, desparramar; (*put to flight*) dispersar ▷ *vi* desparramarse; dispersarse

scenario [sɪ'nɑ:rɪəu] *n* (*Theatre*) argumento; (*Cinema*) guión *m*; (*fig*) escenario

scene [si:n] *n* (*Theatre, fig etc*)

escena; (*of crime etc*) escenario; (*view*) panorama *m*; (*fuss*) escándalo; **scenery** *n* (*Theatre*) decorado; (*landscape*) paisaje *m*

▌ Be careful not to translate **scenery** by the Spanish word *escenario*.

scenic *adj* pintoresco

scent [sɛnt] *n* perfume *m*, olor *m*; (*fig: track*) rastro, pista

sceptical ['skɛptɪkl] *adj* escéptico

schedule ['ʃɛdju:l] (*us*) ['skɛdju:l] *n* (*timetable*) horario; (*of events*) programa *m*; (*list*) lista ▷ *vt* (*visit*) fijar la hora de; **to arrive on ~** llegar a la hora debida; **to be ahead of/behind ~** estar adelantado/en retraso; **scheduled flight** *n* vuelo regular

scheme [ski:m] *n* (*plan*) plan *m*, proyecto, plan; (*plot*) intriga; (*arrangement*) disposición *f*; (*pension scheme etc*) sistema *m* ▷ *vi* (*intrigue*) intrigar

schizophrenic [skɪtzə'frɛnɪk] *adj* esquizofrénico

scholar ['skɔlə*] *n* (*pupil*) alumno/a; (*learned person*) sabio/a, erudito/a; **scholarship** *n* erudición *f*; (*grant*) beca

school [sku:l] *n* escuela, colegio; (*in university*) facultad *f* ▷ *cpd* escolar; **schoolbook** *n* libro de texto; **schoolboy** *n* alumno; **school children** *npl* alumnos *mpl*; **schoolgirl** *n* alumna; **schooling** *n* enseñanza; **schoolteacher** *n* (*primary*) maestro/a; (*secondary*) profesor/a *m/f*

science ['saɪəns] *n* ciencia; **science fiction** *n* ciencia-ficción *f*; **scientific** [-'tɪfɪk] *adj* científico; **scientist** *n* científico/a

sci-fi ['saɪfaɪ] *n abbr* (*inf*) = **science fiction**

scissors ['sɪzəz] *npl* tijeras *fpl*; **a pair of ~** unas tijeras

scold [skəuld] *vt* regañar

scone [skɔn] *n* pastel de pan

scoop [sku:p] *n* (*for flour etc*) pala; (*Press*) exclusiva

scooter ['sku:tə*] *n* moto *f*; (*toy*) patinete *m*

scope [skəʊp] n (of plan) ámbito; (of person) competencia; (opportunity) libertad f (de acción)

scorching ['skɔːtʃɪŋ] adj (heat, sun) abrasador(a)

score [skɔː*] n (points etc) puntuación f; (Mus) partitura f; (twenty) veintena ▷ vt (goal, point) ganar; (mark) rayar; (achieve: success) conseguir ▷ vi marcar un tanto; (Football) marcar (un) gol; (keep score) llevar el tanteo; **~s of** (lots of) decenas de; **on that ~** en lo que se refiere a eso; **to ~ 6 out of 10** obtener una puntuación de 6 sobre 10; **score out** vt tachar; **scoreboard** n marcador m; **scorer** n marcador m; (keeping score) encargado/a del marcador

scorn [skɔːn] n desprecio

Scorpio ['skɔːpɪəʊ] n Escorpión m

scorpion ['skɔːpɪən] n alacrán m

Scot [skɒt] n escocés/esa m/f

Scotch tape® (us) n cinta adhesiva, celo, scotch® m

Scotland ['skɒtlənd] n Escocia

Scots [skɒts] adj escocés/esa;
Scotsman (irreg) n escocés m;
Scotswoman (irreg) n escocesa;
Scottish ['skɒtɪʃ] adj escocés/esa;
Scottish Parliament n Parlamento escocés

scout [skaut] n (Mil: also: **boy ~**) explorador m; **girl ~** (us) niña exploradora

scowl [skaul] vi fruncir el ceño; **to ~ at sb** mirar con ceño a algn

scramble ['skræmbl] n (climb) subida (difícil); (struggle) pelea ▷ vi: **to ~ through/out** abrirse paso/salir con dificultad; **to ~ for** pelear por; **scrambled eggs** npl huevos mpl revueltos

scrap [skræp] n (bit) pedacito m; (fig) pizca; (fight) riña, bronca; (also: **~ iron**) chatarra, hierro viejo ▷ vt (discard) desechar, descartar ▷ vi reñir, armar una bronca; **scraps** npl (waste) sobras fpl, desperdicios mpl; **scrapbook** n

álbum m de recortes

scrape [skreɪp] n: **to get into a ~** meterse en un lío ▷ vt raspar; (skin etc) rasguñar; (scrape against) rozar ▷ vi: **to ~ through** (exam) aprobar por los pelos; **scrap paper** n pedazos mpl de papel

scratch [skrætʃ] n rasguño; (from claw) arañazo ▷ vt (paint, car) rayar; (with claw, nail) rasguñar, arañar; (rub: nose etc) rascarse ▷ vi rascarse; **to start from ~** partir de cero; **to be up to ~** cumplir con los requisitos; **scratch card** n (BRIT) tarjeta f de "rasque y gane"

scream [skriːm] n chillido ▷ vi chillar

screen [skriːn] n (Cinema, TV) pantalla; (movable barrier) biombo ▷ vt (conceal) tapar; (from the wind etc) proteger; (film) proyectar; (candidates etc) investigar a; **screening** n (Med) investigación f médica; **screenplay** n guión m; **screen saver** n (Comput) protector m de pantalla

screw [skruː] n tornillo ▷ vt (also: **~ in**) atornillar; **screw up** vt (paper etc) arrugar; **to screw up one's eyes** arrugar el entrecejo; **screwdriver** n destornillador m

scribble ['skrɪbl] n garabatos mpl ▷ vt, vi garabatear

script [skrɪpt] n (Cinema etc) guión m; (writing) escritura, letra

scroll [skrəʊl] n rollo

scrub [skrʌb] n (land) maleza ▷ vt fregar, restregar; (inf: reject) cancelar, anular

scruffy ['skrʌfɪ] adj desaliñado, piojoso

scrum(mage) ['skrʌm(mɪdʒ)] n (Rugby) melée f

scrutiny ['skruːtɪnɪ] n escrutinio, examen m

scuba diving ['skuːbə'daɪvɪŋ] n submarinismo

sculptor ['skʌlptə*] n escultor(a) m/f

sculpture ['skʌlptʃə*] n escultura

scum [skʌm] n (on liquid) espuma;

(pej: people) escoria

scurry ['skʌrɪ] vi correr; **to ~ off** escabullirse

sea [si:] n mar m; ~ cpd de mar, marítimo; **by ~** (travel) en barco; **on the ~** (boat) en el mar; (town) junto al mar; **to be all at ~** (fig) estar despistado; **out to ~, at ~** en alta mar; **seafood** n mariscos mpl; **sea front** n paseo marítimo; **seagull** n gaviota

seal [si:l] n (animal) foca; (stamp) sello ▷ vt (close) cerrar; **seal off** vt (area) acordonar

sea level n nivel m del mar

seam [si:m] n costura; (of metal) juntura; (of coal) veta, filón m

search [sə:tʃ] n (for person, thing) busca, búsqueda; (Comput) búsqueda; (inspection: of sb's home) registro ▷ vt (look in) buscar en; (examine) examinar; (person, place) registrar ▷ vi: **to ~ for** buscar; **in ~ of** en busca de; **search engine** n (Comput) buscador m; **search party** n pelotón m de salvamento

sea: seashore n playa, orilla del mar; **seasick** adj mareado; **seaside** n playa, orilla del mar; **seaside resort** n centro turístico costero

season ['si:zn] n (of year) estación f; (sporting etc) temporada; (of films etc) ciclo ▷ vt (food) sazonar; **in/out of ~** en sazón/fuera de temporada; **seasonal** adj estacional; **seasoning** n condimento, aderezo; **season ticket** n abono

seat [si:t] n (in bus, train) asiento; (chair) silla; (Parliament) escaño; (buttocks) trasero; (of trousers) culera ▷ vt sentar; (have room for) tener cabida para; **to be ~ed** sentarse; **seat belt** n cinturón m de seguridad; **seating** n asientos mpl

sea: sea water n agua del mar; **seaweed** n alga marina

sec. abbr = **second(s)**

secluded [sɪ'klu:dɪd] adj retirado

second ['sekənd] adj segundo ▷ adv en segundo lugar ▷ n segundo;

(Aut: also: ~ **gear**) segunda; (Comm) artículo con algún desperfecto; (BRIT Scol: degree) título de licenciado con calificación de notable ▷ vt (motion) apoyar; **secondary** adj secundario; **secondary school** n escuela secundaria; **second-class** adj de segunda clase ▷ adv (Rail) en segunda; **secondhand** adj de segunda mano, usado; **secondly** adv en segundo lugar; **second-rate** adj de segunda categoría; **second thoughts**: **to have second thoughts** cambiar de opinión; **on second thoughts** or **thought** (us) pensándolo bien

secrecy ['si:krəsɪ] n secreto

secret ['si:krɪt] adj, n secreto; **in ~** en secreto

secretary ['sekrətərɪ] n secretario/a; **S~ of State (for)** (BRIT Pol) Ministro (de)

secretive ['si:krətɪv] adj reservado, sigiloso

secret service n servicio secreto

sect [sekt] n secta

section ['sekʃən] n sección f; (part) parte f; (of document) artículo; (of opinion) sector m; (cross-section) corte m transversal

sector ['sektə*] n sector m

secular ['sekjulə*] adj secular, seglar

secure [sɪ'kjuə*] adj seguro; (firmly fixed) firme, fijo ▷ vt (fix) asegurar, afianzar; (get) conseguir

security [sɪ'kjuərɪtɪ] n seguridad f; (for loan) fianza; (: object) prenda; **securities** npl (Comm) valores mpl, títulos mpl; **security guard** n guardia m/f de seguridad

sedan [sɪ'dæn] (us) n (Aut) sedán m

sedate [sɪ'deɪt] adj tranquilo ▷ vt tratar con sedantes

sedative ['sedɪtɪv] n sedante m, sedativo

seduce [sɪ'dju:s] vt seducir; **seductive** [-'dʌktɪv] adj seductor(a)

see [si:] (pt **saw**, pp **seen**) vt ver; (accompany): **to ~ sb to the door**

acompañar a algn a la puerta;
(*understand*) ver, comprender ▷ *vi*
▷ *n* (*arz*)obispado; **to ~ that** (*ensure*)
asegurar que; **~ you soon!** ¡hasta
pronto!; **see off** *vt* despedir; **see out**
vt (*take to the door*) acompañar hasta la
puerta; **see through** (*vt fus*) (*fig*) calar
▷ *vt* (*plan*) llevar a cabo; **see to** *vt fus*
atender a, encargarse de

seed [si:d] *n* semilla; (*in fruit*) pepita;
(*fig: gen pl*) germen *m*; (*Tennis etc*)
preseleccionado/a; **to go to ~** (*plant*)
granar; (*fig*) descuidarse

seeing ['si:ɪŋ] *conj*: **~ (that)** visto que,
en vista de que

seek [si:k] (*pt, pp* **sought**) *vt* buscar;
(*post*) solicitar

seem [si:m] *vi* parecer; **there ~s to
be ...** parece que hay ...; **seemingly** *adv*
aparentemente, según parece

seen [si:n] *pp de* **see**

seesaw ['si:sɔ:] *n* subibaja

segment ['sɛgmənt] *n* (*part*) sección
f; (*of orange*) gajo

segregate ['sɛgrɪgeɪt] *vt* segregar

seize [si:z] *vt* (*grasp*) agarrar,
asir; (*take possession of*) secuestrar;
(: *territory*) apoderarse de; (*opportunity*)
aprovecharse de

seizure ['si:ʒə*] *n* (*Med*) ataque *m*;
(*Law, of power*) incautación *f*

seldom ['sɛldəm] *adv* rara vez

select [sɪ'lɛkt] *adj* selecto, escogido
▷ *vt* escoger, elegir; (*Sport*) seleccionar;
selection *n* selección *f*, elección
f; (*Comm*) surtido *m*; **selective** *adj*
selectivo

self [sɛlf] (*pl* **selves**) *n* uno mismo;
the ~ el yo ▷ *prefix* auto...; **self-
assured** *adj* seguro de sí mismo;
self-catering (*BRIT*) *adj* (*flat etc*)
con cocina; **self-centred** (*US*
self-centered) *adj* egocéntrico;
self-confidence *n* confianza en sí
mismo; **self-confident** *adj* seguro
de sí (mismo), lleno de confianza en sí
mismo; **self-conscious** *adj* cohibido;
self-contained (*BRIT*) *adj* (*flat*) con

entrada particular; **self-control** *n*
autodominio; **self-defence** (*US*
self-defense) *n* defensa propia; **self-drive**
adj (*BRIT*) sin chofer or (*SP*) chófer; **self-
employed** *adj* que trabaja por cuenta
propia; **self-esteem** *n* amor *m* propio;
self-indulgent *adj* autocomplaciente;
self-interest *n* egoísmo; **selfish**
adj egoísta; **self-pity** *n* lástima de
sí mismo; **self-raising** [sɛlf'reɪzɪŋ]
(*US* **self-rising**) *adj*: **self-raising flour**
harina con levadura; **self-respect** *n*
amor *m* propio; **self-service** *adj* de
autoservicio

sell [sɛl] (*pt, pp* **sold**) *vt* vender ▷ *vi*
venderse; **to ~ at or** for **£10** venderse a
10 libras; **sell off** *vt* liquidar; **sell out**
vi: **to sell out of tickets/milk** vender
todas las entradas/toda la leche; **sell-
by date** *n* fecha de caducidad; **seller**
n vendedor(a) *m/f*

Sellotape® ['sɛləʊteɪp] (*BRIT*) *n* celo
(*SP*), cinta Scotch® (*LAM*) or Dúrex®
(*MEX, ARG*)

selves [sɛlvz] *npl de* **self**

semester [sɪ'mɛstə*] (*US*) *n*
semestre *m*

semi... [sɛmɪ] *prefix* semi...,
medio...; **semicircle** *n* semicírculo;
semidetached (house) *n* (*casa*)
semiseparada; **semi-final** *n* semi-
final *m*

seminar ['sɛmɪnɑ:*] *n* seminario

semi-skimmed [sɛmɪ'skɪmd] *adj*
semidesnatado; **semi-skimmed
(milk)** *n* leche semidesnatada

senate ['sɛnɪt] *n* senado; **the S~** (*US*)
el Senado; **senator** *n* senador(a) *m/f*

send [sɛnd] (*pt, pp* **sent**) *vt* mandar,
enviar; (*signal*) transmitir; **send back**
vt devolver; **send for** *vt fus* mandar
traer; **send in** *vt* (*report, application,
resignation*) mandar; **send off** *vt*
(*goods*) despachar; (*BRIT Sport: player*)
expulsar; **send on** *vt* (*letter, luggage*)
remitir; (*person*) mandar; **send out**
vt (*invitation*) mandar; (*signal*) emitir;
send up *vt* (*person, price*) hacer subir;

(BRIT: *parody*) parodiar; **sender** n
remitente mf; **send-off** n: **a good
send-off** una buena despedida

senile ['si:naɪl] *adj* senil

senior ['si:nɪə*] *adj* (*older*) mayor, más
viejo; (*: on staff*) de más antigüedad; (*of
higher rank*) superior; **senior citizen** n
persona de la tercera edad; **senior high
school** (*US*) n = instituto de enseñanza
media; *see also* **high school**

sensation [sen'seɪʃən] n sensación f;
sensational *adj* sensacional

sense [sens] n (*faculty, meaning*)
sentido; (*feeling*) sensación f; (*good
sense*) sentido común, juicio ▷ vt
sentir, percibir; **it makes ~** tiene
sentido; **senseless** *adj* estúpido,
insensato; (*unconscious*) sin
conocimiento; **sense of humour** (BRIT)
n sentido del humor

sensible ['sensɪbl] *adj* sensato;
(*reasonable*) razonable, lógico

> Be careful not to translate **sensible**
> by the Spanish word sensible.

sensitive ['sensɪtɪv] *adj* sensible;
(*touchy*) susceptible

sensual ['sensjuəl] *adj* sensual

sensuous ['sensjuəs] *adj* sensual

sent [sent] *pt, pp of* **send**

sentence ['sentns] n (*Ling*) oración
f; (*Law*) sentencia, fallo ▷ vt: **to ~ sb to
death/to 5 years (in prison)** condenar
a algn a muerte/a 5 años de cárcel

sentiment ['sentɪmənt] n
sentimiento; (*opinion*) opinión
f; **sentimental** [-'mentl] *adj*
sentimental

Sep. *abbr* (= *September*) sep., set.

separate [*adj* 'seprɪt, *vb* 'sepəreɪt]
adj separado; (*distinct*) distinto ▷ vt
separar; (*part*) dividir ▷ vi separarse;
separately *adv* por separado;
separates *npl* (*clothes*) coordinados
mpl; **separation** [-'reɪʃən] n
separación f

September [sep'tembə*] n
se(p)tiembre m

septic ['septɪk] *adj* séptico; **septic

tank n fosa séptica

sequel ['si:kwl] n consecuencia,
resultado; (*of story*) continuación f

sequence ['si:kwəns] n sucesión f,
serie f; (*Cinema*) secuencia

sequin ['si:kwɪn] n lentejuela

Serb [sə:b] *adj, n* = **Serbian**

Serbian ['sə:bɪən] *adj* serbio ▷ n
serbio/a; (*Ling*) serbio

sergeant ['sɑ:dʒənt] n sargento

serial ['sɪərɪəl] n (TV) telenovela, serie
f televisiva; (*Book*) serie f; **serial killer** n
asesino/a múltiple; **serial number** n
número de serie

series ['sɪərɪs] n inv serie f

serious ['sɪərɪəs] *adj* serio; (*grave*)
grave; **seriously** *adv* en serio; (*ill,
wounded etc*) gravemente

sermon ['sə:mən] n sermón m

servant ['sə:vənt] n servidor(a) m/f;
(*house servant*) criado/a

serve [sə:v] vt servir; (*customer*)
atender; (*train*) pasar por;
(*apprenticeship*) hacer; (*prison term*)
cumplir ▷ vi (*at table*) servir; (*Tennis*)
sacar; **to ~ as/for/to do** servir
de/para/para hacer ▷ n (*Tennis*) saque
m; **it ~s him right** se lo tiene merecido;
server n (*Comput*) servidor m

service ['sə:vɪs] n servicio; (*Rel*)
misa; (*Aut*) mantenimiento; (*dishes
etc*) juego ▷ vt (*car etc*) revisar;
(*: repair*) reparar; **to be of ~ to sb**
útil a algn; **~ included/not included**
servicio incluido/no incluido
(*Econ: tertiary sector*) sector m terciario
or (de) servicios; (BRIT: *on motorway*)
área de servicio; (Mil): **the S~s** las
fuerzas armadas; **service area** n (*on
motorway*) área de servicio; **service
charge** (BRIT) n servicio; **serviceman**
(*irreg*) n militar m; **service station** n
estación f de servicio

serviette [sə:vɪ'et] (BRIT) n servilleta

session ['seʃən] n sesión f; **to be in ~**
estar en sesión

set [set] (*pt, pp* ~) n juego; (*Radio*)
aparato; (TV) televisor m; (*of utensils*)

batería; (of cutlery) cubierto; (of books) colección f; (Tennis) set m; (group of people) grupo; (Cinema) plató m; (Theatre) decorado; (Hairdressing) marcado ▷ adj (fixed) fijo; (ready) listo ▷ vt (place) poner, colocar; (fix) fijar; (adjust) ajustar, arreglar; (decide: rules etc) establecer, decidir ▷ vi (sun) ponerse; (jam, jelly) cuajarse; (concrete) fraguar; (bone) componerse; **to be ~ on doing sth** estar empeñado en hacer algo; **to ~ to music** poner música a; **to ~ on fire** incendiar, poner fuego a; **to ~ free** poner en libertad; **to ~ sth going** poner algo en marcha; **to ~ sail** zarpar, hacerse a la vela; **set aside** vt poner aparte, dejar de lado; (money, time) reservar; **set down** vt (bus, train) dejar; **set in** vi (infection) declararse; (complications) comenzar; **the rain has set in for the day** parece que va a llover todo el día; **set off** vi partir ▷ vt (bomb) hacer estallar; (events) poner en marcha; (show up well) hacer resaltar; **set out** vi partir ▷ vt (arrange) disponer; (state) exponer; **to set out to do sth** proponerse hacer algo; **set up** vt establecer; **setback** n revés m, contratiempo; **set menu** n menú m

settee [sɛˈtiː] n sofá m

setting [ˈsɛtɪŋ] n (scenery) marco; (position) disposición f; (of sun) puesta; (of jewel) engaste m, montadura

settle [ˈsɛtl] vt (argument) resolver; (accounts) ajustar, liquidar; (Med: calm) calmar, sosegar ▷ vi (dust etc) depositarse; (weather) serenarse; **to ~ for sth** convenir en aceptar algo; **to ~ on sth** decidirse por algo; **settle down** vi (get comfortable) ponerse cómodo, acomodarse; (calm down) calmarse, tranquilizarse; (live quietly) echar raíces; **settle in** vi instalarse; **settle up** vi: **to settle up with sb** ajustar cuentas con algn; **settlement** n (payment) liquidación f; (agreement) acuerdo, convenio; (village etc) pueblo

setup [ˈsɛtʌp] n sistema m; (situation)

situación f

seven [ˈsɛvn] num siete; **seventeen** num diez y siete, diecisiete; **seventeenth** [sɛvnˈtiːnθ] adj decimoséptimo; **seventh** num séptimo; **seventieth** [ˈsɛvntɪɪθ] adj septuagésimo; **seventy** num setenta

sever [ˈsɛvə*] vt cortar; (relations) romper

several [ˈsɛvrl] adj, pron varios/as m/fpl, algunos/as m/fpl; **~ of us** varios de nosotros

severe [sɪˈvɪə*] adj severo; (serious) grave; (hard) duro; (pain) intenso

sew [səu] (pt **-ed**, pp **~n**) vt, vi coser

sewage [ˈsuːɪdʒ] n aguas fpl residuales

sewer [ˈsuːə*] n alcantarilla, cloaca

sewing [ˈsəuɪŋ] n costura; **sewing machine** n máquina de coser

sewn [səun] pp of **sew**

sex [sɛks] n sexo; (lovemaking) **to have ~** hacer el amor; **sexism** [ˈsɛksɪzəm] n sexismo; **sexist** adj, n sexista mf; **sexual** [ˈsɛksjuəl] adj sexual; **sexual intercourse** n relaciones fpl sexuales; **sexuality** [sɛksjuˈælɪtɪ] n sexualidad f; **sexy** adj sexy

shabby [ˈʃæbɪ] adj (person) desharrapado; (clothes) raído, gastado; (behaviour) ruin inv

shack [ʃæk] n choza, chabola

shade [ʃeɪd] n sombra; (for lamp) pantalla; (for eyes) visera; (of colour) matiz m, tonalidad f; (small quantity): **a ~ (too big/more)** un poquitín (grande/más) ▷ vt dar sombra a; (eyes) proteger del sol; **in the ~** en la sombra; **shades** npl (sunglasses) gafas fpl de sol

shadow [ˈʃædəu] n sombra ▷ vt (follow) seguir y vigilar; **shadow cabinet** (BRIT) n (Pol) gabinete paralelo formado por el partido de oposición

shady [ˈʃeɪdɪ] adj sombreado; (fig: dishonest) sospechoso; (: deal) turbio

shaft [ʃɑːft] n (of arrow, spear) astil m; (Aut, Tech) eje m, árbol m; (of mine) pozo;

(of lift) hueco, caja; (of light) rayo

shake [ʃeɪk] (pt **shook**, pp **shaken**) vt sacudir; (building) hacer temblar; (bottle, cocktail) agitar ▷ vi (tremble) temblar; **to ~ one's head** (in refusal) negar con la cabeza; (in dismay) mover or menear la cabeza, incrédulo; **to ~ hands with sb** estrechar la mano a algn; **shake off** vt sacudirse; (fig) deshacerse de; **shake up** vt agitar; (fig) reorganizar; **shaky** adj (hand, voice) trémulo; (building) inestable

shall [ʃæl] aux vb: **~ I help you?** ¿quieres que te ayude?; **I'll buy three, ~ I?** compro tres, ¿no te parece?

shallow ['ʃæləu] adj poco profundo; (fig) superficial

sham [ʃæm] n fraude m, engaño

shambles ['ʃæmblz] n confusión f

shame [ʃeɪm] n vergüenza f; avergonzar; **it is a ~ that/to do** es una lástima que/hacer; **what a ~!** ¡qué lástima!; **shameful** adj vergonzoso; **shameless** adj desvergonzado

shampoo [ʃæm'puː] n champú m ▷ vt lavar con champú

shandy ['ʃændɪ] n mezcla de cerveza con gaseosa

shan't [ʃɑːnt] = **shall not**

shape [ʃeɪp] n forma ▷ vt formar, dar forma a; (sb's ideas) formar; (sb's life) determinar; **to take ~** tomar forma

share [ʃeə*] n (part) parte f, porción f; (contribution) cuota; (Comm) acción f ▷ vt dividir; (have in common) compartir; **to ~ out (among or between)** repartir (entre); **shareholder** (BRIT) n accionista mf

shark [ʃɑːk] n tiburón m

sharp [ʃɑːp] adj (blade, nose) afilado; (point) puntiagudo; (outline) definido; (pain) intenso; (Mus) desafinado; (contrast) marcado; (voice) agudo; (person: quick-witted) astuto ▷ n (: dishonest) poco escrupuloso ▷ n (Mus) sostenido ▷ adv: **a las 2 o'clock ~** a las 2 en punto; **sharpen** vt afilar; (pencil) sacar punta a; (fig) agudizar;

sharpener n (also: **pencil sharpener**) sacapuntas m inv; **sharply** adv (turn, stop) bruscamente; (stand out, contrast) claramente; (criticize, retort) severamente

shatter ['ʃætə*] vt hacer añicos or pedazos; (fig: ruin) destruir, acabar con ▷ vi hacerse añicos; **shattered** adj (grief-stricken) destrozado, deshecho; (exhausted) agotado, hecho polvo

shave [ʃeɪv] vt afeitar, rasurar ▷ vi afeitarse, rasurarse ▷ n: **to have a ~** afeitarse; **shaver** n (also: **electric shaver**) máquina de afeitar (eléctrica)

shavings ['ʃeɪvɪŋz] npl (of wood etc) virutas fpl

shaving cream ['ʃeɪvɪŋ-] n crema de afeitar

shaving foam n espuma de afeitar

shawl [ʃɔːl] n chal m

she [ʃiː] pron ella

sheath [ʃiːθ] n vaina; (contraceptive) preservativo

shed [ʃed] (pt, pp ~) n cobertizo ▷ vt (skin) mudar; (tears, blood) derramar; (load) derramar; (workers) despedir

she'd [ʃiːd] = **she had; she would**

sheep [ʃiːp] n inv oveja; **sheepdog** n perro pastor; **sheepskin** n piel f de carnero

sheer [ʃɪə*] adj (utter) puro, completo; (steep) escarpado; (material) diáfano ▷ adv verticalmente

sheet [ʃiːt] n (on bed) sábana; (of paper) hoja; (of glass, metal) lámina; (of ice) capa

sheik(h) [ʃeɪk] n jeque m

shelf [ʃelf] (pl **shelves**) n estante m

shell [ʃel] n (on beach) concha; (of egg, nut etc) cáscara; (explosive) proyectil m, obús m; (of building) armazón f ▷ vt (peas) desenvainar; (Mil) bombardear

she'll [ʃiːl] = **she will; she shall**

shellfish ['ʃelfɪʃ] n inv crustáceo; (as food) mariscos mpl

shelter ['ʃeltə*] n abrigo, refugio ▷ vt (aid) amparar, proteger; (give lodging to) abrigar ▷ vi abrigarse, refugiarse;

sheltered adj (life) protegido; (spot) abrigado

shelves [ʃɛlvz] npl of **shelf**

shelving [ʃɛlvɪŋ] n estantería

shepherd [ʃɛpəd] n pastor m ▷ vt (guide) guiar, conducir; **shepherd's pie** (BRIT) n pastel de carne y patatas

sheriff [ʃɛrɪf] (US) n sheriff m

sherry [ʃɛrɪ] n jerez m

she's [ʃiːz] = **she is; she has**

Shetland [ʃɛtlənd] n (also: **the ~s, the ~ Isles**) las Islas de Zetlandia

shield [ʃiːld] n (protection) blindaje m ▷ vt: **to ~ (from)** proteger (de)

shift [ʃɪft] n (change) cambio; (at work) turno ▷ vt trasladar; (remove) quitar ▷ vi moverse

shin [ʃɪn] n espinilla

shine [ʃaɪn] (pt, pp **shone**) n brillo, lustre m ▷ vi brillar, relucir ▷ vt (shoes) lustrar, sacar brillo a; **to ~ a torch on sth** dirigir una linterna hacia algo

shingles [ʃɪŋglz] n (Med) herpes mpl o fpl

shiny [ʃaɪnɪ] adj brillante, lustroso

ship [ʃɪp] n buque m, barco ▷ vt (goods) embarcar; (send) transportar or enviar por vía marítima; **shipment** n (goods) envío; **shipping** n (act) embarque m; (traffic) buques mpl; **shipwreck** n naufragio ▷ vt: **to be shipwrecked** naufragar; **shipyard** n astillero

shirt [ʃəːt] n camisa; **in (one's) sleeves** en mangas de camisa

shit [ʃɪt] (inf!) excl ¡mierda! (!)

shiver [ʃɪvə*] n escalofrío ▷ vi temblar, estremecerse; (with cold) tiritar

shock [ʃɔk] n (impact) choque m; (Elec) descarga (eléctrica); (emotional) conmoción f; (start) sobresalto, susto; (Med) postración f nerviosa ▷ vt dar un susto a; (offend) escandalizar; **shocking** adj (awful) espantoso; (outrageous) escandaloso

shoe [ʃuː] n (pt, pp **shod**) n zapato; (for

horse) herradura ▷ vt (horse) herrar; **shoelace** n cordón m; **shoe polish** n betún m; **shoeshop** n zapatería

shone [ʃɔn] pt, pp of **shine**

shook [ʃʊk] pt of **shake**

shoot [ʃuːt] (pt, pp **shot**) n (on branch, seedling) retoño, vástago ▷ vt disparar; (kill) matar a tiros; (wound) pegar un tiro; (execute) fusilar; (film) rodar, filmar ▷ vi (Football) chutar; **shoot down** vt (plane) derribar; **shoot up** vi (prices) dispararse; **shooting** n (shots) tiros mpl; (Hunting) caza con escopeta

shop [ʃɔp] n tienda; (workshop) taller m ▷ vi (also: **go ~ping**) ir de compras; **shop assistant** (BRIT) n dependiente/a m/f; **shopkeeper** n tendero/a; **shoplifting** n mechería; **shopping** n (goods) compras fpl; **shopping bag** n bolsa (de compras); **shopping centre** (US **shopping center**) n centro comercial; **shopping mall** n centro comercial; **shopping trolley** (BRIT) n carrito de la compra; **shop window** n escaparate m (SP), vidriera (LAM)

shore [ʃɔː*] n orilla ▷ vt: **to ~ (up)** reforzar; **on ~** en tierra

short [ʃɔːt] adj corto; (in time) breve, de corta duración; (person) bajo; (curt) brusco, seco; (insufficient) insuficiente; **(a pair of) ~s** (unos) pantalones mpl cortos; **to be ~ of sth** estar falto de algo; **in ~** en pocas palabras; **~ of doing ...** fuera de hacer ...; **it is ~ for** es la forma abreviada de; **to cut ~** (speech, visit) interrumpir, terminar inesperadamente; **everything ~ of ...** todo menos ...; **to fall ~ of** no alcanzar; **to run ~** quedarle a algn poco; **to stop ~** parar en seco; **to stop ~ of** detenerse antes de; **shortage** n: **a shortage of** una falta de; **shortbread** n especie de mantecada; **shortcoming** n defecto, deficiencia; **shortcrust pastry** (BRIT) n pasta quebradiza; **shortcut** n atajo; **shorten** vt acortar; (visit) interrumpir; **shortfall** n déficit m (BRIT)

taquigrafía; **short-lived** adj efímero; **shortly** adv en breve, dentro de poco; **shorts** npl pantalones mpl cortos; (US) calzoncillos mpl; **short-sighted** (BRIT) adj miope; (fig) imprudente; **short-sleeved** adj de manga corta; **short story** n cuento; **short-tempered** adj enojadizo; **short-term** adj (effect) a corto plazo

shot [ʃɒt] pt, pp of **shoot** ▷ n (sound) tiro, disparo; (try) tentativa; (injection) inyección f; (Phot) toma, fotografía; **to be a good/poor ~** (person) tener buena/mala puntería; **like a ~** (without any delay) como un rayo; **shotgun** n escopeta

should [ʃud] aux vb: **I ~ go now** debo irme ahora; **he ~ be there now** debe de haber llegado (ya); **I ~ go if I were you** yo en tu lugar me iría; **I ~ like to** me gustaría

shoulder [ˈʃəʊldə*] n hombro ▷ vt (fig) cargar con; **shoulder blade** n omóplato

shouldn't [ˈʃʊdnt] = **should not**

shout [ʃaut] n grito ▷ vt gritar ▷ vi gritar, dar voces

shove [ʃʌv] n empujón m ▷ vt empujar; (inf: put): **to ~ sth in** meter algo a empellones

shovel [ˈʃʌvl] n pala; (mechanical) excavadora ▷ vt mover con pala

show [ʃəʊ] (pt **~ed**, pp **~n**) n (of emotion) demostración f; (semblance) apariencia; (exhibition) exposición f; (Theatre) función f, espectáculo; (TV) show m ▷ vt mostrar, enseñar; (courage etc) mostrar, manifestar; (exhibit) exponer; (film) proyectar ▷ vi mostrarse; (appear) aparecer; **for ~** para impresionar; **on ~** (exhibits etc) expuesto; **show in** vt (person) hacer pasar; **show off** (pej) vi presumir ▷ vt (display) lucir; **show out** vt: **to show sb out** acompañar a algn a la puerta; **show up** vi (stand out) destacar; (inf: turn up) aparecer ▷ vt (unmask) desenmascarar; **show business** n

mundo del espectáculo

shower [ʃauə*] n (rain) chaparrón m, chubasco; (of stones etc) lluvia; (for bathing) ducha, regadera (MEX) ▷ vi llover ▷ vt (fig): **to ~ sb with sth** colmar a algn de algo; **to have a ~** = ducharse; **shower cap** n gorro de baño; **shower gel** n gel m de ducha

showing [ˈʃəʊɪŋ] n (of film) proyección f

show jumping n hípica

shown [ʃəʊn] pp of **show**

show-off [ˈʃəʊɒf] n (person) presumido/a; **showroom** n sala de muestras

shrank [ʃræŋk] pt of **shrink**

shred [ʃred] n (gen pl) triza, jirón m ▷ vt hacer trizas; (Culin) desmenuzar

shrewd [ʃruːd] adj astuto

shriek [ʃriːk] n chillido ▷ vi chillar

shrimp [ʃrimp] n camarón m

shrine [ʃraɪn] n santuario, sepulcro

shrink [ʃrɪŋk] (pt **shrank**, pp **shrunk**) vi encogerse; (be reduced) reducirse; (also: **~ away**) retroceder ▷ vt encoger ▷ n (inf, pej) loquero/a; **to ~ from (doing) sth** no atreverse a hacer algo

shrivel [ˈʃrɪvl] (also: **~ up**) vt (dry) secar ▷ vi secarse

shroud [ʃraud] n sudario ▷ vt: **~ed in mystery** envuelto en el misterio

Shrove Tuesday [ˈʃrəʊv-] n martes m de carnaval

shrub [ʃrʌb] n arbusto

shrug [ʃrʌg] n encogimiento de hombros ▷ vt, vi: **to ~ (one's shoulders)** encogerse de hombros; **shrug off** vt negar importancia a

shrunk [ʃrʌŋk] pp of **shrink**

shudder [ˈʃʌdə*] n estremecimiento, escalofrío ▷ vi estremecerse

shuffle [ˈʃʌfl] vt (cards) barajar ▷ vi: **to ~ (one's feet)** arrastrar los pies

shun [ʃʌn] vt rehuir, esquivar

shut [ʃʌt] (pt, pp **~**) vt cerrar ▷ vi cerrarse; **shut down** vt, vi cerrar; **shut up** vi (inf: keep quiet) callarse ▷ vt (close) cerrar; (silence) hacer callar;

s

shutter n contraventana; (Phot) obturador m

shuttle ['ʃʌtl] n lanzadera; (also: ~ service) servicio rápido y continuo entre dos puntos; (Aviat) puente m aéreo; **shuttlecock** n volante m

shy [ʃaɪ] adj tímido

sibling ['sɪblɪŋ] n (formal) hermano/a

sick [sɪk] adj (ill) enfermo; (nauseated) mareado; (humour) negro; (vomiting): **to be ~** (BRIT) vomitar; **to feel ~** tener náuseas; **to be ~ of** (fig) estar harto de; **sickening** adj (fig) asqueroso; **sick leave** n baja por enfermedad; **sickly** adj enfermizo; (smell) nauseabundo; **sickness** n enfermedad f, mal m; (vomiting) náuseas fpl

side [saɪd] n (gen) lado m; (of body) costado; (of lake) orilla; (of hill) ladera; (team) equipo m; (of page, door, entrance) lateral m; **to ~ with sb** tomar el partido de algn; **by the ~ of** al lado de; **~ by ~** juntos; **from ~ to ~** de un lado para otro; **to take ~s (with)** tomar partido (con); **sideboard** n aparador m; **sideboards** (BRIT) npl = **sideburns**; **sideburns** npl patillas fpl; **sidelight** n (Aut) luz f lateral; **sideline** n (Sport) línea de banda; (fig) empleo suplementario; **side order** n plato de acompañamiento; **side road** n (BRIT) calle f lateral; **side street** n calle f lateral; **sidetrack** vt (fig) desviar (de su propósito); **sidewalk** (US) n acera; **sideways** adv de lado

siege [siːdʒ] n cerco, sitio

sieve [sɪv] n colador m ▷ vt cribar

sift [sɪft] vt cribar; (fig: information) escudriñar

sigh [saɪ] n suspiro ▷ vi suspirar

sight [saɪt] n (faculty) vista; (spectacle) espectáculo; (on gun) mira, alza ▷ vt divisar; **in ~** a la vista; **out of ~** fuera de (la) vista; **on ~** (shoot) sin previo aviso; **sightseeing** n excursionismo, turismo; **to go sightseeing** hacer turismo

sign [saɪn] n (with hand) señal f, seña;

(trace) huella, rastro; (notice) letrero; (written) signo ▷ vt firmar; (Sport) fichar; **to ~ sth over to sb** firmar el traspaso de algo a algn; **sign for** vt fus (item) firmar el recibo de; **sign in** vi firmar el registro (al entrar); **sign on** vi (BRIT: as unemployed) registrarse como desempleado; (for course) inscribirse ▷ vt (Mil) alistar; (employee) contratar; **sign up** vi (Mil) alistarse; (for course) inscribirse ▷ vt (player) fichar

signal ['sɪgnl] n señal f ▷ vi señalizar ▷ vt (person) hacer señas a; (message) comunicar por señales

signature ['sɪgnətʃə*] n firma

significance [sɪg'nɪfɪkəns] n (importance) trascendencia

significant [sɪg'nɪfɪkənt] adj significativo; (important) trascendente

signify ['sɪgnɪfaɪ] vt significar

sign language n lenguaje m para sordomudos

signpost ['saɪnpəust] n indicador m

Sikh [siːk] adj, n sij mf

silence ['saɪlns] n silencio ▷ vt acallar; (guns) reducir al silencio

silent ['saɪlnt] adj silencioso; (not speaking) callado; (film) mudo; **to remain ~** guardar silencio

silhouette [sɪlu:'et] n silueta

silicon chip ['sɪlɪkən-] n plaqueta de silicio

silk [sɪlk] n seda ▷ adj de seda

silly ['sɪlɪ] adj (person) tonto; (idea) absurdo

silver ['sɪlvə*] n plata; (money) moneda suelta ▷ adj de plata; (colour) plateado; **silver-plated** adj plateado

similar ['sɪmɪlə*] adj: **~ (to)** parecido or semejante (a); **similarity** [-'lærɪtɪ] n semejanza f; **similarly** adv del mismo modo

simmer ['sɪmə*] vi hervir a fuego lento

simple ['sɪmpl] adj (easy) sencillo; (foolish, Comm: interest) simple;

simplicity [-'plɪsɪtɪ] n sencillez f;
simplify ['sɪmplɪfaɪ] vt simplificar;
simply adv (live, talk) sencillamente; (just, merely) sólo
simulate ['sɪmjʊleɪt] vt fingir, simular
simultaneous [sɪməl'teɪnɪəs] adj simultáneo; **simultaneously** adv simultáneamente
sin [sɪn] n pecado ▷vi pecar
since [sɪns] adv desde entonces, después ▷prep desde ▷conj (time) desde que; (because) ya que, puesto que; **~ then**, **ever ~** desde entonces
sincere [sɪn'sɪə*] adj sincero; **sincerely** adv: **yours sincerely** (in letters) le saluda atentamente
sing [sɪŋ] (pt **sang**, pp **sung**) vt, vi cantar
Singapore [sɪŋə'pɔː*] n Singapur m
singer ['sɪŋə*] n cantante mf
singing ['sɪŋɪŋ] n canto
single ['sɪŋgl] adj único, solo; (unmarried) soltero; (not double) simple, sencillo ▷n (BRIT: also: **~ ticket**) billete m sencillo; (record) sencillo, single m; **singles** npl (Tennis) individual m; **single out** vt (choose) escoger; **single bed** n cama individual; **single file** n: **in single file** en fila de uno; **single-handed** adv sin ayuda; **single-minded** adj resuelto, firme; **single parent** n padre m soltero, madre f soltera (o divorciado etc); **single parent family** familia f monoparental; **single room** n cuarto individual
singular ['sɪŋgjʊlə*] adj (odd) raro, extraño; (outstanding) excepcional ▷n (Ling) singular m
sinister ['sɪnɪstə*] adj siniestro
sink [sɪŋk] (pt **sank**, pp **sunk**) n fregadero ▷vt (ship) hundir, echar a pique; (foundations) excavar ▷vi hundirse; **to ~ sth into** hundir algo en; **sink in** vi (fig) penetrar, calar
sinus ['saɪnəs] n (Anat) seno
sip [sɪp] n sorbo ▷vt sorber, beber a sorbitos

sir [sə*] n señor m; **S~ John Smith** Sir John Smith; **yes ~** sí, señor
siren ['saɪərn] n sirena
sirloin ['sɜːlɔɪn] n (also: **~ steak**) solomillo
sister ['sɪstə*] n hermana; (BRIT: nurse) enfermera jefe; **sister-in-law** n cuñada
sit [sɪt] (pt, pp **sat**) vi sentarse; (be sitting) estar sentado; (assembly) reunirse; (for painter) posar ▷vt (exam) presentarse a; **sit back** vi (in seat) recostarse; **sit down** vi sentarse; **sit on** vt fus (jury, committee) ser miembro de, formar parte de; **sit up** vi incorporarse; (not go to bed) velar
sitcom ['sɪtkɔm] n abbr (= situation comedy) comedia de situación
site [saɪt] n sitio; (also: **building ~**) solar m ▷vt situar
sitting ['sɪtɪŋ] n (of assembly etc) sesión f; (in canteen) turno; **sitting room** n sala de estar
situated ['sɪtjʊeɪtɪd] adj situado
situation [sɪtjʊ'eɪʃən] n situación f; **"~s vacant"** (BRIT) "ofrecen trabajo"
six [sɪks] num seis; **sixteen** num diez y seis, dieciséis; **sixteenth** [sɪks'tiːnθ] adj decimosexto; **sixth** [sɪksθ] num sexto; **sixth form** n (BRIT) clase f de alumnos del sexto año (de 16 a 18 años de edad); **sixth-form college** n instituto m para alumnos de 16 a 18 años; **sixtieth** ['sɪkstɪɪθ] adj sexagésimo; **sixty** num sesenta
size [saɪz] n tamaño; (extent) extensión f; (of clothing) talla; (of shoes) número; **sizeable** adj importante, considerable
sizzle ['sɪzl] vi crepitar
skate [skeɪt] n patín m; (fish: pl inv) raya ▷vi patinar; **skateboard** n monopatín m; **skateboarding** n monopatín m; **skater** n patinador(a) m/f; **skating** n patinaje m; **skating rink** n pista de patinaje
skeleton ['skelɪtn] n esqueleto; (Tech) armazón f; (outline) esquema m

skeptical ['skɛptɪkl] (US) = **sceptical**

sketch [skɛtʃ] n (drawing) dibujo; (outline) esbozo, bosquejo; (Theatre) sketch m ▷ vt dibujar; (plan etc: also: ~ **out**) esbozar

skewer ['skjuːə*] n broqueta

ski [skiː] n esquí m ▷ vi esquiar; **ski boot** n bota de esquí

skid [skɪd] n patinazo ▷ vi patinar

ski: skier n esquiador(a) m/f; **skiing** n esquí m

skilful ['skɪlful] (US **skillful**) adj diestro, experto

ski lift n telesilla m, telesquí m

skill [skɪl] n destreza, pericia; técnica; **skilled** adj hábil, diestro; (worker) cualificado

skim [skɪm] vt (milk) desnatar; (glide over) rozar, rasar ▷ vi: **to ~ through** (book) hojear; **skimmed milk** (US **skim milk**) n leche f desnatada

skin [skɪn] n piel f; (complexion) cutis m ▷ vt (fruit etc) pelar; (animal) despellejar; **skinhead** n cabeza m/f rapada, skin(head) m/f; **skinny** adj flaco

skip [skɪp] n brinco, salto; (BRIT: container) contenedor m ▷ vi brincar; (with rope) saltar a la comba ▷ vt saltarse

ski: ski pass n forfait m (de esquí); **ski pole** n bastón m de esquiar

skipper ['skɪpə*] n (Naut, Sport) capitán m

skipping rope ['skɪpɪŋ-] (US **skip rope**) n comba

skirt [skɜːt] n falda, pollera (SC) ▷ vt (go round) ladear

skirting board ['skɜːtɪŋ-] (BRIT) n rodapié m

ski slope n pista de esquí

ski suit n traje m de esquiar

skull [skʌl] n calavera; (Anat) cráneo

skunk [skʌŋk] n mofeta

sky [skaɪ] n cielo; **skyscraper** n rascacielos m inv

slab [slæb] n (stone) bloque m; (flat) losa; (of cake) trozo

slack [slæk] adj (loose) flojo; (slow) de poca actividad; (careless) descuidado; **slacks** npl pantalones m

slain [sleɪn] pp of **slay**

slam [slæm] vt (throw) arrojar (violentamente); (criticize) criticar duramente ▷ vi (door) cerrarse de golpe; **to ~ the door** dar un portazo

slander ['slɑːndə*] n calumnia, difamación f

slang [slæŋ] n argot m; (jargon) jerga

slant [slɑːnt] n sesgo, inclinación f; (fig) interpretación f

slap [slæp] n palmada; (in face) bofetada ▷ vt dar una palmada or bofetada a; (paint etc): **to ~ sth on sth** embadurnar algo con algo ▷ adv (directly) exactamente, directamente

slash [slæʃ] vt acuchillar; (fig: prices) fulminar

slate [sleɪt] n pizarra ▷ vt (fig: criticize) criticar duramente

slaughter ['slɔːtə*] n (of animals) matanza; (of people) carnicería ▷ vt matar; **slaughterhouse** n matadero

Slav [slɑːv] adj eslavo

slave [sleɪv] n esclavo/a ▷ vi (also: ~ **away**) sudar tinta; **slavery** n esclavitud f

slay [sleɪ] (pt **slew**, pp **slain**) vt matar

sleazy ['sliːzɪ] adj de mala fama

sled [slɛd] (US) = **sledge**

sledge [slɛdʒ] n trineo

sleek [sliːk] adj (shiny) lustroso; (car etc) elegante

sleep [sliːp] n (pt, pp **slept**) n sueño ▷ vi dormir; **to go to** n ~ quedarse dormido; **sleep in** vi (oversleep) quedarse dormido; **sleep together** vi (have sex) acostarse juntos; **sleeper** n (person) durmiente m/f; (BRIT Rail: on track) traviesa; (: train) coche-cama m; **sleeping bag** n saco de dormir; **sleeping car** n coche-cama m; **sleeping pill** n somnífero; **sleepover**: **we're having a sleepover at Jo's** nos vamos a quedar a dormir en casa de Jo; **sleepwalk** vi caminar dormido;

(*habitually*) ser sonámbulo; **sleepy** *adj* soñoliento; (*place*) soporífero

sleet [sliːt] *n* aguanieve *f*

sleeve [sliːv] *n* manga; (*Tech*) manguito; (*of record*) portada; **sleeveless** *adj* sin mangas

sleigh [sleɪ] *n* trineo

slender ['slɛndə*] *adj* delgado; (*means*) escaso

slept [slɛpt] *pt, pp of* **sleep**

slew [sluː] *pt of* **slay** ▷ *vi* (BRIT: veer) torcerse

slice [slaɪs] *n* (*of meat*) tajada; (*of bread*) rebanada; (*of lemon*) rodaja; (*utensil*) pala ▷ *vt* cortar (en tajos), rebanar

slick [slɪk] *adj* (*skilful*) hábil, diestro; (*clever*) astuto ▷ *n* (*also:* **oil ~**) marea negra

slide [slaɪd] (*pt, pp* **slid**) *n* (*movement*) descenso, desprendimiento; (*in playground*) tobogán *m*; (*Phot*) diapositiva; (BRIT: *also:* **hair ~**) pasador *m* ▷ *vt* correr, deslizar ▷ *vi* (*slip*) resbalarse; (*glide*) deslizarse; **sliding** *adj* (*door*) corredizo

slight [slaɪt] *adj* (*slim*) delgado; (*frail*) delicado; (*pain etc*) leve; (*trivial*) insignificante; (*small*) pequeño ▷ *n* desaire *m* ▷ *vt* (*insult*) ofender, desairar; **not in the ~est** en absoluto; **slightly** *adv* ligeramente, un poco

slim [slɪm] *adj* delgado, esbelto; (*fig: chance*) remoto ▷ *vi* adelgazar; **slimming** *n* adelgazamiento

slimy ['slaɪmɪ] *adj* cenagoso

sling [slɪŋ] (*pt, pp* **slung**) *n* (*Med*) cabestrillo; (*weapon*) honda ▷ *vt* tirar, arrojar

slip [slɪp] *n* (*slide*) resbalón *m*; (*mistake*) descuido; (*underskirt*) combinación *f*; (*of paper*) papelito ▷ *vt* (*slide*) deslizar ▷ *vi* deslizarse; (*stumble*) resbalar(se); (*decline*) decaer; (*move smoothly*): **to ~ into/out of** (*room etc*) introducirse en/salirse de; **to give sb the ~** eludir a algn; **a ~ of the tongue** un lapsus; **to ~ sth on/off** ponerse/quitarse algo;

slip up *vi* (*make mistake*) equivocarse; meter la pata

slipper ['slɪpə*] *n* zapatilla, pantufla

slippery ['slɪpərɪ] *adj* resbaladizo; **slip road** (BRIT) *n* carretera de acceso

slit [slɪt] (*pt, pp* **~**) *n* raja; (*cut*) corte *m* ▷ *vt* rajar; cortar

slog [slɒg] (BRIT) *n* sudar tinta; **it was a ~** costó trabajo (hacerlo)

slogan ['sləʊgən] *n* eslogan *m*, lema *m*

slope [sləʊp] *n* (*up*) cuesta, pendiente *f*; (*down*) declive *m*; (*side of mountain*) falda, vertiente *m* ▷ *vi*: **to ~ down** estar en declive; **to ~ up** inclinarse; **sloping** *adj* en pendiente, en declive; (*writing*) inclinado

sloppy ['slɒpɪ] *adj* (*work*) descuidado; (*appearance*) desaliñado

slot [slɒt] *n* ranura ▷ *vt*: **to ~ into** encajar en; **slot machine** *n* (BRIT: *vending machine*) distribuidor *m* automático; (*for gambling*) tragaperras *m inv*

Slovakia [sləʊ'vækɪə] *n* Eslovaquia

Slovene [sləʊ'viːn] *adj* esloveno ▷ *n* esloveno/a; (*Ling*) esloveno; **Slovenia** [sləʊ'viːnɪə] *n* Eslovenia; **Slovenian** *adj, n* = **Slovene**

slow [sləʊ] *adj* lento; (*not clever*) lerdo; (*watch*): **to be ~** atrasar ▷ *adv* lentamente, despacio ▷ *vt, vi* retardar; **"~" (road sign)** disminuir velocidad; **slow down** *vi* reducir la marcha; **slowly** *adv* lentamente, despacio; **slow motion** *n*: **in slow motion** a cámara lenta

slug [slʌg] *n* babosa; (*bullet*) posta; **sluggish** *adj* lento; (*person*) perezoso

slum [slʌm] *n* casucha

slump [slʌmp] *n* (*economic*) depresión *f* ▷ *vi* hundirse; (*prices*) caer en picado

slung [slʌŋ] *pt, pp of* **sling**

slur [sləː*] *n*: **to cast a ~ on** insultar ▷ *vt* (*speech*) pronunciar mal

sly [slaɪ] *adj* astuto; (*smile*) taimado

smack [smæk] *n* bofetada ▷ *vt* dar con la mano a; (*child, on face*) abofetear

▷ *vi*: **to ~ of** saber a, oler a

small [smɔ:l] *adj* pequeño; **small ads** (BRIT) *npl* anuncios *mpl* por palabras; **small change** *n* suelto, cambio

smart [smɑ:t] *adj* elegante; (*clever*) listo, inteligente; (*quick*) rápido, vivo ▷ *vi* escocer, picar; **smartcard** *n* tarjeta inteligente; **smart phone** *n* smartphone *m*

smash [smæʃ] *n* (*also*: **~-up**) choque *m*; (*Mus*) exitazo *m* ▷ *vt* (*break*) hacer pedazos; (*car etc*) estrellar; (*Sport: record*) batir ▷ *vi* hacerse pedazos; (*against wall etc*) estrellarse; **smashing** (*inf*) *adj* estupendo

smear [smɪə*] *n* mancha; (*Med*) frotis *m inv* ▷ *vt* untar; **smear test** *n* (*Med*) citología, frotis *m inv* (*cervical*)

smell [smɛl] (*pt*, *pp* **smelt** *or* **~ed**) *n* olor *m*; (*sense*) olfato ▷ *vt*, *vi* oler; **smelly** *adj* maloliente

smelt [smɛlt] *pt*, *pp of* **smell**

smile [smaɪl] *n* sonrisa ▷ *vi* sonreír

smirk [smə:k] *n* sonrisa falsa *or* afectada

smog [smɔg] *n* esmog *m*

smoke [sməuk] *n* humo ▷ *vi* fumar; (*chimney*) echar humo ▷ *vt* (*cigarettes*) fumar; **smoke alarm** *n* detector *m* de humo, alarma contra incendios; **smoked** *adj* (*bacon, glass*) ahumado; **smoker** *n* fumador(a) *m/f*; (*Rail*) coche *m* fumador; **smoking** *n*: **"no smoking"** "prohibido fumar"

▌ Be careful not to translate **smoking** by the Spanish word *smoking*.

smoky *adj* (*room*) lleno de humo; (*taste*) ahumado

smooth [smu:ð] *adj* liso; (*sea*) tranquilo; (*flavour, movement*) suave; (*sauce*) fino; (*person: pej*) meloso ▷ *vt* (*also*: **~ out**) alisar; (*creases, difficulties*) allanar

smother ['smʌðə*] *vt* sofocar; (*repress*) contener

SMS *n abbr* (= *short message service*) (servicio) SMS; **SMS message** *n* (mensaje *m*) SMS

smudge [smʌdʒ] *n* mancha ▷ *vt* manchar

smug [smʌg] *adj* presumido; orondo

smuggle ['smʌgl] *vt* pasar de contrabando; **smuggling** *n* contrabando

snack [snæk] *n* bocado; **snack bar** *n* cafetería

snag [snæg] *n* problema *m*

snail [sneɪl] *n* caracol *m*

snake [sneɪk] *n* serpiente *f*

snap [snæp] *n* (*sound*) chasquido; (*photograph*) foto *f* ▷ *adj* (*decision*) instantáneo ▷ *vt* (*break*) quebrar; (*fingers*) castañetear ▷ *vi* quebrarse; (*fig: speak sharply*) contestar bruscamente; **to ~ shut** cerrarse de golpe; **snap at** *vt fus* (*dog*) intentar morder; **snap up** *vt* agarrar; **snapshot** *n* foto *f* (instantánea)

snarl [snɑ:l] *vi* gruñir

snatch [snætʃ] *n* (*small piece*) fragmento ▷ *vt* (*snatch away*) arrebatar; (*fig*) agarrar; **to ~ some sleep** encontrar tiempo para dormir

sneak [sni:k] (*pt* (*us*) **snuck**) *vi*: **to ~ in/out** entrar/salir a hurtadillas ▷ *n* (*inf*) soplón/ona *m/f*; **to ~ up on sb** aparecérsele de improviso a algn; **sneakers** *npl* zapatos *mpl* de lona

sneer [snɪə*] *vi* reír con sarcasmo; (*mock*): **to ~ at** burlarse de

sneeze [sni:z] *vi* estornudar

sniff [snɪf] *vi* sollozar ▷ *vt* husmear, oler; (*drugs*) esnifar

snigger ['snɪgə*] *vi* reírse con disimulo

snip [snɪp] *n* tijeretazo; (BRIT: *inf: bargain*) ganga ▷ *vt* tijeretear

sniper ['snaɪpə*] *n* francotirador(a) *m/f*

snob [snɔb] *n* (e)snob *mf*

snooker ['snu:kə*] *n* especie de billar

snoop [snu:p] *vi*: **to ~ about** fisgonear

snooze [snu:z] *n* siesta ▷ *vi* echar una siesta

snore [snɔ:*] *n* ronquido ▷ *vi* roncar

snorkel ['snɔ:kl] *n* (*tubo*) respirador *m*

snort [snɔ:t] n bufido ▷ vi bufar

snow [snəʊ] n nieve f ▷ vi nevar;
snowball n bola de nieve ▷ vi (fig)
agrandarse, ampliarse; **snowstorm** n
nevada, nevasca

snub [snʌb] vt (person) desairar ▷ n
desaire m, repulsa

snug [snʌg] adj (cosy) cómodo; (fitted)
ajustado

○ **KEYWORD**

so [səʊ] adv 1 (thus, likewise) así, de este
modo; **if so** de ser así; **I like swimming
– so do I** a mí me gusta nadar – a mí
también; **I've got work to do – so has
Paul** tengo trabajo que hacer – Paul
también; **it's 5 o'clock – so it is!** son las
cinco – ¡pues es verdad!; **I hope/think
so** espero/creo que sí; **so far** hasta
ahora; (in past) hasta este momento
2 (in comparisons etc: to such a degree)
tan; **so quickly (that)** tan rápido (que);
she's not so clever as her brother
no es tan lista como su hermano;
we were so worried estábamos
preocupadísimos
3: **so much** adj, adv tanto; **so many**
tantos/as
4 (phrases): **10 or so** unos 10, 10 o así; **so
long!** (inf: goodbye) ¡hasta luego!
▷ conj 1 (expressing purpose): **so as to** to do
para hacer; **so (that)** para que +subjun
2 (expressing result) así que; **so you see,
I could have gone** así que ya ves, (yo)
podría haber ido

soak [səʊk] vt (drench) empapar;
(steep in water) remojar ▷ vi remojarse,
estar a remojo; **soak up** vt absorber;
soaking adj (also: **soaking wet**)
calado or empapado (hasta los huesos
or el tuétano)

so-and-so [ˈsəʊənsəʊ] n (somebody)
fulano/a de tal

soap [səʊp] n jabón m; **soap opera**
n telenovela; **soap powder** n jabón
m en polvo

soar [sɔ:*] vi (on wings) remontarse;
(rocket: prices) dispararse; (building etc)
elevarse

sob [sɒb] n sollozo ▷ vi sollozar

sober [ˈsəʊbə*] adj (serious) serio; (not
drunk) sobrio; (colour, style) discreto;
sober up vt quitar la borrachera

so-called [ˈsəʊˈkɔ:ld] adj así llamado

soccer [ˈsɒkə*] n fútbol m

sociable [ˈsəʊʃəbl] adj sociable

social [ˈsəʊʃl] adj social ▷ n velada,
fiesta; **socialism** n socialismo;
socialist adj, n socialista mf; **socialize**
vi: **to socialize** alternar; **social life** n
vida social; **socially** adv socialmente;
social networking n interacción
social a través de la red; **social security**
n seguridad f social; **social services**
npl servicios mpl sociales; **social work** n
asistencia social; **social worker** n
asistente/a m/f social

society [səˈsaɪətɪ] n sociedad f;
(club) asociación f; (also: **high ~**) alta
sociedad

sociology [səʊsɪˈɒlədʒɪ] n sociología

sock [sɒk] n calcetín m

socket [ˈsɒkɪt] n cavidad f; (BRIT Elec)
enchufe m

soda [ˈsəʊdə] n (Chem) sosa; (also: ~
water) soda; (US: also: ~ pop) gaseosa

sodium [ˈsəʊdɪəm] n sodio

sofa [ˈsəʊfə] n sofá m; **sofa bed** n
sofá-cama m

soft [sɒft] adj (lenient, not hard) blando;
(gentle, not bright) suave; **soft drink** n
bebida no alcohólica; **soft drugs** npl
drogas fpl blandas; **soften** [ˈsɒfn] vt
ablandar; suavizar; (effect) amortiguar
▷ vi ablandarse; suavizarse; **softly** adv
suavemente; (gently) delicadamente,
con delicadeza; **software** n (Comput)
software m

soggy [ˈsɒgɪ] adj empapado

soil [sɔɪl] n (earth) tierra, suelo ▷ vt
ensuciar

solar [ˈsəʊlə*] adj solar; **solar power**
n energía solar; **solar system** n
sistema m solar

sold [səʊld] *pt, pp of* **sell**

soldier ['səʊldʒə*] *n* soldado; *(army man)* militar *m*

sold out *adj* (Comm) agotado

sole [səʊl] *n (of foot)* planta; *(of shoe)* suela; *(fish: pl inv)* lenguado ▷ *adj* único;**solely** *adv* únicamente, sólo, solamente; **I will hold you solely responsible** le consideraré el único responsable

solemn ['sɒləm] *adj* solemne

solicitor [sə'lɪsɪtə*] (BRIT) *n (for wills etc)* = notario/a; *(in court)* = abogado/a

solid ['sɒlɪd] *adj* sólido; *(gold etc)* macizo ▷ *n* sólido

solitary ['sɒlɪtərɪ] *adj* solitario, solo

solitude ['sɒlɪtjuːd] *n* soledad *f*

solo ['səʊləʊ] *n* solo ▷ *adv (fly)* en solitario;**soloist** *n* solista *m/f*

soluble ['sɒljʊbl] *adj* soluble

solution [sə'luːʃən] *n* solución *f*

solve [sɒlv] *vt* resolver, solucionar

solvent ['sɒlvənt] *adj* (Comm) solvente ▷ *n* (Chem) solvente *m*

sombre, *(US* **somber**) ['sɒmbə*] *adj* sombrío

⬤ **KEYWORD**

some [sʌm] *adj* **1** *(a certain amount or number)*: **some tea/water/biscuits** té/agua/(unas) galletas; **there's some milk in the fridge** hay leche en el frigo; **there were some people outside** había algunas personas fuera; **I've got some money, but not much** tengo algo de dinero, pero no mucho

2 *(certain: in contrasts)* algunos/as; **some people say that ...** hay quien dice que ...; **some films were excellent, but most were mediocre** hubo películas excelentes, pero la mayoría fueron mediocres

3 *(unspecified)*: **some woman was asking for you** una mujer estuvo preguntando por ti; **he was asking for some book (or other)** pedía un libro;

some day algún día; **some day next week** un día de la semana que viene ▷ *pron* **1** *(a certain number)*: **I've got some** *(books etc)* tengo algunos/as **2** *(a certain amount)* algo; **I've got some** *(money, milk)* tengo algo; **could I have some of that cheese?** ¿me puede dar un poco de ese queso?; **I've read some of the book** he leído parte del libro ▷ *adv*: **some 10 people** unas 10 personas, una decena de personas

some: **somebody** ['sʌmbədɪ] *pron* = **someone**;**somehow** *adv* de alguna manera; *(for some reason)* por una u otra razón;**someone** *pron* alguien; **someplace** (US) *adv* = **somewhere**; **something** *pron* algo; **would you like something to eat/drink?** ¿te gustaría cenar/tomar algo?;**sometime** *adv (in future)* algún día, en algún momento; *(in past)*: **sometime last month** durante el mes pasado;**sometimes** *adv* a veces;**somewhat** *adv* algo; **somewhere** *adv (be)* en alguna parte; *(go)* a alguna parte; **somewhere else** *(be)* en otra parte; *(go)* a otra parte

son [sʌn] *n* hijo

song [sɒŋ] *n* canción *f*

son-in-law ['sʌnɪnlɔː] *n* yerno

soon [suːn] *adv* pronto, dentro de poco; ~ **afterwards** poco después; *see also* **as**;**sooner** *adv (time)* antes, más temprano; *(preference: rather)*: **I would sooner do that** preferiría hacer eso; **sooner or later** tarde o temprano

soothe [suːð] *vt* tranquilizar; *(pain)* aliviar

sophisticated [sə'fɪstɪkeɪtɪd] *adj* sofisticado

sophomore ['sɒfəmɔː*] (US) *n* estudiante *mf* de segundo año

soprano [sə'prɑːnəʊ] *n* soprano *f*

sorbet ['sɔːbeɪ] *n* sorbete *m*

sordid ['sɔːdɪd] *adj (place etc)* sórdido; *(motive etc)* mezquino

sore [sɔː*] *adj (painful)* doloroso, que duele ▷ *n* llaga

sorrow ['sɔrəʊ] n pena, dolor m

sorry ['sɔrɪ] adj (regretful) arrepentido; (condition, excuse) lastimoso; **~!** ¡perdón!, ¡perdone!; **~?** ¿cómo?; **to feel ~ for sb** tener lástima a algn; **I feel ~ for him** me da lástima

sort [sɔ:t] n clase f, género, tipo; **sort out** vt (papers) clasificar; (organize) ordenar, organizar; (resolve: problem, situation etc) arreglar, solucionar

SOS n SOS m

so-so ['səʊsəʊ] adv regular, así así

sought [sɔ:t] pt, pp of **seek**

soul [səʊl] n alma

sound [saʊnd] n (noise) sonido, ruido; (volume: on TV etc) volumen m; (Geo) estrecho ▷ adj (healthy) sano; (safe, not damaged) en buen estado; (reliable: person) digno de confianza; (sensible) sensato, razonable; (secure: investment) seguro ▷ adv: **~ asleep** profundamente dormido ▷ vt (alarm) sonar ▷ vi sonar, resonar; (fig: seem) parecer; **to ~ like** sonar a; **soundtrack** n (of film) banda sonora

soup [su:p] n (thick) sopa; (thin) caldo

sour [saʊə*] adj agrio; (milk) cortado; **it's ~ grapes** (fig) están verdes

source [sɔ:s] n fuente f

south [saʊθ] n sur m ▷ adj del sur, sureño ▷ adv al sur, hacia el sur; **South Africa** n África del Sur; **South African** adj, n sudafricano/a m/f; **South America** n América del Sur, Sudamérica; **South American** adj, n sudamericano/a m/f; **southbound** adj (con) rumbo al sur; **southeastern** [saʊθ'i:stən] n sureste, del sureste; **southern** ['sʌðən] adj del sur, meridional; **South Korea** n Corea del Sur; **South Pole** n Polo Sur; **southward(s)** adv hacia el sur; **southwest** n suroeste m; **southwestern** [saʊθ'westən] adj suroeste

souvenir [su:və'nɪə*] n recuerdo

sovereign ['sɔvrɪn] adj, n soberano/a m/f

sow¹ [səʊ] (pt **~ed**, pp **sown**) vt

sembrar

sow² [saʊ] n cerda, puerca

soya ['sɔɪə] (BRIT) n soja

spa [spa:] n balneario

space [speɪs] n espacio; (room) sitio ▷ cpd espacial ▷ vt (also: **~ out**) espaciar; **spacecraft** n nave f espacial; **spaceship** n = **spacecraft**

spacious ['speɪʃəs] adj amplio

spade [speɪd] n (tool) pala; (toy) **spades** npl (Cards: British) picas fpl; (: Spanish) espadas fpl

spaghetti [spə'getɪ] n espaguetis mpl, fideos mpl

Spain [speɪn] n España

spam [spæm] n (junk email) spam m

span [spæn] n (of bird, plane) envergadura; (of arch) luz f; (in time) lapso ▷ vt extenderse sobre, cruzar; (fig) abarcar

Spaniard ['spænjəd] n español(a) m/f

Spanish ['spænɪʃ] adj español(a) ▷ n (Ling) español m, castellano; **the Spanish** npl los españoles

spank [spæŋk] vt zurrar

spanner ['spænə*] (BRIT) n llave f (inglesa)

spare [speə*] adj de reserva; (surplus) sobrante, de más ▷ n = **spare part** ▷ vt (do without) pasarse sin; (refrain from hurting) perdonar; **to ~** (surplus) sobrante, de sobra; **spare part** n pieza de repuesto; **spare room** n cuarto de los invitados; **spare time** n tiempo libre; **spare tyre** (US **spare tire**) n (Aut) neumático or llanta (LAM) de recambio; **spare wheel** n (Aut) rueda de recambio

spark [spa:k] n chispa; (fig) chispazo; **spark(ing) plug** n bujía

sparkle ['spa:kl] n centelleo, destello ▷ vi (shine) relucir, brillar

sparrow ['spærəʊ] n gorrión m

sparse [spa:s] adj esparcido, escaso

spasm ['spæzəm] n (Med) espasmo

spat [spæt] pt, pp of **spit**

spate [speɪt] n (fig): **a ~ of** un

torrente de

spatula ['spætjʊlə] n espátula
speak [spi:k] (pt **spoke**, pp **spoken**)
vt (language) hablar; (truth) decir ▷ vi
hablar; (make a speech) intervenir; **to
~ to sb/of or about sth** hablar con
algn/de o sobre algo; **~ up!** ¡habla
fuerte!; **speaker** n (in public) orador(a)
m/f; (also: **loudspeaker**) altavoz m; (for
stereo etc) bafle m; (Pol): **the Speaker**
(BRIT) el Presidente de la Cámara de los
Comunes; (US) el Presidente del Congreso
spear [spɪə*] n lanza ▷ vt alancear
special ['speʃl] adj especial; (edition
etc) extraordinario; (delivery) urgente;
special delivery n (Post): **by special
delivery** por entrega urgente;
special effects npl (Cine) efectos mpl
especiales; **specialist** n especialista
mf; **speciality** [speʃɪ'ælɪtɪ] (BRIT)
n especialidad f; **specialize** vi: **to
specialize (in)** especializarse
(en); **specially** adv sobre todo,
en particular; **special needs** npl
(BRIT): **children with special needs**
niños que requieren una atención
diferenciada; **special offer** n (Comm)
oferta especial; **special school** n
(BRIT) colegio m de educación especial;
specialty (US) n = **speciality**
species ['spi:ʃi:z] n inv especie f
specific [spə'sɪfɪk] adj específico;
specifically adv específicamente
specify ['spesɪfaɪ] vt, vi especificar,
precisar
specimen ['spesɪmən] n ejemplar m;
(Med: of urine) espécimen m; (: of blood)
muestra
speck [spek] n grano, mota
spectacle ['spektəkl] n espectáculo;
spectacles npl (BRIT: glasses) gafas
fpl (SP), anteojos mpl; **spectacular**
[-'tækjʊlə*] adj espectacular; (success)
impresionante
spectator [spek'teɪtə*] n
espectador(a) m/f
spectrum ['spektrəm] (pl **spectra**)
n espectro

speculate ['spekjʊleɪt] vi: **to ~ (on)**
especular (en)
sped [sped] pt, pp of **speed**
speech [spi:tʃ] n (faculty) habla;
(formal talk) discurso; (spoken language)
lenguaje m; **speechless** adj mudo,
estupefacto
speed [spi:d] n velocidad f; (haste)
prisa; (promptness) rapidez f; **at full** or
top ~ a máxima velocidad; **speed up** vi
acelerarse ▷ vt acelerar; **speedboat**
n lancha motora; **speeding** n (Aut)
exceso de velocidad; **speed limit** n
límite m de velocidad, velocidad f
máxima; **speedometer** [spɪ'dɒmɪtə*]
n velocímetro; **speedy** adj (fast) veloz,
rápido; (prompt) pronto
spell [spel] (pt, pp **spelt** (BRIT) or **~ed**)
n (also: **magic ~**) encanto, hechizo;
(period of time) rato, período ▷ vt
deletrear; (fig) anunciar, presagiar;
to cast a ~ on sb hechizar a algn;
he can't ~ pone faltas de ortografía;
spell out vt (explain): **to spell sth out
for sb** explicar algo a algn en detalle;
spellchecker ['speltʃekə*] n corrector
m ortográfico; **spelling** n ortografía
spelt [spelt] pt, pp of **spell**
spend [spend] (pt, pp **spent**) vt
(money) gastar; (time) pasar; (life)
dedicar; **spending** n: **government
spending** gastos mpl del gobierno
spent [spent] pt, pp of **spend** ▷ adj
(cartridge, bullets, match) usado
sperm [spə:m] n esperma
sphere [sfɪə*] n esfera
spice [spaɪs] n especia ▷ vt
condimentar
spicy ['spaɪsɪ] adj picante
spider ['spaɪdə*] n araña
spike [spaɪk] n (point) punta; (Bot)
espiga
spill [spɪl] (pt, pp **spilt** or **~ed**) vt
derramar, verter ▷ vi derramarse; **to ~
over** desbordarse
spin [spɪn] (pt, pp **spun**) n (Aviat)
barrena; (trip in car) paseo (en coche);
(on ball) efecto ▷ vt (wool etc) hilar; (ball

etc) hacer girar ▷ *vi* girar, dar vueltas

spinach ['spɪnɪtʃ] *n* espinaca; (*as food*) espinacas *fpl*

spinal ['spaɪnl] *adj* espinal

spin doctor *n* informador(a) parcial al servicio de un partido político *etc*

spin-dryer (BRIT) *n* secador *m* centrífugo

spine [spaɪn] *n* espinazo, columna vertebral; (*thorn*) espina

spiral ['spaɪərl] *n* espiral *f* ▷ *vi* (*fig: prices*) subir desorbitadamente

spire ['spaɪə*] *n* aguja, chapitel *m*

spirit ['spɪrɪt] *n* (*soul*) alma; (*ghost*) fantasma *m*; (*attitude, sense*) espíritu *m*; (*courage*) valor *m*, ánimo; **spirits** *npl* (*drink*) licor(es) *m(pl)*; **in good ~s** alegre, de buen ánimo

spiritual ['spɪrɪtjuəl] *adj* espiritual ▷ *n* espiritual *m*

spit [spɪt] (*pt, pp* **spat**) *n* (*for roasting*) asador *m*, espetón *m*; (*saliva*) saliva ▷ *vi* escupir; (*sound*) chisporrotear; (*rain*) lloviznar

spite [spaɪt] *n* rencor *m*, ojeriza ▷ *vt* causar pena a, mortificar; **in ~ of** a pesar de, pese a; **spiteful** *adj* rencoroso, malévolo

splash [splæʃ] *n* (*sound*) chapoteo; (*of colour*) mancha ▷ *vt* salpicar ▷ *vi* (*also: ~ **about**) chapotear; **splash out** (*inf*) *vi* (BRIT) derrochar dinero

splendid ['splendɪd] *adj* espléndido

splinter ['splɪntə*] *n* (*of wood etc*) astilla; (*in finger*) espigón *m* ▷ *vi* astillarse, hacer astillas

split [splɪt] (*pt, pp* ~) *n* hendedura, raja; (*fig*) división *f*; (*Pol*) escisión *f* ▷ *vt* partir, rajar; (*party*) dividir; (*share*) repartir ▷ *vi* dividirse, escindirse; **split up** *vi* (*couple*) separarse; (*meeting*) acabarse

spoil [spɔɪl] (*pt, pp* ~**t** *or* ~**ed**) *vt* (*damage*) dañar; (*mar*) estropear; (*child*) mimar, consentir

spoilt [spɔɪlt] *pt, pp of* **spoil** ▷ *adj* (*child*) mimado, consentido; (*ballot paper*) invalidado

spoke [spəuk] *pt of* **speak** ▷ *n* rayo, radio

spoken ['spəukn] *pp of* **speak**

spokesman ['spəuksmən] (*irreg*) *n* portavoz *m*

spokesperson ['spəukspə:sn] (*irreg*) *n* portavoz *m/f*, vocero/a (LAM)

spokeswoman ['spəukswumən] (*irreg*) *n* portavoz *f*

sponge [spʌndʒ] *n* esponja; (*also: ~ cake*) bizcocho ▷ *vt* (*wash*) lavar con esponja ▷ *vi*: **to ~ off** *or* **on sb** vivir a costa de algn; **sponge bag** (BRIT) *n* esponjera

sponsor ['sponsə*] *n* patrocinador(a) *m/f* ▷ *vt* (*applicant, proposal etc*) proponer; **sponsorship** *n* patrocinio

spontaneous [spon'teɪnɪəs] *adj* espontáneo

spooky ['spu:kɪ] (*inf*) *adj* espeluznante, horripilante

spoon [spu:n] *n* cuchara; **spoonful** *n* cucharada

sport [spɔ:t] *n* deporte *m*; (*person*): **to be a good ~** ser muy majo ▷ *vt* (*wear*) lucir, ostentar; **sport jacket** (US) *n* = **sports jacket**; **sports car** *n* coche *m* deportivo; **sports centre** (BRIT) *n* polideportivo; **sports jacket** (BRIT) *n* chaqueta deportiva; **sportsman** (*irreg*) *n* deportista *m*; **sports utility vehicle** *n* todoterreno *m inv*; **sportswear** *n* trajes *mpl* de deporte *or* sport; **sportswoman** (*irreg*) *n* deportista; **sporty** *adj* deportivo

spot [spot] *n* sitio, lugar *m*; (*dot: on pattern*) punto, mancha; (*pimple*) grano; (*Radio*) cuña publicitaria; (*TV*) espacio publicitario; (*small amount*): **a ~ of** un poquito de ▷ *vt* (*notice*) notar, observar; **on the ~** allí mismo; **spotless** *adj* perfectamente limpio; **spotlight** *n* foco, reflector *m*; (*Aut*) faro auxiliar

spouse [spauz] *n* cónyuge *m/f*

sprain [spreɪn] *n* torcedura ▷ *vt*: **to ~ one's ankle/wrist** torcerse el tobillo/la muñeca

sprang [spræŋ] *pt of* **spring**

sprawl [sprɔ:l] vi tumbarse
spray [spreɪ] n rociada; (of sea) espuma; (container) atomizador m; (for paint etc) pistola rociadora; (of flowers) ramita ▷vt rociar; (crops) regar
spread [spred] (pt, pp ~) n extensión f; (for bread etc) pasta para untar; (inf: food) comilona ▷vt extender; (butter) untar; (wings, sails) desplegar; (work, wealth) repartir; (scatter) esparcir ▷vi (also: ~ **out**: stain) extenderse; (news) diseminarse; **spread out** vi (move apart) separarse; **spreadsheet** n hoja electrónica or de cálculo
spree [spri:] n: **to go on a ~** ir de juerga
spring [sprɪŋ] (pt **sprang**, pp **sprung**) n (season) primavera; (leap) salto, brinco; (coiled metal) resorte m; (of water) fuente f, manantial m ▷vi saltar, brincar; **spring up** vi (thing: appear) aparecer; (problem) surgir; **spring onion** n cebolleta
sprinkle [ˈsprɪŋkl] vt (pour: liquid) rociar; (: salt, sugar) espolvorear; **to ~ water** etc **on, ~ with water** etc rociar or salpicar de agua etc
sprint [sprɪnt] n esprint m ▷vi esprintar
sprung [sprʌŋ] pp of **spring**
spun [spʌn] pt, pp of **spin**
spur [spə:*] n espuela; (fig) estímulo, aguijón m ▷vt (also: ~ **on**) estimular, incitar; **on the ~ of the moment** de improviso
spurt [spə:t] n chorro; (of energy) arrebato ▷vi chorrear
spy [spaɪ] n espía mf ▷vi: **to ~ on** espiar a ▷vt (see) divisar, lograr ver
sq. abbr = **square**
squabble [ˈskwɔbl] vi reñir, pelear
squad [skwɔd] n (Mil) pelotón m; (Police) brigada; (Sport) equipo
squadron [ˈskwɔdrn] n (Mil) escuadrón m; (Aviat, Naut) escuadra
squander [ˈskwɔndə*] vt (money) derrochar, despilfarrar; (chances) desperdiciar

square [skweə*] n cuadro; (in town) plaza; (inf: person) carca m/f ▷adj cuadrado; (inf: ideas, tastes) trasnochado ▷vt (arrange) arreglar; (Math) cuadrar; (reconcile) compaginar; **all ~** igual(es); **to have a ~ meal** comer caliente; **2 metres ~** = 2 metros en cuadro; **2 ~ metres** 2 metros cuadrados; **square root** n raíz f cuadrada
squash [skwɔʃ] n (BRIT: drink): **lemon/orange ~** zumo (SP) or jugo (LAM) de limón/naranja; (US BOT) calabacín m; (Sport) squash m ▷vt aplastar
squat [skwɔt] adj achaparrado ▷vi (also: ~ **down**) agacharse, sentarse en cuclillas; **squatter** n okupa mf (SP)
squeak [skwi:k] vi (hinge) chirriar, rechinar; (mouse) chillar
squeal [skwi:l] vi chillar, dar gritos agudos
squeeze [skwi:z] n presión f; (of hand) apretón m; (Comm) restricción f ▷vt (hand, arm) apretar
squid [skwɪd] n inv calamar m; (Culin) calamares mpl
squint [skwɪnt] vi bizquear, ser bizco ▷n (Med) estrabismo
squirm [skwə:m] vi retorcerse, revolverse
squirrel [ˈskwɪrəl] n ardilla
squirt [skwə:t] vi salir a chorros ▷vt chiscar
Sr abbr = **senior**
Sri Lanka [srɪˈlæŋkə] n Sri Lanka m
St abbr = **saint; street**
stab [stæb] n (with knife) puñalada; (of pain) pinchazo; (inf: try): **to have a ~ at (doing) sth** intentar (hacer) algo ▷vt apuñalar
stability [stəˈbɪlɪtɪ] n estabilidad f
stable [ˈsteɪbl] adj estable ▷n cuadra, caballeriza
stack [stæk] n montón m, pila ▷vt amontonar, apilar
stadium [ˈsteɪdɪəm] n estadio
staff [stɑ:f] n (work force) personal m,

plantilla; (BRIT Scol) cuerpo docente
▷ vt proveer de personal

stag [stæg] n ciervo, venado

stage [steɪdʒ] n escena; (point) etapa; (platform) plataforma; (profession): **the ~** el teatro ▷ vt (play) poner en escena, representar; (organize) montar, organizar; **in ~s** por etapas

stagger ['stægə*] vi tambalearse ▷ vt (amaze) asombrar; (hours, holidays) escalonar; **staggering** adj asombroso

stagnant ['stægnənt] adj estancado

stag night, stag party n despedida de soltero

stain [steɪn] n mancha; (colouring) tintura ▷ vt manchar; (wood) teñir; **stained glass** n vidrio m de color; **stainless steel** n acero inoxidable

staircase ['steəkeɪs] n = **stairway**

stairs [steəz] npl escaleras fpl

stairway ['steəweɪ] n escalera

stake [steɪk] n estaca, poste m; (Comm) interés m; (Betting) apuesta ▷ vt (money) apostar; (life) arriesgar; (reputation) poner en juego; (claim) presentar una reclamación; **to be at ~** estar en juego

stale [steɪl] adj (bread) duro; (food) pasado; (smell) rancio; (beer) agrio

stalk [stɔːk] n tallo, caña ▷ vt acechar, cazar al acecho

stall [stɔːl] n (in market) puesto; (in stable) casilla de establo ▷ vt (Aut) calar; (fig) dar largas a ▷ vi (Aut) calarse; (fig) andarse con rodeos

stamina ['stæmɪnə] n resistencia

stammer ['stæmə*] n tartamudeo ▷ vi tartamudear

stamp [stæmp] n sello (SP), estampilla (LAM), timbre m (MEX); (mark) marca, huella; (on document) timbre m ▷ vi (also: ~ one's foot) patear ▷ vt (mark) marcar; (letter) franquear; (with rubber stamp) sellar; **stamp out** vt (fire) apagar con el pie; (crime, opposition) acabar con; **stamped addressed envelope** n (BRIT) sobre m sellado con las señas propias

stampede [stæm'piːd] n estampida

stance [stæns] n postura

stand [stænd] (pt, pp **stood**) n (position) posición f, postura; (for taxis) parada; (hall stand) perchero; (music stand) atril m; (Sport) tribuna; (at exhibition) stand m ▷ vi (be) estar, encontrarse; (be on foot) estar de pie; (rise) levantarse; (remain) quedar en pie; (in election) presentarse candidatura ▷ vt (place) poner, colocar; (withstand) aguantar, soportar; (invite to) invitar; **to make a ~** (fig) mantener una postura firme; **to ~ for parliament** (BRIT) presentarse (como candidato) a las elecciones; **stand back** vi retirarse; **stand by** vi (be ready) estar listo ▷ vt fus (opinion) aferrarse a; (person) apoyar; **stand down** vi (withdraw) ceder el puesto; **stand for** vt fus (signify) significar; (tolerate) aguantar, permitir; **stand in for** vt fus suplir a; **stand out** vi destacarse; **stand up** vi levantarse, ponerse de pie; **stand up for** vt fus defender; **stand up to** vt fus hacer frente a

standard ['stændəd] n patrón m, norma; (level) nivel m; (flag) estandarte m ▷ adj (size etc) normal, corriente; (text) básico; **standards** npl (morals) valores mpl morales; **standard of living** n nivel m de vida

standing ['stændɪŋ] adj (on foot) de pie, en pie; (permanent) permanente ▷ n reputación f; **of many years' ~** que lleva muchos años; **standing order** (BRIT) n (at bank) orden f de pago permanente

stand: **standpoint** n punto m de vista; **standstill** n: **at a standstill** (industry, traffic) paralizado; (car) parado; **to come to a standstill** quedar paralizado; pararse

stank [stæŋk] pt of **stink**

staple ['steɪpl] n (for papers) grapa ▷ adj (food etc) básico ▷ vt grapar

star [stɑː*] n estrella; (celebrity) estrella, astro ▷ vt (Theatre, Cinema)

s

ser el/la protagonista de; **the stars** npl (Astrology) el horóscopo

starboard ['stɑːbəd] n estribor m

starch [stɑːtʃ] n almidón m

stardom ['stɑːdəm] n estrellato

stare [steə*] n mirada fija ▷ vi: **to ~ at** mirar fijo

stark [stɑːk] adj (bleak) severo, escueto ▷ adv: **~ naked** en cueros

start [stɑːt] n principio, comienzo; (departure) salida; (sudden movement) salto, sobresalto; (advantage) ventaja ▷ vt empezar, comenzar; (cause) causar; (found) fundar; (engine) poner en marcha ▷ vi comenzar, empezar; (with fright) asustarse, sobresaltarse; (train etc) salir; **to ~ doing** or **to do sth** empezar a hacer algo; **start off** vi empezar, comenzar; (leave) salir, ponerse en camino; **start out** vi (begin) empezar; (set out) partir, salir; **start up** vi comenzar; (car) ponerse en marcha ▷ vt comenzar; poner en marcha; **starter** n (Aut) botón m de arranque; (Sport: official) juez m/f de salida; (BRIT Culin) entrante m; **starting point** n punto de partida

startle ['stɑːtl] vt asustar, sobrecoger; **startling** adj alarmante

starvation [stɑːˈveɪʃən] n hambre f

starve [stɑːv] vi tener mucha hambre; (to death) morir de hambre ▷ vt hacer pasar hambre

state [steɪt] n estado ▷ vt (say, declare) afirmar; **the S~s** los Estados Unidos; **to be in a ~** estar agitado; **statement** n afirmación f; **state school** n escuela or colegio estatal; **statesman** (irreg) n estadista m

static ['stætɪk] n (Radio) parásitos mpl ▷ adj estático

station ['steɪʃən] n estación f; (Radio) emisora; (rank) posición f social ▷ vt colocar, situar; (Mil) apostar

stationary ['steɪʃnərɪ] adj estacionario, fijo

stationer's (shop) (BRIT) n papelería

stationery [-nərɪ] n papel m de escribir, artículos mpl de escritorio

station wagon (US) n ranchera

statistic [stəˈtɪstɪk] n estadística; **statistics** n (science) estadística

statue ['stætjuː] n estatua

stature ['stætʃə*] n estatura; (fig) talla

status ['steɪtəs] n estado; (reputation) estatus m; **status quo** n (e)statu quo m

statutory ['stætjutrɪ] adj estatutario

staunch [stɔːntʃ] adj leal, incondicional

stay [steɪ] n estancia ▷ vi quedar(se); (as guest) hospedarse; **to ~ put** seguir en el mismo sitio; **to ~ the night/5 days** pasar la noche/estar 5 días; **stay away** vi (from person, building) no acercarse; (from event) no acudir; **stay behind** vi quedarse atrás; **stay in** vi quedarse en casa; **stay on** vi quedarse; **stay out** vi (of house) no volver a casa; (on strike) permanecer en huelga; **stay up** vi (at night) velar, no acostarse

steadily ['stɛdɪlɪ] adv constantemente; (firmly) firmemente; (work, walk) sin parar; (gaze) fijamente

steady ['stɛdɪ] adj (firm) firme; (regular) regular; (person, character) sensato, juicioso; (boyfriend) formal; (look, voice) tranquilo ▷ vt (stabilize) estabilizar; (nerves) calmar

steak [steɪk] n filete m; (beef) bistec m

steal [stiːl] (pt **stole**, pp **stolen**) vt robar ▷ vi robar; (move secretly) andar a hurtadillas

steam [stiːm] n vapor m; (mist) vaho, humo ▷ vt (Culin) cocer al vapor ▷ vi echar vapor; **steam up** vi (window) empañarse; **to get steamed up about sth** (fig) ponerse negro por algo; **steamy** adj (room) lleno de vapor; (window) empañado; (heat, atmosphere) bochornoso

steel [stiːl] n acero ▷ adj de acero

steep [sti:p] *adj* escarpado, abrupto; *(stair)* empinado; *(price)* exorbitante, excesivo ▷ *vt* empapar, remojar

steeple ['sti:pl] *n* aguja

steer [stɪə*] *vt (car)* conducir (SP), manejar (LAM); *(person)* dirigir ▷ *vi* conducir, manejar; **steering** *n* (Aut) dirección *f*; **steering wheel** *n* volante *m*

stem [stem] *n (of plant)* tallo; *(of glass)* pie *m* ▷ *vt* detener; *(blood)* restañar

step [step] *n* paso; *(on stair)* peldaño, escalón *m* ▷ *vi*: **to ~ forward/back** dar un paso adelante/hacia atrás; **steps** *npl (BRIT)* = **stepladder**; **in/out of ~ (with)** acorde/en disonancia (con); **step down** *vi (fig)* retirarse; **step in** *vi* entrar; *(fig)* intervenir; **step up** *vt (increase)* aumentar; **stepbrother** *n* hermanastro; **stepchild** (*pl* **stepchildren**) *n* hijastro a *m/f*; **stepdaughter** *n* hijastra; **stepfather** *n* padrastro; **stepladder** *n* escalera doble or de tijera; **stepmother** *n* madrastra; **stepsister** *n* hermanastra; **stepson** *n* hijastro

stereo ['steriəu] *n* estéreo ▷ *adj* (*also*: **~phonic**) estéreo, estereofónico

stereotype ['stɪərɪətaɪp] *n* estereotipo ▷ *vt* estereotipar

sterile ['sterail] *adj* estéril; **sterilize** ['sterɪlaɪz] *vt* esterilizar

sterling ['stɜːlɪŋ] *adj (silver)* de ley ▷ *n* (Econ) libras *fpl* esterlinas *fpl*; **one pound ~** una libra esterlina

stern [stɜːn] *adj* severo, austero ▷ *n* (Naut) popa

steroid ['stɪərɔɪd] *n* esteroide *m*

stew [stjuː] *n* estofado, guiso ▷ *vt, vi* estofar, guisar; *(fruit)* cocer

steward ['stjuːəd] *n* camarero; **stewardess** *n (esp on plane)* azafata

stick [stɪk] (*pt, pp* **stuck**) *n* palo; *(of dynamite)* barreno; *(as weapon)* porra; (*also*: **walking ~**) bastón *m* ▷ *vt (glue)* pegar; *(inf: put)* meter; *(: tolerate)* aguantar, soportar; *(thrust)*: **to ~ sth into** clavar or hincar algo en ▷ *vi*

pegarse; *(be unmoveable)* quedarse parado; *(in mind)* quedarse grabado; **stick out** *vi* sobresalir; **stick up** *vi* sobresalir; **stick up for** *vt fus* defender; **sticker** *n (label)* etiqueta engomada; *(with slogan)* pegatina; **sticking plaster** *n* esparadrapo; **stick insect** *n* insecto palo; **stick shift** *(US)* *n (Aut)* palanca de cambios

sticky ['stɪkɪ] *adj* pegajoso; *(label)* engomado; *(fig)* difícil

stiff [stɪf] *adj* rígido, tieso; *(hard)* duro; *(manner)* estirado; *(difficult)* difícil; *(person)* inflexible; *(price)* exorbitante ▷ *adv*: **scared/bored ~** muerto de miedo/aburrimiento

stifling ['staɪflɪŋ] *adj (heat)* sofocante, bochornoso

stigma ['stɪgmə] *n (fig)* estigma *m*

stiletto [stɪ'letəu] *(BRIT)* *n (also*: **~ heel)** tacón *m* de aguja

still [stɪl] *adj* inmóvil, quieto ▷ *adv* todavía; *(even)* aún; *(nonetheless)* sin embargo, aun así

stimulate ['stɪmjuleɪt] *vt* estimular

stimulus ['stɪmjuləs] (*pl* **stimuli**) *n* estímulo, incentivo

sting [stɪŋ] *(pt, pp* **stung**) *n* picadura; *(pain)* escozor *m*, picazón *f*; *(organ)* aguijón *m* ▷ *vt, vi* picar

stink [stɪŋk] *n* hedor *m*, tufo ▷ *vi* heder, apestar

stir [stɜː*] *n (fig: agitation)* conmoción *f* ▷ *vt (tea etc)* remover; *(fig: emotions)* provocar ▷ *vi* moverse; **stir up** *vt (trouble)* fomentar; **stir-fry** *vt* sofreír removiendo ▷ *n* plato preparado sofriendo y removiendo los ingredientes

stitch [stɪtʃ] *n (Sewing)* puntada; *(Knitting)* punto; *(Med)* punto (de sutura); *(pain)* punzada ▷ *vt (Sewing)* coser; *(Med)* suturar

stock [stɔk] *n (Comm: reserves)* existencias *fpl*, stock *m*; *(: selection)* surtido; *(Agr)* ganado, ganadería; *(Culin)* caldo; *(descent)* raza, estirpe *f*; *(Finance)* capital *m* ▷ *adj (fig: reply etc)* clásico ▷ *vt (have in stock)* tener existencias de; **~s and shares** acciones

y valores; **in ~** en existencia or almacén;
out of ~ agotado; **to take ~ of** (fig)
asesorar, examinar; **stockbroker**
['stɔkbrəukə*] n agente mf de corredor
mf de bolsa(a); **stock cube** (BRIT) n
pastilla de caldo; **stock exchange** n
bolsa; **stockholder** ['stɔkhəuldə*] (US)
n accionista m/f

stocking ['stɔkɪŋ] n media
stock market n bolsa (de valores)
stole [stəul] pt of **steal** ▷ n estola
stolen ['stəuln] pp of **steal**
stomach ['stʌmək] n (Anat)
estómago; (belly) vientre m ▷ vt tragar,
aguantar; **stomachache** n dolor m
de estómago
stone [stəun] n piedra; (in fruit) hueso
(= 6.348 kg; 14 libras) ▷ adj de piedra
▷ vt apedrear; (fruit) deshuesar
stood [stud] pt, pp of **stand**
stool [stu:l] n taburete m
stoop [stu:p] vi (also: ~ **down**)
doblarse, agacharse; (also: **have a ~**)
ser cargado de espaldas
stop [stɔp] n parada; (in punctuation)
punto ▷ vt parar, detener; (break)
suspender; (block: pay) suspender;
(: cheque) invalidar; (also: **put a ~
to**) poner término a ▷ vi pararse,
detenerse; (end) acabarse; **to ~ doing
sth** dejar de hacer algo; **stop by** vi
pasar por; **stop off** vi interrumpir
el viaje; **stopover** n parada; (Aviat)
escala; **stoppage** n (strike) paro;
(blockage) obstrucción f
storage ['stɔːrɪdʒ] n almacenaje m
store [stɔː*] n (stock) provisión f;
(depot BRIT: large shop) almacén m; (US)
tienda; (reserve) reserva, repuesto ▷ vt
almacenar; **stores** npl víveres mpl;
to be in ~ for sb (fig) esperarle a algn;
storekeeper (US) n tendero/a
storey ['stɔːrɪ] (US **story**) n piso
storm [stɔːm] n tormenta; (fig: of
applause) salva; (: of criticism) nube f
▷ vi (fig) rabiar ▷ vt tomar por asalto;
stormy adj tempestuoso
story ['stɔːrɪ] n historia; (lie) mentira;

(US) = **storey**

stout [staut] adj (strong) sólido; (fat)
gordo, corpulento; (resolute) resuelto
▷ n cerveza negra
stove [stəuv] n (for cooking) cocina;
(for heating) estufa
straight [streit] adj recto,
derecho; (frank) franco, directo;
(simple) sencillo ▷ adv derecho,
directamente; (drink) sin mezcla; **to
put** or **get sth ~** dejar algo en claro; **~
away**, **~ off** en seguida; **straighten**
vt (also: **straighten out**) enderezar,
poner derecho ▷ vi (also: **straighten
up**) enderezarse, ponerse derecho;
straightforward adj (simple) sencillo;
(honest) honrado, franco
strain [strein] n tensión f; (Tech)
presión f; (Med) tensión; (breed) tipo,
variedad f ▷ vt (back etc) torcerse;
(resources) agotar; (stretch) estirar;
(food, tea) colar; **strained** adj (muscle)
torcido; (laugh) forzado; (relations)
tenso; **strainer** n colador m
strait [streit] n (Geo) estrecho (fig): **to
be in dire ~s** estar en un gran apuro
strand [strænd] n (of thread) hebra;
(of hair) trenza; (of rope) ramal m;
stranded adj (person: without money)
desamparado; (: without transport)
colgado
strange [streindʒ] adj (not known)
desconocido; (odd) extraño, raro;
strangely adv de un modo raro;
stranger n desconocido/a; (from
another area) forastero/a

> ▌ Be careful not to translate **stranger**
> by the Spanish word *extranjero*.

strangle ['stræŋgl] vt estrangular
strap [stræp] n correa; (of slip, dress)
tirante m
strategic [strə'tiːdʒɪk] adj
estratégico
strategy ['strætɪdʒɪ] n estrategia
straw [strɔː] n paja; (drinking straw)
caña, pajita; **that's the last ~!** ¡eso
es el colmo!
strawberry ['strɔːbərɪ] n fresa,

frutilla (SC)

stray [streɪ] adj (animal) extraviado; (bullet) perdido; (scattered) disperso ▷ vi extraviarse, perderse

streak [striːk] n raya; (in hair) raya ▷ vt rayar ▷ vi: **to ~ past** pasar como un rayo

stream [striːm] n riachuelo, arroyo; (of people, vehicles) riada, caravana; (of smoke, insults etc) chorro ▷ vt (Scol) dividir en grupos por habilidad ▷ vi correr, fluir; **to ~ in/out** (people) entrar/salir en tropel

street [striːt] n calle f; **streetcar** n (US) tranvía m; **street light** n farol m (LAM), farola (SP); **street map** n plano (de la ciudad); **street plan** n plano

strength [streŋθ] n fuerza; (of girder, knot etc) resistencia; (fig: power) poder m; **strengthen** vt fortalecer, reforzar

strenuous [ˈstrenjuəs] adj (energetic, determined) enérgico

stress [stres] n presión f; (mental strain) estrés m; (accent) acento ▷ vt subrayar, recalcar; (syllable) acentuar; **stressed** adj (tense) estresado, agobiado; (syllable) acentuado; **stressful** adj (job) estresante

stretch [stretʃ] n (of sand etc) trecho ▷ vi estirarse; (extend): **to ~ to or as far as** extenderse hasta ▷ vt extender, estirar; (make demands) exigir el máximo esfuerzo a; **stretch out** vi tenderse ▷ vt (arm etc) extender; (spread) estirar

stretcher [ˈstretʃə*] n camilla

strict [strɪkt] adj severo; (exact) estricto; **strictly** adv severamente, estrictamente

stride [straɪd] (pt **strode**, pp **stridden**) n zancada, tranco ▷ vi dar zancadas, andar a trancos

strike [straɪk] (pt, pp **struck**) n huelga; (of oil etc) descubrimiento; (attack) ataque m ▷ vt golpear, pegar; (oil etc) descubrir; (bargain, deal) cerrar ▷ vi declarar la huelga; (attack) atacar; (clock) dar la hora; **on ~** (workers)

en huelga; **to ~ a match** encender un fósforo; **striker** n huelguista mf; (Sport) delantero m; **striking** adj llamativo

string [strɪŋ] (pt, pp **strung**) n cuerda; (row) hilera ▷ vt: **to ~ together** ensartar; **to ~ out** extenderse; **the strings** npl (Mus) los instrumentos de cuerda; **to pull ~s** (fig) mover palancas

strip [strɪp] n (of land) franja; (of metal) cinta, lámina ▷ vt desnudar; (paint) quitar; (also: **~ down**: machine) desmontar ▷ vi desnudarse; **strip off** vt (paint etc) quitar ▷ vi (person) desnudarse

stripe [straɪp] n raya; (Mil) galón m; **striped** adj a rayas, rayado

stripper [ˈstrɪpə*] n artista mf de striptease

strip-search [ˈstrɪpsɜːtʃ] vt: **to ~ sb** desnudar y registrar a algn

strive [straɪv] (pt **strove**, pp **striven**) vi: **to ~ for sth/to do sth** luchar por conseguir/hacer algo

strode [strəʊd] pt of **stride**

stroke [strəʊk] n (blow) golpe m; (Swimming) brazada; (Med) apoplejía; (of paintbrush) toque m ▷ vt acariciar; **at a ~** de un solo golpe

stroll [strəʊl] n paseo, vuelta ▷ vi dar un paseo o una vuelta; **stroller** (US) n (for child) sillita de ruedas

strong [strɒŋ] adj fuerte; **they are 50 ~** son 50; **stronghold** n fortaleza; (fig) baluarte m; **strongly** adv fuertemente, con fuerza; (believe) firmemente

strove [strəʊv] pt of **strive**

struck [strʌk] pt, pp of **strike**

structure [ˈstrʌktʃə*] n estructura; (building) construcción f

struggle [ˈstrʌgl] n lucha ▷ vi luchar

strung [strʌŋ] pt, pp of **string**

stub [stʌb] n (of ticket etc) talón m; (of cigarette) colilla; **to ~ one's toe on sth** dar con el dedo (del pie) contra algo; **stub out** vt apagar

stubble [ˈstʌbl] n rastrojo; (on chin)

barba (incipiente)

stubborn ['stʌbən] *adj* terco, testarudo

stuck [stʌk] *pt, pp of* **stick** ▷ *adj* (*jammed*) atascado

stud [stʌd] *n* (*shirt stud*) corchete *m*; (*of boot*) taco; (*earring*) pendiente *m* (de bolita); (*also:* ~ **farm**) caballeriza; (*also:* ~ **horse**) caballo semental ▷ *vt* (*fig*): **-ded with** salpicado de

student ['stju:dənt] *n* estudiante *mf* ▷ *adj* estudiantil; **student driver** (*us*) *n* conductor(a) *m/f* en prácticas; **students' union** *n* (*building*) centro de estudiantes; (*BRIT: association*) federación *f* de estudiantes

studio ['stju:dɪəʊ] *n* estudio; (*artist's*) taller *m*; **studio flat** *n* estudio

study ['stʌdɪ] *n* estudio ▷ *vt* estudiar; (*examine*) examinar, investigar ▷ *vi* estudiar

stuff [stʌf] *n* materia; (*substance*) material *m*, sustancia; (*things*) cosas *fpl* ▷ *vt* llenar; (*Culin*) rellenar; (*animals*) disecar; (*inf: push*) meter; **stuffing** *n* relleno; **stuffy** *adj* (*room*) mal ventilado; (*person*) de miras estrechas

stumble ['stʌmbl] *vi* tropezar, dar un traspié; **to ~ across, ~ on** (*fig*) tropezar con

stump [stʌmp] *n* (*of tree*) tocón *m*; (*of limb*) muñón *m* ▷ *vt*: **to be ~ed for an answer** no saber qué contestar

stun [stʌn] *vt* dejar sin sentido

stung [stʌŋ] *pt, pp of* **sting**

stunk [stʌŋk] *pp of* **stink**

stunned [stʌnd] *adj* (*dazed*) aturdido, atontado; (*amazed*) pasmado; (*shocked*) anonadado

stunning ['stʌnɪŋ] *adj* (*fig: news*) pasmoso; (: *outfit etc*) sensacional

stunt [stʌnt] *n* (*in film*) escena peligrosa; (*publicity stunt*) truco publicitario

stupid ['stju:pɪd] *adj* estúpido, tonto; **stupidity** [-'pɪdɪtɪ] *n* estupidez *f*

sturdy ['stɜ:dɪ] *adj* robusto, fuerte

stutter ['stʌtə*] *n* tartamudeo ▷ *vi*

tartamudear

style [staɪl] *n* estilo; **stylish** *adj* elegante, a la moda; **stylist** *n* (*hair stylist*) peluquero/a

sub... [sʌb] *prefix* sub...;
subconscious *adj* subconsciente

subdued [səb'dju:d] *adj* (*light*) tenue; (*person*) sumiso, manso

subject [n 'sʌbdʒɪkt, vb səb'dʒɛkt] *n* súbdito; (*Scol*) asignatura; (*matter*) tema *m*; (*Grammar*) sujeto ▷ *vt*: **to ~ sb to sth** someter a algn a algo; **to be ~ to** (*law*) estar sujeto a; (*person*) ser propenso a; **subjective** [-'dʒɛktɪv] *adj* subjetivo; **subject matter** *n* (*content*) contenido

subjunctive [səb'dʒʌŋktɪv] *adj*, *n* subjuntivo

submarine [sʌbmə'ri:n] *n* submarino

submission [səb'mɪʃən] *n* sumisión *f*

submit [səb'mɪt] *vt* someter ▷ *vi*: **to ~ to sth** someterse a algo

subordinate [sə'bɔ:dɪnət] *adj*, *n* subordinado/a *m/f*

subscribe [səb'skraɪb] *vi* suscribir; **to ~ to** (*opinion, fund*) suscribir, aprobar; (*newspaper*) suscribirse a

subscription [səb'skrɪpʃən] *n* abono; (*to magazine*) suscripción *f*

subsequent ['sʌbsɪkwənt] *adj* subsiguiente, posterior; **subsequently** *adv* posteriormente, más tarde

subside [səb'saɪd] *vi* hundirse; (*flood*) bajar; (*wind*) amainar

subsidiary [səb'sɪdɪərɪ] *adj* secundario ▷ *n* sucursal *f*, filial *f*

subsidize ['sʌbsɪdaɪz] *vt* subvencionar

subsidy ['sʌbsɪdɪ] *n* subvención *f*

substance ['sʌbstəns] *n* sustancia

substantial [səb'stænʃl] *adj* sustancial, sustancioso; (*fig*) importante

substitute ['sʌbstɪtju:t] *n* (*person*) suplente *mf*; (*thing*) sustituto ▷ *vt*: **to ~ A for B** sustituir A por B, reemplazar B por A; **substitution** *n* sustitución *f*

subtle ['sʌtl] adj sutil

subtract [səb'trækt] vt restar, sustraer

suburb ['sʌbɜːb] n barrio residencial; **the ~s** las afueras (de la ciudad); **suburban** [sə'bɜːbən] adj suburbano; (train etc) de cercanías

subway ['sʌbweɪ] n (BRIT) paso subterráneo or inferior; (US) metro

succeed [sək'siːd] vi (person) tener éxito; (plan) salir bien ▷ vt suceder a; **to ~ in doing** lograr hacer

success [sək'sɛs] n éxito
> Be careful not to translate **success** by the Spanish word *suceso*.

successful adj exitoso; (business) próspero; **to be successful (in doing)** lograr (hacer); **successfully** adv con éxito

succession [sək'sɛʃən] n sucesión f, serie f

successive [sək'sɛsɪv] adj sucesivo

successor [sək'sɛsə*] n sucesor(a) m/f

succumb [sə'kʌm] vi sucumbir

such [sʌtʃ] adj tal, semejante; (of that kind): **~ a book** tal libro; (so much): **~ courage** tanto valor o (of) tan; **a long trip** un viaje tan largo; **~ a lot of** tanto(s)/a(s); **~ as** (like) tal como; **as ~** como tal; **such-and-such** adj tal o cual

suck [sʌk] vt chupar; (bottle) sorber; (breast) mamar

Sudan [su'dæn] n Sudán m

sudden ['sʌdn] adj (rapid) repentino, súbito; (unexpected) imprevisto; **all of a ~** de repente; **suddenly** adv de repente

sudoku [su'dəuku:] sudoku m

sue [su:] vt demandar

suede [sweɪd] n ante m, gamuza

suffer ['sʌfə*] vt sufrir, padecer; (tolerate) aguantar, soportar ▷ vi sufrir; **to ~ from** (illness etc) padecer; **suffering** n sufrimiento

suffice [sə'faɪs] vi bastar, ser suficiente

sufficient [sə'fɪʃnt] adj suficiente, bastante

suffocate ['sʌfəkeɪt] vi ahogarse, asfixiarse

sugar ['ʃugə*] n azúcar m ▷ vt echar azúcar a, azucarar

suggest [sə'dʒɛst] vt sugerir; **suggestion** n [sə'dʒɛstʃən] n sugerencia

suicide ['sʊɪsaɪd] n suicidio; (person) suicida mf; see also **commit**; **suicide attack** n atentado suicida; **suicide bomber** n terrorista mf suicida; **suicide bombing** n atentado suicida

suit [su:t] n (man's) traje m; (woman's) conjunto; (Law) pleito; (Cards) palo ▷ vt convenir; (clothes) sentar a, ir bien a; (adapt): **to ~ sth to** adaptar or ajustar algo a; **well ~ed** (well matched: couple) hecho el uno para el otro; **suitable** adj conveniente; (apt) indicado; **suitcase** n maleta, valija (RPL)

suite [swi:t] n (of rooms, Mus) suite f; (furniture): **bedroom/dining room ~** (juego de) dormitorio/comedor; see also **three-piece suite**

sulfur ['sʌlfə*] (US) n = **sulphur**

sulk [sʌlk] vi estar de mal humor

sulphur ['sʌlfə*] (US **sulfur**) n azufre m

sultana [sʌl'tɑ:nə] n (fruit) pasa de Esmirna

sum [sʌm] n suma; (total) total m; **sum up** vt resumir ▷ vi hacer un resumen

summarize ['sʌməraɪz] vt resumir

summary ['sʌmərɪ] n resumen m ▷ adj (justice) sumario

summer ['sʌmə*] n verano ▷ cpd de verano; **in ~** en verano; **summer holidays** npl vacaciones fpl de verano; **summertime** n (season) verano

summit ['sʌmɪt] n cima, cumbre f; (also: **~ conference, ~ meeting**) (conferencia) cumbre f

summon ['sʌmən] vt (person) llamar; (meeting) convocar; (Law) citar

Sun. abbr (= Sunday) dom

sun [sʌn] n sol m; **sunbathe** vi tomar el sol; **sunbed** n cama solar;

sunblock n filtro solar; sunburn n (painful) quemadura; (tan) bronceado; sunburned, sunburnt adj (painfully) quemado por el sol; (tanned) bronceado

Sunday ['sʌndɪ] n domingo

sunflower ['sʌnflaʊə*] n girasol m

sung [sʌŋ] pp of sing

sunglasses ['sʌnglɑːsɪz] npl gafas fpl (sp) or anteojos fpl (lam) de sol

sunk [sʌŋk] pp of sink

sun: sunlight n luz f del sol; sun lounger n tumbona, perezosa (lam); sunny adj soleado; (day) de sol; (fig) alegre; sunrise n salida del sol; sun roof n (Aut) techo corredizo; sunscreen n protector m solar; sunset n puesta del sol; sunshade n (over table) sombrilla; sunshine n sol m; sunstroke n insolación f; suntan n bronceado; suntan lotion n bronceador m; suntan oil n aceite m bronceador

super ['suːpə*] (inf) adj genial

superb [suː'pɜːb] adj magnífico, espléndido

superficial [suːpə'fɪʃəl] adj superficial

superintendent [suːpərɪn'tɛndənt] n director(a) m/f; (Police) subjefe/a m/f

superior [suː'pɪərɪə*] adj superior; (smug) desdeñoso ▷ n superior m

superlative [suː'pɜːlətɪv] n superlativo

supermarket ['suːpəmɑːkɪt] n supermercado

supernatural [suːpə'nætʃərəl] adj sobrenatural ▷ n: the ~ lo sobrenatural

superpower ['suːpəpaʊə*] n (Pol) superpotencia

superstition [suːpə'stɪʃən] n superstición f

superstitious [suːpə'stɪʃəs] adj supersticioso

superstore ['suːpəstɔː*] n (brit) hipermercado

supervise ['suːpəvaɪz] vt supervisar; supervision [-'vɪʒən] n supervisión f; supervisor n supervisor(a) m/f

supper ['sʌpə*] n cena

supple ['sʌpl] adj flexible

supplement [n 'sʌplɪmənt, vb sʌplɪ'mɛnt] n suplemento ▷ vt suplir

supplier [sə'plaɪə*] n (Comm) distribuidor(a) m/f

supply [sə'plaɪ] vt (provide) suministrar; (equip): to ~ (with) proveer (de) ▷ n provisión f; (of gas, water etc) suministro; supplies npl (food) víveres mpl; (Mil) pertrechos mpl

support [sə'pɔːt] n apoyo; (Tech) soporte m ▷ vt apoyar; (financially) mantener; (uphold, Tech) sostener

▌ Be careful not to translate support by the Spanish word soportar.

supporter n (Pol etc) partidario/a; (Sport) aficionado/a

suppose [sə'pəʊz] vt suponer; (imagine) imaginarse; (duty): to be ~d to do sth deber hacer algo; supposedly [sə'pəʊzɪdlɪ] adv según cabe suponer; supposing conj en caso de que

suppress [sə'prɛs] vt suprimir; (yawn) ahogar

supreme [suː'priːm] adj supremo

surcharge ['sɜːtʃɑːdʒ] n sobretasa, recargo

sure [ʃʊə*] adj seguro; (definite, convinced) cierto; to make ~ of sth/that asegurarse de algo/asegurar que; ~! (of course) ¡claro!, ¡por supuesto!; ~ enough efectivamente; surely adv (certainly) seguramente

surf [sɜːf] n olas fpl ▷ vt: to ~ the Net navegar por Internet

surface ['sɜːfɪs] n superficie f ▷ vt (road) revestir ▷ vi salir a la superficie; by ~ mail por vía terrestre

surfboard ['sɜːfbɔːd] n tabla (de surf)

surfer ['sɜːfə*] n (in sea) surfista mf; web or net ~ internauta mf

surfing ['sɜːfɪŋ] n surf m

surge [sɜːdʒ] n oleada, oleaje m ▷ vi (wave) romper; (people) avanzar en tropel

surgeon ['sɜːdʒən] n cirujano/a

surgery ['sɜːdʒərɪ] n cirugía; (BRIT: room) consultorio

surname ['sɜːneɪm] n apellido

surpass [sɜːˈpɑːs] vt superar, exceder

surplus ['sɜːpləs] n excedente m; (Comm) superávit m ▷ adj excedente, sobrante

surprise [səˈpraɪz] n sorpresa ▷ vt sorprender; **surprised** adj (look, smile) de sorpresa; **to be surprised** sorprenderse; **surprising** adj sorprendente; **surprisingly** adv: **it was surprisingly easy** me etc sorprendió lo fácil que fue

surrender [səˈrendə*] n rendición f, entrega ▷ vi rendirse, entregarse

surround [səˈraund] vt rodear, circundar; (Mil etc) cercar; **surrounding** adj circundante; **surroundings** npl alrededores mpl, cercanías fpl

surveillance [sɜːˈveɪləns] n vigilancia

survey [n ˈsɜːveɪ, vb sɜːˈveɪ] n inspección f, reconocimiento f; (inquiry) encuesta ▷ vt examinar, inspeccionar; (look at) mirar, contemplar; **surveyor** n agrimensor(a) m/f

survival [səˈvaɪvl] n supervivencia

survive [səˈvaɪv] vi sobrevivir; (custom etc) perdurar ▷ vt sobrevivir a; **survivor** n superviviente mf

suspect [adj, n ˈsʌspekt, vb səsˈpekt] adj, n sospechoso a m/f ▷ vt (person) sospechar de; (think) sospechar

suspend [səsˈpend] vt suspender; **suspended sentence** n (Law) libertad f condicional; **suspenders** npl (BRIT) ligas fpl; (us) tirantes mpl

suspense [səsˈpens] n incertidumbre f, duda; (in film etc) suspense m; **to keep sb in ~** mantener a algn en suspense

suspension [səsˈpenʃən] n (gen, Aut) suspensión f; (of driving licence) privación f; **suspension bridge** n puente m colgante

suspicion [səsˈpɪʃən] n sospecha; (distrust) recelo m; **suspicious** adj

receloso; (causing suspicion) sospechoso

sustain [səsˈteɪn] vt sostener, apoyar; (suffer) sufrir, padecer

SUV (esp us) n abbr (= sports utility vehicle) todoterreno m inv, 4x4 m

swallow [ˈswɔləu] n (bird) golondrina ▷ vt tragar; (fig.: pride) tragarse

swam [swæm] pt of **swim**

swamp [swɔmp] n pantano, ciénaga ▷ vt (with water etc) inundar; (fig) abrumar, agobiar

swan [swɔn] n cisne m

swap [swɔp] n canje m, intercambio ▷ vt: **to ~ (for)** cambiar (por)

swarm [swɔːm] n (of bees) enjambre m; (fig) multitud f ▷ vi (bees) formar un enjambre; (people) pulular; **to be ~ing with** ser un hervidero de

sway [sweɪ] vi mecerse, balancearse ▷ vt (influence) mover, influir en

swear [sweə*] (pt **swore**, pp **sworn**) vi (curse) maldecir; (promise) jurar ▷ vt jurar; **swear in** vt: **to be sworn in** prestar juramento; **swearword** n taco, palabrota

sweat [swet] n sudor m ▷ vi sudar

sweater [ˈswetə*] n suéter m

sweatshirt [ˈswetʃəːt] n suéter m

sweaty [ˈswetɪ] adj sudoroso

Swede [swiːd] n sueco/a

swede [swiːd] (BRIT) n nabo

Sweden [ˈswiːdn] n Suecia; **Swedish** [ˈswiːdɪʃ] adj sueco ▷ n (Ling) sueco

sweep [swiːp] (pt, pp **swept**) n (act) barrido; (also: **chimney ~**) deshollinador(a) m/f ▷ vt barrer; (with arm) empujar; (current) arrastrar ▷ vi barrer; (arm etc) moverse rápidamente; (wind) soplar con violencia

sweet [swiːt] n (candy) dulce m, caramelo; (BRIT: pudding) postre m ▷ adj dulce; (fig: kind) dulce, amable; (: attractive) mono; **sweetcorn** n maíz m; **sweetener** [ˈswiːtnə*] n (Culin) edulcorante m; **sweetheart** n novio/a; **sweetshop** n (BRIT) confitería, bombonería

swell [swel] (pt **~ed**, pp **swollen** or **~ed**)

n (of sea) marejada, oleaje *m* ▷ *adj (US: inf: excellent)* estupendo, fenomenal ▷ *vt* hinchar, inflar ▷ *vi (also:* **~ up**) hincharse; *(numbers)* aumentar; *(sound, feeling)* ir aumentando; **swelling** *n (Med)* hinchazón *f*

swept [swɛpt] *pt, pp of* **sweep**

swerve [swəːv] *vi* desviarse bruscamente

swift [swɪft] *n (bird)* vencejo ▷ *adj* rápido, veloz

swim [swɪm] *(pt* **swam**, *pp* **swum**) *n:* **to go for a ~** ir a nadar o a bañarse ▷ *vi* nadar; *(head, room)* dar vueltas ▷ *vt* nadar; *(the Channel etc)* cruzar a nado; **swimmer** *n* nadador(a) *m/f*; **swimming** *n* natación *f*; **swimming costume** (*BRIT*) *n* bañador *m*, traje *m* de baño; **swimming pool** *n* piscina, alberca (*MEX*), pileta (*RPL*); **swimming trunks** *npl* bañador *m* (de hombre); **swimsuit** *n* = **swimming costume**

swing [swɪŋ] *(pt, pp* **swung**) *n (in playground)* columpio; *(movement)* balanceo, vaivén *m*; *(change of direction)* viraje *m*; *(rhythm)* ritmo ▷ *vt* balancear; *(also:* **~ round**) voltear, girar ▷ *vi* balancearse, columpiarse; *(also:* **~ round**) dar media vuelta; **to be in full ~** estar en plena marcha

swipe card [swaɪp-] *n* tarjeta magnética deslizante, tarjeta swipe

swirl [swəːl] *vi* arremolinarse

Swiss [swɪs] *adj, n inv* suizo/a *m/f*

switch [swɪtʃ] *n (for light etc)* interruptor *m*; *(change)* cambio ▷ *vt (change)* cambiar de; **switch off** *vt* apagar; *(engine)* parar; **switch on** *vt* encender (*SP*), prender (*LAM*); *(engine, machine)* arrancar; **switchboard** *n (Tel)* centralita (*SP*), conmutador *m* (*LAM*)

Switzerland [ˈswɪtsələnd] *n* Suiza

swivel [ˈswɪvl] *vi (also:* **~ round**) girar

swollen [ˈswəʊlən] *pp of* **swell**

swoop [swuːp] *n (by police etc)* redada ▷ *vi (also:* **~ down**) calarse

swop [swɒp] *n* = **swap**

sword [sɔːd] *n* espada; **swordfish** *n*

pez *m* espada

swore [swɔːʳ] *pt of* **swear**

sworn [swɔːn] *pp of* **swear** ▷ *adj (statement)* bajo juramento; *(enemy)* implacable

swum [swʌm] *pp of* **swim**

swung [swʌŋ] *pt, pp of* **swing**

syllable [ˈsɪləbl] *n* sílaba

syllabus [ˈsɪləbəs] *n* programa *m* de estudios

symbol [ˈsɪmbl] *n* símbolo; **symbolic(al)** [sɪmˈbɒlɪk(l)] *adj* simbólico; **to be symbolic(al) of sth** simbolizar algo

symmetrical [sɪˈmetrɪkl] *adj* simétrico

symmetry [ˈsɪmɪtrɪ] *n* simetría

sympathetic [sɪmpəˈθetɪk] *adj (understanding)* comprensivo; *(showing support):* **~ to(wards)** bien dispuesto hacia

> Be careful not to translate **sympathetic** by the Spanish word *simpático*.

sympathize [ˈsɪmpəθaɪz] *vi:* **to ~ with** *(person)* compadecerse de; *(feelings)* comprender; *(cause)* apoyar

sympathy [ˈsɪmpəθɪ] *n (pity)* compasión *f*

symphony [ˈsɪmfənɪ] *n* sinfonía

symptom [ˈsɪmptəm] *n* síntoma *m*, indicio

synagogue [ˈsɪnəgɒg] *n* sinagoga

syndicate [ˈsɪndɪkɪt] *n* sindicato; *(of newspapers)* agencia (de noticias)

syndrome [ˈsɪndrəʊm] *n* síndrome *m*

synonym [ˈsɪnənɪm] *n* sinónimo

synthetic [sɪnˈθetɪk] *adj* sintético

Syria [ˈsɪrɪə] *n* Siria

syringe [sɪˈrɪndʒ] *n* jeringa

syrup [ˈsɪrəp] *n* jarabe *m*; *(also:* **golden ~**) almíbar *m*

system [ˈsɪstəm] *n* sistema *m*; *(Anat)* organismo; **systematic** [-ˈmætɪk] *adj* sistemático, metódico; **systems analyst** *n* analista *mf* de sistemas

t

ta [tɑː] (BRIT: inf) excl ¡gracias!
tab [tæb] n lengüeta; (label) etiqueta; **to keep ~s on** (fig) vigilar
table ['teɪbl] n mesa; (of statistics etc) cuadro, tabla ▷ vt (BRIT: motion etc) presentar; **to lay** o **set the ~** poner la mesa; **tablecloth** n mantel m; **table d'hôte** [tɑːbl'dəut] adj del menú; **table lamp** n lámpara de mesa; **tablemat** n (for plate) posaplatos m inv; (for hot dish) salvamantel m; **tablespoon** n cuchara de servir; (also: **tablespoonful**: as measurement) cucharada
tablet ['tæblɪt] n (Med) pastilla, comprimido; (of stone) lápida
table tennis n ping-pong m, tenis m de mesa
tabloid ['tæbloɪd] n periódico popular sensacionalista

TABLOID PRESS

El término **tabloid press** o **tabloids** se usa para referirse a la prensa popular británica, por el tamaño más pequeño de los periódicos. A diferencia de los de la llamada **quality press**, estas publicaciones se caracterizan por un lenguaje sencillo, una presentación llamativa y un contenido sensacionalista, centrado a veces en los escándalos financieros y sexuales de los famosos, por lo que también reciben el nombre peyorativo de "gutter press".

taboo [tə'buː] adj, n tabú m
tack [tæk] n (nail) tachuela; (fig) rumbo ▷ vt (nail) clavar con tachuelas; (stitch) hilvanar ▷ vi virar
tackle ['tækl] n (fishing tackle) aparejo (de pescar); (for lifting) aparejo ▷ vt (difficulty) enfrentarse con; (challenge: person) hacer frente a; (grapple with) agarrar; (Football) cargar; (Rugby) placar
tacky ['tækɪ] adj pegajoso; (pej) cutre
tact [tækt] n tacto, discreción f;
tactful adj discreto, diplomático
tactics ['tæktɪks] npl táctica
tactless ['tæktlɪs] adj indiscreto
tadpole ['tædpəul] n renacuajo
taffy ['tæfɪ] (us) n melcocha
tag [tæg] n (label) etiqueta
tail [teɪl] n cola; (of shirt, coat) faldón m ▷ vt (follow) vigilar a; **tails** npl (formal suit) levita
tailor ['teɪlə*] n sastre m
Taiwan [taɪwɑːn] n Taiwán m; **Taiwanese** [taɪwəniːz] adj, n taiwanés/esa m/f
take [teɪk] (pt **took**, pp **taken**) vt tomar; (grab) agarrar (LAM); (gain: prize) ganar; (require: effort, courage) exigir; (tolerate: pain etc) aguantar; (hold: passengers etc) tener cabida para; (accompany, bring, carry) llevar; (exam) aprobar; **to ~ sth from** (drawer etc) sacar algo de; (person) quitar algo a; **I ~ it that ...** supongo

t

que ...; **take after** vt fus parecerse a; **take apart** vt desmontar; **take away** vt (remove) quitar; (carry) llevar; (Math) restar; **take back** vt (return) devolver; (one's words) retractarse de; **take down** vt (building) derribar; (note) apuntar; **take in** vt (deceive) engañar; (understand) entender; (include) abarcar; (lodger) acoger, recibir; **take off** vi (Aviat) despegar ▷ vt (remove) quitar; **take on** vt (work) aceptar; (employee) contratar; (opponent) desafiar; **take out** vt sacar; **take over** vt (business) tomar posesión de; (country) tomar el poder ▷ vi: **to take over from sb** reemplazar a algn; **take up** vt (a dress) acortar; (occupy: time, space) ocupar; (engage in: hobby etc) dedicarse a; (accept): **to take sb up on** aceptar algo de algn; **takeaway** (BRIT) adj (food) para llevar ▷ n tienda o restaurante m de comida para llevar; **taken** pp of **take**; **takeoff** n (Aviat) despegue m; **takeout** (US) n = **takeaway**; **takeover** n (Comm) absorción f; **takings** npl (Comm) ingresos mpl

talc [tælk] n (also: **~um powder**) (polvos de) talco

tale [teɪl] n (story) cuento; (account) relación f; **to tell ~s** (fig) chivarse

talent ['tælnt] n talento; **talented** adj de talento

talk [tɔːk] n charla; (conversation) conversación f; (gossip) habladurías fpl, chismes mpl ▷ vi hablar; **talks** npl (Pol etc) conversaciones fpl; **to ~ about** hablar de; **to ~ sb into doing sth** convencer a algn para que haga algo; **to ~ sb out of doing sth** disuadir a algn de que haga algo; **to ~ shop** hablar del trabajo; **talk over** vt discutir; **talk show** n programa m de entrevistas

tall [tɔːl] adj (person) alto; (object) grande; **to be 6 feet ~** (person) = medir 1 metro 80

tambourine [tæmbə'riːn] n pandereta

tame [teɪm] adj domesticado; (fig) mediocre

tamper ['tæmpə*] vi: **to ~ with** tocar, andar con

tampon ['tæmpən] n tampón m

tan [tæn] n (also: **sun~**) bronceado ▷ vi ponerse moreno ▷ adj (colour) marrón

tandem ['tændəm] n tándem m

tangerine [tændʒə'riːn] n mandarina

tangle ['tæŋgl] n enredo; **to get in(to) a ~** enredarse

tank [tæŋk] n (water tank) depósito, tanque m; (for fish) acuario; (Mil) tanque m

tanker ['tæŋkə*] n (ship) buque m, cisterna; (truck) camión m cisterna

tanned [tænd] adj (skin) moreno

tantrum ['tæntrəm] n rabieta

Tanzania [tænzə'niːə] n Tanzania

tap [tæp] n (BRIT: on sink etc) grifo (SP), llave f, canilla (RPL); (gas tap) llave f; (gentle blow) golpecito ▷ vt (hit gently) dar golpecitos en; (resources) utilizar, explotar; (telephone) intervenir; **on ~** (fig: resources) a mano; **tap dancing** n claqué m

tape [teɪp] n (also: **magnetic ~**) cinta magnética; (cassette) cassette f, cinta; (sticky tape) cinta adhesiva; (for tying) cinta ▷ vt (record) grabar (en cinta); (stick with tape) pegar con cinta adhesiva; **tape measure** n cinta métrica, metro; **tape recorder** n grabadora

tapestry ['tæpɪstrɪ] n (object) tapiz m; (art) tapicería

tar [tɑː] n alquitrán m, brea

target ['tɑːgɪt] n blanco

tariff ['tærɪf] n (on goods) arancel m; (BRIT: in hotels etc) tarifa

tarmac ['tɑːmæk] n (BRIT: on road) asfaltado; (Aviat) pista de aterrizaje)

tarpaulin [tɑː'pɔːlɪn] n lona impermeabilizada

tarragon ['tærəgən] n estragón m

tart [tɑːt] n (Culin) tarta; (BRIT: inf: prostitute) puta ▷ adj agrio, ácido

tartan ['tɑːtn] n tejido escocés m

tartar(e) sauce ['tɑːtə-] n salsa tártara

task [tɑːsk] n tarea; **to take to ~** reprender

taste [teɪst] n (sense) gusto; (flavour) sabor m; (sample): **have a ~!** prueba un poquito!; (fig) muestra, idea ▷vt probar ▷vi: **to ~ of** or **like** (fish, garlic etc) saber a; **you can ~ the garlic (in it)** se nota el sabor a ajo; **in good/bad ~** de buen/mal gusto; **tasteful** adj de buen gusto; **tasteless** adj (food) soso; (remark etc) de mal gusto; **tasty** adj sabroso, rico

tatters ['tætəz] npl: **in ~** hecho jirones

tattoo [tə'tuː] n tatuaje m; (spectacle) espectáculo militar ▷vt tatuar

taught [tɔːt] pt, pp of **teach**

taunt [tɔːnt] n burla ▷vt burlarse de

Taurus ['tɔːrəs] n Tauro

taut [tɔːt] adj tirante, tenso

tax [tæks] n impuesto ▷vt gravar (con un impuesto); (fig: memory) poner a prueba; (: patience) agotar; **tax-free** adj libre de impuestos

taxi ['tæksɪ] n taxi m ▷vi (Aviat) rodar por la pista; **taxi driver** n taxista mf; **taxi rank** (BRIT) n = **taxi stand**; **taxi stand** n parada de taxis

tax payer n contribuyente mf

TB n abbr = **tuberculosis**

tea [tiː] n té m; (BRIT: meal) = merienda (SP); cena; **high ~** (BRIT) merienda-cena (SP); **tea bag** n bolsita de té; **tea break** (BRIT) n descanso para el té

teach [tiːtʃ] (pt, pp **taught**) vt: **to ~ sb sth**, **~ sth to sb** enseñar algo a algn ▷vi (be a teacher) ser profesor(a), enseñar; **teacher** n (in secondary school) profesor(a) m/f; (in primary school) maestro/a, profesor(a) de EGB; **teaching** n enseñanza

tea: tea cloth n (BRIT) paño de cocina, trapo de cocina (LAM); **teacup** n taza para el té

tea leaves npl hojas de té

team [tiːm] n equipo; (of horses) tiro;

team up vi asociarse

teapot ['tiːpɒt] n tetera

tear[1] [tɪə*] n lágrima; **in ~s** llorando

tear[2] [tɛə*] (pt **tore**, pp **torn**) n rasgón m, desgarrón m ▷vt romper, rasgar ▷vi rasgarse; **tear apart** vt (also fig) hacer pedazos; **tear down** vt +adv (building, statue) derribar; (poster, flag) arrancar; **tear off** vt (sheet of paper etc) arrancar; (one's clothes) quitarse a tirones; **tear up** vt (sheet of paper etc) romper

tearful ['tɪəfəl] adj lloroso

tear gas ['tɪə-] n gas m lacrimógeno

tearoom ['tiːruːm] n salón m de té

tease [tiːz] vt tomar el pelo a

tea: teaspoon n cucharita; (also: **teaspoonful**: as measurement) cucharadita; **teatime** n hora del té; **tea towel** (BRIT) n paño de cocina

technical ['tɛknɪk] adj técnico

technician [tɛk'nɪʃn] n técnico/a

technique [tɛk'niːk] n técnica

technology [tɛk'nɒlədʒɪ] n tecnología

teddy (bear) ['tɛdɪ-] n osito de felpa

tedious ['tiːdɪəs] adj pesado, aburrido

tee [tiː] n (Golf) tee m

teen [tiːn] adj = **teenage** ▷n (US) = **teenager**

teenage ['tiːneɪdʒ] adj (fashions etc) juvenil; (children) quinceañero; **teenager** n adolescente mf

teens [tiːnz] npl: **to be in one's ~** ser adolescente

tee-shirt ['tiːʃɜːt] npl of **tooth**

teetotal ['tiː'təʊtl] adj abstemio

telecommunications [tɛlɪkəmjuː-nɪ'keɪʃənz] n telecomunicaciones fpl

telegram ['tɛlɪgræm] n telegrama m

telegraph pole ['tɛlɪgrɑːf-] n poste m telegráfico

telephone ['tɛlɪfəʊn] n teléfono ▷vt llamar por teléfono, telefonear; (message) dar por teléfono; **to be on the ~** (talking) hablar por teléfono; (possessing telephone) tener teléfono;

telephone book n guía f telefónica; **telephone booth, telephone box** (BRIT) n cabina telefónica; **telephone call** n llamada (telefónica); **telephone directory** n guía (telefónica); **telephone number** n número de teléfono

telesales ['tɛlɪseɪlz] npl televenta(s) (f(pl)

telescope ['tɛlɪskəup] n telescopio

televise ['tɛlɪvaɪz] vt televisar

television ['tɛlɪvɪʒən] n televisión f; **on ~** en la televisión; **television programme** n programa m de televisión

tell [tɛl] (pt, pp **told**) vt decir; (relate: story) contar; (distinguish): to ~ **sth from** distinguir algo de ▷ vi (talk): to ~ (of) contar; (have effect) tener efecto; to ~ **sb to do sth** mandar a algn hacer algo; **tell off** vt: to **tell sb off** regañar a algn; **teller** n (in bank) cajero/a

telly ['tɛlɪ] (BRIT: inf) n abbr (= television) tele f

temp [tɛmp] n abbr (BRIT: inf) n abbr (= temporary) temporero/a

temper ['tɛmpə*] n (nature) carácter m; (mood) humor m; (bad temper) (mal) genio; (fit of anger) acceso de ira ▷ vt (moderate) moderar; to **be in a ~** estar furioso; to **lose one's ~** enfadarse, enojarse

temperament ['tɛmprəmənt] n (nature) temperamento; **temperamental** [tɛmprə'mɛntl] adj temperamental

temperature ['tɛmprətʃə*] n temperatura; to **have** or **run a ~** tener fiebre

temple ['tɛmpl] n (building) templo; (Anat) sien f

temporary ['tɛmpərərɪ] adj provisional; (passing) transitorio; (worker) temporero; (job) temporal

tempt [tɛmpt] vt tentar; to ~ **sb into doing sth** tentar o inducir a algn a hacer algo; **temptation** n tentación

f; **tempting** adj tentador(a); (food) apetitoso/a

ten [tɛn] num diez

tenant ['tɛnənt] n inquilino/a

tend [tɛnd] vt cuidar ▷ vi: to ~ **to do sth** tener tendencia a hacer algo; **tendency** ['tɛndənsɪ] n tendencia

tender ['tɛndə*] adj (person, care) tierno, cariñoso; (meat) tierno; (sore) sensible ▷ n (Comm: offer) oferta; (money): **legal ~** moneda de curso legal ▷ vt ofrecer

tendon ['tɛndən] n tendón m

tenner ['tɛnə*] n (inf) (billete m de) diez libras m

tennis ['tɛnɪs] n tenis m; **tennis ball** n pelota de tenis; **tennis court** n cancha de tenis; **tennis match** n partido de tenis; **tennis player** n tenista mf; **tennis racket** n raqueta de tenis

tenor ['tɛnə*] n (Mus) tenor m

tenpin bowling ['tɛnpɪn-] n (juego de los) bolos

tense [tɛns] adj (person) nervioso; (moment, atmosphere) tenso; (muscle) tenso, en tensión ▷ n (Ling) tiempo

tension ['tɛnʃən] n tensión f

tent [tɛnt] n tienda (de campaña) (SP), carpa (LAM)

tentative ['tɛntətɪv] adj (person, smile) indeciso; (conclusion, plans) provisional

tenth [tɛnθ] num décimo

tent: tent peg n clavija, estaca; **tent pole** n mástil m

tepid ['tɛpɪd] adj tibio

term [tə:m] n (word) término; (period) período; (Scol) trimestre m ▷ vt llamar; **terms** npl (conditions, Comm) condiciones fpl; **in the short/long ~** a corto/largo plazo; **to be on good ~s with sb** llevarse bien con algn; to **come to ~s with** (problem) aceptar

terminal ['tə:mɪnl] adj (disease) mortal; (patient) terminal ▷ n (Elec) borne m; (Comput) terminal m; (also: **air ~**) terminal f; (BRIT: also: **coach ~**)

estación f terminal f

terminate ['tɜːmɪneɪt] vt terminar

termini ['tɜːmɪnaɪ] npl of **terminus**

terminology [tɜːmɪ'nɒlədʒɪ] n terminología

terminus ['tɜːmɪnəs] (pl **termini**) n término, (estación f) terminal f

terrace ['terəs] n terraza; (BRIT: row of houses) hilera de casas adosadas; **the ~s** (BRIT Sport) las gradas fpl; **terraced** adj (garden) en terrazas; (house) adosado

terrain [tɛ'reɪn] n terreno

terrestrial [tɪ'restrɪəl] adj (life) terrestre; (BRIT: channel) de transmisión (por) vía terrestre

terrible ['terɪbl] adj terrible, horrible; (inf) atroz; **terribly** adv terriblemente; (very badly) malísimamente

terrier ['terɪə*] n terrier m

terrific [tə'rɪfɪk] adj (very great) tremendo; (wonderful) fantástico, fenomenal

terrified ['terɪfaɪd] adj aterrorizado

terrify ['terɪfaɪ] vt aterrorizar; **terrifying** adj aterrador(a)

territorial [terɪ'tɔːrɪəl] adj territorial

territory ['terɪtərɪ] n territorio

terror ['terə*] n terror m; **terrorism** n terrorismo; **terrorist** n terrorista mf; **terrorist attack** n atentado (terrorista)

test [test] n (gen, Chem) prueba; (Med) examen m; (Scol) examen m, test m; (also: **driving ~**) examen m de conducir ▷ vt probar, poner a prueba; (Med, Scol) examinar

testicle ['testɪkl] n testículo

testify ['testɪfaɪ] vi (Law) prestar declaración; **to ~ to sth** atestiguar algo

testimony ['testɪmənɪ] n (Law) testimonio

test: test match n (Cricket, Rugby) partido internacional; **test tube** n probeta

tetanus ['tetənəs] n tétano

text [tekst] n texto; (on mobile phone)

mensaje m (de texto); **to ~ sb** vt enviar un mensaje (de texto) or un SMS a algn; **textbook** n libro de texto

textile ['tekstaɪl] n textil m, tejido

text message n mensaje m de texto

text messaging [-'mesɪdʒɪŋ] n (envío de) mensajes mpl de texto

texture ['tekstʃə*] n textura

Thai [taɪ] adj, n tailandés/esa m/f

Thailand ['taɪlænd] n Tailandia

than [ðæn] conj (in comparisons): **more ~ 10/once** más de 10/una vez; **I have more/less ~ you/Paul** tengo más/menos que tú/Paul; **she is older ~ you think** es mayor de lo que piensas

thank [θæŋk] vt dar las gracias a, agradecer; **~ you (very much)** muchas gracias; **~ God!** ¡gracias a Dios! ▷ excl (also: **many ~s, ~ a lot**) ¡gracias! ▷ **~s to** prep gracias a; **thanks** npl gracias fpl; **thankfully** adv (fortunately) afortunadamente; **Thanksgiving (Day)** n día m de Acción de Gracias

○ **THANKSGIVING (DAY)**

En Estados Unidos el cuarto jueves de noviembre es **Thanksgiving Day**, fiesta oficial en la que se recuerda la celebración que hicieron los primeros colonos norteamericanos ("Pilgrims" o "Pilgrim Fathers") tras la estupenda cosecha de 1621, por la que se dan gracias a Dios. En Canadá se celebra una fiesta semejante el segundo lunes de octubre, aunque no está relacionada con dicha fecha histórica.

○ **KEYWORD**

that [ðæt] (pl **those**) adj (demonstrative) ese/a; (pl) esos/as; (more remote) aquel(aquella); (pl) aquellos/as; **leave those books on the table** deja esos libros sobre la mesa; **that one** ése(ésa); (more remote) aquél(aquélla); **that one over there** ése(ésa) de ahí; aquél(aquélla) de allí

▷ pron **1** (demonstrative) ése/a; (pl) ésos/as; (neuter) eso; (more remote) aquél(aquélla); (pl) aquéllos/as; (neuter) aquello; **what's that?** ¿qué es eso (or aquello)?; **who's that?** ¿quién es ése/a (or aquél (aquélla))?; **is that you?** ¿eres tú?; **will you eat all that?** ¿vas a comer todo eso?; **that's my house** ésa es mi casa; **that's what he said** eso es lo que dijo; **that is (to say)** es decir

2 (relative: subject, object) que; (with preposition) (el (la)) que etc, el(la) cual etc; **the book (that) I read** el libro que leí; **the books that are in the library** los libros que están en la biblioteca; **all (that) I have** todo lo que tengo; **the box (that) I put it in** la caja en la que or donde lo puse; **the people (that) I spoke to** la gente con la que hablé

3 (relative: of time) que; **the day (that) he came** el día (en) que vino

▷ conj que; **he thought that I was ill** creyó que yo estaba enfermo

▷ adv (demonstrative): **I can't work that much** no puedo trabajar tanto; **I didn't realise it was that bad** no creí que fuera tan malo; **that high** así de alto

thatched [θætʃt] adj (roof) de paja; (cottage) con tejado de paja

thaw [θɔː] n deshielo ▷ vi (ice) derretirse; (food) descongelarse ▷ vt (food) descongelar

○ KEYWORD

the [ðiː, ðə] def art **1** (gen) el f, la pl, los fpl, las (NB 'el' immediately before f n beginning with stressed (h)a; a+ el =al; de + el = del); **the boy/girl** el chico/la chica; **the books/flowers** los libros/las flores; **to the postman/from the drawer** al cartero/del cajón; **I haven't the time/money** no tengo

tiempo/dinero

2 (+adj to form n) los; lo; **the rich and the poor** los ricos y los pobres; **to attempt the impossible** intentar lo imposible

3 (in titles): **Elizabeth the First** Isabel primera; **Peter the Great** Pedro el Grande

4 (in comparisons): **the more he works the more he earns** cuanto más trabaja más gana

theatre ['θɪətə*] (US **theater**) n teatro; (also: **lecture ~**) aula; (Med: also: **operating ~**) quirófano

theft [θɛft] n robo

their [ðɛə*] adj su; **theirs** pron (el) suyo/(la) suya etc); see also **my; mine¹**

them [ðɛm, ðəm] pron (direct) los/las; (indirect) les; (stressed, after prep) ellos(ellas); see also **me**

theme [θiːm] n tema m; **theme park** n parque de atracciones (en torno a un tema central)

themselves [ðəmˈsɛlvz] pl pron (subject) ellos mismos(ellas mismas); (complement) se; (after prep) sí (mismos(as)); see also **oneself**

then [ðɛn] adv (at that time) entonces; (next) después; (later) luego, después; (and also) además ▷ conj (therefore) en ese caso, entonces ▷ adj: **the ~ president** el entonces presidente; **by ~** para entonces; **from ~ on** desde entonces

theology [θɪˈɒlədʒɪ] n teología

theory ['θɪərɪ] n teoría

therapist ['θɛrəpɪst] n terapeuta mf

therapy ['θɛrəpɪ] n terapia

○ KEYWORD

there [ðɛə*] adv **1 there is, there are** hay; **there is no-one here/no bread left** no hay nadie aquí/no queda pan; **there has been an accident** ha habido un accidente

2 (referring to place) ahí; (distant) allí; **it's**

there está ahí; **put it in/on/up/down there** ponlo ahí dentro/encima/arriba/abajo; **I want that book there** quiero ese libro de ahí; **there he is!** ¡ahí está!

3 there, there (*esp to child*) ea, ea

there: thereabouts *adv* por ahí; **thereafter** *adv* después; **thereby** *adv* así, de ese modo; **therefore** *adv* por tanto; **there's = there is; there has**

thermal [ˈθəːml] *adj* termal; (*paper*) térmico

thermometer [θəˈmɒmɪtə*] *n* termómetro

thermostat [ˈθəːməustæt] *n* termostato

these [ðiːz] *pl adj* estos/as ▷ *pl pron* éstos/as

thesis [ˈθiːsɪs] (*pl* **theses**) *n* tesis *f inv*

they [ðeɪ] *pl pron* ellos(ellas); (*stressed*) ellos (mismos)(ellas (mismas)); ~ **say that ...** (*it is said that*) se dice que ...; **they'd = they had; they would; they'll = they shall; they will; they're = they are; they've = they have**

thick [θɪk] *adj* (*in consistency*) espeso; (*in size*) grueso; (*stupid*) torpe ▷ *n*: **in the ~ of the battle** en lo más reñido de la batalla; **it's 20 cm ~** tiene 20 cm de espesor; **thicken** *vi* espesarse ▷ *vt* (*sauce etc*) espesar; **thickness** *n* espesor *m*; grueso

thief [θiːf] (*pl* **thieves**) *n* ladrón/ona *m/f*

thigh [θaɪ] *n* muslo

thin [θɪn] *adj* (*person, animal*) flaco; (*in size*) delgado; (*in consistency*) poco espeso; (*hair, crowd*) escaso ▷ *vt*: **to ~ (down)** diluir

thing [θɪŋ] *n* cosa; (*object*) objeto, artículo; (*matter*) asunto; (*mania*): **to have a ~ about sb/sth** estar obsesionado con algn/algo; **things** *npl* (*belongings*) efectos *mpl* (personales); **the best ~ would be to ...** lo mejor sería ...; **how are ~s?** ¿qué tal?

think [θɪŋk] (*pt, pp* **thought**) *vi*

pensar ▷ *vt* pensar, creer; **what did you ~ of them?** ¿qué te parecieron?; **to ~ about sth/sb** pensar en algo/algn; **I'll ~ about it** lo pensaré; **to ~ of doing sth** pensar en hacer algo; **I ~ so/not** creo que sí/no; **to ~ well of sb** tener buen concepto de algn; **think over** *vt* reflexionar sobre, meditar; **think up** *vt* (*plan etc*) idear

third [θəːd] *adj* (*before n*) tercer(a); (*following n*) tercero/a ▷ *n* tercero/a; (*fraction*) tercio; (*BRIT Scol: degree*) título de licenciado con calificación de aprobado; **thirdly** *adv* en tercer lugar; **third party insurance** (*BRIT*) *n* seguro contra terceros; **Third World** *n* Tercer Mundo

thirst [θəːst] *n* sed *f*; **thirsty** *adj* (*person, animal*) sediento; (*work*) que da sed; **to be thirsty** tener sed

thirteen [ˈθəːˈtiːn] *num* trece; **thirteenth** [-ˈtiːnθ] *adj* decimotercero

thirtieth [ˈθəːtɪəθ] *adj* trigésimo

thirty [ˈθəːtɪ] *num* treinta

○ **KEYWORD**

this [ðɪs] (*pl* **these**) *adj* (*demonstrative*) este/a *pl*; estos/as; (*neuter*) esto; **this man/woman** este hombre(esta mujer); **these children/flowers** estos chicos/estas flores; **this one (here)** éste/a, esto (de aquí) ▷ *pron* (*demonstrative*) éste/a *pl*, éstos/as; (*neuter*) esto; **who is this?** ¿quién es éste/ésta?; **what is this?** ¿qué es esto?; **this is where I live** aquí vivo; **this is what he said** esto es lo que dijo; **this is Mr Brown** (*in introductions*) le presento al Sr. Brown; (*photo*) éste es el Sr. Brown; (*on telephone*) habla el Sr. Brown

▷ *adv* (*demonstrative*): **this high/long etc** así de alto/largo etc; **this far** hasta aquí

thistle [ˈθɪsl] *n* cardo

thorn [θɔːn] n espina

thorough ['θʌrə] adj (search) minucioso; (wash) a fondo; (knowledge, research) profundo; (person) meticuloso; **thoroughly** adv (search) minuciosamente; (study) profundamente; (wash) a fondo; (utterly: bad, wet etc) completamente, totalmente

those [ðəuz] adj esos(esas); (more remote) aquellos/as

though [ðəu] conj aunque ▷ adv sin embargo

thought [θɔːt] pt, pp of **think** ▷ n pensamiento; (opinion) opinión f; **thoughtful** adj pensativo; (serious) serio; (considerate) atento; **thoughtless** adj desconsiderado

thousand ['θauzənd] num mil; **two ~** dos mil; **~s of** miles de; **thousandth** num milésimo

thrash [θræʃ] vt azotar; (defeat) derrotar

thread [θred] n hilo; (of screw) rosca ▷ vt (needle) enhebrar

threat [θret] n amenaza; **threaten** vi amenazar ▷ vt: **to threaten sb with/ to do** amenazar a algn con/con hacer; **threatening** adj amenazador(a), amenazante

three [θriː] num tres; **three-dimensional** adj tridimensional; **three-piece suite** n tresillo; **three-quarters** npl tres cuartas partes; **three-quarters full** tres cuartas partes lleno

threshold ['θreʃhəuld] n umbral m

threw [θruː] pt of **throw**

thrill [θrɪl] n (excitement) emoción f; (shudder) estremecimiento ▷ vt emocionar; **to be ~ed** (with gift etc) estar encantado; **thrilled** adj: **I was thrilled** Estaba emocionada; **thriller** n novela (or obra or película) de suspense; **thrilling** adj emocionante

thriving ['θraɪvɪŋ] adj próspero

throat [θrəut] n garganta; **to have a sore ~** tener dolor de garganta

throb [θrɔb] vi latir; dar puntadas; vibrar

throne [θrəun] n trono

through [θruː] prep, a través de; (time) durante; (by means of) por medio de, mediante; (owing to) gracias a ▷ adj (ticket, train) directo ▷ adv completamente, de parte a parte; de principio a fin; **to put sb ~ to sb** (Tel) poner or pasar a algn con algn; **to be ~** (Tel) tener comunicación f; (have finished) haber terminado; **"no - road"** (BRIT) "calle sin salida"; **throughout** prep (place) por todas partes de, por todo; (time) durante todo ▷ adv por or en todas partes

throw [θrəu] (pt **threw**, pp **thrown**) n tiro; (Sport) lanzamiento ▷ vt tirar, echar; (Sport) lanzar; (rider) derribar; (fig) desconcertar; **to ~ a party** dar una fiesta; **throw away** vt tirar; (money) derrochar; **throw in** vt (Sport: ball) sacar; (include) incluir; **throw off** vt deshacerse de; **throw out** vt tirar; (person) echar; expulsar; **throw up** vi vomitar

thru [θruː] (us) = **through**

thrush [θrʌʃ] n zorzal m, tordo

thrust [θrʌst] (pt, pp **~**) vt empujar con fuerza

thud [θʌd] n golpe m sordo

thug [θʌg] n gamberro/a

thumb [θʌm] n (Anat) pulgar m; **to ~ a lift** hacer autostop; **thumbtack** (us) n chincheta (SP)

thump [θʌmp] n golpe m; (sound) ruido seco or sordo ▷ vt golpear ▷ vi (heart etc) palpitar

thunder ['θʌndə*] n trueno ▷ vi tronar; (train etc): **to ~ past** pasar como un trueno; **thunderstorm** n tormenta

Thur(s). abbr (= Thursday) juev

Thursday ['θəːzdɪ] n jueves m inv

thus [ðʌs] adv así, de este modo

thwart [θwɔːt] vt frustrar

thyme [taɪm] n tomillo

Tibet [tɪ'bet] n el Tíbet

tick [tɪk] n (sound: of clock) tictac m;

(mark) palomita; (Zool) garrapata; (BRIT: inf): **in a ~** en un instante ▷vi hacer tictac ▷vt marcar; **tick off** vt marcar; (person) reñir

ticket ['tɪkɪt] n billete m (SP), boleto (LAM); (for cinema etc) entrada; (in shop: on goods) etiqueta; (for raffle) papeleta; (for library) tarjeta; (parking ticket) multa de aparcamiento (SP) or por estacionamiento (indebido) (LAM); **ticket barrier** n (BRIT: Rail) barrera más allá de la cual se necesita billete/boleto; **ticket collector** n revisor(a) m/f; **ticket inspector** n revisor(a) m/f, inspector(a) m/f de boletos (LAM); **ticket machine** n máquina de billetes (SP) or boletos (LAM); **ticket office** n (Theatre) taquilla (SP), boletería (LAM) (Rail) mostrador m de billetes (SP) or boletos (LAM)

tickle ['tɪkl] vt hacer cosquillas a ▷vi hacer cosquillas; **ticklish** adj (person) cosquilloso; (problem) delicado

tide [taɪd] n marea; (fig: of events etc) curso, marcha

tidy ['taɪdɪ] adj (room etc) ordenado; (dress, work) limpio; (person) (bien) arreglado ▷vt (also: **~ up**) poner en orden

tie [taɪ] n (string etc) atadura; (BRIT: also: **neck~**) corbata; (fig: link) vínculo, lazo; (Sport etc: draw) empate m ▷vt atar ▷vi (Sport etc) empatar; **to ~ in a bow** atar con un lazo; **to ~ a knot in sth** hacer un nudo en algo; **tie down** vt (fig: person: restrict) atar; (: to price, date etc) obligar a; **tie up** vt (dog, person) atar; (arrangements) concluir; **to be tied up** (busy) estar ocupado

tier [tɪə*] n grada; (of cake) piso

tiger ['taɪɡə*] n tigre m

tight [taɪt] adj (rope) tirante; (money) escaso; (clothes) ajustado; (bend) cerrado; (shoes, schedule) apretado; (budget) ajustado; (security) estricto; (inf: drunk) borracho ▷adv (squeeze) muy fuerte; (shut) bien; **tighten** vt (rope) estirar; (screw, grip) apretar;

(security) reforzar ▷vi estirarse; apretarse; **tightly** adv (grasp) muy fuerte; **tights** (BRIT) npl panti m pl

tile [taɪl] n (on roof) teja; (on floor) baldosa; (on wall) azulejo

till [tɪl] n caja (registradora) ▷vt (land) cultivar ▷ prep, conj = **until**

tilt [tɪlt] vt inclinar ▷vi inclinarse

timber ['tɪmbə*] n (material) madera

time [taɪm] n tiempo; (epoch: often pl) época; (by clock) hora; (moment) momento; (occasion) vez f; (Mus) compás m ▷vt calcular or medir el tiempo de; (race) cronometrar; (remark, visit etc) elegir el momento para; **a long ~** mucho tiempo; **4 at a ~** de 4 en 4; **4 a la vez**; **for the ~ being** de momento, por ahora; **from ~ to ~** de vez en cuando; **any ~** cuando sea; **in ~** (soon enough) a tiempo; (after some time) con el tiempo; (Mus) al compás; **in a week's ~** dentro de una semana; **in no ~** en un abrir y cerrar de ojos; **any ~** cuando sea; **on ~** a la hora; **5 ~ s 5** 5 por 5; **what ~ is it?** ¿qué hora es?; **to have a good ~** pasarlo bien, divertirse; **time limit** n plazo; **timely** adj oportuno; **timer** n (in kitchen etc) programador m horario; **time-share** n apartamento (or casa) a tiempo compartido; **timetable** n horario; **time zone** n huso horario

timid ['tɪmɪd] adj tímido

timing ['taɪmɪŋ] n (Sport) cronometraje m; **the ~ of his resignation** el momento que eligió para dimitir

tin [tɪn] n estaño; (also: **~ plate**) hojalata; (BRIT: can) lata; **tinfoil** n papel m de estaño

tingle ['tɪŋɡl] vi (person): **to ~ (with)** estremecerse (de); (hands etc) hormiguear

tinker ['tɪŋkə*]: **~ with** vt fus jugar con, tocar

tinned [tɪnd] (BRIT) adj (food) en lata, en conserva

tin opener [-əʊpnə*] (BRIT) n abrelatas m inv

tint [tɪnt] n matiz m; (for hair) tinte m; **tinted** adj (hair) teñido; (glass, spectacles) ahumado

tiny ['taɪnɪ] adj minúsculo, pequeñito

tip [tɪp] n (end) punta; (gratuity) propina; (BRIT: for rubbish) vertedero; (advice) consejo ▷ vt (waiter) dar una propina a; (tilt) inclinar; (empty: also: ~ out) vaciar, echar; (overturn: also: ~ over) volcar; **tip off** vt avisar, poner sobreaviso a

tiptoe ['tɪptəu] n: **on ~** de puntillas

tire [taɪə] n (US) = **tyre** ▷ vt cansar ▷ vi cansarse; (become bored) aburrirse; **tired** adj cansado; **to be tired of sth** estar harto de algo; **tire pressure** (US) = **tyre pressure**; **tiring** adj cansado

tissue ['tɪʃu:] n tejido; (paper handkerchief) pañuelo de papel, kleenex® m; **tissue paper** n papel m de seda

tit [tɪt] n (bird) herrerillo común; **to give ~ for tat** dar ojo por ojo

title ['taɪtl] n título

T-junction ['ti:dʒʌŋkʃən] n cruce m en T

TM abbr = **trademark**

🔑 **KEYWORD**

to [tu:, tə] prep 1 (direction) a; **to go to France/London/school/the station** ir a Francia/Londres/al colegio/a la estación; **to go to Claude's/the doctor's** ir a casa de Claude/al médico; **the road to Edinburgh** la carretera de Edimburgo

2 (as far as) hasta, a; **from here to London** de aquí a or hasta Londres; **to count to 10** contar hasta 10; **from 40 to 50 people** entre 40 y 50 personas

3 (with expressions of time) a; **a quarter/twenty to 5** las 5 menos cuarto/veinte

4 (for, of): **the key to the front door** la llave de la puerta principal; **she is secretary to the director** es la secretaria del director; **a letter to his**

wife una carta a or para su mujer

5 (expressing indirect object) a; **to give sth to sb** darle algo a algn; **to talk to sb** hablar con algn; **to be a danger to sb** ser un peligro para algn; **to carry out repairs to sth** hacer reparaciones en algo

6 (in relation to): **3 goals to 2** 3 goles a 2; **30 miles to the gallon** ≈ 94 litros a los cien (kms)

7 (purpose, result): **to come to sb's aid** venir en auxilio or ayuda de algn; **to sentence sb to death** condenar a algn a muerte; **to my great surprise** con gran sorpresa mía

▷ with vb 1 (simple infin): **to go/eat** ir/comer

2 (following another vb): **to want/try/start to do** querer/intentar/empezar a hacer

3 (with vb omitted): **I don't want to** no quiero

4 (purpose, result) para; **I did it to help you** lo hice para ayudarte; **he came to see you** vino a verte

5 (equivalent to relative clause): **I have things to do** tengo cosas que hacer; **the main thing is to try** lo principal es intentarlo

6 (after adj etc): **ready to go** listo para irse; **too old to ...** demasiado viejo (como) para ...

▷ adv: **pull/push the door to** tirar de/empujar la puerta

toad [təud] n sapo; **toadstool** n hongo venenoso

toast [təust] n (Culin) tostada; (drink, speech) brindis m ▷ vt (Culin) tostar; (drink to) brindar por; **toaster** n tostador m

tobacco [tə'bækəu] n tabaco

toboggan [tə'bɔgən] n tobogán m

today [tə'deɪ] adv, n (also fig) hoy m

toddler ['tɔdlə] n niño/a (que empieza a andar)

toe [təu] n dedo (del pie); (of shoe) punta; **to ~ the line** (fig) conformarse:

toenail n uña del pie

toffee ['tɒfɪ] n toffee m

together [tə'geðə] adv juntos; (at same time) al mismo tiempo, a la vez; ~ **with** junto con

toilet ['tɔɪlət] n inodoro; (BRIT: room) (cuarto de) baño, servicio ▷ cpd (soap etc) de aseo; **toilet bag** n neceser m, bolsa de aseo; **toilet paper** n papel m higiénico; **toiletries** npl artículos mpl de tocador; **toilet roll** n rollo de papel higiénico

token ['təʊkən] n (sign) señal f, muestra; (souvenir) recuerdo; (disc) ficha ▷ adj (strike, payment etc) simbólico; **book/record** ~ (BRIT) vale m para comprar libros/discos; **gift** ~ (BRIT) vale-regalo

Tokyo ['təʊkjəʊ] n Tokio, Tokyo

told [təʊld] pt, pp of **tell**

tolerant ['tɒlərnt] adj: ~ **of** tolerante con

tolerate ['tɒləreɪt] vt tolerar

toll [təʊl] n (of casualties) número de víctimas; (tax, charge) peaje m ▷ vi (bell) doblar; **toll call** n (US Tel) conferencia, llamada interurbana; **toll-free** (US) adj, adv gratis

tomato [tə'mɑːtəʊ] (pl ~es) n tomate m; **tomato sauce** n salsa de tomate

tomb [tuːm] n tumba; **tombstone** n lápida

tomorrow [tə'mɒrəʊ] adv, n (also: fig) mañana; **the day after** ~ pasado mañana; ~ **morning** mañana por la mañana

ton [tʌn] n tonelada (BRIT = 1016 kg; US = 907 kg); (metric ton) tonelada métrica; ~**s of** (inf) montones de

tone [təʊn] n tono ▷ vi (also: ~ **in**) armonizar; **tone down** vt (criticism) suavizar; (colour) atenuar

tongs [tɒŋz] npl (for coal) tenazas fpl; (curling tongs) tenacillas fpl

tongue [tʌŋ] n lengua; ~ **in cheek** irónicamente

tonic ['tɒnɪk] n (Med) tónico; (also: ~ **water**) (agua) tónica

tonight [tə'naɪt] adv, n esta noche; esta tarde

tonne [tʌn] n tonelada (métrica) (1.000kg)

tonsil ['tɒnsl] n amígdala; **tonsillitis** [-'laɪtɪs] n amigdalitis f

too [tuː] adv (excessively) demasiado; (also) también; ~ **much** demasiado; ~ **many** demasiados/as

took [tʊk] pt of **take**

tool [tuːl] n herramienta; **tool box** n caja de herramientas; **tool kit** n juego de herramientas

tooth [tuːθ] (pl **teeth**) n (Anat, Tech) diente m; (molar) muela; **toothache** n dolor m de muelas; **toothbrush** n cepillo de dientes; **toothpaste** n pasta de dientes; **toothpick** n palillo

top [tɒp] n (of mountain) cumbre f, cima; (of tree) copa f; (of head) coronilla f; (of ladder, page) lo alto; (of table) superficie f; (of cupboard) parte f de arriba; (lid: of box) tapa; (: of bottle, jar) tapón m; (of list etc) cabeza; (toy) peonza; (garment) blusa; camiseta ▷ adj de arriba; (in rank) principal, primero; (best) mejor ▷ vt (exceed) exceder; (be first in) encabezar; **on ~ of** (above) sobre, encima de; (in addition to) además de; **from ~ to bottom** de pies a cabeza; **top up** vt llenar; (mobile phone) recargar (el saldo de); **top floor** n último piso; **top hat** n sombrero de copa

topic ['tɒpɪk] n tema m; **topical** adj actual

topless ['tɒplɪs] adj (bather, bikini) topless inv

topping ['tɒpɪŋ] n (Culin): **with a ~ of cream** con nata por encima

topple ['tɒpl] vt derribar ▷ vi caerse

top-up card n (for mobile phone) tarjeta prepago

torch [tɔːtʃ] n antorcha; (BRIT: electric) linterna

tore [tɔː*] pt of **tear²**

torment [n 'tɔːment, vt tɔː'ment] n tormento ▷ vt atormentar; (fig: annoy) fastidiar

torn [tɔːn] *pp of* **tear²**

tornado [tɔːˈneɪdəʊ] (*pl* **~es**) *n* tornado

torpedo [tɔːˈpiːdəʊ] (*pl* **~es**) *n* torpedo

torrent ['tɒrənt] *n* torrente *m*; **torrential** [tɒˈrɛnʃl] *adj* torrencial

tortoise ['tɔːtəs] *n* tortuga

torture ['tɔːtʃə*] *n* tortura ▷ *vt* torturar; (*fig*) atormentar

Tory ['tɔːrɪ] (*BRIT*) *adj*, *n* (*Pol*) conservador(a) *m/f*

toss [tɒs] *vt* tirar, echar; (*one's head*) sacudir; **to ~ a coin** echar a cara o cruz; **to ~ up for sth** jugar a cara o cruz algo; **to ~ and turn** (*in bed*) dar vueltas

total ['təʊtl] *adj* total, entero; (*emphatic: failure etc*) completo, total ▷ *n* total *m*, suma ▷ *vt* (*add up*) sumar; (*amount to*) ascender a

totalitarian [təʊtælɪˈtɛərɪən] *adj* totalitario

totally ['təʊtəlɪ] *adv* totalmente

touch [tʌtʃ] *n* tacto; (*contact*) contacto ▷ *vt* tocar; (*emotionally*) conmover; **a ~ of** (*fig*) un poquito de; **to get in ~ with sb** ponerse en contacto con algn; **to lose ~** (*friends*) perder contacto; **touch down** *vi* (*on land*) aterrizar; (*on sea*) amerizar *m*; (*us Football*) ensayo; **touched** *adj* (*moved*) conmovido; **touching** *adj* (*moving*) conmovedor(a); **touchline** *n* (*Sport*) línea de banda; **touch-sensitive** *adj* sensible al tacto

tough [tʌf] *adj* (*material*) resistente; (*meat*) duro; (*problem etc*) difícil; (*policy, stance*) inflexible; (*person*) fuerte

tour [tʊə*] *n* viaje *m*, vuelta; (*also:* **package ~**) viaje *m* todo comprendido; (*of town, museum*) visita; (*by artist*) gira ▷ *vt* recorrer, visitar; **tour guide** *n* guía *mf* turístico/a

tourism ['tʊərɪzm] *n* turismo

tourist ['tʊərɪst] *n* turista *mf* ▷ *cpd* turístico; **tourist office** *n* oficina de turismo

tournament ['tʊənəmənt] *n* torneo

tour operator *n* touroperador(a) *m/f*, operador(a) *m/f* turístico/a

tow [təʊ] *vt* remolcar; **"on** *or* **in** (*us*) **~"** (*Aut*) "a remolque"; **tow away** *vt* llevarse a remolque

toward(s) [təˈwɔːd(z)] *prep* hacia; (*attitude*) respecto a, con; (*purpose*) para

towel ['taʊəl] *n* toalla; **towelling** *n* (*fabric*) felpa

tower [taʊə*] *n* torre *f*; **tower block** (*BRIT*) *n* torre *f* (de pisos)

town [taʊn] *n* ciudad *f*; **to go to ~** ir a la ciudad; (*fig*) echar la casa por la ventana; **town centre** (*BRIT*) *n* centro de la ciudad; **town hall** *n* ayuntamiento

tow truck (*us*) *n* camión *m* grúa

toxic ['tɒksɪk] *adj* tóxico

toy [tɔɪ] *n* juguete *m*; **toy with** *vt fus* jugar con; (*idea*) acariciar; **toyshop** *n* juguetería

trace [treɪs] *n* rastro ▷ *vt* (*draw*) trazar, delinear; (*locate*) encontrar; (*follow*) seguir la pista de

track [træk] *n* (*mark*) huella, pista; (*path: gen*) camino, senda; (*: of bullet etc*) trayectoria; (*: of suspect, animal*) pista, rastro; (*Rail*) vía; (*Sport*) pista; (*on tape, record*) canción *f* ▷ *vt* seguir la pista de; **to keep ~ of** mantenerse al tanto de, seguir; **track down** *vt* (*prey*) seguir el rastro de; (*sth lost*) encontrar; **tracksuit** *n* chandal *m*

tractor ['træktə*] *n* tractor *m*

trade [treɪd] *n* comercio; (*skill, job*) oficio ▷ *vi* negociar, comerciar ▷ *vt* (*exchange*): **to ~ sth** (*for sth*) cambiar algo (por algo); **trade in** *vt* (*old car etc*) ofrecer como parte del pago; **trademark** *n* marca de fábrica; **trader** *n* comerciante *mf*; **tradesman** (*irreg*) *n* (*shopkeeper*) tendero; **trade union** *n* sindicato

trading ['treɪdɪŋ] *n* comercio

tradition [trəˈdɪʃən] *n* tradición *f*; **traditional** *adj* tradicional

traffic ['træfɪk] *n* (*gen, Aut*) tráfico,

circulación f ▷ vi: **to ~ in** (pej: liquor, drugs) traficar en; **traffic circle** (us) n isleta; **traffic island** n refugio, isleta; **traffic jam** n embotellamiento; **traffic lights** npl semáforo; **traffic warden** n guardia mf de tráfico

tragedy ['trædʒədɪ] n tragedia

tragic ['trædʒɪk] adj trágico

trail [treɪl] n (tracks) rastro, pista; (path) camino, sendero; (dust, smoke) estela ▷ vt (drag) arrastrar; (follow) seguir la pista de ▷ vi arrastrar; (in contest etc) ir perdiendo; **trailer** n (Aut) remolque m; (caravan) caravana; (Cinema) trailer m, avance m

train [treɪn] n tren m; (of dress) cola; (series) serie f ▷ vt (educate, teach skills to) formar; (sportsman) entrenar; (dog) adiestrar; (point: gun etc): **to ~ on** apuntar a ▷ vi (Sport) entrenarse; (learn a skill): **to ~ as a teacher** etc estudiar para profesor etc; **one's ~ of thought** el razonamiento de algn; **trainee** [treɪ'niː] n aprendiz(a) m/f; **trainer** n (Sport: coach) entrenador(a) m/f; (of animals) domador(a) m/f; **trainers** npl (shoes) zapatillas fpl de deporte; **training** n formación f; entrenamiento; **to be in training** (Sport) estar entrenando; **training course** n curso de formación; **training shoes** npl zapatillas fpl (de deporte)

trait [treɪt] n rasgo

traitor ['treɪtə*] n traidor(a) m/f

tram [træm] n (BRIT) (also: **~car**) tranvía m

tramp [træmp] n (person) vagabundo/a; (inf: pej: woman) puta

trample ['træmpl] vt: **to ~ (underfoot)** pisotear

trampoline ['træmpəliːn] n trampolín m

tranquil ['træŋkwɪl] adj tranquilo; **tranquillizer** (us **tranquilizer**) n (Med) tranquilizante m

transaction [træn'zækʃən] n transacción f, operación f

transatlantic ['trænzət'læntɪk] adj transatlántico

transcript ['trænskrɪpt] n copia

transfer [n 'trænsfə:*, vb træns'fə:*] n (of employees) traslado; (of money, power) transferencia; (Sport) traspaso; (picture, design) calcomanía ▷ vt trasladar; transferir; **to ~ the charges** (BRIT Tel) llamar a cobro revertido

transform [træns'fɔ:m] vt transformar; **transformation** n transformación f

transfusion [træns'fju:ʒən] n transfusión f

transit ['trænzɪt] n: **in ~** en tránsito

transition [træn'zɪʃən] n transición f

transitive ['trænzɪtɪv] adj (Ling) transitivo

translate [trænz'leɪt] vt traducir; **translation** n [-'leɪʃən] n traducción f; **translator** n traductor(a) m/f

transmission [trænz'mɪʃən] n transmisión f

transmit [trænz'mɪt] vt transmitir; **transmitter** n transmisor m

transparent [træns'pærnt] adj transparente

transplant [træns'plɑ:nt] n (Med) transplante m

transport [n 'trænspɔ:t, vt træns'pɔ:t] n transporte m; (car) coche m (SP), carro (LAM), automóvil m (SP) ▷ vt transportar; **transportation** [-'teɪʃən] n transporte m

transvestite [trænz'vestaɪt] n travestí mf

trap [træp] n (snare, trick) trampa; (carriage) cabriolé ▷ vt coger (SP) or agarrar (LAM) (en una trampa); (trick) engañar; (confine) atrapar

trash [træʃ] n (rubbish) basura; (nonsense) tonterías fpl; (pej): **the book/film is ~** el libro/la película no vale nada; **trash can** (us) n cubo o bote m (MEX) or tacho (SC) de la basura

trauma ['trɔ:mə] n trauma m; **traumatic** [trɔ:'mætɪk] adj traumático

travel ['trævl] *n* el viajar ▷ *vi* viajar ▷ *vt* (*distance*) recorrer; **travel agency** *n* agencia de viajes; **travel agent** *n* agente *mf* de viajes; **travel insurance** *n* seguro de viaje; **traveller** (*us* **traveler**) *n* viajero/a; **traveller's cheque** (*us* **traveler's check**) *n* cheque *m* de viajero; **travelling** (*us* **traveling**) *n* los viajes, el viajar; **travel-sick** *adj*: **to get travel-sick** marearse al viajar; **travel sickness** *n* mareo

tray [treɪ] *n* bandeja; (*on desk*) cajón *m*

treacherous ['trɛtʃərəs] *adj* traidor, traicionero; (*dangerous*) peligroso

treacle ['triːkl] (*BRIT*) *n* melaza

tread [trɛd] (*pt* **trod**, *pp* **trodden**) *n* (*step*) paso, pisada; (*sound*) ruido de pasos; (*of stair*) escalón *m*; (*of tyre*) banda de rodadura ▷ *vi* pisar; **tread on** *vt fus* pisar

treasure ['trɛʒə*] *n* tesoro ▷ *vt* (*value: object, friendship*) apreciar; (*: memory*) guardar; **treasurer** *n* tesorero/a

treasury ['trɛʒərɪ] *n*: **the T~** el Ministerio de Hacienda

treat [triːt] *n* (*present*) regalo ▷ *vt* tratar; **to ~ sb to sth** invitar a algn a algo; **treatment** *n* tratamiento

treaty ['triːtɪ] *n* tratado

treble ['trɛbl] *adj* triple ▷ *vt* triplicar ▷ *vi* triplicarse

tree [triː] *n* árbol *m*; **~ trunk** tronco (de árbol)

trek [trɛk] *n* (*long journey*) viaje *m* largo y difícil; (*tiring walk*) caminata

tremble ['trɛmbl] *vi* temblar

tremendous [trɪ'mɛndəs] *adj* tremendo, enorme; (*excellent*) estupendo

trench [trɛntʃ] *n* zanja

trend [trɛnd] *n* (*tendency*) tendencia; (*of events*) curso; (*fashion*) moda; **trendy** *adj* de moda

trespass ['trɛspəs] *vi*: **to ~ on** entrar sin permiso en; **"no ~ing"** "prohibido el paso"

trial ['traɪəl] *n* (*Law*) juicio, proceso; (*test: of machine etc*) prueba; **trial period** *n* periodo de prueba

triangle ['traɪæŋgl] *n* (*Math, Mus*) triángulo

triangular [traɪ'æŋgjulə*] *adj* triangular

tribe [traɪb] *n* tribu *f*

tribunal [traɪ'bjuːnl] *n* tribunal *m*

tribute ['trɪbjuːt] *n* homenaje *m*, tributo; **to pay ~ to** rendir homenaje a

trick [trɪk] *n* (*skill, knack*) tino, truco; (*conjuring trick*) truco; (*joke*) broma; (*Cards*) baza ▷ *vt* engañar; **to play a ~ on sb** gastar una broma a algn; **that should do the ~** a ver si funciona así

trickle ['trɪkl] *n* (*of water etc*) goteo ▷ *vi* gotear

tricky ['trɪkɪ] *adj* difícil; delicado

tricycle ['traɪsɪkl] *n* triciclo

trifle ['traɪfl] *n* bagatela; (*Culin*) dulce de bizcocho borracho, gelatina, fruta y natillas ▷ *adv*: **a ~ long** un poquito largo

trigger ['trɪgə*] *n* (*of gun*) gatillo

trim [trɪm] *adj* (*house, garden*) en buen estado; (*person, figure*) esbelto ▷ *n* (*haircut etc*) recorte *m*; (*on car*) guarnición *f* ▷ *vt* (*neaten*) arreglar; (*cut*) recortar; (*decorate*) adornar; (*Naut: a sail*) orientar

trio ['triːəu] *n* trío

trip [trɪp] *n* viaje *m*; (*excursion*) excursión *f*; (*stumble*) traspié *m* ▷ *vi* (*stumble*) tropezar; (*go lightly*) andar a paso ligero; **on a ~** de viaje; **trip up** *vi* tropezar, caerse ▷ *vt* hacer tropezar or caer

triple ['trɪpl] *adj* triple

triplets ['trɪplɪts] *npl* trillizos/as *mpl/fpl*

tripod ['traɪpɔd] *n* trípode *m*

triumph ['traɪʌmf] *n* triunfo ▷ *vi*: **to ~ (over)** vencer; **triumphant** [traɪ'ʌmfənt] *adj* (*team etc*) vencedor(a); (*wave, return*) triunfal

trivial ['trɪvɪəl] *adj* insignificante; (*commonplace*) banal

trod [trɔd] *pt of* **tread**

trodden ['trɔdn] *pp of* **tread**

trolley ['trɔlɪ] *n* carrito; (*also:* **~ bus**) trolebús *m*

trombone [trɔm'bəʊn] *n* trombón *m*

troop [truːp] *n* grupo, banda; **troops** *npl* (*Mil*) tropas *fpl*

trophy ['trəʊfɪ] *n* trofeo

tropical ['trɔpɪkl] *adj* tropical

trot [trɔt] *n* trote *m* ▷ *vi* trotar; **on the ~** (*BRIT: fig*) seguidos/as

trouble ['trʌbl] *n* problema *m*, dificultad *f*; (*worry*) preocupación *f*; (*bother, effort*) molestia, esfuerzo; (*unrest*) inquietud *f*; (*Med*): **stomach** *etc* **~** problemas *mpl* gástricos *etc* ▷ *vt* (*disturb*) molestar; (*worry*) preocupar, inquietar ▷ *vi*: **to ~ to do sth** molestarse en hacer algo; **troubles** *npl* (*Pol etc*) conflictos *mpl*; (*personal*) problemas *mpl*; **to be in ~** estar en un apuro; **it's no ~!** ¡no es molestia (ninguna)!; **what's the ~?** (*with broken TV etc*) ¿cuál es el problema?; (*doctor to patient*) ¿qué pasa?; **troubled** *adj* (*person*) preocupado; (*country, epoch, life*) agitado; **troublemaker** *n* agitador(a) *m/f*; (*child*) alborotador *m*; **troublesome** *adj* molesto

trough [trɔf] *n* (*also:* **drinking ~**) abrevadero; (*also:* **feeding ~**) comedero; (*depression*) depresión *f*

trousers ['traʊzəz] *npl* pantalones *mpl*; **short ~** pantalones *mpl* cortos

trout [traʊt] *n inv* trucha

trowel ['traʊəl] *n* (*of gardener*) palita; (*of builder*) paleta

truant ['truːənt] *n*: **to play ~** (*BRIT*) hacer novillos

truce [truːs] *n* tregua

truck [trʌk] *n* (*lorry*) camión *m*; (*Rail*) vagón *m*; **truck driver** *n* camionero

true [truː] *adj* verdadero; (*accurate*) exacto; (*genuine*) auténtico; (*faithful*) fiel; **to come ~** realizarse

truly ['truːlɪ] *adv* (*really*) realmente; (*truthfully*) verdaderamente; (*faithfully*): **yours ~** (*in letter*) le saluda atentamente

trumpet ['trʌmpɪt] *n* trompeta

trunk [trʌŋk] *n* (*of tree, person*) tronco; (*of elephant*) trompa; (*case*) baúl *m*; (*us Aut*) maletero; **trunks** *npl* (*also:* **swimming ~s**) bañador *m* (de hombre)

trust [trʌst] *n* confianza; (*responsibility*) responsabilidad *f*; (*Law*) fideicomiso ▷ *vt* (*rely on*) tener confianza en; (*hope*) esperar; (*entrust*): **to ~ sth to sb** confiar algo a algn; **to take sth on ~** fiarse de algo; **trusted** *adj* de confianza; **trustworthy** *adj* digno de confianza

truth [truːθ, *pl* truːðz] *n* verdad *f*; **truthful** *adj* veraz

try [traɪ] *n* tentativa, intento; (*Rugby*) ensayo ▷ *vt* (*attempt*) intentar; (*test: also:* **~ out**) probar, someter a prueba; (*Law*) juzgar, procesar; (*strain: patience*) hacer perder ▷ *vi* probar; **to have a ~** probar suerte; **to ~ to do sth** intentar hacer algo; **~ again!** ¡vuelve a probar!; **~ harder!** ¡esfuérzate más!; **well, I tried** al menos lo intenté; **try on** *vt* (*clothes*) probarse; **trying** *adj* (*experience*) cansado; (*person*) pesado

T-shirt ['tiːʃəːt] *n* camiseta

tub [tʌb] *n* cubo (*SP*), cubeta (*SP, MEX*), balde *m* (*LAM*); (*bath*) bañera (*SP*), tina (*LAM*), bañadera (*RPL*)

tube [tjuːb] *n* tubo; (*BRIT: underground*) metro; (*for tyre*) cámara de aire

tuberculosis [tjubə:kju'ləʊsɪs] *n* tuberculosis *f inv*

tube station (*BRIT*) *n* estación *f* de metro

tuck [tʌk] *vt* (*put*) poner; **tuck away** *vt* (*money*) guardar; (*building*): **to be tucked away** esconderse, ocultarse; **tuck in** *vt* meter dentro; (*child*) arropar ▷ *vi* (*eat*) comer con apetito; **tuck shop** *n* (*Scol*) tienda ≈ bar *m* (del colegio) (*SP*)

Tue(s). *abbr* (= *Tuesday*) mart

Tuesday ['tjuːzdɪ] *n* martes *m inv*

tug [tʌg] *n* (*ship*) remolcador *m* ▷ *vt* tirar de

tuition [tjuː'ɪʃən] *n* (*BRIT*) enseñanza;

t

(: *private tuition*) clases *fpl* particulares; (*us: school fees*) matrícula

tulip ['tju:lɪp] *n* tulipán *m*

tumble ['tʌmbl] *n* (*fall*) caída ▷ *vi* caer; **to ~ to sth** (*inf*) caer en la cuenta de algo; **tumble dryer** (BRIT) *n* secadora

tumbler ['tʌmblə*] *n* (*glass*) vaso

tummy ['tʌmɪ] (*inf*) *n* barriga, tripa

tumour ['tju:mə*] (us **tumor**) *n* tumor *m*

tuna ['tju:nə] *n inv* (*also*: **~ fish**) atún *m*

tune [tju:n] *n* melodía ▷ *vt* (*Mus*) afinar; (*Radio, TV, Aut*) sintonizar; **to be in/out of ~** (*instrument*) estar afinado/desafinado; (*singer*) cantar afinadamente/desafinar; **to be in/out of ~ with** (*fig*) estar de acuerdo/en desacuerdo con; **tune in** *vi*: **to tune in (to)** (*Radio, TV*) sintonizar (con); **tune up** *vi* (*musician*) afinar (su instrumento)

tunic ['tju:nɪk] *n* túnica

Tunisia [tju:'nɪzɪə] *n* Túnez *m*

tunnel ['tʌnl] *n* túnel *m*; (*in mine*) galería ▷ *vi* construir un túnel/una galería

turbulence ['tə:bjələns] *n* (*Aviat*) turbulencia

turf [tə:f] *n* césped *m*; (*clod*) tepe *m* ▷ *vt* cubrir con césped

Turk [tə:k] *n* turco/a

Turkey ['tə:kɪ] *n* Turquía

turkey ['tə:kɪ] *n* pavo

Turkish ['tə:kɪʃ] *adj*, *n* turco; (*Ling*) turco

turmoil ['tə:mɔɪl] *n*: **in ~** revuelto

turn [tə:n] *n* turno; (*in road*) curva; (*of mind, events*) rumbo; (*Theatre*) número; (*Med*) ataque *m* ▷ *vt* girar, volver; (*collar, steak*) dar la vuelta a; (*page*) pasar; (*change*): **to ~ sth into** convertir algo en ▷ *vi* volver; (*person: look back*) volverse; (*reverse direction*) dar la vuelta; (*milk*) cortarse; (*become*): **to ~ nasty/forty** ponerse feo/cumplir los cuarenta; **a good ~** un favor; **it gave**

me quite a ~ me dio un susto; **"no left ~"** "prohibido girar a la izquierda"; **it's your ~** te toca a ti; **in ~** por turnos; **to take ~s (at)** turnarse (en); **turn around** *vi* (*person*) volverse, darse la vuelta ▷ *vt* (*object*) dar la vuelta a, voltear (LAM); **turn away** *vi* apartar la vista ▷ *vi* rechazar; **turn back** *vi* volverse atrás ▷ *vt* hacer retroceder; (*clock*) retrasar; **turn down** *vt* (*refuse*) rechazar; (*reduce*) bajar; (*fold*) doblar; **turn in** *vi* (*inf: go to bed*) acostarse ▷ *vt* (*fold*) doblar hacia dentro; **turn off** *vi* (*from road*) desviarse ▷ *vt* (*light, radio etc*) apagar; (*tap*) cerrar; (*engine*) parar; **turn on** *vt* (*light, radio etc*) encender (SP), prender (LAM); (*tap*) abrir; (*engine*) poner en marcha; **turn out** *vt* (*light, gas*) apagar; (*produce*) producir ▷ *vi* (*voters*) concurrir; **to turn out to be ...** resultar ser ...; **turn over** *vi* (*person*) volverse ▷ *vt* (*object*) dar la vuelta a; (*page*) volver; **turn round** *vi* volverse; (*rotate*) girar; **turn to** *vt fus*: **to turn to sb** acudir a algn; **turn up** *vi* (*person*) llegar, presentarse; (*lost object*) aparecer ▷ *vt* (*gen*) subir; **turning** *n* (*in road*) vuelta; **turning point** (*fig*) momento decisivo

turnip ['tə:nɪp] *n* nabo

turn: **turnout** *n* concurrencia; **turnover** *n* (*Comm: amount of money*) volumen *m* de ventas; (: *of goods*) movimiento; **turnstile** *n* torniquete *m*; **turn-up** (BRIT) *n* (*Scol* trousers) vuelta

turquoise ['tə:kwɔɪz] *n* (*stone*) turquesa ▷ *adj* color turquesa

turtle ['tə:tl] *n* galápago; **turtleneck** (**sweater**) *n* jersey *m* de cuello vuelto

tusk [tʌsk] *n* colmillo

tutor ['tju:tə*] *n* profesor(a) *m/f*; **tutorial** [tju:'tɔ:rɪəl] *n* (*Scol*) seminario

tuxedo [tʌk'si:dəu] (us) *n* smóking *m*, esmoquin *m*

TV [ti:'vi:] *n abbr* (= *television*) tele *f*

tweed [twi:d] *n* tweed *m*

tweezers ['twi:zəz] *npl* pinzas *fpl* (de depilar)

twelfth [twɛlfθ] num duodécimo

twelve [twɛlv] num doce; **at ~ o'clock** (*midday*) a mediodía; (*midnight*) a medianoche

twentieth ['twɛntɪɪθ] adj vigésimo

twenty ['twɛntɪ] num veinte

twice [twaɪs] adv dos veces; **~ as much** dos veces más

twig [twɪg] n ramita

twilight ['twaɪlaɪt] n crepúsculo

twin [twɪn] adj, n gemelo/a m/f ▷ vt hermanar; **twin(-bedded) room** n habitación f doble; **twin beds** npl camas fpl gemelas

twinkle ['twɪŋkl] vi centellear; (*eyes*) brillar

twist [twɪst] n (*action*) torsión f; (*in road, coil*) vuelta; (*in wire, flex*) doblez f; (*in story*) giro ▷ vt torcer; (*weave*) trenzar; (*roll around*) enrollar; (*fig*) deformar ▷ vi serpentear

twit [twɪt] (*inf*) n tonto

twitch [twɪtʃ] n (*pull*) tirón m; (*nervous*) tic m ▷ vi crisparse

two [tuː] num dos; **to put ~ and ~ together** (*fig*) atar cabos

type [taɪp] n (*category*) tipo, género; (*model*) tipo; (*Typ*) tipo, letra ▷ vt (*letter etc*) escribir a máquina; **typewriter** n máquina de escribir

typhoid ['taɪfɔɪd] n tifoidea

typhoon [taɪ'fuːn] n tifón m

typical ['tɪpɪkl] adj típico; **typically** adv típicamente

typing ['taɪpɪŋ] n mecanografía

typist ['taɪpɪst] n mecanógrafo/a m/f

tyre ['taɪə*] (us **tire**) n neumático, llanta (LAM); **tyre pressure** (BRIT) n presión f de los neumáticos

u

UFO ['juːfəʊ] n abbr (= unidentified flying object) OVNI m

Uganda [juːˈgændə] n Uganda

ugly ['ʌglɪ] adj feo; (*dangerous*) peligroso

UHT abbr (= UHT milk) leche f UHT, leche f uperizada

UK n abbr = **United Kingdom**

ulcer ['ʌlsə*] n úlcera; (*mouth ulcer*) llaga

ultimate ['ʌltɪmət] adj último, final; (*greatest*) máximo; **ultimately** adv (*in the end*) por último, al final; (*fundamentally*) a or en fin de cuentas

ultimatum [ʌltɪ'meɪtəm] (pl **~s** or **ultimata**) n ultimátum m

ultrasound ['ʌltrəsaʊnd] n (*Med*) ultrasonido

ultraviolet ['ʌltrə'vaɪəlɪt] adj ultravioleta

umbrella [ʌm'brɛlə] n paraguas m inv; (*for sun*) sombrilla

umpire ['ʌmpaɪə*] n árbitro

UN n abbr (= United Nations) NN. UU.

unable [ʌn'eɪbl] adj: **to be ~ to do sth**

u

no poder hacer algo

unacceptable [ʌnəkˈseptəbl] adj (proposal, behaviour, price) inaceptable; **it's ~ that** no se puede aceptar que

unanimous [juːˈnænɪməs] adj unánime

unarmed [ʌnˈɑːmd] adj (defenceless) inerme; (without weapon) desarmado

unattended [ʌnəˈtendɪd] adj desatendido

unattractive [ʌnəˈtræktɪv] adj poco atractivo

unavailable [ʌnəˈveɪləbl] adj (article, room, book) no disponible; (person) ocupado

unavoidable [ʌnəˈvɔɪdəbl] adj inevitable

unaware [ʌnəˈwɛə*] adj: **to be ~ of** ignorar; **unawares** adv: **to catch sb unawares** pillar a algn desprevenido

unbearable [ʌnˈbɛərəbl] adj insoportable

unbeatable [ʌnˈbiːtəbl] adj (team) invencible; (price) inmejorable; (quality) insuperable

unbelievable [ʌnbɪˈliːvəbl] adj increíble

unborn [ʌnˈbɔːn] adj que va a nacer

unbutton [ʌnˈbʌtn] vt desabrochar

uncalled-for [ʌnˈkɔːldfɔː*] adj gratuito, inmerecido

uncanny [ʌnˈkænɪ] adj extraño

uncertain [ʌnˈsəːtn] adj incierto; (indecisive) indeciso; **uncertainty** n incertidumbre f

unchanged [ʌnˈtʃeɪndʒd] adj igual, sin cambios

uncle [ˈʌŋkl] n tío

unclear [ʌnˈklɪə*] adj poco claro; **I'm still ~ about what I'm supposed to do** todavía no tengo muy claro lo que tengo que hacer

uncomfortable [ʌnˈkʌmfətəbl] adj incómodo; (uneasy) inquieto

uncommon [ʌnˈkɔmən] adj poco común, raro

unconditional [ʌnkənˈdɪʃənl] adj incondicional

unconscious [ʌnˈkɔnʃəs] adj sin sentido; (unaware) **to be ~ of** no darse cuenta de ▷ n: **the ~** el inconsciente

uncontrollable [ʌnkənˈtrəuləbl] adj (child etc) incontrolable; (temper) indomable; (laughter) incontenible

unconventional [ʌnkənˈvenʃənl] adj poco convencional

uncover [ʌnˈkʌvə*] vt descubrir; (take lid off) destapar

undecided [ʌndɪˈsaɪdɪd] adj (character) indeciso; (question) no resuelto

undeniable [ʌndɪˈnaɪəbl] adj innegable

under [ˈʌndə*] prep debajo de; (less than) menos de; (according to) según, de acuerdo con; (sb's leadership) bajo ▷ adv debajo, abajo; **~ there** allí abajo; **~ repair** en reparación; **undercover** adj clandestino; **underdone** adj (Culin) poco hecho; **underestimate** vt subestimar; **undergo** (irreg) vt sufrir; (treatment) recibir; **undergraduate** n estudiante mf; **underground** n (BRIT: railway) metro; (Pol) movimiento clandestino ▷ adj (car park) subterráneo ▷ adv (work) en la clandestinidad; **undergrowth** n maleza; **underline** vt subrayar; **undermine** vt socavar, minar; **underneath** [ʌndəˈniːθ] adv debajo ▷ prep debajo de, bajo; **underpants** npl calzoncillos mpl; **underpass** (BRIT) n paso subterráneo; **underprivileged** adj desposeído; **underscore** vt subrayar; **undershirt** (US) n camiseta; **underskirt** (BRIT) n enaguas fpl

understand [ʌndəˈstænd] vt, vi entender, comprender; (assume) tener entendido; **understandable** adj comprensible; **understanding** adj comprensivo ▷ n comprensión f, entendimiento; (agreement) acuerdo

understatement [ˈʌndəsteɪtmənt] n modestia (excesiva); **that's an ~!** ¡eso es decir poco!

understood [ʌndəˈstud] pt, pp of

understand ⊳ adj (agreed) acordado; (implied): **it is ~ that** se sobreentiende que

undertake [ʌndəˈteɪk] (irreg) vt emprender; **to ~ to do sth** comprometerse a hacer algo

undertaker [ˈʌndəteɪkə*] n director(a) m/f de pompas fúnebres

undertaking [ˈʌndəteɪkɪŋ] n empresa; (promise) promesa

under: underwater adv bajo el agua ⊳ adj submarino; **underway** adj: **to be underway** (meeting) estar en marcha; (investigation) estar llevándose a cabo; **underwear** n ropa interior; **underwent** vb see **undergo**; **underworld** n (of crime) hampa, inframundo

undesirable [ʌndɪˈzaɪərəbl] adj (person) indeseable; (thing) poco aconsejable

undisputed [ʌndɪˈspjuːtɪd] adj incontestable

undo [ʌnˈduː] (irreg) vt (laces) desatar; (button etc) desabrochar; (spoil) deshacer

undone [ʌnˈdʌn] pp of **undo** ⊳ adj: **to come ~** (clothes) desabrocharse; (parcel) desatarse

undoubtedly [ʌnˈdautɪdlɪ] adv indudablemente, sin duda

undress [ʌnˈdres] vi desnudarse

unearth [ʌnˈɜːθ] vt desenterrar

uneasy [ʌnˈiːzɪ] adj intranquilo, preocupado; (feeling) desagradable; (peace) inseguro

unemployed [ʌnɪmˈplɔɪd] adj parado, sin trabajo ⊳ npl: **the ~** los parados

unemployment [ʌnɪmˈplɔɪmənt] n paro, desempleo; **unemployment benefit** n (BRIT) subsidio de desempleo or paro

unequal [ʌnˈiːkwəl] adj (unfair) desigual; (size, length) distinto

uneven [ʌnˈiːvn] adj desigual; (road etc) lleno de baches

unexpected [ʌnɪkˈspektɪd] adj

inesperado; **unexpectedly** adv inesperadamente

unfair [ʌnˈfeə*] adj: **~ (to sb)** injusto (con algn)

unfaithful [ʌnˈfeɪθful] adj infiel

unfamiliar [ʌnfəˈmɪlɪə*] adj extraño, desconocido; **to be ~ with** desconocer

unfashionable [ʌnˈfæʃnəbl] adj pasado or fuera de moda

unfasten [ʌnˈfɑːsn] vt (knot) desatar; (dress) desabrochar; (open) abrir

unfavourable [ʌnˈfeɪvərəbl] (us **unfavorable**) adj desfavorable

unfinished [ʌnˈfɪnɪʃt] adj inacabado, sin terminar

unfit [ʌnˈfɪt] adj bajo de forma; (incompetent): **~ (for)** incapaz (de); **~ for work** no apto para trabajar

unfold [ʌnˈfəuld] vt desdoblar ⊳ vi abrirse

unforgettable [ʌnfəˈgetəbl] adj inolvidable

unfortunate [ʌnˈfɔːtʃnət] adj desgraciado; (event, remark) inoportuno; **unfortunately** adv desgraciadamente

unfriendly [ʌnˈfrendlɪ] adj antipático; (behaviour, remark) hostil, poco amigable

unfurnished [ʌnˈfɜːnɪʃt] adj sin amueblar

unhappiness [ʌnˈhæpɪnɪs] n tristeza, desdicha

unhappy [ʌnˈhæpɪ] adj (sad) triste; (unfortunate) desgraciado; (childhood) infeliz; **~ about/with** (arrangements etc) poco contento con, descontento de

unhealthy [ʌnˈhelθɪ] adj (place) malsano; (person) enfermizo; (fig: interest) morboso

unheard-of [ʌnˈhɜːdɔv] adj inaudito, sin precedente

unhelpful [ʌnˈhelpful] adj (person) poco servicial; (advice) inútil

unhurt [ʌnˈhɜːt] adj ileso

unidentified [ʌnaɪˈdentɪfaɪd] adj no identificado, sin identificar; see

u

also **UFO**

uniform ['juːnɪfɔːm] *n* uniforme *m*
▷ *adj* uniforme

unify ['juːnɪfaɪ] *vt* unificar, unir

unimportant [ʌnɪm'pɔːtənt] *adj* sin
importancia

uninhabited [ʌnɪn'hæbɪtɪd] *adj*
desierto

unintentional [ʌnɪn'tɛnʃənəl] *adj*
involuntario

union ['juːnjən] *n* unión *f*; (*also*: **trade
~**) sindicato ▷ *cpd* sindical; **Union Jack**
n bandera del Reino Unido

unique [juː'niːk] *adj* único

unisex ['juːnɪsɛks] *adj* unisex

unit ['juːnɪt] *n* unidad *f*; (*section: of
furniture etc*) elemento; (*team*) grupo;
kitchen ~ módulo de cocina

unite [juː'naɪt] *vt* unir ▷ *vi* unirse;
united *adj* unido; (*effort*) conjunto;
United Kingdom *n* Reino Unido;
United Nations (Organization) *n*
Naciones *fpl* Unidas; **United States (of
America)** *n* Estados *mpl* Unidos

unity ['juːnɪtɪ] *n* unidad *f*

universal [juːnɪ'vɜːsəl] *adj* universal

universe ['juːnɪvɜːs] *n* universo

university [juːnɪ'vɜːsɪtɪ] *n*
universidad *f*

unjust [ʌn'dʒʌst] *adj* injusto

unkind [ʌn'kaɪnd] *adj* poco amable;
(*behaviour, comment*) cruel

unknown [ʌn'nəun] *adj*
desconocido

unlawful [ʌn'lɔːful] *adj* ilegal, ilícito

unleaded [ʌn'lɛdɪd] *adj* (*petrol, fuel*)
sin plombo

unleash [ʌn'liːʃ] *vt* desatar

unless [ʌn'lɛs] *conj* a menos que;
~ he comes a menos que venga; **~
otherwise stated** salvo indicación
contraria

unlike [ʌn'laɪk] *adj* (*not alike*) distinto
de or a; (*not like*) poco propio de ▷ *prep*
a diferencia de

unlikely [ʌn'laɪklɪ] *adj* improbable;
(*unexpected*) inverosímil

unlimited [ʌn'lɪmɪtɪd] *adj* ilimitado

unlisted [ʌn'lɪstɪd] (*us*) *adj* (*Tel*) que
no consta en la guía

unload [ʌn'ləud] *vt* descargar

unlock [ʌn'lɔk] *vt* abrir (con llave)

unlucky [ʌn'lʌkɪ] *adj* desgraciado;
(*object, number*) que da mala suerte; **to
be ~** tener mala suerte

unmarried [ʌn'mærɪd] *adj* soltero

unmistak(e)able [ʌnmɪs'teɪkəbl]
adj inconfundible

unnatural [ʌn'nætʃrəl] *adj* (*gen*)
antinatural; (*manner*) afectado; (*habit*)
perverso

unnecessary [ʌn'nɛsəsərɪ] *adj*
innecesario, inútil

UNO ['juːnəu] *n abbr* (= *United Nations
Organization*) ONU *f*

unofficial [ʌnə'fɪʃl] *adj* no oficial;
(*news*) sin confirmar

unpack [ʌn'pæk] *vi* deshacer las
maletas ▷ *vt* deshacer

unpaid [ʌn'peɪd] *adj* (*bill, debt*) sin
pagar, impagado; (*Comm*) pendiente;
(*holiday*) sin sueldo; (*work*) sin pago,
voluntario

unpleasant [ʌn'plɛznt] *adj*
(*disagreeable*) desagradable; (*person,
manner*) antipático

unplug [ʌn'plʌg] *vt* desenchufar,
desconectar

unpopular [ʌn'pɔpjulə*] *adj*
impopular, poco popular

unprecedented [ʌn'prɛsɪdəntɪd]
adj sin precedentes

unpredictable [ʌnprɪ'dɪktəbl] *adj*
imprevisible

unprotected ['ʌnprə'tɛktɪd] *adj* (*sex*)
sin protección

unqualified [ʌn'kwɔlɪfaɪd] *adj* sin
título, no cualificado; (*success*) total

unravel [ʌn'rævl] *vt* desenmarañar

unreal [ʌn'rɪəl] *adj* irreal;
(*extraordinary*) increíble

unrealistic [ʌnrɪə'lɪstɪk] *adj* poco
realista

unreasonable [ʌn'riːznəbl] *adj*
irrazonable; (*demand*) excesivo

unrelated [ʌnrɪ'leɪtɪd] *adj* sin

relación; (family) no emparentado
unreliable [ʌnrɪ'laɪəbl] adj (person) informal; (machine) poco fiable
unrest [ʌn'rɛst] n inquietud f, malestar m; (Pol) disturbios mpl
unroll [ʌn'rəul] vt desenrollar
unruly [ʌn'ru:lɪ] adj indisciplinado
unsafe [ʌn'seɪf] adj peligroso
unsatisfactory ['ʌnsætɪs'fæktərɪ] adj poco satisfactorio
unscrew [ʌn'skru:] vt destornillar
unsettled [ʌn'sɛtld] adj inquieto, intranquilo; (weather) variable
unsettling [ʌn'sɛtlɪŋ] adj perturbador(a), inquietante
unsightly [ʌn'saɪtlɪ] adj feo
unskilled [ʌn'skɪld] adj (work) no especializado; (worker) no cualificado
unspoiled ['ʌn'spɔɪld], **unspoilt** ['ʌn'spɔɪlt] adj (place) que no ha perdido su belleza natural
unstable [ʌn'steɪbl] adj inestable
unsteady [ʌn'stɛdɪ] adj inestable
unsuccessful [ʌnsək'sɛsful] adj (attempt) infructuoso; (writer, proposal) sin éxito; **to be ~** (in attempting sth) no tener éxito, fracasar
unsuitable [ʌn'su:təbl] adj inapropiado; (time) inoportuno
unsure [ʌn'ʃuə*] adj inseguro, poco seguro
untidy [ʌn'taɪdɪ] adj (room) desordenado; (appearance) desaliñado
untie [ʌn'taɪ] vt desatar
until [ən'tɪl] prep hasta ⊳ conj hasta que; **~ he comes** hasta que venga; **~ now** hasta ahora; **~ then** hasta entonces
untrue [ʌn'tru:] adj (statement) falso
unused [ʌn'ju:zd] adj sin usar
unusual [ʌn'ju:ʒuəl] adj insólito, poco común; (exceptional) inusitado; **unusually** adv (exceptionally) excepcionalmente; **he arrived unusually early** llegó más temprano que de costumbre
unveil [ʌn'veɪl] vt (statue) descubrir
unwanted [ʌn'wɔntɪd] adj (clothing)

viejo; (pregnancy) no deseado
unwell [ʌn'wɛl] adj: **to be/feel ~** estar indispuesto/sentirse mal
unwilling [ʌn'wɪlɪŋ] adj: **to be ~ to do sth** estar poco dispuesto a hacer algo
unwind [ʌn'waɪnd] (irreg) vt desenvolver ⊳ vi (relax) relajarse
unwise [ʌn'waɪz] adj imprudente
unwittingly [ʌn'wɪtɪŋlɪ] adv inconscientemente, sin darse cuenta
unwrap [ʌn'ræp] vt desenvolver
unzip [ʌn'zɪp] vt abrir la cremallera de; (Comput) descomprimir

○ **KEYWORD**

up [ʌp] prep: **to go/be up sth** subir/ estar subido en algo; **he went up the stairs/the hill** subió las escaleras/la colina; **we walked/climbed up the hill** subimos la colina; **they live further up the street** viven más arriba en la calle; **go up that road and turn left** sigue por esa calle y gira a la izquierda
⊳ adv **1** (upwards, higher) más arriba; **up in the mountains** en lo alto (de la montaña); **put it a bit higher up** ponlo un poco más arriba or alto; **up there** ahí or allí arriba; **up above** en lo alto, por encima, arriba
2: **to be up** (out of bed) estar levantado; (prices, level) haber subido
3: **up to** (as far as) hasta; **up to now** hasta ahora or hasta la fecha
4: **to be up to**: **it's up to you** (depending on) depende de ti; **he's not up to it** (job, task etc) no es capaz de hacerlo; **his work is not up to the required standard** su trabajo no da la talla; (inf: be doing): **what is he up to?** ¿que estará tramando?
⊳ n: **ups and downs** altibajos mpl

up-and-coming [ʌpənd'kʌmɪŋ] adj prometedor(a)
upbringing ['ʌpbrɪŋɪŋ] n educación

f

update [ʌpˈdeɪt] vt poner al día

upfront [ʌpˈfrʌnt] adj claro, directo
▷ adv a las claras; (pay) por adelantado;
to be ~ about sth admitir algo
claramente

upgrade [ʌpˈgreɪd] vt (house)
modernizar; (employee) ascender

upheaval [ʌpˈhiːvl] n trastornos mpl;
(Pol) agitación f

uphill [ʌpˈhɪl] adj cuesta arriba;
(fig: task) penoso, difícil ▷ adv: **to go ~**
ir cuesta arriba

upholstery [ʌpˈhəʊlstəri] n
tapicería

upmarket [ʌpˈmɑːkɪt] adj (product)
de categoría

upon [əˈpɒn] prep sobre

upper [ˈʌpə*] adj superior, de arriba
▷ n (of shoe: also: ~s) empeine m; **upper-
class** adj de clase alta

upright [ˈʌpraɪt] adj derecho;
(vertical) vertical; (fig) honrado

uprising [ˈʌpraɪzɪŋ] n sublevación f

uproar [ˈʌprɔː*] n escándalo

upset [n ˈʌpset, vb, adj ʌpˈset] n (to
plan etc) revés m, contratiempo m; (Med)
trastorno ▷ vt irreg (glass etc) volcar;
(plan) alterar; (person) molestar,
disgustar ▷ adj molesto, disgustado;
(stomach) revuelto

upside-down [ʌpsaɪdˈdaʊn] adv al
revés; **to turn a place ~** revolverlo
todo

upstairs [ʌpˈsteəz] adv arriba ▷ adj
(room) de arriba ▷ n el piso superior

up-to-date [ˈʌptəˈdeɪt] adj al día

uptown [ʌpˈtaʊn] (us) adv hacia las
afueras ▷ adj exterior, de las afueras

upward [ˈʌpwəd] adj ascendente;
upward(s) adv hacia arriba; (more
than): **upward(s) of** más de

uranium [jʊəˈreɪnɪəm] n uranio

Uranus [jʊəˈreɪnəs] n Urano

urban [ˈɜːbən] adj urbano

urge [ɜːdʒ] n (desire) deseo ▷ vt: **to ~
sb to do sth** animar a algn a hacer algo

urgency [ˈɜːdʒənsɪ] n urgencia

urgent [ˈɜːdʒənt] adj urgente; (voice)
perentorio

urinal [ˈjʊərɪnl] n (building) urinario; n
(vessel) orinal m

urinate [ˈjʊərɪneɪt] vi orinar

urine [ˈjʊərɪn] n orina, orines mpl

US n abbr (= United States) EE. UU.

us [ʌs] pron nos; (after prep) nosotros;
as; see also **me**

USA n abbr (= United States (of America))
EE.UU.

use [n juːs, vb juːz] n uso, empleo;
(usefulness) utilidad f ▷ vt usar,
emplear; **she ~d to do it** (ella) solía or
acostumbraba hacerlo; **in ~** en uso; **out
of ~** en desuso; **to be of ~** servir; **it's
no ~** (pointless) es inútil; (not useful) no
sirve; **to be ~d to** estar acostumbrado
a, acostumbrar; **use up** vt (food)
consumir; (money) gastar; **used** [juːzd]
adj (car) usado; **useful** adj útil;
useless adj (unusable) inservible;
(pointless) inútil; (person) inepto;
user n usuario/a; **user-friendly** adj
(computer) amistoso

usual [ˈjuːʒʊəl] adj normal, corriente;
as ~ como de costumbre; **usually** adv
normalmente

utensil [juːˈtensl] n utensilio;
kitchen ~s batería de cocina

utility [juːˈtɪlɪtɪ] n utilidad f; (public
utility) (empresa de) servicio público

utilize [ˈjuːtɪlaɪz] vt utilizar

utmost [ˈʌtməʊst] adj mayor ▷ n: **to
do one's ~** hacer todo lo posible

utter [ˈʌtə*] adj total, completo
▷ vt pronunciar, proferir; **utterly** adv
completamente, totalmente

U-turn [ˈjuːˈtɜːn] n viraje m en
redondo

V

v. abbr =**verse**; **versus**; (=volt) v; (=vide) véase

vacancy ['veɪkənsɪ] n (BRIT: job) vacante f; (room) habitación f libre; **"no vacancies"** "completo"

vacant ['veɪkənt] adj desocupado, libre; (expression) distraído

vacate [və'keɪt] vt (house, room) desocupar; (job) dejar (vacante)

vacation [və'keɪʃən] n vacaciones fpl; **vacationer** (US **vacationist**) n turista m/f

vaccination [væksɪ'neɪʃən] n vacunación f

vaccine ['væksiːn] n vacuna f

vacuum ['vækjum] n vacío m; **vacuum cleaner** n aspiradora f

vagina [və'dʒaɪnə] n vagina f

vague [veɪg] adj vago; (memory) borroso; (ambiguous) impreciso; (person: absent-minded) distraído; (: evasive): **to be ~** no decir las cosas claramente

vain [veɪn] adj (conceited) presumido; (useless) vano, inútil; **in ~** en vano

Valentine's Day ['væləntaɪnzdeɪ] n día de los enamorados

valid ['vælɪd] adj válido; (ticket) valedero; (law) vigente

valley ['vælɪ] n valle m

valuable ['væljuəbl] adj (jewel) de valor; (time) valioso; **valuables** npl objetos mpl de valor

value ['væljuː] n valor m; (importance) importancia ▷ vt (fix price of) tasar, valorar; (esteem) apreciar; **values** npl (principles) principios mpl

valve [vælv] n válvula f

vampire ['væmpaɪə*] n vampiro

van [væn] n (Aut) furgoneta, camioneta

vandal ['vændl] n vándalo/a; **vandalism** n vandalismo; **vandalize** vt dañar, destruir

vanilla [və'nɪlə] n vainilla f

vanish ['vænɪʃ] vi desaparecer

vanity ['vænɪtɪ] n vanidad f

vapour ['veɪpə*] (US **vapor**) n vapor m; (on breath, window) vaho

variable ['vɛərɪəbl] adj variable

variant ['vɛərɪənt] n variante f

variation [vɛərɪ'eɪʃən] n variación f

varied ['vɛərɪd] adj variado

variety [və'raɪətɪ] n (diversity) diversidad f; (type) variedad f

various ['vɛərɪəs] adj (several: people) varios/as; (diverse) diversos/as

varnish ['vɑːnɪʃ] n barniz m; (nail varnish) esmalte m ▷ vt barnizar; (nails) pintar (con esmalte)

vary ['vɛərɪ] vt variar; (change) cambiar ▷ vi variar

vase [vɑːz] n jarrón m

> Be careful not to translate **vase** by the Spanish word *vaso*.

Vaseline® ['væsɪliːn] n vaselina®

vast [vɑːst] adj enorme

VAT [væt] (BRIT) n abbr (=value added tax) IVA m

vault [vɔːlt] n (of roof) bóveda; (tomb) panteón m; (in bank) cámara acorazada ▷ vt (also: ~ **over**) saltar (por encima de)

VCR n abbr = **video cassette recorder**

VDU n abbr (= visual display unit) UPV f

veal [viːl] n ternera

veer [vɪə*] vi (vehicle) virar; (wind) girar

vegan ['viːɡən] n vegetariano/a estricto/a, vegetaliano/a

vegetable ['vedʒtəbl] n (Bot) vegetal m; (edible plant) legumbre f, hortaliza ▷ adj vegetal

vegetarian [vedʒɪ'tɛərɪən] adj, n vegetariano/a m/f

vegetation [vedʒɪ'teɪʃən] n vegetación f

vehicle ['viːkl] n vehículo; (fig) medio

veil [veɪl] n velo ▷ vt velar

vein [veɪn] n vena; (of ore etc) veta

Velcro® ['vɛlkrəʊ] n velcro® m

velvet ['vɛlvɪt] n terciopelo

vending machine ['vɛndɪŋ-] n distribuidor m automático

vendor ['vɛndə*] n vendedor/a m/f; **street ~** vendedor/a m/f callejero/a

vengeance ['vɛndʒəns] n venganza; **with a ~** (fig) con creces

venison ['vɛnɪsn] n carne f de venado

venom ['vɛnəm] n veneno; (bitterness) odio

vent [vɛnt] n (in jacket) respiradero; (in wall) rejilla (de ventilación) ▷ vt (fig: feelings) desahogar

ventilation [vɛntɪ'leɪʃən] n ventilación f

venture ['vɛntʃə*] n empresa ▷ vt (opinion) ofrecer ▷ vi arriesgarse, lanzarse; **business ~** empresa comercial

venue ['vɛnjuː] n lugar m

Venus ['viːnəs] n Venus m

verb [vəːb] n verbo; **verbal** adj verbal

verdict ['vəːdɪkt] n veredicto, fallo; (fig) opinión f, juicio

verge [vəːdʒ] (BRIT) n borde m; **"soft ~s"** (Aut) "arcén m no asfaltado"; **to be on the ~ of doing sth** estar a punto de hacer algo

verify ['vɛrɪfaɪ] vt comprobar, verificar

versatile ['vəːsətaɪl] adj (person) polifacético; (machine, tool etc) versátil

verse [vəːs] n poesía; (stanza) estrofa; (in bible) versículo

version ['vəːʃən] n versión f

versus ['vəːsəs] prep contra

vertical ['vəːtɪkl] adj vertical

very ['vɛrɪ] adv muy ▷ adj: **the ~ book which** el mismo libro que; **the ~ last** el último de todos; **at the ~ least** al menos; **~ much** muchísimo

vessel ['vɛsl] n (ship) barco; (container) vasija; see **blood**

vest [vɛst] n (BRIT) camiseta; (us: waistcoat) chaleco

vet [vɛt] vt (candidate) investigar ▷ n abbr (BRIT) = **veterinary surgeon**

veteran ['vɛtərn] n excombatiente mf, veterano/a

veterinary surgeon ['vɛtrɪnərɪ-] (us **veterinarian**) n veterinario/a m/f

veto ['viːtəʊ] (pl **~es**) n veto ▷ vt prohibir, poner el veto a

via ['vaɪə] prep por, por medio de

viable ['vaɪəbl] adj viable

vibrate [vaɪ'breɪt] vi vibrar

vibration [vaɪ'breɪʃən] n vibración f

vicar ['vɪkə*] n párroco (de la Iglesia Anglicana)

vice [vaɪs] n (evil) vicio; (Tech) torno de banco; **vice-chairman** (irreg) n vicepresidente m

vice versa ['vaɪsɪ'vəːsə] adv viceversa

vicinity [vɪ'sɪnɪtɪ] n: **in the ~ (of)** cercano/a

vicious ['vɪʃəs] adj (attack) violento; (words) cruel; (horse, dog) resabido

victim ['vɪktɪm] n víctima

victor ['vɪktə*] n vencedor/a m/f

Victorian [vɪk'tɔːrɪən] adj victoriano

victorious [vɪk'tɔːrɪəs] adj victorioso

victory ['vɪktərɪ] n victoria

video ['vɪdɪəʊ] n (video) m, vídeo (SP), (LAM); **video call** n videollamada; **video camera** n videocámara, cámara de vídeo; **video (cassette) recorder** n vídeo (SP), video

(LAM); **video game** n videojuego;
videophone n videoteléfono; **video
shop** n videoclub m; **video tape** n
cinta de vídeo

vie [vaɪ] vi: **to ~ (with sb for sth)**
competir (con algn por algo)

Vienna [vɪˈɛnə] n Viena

Vietnam [vjetˈnæm] n Vietnam
m; **Vietnamese** [-nəˈmiːz] n inv, adj
vietnamita mf

view [vjuː] n vista; (outlook)
perspectiva; (opinion) opinión f, criterio
m; (fig) considerar;
on ~ (in museum etc) expuesto; **in full
~ (of)** en plena vista (de); **in ~ of the
weather/the fact that** en vista del
tiempo/del hecho de que; **in my ~** en
mi opinión; **viewer** n espectador(a)
m/f; (TV) telespectador(a) m/f;
viewpoint n (attitude) punto de vista;
(place) mirador m

vigilant [ˈvɪdʒɪlənt] adj vigilante

vigorous [ˈvɪɡərəs] adj enérgico,
vigoroso

vile [vaɪl] adj vil, infame; (smell)
asqueroso; (temper) endemoniado

villa [ˈvɪlə] n (country house) casa de
campo; (suburban house) chalet m

village [ˈvɪlɪdʒ] n aldea; **villager** n
aldeano/a

villain [ˈvɪlən] n (scoundrel) malvado/
a; (in novel) malo; (BRIT: criminal)
maleante m

vinaigrette [vɪneɪˈɡret] n vinagreta

vine [vaɪn] n vid f

vinegar [ˈvɪnɪɡəʳ] n vinagre m

vineyard [ˈvɪnjɑːd] n viña, viñedo

vintage [ˈvɪntɪdʒ] n (year) vendimia,
cosecha ▷ cpd de época

vinyl [ˈvaɪnl] n vinilo

viola [vɪˈəulə] n (Mus) viola

violate [ˈvaɪəleɪt] vt violar

violation [vaɪəˈleɪʃən] n violación f;
in ~ of sth en violación de algo

violence [ˈvaɪələns] n violencia

violent [ˈvaɪələnt] adj violento;
(intense) intenso

violet [ˈvaɪələt] adj violado, violeta

▷ n (plant) violeta

violin [vaɪəˈlɪn] n violín m

VIP n abbr (= very important person) VIP m

virgin [ˈvɜːdʒɪn] n virgen f

Virgo [ˈvɜːɡəu] n Virgo

virtual [ˈvɜːtjuəl] adj virtual;
virtually adv prácticamente; **virtual
reality** n (Comput) mundo or realidad
f virtual

virtue [ˈvɜːtjuː] n virtud f; (advantage)
ventaja; **by ~ of** en virtud de

virus [ˈvaɪərəs] n (also Comput)
virus m inv

visa [ˈviːzə] n visado (SP), visa (LAM)

vise [vaɪs] (US) n (Tech) = **vice**

visibility [vɪzɪˈbɪlɪtɪ] n visibilidad f

visible [ˈvɪzəbl] adj visible

vision [ˈvɪʒən] n (sight) vista;
(foresight, in dream) visión f

visit [ˈvɪzɪt] n visita ▷ vt (person
(US: also: **~ with**) visitar, hacer una
visita a; (place) ir a, (ir a) conocer;
visiting hours npl (in hospital etc)
horas fpl de visita; **visitor** n (in
museum) visitante mf; (invited to house)
visita; (tourist) turista mf; **visitor
centre** (US) **visitor center**) n centro m
de información

visual [ˈvɪzjuəl] adj visual; **visualize**
vt imaginar

vital [ˈvaɪtl] adj (essential) esencial,
imprescindible; (dynamic) dinámico;
(organ) vital

vitality [vaɪˈtælɪtɪ] n energía,
vitalidad f

vitamin [ˈvɪtəmɪn] n vitamina

vivid [ˈvɪvɪd] adj (account) gráfico;
(light) intenso; (imagination, memory)
vivo

V-neck [ˈviːnek] n cuello de pico

vocabulary [vəuˈkæbjuləri] n
vocabulario

vocal [ˈvəukl] adj vocal; (articulate)
elocuente

vocational [vəuˈkeɪʃənl] adj
profesional

vodka [ˈvɒdkə] n vodka m

vogue [vəuɡ] n: **in ~** en boga

voice [vɔɪs] n voz f ▷ vt expresar;
voice mail n buzón de voz

void [vɔɪd] n vacío; (hole) hueco ▷ adj
(invalid) nulo, inválido; (empty): **~ of**
carente or desprovisto de

volatile ['vɔlətaɪl] adj (situation)
inestable; (person) voluble; (liquid)
volátil

volcano [vɔl'keɪnəu] (pl **~es**) n
volcán m

volleyball ['vɔlɪbɔːl] n vol(e)ibol m

volt [vəult] n voltio; **voltage** n
voltaje m

volume ['vɔljuːm] n (gen) volumen
m; (book) tomo

voluntarily ['vɔləntrɪlɪ] adv
libremente, voluntariamente

voluntary ['vɔləntərɪ] adj voluntario

volunteer [vɔlən'tɪə*] n voluntario/
a ▷ vt (information) ofrecer ▷ vi
ofrecerse (de voluntario); **to ~ to do**
ofrecerse a hacer

vomit ['vɔmɪt] n vómito ▷ vt, vi
vomitar

vote [vəut] n voto; (votes cast)
votación f; (right to vote) derecho
de votar; (franchise) sufragio ▷ vt
(chairman) elegir; (propose): **to ~ that**
proponer que ▷ vi votar, ir a votar; **~
of thanks** voto de gracias; **voter** n
votante mf; **voting** n votación f

voucher ['vautʃə*] n (for meal, petrol)
vale m

vow [vau] n voto ▷ vt: **to ~ to do/
that** jurar hacer/que

vowel ['vauəl] n vocal f

voyage ['vɔɪɪdʒ] n viaje m

vulgar ['vʌlgə*] adj (rude) ordinario,
grosero; (in bad taste) de mal gusto

vulnerable ['vʌlnərəbl] adj
vulnerable

vulture ['vʌltʃə*] n buitre m

waddle ['wɔdl] vi anadear

wade [weɪd] vi: **to ~ through** (water)
vadear; (fig: book) leer con dificultad

wafer ['weɪfə*] n galleta, barquillo

waffle ['wɔfl] n (Culin) gofre m ▷ vi
dar el rollo

wag [wæg] vt menear, agitar ▷ vi
moverse, menearse

wage [weɪdʒ] n (also: **~s**) sueldo,
salario ▷ vt: **to ~ war** hacer la guerra

wag(g)on ['wægən] n (horse-drawn)
carro; (BRIT Rail) vagón m

wail [weɪl] n gemido ▷ vi gemir

waist [weɪst] n cintura, talle m;
waistcoat (BRIT) n chaleco

wait [weɪt] n (interval) pausa ▷ vi
esperar; **to lie in ~ for** acechar a; **I
can't ~ to** (fig) estoy deseando; **to ~
for** esperar (a); **wait on** vt fus servir
a; **waiter** n camarero; **waiting list**
n lista de espera; **waiting room** n
sala de espera; **waitress** ['weɪtrɪs] n
camarera

waive [weɪv] vt suspender

wake [weɪk] (pt **woke** or **~d**, pp **woken**

or **~d**) vt (also: **~ up**) despertar ⊳ vi (also: **~ up**) despertarse ⊳ n (for dead person) vela, velatorio; (Naut) estela

Wales [weɪlz] n País m de Gales; **the Prince of ~** el príncipe de Gales

walk [wɔːk] n (stroll) paseo; (hike) excursión f a pie, caminata; (gait) paso, andar m; (in park etc) paseo, alameda ⊳ vi andar, caminar; (for pleasure, exercise) pasear ⊳ vt (distance) recorrer a pie, andar; (dog) pasear; **10 minutes' ~ from here** a 10 minutos de aquí andando; **people from all ~s of life** gente de todas las esferas; **walk out** n (audience) salir; (workers) declararse en huelga; **walker** n (person) paseante mf, caminante mf; **walkie-talkie** [ˈwɔːkɪˈtɔːkɪ] n walkie-talkie m; **walking** n el andar; **walking shoes** npl zapatos mpl para andar; **walking stick** n bastón m; **Walkman®** n Walkman® m; **walkway** n paseo

wall [wɔːl] n pared f; (exterior) muro; (city wall etc) muralla

wallet [ˈwɒlɪt] n cartera, billetera

wallpaper [ˈwɔːlpeɪpə*] n papel m pintado ⊳ vt empapelar

walnut [ˈwɔːlnʌt] n nuez f; (tree) nogal m

walrus [ˈwɔːlrəs] (pl ~ or ~es) n morsa

waltz [wɔːlts] n vals m ⊳ vi bailar el vals

wand [wɒnd] n (also: **magic ~**) varita (mágica)

wander [ˈwɒndə*] vi (person) vagar por; deambular; (thoughts) divagar ⊳ vt recorrer, vagar por

want [wɒnt] vt querer, desear; (need) necesitar ⊳ n: **for ~ of** por falta de; **wanted** adj (criminal) buscado; **"wanted"** (in advertisements) "se busca"

war [wɔː*] n guerra; **to make ~ (on)** declarar la guerra (a)

ward [wɔːd] n (in hospital) sala; (Pol) distrito electoral; (Law: child: also: **~ of court**) pupilo/a

warden [ˈwɔːdn] n (BRIT: of institution) director(a) m/f; (of park, game reserve)

guardian/ana m/f; (BRIT: also: **traffic ~**) guardia mf

wardrobe [ˈwɔːdrəʊb] n armario, ropero; (clothes) vestuario

warehouse [ˈwɛəhaʊs] n almacén m, depósito

warfare [ˈwɔːfɛə*] n guerra

warhead [ˈwɔːhɛd] n cabeza armada

warm [wɔːm] adj caliente; (thanks) efusivo; (clothes etc) abrigado; (welcome, day) caluroso; **it's ~** hace calor; **I'm ~** tengo calor; **warm up** vi (room) calentarse; (person) entrar en calor; (athlete) hacer ejercicios de calentamiento ⊳ vt calentar; **warmly** adv afectuosamente; **warmth** n calor m

warn [wɔːn] vt avisar, advertir; **warning** n aviso, advertencia; **warning light** n luz f de advertencia

warrant [ˈwɒrnt] n autorización f; (Law: to arrest) orden f de detención; (: to search) mandamiento de registro

warranty [ˈwɒrəntɪ] n garantía

warrior [ˈwɒrɪə*] n guerrero/a

Warsaw [ˈwɔːsɔː] n Varsovia

warship [ˈwɔːʃɪp] n buque m o barco de guerra

wart [wɔːt] n verruga

wartime [ˈwɔːtaɪm] n: **in ~** en tiempos de guerra, en la guerra

wary [ˈwɛərɪ] adj cauteloso

was [wɒz] pt of **be**

wash [wɒʃ] vt lavar ⊳ vi lavarse; (sea etc): **to ~ against/over sth** llegar hasta/cubrir algo ⊳ n (clothes etc) lavado; (of ship) estela; **to have a ~** lavarse; **wash up** vi (BRIT) fregar los platos; (US) lavarse; **washbasin** (US) n lavabo; **wash cloth** (US) n manopla; **washer** n (Tech) arandela; **washing** n (dirty) ropa sucia; (clean) colada; **washing line** n cuerda de (colgar) la ropa; **washing machine** n lavadora; **washing powder** (BRIT) n detergente m (en polvo)

Washington [ˈwɒʃɪŋtən] n Washington m

wash: washing-up (BRIT) n fregado, platos mpl (para fregar); **washing-up liquid** (BRIT) n líquido lavavajillas; **washroom** (US) n servicios mpl

wasn't ['wɒznt] = **was not**

wasp [wɒsp] n avispa

waste [weɪst] n derroche m, despilfarro; (of time) pérdida; (food) sobras fpl; (rubbish) basura, desperdicios mpl ▷ adj (material) de desecho; (left over) sobrante; (: material) baldío, descampado; (land) malgastar, derrochar; (time) perder; (opportunity) desperdiciar; **waste ground** (BRIT) n terreno baldío; **wastepaper basket** n papelera

watch [wɒtʃ] n (also: **wrist ~**) reloj m; (Mil: group of guards) centinela m; (act) vigilancia; (Naut: spell of duty) guardia ▷ vt (look at) mirar, observar; (: match, programme) ver; (spy on, guard) vigilar; (be careful of) cuidarse de, tener cuidado de ▷ vi ver, mirar; (keep guard) montar guardia; **watch out** vi cuidarse, tener cuidado; **watchdog** n perro guardián; (fig) persona u organismo encargado de asegurarse de que las empresas actúan dentro de la legalidad; **watch strap** n pulsera (de reloj)

water ['wɔːtə*] n agua ▷ vt (plant) regar ▷ vi (eyes) llorar; (mouth) hacerse la boca agua; **water down** vt (milk etc) aguar; (fig: story) dulcificar, diluir; **watercolour** (US **watercolor**) n acuarela; **watercress** n berro; **waterfall** n cascada, salto de agua; **watering can** n regadera; **watermelon** n sandía; **waterproof** adj impermeable; **water-skiing** n esquí m acuático

watt [wɒt] n vatio

wave [weɪv] n (of hand) señal f con la mano; (on water) ola; (Radio, in hair) onda; (fig) oleada ▷ vi agitar la mano; (flag etc) ondear ▷ vt (handkerchief, gun) agitar ▷ vi (flag etc) ondear; **wavelength** n longitud f de onda

waver ['weɪvə*] vi (voice, love etc)

flaquear; (person) vacilar

wavy ['weɪvɪ] adj ondulado

wax [wæks] n cera ▷ vt encerar ▷ vi (moon) crecer

way [weɪ] n camino; (distance) trayecto, recorrido; (direction) dirección f, sentido; (manner) modo, manera; (habit) costumbre f; **which ~?** – **this ~** ¿por dónde? or ¿en qué dirección? – por aquí; **on the ~** (en route) en (el) camino; **to be on one's ~** estar en camino; **to be in the ~** bloquear el camino; (fig) estorbar; **to go out of one's ~ to do sth** desvivirse por hacer algo; **under ~** en marcha; **to lose one's ~** extraviarse; **in a ~** en cierto modo o sentido; **no ~!** (inf) ¡de eso nada!; **by the ~ ...** a propósito ...; **"~ in"** (BRIT) "entrada"; **"~ out"** (BRIT) "salida"; **the ~ back** el camino de vuelta; **"give ~"** (BRIT Aut) "ceda el paso"

W.C. n váter m

we [wiː] pl pron nosotros/as

weak [wiːk] adj débil, flojo; (tea etc) claro; **weaken** vi debilitarse; (give way) ceder ▷ vt debilitar; **weakness** n debilidad f; (fault) punto débil; **to have a weakness for** tener debilidad por

wealth [welθ] n riqueza; (of details) abundancia; **wealthy** adj rico

weapon ['wepən] n arma; **~s of mass destruction** armas de destrucción masiva

wear [weə*] (pt **wore**, pp **worn**) n (use) uso; (deterioration through use) desgaste m ▷ vt (clothes) llevar; (shoes) calzar; (damage: through use) gastar, usar ▷ vi (last) durar; (rub through etc) desgastarse; **evening ~** ropa de etiqueta; **sports~/baby~** ropa de deportes/de niños; **wear off** vi (pain etc) pasar, desaparecer; **wear out** vt (use) gastar; (person, strength) agotar

weary ['wɪərɪ] adj cansado; (dispirited) abatido ▷ vi: **to ~ of** cansarse de

weasel ['wiːzl] n (Zool) comadreja

weather ['weðə*] n tiempo ▷ vt (storm, crisis) hacer frente a; **under**

the ~ (fig: ill) indispuesto, pachucho; **weather forecast** n boletín m meteorológico

weave [wiːv] (pt **wove**, pp **woven**) vt (cloth) tejer; (fig) entretejer

web [wɛb] n (of spider) telaraña; (on duck's foot) membrana; (network) red f; **the (World Wide) W~** la Red; **web address** n dirección f de Internet; **webcam** n webcam f; **web page** n (página) web m or f; **website** n sitio web

Wed. abbr (=Wednesday) miérc

wed [wɛd] (pt, pp **~ded**) vt casar ▷ vi casarse

we'd [wiːd] = **we had**; **we would**

wedding ['wɛdɪŋ] n boda, casamiento; **silver/golden ~ (anniversary)** bodas fpl de plata/de oro; **wedding anniversary** n aniversario de boda; **wedding day** n día m de la boda; **wedding dress** n traje m de novia; **wedding ring** n alianza

wedge [wɛdʒ] n (of wood etc) cuña; (of cake) trozo ▷ vt acuñar; (push) apretar

Wednesday ['wɛdnzdɪ] n miércoles m inv

wee [wiː] (SCOTTISH) adj pequeñito

weed [wiːd] n mala hierba, maleza ▷ vt escardar, desherbar; **weedkiller** n herbicida m

week [wiːk] n semana; **a ~ today/on Friday** de hoy/del viernes en ocho días; **weekday** n día m laborable; **weekend** n fin m de semana; **weekly** adv semanalmente, cada semana ▷ adj semanal ▷ n semanario

weep [wiːp] (pt, pp **wept**) vi, vt llorar

weigh [weɪ] vt, vi pesar; **to ~ anchor** levar anclas; **weigh up** vt sopesar

weight [weɪt] n peso; (metal weight) pesa; **to lose/put on ~** adelgazar/engordar; **weightlifting** n levantamiento de pesas

weir [wɪə*] n presa

weird [wɪəd] adj raro, extraño

welcome ['wɛlkəm] adj bienvenido

▷ n bienvenida ▷ vt dar la bienvenida a; (be glad of) alegrarse de; **thank you – you're ~** gracias – de nada

weld [wɛld] n soldadura n ▷ vt soldar

welfare ['wɛlfɛə*] n bienestar m; (social aid) asistencia social; **welfare state** n estado del bienestar

well [wɛl] n fuente f, pozo ▷ adv bien ▷ adj: **to be ~** estar bien (de salud) ▷ excl ¡vaya!, ¡bueno!; **as ~** también; **as ~ as** además de; ~ **done!** ¡bien hecho!; **get ~ soon!** ¡que te mejores pronto!; **to do ~** (business) ir bien; (person) tener éxito

we'll [wiːl] = **we will**; **we shall**

well-behaved adj bueno; **well-built** adj (person) fornido; **well-dressed** adj bien vestido

wellies ['wɛlɪz] (inf) npl (BRIT) botas de goma

well-known adj (person) conocido; **well-off** adj acomodado; **well-paid** adj [wel'peɪd] adj bien pagado, bien retribuido

Welsh [wɛlʃ] adj galés/esa ▷ n (Ling) galés m; **Welshman** (irreg) n galés m; **Welshwoman** (irreg) n galesa

went [wɛnt] pt of **go**

wept [wɛpt] pt, pp of **weep**

were [wə:*] pt of **be**

we're [wɪə*] = **we are**

weren't [wəːnt] = **were not**

west [wɛst] n oeste m ▷ adj occidental, del oeste ▷ adv al or hacia el oeste; **the W~** el Oeste, el Occidente; **westbound** ['wɛstbaʊnd] adj (traffic, carriageway) con rumbo al oeste; **western** adj occidental ▷ n (Cinema) película del oeste; **West Indian** adj, n antillano/a m/f

wet [wɛt] adj (damp) húmedo; (soaked) mojado; ~ **through** (rainy) lluvioso ▷ n (BRIT: Pol) conservador(a) m/f moderado/a; **to get ~** mojarse; "~ **paint**" "recién pintado"; **wetsuit** n traje m térmico

we've [wiːv] = **we have**

whack [wæk] vt dar un buen golpe a

whale [weɪl] n (Zool) ballena

wharf [wɔːf] (pl **wharves**) n muelle m

○ KEYWORD

what [wɒt] adj **1** (in direct/indirect questions) qué; **what size is he?** ¿qué talla usa?; **what colour/shape is it?** ¿de qué color/forma es? **2** (in exclamations): **what a mess!** ¡qué desastre!; **what a fool I am!** ¡qué tonto soy!
▷ pron **1** (interrogative) qué; **what are you doing?** ¿qué haces or estás haciendo?; **what is happening?** ¿qué pasa or está pasando?; **what is it called?** ¿cómo se llama?; **what about me?** ¿y yo qué?; **what about doing ...?** ¿qué tal si hacemos ...?
2 (relative) lo que; **I saw what you did/was on the table** vi lo que hiciste/había en la mesa
▷ excl (disbelieving) ¡cómo!; **what, no coffee!** ¡que no hay café!

whatever [wɒt'evə*] adj: **~ book you choose** cualquier libro que elijas
▷ pron: **do ~ is necessary** haga lo que sea necesario; **~ happens** pase lo que pase; **no reason ~** or **whatsoever** ninguna razón sea la que sea; **nothing ~** nada en lo absoluto
whatsoever [wɒtsəu'evə*] adj see **whatever**
wheat [wiːt] n trigo
wheel [wiːl] n rueda; (Aut: also: **steering ~**) volante m; (Naut) timón m ▷ vt (pram etc) empujar
▷ vi (also: **~ round**) dar la vuelta, girar; **wheelbarrow** n carretilla, **wheelchair** n silla de ruedas; **wheel clamp** n (Aut) cepo
wheeze [wiːz] vi resollar

○ KEYWORD

when [wɛn] adv cuando; **when did it happen?** ¿cuándo ocurrió?; **I know**

when it happened sé cuándo ocurrió
▷ conj **1** (at, during, after the time that) cuando; **be careful when you cross the road** ten cuidado al cruzar la calle; **that was when I needed you** fue entonces que te necesité
2 (on, at which): **on the day when I met him** el día en que le conocí
3 (whereas) cuando

whenever [wɛn'evə*] conj cuando; (every time that) cada vez que ▷ adv cuando sea
where [wɛə*] adv donde ▷ conj donde; **this is ~** aquí es donde; **whereabouts** adv dónde ▷ n: **nobody knows his whereabouts** nadie conoce su paradero; **whereas** conj visto que, mientras; **whereby** pron por lo cual; **wherever** conj dondequiera que; (interrogative) dónde
whether ['wɛðə*] conj si; **I don't know ~ to accept or not** no sé si aceptar o no; **~ you go or not** vayas o no vayas

○ KEYWORD

which [wɪtʃ] adj **1** (interrogative: direct, indirect) qué; **which picture(s) do you want?** ¿qué cuadro(s) quieres?; **which one?** ¿cuál?
2 in which case en cuyo caso; **we got there at 8 pm, by which time the cinema was full** llegamos allí a las 8, cuando el cine estaba lleno
▷ pron **1** (interrogative) cual; **I don't mind which** el/la que sea
2 (relative: replacing noun) que; (: replacing clause) lo que; (: after preposition) (el/la) que etc; **el/la cual etc**; **the apple which you ate/which is on the table** la manzana que comiste/que está en la mesa; **the chair on which you are sitting** la silla en la que estás sentado; **he said he knew, which is true/I feared** dijo que lo sabía, lo cual or lo

que es cierto/me temía

whichever [wɪtʃˈevə*] adj: take ~
book you prefer coja (sp) el libro que
prefiera; ~ book you take cualquier
libro que coja

while [waɪl] n rato, momento ▷ conj
mientras; (although) aunque; for a ~
durante algún tiempo

whilst [waɪlst] conj = while

whim [wɪm] n capricho

whine [waɪn] n (of pain) gemido; (of
engine) zumbido; (of siren) aullido ▷ vi
gemir; zumbar; (fig: complain)
gimotear

whip [wɪp] n látigo; (Pol: person)
encargado de la disciplina partidaria
en el parlamento ▷ vt azotar; (Culin)
batir; (move quickly): to ~ sth out/off
sacar/quitar algo de un tirón; whipped
cream n nata or crema montada

whirl [wəːl] vt hacer girar, dar vueltas
a ▷ vi girar, dar vueltas; (leaves etc)
arremolinarse

whisk [wɪsk] n (Culin) batidor m ▷ vt
(Culin) batir; to ~ sb away or off llevar
volando a algn

whiskers [ˈwɪskəz] npl (of animal)
bigotes mpl; (of man) patillas fpl

whiskey [ˈwɪskɪ] (US, IRELAND) n =
whisky

whisky [ˈwɪskɪ] n whisky m

whisper [ˈwɪspə*] n susurro ▷ vi,
vt susurrar

whistle [ˈwɪsl] n (sound) silbido;
(object) silbato ▷ vi silbar

white [waɪt] adj blanco; (pale) pálido
▷ n blanco; (of egg) clara; whiteboard
n pizarra blanca; interactive
whiteboard pizarra interactiva;
White House (US) n Casa Blanca;
whitewash n (paint) jalbegue m, cal f
▷ vt blanquear

whiting [ˈwaɪtɪŋ] n inv (fish)
pescadilla

Whitsun [ˈwɪtsn] n pentecostés m

whittle [ˈwɪtl] vt: to ~ away, ~ down
ir reduciendo

whizz [wɪz] vi: to ~ past or by pasar a
toda velocidad

○ **KEYWORD**

who [huː] pron 1 (interrogative) quién;
who is it?, who's there? ¿quién es?;
who are you looking for? ¿a quién
buscas?; I told her who I was le dije
quién era yo
2 (relative) que; the man/woman who
spoke to me el hombre/la mujer que
habló conmigo; those who can swim
los que saben or sepan nadar

whoever [huːˈevə*] pron: ~ finds
it cualquiera or quienquiera que lo
encuentre; ask ~ you like pregunta
a quien quieras; ~ he marries no
importa con quién se case

whole [həʊl] adj (entire) todo, entero;
(not broken) intacto ▷ n todo; (all): the
~ of the town toda la ciudad, la
ciudad entera ▷ n (total) total m; (sum)
conjunto; on the ~, as a ~ en general;
wholefood(s) n(pl) alimento(s) m(pl)
integral(es); wholeheartedly
[ˈhəʊlˈhɑːtɪdlɪ] adv con entusiasmo;
wholemeal adj integral; wholesale
n venta al por mayor ▷ adj al por
mayor; (fig: destruction) sistemático;
wholewheat adj = wholemeal;
wholly adv totalmente,
enteramente

○ **KEYWORD**

whom [huːm] pron 1 (interrogative):
whom did you see? ¿a quién viste?;
to whom did you give it? ¿a quién
se lo diste?; tell me from whom you
received it dígame de quién lo recibió
2 (relative) que; to whom a quien(es);
of whom de quien(es), del/de la que
etc; the man whom I saw/to whom
I wrote el hombre que vi/a quien
escribí; the lady about/with whom I
was talking la señora de (la) que/con

quien or (la) que hablaba

whore [hɔ:*] (inf, pej) n puta

○ **KEYWORD**

whose [hu:z] adj 1 (possessive: interrogative): **whose book is this?, whose is this book?** ¿de quién es este libro?; **whose pencil have you taken?** ¿de quién es el lápiz que has cogido?; **whose daughter are you?** ¿de quién eres hija?

2 (possessive: relative) cuyo/a, pl cuyos/as; **the man whose son you rescued** el hombre cuyo hijo rescataste; **those whose passports I have** aquellas personas cuyos pasaportes tengo; **the woman whose car was stolen** la mujer a quien le robaron el coche

▷ pron de quién; **whose is this?** ¿de quién es esto?; **I know whose it is** sé de quién es

○ **KEYWORD**

why [waɪ] adv por qué; **why not?** ¿por qué no?; **why not do it now?** ¿por qué no lo haces or hacemos etc ahora?

▷ conj: **I wonder why he said that** me pregunto por qué dijo eso; **that's not why I'm here** no es por eso (por lo) que estoy aquí; **the reason why** la razón por la que

▷ excl (expressing surprise, shock, annoyance) ¡hombre!, ¡vaya!; (explaining): **why, it's you!** ¡hombre, eres tú!; **why, that's impossible!** ¡pero sí eso es imposible!

wicked ['wɪkɪd] adj malvado, cruel
wicket ['wɪkɪt] n (Cricket: stumps) palos mpl; (: grass area) terreno de juego
wide [waɪd] adj ancho; (area, knowledge) vasto, grande; (choice) amplio ▷ adv: **to open** ~ abrir de par en par; **to shoot** ~ errar el tiro; **widely** adv (travelled) mucho; (spaced) muy;

it is widely believed/known that ... mucha gente piensa/sabe que ...; **widen** vt ensanchar; (experience) ampliar ▷ vi ensancharse; **wide open** adj abierto de par en par; **widespread** adj extendido, general
widow ['wɪdəu] n viuda; **widower** n viudo
width [wɪdθ] n anchura; (of cloth) ancho
wield [wi:ld] vt (sword) blandir; (power) ejercer
wife [waɪf] (pl **wives**) n mujer f, esposa
Wi-Fi ['waɪfaɪ] n wifi m
wig [wɪg] n peluca
wild [waɪld] adj (animal) salvaje; (plant) silvestre; (person) furioso, violento; (idea) descabellado; (rough: sea) bravo; (: land) agreste; (: weather) muy revuelto; **wilderness** ['wɪldənɪs] n desierto; **wildlife** n fauna; **wildly** adv (behave) locamente; (lash out) a diestro y siniestro; (guess) a lo loco; (happy) a más no poder

○ **KEYWORD**

will [wɪl] aux vb 1 (forming future tense): **I will finish it tomorrow** lo terminaré or voy a terminar mañana; **I will have finished it by tomorrow** lo habré terminado para mañana; **will you do it? – yes I will/no I won't** ¿lo harás? – sí/no

2 (in conjectures, predictions): **he will or he'll be there by now** ya habrá or debe (de) haber llegado; **that will be the postman** será or debe ser el cartero

3 (in commands, requests, offers): **will you be quiet!** ¡quieres callarte?; **will you help me?** ¿quieres ayudarme?; **will you have a cup of tea?** ¿te apetece un té?; **I won't put up with it!** ¡no lo soporto!

▷ vt (pt, pp **willed**): **to will sb to do sth** desear que algn haga algo; **he willed himself to go on** con gran fuerza de voluntad, continuó

▷ n voluntad f; (testament) testamento

willing ['wɪlɪŋ] adj (with goodwill) de buena voluntad; (enthusiastic) entusiasta; **he's ~ to do it** está dispuesto a hacerlo; **willingly** adv con mucho gusto

willow ['wɪləu] n sauce m

willpower ['wɪlpauə*] n fuerza de voluntad

wilt [wɪlt] vi marchitarse

wince [wɪns] vi encogerse

wind¹ [wɪnd] n viento; (Med) gases mpl ▷ vt (take breath away from) dejar sin aliento a

wind² [waɪnd] (pt, pp **wound**) vt enrollar; (wrap) envolver; (clock, toy) dar cuerda a ▷ vi (road, river) serpentear; **wind down** vt (car window) bajar; (fig: production, business) disminuir; **wind up** vt (clock) dar cuerda a; (debate, meeting) concluir, terminar

windfall ['wɪndfɔːl] n golpe m de suerte

wind farm n parque m eólico

winding ['waɪndɪŋ] adj (road) tortuoso; (staircase) de caracol

windmill ['wɪndmɪl] n molino de viento

window ['wɪndəu] n ventana; (in car, train) ventanilla; (in shop etc) escaparate m (SP), vidriera (LAM); **window box** n jardinera de ventana; **window cleaner** n (person) limpiacristales mf inv; **window pane** n cristal m; **window seat** n asiento junto a la ventana; **windowsill** n alféizar m, repisa

windscreen ['wɪndskriːn] (US **windshield**) n parabrisas m inv; **windscreen wiper** (US **windshield wiper**) n limpiaparabrisas m inv

windsurfing ['wɪndsəːfɪŋ] n windsurf m

windy ['wɪndɪ] adj de mucho viento;

it's **~** hace viento

wine [waɪn] n vino; **wine bar** n enoteca; **wine glass** n copa (para vino); **wine list** n lista de vinos; **wine tasting** n degustación f de vinos

wing [wɪŋ] n ala; (Aut) aleta; **wing mirror** n (espejo) retrovisor m

wink [wɪŋk] n guiño, pestañeo ▷ vi guiñar, pestañear

winner ['wɪnə*] n ganador(a) m/f

winning ['wɪnɪŋ] adj (team) ganador(a); (goal) decisivo; (smile) encantador/a

winter ['wɪntə*] n invierno ▷ vi invernar; **winter sports** npl deportes mpl de invierno; **wintertime** n invierno

wipe [waɪp] n: **to give sth a ~** pasar un trapo sobre algo ▷ vt limpiar; (tape) borrar; **wipe out** vt (debt) liquidar; (memory) borrar; (destroy) destruir; **wipe up** vt limpiar

wire ['waɪə*] n alambre m; (Elec) cable m (eléctrico); (Tel) telegrama m ▷ vt (house) poner la instalación eléctrica en; (also: **~ up**) conectar

wiring ['waɪərɪŋ] n instalación f eléctrica

wisdom ['wɪzdəm] n sabiduría, saber m; (good sense) cordura; **wisdom tooth** n muela del juicio

wise [waɪz] adj sabio; (sensible) juicioso

wish [wɪʃ] n deseo ▷ vt querer; **best ~es** (on birthday etc) felicidades fpl; **with best ~es** (in letter) saludos mpl, recuerdos mpl; **to ~ sb goodbye** despedirse de algn; **he ~ed me well** me deseó mucha suerte; **to ~ to do/sb to do sth** querer hacer/que algn haga algo; **to ~ for** desear

wistful ['wɪstful] adj pensativo

wit [wɪt] n ingenio, gracia; (also: **~s**) inteligencia; (person) chistoso/a

witch [wɪtʃ] n bruja

○ **KEYWORD**

with [wɪð, wɪθ] prep 1 (accompanying, in the company of) con (con +mí, ti, sí =

w

conmigo, contigo, consigo); **I was with
him** estaba con él; **we stayed with
friends** nos quedamos en casa de unos
amigos; **I'm (not) with you** (don't
understand) (no) te entiendo; **to be
with it** (inf: person: up-to-date) estar al
tanto; (: alert) ser despabilado
2 (descriptive, indicating manner etc)
con; de; **a room with a view** una
habitación con vistas; **the man with
the grey hat/blue eyes** el hombre del
sombrero gris/de los ojos azules; **red
with anger** rojo de ira; **to shake with
fear** temblar de miedo; **to fill sth with
water** llenar algo de agua

withdraw [wɪθ'drɔː] vt retirar,
sacar ▷ vi retirarse; **to ~ money
(from the bank)** retirar fondos (del
banco); **withdrawal** n retirada; (of
money) reintegro; **withdrawn** pp of
withdraw ▷ adj (person) reservado,
introvertido

withdrew [wɪθ'druː] pt of
withdraw

wither ['wɪðə*] vi marchitarse

withhold [wɪθ'həuld] vt (money)
retener; (decision) aplazar; (permission)
negar; (information) ocultar

within [wɪð'ɪn] prep dentro de ▷ adv
dentro; **~ reach (of)** al alcance (de); **~
sight (of)** a la vista (de); **~ the week**
antes de acabar la semana; **~ a mile
(of)** a menos de una milla (de)

without [wɪð'aut] prep sin; **to go ~
sth** pasar sin algo

withstand [wɪθ'stænd] vt resistir a

witness ['wɪtnɪs] n testigo mf
▷ vt (event) presenciar; (document)
atestiguar la veracidad de; **to bear ~ to**
(fig) ser testimonio de

witty ['wɪtɪ] adj ingenioso

wives [waɪvz] npl of **wife**

wizard ['wɪzəd] n hechicero

wk abbr = **week**

wobble ['wɒbl] vi temblar; (chair)
cojear

woe [wəu] n desgracia

woke [wəuk] pt of **wake**

woken ['wəukən] pp of **wake**

wolf [wulf] n lobo

woman ['wumən] (pl **women**) n
mujer f

womb [wuːm] n matriz f, útero

women ['wɪmɪn] npl of **woman**

won [wʌn] pt, pp of **win**

wonder ['wʌndə*] n maravilla,
prodigio; (feeling) asombro ▷ vi: **to ~
whether/why** preguntarse si/por
qué; **to ~ at** asombrarse de; **to ~ about**
pensar sobre or en; **it's no ~ (that)**
no es de extrañarse (que +subjun);
wonderful adj maravilloso

won't [wəunt] = **will not**

wood [wud] n (timber) madera;
(forest) bosque m; **wooden** adj de
madera; (fig) inexpresivo; **woodwind**
n (Mus) instrumentos mpl de viento de
madera; **woodwork** n carpintería

wool [wul] n lana; **to pull the ~
over sb's eyes** (fig) engatusar a algn;
woollen (US **woolen**) adj de lana;
woolly (US **wooly**) adj lanudo, de lana;
(fig: ideas) confuso

word [wɜːd] n palabra; (news) noticia;
(promise) palabra (de honor) ▷ vt
redactar; **in other ~s** en otras palabras;
to break/keep one's ~ faltar a la
palabra/cumplir la promesa; **to have
~s with sb** reñir con algn; **wording**
n redacción f; **word processing** n
proceso de textos; **word processor** n
procesador m de textos

wore [wɔː*] pt of **wear**

work [wɜːk] n trabajo; (job) empleo,
trabajo; (Art, Literature) obra ▷ vi
trabajar; (mechanism) funcionar,
marchar; (medicine) ser eficaz, surtir
efecto ▷ vt (shape) trabajar; (stone etc)
tallar; (mine etc) explotar; (machine)
manejar, hacer funcionar ▷ npl (of
clock, machine) mecanismo; **to be out
of ~** estar parado, no tener trabajo;
to ~ loose (part) desprenderse; (knot)
aflojarse; **works** n (BRIT: factory)
fábrica; **work out** vi (plans etc) salir

bien, funcionar; **works** vt (problem)
resolver; (plan) elaborar; **it works out
at £100** suma 100 libras; **worker** n
trabajador(a) m/f, obrero/a; **work
experience** n: **I'm going to do my
work experience in a factory** voy
a hacer las prácticas en una fábrica.
workforce n mano de obra; **working
class** n clase obrera ▷ adj: **working-
class** obrero; **working week** n
semana laboral; **workman** (irreg)
n obrero; **work of art** n obra de
arte; **workout** n (Sport) sesión f de
ejercicios; **work permit** n permiso
de trabajo; **workplace** n lugar m de
trabajo; **worksheet** n (Scol) hoja
de ejercicios; **workshop** n taller m;
work station n puesto or estación f
de trabajo; **work surface** n encimera;
worktop n encimera
world [wəːld] n mundo ▷ cpd
(champion) del mundo; (power, war)
mundial; **to think the ~ of sb** (fig)
tener un concepto muy alto de algn;
World Cup n (Football): **the World Cup**
el Mundial, los Mundiales; **World Wide
Web** adj mundial, universal; **World-Wide
Web** n: **the World-Wide Web** el World
Wide Web
worm [wəːm] n (also: **earth ~**)
lombriz f
worn [wɔːn] pp of **wear** ▷ adj usado;
worn-out adj (object) gastado; (person)
rendido, agotado
worried [ˈwʌrɪd] adj preocupado
worry [ˈwʌrɪ] n preocupación f ▷ vt
preocupar, inquietar ▷ vi preocuparse;
worrying adj inquietante
worse [wəːs] adj, adv peor ▷ n
lo peor; **a change for the ~** un
empeoramiento; **worsen** vt,
vi empeorar; **worse off** adj
(financially): **to be worse off** tener
menos dinero; (fig): **you'll be worse off
this way** de esta forma estarás peor
que nunca
worship [ˈwəːʃɪp] n adoración f ▷ vt
adorar; **Your W~** (BRIT: to mayor) señor

alcalde; (: to judge) señor juez
worst [wəːst] adj, adv peor ▷ n lo
peor; **at ~** en lo peor de los casos
worth [wəːθ] n valor m ▷ adj: **to be
~ valer; it's ~** vale or merece la pena;
to be ~ one's while (to do) merecer
la pena (hacer); **worthless** adj sin
valor; (useless) inútil; **worthwhile** adj
(activity) que merece la pena; (cause)
loable
worthy [ˈwəːði] adj respetable;
(motive) honesto; **~ of** digno de

○ KEYWORD

would [wʊd] aux vb 1 (conditional
tense): **if you asked him he would do
it** si se lo pidieras, lo haría; **if you had
asked him he would have done it**
si se lo hubieras pedido, lo habría or
hubiera hecho
2 (in offers, invitations, requests): **would
you like a biscuit?** ¿quieres una
galleta?; (formal) ¿querría una galleta?;
would you ask him to come in?
¿quiere hacerle pasar?; **would you
open the window please?** ¿quiere or
podría abrir la ventana, por favor?
3 (in indirect speech): **I said I would do it**
dije que lo haría
4 (emphatic): **it would have to snow
today!** ¡tenía que nevar precisamente
hoy!
5 (insistence): **she wouldn't behave** no
quiso comportarse bien
6 (conjecture): **it would have been
midnight** sería medianoche; **it would
seem so** parece ser que sí
7 (indicating habit): **he would go there
on Mondays** iba allí los lunes

wouldn't [ˈwʊdnt] = **would not**
wound[1] [wuːnd] n herida ▷ vt herir
wound[2] [waʊnd] pt, pp of **wind**[2]
wove [wəʊv] pt of **weave**
woven [ˈwəʊvən] pp of **weave**
wrap [ræp] vt (also: **~ up**) envolver;
(gift) envolver, abrigar ▷ vi (dress

W

warmly) abrigarse; **wrapper** n (*on chocolate*) papel m; (BRIT: *of book*) sobrecubierta; **wrapping** n envoltura, envase m; **wrapping paper** n papel m de envolver; (*fancy*) papel m de regalo

wreath [riːθ, pl riːðz] n (*funeral wreath*) corona

wreck [rɛk] n (*ship: destruction*) naufragio; (: *remains*) restos mpl del barco; (*pej: person*) ruina ▷ vt (*car etc*) destrozar; (*chances*) arruinar; **wreckage** n restos mpl; (*of building*) escombros mpl

wren [rɛn] n (*Zool*) reyezuelo

wrench [rɛntʃ] n (*Tech*) llave f inglesa; (*tug*) tirón m; (*fig*) dolor m ▷ vt arrancar; **to ~ sth from sb** arrebatar algo violentamente a algn

wrestle ['rɛsl] vi: **to ~ (with sb)** luchar (con or contra algn); **wrestler** n luchador(a) m/f (de lucha libre); **wrestling** n lucha libre

wretched ['rɛtʃɪd] adj miserable

wriggle ['rɪɡl] vi (*also: ~ about*) menearse, retorcerse

wring [rɪŋ] (*pt, pp* **wrung**) vt retorcer; (*wet clothes*) escurrir; (*fig*): **to ~ sth out of sb** sacar algo por la fuerza a algn

wrinkle ['rɪŋkl] n arruga ▷ vt arrugar ▷ vi arrugarse

wrist [rɪst] n muñeca

writable ['raɪtəbl] adj (*CD, DVD*) escribible

write [raɪt] (*pt* **wrote**, *pp* **written**) vt escribir; (*cheque*) extender ▷ vi escribir; **write down** vt escribir; (*note*) apuntar; **write off** vt (*debt*) borrar (como incobrable); (*fig*) desechar por inútil; **write out** vt escribir; **write-off** n siniestro total; **writer** n escritor(a) m/f

writing ['raɪtɪŋ] n escritura; (*handwriting*) letra; (*of author*) obras fpl; **in ~** por escrito; **writing paper** n papel m de escribir

written ['rɪtn] pp of **write**

wrong [rɒŋ] adj (*wicked*) malo; (*unfair*) injusto; (*incorrect*) equivocado,

incorrecto; (*not suitable*) inoportuno, inconveniente; (*reverse*) del revés equivocadamente ▷ n injusticia ▷ vt ser injusto con; **you are ~ to do it** haces mal en hacerlo; **you are ~ about that, you've got it ~** en eso estás equivocado; **to be in the ~** no tener razón, tener la culpa; **what's ~?** ¿qué pasa?; **to go ~** (*person*) equivocarse; (*plan*) salir mal; (*machine*) estropearse; **wrongly** adv mal, incorrectamente; (*by mistake*) por error; **wrong number** n (*Tel*) **you've got the wrong number** se ha equivocado de número

wrote [rəʊt] pt of **write**

wrung [rʌŋ] pt, pp of **wring**

WWW n abbr (=*World Wide Web*) WWW m

XL *abbr* = **extra large**
Xmas ['eksməs] *n abbr* = **Christmas**
X-ray ['eksreɪ] *n* radiografía ▷ *vt* radiografiar, sacar radiografías de
xylophone ['zaɪləfəun] *n* xilófono

yacht [jɔt] *n* yate *m*; **yachting** *n* (*sport*) balandrismo
yard [jɑːd] *n* patio; (*measure*) yarda; **yard sale** (*us*) *n* venta de objetos usados (*en el jardín de una casa particular*)
yarn [jɑːn] *n* hilo; (*tale*) cuento, historia
yawn [jɔːn] *n* bostezo ▷ *vi* bostezar
yd. *abbr* (=*yard*) yda
yeah [jeə] (*inf*) *adv* sí
year [jɪə*] *n* año; **to be 8 ~s old** tener 8 años; **an eight-~-old child** un niño de ocho años (de edad); **yearly** *adj* anual ▷ *adv* anualmente, cada año
yearn [jəːn] *vi*: **to ~ for sth** añorar algo, suspirar por algo
yeast [jiːst] *n* levadura
yell [jel] *n* grito, alarido ▷ *vi* gritar
yellow ['jeləu] *adj* amarillo; **Yellow Pages®** *npl* páginas *fpl* amarillas
yes [jes] *adv* sí ▷ *n* sí *m*; **to say/answer ~** decir/contestar que sí
yesterday ['jestədɪ] *adv* ayer ▷ *n* ayer *m*; **~ morning/evening** ayer por la mañana/tarde; **all day ~** todo el

día de ayer

yet [jet] *adv* ya; *(negative)* todavía ▷ *conj* sin embargo, a pesar de todo; **it is not finished ~** todavía no está acabado; **the best ~** el/la mejor hasta ahora; **as ~** hasta ahora, todavía

yew [juː] *n* tejo

Yiddish ['jɪdɪʃ] *n* yiddish *m*

yield [jiːld] *n* (Agr) cosecha; (Comm) rendimiento ▷ *vt* ceder; (results) producir, dar; (profit) rendir ▷ *vi* rendirse, ceder; (us Aut) ceder el paso

yob(bo) ['jɔb(bəʊ)] *n* (BRIT inf) gamberro

yoga ['jəʊɡə] *n* yoga *m*

yog(h)ourt ['jəʊɡət] *n* yogur *m*

yog(h)urt ['jəʊɡət] *n* = **yog(h)ourt**

yolk [jəʊk] *n* yema (de huevo)

○ KEYWORD

you [juː] *pron* **1** (subject: familiar) tú; (pl) vosotros/as (SP), ustedes (LAM); (polite) usted; (pl) ustedes; **you are very kind** eres/es etc muy amable; **you Spanish enjoy your food** a vosotros (or ustedes) los españoles os (or les) gusta la comida; **you and I will go** iremos tú y yo

2 (object: direct: familiar) te; (pl) os (SP), les (LAM); (polite) le/les; (f) la; (pl) las; **I know you** te/le etc conozco

3 (object: indirect: familiar) te; (pl) os (SP), les (LAM); (polite) le; les; **I gave the letter to you yesterday** te/os etc di la carta ayer

4 (stressed): **I told you to do it** te dije a ti que lo hicieras, es a ti a quien dije que lo hicieras; see also **3; 5**

5 (after prep: NB: con +ti =** *contigo*: familiar) ti; (pl) vosotros/as (SP), ustedes (LAM); (: polite) usted; (pl) ustedes; **it's for you** es para ti/vosotros etc

6 (comparisons: familiar) tú; (pl) vosotros/as (SP), ustedes (LAM); (: polite) usted; (pl) ustedes; **she's younger than you** es más joven que

tú/vosotros etc

7 (impersonal one): **fresh air does you good** el aire puro (te) hace bien; **you never know** nunca se sabe; **you can't do that!** ¡eso no se hace!

you'd [juːd] = **you had; you would**

you'll [juːl] = **you will; you shall**

young [jʌŋ] *adj* joven ▷ *npl* (of animal) cría; (people): **the ~** los jóvenes, la juventud; **youngster** *n* joven *mf*

your [jɔː*] *adj* tu; (pl) vuestro; (formal) su; see also **my**

you're [juə*] = **you are**

yours [jɔːz] *pron* tuyo (pl), vuestro; (formal) suyo; see also **faithfully; mine**[1] see also **sincerely**

yourself [jɔː'self] *pron* tú mismo; (complement) te; (after prep) ti (mismo); (formal) usted mismo; (: complement) se; (: after prep) sí (mismo); **yourselves** *pl pron* vosotros mismos; (after prep) vosotros (mismos); (formal) ustedes (mismos); (: complement) se; (: after prep) sí mismos; see also **oneself**

youth [juːθ] *n* juventud *f*; (young man) joven *m*; **youth club** *n* club *m* juvenil; **youthful** *adj* juvenil; **youth hostel** *n* albergue *m* de juventud

you've [juːv] = **you have**

Z

zeal [ziːl] *n* celo, entusiasmo
zebra ['ziːbrə] *n* cebra; **zebra crossing** (BRIT) *n* paso de peatones
zero ['zɪərəʊ] *n* cero
zest [zest] *n* ánimo, vivacidad *f*; (of orange) piel *f*
zigzag ['zɪgzæg] *n* zigzag *m* ▷ *vi* zigzaguear, hacer eses
Zimbabwe [zɪm'bɑːbwɪ] *n* Zimbabwe *m*
zinc [zɪŋk] *n* cinc *m*, zinc *m*
zip [zɪp] *n* (also: **~ fastener**, (US) **~per**) cremallera (SP), cierre (AM) *m*, zíper *m* (MEX, CAM) ▷ *vt* (also: **~ up**) cerrar la cremallera de; (file) comprimir; **zip code** (US) *n* código postal; **zip file** *n* (Comput) archivo comprimido; **zipper** (US) *n* cremallera
zit [zɪt] *n* grano
zodiac ['zəʊdɪæk] *n* zodíaco
zone [zəʊn] *n* zona
zoo [zuː] *n* (jardín *m*) zoo *m*
zoology [zuːˈɒlədʒɪ] *n* zoología
zoom [zuːm] *vi*: **to ~ past** pasar zumbando; **zoom lens** *n* zoom *m*
zucchini [zuːˈkiːnɪ] (US) *n(pl)* calabacín(ines) *m(pl)*